FOR REFERENCE

THE SONG INDEX
OF THE ENOCH PRATT FREE LIBRARY

GARLAND REFERENCE LIBRARY OF SOCIAL SCIENCE
VOLUME 1394

The Song Index
of the Enoch Pratt Free Library
Volume II

Ellen Luchinsky

Garland Publishing, Inc.
A member of the Taylor & Francis Group
New York and London
1998

Library of Congress Cataloging-in-Publication Data

The song index of the Enoch Pratt Free Library / [compiled] by Ellen Luchinsky.
        p.   cm. — (Garland reference library of social science ; vol. 1394)
    A finding aid to the collection of song books in the Enoch Pratt Free Library, Baltimore, Md.; dating from the early 20th century, with various librarians taking responsibility for the indexing.
    Includes bibliographical references (p.   ) and index.
    ISBN 0-8153-2918-0 (v. 1 and 2 : alk. paper)
    1. Songs—Indexes.   2. Enoch Pratt Free Library—Catalogs—Indexes.   I. Luchinsky, Ellen. II. Series.
ML128.S3L665   1998
016.78242—dc21   97–47313
                                            CIP
                                            MN

Printed on acid-free, 250-year-life paper
Manufactured in the United States of America

For Mark Allan Luchinsky
1974-1995
A light that shone briefly but ever so brightly

TABLE OF CONTENTS

Introduction

The *Song Index of the Enoch Pratt Free Library* is a long-term project of the Library's Fine Arts Department. It dates from the early twentieth century, with various librarians taking responsibility for indexing the song books as they arrived in the department. The index grew, at times haphazardly, until the late 1970s, with some control, but little editing. At that time it was noticed how heavily the index was used, and the librarian began to institute rules over what information was entered and how. It continued to expand, as it was put into an electronic database, to about 160,000 entires. This book is the outgrowth of that file.

The Enoch Pratt Free Library has a large collection of song books, upon which this *Index* is based. Every type of song book is collected, including all types of anthologies, school song books, hymnals, single composer, and multiple composers. There are also collections of songs in languages which include African, European, Native American, and Asian. Other anthologies include novelty songs, folk and popular songs, show tunes, children's songs, advertising, protest, and songs of all religions. There are also collections of classical songs including arias from operas and selections from oratorios, symphonies and other larger works.

The *Song Index* is a finding guide for songs of all types. It is not intended as a history of songs or a complete guide to composers or other information. Most of the books indexed herein are owned by the Enoch Pratt Free Library in Baltimore, Maryland. This collection of song books is important because of its wide scope.

The variety of songs available makes the collection useful to every type of musician, amateur and professional. While the Library does not collect every song book, it does attempt to collect every type of anthology. It is important to note that this index includes only songs found in books, not single signature music. In indexing the song books, it became necessary to define "song" in a more general way than the usual "words and music." For example, if a song book contained both songs and instrumental pieces, the latter were not omitted. With demand for popular themes, such as "The Love Theme from St. Elmo's Fire," this made sense. However, books with only instrumental pieces were not included.

Songs are a significant part of many people's lives. Meanings and memories can be attached to them which are deeply personal. For performers, finding just the right song can be important. For weddings, funerals, and other occasions, songs can be a source of celebration and comfort. The intent of this book is to join people with the songs they seek.

Acknowledgments

It is literally impossible to thank everyone involved in the creation of this book. The librarian who began the index is unknown, and the librarians who have worked on it through the decades remain anonymous.

However, the following people have helped tremendously in the recent history and deserve my deepest appreciation: Alprescia Rivers, Ruth Sundermeyer, Natalie Haskins and Daria Phair. Also very important to the project were Elaine Bradtke, Margaret Earickson, Marta Giles, James K. Dickson, Joseph Viviano, Jiton Davidson and especially the late Rita Hollins.

Special thanks go to Joan Stahl, who upon my request assigned the song index to me. Thanks also to John Sondheim, to Carla Hayden, who has been extraordinarily supportive, and to Averil Kadis for her advice. Special thanks to Jana Korman for her patience in editing and proofreading, and to Jeffrey Korman for lugging all those song books back and forth. I am also grateful to Barbara Glassmyer and Gordon Krabbe for the help on the financial and business side of the project.

Wayne Stoler of Letter Perfect has demonstrated great skill and patience in creating the electronic database from which this book was developed.

For their emotional support over a very long haul, my parents, siblings, and nieces and nephews have been wonderful. This book is dedicated to one of those nephews, who unfortunately will never see it.

Financial support for this project was contributed by the late Mrs. Henry A. Rosenberg of the Henry and Ruth Blaustein Rosenberg Foundation, Inc., by the late Lester Levy and the late Katherine Conger.

And finally, thank you Leo Balk and Marie Ellen Larcada, the editors at Garland Publishing, who have waited years for this, and only rarely sounded impatient.

How to Use This Book

The arrangement of the *Index* is alphabetical by title of the song. Each entry contains the song title, the name of the composer in parentheses, alternative titles which might also be checked, and the bibliography number of each book in which the song can be found.

The *Bibliography* is in alphabetical order by either the editor of the book, or if there is no editor, by the title. It gives publishing information for each book listed, with each listing numbered. If Library no longer owns the book, the entry is accompanied by an OCLC number. Readers who do not have access to the OCLC library computer network should contact their local library. There are also some books that might not be completely indexed. These are marked with an asterisk (*).

The *Composer Index* contains two types of entries. Over the years in which this *Index* was compiled, the first names of the composers were often omitted. Where the editor was able to identify individual composers, the full name is listed with those songs. However, many of the entries list the last name only.

The *Source Index* lists larger works from which the songs originated. These include not only stage and movie musicals, but also non-musicals which include songs, television shows, operas, oratorios, symphonies and other classical works, and any source which contains the song indexed.

To find a song, look for the bibliography number(s) next to each entry in the *Index* and find that number in the *Bibliography*. Once you have identified the song book needed, contact the local library, or the Enoch Pratt Free Library, Fine Arts Department, 400 Cathedral Street, Baltimore, Maryland 21201. The telephone number is (410) 396-5490. The fax number is (410) 396-1409. The Song Index has its own e-mail address, which is songs@mail.pratt.lib.md.us.

THE COMPOSERS

COMPOSERS

A 'Becket
See Shaw

Aarons
Capitalistic Boss
Horse With A Union Label, The

Aaronson
Loveliest Night Of The Year, The
Song Angels Sing, The

Abba
Nature Boy

Abbey
I Know Not What The Future Hath
I Worship Thee O Holy Ghost
Life's Railway To Heaven

Abbot
Love's Call'd A Dream

Abbott
Moonlighter, The
Shake You Down

Abdon
To The Loyal Soldier

Abelardo
My Native Land
National Heroes' Day
Song Of The Traveler, The

Abercrombie
Arcade
Foolish Door

Abernathy
Wonderful Time Up There, A

Abert
Romance D'Astorga

Able
Life Of Ages Richly Poured

Abrahams
He'd Have To Get Under Get Out
    And Get Under To Fix His
    Automobile
When The Grown Up Ladies Act
    Like Babies

Abrams & Muir
See Muir

Abreu
Tico Tico

Abt
Abendlied
Ave Maria
Barcarolle
Blissful Dreams Come Stealing O'Er
    Me
Blossoms Close At Eve, The
Class Song At Parting
Dawn
Dearest Now Good-Night
Departing Day
Embarrassment
Evening Song
God Be Our Guide
Good Night
Good Night Good Night
Gruss An Maria
He Giveth His Beloved Sleep

Abt (Cont.)
Ivy Song
Kathleen Aroon
Lesson Of Spring, The
Lo The Great Sun
Milde Dort Oben
Morn Hath Wak'd The World Again
Morning Early
My Native Land
New Year, The
Night
Not A Sparrow Falleth
O Ye Tears
Once Again The Day Hath Flown
Out Walking
Over The Stars
Over The Stars There Is Rest
Rosee Amere
Seek Not Afar For Beauty
Shadows Of Evening
Sonntag, Der
Sunday Morning
Young Postillion, The
Three Rousing Cheers
To Heaven
To Thy Temple I Repair
Toast, A
Ueber Den Sternen
Vater Du In Himmelsauen
Vergiss Ihn Nicht
Verlass Mich Nicht
Vineta
When The Swallows Homeward Fly
Where 'er I Go Thou Goest With Me
Why Should We Parted Be
Winter's Reign Is Past
With Happy Voices Ringing
Wollt Ihr Die Engelein Horen Im
    Chor

Ace
Ready Or Not

Achi
Sons Of The Stanford Red

Ackley
All The Way To Calvary
All Who Will Believe
All Will Be Right
Amazed
Are You Counting The Cost
At The End Of The Road
Be Not Discouraged
Because He Loved Me So
Behold The King
Better Each Day
Calvary
Church By The Side Of The Road,
    The
Drifting
Every Day I Need Thee More
Get Back To The Bible
Glory Of His Presence, The
God Understands

Ackley (Cont.)
God's Tomorrow
He Knows The Way
He Took My Place
He Will Not Let Me Fall
Heartaches
How You Will Love Him
Hymn Of Hope
I Am Coming Home
I Am Ready Are You
I Give Myself To Thee
I Love Jesus
I Never Walk Alone
I Shall Not Be Moved
I Would Be Like Jesus
I'll Decide For Jesus
I've Been Lifted
In The Service Of The King
Jesus I Am Coming Home
Jesus Is Coming Again
Jesus Is Sunshine
Jesus Keeps The Heart Right
Jesus Set The World To Singing
Jesus Will
Just Abide
Just Outside The Door
Land Where The Roses Never Fade
Lean On The Lord
Let My Faith Take Hold On Thee
Light Of His Wonderful Love, The
Love Incarnate
Memory, A
Mother's Prayers Have Followed Me
My Guiding Star
My Heart Belongs To Jesus
My Mother
My Only Hope
Nail In His Hand, A
Old Fashioned Faith, The
Only A Smile
Pardoning Grace
Praises Everywhere
Somebody Knows
Stand By America
Take Up Thy Cross
Tender Care
Under The Blood
Walking With Jesus
We Shall Always Be Happy Over
    There
When At Last We Say Good Bye
When Dreams Come True
When God Is Near
When He Died For Me
When I See The King
When You Know Jesus Too
Where Dreams Come True
Where I Found Him
Will You Be Found Up There
Would You Feel Lost In Bethlehem
You Need The Savior

Ackley & Ackley
Till The Whole World Knows
When I Kneel Down To Pray
Ackley, Alfred
He Lives
Ackley, Bentley
I Walk With The King
If Your Heart Keeps Right
Sunrise
Acosta & Belafonte
Bamba, La
Acqua
Villanelle
Acqua
Provencal Song
Acqua
Country Song, A
Villanelle
Actman
Tree In Tipperaray, A
Acuff
Precious Jewel, The
Adair
Will You Still Be Mine
Adam
Best Friend
Cantique De Noel
Christmas Song
Christmas Song, The
In Vacation
O Holy Night
Standchen
Adams
All In The Name Of Jesus
Artillerist's Oath, The
Bells Of St Mary's, The
Blue Alsatian Mountains
Blue Alsatian Mountains, The
By The Blue Alsatian Mountains
For There Is No Song
God Bless Our Native Land
Growing
Guide Of My Spirit
Have You Got The New Disorder
Heart Of A Sailor, The
Holy City, The
I Doubt It
Jolly Golfing Weather
Midshipmite
Midshipmite, The
Mona
Music Everywhere
Nancy Lee
Nearer My God To Thee
O Thou Almighty God
Pioneers
Portland Town
Praise The Lord
Quaker, The
Remember Now Thy Creator
Somewhere Along The Way
Star Of Bethlehem, The
Story House, The
Holy City, The
They All Love Jack

Adams (Cont.)
Warrior Bold, A
Where The Spirit Of The Lord Is
Young People's Army, The
Adams & Baer & Meyer
There Are Such Things
Adams & Kagna
Straight From The Heart
Adams & Vallance
Edge Of A Dream
Hearts On Fire
Heat Of The Night
Heaven
It's Only Love
One Night Love Affair
Run To You
Somebody
Summer Of '69
Victim Of Love
Adams & Vallance & Giraldo
Back To Paradise
Adams & Vallance & Warren
When The Night Comes
Adams & Vallance & Wayne & Stewart
Another Heartache
Adamson
I Love To Whistle
Adamson & Gordon & Youmans
Time On My Hands
Adcock
One Sole Baptismal Sign
Adderley
Never Say Yes
Nippon Soul
Teaneck
Work Song
Addison
Nero Wolfe TV Theme
Addrisi & Addrisi
Never My Love
Slow Dancin' Don't Turn Me On
Addy
Remember When
There Is No Christmas Like A Home Christmas
Adelson & Livingston
Ten Commandments, The
Ader
Cucaracha, La
Adeyemo & Phillips & Diamond
Object Of My Desire
Adkins
I'll Wish I Had Given Him More
Adler
Nothing More To Look Forward To
So Many Many Years Ago
What's Wrong With Me
Adler & Ross
Heart
Hernand's Hideaway
Hernando's Hideaway
Hey There
I'm Not At All In Love
No Soap No Hope No Mouse No House Blues, The

Adler & Ross (Cont.)
Rags To Riches
Shoeless Joe From Hannibal Mo
Small Talk
Steam Heat
Two Lost Souls
Whatever Lola Wants
Whatever Lola Wants Lola Gets
Admon
Behold This Bread
Bo-I Ha-Malka
Decked With Garlands
Adomian
Negro Mother To Her Child, A
Song To The Soldier
Adu & St John
Smooth Operator
Agay
For You My Love
Old Irish Blessing
Solemn Procession
Ager
There's Something In The Name Of Ireland
Tom Dick And Harry And Jack
Ager, Milton
Ain't She Sweet
Crazy Words Crazy Tune
Forgive Me
Happy Days Are Here Again
Happy Feet
I Wonder What's Become Of Sally
I'm The Last Of The Red Hot Mammas
Lovin' Sam
Mama Goes Where Papa Goes
Ager & Meyer
Everything Is Peaches Down In Georgia
Agter
Louisville Lou
Ahbez, Eden
Nature Boy
Ahle
Blessed Jesu Here We Stand
Blessed Jesus
Blessed Jesus At Thy Word
Blessed Jesus Here Are We
Book Of Books Our People's Strength
Christian Rise And Act Thy Creed
For A Season Called To Part
Gott Ist Getreu
On This Stone Now Laid With Prayer
Saviour Who Thy Life Didst Give
Sing My Soul His Wondrous Love
Thanksgiving
What Thou Wilt O Father Give
Zeuch Hin Mein Kind
Ahlert
It Must Be You
Love You Funny Thing

Ahlert, Fred
I Don't Know Why
I Don't Know Why I Just Do
I'd Love To Fall Asleep And Wake
    Up In My Mammy's Arms
I'll Follow You
I'll Get By
I'll Get By As Long As I Have You
Mean To Me
Moon Was Yellow, The

Ahlert & Crosby & Turk
Where The Blue Of The Night Meets
    The Gold Of The Day

Ahlert & Turk
Mean To Me
Walkin' My Baby Back Home

Ahlert & Young
I'm Gonna Sit Right Down And
    Write Myself A Letter

Ahlf
Lord Whom Winds And Seas Obey

Ahnfelt
Blott En Dag

Aiblinger
Jubilate Deo

Aide
Danube River, The
Maid Of The Mill, The

Ailau
Drowsy Waters

Ainger
Dives And Lazarus
Mary's Child

Ainsworth
Psalm 3

**Aitken & Waterman & Stock & Dallin &
Fahey & Woodw**
More Than Physical

Aitken & Waterman & Summer & Stock
This Time I Know It's For Real

Akeroyd
Behold Us Lord Before Thee Met

Akers
Lead Me Guide Me
Sweet Sweet Spirit

Akst
Travelin' Light

Akst, Harry
Am I Blue
Dinah

Akst & Whiting
Guilty

Aladar
Dialogue, A
Friend Of My Heart
Hajlik A Jegenye

Alau
One Two Three Four

Albanese
Au Bord D'une Fontaine
J'attends Le Soir

Albeniz
Del Salon En El Angulo Oscuro
Love's Own Star
Tango
Tango In D

Alberle
Saludemos La Patria Orgullosos
We're Devoted To Our Wondrous
    Country

Albert
Am Grabe Eines Fruhverstorbenen
Fruhjahrsliedchen
He Is Risen He Is Risen
Im Freien Zu Singen
Jugendmut
Keine Nacht Kein Tag Vergehet
Klage Eines Verliebten Schafers
Lesbia Mein Leben
Lob Der Freundschaft
Maid And The Butterfly, The
Tanzlied
Treue Liebe
Trinklied

Albert & Young
New Beginning, A

Albert, Heinrich
God Who Madest Earth And Heaven

Albert, Morris
Feelings

Albertine
Bandstand Boogie

Albrecht
Bird Calls

Albrecht & Gallop & Jurgens
Elmer's Tune

Albright
Come Thou Holy Spirit Bright
Father We Thank Thee Who Hast
    Planted
Look There The Christ Our Brother

Alcedo
Peru Himno Nacional

Alcock
Duke Or Priest
I Want To Dress
O Maker Of The Mighty Deep
Once In Arcadia
Pray Remember
Troy Town

Alcorn
All I Need Is Jesus

Aldema
Whither's Your Loved One Gone

Alden
Veeda, La

Aldrich
Christchurch Bells
Hark The Bonny Christ Church Bells
O Be Joyful In The Lord
Pals
Tom Jolly's Nose
When Matters Go Wrong

Aldrich, Ronnie
If I Only Had Wings

Aldridge
It Wouldn't Be Enough

Aldrich & Brasfield
No Gettin' Over Me

Aldridge & Brasfield
Holding Her And Loving You
Till You're Gone

Alejandro & Alejandra
Amor Acaba, El
Esa, A
Lagrimas

Alejandro & Magdalena
Esa Triste Guitarra
Lo Dudo
Quiero Dormir Cansado
Todo Se Derrumbo Dentro De Mi

Alexander
Hail Hail Nevonia
I've Already Won The War
Once In Royal David's City
Southern Soldier Boy, The
Stranger Star, The
Sweetheart From Venezuela
Theme From Please Don't Eat The
    Daisies
Theme From The Rounders
You Better Move On

Alexander & Crofter
Do No Sinful Action Speak No
    Angry Word

Alexander, Arthur
Anna

Alfano
Antica Ninna-Nanna Partenopea
Corro Come Il Cervo Muschiato
E Giunto Il Nostro Ultimo Autunno
Egli Mormoro Amor Mio Alza I Tuoi
    Occhi
Felicita
Finisci L'Ultimo Canto
Giorno Per Giorno
I Miei Piedi Son Stanchi
Lungo La Via Del Mare
Mama Il Giovane Principe
Melodia
Non Nascondere Il Secreto
Parlami Amor Mio
Perche Allo Spuntar Del Giorno
Perche Siedi La
Preghiera Alla Madonna
Scrivimi Amor Mio

Alford & Elvey
Come Ye Thankful People Come
Thanksgiving Hymn

Alfred & Allen
Rock And Roll Waltz, The

Alfred & Gibson
Huckle Buck, The

Alfred & Serno
That's It I Quit I'm Movin' On

Alguero
If She Should Come To You

Alison
Sourwood Mountain

Allan
Behind Those Swinging Doors
Strange Fruit
Allegri
Miserere
Allen
Ad Puerum
Alabama Victory Song
Alabama's Day
Any Rags
Ballad Of The Welfare Mother
Bedroom Ballad
Bit-O-Honey
Bury Me Not On The Lone Prarie
Cheer For Lsu
Chloe
Clouds And Sunshine
Confession
Cross And Crown
God Girt Her About With The
    Surges
Golden Days Are Coming Bye And
    Bye, The
Here's To The Women
Hiems
I Found A Friend
In The Valley Of Virginia
Iustitia Et Constantia
Jessie
Jesus United By Thy Grace
Le High Ho
Lullaby, A
Maid Of Athens
March On Cincinnati
Maryland Victory Song
Midnight Oil, The
My Phi Delta Theta Sweetheart
Now I Lay Me Down To Sleep
Orange And Blue, The
Orange And The Black, The
Pal Of My College Days
Pick The Wildwood Flower
Salty Dog
Should I Come Home
Someone Waits For You
Tearing Along
There's A Ship On The Sea
Vanderbilt Forever
Venerable Mother
Victory Song
Wa-Hoo
Whenever A Little Child Is Born
Winter And Summer
Allen & Alton & Vallance
What About Love
Allen & Anderson
I Go To Rio
Allen & Barry
I Honestly Love You
Allen & Cash
Fair Weather Friends
Allen & Hill
Kiss Of Fire
Kiss On My List

Allen & Lay & Lindsey
It Don't Hurt Me Half As Bad
Allen & McHan & Bayless
Pill, The
Allen & Powell
He Did It All For Me
Allen & Robbins & Sheafe
Washington And Lee Swing
Allen & Sager
Don't Cry Out Loud
Everything Old Is New Again
I'd Rather Leave While I'm In Love
Allen & Sheafe
Washington And Lee Swing
Allen, Chester
Praise Him Praise Him
Allen, George
Maitland
Must Jesus Bear The Cross Alone
Must Jesus Bear The Cross Along
Allen, Robert
Chances Are
Everybody Loves A Lover
Home For The Holidays
It's Not For Me To Say
Moments To Remember
No Not Much
Song For A Summer Night
There's No Place Like Home For The
    Holidays
Allen, Steve
Impossible
This Could Be The Start Of
    Something Big
Allen, Thomas
By The Watermelon Vine
Erie Canal, The
Allen, Thornton W.
Big C
Big Red Team, The
Blue And White
Boston University Victory Song
Bow Down To Washington
Brown Cheering Song, The
Cardinal Is Waving, The
Citadel Forever, The
Colgate Fight Song, The
College Years
Down The Field
Drink A Highball
Dukes Of Duquesne
Eyes Of Texas, The
Fair Harvard
Florida Our Alma Mater
For Boston
For Chicago
For Kansas
For The Honor Of Old Purdue
Hail St Mary's
Hail To Georgia
Hail To Old IU
Hail To The Orange
Kentucky Fight Fight Fight
Let's Cheer Again For Temple

Allen, Thornton W. *(Cont.)*
Lord Geoffrey Amherst
Maroon Forever
Matador Song, The
Men Of State
Michigan State Fight Song
Mingle Your Cheers
Mother Of Men
Washington And Lee Swing
Allende
Little Jar, The
Allentini
Sex Appeal
Aller & Esty
Take Me Home
Allison
Bennington Skirmish
Allison, Audrey
He'll Have To Go
Teen-Age Crush
Allison & Abner
Why Do You Have To Go
Allison & Allison
He'll Have To Go
Allison & Muir
Bedroom
Allison & Petty & Holly
Peggy Sue
That'll Be The Day
Allitsen
Lord Is My Light, The
Since We Parted
Song Of Thanksgiving
Song Of Thanksgiving, A
Allman
Nevertheless
Whippin' Post
Allman & Payne
Midnight Rider
Alman
Have You Heard
Worthy The Lamb
Almanac Singers
Belt-Line Girl
Deliver The Goods
Good Reuben James, The
Almaroh
Story Of Love, The
Alpern & Usher
T-U-R-T-L-E Power
Alsop
It's Only A Wee-Wee
My Body
Alster-Yardeni
Hod Ya-Netsah
Alstone, Alex
More
Symphony
Alstone & Bernet
Wise Man
Alter, Louis
Do You Know What It Means To
    Miss New Orleans
Dolores

Alter, Louis (Cont.)
Gotta Feelin' For You
Manhattan Serenade
My Kinda Love
Nina Never Knew
Rainbow On The River
Twilight On The Trail
You Turned The Tables On Me

Alterman & Wilensky
Kolaniyot

Alterman-Zaira
Layla Layla

Altfeld & Christian
Little Old Lady From Pasadena, The

Altman
New Yorker Trern

Altman, Arthur
All Or Nothing At All

Alvarez
Guatemala My Dear Land
Guatemale Feliz
Partida, La

Alves & Dean & Murrah
Southern Star

Alwood
Unclouded Day, The

Alzamora
Little Strawberry Girl, The

Ambrose
If Love Were What The Rose Is
O Come To My Heart Lord Jesus
One Sweetly Solemn Thought
Sweet Is The Solemn Voice That
Calls
Thou Didst Leave Thy Throne

Amdahl
Jorgen Hattemaker
Mari Du Bedare
Marte Og Baldrian

Amerson
Black Woman

Ames
Fire And Ice
Heighho
Musical Yak, The
Patch Of Old Snow, A
Toast, A
When I Get Up In The Morning

Amici
Leif Ericsson

Amiran
Mayim Mayim

Amner
Lift Up Your Heads
Lift Up Your Heads O Gates

Amps
If On A Quiet Sea
O Holy Spirit God
O Saviour Of Our Race

Amram
Theme From Splendor In The Grass

Amstutz
Jesus

Anagni
Ninna Nanna

Anchors
When Came In Flesh The Incarnate
Word

Anderle & Anderle
Greatest Performance Of My Life,
The

Andersen
Holy Night
Marching Down The Avenoo
Rolling Home

Anderson
Get A Little Dirt On Your Hands
Gustavus Adolphus
Key-Stone
Let It Rock
Long Distance Runaround
Lost In The Feeling
Lovely Hula Hands
Malihini Mele
Mele Kalikimaka
More Than A Bedroom Thing
My Life Throw It Away If I Want To
Quits
Shoot First Ask Questions Later
Slippin' Away
Sometimes
Thank God I've Made It
Tip Of My Fingers, The
Whatever Happened To Old
Fashioned Love
Wonderous Stories
World's Desire, The
Yours Is No Disgrace

Anderson & Bruford & Howe & Squire
Apocalypse
Preacher The Teacher, The

Anderson & Delmore
I Wish I Could Write You A Song
Swingin'

Anderson & Foster
Time And A Word

Anderson & Holt
God's Greatest Gift
How Often Do We Say Thank God
There's An Ever Open Door

Anderson & Howard
I Never Once Stopped Loving You

Anderson & Howe
Close To The Edge
I Get Up I Get Down
Roundabout
Seasons Of Man
Total Mass Retain

Anderson & Howe & Moraz & Squire & White
Gates Of Delirium, The
Sound Chaser
To Be Over

Anderson & Howe & Squire
And You And I

Anderson & Howe & Squire & Wakeman
Ancient, The

Anderson & Howe & Squire & White & Wakeman
Remembering, The
Revealing Science Of God, The
Ritual

Anderson & Howe & Wakeman
Siberian Khatru

Anderson & Kelly
Somewhere Down The Line

Anderson & Koller
Will It Be Love By Morning

Anderson & Squire
Dear Father

Anderson & Vangelis
I Hear You Now

Anderson & Weeks
I Wonder Why

Anderson, Bill
River Boat

Anderson, Leroy
Belle Of The Ball
Blue Tango
Forgotten Dreams
Serenata
Sleigh Ride
Syncopated Clock, The

Anderson, R. Alex
Cockeyed Mayor Of Kaunakakai,
The

Andersson & Anderson & Ulvaeus
Dancing Queen
Fernando
Knowing Me Knowing You
Name Of The Game, The
Ring Ring
SOS

Andersson & Rice & Ulvaeus
I Know Him So Well
One Night In Bangkok

Andersson & Ulvaeus
Does Your Mother Know
Take A Chance On Me
Winner Takes It All, The

Andino
Seis Chorreao

Andre
Angels Guard Over All
Rheinweinlied

Andree
Da Lachelt Nun Wieder Der Himmel

Andreoli & Crane
Harem Holiday

Andrews
Kitchen Kalendar, The
Radiant Morn Hath Passed Away,
The
Sea-Fever

Andrews & Davis & Henderson & Uniman
Long Lonely Nights

Andriessen
Divine Praises
Earth Is Full Of The Goodness Of
Christ, The
O Lord With Wondrous Mystery
Androzzo
Babe In The Woods
If I Can Help Somebody
Andulko
Goose Girl, The
Anerio
Christus Factus Est
Angel
Whirly Girl
Angelle & Reid
Love Over Old Times
Angerer
Columbia Columbia
Anglin
Jealousy
Anglin & Wright & Anglin
Ashes Of Love
Angus
Look Up America
Anka, Paul
Diana
Everything's Been Changed
Having My Baby
How Can Anything Be Beautiful
After You
It Doesn't Matter Anymore
Let Me Get To Know You
Lonely Boy
Longest Day, The
One Man Woman One Woman Man
Papa
Puppy Love
Put Your Head On My Shoulder
She's A Lady
Something About You
This Is Your Song
You Are My Destiny
Anka & Carson
Johnny's Theme
Anka & Foster
Hold Me 'Til The Mornin' Comes
Anka & Gosh
We Made It Happen
Anka & Harris
Bring The Wine
Hey Girl
I'm Not Anyone
Jubilation
Love Is A Lonely Song
Anschutz
Io Triumphe
Anstruther
Try Again
Ant & Cymone & Pirroni
Room At The Top
Ant & Pirroni
Antmusic
Goody Two Shoes
Strip

Antes
Go Congregation Go
Anthony
No Power Of My Own
Where Is The Profit
You're Something Special To Me
Anthony & Auletti
Bunny Hop, The
Anthony & Morrison
Midnight Angel
Anthony & O'Brien
Living By Dying
Seedtime And Harvest
Antoinette
Return To France, The
Appelbaum, Stan
Pan Am Makes The Goin' Great
Appenzeller
Je Ne Me Puis D'aimer
Appice & Savigar & Hitchings
Young Turks
Applebaum
Viceroy Gives You All The Taste All
The Time
Appleford
O Lord All The World Belongs To
You
Applegate
Goodbye My Coney Island Baby
Appleton
Mischievous Brownies
Arata
Dance, The
Arberg
Barbershopping Reaches Ev'rywhere
Arcadelt
D'un Extreme Regret
Give Ear Unto My Prayer
Hear Thou My Prayer O Lord
Je Ne Me Confesseray Point
Je Ne Scay Que C'est Qu'il Me Fault
Je Ne Suis Pas Si Sot
Je Ne Veux Plus A Mon Mal
Consentir
Quand Viendra La Clarte
S'infinita Bellezza
Arcadelt, Jacques
Ave Maria
Archangelsky
Glory To God
Hear My Prayer
Nunc Dimittis
O Gladsome Light
O Light Divine
Archer
Easter Secret, An
Magic Vine, The
October's Party
Sleepy Maple Trees, The
Soup Song
Volunteer Boys, The
Archer & Atkins
Would Jesus Wear A Rolex

Archer, Harry
I Love You
Suppose I Had Never Met You
Arditi
Speak
Arditi, Luigi
Bacio, Il
Kiss, The
Kiss Waltz, The
Arensky
Autumn
Bow Down Thine Ear O Lord
But Lately In Dance I Embraced Her
Crystal Brook, The
Eagle, The
Has Your Heart Ever Known
Let The Questions Be
Mystic Stars, The
To Echoes Of Music We Dance
Argent, Rod
She's Not There
Tell Her No
Time Of The Season
Argent & White
Hold Your Head Up
Arkwright
Captive Knight, The
Arlen, Harold
Ac-Cent-Tchu-Ate The Positive
Ain' It De Truth
Andiamo
Anyplace I Hang My Hat Is Home
As Long As I Live
Between The Devil And The Deep
Blue Sea
Blues In The Night
Buds Won't Bud
Circus Day
Cocoanut Sweet
Come Rain Or Come Shine
Ding Dong The Witch Is Dead
Dissertation On The State Of Bliss
Don't Like Goodbyes
Down With Love
Eagle And Me, The
Evelina
Fancy Meeting You
For Every Man There's A Woman
Fun To Be Fooled
Game Of Poker
Get Happy
God's Country
Goose Never Be A Peacock
Guido's Scale
Halloween
Happiness Is A Thing Called Joe
Happy As The Day Is Long
Happy With The Blues
Hit The Road To Dreamland
Hooray For Love
House Of Flowers
I Gotta Right To Sing The Blues

Arlen, Harold (Cont.)
I Had A Love Once
I Had Myself A True Love
I Love A New Yorker
I Love A Parade
I Never Has Seen Snow
I Wonder What Became Of Me
I've Got The World On A String
If I Only Had A Brain
Ill Wind
Ill Wind You're Blowin' Me No
    Good
In The Shade Of The New Apple
    Tree
It Was Written In The Stars
It's Only A Paper Moon
It's So Nice To Have A Man Around
    The House
June Comes Around Every Year
Kickin' The Gong Around
Last Night When We Were Young
Legalize My Name
Let's Fall In Love
Let's Take A Walk Around The
    Block
Let's Take The Long Way Home
Life's Full Of Consequence
Like A Straw In The Wind
Little Biscuit
Little Bug
Little Drops Of Rain
Lose That Long Face
Lullaby
Lydia The Tattooed Lady
Man That Got Away, The
Moanin' In The Mornin'
Money Cat, The
Morning After, The
My Shining Hour
Neighbors
One For My Baby
One For My Baby And One More
    For The Road
Out Of This World
Over The Rainbow
Paris Is A Lonely Town
Pretty To Walk With
Promise Me Not To Love Me
Push De Button
Right As The Rain
Satan's Li'l Lamb
Says Who Says You Says I
Silent Spring, The
Sleepin' Bee, A
So Long Big Time
Stormy Weather
That Old Black Magic
That's A Fine Kind O' Freedom
There's A Sweet Wind Blowin' My
    Way
This Time The Dream's On Me
Today I Love Ev'rybody

Arlen, Harold (Cont.)
Two Ladies In De Shade Of De
    Banana Tree
Wail Of The Reefer Man
Watch Your Step
We're Off To See The Wizard
What Good Does It Do Now
What's Good About Goodbye
When The Boys Come Home
When The Sun Comes Out
When The Wind Blows South
Who Will It Be When The Time
    Comes
With The Sun Warm Upon Me
Woman's Prerogative, A
You're A Builder Upper
You're The Cure For What Ails Me
Armand
Clouds Have Risen Over The City
Armato & Cutler
What Were We Thinking Of
Armbruster
Theme From National Velvet
Armenia
Kher Pan
Armer & Badazz
Rise
Armes
Show Me Thy Hands Blessed Jesus
Soon May The Last Glad Song Arise
Armitage
Lightning Bug
My Morning Star
Stop Look Listen
Two Friends
What I Like
Armstrong
Can't You See I'm Lonely
Do No Sinful Action
Mountain Song Of The Winds
Rose Of Honolulu
Sweet Adeline
Armstrong, Harry
Nellie Dean
Armstrong, Henry
You're The Flower Of My Heart
You're The Flower Of My Heart
    Sweet Adeline
Armstrong & Raye
Just For A Thrill
Arnatt
From God Christ's Deity Came Forth
Arnaud
Bright Summer Days
Bugler's Dream
Arndt, Felix
Nola
Now To Heaven Our Prayer
    Ascending
Arne
A-Hunting We Will Go
Another Year Of Setting Suns

Arne (Cont.)
Bacchus God Of Mirth And Wine
Blow Blow Thou Winter Wind
Buzz Quoth The Blue Fly
By Dimpled Brook
By The Gaily Circling Glass
Cockfight
Come Away Death
Despairing Beside A Clear Stream
Fresh And Strong The Breeze Is
    Blowing
Hark To The Curfew
In Infancy
Jesus I Love Thy Charming Name
Let Zion's Watchmen All Awake
Lo He Comes With Clouds
    Descending
Miller Of Mansfield, The
Now Phoebus Sinketh In The West
O For A Heart To Praise My God
O For A Thousand Tongues
O For A Thousand Tongues To Sing
O Worship The King
Polly Willis
Prostrate Dear Jesus At Thy Feet
Punch
Rubecula
Shepherd, The
Shepherd's Song, The
Soldier Tir'd, The
Soldier Tired, The
Song Of Thanksgiving, A
Spirit Divine
Stand The Omnipotent Decree
Sycamore Shade, The
Thou Soft Flowing Avon
Topsails Shiver In The Wind, The
Under The Greenwood Tree
Water Parted
Water Parted From The Sea
When Daisies Pied
When Daisies Pied And Violets Blue
When Forced From Dear Hebe To
    Go
When I Can Read My Title Clear
When Icicles Hang By The Wall
When Youth's Sprightly Flood
Where The Bee Sucks
Which Is The Properest Day To
    Drink
Which Is The Properest Day To Sing
While You Here Do Snoring Lie
Arne, Michael
Lass With The Delicate Air, The
Arne, Thomas
Am I A Soldier
Am I A Soldier Of The Cross
Arlington
Rule Britannia
Shakespeare's Carol
This Is The Day The Lord Hath
    Made
Arnheim & Tobias & Lemare
Sweet And Lovely

Arnkeitner
Butterfly Waltz
Arnold
Amo Amas
C-H-R-I-S-T-M-A-S
Denison Marching Song
Down And Out Blues
Haste Thee Nymph
He's Got The Whole World In His
  Hands
Highlands Of Heaven
I Wish You Would
John Ran
Milk Cow Blues
No Place To Hide
Sleepyhead
Star Spangled Banner, The
Wayworn Traveller, The
Three Toasts
Arnold & Fowler & Hall
That's How Much I Love You
Arnold & Martin & Morrow
Can't Smile Without You
Let's Be Friends
Arnold & Nelson & Nelson
Will Santy Come To Shanty Town
Arnold, Malcolm
River Kwai March, The
Arnold, Samuel
Way-Worn Traveller, The
Arons
Love's Woe
Aroztegui
Champagne Tango
Arpad
Ossze Tudnek Csokolgatni
Valakinek Muzsikalnak
Valamikor Szerettelek
Arrulo
Lullaby
Art
O Lord Most Holy
Arthur
My Trusty Trot
Vive Purdue
Arthurs
Little Of What You Fancy Does You
  Good, A
Arthurs & Lee
Josh-U-Ah
Aruic
Song From Moulin Rouge, The
Arzonia, Joe
Preacher And The Bear, The
Asaf & Hirsh
Perach Halilach
Asaf & Seltzer
Daber Elai Bifrachim
Ascher
Peace Perfect Peace
Ascher, Joseph
Alice Where Art Thou
Ash & Haskins & Haskins
So Alive

Ashford
Crossing The Bar
My Task
They Who Seek The Throne Of
  Grace
Ashford & Simpson
Ain't No Mountain High Enough
Ain't Nothing Like The Real Thing
I'll Be There For You
Landlord
Onion Song, The
Reach Out And Touch
Reach Out And Touch Somebody's
  Hand
Remember Me
Solid
Surrender
Uh Uh Ooh Ooh Look Out Here It
  Comes
You Ain't Livin' Till You're Lovin'
You're All I Need To Get By
Your Precious Love
Ashford & Simpson & Armstead
I Don't Need No Doctor
Ashford, Emma
My Task
Ashley
Little Sadie
Ashley & Singleton
Laura
Laura What's He Got That I Ain't
  Got
Mental Journey
**Ashman & Gorman & Barbarossa &
Lyin**
Do You Wanna Hold Me
Ashman & Zeira
Ad Or Haboker
Ashwander
Peggy The Pearl Of Pensacola
Asling
Be Not Too Late
Astley
Giving Up On Love
She Wants To Dance With Me
Astol
Borinquena, La
Hymn National De Puerto Rico
Astorga
Immago Tua, L'
Astrop & Shreeve & Harris
Touch Me
Touch Me I Want Your Body
Atchley
New Year
Tender Care
Atherton
Boreen
Oh Like A Queen
Wing Tee Wee
Atherton, John
Brylcreem A Little Dab 'll Do Ya

Atkins
Centipede Boogie
Hark My Soul It Is The Lord
Atkinson
Dear Old Yale
Floating 'Mid The Lilies
Great Truths Are Portions Of The
  Soul
I Am Thinking Love Of Thee
Mrs Craigin's Daughter
Not Worthy Lord To Gather Up The
  Crumbs
O Thou Great Friend To All The
  Sons Of Men
Party At Odd Fellow's Hall, The
Spirit Of God
Spirit Of God Descend Upon My
  Heart
Toboggan Song, A
Violet, The
Atkinson
College Ties Can Ne'er Be Broken
Atterbury
He'll Never Haunt Ye
Hot Cross Buns
Sweet Enslaver
Attey
Sweet Was The Song
Attwood
Creator Spirit By Whose Aid
Teach Me O Lord
Turn Thee Again O Lord
Turn Thy Face From My Sins
Aturov
Song Of The Far Eastern Partisans
Atwood
Upon A Lowly Manger
Auber
Beats There A Heart
Fishermen's Chorus
On Yonder Rock
On Yonder Rock Reclining
Parisienne, La
Romanze Der Zerline
Sail Boat, The
They Who On The Lord Rely
Aubert
On The Railroad Train
Aubrey
Gifts
Power In The Name Of Jesus
Audran
Bob Up Serenely
Coaching Song
Gobble Duet
Gobble Duet, The
Legend Of The Mascots
Now All Is Safely Over
Waltz Song
When In Your Eyes I Look
Audran, Edmond
Torpedo And The Whale, The
Aufderheide
Totally Different Rag, A

Augusto
Bless'd Land Of Love And Liberty
Aunapu
Seminole Indians Of Florida
Auric
Song From Moulin Rouge, The
Austin
Day By Day
Leander
Living On Love
Austin & Bergere
How Come You Do Me Like You Do
Austin & Jordan
Is You Is Or Is You Ain't My Baby
Austin & Lomax
Hey Liley Liley Lo
Austin & Martin
Tonight We Love
Austin & McHugh & Mills
When My Sugar Walks Down The
Street
Austin & Sapaugh
Try A Little Kindness
Austin & Shilkret
Lonesome Road, The
Autry, Gene
You're The Only Star In My Blue
Heaven
Autry & Haldeman
Here Comes Santa Claus
Autry & Pfrimmer & Burgess
Nestor The Long-Eared Christmas
Donkey
Autry & Rose
Tears On My Pillow
Autry & Whitley
Back In The Saddle Again
Avery
Happy Birds
I've Got A Pain In My Sawdust
Song Of The Bell
Avison
Shout The Glad Tidings
Shout The Glad Tidings Exultingly
Sing
Avsec & Iris & Hoenes
Tough World
Axton, Hoyt
Joy To The World
Never Been To Spain
Axton & Durden & Presley
Heartbreak Hotel
Axton & Jackson
No No Song
Axton & Ramsey
Greenback Dollar
Aychel
In Der Kuznye
Ayer
G I Joe
Ayer, Nat
If You Were The Only Girl
If You Were The Only Girl In The
World
Oh You Beautiful Doll

Aylward, Florence
Beloved It Is Morn
Azevedo, Waldyr
Delicado
Aznavour, Charles
And I In My Chair
For Mama
Happy Anniversary
How Sad Venice Can Be
How To Write A Song
I Will Warm Your Heart
It Will Be My Day
Our Love My Love
Plus Bleu Que Tes Yeux
She
Take Me Away
Viens Au Creux De Mon Epaule
Yesterday When I Was Young
You've Got To Learn
Aznavour & Chauvigny
Young Girl, A
Aznavour & Roche
Paris Is At Her Best In May
Poker
Azpiazu
Por Tus Ojos Negros
Babcock
Bryan Leads The Way
Doggone Cowboy
Worlds Fair Rag
Babcock & Sheppard
This Is My Father's World
Baby Mine
Illinois
Babyface
Girlfriend
Roni
Babyface & Reid
Every Little Step
Babyface & Reid & Simmons
Don't Be Cruel
Lover In Me, The
Superwoman
Way You Love Me, The
Babyface & Simmons
In The Mood
My My My
Babyface & Smith
Whip Appeal
Bacage & Piron
Mama's Gone Goodbye
Bach
Ach Gott Und Herr
Ach Gott Vom Himmel Sieh' Darein
Ach Gott Wie Manches Herzeleid
Ach Lieben Christen Seid Getrost
Ach Wie Fluchtig
Ach Wie Fluchtig Ach Wie Nichtig
Air On The G String
All Things Serve Thee
Alle Menschen Mussen Sterben
Allein Gott In Der Hoh' Sei Ehr'
Alleluia

Bach (*Cont.*)
And Now To The Drone Of The
Dudelsack
Arioso
As We Leave This Friendly Place
Auf Christi Himmelfahrt Allein
Aus Liebe Will Mein Heiland
Sterben
Aus Tiefer Noth Schrei Ich Zu Dir
Bache Munter Mein Gemuthe
Bagpipe Chorus
Be Thou Exalted O My God
Be Thou With Me
Begluckt Heerde
Beside The Flood Of Babylon
Beside Thy Cradle
Beside Thy Cradle Here I Stand
Bist Du Bei Mir
Blessed Christ Is Risen Today, The
Blessed Redeemer
Break Forth O Beauteous Heavenly
Light
By Sweet Waters
Child Is Born In Bethlehem, A
Choral
Choral Grace
Christ Jesus Lay In Death's Strong
Bands
Christ Lag In Todesbanden
Christ Unser Herr Zum Jordan Kam
Christe Du Lamm Gottes
Christmas Chorale
Christum Wir Sollen Loben Schon
Christus Der Uns Selig Macht
Come Dearest Lord
Come One And All With Right Good
Will
Come Pure Hearts In Joyful Measure
Come Sing With Us
Come Sweet Death
Come Sweet Peace
Come Sweet Repose
Come Thou O Come
Come Thou Oh Come
Come With Us O Blessed Jesus
Commit Thou All That Grieves Thee
Commit Thy Ways O Pilgrim
Cossack's Farewell
Crucifixus
Cum Sancto Spiritu
Darzu Ist Erschienen Der Sohn
Gottes
Deck Thyself My Soul With
Gladness
Dir Dir Jehovah Will Ich Singen
Du Hirte Israel
Durch Adams Fall Ist Ganz Verderbt
Duteous Day Now Closeth
Duteous Day Now Closeth, The
Dutious Day, The
Each Blade Of Grass
Erfreut Euch Ihr Herzen
Erhalt' Uns Herr Bei Deinem Wort

Bach *(Cont.)*

Ermuntre Dich Mein Schwacher
  Geist
Erschienen Ist Der Herrlich' Tag
Es Ist Genug Herr Wenn Es Dir
  Gefallt
Flosst Mein Heiland
For The Beauty Of The Earth
Freu' Dich Sehr O Meine Seele
Freuet Euch Ihr Christen
Freut Euch Und Jubilirt
From East To West
From God Shall Naught Divide Me
From Ill Do Thou Defend Me
Gelobet Seist Du Jesu Christ
Gloria In Excelsis Deo
Go To Dark Gethsemane
God Is My Strong Salvation
Golden Sun Streaming
Good News From Heaven
Gott Des Himmels Und Der Erden
Gott Ist Mein Lied
Gott Wie Gross Ist Deine Gute
Grant Us To Do With Zeal
Great God Of Nations
Great God We Praise Your Holy
  Name
He That Is Down
Herr Christ Der Ein'ge Gottes-Sohn
Herr Wie Du Willt
Herzlich Thut Mich Verlangen
Holy Holy Holy Lord
How Bright Appears The Morning
  Star
How Brightly Beams The Morning
  Star
How Sleep The Brave
Hush My Dear
Hush My Dear Lie Still And Slumber
I Got Me Flowers
Ich Dank' Dir Lieber Herre
Ich Freue Mich In Dir
Ich Habe Genug
Ich Halte Treulich Still
Ich Steh' An Deiner Krippe Hier
If Fortune You Would Know
If Thou Art Near
If Thou Be Near
If Thou My Heart Wilt Give Me
If You Are Near
In Dich Hab' Ich Gehoffet Herr
In Dulci Jubilo
In Steadfast Faith I Stand
In Washington's Day
Ist Gott Mein Schild Und
  Helfersmann
Jesu Der Du Meine Seele
Jesu Joy Of Man's Desiring
Jesu Leiden Pein Und Tod
Jesu Meine Freude
Jesu Meine Freude Jesus Priceless
  Treasure
Jesu Meiner Seele Wonne

Bach *(Cont.)*

Jesu Meines Glaubens Zier
Jesu Nun Sei Gepreiset
Jesus Is My Joy My All
Jesus Joy Of Man's Desiring
Jesus Lying In The Manger
Jesus Meine Zuversicht
Jesus My Strength My Hope
Jesus Schlaft Was Soll Ich Hoffen
Jesus Shepherd Be Thou Near Me
Joy
Judge Eternal Throned In Splendor
King Of Love My Shepherd Is, The
Klage Am Kreuze Jesu
Komm Gott Schopfer Heiliger Geist
Komm Heiliger Geist Herre Gott
Komm Jesu Komm
Komm O Komm Du Geist Des
  Lebens
Komm Susser Tod
Kommt Her Zu Mir Spricht Gottes
  Sohn
Let Us With A Gladsome Mind
Lieben Sonne Licht Und Pracht, Der
Liebster Gott Wann Werd' Ich
  Sterben
Liebster Herr Jesu
Liebster Immanuel Herzog Der
  Frommen
Lobe Den Herren Den Machtigen
  Konig Der Ehren
Lobt Gott Ihr Christen All Gleich
Lord Bless You, The
Lord Of Our Life
Loving Father Ever Waiting
Mighty Fortress Is Our God, A
Mein Glaubiges Herze Frohlocke
Meine Seel' Erhebt Den Herren
Meine Seufzer Meine Tranen
Meinen Jesum Lass' Ich Night
Minuet
Mit Fried' Und Freud' Ich Fahr'
  Dahin
My Heart Ever Faithful
My Spirit Be Joyful
Neugebor'ne Kindelein, Das
Nicht So Traurig Nicht So Sehr
Now All The Woods Are Sleeping
Now Let All The Heavens Adore
  Thee
Now Let Ev'ry Tongue Adore Thee
Now Let Every Tongue Adore Thee
Now Let Your Happy Voices Ring
Now Thank We All Our God
Now That The Daylight Fills The
  Sky
Now Yield We Thanks And Praise
  To Christ
Nowell Nowell
Nun Bitten Wir Den Heiligen Geist
Nun Danket Alle Gott
Nun Komm Der Heiden Heiland
Nun Lasst Uns Gott Dem Herren
Nun Lob' Mein Seel Den Herren

Bach *(Cont.)*

O Christ The Heaven's Eternal King
O Ewigkeit Du Donnerwort
O Finstre Nacht
O Food To Pilgrims Given
O God Beneath Thy Guiding Hand
O God From Heaven Look Thou
  Down
O God Who Art The Only Light
O Gott Du Frommer Gott
O Grosser Gott Von Macht
O Holy City Seen Of John
O Holy Father
O Infant Sweet
O Jesu So Kind
O Joyous Easter Morning
O Lord Do Not Forget Me
O Love That Casts Out Fear
O My Deir Hert
O Rejoice Ye Christians Loudly
O Sacred Head Sore Wounded
O Saving Victim Opening Wide
O Saviour Sweet
O Spirit Of Life O Spirit Of God
O Welt Ich Muss Dich Lassen
Oh Blest The House Whate'er Befall
On Good Friday
Our God To Whom We Turn When
  Weary
Praise The Lord Rise Up Rejoicing
Praise The Lord Through Every
  Nation
Praise To God
Prayer For Peace
Preise Jerusalem Den Herrn
Puer Natus In Bethlehem
Rejoice Ye Pure In Heart
Schafe Konnen Sicher Weiden
Schauet Doch Und Sehet
Schmucke Dich O Liebe Seele
Schwing' Dich Auf Zu Deinem Gott
Sehet Wir Gehn Hinauf Gen
  Jerusalem
Sei Lob Und Ehr' Dem Hochsten
  Gut
Seufzer Tranen Kummer Not
Sheep And Lambs May Safely Graze
Sheep May Always Graze
Sheep May Safely Graze
Sinfonia
Singen Wir Aus Herzensgrund
Sleepers Wake
Sleepers Wake A Voice Astounds Us
So Du Mit Deinem Munde Bekennest
  Jesum
Song Of Praise
Songs Of Thankfulness And Praise
Spacious Firmament On High, The
Sterbelied
Thanksgiving
There's A Wideness In God's Mercy
Thou To Whom The Sick And Dying
Thy Sweets

Bach (*Cont.*)
Thy Will O Lord Be Done
To Thee Alone Be Glory
To Thee Jehovah
To Thee O Jehovah
Turf Shall Be My Fragrant Shrine,
The
Valet Will Ich Dir Geben
Vater Unser Im Himmelreich
Verleih' Uns Frieden Gnadiglich
Von Gott Will Ich Nicht Lassen
Wachet Auf Ruft Uns Die Stimme
Wachet Betet
War'gott Nicht Mit Uns Diese Zeit
Warum Betrubst Du Dich Mein Herz
Warum Sollt' Ich Mich Denn
Gramen
Was Gott Thut Das Ist Wohlgetan
Was Gott Thut Das Ist Wohlgethan
Was Mein Gott Will Das G'Scheh'
Allzeit
We Give Thee But Thine Own
We Saw Thee In Thy Balmy Nest
Welt Ade Ich Bin Dein Mude
Wenn Mein Stundlein Vorhanden Ist
Wer Weiss Wie Nahe Mir Mein Ende
Wes Mein Gott Wic, Das G'Scheh'
All-Zeit
What Tongue Can Tell Thy
Greatness Lord
When Call'd By Thee I Gain Thy
Portal
When Evening Shadows Fold Us
When To Her Lute Corinna Sings
Where Man Was All Too Marred
While Bagpipes Play
Wie Schon Leuchtet Der
Morgenstern
Wie Sohl Ist Mir O Freund Der
Seelen
Wilt Thou Forgive That Sin
Wilt Thou To Me Thy Heart Give
Wir Christenleut'
Wo Gott Der Herr Nicht Bei Uns
Halt
Bach & Gounod
Ave Maria
Prelude In C Major
Bach & Hintze
Watchman Tell Us Of The Night
Bacharach, Burt
Alfie
Always Something There To Remind
Me
Any Day Now
Any Old Time Of The Day
Anyone Who Had A Heart
April Fools, The
Blob, The
Blue Guitar
Blue On Blue
Casino Royale
Christmas Day
Close To You

Bacharach, Burt (*Cont.*)
Do You Know The Way To San Jose
Don't Make Me Over
Green Grass Starts To Grow, The
House Is Not A Home, A
I Say A Little Prayer
I'll Never Fall In Love Again
Look Of Love, The
Lost Horizon
Magic Moments
Make It Easy On Yourself
Man Who Shot Liberty Valance, The
Message To Michael, A
My Little Red Book
One Less Bell To Answer
Only Love Can Break A Heart
Paper Mache
Promises Promises
Raindrops Keep Fallin' On My Head
Reach Out For Me
Rome Will Never Leave You
This Empty Place
This Guy's In Love With You
Tower of Strength
Trains And Boats And Planes
Twenty Four Hours From Tulsa
Walk On By
What The World Needs Now Is Love
What's New Pussycat
Whoever You Are I Love You
Windows Of The World, The
Wishin' And Hopin'
Wives And Lovers
World Is A Circle, The
You'll Never Get To Heaven
You'll Never Get To Heaven If You
Break My Heart
Bacharach & David
To Wait For Love
Bacharach & Sager
Love Power
On My Own
That's What Friends Are For
Bacharach & Sager & Cross
Chance For Heaven, A
Bacharach & Sager & Cross & Allen
Arthur's Theme
Bacharach & Sager & Roberts
Love Always
Making Love
Bacharach & Williams
Baby It's You
Bachelet
Chere Nuit
Bachelet & Roy
Emmanuelle
Bachman, Randy
Takin' Care Of Business
Bachmann
Pearl Of Madrid, The
Bachmetieff
Cossack's Lullaby

Backer, Bill
If You've Got The Time
If You've Got The Time We've Got
The Beer
It's The Real Thing
Things Go Better With Coke
Backer & Cook & Greenway & Davis
I'd Like To Teach The World To
Sing In Perfect Harmony
Bacon
And This Of All My Hopes
Commonplace, The
Bacon & Tree
You Could Be The One Woman
Badalamenti
Love Theme From Cousins
You'll Come Back You Always Do
Baer
Gee But You're Swell
It's The Girl
Lucky Lindy
Picture From Life's Other Side, A
Baer & Caesar & Schuster
Blue Hawaii
Baer, Abel
June Night
My Mother's Eyes
Baez, Joan
Diamonds And Rust
Song For David, A
Bagdasarian, Ross
Chipmunk Song, The
Bagdasarian & Saroyan
Come On-A My House
Baggett
We Really Want To Thank You Lord
Bagley, E. E.
National Emblem
Bahler, Tom
She's Out Of My Life
Baiggs
Day By Day Dear Lord
Baildon
My Dog And My Gun
Bailes & Bailes
I Want To Be Loved
Bailey
9,999,999 Tears
Dream On My Baby
Ever In Praise
Bailey & Collins & East
Easy Lover
Bailey & Currie
Get That Love
Nothing In Common
Sugar Daddy
Bailey & Currie & Leeway
Hold Me Now
King For A Day
Lay Your Hands On Me
Lies
Love On Your Side
Bain
How Lovely Is Thy Dwelling Place

Baines
    Bagpipe Man, The
    Oh How Lovely
Bainton
    Christmas Carol, A
    Old Winter
    Ye Little Birds That Sit And Sing
Baird
    Keep Your Hands To Yourself
Bairead
    Preab San Ol
Baker
    Art Thou Weary Art Thou Languid
    Art Thou Weary Heavy Laden
    Burman Lover, The
    Do What You Like
    Early In The Mornin'
    Good Assassination Should Be Quiet,
        A
    Happy The Man That Finds The
        Grace
    Jeannie Marsh On Cherry Valley
    Jesus The Calm That Fills My Breast
    Jesus Thou Joy Of Loving Hearts
    Just As I Am Without One Plea
    Let All The World
    Lonely
    Lord Guard And Guide The Men
        Who Fly
    O Love Divine That Stooped To
        Share
    Sailor's Grave, The
    Saviour When Night Involves The
        Skies
    Song Of Peace, A
    Spirit Of Life In This New Dawn
    Status Symbol
    Strong Son Of God Immortal Love
    They Sail'd Away
Baker & Fails
    No One To Blame
Baker & Fails & Powell
    Fairy Tales
    More Than You Know
    Talk To Me
Baker & Johnson & Bias
    Sweet Love
Baker & Scarborough & Holland
    Giving You The Best That I Got
Baker & Seago
    My Baby's Baby
Baker, Henry
    Art Thou Weary
    Art Thou Weary Art Thou Laden
    O God Of Love
    O God Of Love O King Of Peace
Baker, John
    My Trundle Bed
Baker, Yvonne
    Let Me In
Baldwin
    Buried Treasure
    Jesus In Your Heart
    Our Flag

Baldwin *(Cont.)*
    Tarry With Me O My Savior
    Tarry With Me O My Saviour
Baldwin & Borop
    My Soul Desire
Baldwin & Tunney
    Shepherd Of My Heart
Baldwin & Tunney & Smith
    More I Know Of You, The
Bale
    Hail To Mercer
Balee
    Yellow And Blue, The
Bales
    Ozymandias
Balfe, Michael
    Arrow And The Song, The
    By Killarney's Lakes And Fells
    Come Into The Garden Maud
    Excelsior
    Gipsy Song
    Happy And Light
    Heart Bow'd Down, The
    I Dreamt I Dwelt In Marble Halls
    I Dreamt That I Dwelt In Marble
        Halls
    In The Gipsy's Life
    Killarney
    Killarny
    Light Of Other Days
    Oh The Land That We Love
    See At Your Feet
    Then You'll Remember
    Then You'll Remember Me
    Yellow And Blue, The
Balin, Marty
    Miracles
Ball
    Gospel Ship, The
    I Promise You
    You'll Be There
Ball, Ernest
    All The World Will Be Jealous Of Me
    Dear Little Boy Of Mine
    Good-Bye Good Luck God Bless You
    I'll Forget You
    In The Garden Of My Heart
    Isle O' Dreams
    Let The Rest Of The World Go By
    Little Bit Of Heaven, A
    Love Me And The World Is Mine
    West Of The Great Divide
    When Irish Eyes Are Smiling
    Will You Love Me In December
    Will You Love Me In December As
        You Do In May
Ball & Almond
    Say Hello Wave Goodbye
Ball & Drinkard
    Dying Californian, The
Ballard
    Captain Of Sunshine, The
    Carol, A
    Game Of Love, The

Ballard *(Cont.)*
    I Can Hardly Wait
    I Did It For Love
    I Wanna Keep In Touch With
        Heaven All Day Long
    I'll Be Ready
    I'm Alive
    Liar
    Mister Santa
    Oh What A Sunrise
    Safe In His Care
    Venus
Ballard & Chater & Bourke
    You Look So Good In Love
Ballard & Foster & Graydon
    Lady Of My Heart
Ballard & Garrett
    Man In The Mirror
Ballard & James & Otis
    Dance With Me Henry
Ballard & Magness & Pack
    All I Need
Ballard & Phillips
    Hold On
Ballard & Tobias
    Good Timin'
Ballard, Clint
    You're No Good
Ballard, Hank
    Twist, The
Ballard, Pat
    Mister Sandman
Balle
    Det Kimer Nu Til Julefest
    Great God Of Nations
    Happy Christmas Comes Once
        Again, The
    Happy Christmas Comes Once
        More, The
Ballinger
    We Have Come Into His House
    We Have Come Into His House To
        Worship Him
**Baltes & Dirkschneider & Hoffman &
    Kaufmann & Deaffy**
    Balls To The Wall
**Baltes & Dirkschneider & Hoffman &
    Kaufmann & Fischer**
    Metal Heart
Bambridge
    At Thy Feet Our God And Father
    Glorious Things Of Thee Are Spoken
        (First Tune)
    Through The Night Of Doubt And
        Sorrow
Bampton
    I Give Thanks
    O God Whose Law Is In The Sky
Bancroft
    Harvest Fields With Gold Aglow
    There's A Voice In The Wilderness
        Crying
Banister
    Come Unto These Yellow Sands

Banks
God's Goodness
Your Smile
Banks & Collins & Rutherford
Abacab
Behind The Lines
Follow You Follow Me
Illegal Alien
In Too Deep
Invisible Touch
Mama
No Reply At All
Paperlate
Taking It All Too Hard
That's All
Throwing It All Away
Tonight Tonight Tonight
Banks & Collins & Rutherford & Gabr
Lamb Lies Down On Broadway, The
Banks & Crutcher & Davis & Jackson &
Bullard
Who's Making Love
Banks & Jackson & Hampton
I Don't Want To Be Right
Touch A Hand Make A Friend
Bannister
Mountain Top
Nature Of Love
Old Man's Rubble
Bannister & Chapman & Grant & Smith
Angels
Bannister & Grant
Faith Walkin' People
On And On
Bannister & Smith
Stubborn Love
Bannister & Sutter & Rodgers
Sweet Adoration
Bannon
I Wanna Say Yes
Bannon & Spriggs
Goodbye Heartache
Barajas
Queja Pampera
Barak & Paikov
Chag Yovel
Barbaris
Munasterio 'E Santa Chiara
Barber
Clocher Chante, Le
Cygne, Un
Daisies, The
Depart
God Be Merciful Unto Us
I Will Lift Up Mine Eyes
Lord Jesus Christ
My Soul Doth Magnify The Lord
Puisque Tout Passe
Sure On This Shining Night
Tombeau Dans Un Parc
Barberis
Munasterio 'e Santa Chiara

Barbian
Trennung
Barbieri
Last Tango In Paris
Barbosa
Perdicion
Barbour
Joyful Cowboy, The
Like Jesus
Barcelata, Lorenzo
Coconito
Maria Elena
Barclay
Lone Star Forever, The
Bard
Toast To De Pauw, A
Bardos
Night Bells
Bare
All American Boy, The
Hurricane Shirley
Sing A Happy Song
Bare & Lomax
After The Music Has Stopped
Bare & Shaver
Music City U.S.A.
Bare & Williams & West
Five Hundred Miles Away From
Home
Barge & Guida
School Is Out
Baring-Gould
Jesu Gentlest Saviour
Jesus Gentlest Saviour
Jesus Kneel Beside Me
Baring-Gould & Barnby
Now The Day Is Over
Baring-Gould & Sullivan
Onward Christian Soldiers
Baring-Gould, Sabine
Now The Day Is Over
Barkan, Mark
Pretty Flamingo
Barker
Dublin Bay
Irish Emigrant, The
Love Without End Amen
Scottish Blue Bells, The
Silently Tenderly Mournfully Home
Welcome Hymn
Where Are The Friends Of My
Youth
White Squall, The
Why Do Summer Roses Fade
Barker & Lee
Save The Bones For Henry Jones
Barker & Palmer
I Didn't
You Might Want To Use Me Again
Barker & Thomas
Mirror Mirror
Barnaby
Dawn Of God's Dear Sabbath, The

Barnard
Bid Me To Love
But Is That All
Come Back To Erin
Father Bless The Gifts We Bring
Thee
Jesus Loves Me Jesus Loves Me
Jesus Tender Shepherd
Jesus Tender Shepherd Hear Me
Jesus Was A Loving Teacher
Saviour Who Thy Flock Art Feeding
Take Back The Heart
You And I
Barnard, Charlotte
Give Of Your Best To The Master
Barnby
Alleluia
And Is It True As I Am Told
And Must I Be To Judgment Brought
Approach My Soul The Mercy-Seat
Christ Is Coming
Come Ye Sinners Poor And Needy
Cradle Song Of The Blessed Virgin,
A
Cradle Song Of Virgin
Day Of Wrath That Dreadful Day,
The
Did Christ O'Er Sinners Weep
For All Saints
For All The Saints
For All The Saints Who From Their
Labors Rest
God Of Our Fathers Whose
Almighty Hand
God Of The Earth
God Of The Earth The Sky The Sea
Hail The Day When Jesus Rose
Hallelujah Sing To Jesus
Hark The Sound Of Holy Voices
He Hides Within The Lily
He Is Gone A Cloud Of Light
Holy Night Peaceful Night
How Pleasing Is Thy Voice
How Sweetly Flowed The Gospel's
Sound
I Cannot Think Of Them As Dead
I Worship Thee Most Gracious God
Infinite God To Thee We Raise
Is It For Me
Jesus Lover Of My Soul
Jesus My Lord My God My All
Jesus Thou Joy Of Loving Hearts
Jesus Where'er Thy People Meet
Lead Us O Father
Lead Us O Father In The Paths Of
Peace
Lead Us Oh Father
Let Not Thy Hands Be Slack
Light Of Day
Little Jesus Came At Eve
Look Away To Jesus
Look From Thy Sphere Of Endless
Day
Lord Is Come, The

Barnby *(Cont.)*
Lord Is Come On Syrian Soil, The
Lord Is My Shepherd, The
Lord Now Lettest Thou Thy Servant
Lord Of Our Life And God Of Our
    Salvation
Lord Of The Strong When Earth You
    Trod
Mighty God While Angels Bless
    Thee
Morning Walks Upon The Earth, The
My Times Are In Thy Hand
Now God Be With Us
Now God Be With Us For The Night
    Is Closing
Now I Have Found The Ground
    Wherein
O Beautiful My Country
O Blessed Son Of God
O Brother Man Fold To Thy Heart
    Thy Brother
O God In Whose Great Purpose
O God O Spirit
O God Thy Power Is Wonderful
O Hallowed Memories
O Light Whose Beams Illumine All
O Little Town Of Bethlehem
O Lord Of Life Thy Quickening
    Voice
O Lord To Whom The Spirits Live
O Paradise
O Paradise O Paradise
O Stranger With No Place
O Thou Great Friend To All
Our Lord Is Risen From The Dead
Psalm 122
Shepherd Psalm, The
Sing To The Lord A Joyful Song
Still Still With Thee
Still Will We Trust Though
Still Will We Trust Though Earth
    Seem Dark And Dre
Sunset And Evening Star
Talk With Us Lord Thyself Reveal
Teach Me My God And King
There Is A Book Who Runs May
    Read
There Is No Name So Sweet On
    Earth
Thou Didst Leave Thy Throne
Thou Hidden Love Of God
Thy Word O God Declareth
'Tis Finished So The Saviour Cried
To God The Only Wise
Vale
When Morning Gilds The Skies
When Morning Gilds The Skies My
    Heart
When On My Day Of Life
When On My Day Of Life The Night
    Is Falling
Where Is Thy God My Soul
Why Should The Children Of A
    King
Wilt Thou Hear The Voice Of Praise

Barnby *(Cont.)*
With Glorious Clouds Emcompassed
    Round
Ye Holy Angels Bright
Zion Stands With Hills Surrounded
Barnby, Joseph
Carmen Etonense
Crossing The Bar
Just As I Am
Just As I Am Thine Own To Be
Just As I Am Without One Plea
Now The Day Is Over
O Happy Home Where Thou Art
    Loved The Dearest
O Perfect Love
O Perfect Love All Human Thought
    Transcending
Spirit Of God Descend Upon My
    Heart
Sweet And Low
We Give Thee But Thine Own
We March We March To Victory
We Plow The Fields And Scatter
Barnes
Alma Mater
Angels We Have Heard On High
God To The Hungry Child
Home At Twilight
I Cannot Think Or Reason
Lo The Winter Is Past
O Christ Who Holds The Open Gate
Praise To God Immortal Praise
Song Of Then And Now, The
Barnes & Carlisi & Peterik
Hold On Loosely
Barnes & Carlisi & Peterik & Sullivan
Caught Up In You
Barnes & Cornelius & John
Blossom Fell, A
Barnes & Ewing
Coast Of Colorado, The
Barnes & Jones
Thank God For The Radio
Barnes & Richardson
At The Sound Of The Tone
Barnes, Paul
Good-Bye Dolly Gray
Barnet
Being Thankful Every Day
Barnett
Arkansas
Postman, The
Barney
Thousand Leagues Away
Baroni
Soldier Of The Light
Baroni & Borop
Find A Hurt And Heal It
Baroso
Brazil
Barr
Thou Bonnie Wood O' Craigielea
Barraclough
Ivory Palaces

Barratt & Johnstone
Heaven Knows
Barren
Prince Edward Island Murder
Barrett
Look In My Eyes
Maybe
Misty
Barrett-Ayres & Ferguson
Am I My Brother's Keeper
Barretto
El Watusi
Watusi, El
Barri
At Benediction
Good Shepherd, The
Barrie
All That Love Went To Waste
I Surrender Dear
Now That We're In Love
Touch Of Class, A
Barrington
Forward Through The Ages
Barris
Palisades Park
Barris, Harry
I Surrender Dear
Lies
Wrap Your Troubles In Dreams
Wrap Your Troubles In Dreams And
    Dream Your Troubles Away
Barro & Ribeiro
Chiquita Banana
Barron & Long
Cindy Oh Cindy
Barroso, Amy
Baia
Brazil
Barrowes
Swinging 'Neath The Apple-Tree
Barrows
God Who Made The Earth
O North With All Thy Vales Of
    Green
Barrows & Zaritsky
Little White Duck
Barruso
Brazil
Barry
Best Man In The World, The
Music Of Goodbye, The
Reelin' And Rockin'
Somewhere In Time
St Patrick's Day
Theme From The Deep
Barry & Barry
One Day At A Time
Barry & Block
Montego Bay
Barry & Bloom
Montego Bay
Barry & David
Wednesday's Child

Barry & Dubois
Movin' On Up
Barry & Greenwich
Do Wah Diddy Diddy
People Say
Barry & Greenwich & Spector
Da Doo Ron Ron
River Deep Mountain High
Barry & Kim
Sugar Sugar
Barry & McNamara & Cretecos
Lay A Little Lovin' On Me
Barry & Raleigh
Tell Laura I Love Her
Barry, John
All Time High
Born Free
Diamonds Are Forever
Goldfinger
Midnight Cowboy
You Only Live Twice
Barshall
Brunonia
Bart, Lionel
As Long As He Needs Me
Consider Yourself
From Russia With Love
I'd Do Anything
Oliver
Where Is Love
Who Will Buy
Bartenstein
Abe-Iad, The
Barthelemon
All Praise To Thee Who Safe Hast
Kept
Awake My Soul
Awake My Soul And With The Sun
Carmen Vitae
Guide Me O Thou Great Jehovah
Hail Thou Once Despised Jesus
Happy The Souls To Jesus Joined
Hark The Voice Of Jesus Calling
How Bright These Glorious Spirits
Shine
Jesus Spreads His Banner O'Er Us
Lord God Of Morning And Of Night
Mighty God While Angels Bless
Thee
O Jesus Master When Today
Spirit Divine Attend Our Prayers
Bartholemon
Awake My Soul And With The Sun
Bartholomew
Flag Song
Flowers That Blow
Great-Grandmother
Policeman, The
This Is The Day
Wind's Song, The
Bartholomew & King
I Hear You Knocking
One Night

Bartlet
Fortune Love And Time
I Heard Of Late
If There Be Any One
Of All The Birds
Pretty Pretty Ducke, A
Tarry Are You Gone Again
What Thing Is Love
When From My Love I Lookte
Whither Runneth My Sweetheart
Who Doth Behold
Who Doth Behold My Mistress' Face
Bartlett
Boy And The Toot, The
Everybody Will Be Happy Over
There
I Had A Little Pony
Jehovah God Who Dwelt Of Old
Merry Rain, The
O Lord Be Merciful
Punkydoodle And Jollapin
Royal Purple, The
Sweet Red Rose, The
Three Wise Women, The
Thy Dear Eyes
To The Fairest College
Victory In Jesus
Voice That Breathed O'er Eden, The
Wind Is Awake
Wind Is Awake, The
Bartlett, J.C.
Dream, A
Bartlett & Chatham
Christ Lives In Me
Bartok
Gott Ach Gott Im Himmel
Tears Of Autumn
Barton
Gray Sparrow, The
It Was A Lover And His Lass
Texan's Song Of Liberty, The
Two Songs
Bas-Quercy
Come With Us Sweet Flowers
Whence Comes This Rush Of Wings
Basie & Durham
Every Tub
Basie & Gibson
Shorty George
Basie & Livingston & David
Blue And Sentimental
Basie & Livingstone & David
Blue And Sentimental
Basie, Count
Jumpin' At The Woodside
One O'Clock Jump
Theme From M-Squad
Baskette
Dream Pal
Baskette, Billy
Good-Bye Broadway Hello France
Bassani
Bela Dea

Bassett & Werner-Kersten
Jolly Peter
Bassford
Can A Little Child Like Me
For The Fruit Upon The Tree
Bassi
Mia Storia, La
Bassman
I'm Getting Sentimental Over You
Batchelder
Dragon, The
Batchellor
Father We Thank Thee
God Make My Life A Little Light
Morning Hymn
Batchelor
Autumn
Cradle Song
Moon Is Jealous, The
Batchelor & Roberts
Where Do You Come From
Bates
Come Shaker Life
Tramp Tramp Tramp
Bateson
Down From Above
If Love Be Blind
Phyllis Farewell
Sister Awake
Whither So Fast
Batten
Deliver Us O Lord Our God
Let My Complaint Come Before
Thee
Lord We Beseech Thee
O Sing Joyfully
When The Lord Turned Again
Battersby
An Evening Prayer
Battersby & Gabriel
Evening Prayer, An
Battishill
O All Ye Works Of The Lord
O Lord Our Governor
Bauer
Letter, A
Oh Saddle The Roan
Song Of The Wanderer
Baughen
As The Deer Longs For Water
Bless The Lord O My Soul
Blessed Is The Man
Earth Is The Lord's, The
Glory Give To God In Heaven
Go Forth And Tell
God Is King
God Is Our Strength And Refuge
I Thank You Lord
I Waited Patiently For The Lord
If God Has Chosen A Nation
In My Hour Of Grief Or Need
Living Lord
O Lord Our God
O Thank The Lord

Baughen *(Cont.)*
Tell Out My Soul The Greatness Of
  The Lord
When This Land Knew

Baughen & Crocker
I Lift My Eyes
Stars Declare His Glory, The

Baughen & Thornton
Why Do The Heathen Conspire

Baum
Pathway Is Blind, The
We Two
Witching Hour, The
With Muted Strings

Baum & Weiss
Music Music Music

Baumanis
Dievs Sveti Latviju
Latvia

Baumbach
Let The Words Of My Mouth

Baume
Spirit Of God Descend Upon My
  Heart

Baur
It Is The Lord

Baxter
Keep On The Firing Line

Baxter, Phil
Faded Summer Love
I'm A Ding Dong Daddy
I'm A Ding Dong Daddy From
  Dumas
Piccolo Pete

Baxter & Doane
Take The Name Of Jesus With You

Baxter & Moore
Merry Christmas Baby

Bayes-Norworth
Shine On Harvest Moon

Bayly
Gaily The Troubadour
I'm Saddest When I Sing
Isle Of Beauty
Oh 'Tis The Melody
Spanish Serenade
Touch Not The Cup

Bayly, Thomas
I'd Be A Butterfly
Long Long Ago

Beach
Ariette
Concert For Pianoforte And
  Orchestra
Meadow-Larks
O Mistress Mine
Take O Take Those Lips Away
Western Wind, The

Beadell & Tollerton
Cruising Down The River
Cruising Down The River On A
  Sunday Afternoon
Cruising Down The River On A
  Sunny Afternoon

Beal & Boothe
Jingle Bell Rock

Beall
Lift Him Up
Rally Song

Bean & Masters
Scatterbrain

Beasley
One More Time

Beasley & Vester
Love Crazy
Theme From Open House

Beaszley
Wondrous Name Of Jesus, The

Beattie
American Way, The
Bee And The Ant, The
Clouds
Cuckoo Clock, The
Elephant, The
Four Faces
Jack O'Lantern
Lullaby
Milk Wagon, The
My Mother
Our Airplane
Paul Revere's Ride
Questions And Answers
Rainbow, The
Traffic Officer, The
Village Square, The

Beatty
It's Different Now

Beaulaigue
Comme Serait A Moi

Beaumont
Angel Voices Ever Singing
O Praise God

Beauplan
Repos, Le

Beavers & Bristol & Fuqua
Someday We'll Be Together

Beazley
All Is Mine
All Praise To Him Who Built The
  Hills
Am I A Soldier Of The Cross
Awake And Sing The Song
Be In Earnest
Be Ye Therefore Ready
Beyond The Tide
Blest Are The Pure In Heart
Cling To His Hand
Clinging Close To His Hand
Crossing The Bar
Dark Was The Night
Deep Settled Peace
Draw Near To God
Dreaming Still Dreaming
Following On
Glory And Honor
God My King Thy Might Confessing
Going Up And Down The Land
Gospel News, The

Beazley *(Cont.)*
Had It Not Been For The Lord
Hallelujah Jesus Reigns
Head That Once Was Crowned, The
I Want To Serve Him Better
I'll Never Cease To Love Him
I'm A Pilgrim
I'm Willing To Be Thine
In His Name
In The Hollow Of His Hand
In The Resurrection Morning
Jesus Knows
Jesus Meek And Gentle
Jesus The Hope Of The World
Jesus Thou Joy Of Loving Hearts
Join In Exultation
Just To Know
Kept By The Power Of God
King Of Love My Shepherd Is, The
Let The Master Use You
Little Workers
Lo What A Cloud Of Witnesses
Love Divine All Love Excelling
Magnify Jehovah's Name
Majestic Sweetness Sits Enthroned
My God Accept My Heart This Day
My Heaven Song
Naught But The Blood Can Avail
O Come My Soul
O Do Some Good Deed Every Day
O God Of Bethel By Whose Hand
O God Of Love Of King Of Peace
O Love That Cast Out Fear
Oh Bless The Lord My Soul
One Day At A Time
One Touch Of His Hand
Only Sleeping
Orders From The King
Our King Immanuel
Pass Along The Word
Path, The
Praise Him
Recompense
Rejoice In His Great Name
Right Must Win
Roll Billows Roll
Sing His Praises
Something New Each Day
Song Of Wonderful Love, The
Still Small Voice, The
Take Hold Of The Life-Line
Take The Home-Path
To Bless Thy Chosen Race
To See His Face
To Thy Temple I Repair
Walk In The Light Of God
What The Old World Needs
When I Recall Thy Great Blessings
Wonderful Love
Work Must Go On, The
Work On Pray On
Yet There Is Room

Beethoven *(Cont.)*
O Perfect Life Of Love
O Ship Of State
O Sometimes Gleams Upon My Sight
O Spirit Of The Living God
Ode For Washington's Birthday
Ode To Joy
Oh Where Shall Rest Be Found
Opferlied
Partenza, La
Power Of God, The
Praise The Lord Ye Heavens Adore
    Him
Prayer, A
Reveil Des Fleurs, Le
Scale, The
Sehnsucht
Signor Abbate
Sing To God New Songs Of Worship
Sing With All The Sons Of Glory
Singing We Go
Song Of Peace
Summer's Day, The
Symphony No. 5
Take Up Thy Cross
There's A Wideness In God's Mercy
To Maelzel
To The Beloved
To Theo Molt
Tout Passe
Trommel Geruhret, Die
Tune In Parts
Turkish March
Urian's Reise Um Die Welt
Vesper Hymn, The
Vita Felice
Weather Vane, The
Weaving Song
When Jesus Dwelt In Mortal Clay
Where Cross The Crowded Ways Of
    Life
Where Music Grows
Whip-Poor-Will
Wonne Der Wehmuth
World Friendship
Worship Of God In Nature, The
Young Greek's Prayer, The
Zufriedene, Der
Begazzi & Tozzi
Ti Amo
Behan
Oul' Triangle, The
Behr
Tarry But A Little Longer
Behrend
Auntie
Gift, The
Behrend, Arthur
Daddy
Beiderbecke, Bix
In A Mist
Beigelman
Tsigaynerlid

Beirach
Dark Lady
Leaving
October 10th
Stray
Beirly
Landing Of The Pilgrims
Belafonte & Thomas
Suzanne
Belcher
Ionia
My Storehouse Of Blessings
Understanding
Belden
As For Me And My House
Away The Bowl
Glad Crowning Day
Hallelujah Answer We
I Belong To Him
Keep Praying As You Go
Keep Tenting Toward The Highlands
What A Meeting That Will Be
Who Is On The Lord's Side
Who Will Be The Next
Yet There Is Room
Belding
Apple Sass Rag
Belfiore & Genovese
Traditions, Les
Belihu
Good News
Belin
Vray Dieu Qu'amoureux Ont De
    Peine
Bell
Dear Little Boy Of Mine
Didn't I Blow Your Mind This Time
Fling Out The Banner Let It Float
Hail Harbinger Of Morn
Jesus Of Calvary
Bell & Creed
You Are Everything
Bell & Henley
Is It Still Over
Bell & Jones
Born Under A Bad Sign
Everybody Loves A Winner
I Forgot To Be Your Lover
Bell & Kool & The Gang
Celebration
Bell & Kyles & Taylor
Forever
Bell & McGuire
One Man Band
Shine Shine Shine
Bell & Mitchell
Tryin' To Love Two
Bell & Quillen
Jukebox Played Along, The
Bell & Taylor & Kool & The Gang
Cherish
Misled
Victory

Bellak
Carnival Of Venice
Bellamy
For All The Wrong Reasons
Get Into Reggae Cowboy
I Love Her Mind
I Need More Of You
Redneck Girl
You Ain't Just Whistlin' Dixie
You're My Favorite Star
Bellamy, David
If I Said You Had A Beautiful Body
    Would You Hold It Against Me
Belle & Prima & Leonard & Rhodes
Sunday Kind Of Love, A
Bellini
Ah Must Ye Fade
Ah Non Credea Mirarti
Ah Non Credea Mirarti Ah Non
    Giunge
Arie Der Norma
Ascolta
Casta Diva
Castles In Spain
Chaste Enchantress
Deh Tu Deh Tu
Flowers For The Brave
Gentle Maiden
Hour Of Parting, The
Lauriger Horatius
Liberty
O Rendetemi La Speme
Oh Gladly Now We Hail Thee
Oh Recall Not
Son Vergin Vezzosa
Vien Diletto
We Cheer And March Away
Bellis
Fallen Angel
Bellman
Boman's Grave At St Catherine's
    Cemetery
Butterflies At Haga
Elegy To Movitz
Fredman's Farewell To Ulla
Funeral Procession, The
School Days
Bello
Pretty Girls
Bellusci
Robbin' The Cradle
Bellwood
Wotcher 'Ria
Belvin
Guess Who
Bembeg
Creole Song
Bemberg
Arioso
Creole Song
Na-I-Ka
Sultana's Song, The
Venetian Song

Ben
Constant Rain, The
Mas Que Nada
Ben-Haim
Work Of Thy Hand, The
Benbow
Let Thy Blood In Mercy Poured
Bendel
Heart Throbs
Wie Beruhrt Mich Wundersam
Benedict
Blest Be The Home
I'll Be Dar
Moon Has Rais'd Her Lamp Above,
The
Moon Has Raised Her Lamp Above,
The
Our Victorious Banner
Benedict, Julius
By The Sad Sea Waves
Beneken
Gottesacker, Der
Wie Sie So Sanft Ruh'n
Benham
Redemption
Benitez & Garrett & Toni C
Power, The
Benjamin
Shepherd's Holiday
Benjamin & Durham
I Don't Want To Set The World On
Fire
Benjamin & Marcus
Lonely Man
Benjamin & Weiss
Can Anyone Explain No No No
Christmas Time
Cross Over The Bridge
I'll Keep The Lovelight Burning
To Think You've Chosen Me
Wheel Of Fortune
Benjamin & Weiss & Bandini
Girl A Girl Zoom Ba Di Alli Nella, A
Benjamin & Weiss & Carle
Oh What It Seemed To Be
Bennard, George
Old Rugged Cross, The
On A Hill Far Away
Benner
Happy Happy Easter
Oh Shout The News
Bennet
Elves' Dance, The
Falconers' Song, The
Nicholas And Alexandra
Bennet & Toleken
St Patrick Was A Gentleman
Bennett
Cast Thy Bread Upon The Waters
God Is A Spirit
Let Go Why Do You Stay Me
Let Thy Mind
May Dew
Nicholas And Alexandra

Bennett *(Cont.)*
O Sleep Fond Fancy
Still Rolls The Stone
Theme From Nicholas And
Alexandra
Weep O Mine Eyes
Ye Restless Thoughts
Bennett & Aguilar
Come And See
Bennett & Denton
Black Slacks
Bennett & Webster
In The Sweet By-And-By
Sweet By And By
Bennett, Richard R.
Orient Express, The
Too Beautiful To Last
Benoit
Where Charity And Love Prevail
Benshoof
Cow, The
Bensley
Halloween Visitor
Benson
Here's Your Mule
In Lands Across The Sea
Shorty George
White Dove
Benson & Fisher
Your Feet's Too Big
Benson & Wildhorn
Miracles
Bentley
Big Brown Bear
Lullaby
My Fiddle
Who Has Seen The Wind
Whosoever Believeth
Wish, A
Bentley & Gersmehl
We Are One
Benton
How Do You Preach
Live And Let Live
Benton & Williams
Lover's Question, A
Benttonmuller
Seht Ihr Auf Den Grunen Fluren
Beobide
God Our Father Lord Of Heaven
Berat
Ma Normandie
My Normandy
Berbecke
Lord Have Mercy Upon Us
Beresford
Smuggler, The
Beresford & Sanders
If Drinkin' Don't Kill Me Her
Memory Will
Beresovsky
Unter Di Churves Fun Poyln

Berg
Last Letter
Let Us Drink And Be Merry
Not A Day More Than Thirty
Rock With Me
Sing And Be Merry
Berg, David
Quaker Down In Quaker Town
Berge
He Shall Be Great
Love
Slumber My Treasure
Berger
Hail Great Aloha State
Hawaii Ponoi
Neuen Pfingsten, Die
Berger & Klonaris
Little House, The
Berggreen
Master Speak Thy Servant Heareth
One There Is Above All Others
Bergotz & Pulver
Glezele Lechayim, A
Berkeley
How Love Came In
O Mistress Mine
Berkowitz
We Shall Be Free
Berlin
Abraham
Alexander's Ragtime Band
Angels Of Mercy
Antonio
Any Bonds Today
Anything You Can Do
At The Devil's Ball
Back To Back
Be Careful It's My Heart
Becky's Got A Job In A Musical
Show
Before I Go And Marry I Will Have
A Talk With You
Best Things Happen While You're
Dancing, The
Better Times With Al
Blue Skies
Call Again
Call Me Up Some Rainy Afternoon
Change Partners
Cheek To Cheek
Choreography
Coquette
Count Your Blessings Instead Of
Sheep
Couple Of Swells, A
Dat's-A My Gal
Do It Again
Dog Gone That Chilly Man
Doin' What Comes Natur'lly
Dorando
Down In My Heart
Draggy Rag
Easter Parade

Berlin *(Cont.)*
Everybody's Doing It Now
Fella With An Umbrella, A
Follow Me Around
For Your Country And My Country
Freedom Train, The
Get Thee Behind Me Satan
Girl That I Marry, The
Give Me Your Tired Your Poor
God Bless America
Goody Goody Goody Goody Good
He Ain't Got Rhythm
He's A Devil In His Own Home
    Town
He's A Rag Picker
Heat Wave
How Do You Do It Mabel On
    Twenty Dollars A Week
I Can't Do Without You
I Got The Sun In The Morning
I Just Came Back To Say Good Bye
I Left My Heart At The Stage Door
    Canteen
I Like Ike
I Love A Piano
I Never Had A Chance
I Threw A Kiss In The Ocean
I Want To Be In Dixie
I Want To Go Back To Michigan
I'll See You In C-U-B-A
I'm Afraid Pretty Maid I'm Afraid
I'm An Indian Too
I'm Putting All My Eggs In One
    Basket
I've Got My Love To Keep Me
    Warm
If All The Girls I Knew Were Like
    You
If You Believe
Innocent Bessie Brown
International Rag, The
Isn't This A Lovely Day
It Only Happens When I Dance With
    You
It's A Lovely Day Today
It's A Lovely Day Tomorrow
Just Like The Rose
Keep Me Away From The Fellow
    Who Owns An Automobile
Lazy
Let Yourself Go
Let's Face The Music And Dance
Little Bit Of Everything, A
Marie
Marrying For Love
Miss Liberty
My Defences Are Down
My Sweet Italian Man
No Strings
Ocarina, The
Oh How I Hate To Get Up In The
    Morning

Berlin *(Cont.)*
Pick Pick Pick Pick On The
    Mandolin Antonio
Play A Simple Melody
Pretty Girl Is Like A Melody, A
Ragtime Jockey Man, The
Ragtime Soldier Man
Ragtime Violin
Run Home And Tell Your Mother
Russian Lullaby
Sailor's Not A Sailor, A
Shaking The Blues Away
Sisters
Snookey Ookums
Society Bear
Song Of Freedom
Song Of The Metronome, The
Spring And Fall
Steppin' Out With My Baby
Stop Stop Stop
That Mesmerizing Mendelssohn
    Tune
That's How I Love You
There's No Business Like Show
    Business
They Say It's Wonderful
This Is A Great Country
This Is The Army Mister Jones
This Is The Army Mr Jones
This Is The Life
Top Hat White Tie And Tails
True Born Soldier Man, A
Try It On Your Piano
Waltz Of Long Ago, The
We Saw The Sea
We'll Never Know
What'll I Do
When I Leave The World Behind
When I Lost You
When I'm Alone I'm Lonesome
When It Rains Sweetheart When It
    Rains
When The Midnight Choo-Choo
    Leaves For Alabam'
When You Kiss An Italian Girl
When You're In Town
Where Is The Song Of Songs For Me
White Christmas
Who Do You Love I Hope
Won't You Play A Simple Melody
Yiddisha Eyes
Yiddisha Nightingale
Yiddle On Your Fiddle Play Some
    Ragtime
You Can Have Him
You Can't Get A Man With A Gun
You Keep Coming Back Like A Song
You'd Be Surprised
You're Just In Love
You've Got Me Hypnotized

Berlin & Bryan
Ephraim Played Upon The Piano
Woodman Woodman Spare That
    Tree

Berlin & Goetz
Fiddle-Dee-Dee
Lead Me To That Beautiful Band

Berlin & Goetz & Sloane
Alexander's Bag-Pipe Band

Berlin & Leslie
I Didn't Go Home At All
Sadie Salome Go Home
Someone's Waiting For Me

Berlin & Snyder
Kiss Me My Honey Kiss Me
That Mysterious Rag

Berlioz
Absence
Belief
No Joy Could Be More Thrilling

Bermejo
Charreada, La
Tu Solo Tu

Bermudo
Mira Nero De Tarpea

Bernard
Hail And Farewell
When All The World Is Young

Bernard, Felix
Winter Wonderland

Bernard & Smith
Winter Wonderland

Bernie & Pinkard & Casey
Sweet Georgia Brown

Berns
War Is Over, The

Berns & Ragavoy
Piece Of My Heart

Bernstein
Civet A Toute Vitesse
Hawaii
Plum Pudding
Queues De Boeuf
Simple Song, A
Song From Kings Go Forth, The
Spacehunter Adventures In The
    Forbidden Zone
Tavouk Gueunksis
Theme From Stripes
True Grit
Tsum Hemerl
Wishing Doll, The

Bernstein & Adams
After The Lovin'
Kentucky Mornin'
This Moment In Time

Bernstein & Sheldon
Baby The Rain Must Fall

Bernstein, Elmer
Hallelujah Trail
Magnificent Seven, The
Step To The Rear
Walk On The Wild Side

Bernstein, Leonard
America
Ballad Of Eldorado, The
Best Of All Possible Worlds, The
Carried Away

Bernstein, Leonard *(Cont.)*
Cool
Extinguish My Eyes
Glitter And Be Gay
I Am Easily Assimilated
I Can Cook Too
I Feel Like I'm Not Out Of Bed Yet
I Feel Pretty
I Go On
I Hate Music
It Must Be So
It's Love
Little Bit In Love, A
Lonely Town
Lucky To Be Me
Make Our Garden Grow
Maria
My Darlin' Eileen
My House
My Love
My New Friends
Never-Land
New York New York
Oh Happy We
Ohio
One Hand One Heart
One Hundred Easy Ways
Pass That Football
Peter Peter
Piccola Serenata
Quiet Girl, A
Silhouette
So Pretty
Some Other Time
Something's Coming
Somewhere
Swing
Take Care Of This House
Tonight
What's The Use
When My Soul Touches Yours
Who Am I
Wrong Note Rag, The
Ya Got Me
You Were Dead You Know
Berridge
Bearing The Cross
Berry
Back In The USA
Brown Eyed Handsome Man
Bye Bye Johnny
Carol
Come On
Drifting Heart
Johnny B Goode
Little Queenie
Louie Louie
Mabellene
Memphis
Memphis Tennessee
Nadine Is It You
No Particular Place To Go
Palisades Park
Promised Land, The

Berry *(Cont.)*
Reelin' And Rockin'
Rock And Roll Music
Rock & Roll Music
Roll Over Beethoven
Run Around
School Day
Still Got The Blues
Stop And Listen
Surfin' USA
Sweet Little Rock And Roller
Sweet Little Sixteen
Wee Wee Hours
You Can't Catch Me
You Never Can Tell
Berry & Christian & Wilson
Drag City
Berry & Wilson
Surf City
Berryhill
12 Dollar Motel
Baby
Damn I Wish I Was A Man
Indirectly Yours
Me Steve Kirk And Keith
Old Trombone Routine
She Had Everything
Supernatural Fact
Trump
Turn Off The Century
What's Wrong With Me
Yipee
Berstein
Kate McShane
Bert & Gorman & Dobbins & Garrett
Please Mr Postman
Bertei & Kessler
Do It For Love
Berthold
Drift On My Boat
What Is The Law Of Thy Beauty
Berton
Bayard Et La Jeune Fille
Bertrand
Hola Caron
Je Suis Un Demi Dieu
Besancon
Shepherds Shake Off Your Drowsy
Sleep
Beschmitt
Ossian
Beschnitt
Huttelein
Besoyan, Rick
Little Mary Sunshine
Best
For Sentimental Reasons
Best, William
You've Made My Life Worth Living
Bestor, Don
Contented
Betti, Henri
C'est Si Bon

Bettis & Bannon
One Of A Kind Pair Of Fools
Only One Love In My Life
Too Hot To Sleep
Bettis & Lind
Crazy For You
Betts
Jessica
Just Another Love Song
Betts, Dicky
Ramblin' Man
Betts & Cobb
Straight From The Heart
Betts & Cobb & Lawler
Angeline
Beurle
Pilgrim, The
Bevan
Flight Of Ages, The
Bevel & Lafayette
Dog Dog
I Know
Moving On
Bewes
O Lord I Love You
They Are Happy Whose Way Is Pure
Bialik
Ben N'Har P'Rat
Bickersteth & Caldbeck
Peace Perfect Peace
Bickford
Dustin' Off The Piano
Bickhardt
Givers And Takers
Never Been In Love
Bickhardt & Bonagura
Wilder Days
Bickhardt & Collins
You're The Power
Bicknell
Come Faithful People Come Away
Bicknell, G.
You Naughty Naughty Men
Bidoli
Te Voio Ben
Biedermann
Vassar Chant, A
Yellow And The Brown, The
Biencamino
In Lighter Vein
Big Country
In A Big Country
Bigazzi & Riefoli
Self Control
Bigazzi & Tozzi
Gloria
Bigelow
Battle Song Of Liberty, The
Hail The Home Of Freedom
Bigelow, F. E.
Our Director March
Biggs
Day By Day
Day By Day Dear Lord

Biggs *(Cont.)*
Little Boy Blue
Lord Who At Cana's Wedding Feast
Bikel
Mein Kind Musst Beten
Papir Iz Doch Vays
Bilhorn
Afterwhile
Almost
Be Strong
Beautiful Wonderful Story
Believe And Be Saved
Best Friend Is Jesus, The
Bid Him Come In
Blessed Jesus Keep Me White
Call For Volunteers, A
Child Of Mine
Christ Is Coming
Christ Is The Sunny Side
Could I Tell It
Dare To Stand Like Joshua
Do It Now
Do Something Today
Eternity Where
Four Calls, The
Fullness Of Power
Glory For You And For Me
Go In Peace
Go Ye Therefore
Having Done All To Stand
He That Overcometh
I Am On The Right Side
I Know He Is Mine
I Want Everybody To Know
Jesus Christ Is My Savior
Jesus Thou My Only Refuge
Lamb Of God, The
Let Your Light So Shine
Living Where The Healing Waters
    Flow
Longing For The Sweet By And By
Lord Save Me
Message Of Love, A
My Desire
My Lord And I
O Tell Me More Of Christ
Oh 'Tis Glory In My Soul
Precious Blood, The
'Twas For Me
Unto The Uttermost
Vision Of Home, A
Walk And Talk With Jesus
Was It For Me
Wayward Sheep, The
We May Journey With Rejoicing
We Shall Conquer In His Name
What Will Ye Bind
When My Savior I Shall See
When The Beautiful Gates Unfold
Who Will Be The Next
Who Will Join Us
Why Not Receive Him
You Mean To Be Saved But When

Bilhorn, Peter
I Will Sing The Wondrous Story
Sweet Peace The Gift Of God's Love
Bilk
Stranger On The Shore
Bill
Our Friends The Saints
Billeter
Come Sing With Holy Gladness
Our Native Land
Swan Of Peace, The
Billings
Amherst Hymn
David's Lamentation
Easter Anthem
Funeral Anthem
Heavenly Vision
Lamentation Over Boston, The
Let My Name Engraven Stand
Putney Hymn, The
Retrospect
Rose Of Sharon
Shiloh
Union
Virgin Unspotted, A
When Jesus Wept
Billings, William
Amherst
Chester
Binchois
Amours Merchi
Bindi
Arrivederci
Bingham
All Hail Blue And Gold
As I Play On My Old Bass Viol
Mother Of Men
Bingham & Kellie
Autumn Story, An
Bingham & Lohr
Slumber Song, A
Bingham & Molloy
Love's Old Sweet Song
Binion & Nelson
Keep The Flame Burning
Birch
We List To The Sound
With A Down Down Hey Derry
    Down
Birge
At The Airport
Bischoff
Lord Is My Light, The
Bishop
Behold The Royal Cross On High
Bloom Is On The Rye
Bloom Is On The Rye, The
Calm Be Thy Slumbers
Chime Again Beautiful Bells
Come My Gallant Soldier Come
For Common Gifts We Bless Thee
    Lord
Foresters Sound

Bishop *(Cont.)*
Hark From The Midnight Hill
    Around
I Heard The Bells On Christmas Day
Leaf By Leaf The Roses Fall
Mistletoe Bough, The
O Lead My Blindness By The Hand
O Ye That Are Weary
Pretty As A Picture
Somewhere In Between
These Things Shall Be A Loftier Race
We Praise Thee God
White Nights
Bishop & Faragher
So Close To The Fire
Bishop, Elvin
Fooled Around And Fell In Love
Bishop, Henry
Bid Me Discourse
Home Sweet Home
Love Has Eyes
Bishop, Joe
Blue Prelude
Bishop, Stephen
On And On
Save It For A Rainy Day
Separate Lives
Bissell
Ghost-Dance, The
Bitgood
All The Happy Birds Of Spring
As The Wise Men Brought Their
    Treasures
Chinese Children
Christ West Up Into The Hills Alone
Christmas Candle, The
Friends All Over The World
Golden Rule, The
Greatest Of These Is Love, The
I Love My Church
I Was Glad When They Said Unto
    Me
I Will Give Thanks Unto The Lord
In The Beginning
Life Out Of Death
Little King Of The World Came
    Down, The
O God Whose Laws Will Never
    Change
Once There Was A Garden Fair
Ring Out The Joyful News Again
Sing About A Birthday
Bitz
Durch Manche Landerstrecken
Bixby
In Pastures Green
Bixio & Cherubini & Kennedy
Serenade In The Night
Bixio, C. A.
Mama
Tell Me That You Love Me Tonight
Bizet
Absence
After Winter

Bizet *(Cont.)*
Agnus Dei
Beat Out That Rhythm On A Drum
Boys' Chorus
Calm Sea
Carmen's Song And Dance
Castanet Song
Changing The Guard
Chanson D'Avril
Dat's Love
Doubt
Draussen Am Wall Von Sevilla
Dreaming
En Vain Pour Eviter
Fleur Que Tu M'Vais Jetee, La
Gascon, The
Gypsy Girls
Habanera
Habnera
Halte-La
I Vow I'll Do All In My Power
If You Love Me
If You Love Me Carmen
Ja Die Liebe Hat Bunte Flugel
Je Dis Que Rien Ne M'Epouvante
Lady-Bird, The
Lamb Of God
Let Us Not Forget
Love And Dream
Love Song
March Of The Toreadors
Morning
Morning Song
My Dear Old Home
Night
Notte Di Carezze
Open Thy Heart
Ouvre Ton Coeur
Pastel
Prelude From Carmen
Romance
Romance De Nadir
Seguidilla
Serenade
Si Tu M'aimes
Siren, The
Soldier's March
Song At Evening
Song Of April
Song Of Love
Song Of The Castenets, The
Song Of The Madman, The
Song Of The Rose
Song Of The Toreador
Tale
Thine The Glory
This Flower Sweet
Three Kings, The
Toreador Song
Votre Toast
Vous Pouvez M'arreter
Voyage
Who Then Will Love Thee More
Why Need You Weep

Bjoefklund & Evers & Forsey
Boogie Woogie Dancin' Shoes
Bjorkman
Jolly Little Eskimo
Bjorn, Frank
Alley Cat Song, The
Black
Army Air Force Crew Song
Better Every Day
Bluebells And Fairies
Cherry Blossoms
He Saves Me
Holy Spirit Dwell In Me
Long Time Ago
Making Songs
Nobody's Home
Nothing's News
Where Jesus Is Tis Heaven
Black & Barnby
'Twas In The Winter Cold
Black & Bourke
Another Sleepless Night
Shadows In The Moonlight
Black & Bourke & Chater
I Know A Heartache When I See
One
Black & Bourke & Rocco
Little Good News, A
Black & Moret
Moonlight And Roses
Moonlight And Roses Bring
Mem'ries Of You
Black & Moret & Lemare
Moonlight And Roses Bring
Memories Of You
Black & Nicholas & Gay
Walkin' Away
Black & Rocco
Another Motel Memory
Slow Burn
Black, James
When The Roll Is Called Up Yonder
When The Saints Go Marching In
Black, Johnny
Paper Doll
Blackburn & Mitchell & Porter
Need You
Blackburn & Suessdorf
Moonlight In Vermont
Blackith
Gracious Spirit Dwell With Me
Blackley
Stranger In The Straw
Blackman
Everybody Be Dancin'
KC Moan
Blackmar
Cross Of The South, The
For Bales
Goober Peas
Southrons' Chaunt Of Defiance
Sword Of Robert E. Lee, The
Sword Of Robert Lee, The
Upidee Song, The

Blackmer
After
How Far To The City Of Gold
Numberless As The Sands
Oh 'Tis Wonderful
Blackmon & Jenkins
Candy
Word Up
Blackmore & Blackmore
Some Golden Daybreak
Blackmore & Lord & Coverdale & Paice
Burn
Blackwell
Breathless
Lil' Red Riding Hood
Rip It Up
Blackwell & Hammer
Great Balls Of Fire
Blackwell & Jones
Handy Man
Blackwell & Lee
Friends In Low Places
Blackwell & Marascalco
Good Golly Miss Molly
Ready Teddy
Rip It Up
Blackwell & Millet
All Around The World
Blackwell & Presley
All Shook Up
Don't Be Cruel
Don't Be Cruel To A Heart That's
True
Paralyzed
Blackwell & Scott
Easy Question
One Broken Heart For Sale
Please Don't Drag That String
Around
Return To Sender
We're Coming In Loaded
Blackwell & Stevenson
Hey Little Girl In The High School
Sweater
Blackwell & Stone
Handy Man
Blackwell, DeWayne
Make My Day
Mr Blue
Blades
Four In The Morning
Sentimental Street
Blah'a
Musicians Play With Me
Blaikley
Zabadak
Blaine
Trolley Song, The
Blair
O Lamb Of God I Come
Blaisch
Could've Been
Blaisdell
As The Backs Go Tearing By

Blaise
Cerises, Les
Blake
Different From Us
Little Darling
Sidewalks Of New York, The
To Mercy Pity Peace And Love
You Gonna Quit Me Baby
Blake, Charles
Trabling Back To Georgia
Blake, Charlotte
Harbor Of Love, The
Blake, Eubie
I'm Just Wild About Harry
Memories Of You
Blakeman
Alliance Flag-Ship Song
Blamphin
Little Maggie May
Blamphin, Charles
When The Corn Is Waving
When The Corn Is Waving Annie
Dear
Blanche & Orson
Hard Luck Story
Blanchard
Fill My Cup Lord
God Of Our Youth To Whom We
Yield
Blanchard & Malone
Please Love Me Forever
Blanchard & Stewart
My Heart's Prayer
Bland
Carry Me Back
Carry Me Back To Old Virginny
Close Dem Windows
Come Along Sister Mary
Dancing On De Kithchen Floor
Dandy Black Brigade, The
Dem Golden Slippers
Gabriel's Band
Golden Slippers
Golden Wedding, De
Hand Me Down My Walking Cane
In The Ev'ning By The Moonlight
In The Evenin' By The Moonlight
In The Evening By The Moonlight
In The Morning
In The Morning By The Bright Light
Keep Dem Golden Gates Wide Open
Listen To The Silver Trumpet
O Them Golden Slippers
Oh Dem Golden Slippers
Oh Them Golden Slippers
Old Fashioned Cottage, The
Old Homestead, The
Rose Pachoula
Tapioca
Tell All De Children Good Bye
Way Up Yonder
Bland, A. P.
How Beautiful Heaven Must Be

Blandemer
Darlin'
Blandy & Norris
Where He Leads Me I Will Follow
Blane, Ralph
Love
Trolley Song, The
Blangini
Education Des Demoiselles, L'
Blanke
When The Mocking Birds Are
Singing In The Wildwood
Blankenship
Joybells
Blanson & Brookins
She's On The Left
Blanter
Blouse Of Blue, A
Katiusha
Wait For Me
Blaufuss, Walter
Your Eyes Have Told Me So
Blazy & Freeman
You Bring Out The Love In Me
Blazy & Hiter & Mohead
Southern Woman
Bledsoe & Corin & Dobbins & Ri
You Are All I Need
Bleichmann
Pretend
Blewitt
Mama Mama
Bliss
Abundantly Able To Save
Arise And Shine
Being Young And Green
Can It Be Right
Father In Heaven Hear Us Today
Half Was Never Told, The
Hallelujah 'Tis Done
Hi Li'l Feller
Innocent Eyes
Let The Lower Lights Be Burning
Lo The Day Of God Is Breaking
Midsummer Night, A
Precious Promise God Hath Given
Standing By A Purpose True
'Tis The Promise Of God
Waltz Song
Way Of The Cross, The
We Are Marching Onward
Welcome Happy Morning
When Jesus Comes
Windows Open Toward Jerusalem
Bliss & McGranahan
I Will Sing Of My Redeemer
My Redeemer
Bliss, Paul
It Is Well With My Soul
Bliss, Philip
Almost Persuaded
Almost Persuaded Now To Believe
Brightly Beams Our Father's Mercy
Dare To Be A Daniel

Bliss, Philip *(Cont.)*
Eternity
Go Bury Thy Sorrow
Hallelujah What A Savior
Hallelujah What A Saviour
Hold The Fort
I Am So Glad That Our Father In
Heaven
I Gave My Life For Thee
Jesus Loves Even Me
Light Of The World Is Jesus, The
Man Of Sorrows What A Name
More Holiness Give Me
My Prayer
Sing Them Over Again To Me
What Shall The Harvest Be
When Peace Like A River
Whosoever Will
Wonderful Words Of Life
Blitzstein
Cradle Will Rock, The
I Wish It So
Jimmie's Got A Goil
Monday Morning Blues
My True Heart
Nickel Under The Foot
Block
Walkin' After Midnight
Block & Holofcener & Weiss
Mr Wonderful
Blockley
Hearts And Homes
Listen To The Convent Bells
Moon Is Beaming O'Er The Lake,
The
Yesterday
Blodgett
Fair Smith
Blom
Brave Songs Of Norway
Han Skal Apne Perleporten
Bloom
Dear Old White And Blue
Bloom, Rube
Day In Day Out
Don't Worry 'bout Me
Fools Rush In
Fools Rush In Where Angels Fear To
Tread
Give Me The Simple Life
I Wish I Could Tell You
Maybe You'll Be There
Bloom & Cordell & Gentry & James
Mony Mony
Bloomfield & Barnby
O Perfect Love
Bloomfield & Barney
O Perfect Love
Blount
Thou Art My God
Blow
Blessed Be The Lord God Of Israel
Boldly With Mettle
Galloping

Blow *(Cont.)*
Praise The Lord O My Soul
Rarities Of The Fair
Self Banished, The
Blow & Waring & Miller
Fat Boys
Blower
Echo
Blowers
Come Today
Blue
Balintore Fisherman, The
Ballad Of Erica Levine, The
Blume
Grun Ist Die Haide
Blumenthal
Arizona
Lo The Day Of Days Is Here
Loving Shepherd
Sailor Boy's Farewell, The
Saviour When In Dust To Thee
Venetian Boat Song
Boatner
Ain't You Glad
All O' My Sins
Balm In Gilead
Can I Ride
Certainly Lord
Children Don't Get Weary
Couldn't Hear Nobody Pray
Crucifixion
Down By The Riverside
Give Me Your Hand
Glory Glory Hallelujah
God's Going To Set This World On
Fire
Good News
He's Got The Whole World In His
Hand
How Did You Feel
I Know The Lord
I Shall Not Be Moved
I'm A Soldier
I'm So Glad
I've Got A Robe
In My Father's House
Let Me Ride
Let The Words
Listen To The Lambs
Little Talk With Jesus, A
Lord I Want To Be A Christian
My Good Lord's Been Here
My Lord What A Mourning
Now Is The Needy Time
Room Enough
Sit Down Servant
Steal Away
Swing Low Sweet Chariot
There Is Joy In That Land
Time Ain't Long, The
When The Saints Go Marching In
You Must Have That True Religion

Bobo
Long-Sought Home
Boccherini
Menuetto
Bock
Apple Tree, The
Do You Love Me
Fiddler On The Roof
If I Were A Rich Man
Little Tin Box
Matchmaker
Matchmaker Matchmaker
Miracles Of Miracles
One Solitary Life
She Loves Me
Si J'avais Des Millions
Sunrise Sunset
'Til Tomorrow
To Life
Tradition
Tree Of Peace, The
Bock & Harnick
Little Tin Box
Bock & Holofcener & Weiss
Mr Wonderful
Too Close For Comfort
Bode
I Know Not Where The Road Will
Lead
Miss Chickadee
Thanksgiving Morning
Bode & Mann
O Jesus I Have Promised
Body
Gonna Have 'Lasses In The Morning
Boering
Vmi Spirit
Boesel
Take A Look At Your Nickel
Boex
Vot Vos You Up To Uncle Sam
Bofill
Only Love
Bogard & Tweel
Mornin' Ride
Boggs
Tech Triumph
Bogoslavsky
Dark Is The Night
Bohm
Calm As The Night
Friendship's Tree
My All
Still Wie Die Nacht
Bohm, Karl
Still As The Night
Bohme
Sei Still
Boie
Lore Am Tore, Die
Boieldieu
Ballade Of The White Lady
With Joy My Flowing Cup I Bring

Boieldiew
Hunting Song
Bok
Bay Of Fundy
Bolan
Bang A Gong
Boland
I Like It Here
Men Of Pennsylvania
Bolen & Rees
Cuba
Bolin
California Poppies
Bolland & Bolland
Vienna Calling
Bolland & Bolland & Falco
Rock Me Amadeus
Bollback
Ring The Bells
Bolles
Ballad Of The Outland Bowmen
Bolling
Count On Him
From The First Hallelujah To The
Last Amen
Bolton & Goldmark
Soul Provider
Bolton & James
How Am I Supposed To Live
Without You
Bolton & Kaz
That's What Love Is All About
Bolton & Mangold
I Found Someone
Bolton & Stanley
Forever
Bolton & Warren
We're Not Making Love Anymore
Bolton & Warren & Child
How Can We Be Lovers
Bon Jovi
Living In Sin
Silent Night
Bon Jovi & Bryan
Only Lonely
Bon Jovi & Sambora
I'll Be There For You
Lay Your Hands On Me
Never Say Goodbye
Wanted Dead Or Alive
Bon Jovi & Sambora & Child
Bad Medicine
Born To Be My Baby
Livin' On A Prayer
We All Sleep Alone
You Give Love A Bad Name
Bonagura & Baillie & Bickhardt
I Can't Turn The Tide
Bonar & Zundel
I Was A Wandering Sheep
Bond
Bad Dream, A
De Las' Long Res'
Des Hold My Hands Tonight

Bond *(Cont.)*
End Of A Navy Day
Half Minute Songs
Lambkin, The
Mother's Cradle Song
Parting
Still Unexprest
Bond-Jackson
Just A Wearying For You
Bonds
Dream Variation
I Too
Minstrel Man
Bonfa
Samba De Orfeu
Bonfa, Luiz
Day In The Life Of A Fool, A
Bonfire
Born To Be Wild
Bonham & Jones & Plant
D'Yer Mak'er
Boni
Ha Bel Accueil
J'espere Et Crains
Bonnell
Turkey In The Straw
Bonner
Clear Midnight, A
Corn Song, The
Dismantled Ship, The
I Think When I Read That Sweet
Story
My Country Is The World
Phantoms
Bonner & Gordon
Celebrate
Happy Together
Me About You
She'd Rather Be With Me
Bonnet
Francion Vint L'autre Jour
Bono & Nitzsche
Needles And Pins
Bono, Sonny
Baby Don't Go
Beat Goes On, The
I Got You Babe
You'd Better Sit Down Kids
Bonoff
All My Life
Someone To Lay Down Beside Me
Bononcini
Esperto Nocchiero, L'
For The Glory
Per La Gloria D'adorarvi
Since 'Tis Glory
Booker
Ring It Out With A Shout
Boomer
O Come All Ye Children
Boone & Gibson & Hinson
Please Don't Give Candy To A
Stranger

Boone & McQueen
Beautiful Sunday
Boone & Nelson
Roses In December
Boosahda
Comin' Home To You
Let Your Faith Do The Walkin'
Why Choose Me God
You Were There
Boosahda & Stearman
Somewhere It's Snowing
Who Do You Say That I Am
Booth
City Of God How Broad And Far
Cross Is Not Greater, The
God Who Made The Earth
Our Father's God From Out Whose
Hand
Safe Home Safe Home In Port
We Bless Thee For Thy Peace
When Courage Fails And Faith
Burns Low
When Wilt Thou Save The People
Booth & Goff & Hoffman
Run Woman Run
Boothroyd
Powder River
Boott
Bye Baby Birds Are Sleeping
Here's A Health To King Charles
Sands O' Dee, The
Union And Liberty
Borden
When Shall We Meet Again
Borders & Beach
You Lay A Whole Lot Of Love On
Me
Borel-Clerc
Sorella, La
Bornschein
In The Rocky Hills
Borodin, Alexander
Arabian Melody
Dissonance, A
Poisoned
Polovetzian Dance
Prince Igor's Song
Sleeping Princess, The
Song Of The Slave Girls
Borodine
Lovely Garden
Borop
Bread For The World
Borop & Card
Come To The Table
Boroughs
Redeemed
Solemn Warning
Borrelli
Duquesne Pep Song
Bortiniansky
Now On Land And Sea Descending

Bortnianski
Jesus Master Whose I Am
Vesper Hymn
Bortniansky, Dimitri
Before Thy Throne O God We Kneel
Cherubim Song
Ehre Sei Gott
Father We Will Quiet Be
Hark The Vesper Hymn
Hark The Vesper Hymn Is Stealing
I Have Set The Lord Alway Before
Me
Ich Bete An Die Macht Der Liebe
Invocation
Lo A Voice To Heaven Sounding
Peasants' Vesper Song
Savior Breathe An Evening Blessing
Saviour Breathe An Evening Belssing
Saviour Breathe An Evening Blessing
Thou Art With Us
Thou Hast Said Exalted Jesus
Thou Hidden Source Of Calm
Repose
Vesper Hymn, The
Vesper Song
When Gathering Clouds Around I
View
Boshell
I've Got The Music In Me
Bossetti
Would I Were With Thee
Bost
Gratitude
Lord Speak To Me That I May Speak
Boswell, Eric
Little Donkey
Botija
Castigame
Botija & Nunez
Jamas Te Dejare
Botkin
Bless The Beasts And Children
Mork And Mindy Theme
Theme From Mork And Mindy
Theme From Quark
Botkin & Devorzon
Bless The Beasts And Children
Nadia's Theme
Botsford
Pride Of The Prairie
Botsford, George
Black And White Rag
Bottazzo
Popule Meus
Regina Coeli
Vexilla Regis
Bottorf
Conquer In The Savior's Name
I Want To See Jesus Don't You
Wandering Child O Come Home
When The Book Is Opened
Boucicault
Pat Malloy

Boudreau
Hail Crimson Gray
Boughton
Ben Jonson's Carol
Boulanger
Vous M'avez Regarde Avec Toute
Votre Ame
Boulanger & Kennedy
My Prayer
Bounty & Geyer
Hot Rod Hearts
Bourgeois
All Hail Adored Trinity
Ancient Law Departs, The
Before Jehovah's Awful Throne
Bread Of The World
Bread Of The World In Mercy
Broken
Day Thou Gavest, The
Day Thou Gavest Lord Is Ended,
The
Doxology, The
Father We Thank Thee Who Hast
Planted
From All That Dwell Below The
Skies
God Of The Nations Who From
Dawn Of Days
God Of The Prophets Bless The
Prophets' Sons
God's Not Finished With Me Yet
Joy And Triumph Everlasting
Lift Up Your Hearts
Manola
New Songs Of Celebration Render
O Day Of God Draw Nigh In Beauty
O Food Of Men Wayfaring
O Gladsome Light
O Gladsome Light O Grace
O Gladsome Light O Grace Of God
The Father's Face
O Love How Deep How Broad How
High
Rise And Be Healed
Through North And South And East
And West
Turn Back O Man Forswear Thy
Foolish Ways
Veni Creator Spiritus
Virgin Born We Bow Before Thee
When In The Hour Of Utmost Need
When Morning Fills The Sky
With Broken Heart And Contrite
Sigh
Bourgeois & Beckett & Ross
Dare To Fall In Love
Bourgeois & Workman
I Don't Mind At All
Bourgeois, Louis
All People That On Earth Do Dwell
Old Hundred
Old Hundredth
Praise God From Whom All
Blessings Flow

Bourget
You Heavens Open
Bourguignon
Cat, The
Bourke & Black & Pinkard
Blessed Are The Believers
Bourke & Channel & Kane
Doctor's Orders
Bourke & Vanhoy & Allen
Baby I Lied
Let's Stop Talkin' About It
Bourne
Our Father's Care
Bouwens
Paloma Blanca
Bovet
Colin
Bovkin & Anderson
God Answers Every Prayer
Bowen & Knox
I'm Stickin' With You
Party Doll
Bowen, James
Party Doll
Bowering
Vmi Spirit
Bowers
Berkeley Woman
Christopher The Christmas Tree
Oh I'm A Good Old Rebel
Bowers, Frederick
Because
Lucky Jim
Bowie, David
Blue Jean
Let's Dance
Space Oddity
Bowie & Lennon & Alomar
Fame
Bowie & Pop
China Girl
Tonight
Bowles
Ainsi Parfois Nos Seuils
I'm A Jay Hawk
In The Woods
Once A Lady Was Here
Bowles & Robinson
I Know How He Feels
Bowling
Friday Night Fool
Bowling & Bynum
Lucille
Bowling & Wheeler
Coward Of The County
Long Arm Of The Law
Bowman
12th Street Rag
East Of The Sun
East Of The Sun And West Of The
Moon
East Of The Sun West Of The Moon
Lamb, The

Bowman (*Cont.*)
My Pumpkins Are Ripe
Skating
Bowman, Evday
Twelfth Street Rag
Boyarska
Babi Yar
Boyarskaya
Birobizhaner Viglid
Boyce
Alleluia Round
By The Banks Gentle Stour
God Of Saints To Whom The
Number
Heart Of Oak
Hearts Of Oak
In Your Mercy Lord You Called Me
Liberty Song, The
Long Live The King
Lord And Saviour True And Kind
May The Grace Of Christ Our Savior
Now Unto The King Eternal
O Come Let Us Sing
O Come Let Us Sing Unto The Lord
Palms Of Glory Raiment Bright
Providence Alone Secures
Song Of Momus To Mars, The
Thy Kingdom Come O God
Well Judging Phyllis
Boyce & Hart
I Wonder What She's Doing Tonight
Last Train To Clarksville
Monkees, The
Theme From The Monkees
Boyce & Lee
Pretty Little Angel Eyes
Boyd
Albion
God Of The Strong God Of The
Weak
Keep Thyself Pure
New Orleans
Why Should We Start And Fear To
Die
Boyd, William
Fight The Good Fight
Fight The Good Fight With All Thy
Might
Let There Be Light
Let There Be Light Lord God Of
Hosts
Boyden
If I'm Not At The Roll-Call
Boyington
I'm Taking A Flight
Boyle
In Bressilia's Forest Shade
Boyle & Hofmann
To The Castle
Boynton
What's The Matter
Boys
J'Ayme Bien Mon Amy

Bracey
Leavin' Town Blues
Saturday Blues
Bracken
You Gave Me Peace Of Mind
Bracken & Hooker
Dimples
Little Wheel
Bracken & Hudson
Goodnight It's Time To Go
Bracken & Otis
Take Pride In America
Bradbury
Asleep In Jesus
Asleep In Jesus Blessed Sleep
Er Fuhret Mich
Firmly Stand My Native
Flag Of Our Union, The
From Every Stormy Wind
Geheimnisvoll In Tiefer Nacht
Glorious Morning, The
How Blest The Righteous When He
Dies
I've Found A Friend O Such A
Friend
Im Herrn Entschlummert
Inscribed Upon The Cross We See
Lord I Hear Of Showers Of Blessing
Marching Along
My Own Native Land
Never Further Than Thy Cross
Not To Condemn The Sons Of Men
O Give Thanks Unto The Lord
O Love Divine That Stooped To
Share
O Sing Of His Mighty Love
Prince Of Peace Control My Will
Rally Round The Flag
Return O Wanderer Return
'Tis Midnight And On Olive's Brow
Trust His Care
Unfurl The Glorious Banner
We Are Marching On
When As Returns This Solemn Day
Why Should We Start And Fear To
Die
Wicked Polly
Bradbury, William
Brown
Even Me
Even Me Even Me
God Calling Yet Shall I Not Hear
He Leadeth Me
He Leadeth Me O Blessed Thought
I Think When I Read That Sweet
Story Of Old
Jesus Loves Me
Jesus Loves Me This I Know
Just As I Am
Just As I Am Without One Plea
My Hope Is Built
My Hope Is Built On Nothing Less
My Latest Sun Is Sinking Fast
Over The Ocean Wave Far Far Away

Bradbury, William *(Cont.)*
Rest
Savior Like A Shepherd Lead Us
Saviour Like A Shepherd Lead Us
Solid Rock, The
Sweet Hour Of Prayer
Take My Life And Let It Be
There Is No Name So Sweet On
Earth
With Joy We Hail The Sacred Day
Woodworth
Zephyr
Braddock
I Believe The South Is Gonna Rise
Again
Nothing Ever Hurt Me
Would They Love Him Down In
Shreveport
Braddock & Berg
Faking Love
Braddock & Putman
D-I-V-O-R-C-E
He Stopped Loving Her Today
Braddock & Vanhoy
Golden Ring
Bradfield & Meggs
Still Better
Bradford & Lewis
Tears On My Pillow
Bradford, Perry
Crazy Blues
Bradley
Hark The Marning Bell Is Pealing
Bradley & Haskell
Oh Come Angel Band
Bradshaw
Detroit
Mississippi
Palmyra
Bradsky
Thou Art Mine All
Thou Art My All
Braga, Gaetano
Angels' Serenade
Serenata, La
Bragdon
Bow-Wow-Wow
Braham
Adolphus Morning Glory
Anchor's Weigh'd, The
Anchor's Weighed, The
Are You There Moriarity
Green Bush, The
Isle De Blackwell
Little Widow Dunn, The
Major Gilfeather
Mary Kelly's Beau
Over The Hill To The Poor House
Over The Hills To The Poor House
Slavery Days
Widow Nolan's Goat, The
Braham, David
Babies On Our Block, The
Maggie Murphy's Home

Braham, David *(Cont.)*
Mulligan Guard, The
My Dad's Dinner Pail
Never Take The Horse-Shoe From
The Door
Paddy Duffy's Cart
Patrick's Day Parade
Skidmore Guard
Braham, Philip
Limehouse Blues
Brahe
Bless This House
Brahms
Abend, Der
Abendlied
Abendregen
Abschied
Abschiedslied
Ach Wende Diesen Blick
Agnes
Am Sonntag Morgen
An Die Heimat
An Die Stolze
Anklange
Arise Beloved Vision
As The Morning's Crimson Splendor
Auf Dem Schiffe
Barcarole
Bei Dir Sind Meine Gedanken
Bei Nachtlicher Weil
Beim Abschied
Below In The Valley
Beware
Bird Flies Over The Rhine, A
Bird In Air Will Stray Afar
Birds In Air Will Stray Afar
Bitteres Zu Sagen Denkst Du
Blacksmith, The
Botschaft
Brahms Melody
Charm Me Asleep
Christmas Carol, A
Close Your Eyes
Come Let Us Wander
Come Soon
Cradle Song
Da Unten Im Tale
Dammrung Senkte Sich Von Oben
Dein Blaues Auge
Disappointed Serenader, The
Do You Often Call To Mind
Dream Song
Du Mein Einzig Licht
Es Hing Der Reif
Evening Hymn
Faithful Love
Fare Well
Feldeinsamkeit
Fragen
From Yon Hills The Torrent Speeds
Frost Was White, The
Fruhlingslied
Fruhlingstrost
Gang Zum Liebchen, Der

Brahms (*Cont.*)

Gang Zur Liebsten
Gold Uberwiegt Die Liebe
Good Night
Greetings
Guardian Angel
Gute Gute Nacht, Eine
Guten Abend Gut Nacht
Gypsies, The
Gypsy Song
Homeless Man, The
Hungarian Dance
Hungarian Dance No 5
Huntsman, The
I Hear A Harp
Ich Schleich Umher Betrubt
Ich Wandte Mich Und Sahe An Alle
Im Garten Am Seegestade
In Lonely Wood
In Long Green Grass
In Meiner Nachte Sehnen
In Stiller Nacht
In Summer Fields
In Wood Embower'd
In Wood Embowered 'Neath Azure
  Skies
Jager, Der
Juchhe
Jungfraulein Soll Ich Mit Euch Geh'n
Kein Haus Keine Heimat
Klage
Kuss, Der
Lament
Lerchengesang
Liebe Und Fruhling I
Liebe Und Fruhling II
Liebende Schreibt, Die
Liebesglut
Liebesklage Des Madchens
Lied
Lied Vom Herrn Von Falkenstein,
  Das
Lighter Far Is Now My Slumber
Little Dustman, The
Little Sandman, The
Locksmith Ho A Hundred Padlocks
Love Is For Ever
Love Song
Lullaby
Lullaby And Good Night
Madchen, Das
Madchenfluch
Magyarisch
Maid And The Hazel Tree, The
Maiden Rose At Early Dawn, A
Maiden's Curse, The
Maiden's Song
Maiden's Song, A
Maienkatzchen
Mainacht, Die
Marschieren
May Night
Mein Herz Ist Schwer
Mein Madel Hat Einen Rosenmund

Brahms (*Cont.*)

Meine Liebe Ist Grun
Meine Lieder
Mit Vierzig Jahren
Mondenschein
Mondnacht
Morning Song
Murrays Ermordung
My Dear One's Mouth Is Like The
  Rose
My Every Thought Is With Thee
  Love
My Heart Is In Bloom
My Inmost Thoughts Are All Of
  Thee
My Little Queen
My Mother Loves Me Not
My Queen
My Songs
Nachtens
Nachtigall
Nachtigallen Schwingen
Nachtwandler
Nachwirkung
Neckereien
Nightingale
Nightingale Thy Sweetest Song
No There Is No Bearing With These
  Spiteful Neighbors
Now Suffer Me Fair Maiden
Nur Ein Gesicht
Nur Ein Gesicht Auf Erden Lebt
O God We Give Thanks
O Good Morning My Fair One
O Jesu Joy Of Loving Hearts
O Komme Holde Sommernacht
O Kuhler Wald
O Lovely May
O Schone Nacht
O Silent Night
O That I Might Retrace The Way
Oh Death Is Like The Cooling Night
Oh That I Might Retrace The Way
Our Blacksmith
Parole
Quest, The
Quiet Wood, The
Regenlied
Remembrance
Roseate Clouds Of Evening Drift
Salamander
Sandman, The
Sapphic Ode
Sapphische Ode
Saviour Hear Us We Pray
Schoner Augen Schone Strahlen
Schwestern, Die
Secret Nook In Shady Spot
Sehnsucht
Serenade
Silver Moon In Heaven High
Sleep Baby Sleep
Slumber-Song
Smith, The

Brahms (*Cont.*)

So Lass Uns Wandern
Song From Ossian's Fingal
Song From Shakespeare's Twelfth
  Night
Song Of The Skylark
Sonntag
Sounds Of Music
Sower, The
Spatherbst
Standchen
Star Of Joy
Suabian Folk-Song
Sunday
That Night In May
Thought Like Music, A
To A Nightingale
To A Violet
To An Aeolian Harp
To Our Alma Mater
To Part Ah Grief Unending
To The Nightingale
Todessehnen
Trauernde, Die
Treachery
Tremor's In The Branches, A
Trennung
Treue Liebe
Trost In Tranen
True Love
True Lover's Heart
Trysting Place, The
Uber Die Heide
Uber Die See
Unuberwindlich
Vergangen Ist Mir Gluck And Heil
Vergebliches Standchen
Verrat
Versunken
Verzagen
Volkslied
Vom Strande
Vom Verwundeten Knaben
Vorschneller Schwur
Voruber
Wahrend Des Regens
Waltz
Wanderer, Ein
Warum
Was Once A Pretty Tiny Birdie
Watchful Lover, The
Wechsellied Zum Tanz
Weg Der Liebe
Wenn Dunur Zuweilen Lachelst
What Sweeter Music
When Ich Mit Menschen
Wie' Die Wolke Nach Der Sonne
Wie Melodien Zieht Es Mir
Wie Rafft Ich Mich Auf
Wiegenlied
Willie Willie Will
Willst Du Dass Ich Geh
Wir Wandelten
Wondrous Music

Brainard & Kelly & Thayer
  To Canaan
Braine
  Apple Tree, The
Brainin, Jerry
  Night Has A Thousand Eyes, The
Braithwaite & Eastmond & Ocean
  There'll Be Sad Songs To Make You
    Cry
Brambley & Barnby
  Cradle Song Of The Blessed Mother
Bramlett, D.
  Never Ending Song Of Love
Bramley & Smart
  Jesus In The Manger
Brand
  Seven Sleepers, The
Brand, Oscar
  Guy Is A Guy, A
Brandow & Miller & Spotswood
  Hold Tight Hold Tight
Brandstrom
  Sunshine And Rain
Brandt & Haymes
  That's All
  Tht's All
Brannan & Campbell
  Think About Love
Brannan & Crawford & Malloy
  Soldier Of Love
Brannan & Schuyler
  I Could Love You In A Heartbeat
Branscombe
  Draw Night To Thy Jerusalem O
    Lord
  To The Knights In The Days Of Old
Brant
  3-Way Canon Blues, The
Brant & Haymes
  That's All
Brasfield & Byrne
  Get It Up
  Half Past Forever
  I Love The Way He Left You
Brass
  I'm In Your Care
**Brathwaite & Eastmond & Lange &
  Ocean**
  When The Going Gets Tough The
    Tough Get Going
Brathwaite & Eastmond & Ocean
  Love Is Forever
  Love Zone
  There'll Be Sad Songs To Make You
    Cry
Bratta & Tramp
  Little Fighter
  Wait
  When The Children Cry
Bratton
  Good-By Teddy You Must March
    March March
  My Cosey Corner Girl

Bratton, John
  Sunshine Of Paradise Alley, The
  Teddy Bear's Picnic, The
Braun
  All Alone
  Fou D'amour
Braunstein
  I'm In Love With A Big Blue Frog
Bray & Pierce
  Cross My Broken Heart
Bredon
  Babe I'm Gonna Leave You
Bree
  Brooks Shall Murmur
Breedlove
  Charlton
  Cross Of Christ
  Going Home
  Happy Land
  I Would See Jesus
  Mercy's Free
  Victoria
Breese & Jones
  Door Boy's Last Good-Bye, The
Breidenstein
  Wenn Ich Ihn Nur Habe
Breitenfeld
  Last Long Mile, The
Brel & Jouannest
  Marieke
Brel, Jacques
  Days Of The Waltz, The
  If We Only Have Love
  If You Go Away
  Seasons In The Sun
  Valse A Mille Temps, La
Brenner
  Laredo
Brescia
  That Was Then This Is Now
Breuer
  Goo Goo G'Da
Brewer
  Bashfulness
  Blest Is He
  Turn Amarillis To Thy Swain
Brewington
  It Will Be Glory Up There
Brewster
  I'm Getting Nearer To My Home
  Move On Up A Little Higher
  Our Comrade Has Fallen
  These Are They
**Brianbert & Gorman & Dobbins &
  Garrett**
  Please Mr Postman
**Brickell & Withrow & Houser & Bush
  & Aly**
  What I Am
Bricusse & Newley
  Candy Man, The
  Feeling Good
  Gonna Build A Mountain
  Joker, The

Bricusse & Newley *(Cont.)*
  Look At That Face
  Nothing Can Stop Me Now
  Once In A Lifetime
  What Kind Of Fool Am I
  Who Can I Turn To
  Who Can I Turn To When Nobody
    Needs Me
  Wonderful Day Like Today, A
Bricusse, Leslie
  Fill The World With Love
  My Kind Of Girl
  Talk To The Animals
  Thank You Very Much
  You And I
Bridge, Frank
  Adoration
  All Things That We Clasp
  Blow Blow Thou Winter Wind
  Blow Out You Bugles
  Come To Me In My Dreams
  Dawn And Evening
  Devon Maid, The
  E'en As A Lovely Flower
  Evening Primrose
  Fair Daffodils
  Go Not Happy Day
  Into Her Keeping
  Last Invocation, The
  Love Went A-Riding
  Mantle Of Blue
  Pan's Holiday
  So Early In The Morning O
  So Perverse
  Spring Song, A
  Strew No More Red Roses
  Thy Hand In Mine
  'Tis But A Week
  Violets Blue, The
  What Shall I Your True Love Tell
  Where She Lies Asleep
Bridgers
  He Keeps Me Singing
Bridgewater & Bland
  How Beautiful Heaven Must Be
Briegs
  Men Of Rutgers
Brierly
  At The Name Of Jesus
Briggs
  For The Brave Of Ev'ry Race
  Jordan Am A Hard Road To Trabbel
  Lonesome Loser
Briley
  Salt In My Tears, The
Brill, E. S.
  Ma Lady Lu
Brim
  Ice Cream Man
Brimhall
  Christmas Lullaby
Brisker
  Pedlers Brivl, Dem

Bristol
Benediction
Friends In Bethany
Good Samaritan, The
Introit
Lord Make Us Servants Of Your
Peace
O Jesus Joy Of Loving Hearts
On The Road To Emmaus
Prayer Response
Shepherds Of Bethlehem
Ten Lepers, The
Bristol & Bullock & Fuqua
If I Could Build My Whole World
Around You
What Does It Take To Win Your
Love
Bristol & Fuqua & Sawyer & Roach
My Whole World Ended The
Moment You Left Me
Bristol & McLeod
Walk In The Night
Bristol & McNeil
What Is A Man
Bristow
Little John Bottlejohn
Our Noble Land
Rejoice Rejoice The Lost Is Found
Who Are All These Folks I See
Britten
At The Round Earth's Imagined
Corners
Batter My Heart
Charm, A
Choirmaster's Burial, The
Corpus Christi Carol
Death Be Not Proud
Fishing Song
Jazz-Man
Night Song, The
Nocturne
Noel Passee, La
O Might Those Sighes And Teares
Oh My Blacke Soule
Oh To Vex Me
Old Abram Brown
Salley Gardens, The
Sephestia's Lullaby
Since She Whom I Loved
Sweet Was The Song
There Is No Rose
There Was A Man Of Newington
There Was A Monkey
Thou Hast Made Me
Useful Plough, The
Wagtail And Baby
What If This Present
Britten, Benjamin
Fish In The Unruffled Lakes
Britten & Robertson
Carrie
Britten & Shifrin
Show Some Respect

Broadhurst
Cowboy Carol
Broady
Mandy's Broadway Stroll
Brock
Sing And Smile And Pray
Brock & Brock
Beyond The Sunset
Brocklert & Rudolph
Behind The Groove
Brockway
Jockey Hat And Feather
Broderip
When The Full Organ
Brodsky
I'll Walk With God
I've Gotta Hear That Beat
Brodszky, Nicholas
Be My Love
Because You're Mine
I'll Never Stop Loving You
I'll Walk With God
Wonder Why
Broeke
Now Pray We For Our Country
Take Courage Temperance Workers
Bronislau & Jurmann
San Francisco
Bronkema
To Have And To Hold
Brooker, Gary
Conquistador
Brooks
California
Come Share My Love
Grandma Got Run Over By A
Reindeer
If Ever I See You Again
If I Ever See You Again
It Tastes Too Good To Be True
Love And Emotion
Love Me
Mama
Most Misunderstood Soft Drink
Some Of These Days
Walkin' The Dog
Walking With Jesus
Brooks & Barer
I'm Just A Country Boy
Brooks & Blazy
If Tomorrow Never Comes
Brooks & Brooks & Butler
For Your Precious Love
Sweet Was The Wine
Brooks & Butler
For Your Precious Love
Brooks & Cook
Who's Lonely Now
Brooks & Devito
Tennessee Rose
Brooks, Charles
God Bless Our Native Land

Brooks, Joe
Pepsi's Got A Lot To Give You've
Got A Lot To Live
You've Got A Lot To Live
Brooks, John
You Came A Long Way From St
Louis
Brooks, Joseph
You Light Up My Life
Brooks, Shelton
Darktown Strutter's Ball, The
Broonzy
Black Brown And White Blues
Just A Dream On My Mind
Sun's Gonna Shine In My Door
Willie Mae
Broonzy & Segar
Key To The Highway
Brosz
Along The Santa Fe Trail
Brothers, The
When Will I Be Famous
Brothers & Azrael
Shouldn't I Know
Brougham
When I Went Off To Prospect
Broughton
Love Theme From Young Sherlock
Holmes
Main Theme From Silverado
Main Theme From Young Sherlock
Holmes
Theme From The Blue And The
Gray
Theme From The Presidio
We're Home Here
Brounoff
Hand With The Hammer, The
Brourman & Gottlieb
My Favorite Year
Browder, Stony
Cherchez La Femme
Brown
Adieu Sweet Amarillis
Agreement, The
Ah Sorry Poor Frenchmen
All Glory Laud And Honor
Almanac, The
Almanack Catch
Barrier, The
Beautiful Life
Bustin' Loose
Cats Assembled
Children's Hosanna, The
Come Winter Snow
Coral Sea
Daahoud
Day Is Past And Over, The
Don't Sit Under The Apple Tree
Draw Nigh And Take The Body Of
The Lord
Emmanuel Emmanuel
Father We Thank Thee

Brown *(Cont.)*
Foot Washing Song, The
Future Blues
Gentle Like You
Go Right Along Mister Wilson And
    We'll All Stand By You
God The Father God The Son
Going Hollywood
Got A New Pair Of Shoes
Great Round World, The
He Will Carry You
Hundred Years To Come, A
I Knew Love
I'm Going Down The Road
I've Been Treated Wrong
I've Got A Feelin' Your Foolin'
If I Can Dream
If I Had Been There
It Fell Upon A Summer Day
Jesus Name All Names Above
Just As I Am Without One Plea
Let Your Light Shine
Let's Drink To All Our Wives
Let's Drink To Our Wives
Liberty Bell Ring On
Lord Of The Church We Humbly
    Pray
Lord Of The Living Harvest
Lord The Good Shepard, The
Lowly Child, The
Manger Story, The
Mount Zion
My Record Will Be There
My Treasure
O Ring Glad Bells
O Young And Fearless Prophet
O'Er Neptune's Dominions
Off To The Rodeo
Oh Kiddo
On The Prophet's Old Dog
One Day In Your Life
Our Delaware
Panting For Heaven
Prayer For America
Rhode Island
Rock Solid
Rockin' At Midnight
Say It Loud I'm Black And I'm
    Proud
Song Without Words, A
Span Of Life
Sweet The Lesson Jesus Taught
Take My Life Precious Jesus
This Is The Day
Titanic Blues
To Be God's People
Until That Time
Wail From Mortgaged Homes, A
We Weigh The Anchor
When The Lord Of Love Was Here
Wilson That's All
Yard By Yard
Ye Fair Green Hills Of Galilee
Zion's Mount

Brown & Bloodworth
C'Mon Marianne
Brown & Bouton & Burch
Last Resort, The
Brown & Brannan
If You Wanna Talk Love
Brown & Clare
I'd Climb The Highest Mountain
Brown & Craft
I Wanna Be Ready
Brown & Fain
That Old Feeling
Brown & Frey
Take It Easy
Brown & Griffin
My Prerogative
Brown & Hall
What I Want You To Be
Brown & Harvey
Hell And High Water
Brown & Henderson
Life Is Just A Bowl Of Cherries
Thrill Is Gone, The
Brown & Johnson & Kirkland
All In My Mind
Brown & Lehman & Harding
Your Grace Still Amazes Me
Brown & Moore
Tell Me You'll Wait For Me
Brown & Morgan
You Can Call Me Blue
Brown & Naish
Goliath
Jesus I Love You
Brown & Nelson
Somebody's Brother
When Answers Aren't Enough
Brown & Overstreet
He's Gonna Smile On Me
Hold On
In The Middle Of The Night
Soul Set Free, A
Brown & Passe & Long
Here Comes The Judge
Brown & Richards
Jesus Cares For Me
Brown & Rose & Henderson
Dummy Song
Brown & Sansone & Calilli
Walk Away Renee
Brown & Schraubstader
Last Night On The Back Porch
Last Night On The Back Porch I
    Loved Her Best Of All
Brown & Scott
Knights Of The Golden O, The
Brown & Smiley & Gersmehl
Kingdom Of Love
Brown & Sumner
Love Found A Pardon
Brown & Taylor & Kool & The Gang
Emergency
Brown & Timm & Vejvoda & Zeman
Beer Barrel Polka

Brown & Whelan & Evans
Mad About You
Brown & Young
When I Was A Boy From The
    Mountains
Brown & Zachary
Praise His Name
Brown, Arthur
In Excelsis Gloria
When Christ Was Born Of Mary Free
Brown, Charles
America The Beautiful
Reach Out And Touch
Brown, Errol
You Sexy Thing
Brown, Fleta
Under The Stars
Brown, Howard
Follow I Will Follow Thee
Brown, James
I Got You
Papa's Got A Brand New Bag
Brown, Nacio
All I Do Is Dream Of You
Alone
Broadway Melody
Broadway Rhythm
Doll Dance
Good Morning
Love Songs Of The Nile
Make 'em Laugh
Pagan Love Song
Paradise
Should I
Singin' In The Rain
Temptation
Wedding Of The Painted Doll
When Bhudda Smiles
Woman In The Shoe, The
Would You
You Are My Lucky Star
You Stepped Out Of A Dream
You Were Meant For Me
Brown, Peter
Material Girl
Browne
Before The Deluge
Boulevard
Breaking Waves Dashed High, The
Daddy's Tune
Epitaph On Salathiel Pavy
Farther On
For A Dancer
For Everyman
Fountain Of Sorrow
Fuse, The
I Thought I Was A Child
Landing Of The Pilgrims
Landing Of The Pilgrims, The
Late For The Sky
Late Show, The
Lawyers In Love
Linda Paloma
Looking Into You

Browne (*Cont.*)
O Perfect Love
Only Child, The
Our Lady Of The Well
Pretender, The
Ready Or Not
Redneck Friend
Road And The Sky, The
Rock Me On The Water
Running On Empty
Shadow Dream Song
Sing My Songs To Me
Sleep's Dark And Silent Gate
Something Fine
That Girl Could Sing
These Days
Under The Falling Sky
Walking Slow
You Love The Thunder
Your Bright Baby Blues
Browne & Burke
Nothing But Time
Browne & De Vol
Friendly Tavern Polka
Browne & Farnsworth
Here Come Those Tears Again
Browne & Frey
Take It Easy
Taking It Easy
Browne & Garofalo
Load-Out, The
Browne & Kortchmar & Kunkle
Tender Is The Night
Browne & Miller
Rosie
Browning
Sweet Harmony
Brubeck & Jarreau
Blue Rondo A La Turk
Brubeck, Dave
Blue Rondona Ala Turk
Bossa Nova USA
Far More Blue
It's A Raggy Waltz
My One Bad Habit
Summer Song
Unsquare Dance
Bruce
Man That Turned My Mama On,
   The
Scots Wha Hae Wi Wallace Bled
Bruce & Borchers & Bruce
Texas
Bruce & Brown
I Feel Free
White Room
Bruce & Brown & Clapton
Sunshine Of Your Love, The
Bruce & Bruce
Mammas Don't Let Your Babies
   Grow Up To Be Cowboys
Bruce & Bruce & Ray
Ever Never Lovin' You

Bruce & Peterson
Last Cowboy Song, The
Bruce & Rogers
My First Taste Of Texas
Bruce, Gary
Moody River
Bruch
Be Happy
Christ Und Der Tod
In Den Schooss Der Ewigkeiten
In Der Nacht
Bruck
How Happy Is The Child
Turn The Rascals Out
Bruford And Squire
Eclipse
Bruger
Caissons Go Rolling Along, The
Brumley
He Set Me Free
I'll Fly Away
I'll Meet You In The Morning
If We Never Meet Again
Jesus Hold My Hand
Brumley, Albert
Turn Your Radio On
Brun
Ballad Of Davy Crockett, The
Brunel
Listen Now
Brunel & Goyone
Everywhere
Bruni
Voyages, Les
Brunner
Erinnerung
Bruns
I Wonder
Liberty Tree
Love
Theme From Zorro
Toyland March
Westward Ho The Wagons
Yo Ho
Bruns, George
Ballad Of Davy Crockett, The
Brusilovskii
Two Swallows
Bryan
Circus Parade, The
County Fair, The
Old Hickory
Rain
Running Back
Skipping Rope
Snow
Tractor, The
Bryan & Edwards
In My Merry Oldsmobile
Tammany
Wait Till The Sun Shines Nellie
Bryan & Gumble
Winter

Bryant
All I Have To Do Is Dream
Balm Of Gilead
Bird Dog
Calvary
Christofo Columbo
Devoted To You
Hey Joe
I Cheated On A Good Woman's
   Love
It Was Enough
Nothin' Improves My Day Better
   Than Praisin' Him
Sleepy
That's When The Angel Rejoice
Then He Comes
Turkey And The Turk, The
We Could
Bryant & Atkins
Midnight
Bryant & Bryant
Bye Bye Love
Come Live With Me
Country Boy
Have A Good Time
Poor Jenny
Problems
Raining In My Heart
Rocky Top
Shopping List
Wake Up Little Susie
Bryant & Bryant & Franco & Thomas
One Last Goodbye
Bryant, H. T.
Balm Of Gilead
Bryman
Please Go 'way And Let Me Sleep
Bryman & Smith & Burris
Come After Breakfast
Brymn
Please Let Me Sleep
There's A Big Cry Baby In The
   Moon
Bryson
Let The Feeling Flow
Bucalossi
Love I Will Love You Ever
Buccalossi
Hunting Song
Buch
All Glory Be To God Most High
Buchanan
Death Is Only A Dream
Buchanan & Janz & Janz & Taff & Taff
Silent Love
Buck
All Hail Adored Trinity
Capture Of Bacchus, The
Crossing The Bar
Eternal Gifts Of Christ The King,
   The
Freckles Rag
In Thy Dreams
Not Always On The Mount May We

Buck *(Cont.)*
O Lord Most High Eternal King
O Savior Of Our Fallen Race
On The Resurrection Morning
Rock Of Ages
Sing Alleluia Forth In Duteous Praise
Willows By The River

Buck, Percy
Draw Nigh And Take The Body Of The Lord

Buckingham
Big Love
Holiday Road
Ledge, The
Never Going Back Again
Not That Funny
Second Hand News
Tango In The Night
That's Enough For Me

Buckingham, Lindsey
Go Your Own Way
Trouble
Tusk

Buckingham & Gray
'Til You And Your Lover Are Lovers Again

Buckingham & Lorber & Martin
Between Two Fires

Buckingham & McVie & Nicks & Fleetwood & McVie
Chain, The

Buckingham & Stephenson
Modern Day Delilah

Buckingham & Stevenson
Modern Day Delilah

Buckingham & Young
I Don't Mind The Thorns

Buckley
I'm A Good Old Rebel
Jesus The Weary Wanderer's Rest
Kiss Me Quick And Go
Tell Me Is My Father Coming Home
We'll Fight For Uncle Abe

Buckley, R. Bishop
Wait For The Wagon

Budson
Duet Theme

Buell
Family Song, The

Buell & Summer
Child Of The King, A

Buencamino
Malolos Hymn
Woman And A Rose, A

Bufano, Jules
Thanks For The Buggy Ride

Buffett, Jimmy
Captain And The Kid, The
Margaritaville

Buffum
Have You A Friend Like That
I'm Going Through Jesus
Let's Talk About Jesus
When I Take My Vacation In Heaven

Bugatch
Zemer, A

Bugatti & Musker
Every Woman In The World

Buhler & Fennevessey
Waves Of Waikiki, The

Buie & Cobb & Gordy
Traces

Buie & Nix
Neon Nites

Buie & Nix & Daughtry
Imaginary Lover
So Into You

Bulakhov
Do Not Awaken My Memories
Troika Rushing
Village On The Road, The

Bulant
By A Shady Lane

Bull
My Country 'Tis Of Thee
Seterjentens Sondag
Sunday

Bullard
From Age To Age They Gather

Bullinger
Art Thou Weary Art Thou Languid
God Who Touchest Earth With Beauty
I Am Trusting Thee Lord Jesus
When Thy Heart With Joy O'erflowing

Bullock
Tragic Story, A

Bunch & Rose & Kennedy & Cerney
I'll Still Be Loving You

Bungess
Occasional Rose, An

Bunn
Happy And Light Of Heart Are Those

Bunnell, Lee
Horse With No Name, A
Sandman
Tin Man
Ventura Highway

Bunnett, Edward
Shepherd Of Eager Youth

Burch
You Cheated

Burch & Peoples
Out Of Sight And On My Mind

Burch & Woody
My Train Of Thought

Burder
Awake Jerusalem Awake
Let Not The Wise Their Widsom Boast
O Thou To Whom In Ancient Time

Burdett
Building Day By Day
God Will Take Care Of You
Let Us Be Glad And Rejoice Together

Burdett *(Cont.)*
Lift High Your Cheerful Voices
Million Little Diamonds, A
Punkydoodle And Jollapin
Summer Song, A

Burditt
Trusting In His Power Divine

Burdon & Price
I'm Crying

Burgeois
All People That On Earth Do Dwell
Old Hundredth

Burgess
Gospel Ship Is Sailing, The
It Is Strange
Wake Up

Burgie
Angelina
Dolly Dawn
El Matador
I Do Adore Her
Island In The Sun
Jamaica Farewell
Judy Drownded
Kingston Market
Land Of The Sea And Sun
Lead Man Holler
Me Nah Go Married
Millie Gon' A Brazil
Ole San Juan
Solas Market

Burgie & Attaway
Angelique-O
Day-O

Burgie & Attaway & Belafonte
Day-O

Burgmuller
Jerusalem My Happy Home
Thou Dear Redeemer Dying Lamb

Burk & Tobias
Good Night Little Girl Of My Dreams

Burke
Black Coffee
Build Ye On The Rock
Dancing With Tears In My Eyes
For You
I Am He That Liveth
I Am Trusting Thee Lord Jesus
I'm An Old Cowhand From The Rio Grande
In A Little Gypsy Tea Room
It Looks Like Rain In Cherry Blossom Lane
Jesus Is Mine
Kiss Waltz, The
Little Bit Independent, A
Merry Christmas Polka, The
Moon Over Miami
O Saviour Precious Saviour
Oh What A Pal Was Whoozis
One Light In A Dark Valley
Open Wide The Door
Painting The Clouds With Sunshine

Burke *(Cont.)*
Paper Doll
Precious Blood Of Jesus
She Was Just A Sailor's Sweetheart
Tip-Toe Thru' The Tulips With Me
Villanova Anthem
What's New
Whisper Waltz, The
Burke & Gerlach
Daddy's Little Girl
Burke & Hampton
Midnight Sun
Burkhard
Oh My Papa
Burkum
Blessed Be The Lord
Happiness Is Following Jesus
Teach Me To Number My Days
Burleigh
In Christ There Is No East Or West
Swing Low Sweet Chariot
Burleson
I Hope To Meet You There Some
Day
Burnam
Come Away To The Skies My
Beloved
Cripple Creek
Burnap
Light Of The World Whose Kind
And Gentle Care
O Master Workman Of The Race
Our Father While Our Hearts
Unlearn
'Twixt Gleams Of Joy And Clouds
Of Doubt
When Winds Are Raging
Burne
Praise The Grandeur Of Our God
Burnett
My Melancholy Baby
Pillsbury Says It Best
Sitting On Top Of The World
Smokestack Lightning
Burnett & Devorzon
Hey Little One
Burnett & Swan
Drivin' Wheel
Burnette
It's Late
Tall Oak Tree
Burnette & Burnette
Believe What You Say
Burnette & Devorzon
Hey Little One
Burnette & Henley
Out Run The Sun
Burnette & Malloy
Dream You
Burney
Blessed Feasts Of Blessed Martyrs
Forget Them Not O Christ Who
Stand
I Know That My Redeemer Lives

Burney *(Cont.)*
Jack And Jill
Jesus The Truth And Power Divine
Jesus Thou Everlasting King
Lift Up Our Hearts O King Of Kings
O Rugged Master Of The Hills
Our Thought Of Thee
Our Thoughts Of Thee Is Glad With
Hope
Peter White
Thou Lord Of Hosts
Burnham
Campus Song
I Know Not How That Bethlehem's
Babe
I Know Not That Bethlehem's Babe
Burns
Behold O God This Lowly Bread
Christ For Me
Let Us Praise Our Noble God
Lo Our Savior King Is Here
O Lord I Am Not Worthy
O My Luve's Like A Red Red Rose
Burns & Brown
Locked Up In Prison
Burns & Herman
Early Autumn
Burns & Holiday
Who Needs You
Burns & Holiday
Preacher Boy
Burns & Schumann
Still Still With Thee My God
Burr
Burned Like A Rocket
I Won't Let You Down
Love's Been A Little Bit Hard On
Me
Love's Been A Little Hard On Me
Make My Life With You
That's My Job
Burr & Kaz
Vows Go Unbroken, The
Burrage
Cryin' For My Baby
Burrell
Gone Gone Gone
Burrowes
Glory Gilds The Sacred Page, A
How Precious Is The Book Divine
Thou Art The Way To Thee Alone
What Is The Thing Of Greatest Price
Burrows
A
Brooklyn U S A
Carbon Paper
Foolish Memories
Girl With The Three Blue Eyes, The
Gypsy's Violin, The
Happy Days
Happy Days Reprise
I May Be Sick
I Saw You

Burrows *(Cont.)*
Lopin' Along
Memory Lane
Moment, The
My Brain
My Heart
Open Road, The
Pansy In My Garden, The
Ping Pong
Pumpernickel
Rock And The Rose, The
Ron Ron Ron
Sea Chanty
That Train Going South
Tokyo Rose
Upper Peabody
When
When You're In Love
Burt
Caroling Caroling
Infantry Kings Of The Highway, The
O God Of Youth Whose Spirit In
Our Hearts Is Stirr
Prayer Is The Soul's Sincere Desire
Servant Of All To Toil For Man
Silver Dew On The Blue Grass
Tonight
Some Children See Him
Star Carol, The
Wal I Swan
Burtch
Tie That Binds, The
Burtnett
Do You Ever Think Of Me
Burton
I Am Woman
Jesse
My Bark Canoe
Spreading All Over The World
Burton & Goetz
Arise Shine
Burwell
Sweet Lorraine
Busch
America For Me
Christmas Carol, A
Crossing The Bar
Hello Muddah Hello Faddah
Hello Muddah Hello Fadduh
Inclusions
Little Song Of Life, A
Orpheus With His Lute
Sunset And Evening Star And One
Clear Call For Me
Under The Greenwood Tree
Wind, The
Bush
Blue And White, The
Running Up That Hill
Stiil True To Thee
Whiskey River
Bush & Stroud
Whiskey River

Bushby
O Why Not Tonight
Bushell
I Don't Feel No Ways Tired
Surely He Died On Calvary
Bushey
O Why Not Tonight
Oh Why Not Tonight
Bushkin
Oh Look At Me Now
Bushnell
Uncle Sam
Bustini
Esame Di Coscienza
Per Una Strada Ripida
Solo
Butcher
Beautiful Land On High, The
Butler
Gift Of Love, The
Harvest Song
Old Jordan's Waves I Do Not Fear
Sinner Like Me, A
Song Of The Lilies, The
Spring Morning
Thanksgiving
Those Three Blind Mice
What You'll Do When I'm Gone
Wind, The
Butler & Butler & Ely & Ashton
Love My Way
Pretty In Pink
Butler & Butler & Ely & Ashton &
Kilburn & Morris
Pretty In Pink
Butler & Mayfield
Aware Of Love
Find Yourself Another Girl
I Found A Love
I'm Telling You
When Trouble Calls
Butler & Mayfield & Carter
He Don't Love You
He Don't Love You Like I Love You
He Will Break Your Heart
Heartbreaker
Thanks To You
Butler & Moman
Another Somebody Done Somebody
Wrong Song
Butler & Skinner
Lies
Butler & Wilkin & Certain & Stacey
Crying My Heart Out Over You
Butterfield
Taps
When You And I Were Young
Maggie
Buttier & Bell
Tighten Up
Buttolph
Maverick
Buus
Douce Memoire

Buxtehude
It Is Enough
Lord Who At Cana's Wedding Feast
O Father All Creating
Buzzi-Peccia
Colombetta Serenata Veneziana
Lolita Serenata Spagnola
Mariolina
Byelij
Shoulder To Shoulder
Byers
Hard Knocks
Hey Little Girl
I've Got To Find My Baby
Please Don't Stop Loving Me
So Close Yet So Far
So Close Yet So Far From Paradise
Stop Look Listen
Bynum & Reneau
Chains
Byrd
Ave Verum
Come To Me Grief For Ever
Cradle Song
Hey Ho To The Greenwood
I Thought That Love Had Been A
Boy
I Will Not Leave You Comfortless
Iustorum Animae
Little Bitty Pretty One
Lord To Thy Name
Non Nobis Domine
O Mistress Mine
Out Of The Orient
Over And Over
Sacerdotes Domini
This Sweet And Merry Month
Byrd & Hinson
Train Of Memories
Byrne
Book I Read, The
Don't Worry About The
Government
If I Were A Beautiful Twinkling Star
Melt The Bells
Psycho Killer
That Was A Close One
Byrne & Bowles
I Can't Win For Losin' You
Byrne & Fisher
Promises Promises
Byron
Shadows Of The Night
Byron & Evans
Roses Are Red
Roses Are Red My Love
Roses Are Red Ny Love
Byshe
Clean Heart, A
Cables
Ebony Moonbeams
Quiet Fire
Secrets Of Love
Think On Me

Caccini
Amarilli
Amarilli Mia Bella
Wild Woodland Creatures
Caddigan
Rose Of No Man's Land, The
Cadman
At Dawning
Birth Of The World, The
Far Off I Hear A Lover's Flute
From The Land Of The Sky-Blue
Water
Little Road To Kerry, The
Moon Drops Low, The
Moonlight Song, A
My Gift For You
Nature's Orchestra
O Bird In The Dawn
Song Of The Mountains
Spring Exultation
Tallac
White Dawn Is Stealing, The
Caesar
Pledge Of Allegiance To The Flag
Caesar & Lerner & Marks
Is It True What They Say About
Dixie
Cafferty
C-I-T-Y
On The Dark Side
Small Town Girl
Tender Years
Tough All Over
Caffey
We Got The Beat
Caffey & Shipley & Schuckett
Lay Down Your Arms
Caffey & Valentine
Head Over Heels
Cahn & Chaplin
I Could Make You Care
If It's The Last Thing I Do
Please Be Kind
Cahn & Chaplin & Zaret
Dedicated To You
Cahn & Stordahl & Weston
Day By Day
I Should Care
Cahn & Twomey & Walker
Hey Jealous Lover
Cahn & Weston
Indiscretion
Caietain
Puce, Une
Cain
Faithfully
Jesus Name Above All Names
Mist And All, The
Robin's Song, The
Cain & Waite
Price Of Love
Calaway
Guitar Blues
My Two Time Mama

Calaway *(Cont.)*
Prisoner No 999
Written Letter, The
Calbreath
My Love Rode By
Caldara
Alma Del Core
As From The Sun A Ray
Come Raggio Di Sol
Glee
High Spirits
Sebben Crudele
Si Cantemo
Soul Of My Heart
Caldbeck
Peace Perfect Peace
Caldera
Hymn
Calderon
Hymn Of The Cloak
Calderon & Hawker
Eres Tu
Touch Of The Wind
Caldicott
I Cast A Sorrow To The Sea
I Was A Wandering Sheep
Legend Of The Lily, The
Not In Dumb Resignation
Caldwell
Awake My Soul To Joyful Lays
Concord
Funeral Thought
Heard It In A Song
Immensity
Searchin' For A Rainbow
Wakefield
Caldwell & Gordon
Next Time I Fall, The
Cale
After Midnight
Clyde
Cocaine
Calhoun
Shake Rattle And Roll
Calhoun & Turner
Flip Flop And Fly
Calkin
Awake Our Souls Away Our Fears
Breathe On Me Breath Of God
City Of God How Broad And Far
Come Unto Me Ye Weary
Day By Day The Manna Fell
Eternal One Thou Living God
Fling Out The Banner
Fling Out The Banner Let It Float
I Heard The Bells
I Heard The Bells On Christmas Day
I Lay My Sins On Jesus
Jesus Name All Names Above
Lift Up Lift Up Your Voices Now
My Span Of Life Will Soon Be Done
O Beautiful My Country
O Jesus Crucified For Man

Calkin *(Cont.)*
O Lord Of Life Thy Quickening
Voice
O Thou To Whom In Ancient Time
Once More The Liberal Year Laughs
Out
Press On Press On
Ring Out Wild Bells To The Wild
Sky
Sinners The Voice Of God Regard
To Thee O Dear Dear Saviour
Upward Where The Stars
Upward Where The Stars Are
Burning
Welcome Happy Morning
Call
Perfect World
Call & Keller
867-5309-Jenny
Callander & Murray
Billy Don't Be A Hero
Callander & Stephens
Daddy Don't You Walk So Fast
Callcott
Ah How Sophia Can You Leave
Have You Sir John Hawkins' Hist'ry
Mark The Merry Elves
Sentiment I Like A Pretty Girl, A
To All You Ladies Now On Land
When The Weary Seeking Rest
Calleja
Granadinas
Callis
I Can't Stand My Baby
My Baby Does Good Sculptures
Callis & Bakey
Fascination
Calloway
Love Overboard
Calloway & Calloway
Casanova
Jump Start
Calloway & Calloway & Gentry & Lips
I Wanna Be Rich
Calloway & Mills & Gaskill
Minnie The Moocher
Caltabiano
Questi Di Prima Io La Vidi, A
Profonda Solitaria Immensa Notte
Calvi
One Of Those Songs
Calvisius
O God Thou Faithful God
We Sing The Praise Of Him Who
Died
Camarata
No More
Cambissa
Autunno
Primavera
Racconto
Came
Audacia

Cameron
Americas Shake Hands
Autumn Days
Camping Out
Piano Magic
Road Runner, The
Camerota
Los Angeles
Camidge
Lift Up Your Hearts
O Lord Open Thou Our Eyes
Camilieri
Blessed Is He That Considereth The
Poor
Camillo
Dynomite Part I
Camp
Another Year Is Dawning
Living In Laodicea
Since Without Thee We Do No Good
Camp & Frazier
Stranger To Holiness
Camp & Licciardello
Revive Us Oh Lord
Camp & Madeira
Do Something Now
Campana
Only To See Thee
Somewhere
Speak To Me
Campbell
And Can It Be
Be Thou My Vision
Been On The Road So Long
Burgundian Carol
Fairest Flower Of The Southland
I Know Not What The Future Hath
I've Got More To Go To Heaven For
Jesus I Thee Adore
Less Of Me
Oh What A Happy Day
Shew Fly Don't Bother Me
Shoo-Fly Don't Bother Me
Something Within
Thy Palm Trees Fed With Dew And
Sun
When Little Boys Kneel Down To
Pray
Campbell & Harris
I Will Believe
Campbell & Newman
Kisses Sweeter Than Wine
Rock Island Line
Campbell-Tipton
Crying Of Water, The
Campenhout
Belgium
Brabanconne, La
Brabanconne, The
Campian
Hark My Soul It Is The Lord
Jack And Joan
Man Of Life Upright, The
Never Weather-Beaten Sail

Campian (Cont.)
There Is A Garden In Her Face
To His Sweet Lute Apollo Sung
To Music Bent Is My Retired Mind
Tune Thy Music To Thy Heart
Voice Upon The Midnight Air, A
Wise Men Patience Never Want
With Broken Heart And Contrite
    Sigh

Campion
Beauty Is But A Painted Hell
Before Time Was O Word Divine
Breake Now My Heart And Die
Every Dame Affects Good Fame
Her Rosie Cheeks
O Deare That I With Thee Might
    Live
Oft Have I Sighed For Him
Peaceful Westerne Winde
That Day Of Wrath That Dreadful
    Day
There Is A Garden In Her Face
Thrice Tosse These Oaken Ashes In
    The Air

Campo
Casita, La
Chiapanecas
Four Corn Fields
Morir Sonando

Campos
Love Betrayed
Once There Were Happy Days

Campra
Graceful Butterfly

Canal
Espoir Luit Comme Un Brin De
    Paille, L'E

Cananaugh & Kent & Cutter
Gertie From Bizertie

Canario
En Tu Santo
Mi Campesina
Rock In The Lake, The
Song To The Mother

Candlyn
Away In A Manger
God Who Created Me

Canfield
Alma Mater

Canfora
Fortissimo
This Is My Life

Canis
Mariez Moi Mon Pere

Cannel
Party Time

Canning
Just Been Wond'ring
Rock-A-Bye Baby

Cannio
My Carmela
O Surdato 'nnammurato

Cannon
Bill Bailey
Bill Bailey Won't You Please Come
    Home
Bring It With You When You Come
Little Gertie Murphy

Cannon & Dunlap
I Believe In You

Cannon & Squires
Someday This Old Road Won't Be
    So Long

Cannon & Woods
Walk Right In

Cansler
Wildfire

Cantarelli & Armato
I Still Believe

Cantor
As The Dawn
Oh Fair Oh Sweet And Holy

Cantor & Tobias & Mencher
Merrily We Roll Along

Cantoral
Triste, El

Cantu
My Fair Land

Cantwell
I Bowed On My Knees And Cried
    Holy

Capaldi
That's Love

Capehart
Turn Around Look At Me

Capron
Delia

Capua
Ah Marie
Ah Surriento
Down From His Glory

Capua
Golden Sunlight, The
Io Te Vurria Vasa
Maria Mari
Marie Ah Marie
Marie Marie
My Sunlight
My Sunshine
Neapolitan Serenade
O Sole Mio
Oh Marie
Serenade Of The Roses

Caracciolo
Flight Of Clouds, A
From Far Away
Nearest And Dearest
Oh Happy Are The Blind
Streamlet Full Of Flowers, A
Unless
When I Am Dead

Carambula
Mr Bullfrog

Carasone
Vagabond Lover

Caravelli
Let Me Try Again

Carawan & Merrlam & Curtis
Ballad Of The Student Sit-Ins

Carazo
Tiger Team Of LSU

Carbone
Garry's Closing Theme
I Don't Wanna Lose Your Love
It's Garry's Theme
Theme From Star Search

Carcassi
Study

Card
God's Own Fool
I Have Decided
Known By The Scars
Scandalon
This Must Be The Lamb
Wedding, The
Why

Card & Putnam
Forgiving Eyes

Cardillo
Core 'n Grato

Carey
America
Christ The Lord Is Risen Today
Creator Spirit By Whose Aid
Curs'd Be The Wretch
Deus Salva Regem
Easter Anthem
God Bless Our Native Land
God Save The King
I Praised The Earth In Beauty Seen
Learning McFadden To Waltz
Lord My Pasture Shall Prepare, The
Love On My Heart From Heaven
    Fell
My Country 'Tis Of Thee
Sally In Our Alley
Sierra Sue
Spring Morning, A

Carey & Shapiro
Sierra Sue

Carillo
Yellow Days

Carissimi
Deh Contentatevi
Plorate Filii Israel
Victorious My Heart
Vittoria Mio Core
Vittoria Vittoria

Carl & Whitelaw & Bell
Diane

Carle
Sunrise Serenade

Carlebach
Uva-U Ha-Ovdim

Carleton
Ja-Da
Jolly Irishmen

Carleton & Stewart
Cover Them Over With Beautiful
Flowers
Carlisi & Curtis & Carl
Second Chance
Carlisle
Alone And Lonesome
Brakeman's Reply, The
Childhood Dreams
Come Back Sweetheart
Hobo Blues
Hobo Jack's Last Ride
I Don't Mind
I Want A Good Woman
Left All Alone
Lonely Valley
Lonesome Hobo, A
Memories That Make Me Cry
My Carolina Sweetheart
My Dear Old Daddy
My Lonely Boyhood Days
My Mississippi Home
My Rocky Mountain Sweetheart
No Help Wanted
On The Mississippi Shore
Shanghai Rooster Yodel
Where Southern Roses Climb
Carlo & Sanders
That Tumble-Down Shack In
Athlone
Carlson
Bed You Made For Me, The
I'm Gonna Live Forever
If You Want Joy Real Joy
Carlson & Chapman
All The Reasons Why
Carlton
Ja-Da
Carlton & Benton & Sullivan
You'll Never Know How Much I
Needed You Today
Carlton & Kraft
Brand New Life
Carlton & Tunbridge
Mademoiselle From Armentieres
Carmen
All By Myself
Almost Paradise
Maybe My Baby
Never Gonna Fall In Love Again
Carmen & Pitchford
Make Me Lose Control
Carmichael
Baltimore Oriole
Barbaric
Blue Orchids
Can't Get Indiana Off My Mind
Closer Than A Brother
College Swing
Cosmics
Doctor Lawyer Indian Chief
Dreams
Georgia On My Mind
He'll Never Let You Fall

Carmichael *(Cont.)*
Heart And Soul
Hong Kong Blues
How Little We Know
I Get Along Without You Very Well
I Get Along Without You Very Well
Except Sometimes
I Met Him In Paris
I Walk With Music
I'll Dance At Your Wedding
I'll Dance At Your Wedding Honey
Dear
I'm A Cranky Old Yank In A Clanky
Old Tank
In The Cool Cool Cool Of The
Evening
Inbrothered
Ivy
Jubilee
Lamplighter's Serenade
Lazy River
Manhattan Rag
March Of The Hoodlums
May Song, A
Memphis In June
Merry-Go-Round
Mister Bluebird
Moonburn
Morning Glory
Mowing The Hay
My Christmas Song For You
My Friend And I
My Resistance Is Low
Nearness Of You, The
New 23rd, The
Oh I Never Shall Forget The Day
Old Music Master, The
One Morning In May
One Of These Days
Papa Treetop Tall
Poor Old Joe
Prince Charlie
Reach Out To Jesus
Rockin' Chair
Savior Is Waiting, The
Skylark
Small Fry
Star Dust
Two Sleepy People
We're The Couple In The Castle
Wedding Song
Whale Song, The
White World Of Winter, The
Carmichael & Adams
Little Old Lady
Carmichael & Adamson
Just A Shade On The Blue Side
Carmichael & Brooks
Ole Buttermilk Sky
Carmichael & Callahan & Mills
Washboard Blues
Carmichael & Lerner
Judy

Carmichael & Meinardi & Sanford
Manhattan In The Spring
Carmichael & Mercer
Lazybones
Carmichael & Mercer
Moon Country
Carmichael & Mills
Boneyard Shuffle
Carmichael & Torre & Spielman
Who Killed The Black Widder
**Carmichael & Voynow & Mills &
Parish**
Riverboat Shuffle
Carmichael & Webster
Three Rivers, The
Carmines
Promenade Theme
Carnes
Crazy In The Night
It Hurts So Bad
Make No Mistake She's Mine
Carnes & Carnes & Hardy
Pins And Needles
Carnes & Ellingson
Does It Make You Remember
Don't Fall In Love With A Dreamer
You Were A Good Friend
Carnes & Ellingson & Fairweath
Invitation To Dance
Carnes & Ellingson & Hitchings
Voyeur
Carney
Mistaken Identity
Carnicer
Cancion Nacional
Hacesado La Lucha Sangrienta
Carolan
Plearaca Na Ruarcach
Carosone
Torero
Vagabond Lover
Carpenter
Celestial Choirs
Home Road, The
I Am Like A Remnant Of A Cloud
Of Autumn
Light My Light
Looking-Glass River
Man In The Moon's Ball, The
May The Maiden
Merry Christmas Darling
On The Day When Death Will Knock
At Thy Door
On The Seashore Of Endless Worlds
Pools Of Peace, The
Serenade
Sleep That Flits On Baby's Eyes, The
Something In Your Eyes
Top Of The World
Treat Me Nice
When I Bring To You Colour'd Toys
Carpenter & Bettis
Yesterday Once More

Carpenter & Dunlap & Hines
You Can Depend On Me
Carr
Comes The Wondrous Hour
He Wears A Pair Of Silver Wings
How Long How Long Blues
In The Evening When The Sun Goes
   Down
Little Homes Of Ireland, The
Noah's Dove
Old Book And The Old Faith, The
Savior When In Dust To Thee
Saviour When In Dust To Thee
Six Cold Feet Of Ground
Skiddle Diddle Dee-Skiddle Diddle
   Dey
What Would You Give In Exchange
Carr & Corday
See The USA In Your Chevrolet
Carr & Mitchell & Weiss
We Belong Together
Carr & Russell & Havens
We Don't Want The Bacon
Carrack
How Long
Carrack & Difford
One Good Reason
Carradine
I'm Easy
Carrell
Messiah
Carreras & Farver
Cuatro Vidas
Carrillo
Sabor A Mi
Yellow Days
Carroll
By The Beautiful Sea
Down In Bom-Bombay
Elvira
Elvira's Theme
Get Closer
I'm Always Chasing Rainbows
It Takes A Little Rain With The
   Sunshine
Scouts Of The Sea
She Is The Sunshine Of Virginia
Song Of Florida, A
There's A Girl In The Heart Of
   Maryland
This Happy Land Of Mine
Time To Start Building Again
Torch Of Scouting, The
Trail Of The Lonesome Pine, The
When I'm Thru With The Arms Of
   The Army
Carroll & Fairchild
We've Got A Secret
Carroll & Fairchild & Smith
Heaven Fell Like Rain When He
   Spoke
Carroll & Fields
On The Mississippi

Carroll & Manning & Crosby
Learn To Pray Ev'ry Day
Carroll & Moody
Wear My Ring Around Your Neck
Carroll & Payne
Just One Look
Carroll & Taylor
Seven Days
Carron
Clones
Carryl
Capital Ship, A
Carson
Jealous Heart
Let Me Go Lover
Satisfied
**Carson & Chalmers & Barnett &
   Rhodes**
Clown, The
Carste
Those Lazy-Hazy-Crazy Days Of
   Summer
Carte Blanche & Orson
Don't Go Breaking My Heart
Carter
All Around Man
At The Cost Of A Woman's Heart
At The Hop
Augusta
Bell Of Creation, The
Bird Of Heaven
Bitter Was The Night
Carol Of The Universe
Come All You Makers
Come Holy Harlequin
Cook With Honey
Devil Or Angel
Dust Of Snow
East Virginia Blues
Ecstasy
Everyone's Laughing
Exhilaration
Florence
Foggy Mountain Top, The
Gathering Flowers From The Hillside
George Fox
Girl I Loved In Sunny Tenessee, The
God Is Love His Mercy Brightens
Gold Watch And Chain
H20s04 On Kcl03
I Ain't Got You
I'm Thinking Tonight Of My Blue
   Eyes
In The Looking Glass Of Francis
It Just Happened That Way
Jimmy Brown The Newsboy
Judas And Mary
Last Train To Glory
Launch Out
Launch Out Into The Deep
Little Darling Pal Of Mine
Lonely Soldier, A
Lord Of The Dance

Carter *(Cont.)*
Mammy's Lullaby
Moth And The Flame
My Hannah Lady
My Mother Was A Lady
Nose Full Of Nickels, A
O Nannie Wilt Thou Gang Wi'me
On The Rock Where Moses Stood
Once Upon A Time It Happened
Only Trust Your Heart
Orange And The Black, The
Over The Mountain
She Was Bred In Old Kentucky
Son Of Man
Standing In The Rain
Standing On The Promises
Steps Song
Steps Song-Princeton
Rose Family, The
Travelling With God
Used-To-Be
Wabash Cannon Ball
When I Needed A Neighbour
Which One Is Which
Will The Circle Be Unbroken
Worried Man Blues
You Are The Poem
You're Not The Only Pebble On The
   Beach
Young Charlotte
Carter & Erwin
You Are My Music You Are My
   Song
Carter & Hudson
Let's Make Up
Carter & Hudson
Goodnight It's Time To Go
Goodnight Sweetheart Goodnight
Carter & Kilgore
Ring Of Fire
Carter & Koller
Life As We Knew It
Carter & Lewis
Can't You Hear My Heart Beat
Little Bit O' Soul
Carter & Lewis & Ford
Tossing And Turning
Cartwright
Give Me His Last Chance
In My Eyes
Carty & Carty
For Old Manhattan
Carulli
Study
Carus & Leopold & Kahn
John James O'Reilly
Cary
One Sweetly Solemn Thought
Caryll
Goodbye Girls I'm Through
My Beautiful Lady
Casadei
Kiss Me 'N Kiss Me 'N Kiss Me

Case
Be Careful What You Sow
Christ The Fountain
While We Pray And While We Plead
Why Not Now
Casebolt
There's A River Of Life
Casella
Amante Sono Vaghiccia Di Voi
Carita, La
Coccodrillo, Er
Elezzione Der Presidente, L'
Fuor De La Bella Gaiba
Gatto E Er Cane, Er
Giovane Bella Luce Del Mio Core
Sera Fiesolana, Le
Casey
Drill Ye Miners Drill
Drill Ye Tarriers Drill
Mick McGilligan's Ball
Casey & Carter
Give It Up
Casey & Finch
Please Don't Go
Rock Your Baby
Shake Your Booty
That's The Way
Casey & Jacobs
Freddy My Love
Look At Me I'm Sandra Dee
Summer Nights
We Go Together
Cash
Brooklyn's Gift To The Army
Folsom Prison Blues
He Turned The Water Into Wine
I Walk The Line
Over The Next Hill We'll Be Home
Tennessee Flat Top Box
Cash & Crowell
I Don't Know Why You Don't Want
Me
Cash & Williams
I Got Stripes
Cashman & Pistilli & West
Next Man That I Marry, The
What The Hell
Cason & Gayden
Everlasting Love
Cason & Gibb
To Love
Cason & Roberts
I Can Do All Things Through Christ
Jesus
Cason & Weller
Praise The Lord
Cassard
Just For Princeton
Cassard & Brunies & Brunies
Angry
Cassel
King's Business, The
Loyalty To Christ

Cassey
Shadowland
Windflower
Castagne
National Anthem Of
Trinidad-Tobago
Castelnuovo-Tedesco
Barba Bianca, La
Come Away Come Away Death
Er Treno
Grandine
Infinito, L'
O Mistress Mine
Palloncini
Piove
Preghiera Del Mattino
Preghiera Della Sera
Sera
Sogni
Stelle Cadenti
Under The Greedwood Tree
When Daffodils Begin To Peer
When Daisies Pied And Violets
When That I Was A Little Tiny Boy
When That I Was And A Little Tiny
Boy
Where The Bee Sucks
Who Is Sylvia
Castillo
Calandria, La
Castlen
Best Is Yet To Come, The
He Turned My Night Into Day
Castling & Collins
Are We To Part Like This
Are We To Part Like This Bill
Caston & Wakefield
Nathan Jones
Castro
Ah Je Meurs
Je Suis Quasi
Casucci
Just A Gigolo
Caswell & Dykes
Sleep Holy Babe
Catalini
Ebben Ne Andro Lontana
Catel
Military March
Cates
Adios Au Revoir Auf Wiedersehn
Circle Of Two
Man In The Middle
Catlin
Ring The Bell Softly
Caurroy
Las Amour
Cavaliere
Only A Lonely Heart Sees
Cavaliere & Brigati
Girl Like You, A
Groovin'
How Can I Be Sure
People Got To Be Free

Cavalli
Maledetto
Cavanaugh & Barris
Mississippi Mud
Cavanaugh & Kent & Cutter
Gertie From Bizerte
Cavanaugh & Stanton
Roving Kind, The
Cavanaugh & Stock & Morgan
You're Nobody 'Til Somebody
Loves You
Cavendish
Down In A Valley
Cazden
Bombs Away
Left-Handed Song For Human
Rights, The
Celentano
Tar And Cement
Cellar-Door Band
Goin' Or Stayin
Cennick
Jesus My All To Heaven Is Gone
Cermak
Treasurer, The
Ceroni
I've Had It
Cerrone & Ray
Got To Have Lovin'
Certon
J'espere Et Crains
Je Ne Fus Jamais Si Ayse
Je Suis Desheritee
La La La Je Ne Lose Dire
Que N'est Elle Aupres De Moi
Cesario & Collyer & Mullen
Endless Nights
Cesti
Ah Quanto E Vero
E Dove T'aggiri
Cetera
Baby What A Big Surprise
If You Leave Me Now
Wishing You Were Here
Cetera & Foster
Hard To Say I'm Sorry
You're The Inspiration
Cetera & Foster & Nini
Glory Of Love
Cetera & Goldberg
Along Comes A Woman
Cetera & Goldenberg
Along Comes A Woman
Cetera & Leonard
One Good Woman
Chabrier
Espana
Fete Polonaise
Serenade Of The Little Ducks
Chadwick
Across The Hills
Child's American Hymn
Dandelion, The
Easter Canticle, An

Chadwick *(Cont.)*
Euthanasia
Goodnight
I Sought The Lord
Jubilee
O Jesus Youth Of Nazareth
Song To May
There Was A Little Girl
When The Lord Of Love Was Here
Chafer
Road To Eilat
Chaffon
Iraq
Challinor
Stories Of Jesus
Tell Me The Stories Of Jesus
Chalmers & Sosebee
Hollis
Chamberlain
Am I Blue
Am I Blue Yes I'm Blue
Have I Got Some Blues For You
Hurrah For Old New England
Illinois
Chamberlain & Porter
What's Going On In Your World
Chambers
Be Exalted O God
Canyons Of My Mind
Caravanessa
Celebration Song, The
Close Enough To Perfect
Chambers & Jenkins
Old 8x10
Somebody Lied
Chaminade
A L'inconnu
Absence
Amoroso
Angelus, L'
Aubade
Autumn Loves
Ballade A La Lune
Berceuse
Beside My Darling
Broken Blossom
Chanson Groenlandaise
Chant D'amour
Christmas Carol Of The Birds
Colette
Dream Of An Eve
Dreams
Ideal, The
If Thou Dost Say
Love A Captive
Madrigal
Mignonne
On The Shore
Plaints Of Love
Ritournelle
Rosemonde
Serenata
Silver Ring, The

Chaminade *(Cont.)*
Slavonic Song
Soldier's Betrothed
Sombrero
Summer
Trahison
Vieille Chanson
Villanelle
Were I Gard'ner
Wishes
Chaminote
Come My Own Dear Love
Champness
Eternal Light Divinity
Chan & Cunliffe
Double Your Pleasure
Chandler
Beans In My Ears
Father's Grave
Glad She's A Woman
Murder On The Road To Alabama
Right Right
Run Come See The Sun
Turn Around Miss Liberty
Chandler & White & Cohen
Canadian Capers
Chaney
Autumn
Chanler
Lamb, The
Oh Dear
These My Ophelia
Channel
Party Time
Channel & Kane
As Long As I'm Rockin' With You
You're The Best
Channel & Rector & Throckmorton
Stand Up
Chant
Cuckoo Song, The
Good Night
Marching Song, The
Sleigh Song, The
Tip Toe Song, The
Chantey
Rio Grande
Chapin
Better Place To Be, A
Circle
Corey's Coming
Danceband On The Titanic
Dogtown
Dreams Go By
Flowers Are Red
Forest
I Wonder What Would Happen To
  This World
If My Mary Were Here
Last Stand
Mail Order Annie
Mister Tanner
New Britain
Old College Avenue

Chapin *(Cont.)*
Olney
Primrose
Remember When The Music
Rockbridge
Rockingham
Sandy
She Sings Songs Without Words
Shooting Star
Six String Orchestra
Story Of A Life
Sunday Morning Sunshine
Tangled Up Puppet
Taxi
Thirty Thousand Pounds Of Bananas
Tribulation
Vernon
W*o*l*d
When I Look Up
Winter Song
Chapin & Chapin
Cat's In The Cradle
Tangled Up Puppet
Chaplin
I Could Make You Care
If It's The Last Thing I Do
Joseph Joseph
Please Be Kind
Shoe Shine Boy
Smile
This Is My Song
Chapman
Able To Save
Across The Lines
Baby Can I Hold You
Behind The Wall
Betty's Bein' Bad
Fast Car
Father's Eyes
Finally
Five Minutes
Flowers For The Brave
For My Lover
For You
Goblins
If Not Now
Kite
Learning To Play
Lumberjacks
Mountains O' Things
Nothing I Can Do About It Now
Remember Whose Child You Are
Secret Place, The
She's Got Her Ticket
Sincerely Yours
Talkin' Bout A Revolution
Things Are Looking Right
Why
Chapman & Buchanan
It's Not A Song
Chapman & Chinn
Heart And Soul
Living Next Door To Alice
Mickey

Chapman & Chinn *(Cont.)*
  Part Of Me That Needs You Most,
    The
  Ricky
  Stumblin' In
Chapman & Chinn & Knight
  Better Be Good To Me
Chapman & Grant & Buchanan
  Prodigal, The
Chapman & Marsh
  One Day
Chapman & Marsh & Wright
  Who To Listen To
Chapman & Smith
  I Love A Lonely Day
Charden & Dessca
  While We're Still Young
Charig & Meyer
  Fancy Our Meeting
Charlap
  I Won't Grow Up
  I'll Never Go There Anymore
  I'm Flying
  I've Gotta Crow
Charlap & Cooperman
  Nixon's The One
Charles
  Bit Of Soul, A
  And So Goodbye
  Come Back Baby
  Don't You Know
  Fifty Nifty United States
  Hallelujah I Love Her So
  I Got A Woman
  O Lovely World
  Route Four
  Sussex Sailor, The
  Swanee River Rock
  What'd I Say
Charles & King
  Jula Lou
Charlesworth & Harrison & Sadler
  I'm Drifting Back To Dreamland
Charlesworth & Sankey
  Shelter In The Time Of Storm, A
Charpentier
  Glougloux, Les
  Quam Dulces
  Voces Amphorae
Chase
  Clapping Song, The
  Jim Dandy
  Nitty Gritty, The
  Puzzle Song, The
  Such A Night
Chattaway
  Little Black Me
  Mandy Lee
**Chatton & Richards & Seopardi &
  Ramsden**
  I Wanna Be A Cowboy
Chauncey & Byrom & Walker
  I Wanna Go Back

Chausson
  Papillons, Les
  Temps Des Lilas, Le
Chauvigny
  Refrain Courait Dans La Rue, Un
Chavez & Chaney
  Charlena
Chavez-Melo
  Sing Of Mary Pure And Lowly
Chavoit
  Amour Est Passe Pres De Vous, L'
Cheatham
  Aylesbury
Cheeswright
  All Beautiful The March Of Days
  O Master Workman Of The Race
Chenery
  Flag Ever Glorious
  Valiant Boys Of The Army
Cheney
  I'll Change The Thorns To Roses
Chera
  Somebody's Needin' Somebody
  Too Late To Go Home
Chera & Peoples & Morrison
  Now There's You
Cherry
  Dear Little Shamrock, The
  Monarch Of The Woods
  Shells Of Ocean
  Will O' The Wisp
Cherry & McVey
  Kisses On The Wind
**Cherry & McVey & Ramacon &
  Morgan**
  Buffalo Stance
**Cherry & Ramacom & McVey &
  Morgan**
  Buffalo Stance
Cherubini
  Cradle Song
  Dawn, The
  Hymn For A Youth Holiday
  Like As A Father
  Louis Charles Zenobie Salvador
    Maria
  Night Ride
  Sweet Are The Banks When Spring
    Perfumes
  Vieux Vagabond, Le
Chesnut
  Wonders You Perform, The
Chester
  Jesus Calls Us O'er The Tumult
Chestnut
  Four In The Morning
Chetam
  I'm Not Ashamed To Own My Lord
Chetham
  Am I A Soldier Of The Cross
  Aylesbury
  How Great The Wisdom Power And
    Grace
  O God Of Truth Whose Living Word

Chetniks
  Rise Guerillas Rise
Chevalier
  Future Mrs 'Awkins, The
  Knock'd Em In The Old Kent Road
  Our Little Nipper
Chiara
  Spagnola, La
  Spanish Girl, The
Chiate & Garrett & Money & Taylor
  Maybe I'm A Fool
Chihara
  Theme From The Survivors
Child
  If You Were A Woman And I Was A
    Man
Child & Bon Jovi & Samborra
  Livin' On A Prayer
Child & Cooper & McCurry
  Poison
Child & Tyler
  Angel
Child & Warren
  Just Like Jesse James
Childs
  Hearken To The Anthem Glorious
  Virtue
Chirgwin
  My Fiddle Is My Sweetheart
  My Fiddle Was My Sweetheart
Chiriacka & Gantry
  Dear God
Chisholm & Kirkpatrick
  O To Be Like Thee
Chisholm & Lowden
  Living For Jesus
Chisolm & Barbosa
  Let The Music Play
Chisom
  Getting Late In The Evening
  Whose Side Are You On
Chisum & George
  Call To Worship
Chiten & Phillips-Oland
  Come Into My Life
Chope
  Lord Thy Word Abideth
  Praise O Praise Our God And King
Chopin
  Ballade No 1
  Christ Be With Me
  Drinking Song
  Funeral March
  Funeral Song Of The Nation
  Gay Waltz, A
  Invitation Song
  Lithuanian Folk Song
  Lonely Star
  Madchen's Wunsch
  Maiden's Wish, The
  Mist And All, The
  Moonlight Sunlight
  Nocturne
  Piosnka Zegarmistrza

Chopin *(Cont.)*
Polish Song
Polonaise Opus 53
Spring Song
Trees In Winter
Viens Aurore
Waltz
Chorley
Brave Old Oak, The
Chotas
My Yellow Jacket Girl
Christensen
Nidelven
Christian
Funky Broadway
I Don't Need You
Ode To A Gym Teacher
Sail On
Christian & Gaither & Gaither
Not By Might Not By Power
Christian & McSpadden & Smiley
No Other Name But Jesus
Christian & Peek
All Things Are Possible
Christian & Thomas
Without A Doubt
Christiansen
Fairest Lord Jesus
Lullaby On Christmas Eve
Christie & Herbert
Lightnin' Strikes
Christine
She Just Sat There A-Giggling
Christopher
Interrogation
Manic Monday
O Wondrous Love
Wondrous Love
Christy
Carry Me Back To Old Virginny
Farewell Ladies
For Jehovah I Am Waiting
We Have Felt The Love Of Jesus
Chung & Wolf
Everbody Have Fun Tonight
Everybody Have Fun Tonight
Church & Williams
Pretty Girls Everywhere
Churchill
Baby Mine
Casey Jr
Casey Junior
Heigh Ho Heigh Ho
Heigh-Ho
I'm Wishing
Little April Shower
Love Is A Song
Never Smile At A Crocodile
One Song
Put Your Heart In A Song
Silly Song
Some Day My Prince Will Come
Whistle While You Work
Who's Afraid Of The Big Bad Wolf
With A Smile And A Song

Chute
Carradoc Plains
Chwatal
Lovely Night
Ciampi
Fair Nina
Ciccone
Lucky Star
Ciccone & Bray
Angel
Causing A Commotion
Express Yourself
Into The Groove
True Blue
Ciccone & Cole & Rafelson
Open Your Heart
Ciccone & Leonard
Cherish
Like A Prayer
Live To Tell
Oh Father
Where's The Party
Who's That Girl
Ciccone & Leonard & Geitch
Isla Bonita, La
Ciccone & Pettibone
Vogue
Cilia & Duffy
Cry
Cimara
Fiocca La Neve
Cioffi
Stairway To The Sea
Citkowitz
Gentle Lady
Clack & Davidson
Catch Us If You Can
Claiborne
It's My Union
Clampett
Beany And Cecil
Clancy
My Son Ted
Clanton & Matassa
Just A Dream
Clapp
Girl Of My Dreams
Claps & Cicchetti
Beep Beep
Clapton
Bell Bottom Blues
Carnival
Easy Now
Got To Get Better In A Little While
Hello Old Friend
Let It Grow
Presence Of The Lord
Wonderful Tonight
Clapton & Bramlett
Bottle Of Red Wine
Comin' Home
Let It Rain
Lovin' You Lovin' Me

Clapton & Collins & Pappalardi
Strange Brew
Clapton & Gordon
Layla
Clapton & Harrison
Badge
Clapton & Levy & Terry
Lay Down Sally
Clapton & Russell
Blues Power
Clapton & Sharp
Tales Of Brave Ulysses
Clapton & Whitlock
Anyday
Tell The Truth
Why Does Love Got To Be So Sad
Clare & Stept & Palmer
Please Don't Talk About Me When
I'm Gone
Clare & Whiting
On The Good Ship Lollipop
Claribel
Come Back To Erin
Drifting
Five O'Clock In The Morning
I Cannot Sing The Old Songs
Maggie's Welcome
Oh Mother Take The Wheel Away
Strangers Yet
Take Back The Heart
Take Back The Heart That Thou
Gavest
We Sat By The River You And I
We'd Better Bide A Wee
You And I
Clark
Any Way You Want It
Because
Because I Love You
Bohemia Hall
By Cool Siloam's Shady Rill
Call Of The Western Wild, The
Carpenter, The
Closer To You
Come On In
Concha Concepcion
Cow Pony Friend, A
Department Store Cowboy, A
Essay
Floating On A Marcel Wave
For The White And The Blue
Going Back To Nassau Hall
Got My Mind Set On You
Hail The Day That Sees Him Rise
Happy Cowboy, The
Head That Once Was Crowned
Head That Once Was Crowned With
Thorns, The
Heartbroke
Ho For The Kansas Plains
I'd Like To Be In Texas
Immortal Love For Ever Full
Immortal Love Forever Full

Clark *(Cont.)*
It's In His Kiss
Let Us Climb The Hill Together
Lift Up Our Hearts O King Of Kings
Loon Song
Lord Of All Being Throned Afar
Lord Will Come, The
Meet Me By The Running Brook
My Garden
No Longer Forward Nor Behind
Nobody But You
Not Gold But Only Men Can Make
O Blest Creator Of The Light
O Thou Who Didst With Love
    Untold
O Thou Whose Feet Have Climbed
    Life's Hill
O Trinity Of Blessed Light
Orange Moon
Our Faith Is In The Christ
Party Lights
Plenary
Praise The Lord Ye Heavens Adore
    Him
Princeton Forward March
Princeton Jungle March
Princeton That's All
Rags And Tatters
Raindrops
Rodeo Days
Round-Up, The
Saint Who First Found Grace To Pen,
    The
Savin' My Love For You
Shoop Shoop Song, The
Sinful Sighing To Be Blest
Singin' Annie Laurie On Guard
Sos
Swell The Anthem Raise The Flag
Tell Them All
Telling Time
'Tis Winter Now
Trumpet Voluntary
'Twixt Gleams Of Joy And Clouds
    Of Doubt
We've Drunk From The Same
    Canteen
When Courage Fails
You Are Like The Wind
Clark & Abner
Gloria
Clark & Bettis
Heart Of The Night
Slow Hand
Clark & Carter
You're Friends
Clark & Collen & Elliott & Lange &
Love Bites
Pour Some Sugar On Me
Clark & Davidson
Catch Us If You Can
Clark & Gill & Crowell
Oklahoma Borderline

Clark & Hudson
Blessed By The Name
Clark & Leigh
Come From The Heart
Clark & Muldrow & Mann
You Can't Sit Down
Clark & Prim & East
Reservations For Two
Clark & Resnick
Good Lovin'
Clark & Schlitz
True Heart
Clark & Smith
Bits And Pieces
Glad All Over
Clark & Willing
Texas Blues
Clarke
American Flag, The
Chanticleer
Creator Of The Earth And Skies
Head That Once Was Crowned With
    Thorns, The
Heartbroke
Hunter's Song
Hush Somebody's Callin' My Name
Hymn
In The Tree-Top
Into My Heart
Mother
No Hidin' Place Down There
O Very God Of Very God
Trumpet Tune
Trumpet Voluntary
Clarke & Hicks & Nash
Tell Me To My Face
Clarkson & Peterson
So Send I You
Clasen
Lykkeliten
Clasky & Rosenberg
Image Of A Girl
Clattenburg
There's Joy In Giving
Clattenburg & Powell
Chosen Generation
Claude
Hail To New Mexico
Claudin
Il Est En Vous Le Bien Que Je Desire
J'ai Par Trop Longuement Ayme
J'ayme Le Cueur De M'amye
On En Dira Ce Qu'on Vouldra
Claudius
Ruhe Im Grabe, Die
Clawson
Song For You, A
Clawson & Berry
Song For You, A
Clay
Gypsy John
I'll Sing Thee Songs Of Araby
I'll Sing Thee Songs Of Italy

Clay & Crewe
Silhouettes
Clay & Toler
Only Child
Clayton
Avenue C
Come Come Ye Saints
Every Moment Of Every Day
For All My Sin
Gotta Travel On
His Love
I Am Persuaded
I Am The Resurrection And The Life
If We Could See Beyond Today
If You Can Touch Her At All
It Is Faith
Jesus Is All You Need
Jesus My Lord And My God
Ladies Love Outlaws
Now I Belong To Jesus
Safe And Secure
We Shall See His Lovely Face
Wondrous Love
Clayton & Ehrlich & Lazar & Six
Travel On
Clayton & Sigidi
Take Your Time
Clayton-Thomas
Spinning Wheel
Clemenceau
Solitaire
Clemens
Jaquin Jaquet
Smith, The
Clement
Adoramus Te
Guess Things Happen That Way
Clements
Go With Goldwater
Clements & Arnold
Just A Little Lovin' Will Go A Long
    Way
Clements & Danks
No Night There
Clemm
Call For Reapers, The
Clephane & Maker
Beneath The Cross Of Jesus
Clephane & Sankey
Ninety And Nine, The
Clereau
Comme Un Qui Prend
Clesi
I'm Sorry I Made You Cry
Cleveland & Johnson & Robinson
Baby Baby Don't Cry
Cliff
Trapped
Clifford
Rain Upon The Roof
Clifford & Roman & McManus
We Did But Now You Don't

Clifton
I Belong To The King
If Music Be The Food Of Love Play
  On
Long Time Ago
Paddle Your Own Canoe

Climie & Fisher & Morgan
Room To Move

Climie & Morgan
My Heart Can't Tell You No

Clinger & Cymbal
Rock Me Baby

Clinton
Calypso Melody
Dreamy Melody
My Reverie

Clinton & Bernier & Emmerich
Our Love

Clivilles
Could This Be Love

Cloere
Grand Voyage Du Pauvre Negre, Le

Clokey
Concord Hymn
Jesus Lives
Rose, The

Cloninger & Foster
Spirit Wings

Cloninger & Purse
Surrender

Cloninger & Rosasco
Come Celebrate Jesus
Forever

Cloud
Song Of The City

Clough-Leighter
It Was A Lover And His Lass
My Lover He Comes On The Skee

Clunk
See Lord Before Thy Throne

Clydesdale
Empower Me
Forgive Me Lord

Coard
Gipsy's Warning, The

Coates
Praise Him
Sleepy Lagoon

Coats
Invite Him In
Sing Out The Tidings
Where Could I Go

Cobb
Alabama Jubilee
Are You From Dixie
Battle Song Of Liberty, The
Come Pure Hearts
Come Pure Hearts In Sweetest
  Measure
Cries Of London Town
Happy Day O Happy Day
Hark The Sound Of Holy Voices
Round The Lord In Glory Seated
Rubber Plant Rag

Cobb (*Cont.*)
Tinker
Warm O'er The Skies The Sunshine

Cobb & Barnes
Good-Bye Dolly Gray

Cobb & Channel
Hey Baby

Cobb & Edwards
I Can't Tell Why I Love You But I
  Do
School Days
Somebody's Sweetheart I Want To
  Be

Coben
Old Piano Roll Blues, The

Coben & Foree
Nobody's Child

Coben & Grean
Sweet Violets

Cobert
Love Theme From The Winds Of
  War

Cocchi
Busy Curious Thirsty Fly

Cochran
Don't You Ever Get Tired Of
  Hurting Me
Funny Way Of Laughin'
Heartache Away
I Want To Go With You
Little Bitty Tear, A
Make The World Go Away
She's Got You

Cochran & Allison
I'd Fight The World

Cochran & Capehart
Summertime Blues

Cochran & Dillon
Chair, The

Cochran & Dillon & Porter
Ocean Front Property

Cochran & Howard
I Fall To Pieces

Cochran & Kane & Channel
Gonna Have A Party

Cockburn
Feel It Again

Cockshott
Johnny And Jenny

Cocuzzo & Zito
Christmas Time Of Year

Codina
Zacatecas

Codini
C'est Suzette

Coe
Loneliness In Lucy's Eyes, The
Take This Job And Shove It

Coelho
Father I Adore You

Coenen
Come Unto Me
Fruhlingslied
Lovely Spring

Coerne
We Sing Of Sails
Young And Radiant He Is Standing

Coghill & Mason
Work For The Night Is Coming

Cogswell & Harrison & Noble
My Little Grass Shack In Kealakekua
  Hawaii

Cohan
Ethel Levey's Virginia Song
Forty-Five Minutes From Broadway
Give My Regards To Broadway
Good-Bye Flo
Harrigan
I Guess I'll Have To Telegraph My
  Baby
I Want You
I'm A Popular Man
I'm A Yankee Doodle Dandy
I'm Mighty Glad I'm Living And
  That's All
If I'm Going To Die I'm Going To
  Have Some Fun
If Washington Should Come To Life
Life's A Funny Proposition After All
Mary's A Grand Old Name
Molly Malone
Nellie Kelly I Love You
Nothing New Beneath The Sun
Over There
Popularity
So Long Mary
Stand Up And Fight Like H---
Under Any Old Flag At All
When A Fellow's On The Level With
  A Girl That's On
Yankee Doodle Boy, The
Yankee Doodle Dandy
You Can Have Broadway
You Can Tell That I'm Irish
You Can't Deny You're Irish
You're A Grand Old Flag

Cohen
Bird On The Wire
Death Of An Old Seaman
Hey That's No Way To Say
  Goodbye
Stay Close To Someone
Suzanne

Cohen & Mollin
War Of The Worlds' Second Wave

Cohron
City Of Gold

Colacrai
Runaround

Colahan
Galway Bay

Colasse
To Thy Fair Charm

Colbran
Sempre Piu T'amo

Colburn
Dimples
Little Dutch Garden, A
Colcord
There's No Place Like Home
Cole
All That Glitters Isn't Gold
Calypso Blues
Casanova O'Reilly
DC Farewell
Give Me A Heart Like Thine
Harold's House Of Jazz
I'm Never Gonna Give You Up
Love
Maiden With The Dreamy Eyes, The
Mother Mine
New Woman, The
New York Afternoon
On To Victory
Rock Of Ages
Ten Thousand Years
This Is Our Day
Under The Bamboo Tree
What A Day
When All Thy Mercies O My God
White Butterflies
Cole & Campsie & McFarlane
Another Lover
Cole & Cole
Tramp On The Street, The
Cole & Howard
Everything
Cole & Johnson
You're All Right Teddy
Cole & Mills
Straighten Up And Fly Right
Coleman
Baby Dream Your Dream
Best Is Yet To Come, The
Blessing, The
Big Spender
Blame It On Rio
Bread And Roses
Changing Partners
Christmas Lullaby
Colors Of My Life, The
Come Follow The Band
Firefly
Grand Boom Boom, Le
Hey Look Me Over
Hey There Good Times
Humpty Dumpty
I Like Your Style
I Love My Wife
I Rise Again
I Wanna Be Yours
I'm A Brass Band
I've Got Your Number
If My Friends Could See Me Now
In Tune
It's Not Where You Start
Love Makes Such Fools Of Us All
Nobody Does It Like Me

Coleman (Cont.)
On The Twentieth Century
Our Private World
Pass Me By
Real Live Girl
Rhythm Of Life, The
Seesaw
Sweet Charity
Tennessee Wig-Walk, The
There Is A Sucker Born Ev'ry
Minute
Tijuana Taxi
Tin Pan Alley
Una Muy Bonita
What Are Heavy
Where Am I Going
Why Try To Change Me Now
Witchcraft
You There In The Back Row
You're A Lovable Lunatic
Coleman & Darion & Gimble
Ricochet Romance
Coleman & Gibbons
Everytime You Go Outside I Hope It
Rains
Coleman & McCarthy
I'm Gonna Laugh You Out Of My
Life
Coleridge-Taylor
Big Lady Moon
O Mistress Mine
Coleridge-Taylor & Perkinson
Child's Grace, A
Coles
From Every Spire
From Every Spire On Christmas Eve
From Every Spire On Christmas
Even
Jesus My All To Heaven Is Gone
Colin & Isabel
Rossignolet Sauvage
Collazo
Mama Yo Quiero Un Novio
Coller
Christ Is The World's True Light
Collie
Looks Aren't Everything
Collier
Burn Baby Burn
Lead Poison On The Wall
Rent Strike Blues
Collier & Hennesy
Love Our River Again
Collin
Church Bells
We Were Comrades Together In The
Days Of War
Collins
Against All Odds
Angel On My Side
Another Day In Paradise
Born To The Breed
Che
Do You Know Do You Care

Collins (Cont.)
Do You Remember
Don't Let Him Steal Your Heart
Away
Don't Lose My Number
Don't Say Goodbye Love
Dream On
Droned
Farewell To Tarwathie
Fisherman Song, The
Granddaddy
Hand In Hand
Holly Ann
Houses
I Cannot Believe It's Time
I Don't Care Anymore
I Missed Again
I Wish It Would Rain Down
I'm Not Moving
If Leaving 'me Is Easy
If You Ain't Lovin' You Ain't Livin'
In The Air Tonight
Inside Out
It Don't Matter To Me
Life You Dream, The
Like China
Long Long Way To Go
Mama Mama
Misunderstanding
My Father
Nightingale
One More Night
Open The Door
Out Of Control
Rest Of Your Life, The
Roof Is Leaking, The
Running For My Life
Secret Gardens
She's Looking Good
Shoot First
Since You've Asked
Sky Fell
Song For Duke
Song For Martin
Sussidio
Take Me Home
This Must Be Love
Thru' These Walls
Thunder And Lightning
Trust Your Heart
West Side, The
Who Said I Would
Why Can't It Wait Till Morning
You Know What I Mean
Collins & Campbell
Hello Texas
Collins & David & Ling
Eddie My Love
Collins & Davis
Sweet Life
Collins & Harwood & Krantz
Don't Misunderstand Me

Collins & Keach
Easy Times
Collins & Leath
Acapulco
Collins & Leigh
Don't Dilly Dally On The Way
Collins & McDonald
This Is The Day
Collins & Penniman
Lucille
Collins & Pinkard
You're The Reason God Made
Oklahoma
Collins & Pinkard & Garrett
Pecos Promenade
Collins & Stuermer
Doesn't Anybody Stay Together
Anymore
I Don't Wanna Know
Only You Know And I Know
Collins & Van Zant
Free Bird
Colorado School Of Mines
Mining Engineer, The
Colter
I'm Not Lisa
Colton
Ninety-Fifth
Coltrane
Pursuance
Resolution
Straight Street
Thunder And Light'ning
Columbo
Prisoner Of Love
Colyn
Thou'rt Like Unto A Flower
Comden & Green & Edens
French Lesson
Commer
Merry Men
Compton
My Grandfather Had Some Very
Fine Ducks
Comstock
Theme From Adam 12
Comtrack
Real Goodness From Kentucky Fried
Chicken
Conant
Enter Into His Gates With
Thanksgiving
God Is Near
I Bind My Heart This Tide
I Love My Friends And They Love
Me
Now It's Happy Autumn Time
Our World Which Once Was Very
Big
Temper My Spirit O Lord
Concepcion
Lentaments

Concone
Glory To God On High
Lamb Of God
Condray
I Stand Before The Lord
Conet & Austin & Villa
Believe Me
Confrey
Kitten On The Keys
Stumbling
Congden
We Stand At Armageddon
Conkey
God Is Love His Mercy Brightens
In The Cross
In The Cross Of Christ
In The Cross Of Christ I Glory
Conlee & Baber
Rose Colored Glasses
Conley
Stranded On A Dead End Street
When You Were Blue And I Was
Green
Conley & Scruggs
Angel In Disguise
Chance Of Lovin' You
Don't Make It Easy For Me
Love Don't Care Whose Heart It
Breaks
Connell & Drewery
Waiting Game
Connell & Drewery & O'Duffy
You On My Mind
Connelly
Farewell Forever
U Of Toledo
Conniff
Real Meaning Of Christmas, The
Connolly
Drill Ye Tarriers Drill
Connolly & Priest & Tucker & Scott
Action
Fox On The Run
Connor
At My Time Of Life
Fire Was Burning Hot, The
Grandma's Feather Bed
I Saw Mommy Kissing Santa Claus
Peter's Theme
She Was One Of The Early Birds
Connor & Leach & Carr
Little Boy That Santa Claus Forgot,
The
Connors
Tomorrow Is Another Day
Connors & Goldenberg
In Finding You I Found Love
Conrad
Continental, The
Ma
Ma He's Making Eyes At Me
Conrad & Bernie
Co-Ed, The

Conrad & Dubois & Columbo &
Gregory
You Call It Madness But I Call It
Love
Conrad & Friend
Yes Yes
Conrad & Garrett
If Looks Could Kill
Conrad & Kennedy
Every Time I Think Of You
Conrad & Magidson
Here's To Romance
Conrad & Oakland & Drake
Champagne Waltz, The
Conrad & Robinson
Lena From Palesteena
Margie
Conradi
At Sunset
Falcon, The
Conroy
His Lordship Winked At The
Counsel
Constant
Twilight Zone
Conti
Cagney And Lacey Theme
Dynasty
Emerald Point Nas
Falcon Crest
For Your Eyes Only
Gonna Fly Now
Moment Of Truth, The
North And South
Power
Redemption
Right Stuff, The
Theme From An Unmarried Woman
Theme From Broadcast News
Theme From Dynasty
Unmarried Woman, An
You Take My Heart Away
Conti & Lerios & Jenkins
Reach For The Top
Contractus
Hail Blessed Lady
Converse
Aileen Aroon
Alma Mater
Hark Hark My Soul
Hvilken Venn
Just Beyond
Lover's Envy, A
Sound Forth Again The Nation's
Voice
Under The Stars And Stripes
Water Lily, The
What A Friend
What A Friend We Have In Jesus
Conwell
Your Mission
Coogan
Drexel Marching Song

Cook
Bon Bon Buddy
Heavenly Sunlight
I'll Come Running Back To You
Jesus The Resurrection
Jesus Thou Art The Sinner's Friend
Old Arm Chair, The
Over Hill Over Dale
Silvers
You Can Have Her
You Can Have Him
You Send Me
Cook & Hogin
I Believe In You
Cook & Nicholson
Power Of Love, The
Cook & Nicholson & Jarvis
Working Without A Net
Cook & Prine
Love Is On A Roll
Cook & Woods
Talkin' In Your Sleep
Cooke
Another Saturday Night
Around The Family Alter
Bring It On Home To Me
Chain Gang
Cupid
Friend After Friend Departs
Friendship With Jesus
I Do I Do I Do
I Have Redeemed Thee
Laughing Song
Nell Batchelor
Only Sixteen
Strephon's Knell
Time's End
We Got The Whole World Shakin'
Wonderful Love
You Send Me
Cooke & Alpert & Adler
Wonderful World
Cooley
Shame On You
Coonley & Jaspersen
Earth's Resurrection
Cooper
And All The World Resound
Beloved In Story
Cheated Too
Daybreak
Dream Never Dies, The
Easter Lilies
Evening Hymn
Jeff In Petticoats
Jesus Where'er Thy People Meet
Love In On The Line
O Sweet Flower
Song For Canada, A
We Are Riding
What Robin Said
Wonderful Peace
Cooper & Bruce
School's Out

Cooper & Kennedy
Star Of The East
Cooper & Wagner
Only Women Bleed
Coote
Letter In The Candle, The
See Saw
Coots
For All We Know
I Believe In Santa Claus
Love Letters In The Sand
Me And My Teddy Bear
Santa Claus Is Coming To Town
Santa Clause Is Comin' To Town
With God's Hand In Mine
You Go To My Head
Cope
Holy Spirit Be My Guide
World Shut Your Mouth
You Give Good Love
Copeland
Cabbage-Leaf Rag
Copes
For The Bread Which Thou Hast
    Broken
So Lowly Doth The Savior Ride
Copland
Song
That's The Idea Of Freedom
Copper
Ploughshare, The
Coppersmith & Venis
I Don't Have To Go Back To Ireland
Coppes
Onward With Temple
Coquatrix
Comme Ci Comme Ca
Count Every Star
Corbeil
All Are Architects Of Fate
One In Joyful Songs Of Praise
When My Love To God Grows Weak
Corbiel
Soldiers Of The Cross Arise
Corbin
American Family, An
Can't Keep A Good Man Down
On The Wings Of My Victory
Corda
Bittersweet
Cordell
I Think We're Alone Now
Corder & Douglas & Francis & Patter
Walkin' Shoes
Cordero
From The Green Fragrant Meadow
Cordle
Highway 40 Blues
Cordray
You're My Little Indiana Rose
Corea
500 Miles High
Capuccino

Corea *(Cont.)*
Central Park
High Wire
Humpty Dumpty
Inner Space
Now He Sings Now He Sobs
Return To Forever
Samba Song
Sicily
Straight Up And Down
One Step, The
Tones For Joan's Bones
Corea & Rodrigo
Spain
Corfe
O Come Let Us Sing Unto The Lord
Praise The Lord O My Soul
Corfield
Is The World Any Better
Corfts
Agricultural Irish Girl, The
Corigliano
Christmas At The Cloisters
Corin
Aren't You The Girl I Met At
    Sherry's
Corkine
Shall A Smile Or A Guileful Glance
Cormier & Roseland & Van
Hit And Run Affair
Cornelius
Bridal Song
Christmas Song
Christmas Tree
Don't Ever Be Lonely
Grablied
Kings, The
Konige, Die
Mitten Wir Im Leben Sind
Monotone, The
Salamaleikum
Three Kings, The
Ton, Ein
Too Late To Turn Back Now
Treat Her Like A Lady
Voice, The
Cornell
Let Zion's Watchmean All Awake
March
My Faith Looks Up To Thee
Our God Is Love And All His Saints
Cornell & Cooper
Wonderful Peace
Corner
Babe Lies In The Cradle
Baby In The Cradle, A
Kindlein In Der Wiegen, Ein
Cornet
Avecque Vous
Cornett
Wild Stormy Deep
Cornish
May Day Carol

Cornwall & Roberti
Nights, The
Corporation, The
ABC
I Want You Back
Love You Save, The
Mama's Pearl
Corr
Lough Neagh Fishers, The
Correa
Spain
Correll
Mouldering Vine, The
Correlli
Lonsdale
Corrigan
Molly Malone
Cort
Coppersmiths' Song, The
Forced Landing, A
Cortner
World Turns On And On, The
Corton & Franks & Hausey
Honky-Tonk Man
Cory
I Left My Heart In San Francisco
Town's A Christmas Tree, The
Coslow
Daddy Won't You Please Come
Home
Little White Gardenia, A
Coslow & Harling
Sing You Sinners
Coslow & Johnston
Cocktails For Two
Just One More Chance
My Old Flame
Coslow & Whiting
True Blue You
Coslow & Young
Je Vous Adore
Cosson
Voyant Souffrir Celle Que Me
Tormente
Cost
Luna Nova
Costa
Frangesa, A
Caruli
Christmas Mem'ries
French Girl, The
I Will Extol Thee O Lord
Luna Nova
Neapolitan Serenade
New Moon
Oje Caruli
Coste
Celle Fillette
Costeley
Arrete Un Peu Mon Coeur
Mignonne Allons Voir Si La Rose
Your Dancing Fills My Heart With
Joy

Costello
Everday I Write The Book
Cotroumpas
Sons Of Greece
Cotten
Philippine Hombre, The
Cottman
Again The Morn Of Gladness
All As God Wills
All As God Wills Who Wisely Heads
Before Thy Feet I Fall
Blow Winds Of God Awake And
Blow
Come Let Us Join With Faithful
Souls
Make Channels For The Streams Of
Love
O For That Tenderness Of Heart
O It Is Hard To Work For God
Teach Us O Lord True Brotherhood
We Plow The Fields
Who Is Thy Neighbor
Cotton
Freight Train
Under The Gun
Cottrau
Farewell Dear Napoli
Goodbye To Naples
Santa Lucia
Coucy
Morning Song For The Dame De
Fayel
Quand Le Joli Rossignol
When The Sweet Nightingale
Coulston
Folks That Put On Airs
Coulter & Martin
Congradulations
Coulter & Martin
Puppet On A String
Coulthard
Blessed Are Those That Are
Undefiled
Fill You Hearts
Heavens Declare, The
O Be Joyful In The Lord
O Come Let Us Sing Unto The Lord
O Sing Unto The Lord A New Song
Couperin
Fuis Seducteur
Musette
Courage
Star Trek
Theme From Judd For The Defense
Theme From Star Trek
Courage & Roddenberry & Goldsmith
Star Trek The Next Generation
Courteville
Thou Art The Way To Thee Alone
Courtney
Four-F Charlie
My Heart's In The Highlands
Work While The Sun Climbeth High

Courtney & Clawson
Journey, The
Courtville
My God Accept My Heart This Day
Cousin
Beautiful Queen
Cousin & D'urhan
Sands Of Time, The
Cousin-Jacques
L'optimiste
Couture
Verbum Supernum
Covay
Chain Of Fools
Covay & Berry
Pony Time
Coveney
Fordham Ram
Coverdale & Marsden
Here I Go Again
Coverdale & Marsden & Moody
Fool For Your Loving
Coverdale & Sykes
Give Me All Your Love
Is This Love
Covert
Jamie's On The Stormy Sea
Jeff Davis' Dream
Sword Of Bunker Hill, The
Covey & Berry
Pony Time
Cowan
Kisses
Out On The Deep
Waltzing Matilda
Coward
Come The Wild Wild Weather
Dearest Love
I Went To A Marvelous Party
I'll Follow My Secret Heart
I'll Remember Her
I'll See You Again
I'm So Weary Of It All
If Love Were All
Later Than Spring
Mad About The Boy
Regency Rakes
Someday I'll Find You
There's Always Something Fishy
About The French
You Were There
Zigeuner
Cowell
Air Held Her Breath
American Muse
Immensity Of Wheel
March In Three Beats
Spring Comes Singing
Swift Runner
Thy Name Was Once The Magic
Spell
Walk Hand In Hand

Cowen
Angel Came, The
Bloom On My Roses
Children's Home, The
Fountains Mingle With The River, The
In The Chimney Corner
Kissing Gate, The
Left Untold
Love Is A Dream
Love Me If I Live
Mission Of A Rose, The
Snowflakes
Sweet Love Of Mine

Cowles
Forgotten

Cowper & Mason
There Is A Fountain

Cox
It's Real
Life Time Friend
My Lord Knows The Way Through The Wilderness
Nobody Knows You When You're Down And Out
One-Hour Mama

Cox & Cox
I'm Following You

Cox & Waters & Cusic
If He Can Move A Mountain He Can Move A Heart

Coyle
Picket Guard, The

Cozens
Rejoice Again I Say Rejoice

Crafer & Nebb
No Arms Can Ever Hold You
No Arms Can Ever Hold You Like These Arms Of Mine

Craft
Alone
I Wanna Be Ready
One More Day
That's Just Like Jesus

Craig
Near You
When Vandy Starts To Fight

Craighill
Guarded By Encircling Mountains

Cramer
Last Date
March Triumphal
My Last Date With You

Crane
Football
Green Bus, The
Jack And Jill
My Pony
Old Dobbin
Our Story Book
Snowflakes

Crane & Jacobs
Ev'ry Day Of My Life
Hurt
I Need You Now

Crane & Jacobs & Brewster
If I Give My Heart To You

Cranford
This Hour My Bonny Lads

Craven
Oh I Should Like To Marry

Crawford
Alma Mater
Army Air Corps Song
Mechs Of The Air Corps
Metro, The
No More Words
Rebel Song, A

Cray & Amy & Cousins
Smoking Gun

Cray & Harrington
Wounded Hearts

Creamer & Johnson
If I Could Be With You
If I Could Be With You One Hour Tonight

Creamer & King
Go 'Long Mule

Creamer & Layton
After You've Gone
'way Down Yonder In New Orleans

Crean
My Irish Jaunting Car

Creed & Bell
You Make Me Feel Brand New

Crequillon
Un Gai Berger

Creston
Bird Of The Wilderness, The
Psalm Xxiii

Cretry
Du Moment Qu'on Aime

Crewe & Gaudio
Big Girls Don't Cry
Bye Bye Baby Baby Goodbye
Can't Take My Eyes Off Of You
Dawn Go Away
Rag Doll
Ronnie
Silence Is Golden
Sun Ain't Gonna Shine Anymore, The
Walk Like A Man

Crewe & Linzer & Randell
Let's Hang On

Crewe & Nolan
Get Dancin'
Lady Marmalade
My Eyes Adored You

Crewe & Randell
Swearin' To God

Crewe & Slay
Lucky Ladybug
Silhouettes

Crewe & Slay & Piscariello
Tallahassie Lassie

Crider & Neel
Take The Long Way Home

Crisis
Arizona Sky

Crist
April
Blue Bird
Knock On The Door

Cristol & Randall
Tomorrow Doesn't Matter
Tomorrow Doesn't Matter Tonight

Croce
Age
Alabama Rain
Another Day Another Town
Bad Bad Leroy Brown
Big Wheel
Box 10
Careful Man
Dreamin' Again
Five Short Minutes
Good Time Man Like Me Ain't Got No Business, A
Hard Time Losin' Man
Hard Way Every Time, The
Hey Tomorrow
I'll Have To Say I Love You In A Song
In Monte Oliveti
It Doesn't Have To Be That Way
Long Time Ago, A
Lover's Cross
New York's Not My Home
Next Time This Time
One Less Set Of Footsteps
Operator
Photographs And Memories
Rapid Roy
Recently
Roller Derby Queen
Speedball Tucker
Stabat Mater
These Dreams
Time In A Bottle
Tomorrow's Gonna Be A Brighter Day
Top Hat Bar And Grille
Walkin' Back To Georgia
Workin' At The Car Wash Blues
You Don't Mess Around With Jim

Croce & Croce
I Am Who I Am
Just Another Day
Man That Is Me, The
Spin Spin Spin
Vespers
What People Do

Crocker
Angels Bright Heavens High
I Don't Need To Understand

Croegaert
Was It A Morning Like This

Crofford & Durrill & Garrett
Charlotte's Web
Ride Concrete Cowboy Ride
Texas State Of Mind, A

Croft
Blessed Are The Poor In Spirit
Church Triumphant In Thy Love
Dear Newark University
God Be Merciful Unto Us
God Of The Nations
Happy Are They They That Love
   God
It Singeth Low In Ev'ry Heart
O God Help In Ages Past
O God Our Help In Ages Past
O God While Generations Flee
O Light From Age To Age The Same
O Thou Who Art Of All That Is
O Where Are Kings And Empires
   Now
O Worship The King
O Worship The King All Glorious
   Above
O Ye Immortal Throng Of Angels
Our God Our Help
Our God Our Help In Ages Past
Prince Of Peace His Banner Spreads,
   The
Thine Arm O Lord In Days Of Old
To Thee Our God We Fly
While Shepherds Watched Their
   Flocks
Ye Servants Of God Your Master
   Proclaim
Croft & Colbert
He Just Loved Me More And More
Jesus I Love You
Croft & Colbert & Joyce
I Believe He Died For Me
Lord Take The Hand Of This Child
Croft & Croft
First Million Years
Future's Looking Brighter, The
I Believe He Died For Me
I Can't Even Walk Without You
   Holding My Hand
I'm The Reason
Is That Footsteps I Hear
Thanks To Him
Crofts
Evelyn
Ploughman, The
Crolla
Cri Du Coeur
Croly & Atkinson
Spirit Of God Descend Upon My
   Heart
Cronin
Can't Fight This Feeling
Can't Fight This Feeling Anymore
Don't Let Him Go
I Dowanna Know
Keep On Loving You
Keep The Fire Burnin'
Keep The Fires Burnin'
That Ain't Love
Time For Me To Fly

Cronin & Braun
Here With Me
Cronin & Kelly
In My Dreams
Crook
Coster's Serenade, The
Jeerusalem's Dead
What A Beautiful Day For The Lord
   To Come Again
Cropper
In The Midnight Hour
Cropper & Bramlett
I've Told You For The Last Time
Crosby
College Night
Coming Around The Horn
Cut My Hair
Dearest Mae
Deja Vu
Guinnevere
Long Time Gone
Crosby & Allen
Praise Him Praise Him
**Crosby & Croucher & Demartini &
Pearcy**
Lay It Down
Crosby & Demartini & Pearcy
Round And Round
Crosby & Doane
I Am Thine O Lord
Near The Cross
Pass Me Not O Gentle Savior
Rescue The Perishing
Though Your Sins Be As Scarlet
To God Be The Glory
Will Jesus Find Us Watching
Crosby & Kirkpatrick
He Hideth My Soul
Redeemed
Crosby & Knapp
Blessed Assurance
Crosby & Lowry
All The Way My Savior Leads Me
Crosby & Stebbins
Jesus Is Calling
Jesus Is Tenderly Calling
Saved By Grace
Crosby & Stills
Wooden Ships
Crosby & Sweeney
Tell Me The Story Of Jesus
Crosland
Indian Maid, The
Crosley
Navy Blue And Gold
Cross
All Right
Jesus The Calm That Fills My Breast
Never Be The Same
No Time For Talk
Ride Like The Wind
Sailing
Think Of Laura
We Hope In Thee
We Hope In Thee O God

Cross & Cory
I Left My Heart In San Francisco
Cross & Cross
Welcome To Heaven
Cross & Omartian
Charm The Snake
Crossley
Carmen Glenamonense
O God We Praise Thee
Crotch
Blessed Art Thou O Lord
Blessed Be The Lord God Of Israel
Comfort O Lord The Soul Of Thy
   Servant
It Is A Good Thing To Give Thanks
Out Of The Deep
Crouch
Bless The Lord O My Soul
Blood Will Never Lose Its Power,
   The
Broken Vessel, The
Can't Nobody Do Me Like Jesus
I Find No Fault In Him
I'm Gonna Keep On Singin'
I've Got Confidence
If Heaven Never Was Promised To
   Me
It Won't Be Long
Kathleen Mavourneen
My Tribute
My Tribute To God Be The Glory
Soon And Very Soon
Take Me Back
Broken Vessel, The
Through It All
You Don't Have To Jump No Pews
Crouch & Crouch
Jesus Is The Answer
Crow & Goodman & Vowell & Wilburn
You're The Singer
Crowe
Seesaw
Crowell
American Dream, An
Long Hard Road
Crowley & Beckett
Baby Come Back
Crowley & Routh
Paint The Town And Hang The
   Moon Tonight
Crowley & Silbar
I Know What I've Got
Crowninshield
Birds In Flight
Boston Town
Firemen
Crowther-Benyon
Yule Returns Come Christian People
Crudup
Mean Old Frisco Blues
My Baby Left Me
So Glad You're Mine
That's All Right

Crueger
Ah Holy Jesus How Hast Thou
    Offended
Auf Auf Mein Herz Mit Freuden
Deck Thyself My Soul With
    Gladness
Jesu Meine Freude
Jesus All My Gladness
Lamp Of Our Feet Whereby We
    Trace
Let Thy Blood In Mercy Poured
Lord God We Worship Thee
Lord In This Thy Mercy's Day
Now Thank We All Our God
Spirit Divine
Spirit Divine Attend Our Prayers
Wherefore O Father We Thy Humble
    Servants

Crueger & Mendelssohn
Lord God We Worship Thee

Cruger
Ah Holy Jesu How Hast Thou
    Offended
Ah Holy Jesus
Ah Holy Jesus How Hast Thou
    Offended
All My Heart This Night Rejoices
Arise The Kingdom Is At Hand
Calm On The List'ning Ear Of Night
Come Let Us Join Our Cheerful
    Songs
Deck Thyself My Soul With Gladness
Deck Thyself With Joy And Gladness
E'en In Thy Childhood 'mid The
    Desert Places
Frohlich Soll Mein Herze
Hail To The Lord's Anointed
Ich Singe Dir Mit Herz Und Mund
Jesu Priceless Treasure
Jesus All My Gladness
Jesus Christ My Sure Defence
Jesus Christ My Sure Defense
Jesus Meine Zuversicht
Jesus The Name High Over All
Let Thy Blood In Mercy Poured
Light Of The Gentile Nations
Lord In This Thy Mercy's Day
Lord Of Our Life And God Of Our
    Salvation
Love Of Love
Nought On Earth Is Lasting
Now Thank We All Our God
Now Thank We All Our God With
    Heart
Now The Busy Week Is Done
Nun Danket Alle Gott
O God Unseen But Ever Near
O King Of Might And Splendor
Praise To The Holy Trinity
Praise We Our God With Joy
Talk With Us Lord
Thanksgiving
Thy Kingdom Come

Cruger *(Cont.)*
Thy Way Is In The Deep
Up Up My Heart With Gladness
Wherefore O Father We Thy Humble
    Servants
Who Trusts In God A Strong Abode
With Thine Own Pity Savior
World Is Very Evil, The

Cruger & Bach
Now Thank We All Our God

Crumit
O-H And I-O

Cruse
Make A New Me

Cruse & Cruse
New Song, A
Remember Me

Crutchfield
Going Going Gone
Zion's Hill

Cugat
Cui Cui
My Shawl
My Sombrero
One-Two-Three-Kick

Cugat & Rosner
Nightingale

Cui
Cloud Messengers
If Deceits Of Life Are Numbing
Nocturne
Oceano Nox
Radiant Stars Above The Mountains
    Glowing
Spread Your Wings
Statue At Czarskoe-Selo, The
Statue Of Tsarkoe Selo
Three Birds
Your Sparkling Glance

Culiar
I'm A Roaring Repeater
Let's Have A Change

Cull
Open Our Eyes Lord
Welcome To The Family

Culpepper
Show Me The Man Who Never Done
    Wrong

Culross
Calvary

Culter
Son Of God Goes Forth To War, The

Culture Club
Church Of The Poison Mind
Do You Really Want To Hurt Me
I'll Tumble 4 Ya
Miss Me Blind
Mistake No. 3
Time

Culver
Ride Sally Ride

Culverwell
Born Again
Come On Ring Those Bells

Culverwell *(Cont.)*
Cover Me
May This Be The Place

Cumming
Other Loves

Cummings
Hark The Herald Angels Sing
Stand Tall

Cunico
When I Wanted You

Cunningham
Cry Of The People, The
Ha Ha Don't Make Me Laugh
Lift Up Your Hearts
March Of The Hungry Men, The
Mona Lisa Lost Her Smile
My Oklahoma Home It Blowed
    Away
O Valiant Hearts Who To Your
    Glory Came
O Valiant Hearts Who To Your
    Glory Come
Song Of The Lower Classes

Cureil
Full Moon

Cureton
We Shall Reign

Curey
Sally In Our Alley

Curnin
Saved By Zero

**Curnin & Greenall & Woods &
West-Oram & Agius**
One Thing Leads To Another
Saved By Zero

**Curnin & West-Oram & Greenall &
Brown**
Secret Separation

**Curnin & Woods & Greenall & Brown
& West-Oram**
Are We Ourselves

Curran
Hold Thou My Hand
Sonny Boy

Currier
In Christ There Is No East Or West

Curry
Before The Long And Busy Day
Blessed Are The Peacemakers
Boy In Your Home By The Wide
    Blue Sea
For The Silence Of The Snow
For Thy Great Book Of Stories
God Is Watching Over Me
God Made The Golden Sun
Good Night Sweet Jesus
O Jesus We Are Singing
Oh Give Thanks Unto The Lord
Our Happy Land America
Shine Shine Over All The World
Thank You Dear God For Summer
This Is Our Church
We Thank Thee For Our Church
Winter Air Is Crisp And Cold, The

Curry & Cain
He's Gonna Smile On Me
Curschmann
Hark Hark The Lark
Oriole Song, The
Curtis
Carme
Carmela
Come Back To Sorrento
Endymion
Hurrah For The Toiler
I Fought The Law
Love Is All Around
On O Thou Soul
Only Love True Love
Poor Boy
Return To Sorrento
That's My Hope That's My Wish
    That's My Prayer
Voice Of Night
Walk Right Back
Curtis & Allison
More Than I Can Say
Curtis & Hellard
I'm No Stranger To The Rain
Curtis & Military
Christmas Auld Lang Syne
Cusano & Mitchell
Tears
Cushing & Root
Ring The Bells Of Heaven
Cushman & West
Kodak Makes Your Pictures Count
Custance
College Clock, The
Principle's Just The Same, The
Purple Cow, A
Cuthbert
Do Not I Love Thee O My Lord
Cutler
At Length There Dawns The
    Glorious Day
Far Far Away Is Bethlehem
God's Trumpet Wakes The
    Slumb'ring World
Make Large Our Hearts
O Master Workman Of The Race
O Starry Flag
Son Of God Goes Forth To War
Son Of God Goes Forth To War, The
Son Of God The Prince Of Peace
Who Follows
World's Astir The Clouds Of Storm,
    The
Cutter
E Pluribus Unum
Cutts
All Who Love And Serve Your City
Christ Up On The Mountain Peak
God Is Love By Him Upholden
Like The Murmur Of The Dove's
    Song

Cutts *(Cont.)*
Look There The Christ Our Brother
Thanks To God Whose Word Was
    Spoken
Cymbal
Mr Bass Man
Cymone
Better Way
Cymone & Ant & Pirroni
Room At The Top
Czibulka
Among The Lillies
D'Abo
Handbags And Gladrags
D'Albert
Maid And The Butterfly, The
Maiden And The Butterfly, The
D'Ambra
Hunt, The
School Song
D'Anzi
Please Don't Go
D'Arby
Dance Little Sister
If You Let Me Stay
Sign Your Name
To Know Someone Deeply Is To
    Know Someone Softly
D'Arby & Oliver
Wishing Well
D'Arezzo
Ut Queant Laxis
D'Arguto
Tsen Brider
D'Artega
In The Blue Of Evening
D'Esposito
Anema E Core
D'Hardelot
Because
Without Thee
D'Indy
Bergere Avisee, La
Evening Star, The
D'Isle
People's Hymn, The
D'Urhan
For Thee O Dear Dear Country
O God In Restless Living
Da Costa
Two Songs For Julie-Ju
Da Silva
Placid Banks Of Ypiranga Still
    Resound, The
Da Sylva & Meyer
If You Knew Susie
Daasvand & Loveless
After All He's Done For Me
Dabney
S-H-I-N-E
That's Why They Call Me Shine

Dacre
As Your Hair Grows Whiter
Bicycle Built For Two, A
Daisy Bell
Elsie From Chelsea
Playmates
Dadmun
Homeward Bound
In The Christian's Home In Glory
There Is Rest For The Weary
Daffan
Born To Lose
Daggett
Hi Hi For The Scarlet
Rutgers Prayer, A
Dailey
Dreaming
Dain & Dorff & Atchley
Coca Cola Cowboy
Dake
We'll Girdle The Globe
Dalayar
Rien Tendre Amour
Dalayrac
D'un Epoux Cheri
Escouto D'Jeannetto
Hunting Song
J'aimerai Toute Ma Vie
Jour Lisette Allait Au Champ, Un
Notre Meunier Charge D'argent
O Ma Georgette
On Nous Dit Que Dans L'Mariage
Quand De La Nuit Le Voile Tutelaire
Quand Le Bien-Aime Reviendra
Dalayral
Plowman, The
Dalby
Cupid And My Capmaspe
Dalcroze
Arc-En-Ciel, L'
Dale
As Comes The Breath Of Spring
Bird With The Broken Wing, The
I Feel Like Going On
My Jesus As Thou Wilt
No Shadows Yonder
On Jordan's Stormy Banks I Stand
Wine Cup Did It All, The
Dale & Springfield
Georgy Girl
Dalecky
Laughing Blacksmith, The
Daley
When She's In Love
Dall & Deville & Michaels & Rockett
Every Rose Has Its Thorn
Nothin' But A Good Time
Talk Dirty To Me
Unskinny Bop
Dalsheimer
Life On The Vicksburg Bluff, A

Dalton
Doer Of The Word
Looking For A City
Safe
Through His Eyes Of Love
What A Savior
Dalton & McFadden
Crazy Blue Eyes
Don't Fall In Love With Me
Dalton & Worley
Night Has A Heart Of Its Own, The
Dalvimare
Mon Coeur Soupire
Rosette Pour Un Peu D'Absence
Son Que Je Prefere, Le
Daly
Broom And The Shovel, The
Dameron
Fontainebleau
Dameron & Gillespie
Nearness
Damon
Cotton Candy
Jesus The Very Thought Of Thee
My God How Wonderful Thou Art
Damrick
Old Fashioned Boy
Damrosch
Birthday Greeting, A
Easter Carol, An
Far Away
Handel
In Japan
In The Wood
Jessie
Joy Hope And Love
Lord's Day, The
Lost Kingdom, The
Million Little Diamonds, A
Minuet, The
Music Making
Party, The
Proper Way, The
Question, A
Request, A
There's A Ship On The Sea
Thought, A
Valentine, A
World And The Garden, The
Dana
Emilia Polka
Flee As A Bird
Longing For You
Soft Music Is Stealing
Dancz
Raincoat Song, The
Dane
You Don't Know Me
Danes
Beautiful Home
Danhauser
At Close Of School

Daniel
Blue Shadows On The Trail
Freiheit
I Love Lucy
Lavender Blue
Lavender Blue Dilly Dilly
Say It With A Slap
Daniels
Alma Pater
Drinkin' My Baby Goodbye
I Had A Dream Dear
I'm A Believer And Not A Doubter
Long Haired Country Boy
On Mobile Bay
Through The Dark The Dreamers
Came
Willie Jones
You Tell Me Your Dream
You Tell Me Your Dream I'll Tell
You Mine
Daniels & Arnold
I'll Be Forever Loving You
Daniels & Blackton & Brown & Rice
You Tell Me Your Dream I'll Tell
You Mine
Daniels & Crain
In America
Daniels & Crain & Digregorio &
Edwards & Hayward
Devil Went Down To Georgia
Daniels & Crain & Digregorio &
Edwards & Hayward & Marchall
Legend Of Wooley Swamp, The
Daniels & Crain & Digregorio &
Hayward
Boogie Woogie Fiddle Country Blues
Daniels & Digregorio & Gavin &
Hayward
Simple Man
Daniels & Lilly
That's Where My Money Goes
Daniels & Torrence
99 Year Blues
Danko
This Wheel's On Fire
Danks
Amber Tresses Tied In Blue
Do Good To Others
God Of Our Fathers
I Know No Life Divided
In Remembrance Of Me
Japanese Fan, The
Jesus Of Nazareth
My Lord Thy Will Be Done
No Night There
Silver Threads Among The Gold
Unto Thee O Lord
Vale Of Our Own Genesee, The
Waiting At The Gates
We Come O Lord To Thee
We Deck Their Graves Alike Today
Will There Be Light For Me
Dann
Thank You

Danoff
Afternoon Delight
Danoff & Danoff
Flyin' Home To Nashville
Friends With You
Danoff & Danoff & Denver
Take Me Home Country Roads
Danoff & Nivert
Please Daddy Don't Get Drunk This
Christmas
Danvers
Till
Danyel
Eyes Look No More
Now The Earth The Skies The Air
Danzig
Scarlet Ribbons
Scarlet Ribbons For Her Hair
Daraza
Ripe Is The Corn
Darby
'Twas The Night Before Christmas
Darcey
Noah's Ark, The
Dare
Babylonian Captivity
Bugle Song, The
Corn Song, The
Glasgow
Kedon
O Holy City Seen Of John
Sunset To Sunrise Changes Now
Darewski
Sister Susie's Sewing Shirts For
Soldiers
Dargimijsky
Dearest Little Maiden
Darian & Delory & Vanwinkle
Mr Custer
Darin
Dream Lover
Things
Darin & Murray
Splish Splash
Darke
In Stature Grows The Heavenly
Child
In The Bleak Midwinter
Lord Jesus Sun Of Righteousness
Darley
Freuet Euch Der Schonen Erde
Darling & Carey & Arkin
Banana Boat Song
Darms
Getenke Deines Schopfers
Zu Dir Gekreuzigter
Darnley
Swimming Master, The
Darst
Prayer Is The Soul's Sincere Desire
Roll On Big Mama
Darst & Gentry
Lady In The Blue Mercedes, The

Darwall
Before The Lord We Bow
Lord Of The Worlds Above
Rejoice The Lord Is King
Round Me Falls The Night
Shall Hymns Of Grateful Love
Thy Works Not Mine O Christ
Ye Holy Angels Bright
Ye Holy Angels Bright Who Wait

Dauermann
Stephen's Hymn
Who Hath Believed Our Report

Daugherty
Street Of San Antonio, The

Dauvergne
Jour De L'an, Le

Davenport
Cow Cow Blues
Praise Ye The Lord

Davenport & Cooley
Fever

Davey
In The Toy Shop
Spring Song

Davico
Acqua Di Rio
Caccia Di Re Marco, La
Come Un Cipresso Notturno
Commiato
E Vengote A Veder Perla Lizarda
Filtro, Il
Fior D'amaranto
Fior De Pepe
Fiori
Fiorin D'Argento
Gioia Umana
Ho Il Cuor Cosi Greve De Pianto
Incanto, L'A
Luna D'estate
Morte, La
Ninna-Nanna
Ninna-Nanna Abruzzese
Ninna-Nanna Calabrese
O Luna
O Luna Che Fa' Lume
O Maggio Bello
Pioggia
Pioggia D'Ottobre
Plenilunio
Quando Avro Restituito Le Ossa
    Nude
Rondini
Sera D'autunno
Sogno
Ultima Notte, L'
Vascello, Il

David
Charmant Oiseau
Delightful Bird
I Don't Care If The Sun Don't Shine
In Our Time
Sunflower
Where There's Life There's Bud

David & Davis & Kostelanetz
Moon Love

David & Diamond
Tell It Like It Is

David & Edwards
Johnny Get Angry

David & Evans & Hughes
Better Loved You'll Never Be

David & Hampton
Sea Of Heartbreak

David & Hoffman & Livingston
Bibbidi-Bobbidi-Boo
Chi-Baba Chi-Baba
Dream Is A Wish Your Heart Makes,
    A
None But The Lonely Heart
So This Is Love
Unbirthday Song, The
Work Song, The

David & Livingston
Alaskans, The
77 Sunset Strip
Bourbon Street Beat
Hawaiian Eye
Roaring Twenties, The
Surfside 6
This Is It

David & Owens & Altman
American Beauty Rose

David & Peretti & Creatore
Bimbombey

David & Pockriss
My Heart Is An Open Book

David & Reid
To Me

David & Rushing
Hope You're Feelin' Me Like I'm
    Feelin' You

David & Whitney & Kramer
Candy

David & Williams
Whole Lotta Shakin' Goin' On

David-Dixon
Blue And The Gray

Davidica
Christ The Lord Is Risen Today
Jesus Christ Is Risen Today

Davidowits
Wicked King, A

Davidson
Christmas Carol, A

Davie & Moore
Green Door, The

Davies
Cannonball
For All The Blessings Of The Year
God Be In My Head
Good Lovin' Man
Lola
Mercy Blessing Favour Grace
O Come Let Us Sing To The Lord
O King Enthroned On High
Saviour Sprinkle Many Nations
Sing A New Song To The Lord

Davies *(Cont.)*
Song Of Rest, A
Sunny Afternoon
We Give You Praise O God
Well Respected Man, A
Winter Night Was Dark And Still,
    The

Davies & Allen
Hometown Gossip

Davies & Hodgson
Bloody Well Right
Breakfast In America
Crime Of The Century
Dreamer
Even In The Quietest Moments
Goodbye Stranger
It's Raining Again
Logical Song, The
Take The Long Way Home

Davies & Oates
Electric Blue

Davies, Ray
All Day And All Of The Night
Dedicated Follower Of Fashion
Tired Of Waiting For You
You Really Got Me

Davis
At Twelve O'Clock
Baby Don't Get Hooked On Me
Bebop Lives
Bedtime
Bees
Bird Songs
Chimney Sweep
Christ Is The World's True Light
Cocaine
Colly My Cow
Come Raise The Song
Cool Night
Date In '48
Don't Cry Daddy
Down In The Field
Et Bailler Et Dormir
Fatal Wedding, The
From Thee All Skill And Science
    Flow
Gentle Hands
Go Mississippi
God Has Called You
He Carved His Mother's Name
    Upon The Tree
He Knows It All
Holy Ground
I Believe In Music
I Go Crazy
I Won't Get Up
I'll Fly Away
I'll Paint You A Song
I'll Praise My Maker While I've
    Breath
If I Had My Way
In My Birch Canoe
In The Baggage Coach Ahead

Davis *(Cont.)*
In The Ghetto
In Whom I Have Redemption
Is My Name Written There
It's All In The Game
It's Hard To Be Humble
Joyful Tidings, The
Kentucky
Kiss It And Make It Better
Lead Me Savior
Lead Me Saviour
Liverpool
Living Deeper In The Spirit
Living Lamb
Look Away To The Cross
Lookin' Through The Windows
Lullaby
M&O Blues
Nation Once Again, A
Never Can Say Goodbye
Newry
Nobody's Darlin' But Mine
O My Dear Heart
Only The Lonely
Parent's Prayer
Queen Dances, The
Santa Claus Comes
Savior Lead Me Lest I Stray
Saviour Lead Me Lest I Stray
Shame
Sing Again That Sweet Refrain
Sleepin' With The Radio On
Someone To Care
Something's Burning
Suddenly Last Night
Suddenly Last Summer
Take Time To Know Her
Thank You Lord
There Is A Time
Three Sailors, The
Under A Tree
Victory In '56
Washington My Home
We Sat Beneath The Maple On The
    Hill
We'll Endeavor
We'll Win The Day
What A Savior
When Jesus Christ Was Born On
    Earth
Where Do We Go From Here
Where Does It Lead
Wondrous News, The
You're My Best Friend

Davis & Ager & Santly
I'm Nobody's Baby

Davis & Akst
Baby Face

Davis & Baker
Perfect Love Affair

Davis & Burke
Carolina Moon
Yearning

Davis & Calloway
Joy

Davis & Castro
Cose Cose Cose

Davis & Ciani
Have A Coke And A Smile

Davis & Conrad
Lonesome And Sorry

Davis & Diamond
Tell It Like It Is

Davis & Fisher
Honor The Lord
Yeshua Ha Mashiach

Davis & Fletcher & Parks
Dancing Machine

Davis & Greenaway & Backer & Cook
I'd Like To Teach The World To
    Sing

Davis & Jourard
Take The L
Total Control

Davis & Kimball
Bop

Davis & Lewis
Silent Weeper

Davis & Malone & Patrick
Book Of Love

Davis & Mitchell
I Want My Freedom
You Are My Sunshine

Davis & Moore
Green Door, The

Davis & Murry
Don't Break The Heart That Loves
    You

Davis & Oats
Electric Blue

Davis & Onorati & Simeone
Little Drummer Boy, The

Davis & Ramirez & Sherman
Lover Man
Lover Man Oh Where Can You Be

Davis & Sargent
Columbus Stockade Blues

Davis & Severinsen
Stop And Smell The Roses

Davis & Taub
Worry Worry Worry

Davis & Taylor & Hopkins
Wreck Between New Hope And
    Gaethsemane

Davis & Tillman
It Makes No Difference Now

Davis & West
Country Sunshine

Davison
Idumea
Imandra
Sleep Soldier Sleep

Davisson & Houser
Rose Tree, The

Davorin
Yugoslavia

Davorin & Runjanin
God Who From Annihilation Saved
    Us

Davorin & Runjanin & Jenko
Yugoslavia

Davy
Bay Of Biscay
Bay Of Biscay, The
In The Hive Of Deseret

Dawes
Different Bites For Different Likes
Doing What We Do Best
It's All In The Game
Melody In A
Our L'Eggs Fit Your Legs
Plop Plop Fizz Fizz
Transportation Corps March

Dawkins
Christmas Stars Are Shining, The

Dawson
Blue Flowers
Chimes, The

Dawson & Walker
Land Of Pleasure

Day
Come Risen Lord And Deign To Be
    Our Guest
Holy Ghost Dispel Our Sadness
If Love Were What The Rose Is
My Master Was So Very Poor
Not Alone For Mighty Empire
To Every Man There Openeth

Day & Harris & Lewis
Fishnet

Dayton
All Quiet Along The Potomac
Won't You Come Along

Daza
Tierras Agenas, A
Alegrias Alegrias
Cagaleja La De Lo Verde
Callese Ya Mercurio
Dame Acogida En Tu Ato
Enfermo Estaba Antioco
Escrito Esta En Mi Alma
Gritos Dava La Morenica
Mira Juan Lo Que Te Dixe
Nunca Mas Veran Mis Ojos
Quando Las Desdichas Mias
Quien Te Hizo Juan Pastor
Serrana Donde Dormistis

De Achuapa
Venid Pastorcillos

De Apamiguel
Oh Pascua Dichosa

De Barro & Ribeiro
Chiquita Banana

De Benedictus
Theme From McCoy

De Chiara
Spagnola, La

De Chichigalpa
Ninito De Atocha

De Chinandega
Derrama Una Estrella
Ven Dulce Amado Mid
Venid Pastorcillos

De Condega
Derrama Una Estrella
Ven Dulce Amado Mio

De Curtis
Come Back To Sorrento
Surrender
Torna A Surriento
Tu Ca Nun Chiagne

De Dipilto
Venid Pastorcillos

De El Limon De Jalapa
Derrama Una Estrella

De El Viejo
Venid Pastorcillos

De Haven
Busy Milkman
North Wind
Polka And Waltz
Pretender, The
Small Scouts
Together

De Jalapa
Venid Pastorcillos

De Juigalpa
Ven Dulce Amado Mio

De Koven
Cradle Song
Dutch Lullaby
Haymaker's Roundelay, The
Little Doris
Love's Garden
Nita Gitana
O Promise Me
Oh Promise Me
Recessional
Serenade
Song At Evening, A
Song Of The Brown October Ale
Song Of The Water Lily
Tinkers' Song

De La Ceiba
Venid Pastorcillos

De La Paz Centro
Venid Pastorcillos

De Lara
Garden Of Sleep, The
Song Of Farewell

De Lechau
Li'l Liza Jane

De Leon
Derrama Una Estrella
Id A Belen Pastores
Ven Dulce Amado Mio
Venid Pastorcillos

De Leone
Rainbow Trail, The

De Limay
Vamos Pastores Vamos
Ven Dulce Amado Mio

De Los Rios
Song Of Joy, A

De Lulli
Chopsticks

De Macuelizo
Oh Pascua Dichose

De Managua
Venid Pastorcillos

De Marbelle
When They Ring The Golden Bells

De Masaya
Duerme Chiquitito

De Matagalpa
Venid Pastorcillos

De Mozonte
A Las Doce De La Noche
Derrama Una Estrella
Ninito De Atocha
Venid Pastorcillos

De Nagarote
Venid Pastorcillos

De Ocotal
Venid Pastorcillos

De Paulo & Brown
Belle From Barcelona

De Pearsall
Let Us All Go Maying
Meum Erst Propositum

De Posoltega
Venid Pastorcillos

De Pueblo Nuevo
A Las Doce De La Noche
Derrama Una Estralla
Venid Pastorcillos

De Quilali
Venid Pastorcillos

De Rose
Deep Purple
Have You Ever Been Lonely
Have You Ever Been Lonely Have
    You Ever Been Blue
Lilacs In The Rain
Marshmallow World, A
On A Little Street In Singapore
Somebody Loves You
Song Of The Seabees
Starlit Hour, The
Wagon Wheels

De Rose & Shefter
Lamp Is Low, The

De Somoto
Vamos Pastores Vamos
Venid Pastorcillos

DeSylva & Brown & Henderson
Varsity Drag, The

De Telica
A Las Doce De La Noche
Derrama Una Estrella
Ven Dulce Amado Mio

De Telpaneca
Ven Dulce Amado Mio
Venid Pastorcillos

De Totogalpa
Ven Dulce Amado Mio

De Vita
Softly As I Leave You

De Yalaguina
Derrama Una Estrella
Venid Pastorcillos

De Young
Call Me
Don't Let It End
Nothing Ever Goes As Planned

Deacon
Another One Bites The Dust

Dean
Big Bad John
Consolation
Crown, The
Just Over In The Glory-Land
Keep Me Every Day
Ten Thousand Joys

Dean & Dean & Blair
One Has My Name The Other Has
    My Heart

Dean & Glover
You Don't Have To Be A Star
You Don't Have To Be A Star To Be
    In My Show

Dean & Myers
Crossword Puzzle

Dean & Reno
Queen Of The Broken Hearts

Dean & Reno & Dexter & Moore
Heaven In Your Eyes

Dean & Reno & Wray & Cain
This Could Be The Night

Dean & Riser & Weatherspoon
What Becomes Of The Broken
    Hearted

Dean & Strange
Sunny San Juan

Dean & Williams
Walk On

Dean & Wray & Reno
Nothing's Gonna Stop You Now

Deangelis & Deangelis
Yor's World

Dearle
Christ Of The Upward Way
Gather Us In Thou Love That Fillest
    All
Here O My Lord I See Thee Face To
    Face
Take Thou Our Minds Dear Lord

Dearmond & Ackley
If Your Heart Keeps Right

Dearnley
Praise The Spirit In Creation
Sing Ye Faithful Sing With Gladness

Deas
Deep Down In My Heart
Don't Let It Be Said Too Late
Great Camp Meeting
Move Up The King's Highway
Shine For Jesus
Thy Way O Lord
Walk With Me

Deasy & Driscoll
Messiah
Debarge
All This Love
Love Me In A Special Way
Debarge & Debarge
You Wear It Well
Deberiot
Bluebird, The
Debois
Corsair, The
Deburgh
Fatal Hesitation
High On Emotion
Lady In Red, The
Deburgh & Bacharach & Sager
Love Is My Decision
Debussy
At Evening
Beau Soir
Bells, The
C'Est L'extase Langoureuse
Chevaux De Bois
Chevelure, La
Clair De Lune
Cloches, Les
De Fleurs
Fantouches
Faune, Le
Fleur Des Bles
Flute De Pan, La
Il Pleure Dans Mon Coeur
Mandolin
Nuit D'etoiles
O Qu'heureuse Est Ma Fortune
Qui Vauldra Scavoir Qui Je Suis
Reverie
Romance
Tears Fall On My Heart, The
There's Weeping In My Heart
Voici Que Le Printemps
Decall
Silent Evening O'er Us
Decarlo & Leka & Frashuer
Na Na Hey Hey Kiss Him Goodbye
Decius
All Glory Be To God Most High
All Glory Be To God On High
God Is Our Refuge And Defense
To God On High
To God On High Be Thanks And
  Praise
Trinitatisfest
Decker & Rogers
Heart And Soul
Decorbeil
Now The Wings Of Day Are Furled
Sov'reign And Transforming Grace
Deems
May I Hope To Call Thee Friend
Deer
Before Thine Altar

Dees
Disco Duck Part 1
Just The Lonely Talking Again
One In A Million You
Deeves
Stonewall Jackson's Requiem
Stonewall's Requiem
Defaria & Ostwald & Casas
Get On Your Feet
Defaye
Tell Her I Love Her So
Defesch
Tu Fai La Superbetta
Defuentes
In Cuba
Degarmo & Key
Alleluia Christ Is Coming
Blessed Messiah
Destined To Win
Six Six Six
Degarmo & Key & Dixon
Silent Partner
Degarmo & Key & Farrell
Let The Whole World Sing
People In A Box
Degen
Come Unto Me
Trusting And Rejoicing
Degeyter
Arise Ye Slaves Who Know
  Starvation
International
Internationale, L'
Internationale, The
Russia
Dehaven
Country Road
New Shoes
Two Valentines
Deihl
I'm Settled
Deines
Da Droben Muss Christag Sein
Deis
Lover's Lament, A
Waiting
Deiss
All You Nations
Behold Among Men
Child Is Born, A
From The Depths Do I Cry
Have Mercy O Lord
I Want To Sing
Keep In Mind
Longing For God
My Soul Is Longing For Your Peace
O Ever Radiant Virgin
Pasch Of The New Law
Priestly People
Sion Sing
Song Of Joy
Splendor Of Creation
There Is One Lord
Wonderful And Great

Deitz & Schwartz
Alone Together
Dejohnette
Silver Hollow
Del Riego
Art Thou Weary
O Dry Those Tears
Delamar
Are You Snoring
Clanging Bells
Cloud Watching
Dream Of Martin Luther King Jr
Easter Eggs
It Sits On A Shelf
Little Tome Clinker
Loudly Brays The Jackass
Love Grows Old
Marchers' Vigil
Old Glory
Pets
Presidential Cadence With Echo Of
  Taps
Rock Drum Beat
Rockabilly Lullaby
Rockabilly Round
Scale Round
Star Island Chapel Bell
Sweet Beat
This Song Goes Around
Wooden Lady
Delamont
King Jesus
Spirit Of The Dove, The
Delaney
Jazz Me Blues, The
Johnny Appleseed
Delbruck
Tender Ties
Deleopold
Levi
Delerue
Never Gone
Deletre
Hands Across The Table
Delft
Come Down Lord From Your
  Heaven
Delibes
As Falls The Moonlight Gently
Berceuse
Eglogue
Girls of Cadiz, The
Maids Of Cadiz, The
O Mer Ouvre Toi
Ou Va La Jeune Indoue
Regrets
Sylvia
Tramp Tramp Tramp
Delieu
Ni Jamais Ni Toujours
Delius
Aus Deinen Augen Fliessen Meine
  Lieder
Chanson De Fortunio

Delius *(Cont.)*
Dreamy Nights
Fichtenbaum, Der
Hochgebirgsleben
Hor Ich Das Lioedchen Klingen
Longing
Mit Deinen Blauen Augen
Nightingale, The
Nuages
O Schneller Mein Ross
Over The Mountains High
Page Sat In The Lofty Tower, The
Schoner Stern Geht Auf In Meiner
    Nacht
Slumber Song
Summer Eve
Summer Nights
Sunset
Through Long Long Years
To Daffodils
Traum Rosen
Twilight Fancies
Wine Roses
Zwei Braune Augen

Della-Maria
Ariane
Ariette
Oh Ciel Dois-Je En Croire Mes Yeux

Delmarter
I Will Confess Him
I'll Praise Him More And More
Looking To Jesus
Only Believe
Trust The Saviour
Wandering Far

Delmore & Smith & Capehart
Beautiful Brown Eyes

Delugg
Hoop-Dee-Doo
Hoop-Dee-Doo Polka

Demetrius
Hard Headed Woman
Mean Woman Blues

Demetrius & Schroeder
Santa Bring My Baby Back To Me

Dempster
Break Break Break
Rainy Day, The
Sensible Miner, The

Demuth
Brown Owl, The
Still Still With Thee

Dencke
Freuet Euch Ihr Tochter Seines Volks
Gehet In Der Geruch Seines
    Brautigams-Namens
Ich Will Singen Von Einem Konige
Meine Seele Erhebet Den Herrn

Denney
Chimes

Denni
Oceana Roll, The

Denniker
S'posin'

Dennis
Angel Eyes
Angels Eyes
Ballerina
Broken Heart, The
Everything Happens To Me
Grandfather's Clock
He Died Of A Broken Heart
I Like The Look
I've Never Seen The Righteous
    Forsaken
Let's Get Away From It All
Night We Called It A Day, The
Violets For Your Furs
Will You Still Be Mine

Denny
Frankie

Densmore
If God Left Only You
Mother Song
Smoking The Peace Pipe
Starry Night
Unfurling Of The Flag, The

Denver
Annie's Song
Autograph
Back Home Again
Calypso
Dancing With The Mountains
Dreamland
Fly Away
Follow Me
For Baby
For Baby For Bobbie
For You
Goodbye Again
How Can I Leave You Again
I Want To Live
I'm Sorry
Leaving On A Jet Plane
Like A Sad Song
Looking For Space
Love Again
My Sweet Lady
Never A Doubt
Our Father
Perhaps Love
Poems Prayers And Promises
Seasons Of The Heart
Shanghai Breezes
Sweet Surrender
Thought Of You

Denver & Henry
Baby Just Like You

Denver & Taylor
Eagle And The Hawk, The
Rocky Mountain High

Denver & Taylor & Kniss
Sunshine On My Shoulders

Denza
Call Me Back
Funiculi Funicula
Funiculi Funiculi
Harvest Hymn

Denza *(Cont.)*
If
Merry Life, A
Si Vous L'aviez Compris
Sing To Me
Star Of My Heart

Depasquale
We'll Win This World

Depaul
Bless Yore Beautiful Hide
Bless Your Beautiful Hide
Namely You
Teach Me Tonight

Depaul & Mercer
Jubilation T Cornpone

Depew
O Blessed Day Of Motherhood

Dereszynski
Mount Mary March II

Dermer & Galdo & Vigil
Bad Boy
Betcha Say That
Falling In Love
Falling In Love Uh-Oh
Surrender

Derouse & Mende
Power Of Love, The

Derricks
Have A Little Talk With Him
Just A Little Talk With Jesus
My Soul Has Been Set Free
Prescription For Salvation
We'll Soon Be Done With Troubles
    And Trials
When God Dips His Love In My
    Heart

Derricks & Cleavant
Just A Little Talk With Jesus

Deshannon
Bette Davis Eyes
When You Walk In The Room

Deshannon & Holiday & Myers
Brighton Hill
Put A Little Love In Your Heart

Desmond
Take Five

Destri & Harry
I Didn't Have The Nerve To Say No

Desylva
Wishing

Desylva & Brown & Henderson
Aren't We All
Best Things In Life Are Free, The
Button Up Your Overcoat
Good News
I Want To Be Bad
I'm A Dreamer Aren't We All
If I Had A Talking Picture Of You
It All Depends On You
Just Imagine
My Lucky Star
So Blue

Desylva & Brown & Henderson *(Cont.)*
Sunny Side Up
Together
You're The Cream In My Coffee
Desylva & Meyer
If You Knew Susie
If You Knew Susie Like I Know
Susie
Dett
America The Beautiful
I'm So Glad Trouble Don't Last
Alway
Our Country
Somebody's Knocking At Your Door
Deuteromelia
Sing With Thy Mouth
Deutsch & Altman
Play Fiddle Play
Devaney
Someone Loves You Honey
Devere
There Are No Flies On Harrison
Devereux
I Think Of You
Devienne
Chanson De Nemorin, La
Clemence Isaure
Dans L'asile De L'innocence
Fleurs D'Automne
Que J'aime A Voir Les Hirondelles
Regrets, Les
Deville
Storybook Love
Devins
Thy Praise Will We Sing
Devito
Blue Side Of Town, The
Queen Of Hearts
Devito & Cash
If You Change Your Mind
Devito & Flowers
Senorita
Devol
Brady Bunch, The
Brady Bunch Theme, The
Happening, The
Devore
Love And Life
Devorzon
Theme From Swat
Devorzon & Conlan
Renegades
Devorzon & Ellis
Dreamin'
Dewalt
Shotgun
Dewey & Dewey
Heaven's Sounding Sweeter All The
Time
Dewitt
Flowers On The Wall
Dexter
Down At The Roadside Inn
Pistol Packin' Mama

Deyoung
See De Young
Dezede
Chantons L'Hymen Chantons
L'Amour
Eloge Du Temps Present
Je Suis Lindor
Dezso
Szagos Malyva Gyongyvirag
Diamond
America
Cherry Cherry
Cracklin' Rosie
Epitaph
For An Old Man
Headed For The Future
I Am I Said
I'm A Believer
Little Bit Me A Little Bit You, A
Music When Soft Voices Die
Oh Death
Red Red Wine
Song Sung Blue
Story Of My Life, The
Sweet Caroline
Millenium, The
Three Young Rats
Years Of Our Lives, The
Yesterday's Songs
You Don't Bring Me Flowers
Diamond & Bacharach & Sager
Heartlight
Turn Around
Diamond & Becaud
Love On The Rocks
September Morn
Diamond & Bennett
Forever In Blue Jeans
Diamond & Dorff & Loggins
Don't Underestimate My Love For
You
Diamond & Hensley & Lindgren
Headed For The Future
Diamond & Lindgren
Hello Again
Diamond & Ocean
Caribbean Queen
Suddenly
Diamond & Ocean & Woodley
Mystery Lady
Dias
Guantanamera
Dibdin
Blow High Blow Low
Lass That Loves A Sailor, The
Son Of Liberty, The
Tom Bowling
Dichmont
Night Has A Thousand Eyes, The
Peace I Leave With You
Such A Li'l Fellow
Dickens
Rambling Woman

Dickey
Almighty Father Who Dost Give
Princeton Tiger Gridiron March
Dickinson
List To The Lark
Say Not The Struggle Nought
Availeth
Dicus
Our God He Is Alive
Didier
Dames En Qui Reluit Toute Beaute
Diehl
Our Color Guard
Diekema
Friars Song, The
I'll Always Love You
Language Of Love, The
Things They Never Say
Dielman
Bee's Wings And Fish
Diestelhorst
Christmas Eve By The Fireside
Dietz & Schwartz
For The First Time
Louisiana Hayride
Shine On Your Shoes, A
Something You Never Had Before
Diffie & Wilson & Perry
There Goes My Heart Again
Diggle
Lord God Of Hosts Whose Mighty
Hand
My Faith Looks Up To Thee
Safe In The Arms Of Jesus
Salut D'Amour
Dilbeck
My Daddy Is Only A Picture
Dill & Tillis
Detroit City
Dillon
Me And My Uncle Sam
Nobody In His Right Mind
Would've Left Her
Safe Am I
What Good Is A Heart
When The Tingle Becomes A Chill
Dillon & Cannon
I've Come To Expect It From You
Dillon & Cannon & Cochran & Gosdin
Set 'em Up Joe
Dillon & Cannon & Darrell
Country Boy Who Rolled The Rock
Away, A
Dillon & Hargrove
Tennessee Whiskey
Dillon & Huston
Famous Last Words Of A Fool
Dillon & Porter
Homecoming '63
It Ain't Cool To Be Crazy About
You
Dillon & Williams & Stewart & Tucker
Leave Them Boys Alone

Dilworth
Annabel Lee
Dimichino
Vive Regis
Dimirco
Up The Ladder To The Roof
Dimucci & Maresca
Donna The Prima Donna
Lovers Who Wander
Runaround Sue
Dino
24 7
Dipasquale
Cutter To Houston
Dipiero
I Can See Forever In Your Eyes
Dipiero & McManus
American Made
Sentimental Ol' You
Dipiero & Sherrill & Robbins
Church On Cumberland Road, The
Just Say Yes
Too Much Month At The End Of
The Money
Dirksen
Christ Mighty Savior Light Of All
Creation
Come We That Love The Lord
We The Lord's People
Whole Bright World Rejoices Now,
The
Word Of God Come Down On Earth
You Are The Christ O Lord
Dirner
If I Were A Crimson-Rose
It's Nothing New
Discepolo
Esta Noche Me Emborracho
Yira Yira
Distel
Good Life, The
Distler
Weary Of All Trumpeting
Diveroli
Let's Live For Love
Dixon
Babies In The Mill
Big Boat
Give Me O Lord A Heart Of Grace
I Ain't Superstitious
I Just Want To Make Love To You
I Want To Be Loved
I Want You Close To Me
I'm Your Hoochie Coochie Man
Little Red Rooster
My Babe
My God And Father While I Stray
Red Rooster, The
Seventh Son, The
Song To Our Flag
Spoonful
This Pain In My Heart
Tollin' Bells

Dixon (Cont.)
Weave-Room Blues
Whatever I Am You Made Me
When The Lights Go Out
Wreck On The Highway
You Can't Judge A Book By The
Cover
You Need Love
Dixon & Denson
Mama Said
Dixon & Farrell
Boys
**Dixon & Gathers & Pought & Webb &
Pought**
Mister Lee
Dixon & Harrison
Why Baby Why
Dixon & Jackson
I Don't Want To Cry
Dixon & Khent
Sixteen Candles
Dixon & Owens
Tonight's The Night
Dixon & Wylie & Hester
With This Ring
Doane
Another Year Of Labor
Come Great Deliverer Come
Draw Me Nearer
Every Day And Hour
Gently Lord O Gently Lead Us
Give Thy Heart To Me
God Keep Us Till We Meet Again
God Of Our Strength Enthroned
Above
Hark There Comes A Whisper
I Am Thine O Lord
In A Lowly Manger Sleeping
Jesus Is Passing This Way
Jesus Keep Me Near The Cross
Jesus My Redeemer
Jesus Thou Mighty Lord
Jesus Thy Name I Love
Just A Word For Jesus
Keep Your Covenant With Jesus
Labor On
Lord Watch Between Me And Thee,
The
More Like Jesus Would I Be
More Love To Thee O Christ
Near The Cross
O Come Sinner Come
O Light Of Light Shine In
Only A Little Way
Only A Step
Pass Me Not
Pass Me Not O Gentle Savior
Pass Me Not O Gentle Saviour
Precious Name, The
Rescue The Perishing
Safe In The Arms Of Jesus
Sag' Mir Die Heil Ge Kunde
Savior More Than Life To Me
Saviour More Than Life

Doane (Cont.)
Sicher In Jesu Armen
Take The Name Of Jesus With You
Tell Me The Old Old Story
To The Work
Tread Softly
Verlorene Kind, Das
Who Is Ready
Will Jesus Find Us Watching
Doaner
Will Jesus Find Us Watching
Doard
Florian's Song
Dobbins
She's My Rock
Dobkin
My Kind Of Girl
Doche
Champagne, Le
Chiens Savants, Les
Enfants De La France, Les
Dockery
'Twill Be Glory
Dodd
Be Careful Of Stones That You
Throw
Mickey Mouse Alma Mater
Mickey Mouse Club March
Mickey Mouse March, The
Doddridge
Grace 'Tis A Charming Sound
Dodds
Union Label
Dodge
How Westward Ho
Teuton's Tribulation, The
Dodson & Alexander & Beard & Smith
Shake Your Rump To The Funk
Doggett & Butler & Shephard & Scott
Honky Tonk
Honky Tonk Parts 1 And 2
Dokken & Lynch & Brown & Pilson
Burning Like A Flame
Dokken & Lynch & Pilson & Brown
In My Dreams
Tooth And Nail
Dolan
Month Of Sundays, A
Dolby
She Blinded Me With Science
Dolce
Shaddap You Face
Doles
Kindly Spring Again Is Here
Dolphy
Miss Ann
Something Sweet Something Tender
Domingo
Gift Of Love, The
Dominguez
Frenesi
Momento, Un
Perfidia

Domino
I Want To Walk You Home

Domino & Bartholomew
Ain't That A Shame
All By Myself
Blue Monday
Bo Weevil
I Want You To Know
I'm In Love Again
I'm Walkin'
I'm Walking
My Girl Josephine
Poor Me
Valley Of Tears
Whole Lotta Loving

Domino & Bartholomew
Let The Four Winds Blow
When The Saints Go Marching In

Domino & Bartholomew & Hayes
I'm Gonna Be A Wheel Someday

Domino & Bartholomew & Guidry
Walking To New Orleans

Domino & Marascalco & Boyce
Be My Guest

Domnich
Charmant Ruisseau
Wild Rose, The

Donaggio
You Don't Have To Say You Love
Me

Donahue
Loyal Sons Of Illinois

Donald
Hail The Days Of Early Springtime
Memorial Day

Donaldson
At Sundown
Because My Baby Don't Mean
Maybe Now
Beside A Babbling Brook
Bless My Swanee River Home
Borneo
Can't We Fall In Love
Carolina In The Morning
Changes
Close Your Eyes
Clouds
Cottage In The Country That's The
Thing, A
Dancing In The Moonlight
Daughter Of Rosie O'Grady, The
Did I Remember
Don't Be Angry
Don't Do Anything I Wouldn't Do
He's The Last Word
Hello Beautiful
How Ya' Gonna Keep 'em Down On
The Farm

Donaldson *(Cont.)*
How Ya Gonna Keep 'em Down On
The Farm After They've Seen
Paree
How 'Ya Gonna Keep 'em Down On
The Farm After They've Seen
Paree
I Wonder Where My Baby Is Tonight
I'd Be Lost Without You
I'll Be Happy When The Preacher
Makes You Mine
I'm Bringing A Red Red Rose
I've Had My Moments
It's Been So Long
Just Try To Picture Me Back Home
In Tennessee
Just Try To Picture Me Down Home
In Tennessee
Kansas City Kitty
Let Me Day Dream
Little White Lies
Love Me Or Leave Me
Makin' Whoopee
Maybe It's The Moon
Mexico City
Mister Meadowlark
Molly O'Malley
Moonlight And Roses
My Baby Just Cares For Me
My Best Girl
My Blue Heaven
My Buddy
My Little Bimbo Down On The
Bamboo Isle
My Mammy
My Ohio Home
Never A Day Goes By
Nobody Loves No Baby Like My
Baby Loves Me
Oh Baby Don't Say No Say Maybe
Out Of The Dawn
Reaching For Someone And Not
Finding Anyone There
Riptide
Romance
Sail Away For Lullabye Bay
Sam The Old Accordion Man
Sleepy Head
Smarty Pants
Sweet Indiana Home
Sweet Jennie Lee
Taint No Sin To Dance Around In
Your Bones
That Certain Party
That's What I Like Abou You
Thousand Good Nights, A
Tired Of Me
Until You Get Somebody Else
Valentine, A
We'll Have A Jubilee In My Old
Kentucky Home
What Are You Waiting For Mary

Donaldson *(Cont.)*
When My Ship Comes In
Yes Sir That's My Baby
You
You're A Million Miles From
Nowhere
You're Driving Me Crazy
You're Driving Me Crazy What Did
I Do
You've Got A Certain Something
You've Got Ev'rything

Donaldson & Ash
Thinking Of You

Donaldson & Lewis & Young
My Mammy

Donaldson & Lyman
After I Say I'm Sorry
What Can I Say After I Say I'm
Sorry

Donaldson & Straight
Pretty Lips

Donati
Villanella Alla Napolitana

Donato
A Media Luz
People Take Care
When The Lights Are Soft And Low

Donegan
Rock Island Line, The

Donegan & Currie
I'll Never Fall In Love Again

Donida
Al Di La

Donizetti
Ardon Gl'incensi
Arie Der Marie
At Last I'm Thine
Chacun Le Sait
Chi Mi Frena
Child Of The Regiment
Dolce Suono Mi Colpi Di Sua Voce,
Il
Down Her Soft Cheek A Pearly Tear
Elder Blooming
Ensanguined And Lurid
Furtiva Lagrima, Una
Furtive Tear, A
Gentle Breezes Sighing
Greeting And Good-Bye
Hail Rosy Morn
Hail To The Happy Bridal Day
Harp At Nature's Advent Strung,
The
Harp At Nature's Advent, The
Herne The Hunter
I Hear The Breathing
If Thou Plead'st
It Is Better To Laugh Than Be
Sighing
O My Soul Bless Jehovah
O My Soul Bless Thou Jehovah
Oh That I Never More Might See

Donizetti (Cont.)
Sail Away
Sea, The
Sextet
Sextette
Softly Now The Light Of Day
Spirit So Fair
Sunny Italy
Thou Hast Spread Thy Wings To
Heaven
What Restrains Me
When He Is Here
When Twilight Shadows

Donna
Liar Liar

Donovan
Brother Sun Sister Moon
Catch The Wind
Catkin
Colours
Hymn To The Night
Indian Children
Little Church
Mellow Yellow
Molly O'Rourke
Soft White Snow
Sunshine Superman

Doors, The
Hello I Love You Won't You Tell Me
Your Name
LA Woman
Light My Fire
Love Her Madly
Riders On The Storm
Touch Me
Twentieth Century Fox
We Could Be So Good Together

Dorat
Chant Des Francais
Lisette

Dore
Pilot Of The Airwaves

Dore & Littman
Strutt

Doret
All In The Dawn
Bell Tower, The
Frost Flowers
In The Woods

Dorff
As Long As We Got Each Other
Double Or Nothin'
Double Or Nothing
Free Spirit Theme
Room Enough For Two

Dorff & Brown
I'll Wake You Up When I Get Home
Lasso The Moon

Dorff & Brown & Crofford & Garrett
Bar Room Buddies

Dorff & Brown & Garrett
Another Honky-Tonk Night On
Broadway
Any Which Way You Can
Every Which Way But Loose

Dorff & Durrill & Pinkard & Garrett
Beers To You

Dorff & Garrett & Herbstritt & Harju
Cowboys And Clowns

Dorff & Herbstritt
Spenser For Hire Theme

Dorff & Panzer
Through The Years

Doris
Oh Me Oh My
Oh Me Oh My I'm A Fool For You
Baby

Dorman
Mountain Of Love

Dorough
I'm Hip
Small Day Tomorrow

Dorsey
Angels Keep Watching Over Me
Consideration
Crawdad
Diamonds From The Crown Of The
Lord
Down By The Side Of The River
Ev'ry Day Will Be A Sunday By And
By
Gonna Live The Life I Sing About
Gospel Train Is Coming, The
Hide Me In Thy Bosom
I Thought Of God
I'll Tell It Wherever I Go
I'm A Pilgrim I'm A Stranger
I'm Coming Back To Live With Jesus
I'm Going To Live The Life I Sing
About In My Song
If You See My Savior
It Is Thy Servant's Prayer Amen
Jesus Remembers When Others
Forget
Jesus Rose Again
Just Wait A Little While
Lead Me To The Rock That's Higher
Than I
Let The Savior Bless Your Soul Right
Now
Let Us Go Back To God
Lord Has Laid His Hands On Me,
The
My Desire
My Soul Feels Better Right Now
Never Leave Me Alone
Peace In The Valley
Precious Lord Take My Hand
Say A Little Prayer For Me
Someway Somehow Sometime
Somewhere
Take My Hand Precious Lord
That's Good News
There Is No Friend Like Jesus
There'll Be Peace In The Valley For
Me
Today
Walk Close To Me O Lord

Dorsey (Cont.)
Walk Over God's Heaven
Want To Go To Heaven When I Die
What Could I Do If It Wasn't For
The Lord
What Then
When I've Done My Best
When I've Sung My Last Song
While The Evening Shadows Fall
There's Morning In
Windows Of Heaven

Dortch
Ask Seek Knock
I Am Resting In The Savior's Love
I've Been Washed In The Blood

Doster
Old Eli March

Dougall
How Are Thy Servants Blest O Lord
O For A Heart To Praise My God

Dougherty
Across The Field
Beauty Is Not Caused
Love In The Dictionary
Primavera

Dougherty & Ager
Glad Rag Doll

Dougherty & Reynolds
I'm Confessin'

Doughty
One Lonely Night

Douglas
Christian Dost Thou See Them
Eternal Lord Of Love
Follow The Gleam
God Of The Prophets Bless The
Prophets Heirs
He Who Would Valiant Be
He Who Would Valient Be 'gainst
Jesus Is Lord
L-O-V-E
Master Of Eager Youth
Sabbath Day Was By, The
To The Knights In Days Of Old

Douglas & Gersmehl
We Will See Him As He Is

Douglas & Lancy & Rodde
Why Don't You Believe Me

Douglas & Lavere & Rodde
Have You Heard

Douglas & Parman & Lavere
Pretend

Douglas & Redmond & Black & Brown
Rainy Night

Douglas & Weiss
What A Wonderful World

Douglass
I Know My Lord Will Come

Douland
Old Hundred

Dourlen
Je Sais Attacher Des Rubans

Douthit
Land Of Rest, The
Dovaston
Break Of Day, The
Dow
Consolation
I Cannot Always Trace
I Cannot Always Trace The Way
Dowell
Three Little Fishes
Three Little Fishies
Dowland
All People That On Earth Do Dwell
Awake Sweet Love
Awake Sweet Love Thou Are
Returned
Away With These Self-Loving Lads
Burst Forth My Tears
By A Fountain Where I Lay
Can She Excuse My Wrongs
Clear Or Cloudy
Come Again
Come Again Sweet Love
Come Away
Come Away Come Sweet Love
Come Heavy Sleep
Dear If You Change
Disdain Me Still
Far From Triumphing Court
Farewell Unkind
Farewell Unkind Farewell
Fine Knacks For Ladies
Flow My Tears
Flow Not So Fast Ye Fountains
Go Crystal Tears
God And Yet A Man, A
God The Father Seen Of None
Have You Seen But A Whyte Lillie
Grow
Herb Carol, A
If My Complaints Could Passions
Move
If That A Sinner's Sighs
In Darkness Let Me Dwell
It Was A Time When Silly Bees
Lady If You So Spite Me
Love Those Beams
Lowest Trees Have Tops, The
Me Me And None But Me
Mourn Day Is With Darkness Fled
My Heart And Tongue Were Twins
My Thoughts Are Winged With
Hope
Now O Now I Needs Must Part
O What Hath Overwrought
Say Love If Ever Thou Didst Find
Shall I Strive With Words To Move
Shall I Sue
Sorrow Sorrow Stay
Stay Time Awhile Thy Flying
Sweet Stay Awhile
Tell Me True Love
Time Stand Still
Unquiet Thoughts

Dowland *(Cont.)*
Weep You No More Sad Fountaines
Weep You No More Sad Fountains
Were Every Thought An Eye
What If I Never Speed
What If I Never Speede
Where Sin Sore Wounding
White As Lilies Was Her Face
Who Ever Thinks Or Hopes Of Love
Downes
Hark My Soul It Is The Lord
Downey
Where The Western Lights
Downing
I Love My Jean
June
Story Behind The Story, The
Touch Me
Downing & Burdette & Martin
Bring It On Home
Downs
Lord's Prayer, The
Dozier
Invisible
Two Hearts
Without You
Drake
American Flag
Hymn Of Happiness, A
It Was A Very Good Year
Just The Same
My Piano Lesson
Night At Camp
Welfare Cadillac
Drake & Graham & Shirl & Stillman
I Believe
Drake & Hoffman & Livingston
Mairzy Doats
Drake & Shirl
One God
Drake & Thomas & Gresson
Sail On Atlanta
Drake & Wayne
He Believes In Me
Drangosch
Deux Yeux
Two Eyes
Drapkin
Devil In Her Heart
Drdla
Souvenir
Dregert
Spanish Serenade
Dreiser
On The Banks Of The Wabash
Dreist
Was Macht Ihr Dass Ihr Weinet
Drese
Jesus Lead The Way
Jesus Still Lead On
Round Me Falls The Night
Dress
Improperium

Dresser
Here Lies An Actor
In Good Old New York Town
Just Tell Them That You Saw Me
My Gal Sal
On The Banks Of The Wabash
On The Banks Of The Wabash Far
Away
Pardon Came Too Late, The
Parker Parker You're The Moses
Who Will Lead Us Out
Dressner
Just Tell Them That You Saw Me
Drewett
Send Thou O Lord To Every Place
Dreyer
Cecilia
Dreyfus
Non M'Aje Da
Ogni Speranza
Rimprovero
Rondinella
Driftwood
Battle Of New Orleans
Battle Of New Orleans, The
Drigo
Serenade
Driscoll
Irishman's Shanty, The
Driskell
I Want To Know Christ
Jesus Never Fails
We Have Seen God's Glory
Driver
Wonderful Story Of Love
Drizo
Louder Oh Let Me Sing My Song
Drummond
Happy In My Soul Today
Drury
May The Words That We Say
This Is Our Prayer Dear God
This Is The Day Which The Lord
Hath Made
Du Bois
Alma Mater
Chorus Of Seraphim
Du Caurroy
Noel
Dubee
Gold And Olive, The
Dubin & Franklin
Anniversary Waltz, The
Dubin & Gurvitz & Bryant
Love In Your Eyes, The
Dubin & McHugh & Dash
My Kid
Dubin & Rath & Garren
Just A Girl That Men Forget
Dubois
I Know He Cares
On The Dark Shore
She Got The Goldmine And I Got
The Shaft
Thee We Adore

Dubois & Newton
Midnight Hauler
Dubois & Robbins & Stephenson
Let The Heartache Ride
Dubois & Robbins & Stephenson
Big Dreams In A Small Town
Bluest Eyes In Texas, The
Dubois & Stephenson & Lorber & Silbar
Tie Your Dream To Mine
Dubuisson
Autre Jour Jouet M'aloye Parmy Ces
Champs, L'
Duckworth
Jesus Shall Reign Where'er The Sun
Duckworth & Lentz
Sound Off For Chesterfield
Ducray-Duminil
Retour, Le
Dufay
Alons Ent Bien
Belle Se Siet, La
Dufferin
Bay Of Dublin
Irish Emigrant's Lament
Katey's Letter
Duffey & Dixon & Roberts
Schoolhouse Fire, The
Duffield
Blessed Saviour Thee I Love
Duffield & Webb
Stand Up For Jesus
Stand Up Stand Up For Jesus
Dugan
Irish Washer Woman, The
Duguat
Bless Thou The Gifts
Duguet
O God Whose Presence Glows In All
O Saving Victim Opening Wide
O Thou Who Hast At Thy Command
Duke
Acquainted With The Night
Ant, The
April Elegy
April In Paris
Autumn In New York
Babe, The
Bird, The
Brazilian Love Affair
Cabin In The Sky
Calf, The
Centipede, The
Cow, The
Daisy Mae
Elaine
February Twilight
Festival
Fly, The
Fragment
Frog, The
Germ, The
Good Little Girls Go To Heaven
Got A Bran' New Daddy
Grunchin' Witch, The

Duke *(Cont.)*
Here In This Spot With You
Hist Whist
I Can't Be Talkin' Of Love
I Can't Get Started
I Carry Your Heart
I Like The Likes Of You
I Ride The Great Black Horses
I Watched The Lady Caroline
Island In The West Indies
Jelly Fish, The
Kitten, The
Last Word Of A Bluebird, The
Lemme At It
Little Elegy
Love Reborn
Loveliest Of Trees
Mouse, The
Peggy Mitchell
Piper, A
Shelling Peas
Someday
Song Making
Spring Again
Taking A Chance On Love
That's What Makes Paris Paree
Turkey, The
What Is There To Say
When I Was One And Twenty
White Dress, The
Duke & Cody
Doin' It All For My Baby
Dulcina
From Oberon In Fairyland
Dulmage & Clint
When It's Night Time In Nevada
Dumas
Edmonds
Gospel Pool, The
Mullins
Rees
Teacher's Farewell, The
To Die No More
Vain World Adieu
White
Wonder, The
Dumont
Alabama Blossoms, The
Belle Histoire D'amour, La
Dans Leur Baiser
Des Histoires
Gospel Raft, De
Mon Dieu
Mon Vieux Lucien
Mots D'amour, Les
T'es L'homme Qu'il Me Faut
Toi Tu L'Entends Pas
Toujours Aimer
Ville Inconnue, La
Dun
Bonnie Charlie

Dunayevsky
Captain Bold
Heart In My Breast
If The Volga Overflows
Let's Keep In Trim
Loving
My Heart
Oh It Is Joy
Oh Return To Me My Darling
Should The Volga's Banks Be
Flooded
Song Of Our Country
Dunbar
I'll Live For Him
I'll Live For Thee
Walls Of Old Bowdoin
Duncalf
O Christ Who Art The Light And
Day
Duncan
Let Go
My Special Angel
Stay A Little Longer
Duncan & Fender
Wasted Days And Wasted Nights
Dungan
Bring Peace To My Soul
Christ Child, The
Eternal Life
Lift Him Up
Long-Eared Owl
Sea Horse
We Are Boy Scouts
Dunham
Cross, The
Our Father's God To Thee We Raise
Somebody Believed
Dunhill
Hie Away
Lord To Our Humble Prayers Attend
Milkmaid, The
Three Fine Ships
Duni
Ah Que L'amour Est Chose Jolie
Ariette De La Fee Urgele
Helas J'ai Repandu Mon Lait
Joyful Song, A
Duning
Picnic
Dunlap
Flight
Wedding Prayer
Dunlop
I Believe The Answer's On The Way
Our Father Did
Who Is That Movin' My Heart
Dunman
Cradled On A Manager Meanly
Dunn
Come To The Woodlands
Daddy's Hands
Evening Bell
Rest From All Thy Sorrow
Twilight

Dunn & Foster
Love Someone Like Me
Dunn & Little
Ever Joyous
Dunn & Shapiro & Waters
Are You Ever Gonna Love Me
Dunn & Shapiro & Waters
You Really Had Me Going
Dunn & Shapiro & Waters
I'm Not Through Loving You Yet
Only When I Love
Someday
Dunne
Nobody Loves Me Like You Do
Turn Of The Cards
You Look At Me
Dunne & Roberts
When You Put Your Heart In It
Dunnevant
Be Still And Know
Dunning
Picnic
Dunning & Dunning
Earth Is Yours O God, The
Dunson
Goin' Up Side Your Head
You've Got Me Waiting
Dunstedter
One Little Wac
Duny
Fontaine, La
Duparc
Au Pays Ou Se Fait La Guerre
Chanson Triste
Ecstasy
Elegie
Extase
Invitation Au Voyage, L'
Lamento
Manoir De Rosemonde, Le
Phidyle
Rosemond
Serenade Florentine
Soupir
Testament
Vague Et La Cloche, La
Vie Anterieure, La
Dupont
Mandolin
Duprato
Here Below
Dupuis & Chudacoff
Steal Away
Dupuy
Paraguay
Duran Duran
Reflex, The
Save A Prayer Til The Morning After
Wild Boys, The
Duran & Duran & Barry
View To A Kill, A
Durand
All My Love

Durandeau
Ask A P'liceman
Durant
To Charlotte
Durante
Dance Maiden Dance
Danza Danza Fanciulla
Danza Danza Fanciulla Gentile
Misericordias Domini
Vergin Tutto Amor
Durante & Ryan & Donnelly
Inka Dinka Doo
Durham
I Won't Have To Cross Jordan Alone
Promised Land, The
Star Of Columbia
Duringer
Ombre Adoree
Durner
Auf Der Wanderung
Duron
We Come To Worship
Durrill & Crofford & Garrett
Charlotte's Web
Durrill & Garrett
Misery And Gin
Durrner
Lebensregel
Lenz Ist Angekommen, Der
Maientanz
Storm, The
Sturmbeschworung
Dusenbury
Alaska's Flag
Dustable
Quam Pulchra Es
Duthie & Pinsuti
Crusaders, The
Dutton
I Love To Steal Awhile Away
Wood Pigeon, The
Woodstock
Duvernoy
Christ Est Ressuscite
Elle Etait Si Jolie
Dvorak
Als Die Alte Mutter
Around Us Hear The Sound Of Even
Around Us Hear The Sounds Of
Even
As My Aged Mother
Christmas Starlight
Days Of Long Ago
Down De Road
Gefangene
Good Night
Humoreske
Humoresque
Hunting Song
Hush Mah Baby
Hymn Of Love
Lark, The
Lullaby
Massa Dear

Dvorak (Cont.)
Moznost
Requiem For Yesterday
River Road
Sing A New Song
Slavikovsky Polecko Maly
Songs My Mother Taught Me
Songs That My Mother Taught Me
When My Mother Sings
Dwight
Columbia
Dowland
Shall I Sue Shall I Seeke For Grace
Dwyer
Keep The Camp Fires Burning Bright
Sleep Comrades Sleep
Dyckman
I Like To Flop In The Waves That
Slop
Meet Me Mamie On Main Street
Dyer
Come Gracious Spirit Heavenly
Dove
Down Among The Dead Men
I Will Sing I Will Sing
Lord Of All Being Throned Afar
O Thou Who Camest From Above
When Two Become One
Dykema
Carol For Everyman, A
Flags Of All America, The
Great Gray Elephant, A
Precocious Piggy
Where Go The Boats
Dykeman
Christmas Child, The
Dykes
Again As Evening's Shadow Falls
Almighty Father Strong To Save
Arise My Soul Arise
Behold The Lamb Of God
Behold Us Lord A Little Space
Blest Be The Dear Uniting Love
Bring O Morn
By Christ Redeemed
Calm On The List'ning Ear Of Night
Calm On The Listening Ear Of Night
Cast Thy Burden On The Lord
Christ For The World We Sing
Christian Dost Thou See Them
Christians Lo The Star Appeareth
Come Holy Spirit Heav'nly Dove
Come Holy Spirit Heavenly Dove
Come O Lord Like Morning Sunlight
Come Said Jesus' Sacred Voice
Come Unto Me Ye Weary
Come Ye That Love The Saviour's
Name
Day Is Past And Over, The
Day Of Wrath That Day Of
Mourning
Dies Irae
Dost Thou See Them
Eternal Father Strong To Save

Dykes *(Cont.)*

Father In Heaven Whose Love
  Profound
Father Lead Me Day By Day
Fathers Built This City, The
For Those In Peril On The Sea
Forth In Thy Name
Forth In Thy Name O Lord I Go
From Far Away
Gentle Jesus Meek And Mild
Gird Us O God With Humble Might
God Calling Yet Shall I Not Hear
God Send Us Men
Great King Of Nations
Guide Me O Thou Great Jehovah
Hail The Glorious Golden City
Happy The Home When God Is
  There
Hark Hark My Soul
Hark Hark My Soul Angelic Songs
Hark My Soul It Is The Lord
Hark Ten Thousand Voices
Hark The Sound Of Holy Voices
Hark What Mean Those Holy Voices
Hasten Lord The Glorious Time
Head That Once Was Crowned With
  Thorns, The
Holy Holy
Holy Holy Holy
Holy Holy Holy Lord God Almighty
Hosanna To The Living Lord
Hosanna We Sing
Humility
Hymn For The Armed Forces
I Heard The Voice Of Jesus Say
Immortal Love Forever Full
In Evil Long I Took Delight
Into Thy Gracious Hands I Fall
Jesu Lover Of My Soul
Jesus By The Simple Beauty
Jesus Exalted Far On High
Jesus Lover Of My Soul
Jesus Name Of Wondrous Love
Jesus Tender Shepherd Hear Me
Jesus The Very Thought
Jesus The Very Thought Of Thee
Jesus The Very Thought Of You
Jesus Thou Art My Righteousness
Jesus United By Thy Grace
Jesus With Thy Church Abide
King Of Love My Shepherd Is, The
King Of Love, The
Lead Kindly Light
Lead Kindly Light Amid The
  Encircling Gloom
Let Us Sing Again
Lift Up Lift Up Your Voices
Like As A Mother Comforteth
Lord As We Thy Name Profess
Lord God Of Hosts Whose Mighty
  Hand
Lord God Of Hosts Whose Purpose
Lord Is My Shepherd, The
Lord It Belongs Not To My Care

Dykes *(Cont.)*

Lord Of All Being Throned Afar
Lord Of All Power And Might
Lord Of The Living Harvest
Lord To Whom Except To Thee
Lord When I All Things Would
  Possess
Lord With Glowing Heart I'd Praise
  Thee
May The Grace Of Christ Our
  Saviour
'Mid All The Traffic Of The Ways
Morning Hymn
Mourners Came, The
My God How Wonderful Thou Art
My God Is Any Hour So Sweet
My Hope Is Built On Nothing Less
My Hope My All My Saviour Thou
Navy Hymn, The
Nearer My God To Thee
Now Let Us All Arise And Sing
Now On Land And Sea Descending
Now The Laborer's Task Is O'Er
Now The Wings Of Day Are Furled
O Bread To Pilgrims Given
O Brother Man Fold To Thy Heart
O Child Of Lowly Manger Birth
O Christ Our True And Only Light
O Christ The Way The Truth The
  Life
O Come And Mourn With Me
  Awhile
O For A Closer Walk With God
O For A Heart To Praise My God
O God I Love Thee Not That My
  Poor Love
O God Of Gifts Exceeding Rare
O God The Rock Of Ages
O Jesus Crucified For Man
O Jesus When I Think Of Thee
O Joyful Sound Of Gospel Grace
O Lord Of Heav'n And Earth And
  Sea
O Lord Of Heaven
O Lord Of Heaven And Earth And
  Sea
O Love O Life
O Love Who Drew From Jesus' Side
O Master Of The Waking World
O Paradise O Paradise
O Spirit Of The Living God
O Strength And Stay Upholding All
  Creation
O Thou Great Friend To All
O Thou In All Thy Might So Far
O What Their Joy And Their Glory
  Must Be
O Young And Fearless Prophet
Oft As We Run The Weary Way
Oh For A Heart To Praise My God
On Jordan's Stormy Banks I Stand
On The Birthday Of The Lord
On What Has Now Been Sown

Dykes *(Cont.)*

Once More We Come Before Our
  God
One Pray'r I Have
One There Is Above All Others
One Tho't I Have
Osterglocken Klinger, Die
Our Blest Redeemer
Our Blest Redeemer Ere He Breathed
Our Father God Who Art In Heaven
Outside The Holy City
Parise To The Holiest In The Height
Pour Thy Blessings Lord Like
  Showers
Praise The Lord Ye Heavens Adore
  Him
Praise To The Holiest In The Height
Praise To The Holy One
Purer Yet And Purer
Ride On Ride On In Majesty
Saviour Teach Me Day By Day
Shepherd Of Souls Refresh And
  Bless
Shepherds Of Souls Refresh And
  Bless
Show Pity Lord O Lord Forgive
Sing Forth His High Eternal Name
Sing My Soul His Wondrous Love
Sinners Turn Why Will Ye Die
Sleep Holy Babe
Slowly By God's Hand Unfurled
Stabat Mater
Strong Son Of God Immortal Love
Take My Life
Take My Life And Let It Be
Ten Thousand Time Ten Thousand
Ten Thousand Times Ten Thousand
Thou Art Gone Up On High
Thou Bidst Us Seek Thee Early
To Him From Whom Our Blessing
  Flow
Try Us O God And Search The
  Ground
Unseen But Known
We Are The Lord's His All-Sufficient
  Merit
We Bid Thee Welcome In The Name
We Would See Jesus For The
  Shadows Lengthen
When In The Quiet Church I Sit
When Musing Sorrow Weeps The
  Past
When Shadows Gather On Our Way
Where Cross The Crowded Ways Of
  Life
Wherewith O Lord Shall I Draw
  Near
While Life Prolongs Its Precious
  Light
Within Our Quiet Church O God
Dylan
Abandoned Love
Absolutely Sweet Marie
All Along The Watchtower

Dylan (*Cont.*)
All The Tired Horses
Apple Suckling Tree
As I Went Out One Morning
Ballad Of Frankie Lee And Judas
    Priest
Billy
Black Diamond Bay
Blowin' In The Wind
Buckets Of Rain
Catfish
Clothes Line Saga
Country Pie
Crash On The Levee
Day Of The Locusts
Dear Landlord
Dirge
Don't Think Twice It's All Right
Don't Ya Tell Henry
Down Along The Cove
Drifter's Escape
Father Of Night
Forever Young
Fourth Time Around
George Jackson
Get Your Rocks Off
Girl Of The North Country
Goin' To Acapulco
Going Going Gone
Golden Loom
Hard Rain's A Gonna Fall, A
Hard Rain's A-Gonna Fall
Hazel
Hurricane
I Am A Lonesome Hobo
I Dreamed I Saw St Augustine
I Pity The Poor Immigrant
I Shall Be Released
I Threw It All Away
I Wanna Be Your Lover
I Want You
I'll Be Your Baby Tonight
Idiot Wind
If Dogs Run Free
If Not For You
If You See Her Say Hello
Isis
It Ain't Me Babe
It's All Over Now Baby Blue
It's Alright Ma I'm Only Bleeding
Joey
John Wesley Harding
Just Like A Woman
Knockin' On Heaven's Door
Lay Lady Lay
Leopard Skin Pill Box Hat
Like A Rolling Stone
Lily Rosemary And The Jack Of
    Hearts
Living The Blues
Lo And Behold
Long-Distance Operator
Maggie's Farm

Dylan (*Cont.*)
Mama You Been On My Mind
Man In Me, The
Masters Of War
Meet Me In The Morning
Million Dollar Bash
Minstrel Boy
Money Blues
Most Likely You Go Your Way
Mozambique
Mr Tambourine Man
My Back Pages
Nashville Skyline Rag
Never Say Goodbye
New Morning
Nobody 'cept You
Nothing Was Delivered
Obviously Five Believers
Odds And Ends
Oh Sister
On A Night Like This
One More Cup Of Coffee
One More Night
One More Weekend
One Of Us Must Know
Open The Door Homer
Peggy Day
Please Mrs Henry
Pledging My Time
Quinn The Eskimo
Quit Your Low Down Ways
Rainy Day Women
Rainy Day Women #12 & 35
Rainy Day Women #12 And 35
Rita May
Romance In Durango
Sad Eyed Lady Of The Lowlands
Sara
She's Your Lover Now
Shelter From The Storm
Sign On The Window
Silent Weekend
Simple Twist Of Fate
Something There Is About You
Stuck Inside Of Mobile With The
    Memphis Blues Again
Subterranean Homesick Blues
Sweetheart Like You
Tangled Up In Blue
Tell Me Momma
Tell Me That It Isn't True
Temporary Like Achilles
Three Angels
Time Passes Slowly
Times They Are A-Changin', The
Tiny Montgomery
To Be Alone With You
Tomorrow Is A Long Time
Tonight I'll Be Staying Here With
    You
Too Much Of Nothing
Tough Amama
Up To Me
Visions Of Johanna

Dylan (*Cont.*)
Wallflower
Wanted Man
Watching The River Flow
Wedding Song
Went To See The Gypsy
When I Paint My Masterpiece
When The Ship Comes In
Wicked Messenger, The
Wigwam
Winterlude
With God On Our Side
Woogie-Boogie
Yea Heavy And A Bottle Of Bread
You Ain't Goin' Nowhere
You Angel You
You're A Big Girl Now
You're Gonna Make Me Lonesome
    When You Go
Dylan & Harrison
I'd Have You Any Time
Dyson
Let Thy Word Abide In Us
Earl
Beautiful Ohio
Earle
Little Bit In Love, A
Seaweed
Sweet Little '66
Earle & Kling
Nowhere Road
Earnshaw
Lone Wild Fowl In Lofty Flight, The
Eastburn
Little Brown Jug, The
Easterling
When I Wake Up To Sleep No More
Eastmond
You Are My Lady
Eastmond & Diamond
He'll Never Love You Like I Do
**Eastmond & Ocean & Brathwaite &
Skinner**
Colour Of Love, The
Easton
Bricks In My Pillow
Eastwood
There's A Tavern In The Town
Eaton
Adam And Eve
Dude Ranch Cowboy
Ice Cream Man
In The Promised Land
Papa Tony
Eaton & Shand
I Double Dare You
I'm Gonna Lock My Heart And
    Throw Away The Key
Eaton & Taff & Taff
Here I Am
Eaton & Wagner & Hammond
Turn Back The Hands Of Time

Ebeling
All My Heart This Night Rejoices
All The Skies Tonight Sing O'Er Us
At Thy Feet O Christ We Lay
Come Brother-Man Fold
Evening And Morning
Gracious Spirit Dwell With Me
Grateful Hearts And Songs
Guldne Sonne, Die
Holy Father Holy Father
Veiled In Darkness Judah Lay
We Thank You Lord Of Heaven
Work Is Sweet For God Has Blest

Eberling
We Thank You Lord Of Heaven

Eberwein
Ich Liebte Dich
Tischlied

Eccard
Hans Und Grete
O Love Of God
When To The Temple Mary Went

Eckert
Ja Uberselig Hast Du Mich Gemacht
None He Loves But Me
Sailor's Song
Swiss Echo Song

Eddy
Brood O'er Us With Thy Shelt'ring
Wing

Eddy & Hazlewood
Rebel Rouser

Edel & Goldfarb
Sabbath Eve

Edelman
Macgyver
Piano Picker
Weekend In New England

Edelstadt
Arbeter Froyen
In Kamf
Svetshop

Eden
Coloring Song, The

Edens
Hoe Down
In-Between
It's A Great Day For The Irish
Minnie From Trinidad
On The Town
You're Awful

Edmonds & Bristol & Johnson
Two Occasions

Edmonds & Scelsa
I'd Still Say Yes

Edmundson
Come Christians Join And Sing

Edson
Arise My Soul
Arise My Soul Arise
Blow Ye The Trumpet Blow
How Tedious And Tasteless
Lenox

Edwardes
When May Is In His Prime

Edwards
Author Of Life Divine
Big Boots
Black And The Red, The
Broken-Hearted Melody
By The Light Of The Silvery Moon
Cobweb Cradles
Dungaree Doll
Flaming Star
Frankfort Special
Girl Who Cares For Me, The
Guide Me O Thou Great Redeemer
I Can't Tell Why I Love You But I
Do
In My Merry Oldsmobile
In Praise Of Music
Into The Night
Jimmy Valentine
Lady Moon
Mamie Don't You Fee Ashamie
Mule Skinner Blues
National Anthem Of Barbados
Ol' Jim
Once In A While
Our Father By Whose Name
Our Father By Whose Name All
Fatherhood
School Days
See You In September
Sunbonnet Sue
Sunshine Go Away Today
Tammany
Way Down Yonder In The Cornfield
We Want Teddy For Four Years
More
When Jesus Walked On Galilee
When The Roses Bloom Again
Wonderful Wonderful

Edwards & Dixon & Williams
Duke Of Earl

Edwards & Duddy
I Love Bosco

Edwards & Strange
My Own United States

Edwards & Williams & English & Street
Coolin' Out

Eede
Died In Your Arms
I've Been In Love Before
One For The Mockingbird

Eede & Macmichael
Everything But My Pride
Last Thing, The

Effinger
Mary's Soliloquy

Egan
Army Air Cadet, The
First One Ever, The
Maroon Forever

Egerton
We Never Speak As We Pass By

Egli
So Ruhest Du O Meine Ruh
Thou Gracious Pow'r

Egner
Bamsens Fodselsdag
On Brave Old Army Team
Papagoyen Fra Amerika
Rovervise

Eibich
You're My Poem Of Love

Eichberg
To Thee O Country

Eichhorn
Why Not Say Yes Tonight

Eiger & Trenet
We Mustn't Part

Eigg
Mermaid's Croon, The

Eiseman
Army Mule The Navy Goat And The
Kick Of The Kangaroo, The

Eisenstein
Mordecai's Procession

Eisler
Comintern
Forward We've Not Forgotten
From The Aeneid
Herr Doktor Die Periode
In Praise Of Learning
Mother Bloor
Oh Endless Is This Misery
Peace On Earth
Peace Song
United Front
United Front Song
Von Der Freundlichkeit Der Welt
We're Marching O Comrades

Eitner
Hakenkreuz-Lied, Das

Elbel
Toast To Michigan, A
Victors, The

Elbert
University Of Michigan Marching
Song

Elder
I Saw Your Face In The Moon

Elderkin
Jesus The Light Of The World

Eldridge
Thanksgiving
When Good Old Kris Comes 'Round

Elenburg
It's Just The First Farewell

Elfman
Batman Theme, The
Theme From Scrooged

Elgar
Bright Is The World
Is She Not Passing Fair
Land Of Hope And Glory
Land Of Hope & Glory
Love's Greeting

Elgar *(Cont.)*
Love's Tribute Of Flowers
Pomp And Circumstance
See Us Lord About Thine Altar
Speak Music

Elgin & Dixon & Rogers
Hundred Pounds Of Clay, A

Elias & Wilensky
Haro-A Min Hagai

Eliason
Got Any Rivers

Elizondo
Y Andale

Ellerbrock
God Save The South

Ellerton
When Belgium Put The Kibosh On
The Kaiser

Ellington
Birmingham Breakdown
C Jam Blues
Come Sunday
Creole Love Call, The
Do Nothin' Till You Hear From Me
Don't Get Around Much Anymore
Don't You Know I Care Or Don't
You Care To Know
Echoes Of Harlem
Hand-Me-Down Love
I Didn't Know About You
I Got It Bad And That Ain't Good
I Let A Song Go Out Of My Heart
In A Mellow Tone
In A Sentimental Mood
It Don't Mean A Thing
It Don't Mean A Thing If It Ain't
Got That Swing
Lady In Blue
Love You Madly
Mood Indigo
Paris Blues
Prelude To A Kiss
Solitude
Sophisticated Lady
Take Love Easy
That's My Girl
Things Ain't What They Used To Be
Tomorrow Mountain

Ellington & Adamson
Five O'Clock Drag

Ellington & Carruthers & Mills
Black Butterfly

Ellington & David
I'm Just A Lucky So-And-So

Ellington & Dubin
I Never Felt This Way Before

Ellington & Gordon & Mills
Please Forgive Me

Ellington & Hodges
I'm Riding On The Moon And
Dancing On The Stars
Jeep Is Jumping, The

Ellington & Hodges & George
I'm Beginning To See The Light
Wonder Of You, The

Ellington & James & George
Everything But You

Ellington & Kuller
Bli-Blip

Ellington & Lange & Mills
Solitude

Ellington & Mercer & Strayhorn
Satin Doll

Ellington & Mills
Azure
Doin' The Crazy Walk
Gal From Joe's, The
I'm So In Love With You
It Don't Mean A Thing
It Don't Mean A Thing If It Ain't
Got That Swing
Ring Dem Bells

Ellington & Mills & Carney
Rockin' In Rhythm

Ellington & Mills & Stewart
Boy Meets Horn

Ellington & Mills & Tizol & Singer
Gypsy Without A Song
Lost In Meditation

Ellington & Ringle
Alabamy Home

Ellington & Strayhorn
Day Dream
Something To Live For

Ellington & Tizol
Caravan

Ellingwood
Keep On Singing

Elliot
Papa Don't Preach
Sing A Song Of Sixpence
There's A Long Long Trail

Elliot & Bradbury
Just As I Am
Just As I Am Without One Plea

Elliot & Ferguson
Charlie's Angels
Theme From Charlie's Angels

Elliot & Matthews
Thou Didst Leave Thy Throne

Elliott
Air France Makes It Easy To Get
There
Hail Silent Night
Heirs Of Time
Hickory Dickory Dock
Humpty Dumpty
I Love Little Pussy
In Heavenly Love Abiding
Jack And Jill
Jack Horner
Laugh Laugh
Little Bo-Peep
Little Jack Horner
Lord Is King Lift Up Thy Voice, The

Elliott *(Cont.)*
Lullaby
O Day Of Rest And Gladness
O Jesus I Have Promised
Pussy Cat
Ride A Cock Horse
Serenade
Sing A Song Of Sixpence
Somebody's Prayin'
Spider And The Fly, The
Story Book Friends
That's Where The Joy Comes From
Theme From Oh God
There's A Long Long Trail

Elliott & Baldwin
Celebrate The Lord

Elliott & Durand
Just A Little

Elliott & Nelson & Smith & Green
Celebrate His Good Life

Ellis
French Connection Theme, The
In His Presence
Jesus Holds The Keys
Let Me Touch Him
My God Can Do Anything
Untold Millions
What A Day

Ellis & Ellis
Love Is Why

Ellison
Some Kind Of Wonderful

Elliston & Chase
Name Game, The

Ellner & Atkinson & Byrne & Michalski
Psychotic Reaction

Ellor
All Hail The Power Of Jesus 'name

Ellstein & Small & Liebowitz
Wedding Samba, The

Ellsworth
I'm Glad I'm Not Methusalem

Elman
And The Angels Sing

Elsmith
Now Blessed Thou O Christ Jesu

Elson
Daffodils, The

Elton
Hats

Elvey
Blest Jesus Grant Us Strength
Christ The Lord Is Risen To-Day
Come Ye Thankful People
Come Ye Thankful People Come
Crown Him With Many Crowns
Great And Fair Is She
Hail Redeemer King Divine
Hark The Song Of Jubilee
Just As I Am Without One Plea
Let All The World In Every Corner
Sing
Lord Have Mercy Upon Us

Elvey *(Cont.)*
Lord Of All Being Throned Afar
Make Me A Captive Lord
My Soul Doth Magnify The Lord
Nature Wakes And Woodlands
O Grant Us Light That We May
    Know
O Son Of Man
Peace In Our Time O Lord
Round The Lord In Glory Seated
Servant Of God Well Done
Soldiers Of Christ Arise
Sow In The Morn Thy Seed
Strong Son Of God Immortal Love
Watchman Tell Us Of The Night
What Are These In Bright Array
What Various Hindrances We Meet
Elwell
Sailor And The Mermaid, The
Emer
A Quoi Ca Sert L'amour
Accordeoniste, L'
De L'autre Cote De La Rue
Disque Use, Le
Fete Continue, La
Emerson
All People That On Earth Do Dwell
Blood Of Jesus, The
Cast Thy Burden On The Lord
Ever Present Savior
Every Woman I Know
Goodbye Lonesome Hello Baby Doll
Jesus Shall Reign Where'er The Sun
Let Others See Jesus In You
Lord I Am Thine Entirely Thine
Picnic
Sessions
Star Of The Twilight
We Are Coming Father Abra'am
Emerson & Tilden
Calling Home The Cows
Riding My Bike
Emery
Crystal Spring
Emmerich
Doesn't That Mean Anything To
    You
Emmerson
Signs
Emmet
Close Your Eyes Lena My Darling
Dixie
Dixie Land
Emmet's Cuckoo Song
Emmet's Lullaby
Go To Sleep Lena Darling
Jordan Is A Hard Road To Trabel
Lullaby
Emmett
A-Way Down South In Dixie
Big Bill Snyder
Blue-Tail Fly
Boatman Dance, De
Boatman, De

Emmett *(Cont.)*
Boatman's Dance, The
California Bank Robbers
California Humbugs
Cherry Creek Emigrant's Song
Dixie
Dixie Land
Dixie's Land
Emmett's Lullaby
Go To Sleep Lena Darling
Green-Backs
I Wish I Was In Dixie
Old Dan Tucker
Richmond Is A Hard Road To Travel
Seeing The Elephant
Striking A Lead
Sweet Violets
Trip To Salmon, A
Emmett & Levine & Moore
Hooked On You
Emmons & Moman
Luckenbach Texas
Emor
Doonaree
En
Blumchen Wunderhold, Das
Endres
Indian Firefly Song
Endsley
I Like Your Kind Of Love
Singing The Blues
Endsley & Jackson
Why I'm Walkin'
Engel
Roamer, The
Sea-Shell
Engelbrecht
Good-Bye
Engelmann
Melody Of Love
Engelsberg
Love Song
Meine Muttersprache
Englander
Old Before His Time
Song Of The Strollers
Engle
West Virginia Hills
Englemann
Melody Of Love
English
It's A True Story
Quiet Time
Robin In The Rain, The
English & Weiss
Bend Me Shape Me
Enloe
Statue Of Liberty
Entraigues
Complainte De La Tourterelle
Eplett
Huntsman, The

Eppel
Hush-A-Bye Ma Baby
Missouri Waltz, The
Epstein
Revolution, The
Erard & Trafford
Rory O'Mory And Me
Erb
Happy Am I
Erben
Hymn For Whitsunday
Erh
Chee Lai
March Of The Volunteers
Road Building Song
Erickson
Wave The Flag
Wildcat Victory
Erk
Neujahrslied
What A Land
Ertegun & Curtis
Lovey Dovey
Ertegun & Nelson
Don't Play That Song
Ervin
Scoochie
Esch
Hail Thou Once Despised Jesus
Jesus Spreads His Banner O'Er Us
Mighty God While Angels Bless
    Thee
Esenwein
Taps
Esmond
All My Heart This Night Rejoices
Esperon
Borrachita, La
Three Caballeros, The
Espinosa
Altenitas, Las
Gay Ranchero, A
Espinosa & Palacio
Song Of The International Brigade
Esposito
Anema E Core
I Like It
Sunshine
Essex
Rock On
Este
How Merrily We Live
Estefan
Anything For You
Can't Stay Away From You
Cuts Both Ways
Don't Wanna Lose You
Here We Are
No Te Olvidre
Si Voy A Perderte
Words Get In The Way
Estefan & Casas & Ostwald
Oye Mi Canto

Estefan & Garcia
1-2-3
Rhythm Is Gonna Get You
Estella
Delight
Esterling
When I Wake Up To Sleep No More
Estes
Divin' Duck Blues
Girl I Love She Got Long Curly Hair,
The
Milk Cow Blues
Estup & Michael
Heaven Help Me
Etheridge
Angels, The
Bring Me Some Water
No Souvenirs
Sheffield 'Prentice, The
Similar Features
Etris & Harvey
Reuben James
Ett
Blessed City Heav'nly Salem
Blessed City Heavenly Salem
Jesu Meek And Lowly
Laudate Dominum
To The Name Of Our Salvation
To The Name That Brings Salvation
Ettinger & Seltzer
Naara Ush'ma Kinneret
Ettlinger & Brown & Lee
There's A Little Box Of Pine On The
7:29
Eugarps
Hard Times In Dixie
Evans
Belle Ob Baltimore
Bible Tells Me So, The
Build An Ark
By All Your Saints Still Striving
Come Take A Trip In My Air Ship
Death And Resurrection
Down In Arkansaw
Evening Prayer, An
For The Beauty Of The Earth
God Of Mercy God Of Grace
Happy Trails
I'll Be True To My Honey Boy
If
In The Good Old Summer Time
Jesus In Thy Dying Woes
Just For His Sake
Lady Of Spain
Let's All Sing Like The Birdies Sing
O Heav'nly Grace In Holy Rite
Descending
O Heavenly Grace In Holy Rite
Descending
O Jesus Christ May Grateful Hymns
O Son Of Man Our Hero
O Son Of Man Our Hero Strong And
Tender

Evans *(Cont.)*
Once To Every Man And Nation
One Sweetly Solemn Thought
Oregon Pledge Song
Rose With A Broken Stem, A
There I've Said It Again
Twelve Tone Tune
Waltz For Debby
Evans & Hewson
She's A Mystery To Me
Evans & Loeb
Rosie The Riveter
Evans & Mann
No Moon At All
There I've Said It Again
Evans & Reardon
When
Evans & Williams
I Gotta Know
Evart
Barndomshjemmet
Everett
Footprints Of Jesus
Footsteps Of Jesus
Jesus My Strength My Hope
Jesus The All-Restoring Word
Everly
I Kissed You
I Wonder If I Care As Much
So Sad To Watch Good Love Go Bad
When Will I Be Loved
Everly & Everly
Cathy's Clown
Everly & Slater
Bowling Green
Evigan & Macaluso & Jacobs
You Can Count On Me
Ewing
Another Year Is Dawning
How Do I Look Leaving This World
I Love You
If You Had Known Me
It Wasn't His Child
It'll Be Different The Next Time You
Come
Jerusalem The Glorious
Jerusalem The Golden
Your Ride's On The Way
Ewing & Geiger & Mullis
Burnin' A Hole In My Heart
It's You Again
Your Memory Wins Again
Ewing & Sampson
Gospel According To Luke, The
I Don't Have Far To Fall
Excell
All For Jesus
All The Way
All The World For Christ
Amazing Grace
Ashamed Of Jesus
Beacon Of The Cross, The
Because His Name Is Jesus

Excell *(Cont.)*
City Of Beauty
Closing Hymn
Count Your Blessings
Everbody Should Know
God Is Calling Yet
Good Old-Fashioned Way, The
Grace Enough For Me
How Sweet Is His Love
I Am Happy In Him
I Do Don't You
I Have Cast My Anchor
I Will Meet You There
I'll Be A Sunbeam
In The Shadow Of His Wings
In Thy Love
Jesus Bids Us Shine
Let Him In
Let The Saviour In
Little Bit Of Love, A
My Father Knows
My Happy Home
Onward Christian Soldiers
Since I Have Been Redeemed
Sonnenschein Auf Des Bruders Pfad
Under The Cross
Wash Me In The Blood
We Shall Stand Before The King
Will You Be Saved By The Blood
Faben
Gracious God Our Heavenly Father
Faber
Faith Of Our Fathers
Faber & Dykes
O Blest Is He
Faber & Hemy
Faith Of Our Fathers
Faber & Hemy & Walton
Faith Of Our Fathers
Fabor
My Heart Belongs To You
Fabre
Shower, The
Fagan
My Gal Is A High Born Lady
Fagen
I G Y
New Frontier
Fahrenkrog-Peterson & Karges
99 Red Balloons
Fahy
All The Grapes
Fain
Alice In Wonderland
April Love
Are You Havin' Any Fun
Boulevard Of Broken Dream, The
By A Waterfall
Certain Smile, A
Dear Hearts And Gentle People
Eleven O'Clock Song, An
Face To Face
I Can Dream Can't I
I'll Be Seeing You

Fain *(Cont.)*
I'm Late
Lately Song, The
Let A Smile Be Your Umbrella
Let A Smile Be Your Umbrella On A
    Rainy Day
Love Is A Many Splendored Thing
Second Star To The Right, The
Secret Love, A
Someone's Waiting For You
Springtime Cometh, The
Tender Is The Night
Very Good Advice
Very Precious Love, A
Wagon Train
Wedding Bells Are Breaking Up That
    Old Gang Of Mine
Worry Song, The
You Can Fly You Can Fly
You Can Fly You Can Fly You Can
    Fly
Your Mother And Mine

Fain & Kahal
I Left My Sugar Standing In The
    Rain
I'll Be Seeing You

Fain & Kahal & Norman
New Kind Of Love, A
When I Take My Sugar To Tea
You Brought A New Kind Of Love
    To Me

Fain & Lawrence
Once Upon A Dream

Fairchild
Memory, A

Fairlamb
April Girl, An
Carol Carol Joyfully
Cradle Song
Easter Carol, An
Little Mermaid, The
Lullaby, A
Minuet, The
O Star Of Truth Down-Shining
Valentine, A

Fairman
I Don't Know Where I'm Going But
    I'm On My Way
I Think We've Got Another
    Washington And Wilson Is His
    Name

Faith
Brazilian Sleigh Bells
Christmas Is
Swedish Rhapsody
Theme From The Virginian

Falconer & Balfe
By Killarney's Lakes And Fells

Falconieri
O Bellissimi Capelli
Occhietti Amati

Faleni
Capelli Bianchi

Fall
O Katharina
Unter Dem Bluhenden Lindenbaum

Falla
Asturiana
Cancion
Cancion Andaluza El Pan De Ronda
Dios Mio Que Solos Se Quedan Los
    Muertos
Jota
Nana
Olas Gigantes
Oracion De Las Madres Que Tienen
    Sus Hijos En Braz
Pano Moruno, El
Polo
Preludios
Seguidilla Murciana
Tus Ojillos Negros

Fallersleben
O Wie Ist Es Kalt Geworden

Fallersleben & Bruch
Spring Joys

Fallersleben & Schumann
Spring Festival
Spring Greeting

Faltermeyer
Axel F
Heat Is On, The
Love Theme From Thief Of Hearts
Top Gun Anthem

Faltermeyer & Forsey & Seger
Shakedown

Falvo
When I Hold You In My Arms

Faning
I've Something Sweet To Tell You

Faragher & Golden & Baker
With Every Beat Of My Heart

Fargo
Funny Face
Happiest Girl In The Whole USA,
    The
Superman
You Were Always There

Farian & Dalton
Baby Don't Forget My Number

Farian & Nail & Wilder & Thomas
All Or Nothing

**Farian & Reyam & Dowe &
    McNaughton**
Rivers Of Babylon

Farina
Children Of Darkness
Hard Loving Loser
Reno Nevada

Farina & Farina & Farina
Sleepwalk

Farjeon
Mayfair
Our Brother Is Born

Farley
Intoxication Of Love
On The River Tchou

Farley *(Cont.)*
Sapphire, The
Shoreless Sea, The
Young Poet Dreams Of His Beloved,
    A

Farley & Riley
Music Goes 'round And Around,
    The

Farlynne
Schuylkill Rowing Song

Farmer
Ad Hergan
Angels Holy High And Lowly
Fair Phyllis
Herga
In The Field Abiding Their Flocks
In The Field With Their Flocks
    Abiding
Land We Love Is Calling, The
Little Pretty Bonny Lass, A
October
Onward
Take Time While Time Doth Last

Farnaby
Ay Me Poor Heart
Construe My Meaning
Curtain Drawn, The
Psalm 122
Sometime She Would

Farnham & Goble
Playing To Win

Farnie
Scout, The
Up In A Balloon

Farnon
Captain Hornblower Theme
Colditz March

Farnsworth
In Cellar Cool
Who Will Volunteer

Farra
Alleluia Songs Of God Arise
Hallelujah Jesus Is Lord
Lord Hath Put A New Song, The
Oh Mary Don't You Weep

Farrant
Hide Not Thou Thy Face From Us
It Is A Good Thing To Give Thanks
King Shall Come When Morning
    Dawns, The
Lord For The Mercies Of The Night
Lord For Thy Tender Mercies' Sake

Farrar
Don't Stop Believin'
Have You Never Been Mellow
Hopelessly Devoted To You
Little More Love, A
Magic
Music Makes My Day
Sail Into Tomorrow
Something Better To Do
Suddenly
You're The One That I Want

Farrar & Marvin & Black
Sam
Farrell
Earthmaker
Old Zip Coon
Tell Them That You're Irish
Farrell & Helvering & Nelson
There Is A Savior
Farrell & Jansen
Could It Be Forever
Farrell & Janssen
Come On Get Happy
Farrell & Robbins
Hosanna Gloria
Farrely
Isle Of Innisfree
Farrer
Holy Hands
Farres
Acercate Mas
Perhaps Perhaps Perhaps
Without You
Farriss & Farriss & Hutchence & Pengilly
Listen Like Thieves
Farriss & Hutchence
Need You Tonight
What You Need
Farrow
I Have But One Heart
Oh Buddha
Farwell
March March
On A Faded Violet
Fascinato & Ford
What A Friend We Have In Jesus
Fassert
Barbara Ann
Fassone
Margarita
Faure
Absent, L'
Apres Un Reve
Au Bond De L'eau
Aubade
Aurore
Avant Que Tu Ne T'En Ailles
Berceaux, Les
Chanson Du Pecheur
Chant D'Automne
Charite
Charity
Cradles, The
Crucifix
Crucifixus
Dans Les Ruines D'une Abbaye
Donc Ce Sera Par Un Clair Jour D'Ete
En Priere
Hiver A Cesse, L'
Hymne
Ici-Bas
J'ai Presque Peur En Verite

Faure *(Cont.)*
J'allais Par Des Chemins Perfides
Lune Blanche Luit Dans Les Bois, La
Lydia
Mai
Matelots, Les
Moonlight
N'est-Ce Pas
Noel
Palm Branches
Palms, The
Papillon Et La Fleur, Le
Pie Jesu
Puisque L'aube Grandit
Rancon, La
Reve D'amour
Roses Of Ispahan, The
Sainte En Son Aureole, Une
Serenade Toscane
Seule
Sylvie
Tristesse
Fautheree & Gray
Cradle Of Love
Favart
Conseils A Mon Frere
Epicurien, L'
Fawcett
Children Of The Heavenly King
There Is A Book Who Runs May Read
Fawcett & Nageli
Blest Be The Tie That Binds
Fax
Cassandra's Lullaby
Love
Fay
How They Grow
Faye
All In All
Faye & Brown
Don't Ever Let Go Of My Hand
Today's Gonna Be A Brighter Day
Fearis
Beautiful Isle
Beautiful Isle Of Somewhere
Children's Hosanna, The
In The Cleft Of The Rock
Little Sir Echo
Little Stars
'Twill Not Be Long
Feaster & Feaster & McRae & Edwards
Sh-Boom
Feather
Baby Get Lost
Featherstone & Gordon
My Jesus I Love Thee
Fedak
Now Greet The Swiftly Changing Year
Feibel
Come To Me Thou Weary Child
Feist
Does True Love Ever Run Smooth

Fekaris & Perren
I Pledge My Love
I Will Survive
Reunited
Shake Your Groove Thing
Felder
Heavy Metal
Feldman & Goldstein & Gottehrer
My Boyfriend's Back
Feldman & Miran & Kedar
Shiri Li Kinneret
Feldman & Scott
One Lover At A Time
Feliciano
Chico And The Man
Feliz Navidad
It Doesn't Matter
Felipe
Commonwealth Of The Philippines, The
Land Of The Morning
Tierra Adorada
Feller
Makin' The Best Of A Bad Situation
Some Days Are Diamonds
Some Days Are Diamonds Some Days Are Stone
Fellows
Scouts, The
Feltner
I'll See You In The Rapture
Felton
Rose To Remember, A
Fender
Hail To Linfield
Wasted Days And Wasted Nights
Fenne-Vessey
Waves Of Waikiki, The
Fenner
Oh How Pleasant
Small Jesus
When Children Pray
Fenollosa
Spanish National Hymn
Fenstad
Stein Song
Fenton
Turning Japanese
Ferguson
Beautiful Music
Day Is Past And Over, The
Hat My Father Wore, The
It's The Irish In Me
Our Father By Whose Servants
When Our Lord Shall Come Again
Wings Of A Dove
Ferguson & Marshall
Blessed Quietness
Fernandez
Beautiful Heaven
Cielito Lindo
Guantanamera
Oh Brownie Oh Brownie

Ferrabosco
O Eyes O Mortal Stars
Ferrante
Monmouth College Fight Song
Ferrari
Domino
I've A Host Of Things To Tell You
Miroir, Le
Mirror, The
Spring Returns
Ferrata
Unseen Garden, The
Ferre & Marnay
Amants De Paris, Les
Ferrin
There Is Joy In My Soul
Ferris
Behold A Sower From Afar
Some Old Side Road
Ferris & Friedman
Waiting
Ferry
Kiss And Tell
Fesca
Love's Night Watch
Rudelsburg
Soldatenabschied
Fetler
Telling Time
Fettke
Adoration
Empty Hands
He Made Us To Praise Hime
Magnificat
Fettke & Crosby
Give Me Jesus
Fettke & Freud
He Is Risen Hallelujah
Fettke & Hawthorne
Creed, The
Living With The People
Ride The Morning Winds
Fettke & Herklots
Forgive Our Sins As We Forgive
Fettke & Hughes
Beyond The Mist And Doubt
Fettke & Johnson
Changed
Lord Let Me Serve
Majesty And Glory Of Your Name
Words Of Love
Fettke & Leech
I Will Ask My Father
Three Times I Asked Him
Fevin
Fors Seullement La Mort Sans Autre
    Attente
Petite Camusette
Fibich
Mountain Stream
Search, The
You're My Poem Of Love
Fichthorn
Trusting In Thee

Ficsher
Everett The Evergreen
Fiedel
Theme From The Accused
Fieger
Good Girls Don't
Fieger & Averre
Baby Talks Dirty
My Sharona
Fielder
Helen Of Troy
Fielding
Hogan's Heroes Theme Song, The
Theme From McMillan And Wife
Theme From The Bionic Woman
Fields
Chantez Chantez
He's The People's Choice
If My Friends Could See Me Now
It's Not Where You Start
Managua Nicaragua
Miami Beach Rumba
Pay-Day
Pay-Day That Was His Favorite Call
Plymouth Is Out To Win You Over
Fields & Donovan
Aba Daba Honeymoon
Aba Daba Honeymoon, The
Fields & Hague
'Hrbie Fitch's Twitch
Fields & McHugh
I Can't Give You Anything But Love
I'm In The Mood For Love
Fielitz
Oh Irmingard
Fig & Child
Calling It Love
Figueredo
Al Combate Corred Bayameses
Hymn National De Cuba
Rush To Battle All Men Of Bayamo
Filby
Breast The Wave Christian
Lift Your Glad Voices
Lift Your Glad Voices In Triumph
    On High
To Thee O Comforter Divine
Filiberto
Caminito
Filitz
Glory Be To Jesus
God Of Grace And God Of Glory
Gracious Spirit Holy Ghost
Holy Father Cheer Our Way
Lead Us Heavenly Father Lead Us
Three In One And One In Three
Wenn In Leidenstagen
Fillmore
Be Ready When He Comes
Beautiful Flag Of Liberty
Beautiful Garden Of Prayer, The
Blessed Hope
I Am Resolved
I Am Resolved No Longer To Linger

Fillmore *(Cont.)*
I Long To Know Thee Better
I Will Sing Of The Mercies Of The
    Lord
It Is Not Thrown Away
Let Me Go
Oh, The Meetings
Victory May Depend On You, The
We Are Going Down The Valley
Where The Shepherd Leads
Filmore
Do You Know The Song
Finch
As Oft With Worn And Weary Feet
Blessed Morn
By And By
Come And Worship
Evening
Grateful Praise
King Of Glory, The
Looking Unto Jesus
Truth Divine
Finck
I Dont Want To Be A Soldier
I'll Make A Man Of You
Fine
Lullaby
Towers Of Marble
Fink
All Nature's Works His Praise
    Declare
By Law From Sinai's Clouded Steep
O Jesus Once A Nazareth Boy
Our Father Thy Dear Name Doth
    Show
Take Back The Night
Thy Word Is Like A Garden Lord
While Shepherds Watched Their
    Flocks By Night
Finlay
As Pants The Hart For Cooling
    Streams
Immortal Love Forever Full
Jesus Stand Among Us
Finn
Don't Dream It's Over
I Feel Possessed
I Got You
Let Peace Be Yours
Now We're Getting Somewhere
Something So Strong
Finneran & Finneran & Finneran
Dear One
Finney
Words To Be Spoken
Finzi
Channel Firing
Come Away Death
Rollicum-Rorum
Sigh, The
To A Poet A Thousand Years Hence
Fiorentini
Ecce Vidimus
Hosanna Filio David

Fleming & Morgan (*Cont.*)
Morning Comes Too Early
Nobody
Operator Long Distance Please
Sleeping Single In A Double Bed
Smoky Mountain Rain
Snapshot
Sweet Yesterday
Tumbleweed
Years
You Don't Miss A Thing
Fleming & Morgan & Quillen
I Wouldn't Have Missed It For The
World
Fleming & Morgan & Tomlinson
Carolina Dreams
Fleming & Robbins
Easy To Please
Fleming & Schlitz
Give Me Wings
Flemming
Danket Dem Schopfer
Du Bist Der Weg Die Wahrheit Und
Das Leben
Eintracht Und Liebe
He Who Is Upright
Integer Vitae
Lord Of Our Life
Night's Shadows Falling
O Holy Father Bless Us
O Holy Savior Friend Unseen
O Holy Saviour Friend Unseen
O Holy Spirit Friend Unseen
Praise For Peace
Praise Ye The Father
Flemons & Bowser & Moore
That Time Of The Year
That Time Of Year
Flemons & Carter
Here I Stand
Flemons & Miller & Strong
Stay In My Corner
Fletcher
Aunt Dinah's Quilting Party
Gridiron King, The
Hail Hail To Winter Bold
Harvard Reunion Song
Lord Jesus I Long To Be Perfectly
Whole
Quilting Party, The
When I Saw Sweet Nellie Home
Yo Ho
Fletcher & Flett
Just Pretend
Fleyl
Sing To God
Flitz
Glory Be To Jesus
Florence
Bobbin' Around
Sacramento Gals
Florio
Allegro De Concert

Flotow
Ah So Pure
Dawn Of Peace, The
Guide Me O Thou Great Jehovah
Heaven May To You Grant Pardon
How So Fair
Last Rose Of Summer, The
Like A Dream
Lord With Glowing Heart I'd Praise
Thee
M'appari
Maidens Bright And Fair
Martha
Mother's Day
Night So Fair
Nightingale, The
O'er My Head
Spinning Lesson, The
Volkslied
Flowers
Tulsa Time
Floyd & Cropper
Knock On Wood
Flugel
Grace Of Our Lord, The
Stiller Abend Ist Es Worden
Flynn
Down Went McGinty
Duffy's Blunders
Sweet Annie Moore
Where The Columbines Grow
Yip-I-Addy-I-Ay
Flynn & Madden
Maybe
Foerster
Ode To The Patriotic Brave
Fogelberg
Believe In Me
Heart Hotels
Language Of Love, The
Leader Of The Band
Longer
Run For The Roses
Same Old Lang Syne
Sweet Magnolia And The Traveling
Salesman
Fogerty
Bad Moon Rising
Big Train From Memphis
Down On The Corner
Green River
Have You Ever Seen The Rain
Hey Tonight
Lodi
Lookin' Out My Back Door
Midnight Special, The
Old Man Down The Road, The
Proud Mary
Who'll Stop The Rain
Foglia
Down The Line
Foley
Just A Closer Walk With Thee
Old Shep

Foliart & Pearl
Mary
Folk
Police Academy March
Font
Cruz De Mayo, La
Fontane
Give Me Louisiana
Fontenailles
Faithful Love
Obstination
Steadfast Love
Foot
Over The Land In Glory
Foote
Barefooted Maiden, The
Bellman, The
Bells, The
Bright Star
Dandelion, The
Going To London
Knife Grinder, The
Nikolina
See Rock City
Song From The Shore, A
Song Of The Fields
Strawberry Hill
When I See The Blood
Forbert
Romeo's Tune
Forbes
His Love Shines Over All
Texian War Cry, The
Force & Lisa Lisa
Someone To Love Me For Me
Ford
Almighty God Who Hast Me
Brought
In A Simple Way I Love You
Knight To His Lady, A
Magic Sam
Rain
Tee Time For Eric
There Is A Lady Sweet And Kind
Ford & Bratton
Sunshine Of Paradise Alley, The
Ford & Osbourne
Close My Eyes Forever
Fordell
Santa Claus March
Foree
Heartbreak Avenue
Foree & Rose
No One Will Ever Know
Foresythe
Molloy My Boy
Forman
All Things Come Of Thee
Forrest
Crown Of Thorns, The
Night Train
Forsey & Schiff
Don't You Forget About Me

Forshaw
Brush Your Teeth With Colgate
Forster
Book Of Wonders, The
I Love Thee
Im Wunderbuch
Forsyth
Lord's Prayer, The
Forsythe
Born Again
In Thy Steps
Wherever He Leads
Win The One Next To You
Fort
Put Your Shoes On Lucy
Fortgang
Some Girls Have All The Luck
Some Guys Have All The Luck
Fortner
Geh Unter Schone Sonne
Fortune
Am I Crazy
Hurt I Can't Handle, A
My Only Love
Fortune & Rimel
More Than A Name On A Wall
More Than A Name On The Wall
Fosdick & Hughes
God Of Grace And God Of Glory
Foss
1898 And 1562
As I Walked Forth
Foss & Boe
Blaveispike
De Naere Ting
Foster
Alte Neger Joe, Der
Angelina Baker
Annie My Own Love
Away Down Souf
Away Down South
Away Up On The Yuba
Camptown Races, De
Camptown Races, The
Christmas Day In The Morning
Christmas Eve
Come With Thy Sweet Voice Again
Comrades Fill No Glass For Me
Cora Dean
Dearer Than Life
Dolcy Jones
Dolly Day
Don't Bet Your Money On De
Shanghai
Down Among The Cane Brakes
Dusk In June
Ellen Bayne
Eulalie
Eye Hath Not Seen Nor Ear Heard
Fairy-Belle
Farewell My Lilly Dear
Farewell My Lily Dear
Farewell Old Cottage
For Just A Moment

Foster (*Cont.*)
Gambler, The
Gentle Lena Clare
Give The Stranger Happy Cheer
Give Us This Day Our Daily Bread
Glendy Burk, De
Glendy Burk, The
Glendy Burke, The
Got My Mo-Jo Working
Gwine To Run All Night
Handcarts III, The
Happy Hours At Home
Hard Crackers Come Again No
More
Hard Times
Hard Times Come Again No More
I Have Missed You
I Love Him
I Want An Old Fashioned Christmas
I Will Be True To Thee
I Would Not Die In Springtime
I'm Off For California
If Ye Then Be Risen With Christ
Jenny June
Jenny's Coming O'Er The Green
Laura Lee
Leave Me With My Mother
Lift Your Voice Rejoicing
Like Texas In 1880
Lily Ray
Listen To My Story
Little Belle Blair
Little Ella
Little Jenny Dow
Little Mac Little Mac You're The
Very Man
Lou'siana Belle
Love Theme From St Elmo's Fire
Lula Is Gone
Maggie By My Side
Mary Loves The Flowers
Massa's In De Cold Cold Ground
Massa's In De Cold Ground
Massa's In The Cold Cold Ground
Massa's In The Cold Ground
Melanda May
Melinda May
Merry Merry Month Of May, The
Miner's Dream, The
Molly Dear Good Night
Moonlight And Starlight
Mormon Du Dah Song, The
Mother Thou'rt Faithful To Me
Mount Vernon Bells
My Brudder Gum
My Hopes Have Departed Forever
My Log Cabin Home
My Old Kentucky Home
My Old Kentucky Home Good Night
My Sailor Has Gone To The Sea
Nancy's By My Side
National Miner, The
Nell And I

Foster (*Cont.*)
Nelly Bly
Nelly Was A Lady
Night Is Far Spent, The
No Home No Home
Nonsense Song
O California
O Susanna
Oh Boys Carry Me 'long
Oh California
Oh Lemuel
Oh Lemuel Go Down To De Cotton
Field
Oh Susanna
Oh Tell Me Of My Mother
Oh There's No Such Girl As Mine
Oh Why Am I So Happy
Old Black Joe
Old Dog Tray
Old Memories
Old Uncle Ned
On The Banks Of The Sacramento
Once I Loved Thee Mary Dear
Open Thy Lattice Love
Our Bright Summer Days Are Gone
Parthenia To Ingomar
Poor Old Slave
Prospecting Dream
Ring De Banjo
Ring Ring De Banjo
Ring Ring The Banjo
Ring The Banjo
S'Wanee River, The
Shiny Stockings
Soldier In De Colored Brigade, A
Some Folks Do
Song Of All Songs
St Elmo's Fire
Swanee Ribber
Swanee River
Tears Are Not Enough
There Comes A Reckoning Day
There Was A Time
There Were Shepherds
Uncle Ned
Under The Willow She's Sleeping
Unhappy Miner, The
Union Buster, The
Village Maiden, The
Virginia Belle
Voice Of Bygone Days, The
Way Down In Ca-I-Ro
Weep No More
What Must A Fairy's Dream Be
When Old Friends Were Here
Where Has Lula Gone
Where Is Thy Spirit Mary
While The Bowl Goes Round
Why Have My Loved Ones Gone
Why Seek Ye The Living Among The
Dead
Willie Has Gone To The War
Willie My Brave
Willie We Have Missed You
Winter Games

Foster & Graydon & Champlin
After The Love Has Gone
Friends In Love
Foster & Graydon & Goodrum
Who's Holding Donna Now
Foster & Graydon & Jarreau
After All
Foster & Graydon & Osmond & Kipner
Too Young
Foster & Keane
Through The Fire
Foster & Keane & Baskins
Will You Still Love Me
Foster & King
Little Black Mustache, The
Foster & Lloyd
Crazy For You
Crazy Over You
Leave It Alone
Sure Thing
Foster & Lukather & Newton-John
Take A Chance
Foster & Lukather & Waybill
She's A Beauty
Foster & Marolda
Look Out For Number One
Foster & Parr
St Elmo's Fire
Foster & Rice
Easy Part's Over, The
Over
Foster & Vallance & Goodrum
Now And Forever
Now And Forever You And Me
Foster, Stephen
Ah May The Red Rose Live Alway
Beautiful Dreamer
Better Times Are Coming
Come Where My Love Lies
   Dreaming
Gentle Annie
If You've Only Got A Moustache
Jeanie With The Light Brown Hair
Katy Bell
Linger In Blissful Repose
Mr And Mrs Brown
Old Folks At Home, The
Slumber My Darling
Soiree Polka
Some Folks
Sweetly She Sleeps My Alice Fair
Sweetly She Sleeps My Baby Fair
That's What's The Matter
There Are Plenty Of Fish In The Sea
Way Down Upon The Swanee River
We Are Coming Father Abra'am
We Are Coming Father Abraam
   300000 More
We Are Coming Father Abraham
   300000 More
Why No One To Love
Wilt Thou Be Gone Love
Fotine
You Were Only Fooling

Fournier
My Dear
Fouser
Merry Christmas
Foust
Somebody Touched Me
Foust & Shuman
Somebody Touched Heaven For Me
Fowler
Wasted Years
Fowler & Cook
Jesus Is Mine
Fowler & Redman
How 'm I Doin'
Fowler & Sigmon
Champion Of The Battle
Fowler & Sigmon & Snyder
Unveil Your Glory
Fowler & Troccoli
If Only
Fowles
Autumn Wind
Thine Arm O Lord In Days Of Old
Fox
Alamo, The
Different Worlds
Dreams
Gone
Happy Days
Happy Days TV Theme
I Got A Name
I'll Never Ask You To Tell
Killing Me Softly With His Song
Lemon Drops Lollipops And
   Sunbeams
Love Boat, The
Making Our Dreams Come True
Mary Ann I'll Tell Your Ma
My Fair Share
My Heart Is A Silent Violin
Oh My Love Stood Under The
   Walnut Tree
Over The Garden Wall
Penny Whistler
Ready To Take A Chance Again
Sam Houston
Taft The Leader
Through The Years
We Farmers Go To Market
Well Done Thou Good And Faithful
   Servant
Fox & Newmark
Seasons
Fox & Williams
Love Boat, The
Foxx & Foxx
Mockingbird
Fragos & Baker & Gasparre
I Hear A Rhapsody
Fragson
Hello Hello Who's Your Lady Friend
Music-Hall Shakespeare, The

Frampton
Baby I Love Your Way
Show Me The Way
Franc
Before Jehovah's Awful Throne
Buried Beneath The Yielding Wave
Dundee
Great God How Infinite Art Thou
Old Hundred
France
Angelus, The
It Was For Me
Franceschi & Powers
Little Girl
Whoever's In New England
Francis & Williams
O The Deep Deep Love Of Jesus
Francisco
Got To Tell Somebody
He's Alive
Holiness
Franck
America Triumphant
Ave Maria
Chorus Of Camel-Drivers
Danses De Lormont, Les
Father Eternal
From All That Dwell Below The
   Skies
Heavenly Manna
Jerusalem Thou City Fair And High
Lied
Marriage Of Roses
O Bread Of Life From Heaven
O Lord Most Holy
O Lord Most Merciful
O Lord Of Mercy
On Sail On
Panis Angelicus
Sei Nur Still
Star Is Moving Through The Sky, A
Ten Thousand Times Ten Thousand
Thus Saith The Lord Of Nations
Trost Des Sterbenden
Voice Of God Is Calling, The
Franco
Crawl Little Caterpillar
Growing
Francois & Bourtayre
My Boy
Frank & James
After You
Franklin
All Hail Alaska
Franklin & White
Since You've Been Gone
Franks
Monkey See Monkey Do
Popsicle Toes
When I Give My Love To You
When It's Springtime In Alaska
Franks & Horton
I'm A One Woman Man

Franks & Horton & Hausey
Honky Tonk Man
Franz
Abends
As The Moon Her Trembling Image
Aus Meinen Grossen Schmerzen
Bitte
Calm At Sea
Churchyard, A
Colors Of Helgoland, The
Crusade, The
Dancing Song In The May
Dark The Sky The Clouds Are Flying
Dedication
Er Ist Gekommen
Es Hat Die Rose Sich Beklagt
Evening
Evening Song
Farewell
Feast Of Love
For Music
Forebodings
Fur Musik
Good Night
Gute Nacht
Hark How Still
He Is Coming
Hunting Song
I Wander
I Wander This Summer Morning
Ich Hab' In Deinem Auge
Ich Hab' In Deinen Auge
Im Fruhling
Im Herbst
In Autumn
In The Dreamy Wood I Wander
In The Woods
It Was The Rose Herself Who Sigh'd
Knowest Thou
Lassie With The Lips So Rosy
Lieber Schatz Sei Wieder Gut Mir
Little Maid With Lips So Rosy
Lotus Flower, The
Madchen Mit Dem Roten Mundchen
Marie
Mein Schatz Ist Auf Der
    Wanderschaft
Messenger, The
Nachtlied
Nature's Thanksgiving
O Mond O Losch' Dein Gold 'nes
    Licht
O Star Deceive Me Not
Oft On Hidden Paths I Wander
On The Lake So Calm So Placid
On The Sea
Out Of My Soul's Great Sadness
Out Of My Soul's Great Sorrow
Passing Through The Moonlit Woods
Pour Un Regard
Rain And The Sun, The
Request

Franz *(Cont.)*
Rheinweinlied
Rhine The River Of Story, The
Rogue, The
Romance
Rose Complained, The
Rose Complains, The
Rose Was Sad, The
Rose's Complaint, The
Runic Rock, The
Scheiden Und Meiden
Sea Is Shining In The Sun, The
Serenade, The
Sie Liebten Sich Beide
Slumber Song
Spring And Love
Spring Festival
Spring's Blue Eyes, The
Spring's Profusion
Stars With Golden Sandals
Stille Sicherheit
Stormy Night
Sun's Bright Rays, The
Sunset Lights The West
Tempest And Storm Furies Shrieking
Though The Roses Now Flourish
Two Dark Eyes
Um Mitternacht
Up The River
Wand'ring Thro' The Wood
Welcome My Wood
Where Sorrows Touch Me Nearest
Widmung
Woodland Journey, A
Franzel & Forbes
Don't Rush Me
Fras
Beautiful Nebraska
Fraser
Across The Sky And In The Vale
Every Kinda People
Mull Fisher's Love Song
Skye Fisher's Song
Fraser & Shannon
Cowboy
Frazier
Ain't Had No Lovin'
Alley-Oop
Elvira
If My Heart Had Windows
Mohair Sam
Son Of Hickory Holler's Tramp
There Goes My Everything
Frazier & Shafer
Baptism Of Jesse Taylor, The
Dream Painter
I'm Sorry If My Love Got In Your
    Way
Rainbow In Daddy's Eyes, The
Frazier & White & Wilson & Harris
Papa-Oom-Mow-Mow

Frazzini & De Frank & Mills
When Banana Skins Are Falling I'll
    Come Sliding Back To You
Freake
Sweet Slumber Come
Frech
Evening Prayer, An
Fred & Bernard
Judy In Disguise With Glasses
Frederick
Way Of The Dinosaur
Frederick & Salvay
Better Days
Nothing's Gonna Stop Me Now
Fredricks
Texaco Star Theme
Freebairn-Smith
For Love And Honor
Freeburg
Swing Canon
Freed
How Much Farther Must We Go
Verdict, The
Freed & Arnheim & Lyman
I Cried For You
Freed & Brown
Pagan Love Song
Freed & Edens
Our Love Affair
Freedman & Deknight
Rock Around The Clock
We're Gonna Rock Around The
    Clock
Freeds & Eden
Our Love Affair
Freeman
Betty Lou Got A New Pair Of Shoes
Do You Want To Dance
Down Quintana Way
I Will Go With My Father
    A-Ploughing
Mother
Freer
Apparitions
Frehlinghausen
Dir Dir Jehovah
Macht Hoch Die Thur
Morgenglanz Der Ewigkeit
Wie Gross Ist Des Allmachtgen Gute
**Freiberg & McPherson & Chaquico &
Kantner**
Jane
Freilinghausen
Guter Geber Dank Sei Dir
Freire
Ay Ay Ay
My Heart Has A Window
Freisen
Other Mansions
French
Idaho
Out Of Your Pocket
French & Collisson
Mountains O'Mourne, The

Freon
Texian Banner, The

Freud
Lord Has Risen, The
Peter Was A Fisherman

Freudenthal
En Kelohenu

Frew & Hanson & Reid
I'm Still Searching

Frew & Reid & Parker & Connelly & Hanson
I Will Be There

Frey
Adoro Te
All Those Lies
Come By Here
Frankie And Johnny
He Is Lord
How Doth The Little Crocodile
Jesus In The Morning
Marching Song
Old Soldiers Never Die
Singing
Veni Sancte Spiritus
Will You Walk A Little Faster

Frey & Tempchin
I Found Somebody
One You Love, The
Smuggler's Blues
True Love
You Belong To The City

Freylinghausen
Christian Seek Not Yet Repose
Come My Soul Thou Must Be
Waking
Dost Thou Truly Seek Renown
It Is Finished Christ Hath Known
Jehovah Let Me Now Adore Thee
Now The Labourer's Toils Are O'Er
On This Day The First Of Days
Saviour Who Didst Healing Give
Spread O Spread Thou Mighty Word
What Has Drawn Us Thus Apart
Ye Who Own The Faith Of Jesus

Freylingshausen
Let The Earth Now Praise The Lord

Fricker
You Were On My Mind

Friday & Toussaint & Tyler
Java

Friderici
Liebeshoffnung

Frieberg & McPherson & Chaquico & Kantner
Jane

Friebolin
O Ewigkeit O Ewigkeit

Fried
Flamingo Road
Roots
Song Of The Land

Fried & Spencer
Broadway Rose

Friedell
Way To Jerusalem, The

Friedland
My Little Dream Girl

Friedland & Morgan
My Own Iona

Friedlander
Tropical South Sea Isle

Friedman
Down The Field
Fame
Glory For Yale
I Wish I Had Died In My Cradle
I Wish I Had Died In My Cradle
Before I Grew Up To Love You
Let Me Call You Sweetheart
Let Me Call You Sweetheart I'm In
Love With You
Meet Me To-Night In Dreamland
When I Dream Of Old Erin
Whoop It Up
Windy

Friedman & Broeck
Goodbye My Sweet Johnny

Friedman & Minsky
When I Was Young

Friedman & Rich
I Don't Have The Heart

Friedman & Whitson
Let Me Call You Sweetheart

Friend
Give Me A Night In June
Hello Bluebird
Little Boy From The Carpenter Shop,
The
Lovesick Blues
Then I'll Be Happy
When My Dream Boat Comes Home
You Tell Her I Stutter

Friend & Clare & Santly
Big Butter And Egg Man, The

Friend & Franklin
Merry-Go-Round Broke Down, The
When My Dream Boat Comes Home

Friend & Malneck
Love Is Good For Anything That
Ails You

Friend & Tobias
We Did It Before We'll Do It Again

Friesen
Pathway

Friesen & Eklund
Straw Carol, The

Friis
La Oss Leve

Friml
Allah's Holiday
Amour-Toujours-L'amour, L'
Bubble, The
Giannina Mia
I Have The Love
I Love You Dear
Indian Love Call
Katinka

Friml *(Cont.)*
Love Is Like A Firefly
Ma Belle
Madeleine
March Of The Musketeers
My Sword And I
On Hawaiian Shores
Only A Rose
Queen Of My Heart
Rackety Coo
Rose-Marie
Some Day
Something Seems Tingle Ingleing
Song Of The Vagabonds
Sympathy
Trousseau Ball
Vagabond King Waltz, The
We'll Build A Cute Little Nest
We'll Have A Kingdom
When A Maid Comes Knocking At
Your Heart
Woman's Kiss, A
You're In Love

Friml & Stothart
Donkey Serenade, The
Mounties, The

Frisbie
Songs We Sang Upon The Old Camp
Ground, The

Frisch
Two Different Worlds
Why Do They Call 'Em Wild
Women
Wonderful World Of Christmas, The

Frischenschlager
Whirligig

Frishberg
Another Song About Paris
Listen Here
My Attorney Bernie
Slappin' The Cakes On Me
Van Lingle Mungo

Frishberg & Hodges
Little Taste, A

Fritsch
Now Yield We Thanks And Praise
O God Thou Faithful God
Where Is Your God They Say

Fritts
War Baby
You're Gonna Love Yourself
You're Gonna Love Yourself In The
Morning

Frizzell
Mom And Dad's Waltz

Frizzell & Beck
I Love You A Thousand Ways
If You've Got The Money I've Got
The Time

Frizzell & Crawford
Always Late

Froelich
Our Naval Heroes

Frohlich & Bruch
God's Own Temple Is The Wood
Frontier
Hang 'em High
Frontiere
12 O'Clock High
Branded
Matt Houston
Theme From The Immortal
Theme From Vegas
Washington Behind Closed Doors
Frost
Giddy Giddap Go On Go On
Stephen Van Rensselaer
Sweet Hawaiian Moonlight
Frost & Frost
What About Me
Frost & McHugh
When You And I Were Young
  Maggie Blues
Fruhlich
Wem Gott Will Rechte Gunst
  Erwiesen
Fry
Notre Dame Of Paris
We Can Change The World
Fry & Singleton & White
Hey Citizen
Look Of Love
Poison Arrow
That Was Then But This Is Now
Frye
Time Has Made A Change
Fryer
Virgin's Cradle-Hymn, The
Fucik
Thunder And Blazes
Fuentes
Barca De Guyamas, La
Change, A
Cuba
Cubana
En Cuba
Fair Cuba
Fontainailles
Hay Unos Ojos
Lovely Cuba 'Tis You
Resolve, A
Tu
Fuentis
Corrido De Cananea
Fugain
If I Only Had Time
Fuhrman & Goodman
Fan Mail
Full Force
All Cried Out
Head To Toe
Lost In Emotion
Fuller
He Knows
Heavenly Sunshine
Lady Willpower
Little Woman You're So Sweet

Fuller *(Cont.)*
My Bonnie
My Bonnie Is Over The Ocean
San Francisco Bay Blues
Travelin' Man
Weeping Willow Blues
When Jesus Spoke Peace To My Soul
Young Girl
Young World
Fullerton
Halloween Night
Fulmer
Wait Till The Clouds Roll By
Fulson
Reconsider Baby
Fulton
Fool No 1
Fulton & Steele
Wanted
Fuqua & Freed
Most Of All
Sincerely
Furman
Vermont Victorious
Furman & Sharples & Kiljick
Vermont Victorious
Furness
Skating Song
Furth
Budweiser's A Friend Of Mine
No Wedding Bells For Me
Furze
Huntsmen, The
Fyles
Hail Columbia
G, Kenny
Silhouette
Songbird
Gabriel
All Hail Immanuel
Angels' Song, The
Arise My Soul Arise
As A Volunteer
At Sunset
Awakening Chorus
Banner Of The Cross, The
Be A Hero
Be Not Afraid
Because He Loved His Own
Because I Love Jesus
Believe On The Crucified One
Blood Of Jesus Ransomed Me, The
Bridegroom Cometh, The
Brighten The Corner
Brighten The Corner Where You Are
Busy For Jesus
Calling The Prodigal
Carry Your Cross With A Smile
Christ Is All You Need
Christ Shall Be King
Christmas Lullaby
Closer Still
Closer To Jesus
Columbia's Song

Gabriel *(Cont.)*
Come And Take Possession
Come To Him Today
Crown Him
Day Of Glory, The
Dear Little Stranger
Death And Eternity
Diferentes
Do It Today
Do Something For Others
Down The Valley Alone
Earth Is The Lord's, The
Evening Prayer, An
Evergreen Shore, The
Everlasting Father, The
Every Prayer Will Find Its Answer
Everywhere I Go
Games Without Frontiers
Gate Of Blessing, The
Gather We Here
God Knows They Need
Gospel Harvest, The
Great Mediator, The
Growing Dearer Each Day
Hallelujah And Praise
Harbor Lights Of Home, The
Harvest Song
Harvest-Time Is Here
Hasta Que Te Conoci
Have You Forgotten God
He Brightens The Shadows
He Is So Precious To Me
He Lifted Me
He Promised To Keep Me
Help Somebody Today
His Eye Is On The Sparrow
His Eyes On The Sparrow
How Would It Be With You
I Am Happy All The Time
I Am Trusting
I Am With You
I Have Been Born Again
I Have Been To Jesus
I Have Never Found A Friend Like
  Jesus
I Know
I Know Not
I Need Jesus
I Will Not Forget Thee
I Would Be Like Thee
I'm A Saved Sinner
I'm Pressing On The Upward Way
If You Want To Be Happy Take
  Jesus
In His Glory
In The Hollow Of His Hand
It Is Here
It Is Jesus
It Is Thy Blood My Jesus
Jehovah-Jireh
Jesus Has You On His Heart
Jesus Is The Friend You Need
Jesus Met Me There
Jesus Remembered You

Gabriel (*Cont.*)
Joy To Serve Jesus
Just For Today
Just To Know Jesus Cares
Just When I Need Him Most
Keep The Heart Singing
Keep The Vision Of The Cross
Kept Through Faith
Leave It To Him
Let God Use Us
Let The Sunshine In
Let Us Be Lights
Little Sunbeams
Lo A Mighty Army
Look In The Bible
Looking On The Bright Side
Lord Is King, The
Make Somebody Happy Today
More Like The Master
Morning Noon And Night
My Father Planned It All
My Father Watches Over Me
My Only Plea
My Savior's Love
My Saviour's Love
My Tent Is Pitched In Beulah Land
My Wonderful Dream
Near To Jesus
O Jesus Answer Prayer
O Let Him In
O That Will Be Glory
O That Will Be Glory For Me
O What A Change
O What Joy Will Be Ours
Oh It Is Wonderful
Only A Contrite Sinner
Only A Face At The Window
Only In Thee
Only One Way
Onward Christian Workers
Onward Forward
Onward Till The Dawning
Open The Gates Of Prayer
Praise The Lord
Praise Ye The Name Of Jehovah
Quedate Conmigo Esta Noche
Sail On
Send The Light
Since Jesus Came Into My Heart
There's A Call Comes Ringing
They Led Him Away
To The Harvest Field
Toiling For The Master
Way Of The Cross Is The Way, The
Way Of The Cross Leads Home, The
What A Day Of Victory
What A Saviour
When The Comforter Came
Where Jesus Is Is Home To Me
Where My King Leads On
Where The Gates Swing Outward
   Never
Wherever You Wander Come Home
Who Will Gather

Gabriel (*Cont.*)
Why Not Be Saved To Night
Will The Circle Be Unbroken
Win Them One By One
Won't You Come Now
Wonderful Love
Wonderful Power
Wonderful Redeemer, The
Wonderful Story, The
Wonders In Glory
Working Together
Your Light Is Needed

Gabriel-Marie
Folk Dance
Golden Wedding Song

Gabrieli
Ecco L'aurora Con L'aurata Fronte
Jubilate Deo
Quand'io Ero Giovinetto

Gackstatter
Sunday Morning

Gaddis
Bobby Brockett
Down In The Well
Timothy Lee

Gade
Barn Jesus
Child Jesus Came From Heaven
Child Jesus Came To Earth This Day
Christmas Song
Come Prima
Fruhlingsnahen
Gondelfahrt
Jalousie
Lovely Spring Has Come, The

Gadman
Song Of The Mountains

Gadsby
Forward Be Our Watchword

Gagliano
Di Marmo Siete Voi

Gagliardi
My Finest Hour
Words And Music

Gail
Il Est Vrai Que Thibaut
Langueurs, Les
Ma Fanchette Est Charmante
Serment, Le

Gaillard & Ricks
Cement Mixer
Down By The Station

Gaillard & Stewart & Green
Flat Foot Floogee, The

Gaines
This Is Our Homeland

Gaines & Fox & Sweet & Sweet
Always There For You
I Believe In You

Gairdner
New York
New York Oh What A Charming
   City

Gaither & Daniels
I've Just Seen Jesus
Gaither & Gaither
Between The Cross And Heaven
Church Triumphant, The
Family Of God, The
I Will Serve Thee
It Is Finished
My Faith Still Holds
There's Something About That
   Name
This Could Be The Dawning Of That
   Day
Gaither & Gaither & McGuire
We Are Persuaded
Gaither & Gaither & Milhuff
King Is Coming, The
Gaither & George
Bring Back The Glory
Gaither & Huff & Gaither
God Gave The Song
Gaither & Millhuff
All God's Children
Gaither & Wilburn
It's Beginning To Rain
Gaither, Bill
All God's Children
All My Hopes
Because He Lives
Christ Of Every Crisis, The
Come Holy Spirit
Even So Lord Jesus Come
Gentle Shepherd
Get All Excited
He Touched Me
He's Still The King Of Kings
I Am A Promise
I Am Loved
I Believe In A Hill Called Mt
   Calvary
I Came To Praise The Lord
I Just Feel Like Something Good Is
   About To Happen
I've Been To Calvary
If It Keeps Gettin' Better
If It Keeps Getting Better
In The Upper Room
It Is Finished
It's Beginning To Rain
Jesus I Believe What You Said
Jesus Is Lord Of All
Jesus We Just Want To Thank You
Joy Comes In The Morning
Joy Is Serving The Lord, The
King Is Coming, The
Let's Just Praise The Lord
Longer I Serve Him, The
Lovest Thou Me
Lovest Thou Me More Than These
Old Rugged Cross Made The
   Difference, The
Redeeming Love

Gaither, Bill *(Cont.)*
Something Beautiful
Spirit Of Jesus Is In This Place
Spirit Of Jesus Is In This Place, The
Tell Me That Name
Thanks To Calvary
This Is The Time I Must Sing
Why Should I Worry Or Fret
Worthy The Lamb
You're Something Special
Gaito
Flower Of Hope
Mistica
Gaitsch & Marx
Don't Mean Nothing
Nothin' To Hide
Galdieri & Rota
Love Theme From La Strada
Gale
Line Up For Bryan
Galhardo
Lisbon Antigua
Gallagher & Lyle
Stay Young
Gallaher
It's British You Know
Galli
Workers Hymn, The
Gallimore & Mevis & Shore
It Took A Lot Of Drinkin' To Get
That Woman Over Me
Gallimore & Shore
Ev'ry Heart Should Have One
Gallimore & Shore & Mevis & Hobbs
Oklahoma Heart
Gallimore & Shore & Wills
Miss Understanding
Gallo & Potts
Show Me The Way
Gallop & Coquatrix
Count Every Star
Gallop & Saxon
There Must Be A Way
Galloway
Gypsy Trail, The
Gallus
Ecce Quomodo Moritur
Galpaz & Gal
Hal'luya
Galusha
British Soldier, The
British-American Fight, The
Jam On Gerrion's Rock, The
James Bird
Jamie Judge
Lass Of Glenshee
Longshoreman's Strike
Nothing's Too Good For The Irish
Paddle The Road With Me
Plains Of Baltimore
Red White And Red, The
Shanty Boy Farmer Boy
Shanty Man, The

Galusha *(Cont.)*
Springfield Mountain
St Albans Murder, The
This Day
Trip On The Erie, A
Twenty-Third, The
Virginia's Bloody Soil
Waxford Girl, The
Gambardella
O Come Love
O Marenariello
Gambetti
Italian Royal March
Gamble & Butler & Bell
Brand New Me, A
Moody Woman
Gamble & Huff
Give The People What They Want
Hope That We Can Be Together
Soon
Love Train
Sexy
Gamble & Huff & Butler
Hey Western Union Man
Only The Strong Survive
Gamble & Huff & Gilbert
Don't Leave Me This Way
Me And Mrs Jones
Gamble & Williams & Ross
I'm Gonna Make You Love Me
Gambler & Ellington
In A Mellow Tone
Gampian
Thrice Toss These Oaken Ashes In
The Air
Gamse
Comparsa, La
Jamaica Farewell
Gamzu
Efo Habachurot
Gamzu & Braun
Bisharayisch Y'Rushalayim
Ganes
Banner Of The Sea, The
Gannaway & Farrar & Carmichael
Sad Cowboy, The
Ganne
Light Triumphant
March Lorraine
Marche Lorraine, La
Gannon & Kent
Lord Is Good To Me, The
Gannon & Kent & Ram
I'll Be Home For Christmas
Ganss
Banner Of The Sea
Gantry
Dreams Of The Everyday Housewife
Ganz
Memory, A
Garat
Belisaire
Dans Le Printemps De Mes Annees
Il Etait La

Garber & Large
My Dear
Garbett
Glider, The
Garcia
Bertha
Brown-Eyed Woman
Casey Jones
Conga
Cream Puff War
Critical Envelopment
Deal
Dr Beat
Eyes Of The World
He's Gone
If I Had The World To Give
Lady With A Fan
Mountains Of The Moon
Ramble On Rose
Row Jimmy
Scarlet Begonias
Shakedown Street
Ship Of Fools
Stella Blue
Sugaree
Tennessee Jed
Terrapin Station
Touch Of Grey
Uncle John's Band
US Blues
Wharf Rat
Garcia & Dawson
Friend Of The Devil
Garcia & Hart & Kreutzmann & Lesh
Dark Star
Garcia & Kreutzmann
Franklin's Tower
Garcia & Kreutzmann & Lesh & McKern
Golden Road, The
Garcia & Lesh & Weir
Truckin'
Gardane
Douce Memoire
N'avons Point Veu Mal Assenee
Gardiner
All Things Are Thine-No Gift Have
We
Beneath The Forms Of Outward Rite
By Cool Siloam's Shady Rill
God Of The Earth The Sky The Sea
How Precious Is The Book Divine
I Worship Thee Sweet Will Of God
I'm Not Ashamed To Own My Lord
Lord Be With Us, The
Now With Creation's Morning Song
O For A Thousand Tongues To Sing
O How I Love Thy Holy Law
O Thou Whose Bounty Fills My Cup
There Is A Book
Thou Whose Unmeasured Temple
Stands
Walk In The Light

Gardiner *(Cont.)*
When All Thy Mercies O My God
Where Cross The Crowded Ways Of
Life

Gardner
All I Want For Christmas Is My Two
Front Teeth
Autumn Leaves
Christmas Folk-Song, A
I'm Feeling Good About America
Mother's Prayer, A
My Dog And I
My Two Front Teeth
North Wind, The
Softly The Night Is Sleeping
Winter

Gardner & Cosby
Kiss Me

Gari
PM Magazine

Garica
China Cat Sunflower

Garland
Death Of Harry Simms
I Don't Want Your Millions Mister
In The Mood
Leap Frog

Garner
Dreamy
Misty

Garnett
Ode To The Fourth Of July
We'll Sing In The Sunshine

Garratt
Hallelujah Our God Reigns
Owl, The
Winter Rain

Garrels
Song Of The Saddle

Garretson
Merrily We Roll Along

Garrett
Almighty Father God Of Love
Hours Of Day Are Over, The
Nightingale, The
O Fair New Mexico
O The Bitter Shame And Sorrow
Oh My Love's Like A Red Red Rose
You Are Jehovah

Garrick
Liberty Song, The

Garrison
Bondage Of Love, The
Sons Of Ohio
Vale Of Beulah

Garson
Our Day Will Come

Gart & Redmond
Winky Dink And You

Gartlan
Be Sure And Kiss The Blarney Stone
Bit O' The Brogue

Gartlan *(Cont.)*
Don't You Love To Dream Of Dear
Old Ireland
Springtime In Mayo Means Lovetime
With You
Top Of The Mornin', The
What An Irishman Means By
Machree

Gartside & Gamson
Perfect Way

Garvey & Garvey
Ten More Nights In This Old
Barroom

Garvin
Over The Mountain Across The Sea

Garvin & Johns
Desperado Love

Garvin & Jones & Shapiro
Highway Robbery
Your Heart's Not In It

Gascon
Listen Lordlings Unto Me

Gascongne
Beuvons Ma Commere Nous Ne
Beuvons Point

Gaskill & McHugh
I Can't Believe That You're In Love
With Me

Gaskill & McHugh & Mills
I Don't Mind Being All Alone When
I'm All Alone Wi

Gaskin
Bride Coming In, The
Come Morning
I'll Just Lay It Down
Sun's Coming Up, The
What A Singing

Gasso
Mary Ann

Gastaldon
Forbidden Music
Lady Of Light
Musica Proibita

Gastoldi
In Dir Ist Freude In Allem Leide
In Thee Is Gladness
In Thee Is Joy
Maidens Fair Of Mantua's City
Tutti Venite Armati

Gaston
Old North State, The

Gastorius
O Love That Wilt Not Let Me Go
Thou Earth Art Ours
Whate'er My God Ordains Is Right
Whatever God Ordains Is Good

Gates
Baby I'm-A Want You
Been Too Long On The Road
Blue Satin Pillow
Come Again
Diary
Everything I Own

Gates *(Cont.)*
Goodbye Girl
Guitar Man, The
He's A Good Lad
Hooked On You
If
In The Afterglow
It Don't Matter To Me
Let Your Love Go
Lost Without Your Love
Make It With You
Mother Freedom
Other Side Of Life, The
Popsicles And Icicles
She Was My Lady
What A Change

Gatlin
All The Gold In California
Alleluia
Broken Lady
Denver
Help Me
Houston
Houston Means I'm One Day Closer
To You
I Don't Wanna Cry
I Just Wish You Were Someone I
Love
I've Done Enough Dyin' Today
It Don't Get No Better Than This
It Must Have Rained In Heaven
Lady Takes The Cowboy Every
Time, The
Light At The End Of The Darkness
Love Is Just A Game
Mercy River
Night Time Magic
Nothing But Your Love Matters
Runaway Go Home
She Used To Be Somebody's Baby
Statues Without Hearts
Sure Feels Like Love
Take Me To Your Lovin' Place
Taking Somebody With Me When I
Fall
Talkin' To The Moon
We're Number One
What Are We Doing Lonesome
Wind Is Bound To Change

Gatty
Autumn Song
Burial Of The Robin, The
Christmas Carol, A
Christmas Voices
Come Rejoicing Faithful Men
Cradle Song
Cuckoo
Eight Little Birds
Golden Shore, The
Grumbling Joe
Jack
July Song
Lights Far Out At Sea

Gatty *(Cont.)*
Little Girl's Good-Night
May-Day Song
Mud Pies
New Year Carol
New Year Song
North Wind, The
October Song
On The Rocks By Aberdeen
Puff
Rock-A-Bye Baby
Sara Jane's Tea-Party
Sarah Jane's Tea Party
Sing We Triumphant Hymns Of
    Praise
Sister May
Snow Man, The
Springtime, The
Summer Is Coming
Three Little Pigs, The
Twenty Years Ago
Will You Walk A Little Faster
Gaudette
God Has Created A New Day
Gaudio
December 1963
Sherry
Who Loves You
Gaudio & Corbetta
You're Looking Like Love To Me
Gaudio & Linzer
Dawn Go Away
Gaudio & Ruzicka
Night, The
Gaul
Come Ye Blessed
Eye Hath Not Seen
Holy Holy Holy
Holy Holy Holy Lord Of Hosts
List The Cherubic Host
Lord Is Rich And Merciful, The
My Soul Is Athirst For God
No Shadows Yonder
These Are They Which Came
They Shall Hunger No More
Thou Art The Night Wind
Thy Kindom Come On Bended Knee
Gaunt
Bowery, The
Push Dem Clouds Away
Gauntlet
Thou Whose Spirit Dwells In All
Gauntlett
Almighty God Thy Word Is Cast
Brief Life Is Here Our Portion
Christ Is Made The Sure Foundation
Christ The Lord Is Ris'n To-Day
Eternal Spirit Source Of Life
Father O Fall From Land And Sea
For Thy Dear Saints O Lord
Give To The Winds Thy Fears
Gracious Spirit Dove Divine
I Love Thee Lord But Not Because
In His Temple Now Behold Him

Gauntlett *(Cont.)*
Jesus Lives Thy Terrors Now
Jesus Name Of Wondrous Love
Lo What A Cloud Of Witnesses
Lord Jesus Who Our Souls To Save
Make Haste O Man To Live
Mount Up With Wings As Eagles
My God I Love Thee
My God I Love Thee Not Because
Now In The Days Of Youth
O Christ Our King Creator Lord
O Maker Of The Sea And Sky
O That The Lord's Salvation
Oft In Danger Oft In Woe
Once In Royal David's City
Praise My Soul The King Of Heaven
Praise The Lord
Praise We The Lord This Day
Slowly By God's Hand Unfurled
Source Of Light And Life Divine
Think Gently Of The Erring One
Thirsting For A Living Spring
Though Troubles Assail
Voice That Breathed O'er Eden, The
We Give Thee But Thine Own
When All Thy Mercies O My God
Ye Choirs Of New Jerusalem
Gaveaux
Conservez Bien La Paix Du Coeur
Dieu D'Israel Calme Mon Desespoir
Gavitt
I'm So Happy And Here's The
    Reason Why
Things Are Different Now
Gawthorn
Nature With Open Volume
O God Of Love O King Of Peace
Gay
Before The Barn-Door Crowing
Cease Your Funning
Come Sweet Lass
Good Rhine Wine, The
How Happy Could I Be With Either
Lambeth Walk
Leaning On A Lamp-Post
Song Of The Navy, The
There's Something About A Soldier
We Bear The Strain Of Earthly Care
Were I Laid On Greenland's Coast
Youth's The Season
Gaye
Come Get To This
Got To Give It Up
Got To Give It Up Part 1
If This World Were Mine
Mercy Mercy Me
Trouble Man
Gaye & Brown
Sexual Healing
Gaye & Cleveland & Benson
What's Going On
Gaye & Gaye
Baby I'm For Real

Gaye & Nyx
Inner City Blues
Inner City Blues Make Me Wanna
    Holler
Gaye & Stevenson & Gordy
Stubborn Kind Of Fellow
Gaye & Stevenson & Paul
Hitch-Hike
Gaye & Townsend
Let's Get It On
Gaylord
I Will Never Pass This Way Again
Gaynor
Leaves' Party, The
Little Shoemaker, The
Sweet Pea Ladies, The
Swing The Shining Sickle
Gaze
Calcutta
Gear
Sweet Visions
Geary
Man With The Ladder And The
    Hose, The
Gebhardi
Glory To God
Hymnus Angelicus
Gebhardt
O Heiliger Abend
Wie Ist Doch Der Abend So Traulich
Gebirtig
Es Brent
Lidl Fun Goldenem Land
Minutn Fun Bitokhn
Moyshele Mayn Fraynd
S'Brent
Geddins
Haunted House
Geehl
For You Alone
My World
Geffrard
Dessalinienne, La
Dessalinienne, The
National Anthem Of Haiti
Gehricke
Hunter's Life, A
Geibel
All And In All
Blessed Old Banner, The
Blessing For Me, A
Bright World Beyond, A
Easter-Tide
Glory To God
I Was Glad
In The Beautiful Light
Kentucky Babe
Marching On With Gladness
Praise The Lord O My Soul
Sleep My Little Jesus
Sleep Sleep Sleep
Some Day He'll Make It Plain
Stand Up Stand Up For Jesus

Geibel *(Cont.)*
This Day The Sound Upon The
    Street
Trust In The Lord With All Thine
    Heart
Twine The Garland
What Will You Do With Jesus
Who Is This King Of Glory
Wonderful Bible
Work For Jesus Everywhere
Geiger
Just For Tonight
Nur Eine Nacht
Geiger & Hatton
Our Wedding Prayer
Geiger & Mullis
This Missin' You Heart Of Mine
Geiger & Mullis & Rector
In The Middle Of The Night
Geirionnyd
Traditional
Geis
Lament For Brendan Behan
Gelbart
Dray Yingelech
Nakht, Di
Geld
Hurting Each Other
Sealed With A Kiss
Geldof
I Don't Like Mondays
Gelineau
By Gracious Powers So Wonderfully
    Sheltered
Gellert
Look Over Yonder
Genaro & Skylar
You're Breaking My Heart
General Public
Tenderness
Genge
In The Hour Of My Distress
Genns
Palisades, The
Gensler
Keep Smiling At Trouble
Gentry
1959
Drinkin' And Drivin'
Love's Been A Little Bit Hard On Me
Ode To Billy Joe
One I Loved Back Then, The
We Didn't See A Thing
Gentry & Detterline
Ride, The
Gentry & Owen & Fowler
Fallin' Again
Gentry & Scott
Why Lady Why
George
Broken And Spilled Out
Confederate Flag, The

George *(Cont.)*
For Home And Country
I Know
I'll Always Love You
If Ye Love Me Keep My
    Commandments
Mighty Fortress
Ride On Ride On In Majesty
Yellow Rose Of Texas, The
George & Carter & Browne
Love Needs A Heart
George & George & George & Bedeau
Can You Feel The Beat
George & George & George & Bedeau
    & Clark & Charle
I Wonder If I Take You Home
George & Pardini
Just To See Her
Georges
Rain, The
Geppert
Candle, A
Humming Bird, The
Geraci & Richards
Imprevu
Gerard & Armstrong
Sweet Adeline
Gerhardt
Guld'ne Sonne, Die
Gerig
On The Cross Of Calvary
German
Big Steamers
Camel's Hump
First Friend, The
Great And Mighty Wonder, A
I Am The Most Wise Baviaan
I Keep Six Honest Serving-Men
Kangaroo And Dingo
Merrow Down
Of All The Tribe Of Tegumai
Riddle, The
Rolling Down To Rio
There Was Never A Queen Like
    Balkis
This Uninhabited Island
When The Cabin Portholes
Gernhard & Holler
Snoopy Versus The Red Baron
Gernsheim
Gesuhnte Hirsch, Der
Gerovitch
Adon Olom
Sing Now With Joy Unto The Lord
Gerrard
Custom-Made Woman Blues
Gersbach
Getreues Herze Wissen, Ein
Lenz Thut Seinen Freudengruss, Der
Gershe
Born In A Trunk
Gershwin
Across The Sea
All The Livelong Day

Gershwin *(Cont.)*
American In Paris, An
Aren't You Kind Of Glad We Did
Babbitt And The Bromide, The
Back Bay Polka, The
Because Because
Beginner's Luck
Bess You Is My Woman
Best Of Everything, The
Bidin' My Time
Blue Blue Blue
Boy Wanted
Boy What Love Has Done To Me
But Not For Me
By Strauss
Changing My Tune
Cinderelatives
Clap Yo' Hands
Concerto In F Second Movement
Could You Use Me
Dancing Shoes
Delishious
Do It Again
Do-Do-Do
Embraceable You
Fascinating Rhythm
Feeling I'm Falling
Fidgety Feet
Foggy Day, A
For You For Me Forevermore
Funny Face
Half Of It Dearie Blues, The
Hang On To Me
He Loves And She Loves
High Hat
How Long Has This Been Going On
I Can't Be Bothered Now
I Don't Think I'll Fall In Love Today
I Got Plenty O' Nuttin'
I Got Rhythm
I Love To Rhyme
I Love You
I Loves You Porgy
I Need A Garden
I Was Doing All Right
I Was So Young
I'll Build A Stairway To Paradise
I've Got A Crush On You
In The Mandarin's Orchid Garden
Is Wonderful
Isn't It A Pity
It Ain't Necessarily So
Jijibo, The
Jolly Tar And The Milkmaid, The
Just Another Rhumba
K-Ra-Zy For You
Kickin' The Clouds Away
Kongo Kate
Let 'em Eat Cake
Let's Be Lonesome Together
Let's Call The Whole Thing Off
Let's Kiss And Make Up
Limehouse Nights

Gershwin (*Cont.*)
Little Jazz Bird
Liza
Looking For A Boy
Lorelei
Lorlei
Love Is Here To Stay
Love Is Sweeping The Country
Love Of A Wife, The
Love Walked In
Mademoiselle In New Rochelle
Mah-Jongg
Man I Love, The
Maybe
Military Dancing Drill
Mine
Mischa Yascha Toscha Sascha
My Cousin In Milwaukee
My Fair Lady
My Lady
My Man Is Gone Now
My Man's Gone Now
My One And Only
Nice Work If You Can Get It
Night Time In Araby
Nobody But You
Of Thee I Sing
Oh Bess Oh Where's My Bess
Oh Kay
Oh Lady Be Good
Poppyland
Prelude I
Prelude II
Prelude III
Real American Folk Song Is A Rag,
   The
Rhapsody In Blue
Rosalie
'S Wonderful
Sam And Delilah
Shall We Dance
She Hangs Out In Our Alley
Signal, The
Slap That Bass
So Am I
Some Rain Must Fall
Some Wonderful Sort Of Someone
Somebody Loves Me
Someone Believes In You
Someone To Watch Over Me
Soon
Sophia
South Sea Isles
Strike Up The Band
Summertime
Swanee
Sweet And Low-Down
That Certain Feeling
There Is Nothing Too Good For You
There's A Boat Dat's Leavin' Soon
   For New York
They All Laughed
They Can't Take That Away From
   Me
Things Are Looking Up

Gershwin (*Cont.*)
Three Times A Day
Treat Me Rough
Walking Home With Angeline
We're Pals
When Do We Dance
Who Cares
Who Cares So Long As You Care
   For Me
Wintergreen For President
Woman Is A Sometime Thing, A
You Desire To Be Divorce' From Dat
   Man Crown
You've Got What Gets Me
Gershwin & Daly
Innocent Ingenue Baby
Gershwin & Donaldson
Rialto Rag
Gershwin & Green
You And I In Old Versailles
Gershwin & Stothart
Song Of The Flame
Gersmehl
In His Name
Lord Of Glory
Love Them While We Can
We Are In His Hands
Gersmehl & Smiley
Following The King
Quiet Love
Gersmehl & Smiley & Lyles & Green
You Can Be As Full As You Want To
   Be
Gervaise
Si L'on Doit Prendre
Gesangbuch
Praise To The Lord
Gesius
Day Is Past And Over, The
Jesu My Lord My God My All
Light Along The Ages, The
O Beautiful My Country
O Christ Thou Bright And Morning
   Star
O Father All Creating
O God The Rock Of Ages
Our Father By Whose Servants
Gesius & Bach
Our Father By Whose Servants
Gessle
Dressed For Success
It Must Have Been Love
Look, The
Getry
Fievre Brulante, Une
Getz
Bridget Maguire
Getzov
Please Mr Sun
Gevaert
April
Coletta
Sommeil De L'enfant Jesus, Le

Geza
Gyere Cigany
Ghedini
A Un Muover D'Aria
Candida Mia Colomba
Canta Un Augello In Voce Si Suave
Datime A Piena Mano E Rose E Zigli
De' Maria Dolce
Diletto E Spavento Del Mare
Io Mi Viveva Senza Nullo Amore
Mentre Azzurri Splendono I Cieli
O Grande Spirito
Pellegrini Del Mondo
Presenze Naturali
Quiete Della Notte, La
Se Li Arbori Sapesser Favellare
Sia Benedetto Il Giorno Che Nascesti
Tu Te Ne Vai
Vento Rude
Ghys
Drip Drop Falls The Rain
Giacalone
You Were Mine
Gianangelo
Sing
Giant & Baum & Kaye
Do Not Disturb
Down By The Riverside
Everybody Come Aboard
Mirage
Roustabout
Shake That Tambourine
Shout It Out
Sound Of Your Cry, The
Spring Fever
This Is My Heaven
Today Tomorrow And Forever
You're The Devil In Disguise
Giant & Baum & Kaye
Beach Shack
Giardina
Biondina In Gindoleta, La
Come Porti I Capelli
E Come La Marcia Ben
E Le Stellette
Fenesta Che Lucive
Ma Come Bali Bela Bimba
Giardini
Christ For The World We Sing
Come O Thou God Of Grace
Come Thou Almighty King
Come Women Wide Proclaim
Glory To God On High
God Bless Our Native Land
It Came Upon The Midnight Clear
Italian Hymn
Not With Flashing Steel
Strong In The Living God
Thou Whose Almighty Word
Giasson
Cafe Di Roma
Ciao For Now
Holiday Time Of Year, The
Mi Amore Italiano

Gibault
Sing And Dance
Gibb
Band, The
Christmas Bells
Cookies
Dixie Lullaby
Everlasting Love, An
Follow The Flag
For America
Freedom's Torch
Give Us The Wintertime
Golden September
Grease
I Just Want To Be Your Everything
If I Can't Have You
Love Inside, The
Love You Inside Out
Mischievous Trolls, The
Mister Turkey
Morning Hymn
Rest Your Love On Me
Shadow March
She Believes In Me
Sing To The Lord
Squirrel Town
Thanksgiving Day
Gibb & Gibb
Come On Over
How Can You Mend A Broken Heart
New York Mining Disaster 1941
Gibb & Gibb & Gibb
Bodyguard
Chain Reaction
How Deep Is Your Love
Islands In The Stream
Jive Talkin'
Lonely Days
Love So Right
Night Fever
Nights On Broadway
One
Run To Me
Stayin' Alive
Too Much Heaven
Woman In Love
You Should Be Dancing
Gibb & Gibb & Gibb & Gibb
Shadow Dancing
Gibbons
Ages One Great Minster Seem, The
Ah Dear Heart Why Do You Rise
And Now O Father Mindful Of The
    Love
Christmas Day
Completed Lord The Holy Mysteries
Draw Nigh And Take The Body
Drop Drop Slow Tears
Eternal Ruler Of The Ceaseless
    Round
Forth In Thy Name O Lord I Go
Garden In The Rain, A
Gather Us In Thou Love That Fillest
    All

Gibbons *(Cont.)*
Give Me The Wings Of Faith To Rise
Go Labor On Spend And Be Spent
Hail We Now This Happy Morn
How Sweet And Silent Is The Place
In This Peaceful House Of Prayer
Jesu Grant Me This I Pray
Lead Us O Father
Lead Us O Father In The Paths Of
    Peace
Lord For Ever At Thy Side
Lord Jesu Who At Lazarus' Tomb
Lord When Thy Kingdom Comes
    Remember Me
Love Of The Father Love Of God
    The Son
My God Accept My Heart This Day
My Lord My Life My Love
O For A Heart To Praise My God
O Source Divine
O Word Immortal Of Eternal God
Peace Perfect Peace
Peace Perfect Peace In This Dark
    World Of Sin
Psalm 121
Silver Swan
Silver Swan, The
Song Of Deborah, The
Song Of Praise
Spirit Of God
Strong Son Of God
Strong Son Of God Immortal Love
We Are Coming Father Abraham
We Praise Thee Lord
Where Is Death's Sting
Wisdom Hath Treasures Greater
Word Whom Earth And Sea And
    Sky, The
Gibbons & Hill & Beard
Doubleback
Rough Boy
Sharp Dressed Man
Sleeping Bag
Stages
Gibbs
Dream Pedlary
Herrick's Ode
Nod
Runnin' Wild
Ship Of Rio, The
Silver
Slow Horses Slow
Spring
Gibbs & Harrington
Runnin' Wild
Gibney
Sailing Song
Gibson
All Night Long
Cactus Rag, The
Canaanland Is Just In Sight
Electric Youth
Foolish Beat
Give Myself A Party

Gibson *(Cont.)*
I Can't Stop Loving You
I Feel His Promise
Just One Time
Legend In My Time, A
Lonesome Number One
Look Down On Us O Lord
Lost In Your Eyes
National Anthem Of The Bahamas
Oh Lonesome Me
Only In My Dreams
Out Of The Blue
Shake Your Love
Sweet Dreams
There's A Meetin' Here Tonight
There's A Song In The Air
Through The Blood
We Are Those Children
Gibson & Karp
If It Don't Come Easy
**Gibson & Karp & Cook & Jenkins &
McFee**
Honey I Dare You
Gibson & Nelson
House On Old Lonesome Road
Gideon
Gone In Good Sooth You Are
Giefer
Who Threw The Overalls In Mistress
    Murphy's Chowder
Who Threw The Overalls In Mrs
    Murphy's Chowder
Gifford
She Sells Seashells
Smoke Rings
Gifford & Trevor
When It's Apple Blossom Time In
    Normandy
Gil
Dos Arbolitos
Gilbert
Christmas Is A Time
Farmer Went Trotting, A
Hail The Children's Festival Day
Jeannine
John Cook's Little Gray Mare
Lily Of The Valley
Lord Of Earth Thy Forming Hand
Mama Don't Want No Peas An Rice
    An Cocoanut Oil
Man That Broke The Bank At Monte
    Carlo, The
Man Who Broke The Bank At Monte
    Carlo, The
Pirate Song
Pleasant Are Thy Courts Above
Tell Me Where Is Fancy Bred
Whate'er My God Ordains Is Right
Zip-A-Dee Doo-Dah
Gilbert & Friedland
Lily Of The Valley
My Sweet Adair

Gilbert & Morgan
My Hawaiian Sunshine
Gilbert & Perfect
Mighty Oregon
Gilbert & Tek
What Gives
Gilbert & Thielheim & Esposito
We Ain't Got Nothin' Yet
Gilbreath
Lord Hath Done Great Things For
Us, The
Gilchrist
Another Morning Hymn
Bird's Nest, The
Boat Song
Boatman, The
Broken Doll, The
Carpenter, The
Children's Army, The
Dinkey Bird, The
Fairy And Child
Fiddle Dee Dee
Flag, The
Flying Bird, The
Gingham Dog And The Calico Cat,
The
Going To The Fair
Good-Night
If Blue-Birds Bloomed
In The Snowing And The Blowing
Kitty Cat
Little Boy Blue
Little Dance, A
Little John Bottlejohn
Little Window, The
Lullaby
March
Meadow Talk
Midsummer Frolics
Morning Hymn
Morning Song
Mother's Song
O Look At The Moon
Old Mother Hubbard
Our Country Friends
Points Of The Compass, The
Rippling Purling Little River
River Farm, The
Rock A Bye Baby
Seed Babies
Sick Bird, The
Spring
Star, The
Stop Stop Pretty Water
Summer Song
Three Little Kittens
Woodman, The
Gilder & McCulloch
Hot Child In The City
Gilder & Smith
On The Wild Rose Tree
Gilding
Lord My Shepherd Is, The
O Word Of God Above
'Tis Good Lord To Be Here

Giles & Green
Come On In
This Ol' Town
Giles & Longacre
If You Could Only See Me Now
Giles & Montgomery
I Wanna Hear It From You
Gilkyson
Bare Necessities, The
Thomas O'Malley Cat
Gilkyson & Dehr & Miller
Greenfields
Marianne
Memories Are Made Of This
Gill
Battle Of Santwat, The
Gotta Get Away
Gill & Johnson & O'Toole
Relax
Two Tribes
Gillespie
Bebop
Heaven's Just A Sin Away
We Just Gotta Dance
Gillespie & Dillea & Fisher
Absence Makes The Heart Grown
Fonder
Gillespie & Paparelli
And The Melody Still Lingers On
Night In Tunisia, A
Gillespie & Simons & Whiting
Breezin' Along With The Breeze
Honey
**Gillespie & Van Alstyn & Schmidt &
Curtis**
See Van Alstyne
Gillette
Hail Wesleyan
Gillier
Auparavant
Envers Du Th'eatre, L'
Lullaby
Gilliers
Joli Moulin, Le
Gillyard & Morris & Chambliss
Let Me Lay My Funk On You
Gilmore
For Bales
God Save Our Union
I Do Not Ask To Choose My Path
Sad News From Home
We Are Coming Father Abra'am
When Johnny Comes Marching
Home
When Johnny Comes Marching
Home Again
Gilmore & Bradbury
He Leadeth Me
Gilmore & Simon & Allison
What Am I Gonna Do About You
Gilmour
Blessed Hiding
Cleanse And Fill Me
Gospel Feast, The

Gilmour (Cont.)
He Rolled The Sea Away
Like A Mighty Sea
Love Found Me
Gilpin
My Light And My Salvation
My Shepherd's Voice
Gilroy
I Sing A Little Tenor
Gilroy & Bray
Right On Track
Gimbel
Making Our Dreams Come True
Ginastera
North Argentinian Folk-Dance
Giordani
Caro Mio Ben
Dearest Believe
My Own Dear One
Giordano
E L'April Che Torna A Me
March Of The Wildcats
O Pastorelle Addio
Parting Chorus
When You Look At Me
Giorza
Love Me
Giosari & Zwirn
Sorry
Giosasi & Zwirn
Sorry
Sorry I Ran All The Way Home
Giovanelli
You Defy Me Beloved Foe
Giovannini
Wilt Thou Thy Heart Surrender
Giraud
A Propos De Pommier
Under Paris Skies
Girshner
Have A Care
Gist
Our Last Night Together
Gladden
Mountains, The
Gladden & Smith
O Master Let Me Walk With Thee
Gladstone
Dear God The Sun Whose Light Is
Sweet
God Of The Strong God Of The
Weak
Jesus Thou Joy Of Loving Hearts
Glanzberg
Ballet Des Coeurs, Le
Il Fait Bon T'aimer
Glapser & Lillington
Don't Tell Me Lies
Glaser
Azmon
Come Holy Spirit Heavenly Dove
Head That Once Was Crowned, The
Head That Once Was Crowned With
Thorns, The

Glaser *(Cont.)*
In All My Lord's Appointed Ways
Jesus The Name High Over All
Jesus Thine All-Victorious Love
Lange Nacht Entfliehet, Die
My God The Spring Of All My Joys
O For A Faith That Will Not Shrink
O For A Thousand Tongues To Sing
On Top Of Spaghetti
Song Of Hope
Thousand Oracles Divine, A
Through All The Changing Scenes
   Of Love
We Plough The Fields

Glaser & Payne
Woman Woman

Glaser & Wolff
Same Merry-Go-Round, The

Glasper & Lillington
All This I Should Have Known
Don't Tell Me Lies
Hands To Heaven
How Can I Fall

Glass
Broom The Shovel The Poker And
   The Tongs, The
Calico Pie
Courtship Of The
   Yonghy-Bonghy-Bo
Daddy Long-Legs And The Fly, The
Duck And The Kangaroo, The
He Wants My Body
Jumblies, The
Mr And Mrs Spikky Sparrow
Olympian Lighting Of The Torch,
   The
Owl And The Pussy-Cat, The
Quangle Wangle's Hat, The
Table And The Chair, The

Glass & Masser & Goffin
Miss You Like Crazy

Glass & Tiger & Vallance
Don't Forget Me

Glass & Walden & Johnson
Rock-A-Lott

Glasser
O For A Thousand Tongues To Sing

Glassmeyer
One Man's Woman

Glassmeyer & Struble
What A Way To Start The Day

Glazer
Automation
Mill Was Made Of Marble, The
On Top Of Spaghetti
Too Old To Work
We Bear The Strain Of Earthly Care

Gleason
Bivouac Of The Dead, The

Glenn
Crying In The Chapel
In Blossom

Glenn & Quander
Caught In The Rapture
Caught Up In The Rapture

Glenville & Miller
If You're Irish Come Into The Parlor

Glick
Shtil Di Nacht
Shtil Di Nakht Iz Oysgeshternt
Zog Nit Keyn Mol

Gliere
Three Holy Kings, The

Glinka
Doubt
Rejoice And Be Happy
Where Is Our Rose

Glogau
It Takes A Great Big Irish Heart To
   Sing An Irish Song

Glover
Christmas Bells
Do They Think Of Me At Home
Good-Bye At The Door, The
In The Starlight
Loving Voices
Meek And Lowly
Melodies Of Many Lands
Mother Are There Angels Dwelling
Old Familiar Place, The
Rose Of Tralee, The
Wandering In The Maytime
What Are The Wild Waves Saying

Glover & Dee
Peppermint Twist
Peppermint Twist Part I

Glover & Dee & Levy
Hey Let's Twist

Glover & Levy
California Sun

Glover & Robinson & Robinson
Vice

Glover & Spencer
Rose Of Tralee, The

Glover & Spencer & Lawrence
Let The Little Girl Dance

Glover-Kind
I Do Like To Be Beside The Seaside

Gluck
Ah Si La Liberte
Arie Der Alceste
Beloved Strand
Broken Ring, The
Che Faro Senza Euridice
Diruptus Anellus
Divinites Du Styx
From The Realm Of Souls Departed
Gebet
Gracious Saviour
I Have Lost My Euridice
I Have Lost My Eurydice
If Here Where All Is Dark And Silent
J'ai Perdu Mon Eurydice
Laissez-Vous Toucher Par Mes
   Pleurs

Gluck *(Cont.)*
Non Ce N'est Pas Un Sacrifice
Non Ce N'est Point Un Sacrifice
O Del Mio Dolce Ardor
O Du Die Mir Einst Hilfe Gab
O Lasst Mich Tiefgebeugte
O Saviour Hear Me
On S'etonnerait Moins
Par Un Pere Cruel
Saviour Like A Shepherd Lead Us
See What Grace
Sommernacht, Die
Today A Solemn Stillness
Unis Des La Plus Tendre Enfance
Untreue
Vieni Che Poi Sereno
Voici La Charmante Retraite
Why They Sang
Within A Quiet Valley
Ye Awful Stygian Powers

Glynn
Great Creator Of The Worlds, The
O Sometimes Gleams Upon Our
   Sight
Sing Men And Angels Sing

Goate
Trip Along Bright Feet Of May

Gobble
Spirit Of The Hill, The

Gober
We'll Never Turn Back

Goble
Lady
Reminiscing

Gockel-Gussen
Alabama

Godard
Amour, L'
Berceuse
Chanson De Florian
Do You Remember
Florian's Song
Flower Of The Valley
Love
Lullaby
Mother's Prayer
Naught Else
Te Souviens-Tu
Tell Me Now
Tell Me Pray

Godchaux
Sunrise

Goddard
Riding

Godfrey
Curious Things
Gentle Jesus Meek And Mild
Life Of Ages Richly Poured
Lincoln
Parade, The
Take My Life And Let It Be
Washington And Lincoln

Godfrey & Bruce
Sleepy Time Time
Godfrey & Erwin
Christmas Day Is Just Around The
Corner
Godfrey & Gillis & Weeks
Every Christmas Morning
Godfrey & Hatton
Softly Fall The Shades Of Evening
Godfrey & Sheridan
Who Were You With Last Night
Godley & Creme
Cry
Godwin
Ling Ting Tong
Goeckel
Red And Blue, The
Sons Of Commerce
Goemanne
O Love Who Drew From Jesus' Side
Goepp
Fisher Song
Goering & Bernie
Who's Your Little Who-Zis
Goethe
King Of Thule, The
Rattenfanger, Der
Wanderer's Night Song
Goetz
O Holy One
Goetz & Stern
We're Going To Celebrate The End
Of The War In Rag
Goetz & Young & Wendling
Yaaka Hula Hickey Dula
Goetze
O Lovely Day O Happy Day
O Schone Zeit
Goff
Please Search The Book Again
Tears Will Stop This Side Of Heaven
Goffin & King
Can't You Be Real
Chains
Don't Bring Me Down
Down Home
Go Away Little Girl
Halfway To Paradise
Hey Girl
Hi-De-Ho
I Can't Stay Mad At You
It Might As Well Rain Until
September
Keep Your Hands Off My Baby
Loco-Motion, The
On No Not My Baby
One Fine Day
Smackwater Jack
Snow Queen
So Much Love
Some Kind Of Wonderful
Take Good Care Of My Baby
Time Don't Run Out On Me
Up On The Roof

Goffin & King *(Cont.)*
Wasn't Born To Follow
What A Sweet Thing That Was
Where Does Love Go
Will You Love Me Tomorrow
Goffin & King & Wexler
Natural Woman, A
Goffin & Masser
Nothing's Gonna Change My Love
For You
Tonight I Celebrate
Tonight I Celebrate My Love
Tonight I Celebrate My Love For
You
Goguel
Moorsoldaten
Gold
Exodus Song, The
Lonely Boy
Nice To Be With You
Tell Me Why
Thank You For Being A Friend
Theme From Exodus
Gold & Gouldman
Right Between The Eyes
Gold & Mason & Stookey
Hymn
Goldberg
Legion Buddies
Printemps Bien-Aime
Golde
Indian Summer
Own The Night
Golde & McFadden
Fallin' In Love
Golde & Willis
Be There
Golden
It's Not So Easy Leavin'
Goldenberg
Friends Forever
Our House
Soul Kiss
Theme From Alias Smith And Jones
Theme From Banacek
Theme From Columbo
Theme From Kojak
Goldfaden
Rozhinkes Mit Mandlen
Goldfarb
Ark, The
At Dawn I Seek Thee
Foolish Lot
King's Song, The
My Dredl
Roses Raisins And Almonds
Shalom Alechem
Sholom Alehem
Tower Of Babel, The
Goldman
Boy Scouts Of America
How Many Times Can We Say
Goodbye
On The Mall

Goldmark
Beschworung
Er Sagt Mir So Viel
Franz
Herzelied
In The Garden
Kahle Grab, Das
Marie
O Willst Mich Nicht Mitnehmen
Quelle, Die
Schlage Nicht Die Feuchten Augen
Nieder
So Lach Doch Einmal
Song Of Sorrow
Sonntagsruhe
Strom' Leise
Wald Wird Dichter, Der
Weinet Um Sie
Wenn Die Lerche Zicht
Wir Gingen Zusammen
Wollt Er Nur Fragen
Goldmark & Galdston
That's Not The Way
That's Not The Way It's S'Posed To
Be
That's Not The Way It's Supposed
To Be
Goldmark & Roberts
Flames Of Paradise
You Should Be Mine
Goldsboro
Autumn Of My Life
Cowboy And The Lady, The
Cowgirl And The Dandy, The
With Pen In Hand
Goldsborough
Door Is Open, The
Goldsmith
And We Were Lovers
Chinatown
Flying Dreams
Free As The Wind
Gizmo
Moon's A Window To Heaven, The
Nights Are Forever
Patton Theme, The
Piper Dreams, The
Police Story
Theme From Police Story
Theme From Room 222
Theme From The Girl From UNCLE
Theme From The Man From UNCLE
Waltons, The
Goldsmith & Rugolo
Theme From Dr Kildare
Goldsworthy
I Know Not How That Bethl'hem's
Babe
I Know Not How That Bethlehem's
Babe
Golightly
Pacolet
Golmann
Ma Guitare Et Moi

Golson
I Remember Clifford
Whisper Not
Golub
Tanchum
Gombert
Changeons Propos
Vous Etes Trop Jeune
Gonzales
Love's Lament
Gonzalez
Flor De Lodo
Gonzalez & Baskin
Little Girl
Gooch
Reuben And Rachel
Good
Someday When Jesus Comes
Goodale
Where Once The Indian Trod
Goodell
America My Country
Limericks
Mules
On Mules We Find
Goodeve
Fiddle And I
Goodhart
Bells Of Clermont Town, The
God Of Our Fathers Unto Thee
Goodman
Break Down The Walls
City Of New Orleans
Had It Not Been
He Speaks To Me
Headin' Home
I Believe He's Coming Back
Jesus Knows All About It
John The Revelator
Leavin' On My Mind
Look For Me
New York Times Home Delivery,
The
Until You've Known The Love Of
God
Wait'll You See My Brand New
Home
We're Almost Home
Who Am I
Woodsman, The
Goodman & Binion
Darkness Is Under His Feet, The
Friendly Fire
Goodman & Davis
I Wouldn't Take Nothing For My
Journey Now
Goodman & Lehman & Sykes
Fairest Of Ten Thousand
Goodman & Minick
He Keeps Lifting
Goodman & Moore
In The Arms Of My Best Friend
Goodman & Mundy & Christian
Air Mail Special

Goodman & Ross & Sykes
Let Them Go
Goodman & Ryles
Midnight Blue
Goodman & Sampson & Parish
Don't Be That Way
Goodman & Sykes
Help Me Love My Brother
Love Everybody In The World
Love Never Fails
Promises
King Of Who I Am, The
Goodman & Sykes & Goodman
Worthy
Goodman & Toler
Don't Look Back
Goodman & Upson & Poulton
Little Mother Of The Hills
Goodman & Webb & Sampson
Stompin' At The Savoy
Goodrich
After Calvary
O Lord Our God Almighty King
Goodrick
Summer Band Camp
Goodrum
Bluer Than Blue
Broken Hearted Me, A
What Are We Doin' In Love
You Needed Me
Goodrum & Kipner
Hindsight 2020
If She Would Have Been Faithful
Goodrum & Maher
Put You Back On The Rack
Goodrum & Masser
Crazy Love
Goodwin
All Quiet Along The Potomac
Ling Ting Tong
That Wonderful Mother Of Mine
Gordigiani
Benediction, The
Gordon
All My Trials
Don't Take Away My PWA
Fried Bananas
Georgia Rainbow
Here Comes Cookie
In Tenderness He Sought Me
It's Spring Again
Lord Jesus I Love Thee
Mister And Mississippi
My Heart Belongs To Me
My Jesus I Love Thee
Nine-Tenths Of The Tennessee River
Too Fat For The Chimney
Two Brothers
Unforgettable
Gordon & Connor
Down In The Glen
Gordon & Gruska
Friends And Lovers
Friends And Lovers Both To Each
Other

Gordon & Hughes
Dear Ould Dart, The
Gordon & Revel
Goodnight My Love
Meet The Beat Of My Heart
Never In A Million Years
Paris In The Spring
Stay As Sweet As You Are
There's A Lull In My Life
When I'm With You
You Can't Have Everything
Gordon & Rich
M-A-R-Y I Love You
Gordy
Do You Love Me
Try It Baby
Gordy & Bradford
Money
Money That's What I Want
Gordy & Carlo
I'll Be Satisfied
That's Why I Love You So
Gordy & Carlo & Robinson
Got A Job
Gordy & Davis & Hutch & West
I'll Be There
Gordy & Gordy & Carlo
Lonely Teardrops
To Be Loved
You've Got What It Takes
**Gordy & Holloway & Wilson &
Holloway**
You've Made Me So Very Happy
Gordy & Hutch
Hello Detroit
Gordy & Jon
I Love The Way You Love
Gordy & Robinson
Shop Around
Gore
Fame
Out Here On My Own
People Are People
Red Light
Theme From Terms Of Endearment
Goring-Thomas
Midday In The Village
Gorman & McGear & McGough
Lily The Pink
Gorner
An Den Schlaf
Gorney
Brother Can You Spare A Dime
Four Rivers, The
Mister Roosevelt Won't You Please
Run Again
Mr Roosevelt Won't You Please Run
Again
Gorochov
Saleynu
Gorres
Hail Virgin Dearest Mary

Gosdin & Barnes
Chiseled In Stone
That Just About Does It
Gosdin & Barnes & Cochran
This Ain't My First Rodeo
Gosdin & Cochran
Who You Gonna Blame It On This
Time
Gosdin & Cochran & Vickery
Right In The Wrong Direction
Gosdin & Dillon & Cannon
Back In The Swing Of Things
Gosdin & Halupke
Pictures
Gosdin & Le Gosdin & Cannon
I'm Still Crazy
Gosling & Hawkshaw
Country Girl
Goss
Behold A Little Child
Christ Shall Have Dominion
Cornerstone, The
Enkindling Love Eternal Flame
From Out The Rock Whence We
Were Hewn
March On O Soul With Strength
More Than Conquerors
O Master It Is Good To Be
O Saviour Of The World
O Taste And See How Gracious The
Lord Is
Ornerston, The
Praise My Soul The King Of Heaven
See Amid The Winter's Snow
Thanks To God Whose Word Was
Spoken
We Are On The Lord's Side
Weep Not For A Brother Deceased
Who Is On The Lord's Side
Winter's Snow
Gossec
Hymn To Voltaire
Victory March
Gotha
Come Thou Long-Expected Jesus
Gottler
America I Love You
Would You Rather Be A Colonel
With An Eagle On You
Gottschalk
Comes The Pleasant Autumn
God Of Love That Hearest Prayer
Holy Ghost With Light Divine
Holy Spirit Truth Divine
Lord As We Thy Name Profess
Lord Before Thy Presence Come
Mardi Gras
Ninnarella, La
Now The Shadows Of Night Are
Gone
O Loving Heart Trust On
Sinner What Hast Thou To Show
Sleep Be Thine Baby Mine
Softly Now As The Light Of Day

Gottschalk *(Cont.)*
Softly Now The Light Of Day
Souvenir De Porto Rico
Sov'reign And Transforming Grace
Thine Forever God Of Love
Gotze
O Happy Day
Still As The Night
Still Wie Die Nacht
Goudimel
Closing Hymns
Comfort Comfort Ye My People
Old Hundred
Qui Renforcera Ma Voix
Unwise Man, The
Virgin Born We Bow Before Thee
Gould
Again The Lord Of Life And Light
Behold, A Stranger At The Door
Bud Will Soon Become A Flower,
The
Come Gracious Lord Descend And
Dwell
Elder Brother
I Got A One Track Mind
Jesu Heiland Steu're Du
Jesus Savior Pilot Me
Jesus Saviour Pilot Me
Nothin' For Nothin'
O Thou To Whose All Searching
Sight
Oh Cease My Wandering Soul
One Lord There Is
Sing To The Great Jehovah's Praise
Star Of Peace
There Is An Hour Of Peaceful Rest
There Must Be Somethin' Better
Than This
To Thee I Come
Watch America
Who Is Sylvia
Woodland
Goulding
Mam'selle
Gouldman
Bus Stop
For Your Love
Listen People
Gounod
Adore And Be Still
After The Night Dawns The Morrow
Agnus Dei
Ah I Love Thee Only
Ah Je Ris De Me Voir
Ah Je Veux Vivre
Ah The Joy Past Compare
Anges Purs
Avant De Quitter
Ave Maria
Be Mine The Delight
Blessed Is He
Blessed Is He Who Cometh
Canti Ridi Dormi

Gounod *(Cont.)*
Careless Idle Maiden
Cavatina
Chorus Of Bacchantes
Christ Whose Glory Fills The Skies
Christmas Song
Come Unto Him
Cradled All Lowly
Cross Of Calvary, The
Dawn And Twilight
Dio Possente
Dites La Jeune Belle
Domine Salvam Fac
Easter Hymn
Entreat Me Not To Leave Thee
Even Bravest Heart
Even Bravest Heart May Swell
Even The Bravest Heart May Swell
Evening
Fair, The
Faites-Lui Mes Aveux
Flower Song
Forget-Me-Not
From Thee Apart
Funeral March Of A Marionette
Funeral March Of The Marionettes
Gloire Immortelle
Glory To Thee My God This Night
Guardian Angel, The
Houses Of Worship
Hymne A La Nuit
If Happy Fortune
Jahr Ist Nun Zu Ende, Das
King Of Love My Shepherd Is, The
King Of Thule, The
Laisse-Moi
Let Me Gaze
Let Me Gaze On The Vision
Light As Air At Early Morning
Lovely Appear
Lovely Flowers
Lovely Flowers I Pray
Marche
Margherita
Marguerita
Mighty Land Wondrous Land
Nazareth
Ne Permettrez-Vous Pas
Nightingale, The
O Divine Redeemer
O Gentle Nigh
O God Not Only In Distress
O How Can They Look Up To
Heaven
O Tender Moon
O That We Two Were Maying
Oh Tender Moon
Parce Domine
Part In Peace
Peasant Chorus
Praise Ye The Father
Ring Out Wild Bells
Salut Demeure
Saviour Now The Day Is Ending
Scene Et Air Des Bijoux

Gounod (Cont.)
Send Out Thy Light
Serenade
Sing Smile Slumber
Soldier's Chorus
Soldier's Chorus From Faust
Song Jest Perfume And Dances
There Is A Green Hill Far Away
To Spring
Toast To Wisconsin
Unfold Ye Portals
Until The Day Breaks
Vin Ou Biere
Vous Qui Faites L'Endormie
Waltz
Waltz And Chorus
Waltz Song
What Grief Can Try Me O Lord
When Joyous Thoughts

Gourd
Gipsy's Warning, The

Gourley
In The Sunlight Of His Love

Gow
Caller Herrin'
Cam' Ye By Athole
Flora Macdonald's Lament
Hark Alma Mater
On The Chapel Steps
Will Ye No' Come Back Again

Gower
Father Hear Thy Children's Call
God Of Our Fathers Known Of Old
Hail Gladdening Light
Haze On The Far Horizon, A
O God Unseen Yet Ever Near
O Young Meriner
See Israel's Gentle Shepherd Stand
Stand Fast For Christ Thy Saviour
There Is A Green Hill Far Away
Thy Work O God Needs Many
Hands

Graben-Hoffmann
Forget-Me-Not

Gracey
Wonderful Babe, A

Grady & Carlo
That's Why

Graeff & Hall
Does Jesus Care

Graff
Christmas Bells
Happy Happy Easter Day

Grafton & Lauder
Breakfast In My Bed On Sunday
Mornin'
I Love A Lassie
Wee Deoch And Doris, A

Graham
After A Rain At Mokanshan
Dear Old Donegal
Drill Song, A

Graham (Cont.)
Give Me Back That Old Familiar
Feeling
He's Only A Prayer Away
I Ain't Got Nobody
Locomotives' Song, The
Old Account Settled, An
Picture That Is Turned Toward The
Wall, The
Prospect
Two Little Girls In Blue
When Witches Ride
You Better Go Now

Graham & Good
Through His Eyes

Graham & Richmond
Shining Star

Grahame Of Claverhouse
Bonnie Dundee

Grainer
That Was The Week That Was

Grainger & Robbins
'Tain't Nobody's Biz-Ness If I Do

Gramblin
Pilgrim's Lot, The

Grambling
Milledgeville
Mission
Narrow Way, The
Prospect Of Heaven

Gramm
Up Socialist Comrades

Gramm & Knight
Just Between You And Me

Gramm & Turgon
Midnight Blue

Granada
Humildes Peregrinos

Granados
Amor Y Odio
Callejeo
Canto Gitano
Currutacas Modestas, Las
Descubrase El Pensamiento De Me
Secreto Cuidado
Elegia Eterna
Gracia Mia
Iban Al Pinar
Llorad Corazon Que Teneis Razon
Maja De Goya, La
Maja Dolorosa No. 1, La
Maja Dolorosa No. 2, La
Maja Dolorosa No. 3, La
Majo Discreto, El
Majo Olvidado, El
Majo Timido, El
Mananica Era
Mirar De La Maja, El
No Lloreis Ojuelos
Ocell Profeta, L'G
Playera
Si Al Retiro Me Llevas
Tra La La Y El Punteado, El
Villanesca

Granata
Marina

Grand & Boyd
Guess Who I Saw Today

Grandval
Vendanges, Les

Granier
Hosanna

Grannis
Do They Miss Me At Home
Do They Miss Me In The Trenches
Vocal Miner, The
Your Mission

Grant
Arrah Go On I'm Gonna Go Back To
Oregon
Baby Come Back
Brand New Start
Election In Jungle Town, The
Entreat Me Not To Leave Thee
I'm Gonna Fly
If I Could've Been
If I Knock The L Out Of Kelly It
Would Still Be Kelly To Me
My Barney Lies Over The Ocean Just
The Way He Lied
Thank Heaven For You

Grant & Bannister & Christian
So Glad
Too Late

Grant & Bannister & Keister & Smith
Got To Let It Go

Grant & Chapman
Don't Run Away
Tennessee Christmas

Grant & Chapman & Hibbard
Open Arms
Tomorrow

**Grant & Chapman & Keister &
Bannister**
In A Little While

Grant & Chapman & McPherson
1974

Grant & Christian
Too Late

Grant & Cole
Say Once More

Grant & Eaton
Sharayah

Grant & Farrell & Bannister
Heirlooms

Grant & Huff & Naish
All Right

**Grant & Kirkpatrick & Chapman &
McP**
Wait For The Healing

Grant & McPherson
If You Have To Go Away

Grant & Peris & Peris
Shadows

Grant & Smith
Christmas Hymn
Faithless Heart
Find A Way

Grant & Smith (Cont.)
I Love You
Thy Word
Where Do You Hide Your Heart
Grant & Smith & Kirkpatrick
Lead Me On
Grant & Smith & Peters
Saved By Love
Grant & Troccoli
Raining On The Inside
Grant & Whitfield & Holland
I'm Losing You
Grant-Schaefer
Airships
Attic, The
Cuckoo Clock, The
Twilight Song
Wind Speaks, The
Granville
Baby, The
Lady-Bird
Grape
All To Christ I Owe
I Hear The Savior Say
I Hear The Saviour Say
Jesus Paid It All
Grasmuck & Gruber & Pfleger
Live Is Life
Grasmuck & Gruber & Pfleger &
Plisnier & Tremschni
Live Is Life
Grason
Southern Song
Graun
Auferstehung, Die
Graves
Boatman's Baby, The
Carol Of The Mouse, The
Dawn On The River
Good Sailing
Moon And Stars, The
Not Much To Eat
Poet Aboard
Race Of The Dragon Boats, The
Rain On A Winter Night
Raising The Anchor
Gray
Church Across The Way, The
Dream Of Paradise, A
In Exchange
Pennsylvania 6-5000
She Is More To Be Pitied
She Is More To Be Pitied Than
Censured
String Of Pearls, A
When Christ Was Born In Bethlehem
Gray & Buckingham & Buckingham
Nice Girls Think About It
Gray & Elms
Theme From Space 1999
Gray & Harrington
Wounded Hearts
Gray & Harrington & Taylor
It Ain't Easy Bein' Easy

Gray & Lemaire & Woods
Left Side Of The Bed
Gray & Pennington
Closer You Get, The
Take Me Down
Gray & Tipton & Karp
Second Hand Heart
Graydon & Champlin
Smile Again
Graydon & Foster & Kipner
Nothing You Can Do About It
Graydon & Jarreau & Foster
Mornin'
Graydon & Mathieson & Veitch
Trouble In Paradise
Graydon & Nevil & Mueller
Someone
Graydon & Page
On The Boulevard
Ready For Anything
Graydon & Paul
Twilight Tone
Grayson
Handsome Molly
Grean
Thing, The
Greatorex
Defend Us Lord From Every Ill
Gloria Patri
Glory Be To The Father
Great God Of Nations
Great God Of Nations Now To Thee
How Rich Thy Bounty King Of
Kings
Laborers Of Christ Arise
Land Of Our Hearts
Lift Up Your Hearts
Lord When We Bow Before Thy
Throne
My God I Love Thee
My Soul Be On Thy Guard
O For A Heart Of Calm Repose
Rise Crowned With Light Imperial
Salem Rise
Strong Son Of God Immortal Love
Tell Out My Soul The Greatness Of
The Lord
There Is A Name I Love To Hear
Greco
Gloria
Green
Asleep In The Light
Betty Boop
Black Magic Woman
Body And Soul
Come To Me
Gifts
Good Man Is Hard To Find, A
Great Washington
How Can They Live Without Jesus
I Cover The Waterfront
I Loved My Friend
I Wanna Be Loved
I'm Going Back To Old Kentucky

Green (Cont.)
I'm Yours
It's Almost Time
Lonely Yukon Stars
Love With Me
O Thou In All Thy Might So Far
Oh Lord You're Beautiful
Out Of Nowhere
Song Of Raintree County
That's How The Yodel Was Born
There's A River Rolling Deep
We're The Light
Green & Brown
Sentimental Journey
Green & Brown & Homer
Sentimental Journey
Green & Hodges
Take Me To The River
Green & Mohr & Lyles & Naish
Other Side Of The Grave
Green & Ruby & Stept
I'll Always Be In Love With You
Green & Step
It's A Swingy Little Thingy
That's My Weakness Now
Greenaway & Cook
You've Got Your Troubles
Greenaway & Mason
Say You'll Stay Until Tomorrow
Greenaway & Stephens
It's Like We Never Said Goodbye
Greenberg
Funkytown
Greene
Across The Alley From The Alamo
Come All Noble Souls
Eheu Fugaces
Integer Vitae
So Peaceful Rests
Greene & Beal
Softly
Greenebaum & Seals & Setser
Down On The Farm
Greenfield & Keller
Bewitched
Ev'rybody's Somebody's Fool
Hazel
My Gidget
Venus In Blue Jeans
Greenhill
Autolycus' Song
Time You Old Gipsy Man
Greenwich
God Bless The USA
Greenwood
By Your Stripes
God Bless The USA
Greer
Freshie
Just You Just Me
You Can't Tell A Lie To Your Heart
Gregh
Fatma

Gregor
  Hosanna
  Segne Und Behute Uns
Gregorian
  Lord's Prayer, The
Greig
  Alte Lied, Das
  Alte Mutter, Die
  Am Schonsten Sommerabend Wars
  An Den Bahre Einer Jungen Frau
  An Einem Bache
  Bursch, Der
  Traum, Ein
Grein
  Bread Upon The Water
  More Than Conquerors
Grein & Grein
  By His Word
Greiter
  O Faith Of England Taught Of Old
Greith
  O Sanctissima
  Schweizerknabe, Der
Grenet
  Amor Sincero, El
  Asuncion
  Clave De Oro, La
  Conga, La
  Mama Inez
  Maraquero, El
  Marimbulero, El
  Rosita La Bonita
  Viene La Conga
Gretchani
  Autumn
Gretchaninov
  Ai-Doo-Doo
  Autumn
  Calling Of The Spring, The
  Cherubic Hymn, The
  Cherubim Song
  Hymn Of Free Russia
  Kolibelnaya
  Over The Steppe
  Slumber Song
  Styepyoo Eedoo
  Sun And Moon
Gretry
  Bon Dieu Bon Dieu Comme A C'Te
    Fete
  Danse N'est Pas Ce Que J'aime, La
  De Ma Barque Legere
  Du Destin Qui T'accable
  Garde Passe, La
  Je Crains De Lui Parler La Nuit
  Laisse En Paix Le Dieu Des Combats
  Ma Barque Legere
  Plus De Depit Plus De Tristesse
  Rose Cherie
  Si Des Tristes Cypres
  Tandis Que Tout Sommeille
  To Norway
  Veillons Mes Soeurs
  Vous Etiez Ce Que Vous N'etes Plus
  Watch Is Passing, The

Grever
  C'est Ma Vie
  Jurame
  Magic Is The Moonlight
  Rataplan
  What A Diff'rence A Day Made
  What A Difference A Day Made
Grey
  Roses In The Garden, The
Grieg
  Am Grabe Der Mutter
  Auf Der Reise Zur Heimat
  Auf Der Reise Zur Heimath
  Boat Song
  Brothers Sing On
  By The Brook
  Cottage, The
  Dairymaid, The
  Day In The Country, A
  Dereinst Gedanke Mein
  Des Dichters Herz
  Down The Dark Future
  Dream, A
  Echo Song
  Eros
  Erste, Das
  Erstes Begegnan
  Erstes Begegnen
  Farmyard
  Farmyard Song
  First Meeting, The
  First Primrose
  Freundschaftsstuck, Ein
  Fruhling, Der
  Garden Sleeps, The
  Good Morning
  Gruss
  Guten Morgen
  Hail To Tomorrow
  Herbststurm
  I Love Thee
  I Love You
  Ich Liebe Dich
  Im Kahne
  In The Boat
  In The Hall Of The Mountain King
  Kind Der Berge, Das
  Lauf Der Welt
  Lenz Soll Mein Lied Erklingen, Der
  Lichte Nacht
  Liebe
  Loyal Sons Of Glockenheim
  Margarethens Wiegenlied
  Mein Sinn Ist Wie Der Macht'ge Fels
  Millom Rosor
  Mit Einer Primula Veris
  Mit Einer Wasserlilie
  Morgenthau
  Morning
  Mother's Sorrow, A
  Mutter Singt, Die
  Mutterschmerz
  My Native Land
  National Song

Grieg *(Cont.)*
  Norwegian Dance
  Norwegian Song
  O Happy Happy Children
  O Native Land How Fair You Seem
  Oh Lord So Wondrous
  Old Mother
  One Summer Night
  Onward The Brood
  Our Native Land
  Pretty Margaret
  Princess, The
  Prinzessin, Die
  Ragna
  Ragnhild
  Return To The Mountain Home
  Schwan, Ein
  Sieh' Dich Vor
  Solvejg's Song
  Solvejgs Lied
  Solvejgs Wiegenlied
  Song To The Christmas Tree
  Spielmannslied
  Springtide
  Stately Dance, A
  Stelldichein
  Sunshine Song
  Swan, A
  Traume
  Two Brown Eyes
  Vaaren
  Verborg'ne Liebe
  Verschwiegene Nachtigall, Die
  Verwundete, Der
  Vom Monte Pincio
  Waldwanderung
  Wandering In The Woods
  Was Ich Sah
  Watchman's Song
  Who Goes There In The Night
  Wiegenlied
  With A Violet
  With A Water Lily
  Zur Rosenzeit
Griesenbeck
  Song Of The Cowboy, A
Griffes
  Auf Geheimem Waldespfade
  Auf Ihrem Grab
  Ballons, Les
  Cleopatra To The Asp
  In The Harem
  Lament Of Ian The Proud, The
  Phantoms
  Pierrot
  Two Birds Flew Into The Sunset
    Glow
  Water-Lily, The
  Wohl Lag Ich Einst In Gram Und
    Schmerz
Griffin
  Changing Keys
  I Love My Love In The Morning
  Jeopardy Theme

Griffin *(Cont.)*
 My Greenwood Home
 Place In Thy Memory, A
Griffin & Gordon
 Apologize
Griffith
 Art Thou Weary Art Thou Languid
Griffiths
 Most Holy God The Lord Of Heaven
 O Love Of God How Strong And
  True
Griggs
 My Sins Are Gone
Grill
 Julida Polka
Grille
 Shine Glorious Sun
Grime
 Children Who Live Across The Sea
Grimes
 What Shall I Give Thee Master
Grimley
 Backward We Look O God Of All
  Our Days
 God Of The Nations Who From
  Dawn
Grimm
 Ewige Stern, Der
 Min Annamedder
 Prinzessin
 Whoin
Grine & Grine
 Bread Upon The Water
Grinnell
 Just Cling To The Word Of God
Griswold
 What The Chimney Sang
Grobe
 Mit Dem Herrn Fang Alles An
Grofe
 Daybreak
 Mardi Gras
Grolnick
 Pools
Groos
 Freedom
 Freiheit
 If I Were A Sunbeam
 Mountain Shepherd Boy, The
Grose & Barnard
 Give Of Your Best To The Master
Gross
 Freiheit Die Ich Meine
 Shannon
 Tenderly
Grossman
 Hal 'lu Saa Bhu Sh 'mo
 Ivdu Avde
 Just One Person
Grossman & Lange
 We 're Going Over
Grossmith
 Baby On The Shore, The

Grosz
 Along The Santa Fe Trail
 In An Old Dutch Garden
 Isle Of Capri
 Red Sails In The Sunset
Grothe
 An Der Donau Wenn Der Wein
  Bluht
Grothe & Helichar
 An Der Donau Wenn Der Wein
  Bluht
Grouya
 I Heard You Cried Last Night And
  So Did I
Grove
 Rose, The
Gruber
 Caisson Song, The
 Caissons Go Rolling Along, The
 Glade Jul
 Holy Night
 Holy Night Peaceful Night
 'S Wird Schone Maderln Geb 'n Und
  Mir Werd 'n Nimmer
 Silent Night
 Silent Night Holy Night
 Silent Tears Holy Night
 Stille Nacht
 Stille Nacht Heilige Nacht
Grum
 Elijah 's God Still Lives
Grunn
 God Answers Prayer
Grusin
 Absence Of Malice
 Baretta 's Theme
 Capital News
 It Might Be You
 On Golden Pond
 Phantazia
 St Elsewhere
 Theme From It Takes A Thief
 Theme From Name Of The Game
 Theme From Racing With The Moon
 Theme From The Goonies
 There 's Something Funny Going On
Gruska & Williams
 So Glad I Know
Guant
 Bowery, The
Guaraldi
 Cast Your Fate To The Wind
 Linus And Lucy
Guard
 Scotch And Soda
Guard & Glazer
 Worried Man, A
Guedron
 Aux Plaisirs Aux Delices
Guefen & Mandeville & Cacavas
 Lady Blue
Guest
 Onward

Guevara
 Nice Dreams
Guglielmo
 Italian Barcarolla, An
Guida & Anderson & Barge & Royster
 Quarter To Three
Guida & Guida & Royster
 If You Wanna Be Happy
Guida & Royster
 New Orleans
Guidetti
 Eternal Gifts Of Christ The King
Guidry
 See You Later Alligator
Guidry & Gayten
 But I Do
Guiffria & Eisley
 Call To The Heart
Guilbeau
 Sweet Susannah
Guilbert
 Absence
Guild
 Illinois Loyalty
Guilmant
 Wedding March
Guinand
 Serenade Sevillane
Guion
 Mary Alone
Guire
 Three Leaves Of Shamrock, The
Guizar
 Guadala Jara
Gulino & Lagueux
 Baby Blue
Guller
 My Bonnie
Gullicksen
 Charity
Gullivan
 I Am The Very Pattern
Gumbert
 Larmes Et Pleurs
 Refrain D 'amour
 Si Je T 'adore
Gumble
 Alexander 's Band Is Back In
  Dixieland
 Rebecca Of Sunny Brook Farm
Gummoe
 Rhythm Of The Rain
Gunn
 Jesus Reigns
Gunter
 Baby Let 's Play House
Gunter-Neumann
 Wonderland By Night
Gurley & Tunney
 On One Condition
Gurley & Weber & Sprague
 Every Step Of The Way
 Trust The Lord

Gurney
Carol Of The Skiddaw Yowes
Epitaph, An
I Will Go With My Father
    A-Ploughing
Sleep
Spring
Guthrie
Alice's Restaurant
Bling Blang
Do Re Mi
Don't You Push Me
Farmer Labor Train, The
Goin' Down The Road
Hard Travelin'
Hard Traveling
Jig Along Home
Kisses Sweeter Than Wine
Mail Myself To You
Oklahoma's Calling
Pastures Of Plenty
Pretty Boy Floyd
Put Your Finger In The Air
Roll On Columbia
So Long
So Long It's Been Good To Know
    You
So Long It's Been Good To Know
    Yuh
Take Me A Ride In The Car Car
Talking Fishing Blues
Talking Merchant Marine
This Land Is Your Land
Tom Joad
Union Maid
You Gotta Go Down
Guthrie & Guthrie
Oklahoma Hills
Gutierrez
Costa Rica Himno Nacional
Noble Country Your Beautiful
    Banner
Noble Patria Tu Hermosa Bandera
Gwent
Musicians' Serenade, The
Gwyllt
God Be With Thee
Gyorgy
H Ogyh A Olykor Ej Fectajban
Haagen
Jesus Ist Mein A Und O
Haas
Nearer My God To Thee
O Christians Leagued Together
Haavie
Blamann Blamann
Hackleman
Drifting Down
Hadar
Al Harim
Hadden
Bells Must Ring, The

Haden
Silence
Song For Che
Hadjidakis
Never On Sunday
Hadley
Garden Old, The
Il Pleut Des Petales De Fleurs
Love's Matins
Old Gaelic Lullaby
What The Flowers Say
Hadow
O Lord To Whom The Spirits Live
Haendel
Thou Shalt Give Him Everlasting
    Felicity
Hagan
Bright Banner Of Freedom
Hurrah For Old Glory
Lightly Row
Proud Flag Of The Free
Soldier's Song, The
Hagar
Give To Live
I Can't Drive 55
I've Done Everything For You
Two Sides Of Love
Your Love Is Driving Me Crazy
Hagar & Cartier
Keep On Rockin'
Hage
My Little Heaven Down In Devon
Hageman
At The Well
Do Not Go My Love
Hagen
Cowboy And His Love, The
Cowman's Loss
Dick Van Dyke Theme
Gomer Pyle
Harlem Nocturne
I Spy
Let Us Ride Together
Mod Squad, The
That Girl
Hagen & Spencer
Andy Griffith Show, The
Theme From Andy Griffith Show
Theme From The Andy Griffith
    Show, The
Haggard
Are The Good Times Really Over
Chill Factor
Fightin' Side Of Me, The
I Take A Lot Of Pride In What I Am
Mama Tried
Silver Wings
Twinkle Twinkle Lucky Star
Workin' Man Blues
Haggard & Burris
Okie From Muskogee
Haggard & Owens
Legend Of Bonnie And Clyde, The
Today I Started Loving You Again

Haggard & Powers & Rodgers
Let's Chase Each Other Around The
    Room
Haggart
What's New
Haggart & Bauduc
Big Noise From Winnetka
Hagman
Little Tyke
Hague
Follow Your Heart
It Wonders Me
Lifetime Love, A
My Girl Is Just Enough Woman For
    Me
Welcome Christmas
Young And Foolish
Hague & Humphries & McClusky
So In Love
Hahn
Amazon Rag, The
Could My Songs Their Flight Be
    Winging
D'une Prison
Dreary Landscape
Enchanted Hour
Exquisite Hour
Green Cathedral, The
Happy Song, The
Heure Exquies, L'
If My Song Had Wings For Flying
If My Songs Had Wings
My Song On Wings
Offrande
Paysage
Perfect Hour, The
Pholoe
Reverie
Si Mes Vers Avaient Des Ailes
Song Of Autumn
Were My Songs With Wings
    Provided
Hahr
Bye Baby Bye
Haibel
Tyrolese, The
Haidra
Hail Mother India
Hailstork
Charm At Parting, A
I Loved You
Hainsworth
Jesus Is My Friend
Hairston
Amen
Mary's Little Boy Child
Haker
O Loving Father Keep Me
Haldeman & Trace & Lee
Brush Those Tears From Your Eyes
Hale
Marion's Song
Old North State, The

Hale *(Cont.)*
Robin M'aime
Rondeau-Tant Com
Halevy
Call Me Thine Own
Little Owl
Haley
Fountain In The Park, The
While Strolling In The Park
While Strolling In The Park One Day
While Strolling Through The Park
While Strolling Through The Park
   One Day
While Strolling Thru The Park One
   Day
Hall
Abide With Me
All Across The City
American Cadets March
As The Hart
Christ Keeps His Own
Count On Me
Does Jesus Care
Ever Of Thee
Ever Of Thee I'm Fondly Dreaming
Everything Your Heart Desires
Everytime You Go Away
Foolish Pride
Greater Is He That Is In You
Hall Or Nothing
Harper Valley PTA
He Is Mine
I Heard The Bells Of Christmas Day
I Love
I Will Feed My Flock
I Will Praise Thee
I'm A Pilgrim
It Ain't Gonna Rain No Mo'
It Looks Like Rain
Jesus Comes To Save
Jesus Is The Man For The Hour
Jesus Lover Of My Soul
John Brown's Body
Joys That We've Tasted
Looking Beyond
Marching Song
Master Wants Workers, The
Me And Jesus
Method Of Modern Love
Missed Opportunity
My Jesus I Love Thee
Not Always On The Mount May We
Now And The Not Yet, The
O Lord Abide With Me
O Lord How Manifold Are Thy
   Works
Oil And Vinegar
Old Dogs Children And Watermelon
   Wine
One More Song For Jesus
Ordinary People
Organic
Osaka Express
Ravishing Ruby

Hall *(Cont.)*
Rich Girl
Romaine
Saviour Breathe An Evening Blessing
Sling Your Pack
Some Things Are Better Left Unsaid
Someone Like You
Sons Of Old Grinnell
True-Blue Elihu
What Are You Doing For Jesus
What Month Was Jesus Born In
Young One
Hall & Allison & Cody
I Am The Dreamer
Hall & Beebe
Dreamtime
Hall & Grape
Jesus Paid It All
Hall & Hall
Still The One
Hall & Kleinkauf
Johnson Rag
Hall & Laughery
Blessing
Hall & Mullins
Sparrow Watcher
Hall & Oates
Maneater
Out Of Touch
Possession Obsession
Sara Smile
She's Gone
Hall & Oates & Allen
I Can't Go For That
Possession Obsession
Hall & Oates & Iantosca
Downtown Life
Hall & Pash & Allen & Allen
Private Eyes
Hall & Temple & Johnson
Watusi, The
Halle
Below And Above
Fairest Chiquita
Harp Of The Winds, The
May The Grace Of Christ Our
   Saviour
Hallet
Thank You Jesus
Hallett
My Song Of Songs
Halley
Hard Livin'
Halligan
Some Heads Are Gonna Roll
Hallock
This Is The Feast Of Victory
Hallstrom
Give Peace O God The Nations Cry
Halvorson
Indian Summer Day On The Prairie,
   An
Ham
Music Of Your Life, The

Ham & Evans
Without You
Hamblen
Day Of Golden Promise, The
God Is A Good God
Hardrock Coco And Joe
His Hands
How Big Is God
I Want To Be There
It Is No Secret
It Is No Secret What God Can Do
Lord Is Counting On You, The
Rose Of Love, The
Teach Me Lord To Wait
They That Wait Upon The Lord
This Ole House
Until Then
Hamerton
Waken Christian Children
Hamilton
Cry Me A River
If On A Quiet Sea
In Search Of Silver And Gold
It's Time To Say So Long
Kings Of The East Are Riding, The
Kings Of The East, The
Lord Geoffrey Amherst
Lord Jeffery Amherst
Hamilton & Gorman
Romeo And Juliet
Hamilton & Starr & Morris
Stop Her On Sight
Hamilton-Geil
Earth Below Is Teeming
Hamlin
Angel Baby
Hamlisch
At The Ballet
Better Than Ever
Dance Ten Looks Three
Disneyland
Fallin'
Girl Who Used To Be Me, The
I Can Do That
If You Really Knew Me
If You Remember Me
In Our Hands
Last Time I Felt Like This, The
Music And The Mirror, The
Nobody Does It Better
One
One Hello
Seems Like Old Times
Smile
Somewhere I Belong
Sophie's Choice
Starting Over
Sunshine Lollipops And Rainbows
Sweet Alibis
Theme From Ice Castles
Theme From Sophie's Choice
They're Playing My Song
Through The Eyes Of Love
Way We Were, The

Hamlisch *(Cont.)*
What I Did For Love
Winners All
Hamlisch & Sager
I'm On Your Side
If You Remember Me
Hamlisch & Sager & Bacharach
Maybe
Hamm & Bennett & Lown & Gray
Bye Bye Blues
Hamma
O Bone Jesu
Hammer
Evan
Flashback
Miami Vice
Hammerel
Doll's House, The
Glow Worm, The
Lullaby
Hammerschmidt
Jesus Sinners Doth Receive
Hammerstein & Wilkinson
Because Of You
Hammitt
Hail South Dakota
Hammond
Far From My Heavenly Home
Highways And Byways
O Breath Of Life
To All The Girls I've Loved Before
When I Need You
Hammond & Bettis
One Moment In Time
Hammond & Hazlewood
Air That I Breathe, The
It Never Rains In Southern
California
Hammond & Warren
I Don't Wanna Live Without Your
Love
Nothing's Gonna Stop Us Now
Through The Storm
Hampton
Let All The World In Every Corner
Most High Omnipotent Good Lord
My Mother The Car
O Love Of God How Strong And
True
O Master Let Me Walk With Thee
There's A Wideness In God's Mercy
Hampton & Arr
World's Most Precious Thing, The
Hanby
Darling Nellie Gray
Darling Nelly Gray
Ole Shady
Santa Claus
Up In The House Top
Up On The Housetop
Who Is He
Who Is He In Yonder Stall

Hancke
Jagerlied
Hancock
4 Am
Absalom
Come Running To Me
Driftin'
Little One
Maze, The
Nunc Dimittis
O God Of Love To Thee We Bow
Oliloqui Valley
See The Farmer Sow The Seed
Tell Me A Bedtime Story
Watermelon Man
What Would You Give In Exchange
For Your Soul
Hancock & Laswell & Beinhorn
Rock It
Hancock & Laswell & Suso & Dien
Junku
Hancock & Ragin
I Thought It Was You
Hancort
Goosie-Goosie-Gander
My Pumpkin Pie
Susie Sue
Hancourt
Pretty Little Robin
Handel
Air
Allurements The Dearest
Alma Mia
Am I A Soldier Of The Cross
And Have The Bright Immensities
And The Glory Of The Lord
Angels Ever Bright And Fair
Antioch
Arm Arm Ye Brave
Art Thou Troubled
As The Sun Doth Daily Rise
As With Rosy Steps The Morn
Author Of Faith Eternal Word
Awake My Soul
Awake My Soul Stretch
Awake My Soul Stretch Ev'ry Nerve
Awake My Soul Stretch Every Nerve
Blest Be The Lord
But Thou Didst Not Leave His Soul
In Hell
But Who May Abide
But Who May Abide The Day Of His
Coming
By This Falchion
Lightning-Garnished
Calm Repose Contentment Smiling
Care Selve
Chi Scherza Colle Rose
Christian Rise And Act Thy Creed
Come Ever Smiling Liberty
Come See Where Golden-Hearted
Spring
Come Unto Him
Come Ye That Love The Lord

Handel *(Cont.)*
Comfort Ye Comfort Ye My People
Comfort Ye My People
Convey Me To Some Peaceful Shore
Crushed By Fate
Dank Sei Dir Herr
Dedication
Deeper And Deeper Still
Dem Helden
Dismiss Me Not Thy Service Lord
Dove Sei
Dove Sei Amato Bene
Er Weidet Seine Herde
Eternal God Whose Power Upholds
Every Valley Shall Be Exalted
False Destructive Ways Of Pleasure
Farewell Ye Limpid Springs
For Ever Blessed
For Unto Us A Child Is Born
Frag' Ob Die Rose
Freue Dich Welt
Funeral Dirge
Gentle Airs Melodious Strains
Go Call Irene
Go My Faithful Soldiers Go
God Of Eternal Love
God Of My Life Whose Gracious
Power
Grace Thy Fair Brow
Great God Who Yet But Darkly
Known
Hail Hero Workers
Hallelujah
Hallelujah Amen
Hallelujah Chorus
He Shall Feed His Flock
He Was Despised
He Was Despised And Rejected
He Who Himself And God Would
Know
Heroes When With Glory Burning
Honor And Arms
Honour And Arms
How Beauteous Are Their Feet
How Beautiful Are The Feet
How Beautiful Are The Feet Of
Them
How Charming Is The Place
How Shall I Find Thee
How Willing My Paternal Love
Hymen Haste Thy Torch Prepare
I Know That My Redeemer Lives
I Know That My Redeemer Liveth
I Love Thy Kingdom Lord
I Press Thee To My Bosom
I'll Hear No More
Ich Weiss Dass Mein Erloser Lebet
If God Be For Us Who Can Be
Against Us
If Manly Valor
In Deinem Namen Jesus Christ
In Gentle Murmurs
In The Battle Fame Pursuing
In Thee O Lord Have I Trusted

Handel *(Cont.)*

It Must Be So
Joy To The World
Joy To The World The Lord Is Come
Largo
Largo In G
Lascia Ch'io Pianga
Lass Mich Mit Tranen
Leave Me In Anguish
Leave Me In Sorrow
Leave Me Loathsome Light
Leave Me To Languish
Let Other Creatures Die
Let The Bright Seraphim
Let Their Celestial Concerts All
   Unite
Life Of A Vassal, The
Like Noah's Weary Dove
Lo Here My Love
Loathsome Urns Disclose Your
   Treasure
Lord Guard And Guide The Men
   Who Fly
Lord In The Hollow Of Thy Hand
Lord Is My Strength, The
Lord Of The Universe
Lord To Thee Each Night And Day
Lord Worketh Wonders, The
Lost Princess, The
Love In Her Eyes Sits Playing
Love Sounds Th' Alarm
Love Ye The Lord
Love's Richest Dower
Lusinghe Piu Care
My Cup Is Full
My God I Love Thee Not Because
My Hope Star Royal
My Plane Tree
My Pray'rs Are Heard
My Shepherd
Ne'er Could There Be
Ne'er Shade So Dear
Now Behold The Car Advances
Now On Land And Sea Descending
Now That The Sun Is Beaming
   Bright
O Beauteous Queen
O Bless The Lord My Soul
O Come Let Us Worship
O God Before Thy Sun's Bright
   Beams
O Hatt Ich Jubals Harf
O Liberty Thou Choicest Treasure
O Lord Correct Me
O Lord Whose Mercies
O Lord Whose Mercies Numberless
O Lovely Peace
O Ruddier Than The Cherry
O Sacred Oracles Of Truth
O Sleep
O Sleep Why Dost Thou Leave Me
O Thou That Tellest Good Tidings
   To Zion
Oh Had I Jubal's Lyre

Handel *(Cont.)*

Oh Sleep Why Dost Thou Leave Me
Oh Worse Than Death Indeed
Ombra Mai Fu
Ominous A Storm Upsurging
Or Let The Merry Bells
Overture
Overture Messiah
Pastoral Symphony
People That Walked In Darkness,
   The
Piangero La Sorte Mia
Pluck Root And Branch
Pour Forth No More
Rejoice My Countrymen
Rejoice The Lord Is King
Rend'il Sereno Al Ciglio
Return O God Of Hosts
Revenge Timotheus Cries
Ruddier Than The Cherry
Sadly I Languish
Scenes Of Horror
See Me In Anguish
See The Conquering Hero Comes
See The Raging Flames Arise
Shade Departed
Shall I In Mamre's Fertile Plain
Si Tra I Ceppi
Sieh Der Winter Ist Vergangen
Sighing Lamenting
Sin Not O King
Sing Songs Of Praise
Sing Unto The Lord
Sorge Nel Petto
Sound An Alarm
Te Deum
Tears Such As Tender Fathers Shed
Tempeste, Da
Thanks Be To Thee
Thatcher
Then Round About The Starry
   Throne
Then Will I Jehovah's Praise
Thine Be The Glory
Thine Is The Glory
Thou Shalt Bring Them In
Thus Saith The Lord To Cyrus His
   Anointed
Thy Glorious Deeds Inspired My
   Tongue
To Thee Eternal Soul
To Thee Eternal Soul Be Praise
Tornami A Vagheggiar
Total Eclipse
Trostung
Trumpet Shall Sound, The
Turn Not O Queen Thy Face Away
'Twill Be A Painful Separation
Under Your Shade
Unveil Thy Bosom Faithful Tomb
Verdant Meadows
Verdant Meadows Groves
   Enchanting
Verdi Prati

Handel *(Cont.)*

Vessel Storm-Driven, The
Vouchsafe O Lord
Waft Her Angels
We Limit Not The Truth Of God
We Thank Thee For Music
Welcome Mighty Chief
Wenn Christus Der Herr
Wenn Christus Der Herr Zum
   Menschen Sich Neigt
Werbung
What Though I Trace
What Though I Trace Each Herb
   And Flower
When Golden Sunbeams
When His Loud Voice In Thunder
   Spoke
Where Now Art Thou My Own
   Beloved One
Where'er You Walk
While In Spirit Lord To Thee, A
While Shepherds Watched
While Shepherds Watched Their
   Flocks
While Shepherds Watched Their
   Flocks By Night
Why Do The Nations
Wie Lieblich Ist Der Boten Schritt
Will God Whose Mercies Ever Flow
With Mournful Sounds Of Weeping
With Thee Th' Unsheltered Moor I'd
   Tread
With Thee Th'Unshelter'd Moor I'd
   Tread
Would You Gain The Tender
   Creature
Yea Mid Chains
Yes Through All My Pains
Your Voice Raise
Zur Totenfeier

Handel & Mason
Joy To The World

Handl
Alleluia Today Is Christ Risen

Handman
You've Got Those Wanna Go Back
   Again Blues

Handy
Aunt Hagar's Children
Basement Blues, The
Beale Street Blues
Blue Gummed Blues
Careless Love
Chantez-Les Bas
Chicago Gouge, The
Darling Nelly Gray
Deep River Blues
Friendless Blues
Golden Brown Blues
Got No Mo' Home Dan A Dog
Gouge Of Armour Avenue, The
Harlem Blues
Hesitating Blues, The
Hooking Cow Blues, The

Handy *(Cont.)*
Joe Turner Blues
Jogo Blues, The
John Henry Blues
Long Gone
Loveless Love
Memphis Blues, The
Oh Didn't He Ramble
Ole Miss
Shoeboot's Serenade
St Louis Blues, The
Sundown Blues
Wall Street Blues
Way Down South Where The Blues
    Began
Yellow Dog Blues
Handy & Elman
Atlanta Blues
Handy & Williams
Careless Love
Hanemann
Before You Asked Me To Believe
Bootlegger's Child, The
Don't Put Your Foot In My Face
    Dear
I'll Be Back
It's On The Right Finger
Just A Frowsy Little Dump
Never Hit Your Grandma With A
    Shovel
Put Away The Moustache Cup
Slug In The Slot Machine, The
You Told Me
Hanford
I Am A Suffragette
I'm A Suffragette
Hanighen
Bob White
Bob White Whatcha Gonna Swing
    Tonight
Hanisch
Bedroom Backlash
I Gotta Learn To Sing
Hanitsch
Bundeslied
Hankey & Doane
Tell Me The Old Old Story
Hankey & Fischer
I Love To Tell The Story
Hanley
Indiana
Just A Cottage Small By A Waterfall
Rose Of Washington Square
Second Hand Rose
Zing Went The Strings Of My Heart
Hann
Here You Come Again
O God Of Truth Whose Living Word
Hanna
My Ain Countrie
Serenade
Hanna & Barbera & Curtin
Flintstones, The
Huckleberry Hound Song

Hanna & Barbera & Curtin *(Cont.)*
Jetsons, The
Magilla Gorilla
Scooby Doo
Yogi Bear Song
Hanna & Barbera & Curtin & Timmens
Top Cat
Hanna & Hathaway & Carpenter
Make A Little Magic
Hanner
Beautiful You
Lord I Hope This Day Is Good
Hansen
Michael
Hansen & Brimhall
Christmas Snow
My Love Is Like A Rose
O Thou Blessed Day
Hansen & Marchetti
Fascination
Hanson
Drink A Highball
Hapkins
Dartmouth's In Town Again
Harbison
You Know Who
Harcourt
All Patrols Look Out
Hardcox & Cunningham
There Is Mean Things Happening In
    This Land
Hardelot
Without Thee
Hardeman & Hardeman
I Feel Good All Over
Harder
Raindrops
Winter Song
Hardin
Every Day
If I Were A Carpenter
Misty Roses
Harding
Brighest And Best Of The Sons
Brightest And Best
Brightest And Best Of The Sons Of
    The Morning
Brightest And Best Of The Stars Of
    The Morning
Here We Tread With Hallowed Feet
Highest And Best Of The Songs Of
    The Morning
Love Thyself Last
Pretty Kitty Doyle
Harding & Lehman
Sailing On The Sea Of Your Love
Hardy
Homecoming, The
Something I've Been Meaning To
    Tell You
Hargrove
Let It Shine
Lilies Of The Field

Harington
O Thou From Whom All Goodness
    Flows
Harker & King
Indiana Our Indiana
Harkins
Jesus Is The Bridge Over Troubled
    Water
Harkness
Afar From God
Are We Downhearted
At Your Door
Bearing His Cross
Beyond
But I Know
Bye And Bye
Can The Lord Depend On You
Children's Friend Is Jesus, The
Come Ye Yourselves Apart
Does Jesus Care
Gethsemane
Give Me Jesus
Go Home And Tell
He Does It All In Love
He Will Hold Me Fast
He Will Not Let Me Go
I Am With You
I'm A Poor Sinner
I'm A Subject Of The King
In Jesus
Is He Yours
Just Where I Am
Led By Jesus
Longing For Jesus
Lord Is It I
Memories Of Mother
My Father's Love
My Ransom
My Sins Are Forgiven
Oh What A Change
Only Jesus
Onward Christian Soldiers
Pardoned
We Meet Again
What Will It Be
When He Shed His Blood
When I See My Saviour
Who Could It Be
Why Should He Love Me So
Win Someone
You Must Do Something Tonight
Harline
From This Day Forward From This
    Day On
Give A Little Whistle
Hi-Diddle-Dee-Dee
I've Got No Strings
When You Wish Upon A Star
World Owes Me A Living, The
Harling
Contemplation
Harlow
Suffolk Hail

Harmati
Blue Bird Of Happiness
Harmon
Reach Out And Touch The Lord
Harms
Walk On Water
Harney
Mister Johnson
Harper
Above The Clear Blue Sky
Following You
Freedom Road
From This Moment On
I Know Not How That Bethlehem's
Babe
John III 16
Keep Cool And Keep Coolidge
See What God Can Do
World Must Be Bigger Than An
Avenue, The
Harrah
No More Night
Harrigan
Little Fraud
My Johanna
Pat Maloney's Family
Harrington
Assignation, The
Beyond The Smiling And The
Weeping
Christ's Life Our Code
Fair Harvard
Give Me The Sweet Delights Of Love
How Great Is The Pleasure
I Cannot Sing This Catch
I Do Not Ask O Lord That Life May
Be
In The Cross Of Christ I Glory
Jesus Immortal King Arise
Jesus Meek And Gentle
Long Years Ago O'Er Bethlehem's
Hills
Look At The Ears On Him
Lord Is In His Holy Temple, The
My Bark Is Wafted To The Strand
Now From The Altar Of My Heart
Praise Ye Jehovah Praise The Lord
Most Holy
She Loved Her Saviour And To Him
Sweet Delights Of Love
There Was A Time When Children
Sang
There's A Song In The Air
Three Old Women In A Country
Churchyard
'Tis Hum Drum
To Thee Eternal Soul Be Praise
Yawning Round, A
Harrington & Adams
For Love Of Wooster U
Harris
After The Ball
After The Ball Is Over
All That Thrills My Soul

Harris *(Cont.)*
All The Time In The World
Break The News To Mother
Claribel
Gardens Of The Sky
God Save Our King
Hello Central Give Me Heaven
Hide Thou Me
I've A Longing In My Heart For You
Louise
I've Got Jesus In My Heart
Just As It Used To Do
Keep That Moment Alive
Kiss And Let's Make Up
Lead Them To Thee
Looking Beyond
Mirror
Orient
Pathway Divine, The
Praise The Lord He Never Changes
Put Jesus First In Your Life
Scab's Lament, The
Steppin Out On Faith
Tie Me Kangaroo Down Sport
Upper Room, The
Venetian Serenade
We Are Sailing
When Marshaled On The Nightly
Plain
Who Could It Be But Jesus
Harris & Gilbert
Isn't That Just Like Jesus
Harris & Harris
Friend Of The Father
In This Very Room
Mirror
Over And Over And Over Again
Special Delivery
Tell All The World About Love
Harris & Lewis
Diamonds
Fake
Human
I Didn't Mean To Turn You On
If It Isn't Love
Just The Facts
Making Love In The Rain
Miss You Much
Tender Love
What Have You Done For Me Lately
When I Think Of You
Harris & Lewis & Jackson & Andrews
Let's Wait Awhile
Harris & McBride
Rose In Paradise
Harris & McClain & Harrison
Hotspot
Harris & McKee
Just A Woman
Harris & Rosasco
Juke Box Saturday Night
Harris & South
I Beg Your Pardon

Harris & Terry
I'm Leaving It All Up To You
Justine
Harrison
Blest Are The Moments Doubly Blest
Blow Away
Dippers And Bears
Dove Of Mine
Hallelujah
In Pleasant Lands Have Fall'n The
Lines
In The Gloaming
It's All Too Much
Long Long Long
Morning Walks Upon The Earth, The
Only A Northern Song
Peterboro
Philomel
Rise O My Soul Pursue The Path
Spirit Of Truth
Voice By Jordan's Shore, A
Harrison & Harris
Let It All Blow
Harrison & Lynne
This Is Love
When We Was Fab
Harrison & Martin
Domestic Life
Two Car Garage
Harrison & Miles
On My Word Of Honor
Harrison & Staley
Face In The Crowd, A
Harrison, George
All Those Years Ago
Blue Jay Way
Crackerbox Palace
Don't Bother Me
For You Blue
Give Me Love
Here Comes The Sun
I Me Mine
I Need You
I Want To Tell You
If I Needed Someone
Inner Light, The
Love You To
My Sweet Lord
Old Brown Shoe
Piggies
Savoy Truffle
Something
Taxman
Think For Yourself
This Song
While My Guitar Gently Weeps
You Like Me Too Much
Harriss
I Heard The Voice Of Jesus Say
Harry & Stein
Heart Of Glass
In The Flesh
Harry & Valentine
X Offender

Hart
At A Siding
Easy Loving
Fire On The Mountain
Good Sweet Ham
I Am By Your Side
It Never Entered My Mind
My Hang-Up Is You
Never Surrender
Song Of The Tangier Gold Mines
Hart & Lucas
Loose Talk
Hart & Portnoy
Cheers
Every Time I Turn Around
Hart & Teel
Go To All The World
Hart & Weir
France
Playing In The Band
Hartel
I Long For Thee
Harter
Erasmus Hall
Hartford
Autumn Breezes
Gentle On My Mind
In The Park
Spring Is Here
Hartlan
Sable Island Song
Hartling
India Virgen Y Hermosa Dormias
Oh Your Banner
Hartman
Beat The System
Christ For The World We Sing
Grave Robber
Hollow Eyes
I Can Dream About You
More Power To Ya
Not Of This World
Why Should The Father Bother
Hartman & Midnight
Living In America
Second Nature
Waiting To See You
Hartmann
King Christian
Hartmann & Kamano
I'm A Lonely Little Petunia In An
   Onion Patch
Hartog
Swinging
Hartsough
I Am Coming Lord
I Hear Thy Welcome Voice
My Love's Own
Hartsough & Fillmore
I Am Resolved
Harty
Lullaby, A
Scythe Song
Sea Wrack

Harussi & Zeira
Al Tira Avdi Yaakov
Harvey
Daily Express, The
Have We Changed
Love Your Hair
Someone Who Cares
Wreck Of The Virginian No 3, The
Harvey & Collins
Delta Dawn
Harwood
Blessed By The God Of Israel
Come Along Sing
Lord Keep Us Safe This Night
Thy Hand O God Has Guided
Haselden
It Ain't Nothin'
Nobody Said It Was Easy
Hasler
An Die Hartherzige
Jungfrau Dein Schon Gestalt
Scheiden Und Leiden
Tanzliedchen
Trost In Todesnot
Haslip & Ferrante
Man In The Moon
Hassler
All Who Believe And Are Baptized
Cantate Domino
Commit Thou All That Grieves Thee
How Shall I Fitly Meet Thee
In Heavenly Love Abiding
My Soul There Is A Country
O Beautiful My Country
O Bleeding Head
O Sacred Head
O Sacred Head Now Wounded
O Sacred Head Sore Wounded
O Sacred Head Surrounded
Hastings
Amazing Sight The Savior Stands
Come Holy Ghost In Love
From Ev'ry Stormy Wind That
   Blows
From Every Stormy Wind That
   Blows
Give Me The Wings Of Faith To Rise
Guide Me O Thou Great Jehovah
How Sweet The Name Of Jesus
   Sounds
Iesu Pro Me Perforatus
Luther
Majestic Sweetness
Majestic Sweetness Sits Enthroned
Mercy-Seat, The
My God How Endless
New Haven
O For A Faith That Will Not Shrink
O God Our Help In Ages Past
O God We Pray For All Mankind
On The Mountain's Top Appearing
Plunged In A Gulf Of Dark Despair
Retreat
Rock Of Ages

Hastings *(Cont.)*
Rock Of Ages Cleft For Me
So Wie Ich Bin
What Of The Night
Zion
Zion Stands With Hills Surrounded
Hatch
Call Me
Downtown
My Love
Hatch & Dean
Don't Your Mem'ry Ever Sleep At
   Night
Hatch & Jackson
Breathe On Me Breath Of God
Hatch & Trent
Don't Sleep In The Subway
Hatfield
Bible Satisfies, The
Forward To The Goal
Glorious Tidings, The
Hatton
Abide Not In The Realm Of Dreams
April Showers
Baker University Hymn
Before Jehovah's Throne
Beneath Thy Guiding Hand
Beschirm' Uns Herr Bleib' Unser
   Hort
Beware
Evening Hymn
From All That Dwell Below The
   Skies
Give To Our God Immortal Praise
Good News On Christmas Morning
Goodbye Sweetheart Goodbye
Goodnight
Hail Thou Whose Sin-Atoning Blood
Jesus Shall Reigh Where'er The Sun
Jesus Shall Reign
Jesus Shall Reign Where'er The Sun
Now To The Lord A Noble Song
O God Beneath Thy Guiding Hand
O Happy Holy Easter Morn
Our Lord Is Risen From The Dead
Perfect World By Adam Trod, The
Pour Out Thy Spirit From On High
Simon The Cellarer
Stand Up My Soul Shake Off Thy
   Fears
Unto Thy Temple
Veni Creator Spiritus
When Evening's Twilight Gathers
   Round
Wild Roars The Blast
Willkommen Lieber Ostertag
With Loyal Hearts
Yes God Is Good
Hauger
Blaklokker
Haupt
Fairest Lord Jesus

Hauptmann
Aus Der Jugendzeit
Birthday Greeting, A
Mule, The
O How Sweet
Sommermorgen
Wunderbar Ist Mir Geschehn

Hauser
Clouds
Gaines
Mocksville
Thomasson
Zellville

Hausman
Suffer The Little Children

Havergal
According To They Gracious Word
All The Happy Children
Blest Are The Pure In Heart
City Of God How Broad And Far
Come Thou Long Expected Jesus
Earth Has Many A Noble City
God My King Thy Might Confessing
Golden Harps
Golden Harps Are Sounding
Hail To The Lord's Anointed
Harp At Nature's Advent Strung,
    The
How Sweet The Name Of Jesus
    Sounds
I Heard The Voice Of Jesus Say
Lamp Of Our Feet
Lord I Believe A Rest Remains
Lord Is Risen Indeed, The
Lord's My Shepherd I'll Not Want,
    The
O That The Lord Would Guide My
    Ways
On Our Way Rejoicing
On This Day The First Of Days
Remember Thy Creator
Take My Life And Let It Be
There Came A Little Child To Earth
There Is A Fountain Filled With
    Blood
There Is A Name I Love To Hear
Welcome Happy Morning
When Wounded Sore The Stricken
    Soul
Why Do We Mourn Departing
    Friends
Ye Servants Of The Lord

Havergal & Bliss
I Gave My Life For Thee

Havergal & Herold
Take My Life And Let It Be

Havergal & Malan
Take My Life And Let It Be

Havergal & Mountain
Like A River Glorious

Havergal & Stebbins
Truehearted Wholehearted

Havez
Everybody Works But Father

Haweis
Awake Arise Lift Up Your Voice
City Of God
City Of God How Broad And Far
I'm Not Ashamed To Own My Lord
Joy To The World
Joy To The World The Lord Is Come
My God The Spring Of All My Joys
O Thou In All Thy Might So Far
Our Glad Hosannas Prince Of Peace
Praise To The Holiest In The Height
What Shall I Do My God To Love
What Shall I Render To My God

Hawes
Mad As I Can Be
UAW-CIO

Hawkes
God Is In His Holy Temple

Hawkins
All Your Need
Be Grateful
Easter Bells Are Ringing
Goin' Up Yonder
Honest Money
I Put A Spell On You
Jesus Christ Is The Way
Jesus Meek And Gentle
Let Thy Mantle Fall On Me
Lilies Tell The Story, The
Oh Happy Day
On Ben Jonson
Thrill Is Gone, The
Willing To Take The Cross

Hawkins & Darnel
Thrill Is Gone, The

Hawkins & Johnson & Dash
Tuxedo Junction

Hawkins & Lewis & Broadwater
Susie-Q

Hawks & Lowry
I Need Thee

Hawley
Ashes Of Roses
My Little Love
See Amid The Winter's Snow
Song Of Winter, A

Haworth
Technology

Hawthorne
Listen To The Mocking Bird
Out Of Work
What Is Home Without A Mother
Whispering Hope

Hay
Dr Heckyll And Mr Jive
Everything I Need
High Wire
It's A Mistake
Overkill
Who Can It Be Now

Hay & Ham
Be Good Johnny

Hayden
Model College Girl, A

Haydn
Alleluia Song Of Gladness
An Die Freundschaft
Antidotium Contra Tyrannidem
    Peccati
Ark Of Freedom
As Down In The Sunless Retreats
Auf Starkem Fittich
Austrian National Hymn
Bald Wehen Uns Des Fruhlings Lufte
Begin My Tongue Some Heavenly
    Theme
Beredsamkeit, Die
Beware Comrades
Bose Weib, Das
Brightly
Brightly Brightly Gleam The
    Sparkling Rills
Brightly Gleam
Brightly Gleams Our Banner
Christi Todesstunde
Christmas Eve Canon
Columbia God Preserve Thee Free
Come Gentle Spring
Come My Soul Thou Must Be
    Waking
Content
Country Delight
Crown His Head With Endless
    Blessing
Death Is A Long Long Sleep
Death Is A Long Sleep
Despair
Deutschland Uber Alles
Dir O Jesu Heil Der Sunder
Earth Below Is Teeming
Eine Sehr Gewohnliche Geschichte
Emperor's Hymn, The
Equals
Fidelity
Forward Be Our Watchword
Forward Be Watchword
Forward Through The Ages
From The Eastern Mountains
Gegenliebe
Gloria Gloria
Gloria In Excelsis
Glorious Things Of Thee Are Spoken
God Moves In A Mysterious Way
Hail The Glorious Golden City
Hail The Hero Workers
How Firm A Foundation
How Firm A Foundation Ye Saints
    Of The Lord
How Lovely Is Thy Dwelling Place
How Wondrous And Great Thy
    Works
I Know That My Redeemer Lives
I Live For Those Who Love Me
I Will Not Plead
In Memory Of The Savior's Love
In The Country
Interrupted Serenade, The
Jerusalem My Happy Home

Haydn (*Cont.*)

Jolly Month Of May
Joy
Land Of Greatness Home Of Glory
Landlust, Die
Lead Us Heavenly Father
Lead Us Heavenly Father Lead Us
Leben Ist Ein Traum, Das
Let There Be Light
Liebes Madchen Hor' Mir Zu
Lied Der Deutschen, Das
Light Of Ages And Of Nations
Light Thou For Us O God A Candle
Litany
Lob Der Faulheit
Lord My Pasture Shall Prepare, The
Lord While For All Mankind We
    Pray
Lully Lullay
Man's Fate
Mermaid's Song, The
Merry-Go-Round, The
My Mother Bids Me Bind My Hair
Mysterious Presence Source Of All
Night And Day
Not Alone For Mighty Empire
Now While We Sing Our Closing
    Psalm
Nun Beut Die Flur
O God I Thank Thee
O To See A Giant
O Worship The King
O Worship The King All-Glorious
    Above
Oh Worship The King
Onward Christian Soldiers
Our Land O Lord
Pange Lingua
Piercing Eyes
Pleasing Pain
Praise The Lord Ye Heavens Adore
    Him
Recollection
Rejoice Rejoice Believers
Sach Ist Dein, Die
Sailor's Song
Sailor's Song, The
Scale Syllables
Schon Eilet Froh Der Akkersmann
See The Conquerer Mounts In
    Triumph
Sehr Gewohnliche Geschichte
Serenade
Serenader, The
She Never Told Her Love
Shepherd's Song
Silent Night
Sister Ruth
Song Of Columbus Day
Song Of Praise
Sorrow
Spacious Firmament On High, The
Spacious Firmament, The
Standing At The Portal

Haydn (*Cont.*)

Stoic's Creed, A
Strategy
Surprise
Sympathy
Tenebrae Factae Sunt
This Is The Day
Thou Art O God The Life And Light
To Friendship
Tod Und Schlaf
Very Kind Young Couple, A
Very Ordinary Story, A
Voice Of God Is Calling, The
Walk In The Light
Wanderer, The
We Are Living We Are Dwelling
We Thy People Praise Thee
Welche Labung Fur Die Sinne
Welcome Happy Morning
When All Thy Mercies
When All Thy Mercies O My God
Will I Get A Christmas Present
With Verdure Clad
Woman Of Canaan, The
Wort Des Lebens Lautre Quelle
Ye Servants Of God
Ye Servants Of God Your Master
    Proclaim

Haydn & Mehul

Walk In The Light

Hayes

Ars Longa Vita Brevis
Beat Your Pate
Bring Thy Treasures
Catch
Cock-A-Doodle-Doo
Deja Vu
English And French
Epitaph
Fine Oranges
Friend A Friend, A
Frog He Would A-Wooing Go, A
Gently Flow
It's Hard Ain't It Hard
Jesse James
John Henry
O Lord How Happy Should We Be
Old Chairs To Mend
Old Mountain Dew
On Alexander Pope
On The Poet
Poet's Lament
Ripe 'Sparagrass
Roll Out Heave Dat Cotton
Rose's Age, The
Salty Dog
Sliding
Some Women
Sophocles' Tomb
Spring Is Come
Spring, The
Sweetly Flow
Thou Art O God The Life And Light

Hayes (*Cont.*)

Three Oxford Cries
To Newton
Walk On By
We Sing Of God The Mighty Source
Who's Cheatin' Who
Would You Sing A Catch
Would You Sing A Round With
    Pleasure

Hayes & Johnson

Blue Christmas

Hayes & Lewis

Small World

Hayes & Porter

Hold On I'm Comin'
Hold On I'm Coming
Soul Man
When Something Is Wrong With My
    Baby
Wrap It Up

Hayford

Nobody Cared
Tell Ye This Story
This Is My Body
Until He Comes Again

Hayford & Stone

Come On Down

Hayman

Love Thyself Last
O Son Of God Our Captain Of
    Salvation

Hayman & Daniels & Parker

Dansero

Haymes & Acquaviva

My Love My Love

Hayne

Jesus My Strength My Hope
Jesus Thy Boundless Love To Me
O Draw Me Saviour After Thee
O Love Who Formedst Me To Wear
Saviour Teach Me Day By Day
Thy Kingdom Come O God
Thy Kingdom Come O Lord
When Jesus Was On Earth

Haynes

Christ Whose Glory Fills The Skies
He Is Lord
Sherman The Brave
Yellow And Blue, The

Hayon

O Blest Creator Source Of Light
O Trinity Of Blessed Light
Praise The Lord

Hays

Angels Meet Me At De Cross-Roads
Angels Meet Me At The Cross Roads
Cleveland Is The Man
Drummer Boy Of Shiloh, The
Early In De Mornin
Keep In De Middle Ob De Road
Keep In De Middle Of De Road
Little Joe The Wrangler
Little Old Cabin In The Lane, The
McClellan Is The Man

Hays (*Cont.*)
Mollie Darling
Nobody's Darling
Nora O'Neal
Number Twenty-Nine
O'Grady Goat
Oh Sam
Roll Out Heave Dat Cotton
Shamus O'Brien
Susan Jane
Turnpike Gate, The
We Parted By The River Side

Hays & Lowenfels
Ballad For Un-American Blues, The
Rankin Tree, The
Wasn't That A Time

Hays & Rhodes
Satisfied Mind, A

Hayward
I Know You're Out There
Somewhere
Nights In White Satin
Tuesday Afternoon
Your Wildest Dreams

Hayward & Lodge
Gemini Dream

Haywood
She's A Bad Mama Jama

Hazard
Girls Just Want To Have Fun

Hazlewood
Houston
Sugar Town
These Boots Are Made For Walkin'

Hazlewood & Cook & Greenaway
Freda Comes Freda Goes

Heacox
Terre Nationale, La

Head
Estuary, The
Green Cornfield, A
Lavender Pond
Money-O
Sweet Chance
Treat Her Right

Healy
Andy Adams
Annie Rooney-Ryan
At Custer's Last Battle
Buffalo Bill
Down The Old Street Of My Dreams
Ed Corbin On Weary Hill
I'm Going Back To The Smokys
I'm Rarin' To Go
On A Lonely Road They Found Him
Whistling Mike O'Connor
Wild Sam Brown

Heath
Big P
Easter Time
New Blue, A
Sassy Samba, A
Snow Storm, The
Sound For Sore Ears, A

Heath & Marr & Fletcher
Organize Unions

Heath & Solman
In The Sweet Long Ago

Heather
I've Got A Lovely Bunch Of
Cocoanuts
Phfft You Are Gone
Phfft You Were Gone

Heatlie
Cry Just A Little Bit

Hebb
Sunny

Heber
From Greenland's Icy Mountains
Son Of God Goes Forth To War, The

Heber & Dykes
Holy Holy Holy Lord God Almighty

Heeney & Moffat
Still Doin' Time

Hefer & Wilensky
Hayu Z'Manim

Hefferman
Watchman's Song

Hefti
Batman Theme
Cherry Point
Cool Blue
Coral Reef
Cute
Girl Talk
In Veradero
Kiss Me First
Li'l Darlin'
Little Pony
Odd Couple, The
Repetition
Scoot
Teddy The Toad

Hegar
Deutsches Lied
Gang Zur Liebsten
Muttersprache
Trompete Von Gravelotte, Die

Hegel & Wagner
Just As I Am

Heider
Christmas Chopsticks

Heilner
Tide Rises, The

Heim
In Die Ferne

Heindorf
Melancholy Rhapsody

Heindorf & Steiner
Sugarfoot

Heindorg
Some Sunday Morning

Heinlein
Bread Of Heaven On Thee We Feed
God The Father God The Son

Heins
Spirit Divine Attend Our Prayer
There's A Voice In The Wilderness
Crying

Heinzerling
Ehre Sei Gott

Heise
Husker Du I Hoest

Held
Chromatic Rag
In Bethlehem A New-Born Boy

Helder
Lord And King Of All Things, The
Lord My Shepherd Is, The

Helf
Ain't You Coming Back To Old New
Hampshire Molly
How'd You Like To Be The Ice-Man
Make A Noise Like A Hoop And
Roll Away
Picture No Artist Can Paint, A

Helf & Gardenier
Fatal Rose Of Red, The

Hell
Blank Generation
Love Comes In Spurts

Hellard & Garvin & Jones
I Tell It Like It Used To Be

Heller
O Starry Flag
That Horn

Hellerman & Barer
I'm Just A Country Boy

Helm
Dona Nobis Pacem

Helmar
Can Dubinsky Do It

Helmore
O Come O Come Emmanuel

Helvering
In The Name Of The Lord

Hemans
Landing Of The Pilgrims
'Twas A Trumpet's Pealing Sound

Hemby
I Give It All To You
Living Without Your Love

Hemmerel
Doll's House, The

Hemphill
He's Still Working On Me
I Came On Business For The King
I'm In This Church
Ready To Leave
Sing The Glory Down

Hemphill & Hemphill
I'm So Excited

Hemsworth
Black Fly, The

Hemy
City Of God
Come Father Son And Holy Ghost
Faith Of Our Fathers
Faith Of Our Fathers Living Still

Hemy (*Cont.*)
God Of The Earth The Sky The Sea
God Of The Living In Whose Eyes
Jesus Thy Boundless Love To Me
O Jesus Christ Our Lord Most Dear
Our Father As We Start The Day
Paradise
Since Jesus Freely Did Appear
There Is A Blessed Home
Thou Hidden Love Of God
Thou Hidden Love Of God Whose
    Height
Henderson
Alabamy Bound
Birth Of The Blues, The
Black Bottom
Bye Bye Blackbird
Deep Night
Don't Bring Lulu
Five Foot Two Eyes Of Blue
Go On Train
Golden Slumbers Kiss Your Eyes
He Ransomed Me
I'm Sitting On Top Of The World
Just A Memory
Lucky Day
Lucky In Love
Nasty Man
Out Of This World Birth Of The
    Blues, The
That Old Gang Of Mine
Thrill Is Gone, The
Henderson & Fishman
Why Don't They Understand
Henderson & Scott & Robin
I Miss You So
Hendorf
Melancholy Rhapsody
Hendorf & Steiner
Sugarfoot
Hendricks & Adderley
Sermonette
Hendrickson
Spanish Cavalier, The
Hendrix
Are You Experienced
Fire
Foxy Lady
I Don't Live Today
Little Wing
Love Or Confusion
Manic Depression
May This Be Love
Purple Haze
Third Stone From The Sun
Wind Cries Mary, The
Heneker
If The Rain's Got To Fall
Money To Burn
Henley & Boatwright & Hurt
You're Welcome To Tonight
Henley & Campbell
Boys Of Summer, The

Henley & Campbell & Souther
Heart Of The Matter, The
Henley & Corey & Lynch
Last Worthless Evening, The
Henley & Frey
After The Thrill Is Gone
Desperado
Long Run, The
Lyin' Eyes
One Of These Nights
Tequila Sunrise
Wasted Time
Henley & Frey & Felder
Hotel California
Henley & Frey & Meisner
Take It To The Limit
Henley & Frey & Schmit
I Can't Tell You Why
Henley & Frey & Seger & Souther
Heartache Tonight
Henley & Frey & Souther
Best Of My Love, The
New Kid In Town
Henley & Heimermann
Throw Me The Keys
Henley & Hornsby
End Of The Innocence, The
Henley & Kortchmar
Dirty Laundry
Johnny Can't Read
Henley & Kortchmar & Tench
Not Enough Love In The World
Sunset Grill
Henley & Silbar
Wind Beneath My Wings, The
Henneke
Hurricane Spirit Song
Hennessy
Colored Leaves
Grasshopper, The
Henning
Ballad Of Jed Clampett, The
Henrich
Musical Bachelor, The
Henry
Ain't Got No Home
Down In The Cherry Orchard
Evil Ways
Faith Of Our Fathers
He Did So Much For Me
I Know I Am Saved
Land We Love, The
Make Jesus Yours Today
Trust Song, A
When A Wicked Man Dieth
When The Shout Of Battle Dies
    Away
Henry IV
In Praise Of Gabrielle D'Estree
Henry VIII
Green Groweth The Holly
Green Grows The Holly
Henschel
Morning Hymn

Hensel
Fruhling
Nach Suden
Schwanenlied
Hensley & Clarke
Wizard, The
Henson & Pottle
Muppet Show Theme, The
Herald
Take My Life And Let It Be
Herbeck
Lied Jung Werners
Herbert
Absinthe Frappe
Al Fresco
All For The Sake Of A Girl
All For You
Always Do As People Say You
    Should
Angel Of The Lord, The
Angelus
Ask Her When The Band Is Playing
Ask Her While The Band Is Playing
At The Rain-Bow's End
Away In A Manger
Blasting At The Rock Of Ages
Call Around Again
Cricket On The Hearth, The
Cupid Will Guide
Dagger Dance
Dance Of The Marionettes
Eileen
Every Lover Must Meet His Fate
Good Cigar Is A Smoke, A
House That Stood The Storm, The
I Might Be Your Once In A While
I'm A Pilgrim
If I Were On The Stage
In Old New York
Indian Summer
Irish Have A Great Day Tonight, The
Jeannette And Her Little Wooden
    Shoes
Keep Me As The Apple Of The Eye
Knot Of Blue, The
Little Old New York
Love Is A Story That's Old
Love Is Like A Cigarette
Love Is The Best Of All
Love Laid His Sleepless Head
Luther's Cradle Hymn
My Dream Girl
Native Music
Neapolitan Love Song
O Love That Will Not Let Me Go
O My Soul Bless Thou Jehovah
O 'Tis A Great Change For Me
Only One, The
Pretty As A Picture
Rose Of The World
Serenade
Someday
Star Of Love

Herbert *(Cont.)*
When Our Hosts To Battle Go
When Shall I Again See Ireland
When The Maytime Comes Again
When You're Pretty And The World
  Is Fair
When You're Wearing The Ball And
  Chain
Whiter Than Snow
Why Will You Do Without Him
Will O' The Wisp, The
Woman Is Only A Woman, A

Herbert & Bruns
March Of The Toys
Toyland March

Herbert, Victor
Ah Sweet Mystery Of Life
Badinage
Because You're You
Every Day Is Ladies' Day With Me
Fairy Tales
Go To Sleep Slumber Deep
Gypsy Love Song
I Can't Do The Sum
I Want What I Want When I Want It
I'm Falling In Love With Someone
In Dreamland
Isle Of Our Dreams, The
Italian Street Song
Jane
Kiss In The Dark, A
Kiss Me Again
March Of The Toys
Moonbeams
My Angeline
Naughty Marietta
'Neath The Southern Moon
One For Another
Romany Life
Star Light Star Bright
Streets Of New York, The
Sweethearts
Tattooed Man, The
Thine Alone
Time Will Come, The
To The Land Of My Own Romance
Toyland
Tramp Tramp Tramp
When You're Away

Herbst
Forty Days And Forty Nights
Ich Gehe Einher In Der Kraft Des
  Herrn

Herbstritt & Dorff & Sklerov & Lloyd
I Just Fall In Love Again

Hering
At The Spinning-Wheel
Midnight Calm

Heritage
Saviour's Call, The

Herman
Dear World
Du Schone Lilie
Milk And Honey
Night Time Is The Right Time, The
To Mercy Pity Peace And Love
Your Morning Tribute Bring

Herman, Jerry
Before The Parade Passes By
Best In The World, The
Best Of Times, The
Hello Dolly
Hello Lyndon
I Won't Send Roses
If He Walked Into My Life
It Only Takes A Moment
Look Over There
Mame
Shalom
Song On The Sand
Time Heals Everything
We Need A Little Christmas

Hermann
Dear Lord And Father
Dear Lord And Father Of Mankind
Joy To The World
Let All Together Praise Our God
Not Only Where God's Free Winds
  Blow
O God We Praise Thee
On Earth Has Dawned This Day Of
  Days
Sing To The Great Jehovah's Praise
Thy Kingdom Come
Ye That Have Spent The Silent Night

Hermes
Woodland Rose, The

Hernandez
Cumbanchero, El
Lamento Borincano
Where Is The Land Of Joy
Yaller Gal That Winked At Me, The

Herold
Guide Me Great Jehovah
Hour Of Prayer, The
See How Great A Flame Aspires
Swell The Anthem Raise The Song
Take My Life And Let It Be
  Consecrated

Heron-Maxwell
Keep On Hopin'

Herpin
Ma Mie

Herrell
Unveiled Christ, The

Herrero
Corazon De Piedra
Gal With The Balmoral, The

Herring
Easter Song
Mansion Builder
Takin' The Easy Way

Herrington & Foley
Lord As I Wake I Turn To You

Herrington & Jamieson
Care For My Lambs

Herrington & Wren
Bible Story, The

Herrmann
I Know That My Redeemer Lives
Praise God The Lord Ye Sons Of
  Men
Theme From Taxi Driver

Herscher
Daddy's Darling College Boy
Good Morning Good Evening Good
  Night
I Love My Ukulele
I Wish I Weren't A Princess
I'm Glad That I Am A Princess
It Serves Me Right
Lilac Song, The
My High-Brow Love Affair
My Princess Share Your Happiness
  With Me
My Thrill From Seville
Ooh Ooh Georgie
Pinto Minto And Quinto
Sample Of Simpletomania, A
Song Of Woe
Teacher Put Me Among The Girls
That's My Sorority Sweetheart
We Can Run Away To Iceland
We Hope You Liked It We Do
We Want What We Want
What You Turned Out To Be
Where Were You
Why Oh Why Oh Why
You're So Cute

Herst
So Rare

Hertsert
Indian Summer

Herubini
So Come So Come

Hervey
Jesus With Thy Church Abide

Herzig & Watkins
Right From The Start

Herzog & Holiday
Don't Explain
God Bless' The Child

Hesdin
Il N'est Soulas Qui Soit Meilleur A
  Suyvre
Mon Pere M'a Tant Batu

Hess
And I'm A Child Of The King
Come Along
Little Charley Went A Fishing
Monsieur Saint-Pierre
Rendez-Vous Sous La Pluie
Sweet Happiness
Sweeter Gets The Journey
What Would I Do Without Him

Hess & Lewis & Young
Huckleberry Finn

Hess & Misraki
Vous Qui Passez Sans Me Voir
Hessler
Whole Wide World Around, The
Hester & Parenti
When God Ran
Hetherington
I Will Bless The Lord
Heuberger
Auf Dich Seh Ich
Hewitt
All Quiet Along The Potomac
All Quiet Along The Potomac
   Tonight
All Quiet On The Potomac
American Star, The
Attache, The
Aunt Harriett Becha Stowe
Battle Of Trenton, The
Come Ye Men Of Princeton
Dixie The Land Of King Cotton
Maid Of Monterey, The
Rock Me To Sleep Mother
Somebody's Darling
When Upon The Field Of Glory
You Are Going To The Wars Willie
   Boy
Young Volunteer, The
Hewitt & Kirkpatrick
Stepping In The Light
Hewitt & Le Boutillier
Princeton Stadium Song
Hewitt & Osborn
Guard Of Old Nassau, The
I'm Saving A Place For You
Hewitt & Osburn
Princeton Cannon Song, The
Hewitt & Sweeney
More About Jesus Would I Know
Sunshine In The Soul
Hewitt & Wilsen
When We All Get To Heaven
Hewlett
Seek Not Afar For Beauty
Hews
Again As Evening's Shadow Falls
Bread Of Heaven On Thee We Feed
Lord Speak To Me
Lord Speak To Me That I May Speak
Softly Fades The Twilight Ray
Softly Now The Light Of Day
Thou Lord Of Life Our Saving
   Health
Hewson & Evans & Clayton & Mullen
New Years Day
Heyden
Yo Ho Ahoy
Heyman & Green
Out Of Nowhere
Heyman & Young
Love Letters
Heyne
Petite Waltz, The

Heyward
Love Plus One
Heywood
Canadian Sunset
I'm Coming Virginia
Soft Summer Breeze
Heywood & Gimbel
Canadian Sunset
Hiatt
Sure As I'm Sittin' Here
Thing Called Love
Hibbs
God Made A Rose
Hickey
Bluebirds Over The Mountain
Hickman
Lindenwood We're Loyal
Rose Room
Hicks
I'm Happy In Jesus Today
Mathy Grove
Palms Of Victory
Poor Wayfaring Pilgrim, A
Praise The Name Of Jesus
Rude And Rambling Boy, A
Voice From The Tombs
Way Up In Sofield
When Sorrows Encompass Me
   'Round
Where The Sun Don't Never Go
   Down
Hicks & Murrah & Dean
It Takes A Little Rain To Make Love
   Grow
Hickson
O Come Come Away
Oh Come Come Away
Hidaka
In That Cursed Morning Of
   Hiroshima
Hidalgo & Perez
Will The Wolf Survive
Higgenbotham
Hi-Heel Sneakers
Higgins & Limbo
Key Largo
Higgins & Limbo & Jones
Just Another Day In Paradise
Higley
Western Home
Hild
You Don't Know
Hildach
Abschied Der Vogel
Folk-Song
Hildebrand
All He Ever Wants
Childhood Joys
He's Been Wonderful
Hey Paula
I Know Now
Say I Do
We Really Do

Hilderbrand
Hey Paula
Hildreth
Bought By The Blood
Hildt & Nicholo & Warner & Levinson
Put A Tic Tac In Your Mouth
Hiles
How Blessed From The Bonds Of Sin
I Bow My Forhead In The Dust
Jesus Thy Name I Love
O Gracious Father Of Mankind
O Thou Who By A Star Didst Guide
O Zion Blest City
Shadows Of The Evening Hours, The
Thy Word O Lord Like Gentle Dews
Hiliday
Somebody's On My Mind
Hill
Beatrice
Can't We Try
Cucaracha, La
Empty Saddles
For God So Loved
Glory Of Love, The
Hail To The Orange
In The Chapel In The Moonlight
Last Round Up, The
Lights Out
March On Brave Lads March On
My College Girl
Never Thought
Never Thought That I Could Love
Old Spinning Wheel, The
Ooh Poo Pah Doo
Rebel Girl, The
Tramp Tramp Tramp
West A Nest And You, The
What A Day That Will Be
Young Convert, The
Hill & Bays
Card Carryin' Fool
Hill & Derose
There's A Home In Wyomin'
Hill & Hill
Can't We Try
Happy Birthday To You
Birthday Song, The
Hill & Knutson
Out Of Your Mind
Hill & Pierce
Slowly
Hill & Regan
Til Love Comes Again
Hill & Sinfield
Heart Of Stone
Keep Each Other Warm
Peace In Our Time
Hill & Wooley
Two Strong Hearts
Hille
Our Colorado
Hillebrand
Sunday Morning Quarterback

Hillebrand & Michelena
It's A Great Country Over Here
Little Mandy
Theatre In The Sky, The
There's Nothin' Like A Minstrel
    Show
Hiller
Be Near Me Still
Be Thou With Me
Era Of The Era, The
In May-Time
Jumping The Rope
O Woodman Spare That Tree
Wenn Ich Ein Voglein War
Wittenberg Hymn
Hiller & Simons
United We Stand
Hillert
Worthy Is Christ The Lamb Who
    Was Slain
Hilliard & Bacharach
Any Day Now
Hilliard & Deluca
Shanghai
Hilliard & Garson
Our Day Will Come
Hilliard & Miles
Coffee Song, The
Hilliard & Pockriss
Seven Little Girls Sitting In The Back
    Seat
Sitting In The Back Seat
Hilliard & Sanford & Mysels
Mention My Name In Sheboygan
Hilliard & Sigman
Civilization
Hillis
Let Thy Blessing Rest On Me
Will I Empty-Handed Be
Hillman & Hill
I Still Believe In You
Hillman & Napton
My Devotion
Hillmer
Gnade Unsers Herrn Jesu, Die
Hills
O Lovely Night
Hilton
Adieu Deer
Bless Them That Curse You
Cold Winter Now Appears
Come Follow
Come Follow Follow
Come Follow Follow Follow
Come Follow Me
Come Hither Boy
Dungeon Deep
Follow Me
He That Killed The Deer
Here Lies A Woman Tread Soft
I Poor And Well
Invisible Fox Visible Geese
John The Boatman
Let Us All A-Maying Go

Hilton *(Cont.)*
Let Us Go A Maying
Pratty Naun
Reapers
She That Will Eat Her Breakfast In
    Her Bed
Simon's Beard
There Was Three Cooks In
    Colebrook
Three Blewe Beans
To The Greenwood Tree
Turn Amarillis
Wilt Thou Forgive That Sin
Himber
Tonight
Himmel
Ewiger Wechsel
Gebet Wahrend Der Schlacht
Incline Thine Ear
Light Of Those Whose Dreary
    Dwelling
Message Of The Rose, The
Mignon
Prayer, A
Hindemith
Oh Threats Of Hell
Romance
Sea Gypsy, The
Spider's Web, The
Thrush Song
Young And Old
Hine
How Great Thou Art
Hinga
Coasting
Moon, The
My Kite
Hinkle
Indiana Fight
Hinsch
O Susanna Wie Ist Das Leben Doch
    So Schon
Hinson
God's Gonna Do The Same
Let Me Tell You His Name Again
Lighthouse, The
Soldier In The Army
Till The Land
Hinson & August
Fancy Free
Hintze
At The Lamb's High Feast We Sing
Lo The Day Of Days Is Here
Men Whose Boast It Is
Songs Of Thankfulness And Praise
Take My Life And Let It Be
Watchman Tell Us Of The Night
Hirsch
Boola Boola
Can't We Try
Gaby Glide, The
Hello Frisco
I've Never Been To Me

Hirsch *(Cont.)*
Love Nest, The
No One In The World
Two Less Lonely People In The
    World
Used To Be
Hirsch & Rose
Deed I Do
Hirschhorn
Dance A Revolution For Emma
    Goldman
Hirsh
Al Chomotayich Y'Rushalayim
Bashana Haba-A
Boola
Boola Song
O'Se Shalom
Sason Vikar
Yale Boola
Hirtz
Bambaloo
Hitman
Adon Olom
Nolad'ti L'Shalom
Hjelmervik
Morning Song
Hoad & Hoad
Black Leather
Hobbs
Do You Feel The Same Way Too
I Learned All About Cheatin' From
    You
I'm Going To Plant Me A Garden
Phyllis Is My Only Joy
Hobbs & Vickery & Goodman
Jones On The Jukebox
Hobson
Paddle Your Own Canoe
Hodges
Bread Of The World
Bread Of The World In Mercy
    Broken
Buffalo Gals
Come My Soul Thou Must Be
    Waking
Come On My Partners In Distress
How Happy Is The Pilgrim's Lot
Now While The Day In Trailing
    Splendor
O Love Divine How Sweet Thou Art
Someday
Someday You'll Want Me To Want
    You
Hodgson
Daffodil Gold
In Jeopardy
Hoefle
Ma And Pa
Hofer
Sieh Wie Lieblich Und Wie Fein
Wasserstrome Will Ich Giessen
Hoffman
Are You Washed In The Blood
Christ Has For Sin Atonement Made

Hoffman *(Cont.)*
Ding Dong
Enough For Me
Follow All The Way
God Is On His Throne
Good News Must Be Told, The
He Loves Me
Heartaches
How Can I But Love Him
I Am The Lord's Forever
I Have Precious News To Tell
I Have Wonderful Peace
I Must Tell Jesus
I've Had A Glimpse Of Jesus
Is It Not Wonderful
Is Thy Heart Right With God
Is Your All On The Altar
Jesus Shall Have It All
Jesus The Wonderful Savior
Lay Hold On The Life Line
Linger No Longer
May The Master Count On You
More Would I Love Thee
Oh It Is Wonderful
Oh The Glad Good News
Old Memories
Sparkling And Bright
Toil Faithfully On
Trust And Be Encouraged
Unspeakably Precious Is He
Washed In The Blood
We Will Scatter Sunshine
What A Wonderful Savior
What A Wonderful Saviour
When We Reach Our Home
While The Days Are Passing By
Why Are You Waiting
Why Stand Ye Idle
Winning Precious Souls To Thee
Wondrously Redeemed
Hoffman & Curtis & Livingston
Story Of A Starry Night, The
Hoffman & Gimbel
Whale Of A Tale, A
Hoffman & Goodhart
Fit As A Fiddle
Hoffman & Goodhart & Ager
Auf Wiedersehen My Dear
Hoffman & Klein
Bobby's Girl
Hoffman & Livingston
So This Is Love
Hoffman & Livingston & Lampl
Close To You
Hoffman & Manning
Allegheny Moon
Gilly Gilly Ossenfeffer Katzenellen
    Bogen By The Sea
Hot Diggity Dog Ziggity Boom
Takes Two To Tango
Hoffman & Manning & Markwell
Are You Really Mine
Make Me A Miracle
Oh-Oh I'm Falling In Love Again
Secretly

Hoffman & Manning & Reichner
Papa Loves Mambo
Hoffman & Merrill & Watts
I'd've Baked A Cake
Hoffman & Nelson & Goodhart & Ager
Auf Wiedersehn My Dear
Hoffman & Stockton
Down At The Cross
Hoffman & Stork & Fuhrman
Click With Dick
Hoffmann
By The Sycamore Tree
Lord Is Coming, The
Old New Hampshire
Yankee Land
Hoffmann & Macdonald
One Step
Hoffmeister
Arise O Lord
Because Of Thy Great Bounty
Hoffs & Gutierrez & Kahne
Walking Down Your Street
Hofmann
Song Of Praise
Hofmann-Siegen
Wenn Du Ein Herz Gefunden
Hogan
All Coons Look Alike To Me
Army Of Progress
Good Morning Mr Zip
Simple Song Of Love
Hogarty
Sound The Clarion
Hogin & Gillon
Shoe String
Hohmann
Bee, The
Hoiby
Christmas Song, A
River-Merchant's Wife A Letter, The
Hoitsma
Share Your Love
Hol
Child Jesus Comes
Holbrook
Christian Dost Thou See Them
I Heard The Voice Of Jesus Say
Jesus Lover Of My Soul
Jesus Thy Name I Love
O Sacred Head Now Wounded
Holden
All Hail The Pow'r Of Jesus' Name
All Hail The Power
All Hail The Power Of Jesus' Name
Coronation
Crown Him Lord Of All
Ich Sag' Es Jedem Dass Er Lebt
Jesus The Name High Over All
Our God Our God
Paradise
Holden & Bunetta & Chudacoff
Look What You Started
Holder & Lea
My Oh My

Holding & Nevil & Pain
C'est La Vie
Holdrayd
God Of My Life What Just Return
Holdridge
Eight Is Enough
First Time I Loved Forever, The
It's Christmas Time This Year
Lime Street
Love Came For Me
Love Until The End Of Time, A
Moonlighting
O Joyful Children
Theme From Beauty And The Beast
Theme From Sierra
Holdroyd
Wells
Holiday
Billie's Blues
Don't Explain
Fine And Mellow
Long Gone Blues
Second Time You're Born, The
Tell Me More And More And Then
    Some
You're A Flower In The Wildwood
Holiday & Charles
Understanding Is The Best Thing In
    The World
Holiday & Harding
Please Don't Do It In Here
Holiday & Reeves
All I Ever Need Is You
Don't Change On Me
Holiner & Nichols
Look Ahead Neighbor
**Holiner & Nichols & Cahn & Chaplin
& Freeman**
Until The Real Thing Comes Along
Hollaender
Winter Night
**Holland & Bateman & Gorman &
Dobbins & Garrett**
Please Mr Postman
**Holland & Bateman & Stevenson &
Horton**
Playboy
Holland & Dozier & Holland
7 Rooms Of Gloom
Baby Don't You Do It
Baby I Need Your Lovin'
Baby Love
Back In My Arms Again
Bernadette
Can I Get A Witness
Come See About Me
Heat Wave
Heaven Must Have Sent You
How Sweet It Is
How Sweet It Is To Be Loved By
    You
I Can't Help Myself
I Guess I'll Always Love You

Holland & Dozier & Holland (*Cont.*)
I Hear A Symphony
I'm Ready For Love
I'm The One You Need
In And Out Of Love
It's The Same Old Song
Jimmy Mack
Love Is Here And Now You're Gone
Love Is Like An Itching In My Heart
Mickey's Monkey
My World Is Empty Without You
Nothing But Heartaches
Nowhere To Run
Quick Sand
Reach Out I'll Be There
Reflections
Road Runner
Shake Me Wake Me When It's Over
Something About You
Standing In The Shadows Of Love
Stop In The Name Of Love
When The Love Light Starts Shining
    Through His Eye
Where Did Our Love Go
Where Did Your Love Go
You Can't Hurry Love
You Keep Me Hangin' On
You're A Wonderful One
Holland & Dozier & Holland & Moy
This Old Heart Of Mine Is Weak For
    You
Holland & Dozier & Holland & Taylor
There's A Ghost In My House
**Holland & Dozier & Holland &
    Thornton**
Ain't Too Proud To Beg
Put Yourself In My Place
Holland & Harrington
There's A Song In The Air
Holland & Whitfield
Ain't That Peculiar
Ain't Too Proud To Beg
Beauty Is Only Skin Deep
Too Many Fish In The Sea
Holland & Wilson & Taylor
All I Need
Hollander
Falling In Love Again
You Leave Me Breathless
Hollander & Lerner
Falling In Love Again
Holler
Abraham Martin And John
Jesus Meek And Gentle
Lead Us Heavenly Father
Holliday
Evening Bells
Hollingsworth
Stand Beneath The Mistletoe
Hollins
Holy Was That Night So Fair
Hollis & Douglas
Do Anything You Wanna Do

Hollis & Friese-Greene
It's My Life
Holloway
Fish Pond
Precious Saviour
Holly
Crying Waiting Hoping
Words Of Love
Holm
He Means All To Me
Jesus Got Ahold O' My Life
Jesus Got Ahold Of My Life
Losing Game
Rise Again
Holm & Johnson
Tell 'Em Again
Holmes
America's Getting Into Training
Answering Machine
Anytime
Escape
Ev'ry Fat Man
Give Us A Flag
God Of The Circling Realms Of
    Space
God Of The Earth The Sky The Sea
Have You Observed
Him
I'm A Pepper
Irish Noel, An
Love
Money Money
Morning Man
Of All The Thoughts Of God That
    Are
On The Road
Prepare Your Hearts
Rock The Boat
This Gear Goes Hard
Thou Hidden Source Of Calm
    Repose
Weep For The Slain
Who So Free
You Got It All
Holmes & Watkins
Sooner Or Later
Holmes, Rupert
Moonfall
There You Are
Holmquist & Sweet & Sweet
Go On Bruins
Holst
From Glory To Glory Advancing We
    Praise Thee O Lor
Hark The Voice Eternal
I Vow To Thee My Country
In A Bleak Mid-Winter
In Loyal Bonds United
In The Bleak Mid-Winter
Indra God Of Storm And Battle
Lullay My Liking
Maruts
Mid-Winter

Holst (*Cont.*)
O Valiant Hearts Who To Your
    Glory Came
O Valiant Hearts Who To Your
    Glory Come
Song Of The Frogs
Song Of The Ship Builders, The
Song Of The Shoemakers
Terly Terlow
Ushas
Varuna I
Varuna II
Holt
Antioch Church House Choir
I'll Walk Dem Golden Stairs
Lemon Tree
Holvay
Kind Of A Drag
Holvay & Beisber & Guercio
Don't You Care
Holyfield
Down In Tennessee
I'm Gonna Love You Tonight In My
    Dreams
New York Wine And Tennessee
    Shine
You're My Best Friend
Holyfield & Brown & Wilson
When You Get To The Heart
Holyfield & House
Could I Have This Dance
Holyfield & Williams
'Till The Rivers All Run Dry
Holzel
Sing
Holzman
Get On The Raft With Taft
Spirit Of Independence
Home
When I'm Gone
Homer
Barber Barber Shave A Pig
Dance To Your Daddy
Ding Dong Bell
Down Bye Street
Hickory Dickory Dock
House That Jack Built, The
Humpty Dumpty Sat On A Wall
I Had A Little Husband
I Love Six-Pence Pretty Little
    Six-Pence
I Went Up One Pair Of Stairs
If All The World Were Apple-Pie
Little Boy Blue
Little Jack Horner
Little Miss Muffet
Little Polly Flinders
Little Willie Winkle
Mar'gret Wrote A Letter
Mistress Mary Quite Contrary
North Wind Doth Blow, The
Old Father Gray Beard
Old King Cole
One Misty Moisty Morning

Homer *(Cont.)*
Pease-Pudding Hot Pease-Pudding
Cold
Poor Dog Bright
Pussy Cat Pussy Cat Where Have
You Been
Queen Of Hearts, The
Requiem
Rock A-Bye Baby
See-Saw Sacradown
Simple Simon
There Was A Crooked Man
There Was A Little Man
To Market To Market
Tommy Snooks And Bessie Brooks

Honeytree
Clean Before My Lord
Known By Heart
Live For Jesus
Pilgrim, The

Hook
Lass Of Richmond Hill, The
Within A Mile Of Edinboro

Hook & O'Kane
Guaranteed For Life

Hooker
Alimonia Blues
Angeline
Apologize
Big Legs Tight Skirt
Bluebird
Blues Before Sunrise
Boom Boom
Born In Mississippi Raised Up In
Tennessee
Dimples
Down At The Landing
Drifter
Dusty Road
End Of The Blues
Feelin' In Gone, The
Five Long Years
Frisco Blues
Hold On I'm Coming
I'm Leaving
I'm Mad Again
If You Got A Dollar
Let's Make It
Letter To My Baby
Little Wheel
Long Gone
Maudie
Mean Woman Blues
My First Wife Left Me
Night Life Women And Whiskey
No Shoes
Not Yet But Soon
Process
Send Me Your Pillow
She's Mine
Standin' At The Crossroads
Trouble Blues
Tupelo

Hooker *(Cont.)*
Two Bugs In A Rug
Want Ad Blues
Wednesday Evening Blues
What's The Matter Baby
Whiskey And Wimmen
You Talk Too Much
You're Looking Good Tonight

Hooker & Steele
Don't Swat Yer Mother Boys

Hoon & Carney
'Twas Her First

Hooper & Romeo & Wheeler & Law
Back To Life

Hoor
Roll On Tulane

Hoover
Flag Song
Happy Builders
Running
Song Of The Shell

Hope
Lullay Thou Little Tiny Child

Hopfensperger
Red Raven Polka

Hopkins
Adios Ke Aloha
Appetite Blues
Because I Knew Not
Black Cat
Breakfast Time
Cherry Trees, The
Christ's Prayer In Gethsemane
Christmas Comes Again
Christmas Tree, The
Come Holy Ghost Our Souls Inspire
Corrina Corrina
Every Morning Mercies New
Father Again To Thy Dear Name
Father Again To Thy Dear Name We
Raise
Forward Through The Ages
From Thee All Skill And Science
Flow
Gather Around The Christmas Tree
Gather Round The Christmas Tree
Glory Be To God The Father
Go Ye Messengers Of God
God That Madest Earth And Heaven
God The Father God The Son
Holy Holy Holy
House Upon The Hill
I Look To Thee In Every Need
I Sing A Song Of The Saints Of God
I Sought The Lord And Afterward I
Knew
I'm Comin' Home
I'm Tired Of Trouble
Jesu Lord Of Life And Glory
Jesus Lord Of Life And Glory
Kings Of Orient
Little Doves, The
Lonesome Dog Blues
Long Way From Home

Hopkins *(Cont.)*
Lord We Come With Hearts Aflame
Love Me This Morning
Lovin' Arms
My Suggestion
O Can You Play The Clarinet
O God Whose Love Is Over All
Ride In Your New Automobile
Rock Me Mama
Savior Again To Thy Dear Name
Savior Again To Thy Dear Name We
Raise
Saviour Again To Thy Dear Name
Saviour Again To Thy Dear Name
We Raise
Saviour Like A Shepherd Lead Us
Some Day Baby
Talkin' Some Sense
Tell The Blessed Tidings
Theme From Baby Doll
Thou Life Within My Life
Three Kings Of Orient
Ticket Agent
Waipoi
We Praise Thee Lord
We Three Kings
We Three Kings Of Orient Are
Where Lies Our Path We Seek To
Know
You're Too Fast

Hopkins & Lewis
Back Door Friend
Found My Baby Crying
Gambler's Blues
Morning Blues

Hopkins & Taub
Bad Luck And Trouble
Candy Kitchen
Don't Keep My Baby Long
Jake Head Boogie
Last Affair
Mistreated Blues
One Kind Favor

Hopkins & Young
Marching Oregon

Hopkinson
Battle Of The Kegs
Beneath A Weeping Willow
Beneath A Weeping Willow's Shade
Come Fair Rosina
Enraptured I Gaze
Garland, The
Give Me Thy Heart
Hail Columbia
My Days Have Been So Wondrous
Free
My Love Is Gone To Sea
See Down Maria's Blushing Cheek
Toast, The
With Pleasures Have I Passed My
Days

Hopkirk
O Day Of God Draw Nigh
O Day Of God Draw Nigh In Beauty

Hopper
Colt 45
There's No You
Hopper & Gould
Jesus Savior Pilot Me
Hoppin
Campfire Circle
Dnieper, The
Lazy River
Massasoit
Old Bookshop, The
Horatii Flacci
Integer Vitae
Horn
Allan Water
Cherry Ripe
I Know A Bank
I've Been Roaming
Horne
Come Ye Faithful Raise The Strain
For The Might Of Thine Arm
I Know Jesus Will Always Be There
I'll Keep Holding On To Jesus
I'm One Of His Own
Snow, The
Someday
Horner
Giver Of Concord Prince Of Peace
Main Theme From Star Trek II
Main Theme Star Trek II
Search For Spock, The
Though Fatherland Be Vast And Fair
Hornsby
Every Little Kiss
Way It Is, The
Hornsby & German
Schaefer Is The One Beer
Hornsby & Hornsby
Mandolin Rain
Valley Road
Horrocks
Bird And The Rose, The
Horsley
Church Of God A Kingdom Is, The
Lord It Belongs Not To My Care
Mid All The Traffic Of The Ways
There Is A Green Hill Far Away
When All Thy Mercies
When All Thy Mercies O My God
Horsman
Bird Of The Wilderness, The
Stand Stand Up America
Horson
Paddle Your Own Canoe
Horton
Fuglevise
I Don't Want To Live No More
Without Jesus
Mockin' Bird Hill
Old Christmas Card
Teardrops In My Heart
Horton & Hamilton & Carawan & Seeger
We Shall Overcome

Hoschna
Birth Of Passion, The
Cuddle Up A Little Closer
Cuddle Up A Little Closer Lovey
Mine
Every Little Movement
Yama-Yama Man, The
Hosmer
And Then
There's A Friend For Little Children
Hou
Grazing In The Grass
House
Dry Spell Blues
Fa Sol La
My Black Mama
Houser
Behold The Lamb Of God
Calhoun
Chalmers
Crumly
Isles Of The South
My Baby's Gone
Palmetto
Sons Of Sorrow
Sweet Gliding Kerdron
Wheeling
Wilson
Houston
It Was A Dark And Stormy Night
Hovey & Bullard
Hanover Winter Song
Howard
Above And Beyond
Ah How Shall Fallen Man
And Wilt Thou Pardon Lord
Breathe On Me Breath Of God
Busted
Butterfly Song, The
Call Me Mr In-Between
Canticle Of The Gift, The
Chokin' Kind, The
Digging Your Scene
Fly Me To The Moon
From Foes That Would The Land
Devour
Give To The Winds Thy Fears
God Of The Earnest Heart
Good Bye My Lady Love
Have Mercy Lord On Me
Heartaches By The Number
Hello Ma Baby
Hello My Baby
His Are The Thousand Sparkling
Rills
I Believe In The Man In The Sky
I Don't Know A Thing About Love
I Wish That I Could Fall In Love
Today
I Wonder Who's Kissing Her Now
I'm Always On A Mountain When I
Fall
In The Lonely Midnight

Howard *(Cont.)*
Kingdom Of God, The
Let Us Give Thanks
Life Turned Her That Way
Lord Jesus Think On Me
Lord Of The Harvest
Lord Of The Harvest Hear
Mary's Wise Little Lamb
Montana
My Love Is A Wanderer
Not All The Blood Of Beasts
Now That The Sun Is Beaming
Bright
O Pure Reformers
Oh I'se So Wicked
On A Saturday Night
Out Of The Deep I Call
Out Of The Depths I Call To God
Pick Me Up On Your Way Down
Second Hand Rose
Too Many Rivers
When The Robins Nest Again
Wonderful Night
You Never Miss The Water Till The
Well Runs Dry
Howard & Blaikley
Flame Trees Of Thika, The
Howard & Braddock
I Don't Remember Loving You
Howard & Ellsworth & Morgan
Somebody Else Is Taking My Place
Howard & McDonald & Stewart
You Took Her Off My Hands Now
Please Take Her Off My Mind
Howard & Orlob
I Wonder Who's Kissing Her Now
Howard & Owens
Foolin' Around
I've Got A Tiger By The Tail
Howard & Rains
Somebody Should Leave
Howard & Throckmorton & Maher
Why Not Me
Howard & Vincent
My Dear Old Arizona Home
Howard & Walker
I'm Down To My Last Cigarette
Howard & Weston
Shrimp Boats
Howe
Battle Hymn Of The Republic
I Sing Of A Kingdon
Howe & Burns
Down The Lane
Howe & Hackett
When The Heart Rules The Mind
Howell
By The Waters Of Babylon
Young May Moon, The
Howells
All My Hope On God Is Founded
Gavotte
Girl's Song
Holly Song

Howells (*Cont.*)
King David
Madrigal, A
O Holy City Seen Of John
When Cats Run Home

Howliston
Cover Them Over With Flowers

Hoyland
Julekveldsvise

Hoyos
Carrerito, El

Hoyte
From Glory Unto Glory
Rejoice Rejoice Ye Christians

Hsuch-An
Song Of The Great Wall

Hu Jan
Little Blacksmith

Hubbard
Hot Stuff
Love Connection, The
Neo Terra
One Of A Kind
Povo
Texas Bound And Flyin'
Thermo
Thing Called Love, A
'Twas Off The Blue Canaries

Hubbard & Smith
Colgate Fight Song, The

Hubbell
Poor Butterfly

Huber
Gemsjager, Der
Sommers Anfang

Hubert
Sehnsucht Nach Der Heimat
Swiss Evening Song

Hubre
Greeting Song

Hucknall
Right Thing, The

Hucknell & Moss
Holding Back The Years

Huddleston & Colby
I'm A Fool For You

Huddleston & Rinker
Ev'rybody Wants To Be A Cat

Hudson
At The Cross
Benny Havens Oh
Blessed Be The Name
Half Has Never Been Told, The
His Yoke Is Easy
I Know I Love Thee Better Lord
Jesus Now Is Calling
Road To Zion, The
Take Me Home
Tormented

Hudson & Card & Meece
You Can Go

Hudson & Delange & Mills
Moonglow

Hudson & Driskell
Born In Zion

Hudson & Gregory & Bracken
Baby It's You

Hudson & Mills
You're Not The Kind

Hue
A Des Oiseaux
In A Dream I Sorrowed
In My Dreams I Sorrowed
J'ai Pleure En Reve
To The Birds

Huelani
Violeta

Huerter
Pirate Dreams
There's That About A Rose

Huerto
We Soldiers Proud And Faithful

Hues
Dance Hall Days

Hues & Feldman
Let's Go
To Live And Die In LA

Hues & Feldman & Wolf
Everybody Have Fun Tonight

Huff
Do It Anyway You Wanna

Huffam
It's Not Over
Power And The Holy Ghost
This Coming King

Huffhines
Christmas Elf, The

Huffman
Tight Fittin' Jeans

Huffman & Brown
Beautiful Savior

Huffman & Lehman
Right Direction

Huffman & Waters
When You're Following Jesus

Hugg
Adoration
At Anchor Riding
At Last
Bells Across The Snow
Beyond
Bonar
Callest Thou
Cheering Light
Children Come
Come To Me
Coming
Enter In
Even So Amen
Fresh Springs
Galilee
Glad Bells
Going Up To Zion
Gospel Armour
Green Hill, A
Have You Not A Word
Healer, The

Hugg (*Cont.*)
In The Happy Land
Jesus Knows
Joy Joy Joy
Just The Same
Land Of Promise
Lean On Me
Lift Me Higher
Light Divine
List The Notes
Living Water
Make Room
Master Is Come, The
Morning, The
No Not One
Our Cheerful Song
Praise Ye
Trusting Jesus
Turning To God
Under His Shadow
Victory
Wait Patiently
Walk In The Light
Wandering Sheep
Watchers, The
We'll Never Say Good Bye
Worker's Prayer, The
Yes We Have A Word

Huggins
Blessed Hour Of Prayer

Hughes
All As God Wills
Blessed
God Of Grace And God Of Glory
Guide Me O Thou Great Jehovah
I Know Someone
I Seek Not Life's Ease And Pleasure
Island Song
O Men From The Fields
Tennessee Saturday Night
Up Up Ye Dames And Lasses Gay
What Does He Plant Who Plants

Hughes & Lake & Stillman
Bless 'Em All

Hughes & McConnell
Mickey Donohue

Hugo & Luigi & Weiss
Hey Girl Come And Get It

Hull
Remember Me

Hullah
I Know No Life
Sometimes A Light Surprises
Three Fishers

Hulse
Behold O God This Lowly Bread

Hume
Afton Water
Dare To Be Brave Dare To Be True
Flow Gently Sweet Afton

Hume-Douglas
Here We Have Idaho

Humfrey
Hymn To God The Father, A
Where The Bee Sucks
Willow Song, The

Hummel
Ausfahrt
Streitgegang

Humperdinck
Brother Come And Dance
Children's Prayer, The
Dance With Me
Dancing Lesson, The
Evening Prayer
Little Man, A
Little Man, The
Magic Castle, The
Oh Happy Be And Gay And Free
Prayer From Hansel And Gretel, The
Sandman's Song, The
Suse Little Suse
Susie Little Susie
Susy Little Susy
There Stands A Little Man
Tiny Little Man, A

Humphreys
Christ Our Passover
Exultation
He Shall Teach You All Things
Kingwood

Humphreys & McCluskey
If You Leave
Secret

Humphreys & McCluskey & Hague
So In Love

Hunemann
Jesus Lebt Frohlockend Sing' Ich

Hunnicutt & Gilmore & Vincent
Doo-Wah Days

Hunt
Bell Goes A-Ringing For Sai-Rah
Blessed Be The Name
Bold Fisherman, The
Dear Old Pals
Macdermott's War Song
Starlight In Thine Eyes, The
Up In A Balloon

Hunter
Cosmic Charlie
I Almost Lost My Mind
I Feel Like Traveling On
I Need You So
It Must Have Been The Roses
My Wish Came True
Once Bitten Twice Shy
Out Of Sight Out Of Mind
Queen Of Love
Ships
Since I Met You Baby
St Stephen
Tragedy
Why We Smile

Hunter & McKernan
Alligator

Hunter & Otis
Ain't That Loving You Baby
Out Of Sight Out Of Mind

Hunter & Pigott & Hunter
Rain

Hunter & Verdi
Behind A Painted Smile

Huntington
Over There

Huntsinger
Everlasting Peace

Hupfeld
As Time Goes By
Let's Put Out The Lights And Go To
Sleep
Sing Something Simple
When Yuba Plays The Rhumba On
The Tuba
When Yuba Plays The Rumba On
The Tuba

Hupfield
As Time Goes By

Hupp & Macrae & Morrison
Don't Call Him A Cowboy

Huppfeld
As Time Goes By

Hurd
Christ Mighty Savior Light Of All
Creation
Creating God Your Fingers Trace
He Is The Way
Jesus Calls Us O'Er The Tumult
O Christ You Are Both Light And
Day
Praise The Spirit In Creation
Stable Lamp Is Lighted, A
When Jesus Dies To Save Us
Ye Who Claim The Faith Of Jesus

Hurlebusch
Bescheidne Liebe

Hurley
For Boston
Marching Song

Hurley & Wilkins
Love Of The Common People
Son-Of-A-Preacher Man

Hurt
Spike Driver Blues

Hurt & Dubois
Love In The First Degree

Husband
Coming Coming Yes They Are
Live Out Thy Life Within Me
O Jesus Thou Art Standing
Revive Us Again
We Praise Thee O God

Huston
Beloved Old Purdue
For The Honor Of Old Purdue
It Pays To Serve Jesus
Purdue Hymn
Word Of God Shall Stand, The

Hutch
Keep On Jammin'

Hutch & Johns
Sexy Ways

Hutcherson
Highway One
I Wanna Stand Over There
Littlest One Of All, The

Hutcheson
And Now The Wants Are Told That
Brought
Go Not My Soul
O For A Thousand Tongues
O Thou Whose Spirit Witness Bears
Though Lowly Here Our Lot May Be
Twenty-Third Psalm, The

Hutchinson
Dream Faces
Excelsior
Fetters Of Gold
Go Call The Doctor And Be Quick
Kind Words Can Never Die
Little Topsy's Song
Mountain Echo
My Mother's Bible
Sweet Dreamland Faces
Uncle Sam's Farm

Hutchison
Pierrot
Sammy

Hutsell
U Of M Rouser, The

Hutson
Easter Alleluia
O Lamb Of God

Hutton
Duke Street

Hyatt
Pass On The Torch
Touch Of Human Hands, The

Hyde
Sixty
You're Only Young Once

Hyde & Henry
Little Girl

Hye-Knudsen
Catkin
Rabbit, The

Hynde
Back On The Chain Gang
Don't Get Me Wrong

Hynde & Honeyman-Scott
Brass In Pocket

Ian
At Seventeen
Society's Child

Icini
Believe In Me
Summertime In Venice

Idol
White Wedding

Iglesias
Mes 33 Ans
Pauvres Diables

Iglesias & Arcusa & Calva
Aimer La Vie

Iglesias & Belfiore & Balducci & AR
Il Faut Tourjours Un Perdant
Iglesias & Ferro
Viens M'embrasser
Iglesias & Ferro-Cecilia
Quiero
Iglesias & Navarro & Calva & Arcusa
Souriez Madame
Iglesias & Sobredo
A Veces Tu A Veces Yo
Ilsley
Cradle Song
Soldier's Suit Of Grey, The
Imagawa
In The Sky A Bright Star Gleaming
We Thank Thee God
Imber
Hatikvah
Hatikvoh
Immel
Dallas
King's Crossing
Knot's Landing
Yellow Rose, The
Imre
Megallok A Keresztutnal
Indy
Buvons Bien
Ingalls
And Can It Be That I Should Gain
Come Ye Sinners
New Jerusalem
Northfield
O For A Thousand Tongues
Turn To The Lord
Ingham
High O'er The Lonely Hills
Ingle
In-A-Gadda-Da-Vida
My Old Dutch
Nasty Way 'E Sez It, The
Our Little Nipper
Sich A Nice Man Too
Wot Cher
Wot's The Good Of Hanyfink
Why-Nuffink
Ingler
Pearly White City, The
Ingles
Garment Of Praise
I Am Healed
I Am The Righteousness Of God In
Christ
Oasis Of Love
Paralyzed
That Name
There's A Whole Lot Of People
Going Home
Thomas Kind Of Faith, The
Wonderful Excellent Mighty
Ingraham
All That I Ask Of You Is Love
Because I'm Married Now

Ingraham *(Cont.)*
Don't Wake Me Up I Am Dreaming
Good-Bye Rose
Little Miss Clover
Roses Bring Dreams Of You
Sweet Red Rose, The
When I Dream In The Gloaming Of
You
Won't You Waltz Home Sweet
Home With Me
You Are The Ideal Of My Dreams
Ingram & Jones
PYT
PYT Pretty Young Thing
**Ingram & McDonald & Jones &
Temperton**
Yah Mo B There
Inini
Believe In Me
Innes
At The Bakery
Whip-Poor-Will
Insetta
Sitting By The Window
Inzenga
Canto De La Trilla
Iommi & Osbourne & Ward & Butler
Paranoid
Ippolitof-Ivanof
Bless The Lord
In A Manger
Incline Thine Ear
When We Parted Alma Mater
When We Parted
Irby
Apples Peaches Pumpkin Pie
Ireland
Encounter, The
Epilogue
Goal And Wicket
Holy Boy, The
In Praise Of May
Ladslove
Lent Lily, The
Love Is A Sickness
My Song Is Love Unknown
New Prince New Pomp
Spring Sorrow
Summer Schemes
Vain Desire, The
Irons
How Sad Our State By Nature Is
Hymn Of Praise
Jerusalem My Happy Home
O Mother Dear Jerusalem
Sun Is Sinking Fast, The
Irvine
Lord My God My Shepherd, The
Lord's My Shepherd, The
Irwin
Healer, The
Irwin & Owens & Simmons
Oh Baby

Isaac
Communio
Dear Love Now I Must Leave Thee
Duteous Day Now Closeth, The
Farewell To Innsbruck
Innsbruck Ich Muss Dich Lassen
Lord God By Whom All Change Is
Wrought
Now Are The Woodlands Resting
Now Rest Beneath Night's Shadows
O Welt Ich Muss Dich Lassen
To Sleep
Whole World Lies In Shadows, The
Woods Are Hushed, The
Isaacs
Write A Letter To My Mother
Isaak
Now All The Woods Are Sleeping
Now Rest Beneath Night's Shadow
O Bread Of Heaven
O Sacred Heart All Holy
O Welt Ich Muss Dich Lassen
Isawa
Tencho Setsu No Uta
Isbell
Mexico
Isenmann
Cheerful Heart, A
Isley & Isley & Isley
Nobody But Me
Respectable
Shout
Isley & Isley & Isley & Isley & Isley
Between The Sheets
Choosey Lover
Isley & Isley & Isley & Jasper
Need A Little Taste Of Love
Israel
ABC 20 20
ABC Monday Night Football
Olympic II USA Vs The World
Iszlai
All Beautiful The March Of Days
Hours Of School Are Over, The
We Come O God With Gladness
Ivanoff
Praise The Name Of The Lord
Ivanovici
Danube Waves
Silver Wedding Song
Wedding Waltz, The
Iverson
Spirit Of The Living God
Ives
Christmas Carol, A
Cumberland Crew, The
Evening
Peaks
Pictures
Psalm 67
Sea Dirge, A
Serenity
See 'r, The
Vote For Names

Ives (*Cont.*)
Waltz
Where The Eagle
Ivey
I Would Live In Your Life
To One Away
Ivey & Woodford & Brasfield
Angel In Your Arms, The
Izlai
Sing Forth His High Eternal Name
Jabara
Last Dance
Jabara & Esty
Fight
Jabara & Roberts
Enough Is Enough
Main Event, The
No More Tears
Jachet
Fisherman, The
Jachino
Santa Orazione Alla Vergine Maria
Jackson
Another Patriot Claims The Votive
Strain
Be Not Always
Behold Us Lord A Little Space
Body
Breathe On Me Breath Of God
Captain Of Industry
Centipede
Control
Ever True To Brown
For The Fruit Of All Creation
God Bless Our Native Land
Great And Fair Is She Our Land
Happy Rest In Jesus
He Saves Me Today
Hearts Of Stone
I Am A Union Woman
Kansas City Blues
Let The Joy Overflow
Lovely One
Muscles
Parting Hymn
Poor Miner's Farewell
Right Or Wrong
Salty Dog Blues
Shower Me With Your Love
State Of Shock
Steppin' Out
Tawny Lass
This Is The Way That I Feel
Torture
When A Woman That's Buxom
When Father Laid The Carpet On
The Stairs
Would You Be Saved
You Can't Get What You Want
Jackson & Bono
She Said Yeah
Jackson & Harris & Lewis
Alright
Escapade
Rhythm Nation

Jackson & Jackson
Lovely One
Turn The Beat Around
Jackson & Jones
Old Time Rock And Roll
Jackson & Molinary & Foelber
Burning Hot
Jackson & Omartian & Wonder
I Think It's Love
Jackson & Omartin & Wonder
I Think It's Love
Jackson & Ray
Hearts Of Stone
Jackson & Richie
We Are The World
Jackson & Seymour
Christmas Will Be Just Another
Lonely Day
Jackson & Smith & Miner
Higher And Higher
Jackson & Straigis & Williams
So Much In Love
Jackson & Townsend
Closer Than Friends
Jackson & Van Alstyne
Pretty Baby
Jackson & Yancy
I've Got Love On My Mind
Our Love
Jackson, Michael
Another Part Of Me
Bad
Beat It
Billie Jean
Dirty Diana
Don't Stop Till You Get Enough
Girl Is Mine, The
I Just Can't Stop Loving You
Leave Me Alone
Liberian Girl
Smooth Criminal
Speed Demon
Wanna Be Startin' Somethin'
Way You Make Me Feel, The
Jacob
Lord You've Tested Me
Pretty Pollie Pillicote
Rejoice Rejoice You Men Of God
Jacobi
Elegy
Ode To Freedom
On The Sleep Of Plants
You Are Free
Jacobowski
Lullaby
Parade, The
Jacobs
Blues With A Feeling
This Is My Country
Jacobs & Olshanetsky
Belz
Jacobs-Bond
Birds
Forget-Me-Not, The

Jacobs-Bond (*Cont.*)
God Remembers When The World
Forgets
Golden Key, The
Good Night
Hand Of You, The
Her Greatest Charm
His Lullaby
Hush-A-By
I Love You Truly
I've Done My Work
In The Meadow
Is Yo' Yo' Is
Just A Wearyin' For You
Just Lonesome
Lazy River
Life's Garden
Little Bit O'Honey, A
Little Pink Rose, A
O Time Take Me Back
Perfect Day, A
Sandman, The
Shadows
Song Of The Hills, A
Study In Symbols, A
Through The Years
Until God's Day
Were I
When Church Is Out
When God Puts Out The Light
Jacobsen
Little Ole
Jacobson
Marie Antoinette's Song
Jacobus
O Lamb Of God
Jacotin
A Paris A Trois Fillettes
Amor Me Poingt Et Si Ne Me Veulx
Plaindre
Dame D'honneur Princesse De
Beaulte
Qui Veult Aimer Il Fault Estre
Joyeulx
Jacques-Dalcroze
Bluebird, The
Jacquet
Funny Mandarin, A
Zoo, The
Jadin
Colas Colas Sois-Moi Fidele
Jaeggi
O Christians Let Us Join In Song
Jaffe & Bonx
Collegiate
Jaffe & Fulton & Bonx
If You Are But A Dream
Jagger
Just Another Night
Throwaway
Jagger & Alomar
Lucky In Love
Jagger & Richards
All Sold Out

Jagger & Davies
Have You Seen Your Mother Baby
    Standing In The Sha
Jagger & Richards & Oldham
As Tears Go By
Jagger & Richards
100 Years Ago
19th Nervous Breakdown
2000 Light Years From Home
2000 Man
All About You
All Down The Line
All Together
Angie
Back Street Girl
Beast Of Burden
Before They Make Me Run
Bitch
Blue Turns To Grey
Brown Sugar
Can You Hear The Music
Can't You Hear Me Knocking
Casino Boogie
Child Of The Moon
Citadel
Coming Down Again
Complicated
Congratulations
Connection
Cool Calm Collected
Country Honk
Crazy Mama
Dance Little Sister
Dancing With Mr D
Dandelion
Dead Flowers
Dear Doctor
Don't Lie To Me
Doncha' Bother Me
Doo Doo Doo Doo
Down In The Hole
Each And Every Day Of The Year
Emotional Rescue
Factory Girl
Family
Far Away Eyes
Fingerprint File
Flight 505
Fool To Cry
Get Off My Cloud
Gimme Shelter
Goin' Home
Gomper
Good Times Bad Times
Gotta Get Away
Grown Up Wrong
Hand Of Fate
Happy
Have You Seen Your Mother Baby
    Standing In The Shadows
Heart Of Stone
Hey Negrita
Hide Your Love
High And Dry

Jagger & Richards *(Cont.)*
Honky Tonk Women
Hot Stuff
I Am Waiting
I Got The Blues
I'm Free
I'm Going Down
If You Can't Rock Me
If You Let Me
If You Really Want To Be My Friend
Indian Girl
It's Not Easy
It's Only Rock 'n Roll
It's Only Rock 'n' Roll But I Like It
Jigsaw Puzzle
Jiving Sister Fanny
Jumpin' Jack Flash
Just Want To See His Face
Lady Jane
Lantern, The
Last Time, The
Let It Bleed
Let It Loose
Let Me Go
Let's Spend The Night Together
Lies
Live With Me
Long Long While
Love In Vain
Loving Cup
Luxury
Melody
Memo From Turner
Memory Motel
Midnight Rambler
Miss Amanda Jones
Miss You
Mixed Emotions
Monkey Man
Moonlight Mile
Mother's Little Helper
My Obsession
No Expectations
Off The Hook
On With The Show
One More Try
Out Of Time
Paint It Black
Parachute Woman
Please Go Home
Respectable
Ride On Baby
Rip This Joint
Rock And A Hard Place
Rocks Off
Ruby Tuesday
Sad Day
Salt Of The Earth, The
Satisfaction
Send It To Me
Shattered
She Smiled Sweetly
She Was Hot

Jagger & Richards *(Cont.)*
She's A Rainbow
She's So Cold
Shine A Light
Short And Curlies
Silver Train
Singer Not The Song, The
Sister Morphine
Sittin' On A Fence
Sleepy City
So Much In Love
Some Girls
Some Things Just Stick In Your Mind
Something Happened To Me
    Yesterday
Soul Survivor
Spider And The Fly, The
Star Star
Start Me Up
Stray Cat
Street Fighting Man
Stupid Girl
Summer Romance
Surprise Surprise
Sway
Sweet Black Angel
Sweet Virginia
Sympathy For The Devil
Take It Or Leave It
Tell Me You're Coming Back
Think
Till The Next Goodbye
Time Waits For No One
Torn And Frayed
Try A Little Harder
Tumbling Dice
Turd On The Run
Under My Thumb
Undercover
Undercover Of The Night
Waiting On A Friend
Wasting Time
We Love You
What A Shame
What To Do
When The Whip Comes Down
Where The Boys Go
Who's Been Sleeping Here
Who's Driving Your Plane
Wild Horses
Winter
Yesterday's Papers
You Can't Always Get What You
    Want
You Got The Silver
You Gotta Move
You Must Be The One
Jagger & Richards & Jones & Wyman & Watts
I'm All Right
Jagger & Richards & Jordan
Almost Hear You Sigh

Jagger & Richards & Oldham
As Tears Go By
Jagger & Richards & Taylor
Ventilator Blues
Jagger & Richards & Wood
Dance
One Hit To The Body
Jagger & Stewart
Let's Work
Say You Will
Jakobowski
Birds Of A Feather
Dream Song
Good Night
Lullaby
Jal
C'etait Une Histoire D'amour
James
All For Jesus
American Anthem
And Have The Bright Immensities
Angela
Boogaloo Down Broadway
Courtship
Cut Yourself A Piece Of Cake
Cypress Grave
Dear Ole Duke
Ebony Eyes
Freight Train
Hooked On A Feeling
I'm Beginning To See The Light
In My House
Moody Blue
O Nightingale
Party All The Time
Raised On Rock
Suspicious Minds
Wait's Carol, The
Where Can My Baby Be
Wild And Crazy Love
James & Grasso
Sweet Cherry Wine
James & Josea
Please Find My Baby
Rock My Baby Right
Standing At The Crossroads
James & King
Gotta Get Back To You
James & Lucia
Crimson And Clover
James & McClintock
All This Time
James & Miller
Come To Baby Do
James & Miller & Hammer
U Can't Touch This
James & Organ
I'll Go Stepping Too
James & Taub
Mean And Evil
James & Vale & Gray
Crystal Blue Persuasion
James & Williams
Freight Train

Jameson
Landing Of The Pilgrims, The
Lord's Prayer, The
March Of Labor, The
Jameson & Feller
Summertime Summertime
Jameson & O'Leary
Weatherman Says
Janacek
Moo Moo Two By Two
Janequin
Au Joli Jeu De Pousse Avant
Chant Des Oiseaux, Le
Or Vien Ca Vien M'amie
Plus Belle De La Ville, La
Pourquoi Tournez Vous Vos Yeux
Janis
Nanu Nanu I Wanna Funky Wich
You
Jannequin
Month Of May, The
Janos
Bakony Erdon Sir A Gerle
Ha Eler Hoszad
Jansch
Needle Of Death
Janssen
At The End Of Day
Liners
Little Brown Bug
Mary Call The Cattle Home
Janssen & Hart
Somethin's Wrong With Me
Janz
Believe In Me
Enemies Like You And Me
Janz & Janz
Leaving LA
Janza
Lion Tamer Rag, The
Jararaca & Paiva
I Want My Mama
Jarman
O For A Thousand Tongues
Jaroff
Heave Ahoy Ho
Jarrard & Martin
Lonely Alone
Jarrard & Nicholson
I Wonder What She's Doing Tonight
Jarrard & Palas & Aldridge
They Only Come Out At Night
Jarrard & Quillen
What's A Memory Like You
What's A Memory Like You Doing
In A Love Like This
Jarre
Forbidden
It Was A Good Time
Lawrence Of Arabia
Main Theme From Witness
Somewhere My Love
Theme From Fatal Attraction

Jarre (Cont.)
Theme From Lawrence Of Arabia
Theme From Lion Of The Desert
Jarreau
Spirit
Jarreau & Graydon & Canning
Breakin' Away
Roof Garden
Jarreau & Graydon & East & East
Fallin'
Jarreau & Graydon & Foster
After All
Mornin'
Jarreau & Graydon & Lyle
High Crime
Jarreau & Klugh
This Time
Jarreau & Omartian
Boogie Down
Jarrett
You Can Make It If You Try
Jarrett & Charles
I'm Leavin'
Jarvis
Good Three Bells, The
Greatest Gift Of All, The
Lift Him Up
Quiet Place
Jarvis & Cook
Julia
Small Town Girl
Jason & Burton
Penthouse Serenade
Jaspers
Jerusalem Surge
Jaspersen
Say Not The Struggle Nought
Availeth
Voice Of Truth, The
Welcome Wild Northeaster
Javits & Springer & Springer
Santa Baby
Jay
Cross My Heart
Westinghouse Makes It Happen
Jay & Cruz
Right Combination, The
Jay & Martika
Toy Soldiers
Jay & Morrow
If I Say Yes
Jay & Palombi
Mind Over Matter
Jay & Reid & Abrams
Johnny Be Smart
Jay & Smith
Bounce Back
Jayne
Oh What A Night It Must Have
Been
Jazzini
Holy Mary
Jeboult
Forgive Them O My Father

Jefferson
Match Box Blues
One Dime Blues
Rabbit Foot Blues

Jeffery
Ancient Of Days
Ancient Of Days Who Sittest
Throned
Ancient Of Days Who Sittest
Throned In Glory
Father Of Lights
Inauguration Day Hymn
Lord God Of Hosts Whose Purpose
O God Of God O Light Of Light

Jefferys
Chosen Three On Mountain Height,
The
We Have Lived And Loved Together

Jeffreys
Summer Days Are Coming

Jenkin
Frogs At Night

Jenkins
All Over This World
Boat A Boat, A
Come Pretty Maidens
Fire Ball Mail
Night In The Desert
Ps I Love You
Sweet Sexy Eyes
This Is All I Ask

Jenko
God Of Justice
Jugoslav National Anthem

Jenks
Alas And Did My Saviour Bleed

Jenner
Lord Be Thy Word My Rule
My Father Hear My Prayer
We Love The Place O God

Jennings
Are You Sure Hank Done It This
Way
Don't You Think This Outlaw Bit's
Done Got Out Of Hand
Good Ol' Boys
I've Always Been Crazy
Love Came For Me
Never Could Toe The Mark
People Up In Texas
Shine

Jennings & Bowman
Just To Satisfy You

Jennings & Buffett & Utley & Leo
Who's The Blonde Stranger

Jennings & Emmons
Women Do Know How To Carry On

Jennings & Murrah
How Much Is It Worth To Live In La
Somewhere Between Ragged And
Right

Jennings & Murrah & Jennings
If Ole Hank Could Only See Us Now

Jennings & Nelson
Good Hearted Woman

Jenny
We Praise Thee Lord Whose Life We
Are

Jeno
Az A Szep
Halvany Sarga Rozsat
Minek Turbekoltok

Jensen
Barcarole
Bigger Than Any Mountain
Blossoms And Flowers
Breath Of Spring, A
Busy Clock, A
Coming Of The Lord, The
Departure
Ere Long O Heart Of Mine
Forest Voices
Forever Is A Long Long Time
From Slumber Awaken
Futile Candle Flame Am I, A
Here Where Rose And Grape
Entwine
I Should Have Been Crucified
In The Hills
In The Mountains
In The Shadow Of My Tresses
It Made News In Heaven
It Made News In Heaven When I
Got Saved
It Seemed In My Dream
Jesus Will Outshine Them All
Jock Of Hazeldean
Last Wish
Leafy Trees With Boughs Entwining
Lehn' Deine Wang'
Lehn' Deine Wang' An Meine
Wang'
Lehn's Deine Wang' An Meine
Wang'
Linden, The
Lullaby Of An Infant Chief
Margreta
Marie
Mother Mine Nor Rain Nor Dew
Murmuring Breezes
Murmuring Zephyr
Now Are The Glorious Halcyon
Days
Now The Shadows Darken
O Faster My Steed
O Lay Thy Cheek On Mine Dear
Love
O Stay Thou Golden Moment
O Stay Thy Passing Golden
Moments
Oh Press Thy Cheek Against Mine
Own
Old Assyrian Song
Old Heidelberg Thou Fairest
Once By Thy Beauty Kindled
Play Away Oh My Pandora
Press Thy Cheek Against Mine Own

Jensen (*Cont.*)
Puritan Maid, The
Redemption Draweth Nigh
Song Holy Angels Cannot Sing
Song To Sing At Midnight, A
Spring Night
Sweet And Low
Swiss Song
Thou Gentle Night Of Springtime
Tinkle Gaily My Pandero
Two Sparkling Eyes I've Seen
Und Schlafst Du Mein Madchen
We'll Cast Our Crowns At His Feet
We're Together Again
What Wrong My Father
When Through The Piazzetta
Where Flows The Bright River
Why So Pale

Jentes
I Don't Want To Get Well

Jerome
Just A Baby's Prayer At Twilight
Lam' Lam' Lam'
Mi Caballero
My Little Buckaroo
Old Pal Why Won't You Answer Me
Sweet Dreams Sweetheart

Jerome & Heindorf
Some Sunday Morning

Jessel
Parade Of The Wooden Soldiers

Jessop
Anywhere With Jesus

Jett & Child
I Hate Myself For Loving You
Little Liar

Jeune
Ce N'est Que Fiel
J'aime La Pierre Precieuse
Jerusalem The Golden
Revoice Venir Du Printemps
Susanne Un Jour

Jewitt
Comfort Ye One Another
Father We Thank Thee
I Am Thy God
Teach Me To Pray

Jezek
Against The Storm
V Song

Jimenez
Adios Mariquita Linda

Job & Dawson & Hagans
Whenever You're Ready

Jobim
Desafinado
Dindi
Girl From Ipanema, The
Goodbye Tristesse
How Insensitive
Meditation
No More Blues
Once I Loved

Jobim *(Cont.)*
One Note Samba
Quiet Night Of Quiet Stars
Slightly Out Of Tune
Someone To Light Up My Life
Wave

Joel
52nd Street
Ain't No Crime
All For Leyna
All You Wanna Do Is Dance
Allentown
Angry Young Man
Baby Grand
Ballad Of Billy The Kid, The
Big Man On Mulberry Street
Big Shot
C'etait Toi
Captain Jack
Careless Talk
Christie Lee
Close To The Borderline
Code Of Silence
Don't Ask Me Why
Easy Money
Entertainer, The
Everybody Has A Dream
Everybody Loves You Now
Get It Right The First Time
Getting Closer
Goodnight Saigon
Great Suburban Showdown, The
Half A Mile Away
Honesty
I Don't Want To Be Alone
I Go To Extremes
I've Loved These Days
If I Only Had The Words To Tell
    You
Innocent Man, An
It's Still Rock And Roll To Me
James
Just The Way You Are
Keeping The Faith
Last Of The Big Time Spenders
Laura
Leave A Tender Moment Alone
Longest Time, The
Los Angelenos
Matter Of Trust, A
Mexican Connection, The
Miami 2017
Modern Woman
Movin' Out
My Life
New York State Of Mind
Night Is Still Young, The
Only The Good Die Young
Piano Man
Prelude
Pressure
Roberta
Room Of Our Own, A

Joel *(Cont.)*
Root Beer Rag
Rosalinda's Eyes
Running On Ice
Say Goodbye To Hollywood
Scandanavian Skies
Scenes From An Italian Restaurant
She's Always A Woman
She's Got A Way
She's Right On Time
Sleeping With The Television On
Sometimes A Fantasy
Somewhere Along The Line
Souvenir
Stiletto
Stop In Nevada
Stranger, The
Streetlife Serenader
Summer Highland Falls
Surprises
Tell Her About It
Temptation
This Is The Time
This Night
Through The Long Night
Travelin' Prayer
Until The Night
Uptown Girl
Vienna
We Didn't Start The Fire
Weekend Song
Where's The Orchestra
Worse Comes To Worst
You May Be Right
You're My Home
You're Only Human
Zanzibar

John
I Need You To Turn To
Is Thy Cruse Almost Exhausted
Nikita
Reverie
Sad Eyes
Song For Guy
Triumphal Song

John Alexander Band, The
No More Commercials
We're Comin' Back

John & Osborne
Big Dipper
Blue Eyes
I Don't Care
It Ain't Gonna Be Easy
Little Jeannie
Madness
Oh Georgia
Part-Time Love
Return To Paradise
Shine On Through

John & Osbourne
Shooting Star

John & Taupin
Levon
Tower Of Babel

John & Taupin
Bennie And The Jets
Better Off Dead
Billy Bones And The White Bird
Bitch Is Back, The
Bite Your Lip Get Up And Dance
Bitter Fingers
Candle In The Wind
Captain Fantastic And The Brown
    Dirt Cowboy
Chameleon
Club At The End Of The Street
Country Comfort
Crazy Water
Crocodile Rock
Curtains
Daniel
Dixie Lily
Don't Let The Sun Go Down On Me
Feed Me
Goodbye Yellow Brick Road
Grimsby
Grow Some Funk Of Your Own
Healing Hands
I Don't Wanna Go On With You
    Like That
I Feel Like A Bullet In The Gun Of
    Robert Ford
I've Seen The Saucers
Idol
In Neon
Island Girl
Meal Ticket
Nikita
Out Of The Blue
Philadelphia Freedom
Pinky
Rocket Man
Sacrifice
Sad Songs
Salvation
Shoulder Holster
Solar Prestige A Gammon
Someone Saved My Life Tonight
Someone's Final Song
Sorry Seems To Be The Hardest
    Word
Stinker
Street Kids
Tell Me When The Whistle Blows
Theme From A Non-Existent TV
    Series
Ticking
Tiny Dancer
Tonight
We All Fall In Love Sometimes
Where's The Shoorah
Writing
You're So Static
Your Song

John & Taupin & Johnstone
Cage The Songbird
I Guess That's Why They Call It The Blues
If There's A God In Heaven What's He Waiting For
Wrap Her Up
John & Taupin & Johnstone & Quaye
Between Seventeen And Twenty
Boogie Pilgrim
John & Taupin & Johnstone & Quaye & Newton-Howard
Wide Eyed And Laughing, The
John & Taupin & Newton-Howard
One Horse Town
Johns
Barefoot Boy
Common Man
Echo Song
Tessie
Where Blooms The Rose
Johnson
32-20 Blues
Almighty God Your Word Is Cast
Band O' Gideon, De
Believe I'll Dust My Broom
Bible A-B-C, The
Blame It On The Union
Bye Bye Blues
Canned Heat Blues
Carrier Dove, The
Come On In My Kitchen
Company Unions
Congo Love Song
Crossroad Blues
Day By Day I'll Follow Jesus
Day He Wore My Crown, The
Dead Shrimp Blues
Drawin' From The Well
Drunken-Hearted Man
Earth And All Stars Loud Rushing Planets
Everybody Dance
Florida Cakewalk
Followin' You
Following You
From Four Until Late
Full Fathom Five Thy Father Lies
Give Them All To Jesus
Harvest Is Plentiful, The
He Didn't Lift Us Up To Let Us Down
He Speaks To Me
Hell Hound On My Trail
His Sheep Am I
His Sheep I Am
His Thought Toward Me
Honeymoon Blues
I Believe I'll Dust My Broom
I Still Believe
I'm A Pilgrim
I'm A Steady Rollin' Man
I've Been Touched

Johnson *(Cont.)*
If I Had Possession Over Judgement Day
If I Had Possession Over My Judgement Day
Illinois
In Remembrance Of Me
Indian Convert
Iola
It Is Summertime In My Heart
Joe Bowers
Katy Avourneen
Kindhearted Woman Blues
Last Fair Deal Gone Down
Lazy Moon
Learn To Croon
Li'l Gal
Lift Ev'ry Voice And Sing
Lift Every Voice And Sing
Lift Up The Name Of Jesus
Little Queen Of Spades
Lord Take Control Of Me
Love In Vain
Love Theme
Love's Redeeming Work Is Done
Make Us One
Make Us One Father
Malted Milk
Mary Had A Baby
Me And The Devil Blues
Mike Fink
Milkcow's Calf Blues
More Than You'll Ever Know
Mr Moonlight
My Castle On The Nile
My Lord What A Mornin'
My Party Led Me
Nashville
Never Be
Nothing Seems Better To Me
O Breath Of Life
Oh For A Thousand Tongues
Oh Freedom
Old Flag Never Touched The Ground, The
Paul Bunyan
Phonograph Blues
Porter's Love Song To A Chambermaid, A
Praise The Lord Ye Heavens Adore Him
Preachin' Blues
Ragged Coat, The
Ramblin' On My Mind
Rest Of The Way, The
Rock 'n Roll I Gave You The Best Years Of My Life
Since I Fell For You
Song For June
Stone's Throw Away
Stones In My Passway
Stop Breakin' Down Blues
Sweet Home Chicago

Johnson *(Cont.)*
Take My Mother Home
Terraplane Blues
That The World May Know
Them Lonesome Moanin' Blues
Theme From Dr Strangelove
There Is A Light
They're Red Hot
Travelin' Riverside Blues
Traveling Riverside Blues
Under The Bamboo Tree
Vacation Days
Vacation Days Are Here
Walkin' Blues
What Would He Say
When I Say Jesus
When You Got A Good Friend
Where The Bee Sucks
Where'er You And I Were Young Maggie
You Took My Heart By Surprise
You're Gonna Love Your New Life With The Lord
Johnson & Barnum
Your Love
Johnson & Benson
Give Them All To Jesus
Johnson & Butterfield
When You And I Were Young Maggie
Johnson & Chaplin
Anniversary Song
Johnson & Dixom
Baby That's Love
Johnson & Hubbard
Affection
Johnson & Johnson
Lift Ev'ry Voice And Sing
Johnson & Johnson & Johnson & Temperton
Stomp
Johnson & Johnson & Sam
I'll Be Good To You
Johnson & Kibble
Boogie Oogie Oogie
Johnson & Klein & Cavanaugh
Since O'Keefe Is On Relief
Johnson & McFadden & Brooks
Bosom Of Abraham
I John
Johnson & Moll & King
I Scream You Scream We All Scream For Ice Cream
Ice Cream
Johnson & Paxton
He Alone
Johnson & Steele & Lang
Rock-A-Bye Moon
Johnson & Wenrich
Where Do We Go From Here
Johnson & Wilson
Full Fathom Five
Lawn As White As Driven Snow
Lovers Never Say Goodbye

Johnston
Another Park Another Sunday
Baby Mine
Best Of Friends
China Grove
I Write The Songs
Illinois
Listen To The Music
Long Train Runnin'
Pennies From Heaven

Johnston & Henderson
He Ransomed Me

Johnstone
Air Ride, An
Indian Lullaby
John-John-Johnny
Lady Moon
Land Of Nod, The
My Native Land
Our Flag
Salute To The Flag
Santa Claus
Seasons, The
St Valentine's Day
When Things Grow Up

Joiner
Fallen Star, A

Joio
Railroad Cars Are Coming, The

Jolley
Fat Old Toad, The
Glad I Am To Grow
Memorial Day
Prayer For Freedom
Texas Trail, The
Tugboats

Jolley & Swain
Cruel Summer

Jolson
Harding You're The Man For Us
Yoo-Hoo

Jolson & Chaplin
Anniversary Song

Jolson & Chaplin & Akst
All My Love

Jolson & Desylva & Brown & Henderson
Sonny Boy

Jolson & Desylva & Meyer
California Here I Come

Jolson & Dreyer
Me And My Shadow

Jolson & Rose & Dreyer
Back In Your Own Backyard
There's A Rainbow 'round My Shoulder

Jones
All I Need
Amorous Goldfish, The
Be Ready When He Comes
Beautiful Land, The
Blessed Sabbath Day
Blow Bugle Blow
Blue Morning Blue Day

Jones *(Cont.)*
Blue Of The Hudson, The
Bob White
Bonds Of Love, The
Borderlines
Break Forth O Living Light Of God
Broke Broke Broke
Centipede And The Frog, The
Christ The Lord Is Ris'n Today
Christ The Lord Is Risen Today
Chuck E's In Love
Cold As Ice
Cow With A Brindle Tail
Crimson Wave, The
Dark The Night
Dear Aunt May
Del Sasser
Demonstrating Gi
Demonstration, A
Do Not O Do Not
Doctor Peter Price's Permanent Panacea
Double Vision
Easy Street
Eight Hours
Farewell Dear Love
Feels Like The First Time
Filthy Rich
For God So Loved The World
Get Lost My Love
Glory Be To God On High
God Is Love
God Moves In A Mysterious Way
God Our Father Cares
God's Glory Is A Wondrous Thing
Haven't Stopped Dancing Yet
He Healeth Today
He That Goeth Forth With Weeping
Head Games
Here In My Heart
Hopewell
Hot Blooded
I Believe
I Believe In God The Father
I Don't Want To Live Without You
I Go To Prepare A Place
I Want To Know What Love Is
I Wish You'd Shave
I'll Never Have To Dream Again
I'll See You In My Dreams
I'm Happy With Jesus
I'm Happy With Jesus Alone
If You Were Only Mine
Illinois
Immortal Love Forever Full
In Booger-Man's Land
In Sherwood Lived A Stout Robin Hood
In The Heat Of The Night
In Times Like These
In Token That Thou Shalt Not Fear
Isn't He Wonderful
It Had To Be You

Jones *(Cont.)*
Jesus Sets The Joy-Bells Ringing
Jesus Will Step Right In On Time
King Of Glory King Of Peace
King Shall Come, The
King Shall Come When Morning Dawns, The
Lean On His Arms
Legend Of Danville
Let The Beauty Of Jesus
Let The Beauty Of Jesus Be Seen In Me
Let Us Go Into The House Of The Lord
Life In One Day
Mabel's Coming Home From College
Mammy Sings The Boy To Sleep
May Thy Blessing Rest Upon Them
Mellow Horn, The
My God How Wonderful Thou Art
New Song
No Greater Love
No One Is To Blame
Nothing But Another Girl
O Pendry You Are Such A Fool
Oginga Odinga
Oh What Wilt Thou Do
Old Book Stands, The
Ole Man Dark 'ill Git You
On Days Like These
One Holy Church Of God Appears
One I Love Belongs To Somebody Else, The
One I Love, The
Our Journey Home
Play You's Er Squirrel Chile
Prophecy Of A Sncc Field Secretary
Quintessence
Rama Lama Ding Dong
Remember Me
Riders In The Sky
Rocky By Baby By-0
Sanford And Son
Sayin' Ter You Good Night
Send For Me
Silently The Shades Of Evening
Since First Disdain Began To Rise
Sleet An' De Snow, De
Street Thunder
Sweet Kate
Swingin' Down The Lane
Taxi Song, The
Theme From Ironside
There Is Pow'r In The Blood
There Is Power In The Blood
Things Can Only Get Better
Though Your Strangeness Frets My Heart
Throw Me Anywhere Lord
Thy Gospel Jesus We Believe
Treasure Up The Sunbeams
Trouble In Mind
Urgent

Jones (Cont.)
Vacant Stare, The
Wake O Wake You Drowsy Sleeper
We Praise And Bless Thee Gracious
     Lord
We Shall See The King Some Day
What If I Speede
When First I Kissed Sweet Margaret
When You Dance
Where Shall I Be
While The Christmas Stars Are
     Shining
Who-Tu-Whoo-Whoo
Window Up Above, The
Wringle Wrangle
You Know I Love You Don't You

Jones & Bryant
There's Hope For This World

Jones & Cole
Strange But True

Jones & Cropper & Steinberg & Jackson
Green Onions

Jones & Garrett & Temperton & Debar
Secret Garden, The

Jones & Garvin
Only One You

Jones & Gramm
Heart Turns To Stone
Say You Will
That Was Yesterday
Waiting For A Girl Like You

Jones & Grammatico
Dirty White Boy

Jones & Hainsworth
Let The Beauty Of Jesus

Jones & Hall
You Talk Too Much

Jones & Hugg & Mann
5-4-3-2-1

Jones & Jones
Finders Keepers Losers Weepers

Jones & Jones & Jones & Thomas
Iko Iko

Jones & Lantrip
I Just Cut Myself

Jones & Laron
Brother That Ain't Good

Jones & Lubbock
Grace

Jones & Plant
All My Love

Jones & Salvador
Midnight Sun Will Never Set, The

Jones & Sawyer & McMurray
If I Were Your Woman

Jones & Schmidt
Try To Remember

Jones & Shade
Overseas Stomp

Jones & Smith
I Wouldn't Change You If I Could
Step By Step

Jones & Temperton
Miss Celie's Blues

Jones & Temperton & Lubbock
Color Purple, The

Jong
Eternal Rest
Glorious Mysteries
O Sacrament Most Holy

Joplin
Antoinette
Crush Collision March, The
Leola
March Majestic
Pleasant Moments
Preaching Rag
Sycamore, The

Joplin & Chauvin
Heliotrope Bouquet

Joplin & Hayden
Felicity Rag
Kismet Rag
Something Doing
Sun Flower Slow Drag

Joplin & Marshall
Lily Queen

Joplin, Janis
Down On Me

Joplin, Scott
Breeze From Alabama, A
Cascades, The
Chrysanthemum, The
Cleopha
Combination March
Easy Winners, The
Elite Syncopations
Entertainer, The
Eugenia
Favorite, The
Maple Leaf Rag
Nonpareil, The
Original Rags
Palm Leaf Rag
Peacherine Rag
Rag-Time Dance
Reflection Rag
Rose-Bus March, The
Solace
Strenuous Life, The
Swipesy
Weeping Willow

Jorda
Amar Y Sufrir
Love And Sorrow

Jordan
Blue Bell Of Scotland, The
Cocaine Blues
Down By The Riverside
English Country Garden
How Can A Sinner Know
It Was Almost Like A Song
Jesus Is Your Ticket To Heaven
Jose Cuervo
Lullaby
Santa Claus Blues
Still With Thee O My God
What A Difference You've Made In
     My Life

Jordan & Cloninger
You Gave Me Love

Jordan & David
Happy Birthday Dear Heartache

Jordan & Martin
Let's Take The Long Way Around
     The World

Jordan & Wilson
Shake Some Action
Yes It's True
You Tore Me Down

Jordon & Capek
Pieces Of Ice

Jorge
Alcanzamos For Fin La Victoria
Now With Victory We Are
     Rewarded

Jorris
Ortergruss

Josea & Phillips
Cherry Pie

Joseph
At Even Ere The Sun Was Set
At Even When The Sun Was Set
Be Still My Soul For God Is Near
Shepherd Of Souls In Love Come
     Feed Us
Sinner Kissed An Angel, A
Thursday

Josephi
O Thou Who Camest From Above

Josie
Midnight Confessions

Joslyn
Alma Mater

Josquin Des Pres
Ave Verum Corpus Christi
Ecce Maria Genuit
En L'ombre D'un Buissonet
Petite Camusette

Josquin Du Prez
Faute D'argent
Mille Regrets

Joy
Streets Of Bakersfield

Joy & Lewis
Take My Ring Off Of Your Finger

Joyce
Onward For Cuba

Jozsef
Kanyargo Tisza Partjan Ott
     Szulettem, A
Szeretot Keresek
Vett A Rozsam Piros Selyem Viganot

Judassohn
When The Evening Shadows Gather

Judd
Old Woman Of The Roads, An

Jude
Bells Of Seville, The
Jesus Calls Us
Jesus Calls Us O'er The Tumult
Mighty Deep, The
There's A Wideness In God's Mercy

Judge & Williams
It's A Long Long Way To Tipperary
It's A Long Way To Tipperary
Judson
Come Ye Disconsolate
Julia & Jay
I Cried A Tear
Jungst
Gesellen-Wanderlied
Mullers Abschied
Spinn Spinn
Spinning Maiden, The
Two Songs, The
Withered Wreath, A
Junior & Funches
Oh What A Night
Pain In My Heart
Juravich
Putting The Blame On Me
Rise Again
Jurgens
Im Mai
Jurgens & Donovan
One Dozen Roses
Jurmann
When I Look At You
You And The Waltz And I
Justman
Angel In Blue
Centerfold
Kaai & Kinney & Noble
Across The Sea
Kabalevsky
Campfire Song
Kacherginsky
Itsik Vitnberg
Kaempfert & Gabler
L-O-V-E
Kaempfert & Singleton & Snyder
Spanish Eyes
Strangers In The Night
Kahle
Way Down South In Mississippi
Kahn
Beautiful Friendship, A
Hollywood
Little Street Where Old Friends Meet,
A
People Like You
Truck Driving Woman
Kahn & Akst & Whiting
Guilty
Kahn & Burke
Oh What A Pal Was Whoozis
Kahn & Daniels
You Tell Me Your Dream I'll Tell
You Mine
Kahn & Donaldson
Love Me Or Leave Me
Makin' Whoopee
Kahn & Erdman & Meyers & Schoebel
Nobody's Sweetheart

Kahn & Erdman & Russo & Fiorito
Toot Toot Tootsie
Toot Toot Tootsie Goodbye
Kahn & Fiorito
I Never Knew
Kahn & Flindt & King
Waltz You Saved For Me, The
Kahn & Jones
I'll See You In My Dreams
Kahn & Leonard & Greene
Leave It To Beaver
Kahn & Malneck & Signorelli
I'll Never Be The Same
Kahn & Woods
Little Street Where Old Friends
Meet, A
Kaihan & Scott & Stewart
Now Is The Hour
Kaillmark
Old Oaken Bucket, The
Kailmai
On The Beach At Waikiki
Kaiser
Bring Back The Springtime
He Careth For You
Hush The Baby Is Sleeping
I Am Willing Lord
O How He Loves You And Me
Oh How He Loves You And Me
Pass It On
Reach Your Hand
Sunday Mornin'
That's For Me
Lord Whom We Love, The
Kalaff
Empaliza
Kalakaua
Sweet Lei Lehua
Kalb
It Is Jesus
Kalb & Kalb
Mississippi Squirrel Revival, The
Kalfin
Just To Be With You
Kalinnikoff
To Thee O Lord Do I Lift Up My
Soul
Kalisch
Ballad Of Crystal Night, The
Kalliwoda
Deutsche Lied, Das
Kalman
Love's Own Sweet Song
Play Gypsies Dance Gypsies
Kalmar & Ruby
America I Love You
Captain Spalding
Hooray For Captain Spaulding
Love Is Like A Rose
Musketeers, The
My Dream Of The South Of France
My Love Is Waiting
Never The Less I'm In Love With
You

Kalmar & Ruby *(Cont.)*
Nevertheless
Show Me A Rose
So Long Oo-Long
Songs My Mother Used To Sing To
Me, The
There Were Three Little Fishes That
Lived In The Sea
Three Little Fishes, The
Tulip Told A Tale, A
Whoopee
You Said Good-Bye
Kalmar & Ruby & Hammerstein
Kiss To Build A Dream On, A
Kalmar & Ruby & Snyder
Who's Sorry Now
Kamosi & Dequincey
Pump Up The Jam
Kandall
All Of My Life
Kander
After All These Years
And All That Jazz
Best Of Everything, The
But The World Goes 'round
Cabaret
City Lights
Grass Is Always Greener, The
Happy Ending
Happy Time, The
Home
How Lucky Can You Get
I Don't Remember You
I Wrote The Book
Isn't This Better
Life Is
Married
Marry Me
Maybe This Time
Money Money
My Coloring Book
My Own Space
Nowadays
One Of The Girls
Only Love
Quiet Thing, A
Show Stopper
Sing Happy
Sometimes A Day Goes By
Theme From New York New York
There Goes The Ball Game
We Can Make It
Willkommen
Woman
Yes
Kane
Dedicate
Kane & Allen & Channel
Don't Worry 'Bout Me Baby
Kane & Hill & Lee
Speedy Gonzales
Kane & Kane
Play Another Slow Song

Kane & O'Hara
Can't Stop My Heart From Lovin'
    You
Oh Darlin' Why Don't You Care For
    Me No More

Kane & Sparks
One Star

Kanoa
Ua Like No A Like

Kaper
Hi-Lili Hi-Lo
Invitation
On Green Dolphin Street
Take My Love

Kaper & Jurmann
Cosi Cosa
San Francisco

Kaplan
Rifkele Di Shabesdike

Kapp
For The First Time I've Fallen In
    Love

Kaproff
Starman

Karajian
Your Lovely Lips

Karas
Third Man Theme, The

Karchevsky
By The Shores Of Kineret

Karen
Jerusalem Is Mine

Karg-Elert
Come Follow Me The Savior Spake

Karger
From Here To Eternity

Karger & Gottlieb & Weisman
Frankie And Johnnie

Karger & Wayne & Weisman
I'll Never Know

Karlin
Come Saturday Morning
For All We Know

Karlo
Flores Negras

Karmen
Aren't You Glad You Use Dial
At Beneficial Doot Doot You're
    Good For More
Breakaway In A Wide-Trackin'
    Pontiac
Bud Is The King Of Beers But You
    Know That
Burry's Blues, The
Call Nationwide 'cause Nationwide
    Is On Your Side
Carry The Big Fresh Flavor
Chrysler Plymouth Comin' Thru
Comfortable Life, The
Completely Unique Experience, A
Don't Compromise Midasize
Doublemint Will Do It

Karmen *(Cont.)*
Energy For A Strong America
Everybody Likes It
Farrell's Is Fabulous Fun
Feelin' Like A Million Bucks
First Malt Liquor Good Enough To
    Be Called Budweiser
Ford That's Incredible
Give That Man A Blue Ribbon
Good Taste Runs In The Family
Great American Chocolate Bar, The
Greatest Day In Your Life
Here Comes The King
Hush Puppies Are Dumb
I Can Be Very Friendly
I Love New York
It's Great To Know You're Good For
    More
It's Our Flavor That Makes Us
    Special
It's Right For You
It's Time For A Tic Tac
Ji-Ji-Jack Ji-Ji-Jack Jack In The Box
Land Of Pleasant Living
Let's Pick A Pack
Michelob Drinking Song, The
More You Know The More You'll
    Want Delco, The
Pitch In To Clean Up America
Plymouth Makes It
Purina In The Little Blue Can
Sooner Or Later You'll Own
    Generals
Stand Up
Standard For The World, A
Sunoco Is Making Every Drop Count
Sunwich Is Better Than A Sandwich,
    A
Take A Natural Break
Taste Of Europe Trans World
    Service, A
Tastes Like A Soft Drink
That's What It's All About
There's Nothing Like The Face Of A
    Kid Eating A Hershey Bar
We Better Be Better
We Give You Half The World
We Made It First We Make It Last
Weekend Pops
Weekends Were Made For Michelob
What Else Is So Nice For The Price
When Do You Say Budweiser
When You Say Budweiser You've
    Said It All
Won't Fill You Up So It Won't Slow
    You Down
You Can Take Salem Out Of The
    Country But
You Haven't Read The Paper Until
    You've Read The N
You Know It Protects
You Know Who You Are

Karmen *(Cont.)*
You'll Be Sorry For All The Time
    You Wasted
You'll Like The Big Long-Lasting
    Flavor
Your Next Car Is Chrysler

Karr
How Does The Wine Taste
Mutual Admiration Society
Wedded Man, A

Kasha & Hirschhorn
Brazzle Dazzle Day
Candle On The Water
I'd Like To Be You For A Day
It's Not Easy
Morning After, The
We May Never Love Like This
    Again

Kasha & Hunter
My Empty Arms

Kashani
He's A Joy And A Wonder To My
    Soul

Kashtan & Alderna
Ki Tinam

Kassel
Around The Corner
Doodle Doo Doo

Kastalsky
God Is With Us

Katcher
When Day Is Done

Katz
Beloved Comrade

Kauffman
Keep In Touch With Jesus

Kauflin
Maker Of My Heart

Kaufman
How Many Hearts Have You Broken
    With Those Great Big Beautiful
    Eyes
Stop It

Kaufman & Anthony
Poetry In Motion

Kaun
My Native Land
Patria
With The Goslings

Kavanaugh
Virginia Rose Bud, The

Kavelin & Lyn
I Give You My Word

Kawohl & Farian & Bischof-Fallenste
Girl I'm Gonna Miss You

Kawohl & Farian & Bischof-Fallensti
Girl I'm Gonna Miss You

Kay & Bruce
Forgetting You

Kay & Gordon
That's Life

Kay & O'Dea & Clinton
Christmas Candles

Kaye & Care
Penny A Kiss A Penny A Hug, A
Kaye & Loman
Christmas Alphabet
Kaye & Montenegro
Jeannie
Kaye & Mossman
Full Moon And Empty Arms
Till The End Of Time
Kaye & Rabin & Anderson & Squire
Rhythm Of Love
Kaye & Springer
Never-Ending
Kaye & Starr
Once Upon A Nickel
Kaye & Weisman & Fuller
Cindy Cindy
Kaye & Wise & Lippman
A You're Adorable
Kaylan & Volman & Pons & Nichol & Barbata
Elenore
Kaz & Waldman
Heartbeat
Keaggy
Rejoice
Keagy
Sister Christian
Kealamakia
E Honi Mai Ku'u Ipo
Kealoha
To Thee Forever
Kean & Smith & Sayers
It's Howdy Doody Time
Kean & Unger & Smith
Where Is Sam
Kearney
Whack Fol-The-Diddle
Kearney & Ryan
Down By The Glenside
Keating
I Love To See My Poor Old Mother Work
Keble Barr
New Every Morning Is The Love
Keefer & Amway
Dog-Gone It Baby I'm In Love
Keegan
Jesus Is Coming
Keel
You Spotted Snakes
Keel & Coe & Latimer
Need A Little Time Off For Bad Behavior
Keen & Pritchard & Brooks
Love Has Taken Its Time
Keen & Tunney
What Can I Do
Keenan
Hello Patsy Fagan
My Kathleen
Keene-Bean & Masters
Scatter-Brain

Kees & Rakes & Larkin
Searchin' For Some Kind Of Clue
Kehrein
Glorious Hope, The
Keifer
Don't Know What You Got Till It's Gone
Nobody's Fool
Somebody Save Me
Keiser
Be Good To California Mr Wilson
California Was Goo
Has Your Mother Any More Like You
Musket Or The Sword, The
Keister & Morrison & Macrae
Some Love Songs Never Die
Keith
Before The Next Teardrop Falls
Free The People
Kellaway
Remembering You
Kellem
Gonna Get Along Without Ya Now
Gonna Get Along Without You Now
Keller
American Hymn, The
Angel Of Peace
Blessing And Honor And Glory And Power
Exile, The
Hail To Our Country
Here Comes Summer
Keller's American Hymn
Land Of Our Heroes
Marche Eternel Voyageur
Our Braves
Speed Our Republic
Keller & Hilderbrand
Easy Come Easy Go
Keller & Shayne
Almost There
Kelley
Home On The Range
Ode To Quinbus Flestrin
Kelley & Wyatt
Tangleweed 'Round My Heart
Kellie
Independent Man, The
Is It Too Late
Kellis
Pledge Of Allegiance To The Flag, The
Kellogg
Cow, The
Crew Song
It's Good To Share
Movies, The
Kells
Pledge Of Allegiance To The Flag, The
Kelly
32-20 Blues
Dancin' In The Moonlight

Kelly *(Cont.)*
Ode To Quinbus Flestrin
Personally
Throw Him Down M'Closkey
Throw Him Down McCloskey
Kelly & Didier
I'd Do Anything For You
Kelly & Randolph
You And Me Tonight
Kelly & Sheets & Benatar
Fire And Ice
Kelso
Lily Bells
My Pinto Pal
On Easter Day
Ridin' Round The Range
Ring Easter Bells
Wake Up Song
Kemp
I'll Leave This World Loving You
Stingaree Blues
Tell Old I Ain't Here To Get On Home
Kemp & Griffin
Just Got Paid
Kemp & Ross
Your Wife Is Cheatin' On Us Again
Kenbrovin & Kellete
I'm Forever Blowing Bubbles
Kenbrovin & Kellette
I'm Forever Blowing Bubbles
Kendall
April's Here Again
Love Seeds
Kendall & Niven
Angel Song, The
Kendel
Penguin, The
Kendis
If I Had My Way
Kendis & Brockman & Johnson
Feather Your Nest
Kendis & Brockman & Vincent
I Know What It Means To Be Lonesome
Kendis & Paley
Billy
Cheer Up Mary
I Couldn't Make A Hit With Molly
Just A Little Fond Affection
Sympathy
Won't You Fondle Me
Kendrick
My Flo
Kenley & Kortchmar
I Can't Stand Still
Kenna
Down In The Old Neighborhood
Kennedy
Acushla Mine
Flower From Mother's Grave, A
I Had Fifteen Dollars In My Inside Pocket

Kennedy *(Cont.)*
Molly And I And The Baby
Say Au Revoir But Not Good Bye
Star Of The East

Kennedy & Carr
Did Your Mother Come From
Ireland
Ole Faithful

Kennedy & Carr
South Of The Border
Washing On The Siegfried Line

Kennedy & Goodman
Hey Jesus You're My Best Friend

Kennedy & Rose & Goodman
Dixie Road

Kennedy & Rose & Schuyler
Little Bit Closer, A

Kennedy & Williams
Harbor Lights

Kennedy-Fraser
Seagull Of The Land Under Waves,
The
Spinning Song

Kenner
Something You Got

Kenner & Domino
Freedom Now
Land Of A Thousand Dances

Kenner & Toussaint
I Like It Like That

Kennerley
Born To Run
Chains Of Gold
Cry Myself To Sleep
First In Line, The
Give A Little Love
Have Mercy
Heaven Only Knows
Hillbilly Rock
One Man Woman
Walking Shoes

Kennerley & Harris
Heartbreak Hill

Kennerley & Maher
Tell Me True

Kennerley & Maher & Perkins
Let Me Tell You About Love

Kennerley & Stuart
Western Girls

Kennerly
Have Mercy
In My Dreams

Kennerly & Crowell
Had My Heart Set On You
I Had My Heart Set On You

Kennerly & Maher & Perkins
Let Me Tell You About Love

Kennett & Udall
Stay In Your Own Back Yard

Kenny & Kenny
Cathedral In The Pines

Kenoa
Nuuanu Waipuna

Kent
Alliance Song
End Of The World, The
Gentle Rain
I Taught Her Everything She Knows
I'll Be Home For Christmas
We Wish You A Merry Christmas
White Cliffs Of Dover, The

Kent & Amnn
Don't Go To Strangers

**Kent & Brandow & Robinson &
Spottswood & Ware**
Hold Tight Hold Tight

Kent & Mann
Don't Go To Strangers

Kent & Ram & Gannon
I'll Be Home For Christmas

Kenton & Lawrence
And Her Tears Flowed Like Wine

Kentucky
Jesus Born In Bethlehem

Keolling
Before All Lands In East Or West

Keppel
Robin Adair

Kerker
Little Birdies Learning How To Fly
Purity Brigade, The
She Is The Belle Of New York

Kern
All In Fun
All Praise To Thee
All Through The Day
Am Hohen Himmel
Busy Bonnet, The
Butterflies
Can I Forget You
Can't Help Singing
D'Ye Love Me
Freckles
Fruhling Ist Nah, Der
Go Little Boat
I Dream Too Much
I Watch The Love Parade
I've Told Ev'ry Little Star
I've Told Every Little Star
In Love In Vain
Ka-Lu-A
Night Winds
Old Country, The
Old-Fashioned Wife, An
One Moment Alone
Postillion, The
Reckless
Scissors-Grinder, The
Scouting Ants, The
Siren's Song, The
Spring Delight
Stille Stille Stille Ist Die Nacht
Sure Thing
'Twas Not So Long Ago
Ups And Downs
Waltz In Swing Time

Kern *(Cont.)*
Winter's Going
Woodpecker, The
You Were Never Lovelier
You're Here And I'm Here

Kern & Muller
Da Droben Da Droben Muss

Kern, Jerome
All The Things You Are
Bill
Can't Help Lovin' Dat Man
Cleopatterer
Cotton Blossom
Dearly Beloved
Don't Ever Leave Me
Fine Romance, A
Folks Who Live On The Hill, The
How'd You Like To Spoon With Me
I Won't Dance
I'm Old Fashioned
In Egern On The Tegern See
In The Heart Of The Dark
Just Let Me Look At You
Last Time I Saw Paris, The
Life Upon The Wicked Stage
Long Ago And Far Away
Look For The Silver Lining
Lovely To Look At
Make Believe
Night Was Made For Love, The
Ol' Man River
Pick Yourself Up
Remind Me
Sally
She Didn't Say Yes
Smoke Gets In Your Eyes
Song Is You, The
Sunny
They Didn't Believe Me
Till The Clouds Roll By
Touch Of Your Hand, The
Way You Look Tonight, The
Whip-Poor-Will
Who
Why Do I Love You
Why Was I Born
Wild Rose
Yesterdays
You Are Love
You Couldn't Be Cuter

Kerner
Jesus

Kerr
I'll Never Love This Way Again
In Love With The Lover Of My Soul
Looks Like We Made It
Riding To Town
Somewhere In The Night
Where Are They Now

Kerr & Burchill & Macneil
Alive And Kicking
Sanctify Yourself

Kerr & English
Mandy
Kerr & Jennings
No Night So Long
Kershaw
Louisiana Man
Kesler
Playin' For Keeps
Kesler & Feathers
I Forgot To Remember To Forget
Kesler & Taylor
I'm Left You're Right She's Gone
Kessler & Richards & Bray
Baby Love
Kettle
I Bow My Forehead
When On My Day Of Life
Kettring
Forward Be Our Watchword
Grant Us Hearts Thy Name To
    Praise
Offering Sentence, An
Keyes
Sweet Someone
Keyes & Feaster & McRae & Edwards
Sh-Boom
Keys
Give Thanks To God
Lord Is King, The
Sweet Someone
Khoury & Bastiste
Sea Of Love
Khoury & Thierry
Mathilda
Kiallmark
Araby's Daughter
Old Oaken Bucket, The
Kicken
Cueillons Les Roses De L'amour
Kidd
Shakin' All Over
Kidder & Tucker
Cottage Round The Corner, The
Kieffer
City Of Light, The
It Is I
Jesus Will Let You In
Morning Light, The
Nearer Yet Nearer
Pilgrim's Song, The
Redeeming Love
Kiely
Bye-Bye Landon Goodbye
Kienzi
Little Sandman, The
Kienzl
Volkslied, Das
Kieserling
Spring Song
Kihn & Wright
Lucky
Kihn & Wright & Phillips
Break Up Song, The

Kilgore
She Understands Me
Kilgore & King
Wolverton Mountain
Kilgore & Thomas
Old Records
Killen
We Love Each Other
Killen & McDowell
Lovin' A Livin' Dream
Never Seen A Mountain So High
Watchin' Girls Go By
Killen & Miller
Open Up Your Heart
Killian
Hands To The Mainsail
Killion & McMichael & Owens
Hut-Sut Song, The
Kim
Rock Me Gently
Kimball
Paddle And Sing
Kimball & Sherrill & Whitmore
You're My Kind Of Woman
Kindt
Wabash Cannon Ball, The
King
Ain't Gonna Worry My Life
    Anymore
Back To California
Being At War With Each Other
Believe In Humanity
Bonaparte's Retreat
Bound For Canaan
Brother Brother
Canaan's Land
Carnsville
Chicken Soup With Rice
Child Of Grace, The
Children's Hosanna
Come O Thou Traveller Unknown
Corazon
Country Girl
Dancin' With Tears In My Eyes
Dancing Boilerman, The
Dull Care
Dying Christian, The
Eve's Lamentation
Everyone's Gone To The Moon
Give Me The Mouth That Never Had
    The Toothache
God Only Knows
Gospel Trumpet
Hail U B C
Hard Rock Cafe
Hawaiian Wedding Song, The
Honey Honey
How Am I To Know
I Ain't Nobody's Darling
I Believe I've Been Blue Too Long
I'm Not Wanted Anymore
Ich Vil Zich Shpilen

King *(Cont.)*
Israfel
It's Good News Week
Josephine
Let's Get Down To Business
Lord Of All Majesty And Might
Lucille
Lullaby For Christmas Eve
Main Street Saturday Night
Midnight
Mr Hoover And Mr Smith
Music
On That Hill By The Tennesse
Only Love Is Real
Show Me The Way To Go Home
So Many Ways
Song Of The Islands
Songs Of Praise The Angels Sing
Sweet Canaan
Thank You For Loving The Blues
That's Wrong Little Mama
Time Gone By
Time Won't Let Me
Tom Kisses John's Wife Every Night
Union
Weeping Saviour
Welcome Home Children
Where The Sun Has Never Shone
While Strolling Thru' The Park One
    Day
Yankee Ship And A Yankee Crew, A
You Light Up My Life
You're The One Who Knows
Young Men Taken In And Done For
King & Bivens
Josephine
King & Clark
Can't You Hear Me Talking To You
Ghetto Woman
Why I Sing The Blues
King & Elliott
There's A Long Long Trail
King & Evers
Simple Thngs
King & Flindt
Waltz You Saved For Me, The
King & Glick
Stand By Me
King & Goffin
Ferguson Road
High Out Of Time
King & Gould & Badaou
Lessons In Love
King & Gould & Gould & Lindup &
Badarou
Something About You
King & Greenfield
Crying In The Rain
King & Hudson & King
Lady
Lady You Bring Me Up

King & Josea
Rock Me Baby
Sweet Sixteen
That Evil Child
King & Leiber & Stoller
Stand By Me
King & Levy
Dance Dance Dance
King & Palmer
Paradise Alley
King & Stern
Come Down Easy
It's Going To Take Some Time
It's Too Late
Now That Everything's Been Said
Sweet Seasons
Too Much Rain
Where You Lead
King & Stewart
Bonaparte's Retreat
King & Taub
Darlin' You Know I Love You
Three O'Clock Blues
Woke Up This Morning My Baby
    She Was Gone
King & Walker
Saints Bound For Heaven, The
King & Weil
One To One
King & Williams
Peace Will Come
King, Carole
Beautiful
Been To Canaan
Bitter With The Sweet
Home Again
I Feel The Earth Move
It's Too Late
Really Rosie
So Far Away
Stand Behind Me
Tapestry
Way Over Yonder
You've Got A Friend
Kingham
God Is Working His Purpose Out
Kingsbery
When Your Heart Is Weak
Kingsford
Wall-Paper For A Little Girl's Room
Kingsley
Elizabethtown
Give Me The Wings Of Faith To Rise
How Beauteous Are Their Feet
I Would Not Live Alway
Jesus My Truth My Way
Jesus The Conqueror Reigns
Joy Is A Fruit That Will Not Grow
Lord Our God Is Clothed With
    Might, The
O For A Faith That Will Not Shrink
Prayer Is The Soul's Sincere Desire
Yield Not To Temptation

Kingston & Nix
Thank God And Greyhound
Kingston & Sutton
Pair Of Old Sneakers, A
Kingston & Thomas & Lathan
I'm In Turn
That's Wrong With The World
    Today
Kinkel
Knights' Farewell, The
No Power On Earth Shall Sever
Soldier's Farewell, The
Wie Bringt Uns Doch Das Scheiden
Kipner & Beckett
Twist Of Fate
Kipner & Bliss
Heart Attack
Kipner & Parker
Hard Habit To Break
Kipner & Shaddick
Physical
Kipner & Vallins
Too Much Too Little Too Late
Kirby
When It's Reveille Time In Heaven
Kirby & Bynum
There Ain't No Good Chain Gang
Kirby & Martin
Is Anybody Goin' To San Antone
Kirbye
Join All Ye Ransomed Sons Of Grace
Kirch
Keine Frede
Kirchl
Indian Village, The
Kirchner
Auctioneer, The
Crickets Sang, The
He Scanned It
Much Madness
Partake As Doth The Bee
There Came A Wind
Kirk
Cal-Lib-Song
Our Love Is On The Faultline
Kirk & Tullar
Our Best
Kirkland & Harris
Cloudburst
Kirkman
Cherish
Kirkpatrick
As The Apple Of His Eye
Away In A Manger
Away In A Manger No Crib For His
    Bed
Because He First Loved Me
Beyond The Shadows
Blessed Be The Name
Bolted Door, The
Cast Thy Bread Upon The Waters
Comforter Has Come, The
Entire Consecration
Ere The Sun Goes Down

Kirkpatrick *(Cont.)*
Everybody's Got A Right To Live
For Christ And The Church
Go Tell The World Of His Love
God Is Able To Deliver
God's Promises
Good Morning Brother Hudson
Good Night
Have You Found The Savior
    Precious
He Hideth My Soul
He Is Able
He Never Will Forsake Me
He Never Will Turn Me Away
I Will Follow On
It Just Suits Me
It Was Spoken For The Master
Jesus Comes
Jesus For Me
Jesus Saves
Jesus Wills Save You Now
Just A Little Sunshine
Lead Me To Calvary
Let Me Lean Harder On Thee
Lo The Golden Fields Are Smiling
Look Beyond
Lord I'm Coming Home
Loyalty To The Master
Meet Me There
Mercy Is Boundless And Free
My Saviour
O For A Heart Whiter Than Snow
Old Fountain, The
Saved To The Uttermost
'Tis So Sweet To Trust In Jesus
Very Same Jesus, The
Wait And Murmur Not
Watch And Pray
We Are Passing Away
We Have An Anchor
Welcome For Me
What Will It Matter
When Love Shines In
Where His Voice Is Guiding
Wilt Thou Be Made Whole
Work For The Master
You May Have The Joybells
Kirkpatrick & Brignardello & Keiste
Sure Enough
Kirksen
Rejoice Ye Pure In Heart
Kirmar
Vuelo Del Abispon Cojo, El
Kirwan
Bare Trees
Kisco
Daughter Of Peggy O'Neil, The
Song Of Troy
Kiser
'Twas The Night Before Christmas
Kistler
Alma Mater

Kitchings
Ghost Of Yesterday
I'm Pulling Through And It's
    Because Of You
Some Other Spring

Kittel
Auferstehn Ja Auferstehn
O Father Son And Holy Ghost
Stars Of The Morning So Gloriously
    Bright

Kittredge
Tenting On The Old Camp Ground
Tenting Tonight
Tenting Tonight On The Old Camp
    Ground
We're Tenting Tonight

Kjerulf
Afar In The Wood
Alone
Beating Of My Own Heart, The
Bygone Days
Divided Love
Elfenland
Evensong
Good Morning
Good Night
Have You Forgotten That Day
I Hardly Know
In The Forest
Last Night
Last Night The Nightingale Woke
    Me
Longing
Love Song
Love Thee Dearest Love Thee
Love Voices
Morning Song
Mountains Of Norway, The
My Heart And Lute
My Pretty Bird
Never Laugh At Love
Night On The Fjord
O Why
On The Hillside
On The Ling Ho
Queen Red Rose
Search, The
Secret, A
Sehnsucht
Separation
Silent Love
Simile, A
Sing Sing
Song
Spanische Romanze
Spring Song
Summer Ecstasy
Summer Sadness
Sunlight Song
Surrender
Swallow Where Flyest Thou
Synnove's Song
Tell Me
To A Portrait

Kjerulf *(Cont.)*
When You Slept
Where Are They
Woodland Well, The
Young Venevil

Klaking
Up And At 'Em Navee

Klarmann & Weber
Symptoms Of True Love

Klatzkin
Sleep Well Little Children

Klein
Ah Once I Lay In Grief And Pain
Be Thou Consoled O Quiet Heart
Christ Is Arisen
Cradle Song
Evening Bells, The
Forsaken
Fruhlingsgruss An Das Vaterland
In Silent Night
Irma
Love Song
Love's Parting
Moon Dear
My Fate I Cannot Banish
My Lovely Beloved
On A Night In Spring
Parting
Sailing
Song Of The Harp Girl
There's A Fly On Aunty's Nose
To The Loved One Far Away
Wanderer's Night Song

Kleinman
Union Man, The

Kleinsinger
Pass It On
Way Down Blues

Klemm
Flower And Tree
Joy And Pain
Lullaby Of The Bells
Old Tale, An
Sounds

Klenner
Just Friends

Klickman
'Twas The Night Before Christmas

Klickmann
Floatin' Down To Cotton Town
In Flanders Fields
It's For You Old Glory It's For You
Keep Your Face To The Sunshine
Old Glory Goes Marching On
Tears Of The Shannon
There's A Little Blue Star In The
    Window
When The Little Blue Star In The
    Window Has Turned

Kline
Lilac, The
Pennsylvania Dutch, The
Shoo Fly Pie

Klingstedt
Alma Mater Hymn

Klohr
Billboard March, The

Klug
Glory Of These Forty Days, The

Klughardt
Kamerad Komm

Kmora
Kathleen

Knapp
And Faithful Hearts Are Raised On
    High
Awake My Soul And With The Sun
Awake My Soul To Joyful Lays
Blessed Assurance
Blessed Assurance Jesus Is Mine
Cleansing Wave, The
Come Gracious Spirit Heavenly
    Dove
Consecration
Eternal Source Of Every Joy
Great God Attend While Zion Sings
Great God We Sing That Mighty
    Hand
He Has Come
House For God, A
How Happy Is He Born
How Happy Is He Born Or Taught
How Pleasant How Divinely Fair
Let The Saviour In
My Body Soul And Spirit
Mysterious Presence
Nearer The Cross
O Jesus Lord Of Heavenly Grace
O Sometimes Gleams Upon Our
    Sight
O Splendor Of God's Glory Bright
O Thou To Whom In Ancient Time
O Wondrous Type
O Wondrous Type O Vision Fair
Open The Gates Of The Temple
Rejoice O Land
Rejoice O Land In God Thy Might
Triumphant Sion Lift Thy Head
We Sing The Praise Of Him Who
    Died
Wyoming
Your Love O God Has Called Us
    Here

Knauff
California Ball
Wait For The Wagon

Kneass
Ben Bolt
Shady Old Camp, The
Sonora Filibusters, The
Sweet Alice Ben Bolt

Knecht
Children Of The Heavenly King
Draw Us To Thee Lord Jesus
God My Father Loving Me
Great And Mighty Wonder, A
Let The Whole Creation Cry

Knecht (*Cont.*)
Life Of Ages
Lord Jesus Thou Are Standing
Loving Jesus Gentle Lamb
Now May He Who From The Dead
O Happy Band Of Pilgrims
O Jesus Thou Art Standing
Willkommen Held Im Streite

Knecht & Husband
I Lay My Sins On Jesus
O Jesus Thou Art Standing

Knig
Werde Licht Du Stadt Der Heiden

Knight
Change
Have A Little Regiment Of Your
Own
Henrietta
Lonesome Town
Near The Cross Was Mary Weeping
Never Be Anyone Else But You
One Of The Living
Poet And Lark
Ring My Bell
Rock'd In The Cradle Of The Deep
Rocked In The Cradle Of The Deep
Rosalie
Say What Shall My Song Be Tonight
They Whose Course On Earth Is
O'Er
Welcome
Where Hudson's Wave
Wonder Of You, The

Knight & Barres
Obsession

Knight & Bloch & Connie
Never

Knight & Bloch & Wilson & Wilson
Never

Knight & Brown
There's No Stopping Us

Knight & Chapman
Best, The
Hanging On A Heart Attack
Love Is A Battlefield
Pleasure And Pain

Knight & Chapman & Black
Love Touch

Knight & Chapman & Taupin
I Engineer

Knight & Climie
Invincible

Knight & Gilder
Warrior, The

Knight & Lyle
Here We Are Here We Are Here We
Are Again

Knight & Whitsett
Sure Feels Good

Knight & Wilson
There's The Girl

Knight & Zigman
Crush On You
Curiosity

Knight & Zigman (*Cont.*)
Private Number
Save The Best For Me

Knipe
Listen To The Radio

Knipper
Cavalry Of The Steppes
In Meadowland
Meadowland
Song Of The Meadow Land
Song Of The Plains

Knoblock & Whitsett
Why Not Me

Knopfler
Money For Nothing
Private Dancer
Setting Me Up
So Far Away
Sultans Of Swing
Walk Of Life

Knowles
Lord Will Come And Not Be Slow,
The

Knowlton
Even Song
For Sowing And Reaping
Patriotic Hymn

Knox
Hula Love

Knudsen
I Am So Glad On Christmas Eve
Jeg Er Sa Glad Hver Julekveld
Jeg Er Saa Glad Hver Julekveld

Knudsen & McFee & Carter
One Step Closer

Knutson & Owens
Bird, The
Right Left Hand, The
Somebody Wants Me Out Of The
Way

Knutson & Shaw
41st Street Lonely Hearts Club

Knyvett
Bells Of Saint Michael's Tower

Koch
Calico Pie
Immortality, An
Tame Cat
This Is Where The Candle Glows

Kocher
Ad Sanctum Spiritum
As With Gladness Men Of Old
For The Beauty Of The Earth
For The Joy Of Human Love
Geist Des Lebens
Holy Spirit Lord Of Love
Praise To God Immortal Praise
Without Haste And Without Rest
Ye Who Claim The Faith Of Jesus

Kodaly
Fancy
Viennese Musical Clock

Koehlei
Columbian Doxology No. 1

Koehler
Hollywood Canteen

Koehler & Arlen
Between The Devil And The Deep
Blue Sea
Get Happy

Koehler & Bloom
Truckin'

Koelling
Patriotic Boys And Girls

Koenig
My Soul With Patience Waits

Koerner
Lord's Prayer, The

Koert
Sing To The Lord A Joyful Song

Koffman
Swingin' Shepherd Blues, The

Kohl
Church, The

Kohlman
Cry
She's Sleeping By The Silv'ry Rio
Grande

Kohlmann
Church, The
In The Starlight

Kohlsaat
Bread And Roses

Kolisi
Nkosi Nkosi

Kolmanovsky
Do Russian People Stand For War
Silently

Kolsrud & Ovland & Black
Downtown

Kompaneetz
Varshavianka

Konig
All Depends On Our Possessing
Blest Are The Pure In Heart
Have Faith In God My Heart
Jesus Jesus Jesus Only
Lord In The Strength Of Grace
O Dass Ich Tausend Zungen Hatte
O That I Had A Thousand Voices

Koninkx
Bread Of Heaven On Thee We Feed

Koninsky
Eli Green's Cake-Walk

Kook
Zol Shoyn Kumen Di Geule

Kooymans
Twilight Zone

Kopolyoff
Alleluia Christ Is Risen

Kopylov
God Is A Spirit

Korn-Teuer & Strock
Tell Me Where Can I Go

Korner
Battle Prayer, The

Kortchmar
All She Wants To Do Is Dance
Shaky Town
You're Not Drinking Enough
Kortes
Everywhere I Go
Kosakoff
Ki L'Olam Hasdo
To The Red Sea
Koschat
Forsaken
In Exile
Karntnergmuat
Lord Is My Shepherd, The
My Mother
Sakrische Bass, Der
Twilight
Verlassen
Young Lover, The
Kosloff
I Want You I Need You I Love You
Kosma & Prevert & Mercer
Autumn Leaves
Kost
Trautes Wort Mit Jesu, Ein
Kostas
Timber I'm Falling In Love
Kotchetoff
Tell O Tell Her
Kotscher & Lindt
Liechtensteiner Polka
Kotzschmar
Come Forth And Bring Your
  Garlands
Merry Christmas Bells Are Ringing
Kountz
Carol Of The Questioning Child
Kovanovski
Shlof Mayn Kind
Krallmark
Old Oaken Bucket, The
Kramer
I Have Seen Dawn
In Explanation
Phantasy, A
Kramer & Clausen
Theme From Alf
Kramp
Touch Of The Master's Hand, The
Krauth
Rest Of The Weary Thou
Kreckel
Hail Mary
Hodie Christus Natus Est
Jesu Dulcis Memoria
O Jesus Thou The Beauty Art
O Salutaris Hostia
Kreipl
May Breezes
May-Breeze, The
Krekel
Turning Away
Kremer
I Will Sing To The Lord

Kremser
Braune Gesellen
Hymn Of Thanksgiving
Volkslied, Das
We Gather Together
Wenn Zweie Sich Gut Sind
Krenek
O Would I Were
Krenski & Krenski
Cheater, The
Kreso
That's My Desire
Kretz
Thou Wilt Keep Him In Perfect
  Peace
Kreutzer
An Das Vaterland
Evening Chorus
Evening Shades
Fruhlingsnahen
Kapelle, Die
Mon Habit
Morning
Oiseaux, Les
Our Flag Is There
Parting, The
Practicing
Sabbath Day, The
Schafers Sonntagslied
Serenade
Song To Light
Sur La Terre D'exil
Kreutzmann & Weir
Other One, The
Kricka
April
Krieger
Ergotzlichkeit Zur Rechten Zeit
I Heard The Lord
Nun Sich Der Tag Geendet Hat
Rheinische Wein, Der
Shine On Our Souls Eternal God
Krieger, Harvey
And I Am Telling You I'm Not
  Going
Dreamgirls
I Am Changing
Krise & Dorsey
John Silver
Kristofferson
Come Sundown
For The Good Times
Help Me Make It Through The Night
I'd Rather Be Sorry
Loving Her Was Easier Than
  Anything I'll Ever Do A
Me And Bobby McGee
Nobody Wins
Please Don't Tell Me How The Story
  Ends
So Help Me Make It Through The
  Night
Stranger

Kristofferson (*Cont.*)
Sunday Mornin' Comin' Down
When I Loved Her
Why Me
Why Me Lord
Kristofferson & Foster
Me And Bobby McGee
Kristofferson & Silverstein
Once More With Feeling
Kristofferson & Utley & Bruton
How Do You Feel About Foolin'
  Around
Kristofferson & Wilkin
One Day At A Time
Kroeger
Song Of The Cherry Blossoms
Tulips
Kromer
Grusse An Die Heimat
Krondes
End, The
End Of A Rainbow
Krone
Bluebonnets Of Texas
Johnny Appleseed
Paul Bunyan
Singing Together
What Did You Do Last Summer
Kronenberg
Chicken Talk
Lazy Clouds
Mister Bear
Thanksgiving Day
Krupa & Eldridge
Drum Boogie
Kubik
Sailor He Came To Court Me, A
Kucken
All Praise And Thanks Be Unto God
Captive, La
Chant Du Retour
Confidence
Depth Of Mercy
Fleur Du Vallon, La
Good-Night Farewell
Heup Trilby
Hiron Delle, L'
How Can I Leave Thee
Jeannette
Larme, Une
Lizette
Loyal Song
Mois De Mai, Le
Naufrage Au Port
Serenade
Slumber Song
There's One I Love Dearly
Ton Nom
Treue Liebe
Young Recruit, The
Kudirka
Lietuva Tevyne Musu
Lithuania

Kugelman
All Ye Nations Praise The Lord
Kuhlau
Nachtlied
Ueber Allen Gipfeln Ist Ruh
Unter Jesu Kreuze Ist Ruh'
Kuhmstedt
Meeting House Bell, The
Kuhn
Random Thoughts
Something Everywhere
Kummer
Dearie
Kunkel
Soldier's Vote, The
Veteran's Vote, The
Kurpinski
God For Poland
Kurtz
Du Bachlein Silberhell Und Klar
Grosser Immanuel
Ich Geh' Durch Einen Grasgrunen
Walk
Ihr Kinderlein Kommet
Kusik & Snyder
Making Memories
L'Heureux
East Is East
L'Isle
Ye Sons Of Freedom
L'Isle
Marseillaise Hymn, The
Marseillaise, La
Marseillaise, The
Virginia Marseillaise
La Feillee
O What The Joy And The Glory
Must Be
La Forge
Chant De Joie Libre
La Trobe
Son Of Man To Thee I Cry
Labaky
Holy Mary
Look Upon Your Son
O Bread Of Life
Laborde
Ma Philosophie
Labotna
Dime Si Tu Me Extranas
Labounty & Foster
Weekend, The
Labounty & Foster & Swilley
Heart Don't Fall Now
Labounty & Freeland
This Night Won't Last Forever
Labounty & Geyer
Hot Rod Hearts
Labounty & McLaughlin
Lynda
Labriola
Goldfinch, The

Laburda
Little Bee, The
Robin, The
White Butterfly, The
Wren, The
Lacalle
Amapola
Lacalle & Gamse
Amapola
Lacey
Beyond The Smiling
Cheer Up Chillun
Great Is The Lord
I Am On My Way To Heaven
O Be Joyful In The Lord
O Come Let Us Sing
Lachau
Lil Liza Jane
Lachner
Allmacht, Die
Evening Star, The
Hymne An Die Musik
Kanon
Lenz Fragen
Mon Etoile
Lacome
Estudiantina
On A Nameless Hill Top
Rose
Lacovacci
Miserere
Lafarge
Ballad Of Ira Hayes
River Seine, The
Lafferty
Seek Ye First
Seek Ye First The Kingdom Of God
Laforge
Retreat
Lagergren
Jesus Master Son Of God
Lahache
Conquered Banner, The
Lahee
Hark The Glad Sound
Jesus Let All Thy Lovers Shine
Joy To The World The Lord Is Come
Ring Out Wild Bells
Workman Of God O Lose Not Heart
Lai
Imagine
Live For Life
Love Story
Love Story Theme
Man And A Woman, A
Music's Too Sweet Not To Dance,
The
Theme From Love Story
Where Do I Begin
Laird-Clowes & Gabriel
Life In A Northern Town
Lajos
En Nem Szeretek Mast Csak Teged

Lake
Have You Ever Been To Texas In
Spring
Therefore The Redeemed
Lalo
A Celle Qui Part
A Une Fleur
Amis Vive L'Orgie
Aubade
Aube Nait, L'
Ballade A La Lune
Captive, The
Chanson A Boire
Chanson De Barberine
Chanson De L'alouette, La
Chant Breton
Comment Disaient Ils
Dieu Qui Sourit
Esclave, L'
Fenaison, La
Marine
Oh Quand Je Dors
Priere De D'enfant A Son Reveil
Puisqu'ici-Bas Toute Ame
Rouge-Gorge, Le
Souvenir
Tristesse
Viens
Zuecca, La
Lama
Tic-Ti Tic-Ta
Tic-Tock Polka
Lamb
Army Of The Lord
Bohemia
Champagne Rag
Contentment Rag
Excelsior Rag
Government Issue
Patricia Rag
Ragtime Nightingale
Reindeer Rag
Sensation
Lambert
Billy Magee Magaw
De Ma Celine Amant Modeste
Great-Granddad
When Johnny Comes Marching
Home
When Johnny Comes Marching
Home Again
Lambert & Golde & Hitchings
Don't Look Any Further
Lambert & Golde & Orange
Nightshift
Lambert & Potter
Country Boy You Got Your Feet In
La
Don't Pull Your Love
One Tin Soldier
Lambert & Reynolds & Golde
Take It From Me
Lambertson
Alberta

Lambillotte
Come Holy Ghost
Panis Angelicus

Lamkin & Andrews
Zeb Turney's Gal

Lamm
25 Or 6 To 4
Does Anybody Really Know What
Time It Is
Saturday In The Park

Lamm & Seraphine & Cetera
Thunder And Lightning

Lamothe
Breeze Of The Night

Lampe
Hot Mutton Pies
How Blessed Is This Place
If You Trust Before You Try
O Thou Who Gavest Power To Love
To Us A Child Of Royal Birth
Who's Lead A Happy Life

Lampert
On On U Of K

Lancaster
Last Words Of Copernicus
New Harmony
Sardis

Lance & Mayfield & Cobb
I'm A Soldier Boy

Lancelot
Walk In Peace

Land
When Sorrow Sleepeth

Landaeta
Gloria Al Bravo Pueblo

Landahl
Thy Mercy O Lord

Landau & Ross
Sacred

Landesman & Wolf
Ballad Of The Sad Young Men

Landino
Ballad

Landon
Band Music
Betsy Ross

Landrum & Walker
Martial Trumpet, The

Lane
Begat, The
Church Of The Living God, The
Everybody Loves Somebody
House Of The Lord
How Could You Believe Me When I
Said I Love You When You
Know I've Been A Liar All My
Life
I'm Standing On Solid Rock
I'm Standing On The Solid Rock
In The Hour Of The Trial
In The Hour Of Trial
In The Hour Of Trial Jesus Plead For
Me

Lane *(Cont.)*
Lady's In Love With You, The
Life's Lullaby
Mississippi Woman
Oh Land Of Rest
Standing On The Solid Rock
They Don't Make Love Like They
Used To
Touring That City
Warren
When The Lights Are Low

**Lane & Allen & Dixon & Sweet &
Turner**
Heaven
Sometimes She Cries

Lane & Haggard
My Own Kind Of Hat

Lane & Hanley & Slate
World Needs A Melody, The

Lane & Henley
Till I Get It Right

Lane & Morrison
Yours For The Taking

Lane & Prentiss
Lead Me Into Love

Lane & Speer
What Sins Are You Talking About

Lane, Burton
Babes On Broadway
Come Back To Me
Don't Let It Get You Down
Everything I Have Is Yours
Feudin' And Fightin'
How About You
How Are Things In Glocca Morra
How'dja Like To Love Me
Hurry It's Lovely Up Here
I Hear Music
If This Isn't Love
It's Time For A Love Song
Look To The Rainbow
Love With All The Trimmings
Melinda
Moments Like This
Necessity
Old Devil Moon
On A Clear Day You Can See
Forever
On The SS Bernard Cohn
One More Walk Around The Garden
She Wasn't You
Something Sort Of Grandish
That Great Come-And-Get-It Day
There's A Great Day Coming
Manana
Too Late Now
Wait Till We're Sixty-Five
What Did I Have That I Don't Have
When I'm Not Near The Girl I Love
World Is In My Arms
You're All The World To Me

Laney
I'll Live On

Lang
Fear Not Said He
For Kansas
From Glory To Glory Advancing
I Knew The Flowers Had Dreamed
Of You
In The Shadow Of The Pines
Love's Gifts
On An April Apple Bough

Langdon
Let The Words Of My Mouth
O Sing Unto The Lord

Lange
All I Wanna Do Is Make Love To
You
America Here's My Boy
Do You Believe In Love
Flower Song
He Loves Everybody
I Found The Answer
Lovin' Every Minute Of It
Take The Children And Run
There's Someone To Help You
When I Made My Decision

Lange & Duncan
I Asked The Lord

Lange & Graham
He's Only A Prayer Away

Lange & Heath
Clancy Lowered The Boom
Keep The Bible In Your Heart

Lange & Heath & Burke
Somebody Bigger Than You Or I

Lange & Heath & Glickman
Mule Train

Lange & Heath & Solman
In The Sweet Long Ago

Lange & Merrill & Ballantine
First Thing I Do Every Morning, The
I Am Not Alone

Lange & Ocean
Get Outta My Dreams Get Into My
Car
Licence To Chill

Lange & Porter & Heath
You Gotta Quit Cheatin' On Me

Lange & Weisman
Miracle Happened To Me, A

Langer
Grossmutterchen

Langley
Ensign Of Our Liberty, The
Old-Time Woman

Langlotz
Old Nassau

Langlotz & Carter
Old Nassau

Langran
All Souls O Lord Are Thine
Gather Us In Thou Love That Fillest
All
Hail Thou Source Of Every Blessing
It Is So Long A Way That I Must Go
Lead Us O Father

Langran *(Cont.)*
Lead Us O Father In The Paths Of
Peace
O Thou Great Friend
Seek Not Afar For Beauty
Watching Church, The
Weary Of Earth And Laden With My
Sin
Weary Of Earth Laden With My Sin

Laning
Legionaires

Lankey
Michigan State Fight Song

Lanni
When I'm With You

Lapread & Richie
Fancy Dancer

Lara
Be Mine Tonight
Cocoa Trees In Blossom
Granada
Marimba
Mine Today
My Rival
Solamente Una Vez
Time Has Wings
You Belong To My Heart

Lardner
Mountain Cottage, The
Old Ironsides

Large
Hayride

Larrieu
Hantise

Larsen
Jungle Fever

Larson
Theme From McCloud
Vict'ry For Washington

Larson & Somerville & Jensen
Ballad Of The Unknown Stuntman

Larsson
Norge I Rodt Hvitt Og Blatt

Lasher
Champotch
Night Flower

Lasley
You Bring Me Joy

Lasley & Goodrum
Tell Me Tomorrow

Lassen
Ah Tis A Dream
All Souls' Day
At Evening
Avec Tes Yeux Mignonne
Be Thou Still
Blue Eyes
Cheerless Morn
Ever With Thee
Gipsy Boy In The North, The
Glaciers By Moonlight, The
Greeting
I Feel Thy Angel Spirit
I Wept One Night While Dreaming

Lassen *(Cont.)*
Ich Fuhle Deinem Odem
Ich Hatt Einst Ein Vaterland
In April
In Autumn
It Was A Dream
Lily Blossom
Lullaby
My Device
My Heart Is Like The Silent Night
Near Thee
Nest, The
O Were I You
Old Song, The
Once Again
Poet, The
Prithee Maiden
Resolution
Romance
Sabbath Rest
Silence
Solitude
Spring
Spring Greeting
Spring Song
Spring Time
Sun's Bright Beams, The
Thine Eyes So Blue
Thine Eyes So Blue And Tender
Thine Image
Thou Fairest Vision Of My Soul
Thy Bright Eyes
Vorsatz
Weary My Heart With Thee Doth
Plead
When The Springtide O'Er The Hills
Is Seen
Whither

Lasso
Ah Could My Eyes Behold Thee
Canst Thou Say The Ave
Celebrons Sans Cesse
Echo-Song
Good-Day Dear Heart
Good-Day Sweetheart
I Know A Young Maiden Wondrous
Fair
Inimici Autem
Into Your Hands I Give My Heart
Ipsa Te Cogat Pietas
Liebesbeteuerung
Liebesklage
Madrigal
Mailied
Matona Lovely Maiden
My Heart Doth Beg You'll Not
Forget
O Eyes Of My Beloved

Lassus
Bonjour Mon Coeur
Matona
Nuit Froide Et Sombre, La
Puce, Une
Quand Mon Mari

Last
Fool
Games That Lovers Play
Happy Heart
When The Snow Is On The Roses

Latham
Broadway Sights

Lathbury
Day Is Dying In The West

Lathbury & Sherwin
Break Thou The Bread Of Life

Latino
Holly Boy With The Christmas Ball
Nose, The

Latrobe
Throned Upon The Awful Tree

Laubenstein
Now Is The Time

Lauder
I Love A Lassie
Nanny
Roamin' In The Gloamin'
She Is Ma Daisy
Stop Yer Tickling Jock
That's The Reason Noo I Wear A
Kilt

Laudes
As Tranquil Streams That Meet And
Merge

Laufer
V'Karev P'Zurenu
We Thank Thee Lord
We Thank Thee Lord Thy Paths Of
Service
We Thank Thee Lord Thy Paths Of
Service Lead
When The Golden Evening Gathered

Laughlin
Have You Never Heard Of Holyoke

Laujon
Origine De La Danse

Lauper & Hyman
Time After Time

Lauper & Lunt & Stead
Goonies 'r' Good Enough, The

Lauridsen
As Birds Come Nearer
When Frost Moves Fast

Lava
Cheyenne
Secret Of Silent Hills, The
Theme From F Troop

Lavallee
Lord Of The Lands
O Canada
O Canada Terre De Nos Aieux

Lavoie
Ginger Bread House, The
Me And You And A Dog Named
Boo

Law
Bunker Hill
On Iowa

Lawes
Angler's Song, The
Bid Me To Live
Blessed Be The Lord Our God
Candlemas Eve
Captive Lover, The
Cawood's Dragon
Chast'ned With Fasting
Cobbler's Thumb
Drink To The Fat Man
Gather Ye Rosebuds
Goose Law'd With Goose
Great 'tom' Is Cast
I Prethee Send Me Back My Heart
I'll Marry A Maid
Join In This Round
Long Did I Toil And Knew No
    Earthly Rest
Lord God Of Hosts Within Whose
    Hands
Most Glorious Lord Of Life
New Year's
Now The Last Load
O God I Thank Thee
Reapers Singing
She Weepeth Sore
Sing Tonight
Sweet Echo
Tar's Devotion
Three Merry Boys And Girls
Thy Way Not Mine O Lord
To Anthea
To The Other World
Wars Are Our Delight
Wise Men Were But Sev'n, The
Wisemen Were But Seven, The
Woe's Au Be

Lawler
Irish Jubilee, The

Lawlor & Blake
Sidewalks Of New York, The

Lawreer
Who's That A Calling

Lawrence
He Grew The Tree
Honolulu Moon
If I Didn't Care
Linda
That's What I Want For Christmas
Whippoorwill
You Take My Breath Away

Lawrence & Carle
Sunrise Serenade

Lawrence & Desautels
Love Theme From Eyes Of Laura
    Mars

Lawrence & Edwards
With The Wind And The Rain In
    Your Hair

Lawrence & Tinturin
Foolin' Myself

Lawson
Any Time
Loch Lomond

Lawton
Jesus Jesus Wonderful Lord

Layriz
There Comes A Galley

Layton
After You've Gone
Way Down Yonder In New Orleans

Lazaros
Big City Miss Ruth Ann

Lazarus
It All Comes Out Of The Piano
Natasha
Night In The Ukraine, A

Lazzaro
Ferry-Boat Serenade

Lazzaro
Mariarosa Alla Festa Va
Woodpecker Song, The

LeBrunn
If It Wasn't For The 'ouses In
    Between
It's A Great Big Shame
Oh Mr Porter

LeCocq
Legend Of Madame Angot, The

Le Gallienne
At The Round Earth's Imagin'd
    Corners
Batter My Heart Three Person'd God
Death Be Not Proud
Hymne To God The Father, A
Solveig's Song

Le Grand
Vetus Abit Littera

Leach
Ain't That Enough
All Those In Favor Of Having A
    Drink
Bible Stories
Greenhouse, The
Highballs Rolling On The Ground
Lydia Pinkham
Tattooed Lady, The
We Didn't Mean No Harm
Why Men Drink

Leadon & Henley
Witchy Woman

Leake
Excuses

Leander
We Will Stand The Storm

Leander & Mills
Lady Godiva

Leary & Taylor
Ageless Dancer

Leavitt
Blest Be The Ground
I Hear The Whispering Wind
Otherwise
Rain Feathers
Storm Winds, The
Sunset

Lebedeff
Rumania Rumania

Lebieg
Sleep

Lebish & Treadwell & Nahan & Glick
Dance With Me

Leblanc & Aldridge
Somebody Send My Baby Home

Lebowsky
Don't Go Home
Don't Go Home My Little Darlin'

Leboy
I Wish I Had A Girl

Lebrunn
I've Never Lost My Last Train Yet
If It Wasn't For The 'Ouses In
    Between

Lechner
Gott Bhute Dich

Leclere
Triangle Jazz Blues

Lecocq
Chimney Swift, The
Son Of A Wealth House, The
Youth

Lecuona
Always In My Heart
Andalucia
As We Are Today
At The Crossroads
Babilu
Breeze And I, The
Four Winds, The
Jungle Drums
Malaguena
Maria-La-O
Mi Vada
Noche Azul
Para Vigo Me Voy
Pavo Real
Say Si Si
Siboney
Taboo

Ledbetter
Ain't It A Shame
Ain't You Glad
Almost Day
Army Life
Backwater Blues
Birmingham Jail
Black Betty
Black Girl
Boll Weevil Blues
Borrow Love And Go
Bourgeois Blues
Bring Me A Little Water Silvy
Bring Me L'il Water Silvy
Christmas Is A-Coming
Come Along All You Cowboys
Corn Bread Rough
Cotton Fields
Cotton Song
Cow Cow Yicky Yicky Yea

Ledbetter (Cont.)
Dekalb Blues
Didn't Old John
Don't Sleep Too Long
Duncan And Brady
Easy Rider
Fannin Street
Gallis Pole
Go Down Old Hannah
Good Morning Blues
Green Corn
Ha-Ha This A-Way
Ham And Eggs
Happy Birthday
Haul Away Joe
Hitler Song
House Of The Rising Sun
Irene
Jailhouse Blues
Jean Harlow
Jim Crow Blues
John Henry
Julie Ann Johnson
Keep Your Hands Off Her
Leavin' Blues
Little Children's Blues
Little Sally Walker
Look Away In The Heaven
Looky Looky Yonder
Meeting At The Building
More Yet
National Defense Blues
Old Man Will Your Dog Catch A
   Rabbit
Old Riley
On A Monday
Pigmeat
Poor Howard
Pretty Flower
Red Bird
Rock Island Line
Salty Dog
Shorty George
Silver City Bound
Skip To My Lou
TB Blues
There's A Man Goin' Round Takin'
   Names
They Hung Him On A Cross
Titanic
We Shall Be Free
We Shall Walk Through The Valley
Yellow Gal
You Can't Lose-A Me Cholly
Ledbetter & Campbell
Sylvie
Ledbetter & Lomax
Goodnight Irene
Irene Goodnight
Ledbetter, Huddie
Alabama Bound
Can't You Line 'em
Good Mornin' Blues

Ledbetter, Huddie (Cont.)
Grey Goose
Midnight Special
Pick A Bale Of Cotton
Stewball
Take This Hammer
Whoa Buck
Lee
Champagne Charlie
Come Back And Stay
Down By The Flowing River
Dream Seller, The
Flying Trapeze, The
Give Me Wings Lord
Independence Day
Jesus He Is The Son Of God
Let The Good Times Roll
Macgregor's Gathering
Man On The Flying Trapeze, The
O Zion Tune Thy Voice
Our Mother's Way
Soldier's Tear
That's The Man I'm Looking For
This Is A Very Special Day
We're Not Strangers Anymore
Who Is Building That Boat
Lee & Barbour
I Don't Know Enough About You
It's A Good Day
Manana
Lee & Burke
Bella Notte
He's A Tramp
La-La-Lu
Siamese Cat Song, The
Lee & Cash
If I Only Knew
Jackie Blue
Lee & Duffy
She Thinks I Still Care
Lee & Jones
He Broke Your Memory Last Night
Lee & Lifeson
Big Money, The
Body Electric, The
Closer To The Heart
Distant Early Warning
New World Man
Red Barchetta
Spirit Of Radio, The
Tom Sawyer
Lee & Manners
Pennsylvania Polka
Lee & Mullan
I Don't Work For A Living
Leech
He Rescued Me
Hiding Place, The
Lately Have You Seen The Sun
Little Hearts Are Happy
Leeuwen
Mighty Joe
Venus

Lefebvre
Christmas Eve
Lefevre
Without Him
Leffler & Schuckett
Another World
Another World Theme
Friends
Lefort
Negros Diamantes, Los
Leftwich
Blue And White
Legassick & Ray
One Heartbeat
Legrand
After The Rain
Ask Yourself Why
Blue Green Grey And Gone
Breezy's Song
Brian's Song
Catch A Pebble
Faded Roses
Hands Of Time, The
Happy
Her Hair
His Eyes Her Eyes
How Do You Keep The Music
   Playing
I Was Born In Love With You
I Will Say Goodbye
I Will Wait For You
Little Boy Lost
Loving Me Loving You Loving Me
Make Me Forget
No Matter What Happens
Nobody Knows
Noelle's Theme
On My Way To You
Once You've Been In Love
One At A Time
One Day
Orson's Theme
Papa Can You Hear Me
Piece Of Sky, A
Pieces Of Dreams
Rose In The Snow, A
Some Day
Something New In My Life
Summer Knows, The
Summer Me Winter Me
Sweet Gingerbread Man
There'll Be Time
This Quiet Room
Watch What Happens
Way He Makes Me Feel, The
What Are You Doing The Rest Of
   Your Life
Where Do The Balloons Go
Where Is It Written
Where's The Love
Will Someone Ever Look At Me That
   Way
Windmills Of Your Mind, The

Legrand (Cont.)
World Of You And I, The
Years Of My Youth, The
You Must Believe In Spring
You're Gone
Legrand & Barclay
Once Upon A Summertime
Legrand & Burr
Place Of Bittersweet
Legrand & Connors
Yesterday's Dreams
Legrand & David
Everything That Happens To You
Happens To Me
First Time I Heard A Bluebird
Let Me Be Your Mirror
Legrand & Gimbel
I Will Wait For You
Legrand & Gimbel & Marnay
Love And Learn
Legrand & Harnick
Penny By Penny
Legrand & Lambert
First Time, The
You Had To Be There
Legrand & Lee
Mon Amour
Legrand & Shaper
I Still See You
Paris Was Made For Lovers
Legrand & Shaper & Marnay
Martina
Legrand & Shuman & Marnay
Look
Legrenzi
Che Fiero Costume
Lehar
Girls Girls Girls
I Love You So
Maxim's
Merry Widow Waltz
My Little Nest Of Heavenly Blue
Oh Fatherland
Study Of Woman, The
Valse-Song
Vil Ja-Lied
Vilia
Vilia Song
Waltz Song
Wenn Zwei Sich Lieben
Yours Is My Heart Alone
Lehman
Ev'rybody Works But Father
Everybody Works But Father
Love Of God, The
Royal Telephone, The
Lehman & Edwards & Rodgers
Dance Dance Dance
Lehman & Michael & Harding
You're The Reason
Lehman & Turner
Think Big
Lehman & Wilburn & Wilburn
Who Is He

Lehmann
Alone At Last
At The Making Of The Hay
Myself When Young
Titania's Cradle
Woodpigeon, The
Wren, The
Yellowhammer, The
Lehmann & Black
Leave It In The Hands Of The Lord
Lehmann & Lebowsky & Clarke
TLC
Lehmann & Miller
Night
Leiber
Forever Your Girl
Opposites Attract
Way That You Love Me, The
Leiber & Spector
Spanish Harlem
Leiber & Stoller
Baby I Don't Care
Bossa Nova Baby
Charlie Brown
Don't
Framed
Girls Girls Girls
Hot Dog
Hound Dog
I Want To Be Free
I'm A Woman
Is That All There Is
Jailhouse Rock
Just Tell Her Jim Said Hello
Kansas City
King Creole
Love Me
Love Potion No. 9
Love Potion Number Nine
Loving You
One Bad Stud
Poison Ivy
Ruby Baby
Santa Claus Is Back In Town
Searchin'
Smokey Joe's Cafe
Steadfast Loyal And True
Treat Me Nice
Trouble
Yakety Yak
Leiber & Stoller & Pomus
She's Not You
Young Blood
Leibling & Hamlisch
Sunshine Lollipops And Rainbows
Leigh
Best Minute Of The Day, The
Don't It Make My Brown Eyes Blue
Dulcinea
Hey Look Me Over
I'll Get Over You
Impossible Dream, The
It Ain't Gonna Worry My Mind

Leigh (Cont.)
Man Of La Mancha
Put On Your Tat-Ta Little Girlie
Sarava
Your Old Cold Shoulder
Leigh & Bastow
Galloping Major, The
Leigh & Blackford
Heart Mender
Leigh & Jordan
It's All I Can Do
Leigh & Nicholson
That's The Thing About Love
Leighton
Steamboat Bill
Leiken & Gassman
Step Into The Sunshine
Leisring
O Filii Et Filiae
Leitch
Mellow Yellow
Season Of The Witch
Sunshine Superman
Lejeune
Awake Glad Soul Awake
Jesus Thou Divine Companion
Love Divine All Loves Excelling
Our Saviour Bless The Food
Lemaire
Countess You Dance Sprightly
Lemaire & Gray
Diamond In The Dust
LeMaire & Pennington
Crazy For Your Love
Lemaire & Pennington
Give Me One More Chance
Hang On To Your Heart
I Could Get Used To You
I Don't Want To Be A Memory
It'll Be Me
It's You Again
Just In Case
Just One Kiss
She's A Miracle
She's Too Good To Be True
Super Love
Lemare
Andantino
Deep In My Heart
Moonlight And Roses
Night Song
Nocturne
Lemcke
In Lonely Wood
Lemmel
Children's Friend, The
Turn Your Eyes Upon Jesus
Lemon
My Ain Folk
Lems
Farmer
My Mom's A Feminist
Lendhurst
Be-Bop Baby

Leng & May
Closest Thing To Heaven

Lengsfelder & Drake & Tizol
Perdido

Lennon
Beautiful Boy Darling Boy
Clean Up Time
Cold Turkey
Crippled Inside
Dear Yoko
Gimme Some Truth
God
Grow Old With Me
How
How Do You Sleep
I Don't Wanna Be A Soldier
I Found Out
I'm Losing You
Imagine
Instant Karma
Isolation
It's So Hard
Jealous Guy
John Sinclair
Just Like Starting Over
Look At Me
Love
Mind Games
Mother
My Mummy's Dead
Oh Yoko
Power To The People
Remember
Say You're Wrong
Starting Over
Too Late For Goodbyes
Watching The Wheels
Well Well Well
Whatever Gets You Through The
    Night
Woman
Working Class Hero

Lennon & Clayton & Morales
Valotte

Lennon & McCartney
Across The Universe
All I've Got To Do
All My Loving
All Together Now
All You Need Is Love
And I Love Her
And Your Bird Can Sing
Another Girl
Anytime At All
Ask Me Why
Baby You're A Rich Man
Baby's In Black
Back In The USSR
Bad To Me
Ballad Of John And Yoko, The
Because
Being For The Benefit Of Mr Kite
Birthday

Lennon & McCartney *(Cont.)*
Blackbird
Can't Buy Me Love
Carry That Weight
Come And Get It
Come Together
Continuing Story Of Bungalow Bill
Cry Baby Cry
Day In The Life, A
Day Tripper
Dear Prudence
Dig A Pony
Do You Want To Know A Secret
Doctor Robert
Don't Let Me Down
Drive My Car
Eight Days A Week
Eleanor Rigby
End, The
Every Little Thing
Everybody's Got Something To Hide
    Except Me And My Monkey
Fixing A Hole
Fool On The Hill, The
For No One
From Me To You
Get Back
Getting Better
Girl
Give Peace A Chance
Glass Onion
Golden Slumbers
Good Day Sunshine
Good Morning Good Morning
Good Night
Goodbye
Got To Get You Into My Life
Happiness Is A Warm Gun
Hard Day's Night, A
Hello Goodbye
Help
Helter Skelter
Her Majesty
Here There And Everywhere
Hey Bulldog
Hey Jude
Hold Me Tight
Honey Pie
I Am The Walrus
I Call Your Name
I Don't Want To See You Again
I Don't Want To Spoil The Party
I Feel Fine
I Saw Her Standing There
I Saw Him Standing There
I Should Have Known Better
I Wanna Be Your Man
I Want To Hold Your Hand
I Want You
I Will
I'll Be Back
I'll Cry Instead
I'll Follow The Sun

Lennon & McCartney *(Cont.)*
I'll Get You
I'm A Loser
I'm Down
I'm Happy Just To Dance With You
I'm Looking Through You
I'm Only Sleeping
I'm So Tired
I've Got A Feeling
I've Just Seen A Face
If I Fell
In My Life
It Won't Be Long
It's Only Love
Julia
Lady Madonna
Let It Be
Little Child
Long And Winding Road, The
Love Me Do
Lovely Rita
Lucy In The Sky With Diamonds
Magical Mystery Tour
Martha My Dear
Maxwell's Silver Hammer
Mean Mr Mustard
Michelle
Misery
Mother Nature's Son
Night Before, The
No Reply
Norwegian Wood
Not A Second Time
Nowhere Man
Ob-La-Di Ob-La-Da
Oh Darling
One After 909
Paperback Writer
Penny Lane
Please Please Me
Polythene Pam
PS I Love You
Rain
Revolution
Ringo's Theme
Rocky Raccoon
Run For Your Life
Sexy Sadie
Sgt Pepper's Lonely Hearts Club
    Band
She Came In Through The Bathroom
    Window
She Loves You
She Said She Said
She's A Woman
She's Leaving Home
Strawberry Fields Forever
Tell Me What You See
Tell Me Why
Thank You Girl
There's A Place

Lennon & McCartney *(Cont.)*
Things We Said Today
This Boy
Ticket To Ride
Tomorrow Never Knows
Twist And Shout
Two Of Us
Wait
We Can Work It Out
What You're Doing
When I Get Home
When I'm Sixty-Four
Why Don't We Do It In The Road
Wild Honey Pie
With A Little Help From My Friends
Within You Without You
Word, The
World Without Love, A
Yellow Submarine
Yer Blues
Yes It Is
Yesterday
You Can't Do That
You Know My Name Look Up My
    Number
You Never Give Me Your Money
You Won't See Me
You're Going To Lose That Girl
You've Got To Hide Your Love
    Away
Your Mother Should Know
Lennon & McCartney & Harrison &
    Starkey
Dig It
Flying
Lennon & McCartney & Starkey
What Goes On
Lennon & Ono
Happy Xmas
Luck Of The Irish, The
Oh My Love
Sunday Bloody Sunday
Lennox
Love's Golden Dream
Lennox & Stewart
Don't Ask Me Why
Here Comes The Rain Again
Love Is A Stranger
Missionary Man
Right By Your Side
Sisters Are Doin' It For Themselves
Sweet Dreams
Sweet Dreams Are Made Of This
There Must Be An Angel Playing
    With My Heart
Thorn In My Side
Who's That Girl
Would I Lie To You
You Have Placed A Chill In My
    Heart
Lenoir
Speak To Me Of Love

Lenore
Prayer For Advent, A
Lenox & Sutton
I Don't Care
Lenton
Let Us Love And Drink
Love And Drink
Mate To A Cock, The
Rebus On The Late Mr Henry
    Purcell's Name
Lentz
Our Country Fair
Leo & Waldman
Baby What About You
Home Again In My Heart
Leonard
Du Bist Wie Eine Blume
Ida Sweet As Apple Cider
Mazurka
Roll Them Roly Boly Eyes
Leoncavallo
Arioso
Dawn
E Allor Perche
Guarda Amor Mio
Mattinata
O Colombina
Serenade
Si Puo
Stridono Lassu
Vesti La Giubba
Leoni
We Sing Our Praise To God
Leontovich
Carol Of The Bells
Leontovich-Gnotov
Come Dance And Sing
Leopoldi
In Einem Kleinen Cafe In Hernals
Lerman
O Brother Man Fold To Thy Heart
Lerner
Dance A Little Closer
Gigi
I'm Popeye The Sailor Man
On The Street Where You Live
Lerner & Loewe
Adlai's Gonna Win This Time
Leroy
Can't I
Lesh
Box Of Rain
New Potato Caboose
Passenger
Leslie
Annabelle Lee
By The River Sainte Marie
Flag They Loved So Well, The
How Sweet The Moonlight Sleeps
It Looks Like Rain In Cherry
    Blossom Lane
Let The Words Of My Mouth
Rock Me To Sleep Mother

Leslie & Young & Jentes
Now She Knows How To Parle-Voo
Lesneven
Winds Were Wailing, The
Lester
Behold A Stranger At The Door
Delta Blues
I Vow To Thee My Country
If All The Magic Is Gone
When Through The Whirl Of Wheels
Lester & Dubois
Good Night's Love, A
Leston
Evening Twilight Gathers
Lesueur
France's Triumphal Song
Letford
To The Legion
Levant
Blame It On My Youth
Pitt Victory Song
Levay & Prager
Fly Robin Fly
Get Up And Boogie
Leven
Are My Ears On Straight
Cruella De Ville
Levenson
Let's Do Something Cheap And
    Superficial
Levenson & Garton
My Belgian Rose
Leveridge
Love Is A Bauble
Sweet Rosy Morning, The
Who Is Sylvia
Levert & Gordon & Baker
Whatever It Takes
Levey
Two Roses
Levi
Belle Of Murray Hill, The
Levine
Gino's Gives You Freedom Of
    Choice
Serengeti
Something Old Something Blue
Levine & Brown
Knock Three Times
Tie A Yellow Ribbon Round The Ole
    Oak Tree
Levinson
Denise
Let's Do Something Cheap And
    Superficial
Levinson & Warner
Nothing Goes With Everything Like
    Mueller's
Levy
Abc's Of Love
I Want You To Be My Girl
Levy & Callender & Peabody
Little Star

Levy & Cox
Little Girl Of Mine
Levy & Davis
Gee
Levy & Roberts
My Boy Lollipop
Lewars
God Of Heaven Hear Our Singing
Jesus In Thy Dying Woes
O Ye Heavens Bend And See
Royal Standard Forward Goes, The
Wide Open Are Thy Hands
Lewis
Ant Reporter Interviews The Bees,
The
Blackbeard
Bring Back My Wandering Boy
Down The Field
Dryland Blues
Dunlap's Creek
Farewell My Summer Love
For Thy Blest Saints A Noble Throng
Going To Germany
Great Redeemer Lives, The
Hello Stranger
Honky-Tonk Train
How High The Moon
I Had But Fifty Cents
I'm A Citizen Of Two Worlds
It Ain't Gonna Rain No More
Minglewood Blues
Now Let Us All With One Accord
O Thou In Whose Presence
Old Soft Shoes, The
Sailing
Star
Teenage Idol
Versatile Baby, The
Lewis & Colla
Trouble In Paradise
Lewis & Levy
Ya Ya
Lewis & Lewis
Secret Lovers
Lewis & Lewis & Lewis
Always
Lewis & Perren
Heaven Must Be Missing An Angel
Lewis & Ross
Judy's Turn To Cry
Lewis & Schindler & Adams
Mother Pin A Rose On Me
Lewis & Smith
I Almost Called Your Name
Lewis & Stock & Rose
Blueberry Hill
Lewis & Waring
'Way Back Home
Lewis & Wright
When A Man Loves A Woman
Lewis & Young
Sam You Made The Pants Too Long
Lewis & Young & Fiorito
Laugh Clown Laugh

Lewis & Young & Grant
If I Knock The L Out Of Kelly
If I Knock The L Out Of Kelly It
Would Still Be Kelly To Me
Lewis & Young & Henderson
I'm Sitting On Top Of The World
Lewis & Young & Jerome
Just A Baby's Prayer At Twilight
Lewis & Young & Schwartz
Rock-A-Bye Your Baby With A Dixie
Melody
Lewis & Young & Wayne
In A Little Spanish Town
Lewisham
I Know A Fount
Ley
Fight The Good Fight With All Thy
Might
Saylor's Song, The
Song Of The Cyclops
This Day At Thy Creating Word
Leyden
Boston University Victory Song
Victory
Leyerle
Treasure Chest, The
Liang
Midnight Sleeping Bethlehem
Libbey
Mangos
Libornio
Maui Girl
Licciardello
Champion, The
Lazarus Come Forth
Lidarti
Envy Not The Mighty Great
I Envy Not The Mighty Great
Su Cantiamo Su Beviamo
Wise Old Owl
Liddle
How Lovely Are Thy Dwellings
Lideman
Babe Is Born In Bethlehem, A
Lidgey
See Where My Love A Maying Goes
Sunny March
Liebe
Nature's Orchestra
Lieberman
Brite Piece, A
Liebich
To Labor
We Have Fed You All For A
Thousand Years
Workers' Memorial Song
Liebick
Advancing Proletaire, The
Liebman
Brite Piece, A
Dance For Your Thoughts, A
New Breed
Liessin & Weiner
Frayhayt Statue

Lieurance
By The Waters Of Minnetonka
By The Waters Of The Minnetonka
Hail Wichita
Lightbourne
National Anthem Of Jamaica
Lightfoot
Affair On Eighth Avenue
Baby Step Back
Beautiful
Bend In The Water
Bitter Green
Canadian Railroad Anthology
Canadian Railroad Trilogy
Carefree Highway
Christian Island
Circle Is Small, The
Circle Of Steel
Cold On The Shoulder
Cotton Jenny
Crossroads
Daylight Katy
Did She Mention My Name
Don Quixote
Dream Street Rose
Early Mornin' Rain
Ecstasy Made Easy
For Lovin' Me
For Loving Me
Go My Way
I'll Be Alright
I'll Tag Along
I'm Not Sayin'
If You Could Read My Mind
Leaves Of Grass
Minstrel Of The Dawn
Old Dan's Records
Pussywillows Cat Tails
Race Among The Ruins
Rainy Day People
Ribbon Of Darkness
Rich Man Spiritual
Salute
Sea Of Tranquility
Second Cup Of Coffee
Shadows
Sit Down Young Stranger
Softly
Song For A Winter's Night
Spin Spin
Stay Loose
Steel Rail Blues
Summer Side Of Life
Summertime Dream
Sundown
Sweet Guinevere
Talking In Your Sleep
Tattoo
Walls
Way I Feel, The
Wherefore And Why
Wreck Of The Edmund Fitzgerald,
The

Lightwood
Little Ship Was On The Sea, A
Lord When We Have Not Any Light
Liguori
Tu Scendi Dalle Stelle
Lilenas
Everbody Ought To Love Jesus
Liles & Borop
Only God Could Love You More
Proclaim The Glory Of The Lord
Liles & Gersmehl & Borop
Pour On The Power
Liles & Liles
Make Us One
Liliuokalani
Aloha Oe
Hawaiian Farewell Song
Queen's Prayer, The
Lillenas
Abundant Entrance, An
All For Me
All We Can
At The Feet Of Jesus
Beautiful Lilies Of Easter
Calvary Road, The
Easter Joy
Gates Of Life, The
Glory Of Easter, The
Go To Thy Father In Prayer
Hallelujah All The Way
He Always Knows
He Is Not Here He Is Risen
He Is Risen
He Keeps On Loving Us Still
In A Lovely Garden
It Is Glory Just To Walk With Him
It Was Jesus Who Set Me Free
Jesus Took My Burden
Jesus Will Walk With Me
O Living Redeemer
Such Is Love Divine
Well Springs Up In My Soul, A
Will The Circle Be Broken
Will You Be Ready
Lilley
Jingle Jangle Jingle
Lilliburlero
Marchin Along
Limahl
Only For Love
Limscomb & Duffy
She Thinks I Still Care
Linblad
Hermeline
Ruisseau, Le
Lincke
Glow-Worm, The
Glowworm Rock
Lincoln
Midnight Fire-Alarm
Repasz Band
Wellcome Evening Shadows

Lind
Elusive Butterfly
I Cannot See But I Can Trust
We Invoke Thee Holy Spirit
Yes For Me He Careth
Yet There Is Room
Lind & Galdston
Reason To Try
Lind & Goldenberg
Skin Deep
Linda & Campbell & Peretti & Creato
Lion Sleeps Tonight, The
Lindblad
From The Depths Of Swedish Hearts
Swallow, The
Linde
Burning Love
For The Heart
In A Letter To You
Linde & Morrison
Love She Found In Me, The
Lindeman
Babe Is Born In Bethlehem, A
Et Barn Er Fodt I Betlehem
Friend Of The Weary O Refresh Us
Long Hast Thou Stood O Church Of
God
Lord Christ When First Thou Cam'st
Suffering Son Of Man Be Near Me
Lindeman & Stutz
Little Things Mean A Lot
Lindenfeld
Cow, The
Dolor
Lindpaintner
Porte-Etendard Et Menestrel
Lindsay
Always Take Mother's Advice
Bridge, The
Far Away
Tired So Tired
Too Late Too Late
Lindsey
Lorna
Lindsey & Tubb & Wynette
Two Story House
Lingenfelter
Invasion Song, The
Link
No One Loves You Any Better Than
Your M-A-Double-My
Linley
Lord Of All Being
Now The Hungry Lion Roars
Switzer's Farewell, The
Linton & Huff
Easier Said Than Done
Linwood
Lord Is God And King, The
Linzer & Levine
Talk It Over
Linzer & Randell
Workin' My Way Back To You

Lippe
How Do I Love Thee
Lippman
Chickery Chick
My Sugar Is So Refined
These Things You Left Me
Too Young
Lipsky
Lilac-Time
Lisette
Lisette
Lister
All Of Me
All The Way
And Even I
At The Right Time
Behold He Comes
Behold He Stands And Knocks
Believe On The Lord
Bring Us Back
Celebrate The Coming
Coming Again
Day Of Miracles, The
Gentle Stranger, The
God Loved The World So Much
Goodbye World Goodbye
He Has Time
He Knows Just What I Need
His Grace Is Sufficient For Me
His Hand In Mine
Hold On
Hold On To Love
Holy Holy
Holy Savior
How Long Has It Been
I Choose Jesus
I Surrender All
I Won't Turn Back
I'm Bound For The Kingdom
I've Been Trying Lord
In My Risen Lord
In The Springtime Of My Years
Jesus Come On In
Jesus My Everything
Jesus Only Lord
King And I, The
Led By The Master's Hand
Light Up The Sky
Lord Is In This Place, The
Love Of God Will Live Forever, The
One More Voice
One Of Your Children Needs You
Lord
Prayer Of Faith, The
Reaching
Restore My Soul
Shoutin' Ground
Something Exciting
Sound Of His Name, The
Storm Now And Then, A
Surrender
Take Me To The Fountain
That Says It All

Lister *(Cont.)*

This Love Is Mine
Though Unworthy Am I
'Til The Storm Passes By
Touched By The Hand Of The Lord
Turning Point
Very Uncommon Man, A
We Shall Rise
What Love Can Do
Where Jesus Is
Where No One Stands Alone
While Ages Roll
World Needs Love, The

Liszt

Angel Fair With Golden Hair
Angiolin Dal Biondo Crin
Ave Maris Stella
Comment Disaient-ils
Could I Ever Hope To Endure It
Dear Love Thou'rt Like A Blossom
Dis Vatergruft
Du Bist Wie Eine Blume
I Love But Thee
In Love's Bright Joy
It Must Be Wonderful Indeed
Liebestraum
Loreley, The
Love Divine
Love's Dream
Love's Sweet Mystery
Mignon's Song
O Thou That From Heaven Art
Oh Love
Oh Quand Je Dors
Once Again I Fain Would Meet Thee
Sacred Love
Song Of Mignon
Sound Softly My Lay
Sunrise
There Reigned A King In Thule
Thou'rt Like A Flower
Veilchen, Das
Vereinslied
Violet, The
Wanderers Nachtlied
While Jesus Sleeps
Wieder Mocht' Ich Dir Begegnen
Wir Sind Nicht Mumien
Wondrous Thing 'T Must Be Indeed
Ye Sons And Daughters Of The King

Little

Because They All Love You
Jealous
My Lord And I
Nice Situation For A Girl, A

Little & Malie & Finch

Jealous

Little & Oppenheim & Schuster

Hold Me

Little & Siras

In A Shanty In Old Shanty Town

Liubin

May You All Prosper

Liuzzi

Canto D'Amore
Canto Di Falciatrici
Canto Di Pescatori
Crepuscolo
Di Notte
Solitudine

Livgren

Carry On Wayward Son
Dust In The Wind

Livingston

Ballad Of Cat Ballou, The
Blues Country Style, The
Bronco
Casper The Friendly Ghost
Hanging Tree, The
It's The Talk Of The Town
Lawman
My Destiny
Twelfth Of Never, The
Under A Blanket Of Blue
Wake The Town And Tell The
People

Livingston & Evans

Bonanza
Buttons And Bows
Mister Ed
Mona Lisa
My Love Loves Me
Never Let Me Go
Que Sera Sera
Silver Bells
Streets Of Laredo, The
Sugar Baby Bounce
Tammy
To Each His Own
Whatever Will Be Will Be
Wish Me A Rainbow

Lloyd

B-I-Double L-Bill
For Thee O Dear Dear Country
God Laid His Rocks In Courses
Good Morning All You Jolly Friends
Good Morning Mr Zip-Zip-Zip
Handsome Cabin Boy, The
In The Early Morning
Monst'rous Drefful Bogie Man
Morning Hangs A Signal, The
O Lamb Of God Still Keep Me
O Young And Fearless Prophet
Pray When The Morn Is Breaking
Sons Of Britain
Strong Son Of God Immortal Love
They're Talking War
Thou Who At Thy First Eucharist
Didst Pray
Voice Of God Is Calling, The

Lloyd & Foster & Clark

Fair Shake

Lloyd

Bonnie Blue Flag, The

Lloyd & Tillis

Goin' To Work

Lloyd Webber & Rice

Christmas Dream

Lloyd Webber, Andrew

All I Ask Of You
Another Suitcase In Another Hall
Any Dream Will Do
Close Every Door
Don't Cry For Me Argentina
Gus The Theatre Cat
Herod's Song
High Flying Adored
I Don't Know How To Love Him
Jesus Christ Superstar
Last Man In My Life, The
Make Up My Heart
Memory
Mr Mistoffelees
Music Of The Night
Only You
Phantom Of The Opera, The
Pie Jesu
Rainbow High
Starlight Express
Superstar
Take That Look Off Your Face
Take That Look Off Your Face
Reprise
Tell Me On A Sunday
There's Me
Unexpected Song
Wishing You Were Somehow Here
Again

Lobo

How Can I Tell Her About You

Locke

Believe Me If All Those Endearing
Young Charms
Equal Rights
Up And Down
We Are Marching On To Richmond

Lockhart

All Praise To You O Lord
From Homes Of Quiet Peace
My Soul Be On Thy Guard
O Come And Dwell In Me
O Shepherd Of The Sheep
Rejoice Ye Pure In Heart
Still Ain't Satisfied
Teach Me My God And King
'Tis Good Lord To Be Here
Witch Song, The

Lockheart

Rejoice Ye Pure In Heart

Locklin

Send Me The Pillow You Dream On

Lockwood

Don't You Go Tommy
Joseph Dearest Joseph
Song Of An Old Fisherman

Loder

Brave Old Oak, The
Church Without A Prophet
Eliza's Flight
I Heard A Brooklet Gushing

Loder *(Cont.)*
Rose That All Are Praising, The
Upper California

Lodge
Black Diamond Rag
Ride My See-Saw
Sure Fire Rag

Loeb
Masquerade
Reflections In The Water

Loeffler
Adieu Pour Jamais
Paons, Les
Prayer

Loenholdt
Woodpecker, The

Loes
Blessed Redeemer
For Me
Saviour Lives, The

Loesser
Abbondanza
Adelaide
Adelaide's Complaint
Adelaide's Lament
All Is Forgiven And All Is Forgotten
Anywhere I Wander
Baby It's Cold Outside
Big D
Bloop Bleep
Brotherhood Of Man
Bushel And A Peck, A
Can't Get Out Of This Mood
Cinderella Darling
Coffee Break
Company Way, The
Don't Cry
Faraway Boy
Feathery Feelin', The
First Class Private Mary Brown
Follow The Fold
Fugue For Tinhorns
Gideon Briggs I Love You
Grand Old Ivy
Greenwillow Christmas
Guys And Dolls
Happy To Keep His Dinner Warm
Happy To Make Your Acquaintance
Have I Stayed Away Too Long
Hoop-Dee-Doo
How To Succeed In Business
    Without Really Trying
I Believe In You
I Like Ev'rybody
I Wish I Didn't Love You So
I'll Know
I'm Hans Christian Andersen
I've Never Been In Love Before
If I Were A Bell
Inch Worm, The
Joey Joey Joey
King's New Clothes, The

Loesser *(Cont.)*
Last Thing I Want Is Your Pity, The
Love From A Heart Of Gold
Lovelier Than Ever
Luck Be A Lady
Make A Miracle
Marry The Man Today
More I Cannot Wish You
Most Happy Fella, The
Music Of Home, The
My Darling My Darling
My Heart Is So Full Of You
My Time Of Day
Never Will I Marry
New Ashmolean Marching Society
    And Students Conser
No Two People
Now That I Need You
Oldest Established, The
On A Slow Boat To China
Once In Love With Amy
Paris Original
Pernambuco
Pet Me Poppa
Praise The Lord And Pass The
    Ammunition
Road To Victory, The
Rodger Young
Roseanna
Rosemary
Secretary Is Not A Toy, A
Sit Down You're Rockin' The Boat
Somebody Somewhere
Spring Will Be A Little Late This
    Year
Standing On The Corner
Sue Me
Summertime Love
Take Back Your Mink
Tallahassee
Tune For Humming, A
Three Cornered Tune
Thumbelina
Ugly Duckling, The
Walking Away Whistling
Warm All Over
What Are You Doing New Year's
    Eve
What Do You Do In The Infantry
Where's Charley
Woman In Love, A
Wonderful Copenhagen

Loesser & Calame & Welk
Bubbles In The Wine

Loesser & Carmichael
Heart And Soul

Loesser & Delugg
Just Another Polka

Loesser & Grouya
In My Arms

Loesser & Lilley
Jingle Jangle Jingle

Loewe
A Toujours
Almost Like Being In Love
Another Autumn
Brigadoon
Camelot
Come To Me Bend To Me
Day Before Spring, The
Edward
Erl-King, The
Fridericus Rex
Get Me To The Church On Time
Gigi
Heather On The Hill, The
Heinrich Der Vogler
How To Handle A Woman
I Could Have Danced All Night
I Love You This Morning
I Loved You Once In Silence
I Still See Elisa
I Talk To The Trees
I'll Go Home With Bonnie Jean
I've Grown Accustomed To Her
    Face
If Ever I Would Leave You
Just You Wait
Kloster Grabow
Little Prince
Nachtlied
Night They Invented Champagne,
    The
On A Clear Day You Can See
    Forever
On The Street Where You Live
Parisians, The
Rain In Spain, The
Show Me
Simple Joys Of Maidenhood, The
Song Of The Night, A
Thank Heaven For Little Girls
They Call The Wind Maria
Unzerstorbare Liebe
Waitin' For My Dearie
Wand'rin' Star
With A Little Bit Of Luck
Without You
Wouldn't It Be Loverly

Lofton
I Don't Know

Logan
Marrow Of My Bone
Missouri Waltz, The

Logan & Price
Personality
Stagger Lee
You've Got Personality

Logatti
Irresistible, El

Loge
Across The Still Lagoon

Loggins
Danny's Song
Footloose

Loggins *(Cont.)*
I Believe In Love
I'm Alright
I'm Free
Keep The Fire
Morning Desire
Roll On
She And I
Vox Humana
Welcome To The Heartlight
Wheels
Whenever I Call You Friend
You Make Me Want To Make You
  Mine
Loggins & Foster
Forever
Loggins & Macdonald
This Is It
What A Fool Believes
Loggins & Martin
Everday
I'll Never Stop Loving You
Love Will Find It's Way To You
Loggins & Morris
Makin' Up For Lost Time
Loggins & Perry & Pitchford
Don't Fight It
Loggins & Pitchford
Footloose
Loggins & Schlitz & Silver
Forty Hour Week For A Livin'
One Promise Too Late
Loggins & Smith
Heartbeat In The Darkness
Loggins & Towers
Nobody's Fool
Loggins & Wilkins
Growin'
Loggins & Wolf & Wolf
Playing With The Boys
Loh
For The Bread Which You Have
  Broken
Lohe
Biondina
Lohr
Crown Of Love, The
Little Grey Home In The West
Love's Proving
Margarita
Out On The Deep
You Are Mine
Loland
God Isn't Dead
Teach Me Thy Way O Lord
Lomas
From North And South And East
  And West
Lombard
Teddy Come Back
Lombarde & Green
Coquette

Lombardo
Sweethearts On Parade
Lombardo & Green
Coquette
Lombardo & Loeb
Boo-Hoo
Sailboat In The Moonlight, A
Seems Like Old Times
London
It Hurts Me Too
To Sir With Love
Long
Jesus Is The Sweetest Name I Know
Long & Scott
Oh Its A Lovely War
Long & Sumner
Jesus Is The Sweetest Name I Know
Longacre
Dear God Our Father
Four Little Grasshoppers
Lord Of Might And Lord Of Glory
Longas
Cielo Azul
Gitana
Ronda
Longfellow
Night
Longstaff & Stebbins
Take Time To Be Holy
Loomis
Air Liner, The
Air Music
And Let Me The Canakin Clink
Antiphon
At Daylight's Close
Baby Bye Here's A Fly
Bees' Party, The
Birds' Singing Lesson, The
Blacksmith
Cheery World, The
Chimes, The
Cotton Song, A
Country Circus
Cozy Homes
Crabbed Age And Youth
Cruel Miss Newell
Day And Night
Down In Dixie
Drip Drip
Enchantment
Foolish Question, A
Gay October
Guess Who I Am
Hallowe'en
Happy Secret, A
Hark Hark The Lark
Harvest Moon
In The Rain
Jolly Tar, A
June
Lady Mood
Lady Moon
Lasting Treasures

Loomis *(Cont.)*
March Wind
Marco Polo
Mayday Song
Mince Pie
Morning Prayer
Moving Day
My Funny Jumping Jack
My Humming Top
New Year
Night Wind, The
Nosiy Bird, A
Now-A-Days And Then-A-Days
Nutting Song
Orange Moon
Our Carol
Outing, An
Piper, The
Queer Names
Ragtag And Bobtail
Rest Tune
Satisfied Singer, The
See That Elephant
Sing A Song Of Seasongs
Singing
Sleep Song
Slight Mistake, A
Sparrow In The Garden
Strange
Such A Difference
Tailor And Sailor
Tale Of The Tailless Rabbit, The
Tower Music
Traveler, The
Tribute, A
Water Lilies
Waterproof Gowns
We Sing As We March
Weather Vane
Which Is Better
William Penn
Winter
Lopatnikoff
Time Is Infinite Movement
Lopez
Hymn To Barrios
Los Laureles
Lopez & Nunez
Livery Stable Blues
Lorand
Elmegyek Ablakod Elott
Szaz Szal Gyertyat Szaz Itce Bort
Lorber
Katherine
Magic Lady
Water Sign
Lorber & Innis
Dare Me
Lorber & Silbar
Come To My Love
Perfect Strangers
Lorber & Silbar & Dubois
Love Will Get You Through Times
  With No Money

Lord & Bereen & Derose
Back In The Old Sunday School
Lordsby
Can You Dance
Lore
That's What Made Me Love You
Lorens
Mir Gengan Heut' Nach Nussdorf
H'Naus
Lorenz
I'm A Pilgrim
Joy Cometh In The Morning
Lenzeszeit Weit Und Breit
Lifetime Is Working Time
Name Of Jesus, The
Ninety And Nine, The
Resting In His Love
Thou Thinkest Lord Of Me
Wonderful Love Of Jesus
Young Men And Maidens
Lorenze
Fruhlings-Wonne
Lorenzo & Whiting
Sleepy Time Gal
Loretz
Uncle Sam What Ails You
Loring
This Tiny Flower
Lortzing
Arie Der Marie
Arie Der Undine
Ariette Der Marie
Maries Brautlied
With Dark Suspicions
Loth
Merry Merry May Day
My Little Brown Hen
My Merry Canary
Our Country's Flag
Rockaby Baby Bird
Song Of The Seasons
Lott
Scatter Flowers
Lotti
Crucifixus
Kyrie
Pur Dicesti
Pur Dicesti O Bocca Bella
Surely He Hath Borne Our Griefs
Vere Languores Nostros
Louchheim
What Christmas Means To Me
Louden
Living For Jesus
Loudermilk
Big Daddy
Break My Mind
I Wanna Live
Indian Reservation
Norman
Sad Movies Make Me Cry
Then You Can Tell Me Goodbye
Tobacco Road

Loudermilk & Brown & Gibson
Abilene
Loudermilk & Wilkin
Waterloo
Loughborough
How Lovely Is The Hand Of God
Loughlin
Little Turtle, The
Louiguy
Cherry Pink And Apple Blossom
White
Simple Comme Bonjour
Vagabond, Le
Vie En Rose, La
Louis XIII
Amaryllis
**Love & Love & Love & Love & Judy &
Phillips**
Shake Your Tail Feathers
Love & Melcher
Getcha Back
Rock 'n' Roll To The Rescue
Love & Melcher & Philips & McKenzie
Kokomo
Lovejoy
Upon A Quiet Hill
Lovelace
Carol Of The Mother
Come Bless The Lord
I Was Glad
My Beloved
O Send Out Thy Light
Shepherd Of Eager Youth
Loveless
Lead Me To Some Soul Today
Lover
Bowld Sojer Boy, The
Girl I Left Behind Me, The
I Goes To Fight Mit Sigel
Low Back'd Car, The
Low Backed Car, The
Low-Backed Car, The
Rory O'Moore
Sambo's Right To Be Kilt
What Will You Do Love
When First I Saw Sweet Peggy
Widow Machree
Young Rory O'More
Lovesmith
Break The Ice
Lovesmith & Holland
All I Do Is Think Of You
Lovett
Kiss And Say Goodbye
Lowden
Bless The Lord O My Soul
Christ Is Not A Disappointment
God Who Touchest Earth With
Beauty
I Will Extol Thee
Living For Jesus
Make A Joyful Noise
What A Friend We Have

Lowe
Angels From The Realms Of Glory
I'll Never Smile Again
I'll Never Smile Again Until I Smile
At You
O Come To The Saviour
Salvum Fac Regem
Take Me Back To Toyland
Lowe & Gomm
Cruel To Be Kind
Lowe & Mann & Appell
Wild One
Lowe & Tennant & Willis
What Have I Done To Deserve This
Lowell & Williams
Once To Every Man And Nation
Lowen & Navarro
We Belong
Lowens
O Omega Invocation
Old Christmas Returned
Rune Of Hospitality, The
Lowenstern
Ich Hab Von Ferne Herr
Lower
Go Tell It To Jesus
Lowery & McAnally
Old Flame
Lowing
Captain Of Salvation
Happy In Jesus
He Leadeth Me
Lowrance
Vesper Song
Lowry
Alas And Did My Saviour Bleed
All The Way My Savior Leads Me
All The Way My Saviour Leads
All The Way My Saviour Leads Me
Anywhere Everywhere
Arise Young Men Arise
Beautiful River
Christ Arose
Come Unto Me
Come We That Love The Lord
Florida Rag
Follow On
Fresh From The Throne Of Glory
God Is Good To You And Me
I Need Thee Ev'ry Hour
I Need Thee Every Hour
In Thy Cleft O Rock Of Ages
Jesu Aus Lieb' Konnt'st Du Sterben
Fur Mich
Jesus Will Help You
Keep The Banner Flying
Low In The Grave He Lay
Morning Star
My Soul Will Overcome
Nothing But The Blood
Nothing But The Blood Of Jesus
One More Day's Work For Jesus
Pisgah
Savior Thy Dying Love

Lowry (*Cont.*)
Savior Thy Dying Love Thou Gavest
Me
Saviour Thy Dying Love
Shall We Gather At The River
Shall We Know Each Other There
Traveller
We'll Meet Each Other Over There
We're Marching To Zion
When I Can Read My Title Clear
Where Is My Boy Tonight
Where Is My Wand'ring Boy
Tonight
Where Is My Wandering Boy
Tonight
Who'll Be The Next

Lowry & Quick
Whispering Bells

Loy
Bring O Morn Thy Music

Lozier
Do I Love Her
In The Old Porch Chairs
My Dear Old Looking Glass
Polyglot's Wooing, The

Luboff
Yellow Bird

Luboff & Belafonte & Attaway
Jump Down Spin Around

Luca
Non Posso Disperar

Lucantioi
Fairest Maiden I Behold Thee Ever

Lucas
Aren't You Hungry For Burger King
Now
Borderline
Carve Dat Possum
Catch That Pepsi Spirit
Good Things To Life
Jesus You Are My Friend

Lucchesi
Ah

Luckstone
May

Luders
Heidelberg
Message Of The Violet, The
Tale Of A Bumble-Bee, The
Tale Of The Turtle Dove, The

Ludt
Vandringsvise

Luening
Farm Picture, A

Lukather
I Won't Hold You Back

Lukather & Goodrum
I'll Be Over You

Lukather & Paich & Porcaro & Porcaro
Moodido

Luke
Susie Darlin'

Lulli
Au Clair De La Lune
Bring Me No Lily
See How The Universe

Lully
Ariette De La Princesse D'elide
Au Clair De La Lune
Bois Epais
Bois Epais Redouble Ton Ombre
By The Light Of The Moon
Christmas Lullaby, A
Close Thee Now And For Aye
Forest Gloom Lend Darkness To
Hold Me
Heros Que Jiattends, Le
Ma Petite Revue
Shaded Grove
Suivons L'amour

Lunceford & Cahn & Kaplan
Rhythm Is Our Business

Lunceford & Chaplin
If I Had Rhythm In My Nursery
Rhymes
Rhythm In My Nursery Rhymes
Rhythm Is Our Business

Lundberg
You Call And Create From Blindness
And Death

Lundell
Mount Mary March

Lundstrom
Walkin' In The Sunshine Of His
Love

Lunsford & Belle & Scotty
Mountain Dew

Lupi
Dame Pour Mieux Venir, Une

Lupus
Je Suis Desheritee

Lurie
Brandy You're A Fine Girl

Lush
These Times God Is Able

Lussier
Doobedood'ndoobe
I'm Still Waiting

Luther
Away In A Manger
Barnacle Bill The Sailor
Before Thy Throne O God We Kneel
Beside Thy Manger Here I Stand
Down In The Valley
From Heav'n Above
From Heaven Above
From Heaven Above To Earth
From Heaven Above To Earth I
Come
From Heaven High I Come To You
Give Heed My Heart
God Is Our Hope And Strength
Ida Red
Jesus Never Fails
Mighty Fortress, A

Luther (*Cont.*)
Mighty Fortress Is Our God, A
Mighty Fortress Is Our Lord, A
O Let Us All Be Glad Today
Out Of The Depths I Cry To Thee
Reformation
Rejoice Today With One Accord
Safe Stronghold Our God Is Still, A
Vom Himmel Hoch Da Komm Ich
Her
We Wait Beneath The Furnace Blast
What Means This Glory

Luther & Bach
From Heaven High

Lutken
Lord Bless You And Keep You, The

Lutkin
Almighty Lord With One Accord
Come My Soul Thou Must Be
Waking
Deem No That They Are Blest Alone
Defend Us Lord From Every Ill
I Weave You A Rhyme For
Christmas Time
If I Can Stop One Heart From
Breaking
Into The Woods My Master Went
Jesus Thou All-Redeeming Lord
Joy To The World
Little Things That Run And Quail
Lord Bless You And Keep You, The
Lord Our God Alone Is Strong, The
Lord Thou Hast Promised Grace For
Grace
My Dear Redeemer And My Lord
O God Great Father Lord And King
O How Happy Are They
O Love O Life Our Faith And Sight
O Thou In All Thy Might So Far
Our Fathers' God To Thee We Raise
Our Thought Of Thee Is Glad With
Hope
Slowly Slowly Darkening
There's A Song In The Air

Luttazzi
Souvenir D'Italie

Lutz
Lord Is Come On Syrian Soil, The
May The Grace Of Christ Our
Saviour

Lutz & Koda
Smokin' In The Boys Room

Luzzaschi
Quivi Sospiri

Luzzi
Ave Maria Op. 80

Lvoff
Give Peace In Our Time O Lord
Hail Pennsylvania
Of Thy Mystical Supper
Rise Crowned With Light
Russian Hymn
Russian National Anthem

Lvov
Christ The Victorious Give To Your
Servants
God Ever Glorious
God Save America
God The All-Merciful
God The All-Merciful Earth Hath
Forsaken
God The All-Powerful
God The All-Terrible
God The Almighty One
God The Omnipotent
God The Omnipotent King Who
Ordainest
Praise Ye Jehovah
Russian Hymn

Lvovsky
Hospodi Pomilui

Lyle
Army Of Todays Alright, The
Jolly Good Luck To The Girl Who
Loves A Soldier

Lyle & Britten
Just Good Friends
Sou Inspiration
Straight To The Heart
Toughen Up
Two People
Typical Male
We Don't Need Another Hero
What You Get Is What You See
What's Love Got To Do With It

Lyle & Kennerley
Rock And Roll Shoes

Lyle & Kennerly
Rock And Roll Shoes

Lyman
Arion
In A Silent World

Lyman & Waggner & Robinson
Mary Lou

Lymon & Levy
Why Do Fools Fall In Love

Lynch & Pilson
Mr Scary

Lynes
God Of Our Youth To Whom We
Yield

Lynne
Calling America
Can't Get It Out Of My Head
Don't Bring Me Down
Xanadu

Lynot
Boys Are Back In Town

Lyoff
Glorious Yuletide Glad Bells
Proclaim It

Lyon
God Of Abraham Praise, The
Praise To The Living God

Lyon & McIntire
One Rose, The
One Rose That's Left In My Heart,
The

Lyons
Merry Merry Merry Merry
Christmas

Lyons & Hart & The Vagabonds
When It's Lamp Lightin' Time In
The Valley

Lyra
Meine Muse
Wanderschaft

Lysaght
Kitty Of Coleraine

Lysberg
Almighty Father Hear Our Prayer
God Shall Charge His Angel Legions

Lyte
Beautiful Bells
Row Row Row Your Boat
Row Your Boat

Lyte & Monk
Abide With Me

M'Intosh
Gathering Home

Maas
Poor Old Uncle Rufe

Mabry
Golden Street Parade, The

Mabte
Unity

Macarthy
Bonnie Blue Flag, The
It Is My Country's Call
Volunteer, The

Macaulay
I Didn't Get To Sleep At All

Macaulay & Cook & Greenaway
Here Comes That Rainy Day Feeling
Again

Macaulay & Mason
Love Grows Where My Rosemary
Goes

Macaulay & Stephens
Smile A Little Smile For Me

Macauley
Can't We Just Sit Down And Talk It
Over

MacCall
Shoals Of Herring, The

MacCarthy
Night Will Never Stay, The

MacColl
First Time Ever I Saw Your Face,
The
They Don't Know

MacColl & Seeger
Ballad Of Springhill

MacDonald
It Keeps You Runnin'
Minute By Minute
Takin' It To The Streets

MacDermot
Aquarius
Aquarius Let The Sun Shine In
Easy To Be Hard
Frank Mills
Good Morning Starshine
Hair
Let The Sunshine In
Manchester England
Where Do I Go

MacDonald
God's Trumpet Wakes The
Slumbering World
You Belong To Me

MacDonald & Salter
Where Is The Love

MacDonald & Salter & Withers
Just The Two Of Us

MacDonough & Herbert
Toyland

MacDougall
In Heavenly Love Abiding

MacDowell
Blue-Bell, The
Clover, The
Confidence
For Sweet Love's Sake I Pray Thee
Take
I Ask But This
In The Woods
Is It The Shrewd October Wind
Brings The Tears
Long Ago
Maid Sings Light, A
Midsummer Lullaby
Mignonette, The
Myrtle, The
O Lovely Rose
Pansy, The
Robin Sings In The Apple Tree, The
Sea, The
Sweet Blue-Eyed Maid Where Goest
Thou
Sweetheart Tell Me What Befell Thee
Sea, The
Through The Meadow
Thy Beaming Eyes
Thy Beaming Eyes Are Paradise To
Me
To A Wild Rose
West-Wind Croons In The Cedar,
The
Yellow Daisy, The

MacFarren
Light
My Own My Guiding Star
There's Not A Bird With Lonely
Nest
This Day The Light Of Heavenly
Birth

MacGimsey
Shadrach
Sweet Little Jesus Boy
Swing Low Sweet Chariot

MacGregor
 Twenty-Seven Bells By The
   Waterbury Watch
MacHault
 Douce Dame Jolie
Mack
 Down Among The Sugar Cane
 Drinking Champagne
 Heart Of My Heart
 I Married Joan
 Story Of The Rose, The
 When Sherman Marched Down To
   The Sea
Mack & Johnson
 Charleston
MacKay
 Miller Of The Dee, The
 Winning Souls For Jesus
MacKay & Husband
 Revive Us Again
MacKenzie
 Chanson
 Feste's Song
 King Charles
 Simeon's Song
 To Daffadills
MacKenzie & Montgomery & Wirges
 Chiquita Banana
 I'm Chiquita Banana
MacKinnon
 Christ Is Born Of Maiden Fair
MacLachlan
 Dark Island, The
MacLagan
 Bread Of Heav'n On Thee We Feed
 Captain Jinks
 Captain Jinks Of The Horse Marines
 Gracious Spirit Dwell With Me
 Jesus Truest Friend Unite
 Thine Forever God Of Love
MacLean & Richardson
 Too Fat Polka
Maclellan
 Put Your Hand In The Hand
 Snowbird
MacLeod
 Skye Boat Song
MacManus & McCartney
 Veronica
MacMurrough
 Macushla
MacNeil & Kraemer
 Hello Hello
Macrae
 I'd Just Love To Lay You Down
Macrae & Clark
 Living Proof
Macy
 Night Of Joy
 Simple Simon
Madara & White
 You Don't Own Me
Madeira
 Mighty Lord

Madeira & Dorsey
 I'm Glad There Is You In This World
   Of Ordinary People
Madgeburg
 From God Shall Nought Divide Me
Madonna
 Sidewalk Talk
Madriguera
 Adios
Maeder
 Let Us All Speak Our Minds
 Let Us All Speak Our Minds If We
   Die For It
Mael & Mael
 Cool Places
Maesch & Trezise
 Viking Song
Magann
 Precious Treasure Thou Art Mine
Maggio
 I Got The Blues
Magid & Gertsman
 In Kriuvke
Magidson & Wrubel
 Gone With The Wind
Magnusson
 Revelation 21-4
Maguinnis
 Irish Wedding, The
Mahaffey
 Weighed In The Balance
Mahler
 Comfort In Sorrow
 Far Over The Hill
 Geing Heut Morgen Uber's Feld
 Hans Und Grethe
 Ich Hab' Ein Gluhend Messer
 In Diesem Wetter
 Liebst Du Um Schonheit
 Life On Earth
 Man Oh Manischewitz
 Nun Seh' Ich Wolh Warum So
   Dunkle Flammen
 Nun Will Die Sonn' So Hell
   Aufgehn
 Oft Denk' Ich Sie Sind Nur
   Ausgegangen
 Sentinel's Night Song
 Wenn Dein Muetterlein
 Wenn Mein Schatz Hochzeit Macht
 Where The Shining Trumpets Blow
 Zwei Blauen Augen, Die
Mahlmann
 German Students' Song
Mahony
 Bells Of Shandon
Mai-Hsin
 Sword Blade March
Maiden & Washburn
 At Midnight
Maier
 Strolling Musician, The
 Young Niclas

Maillart
 Arie Der Rose
 Morning By The Lake
 Winter Sports
Maille
 Qui Me Dois Je Retirer, A
Main
 Calling To Thee
 Come Come To Jesus
 Come To Jesus Now
 God Heareth Prayer
 Happy Resting
 I Came To The Fountain
 Jesus Saviour On Thy Breast
 Lo The Day Is Over
 My Lord And I
 O Rock Of Ages
 O Thou Great Friend To All The
   Sons
 Rejoice Rejoice Believer
 We Never Grow Weary Of Telling
 We Shall Meet Beyond The River
 We Shall Meet By And By
 Wonderful Love
Mainegra & Roberts
 Here's Some Love
Mainegra & Yancey & Griffin
 Who's Gonna Know
Mainzer
 Author Of Faith Eternal Word
 O God Above The Drifting Years
 They Come God's Messengers Of
   Love
Mair
 Antoinette
 Down The Road We Swing
 Like The Woodland Roses
Maire
 Matador Song, The
Maitland
 Must Jesus Bear The Cross
 Ring Out Ye Wild And Merry Bells
Maitland & Maitland
 Magnificat And Nunc Dimittis
Maitrier
 Elle Frequentait La Rue Pigalle
Makarov
 Angel Said To Mary, An
Makeba
 Bamotsweri
Makem
 Blow Ye Winds
 Curlew's Song, The
 Ever The Winds
 Four Green Fields
 Freedom's Sons
 Lord Nelson
 Month Of January, The
 Redmond O'Hanlon
 Sally-O
 William Bloat
 Winds Of Morning
Maken
 Johnny Is A Roving Blade

Maker
Begin My Tongue Some Heavenly
Theme
Beneath The Cross Of Jesus
Christ Is Risen Alleluia
Dear Lord And Father
Dear Lord And Father Of Mankind
For Mercy Courage Kindness Mirth
God Send Us Men Whose Aim'
Twill Be
Lord God Omnipotent
My God I Thank Thee
My God I Thank Thee Who Hast
Made
O Blessed Sun Whose Splendor
O Lamb Of God Still Keep Me
O Thou Not Made With Hands
O Thou Whose Gracious Presence
Blest
Ocean Hath No Danger, The
Our God We Thank Thee
Peacefully Round Us The Shadows
Peacefully Round Us The Shadows
Are Falling
Return Dear Lord To Those Who
Look
Malan
Ask Ye What Great Thing I Know
Come My Soul
Come My Soul Thy Suit Prepare
God Of My Life Through All My
Days
Harre Des Herrn
Harre Meine Seele
Hendon
Lord We Come Before Thee Now
Take My Life And Let It Be
Till He Come O Let The Words
Weary Souls That Wander Wide
Welton
What Thou Wilt
Malcomson
Castles Fairy Castles
Malderen
Dream Tango
Tange De Reve, El
Malie & Steiger
Looking At The World Through
Rose Colored Glasses
Malin
My Pretty Maid
Malipiero
Ballata
Eco, L'
Eliana
Grasinda
Inno A Maria Nostra Donna
Melusina
Mirinda
Morgana
Oriana Infedele
Oriana Oriana Infedele
Mallah & Kelly & Powell
Make It Real

Mallett
Gaarden Song
Mallette & Ryan & Morrison
Lookin' For Love
Malloy & Brannan & McCormack
Real Love
Malloy & Brannan & McCormick
Real Love
Malneck
Goody Goody
Shangri-La
Malneck & Livingston
I'm Thru With Love
Malneck & Maxwell
Shangri La
Malneck & Signorelli
I'll Never Be The Same
Stairway To Heaven
Stairway To The Stars
Malone & Braggs
Share Your Love With Me
Maloo & Haug
Captain Of Her Heart, The
Malotte
Homing Heart, The
Lord's Prayer, The
Twenty-Third Psalm, The
Upstream
Malsby
I Miss You
Maltby & Shire
Starting Here Starting Now
Malvern
Father We Thank Thee
Mana-Zucca
My Garden
Queer Facts
Rachem
Visitor, The
Manchester & Sager
Come In From The Rain
Midnight Blue
Manchicourt
Doux Regard, Un
Mancini
All His Children
Anywhere The Heart Goes
Arabesque
Ask Me No Questions
Baby Elephant Walk
Bachelor In Paradise
Blackie's Tune
Blue Roses
Brass On Ivory
Breakfast At Tiffany's
Brothers Go To Mother's, The
Charade
Cool Shade Of Blue, A
Cow Bells And Coffee Beans
Crazy World
Dancing Cat, The
Darling Lili
Days Of Wine And Roses
Dear Heart

Mancini *(Cont.)*
Don't You Forget It
Dreamsville
Every Christmas Eve
Experiment In Terror
Fine Mess, A
Fluter's Ball
Giving
Great Mouse Detective, The
Greatest Gift, The
Harry's Theme
How Soon
I Like The Look
I'll Give You Three Guesses
In The Arms Of Love
Inspector Clouseau Theme, The
It Had Better Be Tonight
Jazz Hot, Le
Joanna
Just You And Me Together Love
Life In A Looking Glass
Little Boys
Little Man Theme, The
Loss Of Love
Love Theme From The
Moneychangers
Man's Favorite Sport
Mancini Generation, The
March Of The Cue Balls
Moment To Moment
Mommie Dearest
Moon River
Mostly For Lovers
Mr Lucky
Mystery Movie Theme
Natalie
Natasha's Theme
Nbc Nightly News Theme
Newhart
Nothing To Lose
Oklahoma Crude
Once Is Not Enough
Peter Gunn
Peter Gunn Style
Physical Evidence
Pink Panther, The
Powdered Wig, A
Raindrops In Rio
Remington Steele
Send A Little Love My Way
Shot In The Dark, A
Slow Hot Wind
Smile Away Each Rainy Day
Softly
Soldier In The Rain
Sometimes
Song About Love
Song From 10
Sweetheart Tree, The
Theme For Laura
Theme From Cades Country
Theme From Cades County
Theme From Hotel

Mancini *(Cont.)*
Theme From Mommie Dearest
Theme From Ripley's Believe It Or
  Not
Theme Song From The Molly
  Maguires
There's Enough To Go Around
Thief Who Came To Dinner, The
Thorn Birds Theme, The
Timothy
Tom's Theme
Tomorrow Is My Friend
Two For The Road
We
We've Loved Before
What's Happening
What's Happening Theme
Whistling Away The Dark
White On White
Who Is Killing The Great Chefs Of
  Europe
You And Me
Your Good-Will Ambassador

Mancini & Merrill & Rubicam
Simply Meant To Be

Mandel
Cinnamon And Clove
Emily
Shadow Of Your Smile, The
Song From M*A*S*H
Suicide Is Painless
Time For Love, A
Where Do You Start

Mandell & Jacobs
Santa Claus Indiana USA

Mangold
Sans Souci

Mangum
Way Of The Lord, The

Mangun
Only The Sound Of His Trumpet

Manilow
Copacabana
Even Now
It's A Miracle
Like A Good Neighbor
One Voice
Some Kind Of Friend
Stuck On Me
This One's For You

Manilow & Anderson
Could It Be Magic

Manilow & Panzer
All The Time

Manly
Realms Of The Blest

Mann
Blooming Youth
Don't Jump Me Mother
Fleeting Days
From The Eastern Mountains
Gift Of Love, The
Here You Come Again
I Love To Hear The Story

Mann *(Cont.)*
In The Wee Small Hours Of The
  Morning
Jesus Stand Among Us
Journey Home
Just A Little Lovin' Early In The
  Mornin'
Just Once
Kingdom Of Light Whose Morning
  Star
Let The Song Last Forever
Lonesome Valley
Lord Jesus I Have Promised
Mighty Idy
Never Gonna Let You Go
O Jesus I Have Promised
O Saviour Precious Saviour
O There's A Call For Service
Sacred Music
Sacred Stream
Sometimes When We Touch
Standing At The Portal
There's No Easy Way
We're Over
Why Do We Mourn Departing
  Friends

Mann & Appell
Bristol Stomp
Don't Hang Up
Let's Twist Again
South Street
Wah-Watusi, The

Mann & Floreale & Farrington
Heaven Knows
Promise, The

Mann & Goffin
Who Put The Bomp In The Bomp Ba
  Bomp Ba Bomp

Mann & Kolber
I Love How You Love Me

Mann & Lowe
Butterfly
Let Me Be Your Teddy Bear
Teddy Bear

Mann & Phillips
Hold On To The Night

Mann & Weil
Blame It On The Bossa Nova
I Just Can't Help Believin'
Make Your Own Kind Of Music
Soul And Inspiration
We Gotta Get Out Of This Place

Mann & Weil & Horner
Somewhere Out There

Mann & Weil & Leiber & Stoller
On Broadway

Mann & Weil & Snow
Don't Know Much

Mann & Weil & Spector
You've Lost That Lovin' Feelin'

Mann & Weiss
Put Your Dreams Away
Put Your Dreams Away For Another
  Day

Manners
Don't Do It Darling

Manney
Old Glory Is Waving
Orpheus With His Lute
Pine Tree, The

Manning
Easter Greeting
Monk Of Siberia, The
Our Domestic Was Called Mary Ann
Pussy Cat Song, The
Shoes
Sweet Girl Of Hoboken, The
There Was A Gay Maiden Named
  Fanny
Young Lady Of Niger, The
Young Lady Who Sailed From
  Ostende, A

Mannino
Ecco La Notte

Mannsell
Jesus Is Lord

Manoloff
Texas Cowboy, The
Traveling Yodler

Manor & Toledano
Chai

Manson
Newburgh

Mantzaroy
Well I Know Thee By The Keen
  Edge

Manuel
Tears Of Rage

Manzanero
It's Impossible
Somos Novios
Yesterday I Heard The Rain

Manzaros
Hymn To Freedom

Manzer
With Happy Voices Singing

Manzuro
Hymn Of Freedom

Mao-Yun
San Min Chu I

Mar
Heart Of A King

Marais
In The Marshes
Si J'etais Petit Oiseau

Marais & Diggenhof
Henrietta's Wedding

Marcello
Arietta
As Pants The Wearied Hart
Il Mio Bel Foco
Psalm XVIII

March
Thou Who Taught The Thronging
  People

Marchant
Traction Engine, The

Marchello
Love Makes You Blind
Marchetti
Fascination
Marcucci & De Angelis
Why
Marcus & Seiler & Benjemen
When The Lights Go On Again
Mardones & Tepper
Into The Night
Marella
Catch Of Catches
Coach Coach
Half An Hour Past Twelve O'Clock
Marenzio
Fiere Silvestre
Spring Returns
Maresca
Wanderer, The
Maresca & Bogdani
Come On Little Angel
Marf & Mascheroni
Music Played On A Heartstring
Non 'e Per Gelosia
Serenade Music Played On A
Heartstring
Margetson
Sing We A Joyous Measure
Margis
Valse Bleue
Margola
Possa Tu Giungere
Margolin & Fox
Love American Style
Mariani
Bongo, El
Mariash & Berg
Last One To Know, The
Marie
Lovergirl
Marie Antoinette
'Tis My Friend
Marin & Delorme
Chilly Winds
Mario
Apaga La Vela
Marion
Her Eyes Don't Shine Like
Diamonds
It's Not What You Were It's What
You Are Today
Only One Girl In The World For Me
Mark
Entertainment Tonight
Markes & Charles
Mad About Him Sad Without Him
How Can I Be Glad Without
Him
May You Always
Markes & Charles & DeLange
Along The Navajo Trail
Markie
Just A Friend

Markowitz
Rebel, The
Theme From Hondo
Wild Wild West
Markowitz & Fenady
Rebel, The
Marks
A-Caroling We Go
Everyone's A Child At Christmas
For Once In Your Life
Holly Jolly Christmas, A
I Heard The Bells On Christmas Day
Is It Only Cause You're Lonely
Jingle Jingle Jingle
Joyous Christmas
Last Mile Of The Way, The
Merry Merry Christmas To You, A
Most Wonderful Day Of The Year,
The
Night Before Christmas Song, The
Night Before Christmas, The
Now The Day Is Over
Old Fashioned Christmas, An
Remember Your Name And Address
Rockin' Around The Christmas Tree
Rockin' Around The Clock
Rudolf Er Rod Pa Nesen
Rudolf The Red-Nosed Reindeer
Rudolph The Red-Nosed Reindeer
Sailing
Sailing Sailing
Sailing Sailing Over The Bounding
Main
Silver And Gold
That's What I Want For Christmas
We Are Santa's Elves
We Will Carol Joyfully
When Santa Claus Gets Your Letter
Marks & Stern
Mother Was A Lady
Markush
Take Me In Your Arms
Marlatt & Mason
Are Ye Able
Marley
I Shot The Sheriff
Marley & Daly
Chicken Reel
Marlow & Scott
Taste Of Honey, A
Marlowe & Maxwell
Let's Be Sweethearts Again
Marple
Hawaiian Dreams
Marriott
Thy Face Is Always Near To Me
Marsala
Don't Cry Joe
Marschner
An Deutschland
Donne-Moi Ton Coeur
King Richard Lion-Heart
Liedesfreiheit
Song Of The Oak, The

Marschner *(Cont.)*
Trinklied
Tunnel-Festlied
Vaterlandslied
Marsden
Don't Let The Sun Catch You Crying
Ferry Cross The Merry
Marsh
All Hail To Massachusetts
Are You Counted In
At Thy Cross
How Could It Be
Hymnus Guesleianus
Is It The Crowning Day
Jesus Ist Der Kern Der Schrift
Jesus Lover Of My Soul
Martyn
Texas Our Texas
Marsh & Marsh
Ode To The Georgia Farmer
Marsh & Ware & Gregory
Let Me Go
Marshall
Almighty God Your Word Is Cast
Be My Little Baby Bumble Bee
Boston University Hymn
Eternal Light Shine In My Heart
God Is So Wonderful
How Oft O Lord Thy Face Hath
Shone
I Am Listening
I Cried To God
I Hear You Calling Me
Joys Are Flowing Like A River
Mary You're A Little Bit Old
Fashioned
Munsters Theme, The
Peach, The
Roarious
Venus
What's The Matter With Hanna
You Can't Stop Me From Loving
You
Martell
Dear Refuge Never Failing
Martika & Jay & Morrow
More Than You Know
Martin
Adonai
Ah Whither Should I Go
Aspiration
Awake Arise
Bad Case Of Lovin' You
Be Not Dismayed
Be Not Dismayed Whate'er Betide
Brown Thrush, The
Clouds
Could It Have Been A Shadow
Day Of Resurrection, The
God Will Take Care Of You
He Took My Place
I Would Not Live Without Thee
I'm Not So Bright

Martin *(Cont.)*
It's Christmas Time All Over The
    World
Jesus King Of Glory
Land We Love Is Calling, The
Make Me A Captive Lord
O Heavenly Jerusalem
Opening Song
Out Of Bounds
Prayer To The Angels, A
Rolene
S E's Dream
Take Him To Heart
Take Me For A Little While
Til We Two Are One
Victory Is Sure
Wandering Hobo, The
Wasn't It Romantic
Wind, The
Martin & Anderson
Our Finest Hour
Martin & Blane
Boy Next Door, The
Buckle Down Winsocki
Ev'ry Time
Have Yourself A Merry Little
    Christmas
Just A Little Joint With A Juke Box
Meet Me In St Louis Louis
Trolley Song, The
Martin & Christian
Mirror Of Your Heart
Martin & Cochran
It's Not Love But It's Not Bad
Martin & Gabriel
His Eye Is On The Sparrow
Martin & Gray
You'd Better Love Me
Martin & Liles
Stronger Than The Weight
Martin & Lorenz
Name Of Jesus, The
Martin & Martin
God Will Take Care Of You
Till We Two Are One
Martin & McKee
When It's Harvest Time In Peaceful
    Valley
Martin & Mortimer
For The Love Of Him
Martin & Naish
Let The Wind Blow
Martin & Parr & Astley
Night Moves
Martin & Reid
I'd Fall In Love Tonight
Martin & Trace & Watts
You Call Everybody Darling
Martin & Zinetis
Snap Your Fingers
Martine
Way Down

Martinee
Come Go With Me
Let Me Be The One
Point Of No Return
Seasons Change
Tell Me Why
What You Don't Know
When I Looked At Him
Martinez
Adios Vida Mia
Bamba, La
Martini
Amour Est Un Enfant Trompeur,
    L'C
Gavotte
In Monte Oliveti
Joys Of Love, The
Mary Stuart's Lament
Piacer D'amor
Plaintes De Marie Stuart
Plaisir D'amour
River That In Silence Windest
Tickling Trio, The
Tristis Est Anima Mea
Vieux Robin Gray, Le
Martyn
May You Never
Marvin
This Is Princeton
Marx
Ask Any Mermaid
Children Of The Night
Edge Of A Broken Heart
Endless Summer Nights
Hold On To The Nights
Right Here Waiting
Satisfied
Sears Where America Shops
Should've Known Better
Too Late To Say Goodbye
Marx & Lamm & Foster
Good For Nothing
Marx & Vannelli
Surrender To Me
Surrender To Time
Marzials
Ask Nothing More
Friendship
Go Pretty Rose
Go Where Glory Waits Thee
Leaving Yet Loving
Night Was Still, The
Three Sailor Boys, The
Twickenham Ferry
Marzo
Easter Song, An
Mascagni
Ave Maria
Drinking Song
Intermezzo
Lola's Ditty
Lola's Song
Music Of Nature

Mascagni *(Cont.)*
Siciliana
Thy Star
Mascheroni
For All Eternity
Maschwitz & Sherwin
Nightingale Sang In Berkeley Square,
    A
Mason
Across The Snow-Clad Waste
All Rise
And Are We Yet Alive
And Can I Yet Delay
Are Ye Able
Are Ye Able Said The Master
Ariel
At Even Ere The Sun Was Set
Awaked By Sinai's Awful Sound
Bei Dir O Gotteslamm
Beset With Snares On Every Hand
Bethany
Blest Be The Dear Uniting Love
Blest Be The Tie That Binds
Boylston
Breathe On Me Breath Of God
Charge To Keep, A
Charge To Keep I Have, A
Christ Is Alive Let Christians Sing
Come Brothers Let Us Go
Come Father Son And Holy Ghost
Come Gracious Spirit Heavenly
    Dove
Come Sinners To The Gospel Feast
Come Unto Me
Come Unto Me When Shadows
    Darkly Gather
Come Ye That Know
Come Ye That Love The Lord
Did Christ O'Er Sinners Weep
Downs
Eltham
Entirely Thine
Eternal Son Eternal Love
Father Whate'er Of Earthly Bliss
Forever With The Lord
Friendship
From Greenland's Icy Mountains
Glory Gilds The Sacred Page, A
Go Labor On Spend And Be Spent
God In The Gospel Of His Son
God Is The Refuge Of His Saints
God Moves In A Mysterious Way
God Of The Ages By Whose Hand
God Of The Earth
Grace Before And After Meat
Great God And Wilt Thou
    Condescend
Great God The Followers Of Thy
    Son
Hail Thou Long-Expected Jesus
Hail To The Brightness
Hail To The Brightness Of Zion's
    Glad Morning
Hark Ten Thousand

Mason *(Cont.)*

Hark Ten Thousand Harps And
  Voices
Hark The Sound Of Holy Voices
Hark What Mean Those Holy Voices
Hath Not Thy Heart Within Thee
  Burn'd
He Who Himself And God Would
  Know
Heaven Is My Home
Hebron
How Beauteous Were The Marks
  Divine
How Gentle God's Commands
How Happy Is He Born Or Taught
How Oft Alas This Wretched Heart
Hurdy-Gurdy Man, The
I Love Thy Kingdom Lord
I Strove With None
I'm But A Stranger Here
In All My Vast Concerns With Thee
Jesus Thou Joy Of Loving Hearts
Jesus Thy Blood And Righteousness
Jesus Where'er Thy People Meet
Joy To The World
Let All On Earth Their Voices Raise
Let It Go Let It Flow
Light Pours Down From Heaven,
  The
Lo On A Narrow Neck Of Land
Long Life To The Friend
Lord Jesus Thou Dost Keep
Lord Of All Being Throned Afar
Lord Pour Thy Spirit From On High
Lord Thou Hast Searched And Seen
  Me Through
Lynn
Many Many Children, The
May We Thy Precepts Lord Fulfil
Meadow, The
Missionary Hymn
Mount Vernon
Mourn For The Thousands Slain
My Faith Looks Up To Thee
My Faith Looks Up To You
My God My Father Blissful Name
My God My King Thy Various
  Praise
My Soul Be On Thy Guard
Naher Mein Gott Zu Dir
Nearer My God To Thee
Not All The Blood Of Beasts
O All Ye Nations Of The Earth
O Come And Dwell
O Could I Speak
O Could I Speak The Matchless
  Worth
O Day Of Rest And Gladness
O For A Heart To Praise My God
O Glorious Hope Of Perfect Love
O Happy Day That Fixed My Choice
O Jesus I Have Promised
O Lord How Happy Should We Be
O Sacred Head Now Wounded

Mason *(Cont.)*

O Sometimes Gleams Upon Our
  Sight
O That I Could Repent
O That My Load Of Sin Were Gone
O Thou To Whose All Searching
  Sight
Of Him Who Did Salvation Bring
Olivet
Only You Know And I Know
Our Father Unto Thee
Our Father Who Art In Heaven
Parting Hymn We Sing, A
Pity Of The Lord, The
Praise The Saviour All Ye Nations
Prayer Is Appointed To Convey
Prisoner To The Singing Bird, The
Psalm 23
Race That Long In Darkness Pined,
  The
Return My Wandering Soul Return
Ripley
Rise Glorious Conqueror
Rising Day, The
Rockingham
Safely Thro' Another Week
Safely Through Another Week
Serenade
Servant Of God Well Done
Shall I For Fear Of Feeble Man
Shepherd Of Tender Youth
Show Pity Lord O Lord Forgive
Silver Spring
Sing Good Night
Sister Thou Wast Mild And Lovely
Soldiers Of Christ Arise
Soon May The Last Glad Song Arise
Sow In The Morn Thy Seed
Spirit Of Faith Come Down
Spirit Of Holiness Descend
Stay Thou Insulted Spirit Stay
Strew All Their Graves
Strong Son Of God
Sweet Is The Memory Of Thy Grace
Sweet Is The Work
There Is A Fountain
There Is A Fountain Filled With
  Blood
There Is A Happy Land
Thou Mighty God Who Didst Of Old
Thou Whose Almight Word
Thou Whose Almighty Word
Thus Far The Lord Has Led Me On
Thus Far The Lord Hath Led Me On
To Thee Be Glory Honor Praise
To Thee O God In Heaven
Today
Today The Savior Calls
Today The Saviour Calls
Triumphant Zion Lift Thy Head
Von Gronlands Eisgestaden
Watchman Of The Night
Watchman Tell Us Of The Night

Mason *(Cont.)*

What Grace O Lord And Beauty
  Shone
When I Survey
When I Survey The Wonderous
  Cross
When I Survey The Wondrous Cross
When Thou My Righteous Judge
  Shalt Come
When Thou Salt Come
Wherever Through The Ages Rise
Whither O Whither Should I Fly
Wildwood Flower
Wildwood Flowers
Work For The Night Is Coming
Write Thy Law
Yes I'm Ready

Mason & Adams

We Don't Have To Hold Out

Mason & Medley

O Could I Speak

Mason & Webb

We Give Thee But Thine Own

Mass Insti Tech

Take Me Back To Tech

Massek

What She Aims To Be

Massenet

Aragonaise
Dost Thou Know
Down Through The Path Fragrant
  With Roses
Dream Song
Elegie
Elegy
Gavotte
Good Night
He Is Kind He Is Good
Il Est Doux Il Est Bon
Meditation
Ne Me Refuse Pas
Open Thou My Love Thy Blue Eyes
Open Thy Blue Eyes
Open Your Blue Eyes
Ouvre Tes Yeux Bleus
Provence Song
Reve, Le
Serenade Du Passant
Twilight

Massengale

Corinth
Lord Save
Mount Zion
Oxford

Masser

All At Once
Do You Know Where You're Going
  To
Greatest Love Of All, The
Home Again
In Your Eyes
It's My Turn
Last Time I Saw Him
Long And Lasting Love, A

Masser (*Cont.*)
Nobody Wants To Be Alone
Saving All My Love For You
Someone That I Used To Love
Theme From Mahogany
Touch Me In The Morning
Masser & Creed
Hold Me
Hold Me In Your Arms
You Are The Love Of My Life
Masser & Jennings
Didn't We Almost Have It All
Masser & Sawyer
I Thought It Took A Little Time But
    Today I Fell In Love
Masser & Snow & Weil
If Ever You're In My Arms Again
Massey
Petticoat Junction
Prisoner's Song, The
Massey & Gawenda & Massey
She's Only Twenty
Massey & Penny
My Adobe Hacienda
Massingham
Dear Land So Fair
Flag Of The Golden Age
School-House And The Flag, The
Voice Of Freedom, The
Masson
O Could I Speak
Mather & Stegall & Waters
Sexy Eyes
Matheson
Polar Bear
Raindrops
Tum Tum Tiddy Tum
Wake Up Mandy
Matheson & Peace
O Love That Will Not Let Me Go
Mathews
Around The Throne Of God
Around The Throne Of God In
    Heaven
Can't Wait Till He's Here
Free Indeed
Hallelujah Celebration
Liftin' Up Christ
We're Getting All Excited
Mathieson
I'm Home
Mathieson & Veitch
Telefone
Mathieu
Poor Fly
Mathison-Hansen
Tulla
Mattei
Dear Heart
Non E Ver
Slumber Song
'Tis Not True
Matteini
Gondola Va, La

Matteson
Flag Of '76
Matthew & Turner
Keep On Dancin'
Matthews
Creature Praise
Day Of Wrath O Dreadful Day
Father In Heaven Who Lovist All
God Of The Nations Hear Our Call
He Dies The Friend Of Sinners Dies
I Ask None Else Of Thee
Jesus High In Glory
Lord Jesus When We Stand Afar
Love Come Down At Christmas
Make Christ King
O Light O Trinity Most Blest
O Word Of God Incarnate
There Came A Little Child To Earth
Thou Didst Leave Thy Throne
Thou Didst Leave Thy Throne And
    Thy Kingly Crown
We Praise Thee God For Harvests
    Earned
Weary Blues
Where High The Heavenly Temple
    Stands
Matthews & Hart
White Silver Sands
Matthias
Deliverance Will Come
Mattiello
Marianna
Mattson
Rich Man
Maud
Olden Days
Maude
Evensong Is Hushed In Silence
Magdalen
Mauduit
Voici Le Vert Et Beau Mai
Maunder
Christ Our King
I Love To Hear The Story
Lord Of The Sabbath Hear Our
    Vows
O Love Of God How Strong And
    True
Maurer
Get Wildroot Cream-Oil Charlie
Mauri
Tropical Maid, The
Maxwell
All Hail O Davidson
Are You Groping For An Answer
Blessed Are They
Can It Be True?
Cast Your Bread Upon The Waters
Christmas Candy Calendar, The
Counting Song
Daily Affirmation
Ebb Tide
First Supper, The
Give Me A Burden Lord

Maxwell (*Cont.*)
Have You Watched
Hawaiian Christmas Song, The
How Can I Tell Right From Wrong
How Shall I Know Him
I'd Rather See A Sermon
If I Were A Voice
Is He Satisfied With Me
Just Because
Kindness
Live Today
Lord Is My Refuge, The
My Father's Hand
My Prayer
What If The Savior Had Never Been
    Born
What Shall I Do
What Shall I Take With Me
Where Can I Go
You Have A Follower
Maxwell & Gibbs
Channels Only
Maxwell & Wirges
Will He Answer
May
Green Hornet Theme
Lean Baby
We Bring These Our Gifts For Thy
    Service
We Will Rock You
Mayer
Boys Keep Your Powder Dry
Dar Song
For Me And My Gal
I'm Labor
My Melody Of Love
Summer Wind
Mayfield
Gonna Be A Meetin' Over Yonder
Hit The Road Jack
Keep On Pushing
Let's Do It Again
Man's Temptation
Need To Belong To Someone
Never Too Much Love
People Get Ready
Please Send Me Someone To Love
Praise The Lord
Rainbow
When Jesus Comes Again
Mayfield & Dixon
Rainbow
Mayhew
All Over Now
It's A Sin To Tell A Lie
Serenade
Maynard
Lost Is Found, The
My Neighbour
Song And Dance
Tree Once Grew In Galilee, A
Mayo & Chater
If I Had You

Mays
Are You Growing
I'm Too Busy Followin' Footsteps
Take Some Time To Walk With The
   One You Love
Mazak
Jesus Is A Friend Of Mine
Mazzaferrata
Presto Presto Io M'Innamoro
Mazzinghi
Monroe Is The Man
McAardle
I Point My Right Foot So
McAfee
Heart Of God, The
Near To The Heart Of God
McAlpin & Toombs
Almost
McAnally
You're My First Lady
McAnally & Brasfield
I'm Gonna Love Her On The Radio
McAnally & Byrne
She Put The Sad In All His Songs
Two Dozen Roses
McAnally & Lowery
I Want To Go Somewhere
McAnally & Schlitz
Written In Stone
McArdle
American Boy, An
I'll Wear A Shamrock
Magic Snow
My Zipper Suit
Ring Around The World
Sea Shell
Singing
McArthur
Night
McBride
Love You To The Letter
McBride & Mason
Guilty Eyes
McBroom
Rose, The
McCabe
O'Connell's Dead
McCall
Chanson Triste
I've No Time To Be A Sighin
Sweet Sorrow
McCall & McCall
On The Water
McCandless
Hungry Heart
Moon And Mind
McCann
Do You Wanna Make Love
Right Time Of The Night
McCann & Leigh
Wall Of Tears
McCann & McBride
Do I Have To Say Goodbye

McCann & Wright
Nobody Falls Like A Fool
McCarron & Morgan
Oh Helen
McCarthey
Light Of God Is Falling, The
McCarthy
Bonnie Blue Flag, The
Garden In Connemara, A
Southern Girl, The
McCarthy & Doehing
Houston Knights
McCarthy & Johnson & Fisher
Ireland Must Be Heaven
Ireland Must Be Heaven For My
   Mother Came From There
McCartney
Band On The Run
Come And Get It
Ebony And Ivory
It Won't Be Long
Listen To What The Man Said
Maybe I'm Amazed
My Love
O Beautiful My Country
Silly Love Songs
Uncle Albert/Admiral Halsey
With A Little Luck
McCartney & Jackson
Say Say Say
McCartney & McCartney
Live And Let Die
McCarty
Forward Loretto
McClagan
Bread Of Heaven On Thee We Feed
McClary & Richie
High On Sunshine
McClatchy
Best Of Friends
McClintock
Big Rock Candy Mountain, The
Halleluja I'm A Bum
Until Tonight
McCloud & Walker
Trumpeters, The
McCollin
April Harpist
Ben Franklin Esq
Ice Box, The
University Hymn, A
Woodcutter, The
McCollins
Pennsylvania Girl, The
McConnell & Downey & Sanford
That's How I Spell I-R-E-L-A-N-D
McConnell & Sanford & Luther
Chuck Goes The Woodchuck
Cowboys Midnight Song, The
Flies Are In Again, The
Forgotten Road, The
Gal From Tennessee, The
I Wish I Was Back Home Tonight
I'm Bummin' For My Health

McConnell & Sanford & Luther *(Cont.)*
Keep The Bible Handy
King Of The Bums, The
Light On The Golden Shore, The
Lonely Mountaineer, The
Mary Left A Year Ago Today
On The Banks Of The Old Rio
   Grande
Poor Lonely Widow, A
Prisoner's Mother, The
There's A Shack On The Back Of A
   Mountain
Train That Never Came In, The
Vine Covered Grave On The Hill,
   The
When You're Twenty Miles From
   No-Where
You Don't Miss Your Mother 'Til
   She's Gone
McCorkle
Fire On The Mountain
McCormack & Voss
Sugar Shack
McCormick
Advance Australia Fair
Australia
McCosh
Hear Dem Bells
Hear Them Bells
McCoy
Baby I'm Yours
Change With The Times
Hustle, The
Walk Softly
Why Don't You Do Right
McCoy & Maguire
Hee Haw
McCoy & Owens
I Beg Of You
McCracklin
Walk, The
McCurdy
Last Night I Had The Strangest
   Dream
McCurry
Raymond
McCusker
Hats Off To The Band
State Of The Heart
McCusker & Springfield & Pierce
State Of The Heart
McCutchan
Let All The World In Every Corner
   Sing
McDaniel
Bo Diddley
I'm A Man
Road Runner
Who Do You Love
McDaniel & Gabriel
Since Jesus Came Into My Heart
McDaniel & Linde
Goodbye Marie

McDaniel & Morrison
Grandest Lady Of Them All, The
McDaniels
Feel Like Makin' Love
McDill
Amanda
Baby's Got Her Blue Jeans On
Come Early Mornin'
Don't Close Your Eyes
Falling Again
Good Ole' Boys Like Me
I Call It Love
I May Be Used But Baby I Ain't
Used Up
I Never Made Love Till I Made It
With You
I'm Already Blue
If Hollywood Don't Need You
Honey I Still Do
It Must Be Love
Louisiana Saturday Night
Love Me Tonight
Rake And Rambling Man
Right In The Palm Of Your Hand
Save Your Heart For Me
Say It Again
Somebody's Always Saying
Goodbye
Song Of The South
Starting Over
We Believe In Happy Endings
What'll I Tell Virginia
Why Don't You Spend The Night
You Never Miss A Real Good Thing
Till He Says Good
McDill & Bourke
Too Good To Stop Now
McDill & Harrison
Another Place Another Time
What She Is Is A Woman In Love
McDill & Holyfield
I Met A Friend Of Yours Today
I'll Do It All Over Again
I'll Need Someone To Hold Me
When I Cry
I've Never Seen The Likes Of You
Nobody Likes Sad Songs
She Never Knew Me
McDill & Holyfield & Neese
Red Necks White Socks And Blue
Ribbon Beer
McDill & Lee
Door Is Always Open, The
I've Been Around Enough To Know
McDill & Reynolds
Catfish John
I Recall A Gypsy Woman
McDill & Seals
Big Wheels In The Moonlight
Everything That Glitters Is Not Gold
My Baby's Got Good Timing
McDill & Weatherby
All Tangled Up In Love

McDill & Weatherly
You Turn Me Like A Radio
McDonald
In The Christian's Home In Glory
My Heavenly Home
There Is Rest For The Weary
McDonald & Henderson
Real Love
McDonald & Loggins & Sandford
No Lookin' Back
McDuffie
Between Blue Eyes And Jeans
McEastland
Spirit
McElhone & Spiteri
I Don't Want A Lover
McEnery
Amelia Earhart's Last Flight
Cotton-Eyed Joe
McEntire
Only In My Mind
McEwan
To The Field
McFaddin & Brown & Perry
One Love In My Lifetime
McFall
Thank God I Am Free
McFaul
Meow Mix Theme
McFee & Pessis
Any Way The Wind Blows
McFerrin
All I Want
Come To Me
Don't Worry Be Happy
Drive
Jubilee
Simple Pleasures
McGee
Canoe Round
I'd Really Love To See You Tonight
McGee & Gundry
If You Ever Change Your Mind
McGhee
Wreck Of The Virginian No 3, The
McGheen
Sporting Life Blues
McGinn
Dundee Ghost, The
Pill, The
Red Yo-Yo, The
McGiveran & Zoob
Fight On Pennsylvania
McGlasson
Head
McGlennon
And Her Golden Hair Was Hanging
Down Her Back
Comrades
Her Golden Hair Was Hanging
Down Her Back
Mr Captain Stop The Ship

McGlohon
I Wish I Had The Blues Again
Songbird Thank You For Your
Lovely Song
McGranahan
Afterward
All For Jesus
Anchor Holds, The
Are You Coming Home To-Night
As Pants The Hart
At That Day Ye Shall Know
Awake Awake O Christian
Banner Of The Cross, The
Be Near Me O My Saviour
Be Ye Also Ready
Beautiful City Of God
Behold What Love
Believe And Keep On Believing
Believe Ye That I Am Able
Beloved Now Are We
Beseechings Of Jesus
Bless The Lord
Blessed Saviour Ever Nearer
Bring Him Unto Me
By The Beautiful Gate
Carried By The Angels
Casting All Your Care Upon Him
Christ Is My Redeemer
Christ Liveth In Me
Christ Receiveth Sinful Men
Christ Returneth
Come
Come Near
Come On The Wings Of The
Morning
Comfort My People
Create In Me A Clean Heart
Crowning Day, The
Eternity Draws Near
Every Day Will I Bless Thee
Glorious And Victorious
Glory To God The Father
Go Ye Into All The World
God Bless You
God Is Now Willing Are You
Greatest Thing, The
Hallelujah Bless His Name
Hallelujah Christ Is Risen
Hallelujah For The Cross
Have Faith In God
He Shall Reign From Sea To Sea
How Can You Live Without Jesus
How Shall I Know That I Am His
How Shall We Escape
I Am The Light
I Am The Way
I Know Whom I Have Believed
I Looked To Jesus
I Will
I Will Give Let Him Take
I Will Lift Up Mine Eyes
I Will Pass Over You
I Will Praise Thee
I Will Trust And Not Be Afraid
If God Be For Us

McGranahan *(Cont.)*
In God Is My Salvation
In His Presence Is Fulness Of Joy
In Jesus' Face
It May Be At Morn
Jesus Christ Our Saviour
Jesus Has Taken Them All
Jesus Is Coming
Jesus Of Nazareth
Jesus Only Jesus Ever
Jesus Our Saviour And King
Let Us Crown Him
Let Us Go Forth
Little Lights
Look Unto Me
Lord Keep Watch Between Us, The
Love That Gave Jesus To Die, The
Morning Breaks Upon The Gloom
My Grace Is Sufficient
My Offering
My Redeemer
My Saviour Tells Me So
Not Now But In The Coming Years
O Glad And Glorious Gospel
O Glorious Fountain
O How Love I Thy Law
O Paradise
O Praise Him
O The Crown The Glory Crown
O Who Will Go Forth
Our Church Home
Our Lord Is Now Rejected
Pass It On
Preach The Gospel
Resting On Jesus
Sinners Jesus Will Receive
Thy Will Be Done
Waiting For The Promise
We Lift Our Songs To Thee
We Will Bless The Lord
What A Gospel
When Jesus Comes Again
McGrane
Juke Box Saturday Night
McGrannahan
Hallelujah Praise Jehovah
McGranshan
Casting All Your Care Upon Him
McGrath
On And On
McGrath & Brett & O'Brian & English
Rapparee
McGraw & Schaeffer
We're All Going Out To Vote For
Wilkie
McGuire
Communion Song
Upon This Rock
McGuire & Gaither
All The Way Home
McGuire & McGuire
Wounded Soldier

McHan & Taylor
His Great Plan
O City Eternal
Sing God's Children Sing
McHose
Light Is Shining
Look To The Hill-Tops
Meet Me Over There
Oh Such Wonderful Love
'Tis Better On Before
Wonder Of Wonders
McHugh
Comin' In On A Wing And A Prayer
Diga Diga Doo
Don't Blame Me
Down Deep In An Irishman's Heart
Exactly Like You
Freedom
God And God Alone
I Can't Give You Anything But Love
I Couldn't Sleep A Wink Last Night
I'm In The Mood For Love
I'm Sitting On Top Of The World
It's A Most Unusual Day
Let's Get Lost
Lovely Way To Spend An Evening,
A
My Dream Of The Big Parade
Nobody's Perfekt
On The Sunny Side Of The Street
Peaceable Kingdom Theme
Say It Over And Over Again
South American Way
Spreadin' Rhythm Around
Thank You For A Lovely Day
Where Are You
You're A Sweetheart
McHugh & Fields & Oppenheimer
I Feel A Song Comin' On
McHugh & Gaither & Helvering
In The Name Of The Lord
McHugh & Livingston & Evans
Warm And Willing
McHugh & Mills
Lonesomest Girl In Town
McHugh & Naish
Above The Storm
McHugh & Nelson
All Over The World
Calvary's Love
Lamb Of Glory
Love Found A Way
Only Jesus
People Need The Lord
Red Sea Parted, The
Where There Is Love
McHugh & Peters
Believers
McIlhargey & Sheridan
Detroit Victory March

McIntosh
For Me To Live Is Christ
From All The Dark Places
God's Matchless Love
Kingdom Is Coming, The
Mustard Seed, The
Tell It Again
McIntosh & Eugene & Nichol
Hangin' On A String
McKay
Great Grand Coulee Dam, The
Humpty Dumpty's Song
Indian Names
Meadow Brook, The
Moon Is Up, The
Morning Prayer, A
Necklace, The
Song Of The Lone Prairie
Sunrise At Grand Canyon
Tall Pine Tree, The
Western Horizon
Witch-Hazel Bough
McKay & Maxwell
Old Scotch Mother Mine
McKellar
Tartan, The
McKenna
We've Only Just Begun
McKernan
Operator
McKinney
Breathe On Me
Dolly's Lullaby
Fall Fresh On Me
Follow The Living Christ
Glorious Is Thy Name
Have Faith In God
He Died But Not In Vain
He Is Mine
He's Done So Much For Me
Hymn To Queens, A
I Am Redeemed
I'll Be One To Win One
In The Old Time Way
Jesus Is Mighty To Save
John Three Sixteen
Make My Life Beautiful
Nail Scarred Hand, The
Never Lose Sight Of Jesus
New Year's Bells
Singing
When The Morning Comes
Wherever He Leads I'll Go
Win One Today
Winter Fun
McKuen
I'll Catch The Sun
Jean
Love's Been Good To Me
Pastures Green
World I Used To Know, The

McLaughlin
Birds Of Fire
Morning, The
McLaurin
Blind Man Blues
McLean
American Pie
And I Love You So
Hudson Song, The
Orphans Of Wealth
Plenty Of Time
Tapestry
Vincent
McLeod
Scotland Yet
McMahon
Old Double Diamond, The
Real Live Buckaroo
McManus
If I Could Only Dance With You
Mr Harding We're All For You
Somethin' On The Radio
Trail End
McManus & Bomar
You're Gettin' To Me Again
McManus & Dipiero & House
Little Rock
McNaughton
Belle Mahone
Faded Coat Of Blue, The
Three Trees, The
When There's Love At Home
McNeely
Burgundy And The Virgin Snow
Plot Thickens, The
Stand Up And Cheer
There's Something On Your Mind
McPhail
Follow All The Way
Fullness Of Blessing
Go Quickly
Hallelujah For The Prospect
I Am Now A Child Of God
I Heard The Voice Of Jesus Say
In That Day
Jesus Alone Can Save
Jesus Hath Done All Things Well
Just The Same Today
Love's Reason
Praise His Name
Would You Shine For Jesus
McPherson & Harden
Backfield In Motion
McRae & Wyche & David
Love Love Love
McShann & Bowman
Hands Off
McSpadden & Goss
Glorious Morning
McTell
Ferryman, The
Searching The Desert For The Blues
Statesboro Blues

McTell (*Cont.*)
Streets Of London
Terminus
McVea & Howell
Open The Door Richard
McVie
Brown Eyes
Don't Stop
Everywhere
Oh Daddy
One More Night
Over And Over
Over My Head
Say You Love Me
Songbird
Think About Me
You Make Lovin' Fun
McVie & Patton
Hold Me
McVie & Quintela
As Long As You Follow
Little Lies
Save Me
McVie & Recor
Love In Store
McVie & Sharp
Got A Hold On Me
Meacham
American Patrol, The
Music On Parade
Meade
Time Is On My Side
Mealand
Morning Song
Means
Creation's Lord We Give Thee
Thanks
Mears
Always Have Always Will
Medd
All Hallow's Eve
Bonfire Carol
Medema
Every Day Is A Victory
Gentle As Morning
Shall We Learn To Be Friends
Medina
Kinor David
Laner V'Livsamim
Medley
Million To One, A
Meece
Forgiven
I Can See
We Are The Reason
Meek
Telstar
Meekins
Walkin' In The Parlor
Meen
O Fred Tell Them To Stop
Oh Fred Tell Them To Stop
Meher
Was Macht Ihr Dass Ihr Weinet

Mehrtens
Two Stalwart Trees Both Rooted In
The Faith
Mehul
Adieux
Chant Du Depart, Le
Departure Song
En Vain Le Coeur Veut Se Defendre
Hymn Sung By The People At The
Festival Of Bara An
Ociel Que Faire
Off For The Front
Meidell
Oleanna
Meigret
Doux Regard, Un
Puis Que De Vous Je N'ay Aultre
Visaige
Meiler
Flyers' March
Meinecke
Glory Be To The Father
Meineke
Gloria Patri
Meinke
Glory Be To The Father
Meinken
Wabash Blues
Meir
I'll Never Be Lonely Again
Meisner & Kaz
Deep Inside My Heart
Hearts On Fire
Mejer
For All The Blessings Of The Year
Melamet
Alles Was Dein Gott Dir Gibt
Mellencamp
Authority Song
Check It Out
Cherry Bomb
Hand To Hold On To
Hurt So Good
Jack And Diane
Lonely Ol' Night
Paper In Fire
Pink Houses
Pop Singer
ROCK In The USA
Small Town
Mellencamp & Green
Crumblin' Down
Hurts So Good
Mellor & Gifford & Trevor
When It's Apple Blossom Time In
Normandy
Melone
To You Muskingum
Melrose & Morton
Sidewalk Blues
Melvill
To Portsmouth
Melville
Banks Of The Genesee, The

Memphis Minnie
Meningitis Blues
Where Is My Good Man
Men Without Hats
Pop Goes The World
Mencher
I See God
Mendelsohn
Be Not Afraid
Mendelssohn
A Toi Les Songes De Bonheur
Abendlied
Almighty Father Hear Our Prayer
Ambitious Clover, The
America Our Homeland
An Des Lust'gen Brunnens Rand
Arise Ye Lands
As Pants The Wearied Heart
Auf Flugeln Des Gesanges
Autumn Song
Ave Maria
Bird Let Loose, A
Blessed Are The Men
Boating
Brightest And Best
Broken Heart, The
But The Lord Is Mindful
But The Lord Is Mindful Of His
   Own
By Cool Siloam's Shady Rill
By The Cradle
Call Jehovah Thy Salvation
Cast Thy Burden
Cast Thy Burden On The Lord
Cast Thy Burden Upon The Lord
Clear Is The Trumpet
Come Saviour Jesus From Above
Come Thou Long-Expected Jesus
Comitat
Confession
Das Waldschloss
Dear God Our Father At Thy Knee
Dear Ties Of Mutual Succor Bind
Death Song Of The Boyard
Denn Also Hat Uns Der Herr
   Geboten
Denn In Seiner
Deutschland
Dimanche De La Promise, Le
Doux Nom D'Amour
Drum Sing Ich Mit Meinem Liede
E'Er Fadeless Be Their Glory
Earth Is Hushed In Silence, The
Eden Aux Bords Du Gange, L'E
Elegy
Elfes, Les
Es Ist Bestimmt In Gottes Rat
Evensong
Ever-Changing Seasons, The
Fair-Tinted Primrose
Fairies
Fleurs Messageres
Frohe Wandersmann, Der

Mendelssohn (Cont.)
From Heaven Above To Earth I
   Come
Fruhling Naht Mit Brausen, Der
Garland, The
God Is Love His Mercy Brightens
God Reigns
Greeting
Gruss
Hail To The Day
Happy Sunday Bells
Hark The Herald Angels Sing
Hark What Means Those Holy
   Voices
Harvest Hymn
He Sat To Watch O'Er Customs Paid
Hear My Prayer
Hear Thou In Love O Lord Our Cry
Herbstlied
How Lovely Are The Messengers
Hunter's Farewell, The
Huntsman's Song
I Waited For The Lord
I Would Be True
I Would That My Love
Ich Harrete Des Herrn
Ich Wollt' Meine Lieb
If With All Your Heart
In Heavenly Love Abiding
In Memory
In Spring
In The Woods
It Is Enough
Italy
Jager Abschied, Der
Jerusalem Thou That Killest The
   Prophets
Jesus Thy Boundless Love To Me
Lass Dich Nur Nichts Nicht Dauern
Leise Zieht Durch Mein Gemuth
Lied An Die Deutschen In Lyon
Lift Thine Eyes
Lift Thine Eyes To The Mountains
Light Of Conscience Clear And Still
Lord's Prayer, The
Lord Guard And Guide The Men
   Who Fly
Love Song
Love Song In May
Lovely Messengers
Lullaby
Maienlied
Maiglockchen Und Die Blumelein
May Song
Maybells And The Flowers, The
Midsummer Night
Minnelied Im Mai
Mond, Der
Moon, The
Morning
Morning Song
My Song Shall Be Alway
My Soul Before Thee Prostrate Lies
Nightingale, The

Mendelssohn (Cont.)
Nocturne
Now Thank We All Our God
O For The Wings Of A Dove
O Rest In The Lord
O Sacred Head Now Wounded
O Sah Ich Auf Der Haide
O Wert Thou In The Cauld Blast
O Wie Selig Ist Das Kind
Ode Valedictoria
Oh Wert Thou In The Cauld Blast
On Wings Of Love
On Wings Of Song
Ou S'En Vont Mes Reves
Petition
Plaintes De Suleika, Les
Praise The Lord
Premiere Violette, La
Prends Garde A Tol
Quand Tu M'Aimais
Reflections
Resignation
Rheinweinlied
Rhine-Wine Song
Ring O Ring Ye Christmas Bells
Robin, The
Sehnsucht
Selig Sind Die Toten Beati Mortui
Slumber Song
Softly Distant Chime Of Bell
Song Of Home
Song Of Spring
Sonntagsmorgen
Sous L'eglantier
Souviens-Toi
Spring Greeting
Spring Song
Stiftungsfeier, Die
Still Still With Thee
Student's Farewell
Thanks Be To God
Them Shall The Righteous Shine
   Forth
Thy Will Be Done
Trinklied
Tristesse
Turkisches Schenkenlied
Venetian Boat Song
Vieux Refrain
Villanelle
Vogue Leger Zephyr
Wasserfahrt
We Come Unto Our Fathers' God
We Sing The Glorious Conquest
   Before
We Would See Jesus
Wedding March
Welcome To Spring
When The Weary Seeking Rest
Wirf Dein Anliegen Auf Den Herrn
Wohin Habt Ihr Ihn Getragen
Woods, The
Ye People Rend Your Hearts
Zuleika And Hassan

Mendelssohn & Heber
New Year, The
Mendez
Cu-Cu-Rru-Cu-Cu Paloma
Mendoza Y Cortez
Cielito Lindo
Menegger
Hello Trees
Menendez
Aquellos Ojos Verdes
Green Eyes
Menescal
Little Boat
Mengerlein
Wie Ist Der Abend So Traulich
Menken
Everlasting
Little Shop Of Horrors
Prologue
Suddenly Seymour
Mentel
Gasoline Rag
Menten
Scrumpdillyishus Day, A
Merbecke
Glory Be To God
Glory Be To God On High
Lift Up Your Hearts
O Lamb Of God
Praise Be To Thee
Mercadante
Rose, The
Mercer
Dream
Dream When You're Feeling Blue
Each Step I Take
GI Jive
Greensborough
Harlem Butterfly
I'm An Old Cowhand
I'm An Old Cowhand From The Rio
Grande
My New Celebrity Is You
Something's Gotta Give
Waiter And The Porter And The
Upstairs Maid, The
Way That He Loves, The
Mercer & Berstein
Love With The Proper Stranger
Mercer & Bloom
Fools Rush In
Mercer & Burke & Hampton
Midnight Sun
Mercer & Malneck
Goody Goody
Mercer & Vimmerstedt
I Wanna Be Around
Mercury
Body Language
Bohemian Rhapsody
Crazy Little Thing Called Love
Play The Game
We Are The Champions

**Mercury & Deacon & May & Taylor &
Bowie**
Under Pressure
Meredith
Blessed Is He That Endureth
Christmas
For The Man Of Galilee
I Heard The Bells On Christmas Day
Mergner
Gib Mir Ein Frommes Herz
Merlino & Babylon
Kissing
Merrick
Gillette Look Sharp March, The
My Times Are In Thy Hands
Sterling
To Look Sharp
Merril
Old Hickory Cane, The
Merrill
Braving The Wilds All Unexplored
Cheerfully Cheerfully
Doggie In The Window
Honeycomb
If That Was Love
It's Good To Be Alive
Let Us Be Tender
Love Makes The World Go 'Round
Mira
O Lord Our God Thy Mighty Hand
Sunshine Girl
Take Your Gun And Go John
That Doggie In The Window
Merrill & Hooker
I Love Rock 'n Roll
Merrill & Rubicam
Bring Down The Moon
I Wanna Dance With Somebody
I Wanna Dance With Somebody
Who Loves Me
Waiting For A Star To Fall
Merrill & Rubicam & Pitchford
I Know You By Heart
Merrill & Rubicam & Walden
How Will I Know
Merrill & Shand
Chicken Song, The
You Don't Have To Be A Baby To
Cry
Merrily
Merrily Merrily
Merritt
May The Bird Of Paradise Fly Up
Your Nose
Merson
On The Good Ship Yacki Hicki Doo
La
Spaniard That Blighted My Life, The
Merulo
Quand'io Pens'al Martire
Mescoli
My Love Forgive Me
Mesquido
Boating Song

Mesquita
Esmeralda
Messager
Villanelle
Messina & Garth
Listen To A Country Song
Messina & Loggins
Angry Eyes
Watching The River Run
Your Mama Don't Dance
Messiter
Rejoice Give Thanks And Sing
Rejoice Ye Pure In Heart
Metheny & Mays & Bowie
This Is Not America
Methfessel
Deutsches Weihelied
Gesang Ausziehender Kreiger
Our Native Land
Vaterlandslied
Metra
Valse Espagnole
Metz
Citadel Forever, The
Hot Time In The Old Town, A
Hot Time In The Old Town Tonight,
A
Kansas Jayhawker
There'll Be A Hot Time In The Old
Town Tonight
Metzger
When She Is Gone
Metzger & Lewis
Joy
Mevis & Hobbs & Gallimore & Shore
Oklahoma Heart
Mevis & Shore
Wishful Drinkin'
Meyer
Body Lord Is Ours To Keep, The
Brown Eyes Why Are You Blue
Clap Hands Here Comes Charley
Cup Of Coffee A Sandwich And
You, A
For Me And My Gal
Good-Bye God Bless You
Homeward Bound
It's An Old Southern Custom
Junk Man
Looking Unto Jesus Makes It Right
Lord Bless Thee And Keep Thee, The
My Honey's Lovin' Arms
My Mother's Rosary
Where Did Robinson Crusoe Go
With Friday On Saturday
Meyer & Kahn
Crazy Rhythm
Meyer-Helmund
Daily Question, The
Flirtation
Madchenlied
Magic Song, The
Maiden's Song, A
Of Thee I'm Thinking Margareta

Meyer-Helmund *(Cont.)*
Old German Love Rhyme
On Memorial Day
Swabian Folk-Song
Sweetheart Adieu
Thou Art Near Me Margarita
Vow, The
Meyer-Helmund
Absence
Meyerbeer
Ah My Son
Light-Flitting Shadow
Page's Song, The
Meyerowitz
Kinder Yoren
Meyers
You And I
Meyorowitz
Kolombus Ich Hob Tsu Dir Gornit
Michael
Different Corner, A
Edge Of Heaven, The
Everything She Wants
Faith
Father Figure
Freedom
I'm Your Man
Kissing A Fool
Mission Bell
One More Try
Wake Me Up Before You Go-Go
Michael & Ridgeley
Careless Whisper
Michaeloff
Praise The Lord From Heaven
Michaels
Columbus
Crooked Man, The
Early Bird
Fuzzy-Wuzzy Caterpillar
Morning Song
Mother Of The Infant Jesus
Our Lady Of The Trails
Pumpkin's Prayer, The
Quail's Call, The
Rainbow, The
Stars
Tired Caterpillar, The
To Saint Joseph
What I Like
When Our Flag Goes By
When Spring Comes
Michaels & Gorman
Happy
Michels
San
Middleton
Alma Mater
Midgette
Tommy
Wallabug
Midnight & Schwartz & Johnston
Doctor, The

Mieir
All He Wants Is You
His Name Is Wonderful
No More
When You Pray
Miers & Walter
Seventeen Sixty Six
Miessner
Alphabet Soup
Daffydowndilly
Dear Land I Adore
God Save America
Marching Here We Come
Marching Song
Michigan My Michigan
My Country
My Singing Friends
New Year's Greeting
To A Star
When Ships Put Out To Sea
Mihaly
Szeret-E Meg
Tizenhat Esztend Os Barna Kis Lany
Milan
Amor Que Tan Bien Sirviendo
Miles
All Alone
Anchors Aweigh
Angels Get My Mansion Ready
Dear Spirit Lead Thou Me
Dwelling In Beulah Land
Faith
Give Unto The Lord
How Sweet The Name Of Jesus
    Sounds
If Jesus Goes With Me
In The Garden
Let Him In
Lord Is My Light, The
New Name In Glory, A
On Jordan's Bank
Them Changes
Wide As The Ocean
Miles & Robi
One In A Million
Miles & Robi & Taylor
He's Mine
Miles & Zimmerman
Anchors Aweigh
Milete
My Little Friend
When I'm Over You
Milete & Fowler
It's Your Baby You Rock It
Milford
We Never Speak As We Pass By
Milgrove
Captains Of The Saintly Band
For All Thy Saints O Lord
Spirit In Our Hearts, The
Milhaud
Ardeur
Chant D'amour
Chant De Forgeron

Milhaud *(Cont.)*
Chant De La Pitie
Chant De Nourrice
Chant De Resignation
Chant De Sion
Chant Du Laboureur
Decembre
Great Big Boy
Lamentation
Mililotti
Cade La Sera
Night, The
Millar
Bonnie Doon
Millard
Flag Of Columbia, The
Long Live America
Undying Love
Viva L'America Home Of The Free
Miller
Abracadabra
Abraham Lincoln
And Will The Great Eternal God
Awake O Sleeper Rise From Death
Bernie's Tune
Blood Is All My Plea, The
Cat Came Back, The
Chug-A-Lug
Cleansing Blood, The
Come Gracious Spirit Heav'nly
    Dove
Come Gracious Spirit Heavenly
    Dove
Come To The Arms Of Jesus
Come Ye That Love The Lord
Corn Likker Corn Likker
Creation's Lord
Dang Me
Don't We All Have The Right
Engine Engine Number Nine
England Swings
Eternal Power Whose High Abode
Evening Hymn
Fly Like An Eagle
Forth In Thy Name O Lord I Go
From A Jack To A King
Give Peace O God The Nations Cry
Good Old Beer
Hail West Virginia
Heaven Help Us
Husbands And Wives
I'm Going Home
I've Been A Long Time Leaving But
    I'll Be A Long Time Gone
It Wasn't God Who Made Honky
    Tonk Angels
Johnny Green
Joker, The
Kansas City Star
King Of The Road
Last Word In Lonesome Is Me, The
Marching Song

Miller *(Cont.)*
Marching Thru Berlin
Moonlight Serenade
My God Thy Table Now Is Spread
My Heavenly Home Is Bright And
    Fair
My Home Is A Prison
My Uncle Used To Love Me But She
    Died
O Land Of Rest For Thee I Sigh
Oo-De-Lally
Quicksilver Girl
River In The Rain
Rock 'n Me
Sail For The Other Side
Singer, The
Slogan
Solid Gold
Step That Step
Walking In The Sunshine
We'll Work Till Jesus Comes
What Shall I Do My Lord My God
When I Survey
When I Survey The Wondrous Cross
Worlds Apart
You Can't Roller Skate In A Buffalo
    Herd
You Don't Want My Love

Miller & Allison
I Can See Forever Loving You

Miller & Anderson
When Two Worlds Collide

Miller & Cohn & Stein & Krueger
Sunday

Miller & Conn
Why Should I Cry Over You

Miller & Jackson
Let There Be Peace On Earth
Let There Be Peace On Earth Let It
    Begin With Me

Miller & Miller
Behind The Tear

Miller & Riordan & Satchwell
Madame's Place

Miller & Scruggs
Out Goin' Cattin'

Miller & Stevenson
Release Me

Miller & Taylor
Gotta See Jane

Miller & Williams & Yount
Release Me

Millet
I Want To Walk Walk With Him

Millhuff
Brush, The

Millikan & Robison
Fat Baby

Millikin
Groves Of Blarney, The

Millocker
Belles Of Poland
Entrance Song

Millot
O Ma Belle Maitresse

Mills
At A Georgia Camp-Meeting
Dream On Texas Ladies
He Loves You
Holy Spirit Flow Through Me
I Have
In The City Of Sighs And Tears
Little Music Box Dancer
Meet Me In St Louis
Meet Me In St Louis Louis
Moon Shines Bright On Charlie
    Chaplin, The
Music Box Dancer
Red Wing
Thou Art Worthy
Top Of The Mountain
When The Bees Are In The Hive
Will The Circle Be Unbroken

Mills & Bonne
I Know An Old Lady

Mills & Carter
You've Got A Long Way To Go

Mills & Friend
Lovesick Blues

Mills & Godfrey & Scott
Take Me Back To Dear Old Blighty

Mills & Reed
It's Not Unusual

Mills & Scott
When I Take My Morning
    Promenade

Milman & Dykes
Ride On Ride On In Majesty

Milner
In Cheider

Milns
Federal Constitution And Liberty
    Forever

Milton
How Lovely Are Thy Dwellings Fair
O Had I Wings Like To A Dove

Milveden
Time Is Full To Overflowing

Minard
Morning Bell

Mingus
Free Cell Block F 'Tis Nazi USA
I X Love

Mingus & Davis
Smooch

Miniscalchi
Wanderer's Night Song

Mink
Faith
Hosanna
I Will Song Unto The Lord
Precious Little Baby

Minkler
In The Shady Green Pastures

Minkowsky
Sabbath Queen

Minnigerode & Pomeroy & Galloway
Whiffenpoof Song, The

Minns
There's Not A Bird With Lonely
    Nest

Minor
Bringing In The Sheaves
Going Dry

Miranda
Fairest Beloit

Mireille
Ce Petit Chemin
Couches Dans Le Foin
Puisque Vous Partez En Voyage
Quand Un Vicomte

Miron & Grossman
Tzena Tzena Tzena

Misraki
Ah Vivement Dimanche
Au Vent Leger
Bateau De Peche, Le
Chacun A Sa Place
Domino
Elle Est Laide
J'ai Besoin De Vous
Paulette

Mitchell
Ace In The Hole
Chinese Cafe
Dancin' Round And Round
He Comes For Conversation
I Don't Know Where I Stand
I'm Don Juan's Reckless Daughter
Michael From The Mountains
Out Among The Stars
Pilesgrove
Solid Love
Song To A Seagull
Wild Things Run Fast

Mitchell & Graham
Flame, The

Mitchell & Green & Jackson
Let's Stay Together

Mitchell, Joni
All I Want
Big Yellow Taxi
Blue
Both Sides Now
California
Car On A Hill
Carey
Case Of You, A
Chelsea Morning
Circle Game, The
Coyote
Free Man In Paris
He Played Real Good For Free
Help Me
In France They Kiss On Main Street
Jericho
Ladies Of The Canyon
Morning Morgantown
My Old Man

Mitchell, Joni *(Cont.)*
　Rainy Night House
　Raised On Robbery
　River
　Willie
　Woodstock
　You Turn Me On I'm A Radio
Mitchell & Alter
　Twilight On The Trail
Mittantier
　Moins Je La Veux
Mizzy
　Addams Family, The
　Green Acres
　Moment Of Fear
　My Dreams Are Getting Better All
　　The Time
　With A Hey And A Hi And A Ho
　　Ho Ho
Moberly
　Floreat Rugbeia
Mockel
　Soldier's Farewell, The
Modugno
　Addio Addio
　Ciao Ciao Bambina
　Ciao Ciao Bambino
　I'm Longin' For Love
　If This Is Love I've Had It
　Pitter Patter Serenade, The
　Stay Here With Me
　Volare
Moe
　Gracious Spirit Holy Ghost
Moeran
　Come Away Death
　Diaphenia
　Lover And His Lass, The
Moeulle
　Si Je Maintiens Ma Vie
Moffat
　Timothy Tippen's Horse
Moffatt & Sebert
　Wild Turkey
Moffett
　Intercession
Moffitt & Ball
　Oh Julie
Moghadam
　Iran
Mogulesco
　Mazel Tov
Mohar & Wilensky
　Shir Eres Negbi
Mohaupt
　Unterm Machandelbaum
Mohawk
　Change Of Heart
　Change Of Hearts
Mohr
　7 O'Clock News Silent Night
　Cherish The Treasure
　He Holds The Keys
　Higher Ground

Mohr *(Cont.)*
　Liberty Bell
　Lookout Mountain
　Lord Is My True Shepherd, The
　O Salutaris Hostia
　Passin' The Faith Along
　Silent Night
　They're Wearing 'Em Higher In
　　Hawaii
　When I Behold The Wondrous Cross
　You Want To Now Will You
Mohr & Green & Nelson
　Enter In
Mohr & Gruber
　Silent Night
Mohr & Mays
　Love In Any Language
Mohring
　Drum Now Calls, The
　Engineer's Song
　O Tender Buds
Moir
　Best Of All
　Dreams Of Gladness
　Only Once More
　Pleasure Principle, The
Moki
　He Lei No Kaiulani
Mokrousov
　Lonely Accordion
　Wait For Your Soldier
Molique
　Du Bist O Gott
　It Is Of The Lord's Great Mercies
　Jahreszeiten, Die
　Seine Macht Ist Unerforschlich
　Weint Kinder Von Israel
Molitor
　Ave Maria
Moller
　Glade Vandere, Den
　Happy Wanderer, The
Mollin
　Friday The 13th The Series
Molloy
　Ching-A-Ring-A-Ring
　Clochette
　Darby And Joan
　Ding Dong
　Dustman, The
　Just A Song At Twilight
　Kerry Dance, The
　Little Tin Soldier, The
　Love's Old Sweet Song
　O The Days Of The Kerry Dancing
　Only Tonight
　Punchinello
　Sing A Song At Twilight
　Sweet Song-Bird
　We've Hit The Trail Again
Moloney & Pilger & Polen
　Miss Jones
Molzer
　Autumn

Moman
　This Time
Mompoo
　Fausse Morte, La
　Fes-Me La Vida Transparent
Mompou
　Aquesta Nit Un Mateix Vent
　Aserrin Aserran
　Aureana Do Sil
　Canco De La Fira
　Canconeta Incerta
　Cantar Del Alma
　Cortina De Fullatge
　Damunt De Tu Nomes Les Flors
　Hora Grisa, L
　Hoy La Tierra Y Los Cielos Me
　　Sonrien
　Incertitud
　Insinuant, L'
　Invisibles Atomos Del Aire, Los
　Jo Et Pressentia Com La Mar
　Llueve Sobre El Rio
　Neu
　Nuage, Le
　Olas Gigantes
　Pas, Les
　Pastoral
　Petite Fille De Paris
　Pito Pito Colorito
　Primeros Pasos
　Rosa Del Cami
　Sant Marti
　Sylphe, Le
　Tres Comptines
　Vin Perdu, Le
　Volveran Las Oscuras Golondrinas
　Yo Se Cual El Objeto
　Yo Soy Ardiente Yo Soy Morena
Monaco
　Dear Mr Gable
　I Can't Begin To Tell You
　I'll Take Care Of Your Cares
　I'm Making Believe
　I've Got A Pocketful Of Dreams
　If We Can't Be The Same Old
　　Sweethearts
　If We Can't Be The Same Old
　　Sweethearts We'll Just Be The
　　Same Old Friends
　Only Forever
　Row Row Row
　Torpedo Jim
　What Do You Want To Make Those
　　Eyes At Me For
　You Made Me Love You
　You Made Me Love You I Didn't
　　Want To Do It
　You're Gonna Lose Your Gal
Monath
　Magic Of Believing, The
Monckton
　Rhoda And Her Pagoda
　Soldiers In The Park

Moncrief
Tongo Island
Moncrieff
Creole Love-Song, A
Parting Kiss, The
Moncur
Frankenstein
Monday
Knoxville
Mondugno
If This Is Love I've Had It
Volare
Money & Carter & Myers
Shakin'
Money & Oda
Think I'm In Love
Monk
Abide With Me
Abide With Me Fast Falls The
Eventide
All Things Bright And Beautiful
And Now O Father Mindful Of The
Love
At The Name Of Jesus
Before The Lord's Eternal Throne
Boating Song
Charge To Keep I Have, A
Christian Seek Not Yet Repose
For The Beauty Of The Earth
God That Madest Earth And Heaven
Good-Night Beloved
Guide Of My Spirit On Its Devious
Way
Hail The Day That Sees Him Rise
Hark A Herald Voice Is Calling
Hark A Thrilling Voice Is Sounding
Help Us O Lord To Learn The
Truths
How Swift The Torrent Rolls
Jesus Meek And Gentle
Jesus With Thy Church Abide
Let Us With A Gladsom Mind
Look Ye Saints The Sight Is Glorious
Lord In This Thy Mercy's Day
Lord Jesus Christ Our Lord Most
Dear
Lord Of Nations Bless In Kindness
Lord Thy Word Abideth
Lord Who At Thy First Eucharist
Didst Pray
My Soul Be On Thy Guard
My Soul Repeat His Praise
Now Let The Heavens Joyful
O God We Pray For Faithful Wills
O Master Of The Waking World
O Perfect Life Of Love
O Saviour Bless Us Ere We Go
On Jordan's Bank The Baptist's Cry
Praise To God Immortal Praise
Reste Avec Nous Seigneur
Safely Through Another Week
Send Down Thy Truth O God
Sing Alleluia Forth In Duteous Praise

Monk *(Cont.)*
Soldiers Of Christ Arise
Son Of God Eternal Saviour
Song Of Mercy
Soon Shall Each Raptured Tongue
Spirit Of God For Every Good
Strife Is O'er, The
Strife Is O'er The Battle Done, The
Sun Of My Soul
Sweet Saviour Bless Us
Thy Life Was Given For Me
Voices Of Duty
Wakened By The Solemn Warning
We Praise Thee O God
Who Are These Like Stars Appearing
Monk & Dretzel
Through The Day Thy Love Has
Spared Us
Monks & McCourt
On Saxon Warriors
Monnikendam
O Heart Of Christ
Monnot
Amants D'un Jour, Les
C'est Merveilleux
Chant Du Pirate, Le
Comme Moi
From A Prison Cell
Histoires De Coeur, Les
If You Love Me Really Love Me
Irma La Douce
Je M'imagine
Je N'en Connais Pas La Fin
Milord
Our Language Of Love
Poor People Of Paris, The
Salle D'attente
Y'a Pas D'Printemps
Monnoye
Patapan
Monro
My Lovely Celia
Monroe
All Hail Arizona
Blue Moon Of Kentucky
Kentucky Waltz
Ma Ma Where's My Pa
Red Rocking Chair
Uncle Pen
Will You Be Loving Another Man
Monsell & Smart
Sing To The Lord Of Harvest
Monsigny
C'est Ici Que Rose Respire
Ce N'est Qu'ici Ce N'est Qu'au
Village
Gentle And Sweet Musette
Il Etait Un Oiseau Gris
Il Regardait Mon Bouquet
Non Vous Ne M'avez Jamais Traitee
Ainsi

Monsigny *(Cont.)*
O Ma Tendre Musette
Si L'eclat Du Diademe
Montague
Home
Sunset
Time
Montague & Abner
Up On The Mountain
Monte
Bonjour Mon Coeur
Verament 'in Amore
Monteverde
O Death Pray Come And Save Me
O Let Me Perish
Monteverdi
Ardo E Scoprir
Lasciatemi Morire
Ohime Ohime
Montgomery
Angels From The Realms Of Glory
First Time I Met The Blues
Gift, The
Sos
Vicksburg Blues No 2
Watch And Ward
Montgomery & Jones
We're Gonna Hold On
Montgomery & Koschat
Lord Is My Shepherd, The
Montgomery & Paschal
Dreamin'
Montgomery & Richards
Let's All Go Down To The River
Let's All Go Down To The River
There's A Man Walking On The
Water
Montrose
Caesar's Triumph
Clementine
My Darling Clementine
Oh My Darling Clementine
Montross
Clementine
Moody
God Is Love
Is It Nothing To You
Moment By Moment
Moody & Lehman
Walking On The Water
Moolai
All Hail To Thee
Mooney & Seals
Crazy Arms
Moonie
Song For The Flag, A
Moore
Baby Scratch My Back
Blue Book Man
Brethren We Have Met To Worship
Bum Army, The
Burdens Are Lifted At Calvary

Moore *(Cont.)*
Caldonia What Makes Your Big
    Head So Hard
Caldonia What Makes Your Head So
    Big
College Days
Dashing On Before The Gale
Dear Gc
Dreaming Alone In The Twilight
Good Night Poor Harvard
Haven Of Rest, The
Hymn To Skidmore
I Want To Be A Foot Ball Man
I'll Love You 'Till The Next One
    Comes
I'm A King Bee
I'm So Sorry
Just A Little Bit Too Far
Just For A Smile
Last Rose Of Summer, The
Letter Song
Love Let The Wind Cry How I
    Adore Thee
Michigan Goodbye
Midnight Love
Motherhood Sublime
My Soul In Sad Exile
Oft In The Stilly Night
Restore The Joy
Rise
Shake Your Hips
Strolling On The Boulevard
Sweet Marie
Sweet Rivers
Take Me Back To Collerradda Fer To
    Stay
Varsity
Way We Have At Michigan, A
Weary Blues
Western Winde
When The Drive Goes Down
Where We'll Never Grow Old
Whole World Is A Christmas Tree,
    The
Willow Song
Moore & Abner
At My Front Door
Moore & Campbell
Four Walls
Moore & Griffin
Love Machine
Moore & Penner
Ooby-Dooby
Moore & Raymond
Some Hearts Get All The Breaks
Moore & West
Buzz Me Babe
Rainin' In My Heart
Moore & Williams
One For The Money
Moore, Thomas
Harp That Once Through Tara's
    Halls

Moore, Thomas *(Cont.)*
Minstrel Boy, The
'Tis The Last Rose Of Summer
Moorman
Little Talk With Jesus, A
Moraine
Christmas Island
Morales
Chiflido, El
Me Ye Have Bereaved
Morali & Belolo & Willis
In The Navy
YMCA
Moran
Chit Chat
Pray Papa
Moran & Tubb
Skip A Rope
Morbelli & Astore & Stanley
Botch-A-Me
More
Farewell
Holy Manna
Montgomery
Sweet Rivers
Wesley
Morehead
Sentimental Me
Moreland
I Might
I'm A College Man
Little Old Red Shawl My Mother
    Wore, The
Take Me Back To College
When All The World's Asleep
Morely
Dainty Fine Sweet Nymph
Moret
Hiawatha
She's Funny That Way
Silver Heels
Moreve & Kay
Magic Carpet Ride
Morey
All Things Come Of Thee
Fugitive Breakdown
Morey & Daniel
Lavender Blue
Morgan
Candy Kisses
Cumberland Mountain Deer Chase
Don't Bite The Hand That's Feeding
    You
Hail To Our School
Hawaiian Bluebird
Jesus Christ Is Risen Today
Marita
Ours Is The World
Song Of Friendship, A
Sweet Eloise
Morgan & Climie
I Knew You Were Waiting
I Knew You Were Waiting For Me
My Heart Can't Tell You No

Morgan & Climie & Fisher
Love Changes Everything
Room To Move
Morgan & David
Sipping Cider Thru A Straw
Suckin' Cider Through A Straw
Morgan & Davis
Just A Little Love
Only A Lonely Heart Knows
Radio Heart
So This Is Love
When It's Down To Me And You
Morgan & Harris & Melsher
So Long
Morgan & Johnson
Does Your Heart Beat For Me
Morgan & Malkin
Hey Mr. Banjo
Morgan & Pfrimmer
Victims Of Goodbye
Morgan & Pfrimmer & Reid
She Keeps The Home Fires Burning
Morganfield
Baby Please Don't Go
Clouds In My Heart
Cold Weather Blues
Trouble No More
Morley
April Is In My Mistress' Face
Canzonet
Die Now My Heart
Fire Fire My Heart
Flora Wilt Thou Torment Me
Go Ye My Canzonets
I Go Before My Charmer
I Go Before My Darling
In Life's Earnest Morning
In Thy Name O Lord Assembling
It Was A Lover And His Lass
Lord Thou Hast Been Our Dwelling
    Place
Madrigal
My Bonny Lass
Nolo Mortem Peccatoris
Now Is The Gentle Season The
    Fields Abroad
Now Is The Month Of Maying
Praise The Lord Of Heaven
Saviour Blessed Saviour
Say Gentle Nymphs
See Lovely Day Is Dawning
Shoot False Love I Care Not
Sing We And Chant It
Those Eternal Bowers
Though Philomela Lost Her Love
Zion Stands With Hills Surrounded
Mornable
Je Ne Me Confesserai Point
Mornington
Cheap Jack
It Was You
Maid's Wish, The
Teach Me My God And King
Tomorrow Lord Is Thine

Mornington *(Cont.)*
'Twas You Sir
We Lift Our Hearts To Thee

Moroder
Breakdance
Call Me
Flashdance What A Feeling
Love Theme From Flashdance
Love Theme From Superman III
Love's Theme
Meet Me Half Way
Reach Out
Theme From Midnight Express
Wanderer, The
Winner Takes It All

Moroder & Forsey
Never Ending Story

Moroder & Forsey & Cara
Why Me

Moroder & Summer
On The Radio

Moroder & Whitlock
Danger Zone
Take My Breath Away

Moross
I've Got Me
It's The Going Home Together
Lazy Afternoon
Theme From Wagons Ho
Windflowers

Morrey
Flag March, The
Raising The Flag

Morricone
Good The Bad And The Ugly, The
Once Upon A Time In America
Theme From Once Upon A Time In
America
Untouchables Theme, The

Morris
All On The Altar For Jesus
Almost Decided
Blazing Saddles
Broken For You
Can The Lord Depend On You
Can The World See Jesus In You
Choosing
Confess Him Today
Crown Him
Day After Day
Dig A Little Deeper In God's Love
Flag Of Our Union, The
Hallelujah Song, The
Have You
How Green Was My Valley
I Can Put My Trust In Jesus
Is It I Is It You
Jesus Lives
Jesus Met The Woman At The Well
Just A Closer Walk With Thee
Leave Me Lonely
Let All The People Praise Thee
Let Jesus Come Into Your Heart
Let Me Love You

Morris *(Cont.)*
My God Is Real
My Mother's Bible
Nearer Still Nearer
Onward To Victory
Row Me Over The Tide
Same Old Way, The
Shake A Hand
Step Back
Sweet Will Of God
Sweeter As The Years Go By
Theme From Blazing Saddles
Theme From Clue
When He Is Come To You
Winter's Snow
Woodman Spare That Thee
Wounded For Our Transgressions
Yes There's One

Morris & Brantley
Baby Bye Bye

Morris & Greenberg & Baer & Schwartz
Sweet Talkin' Guy

Morris & Hughes & Ishmall
Here I Am In Dallas

Morris & Morris
Made In Japan

Morris & Moy
Forget Me Not

Morris & Setser
Anything Goes
Why Lady Why

Morris & Welch
Plain Brown Wrapper

Morrison
Born To Love Me
Brown Eyed Girl
Domino
Easy Ride
Gloria
I Shall Sing
Into The Mystic
Moondance
Mystic Eyes
River's Too Wide, The
Tupelo Honey
Warm Love
What A Joy
Wild Night
You're The One

Morrison & Crabb
Trouble

Morrison & Fielder & Betts
Your Memory Ain't What It Used To
Be

Morrison & Hupp
Are You On The Road To Lovin' Me
Again
You Decorated My Life

Morrison & Keith
Little By Little

**Morrison & Kennedy & Grundland &
Steels**
How Can You Buy Killarney

Morrison & Kirby
Too Old To Play Cowboy

Morrison & Lester
Bedtime Stories

Morrison & Macrae
I'll Love Away Your Troubles For
Awhile
One-Night Fever
Shine On
Stuck Right In The Middle Of Your
Love

Morrison & Russell
Act Naturally

Morrison & Slate
Friends
I Ain't Got No Business Doin'
Business Today
I Can't Get Enough Of You
Loving Up A Storm

Morrison & Stephenson & Silbar
You've Got A Good Love Coming

Morrow
Virginia Hail All Hail

Morrow & Arnold & Pomerov
Open Letter To The President, An

Morse
Ask The Man In The Moon
Blue Bell
Dear Old Girl
God Be With You Till We Meet
Again
Hail Hail The Gang's All Here
Hail To California
Hurrah For Baffin's Bay
M-O-T-H-E-R
M-O-T-H-E-R A Word That Means
The World To Me
O Love That Will Not Let Me Go
O Love That Wilt Not Let Me Go
Pretty Girl A Summer Night, A
We'll Knock The Heligo Into Heligo
Out Of Heligola
You Don't Have To Be Irish To Be
Welcome In An Irishman's
Home

Mortari
El Ueselin Del Basco, L'

Morton
Air Is Filled With The Echoes, The
Can It Be
Chicago Breakdown
First Christmas, The
If I Could But Tell It All
Jelly Roll Blues
King Porter Stomp
Touch Of His Hand On Mine, The

Morton & Barry & Greenwich
Leader Of The Pack

Morton & Putman
Smooth Sailing

Mosenthal
Minuet, The
Punkydoodle And Jollapin
Sweet Red Rose, The

Moses
It Is Not Dying
Moses-Tobani
Hearts And Flowers
Mosigny
Adieu Chere Louise
Mosley & Taylor
Sha-La-La
Moss
Circles
Everyone Makes Mistakes
Five People In My Family
Grouch Song, The
I Love Trash
People In Your Neighborhood, The
Rubber Duckie
Someday Little Children
Stand Up And Cheer Ronald Reagan
Still Still With Thee
Up And Down
What Do I Do When I'm Alone
What Is Our Calling's Glorious
Hope
Word Family Song, The
Moss & Collins
Until Sunrise
Moszkowski
Guitarre
I Ask Thee Not
Serenade
Spanish Dance No. 5
Mote & Bradbury
My Hope Is Built
Mothersbaugh & Casale
Freedom Of Choice
Whip It
Motola & Marascalco
Goodnight My Love Pleasant
Dreams
Mouhl
Believe Me If All Those Endearing
Young Charms ,
Moulds & Bergsnes & Eatherly
Ring Where A Ring Used To Be, A
Moulu
Amy Souffrez Que Je Vous Aime
Mounsey
Theme From Guiding Light
Mountain
I Am His And He Is Mine
Jesus I Am Resting
Like A River Glorious
Midnight Special
Mouret
Baroque Fanfare
Rondeau
Mouret & Parnes
Masterpiece, The
Moussorgsky
By The River Don
Classic
Cradle-Song Of The Poor
Marina's Song
Mushrooms

Moussorgsky *(Cont.)*
Seminarian, The
Song Of Khivria, The
Moustaki & Chavigny
Etranger, Un
Mouton
En Venant De Lyon
Movie & Patton
Hold Me
Moy & Cosby & Stevenson
Nothing's Too Good For My Baby
Moy & Stevenson & Hunter
My Baby Loves Me
Moya
Chanson Du Coeur Brise
Moyer
I Sought The Lord And Afterward
Mozart
Abendempfindung
Ach Ich Fuhl's
Adoramus Te Christe
All-Wise Nature
Alleluia
Alleluja
Alphabet, The
An Cloe
Aria
Arie Der Constanze
Autumn Comes
Ave Maria
Ave Verum
Ave Verum Corpus
Away With Melancholy
Batti Batti
Berceuse
Bird-Catcher, The
Blacksmith, The
Bona Nox
Breaks The Joyful Easter
Brightest And Best Of The Sons Of
The Morning
Bundeslied
Cherubino's Song
Chide Oh Chide Me
Christmas
Ci Darem La Mano, La
Contentment
Cradle Song
Dalla Sua Pace
Dancing Of Long Ago
Das Veilchen
Day Dreams
Deh Per Questo Istante
Deh Vieni Alla Finestra
Deh Vieni No Tardar
Der Holle Rache
Don Giovanni's Serenade
Dove Sono
Drink To Me Only With Thine Eyes
Ein Loser Dieb Ist Amor
Endlich Naht Sich Die Stunde
Even Song
Fairy Flute, The
Friendship

Mozart *(Cont.)*
Gebet
Go Forget Me
God Is The Name My Soul Adores
God Of All Power And Truth And
Grace
God Of The Strong God Of The
Weak
Hark The Voice Of Jesus Calling
Hor Mein Flehn
How Cavaliers Have Changed
Ich Grausam O Nein Geliebter
Ich Weiss Nicht Wo Ich Bin Was Ich
Tue
In The Army
Jesu Holy Spirit
Jesu Son Of God
Jesu Word Of God Incarnate
Jesus I My Cross Have Taken
Joy Flies Away
Kanon
Lady May
Let Precious Truth And Honesty
Light For Him A Candle
Little Spinner, The
Long Ago In Olden Times
Longing For Spring
Looking Upward Day By Day
Lullaby
Magic Flute, The
Melancholy Folly
Mine Be The Tongue
Minuet
Minuet Of Long Ago, The
Minuet, The
Minuetto, The
Mio Tesoro, Il
Moto Di Gioja, Un
Music Magic
Nachtigallenkanon
Nay Bid Me Not
New Year, The
Night And The Grasses Grow
Non Mi Dir
Non So Piu
Northern Lights, The
O Jesu Name
O Lord On High
O Wie Ist Die Welt So Schon
Of Selim Mighty Great And
Powerful
Old Woman, The
One There Is Above All Others
Orpheus With His Lute
Papageno's Aria
Pledge Now Thy Hand
Porgi Amor
Praise The Lord
Praise To God
Prayer, A
Queen Of Night's Vengeance Aria,
The
Ring Out Wild Bells
Romance

Mozart *(Cont.)*
Sagt Holde Frauen
Schmale Tobe Lieber Junge
Schon Ein Madchen Von Funfzehn
    Jahren
Serenade
Ships
Shir Yayin
Silently Blending
Skylark And Nightingale
Sleep And Rest
Sleep Baby Sleep
Song Of Praise
Song Of The Fowler
Song Of The Three Youths
Speak Gently
Spring Carol
Spring The Charmer
Such Chiming Melodious
Summer Days Once More
Sweet Bells
Sweet Music Enchanting
Tell Me Fair Ladies
Tell Me O Fair Ones
That Music Enchanting
Theme
Theme From Symphony In G Minor
Things I Like Best
Thoughts At Eventide
Three Faithful Youths We Now Will
    Lend You
To Night
Trink-Kanon
Twilight
Twinkle Little Star
Two Rounds
Unsre Wiesen Grunen Wieder
Vedrai Carino
Veilchen, Das
Verheissung
Violet, The
Voi Che Sapete
Waltz In A
Waltz In D
We Hail Thee With Rejoicing
Weihelied
Welche Wonne Welche Lust
Wenn Du Fein Artig Bist
What Is This Splendor
When Jesus Was A Child Like Me
Wie Wohl Ist Mir O Freund Der
    Seelen
Within This Sacred Dwelling
Wohin Flohen Die Wonnestunden
Wood Wind Duet, A
Ye Who Love's Power
Youth's Journey
Zufriedenheit, Die

Mraks
I Heard The Bells On Christmas Day

Mraz
Blues For Sarka
What Does It Matter

Mtume & Lucas
Back Together Again
Closer I Get To You, The
What Cha Gonna Do With My
    Lovin'

Muck
Morning Prayer

Mudarra
Claros Y Frescos Rios
Dulces Exuviae
Durmiendo Yva El Senor
Isabel Perdiste La Tu Faxa
Israel Mira Tus Montes
Por Asperos Caminos
Recuerde El Alma Dormida
Si Por Amar El Hombre
Triste Estava El Rey David
Vita Fugge, La

Muehleisen
Salon And Saloon

Mueller
Away In A Manger
Glad New Day, A
I Give Thee Thanks With All My
    Heart
Just Before I Sleep Tonight
Lord Let Us Now Depart In Peace
Love Came Down At Christmas
Nothin' At All
So Arm In Der Krippe
When Jesus Was A Little Lad
With Heart And Voice

Mueller & Johnson & Busse
Wang Wang Blues, The

Muhling
Froh Zu Sein
Lightsome Heart

Muhoberac
No One Like You

Muir
Canada's National Hymn
I Had A Gal I Had A Pal
Mammy Jinny's Jubilee
Maple Leaf For Ever, The
Play That Barber Shop Chord
Take Me To That Swanee Shore
Trail To Sunset Valley
Waiting For The Robert E Lee

Muir & Abrahams
Hitchy Koo
Ragtime Cowboy Joe

Mullen
Afterwards
Silence And Fun

Muller
Afterwards
Away In A Manger
I Sing Of Thee
In Orchard Green
Mein Heiland Geht Ins Leinden
Rousing Cheer, A

Mullican
Jole Blon

Mullins
Doubly Good To You
Elijah
Guiding Star, The
O Come All Ye Faithful
Sing Your Praise To The Lord

**Mullins & Kirkpatrick & Grant &
Chapman**
Love Of Another Kind

Muloch
Douglas Tender And True
Stars Trembling O'er Us

Mulock
Row Row Cheerly Row

Mulso
What Diff'ring Beauties

Munday
New Topia

Mundy
My Prime Of Youth

Mundy & Mason
Schneider's Band

Mundy & Young
Trav'lin' Light

Munsey
Here Comes The Bride

Munson
Ida Sweet As Apple Cider
Newburg

Munz
Du Heil'ger Tag Du Tag Des Herrn

Murchison
Colonel Rutgers

Murden
For Once In My Life

Murdock
For The Love Of It
Stella The Belle Of Fedela

Murphey
Carolina In The Pines
Rollin' Nowhere
Talkin' To The Wrong Man

Murphey & Quatro
Geronimo's Cadillac

Murphey & Rains & Norman
Disenchanted

Murphy
Constantly Abiding
Coortin' In The Kitchen
Curly Locks And The Chestnut Man
Darker The Night, The
Fifth Of Beethoven, A
Handful Of Earth, A
I Live In Trafalgar Square
Lady-Lady
Moonshiner, The
Nicodemus Johnson
Thanksgiving Day
Thing He Had Never Done Before, A

Murphy & David
Keep Your Head Down Fritzie Boy

Murphy & Frank
Don't Disturb This Groove

Murphy & Kavanaugh
Three Lovely Lasses In Bannion
Murphy & Letters & McKenna
Has Anybody Here Seen Kelly
Murphy & Turner
Shutters And Boards
Murphy & Walden & Cohen
Put Your Mouth On Me
Murphy & Wood
Half The Way
Murrah
Good Love Died Tonight, A
Murrah & Anders
Ozark Mountain Jubilee
Murrah & Dean
Fast Lanes And Country Roads
Hearts Aren't Made To Break
Hearts Aren't Made To Break
They're Made To Love
Now And Forever Fast Lanes And
Country Roads
Murrah & Hicks
Goodbye This Time
This Crazy Love
Murrah & Leigh
Life's Highway
Murrah & Murrah & Burch
You Can't Keep A Good Memory
Down
Murrah & Van Warmer
Bridges And Walls
Murray
Away In A Manger
Cling To The Bible
Eternal Gifts Of Christ The King, The
Hallowed Memories
Here In Christ We Gather
How Do You Do It
How Strong And Sweet My Father's
Care
It Ain't All Honey And Ain't All
Jam
Jesus Saves O Blessed Story
Lamb's High Banquet Called To
Share, The
Mama Don't 'Low
My God And My All
Night Chicago Died, The
Terrible Tale, A
Waltz Song
Murray & Everard
It's Alright In The Summertime
Murray & Leigh
Little Bit Off The Top, A
Murray & Weston
I'm Henery The Eighth
I'm Henry VIII I Am
Murry
I'll Walk Beside You
Murtaugh
Oregon State Song

Muscarella
Sweet And Sorrowful Fantasy, A
Muse
Dying Volunteer, The
When It's Sleepy Time Down South
Muset
Lai
Musgrave
Thou Say'st Take Up Thy Cross
Musorgski
Child's Song, A
Musorgskii
Evening Prayer, The
Musorgsky
In My Attic
Long Live And Reign Great Boris
Mussorgsky
Dolly's Lullaby
Hopak
Lied Vom Floh, Das
Song Of The Hebrew Maiden
Myddleton
Down South
Myerowitz
Vus Geven Iz Geven
Myers
California Stage Company
Cavatina
Christmas People
I Am Certain
I'm Always Rejoicing
If Santa Were My Daddy
Jesus Lives
Jesus Will Carry Me Over The River
Look Up Lift Up
This Christmas Eve
You And I
Myers & Giles
You're Never Too Old For Young
Love
Myers & Pfrimmer & Raven
You Should've Been Gone By Now
Myers & Raven
I Got Mexico
Sometimes A Lady
Myles
Chapel Of Dreams
Have You Ever Loved A Woman
Myrow
Autumn Nocturne
Fable Of The Rose, The
If I'm Lucky
On The Boardwalk
Velvet Moon
You Make Me Feel So Young
Mysels
We Three
Naci
Erdoszelen Nagy A Zsivaj
Hogyha Szeretnelek
Nador
It Is Hard To Hide Love

Nageli
And Are We Yet Alive
Blest Feast Of Love Divine
Blest Be The Tie
Blest Be The Tie That Binds
Come To The Wood
Dennis
Firmly Stand O Native Land
France Est Belle, La
Freut Euch Des Lebens
Gardening
Gesegnet Sei Das Band
How Gentle God's Commands
Jesus Invites His Saints
Lehr Mich Beten
Lied Vom Rhein, Das
Lobt Froh Den Herrn
Morning
Motette
Mourn For The Thousands Slain
Nacht Und Still Ists Um Mich Her
Nachtgesang
Now From The Altar Of My Heart
O For A Closer Walk With God
Our Father
Out Of The Depths To Thee I Cry
Song Of Praise
Summer Evening Twilight
Sunset Song
Teach Me O God And King
Naginski
Pasture, The
Nagle
Lord And Master Lead Us Onward
Nairn
Land O' The Leal, The
Nairne
Rowan Tree, The
Naish & Smiley & Gersmehl & Elliott
Where Are The Other Nine
Nakamura & Rokusuke
Sukiyaki
Nalbandian
Hail Ethiopia Hail Rejoice
Nalyor
Now In The Days Of Youth
Namur
Dear Heart Of Jesus
Guardian Angel
Little Golden Door
Mary Mother Sweet
Saint Joseph
Nanino
Diffusa Est Gratia
Naor & Hirsh
Makhela Aliza
Nape
Old Plantation, The
Napoleon
Corazon Corazon
Tiempo Al Tiempo
Naravaez
Paseavase El Rey Moro

Nares
Rise My Soul
Rise My Soul And Stretch Thy
    Wings
Wilt Thou Lend Me Thy Mare

Narvaez
Ay Arde Coracon Arde
Con Que La Lavare
Sy Tantos Halcones
Ya Se Asienta El Rey Ramiro

Nascimento & Brant
Exits And Flags

Nascimento & Moore
One Coin

Nash
Glad Cat Rag
Goin' Down That Long Long
    Lonesome Road
Hold Me Tight
I Can See Clearly Now
In Thee Our Father Are We All At
    Home
Jersey Legionaire, The
Keep Them Burning
Lady Of The Island
Marrakesh Express
Our House
Pre-Road Downs
Snakey Blues, The
Teach Your Children Well
Wasted On The Way
What Kind Of Love Is This

Nason
Battle Song

Nathan
Man Who Fights The Fire, The
Pal Of Mine

Nathan & McGranahan
I Know Whom I Have Believed
There Shall Be Showers Of Blessing

Nathanson
L'Shana Ha-Ba'a

Naughton
Faded Coat Of Blue, The

Naumann
Bleibe Bei Mir
Sie Ist Da Die Schone Stunde

Navarro
Que Razon Podeys Vos Tener
Speedoo

Nayarro
Homage To Rizal

Naylor
Beneath The Shade Of The Cross
Oh The Blood

Nazereth
Dengozo

Neal & Andrews & King
Engineer's Child, The

Neale
Christ Was Born On Christmas Day
January Carol

Neander
Come Ye Faithful Raise The Anthem
God Himself Is With Us
God Of Love And God Of Power
He Is Risen He Is Risen
Open Now Thy Gates Of Beauty
Rise Ye Children Of Salvation
See The Morning Sun Ascending
Tut Mir Auf Die Schoene Pforte
Weicht Ihr Berge

Near
Hay Una Mujer
Jesus Came Adored By Angels
O Brightness Of The Immortal
    Father's Face

Neary & Photoglo
20th Century Fool
We Were Meant To Be Lovers

Neck & Maxwell
Shangri-La

Nedelmann
O The Summer It Has Flown

Neefe
Contented Heart
Let Songs Of Praises Fill The Sky

Neel & Giles
When Somebody Loves You

Neeman
Hana'ava Babanot

Neiburg & Dougherty & Reynolds
I'm Confessin'
I'm Confessin' That I Love You

Neiburg & Fleischer & Timburg
Raggedy Ann

Neidlinger
Birthday Of A King, The
Boat Song
Pine-Tree, The
Serenade
Shepherd's Song
Sweet Miss Mary
Weary Hours, The
Where Did You Come From Baby
    Dear

Neighbours
Spiritual Sailor, The

Neil
Everybody's Talkin'
Just A Little Bit Of Rain
Other Side Of This Life, The

Nelham
All Must Die
Cuckoo Hark
Drink Is A Thing
Follow Me Merrily
He That Buys Good Ale
Hedge In The Cuckoo
How Merrily Looks The Man That
    Hath Gold
Lend Me Thy Mare
Slaves To The World
Tinker's Cry
Weary Of My Groaning

Nelham *(Cont.)*
Wily Fox
Yonder He Goes

Nelon
We Shall Wear A Crown

Nelson
111-444
Angel Flying Too Close To The
    Ground
Christmas In Alaska
Crazy
Forgiving You Was Easy
Funny How Time Slips Away
Garden Party
God Be Merciful Unto Us
Good Times
Hello Walls
I'm A Memory
If Thou Wert By My Side
Images
Island In The Sea
Little Old Fashioned Karma
Mary Of Argyle
On The Road Again
Pretty Paper
Remember The Good Times
Rose Of Allandale, The
Songwriter
Spirit Of Old NU, The
Theme From Six Million Dollar Man
Then Came You
Vesper Song
Yesterday's Wine

Nelson & Boone & Nelson
Burnin' Old Memories
Old Coyote Town

Nelson & Buskirk & Breeland
Night Life

Nelson & Egnolan
Teen Beat

Nelson & Gaither
I Walked Today

Nelson & Gaither & Gaither
We Are So Blessed

Nelson & Hilliard
Bouquet Of Roses

Nelson & McHugh & Green & Goss
His Grace Is Greater

Nelson & McSpadden
Jesus Lord To Me

Nelson & Nelson
Eighteen Wheels And A Dozen
    Roses
I Have You

Nelson & Rollins
Frosty The Snow Man
Peter Cottontail

Nelson & Smith
Dyin' Rider Blues

Nemo
Don't Take Your Love From Me
'Tis Autumn

Nepomuceno
Cantigas
Coracao Indeciso
Indecision
Trovas
Nero
Hot Canary
Nesbit & Macdermid
Land Of Mine
Nesbitt
Christmas Is Coming
Little Miss Muffett
Nesmith
Different Drum
Nesmith & Hargrove
I've Never Loved Anyone More
Nessler
Abschiedslied
It Was Not So To Be
It Was Not Thus To Be
Withered Wreath, The
Nestler
Entschuldigung
Neswick
In The Cross Of Christ I Glory
Neufeld
We've Come O Lord
Neukomm
O Saving Victim Opening Wide
Neuman
Wonderland By Night
Neumane
Primeros Los Hijos Del Suelo, Los
Neumark
If Thou But Suffer God To Guide
Thee
If Thou But Trust In God To Guide
Thee
Leave God To Order
Leave God To Order All Thy Ways
O Lord Of Hosts All Heaven
Possessing
Wer Nur Den Lieben Gott Lasst
Walten
Nevada
Letter Edged In Black, The
Nevermind
Sugar Walls
Nevia
Mill, The
Nevil & Eastman & Hart
Dominoes
Nevil & Mueller
Just A Little Closer
Nevil & Pescetto & Feldman
Somebody Like You
Nevil & Tongeren & Galdston
It's Not Over 'Til It's Over
Nevin
Bed In Summer
Little Boy Blue
Might Lak' A Rose
Mighty Lak A Rose
Narcissus

Nevin *(Cont.)*
Nocturne
Oh That We Two Were Maying
One Spring Morning
Orsola's Song
Rosary, The
Singing
Tell Me Bewitching Maiden
Venetian Love Song
Nevin-Leavitt
Deep In The Rose
Nevins
I Believe In Santa Claus
Twilight Time
Nevins & Benjamin & Weiss
These Things I Offer You For A
Lifetime
Nevins & Nevins
Twilight Time
Nevins & Nevins & Dunn & Ram
Twilight Time
New
Tapping At The Garden Gate
New Orleans Rhythm King
Tin Roof Blues
Newberry
Sunshine
Newborn
Theme From The Naked Gun From
The Files Of Police
Newbury
Advent Of Our God, The
Alleluia Jesus Lives
American Trilogy, An
Ask And It Will Be Given You
Blessing And Glory
Communion Prayer
Go To Dark Gethsemane
I Give Thee Thanks O Lord
Jesus Is Born
Just Dropped In
My Burden Is Light
San Francisco Mabel Joy
Sing Hosanna
Newcomb
Big Sunflower, The
Swing, The
Newell & Towner
At Calvary
Newman
Adventures In Paradise
Again
Airport Love Theme
Back On My Feet Again
Best Of Everything, The
Birds And The Bees, The
Cowboy And The Lady, The
Daniel Boone
Dobie
Follow The Flag
Georgie Porgie
God's Song
Guilty
He Believes In Me

Newman *(Cont.)*
I Love LA
It's Money That Matters
Kisses Sweeter Than Wine
Little Kingdom I Possess, A
Louisiana 1927
Love Theme From The Robe
Mama Told Me Not To Come
Moon Of Manakoora, The
Most Original Soft Drink Ever
Natural, The
One More Hour
Rednecks
Roll With The Punches
Sail Away
Short People
So This Is Love
Summer Days Are Come Again, The
When It's Iris Time In Tennessee
Newman & Dykes
Lead Kindly Light
Newman & Lebowsky
Wayward Wind, The
Newman & Miller
Cry Cry Darling
Newman & Newman
Be A Friend
Great Reward, The
He Believes In Me
Spreadin' Like Wildfire
Turn To Jesus
Newman & Oldham
He's Only A Prayer Away
Newport
Lo A Star Ye Sages Hoary
Newsom
O Clap Your Hands Together
Newton
Amazing Grace
Casey Jones
Eastern College Boating Song, An
Newton & Noble
I Want Everyone To Cry
What I Didn't Do
Newton & Reinagle
How Sweet The Name Of Jesus
Sounds
Newton & Tyler & Tyler
Bobbie Sue
Newton-John
Changes
Rosewater
Nichol
Hark To The Sound Of Voices
Nearer My God To Thee
We've A Story To Tell
We've A Story To Tell To The
Nations
Nicholas
We've Only Just Begun
Nicholls
Among My Souvenirs
Kentucky Fight Fight Fight

Nichols
Among My Souvenirs
I Won't Last A Day Without You
I've Waited Honey Waited Long For You
Lady Sings The Blues
Let Me Be The One
Rainy Days And Mondays
Times Of Your Life
We've A Story To Tell To The Nations
We've Only Just Begun

Nicholson
God Be In My Head
God Be In My Head And In My Understanding
Lift High The Cross
Welcome Yule

Nicholson & Fischer
White Than Snow

Nicholson & Holyfield
Break Away

Nichtern
Midnight At The Oasis

Nickens
Comfort In Trouble
Magnitude Of Mercy, The

Nickle
Grace Abounding
I Long To Work For Thee
I'll Work For Thee
Meet Mother In The Skies
What Then
Working And Waiting

Nicks
Angel
Dreams
Edge Of Seventeen
Gold Dust Woman
Gypsy
I Don't Want To Know
Landslide
Leather And Lace
Rhiannon
Sara
Sisters Of The Moon
Stand Back

Nicks & Johnston
No Questions Asked

Nicks & Nowels & Pressly
I Can't Wait

Nicks & Stewart
If Anyone Falls
Seven Wonders

Nicolai
Adieu, The
Angel Song
Arie Der Anna
Arie Der Frau Fluth
God's Holy Mountain We Ascend
How Bright Appears The Morning Star
How Brightly Beams The Morning Star

Nicolai *(Cont.)*
How Brightly Shines The Morning Star
How Lovely Now The Morning Star
O Holy Spirit Enter In
O Morning Star How Fair And Bright
O Morning Star So Pure So Bright
Praise The Lord Through Every Nation
Sleepers Wake A Voice Astounds Us
Wachet Auf Ruft Uns Die Stimme
Wake Awake For Night Is Flying
Wake Awake The Night Is Dying
Wake O Wake For Night Is Flying
Wake O Wake With Tidings Thrilling
Wie Schon Leucht Uns Der Morgenstern
Wie Schon Leuchtet Der Morgenstern

Niebergall
Horseshoe Rag

Niedt
Now Come All Ye People

Nieh-Erh
March Of The Volunteers

Niel
O Love That Casts Out Fear

Nielsen
Du Ska Fa En Dag I Mara
I Want You To Want Me
Spring Break
Surrender

Nielsen & Pearson
If You Should Sail

Nielsen & Warren
Ghost Town

Nielsen & Zander & Brant & Radice
Tonight It's You

Nielson
She's Tight
Spring Break
Surrender

Nightingale
All Hail To You
Three Court Jesters

Nikolayef
Dawn Of Night

Nikolsky
O Taste And See How Gracious Is The Lord

Nikorowicz
'Mid Fire And Smoke

Niles
Go Way From My Window
Grace Before Meals
I Wonder As I Wander
Kentucky Wassail Song, The
My Horses Ain't Hungry
My Little Mohee
Three Little Pigs

Nilsen
Regnvaersangen

Nilson
White Butterflies

Nilsson
My Best Friend

Nims
Precious And Few

Ninot
Et La La La

Nish
Hoop De Dooden Do

Nitzsche
One Flew Over The Cuckoo's Nest

Nixon
Mother Country Music
Pleasure's Been All Mine, The

Noack
These Hands

Noble
Cherokee
Come Labor On
Dost Thou In A Manger Lie
Fair The Night In Bethlem Land
Fairest Lord Jesus
Fairest Lord Jesus Ruler Of All
For Thee O Dear Dear Country
For You A Lei
Good Night Sweetheart
Hold Me Thrill Me Kiss Me
I Want To Learn To Speak Hawaiian
Love Is The Sweetest Thing
Love Locked Out
Manuela Boy
O Beautiful For Spacious Skies
O Who Shall Roll Away The Stone
Old Hawaiian Custom, An
Out Of The East
Very Thought Of You, The

Noble & Campbell & Connelly
Good Night Sweetheart

Noble & Carlson
Flower Lei, A

Noble & Leleiohaku
Hawaiian War Chant
Ta-Hu-Wa-Hu-Wai

Noble & Long
My Sweetheart

Noble & Malani
Maori Brown Eyes

Noble & Peterson & George
Tropic Trade Winds

Noble & Rito
King Kamehameha

Noble & Spriggs & Colton
If There's Any Justice In This World

Noble & Wolf
Pretty Red Hibiscus

Nock
Dark Light
In Out And Around
Love Child

Noel
Lend A Hand

Noelsch
Halleluja Schoner Morgen
Mein Gott Das Herz Ich Bringe Dir
Noiman
Talit
Noir
Beauregard Manassas Quickstep, The
Nolan
Cool Water
I Like Dreamin'
I Whistle And Wait For Katie
Little Annie Rooney
Lonely Together
Love's Grown Deep
Swing Your Daddy
Touch Of God's Hand, The
Tumbling Tumbleweeds
Nordoff
Embroidery For A Faithless Friend
Nordraak
Ja Vi Elsker
Norway
Norwegian Hymn
Norwegian National Hymn
Norlin
Airplane, The
Davy Crockett
Dream Ryhmes
Skating Song
Village Band, The
Winter Winds
Wise Ben Franklin
Norman
I Wish We'd All Been Ready
Sweet Sweet Song Of Salvation
Norris
Alma Mater
Grace Is Free
I Can Hear My Savior Calling
I Can Hear My Saviour Calling
Where He Leads Me
Norris & Simon
Down On My Knees
North
Agony And The Ecstasy Theme, The
Autumn's Ballad
Dragonslayer-Romantic Theme
Green Glens Of Antrim, The
Hark The Voice Of Love And Mercy
Long Hot Summer, The
O'er The Gloomy Hills Of Darkness
Romantic Theme
Someday Soon
Theme From Rich Man Poor Man
Unchained Melody
Northrup
Slumbering In The Dusk Twilight
Norton
Arise Christian Soldier
For Her Lover Who Was Far Way
Juanita
Nuit De Carnaval, Une
Paloma Blanca

Norton *(Cont.)*
Round Her Neck She Wears A Yeller
    Ribbon
Nosov
Far Away Far Away
Novaro
Italian National Anthem
Novello
From Thee All Skill And Science
    Flow
Glory Be To The Father Almighty
    God
Immortal Love Forever Full
Keep The Home Fires Burning
Lo He Comes With Clouds
    Descending
Now From The Altar Of Our Hearts
O Sing Unto The Lord
Once Only Once And Once For All
Novikov
On The River
Strains Of Guitar On The River
Strains Of The Guitar
Nowels & Shipley
Leave A Light On
Nowels & Shipley
Circle In The Sand
Heaven Is A Place On Earth
Nugent
Cat Scratch Fever
Sweet Rosie O'Grady
Nugetre
Chains Of Love
Don't You Know I Love You
Fool Fool Fool
Hey Miss Fannie
Null
I Forgot More Than You'll Ever
    Know
Nuno
Mexicanos Al Grito De Guerra
Valiant Mexicans Bring To Battle
Nusbaum
His Way With Thee
Nutt
Eating Goober Peas
Nutting
Carmen Horae Vespertinae
Nykerk
Collegium
Nyro
And When I Die
Eli's Comin'
Save The Country
Stoned Soul Picnic
Stoney End
Sweet Blindness
Wedding Bell Blues
Nyvall
Idaho Mother Of Mine
O'Brien
Rag Pickers Rag, The
Untold Stories
Walk The Way The Wind Blows

O'Brien & Wallace
With My Shillelagh Under My Arm
O'Bryant
Those Memories Of You
O'Callaghan
Fair Day To-Morrah
O'Casey & O'Casey
Mush Mush Mush Tural-I-Addy
O'Conner
K-K-K-Katy
O'Daniel
Beautiful Texas
O'Day
Angie Baby
Undercover Angel
O'Dea & Clinton
Christmas Candles
O'Dell
Behind Closed Doors
Mama He's Crazy
Thank You Ever-Lovin
Too Much Is Not Enough
O'Donnell
My Pony Boy
O'Donoghue
Single Women
**O'Dowd & Moss & Hay & Craig &
Pickett**
Gusto Blusto
It's A Miracle
Karma Chameleon
Move Away
O'Hara
Art Thou The Christ
At The Rainbow's End
Drop A Little Letter In Your Heart
God's Other Room
Grace Before Meals
Grandpa Tell Me 'Bout The Good
    Old Days
Happy Sheep, The
I Would Weave A Song For You
Isle Of Beautiful Dreams, The
K-K-K-Katy
Let Him In
Man In The Moon, The
O Thou Blessed Christ Our Saviour
Older Women
One More Song For Jesus
Power
Somewhere In The World
Tadpoles
Thanks
There's A Light In The Window
Today Is Mine
United We Stand
O'Hara & Brown & McKinney
Just Because
O'Kane
Enthroned Is Jesus Now
Glorious Fountain
My Mother's Prayer

O'Kane *(Cont.)*
O Think Of The Home Over There
Waiting At The Door
We'll Stand The Storm

O'Keefe
Always A Bridesmaid But Never A
    Bride
Bearded Lady, The
Gambler's Wife, The
Good Time Charlie's Got The Blues
Man On The Flying Trapeze, The
Road, The
Tattooed Lady, The

O'Leary
Teddy O'Neil

O'Malley
Twinkle Twinkle Little Me

O'Mullain
An Poc Arbuile

O'Neal
Back In Town
Shenandoah

O'Neill & Burns
Painted Moon

O'Rourke
Honky Tonk Moon

O'Shay
Paddy Upon The Canal

O'Steen
Oh Sing To The World

O'Sullivan
Alone Again Naturally

Oakeley
Again As Evening's Shadow Falls
All Things Are Thine No Gifts Have
    We
Around The Throne Of God
Around The Throne Of God A Band
At Even Ere The Sun Was Set
It May Not Be Our Lot To Wield
Jesus Thou Joy Of Loving Hearts
O Holy Lord Content To Fill
O Lord Thy Benediction Give
Saviour Blessed Saviour
This Is The Day Of Light

Oakey & Burden
Love Action

Oakey & Callis & Burden
Mirror Man

Oakey & Wright & Callis
Don't You Want Me

Oakland
I'll Dance At Your Wedding
I'll Take Romance
If I Love Again
Java Jive

Oakley
At Even Ere The Sun Was Set
Jesus Let Thy Pitying Eye

Oatman & Excell
Count Your Blessings

Oatman & Gabriel
Higher Ground

Oatman & Hugg
No Not One

Oatman & Marks
Last Mile Of The Way, The

Oatman & Sewell
He Included Me

Obiedo
True Or False

Ocasek
Drive
Emotion In Motion
Good Times Roll
I'm Not The One
Just What I Needed
Let's Go
Magic
My Best Friend's Girl
Shake It Up
Tonight She Comes
Touch And Go
Why Can't I Have You
You Are The Girl
You Might Think

Ocean & Diamond & Lange
Loverboy

Ochs
Bracero
Cops Of The World
I Ain't Marchin' Any More
I Declare The War Is Over
It Must Have Been Another Country
There But For Fortune

Ockeghem
Kyrie

Offenbach
Barcarolla
Barcarolle
Belle Nuit
Belle Nuit O Nuit D'Amour
Can Can
Chanson De Fortunio
Couplets Of The Kings
Fellowship
Garden In The Snow
Gendarmes' Duet
Hammering Nails
Letters From Lovers
Little Doll With China Eyes, A
Lovely Night
Lovely Night O Night Of Love
Marine's Hymn, The
Morning Serenade
O Lovely Night
Rondo
Sabre Of My Father, The
Shoulder To Shoulder
Skating
Song At Dawn
Song Of The Saber
Song Of The Sabre
Summer Song, A

Offenbach *(Cont.)*
Tu N'est Pas Beau
Waltz Song

Ogden
Able To Deliver
Again We'll Never Pass This Way
Bells Of Easter-Time
Bring Them In
Children Of The King
Christ Jesus Died For Sinners
Come To The Feast
Come To The Living Water
Ere On My Bed My Limbs I Lay
Everlasting Life
Eye Of Faith, The
Glory In The Highest
He Calleth Thee
He Is Able To Deliver Thee
I'm So Glad
Idle Stand Not All The Day
Jesus Is Able To Save
Look And Live
Lovingly Tenderly Calling
Marching On To Canaan
More Than Conquerors
My Rock And Shield
O Light Of Light Shine In
Only A Look
Resting Safe With Jesus
Seeking The Lost
Toiling For Jesus
Two Little Hands
Unto You Is Everlasting Life
Welcome Easter Morning
What Shall It Profit Thee
When A Sinner Comes As A Sinner
    May
When Thou Comest
Where He Leads I'll Follow
Who Can It Be
Who Shall Abide
Workers For The Master

Ogden & Gabriel
Brighten The Corner Where You Are

Oginski
Polish National Anthem
Polish National Song

Ogletree
Gethsemane
Heavenly Dove

Oglevee
For The Bible We Thank You

Ohl
Come And Hear The Grand Old
    Story
Daylight Fades, The
Dear Father For Thy Gifts To Me
Guide Me O Thou Great Jehovah
Jesus Master Whose I Am
Love Divine All Love Excelling
Nearer My God To Thee (First Tune)
Thou Art My Hiding Place O Lord
Through The Day Thy Love Hath
    Spared Us

Oiantadosi
In All My Dreams I Dream Of You
Ojea
One Star At Twilight
Okegehm
Benedictiner Munklikor
Olcott
My Beautiful Irish Maid
My Wild Irish Rose
Olcott's Lullaby
Olcott & Ball
Mother Machree
Oldberg
To Thee Eternal Soul Be Praise
Oldfield
Tubular Bells
Oldham & Gaither
Something Worth Livng For
Oldham & Richards
I'd Much Rather Be With The Boys
Olds
All The Past We Leave Behind
As Torrents In Summer
Brave Songs
Burro, The
Come Ye Back To Old Grinnell
Hail Beloit
Trains Up In The Sky
Western College Boating Song, A
Oliphant
Santa Lucia
Oliver
Almighty Builder Bless We Pray
Behold A Stranger
Behold A Stranger's At The Door
Come Gracious Spirit
Dream Of You
Get Right With God
God Calling Yet Shall I Not Hear
Hallelujah
Ihr Kinder Lernt Von Anfang Gern
Itchy Twitchy Feeling
Jesus And Shall It Ever Be
Jesus The Sinner's Friend
Jesus The Sinner's Friend To Thee
My Dear Redeemer And My Lord
O Love Divine
O Sometimes Gleams Upon Our
Sight
O Suff'ring Friend Of Human Kind
Old Glory
Opus One
Past Is Dark With Sin And Shame,
The
Spirit Of Mercy Truth And Love
Sugarfoot Stomp
There Is A Land Mine Eye Hath
Seen
Unto The Calmly Gathered Thought
We Bless Thee Lord
What If
Yes Indeed

Oliver & Carter
Cling A Ling
You're Looking Good
Oliver & Garris
Opus One
Oliver & Wild & Wright
Fire
Oliver & Young
'tain't What You Do
Olivieri
Garibaldi Hymn, The
Garibaldi's Hymn
Garibaldi's War Hymn
Quanno Staje Cu Mme'
Till Good Morning Good Night
Oliviero
Quanno Staje Cu Mme'
Olman
Down Among The Sheltering Palms
Oh Johnny Oh
Oh Johnny Oh Johnny Oh
Olman & Yellen
Down By The O-Hi-O
Olsen & Johnson & Levison & Evans
G'bye Now
Olude
Jesus We Want To Meet
Olvirades
Conga Sabrosa, La
Flor De Lima
Omartian
All My Life
Believing For The Best In You
I'd Rather Believe In You
One More Song For You
Trumpet Of Jesus, The
Omartian & Harris
Praise The Lord He Never Changes
Omartian & Hibbard & Hockensmit
I'm Forgiven
Omartian & Omartian
Time Is Now, The
Trumpet Of Jesus, The
Omartian & Sudano & Gruska
Tell Me I'm Not Dreamin'
Tell Me I'm Not Dreaming
Omartian & Sudano & Jackson
Perfect
OMD
Dreaming
Ondracek
E Flat A Flat
Ono
Beautiful Boys
Every Man Has A Woman Who
Loves Him
Give Me Something
I'm Moving On
Kiss Kiss Kiss
Openshaw
June Brought The Roses
Love Sends A Little Gift Of Roses

Opeskin
Geto Lid
Opie
Communion Hymn
Opler
While We Danced At The Mardi
Gras
Oppleman
Victory Swing, The
Or & Hirsh
Haderech, El
Orange
Hole In My Heart
Oh Wallace
Orbison
Claudette
Falling
In Dreams
Leah
Working For The Man
Orbison & Dees
Breakin' Up Is Breakin' My Heart
Goodnight
It's Over
Oh Pretty Woman
Ride Away
Twinkle Toes
Orbison & Lynne & Petty
California Blue
You Got It
Orbison & Melson
Blue Angel
Blue Bayou
Crowd, The
Crying
I'm Hurtin'
Only The Lonely
Only The Lonely Know The Way I
Feel
Running Scared
Up Town
You're My Girl
Ordonez
Ay Fortuna Cruel
Ay Mudo Soy
Ordway
Dreaming Of Home And Mother
Twinkling Stars Are Laughing Love
Orender & Ware
Midnight Rodeo
Oreste Sindici
Himno Nacional
Original Dixieland Jazz Band
Tiger Rag
Orland & Zeira
Shne Shoshanim
Orland & Zeria
Shir Same-Ach
Orlansky
Tell Me Why
Ormiston
Little Sailors' Song, The

Ornadel
  If I Ruled The World
  Portrait Of My Love, A
Orozco
  Corrido De Dolores Huerta
Orr
  Gonzaga Glorius
  Stay The Night
Orrall & Wright
  Next To You Next To Me
Ortolani
  Forget Domani
  Great Dreamer, The
  Lesson In Love, A
  She's Just A Quiet Girl
Ortolani & Oliviero
  More
Ory
  Muskrat Ramble
Orzabal
  Woman In Chains
Orzabal & Holland
  Advice For The Young At Heart
Orzabal & Smith
  Head Over Heels
  Sowing The Seeds Of Love
Orzabal & Stanley
  Mothers Talk
  Shout
Orzabal & Stanley & Hughes
  Everybody Wants To Rule The
    World
Osborn
  Great Speckled Bird, The
  Just A Closer Walk With Thee
Osborne
  On The Wings Of Love
Osborne & Rogers
  Between 18th And 19th On Chestnut
    Street
Osborne & Sembello & Freeman
  Don't You Get So Mad
Osbourne
  Bark At The Moon
  So Tired
Osgood
  From A By-Gone Day
  Wake Not But Hear Me Love
Osgood & Kienzi
  Old German Shepherd's Song
Oshrat
  Hal'luya
Oshrat & Orr
  Halleluja
Oslin
  Do Ya'
  Hold Me
Oslin & Bourke & Black
  Come Next Monday
Osmond & Sturken & Rogers
  Hold On
Ostlere
  Dutch Dolls

Oteo
  Sierras Of Chipas, The
Other Ones, The
  Holiday
  We Are What We Are
Otis
  So Fine
  Willie And The Hand Jive
  Willie And The Hand-Jive
Otis & Benton
  Endlessly
  Boll Weevil, The
Otis & Benton & Hendricks
  It's Just A Matter Of Time
  Looking Back
Otis & Byers
  What's A Matter Baby
Otis & Corso
  Ties That Bind, The
  This I Promise You
  With This Ring
Otis & Dixon
  Doncha' Think It's Time
Otis & Hendricks
  Call Me
Otis & Lee
  Stroll, The
Otis & Stein
  Baby You've Got What It Takes
  Smooth Operator
Otten & Griffin
  You Can't Be True Dear
Otto
  Contented Heart, A
  Das Treue Deutsche Herz
  Flag Of The Free
  Forget-Me-Not
  Reiterlied
  Standchen
  Treue Deutsche Herz, Das
Ouseley
  Angels Holy
  Easter Flowers Are Blooming Bright
  God Of All Grace Thy Mercy Send
  Jesus Name All Names Above
  O Love Who Formedst Me To Wear
  O What If We Are Christ's
  Radiant Morn Hath Passed Away,
    The
Overholt
  Hallelujah Square
  Ten Thousand Angels
Overstreet
  There'll Be Some Changes Made
Overstreet & Davis
  One Love At A Time
  You're Still New To Me
Overstreet & Gore
  Diggin' Up Bones
Overstreet & Schlitz
  Deeper Than The Holler
  Forever And Ever Amen
  Houston Solution

Overstreet & Schlitz *(Cont.)*
  I Won't Take Less Than Your Love
  I'll Be Loving You
  Like Father Like Son
  My Arms Stay Open All Night
  On The Other Hand
  Richest Man On Earth
  Sowin' Love
  When You Say Nothing At All
  You Again
Overstreet & Stevens
  Cotton Pickin' Time
Owain
  All Through The Night
Owen
  Choose Now
  Come Risen Lord And Deign To Be
    Our Guest
  Daisies Won't Tell
  Face To Face
  Feels So Right
  I Lay My Sins On Jesus
  Lady Down On Love
  Lo He Comes With Clouds
    Descending
  Look Ye Saints The Sight Is Glorious
  Lord Enthroned In Heavenly
    Splendour
  Lord Enthroned In The Heavenly
    Splendor
  Mountain Music
  Open Wide Thy Heart
  Same Old Me, The
  Sweet Bunch Of Daisies
  Tar Top
  What Did He Do
Owen & Gentry
  My Home's In Alabama
Owens
  Behold The Man
  Cocoanut Grove
  Crying Time
  Genius Child
  Hawaiian Paradise
  He's My Friend
  Hi Neighbor
  Holy Holy
  If My People Will Pray
  Just Ask Him
  Linger Awhile
  Lord Is My Shepherd, The
  Once More
  Together Again
Owens & Frazier
  Wearin' That Loved On Look
  Where Did They Go Lord
Owens & Harris & Coley & Lee
  I Met Him On A Sunday
Owens & Kirkpatrick
  Jesus Saves
Owens & Moore
  Sweet Rosanna

Owens & Noble
I've Found A Little Grass Skirt For
My Little Gras
Owens & Owens
Warrior, The
Owens-Collins
How Could I Ever Say No
Owens-Collins & Christian
Look How Far You've Come
Oxenford
Merry Heart, A
Merry June
Oxenford & King
Cricket, The
Oxenford & Trotere
No Lips Can Tell
Oxenham & Reinagle
In Christ There Is No East Or West
Oyler
My Chains Are Broken
Pace
Happy Jubilee, The
It's Not The First Mile
Jesus The Master
Saviour Came In Search Of Me, The
That Glad Reunion Day
Pace & George & Lang
Kyrie
Pace & Paglia & Rekers
Sailing Ships
Pace & Panzeri & Livraghi
Man Without Love, A
Pache
Mag Auch Die Liebe Weinen
Pachelbel
Canon
Canon In D
Pachelbel Canon In D
Theme From Ordinary People
Pacius
Mu Isamaa Mu Onn Jo Roem
My Native Land
Our Land
Pack
Biggest Part Of Me
You're The Only Woman
Pack & Howard
Prove Me Wrong
Paden & Hurt
Show Me The Way
Padilla
Buy My Violets
Princesita
Relicario, El
Valencia
Violetera, La
Who'll Buy My Violets
Paer
Helas Ciest Pres De Vous
Si L'hymen A Quelque Douceur
Page
Shoulder To Cry On, A
Page & Cox & Drummie
King Of Wishful Thinking

Page & Funderburk
It's Not Enough
Page & George & Lang
Broken Wings
Kyrie
Kyrie Eleison
Stand And Deliver
Page & George & Lang & Mastelotto
Is It Love
Page & Jones & Bonham
Good Times Bad Times
Page & Knight & Wood
I'll Be Your Everything
Page & Panzeri & Livraghi
Man Without Love, A
Page & Plant
Immigrant Song
Living Loving Maid
Song Remains The Same, The
Stairway To Heaven
Page & Plant & Jones
Black Dog
Page & Plant & Jones & Bonham
Heartbreaker
Rock And Roll
Whole Lotta Love
Paich
Hold The Line
Make Believe
Miss Sun
Rosanna
Stranger In Town
Paich & Howard
Lady Love Me
Lady Love Me One More Time
Paich & Porcaro
Africa
Paich & Porcaro & Porcaro & Porcaro & Lukathe
Dune
Paich & Williams
Pamela
Paikov
Eretz Eretz
Eretz Yisrael Yafa
Sim Shalom
Paine
Azara
Commencement Hymn
Not Alone For Mighty Empire
St Peter
Through The Night Of Doubt And
Sorrow
Paisielllo
Nel Cor Piu Non Mi Sento
Paisiello
Forever With The Lord
Je Suis Lindor
My Heart No Longer Dances
Nel Cor Piu Non Mi Sento
Why Is My Heart So Heavy
Paisley
Razorback Pep Song

Palacio
Steel Battalions, The
Palacios
Granada, A
Paladilhe
Mandolin Song, The
Mandolinata
Psyche
Russian Song
Palas & Robinson & Jarrard
There's No Way
You've Got The Touch
Palestrina
Adoramus Te
Adoramus Te Christe
Agnus Dei
Alleluia
Alleluia The Strife Is O'Er
Benedictus Qui Venit
Come Holy Ghost
Dona Nobis Pacem
Ecce Quomodo Moritur
Gloria Patri
Glory To God
Good Christian Men Rejoice And
Sing
Holy Holy Holy
Illumina Oculos Meos
Improperia
Jesu Rex Admirabilis
Lord Of Mercy
Morning Hymn
O Bone Jesu
O Holy Jesu
Strife Is O'er, The
Strife Is O'er The Battle Done, The
Tenebrae Factae Sunt
Thy Grace Impart
Ye Sons And Daughters Of The Lord
Paley
Keep On Smiling
Sweet Little Buttercup
Palmer
Addicted To Love
Angry Words
Angry Words Oh Let Them Never
Aunt Jemima Jingle
Band Played On, The
Childhood's Gold
Come Close To The Saviour
Come Sinner Come
Come Where Joy And Gladness
God Of Our Fathers Known Of Old
Hark The Voice Of Jesus Calling
Haste Traveller Haste The Night
Comes On
Have Courage My Boy To Say No
Have You Seen That Maid Of Mine
Just For To-Day
Keep Step Ever
Little Maid Margery
Lord For Tomorrow And Its Needs
Master The Tempest Is Raging
Memories Of Galilee

Palmer *(Cont.)*
Morning Train
Peace Be Still
Praise Ye The Lord
Sensible Girl, The
Simply Irresistible
Stonewall Jackson's Way
Way-Side Cross, The
While Jesus Whispers
While Jesus Whispers To You
Yield Not To Temptation

Palmer & Bugatti
When He Shines

Palmer & King
Jazzman
Nightingale
Wrap Around Joy
You Go Your Way I'll Go Mine
You're Something New

Palmer & Mason
My Faith Looks Up To Thee

Palmer & Spencer
Everybody Loves My Baby But My
Baby Don't Nobody But Me

Palmer & Taylor & Taylor
Some Like It Hot

Palmer & Taylor & Taylor & Bramble
Communication

Palmer & Van Ness
Silver Dollar

Palmer & Williams
Everbody Loves My Baby

Palmgren
Birds' Winter Song
Boat Glides Slowly, A
Mother
Song Of The Ants

Palumbo & Purnell & Halligan
Don't Close Your Eyes

Pammelia
Follow Me Quickly
Sing After Me
Sing We This Roundelay
We Lack Money To Make Us Merry

Pankov
You Are On My Mind

Pankow
Colour My World
Make Me Smile
Old Days
Searchin' So Long
Searching So Long
White Easter Lilies, The
You Are On My Mind

Pantchenko
Star, The

Panzuti
Echoes In The Night
Only Love Me

Papale
Cup Of Blessing That We Share

Paper & Jurmann
San Francisco

Paradies
Brooklet, The

Pardove
Negra Consentida

Pare
Weary Pilgrim's Consolation, The

Paris
Do I Trust You
I Will Never Go
Keepin' My Eyes On You
Lamb Of God
Runner
Warrior Is A Child, The

Park
Fair Radcliffe

Parker
All My Heart This Night Rejoices
Baby Sittin' Boogie
Barefootin'
Beneath The Shadow Of The Cross
Blues Get Off My Shoulder
Christ Is Our Cornerstone
Come O Come My Life's Delight
Complacent Lover, The
Forth In Thy Name O Lord I Go
Ghostbusters
Girls Are More Fun
God Hath Sent His Angels
God Hath Sent His Angels To The
Earth Again
God Moves In A Mysterious Way
God Of The Nations Who From
Dawn
Gold And Blue
Good Night Song, A
He That Loves A Rosy Cheek
How Firm A Foundation
I Still Can't Get Over Loving You
I'll Be A Voice
Jamie
Jerusalem
Just The Old Story Soft And Low
Lark Now Leaves His Watery Nest,
The
Love Is A Sickness Full Of Woes
Master No Offering
Master No Offering Costly And
Sweet
Morning Song
Mr Telephone Man
National Hymn
O 'Twas A Joyful Sound To Hear
Oh Where Do Fairies Hide Their
Heads
On Wings Of Living Light
Other Woman, The
Our Day Of Praise Is Done
Praise The Lord
Quasimodo
Recruit, The
Rejoice The Lord Is King
Rejoice The Lord Of Life Ascends
Rowing

Parker *(Cont.)*
Royal Banners Forward Go, The
Scrapple From The Apple
Send Down Thy Truth O God
Theme From Chips
Trapper John Md
Two Places At The Same Time
Up Front
Village Of St Bernadette, The
We Old Boys
When The King Enjoys His Own
Again
When The King Shall Enjoy His
Own
You Can't Change That
Your Love For Me

Parker & Challinor
Tell Me The Stories Of Jesus

Parker & Charles
We'll Meet Again

Parker & Harris
Ornithology

Parker & Rainger
I Wished On The Moon

Parker & Sanicola
This Love Of Mine

Parkhurst
Drunkard's Child, The
Father's A Drunkard And Mother Is
Dead
Katy Did Katy Didn't
Open Door, The
Psalm Of Praise, A

Parkins
By Thy Spirit Lead Me

Parks
Boys Who Wear The Blue
Cab Driver
How It Happened
Lord's Prayer, The
My Pony
Somethin' Stupid

Parks & Turnbow
Bread And Butter

Parnell
Blackbird Of Sweet Avondale, The
House Of Peers And The Home Rule
Bill, The
Lines On The Phoenix Park Tragedy
Lisnagade
We Won't Let Our Leader Down

Parnes & Evans
Happiness Is

Parody
Frisco Strike Saga

Parr
Naughty Naughty
Two Hearts

Parra
Por Un Amor

Parratt
I Need Thee Ev'ry Hour

Parris
In The Still Of The Night

Parry
ABC
And Did Those Feet In Ancient Time
Bard's Visit, The
By Gracious Powers So Wonderfully
    Sheltered
Cambrian Triplet, The
Cymru Fydd
Dear Lord And Father
Dear Lord And Father Of Mankind
Eiluned
Fear No More The Heat O' The Sun
Flow Gently Deva
Great Western Land
Holy Spirit Lord Of Love
Huntsmen's Chorus
Jenny Jones
Jesu Lover Of My Soul
Jesus Lover Of My Soul
Lullaby
Mary's Song
Minstrel's Desire, The
My Blodwen
Norah The Pride Of Kildare
O Brother Man Fold To Thy Heart
O Brother Man Fold To Thy Heart
    Thy Brother
O Day Of Peace That Dimly Shines
O Lord Abide With Me
O Praise Ye The Lord
Old Blind Harper, The
Our Fathers Where Are They
Place Where We Met, The
Round The Lord In Glory Seated
Sailor' Glee
Sailor's Song, The
Saint David
Saint Gwyndav
Saviour When In Dust To Thee
Sing We Of The Blessed Mother
Song Of Joy, A
Spring Song, A
Watchman Tell Us Of The Night
Parsons
Christ Leads Me Through No Darker
    Rooms
He Made A Way
Old Time Way
Sweet Beulah Land
Partichela
Jarabe Tapatio
Mexican Hat Dance
Partlow
Talking Atomic Blues
Parton
Coat Of Many Colors
Daddy Was An Old Time Preacher
    Man
Everything's Beautiful In Its Own
    Way
God Won't Get You
I Believe In Santa Claus
I Will Always Love You

Parton *(Cont.)*
Jolene
Kentucky Gambler
Light Of A Clear Blue Morning
Love Is Like A Butterfly
Nine To Five
Seeker, The
Tennessee Homesick Blues
Traveling Man
Two Doors Down
Waltz Me To Heaven
Wildflowers
Yellow Roses
Parton & Davis
White Limozeen
Parton & Hobbs
I Want To Know You Before We
    Make Love
Parton & Owens
Put It Off Until Tomorrow
Partridge
Mayor Of Simpleton, The
Partridge & Seaver
Just For Today
Pascoe & Carlo & Sanders
When I Dream Of My Ould Kerry
    Home
Pasqua & Spiro
I'll See You In My Dreams
Pasquale
I Remember Holding You
Passereau
Il Est Bel Et Bon
Pastor
Hymn At Nightfall
Plegaria
Pastorius
Punk Jazz
Teen Town
Patillo
Cornerstone
Go
I've Heard The Thunder
Love Calling
One Thing Leads To Another
Star Of The Morning
The Sky's The Limit
Paton & Lyall
Magic
Patrichala
Mexican Hat Dance
Patterson
Billy The Kid
Dry-Landers, The
I'd Like To Be In Texas When They
    Round Up In The
Lone Driftin' Riders
Make Me A Cowboy Again For A
    Day
Old Black Outlaw Steer
On The Red River Shore
Roll Out Cowboys
Roy Bean
Utah Carl's Last Ride

Patterson *(Cont.)*
Wandering Cow Boy, The
Whoa Skew 'Til I Saddle Yea Whoa
Willie The Whistling Giraffe
Patterson & Heyward
Mary's Little Boy
Patterson & Treadwell & Nelson
There Goes My Baby
Pattison
Hancock Is Coming
Patton
Down The Dirt Road Blues
High Water Everywhere
March Of The Armored Corps
Pony Blues
Patty
Coe Loyalty
Paul
All My Children
Broken Doll, The
Cardinal Is Waving, The
Namely You
Poets
Rain Song
Ten Commandments Of Love, The
Where
Paul & Cosby
Fingertips Part 2
Pauling & Bass
Dedicated To The One I Love
Paulter
I Watched One Hour With The
    Savior
I Watched One Hour With The
    Saviour
Paxton
Fare The Well Cisco
Happy Anniversary
He Was There All The Time
Hey You Little Brand New Baby
How Sweet How Fresh This Vernal
    Day
I Can't Help But Wonder Where I'm
    Bound
I Can't See Me Servin' Nobody But
    Jesus
Lord I Need You Right Now
No Shortage
Pictures On Paper
Talking Death Of God
We Didn't Know
What Did You Learn In School
    Today
Willing Conscript, The
Woman
Paxton & Gaither
More Of You
Paxton & Gaither & Gaither
Learning To Live Like A Child Of
    The King
World Didn't Give It To Me And
    The World Can't Tak

Paxton & Hellard
Great Divide, The
Honeymoon Feelin'
Paxton & Paxton
I'm Anchored In The Rock Of Ages
Paxton, Tom
Bottle Of Wine
Going To The Zoo
Last Thing On My Mind, The
Marvelous Toy, The
My Dog's Bigger Than Your Dog
My Ramblin' Boy
Whose Garden Was This
Payne
Baylor Bears, The
Beautiful Nazarene, The
Cloud He's Comin' Back On, The
I Love You Because
Just In Case Of Rapture
Lather And Shave
Lost Highway
Ready Or Not
They'll Never Take Her Love From
   Me
You've Still Got A Place In My
   Heart
Payne & Bishop
Home Sweet Home
Payne & Hinson
Who But God
Paz
Me Di Jiste Cierto Dia
Peace
And Now My Soul Another Year
Beneath The Shadow Of The Cross
Breathe On Me Breath Of God
Darling I Am Coming Back
Immortal Love Within Whose
   Righteous Will
Love That Wilt Not Let Me Go
Majestic Sweetness Sits Enthroned
O Love That Will Not Let Me Go
Religion Is The Chief Concern
Salvete Cives Nostri
Why Should Our Tears In Sorrow
   Flow
Peacock
Vignette
Pearce
Gloria Tibi
It's My Desire
Men Of England
Pearl
You Never Gave Up On Me
Pearsall
Before The Cross Of Jesus
Beneath The Cross Of Jesus
Christmas Holly
In Dulci Jubilo
O Who Will O'er The Downs
O Who Will O'er The Downs So
   Free
Sing We And Chaunt It

Pearsall *(Cont.)*
When Allen A Dale Went A Hunting
World Is Very Evil, The
Pearson
Jeannine
Ploughboy, The
Plowboy, The
Red River Valley
Thousand Stars, A
Pease
Break Break Break
Charles E Hughes The American
Dash Away Boat
Princeton Days
Stars Of The Summer Night
Pease & Nelson & Dodge
Peggy O'Neil
Pease & Nelson & Fier
My Name Is Kelly But I'm Living
   The Life Of Reilly
Pease & Nelson & Johnson
In The Old Town Hall
Peavey
Men Of State
Pecha
There Is No Place Like Nebraska
Peck
Sister Carrie
Pedrell
Dreaming And Waking
If He Should Return
J'ai Pleure En Reve
Ma Mere L'oie
Yeux Qui Songent, Les
Pedrette
O Perfect Love
Pedro
Hasta La Vista
Pedro IV
National Hymn Of Portugal
Peek
Don't Cross The River
I Would Be True
Lonely People
Peel
In The Highlands
Sorrow And Spring
Peels & Manigo
Lover's Island
Peery
Dear Lord Who Sought At Dawn Of
   Day
God Shall Wipe Away All Tears
Peeters
Joyful Mysteries, The
Pegram
Bleached Shirt, The
Pelay & Le Govic
Do I Love You Yes In Every Way
Pelz
Come Let Us With Our Lord Arise
Pena
Basta Ya
Jet Airliner

Pendarvis & Carnes
After Hours
Pendergrass
Greatest Thing, The
Pendleton & Seal & Dandrige
In Your Heart
Penet
Au Joly Bois A L'ombre D'un Soucy
Il Fait Bon Aimer L'oisillon
Penick
Loving Kindness
Penn
Carissima
Honeysuckle And The Bee, The
Lamplit Hour, The
Leave It All With Jesus
No Myth
Others
Overtime
Smilin' Through
They Will Be Done
Union Man
Walking And Talking With Jesus
Penn & Oldham
Cry Like A Baby
I'm Your Puppet
Sweet Inspiration
Penney & Oates
Welcome Stranger
Pennig & Harrington
Killin' Time
Penniman
Bama Lama Bama Loo
Boo Hoo Hoo Hoo
Hey Hey Hey
Hey Hey Hey Hey
Penniman & Johnson
Jenny Jenny
Penniman & Bocage & Collins & Smith
Slippin' And Slidin'
Penniman & Johnson
Miss Ann
Penniman & Johnson & Blackwell
Long Tall Sally
Penniman & La Bostrie
Tutti Frutti
Pennington
Ramblin' Man
Walking On New Grass
Woke Up In Love
Pennington & Marcum
Don't Cheat In Our Home Town
Pennino
Pecche
Penny & Gillespie
Somebody's Knockin'
Pennywacker
Dogwood Dell
Penrose
Whitman Here's To You
Pepper
We're Soldiers With Wings

Percival
Carol For The Sunday After
Christmas, A
God's Own Son
Longfellow's Carol
Troubador's Carol, A

Percy & Coy & Burns & Lever
You Spin Me Round Like A Record

Peretti & Creatore & Weiss & Stanton
Lion Sleeps Tonight, The

Peretz & Aharoni
En Gedi

Perez
Se Me Sigue Olvidando
Te Amare

Perez Freire
Ay Ay Ay

Perez Y Soto
Cigarra, La

Pergolesi
Glory To God In The Highest
If Thou Love Me
If 'Tis For Me
Nina
On Serpina Think With Pleasure
Que Ne Suis Je La Fougere
Se Tu M'ami Se Sospiri
Tre Giorni Son Che Nina

Peri
Invocation Of Orpheus

Perkins
As Stars Come With The Night
Battling For The Lord
Beautiful Land
Beyond The Smiling And The
Weeping
Blessed Be The Fountain
Blessed Redeemer
Blue Suede Shoes
Bolero
Bye-Lo
Cabin In The Cotton
Calling Thee Home
Carol Sweetly Carol
Christ Is Coming
Christ Is Risen
City Of Our God, The
Cling Close To The Rock
Come With Thy Broken Heart
Daddy Sang Bass
Dixiefried
Even Me
Everybody's Trying To Be My Baby
Fade Fade Each Earthly Joy
Gospel Light, The
Honey Don't
I'm A Pilgrim Going Home
I'm Kneeling At The Door
Is It Nothing To Me
Jesus Calls Thee
Jesus I Long For Thee
Jesus Is Mine
Jesus My All

Perkins (Cont.)
Jesus Of Nazareth Passeth By
Jesus Still Lead On
Jesus Then I Know
Keep Thou My Way
Light Of God Is Falling
Love Of Jesus
Master Is Calling, The
Matchbox
Mine The Cross
Morning Light Is Breaking, The
My Saviour Knows
Nearer My Home
Nearer The Fount
O Thou My Soul Forget No More
Oh To Be Nearer Thee
Only Here For A Little While
Praise Ye Jehovah
Resting By The Well
Return O Wanderer
Sentimental Gentleman From
Georgia
Stars Fell On Alabama
Upon The Solid Rock
Wanderer, The
What Then
Whiter Than Snow
Who Will To The Greenwood Hie
Will That Not Joyful Be
Work For The Master

Perkins & Parish
Stars Fell On Alabama

Perkinson
Melancholy

Perlmutter & Wohl
Lebn Zol Kolombus

Pero
Burning Bush, The
Memories

Peron
To Thee We Sing O Columbia

Perosi
Jesus Lord Be Thou Mine Own

Perper & Gasper & Aranda
Still Waters Run Deep

Perre
Pep Song

Perren
Hallelujah Day

Perren & Yarian
It's So Hard To Say Goodbye To
Yesterday

Perronet & Holden
All Hail The Power Of Jesus' Name

Perry
Angels Praise Him
By Flowing Waters Of Babylon
Calypso Carol
Come Sing Praises To The Lord
Above
Father In Thy Mysterious Prescence
Kneeling
Hail Vermont
I Never Will Marry

Perry (Cont.)
I Will Never Marry
Jubilate Everybody
Let Me Now Depart In Peace
Lonesome Tunes
Lovin' Touchin' Squeezin'
Mary Sang A Song
Night Flight
O Happy Home Where Thou Art
Loved
Oberlin Pep Song
Party's Over, The
Sound Loud The Trumpet
Time The Fiddler
To The Praise Of God The Father
Where Would We All Be Now

Perry & Cain
Open Arms
Send Her My Love
Separate Ways
Suzanne
Who's Crying Now

Perry & Candullo & Ceade
Christmas Symphony, The

Perry & Cuomo & Krampf
Oh Sherrie

Perry & Goodrum
Foolish Heart
If Only For The Moment Girl

Perry & Schon
Dixie Highway
Good Morning Girl
Stay Awhile

Perry & Schon & Cain
Be Good To Yourself
Don't Stop Believin'
Escape
Girl Can't Help It
I'll Be Alright Without You
Only The Young
Still They Ride

Perry & Young
Tattletale Tears

Persichetti
Hallelujah Bum Again
Preface To Canons
Should Fancy Cease

Persico
Rota Si Fa In Cielo, Una

Person
How Long O Lord How Long
What Shall I Do

Perti
Dolce Scherza

Peruchino
Gondolier, The

Pessard
Good-Day Marie

Pessis & Wells
Never Get Enough Of You

Pestalozza
Ciribiribin

Peter
Bread Of Heaven On Thee We Feed
Gott Ist Mein Hort
Jolly Coppersmith, The
Leite Mich In Deiner Wahrheit
O Anblick Der Mirs Herze Bricht

Peterik & Sullivan
American Heartbeat
Burning Heart
Eye Of The Tiger
I Can't Hold Back
Is This Love
Search Is Over, The

Peterik & Sullivan & Smith
Rockin' Into The Night

Peters
Daytime Friends
Draw Us To Thee
Fourteen Ninety-Two
Frog And Owl
Kiss An Angel Good Mornin'
Let Me Live
Lost My Baby Blues
Misty Memories
One More Time For Love
Prayer For All Airmen, A
Rah For The Black And Blue
Turn The World Around
You're So Good When You're Bad

Peters & Keith
Before The Next Teardrop Falls

Peters & McDonald
Walk Forever By My Side

Peterson
Blues Of The Prairies
But Jesus Would
Calling
Don't Let The Song Go Out Of Your
    Heart
He Owns The Cattle
He Walked That Lonesome Road
Heaven Came Down And Glory
    Filled My Soul
Hogtown Blues
I Believe In Miracles
I Surrender All
In The Garden Of Gethsemane
It Took A Miracle
It's A Wonderful Wonderful Life
It's Not An Easy Road
Jesus Is Coming Again
Lady Moon
Like Him
Looking For Jesus
No One Understands Like Jesus
O That You Would Meet My Jesus
Over The Sunset Mountains
Share Jesus With Others
So Send I You-By Grace Made
    Strong
Springs Of Living Water
There Is No Greater Love
Who Cares
Will You Be Ready

Peterson & Igleheart
Be With You

Peterson & Smith
Surely Goodness And Mercy
Why Worry When You Can Pray

Pether
Poor John
Waiting At The Church

Petkere
Close Your Eyes
Lullaby Of The Leaves

Petrassi
Alla Sera
Benedizione
Invito All'erano
Io Qui Vagando
Keepsake
Lamento D'arianna
Tramontata E La Luna

Petrie
Asleep In The Deep
At Rest In Thee
I Don't Want To Play In Your Yard
Roll On Thou Deep And Dark Blue
    Ocean
Where The Sunset Turns The
    Ocean's Blue To Gold

Petrillo & Samuels
Jim

Petrocokino
Workers Carol

Petteteri
I Beg Your Pardon Dolly Parton

Pettinos & Hutchinson
Song Of Arbor Day

Pettis & Meyers & Schoebel
Bugle Call Rag

Pettman
Angel Gabriel From Heaven Came,
    The

Petty
Change Of Heart
Don't Do Me Like That
Waiting, The
Wheels

Petty & Campbell
Stop Draggin' My Heart Around
You Got Lucky

Petty & Dylan & Campbell
Jammin' Me

Petty & Hardin
Every Day
Not Fade Away

Petty & Holly
True Love Ways

Petty & Lynne
Face In The Crowd, A
Free Fallin'
I Won't Back Down
Yer So Bad

Petty & Lynne & Campbell
Runnin' Down A Dream

Petty & Stewart
Don't Come Around Here No More

Peuschel
Edelweiss

Pevernage
D'etre Amoureux

Peyce
Five Fat Turkeys

Peyretti
O Notte
Ora Che Sale Il Giorno

Pfautsch
Christian Dost Thou See Them
I Want A Principle Within

Pfeifer
Free To Be Lonely Again
Perfect Fool
Play Something We Could Love To

Pfeil
At Evening
Serenade
Still Is The Lake

Pfitzner
Gartner, Der
Gewalt Der Minne
Ich Aber Weiss
Im Herbst
Klage
Mude
Nachts
Sehnsucht
Sonst
Untreu Und Trost
Zorn
Zum Abschied Meiner Tochter

Pflueger
When All The World Is Young Lad

Pfrimmer & Giles
You Put The Beat In My Heart

Pfrimmer & Morris
Matador, The

Pfrimmer & Reid
I Never Quite Got Back
I Never Quite Got Back From Loving
    You

Pheatt
Bumblebee, A

Phelge (see also Jagger & Richards)
2120 South Michigan Avenue
Empty Heart
Play With Fire
Stoned
Under Assistant West Coast
    Promotion Man, The

Phelps
Annie And I
Female Suffrage
Gaining Ground
O Morning Land
Over The Line
Sure Of It All

Phile
Hail Columbia
President's March, The

Philidor
Brilliant Dans Mon Emploi
Chanter Rire Et Boire, A
Petits Enfants, Les

Philippe-Gerard
When The World Was Young

Philips
One Sweetly Solemn Thought
San Francisco

Philips & Hinsche
Automan

Phillips
Birds' Picnic
By My Spirit
Charioteers, The
College Hymn
Florida Blues, The
Hands Of Jade
Here He Comes With My Heart
I Will Sing You A Song
Marines' Hymn, The
McSorley's Twins
Pray Brethren Pray
Rumpelstiltzkin
Son Of The Desert Am I, A
Strength Of My Life
Strings In The Earth And Air
Your Kindness

Phillips & Diamond
Restless

Phillips & Parker
Mystery Train

Phillips & Phillips
California Dreamin'

Phillips, John
Monday Monday
San Francisco

Philp
Jewel Of Asia, The

Philpot
Lazy Luke

Phinot
Pleurez Me Yeux

Phippen
Message, The

Phyle
Hail Columbia

Piantadosi
Baby Shoes
Curse Of An Aching Heart, The
I Didn't Raise My Boy To Be A
Soldier
In All My Dreams I Dream Of You
My Mariuccia Take A Steamboat
That's How I Need You

Piccini
Ah Que Je Fus Bien Inspiree
Depart Des Cavaliers, Le
Eloge Du Temps Passe
Je Mourrai
Objets Perdus, Les

Pick
Wiener Fiakerlied

Picket & Capizza
Monster Mash

Pickett
Abiding And Confiding
Great Judgement Morning, The
Great Judgment Morning, The
In The Midnight Hour

Pickett & Cropper
In The Midnight Hour
Midnight Hour, The

Pieraccini
O Maker Of The Sea And Sky

Pierce
Behold I Will Show
Cheer For Old Amherst
Horse To Trot

Pierce & Louie Louie
Sittin' In The Lap Of Luxury

Pierne
En Barque
Serenade

Pierpont
Bjelleklang
Chinatown
Dancing
Happy Song, A
In A Hickory Nut
Jingle Bells
Joe Hardy
Little Rippling Brook
Scissors Grinder, The
Silver Maple Leaves
Song Without Words
Strike For The South
Tick Tock
We Conquer Or Die

Pierpont & Kocher
For The Beauty Of The Earth

Pierson & Schneider & Strickland & Wilson
Love Shack
Roam

Piety
O Bethlehem Beloved

Pigott & Mountain
Jesus I Am Resting

Pike
Bless The Lord
Gentle Nettie Moore
Grave Of Washington
Happy Are We Tonight
Home Again

Pilat & Panzeri
Love Me Tonight

Pilkington
Amynatas With His Phyllis Fair
Downe-A-Downe
Have I Found Her
Look Mistress Mine
Palaemon And His Sylvia
Rest Sweet Nymphs
What Though Her Frowns
Why Should I Grieve

Pillar & Gruska & Cain
He'll Shine His Light On You

Pillar & Laird
I Want To Make A Difference

Pinard
Walk In Peace

Pinette
King Of The Hill

Pingree
Good-Night

Pinkard
Mammy O Mine

Pinkard & Tracey & Tauber
Them There Eyes

Pinna
What Fairy-Like Music

Pinsuti
Bedouin Love Song
Bugler, The
I Fear No Foe
I Love My Love
If
If Love Were What The Rose Is
Lead Kindly Light
Queen Of The Earth
Sovvenir
There Is A Reaper
Welcome Pretty Primrose
What Jack Will Say

Pinz & Leka
Green Tambourine

Pippa & Dipaolo
Lonely Teenager

Pippin & Hurt
Ain't No Trick
Ain't No Trick It Takes Magic

Pippin & Keith
My World Begins And Ends With
You

Pippin & Newton
Girl Most Likely To, The

Pippin & Spriggs
Runaway Heart

Piron
I Wish I Could Shimmy Like My
Sister Kate

Piroznikov
Concerning A Kid

Pisador
A Las Armas Moriscote
Aquellas Sierras Madre
Flerida Para Mi Dulce
Gentil Cavallero
Guarte Guarte Rey Don Sancho
Mal Ferida Va La Garca
Manana De Sant Juan, La
Para Qu'es Dama
Partense Partiendo Yo
Passando El Mar Leandro
Pues Te Partes Y Te Vas
Quien Huviesse Tal Ventura
Quien Tuviesse Tal Poder
Si La Noche Haze Escura
Si Te Quitasse Los Hierros

Pisador *(Cont.)*
Si Te Vas A Banar Juanica
Y Con Que La Lavare
Pisani
Strong Of Body High Of Spirit
Pisek
Lovers' Quarrel, The
Pistilli
Too Gone Too Long
Pistilli & Seals
Baby You'll Be My Baby
Pitcher
Breakfast Time
Down And Back
Forest Ranger, The
Good Morning
Great River
Little Turtle, The
Long Trip, A
Look Both Ways
Lovely Color, A
Mary's Lamb
Musical Mix Up, A
My Quiet Place
My Radio
New Simple Simon
On Parade
Plan, A
Rainbow
Russian Cradle Song
Song
Subtraction
Telltale, The
They're Useful
Three Sailors
Trapeze Man, The
Tree Toad, The
Two To One
Under-The-Table Manners
Waves And I, The
We Give Thanks
Whistling Boy, The
Willow Plate, The
Young Puss
Pitchford
Almost Paradise
Let's Hear It For The Boy
Pitchford & Cain & Page
Sing
Pitchford & Lawrence
Birthday Suit
Pitchford & Leonard
Romance
Pitchford & Snow
After All
Pitchford & Wolfer
One Sunny Day
Pitman
Balm
Pitney
He's A Rebel
Pitt & Waltzer
My True Story

Pittari
Sciuri Sciuriddu
Pitts
Church In The Wildwood, The
Little Brown Church In The Vale,
The
Little Brown Church, The
Pitts & Egan & Marsh
I Never Knew I Could Love
Anybody Like I'm Loving You
Piufsich
I Have No Tiled Hut
Pizzetti
Augurio
Canzone Per Ballo
Clefta Prigione, Il
Donna Lombarda
E Il Mio Dolore Io Canto
Erotica
Levommi Il Mio Pensier In Parte
Ov'era
Madre Al Figlio Lontano, La
Mirologio Per Un Bambino
Oscuro E Il Ciel
Passeggiata
Pastori, I
Pesca Dell'anello, La
Prigioniera, La
Quel Rosignuol Chese Soave Piagne
San Basilio
Vita Fugge E Non S'Arresta Un'ora,
La
Planche
Far O'er Hill And Dell
Love's Ritornella
Spring Gentle Spring
Plank
Lord Is My Light And Salvation, The
Planquette
In The Armor
Legend Of Normandy, A
Legend Of The Bell, The
Legend Of The Bells
On Billow Rocking
Regiment De Sambre Et Meuse, Le
Regiment Of The Sambre And
Meuse, The
Regiment Of The Sambre And The
Meuse, The
Silent Heroes
Waltz Song
Planson
Puis Que Le Ciel Veut Ainsi
Plant & Blunt
Pledge Pin
Plant & Blunt & Woodroffe
Burning Down One Side
Plant & Johnstone
Shop Of Fools
Tall Cool One
Plater & Bradshaw & Johnson
Jersey Bounce

Playford
God Moves In A Mysterious Way
O God Whom Neither Time Nor
Space
This Is The Day The Lord Hath
Made
Plaza
Cancioncilla Romantica Venezolana
Four Birds
Golpe
Green Palm, The
Night Comes To The Valley
Shadow Came Down The Mountain,
The
Shroud For Love, A
While My Horse Tarries
Yet Was I Gloomy And Silent
Pleyel
Child's Prayer, A
Children Of The Heav'nly King
Children Of The Heavenly King
Come My Soul Thy Suit Prepare
Geist Vom Vater Und Vom Sohn
Hasten Sinner To Be Wise
In Quiet Hours The Tranquil Soul
Life Of All That Lives Below
Lord We Come Before Thee Now
O Come Creator Spirit
O Come Creator Spirit Come
O Thou To Whose All Searching
Sight
O Thou To Whose All-Searching
Sight
On This Stone Now Laid With
Prayer
Pleyel's Hymn
Praise Lord For Thee In Zion Waits
Praise To God Immortal Praise
Sinners Turn Why Will Ye Die
Sovereign Ruler Of The Skied
Thirsting For The Living Spring
Thou Lord Of Life
Thou One In All
To Thy Temple I Repair
While Thee I Seek Protecting Power
With All The Powers My Poor Heart
Hath
Plotz
'S Bluemli
Plumer
To Wooster U
Plummer
Right To Work Lie, The
Plumptre & Messiter
Rejoice Ye Pure In Heart
**Plunkett & Isham & Rand & Richards &
Lynch**
Turn Up The Radio
Pober
Tiny Bubbles
Pockriss
Big Daddy
Happy Birthday Jesus

Pockriss *(Cont.)*
Johnny Angel
My Little Corner Of The World
Poe & Grier
Object Of My Affection, The
Poirier
Walkin' Sinai
Pokrass
Moscow
Should Our Land Be Attacked
Pola & Steininger
Marching Along Together
Pola & Wyle
I Love The Way You Say Goodnight
I Said My Pajamas
Poldowski
Crepuscule Du Soir Mystique
Mandoline
Polikarp
I Will Go To The Swift River
Politi & Curinga
Those Oldies But Goodies
Polk
Dandelion
Dandelion Seed
Polla
Gondolier, The
Pollack
Cheatin' On Me
Sing Baby Sing
That's A Plenty
Two Cigarettes In The Dark
You Do The Darn'dest Things Baby
Pollard
Last Safe Place On Earth, The
Pollard & Stebbins
Have Thine Own Way Lord
Pollock
Jesus I Love Thy Charming Name
O Come Weary One
Remember Me
Polnareff
Lipstick
Pomeranz
It's In Every One Of Us
Tryin' To Get The Feeling Again
Pomeranz & Kaye
Old Songs, The
Pomus
Lonely Avenue
Pomus & Jeffreys
I Feel That I've Known You Forever
Pomus & Meade
Girl Happy
Pomus & Shuman
Double Trouble
Gonna Get Back Home Somehow
His Latest Flame
Hushabye
Kiss Me Quick
Little Sister
Mess Of Blues, A
Never Say Yes
Night Rider

Pomus & Shuman *(Cont.)*
No One
Save The Last Dance For Me
Suspicion
Teenager In Love, A
This Magic Moment
True Love True Love
Viva Las Vegas
What Every Woman Lives For
Ponce
Estrellita
Serenata
Ponchielli
Dance Of The Hours
Poncia & Starr
Oh My My
Pond
All Praise To Our Redeeming Lord
Missionary Song
What Shall I Render To My God
Poniatowski
Yeoman's Wedding Song, The
Pontius
O Thou Whom All Thy Saints Adore
Oft In Danger Oft In Woe
Waiting And Watching
Poole
Brush Creek
From Many Ways And Wide Apart
God Of The Nations Near And Far
Poole & Gabriel
Just When I Need Him Most
Popp
Love Is Blue
Popp & Lucchesi
Portuguese Washerwomen, The
Porcaro & Bettis
Human Nature
Porta
Erasi Al Sole Il Mio Bel Sole Assiso
Portnoy & Angelo
Every Time I Turn Around
Portal
Sweet And Gentle
Porter
Annabelle Birby
Barnyard Cogitations
Bingo That's The Lingo
Buddy Won't You Roll Down The
Line
Could It Be You
Ella Ree
Far Away
Football King, A
Happy Heaven Of Harlem
I Loved Him But He Didn't Love Me
I'm Getting Myself Ready For You
I'm In Love
I'm In Love With A Soldier Boy
Kling-Kling Bird On Top Of The
Divi-Divi Tree, The
Laziest Gal In Town, The
Leave It To Me

Porter *(Cont.)*
Looking At You
Love Letter Words
Make It Another Old Fashioned
Please
Me And Marie
My Long Ago Girl
Now You Has Jazz
O God Thou Canst Not Hide From
Me
Ours
Paree What Did You Do To Me
Queen Of Terre Haute, The
Suffer The Children
Take Me Back To Manhattan
Wait For The Moon
Wake Up And Dream
You Don't Remind Me
You're On Top
Porter & Goetz
Washington Square
Porter & Wilson & Levy
Ko Ko Mo I Love You So
Porter, Cole
Ace In The Hole
After You
Agua Sincopada
All Of You
All Through The Night
Allez-Vous-En Go Away
Another Op'nin' Another Show
Anything Goes
As On Through The Seasons We Sail
At Long Last Love
Be A Clown
Begin The Beguine
Between You And Me
Blow Gabriel Blow
Brush Up Your Shakespeare
Buddie Beware
Bull-Dog
But In The Morning No
C'est Magnifique
Ca C'est L'amour
Can-Can
Do I Love You
Don't Fence Me In
Don't Look At Me That Way
Down In The Depths On The
Ninetieth Floor
Dream Dancing
Easy To Love
Ev'ry Time We Say Goodbye
Ev'rything I Love
Experiment
Find Me A Primitive Man
Friendship
From Alpha To Omega
From This Moment On
Get Out Of Town
Goodbye Little Dream Goodbye
Great Indoors, The

Porter, Cole *(Cont.)*
I Am Loved
I Concentrate On You
I Get A Kick Out Of You
I Happen To Like New York
I Hate You Darling
I Love Paris
I Love You
I'm Going In For Love
I've Got My Eyes On You
I've Got You On My Mind
I've Got You Under My Skin
I've Still Got My Health
In The Still Of The Night
Information Please
It's All Right With Me
It's Bad For Me
It's De-Lovely
Just One Of Those Things
Katie Went To Haiti
Let's Be Buddies
Let's Do It
Let's Do It Let's Fall In Love
Let's Misbehave
Let's Not Talk About Love
Longing For Dear Old Broadway
Love For Sale
Mind If I Make Love To You
Miss Otis Regrets
Missus Lowsborough-Goodby
Mister And Missus Fitch
Most Gentlemen Don't Like Love
My Heart Belongs To Daddy
Night And Day
Old Fashioned Garden
Paree
Paris Loves Lovers
Physician, The
Picture Of Me Without You, A
Ridin' High
Rosalie
Silk Stockings
So In Love
So Near And Yet So Far
Stereophonic Sound
Tale Of The Oyster, The
True Love
Two Little Babes In The Wood
Use Your Imagination
Vite Vite Vite
Well Did You Evah
Weren't We Fools
What Is This Thing Called Love
When Love Comes Your Way
Where Have You Been
Where Oh Where
Why Shouldn't I
Wouldn't It Be Fun
Wunderbar
You Do Something To Me
You Don't Know Paree

Porter, Cole *(Cont.)*
You'd Be So Nice To Come Home
   To
You're Sensational
You're The Top
You've Got That Thing
Portnoy & Angelo
Theme From Cheers
Where Everybody Knows Your
   Name
Portogallo
Earth And The Fulness With Which
   It Is Stored, The
How Firm A Foundation
Posner
Workmen's Circle Hymn
Posselt
I Want A Life
Lydia Pinkham
Posselt & Erich
I Want To Go Home
Post
Doogie Howser Md
Greatest American Hero, The
Hill Street Blues Theme, The
Nevada Hail Song
Theme From Hooperman
Theme From The Greatest American
   Hero
Theme From The Joan Rivers Show
Post & Carpenter
Hunter
Theme From The A Team
Theme From The Rockford Files
Post & Post
Sixteen Reasons Why I Love You
Pothier
Sing To Mary Mother Most Merciful
Potter
CC Rider
Hymn Of The Alamo
National Anthem Of Guyana
Private Tommy Atkins
See See Rider
Swell Affair, A
Potts
Digital Display
Poulenc
Attributs
Aussi Bien Que Les Cigales
Belle Jeunesse, La
Chanson A Boire
Chanson De L'oranger Sec
Couplets Bachiques
Enfant, L'
Espionne, L'
Fancy
Grace Exilee, La
Il Pleut
Invocation Aux Parques
Je N'ai Plus Que Les Os
Mais Mourir
Mutation

Poulenc *(Cont.)*
Tombeau, Le
Ver Le Sud
Voyage
Poulton
Aura Lee
Pound & Whitten
Loved Ones, The
Pounds & Fearis
Beautiful Isle Of Somewhere
Pounds & Fillmore
I Know That My Redeemer Liveth
Pounds & Gabriel
Way Of The Cross Leads Home, The
Pounds & Towner
Anywhere With Jesus
Poupe
Little Chimney Sweeper, The
Powell
Author Of Life Divine
Blacksmith's Daughter, The
Clarinade
Earl, The
Funny Folks
Heartsease
Herald Sound The Note Of
   Judgment
King's Highway, The
Knightsbridge
Once To Every Man And Nation
Pack Up Your Troubles In Your Old
   Kit Bag
Pack Up Your Troubles In Your Old
   Kit Bag And Smile Smile Smile
Pearls On Velvet
Romans 8:28
Power
Dearest Mae
Royal Band, The
Powers
Friend In California, A
Get Together
Let's Get Together
Mother Judson
Powers & Church & Whitson & Ha
I Always Get Lucky With You
Poyser
Ambition
Ballad Of John Silver, A
Battle Of Waterloo
Be Prepared
Ben Battle
Bold Robin Hood
Bonnet O' Blue
Bowmont Water
Boy From Ballytearim
Brigands
Buttered Toast
Camping
Captain Barnard's Grenadier
Changed
Chief, The
Christmas Eve
Compleat Angler, The

Poyser *(Cont.)*
Coridon's Song
Dagonet
Davie
Day Is Coming, The
Down The Road To Nineveh
Drummer, The
Dumb Dumb Dumb
Epping Hunt
Essentials
Faithless Sally Brown
Farmer's Daughter, The
Galleons Of Spain, The
Galloping Squire, The
Gilbert And Sullivan
Gude Gaun Game O' Curlin', The
Hallucinations
Hot Stuff
Howe O' The Mearns, The
Innisfree
Irish Schoolmaster, The
John Trot
Johneen
Kinmont Willie
Lands Across The Sea
Lydford Law
Morning
Noble Earl Of Salisbury, The
Old Angler's Triumph, The
Old England
Old Navy, The
Old Superb, The
On The Beach
Parting Song, The
Pater's Bathe
Plato
Private Of The Buff, The
Richmond Park
Road To Maresfield, The
Rover, The
Royal Game Of Golf
Scout Law, The
South Country, The
St Valentine's Day
Surnames
Teddy
Tigers, The
Tom Brown
Treasure Island
Wanderer's Song, A
War Song Of Dinas Vawr
When All The World Is Young Lad
Yorkshire Boy, A
Prado
Duerme
Patricia It's Patricia
Praetorius
Behold A Branch Hath Flowered
Behold A Rose Of Beauty
Canon Of The Mimes
Christmas Hymn
Christo Incarnato
Come Sing Ye Choirs Exultant

Praetorius *(Cont.)*
Erstanden Ist Der Heilig Christ
Great And Mighty Wonder, A
I Know A Rosetree Springing
In Another Land And Time
Lo How A Rose
Lo How A Rose E'er Blooming
Lord Ascendeth Up On High, The
Make A Joyful Noise Unto The Lord
Nobis Est Natus
Noble Stem Of Jesse, The
O Lord Thy People Gathered Here
O Love Divine
O Splendor Of God's Glory Bright
O Thou Whose Gracious Presence
  Shone
Parvulus Nobis Nascitur
Psallite Unigenito
Psalm 66
Puer Nobis Nascitur
Rise Up O Flame
She Is So Dear
Shepherd Band Their Flocks Are
  Keeping, A
Son Of God Is Born For All, The
That Easter Day With Joy Was Bright
This New Day
Today
Universi Populi
Viva La Musica
We Will Be Merry
We Will Be Merry Far And Wide
What Star Is This
What Star Is This With Beams So
  Bright
World One Neighborhood, The
Pratt
At The Window
Hot-House Rag
My Bonnie Lies Over The Ocean
Sparkling Piper Heidsieck
Walking Down Broadway
Prentice
Acushla My Darling
Prentiss & Doane
More Love To Thee
Pres
Miserere
Tu Pauperum Refugium
Presley
Amazing Grace
I'll Have A New Life
Presley & Matson
Love Me Tender
Poor Boy
Presnell
My Grandmother's Chair
Pretty Crowin' Chickens
Rambling Boy, The
Talking With The Social Union
Press
Breathless
Pressis & Wells (see also Wells)
Walking On A Thin Line

Preston
I Wonder
Preston & Fisher
Nothing From Nothing
You Are So Beautiful
Prestwood
Hard Rock Bottom Of Your Heart
Hard Times For Lovers
Sound Of Goodbye
Previn
Coco
I Like Myself
Money Rings Out Like Freedom, The
Theme From Valley Of The Dolls
You're Gonna Hear From Me
Previte & Denicola
Hungry Eyes
Previte & Elworthy
Sweetheart
Previte & Markowitz & Denicola
I've Had The Time Of My Life
Time Of My Life, The
Price
Alone
Be Strong We Are Not Here To Play
Evening Campus Song
House Of The Rising Sun, The
Just Because
King Of Peace
Lawdy Miss Clawdy
My Hope My All My Saviour Thou
Night
Saint's Delight, The
Soft Rain
Solemn Thought
Song To The Dark Virgin
When Cometh The End Of The War
Price & Logan
I'm Gonna Get Married
Price & Marascalco
Send Me Some Lovin'
Price & Sandstrom
Indestructible
Prichard
Alleluia Sing To Jesus
Alleluya Sing To Jesus
Blow Thou Cleansing Wind
Come Thou Long-Expected Jesus
Love Divine All Loves Excelling
Not Alone For Mighty Empire
Praise The Lord Ye Heavens
Topsy-Turvery World
Prieto
Wedding, The
Prima
Hitsum Kitsum Bumpity Itsum
Sing Sing Sing
Primrose
St James Infirmary
Prince
1999
4 Tears In Your Eyes
Alphabet St
Batdance

Prince (Cont.)
I Could Never Take The Place Of
Your Man
I Feel For You
I Wanna Be Your Lover
I Would Die 4 U
Kiss
Let's Go Crazy
Little Red Corvette
Mandalay
Nothing Compares 2 U
Purple Rain
Take Me With U
U Got The Look
When Doves Cry
Prince & Brown & Armato
She Ain't Worth It
Prince & Easton
Arms Of Orion, The
Prince & Neil & Broughton
Funny
Prince & Nelson
Scandalous
Prince & Rogers & Kanner
I Guess I'll Get The Papers
Prince & The Revolution
Pop Life
Respberry Beret
Prine
Angels From Montgomery
Blue Umbrella
Donald And Lydia
Far From Me
Flashback Blues
Hello In There
Illegal Smile
Paradise
Pretty Good
Quiet Man
Sam Stone
Six O'Clock News
Spanish Pipe Dream
Your Flag Decal Won't Get You Into
Heaven Anymore
Prins-Buttle
Easter Carol
Prior
Are You Growing
Pritchard
Love Divine All Loves Excelling
Proch
Beaux Jours Passes
Plaintes D'Amour
Procter & Giorza
Because
Proffer & Pomeranz
Daybreak
Proffitt
Don Kelly's Girl
Groundhog
Hang Man
I Wish I Was A Single Girl Again
I'm Goin' Back To North Carolina

Proffitt (Cont.)
I'm Goin' To Pick My Banjo
James Campbell
Jimmy Ransome
Johnson Boys
Lawson Family Murder, The
Lord Randall
Lowland Low
Marching On
Moonshine
Poor Soldier
Pretty Fair Widow, The
Reuben's Train
Rose Connally
Shulls Mills
This World Is Not My Home
Tom Dooley
Trifling Woman
'Way Down In Columbus Georgia
When I Was Single
Wild Bill Jones
WP And A
Prokofieff
Snowdrops
Snowflakes
Prothero
Father Dearest Father
Protheroe
My Shadow And I
Song Of Redemption, A
When In Twilight
Proulx
Here In Christ We Gather
Stars Declare His Glory, The
To God With Gladness Sing
Prout
Come Thou O Come
Holy Father In Thy Mercy
Provenzale
Deh Rendetemi
Provost
Intermezzo
Pruett & Glaser
Fastest Gun Around, The
Prutting
Chartles
Pryor
Razzazza Mazzazza
Whistler And His Dog, The
Puccini
Bel Di Vedremo, Un
E L'Uccellino
Entrata De Butterfly
Forget-Me-Nots
Humming Chorus
Musetta's Waltz
Musetta's Waltz Song
Vissi D'arte Vissi D'amore
Puck
Little House Upon The Hill, The
Where Did You Get That Girl
Puckett & Dickerson
Unblind Yourself

Puente
Oye Como Va
Para Los Rumberos
Puerner
Full Dinner Pail, The
Pugh
Hallelujah Crown Him
Land Beyond
When Fades The Light
Wonderful Story Is True, The
Pugh & Marshall
Then Came You
Pulkingham
Bless Thou The Lord
Body Song, The
Hallelujah Today
In Babilone
Jesus Jesus Is My Lord
Wake Up
We Love The Lord
Pullen
For Man's Unceasing Quest For God
Purcell
Ah How Gladly We Believe
Ah How Pleasant 'Tis To Love
Answer Of The Ocean, The
Ape A Lion A Fox And An Ass, An
Bubbling And Splashing
Children Of The Heavenly King
Chorus Of Sprites
Christ Is Made The Sure Foundation
Close Of The Day, The
Come Unto These Yellow Sands
Corinna Is Divinely Fair
Euclid Before 'em
Evening Hymn
Fairest Isle
Festival Rondo
Fie Nay Prithee John
Five Reasons
Full Fathom Five
Full Fathom Five Thy Father Lies
Gabriel John
Glory And Worship Are Before Him
Hark Hark How All Things In One
Sound Rejoice
Harvest Home
He That Drinks Is Immortal
Humours Of Bartholomew Fair
I Attempt From Love's Sickness To
Fly
I'll Sail Upon The Dog Star
If Music Be The Food Of Love
In These Delightful Pleasant Groves
Invitation
Jack Thou'rt A Toper
Knotting Song, The
Life Span
Lilliburlero
Lost Is My Quiet
Macedon Youth, The
Mavis, The
Mingle Voices And Souls

Purcell *(Cont.)*
Moon Reappears, The
Music For A While
Nymphs And Shepherds
Nymphs And Shepherds Come
  Away
On The Brow Of Richmond Hill
Once In Our Lives
One Industrious Insect
One Night
One Two Three
Out Of The Deep Have I Called
Passing By
Passing Of The Moon, The
Pious Celinda
Pleasures Are Few
Pretty Maid
Prithee Ben't So Sad And Serious
Questioning Of The Ocean, The
Rebus On Mr Anthony Hall
Rebus On Roman Numerals
Rejoice In The Lord Alway
Search, The
Shepherd Shepherd Leave Decoying
Sing On
Sound The Trumpet
Thou Knowest Lord
Thou Knowest Lord The Secrets Of
  Our Heart
Thrice Blest Is He To Whom Is
  Given
Thy Hand Belinda
Time So Kind
'Tis Too Late For A Coach
'Tis Women
Trumpet Tune
Trumpet Voluntary In D Major
Turn Then Thine Eyes
Under This Stone
Upon A Quiet Conscience
We Merry Minstrels
What Shall I Do To Show
When I Am Laid In Earth
When V And I Together Meet
Who Can Swim
With Drooping Wings
With Drooping Wings Ye Cupids
  Come
Woodland Dark, The
Would You Know How We Meet

Purday
God Of Our Life
God Of Our Life Through All The
  Circling Years
Lead Kindly Light

Purdy
Dartmouth Drinking Song
March Of The Maroons, The
On Wisconsin

Purse
Jesus Call Your Lambs

Purse & Purse
Celebrate
I Dedicate All My Love To You
Tapestry

Purse & Purse & Cason
Battleline

Putman
Blood Red And Going Down
Green Green Grass Of Home
Older The Violin The Sweeter The
  Music, The
Set Me Free

Putman & Jones
Do You Wanna Go To Heaven

Putman & Throckmorton
What I Had With You

Putman & Throckmorton
Smooth Sailing

Putman & Whipple
I'll Be Coming Back For More

Putman & Wilson & Jones
I Would Crawl All The Way To The
  River
War Is Hell On The Homefront Too

Putnam
Champlain
Evening On The Lake
North Dakota Hymn

Putnam & Vanhoy
Let's Keep It That Way

Quadling & Howard & Jurgens
Careless

Quaile
O Lord Of Heaven And Earth And
  Sea

Quaranta
Notti Di Mergellina

Quarles
Alma Mater
Sleep Fairy, The

Quaye
Your Starter For

Queen & Cannon
Just Because She Made Dem
  Goo-Goo Eyes

Quick
Come Go With Me

Quigley
Dukes Of Duquesne

Quijano & Debaly
Libertad Libertad Orientales

Quillen & Perimmer
My Heart

Quilter
April
Autumn Evening
Blow Blow Thou Winter Wind
Come Away Death
Fair House Of Joy
Last Year's Rose, A
Love's Philosophy
Now Sleeps The Crimson Petal
O Mistress Mine
Song Of The Blackbird
To Daisies
Weep You No More

Quiroga
Maria De La O

Quiroga Moro
Ingratitud

Qunta Davies & Kretschmer
Crazy

Qunta & Thompson & Ryder & Reid
You're The Voice

Rabbitt
On Second Thought
Pure Love

Rabbitt & Bourke
Patch It Up

Rabbitt & Heard
Kentucky Rain

**Rabbitt & McCormick & Malloy &
Stevens**
Suspicions

Rabbitt & Neilsen & Landis
Gotta Have You

Rabin
Love Will Find A Way
Your Body Is An Outlaw

Rabin & Anderson & Squire & Horn
Owner Of A Lonely Heart

Rabinowitz
Reilly

Rachmaninoff
All Once I Gladly Owned
All Things Depart
Arion
Ave Maria
Before My Window
Beloved Let Us Fly
Christ Is Risen
Come Let Us Rest
Corn Field, The
Daisies
Day To Night Comparing Went The
  Wind Her Way
Dissonance
Dreams
Forsake Me Not My Love I Pray
Fountains, The
Fruhlingsfluthen
Heart's Secret, The
I Long For Thee
In My Garden At Night
In The Silence Of Night
In The Silent Night
Island, The
Let Me Rest Here Alone
Lilacs
Morn Of Life, The
Muse, The
Music
Night Is Mournful
O Do Not Grieve
Oft In The Silent Night
Pied Piper, The
Poet, The
Quest, The
Rachmaninoff Concerto Theme
Raising Of Lazarus, The
Ring, The
So Dread A Fate I'll Ne'er Believe

Rachmaninoff *(Cont.)*
Soul's Concealment, The
Storm, The
Thy Pity I Implore
To Her
To The Children
To Thee O Lord Do I Lift Up My
Soul
Triumph Thanksgiving
Two Partings
Vocalise
What Wealth Of Rapture
When Yesterday We Met
With Holy Banner Firmly Held

Racz
Autumns Come

Radebaugh
At The Dawn Of The Day
In That Day

Radecke
Aus Der Jugendzeit
By-Gone Days

Rader
Only Believe

Rader & Presley
Only Believe

Raderbaugh
Keep On Praying

Radicke
Days Of Youth, The

Raff
Be Still
Serenade
Wie Heimlicherweise Ein Engelein
Leise

Rafferty
Baker Street

Raffetto
Home Means Nevada

Raffi
Bathtime
Eight Piggies In A Row
Everything Grows
Just Like The Sun
Let's Make Some Noise
Saturday Morning

Raffi & Simpson
Teddy Bear Hug

Ragan
Alma Mater

Ragland
I Hear A Sweet Voice

Ragovoy
Time Is On My Side

Ragovoy & Laurie
You Got It

Ragsdale
Let Your Love Be A Light Unto The
People

Raif
My Spirit Shall Be Transplanted
Old French Sonnet

Rainey
See See Rider

Rainger
Here Lies Love
Moanin' Low
Please

Rains
Way I Want To Go, The
What More Could A Man Need

Rains & Caswell
That's What Your Love Does To Me

Rains & Cook
Cowboy Logic

Rainwater
Gonna Find Me A Bluebird

Raitt
Nick Of Time

Raksin
Bad And The Beautiful, The
Kretchma
Laura
Those Were The Days
You Above All

Raleigh
Laughing On The Outside Crying
On The Inside

Raleigh & Barkan
How Would You Like To Be

Raleigh & Edwards
Wonderful Wonderful

Raleigh & Linden
Love Is A Hurtin' Thing

Raleigh & Wayne
You Walk By

Raleigh & Wolf
Love Is All We Need

Ram
Enchanted
Great Pretender, The
Helpless
Magic Touch, The
My Dream

Ram & Madi
I Wish
It's Raining Outside

Ram & Nevins & Nevins
Twilight Time

Ram & Ram
Only You
Only You And You Alone

Ram & Rand
Only You
Only You And You Alone

Ram & Tinturin & White
I'm Sorry

Ramann
Warily

Rambo
Behold The Lamb
Build My Mansion
Build My Mansion Next Door To
Jesus
He Looked Beyond My Fault
I Go To The Rock

Rambo *(Cont.)*
I've Never Been This Homesick
Before
If That Isn't Love
In The Valley He Restoreth My Soul
Just In Time
Tears Will Never Stain The Street Of
That City
Tears Will Never Stain The Streets
We Shall Behold Him
What You Say Is What You Get

Rambo & Davis
Sheltered In The Arms Of God

Rambo & Huntsinger
Holy Spirit Thou Art Welcome

Rambo & McGuire
Teach Us To Pray
When His Kingdom Comes

Rameau
A L'amour Rendez Les Armes
Arrachez De Mon Coe Ur Un Trait
Qui Le Dechire
Ave Maria
Gavotte, The
Grillon, Le
Musette
Nightingales Passion-Stirred
Pourquoi Leur Envier
Seamen's Chorus
To The Bagpipe

Ramin
Music To Watch Girls By
Patty Duke Theme, The

Ramones
Blitzkrieg Bop
I Wanna Be Your Boyfriend
Judy Is A Punk
Oh Oh I Love Her So
Ramona
Rockaway Beach
Sheena Is A Punk Rocker
Swallow My Pride

Ramos
Alla En El Rancho Grande
Hymn To The Pine
Je N'ai Pas Change
My Dreams
Rancho Grande, El

Ramsay
Christ Rescued Me
My Heart Is Fixed On Jesus

Ramsey
Muskrat Love
We Can Make The Morning

Rand
Let There Be Love

Randall
God Of Love My Shepheard Is, The
Hail Alma Mater
If There Be That Skills To Reckon
Libertas Et Patria
Lo What A Glorious Sight Appears
Maryland My Maryland

Randall *(Cont.)*
My Soul Doth Magnify The Lord
Salvation O The Joyful Sound
Randazzo & Hart & Wilding
Hurts So Bad
Randazzo & Pike & Joyce
It Feels So Good To Be Loved So Bad
Randazzo & Weinstein
Goin' Out Of My Head
I'm On The Outside Looking In
Pretty Blue Eyes
Randazzo & Weinstein & Barberis
Have You Looked Into Your Heart
Randazzo & Weinstein & Stallman
It's Gonna Take A Miracle
Randegger
As The Storm Retreating
God Of Heaven Hear Our Singing
Harken O Lord
I Ought To Love My Saviour
Take The Fruit I Give You
Randell
My Soul Doth Magnify The Lord
Randle
I'm Gonna Tear Your Playhouse
Down
Randolph
Happy Home Of Mine
Randolph & Rich
Yakety Sax
Raney
Laziest Man In The World, The
Motion
Rankin
Baby Come Back
Rapee & Pollack
Charmaine
Diane
Raposo
Everybody Wash
Face, A
Garden, The
Green
Has Anybody Seen My Dog
I'm Pretty
J Jump
Picture A World
Rub Your Tummy
Sesame Street
Sing
Somebody Come And Play
Three's Company
What Are Kids Called
You Will Be My Music
Rappard
Aufmunterung
Rascel
Arrivederci Roma
Ratcliff
O Light Of Light
Rathbone
Nineteen Birds
Windmill, The

Rathgeber
Bruder Liederlich
Ich Weiss Nit Wie Mir Ist
Von Allerhand Nasen
Von Erschaffung Adam Und Eva
Ravel
Chanson A Boire
Chanson Epique
Chanson Romanesque
D'Anne Jouant De L'espinette
D'Anne Qui Me Jecta De La Neige
Sur L'herbe
Raven
Thank God For Kids
Ravenscroft
Hey Down
How Wondrous And Great Thy
Works
O God We Praise Thee And Confess
People Who In Darkness Walked,
The
Remember O Thou Man
Three Blind Mice
When All Thy Mercies O My God
While Shepherds Watched Their
Flocks By Night
Ravina
Almond Tree, The
Rawles & Glover
Merry Christmas Time-Ee-O
Rawls & Neel
Majestic Rag
Rawson
Keuka Mother
Ray
Sunshine Of Your Smile, The
Ray & White & Holmes
House Of The Rising Sun
Raye
We're In The Navy
Raye & De Paul & Johnston
I'll Remember April
Raye & Depaul
He's My Guy
Mister Five By Five
You Don't Know What Love Is
Raye & Depaul & Carter
Cow-Cow Boogie
Raye & Depaul & Johnson
I'll Remember April
Raye & Prince
Boogie Woogie Bugle Boy
Raye & Prince & Sheehy
Beat Me Daddy Eight To The Bar
Raye & Slack
House Of Blue Lights
Rayford
Promised Day
Raymond
Beer Garden Blues
Dear Land Of The South
Raymonde & Hawker
I Only Want To Be With You

Razaf & Blake & Cooke
We Are Americans Too
Rea
Fool If You Think It's Over
Read
Broad Is The Road
Broad Is The Road That Leads To
Death
Day Of Wrath, The
How Beauteous Were The Marks
Lisbon
My Dear Redeemer And My Lord
Nocturne
Welcome Sweet Day Of Rest
Whoa Emma
Windham
Read & Watts
Broad Is The Road
Reading
Adeste Fideles
Come All Ye Faithful
Dulce Domum
How Firm A Foundation
In Praise Of White Wine
Lord Is My Shepherd, The
O Come All Ye Faithful
Oh Come All Ye Faithful
Rogue On Trial
Sound Over All Waters
Two Lawyers
Reagon
Give Your Hands To Struggle
Oughta Be A Woman
Reay
At Length There Dawns The
Glorious Day
Let All The World In Every Corner
Sing
Reb
Goober Peas
Rebikof
Christmas Bells
Recli
Bela Bellina
Record
Oh Girl
Record & Acklin
Have You Seen Her
Recunda
Bei Mir Bist Du Schon Means That
You're Grand
Red
Would You
Reddick
Prayer In One Accord, A
Redding
End Of A Love Affair, The
Love Man
Respect
Thou Art My Own Love
Redding & Cropper
Dock Of The Bay, The
Redford
Annie McGuire

Redhead

All That I Was My Sin My Guilt
Bread Of Heaven On Thee We Feed
Bright The Vision That Delighted
By Thy Birth And By Thy Tears
Chief Of Sinners Though I Be
Go To Dark Gethsemane
Gracious Spirit Dwell With Me
Hearken To The Anthem Glorious
Holy Off'rings Rich And Rare
Lord With Glowing Heart
Lord With Glowing Heart I'd Praise
　Thee
O Christ Our Hope Our Heart's
　Desire
O Thou From Whom All Goodness
　Flows
Rock Of Ages
Rock Of Ages Cleft For Me
When Our Heads Are Bowed With
　Woe

Redi

Non Dimenticar

Redington

Dare To Do Right
You You're The One

Redman

Cherry
Cradle Song
Gee Baby Ain't I Good To You
I Feel So Good About It

Redmond & Cavanaugh & Weldon

Christmas In Killarney
Thirty-Two Feet And Two Little
　Tails

Redner

Everywhere Everywhere Christmas
　Tonight
O Little Town Of Bethlehem

Reece

Which Side Are You On

Reed

Ain't No Big Deal
Ain't That Lovin' You Baby
Aw Shucks Hush Your Mouth
Baby What You Want Me To Do
Baby What's Wrong
Bright Lights Big City
Busload Of Faith
Calvary
Can't Stand To See You Go
Caress Me Baby
Close Together
Cold And Lonesome
Dime Store Mystery
Dirty Blvd
Endless Cycle
Found Love
Going To New York
Good Evening Mr Waldheim
Good Lover
Guitar Man
Halloween Parade

Reed (*Cont.*)

Hold On
Hush Hush
I Wanna Be Loved
I'm Trying To Please You
In The Bleak Midwinter
Jesus We Love To Meet
Last Great American Whale
Little Child There Is Born, A
Lord Jesus Christ We Humbly Pray
Lullay My Liking
Misery Loves Company
My Hannah Lady Whose Black Baby
　Is You
New Leaf
O My Dear Heart Young Jesus Sweet
Over Yonder's A Park
Remember
Ritual
Romeo Had Juliette
Shame Shame Shame
Sick Of You
Stafford
Strawman
That's All You Gotta Do
There Is No Time
There'll Be A Day
US Male
Windham
Winter
Wreck Of The Virginian No 3, The
Xmas In February
You Don't Have To Go

Reed & Abner

Baby What's On Your Mind
Honest I Do
You Got Me Dizzy

Reed & Bracken

High And Lonesome

Reed & Mason

Bicyclettes De Belsize, Les
Delilah
I Believe In Miracles
Last Waltz, The
Winter World Of Love

Reed & Neal

Blues I've Got, The

Reed & Rae

Please Don't Go

Reed & Rathke

Beginning Of A Great Adventure

Reed & Reed

Going To New York
I'm Gonna Get My Baby

Reed & Smith

I'm Gonna Help You
Tell Me That You Love Me

Reed & Stephens

Tell Me When

Reed & Stephens

There's A Kind Of Hush
There's A Kind Of Hush All Over
　The World

Rees

Can I Leave You
Eternal Day
Eureka
Golden Harp, The
Humble Penitent
Jesus Is My Friend
Mulberry Grove
Newman
O Thou Best Gift Of Heaven
Struggle On
Traveling Pilgrim
Weeping Sinners
When First We Met

Rees & Shell

Sharpsburg

Reese

Build Right On That Shore
He's Got His Eyes On Me
Tall In The Saddle
Walla Walla College
We've Got A Job
Weeping Pilgrim
Which Side Are You On

Reeves

Love Will Roll The Clouds Away

Refice

Ombra Di Nube

Reger

Virgin's Slumber Song, The
Waldeinsamkeit

Regnard

Gay Little Nymph
Las Je Me Plains

Regnart

Geluld
Venus Du Und Dein Kind

Reichard

Wer Hat Die Schonsten Schafchen

Reichardt

Birds And Flowers
Bleibe Bei Uns Denn Es Will Abend
　Werden
Des Deutschen Vaterland
Dustre Nebel Ziehen
Einst Unser Herr Auf Erden War
Fruhling Hat Sich Eingestellt, Der
Giusto Amor
Immer Muss Ich Wieder Lesen
In The Time Of Roses
Lied Der Parzen
Mensch Hat Nichts So Eigen, Der
Reiters Abschied
Rhapsodie
Schone Nacht, Die
Sleep Baby Sleep
Sleep My Saviour Sleep
Tageweise
Vanne Felice Rio
Wach Auf Mein Herzensschone
Wachter Mit Dem Silberhorn, Der
Wechsellied Zum Tanze
Welche Morgenroten Wallen

Reichardt *(Cont.)*
When The Roses Bloom
Wie Mit Grimm'gen Unverstand
Reichenbach
Catch
Shepherd, The
Reichhart
In The Time Of Roses
Reichner
I Need Your Love Tonight
Reid
Best I Know How, The
Everybody's Crazy 'bout My Baby
Glamour Boys
Gypsy, The
I Was There
I'll Go To My Grave Loving You
I'm Walking Behind You
Inside
It's A Pity To Say Goodnight
Old Folks
Onward Forward
Our Chicago
Prisoner Of The Highway
Show Her
Still Losing You
Stranger In My House
Susan When She Tried
Tree In The Meadow, A
Reid & Babyface & Simmons
Dial My Heart
Knocked Out
On Our Own
Reid & Bourke
Back In The Fire
Hurtin' Side, The
I Wouldn't Be A Man
It's Only Over For You
Reid & Brooker
Whiter Shade Of Pale, A
Reid & Byrne
How Do I Turn You On
Reid & Dees
In Love
Reid & Glover & Calhoun & Skillings
Cult Of Personality
Reid & Maher & David
Born To Be Blue
Reid & Manning
I Still Feel The Same About You
Reid & Reid
All Because Of Jesus
Do You Know You Are My Sunshine
I'll Be The One
We Belong To The Family
What A Time Over There
Whatever Happened To Randolph
Scott
Reid & Reid & Reid
Let's Get Started If We're Gonna
Break My Heart

Reid & Robbins
One Good Well
When He Leaves You
Reid & Seals
Back When Love Was Enough
Call Home
Fallin' For You For Years
Reid & Seals & Parris
Lost In The Fifties Tonight
Reif
Dirty Gertie From Bizerte
Flirty Gertie From Bizertie
Reimann
All Hail, The Pageant Of The Years
I Look To Thee In Every Need
O Sing With Loud And Joyful Song
Shepherd's Christmas Song
Reinach & Rene
Liberation Now
Reinagle
All Hidden Lie The Future Ways
Awake My Soul
Come O Thou All-Victorious Lord
How Shall I Follow Him I Serve
How Sweet The Name Of Jesus
Sounds
In Christ There Is No East Or West
It Is Not Death To Die
Lord Be With Us, The
My God Accept My Heart This Day
My Soul Repeat His Praise
O God Of Jacob By Whose Hand
O Living Christ Chief Cornerstone
O Lord May Church And Home
Combine
While Thee I Seek
World Wide Church, The
Reinecke
Dancing Song
Reine & North & Harper
Tobermory Bay
Reinecke
Auf De Wacht
Aus Dem Schenkenbuche
Christmas At The Door
Christmas Carol, A
Dancing Lesson, The
Even-Song
Evening
Father From Thy Throne On High
Foreign Language, A
From The Bright Blue Heavens
Fruhlingsblumen
Good King Arthur
I Live For Those Who Love Me
In Summer Go Thy Love To Seek
Jesus Master Whom I Serve
Morning Star, The
Mother's Birthday
On Weary Hearts Descending
Snowflake, A
Spinning Song
Sunbeams In Winter
To The Nightingale

Reinecke *(Cont.)*
Up Yonder On The Mountain
Weary Am I Go To Rest
When Little Children Sleep
When The Little Children Sleep
Woe To Him
Reingold
Vos Vet Zayn Der Sof
Reinick
To The Sunshine
Reinmann
I Look To Thee In Ev'ry Need
Reisch & Robinson
Two Hearts In 3-4 Time
Reisfeld
Chupadero, La
Reisfeld & Fryberg & Marbot
Call Me Darling
Reissiger
Blucher Am Rhein
Doux Foyer Sois Beni
Lord Jesus When We Stand Afar
O Father Thou Who Givest All
One Lord There Is
Put Thy Trust In God
Relf & Nelson
Harlem Shuffle, The
Rendall & Thomas
Dance Little Bird
Rendine
Pansy
Vurria
Rendle
Day Is Slowly Wending, The
God Of The Shining Hosts
Where The Great Ship Passing
Rene
Gloria
When The Swallows Come Back To
Capistrano
Rene & Adams
Tossin' And Turnin'
Rene & Lewis
One-Track Mind
Rene & Rene & Muse
When It's Sleepy Time Down South
Rene & Scott & Rene
Someone's Rocking My Dream Boat
Renehan
By George's Bank
River Lullaby
Renis
Quando Quando Quando
When I Tell You That I Love You
Renis & Guantini & Lawrence
Ae Ao
Renis & Iglesias
All Of You
Rennes
And Are You In The Stars
Go When The Morning Shineth
God Helps Those That Help
Themselves

Rennes *(Cont.)*
Great God And Wilt Thou
  Condescend
In His Name My Brother
O God I Thank Thee That The Night

Renstrom
Indian Lullaby
Little Ducky Duddle
Summer Showers
Turkey Talk

Repp
Allelu

Repper
Down In The Valley
Plains Of Uruguay, The

Resnick & Young
Under The Boardwalk

Respighi
Abbandono
Acqua
Au Milieu Du Jardin
Ballata
Bella Porta Di Rubini
Canto Funebre
Canzone De Re Enzo
Contrasto
Crepuscolo
E Se Un Giorno Tornasse
Egle
Fine, La
Giardino, Il
I Fauni
In Alto Mare
Invito Alla Danza
Io Sono La Madre
Ma Come Potrei
Mamma E Come Il Pane Caldo, La
Mattinata
Mattino Di Luce
Musica In Horto
Najade, La
Nebbie
Nevicata
No Non E Morto Il Figlio Tuo
Noel Ancien
Notte
O Falce Di Luna
Piccola Mano Bianca
Pioggia
Povero Core
Scherzo
Sera, La
Serenata Indiana
Sogno, Un
Sopra Un'aria Antica
Stornellatrice
Su Una Violetta Morta
Tempi Assai Lontani
Udir Talvolta, L'
Van Li Effluvi De La Rose

Resta
Hail To The U Of L

Reswick & Werfel & Rich
I Live For Your Love

Reuental
May Flight

Reuter & Howell & Farian & Dalton
Baby Don't Forget My Number

Revaux & Francois
My Way

Revel
Did You Ever See A Dream Walking
I'd Like To Set You To Music
Love Thy Neighbor
When There's A Breeze On Lake
  Louise

Revil
Il Pleurait

Rew
Walking On Sunshine

Reyes
Hymn National De Republic
  Dominican
Quisqueyanos Valientes Alcemos
Valiant Men Of Quisqueya Don't
  Tarry

Reynolds
All Through The Night
Give Me The Wings Of Faith
God Bless The Grass
I'm Goin' Back To The Prairie
If God Is Dead
If God Is Dead Who's That Living In
  My Soul
If You Love Me
Jesus Is Just Alright
Jesus My Lord Is Real To Me
Little Boxes
Mario's Duck
Peace Isn't Treason
Playing War
Ready For The Times To Get Better
Round About Christmas, A
Saigon Children, The
Share His Love
We Don't Need The Men
What Have They Done To The Rain
When The Sun Shines Bright
Wise Men, The
You Can't Eat The Oysters

Reynolds & Dane
It Isn't Nice

Reynolds & Greene & Belafonte
Turn Around

Reynolds & Nance
Endless Sleep

Reynolds & Pafumi
May God Bless You On Easter
  Sunday

Reynolds & Rhodes
Silver Threads Among The Gold

Rhea
Christmas Carol
Jolly Cowboy, The
Land We Love Is Calling, The
O Joyous Easter Morning
Surely It Is God Who Saves Me

Rheinberger
Evening Hymn
Morning Hymn

Rhody
I'll Be True To You

Rhys-Herbert
Moon-Man, The
Playtime Land
School Festival Song

Ricardel
Wise Old Owl, The

Ricardel & Evans
Frim Fram Sauce, The

Riccius
Lustgen Musikanten, Die

Rice
Clare De Kitchen
Golden Chains
I Want To Go Home
Jim Crow
Mustang Sally
Shall We Meet
Shall We Meet Beyond The River
Thinking Love Of Thee
We Stopped Them At The Marne

Rice & Gitz
I Want To Go Home

Rice & Ingram
Respect Yourself

Rice & Prince
Boogie Woogie Bugle Boy

Rice & Rice
I Could 'A Had You
There Ain't No Future In This
Till Your Memory's Gone

Rich
American Lullaby
Life Goes On
Lonely Weekends
Smile Darn Ya Smile

Rich & Sherrill
Every Time You Touch Me I Get
  High

Richafort
Rousee Du Mois De May, La
Trut Avant Il Faut Boire

Richard
Greenbacks
King Richard's Prison Song

Richards
Bless Thou The Gifts We Bring
Christmas Chimes
Dear God We Thank You
Go Tell Everyone
God Bless The Prince Of Wales
He
He Was There When I Needed You
Let The Hills And Vales Resound
O Whisper What Thou Feelest
Oklahoma Hail
Our Part
Young At Heart

Richardson
Chantilly Lace
Evening Song
Lambs In The Valley
Mary
Men Whose Boast It Is That Ye
My God I Love Thee
Running Bear
Thou Art The Way
Thou By Heav'nly Hosts Adored
White Lightning
Richardson & Edwards
Wildflower
Richardson & Lomax
If You Can't Find Love
Richberg
Flag Of Maroon
For Chicago
For Chicago Alma Mater
Richerson & Walker
Bower Of Prayer
Richey & Sherrill & Wilson
Soul Song
Richie
Ballerina Girl
Deep River Woman
Easy
Endless Love
Hello
Jesus Is Love
Just Put Some Love In Your Heart
Just To Be Close To You
Lady
Lucy
My Love
Oh No
Sail On
Say You Say Me
Serves You Right
Still
Stuck On You
Sweet Love
This Is Your Life
Three Times A Lady
Tonight Will Be Alright
Truly
Wandering Stranger
You Mean More To Me
Richie & Barnes
Don't Stop
Richie & Cochrane
Can't Slow Down
Round And Round
Tell Me
Richie & Foster
Only One, The
Richie & Harvey-Richie
Penny Lover
You Are
Richie & Jones
Heroes
Richie & Lapread & Orange & Williams & McClary & King
Brick House

Richie & Phillinganes
Love Will Conquer All
Love Will Find A Way
Sela
Richie & Phillinganes & Maclain
Serves You Right
Richie & Richie
You Are
Richie & Rios & Frenchik
Dancing On The Ceiling
Richie & Weil
All Night Long
Running With The Night
Richmond
White And The Blue, The
Richrath
In Your Letter
Take It On The Run
Richter
By The Fireside
Winds, The
Rickard
Hail Minnesota
Riddle
New Naked City Theme
Theme From Emergency
Theme From Route 66
Theme From Sam Benedict
Riegger
Dying Of The Light, The
Ye Banks And Braes O'Bonnie Doon
Ries
Call To The Colors, The
Cradle Song
From Out Thine Eyes My Songs Are
Flowing
Most Wondrous It Must Be
Riesa & Bancroft
At Evening
Riesenfeld
One For All All For One
Rietz
Maienzeit
Morgenlied
Rigel
Petits Oiseaux
Riggs
Mormon Love Serenade
Righini
Thou Whose Almighty Word
Rigual & Martinoli
Cuando Calienta El Sol
Love Me With All Your Heart
Riley
Love You Down
Riley & Bragg
Just Walkin' In The Rain
Just Walking In The Rain
Riley & Strozier & Valentine
Oh Sheila
Rimbault
Happy Day
How Dry I Am
O Happy Day

Rimbault *(Cont.)*
O Happy Day That Fixed My Choice
O Ye Who Taste That Love Is Sweet
Oh Happy Day
Oh Happy Day That Fixed My
Choice
Rimskii-Korsakov
As The Fair Skies Your Eyes Are
Shining
Chanson Du Marchand Hindou
Chanson Indoue
Cradle-Song
Hymn To The Sun
Nightingale And The Rose, The
River Of Sleep
Snow Maiden's Aria, The
Song Of India, A
Song Of Scheherezade
Song Of The Shepherd Lehl
Sonnent Les Cloches A Novgorod
Rinck
Murmur Gentle Lyre
Night
Our Dear Church
Selig Sind Des Himmels Erben
Rines
Halo Everybody Halo
Use Ajax The Foaming Cleanser
Ringhardt
Anew We Lift Our Song
Rink
Alle Jahre Wieder Kommt Das
Christuskind
As Each Happy Christmas
Give Me A New A Perfect Heart
I Heard The Voice Of Jesus Say
There Is A Land Of Pure Delight
Rio
Tequila
Riperton & Rudolph
Lovin' You
Rippon & Holden
All Hail The Power
Riso
Gotta Have The Real Thing
Rist
O Traurigkeit O Herzeleid
Ritchie
Black Waters
Holly Tree Carol, The
Still
Ritenour & Watts
Bullet Train
Rittenhouse
Love Came Down At Christmas
Ritter
Freedom
Grosser Gott Wir Loben Dich
Holy God We Praise Thy Name
O Bearer Of The Cross
O For A Glance Of Heav'nly Day
Sun Of My Soul
Sun Of My Soul Thou Savior Dear
Sun Of My Soul Thou Saviour Dear

Rivers
Bless The Lord
God Is Love
Midnight Special
Riviere
Spring Gentle Spring
Rivinac
Our First President's Quickstep
Rizo
Blue Havana Moon
Rizzio
Ah For My Peaceful Prime
Roach & Mysels
One Little Candle
Roachford
Cuddly Toy
Roat
Pal Of My Dreams
Robb
Walking Away
Robb & Kirby
Forever Again
Memories To Burn
Robbins
Any Poet To Posterity
Atlanta
Ave Atque Vale
Belle Dame Sans Merci, La
Canzonet
Certain One Who Died, A
Dover Beach
Dreams Of The Sea
El Paso
Epilogue Frost At Midnight
Evening
Forsaken Merman, The
Great Misgiving, The
I Don't Think She's In Love
    Anymore
I'll Go On Alone
If You Still Want A Fool Around
Last Faun Seeks, The
Last Faun Thinks Of Death, The
Last Faun Wakes, The
Love Is Alive
Master's Call, The
My Lost Youth
My Song
Nightingales
Nymph Of The Downward Smile
Ode In May
Ode On A Grecian Urn
Ode To A Nightingale
Ode To Autumn
Ode To Duty
Ode To Psyche
Ode To The West Wind
Passer By, A
Ploughman, The
Psalm 18
Psalm 68
Put Forth O God Thy Spirit's Might
Red Hills Of Utah
Shepherdess, The

Robbins *(Cont.)*
Shrine By The Sea, A
Sohrab And Rustum
Song To David
Sonnet From The Portuguese
Sonnet The Sea
Wanderers, The
White Sport Coat And A Pink
    Carnation, A
You Gave Me A Mountain
Robbins & Carpenter
I'll Come Back As Another Woman
Robbins & Gibson
Heart Trouble
Robbins & Johnson
Gotta Learn To Love Without You
Robbins & Kennerley
Young Love
Robert
Angelina
Belle Boulangere, La
Madelon
Quand Madelon
Roberts
Give It What You Got
Goodbye I Love You
Headed For A Fall
Hey Joe
Just Remember I Love You
Love That Got Away
Lucky One, The
Moonlight Cocktail
O God Of Mercy God Of Might
O Thou The Contrite Sinners' Friend
O Thou Who Driest The Mourner's
    Tear
Real Love
Same Old You, The
Smiles
Strange Way
You Are The Woman
Roberts & Barrand
Strike The Bell
Roberts & Black
100% Chance Of Rain
Roberts & Bronfman
Whisper In The Dark
Roberts & Chater
IOU
Roberts & Darnell
There's A Star Spangled Banner
    Waving Somewhere
Roberts & Fischer & Black
You Lie
Roberts & Fisher
Into Each Life Some Rain Must Fall
Put The Blame On Mame
That Ole Devil Called Love
You Always Hurt The One You Love
Roberts & Gannon
Moonlight Cocktail
Roberts & Goldman
Oh People

Roberts & Hart
Over You
Roberts & Jacobson
His Invisible Hand
Roberts & Katz
Nina The Pinta The Santa Maria, The
Roberts & McLeod
Same Ole Love
Roberts & Ovens
Wounded For Me
Roberts & Piller & Katz
Red Leaves On The Campus Green
Roberts & Warren
God Of Our Fathers
God Of Our Fathers Whose
    Almighty Hand
Roberts & Weiss
Sugar Don't Bite
Robertson
Anything That's Part Of You
I Don't Hurt Anymore
I Think I'm Gonna Like It Here
I'm Falling In Love Tonight
Night They Drove Old Dixie Down,
    The
Please Help Me I'm Falling
Starting Today
Weight, The
Wild Cat Song
Wild Cats
Robertson & Blair
I'm Yours
No More
Please Help Me I'm Falling In Love
    With You
Robertson & Cavanaugh & Weldon
Little On The Lonely Side, A
Robertson & Cogane & Mysels
We Three
Robertson & Goldmark
Flames Of Paradise
Robertson & Hoffman & Weldon
Good Night Wherever You Are
Robertson & Rutherford
Living Years, The
Other Side Of The World, The
Silent Running
Robey & Washington
Pledging My Love
Robi & Miles & Williams
You'll Never Never Know
Robin
Christmas Present
Robin & Gaskill & Columbo
Prisoner Of Love
Robin & Gensler
Love Is Just Around The Corner
Robin & Hollander
Moonlight And Shadows
Robin & Rainger
Blue Hawaii
Easy Living
If I Should Lose You
June In January

Robin & Rainger (*Cont.*)
 Love In Bloom
 Thanks For The Memory
Robin & Von Tilzer
 My Cutey's Due At Two-To-Two
  Today
Robin & Whiting
 Louise
Robin & Whiting & Rainger
 Miss Brown To You
Robinson
 Automatically Sunshine
 Black And White
 Carry Me Back To The Lone Prairie
 Death House Blues
 Don't Mess With Bill
 Floy Joy
 Free
 Get Ready
 Harriet Tubman
 He Gave Himself
 He Never Gave Up On Me
 House I Live In, The
 I Don't Blame You At All
 Jesus Is Alive And Well
 Joe Hill
 Keep It A Secret
 Learning To Serve
 Little Fishermen Are We
 Man's A Man For A' That, A
 Memories Of France
 My Baby Must Be A Magician
 O Be Joyful In The Lord
 On The Way Home
 Other Woman, The
 Party
 Two Lovers
 What's So Good About Goodbye
 While Shepherds Watched Their
  Flocks By Night
 Will You Go
 Woman Alone With The Blues, A
Robinson & Byrne
 What I'd Say
Robinson & Cleveland
 I Second That Emotion
Robinson & Moore
 Ooh Baby Baby
 Ooo Baby Baby
 Since I Lost My Baby
Robinson & Moore & Rogers & Tarplin
 Going To A Go-Go
 Ain't That Peculiar
Robinson & Moore & Tarplin
 I'll Be Doggone
 Take This Heart Of Mine
 Tracks Of My Tears, The
Robinson & Rogers
 Way You Do The Things You Do,
  The
Robinson & Tarplin
 I Like It Like That

Robinson & White
 My Girl
 My Guy My Girl
 You Beat Me To The Punch
Robinson & White & Moore & Tarplin
 One More Heartache
Robinson & Wonder & Cosby
 Tears Of A Clown, The
Robinson, Smokey
 Being With You
 One Who Really Loves You, The
 You Really Got A Hold On Me
 You've Really Got A Hold On Me
Robison
 Behind These Gray Walls
 Cottage For Sale, A
 Fiducia
 Old Folks
 Peaceful Valley
 Way Out West In Kansas
 Woman Alone With The Blues
Robison & Pepper
 Sorry 'Bout The Whole Darned
  Thing
Robledo
 It's Seven O'Clock
 Three O'Clock In The Morning
Robles
 Condor Pasa, El
Robyn
 Ain't It Funny What Difference Just
  A Few Hours Make
 Varsity Song
 You
Rocco & Black & Roberts
 Strong Heart
Rocco & Bogard & Black
 All Heaven Is About To Break Loose
Rocco & Bourke & Black
 Little Good News, A
Rocco & Lee & Russell
 Let's Fall To Pieces Together
Rochberg
 Set Me As A Seal
Roche
 Oublie Loulou
Rock & Martin
 Since I Don't Have You
 This I Swear
Rockefeller
 God Is With Me Every Day
 God Made Us A Beautiful World
 Jesus Went Alone To Pray
Rockstro
 For The Bread Which You Have
  Broken
 Reefer, The
Rockwell
 Sherman's March To The Sea
 Somebody's Watching Me
 We Are Soldiers Of The Cross
Rockwell & Cole & Greene
 Peeping Tom

Rodeheaver
 Confidence
 Good-Night And Good-Morning
 How It Saves
 Somebody Cares
 Then Jesus Came
Roders
 Johnny One Note
 This Can't Be Love
Rodgers
 Daddy And Home
 In The Jailhouse Now
 My Best Love
 Old Fashioned Girl
 Radioactive
 Rock 'n' Roll Fantasy
 Wedding Processional
 Wonderful Guy, A
 Yesterday I Loved You
 You Are Too Beautiful
Rodgers & Edwards
 Freak, Le
 Good Times
 He's The Greatest Dancer
 I Want Your Love
 I'm Coming Out
 My Forbidden Lover
 Rebels Are We
 Upside Down
 We Are Family
Rodgers & Fraser
 All Right Now
Rodgers & Huang
 Coming To America
Rodgers & Vaughn
 Mule Skinner Blues
Rodgers & Walker
 Baruch Hashem Adonai
Rodgers, Jimmie
 It's Over
Rodgers, Mary
 Boy From..., The
Rodgers, Richard
 All At Once You Love Her
 Babes In Arms
 Bali Ha'i
 Bewitched
 Big Black Giant, The
 Blue Moon
 Blue Room, The
 Climb Ev'ry Mountain
 Cock-Eyed Optimist, A
 Dancing On The Ceiling
 Do I Hear A Waltz
 Do I Love You Because You're
  Beautiful
 Do-Re-Mi
 Don't Marry Me
 Down By The River
 Edelweiss
 Everybody's Got A Home But Me
 Falling In Love With Love
 Gentleman Is A Dope, The

Rodgers, Richard *(Cont.)*
Getting To Know You
Happy Talk
Have You Met Miss Jones
Hello Young Lovers
Honey Bun
I Cain't Say No
I Could Have Danced All Night
I Could Write A Book
I Didn't Know What Time It Was
I Enjoy Being A Girl
I Have Dreamed
I Married An Angel
I Whistle A Happy Tune
I Wish I Were In Love Again
I'm Your Girl
I've Got Five Dollars
If I Loved You
In My Own Little Corner
Isn't It Romantic
It Might As Well Be Spring
It Never Entered My Mind
It's A Grand Night For Singing
It's Easy To Remember
Johnny One Note
June Is Bustin' Out All Over
Lady Is A Tramp, The
Little Girl Blue
Lonely Room
Lovely Night, A
Lover
Man I Used To Be, The
Manhattan
Many A New Day
Mimi
Most Beautiful Girl In The World,
    The
Mountain Greenery
My Favorite Things
My Funny Valentine
My Heart Stood Still
My Lord And My Master
My Romance
Next Time It Happens, The
No Other Love
Oh What A Beautiful Mornin'
Oklahoma
People Will Say We're In Love
Pore Jud
Sentimental Me
Shall We Dance
Ship Without A Sail, A
Sing For Your Supper
So Far
Some Enchanted Evening
Sound Of Music, The
Spring Is Here
Sunday
Surrey With The Fringe On Top, The
Sweetest Sounds, The
Ten Cents A Dance
Ten Minutes Ago
There Is Nothing Like A Dame

Rodgers, Richard *(Cont.)*
There's A Small Hotel
This Can't Be Love
This Nearly Was Mine
Thou Swell
To Keep My Love Alive
Very Special Day, A
Wait Till You See Her
We Kiss In A Shadow
When The Children Are Asleep
Where Or When
With A Song In My Heart
You Are Beautiful
You Are Never Away
You Took Advantage Of Me
You'll Never Walk Alone
Younger Than Springtime
Zip

Rodney
Calvary
Clang Of The Forge, The
Ferryman John
Sion
Time And Tide

Rodriguez
Cumparsita, La

Rodwell
Hudson Side, The

Roe
Abiding Love
Does It Make Any Diff'rence To You
Friend Of Sinners Lord Of Glory
From The Eastern Mountains
Hallelujah Praise Jehovah
Love Divine All Loves Excelling
My Prayer
Sheila
So Great Salvation
Souls Of Men Why Will Ye Scatter
There's Something Special
Unworthy

Roeckel
Cherette
Faithful

Roeder
Child's Dreamland
On Venice Waters

Roeder & Allen
She's My Sorority Girl

Roemheld
Ruby

Roger
I May Be Crazy But I Ain't No Fool

Rogers
Armoraider's Song, The
Clock Store, The
Cloud-Shadows
Cock-A-Coodle-Do
Dixieland Delight
Following In Father's Footsteps
Gone
Good Old Ben

Rogers *(Cont.)*
I'm A Jonah Man
Morgana Jones
Rockin' Little Angel
Rowing
See Father Thy Beloved Song
Shot In The Dark
Stretching
Sweet Music Man
Te Deum Patrem Colimus
Time For Making Songs Has Come,
    The
Try Smiling
When Pershing's Men Go Marching
    Into Picardy
Won't You Be My Neighbor

Rogers & Glassmeyer
Love Or Something Like It
Starting Again

Rogers & Marx
Crazy

Rogers & Marx & Foster
What About Me

Rogers & Morrison & Macrae
Let's Put Our Love In Motion

Rogers & Nevin
Rosary, The

Rogers & Stevens & Schuyler & Malloy
Love Will Turn You Around

Rogers & Timm & Bernard
Silver Shenandoah, The

Rogers & Williams
Nobody

Rogert
Kong Kristian Stod Ved Hojen Mast

Rohmer
Bang Went The Chance Of A
    Lifetime

Roig
Yours

Roland
Big Fat Mama

Rolfe
Closer Still With Thee

Rolle
Lobt Den Herrn

Rolling Stones
Little By Little

Rollins
Race Is On, The

Rolmaz
Where Did You Get That Hat

Roma
Can't Yo' Heah Me Callin'
Can't Yo' Heah Me Callin' Caroline
God Shall Wipe Away All Tears
Grateful O Lord Am I
I Come To Thee
Silent Voice, The

Romagnesi
Adieux De Nemorin, Les
Gypsy Life
Prisonniere Et Le Chevalier, La

Romaine
Georgia Cotton Mill Woman
Roman
Ramblin' Wreck
Rambling Wreck From Georgia Tech
Roman & Swirsky
Prove Your Love
Romani
Lover's Holiday, A
Romano
Amaryllis
Romberg
Carousel In The Park
Close As Pages In A Book
Deep In My Heart Dear
Desert Song, The
Drinking Song
Faithfully Yours
French Military Marching Song
Girl On The Prow, The
Golden Days
I Bring A Love Song
Just We Two
Lost In Loveliness
Lover Come Back To Me
Marianne
One Alone
One Flower Grows Alone In Your
Garden
One Kiss
Riff Song, The
Road To Paradise, The
Romance
Serenade
Silver Moon
Softly As In A Morning Sunrise
Song Of Love
Stouthearted Men
Students March Song
Wanting You
When I Grow Too Old To Dream
Will You Remember
You Will Remember Vienna
Your Land And My Land
Zing Zing Zoom Zoom
Romberg & Goodman
When Hearts Are Young
Rome
Anyone Would Love You
Fanny
I Have To Tell You
I Know Your Kind
Investigator's Song, The
Miss Marmelstein
My Friend Franklin
Nobody Makes A Pass At Me
Sing Me A Song With Social
Significance
South America Take It Away
Wish You Were Here
Rome & Jamblan & Herpin
My Heart Sings

Romeo
Blessed Is The Rain
Candy Kid
Keep On Movin'
Romeo & Law & Calvin
Dream's A Dream, A
Romer
New Heaven New Earth
O Would I Were A Boy Again
Romer & Smith
Gift
Romera
Hippy Hippy Shake, The
Romero
Ay Casimira
Bogota
Candy Kid
Capricho
Capuli, El
Conga Pasa, La
Eco De Los Andes
I Just Came To Praise The Lord
Linda Provincianita
Llanero, El
Mulatinha
No Llores Corazon
Para Balar La Cueca
Quiero Morir
Sone
Tango Divino
Romm
Lord's Prayer, The
Romualdez
Sleep Song
Ronell
Willow Weep For Me
Roodney
Rochester Marching Song
Rooney
Are You The O'Reilly
Oceans Apart
Root
At My Work I'm Always Singing
Away The Track Is White
Battle Cry Of Freedom, The
Beautiful Evening Star
Boys Of Sanpete County, The
Brother Tell Me Of The Battle
Bugle Call, The
Call 'Em Names Jeff
Can The Soldier Forget
Columbia's Call
Come Hearts In Whose Pulses
Come To The Savior
Come To The Saviour
Cruising Boys Of Subdivision Nine,
The
Drummer Boy
Fair As The Morning
Farewell Father Friend And
Guardian
Foes And Friends
Glory Glory

Root *(Cont.)*
God Bless Our Brave Young
Volunteers
Good-Bye Old Glory
Hazel Dell, The
Honor To Sheridan
Housatonic Valley, The
I Will Lift Up Mine Eyes
In Heavenly Pastures
In His Name We Meet
Jesus Loves The Little Children
Jewels
Johnny Schmoker
Just After The Battle
Just Before The Battle Mother
Knocking Knocking
Knocking Knocking Who Is There
Lay Me Down And Save The Flag
Lord Is In His Holy Temple, The
Lord Is Ris'n, The
Lord Is Risen Indeed, The
Minnehaha
Music In The Air
My Days Are Gliding Swiftly By
Narrow And Straight
National Song
Never Forget The Dear Ones
Never Give Up The Right Way
Now May Awakes
Oh Where Are The Reapers
On On On The Boys Came Marching
Our Leaky Tents
Peaceful The Morning
Pilgrim's Vesper Song
Prisoner Free, The
Reaper On The Plain, The
Ring The Bells Of Heaven
River's Laughing Song, The
Shall Man O God Of Light And Life
Shining Shore
Stand Up For Uncle Sam
There Is A Land Of Pure Delight
There's Music In The Air
Tramp, The
Tramp Tramp Tramp
Tramp Tramp Tramp The Boys Are
Marching
Vacant Chair, The
Voice In The Air, A
Vote For Prohibition
When He Cometh
When The Heart Is Young
Where Are The Reapers
Why Do You Wait
With Joy We Greet
Within The Sound Of The Enemy's
Guns
Yes We'll Meet In The Morning
Root & Fosdick
Independent Farmer, The
Root & Funderburgh
Guide Of La Verne
Rootham
How Sleep The Brave

Roper & Wills
Love Struck

Roppolo & Mares & Morton & Melrose
Milenberg Joys

Rore
O Morte Eterno Fin

Rorem
Silver Swan, The
Song Of David, A
Youth With The Red-Gold Hair, The

Rosa
Star Vicino
Star Vicino Al Bell' Idolo
To Be Near The Fair Idol
To Be Near Thee
Vado Ben Spesso

Rosas
Loveliest Night Of The Year
Over The Waves
Sobre Las Olas

Rosasco
Come Celbrate Jesus
Household Of Faith

Rosche
Crown Him
He Keepeth Me Ever

Rose
Abiding Love
Avalon
Blue Eyes Crying In The Rain
Coming Into My Years
Deep Water
End Of The World, The
Foggy River
Holiday For Strings
Linger Awhile
Stripper, The
Theme From My Dad Can't Be
   Crazy Can He
Theme From The Monroes
Waltz Of The Wind
Worlds
Young And Alive

Rose & Bloom & Breuer
Does Your Chewing Gum Lose Its
   Flavor On The Bedpost
   Overnight

Rose & Cavanaugh & Stock
Umbrella Man, The

Rose & Conrad
Barney Google

Rose & David
Tonight You Belong To Me

Rose & Dixon & Henderson
That Old Gang Of Mine

Rose & Heath
Take These Chains From My Heart

Rose & Heyman & Green
I Wanna Be Loved

Rose & Kennedy & Bunch
First Word In Memory Is Me, The
He's Letting Go
Somebody Else's Fire

Rose & Nelson & Nelson
Hang Your Head In Shame

Rose & Slash & Stradlin' & McKagan
Sweet Child O' Mine

Rose & Slash & Stradlin & McKagan & Adler
Patience

Rose & Turner
It's A Sin

Rosenberg & Weinman
Too Much

Rosenfeld
Don't Be Angry With Them Dear
I'll Marry The Man I Love
Just Tell Them That You Saw Me
Mayn Rue Plats
She Was Happy Till She Met You
Take Back Your Gold
Those Wedding Bells Shall Not Ring
   Out
When Bob White Is Whistling In The
   Meadow
With All Her Faults I Love Her Still

Rosenfeld & Graham
She Was Happy Till She Met You

Rosenfeld & Williams
Let Me Shake The Hand That Shook
   The Hand Of Sullivan

Rosenman
Theme From East Of Eden
Theme From Marcus Welby Md
Theme From Rebel Without A Cause
Theme From Star Trek IV The
   Voyage Home

Rosenmuller
Till He Come O Let The Words

Rosenthal
Imagine That
Man Who Couldn't Walk Around,
   The
Maybe It's Time For Me
Theme From Fantasy Island

Rosette
Sailor Or Soldier

Rosey
Handicap March, The

Rosier
Alabama, The

Ross
Curtain In The Window
Find Another Fool
Goin' For A Ride
Harden My Heart
Join All The Glorious Names
Mademoiselle From Armentieres
Mama's Christmas Song
Take Another Picture
Take Me To Heart
We Shall Overcome

Ross & Abel
Let's Go

Ross & Adler & Howell
Even Now

Ross & Bobrick
Girl Of My Best Friend, The

Ross & Byers
Girls Nite Out

Ross & Dixon
Lollipop

Ross & Neil
Candy Man

Rosseau
Come Thou Fount

Rosseter
And Would You See My Mistress'
   Face
Let Him That Will Be Free
What Heart's Content Can He Find
What Is A Day
When Laura Smiles
Whether Men Do Laugh Or Weep

Rossi
If You Should Leave Me
Na Voce 'Na Chitarra E'o Poco 'E
   Luna
One Day I'll Buy A Trumpet
Only With You
Without You
You Could've Heard A Heart Break

Rossi & Testa & McCreery
One Day I'll Buy A Trumpet

Rossini
Ah Quel Giorno
Assisa Aun Pie D'Un Salice
At Last Hope's Cheering Ray
Barber Of Seville Overture, The
Belraggio Lusinghier
Cavatina
Charity
Cujus Animam
Di Piacer Mi Balza Il Cor
Frag Ich Mein Beklommes Herz
Inflammatus
Lord While For All Mankind We
   Pray
Mira La Bianca Luna
O God Who Givest All Things
O Thou From Whom All Goodness
   Flows
O Thou In All Thy Might
Oh Patria
Pastorella Delle Alpi, La
Promessa, La
Pull Away Brave Boys
There's A Voice That I Enshrine
To Him From Whom Our Blessings
   Flow
Una Voce Poco Fa
Up The Hills
Vesper Bells
Voce Poco Fa, Una
Walk In The Light So Shalt Thou
   Know
What Various Hindrances We Meet
When To Danger Duty Calls Me

Rossini *(Cont.)*
Whene'er The Household Board Is
Spread
William Tell Overture
Willow Song, The
Rossman
Copying Mother
Dream-Man
Geese
Grocer Man, The
I'm A Duck
Jumping Rope, The
Little Bunny Hops
Little Wind
My Daddy's Watch
Policeman, The
Robin In The Rain
Snowflakes
Song Of The Meadowlark
Swinging
Swish
Trot Trot Trot
Wave Your Hand Policeman
Wonderful Man Of Snow, A
Year's At The Spring, The
Rost
Umtrunk, Der
Rostill
If You Love Me
If You Love Me Let Me Know
Let Me Be There
Rota
Dolce Vita, La
Godfather Waltz, The
Love Said Goodbye
Romeo And Juliet
Speak Softly Love
Theme From Godfather II
Time For Us, A
Rotella
Abbracciami
Baby-O
Roth
Over The Chaos Of The Empty
Waters
Rosa Lee
Thou Who Sentest Thine Apostles
You Painted Pictures
Roth & Tuggle
Just Like Paradise
Stand Up
Roth & Vai
Yankee Rose
Rothrock & Yakus & Jeffrey
Old Cape Cod
Rothschild
If You Have Naught To Tell Me
Truly
Rotoli
Fiore Che Langue
Love Song

Rotten & Jones & Cook & Matlock
Anarchy In The U K
God Save The Queen
Pretty Vacant
Rotten & Vicious & Jones & Cook
Holidays In The Sun
Roubanis
Misirlou
Rounsefell
I'll Go Where You Want Me To Go
It May Not Be On The Mountain's
Height
Rouse
Orange Blossom Special
Roush
Far Out On Cedar Crest
Rousseau
Come Sinners Poor And Needy
Come Ye Sinners Poor And Needy
Cradle Hymn
Cradle Hymns
Evening And Morning
Hark The Vesper Hymn
Hark 'Tis The Breeze
Hush My Babe
I Love Jesus He's My Savior
Lord Dismiss Us
Lord Dismiss Us With Thy Blessing
Que Le Jour Me Dure
Rose Tree, The
Rosier, Le
Thoughts Of Wonder
When The Mists Have Rolled Away
Roussel
Mon Coeur A Vous Belle Se
Recommande
Routley
Come O Thou Traveler
Go Forth For God Go To The World
Heavens Are Not Too High, The
What Does The Lord Require
Rowan
You Make Me Feel Like A Man
Rowand
Far Above The Winding Coosa
Rowe
All Is Well
Dewdrop, A
Good Resolution, A
Jack Frost
Merry-Go-Round
Song In My Heart, The
Spring
Stand On His Promises
Starlight Starbright
There Was A Little Girl
Rowe & Ackley
I Would Be Like Jesus
Rowe & Dotson & Stevens & Carter
Sweet Country Music
Rowe & Smith
Love Lifted Me

Rowen
Coronation March
Friends On The Farm
My Shadow
Sing A Song
Rowland
He Will Roll You Over The Tide
Jessica's Theme
Man From Snowy River, The
We Are A Race Of Freemen
Wedding Invitation, A
Rowland & Adams & Patterson
Come On Eileen
Rowlands & Parry
Maid Of Mona's Isle
Winnie's Primrose
Rowles
Peacocks
Rowley
I Have An Apple Tree
Mister Sailorman
Service
There Was An Old Man
Rowley & Bilhorn
I Will Sing The Wondrous Story
Rox
It's A Big Wide Wonderful World
Roy
Fire Brigade, The
Mill, The
This Little Rose
Royal & Burnette & Sovine & Hill
Teddy Bear
Roze
Voici Le Printemps
Rozsa
Love Theme From Ben-Hur
Love Theme From El Cid
Lygia
Robbins
She Just Started Liking Cheatin'
Songs
Ruark & Kirkpatrick
You May Have The Joy-Bells
Rubbra
Virgin's Cradle Hymn, The
Rubens
Your King And Country
Rubenstein
Angel, The
Gelb Rollt Mir Zu Fussen
Gold Rolls Here Beneath Me
Theme From Blue Thunder
Video Fever
Wanderer's Night Song
Rubin
Ballad Of The Triangle Fire, The
Happy Birthday To Me
Yugnt-Himen
Rubin & Mills & McHugh & Dash
What Has Become Of Hinky Dinky
Parlay Voo

Rubinshtein
Du Bist Wie Eine Blume
Thou'rt Like Unto A Flower

Rubinstein
Am Abend
Angel, The
Asra, Der
Asra, The
At Saint Blaize
Autumnal Fancies
Barberine's Song
Be Not So Coy Beloved Child
Beim Scheiden
Bird, The
Bring 'em Back Alive
Clara's Song
Clouds
Dawn, The
Dew Is Sparkling, The
Dew-Drop, The
Dream, A
Drinking Song
Du Bist Wie Eine Blume
Earth Has Rest, The
Easter Morn With Gladness Shine
Engel, Der
Entomb Me Neath Roses
Fair Bud
Fatme
Flower, The
Fly Away Nightingale
Forest Solitude
Fruhlingsglaube
Fruhlingslied
Gelb Rollt Mir Zu Fussen
Glistening Dew, The
God Bade The Sun
Golden Sun It Shineth, The
Good Night
I Feel Thy Breath In Sweetness
Just As A Lark In Ether Trills
Lark, The
Lay Thy Tschadra Aside
Leaflet, The
Lied Der Vogelein
Longings
Loss
Lotusblume, Die
Love's Wonders
Mariner, The
Meeresabend
Melody In F
Modern Greek Song
Morning
Morning Song
My Heart Is Bright With Thee
Nacht, Die
Nightingale And The Rose
Not E'en Angels
Now The Shades Are Deepening
O Ask Not Why
O Fair And Sweet And Holy
O Sweetheart Mine
O When She Sings

Rubinstein (*Cont.*)
Page, The
Ravens, The
Remember Me
Ring Ring
Ringlet, The
Rock, The
Romance
Sang Das Voegelein
Scarecrow And Mrs King
Sehnsucht
Since First I Met Thee
Theme From Blue Thunder
Thine Eyes So Blue
Thou Art Like Unto A Flower
Thou Art So Like A Flower
Thou'rt Like A Tender Flower
Thou'rt Like Unto A Flower
Three Pictures
To Thy Health Drink I
Traum, Der
Traum, Ein
Turteltaube Und Der Wanderer, Die
Twilight
Video Fever
Voglein, Das
Voices Of The Woods
Volkslied
Voruber
Waldlied
Wanderer's Night Song
Wanderers Nachtlied
Welcome Sweet Springtime
When Thy Soft Voice I Hear
When Thy Tiny Feet I See
Witch Of The Forest, The
Wolke, Die
Woman's Prayer, A
Yearnings
You Are Like A Lovely Flower

Ruby
Real McCoys, The
Thinking Of You
This Heart Of Mine
Three Little Words
Whatever It Is I'm Going Against It

Rudisill
Eight O'Clock Rush, The

Rudnitska
Dremlen Feygl

Rudnitzky
S'Dremlin Feygl

Rudolf
Honnan Jo A Feny
Mezei Bokreta

Rudorff
Treue Liebe

Ruebush
Are You Living A Life That Counts
Have You Saved One Today

Rueyan
Birdlings Sweet Did Sing

Ruff
Envoi

Ruggles
Our College Home

Rugulo
Fugitive, The

Ruhn
Nun Schlafen Die Voglein

Ruiz
Amor
Cuanto Le Gusta
Sway

Rule
All Over Nothing At All
Have A Smile

Rumshinsky & Lilliam
Shloimele Malkele

Rumshinsky & Tauber
Shen Vi Di L'Vone

Rundgren
Hello It's Me

Runkel
Eternal Light Eternal Light

Runkle
Love Song

Runyan
Forward Still With Face Full
   Forward
Great Is Thy Faithfulness
Lord I Have Shut The Door
Saviour For Me, The
We Thank Thee For The Brawny
   Arm

Runyon
Keep Cool

Rupert
O Katy O'Neil

Rusch
Christmas Greeting

Rush
All Your Love
Double Trouble
Whiskey River

Rush & Linde
Walkin' A Broken Heart

Rushing
Cajun Moon
Jimmy's Blues

Russel
Ole Dan Tucker

Russel & James & Pepper
Vaya Con Dios

Russell
All Out Of Love
Bluebird
Cheer Boys Cheer
Deseret
From The Eastern Mountains
Honey
I Cannot Find Thee
If Only For One Night
Ivy Green, The
Lamb Of God Our Saviour
Life By The Cabin Fire, A
Life On The Ocean Wave, A
Life On The Vicksburg Bluff, A

Sammartini
Bells In The Steeple, The
Sammis
Horned Frogs We Are All For You
Sammis & Towner
Trust And Obey
Samoht & Wilson
Stoned Love
Samoset & Berg
Mining For Coal
Sampson
Hey Dog
I Loved 'em Every One
Sailor's Consolation, The
Under The Greenwood Tree
Samudio
Wooly Bully
Samuel
Diaphenia
Nanny
Oh My Swetynge
Samuels
Good-Night
Sanchez De Fuentes
Fair Cuba
Tu
Sandburg
Hail To The Chief
Sandell
Children Of The Heavenly Father
Sandell & Ahnfelt
Day By Day
Sander
When Thy Heart With Joy O'er
Flowing
Sanders
Adios Muchachos
He Leads Us On
Millennium
Mole End Carol, The
When The Lord Of Love Was Here
Sanders & Pate
When I Didn't Have A Prayer
Sanders & Stevens
Sally Go Round The Roses
Sanderson
Great Master Touch Us
Hail To The Chief
Sandfer
On My Way
Sandford
Talk To Me
Sandor
Angel With Eyes That Are Blue And
Bright
Thou Believest That It Is Love
Sandoval
Serenata Gitana
Sin Tu Amor
Sandrin
Douce Memoire
Puisque Vivre En Servitude

Sands
Mount The Barricades
Not If But When
Song Of The Builders
We'll Sing Her Praises
Sandstrom & Price & Steele
Save The Night For Me
Sanford
Lubly Dine
Miss Lucy Neale
Talk To Me
Sankey
Able To Deliver
After The Darkest Hour
At The Cross
At The Door
Be Ye Strong In The Lord
Beyond The Sea
Bless This Hour Of Prayer
Blessed Be The Name
Calm Me My God
Cast Thy Bread Upon The Waters
Christian's Good-Night, The
Clanging Bells Of Time, The
Cleansing Fountain, The
Come And Let Us Worship
Come Up Higher
Encamped Along The Hills Of Light
Evening Hymn, An
Evening Prayer, An
Everlasting Hills, The
Fading Away Like The Stars Of The
Morning
Full Assurance
Gather In The Sheaves
Glory Ever Be To Jesus
God Is Love
God Whose Farm Is All Creation
God's Time Now
Grand Is The Song
Harbor Bell, The
Have You Sought
He Is Coming
He Will Hide Me
Hiding In Thee
How Dear To My Heart
How Long
How Precious The Promise
I Am Praying For You
I Am Redeemed
I Come O Blessed Lord
I Have A Saviour
I Have A Saviour He's Pleading
I Will Bow And Be Simple
If I Were A Voice
It Came To Me
It Passeth Knowledge
Jesus I Will Trust Thee
Jesus Knows Thy Sorrow
Lead Me On
Let Us Stand Up For Jesus
Light After Darkness
Lily Of The Valley, The
Lord Is My Refuge, The

Sankey *(Cont.)*
Love Of Jesus, The
Many Mansions, The
Mission Hymn
My Hiding Place
Near To Thee
Ninety And Nine, The
O Blessed Word
O Brother Life's Journey Beginning
O Child Of God
O Come To The Merciful Saviour
O Give Thy Heart To Jesus
O Land Of The Blessed
O Precious Word
O Safe To The Rock
O To Be Nothing
O What A Saviour
O Wondrous Land
O World Of Joy Untold
Oh Wonderful Word
Oh Wondrous Name
Only Remembered
Onward Onward
Onward Upward Homeward
Praise The Lord And Worship Him
Precious Thoughts
Press Forward O Soldiers
Press On
Resurrection Morn
There Were Ninety And Nine That
Safely Lay
Trusting Jesus
Trusting Jesus That Is All
Under His Wing
Under His Wings
Waiting For Thy Coming
Walking In The Sunshine
We Praise Thee We Bless Thee
Welcome Wanderer Welcome
Wells Of Salvation
What A Gathering
When The King Shall Come
When The Mists Have Rolled Away
Where My Saviour Leads
Where The Savior Leads
While The Days Are Going By
Who Is On The Lord's Side
Whoever Will
Whosoever Calleth
Whosoever Shall Call
Whosoever Will May Come
Wondrous Cross, The
Year Of Precious Blessings, A
Yet There Is Room
Santiago
Alma Mater
Ave Maria
Bagumbayan
Commencement March
Dignity Of Labor, The
Peace Of Night, The
Philippines My Philippines
Rizal's Birthday

Santiago *(Cont.)*
Song Of Hope, A
To The Banner Of Learning
Santiago & Vermelho
Rio
Santly
There's Yes Yes In Your Eyes
Santner
Tantum Ergo
Santoliquido
Tre Poesie Persiane
Sarde
Tess
Sargent
Building For Eternity
Life On The Ocean Wave, A
Manhattan Joy Ride
Yankee Thunders
Sarig
Or Virushalayim
Sarjeant
Watchman What Of The Night
Sarona
Dip Boys Dip The Oar
Sarradel
La Golondrina
Sarradell
Swallow, The
Sarson
King's Men, The
Sarti
Lungi Dal Caro Bene
Sass
Harvest Time
Sattler
Hay-Ride, The
Saudill & Walker
Sailor's Home, The
Sauer
Ich Mache Alles Neu
Siegesfurst, Der
When It's Springtime In The Rockies
Saunders
Lost Lost Undone
Saunders & Sell
Cha Cha In The Park
Saunderson & Grey & Holman
Good Life
Sauter
All The Cats Join In
Savage
At Our House
Grace
Poor Ralpho
Walking With Jesus
Savigar & Cregan
Tonight I'm Yours
Savigar & Stewart & Cregan
Forever Young
Saville
Waits, The
Savino
Santa Lucia

Savino & Derose
March Of The Marionettes
Savitt & Watson
It's A Wonderful World
Savona
Ricordate Marcellino
Saward
I Thank You Lord
Sawtell
Theme From Voyage To The Bottom
Of The Sea
Sawyer
I Hae A Curl
Mother Would Comfort Me
National Thanksgiving Hymn
Who Will Care For Mother Now
Sawyer & Burton
Ain't Gonna Eat Out My Heart
Anymore
Sawyer & Hunter & Bullock & Goga
Yesterday's Dreams
Sawyer & McLeod
Love Hangover
**Sawyer & Taylor & Wilson & Cosby &
Ceordy**
I'm Livin' In Shame
Sawyer & Taylor & Wilson & Richards
Love Child
Sawyer & Ware & Bristol
Take Me Girl I'm Ready
Saxe
Railroad Chorus
Saxe & David
Rose In A Garden Of Weeds, A
Saxon
There Must Be A Way
Sayer & Poncia
You Make Me Feel Like Dancing
Sayers
Ta-Ra-Ra Boom-Der-E
Ta-Ra-Ra-Boom-De-Ay
Sayles
Beautiful Star In Heaven So Bright
Sayne
Oh What A Night It Must Have
Been
Scaggs
We're All Alone
Scaggs & Foster
Breakdown Dead Ahead
Jojo
Look What You've Done To Me
Scaggs & Paich
Lido Shuffle
Lowdown
Scaife & Scaife & Thomas
Drinkin' My Way Back Home
Scandello
Little White Hen, The
Scanlan
Bye Bye Baby Bye Bye
Gathering The Myrtle With Mary
I Love Music
Live My Love Oh Live

Scanlan *(Cont.)*
Molly O
Moonlight At Killarney
My Maggie
My Nelly's Blue Eyes
Over The Mountain
Peek-A-Boo
Remember Boy You're Irish
Scanlan's Rose Song
Scanlan's Swing Song
There's Always A Seat In The Parlor
For You
What's In A Kiss
You And I Love
Scaramuzza
I Love A Flower
Scarano & Skorsky & Gomez
You're My Everything
Scarlatti
Ah If Thou Would'st Cease To
Wound
Cara E Dolce
Cease Oh Cease
Hark The Voice Of Jesus
Non Vogl' Io Se Non Vederti
Sento Nel Core
Sun O'er The Ganges, The
Violette, Le
Scarlatti, Allessandro
Gia Il Sole Dal Gange
O Cessate Di Piagarmi
Se Florindo E Fedele
Schaab
Geh Aus Mein Herz
Schaefer
Boat Song
Schaeffer
Hunger March
Lenin Our Leader
Strife Song
Schafer
Thine Arm O Lord In Days Of Old
Schafer & Levin
I Like Him
She Touched Me
Schaffer
Gift Of Wheat From Thy Teeming
Fields
Schalchlin
I Will Trust The Lord
Schalk
Eternal Spirit Of The Living Christ
Now The Silence Now The Peace
Schaller
Magnificat
Scharf
Ben
Like To Get To Know You
Schauffler
Happy Landing
Scheff & Dexter
We Can Last Forever

Scheff & Sandford & Caldwell
What Kind Of Man Would I Be
Scheffler
Life Of Ages Richly Poured
Scheib & Barer
Mighty Mouse Theme Song, The
Scheidemann
Puer Nobis Nascitur
Scheidt
Eternal Light Shine In My Heart
O Jesu Sweet
O Little One Sweet
Schein
Captain Of Israel's Host
Cloud And Sunshine
Columbian Doxology No. 2
God Whom Earth And Sea And Sky
Lo God Is Here
Mir Nach Spricht Christus
O Lord All Glorious Life Of Life
O Love How Deep How Broad How
High
O Thou Who Camest From Above
Sollt Ich Mein Freud Verschweigen
Thou Art O God
Thou Hallowed Chosen Morn Of
Praise
What Means This Glory 'Round Our
Feet
Scheinert
Slugger Theme, The
Schelling
Blue And The Gray, The
Schemelli
Sing Praise To God
Schenkendorf
Habt Ihr Nimmer Noch Erfahren
Schenker
Big City Nights
I'm Leaving You
Rhythm Of Love
Rock You Like A Hurricane
Still Loving You
Schertzinger
Chalita
I Remember You
Marcheta
Tangerine
Scheu
Sleepy Sidney
Schew
Hail Working Class
Schicht
Now When The Dusky Shades Of
Night
When Winds Are Raging
Schien
Lotha
Schifrin
Burning Bridges
Down Here On The Ground
Fox, The
Love Theme From The Competition
Mannix

Schifrin *(Cont.)*
Mission Impossible
Mission Impossible Theme
That Night
Theme From Petrocelli
Schilitz & Maher & Bickhardt
Turn It Loose
Schilling
Come O Come With Harp And
Timbrel
God Is Everywhere
Hark A Burst Of Heavenly Music
His Glory Crowns The Year
Out Of Every Clime And People
There's A Beautiful Star
Schimmel
Turkeys
Schimmerling
Easter
Hymn Of Glory Let Us Sing, A
Hymn Of The Saviour, The
Hymn Of The Trinity, The
Lord Jesu Think On Me
O Soul Of Mine
O Unity Of Threefold Light
Royal Banners Forward Fly, The
Safe Home
Whence Shall My Tears Begin
Schinelli
Grape Gathering
Schipiro
For God And Country
Schlesinger
Bronze-Brown Eyes
Schless
On The Wings Of Love
Schletterer
Wir Wollen Ihm Die Krippe
Schlitz
Gambler, The
Midnight Girl Sunset Town
Schlitz & Bellamy & Bellamy
Center Of My Universe, The
I Could Be Persuaded
You'll Never Be Sorry
Schlitz & Bonagura & Baillie
She Deserves You
Schlitz & Cartwright
I Watched It All On My Radio
Schlitz & Chapman
Strong Enough To Bend
Schlitz & Fadden
When It's Gone
Schlitz & Gill
Satisfy You
Schlitz & Jarvis & Judd
Guardian Angels
Schlitz & Lowery
Say What's In Your Heart
Schlitz & Maher
Rockin' With The Rhythm Of The
Rain

Schlitz & Maher & Bickhardt
I Know Where I'm Going
Turn It Loose
Schloeder
Christus Factus Est
Sleep Holy Babe
Schlos
Peace Of Mind
Schlosser
He That Keepeth Israel
Schmertz
Noah Found Grace In The Eyes Of
The Lord
Schmidt
Celebration
Earthly Paradise
Everything Beautiful Happens At
Night
Fifty Million Years Ago
Gonna Be Another Hot Day
Greatest Of These, The
Hark Ye Ransomed Nations
Honeymoon Is Over, The
I Can See It
I Do I Do
I Love His Face
I'm Glad To See You Got What You
Want
I'm Gonna Wear Your Love
Is It Really Me
Love Don't Turn Away
Love Isn't Everything
Love Song
Man And A Woman, A
Much More
My Cup Runneth Over
My Garden
Never Say No
Oil Well Song, The
Postcards
Raunchy
Roll Up The Ribbons
Room Is Filled With You, The
Simple Little Things
Somebody
Soon It's Gonna Rain
Thank You For Your Love
They Were You
Together Forever
Try To Remember
Under The Tree
Ungeduldige Liebhaber, Der
What Is A Woman
Where Are The Snows
Wonderful Way To Die, A
Schmidt & Schulz
O Come Little Children
Schmit & Jennings & Gaitsch
Boys Night Out
Schmolzer
When Far On The Hillside
Schnaars & Schuyler
Nothing Like Falling In Love

Schubert (*Cont.*)

Allmacht, Die
Almighty, The
Alpenjager, Der
Alpine Hunter
Als Ich Sie Errothen Sah
Alte Liebe Rostet Nie
Altschottische Ballade, Eine
Am Bach Im Fruhling
Am Brunnen Vor Dem Thore
Am Feierabend
Am Fenster
Am Flusse
Am Grabe Anselmo's
Am Meer
Am See
Am Strome
Amalia
Ammenlied
Amphiaraos
An Chloen
An Dem Mond
An Den Fruhling
An Den Mond
An Den Mond In Einer Herbstnacht
An Den Schlaf
An Den Tod
An Die Apfelbaume Wo Ich Julien
    Erblickte
An Die Entfernte
An Die Freude
An Die Freunde
An Die Geliebte
An Die Laute
An Die Leier
An Die Leyer
An Die Musik
An Die Nachtigall
An Die Natur
An Die Sonne
An Die Untergehende Sonne
An Eine Quelle
An Emma
An Mein Clavier
An Mein Herz
An Mein Klavier
An Mignon
An Rosa I
An Rosa II
An Schwager Kronos
An Sie
An Silvia
An Sylvia
Andenken
Anselmo's Grave
Antigone Und Oedip
Atlas
Atys
Auf Bethlems Stillen Auen
Auf Dem Flusse
Auf Dem See
Auf Dem Strom
Auf Dem Wasser Zu Singen
Auf Den Tod Einer Nachtigall

Schubert (*Cont.*)

Auf Der Bruck
Auf Der Brucke
Auf Der Donau
Auf Der Riesenkoppe
Auf Einen Kirchhof
Aufenthalt
Auflosung
Augenlied
Aus Der Deutschen Messe
Aus Diego Manazares
Aus Heliopolis I
Aus Heliopolis II
Ave Maria
Ballade
Bei Dem Grabe Meines Vaters
Bei Dir
Beim Winde
Berge, Die
Bertha's Lied In Der Nacht
Betende, Die
Birds, The
Blanka
Blinde Knabe, Der
Bliss
Blondel Zu Marien
Blumen Schmerz, Der
Blumenbrief, Der
Blumenlied
Blumensprache, Die
Bootgesang
Bose Farbe, Die
Boy And The Rose, The
Brooklet , The
Bundeslied
Burgschaft, Die
Butterfly, The
By Murmuring Brook
By The Sea
By The Stream
Calm At Sea
Carrier Dove, The
Chorus Of The Angels
Confidential
Cora An Die Sonne
Coronach
Courage
Cradle Song
Credo
Cronnan
Danksagung An Den Bach
Daphne Am Bach
Dass Sie Hier Gewesen
De'il's Awa', The
Death And The Maiden
Dem Unendlichen
Des Baches Wiegenlied
Des Madchens Klage
Des Mullers Blumen
Dithyrambe
Doppelganger, Der
Dradle Song
Drang In Die Ferne
Du Bist Die Ruh

Schubert (*Cont.*)

Du Liebst Mich Nicht
Echo, Das
Edone
Edward Edward
Eifersucht Und Stolz
Einsame, Die
Einsamkeit
Einsiedelei, Die
Ellen's Gesang
Ellen's Gesang I
Ellen's Gesang II
Ellen's Gesang III
Elysium
Emma
Entfernten, Der
Entsuhnte Orest, Der
Entzuckung
Entzuckung An Laura, Die
Erelafsee
Erinnerungen
Erl King, The
Erlafsee
Erlkonig
Erntelied
Erscheinung, Die
Erstarrung
Erster Verlust
Erwartung, Die
Estarrung
Evening Glow
Fahrt Zum Hades
Faith In Spring
Farewell
Favorite Color, The
Fee, La
Finden, Das
Fischer, Der
Fischerlied
Fischermadchen
Fischers Liebesgluck, Des
Fischerweise
Fluchtling, Der
Flug Der Zeit, Der
Fluss, Der
Forelle, Die
Fragment Aus Dem Aeschylus
Freiwilliges Versinken
Freude Der Kinderjahre
Frohlichkeit, Die
Frohsinn
Frozen Heart, The
Fruhe Liebe, Die
Fruhen Graber, Die
Fruhlingsglaube
Fruhlingslied
Fruhlingssehnsucht
Fruhlingtraum
Fulle Der Liebe
Furcht Der Geliebten
Ganymed
Garden Musician, A
Gebet Wahrend Der Schlacht
Gebusche, Die

Schubert *(Cont.)*

Gefangenen Sanger, Die
Gefrorne Tranen
Geheimes
Geheimniss
Geheimniss, Das
Geist Der Liebe
Geistegruss
Geisternahe
Geisterstimme, Eine
Geistertanz, Der
Geistes-Gruss
Genugsamkeit
Gesang An Die Harmonie
Gesang An Sylvia
Gesang Der Norna
Gesange Des Harfners
Gestirne, Die
Gestorte Gluck, Das
Getauschte Verrather, Der
Glaube Hoffnung Und Liebe
Goldschmiedsgesell, Der
Gondelfahrer
Good Night
Gott Im Fruhling
Gott Im Fruhlinge
Gott Und Die Bajadere, Der
Gotter Griechenlands, Die
Grab, Das
Grab Und Mond
Grablied
Grablied Auf Einen Soldaten
Grablied Fur Die Mutter
Gravedigger
Gray Head, The
Greise Kopf, Der
Greisengesang
Grenzen Der Menschheit
Gretchen Am Spinnrade
Gretchen At The Spinning Wheel
Gretchen's Bitte
Grosse Halleluja, Das
Group From Tartarus
Gruhlingstraum
Gruppe Aus Dem Tartarus
Guide-Post, The
Gute Hirte, Der
Gute Nacht
Gypsy Song
Hagars Klage
Halt
Hanflings Liebeswerbung
Harfenspieler
Harfenspieler III
Hark Hark The Lark
Hedge-Rose, The
Hedge-Roses
Heidenroslein
Heimliches Lieben
Heimweh, Das
Hektors Abschied
Her Image
Her Portrait
Herbst

Schubert *(Cont.)*

Herbstabend, Der
Herbstlied
Hilltop Song, A
Hirt, Der
Hoffnung
Holy Holy Sholy
Huldigung
Hunter's Evening Song
Hurdy-Gurdy Man
Hurdy-Gurdy Man, The
Hymn Of Praise
Hymne I
Hymne II
Hymne III
Hymne IV
Ideal Longing
Idens Nachtgesang
Idens Schwanenlied
Ihr Bild
Ihr Grab
Il Modo Di Prender Moglie
Il Traditor Deluso
Im Abendrot
Im Abendroth
Im Dorfe
Im Freien
Im Fruhling
Im Haine
Im Walde
Impatience
In Der Ferne
In Der Mitternacht
In Evening's Glow
In Praise Of Tears
In Springtime
In Stillness Night Surrounds Us
In The Village
Incanto Degli Occhi, L'
Inn, The
Inquirer
Inquirer, The
Iphigenia
Irdisches Gluck
Irrlicht
Jagdlied
Jager, Der
Jager Ruhe Von Der Jagd
Jagers Abendlied
Jagers Liebeslied
Jock Of Hazeldean
Jolly Miller, The
Journey To Hades
Julius An Theone
Junge Nonne, Die
Jungling Am Bache, Der
Jungling An Der Quelle, Der
Jungling Auf Dem Hugel, Der
Jungling Und Der Tod, Der
Junglingswonne
Kampf, Der
Kennst Du Das Land
Klage
Klage Der Ceres

Schubert *(Cont.)*

Klaglied
Knabe, Der
Knabe In Der Wiege, Der
Knabenzeit, Der
Kolma's Klage
Konig In Thule, Der
Konig Von Thule, Der
Krahe, Die
Kreuzzug, Der
Kreuzzung, Der
Kriegers Ahnung
Labetrank Der Liebe
Lachen Und Weinen
Lad And The Stream
Lambertine
Last Greeting, The
Laube, Die
Laura Am Klavier
Lebenslied
Leichenphantasie, Eine
Leiden Der Trennung
Leidende, Der
Leiermann, Der
Letzte Hoffnung
Liane
Licht Und Liebe
Lieb Minna
Liebe
Liebe, Die
Liebe Farbe, Die
Liebe Hat Gelogen, Die
Liebende, Der
Liebende Schreibt, Die
Liebesbotschaft
Liebesgotter, Die
Liebeslauschen
Liebesrausch
Liebestandelei
Liebhaber In Allen Gestalten
Liebliche Stern, Der
Liebst Mich Nicht, Du
Lied
Lied Aus Der Ferne
Lied Der Anna Lyle
Lied Der Anne Lyle
Lied Der Liebe
Lied Der Mignon
Lied Des Gefangenen Jagers
Lied Des Orpheus Als Er In Die
    Holle Ging
Lied Eines Kriegers
Lied Eines Schiffers An Die
    Dioskuren
Lied Im Grunen, Das
Lied Vom Reifen, Das
Liedesend
Liedler, Der
Lilla An Die Morgenrothe
Linden Tree, The
Lindenbaum, Der
Litanei Auf Das Fest Aller Seelen
Litaney
Litaney Auf Das Fest Aller Seelen

Schubert *(Cont.)*

Litany
Litany For The Feast Of All Saints
Lob Der Thranen
Lob Der Tranen
Lob Des Tokayers
Loda's Gespenst
Love's Message
Luisens Antwort
Macht Der Augen, Die
Macht Der Liebe, Die
Madchen Aus Der Fremde, Das
Madchen, Das
Madchen Von Inistore, Das
Madchens Klage, Des
Maiden's Lament, The
Mainacht, Die
Manner Sind Mechant, Die
March Militaire
Margaret At The Spinning-Wheel
Marie
Marienbild, Das
Maudit, Le
May Peace Abide With You
Meeres-Stille
Mein
Mein Gruss An Den Mai
Memnon
Mignon
Mignon I
Mignon II
Mignon Und Der Harfner
Mignon's Song
Mignonne Eveille-Toi
Miller's Flower, The
Minnelied
Minona
Misero Pargoletto
Mit Dem Grunen Lautenbande
Mock Suns, The
Moment Musicale
Mondabend, Der
Mondnacht, Die
Moon Of Silver White
Moon, The
Morgengruss
Morgenkuss, Der
Morgenkuss Nach Einem Ball, Der
Morgenlied
Morning Greeting
Muller Und Der Bach, Der
Musensohn, Der
Mut
My Abode
My Double
My Lone Abode
My Peace Thou Art
My Phantom Double
My Sweet Repose
Nach Einem Gewitter
Nacht, Die
Nacht Und Traume
Nachtgesang
Nachthymme

Schubert *(Cont.)*

Nachtstuck
Nachtviolen
Nahe Des Geliebten
Namenstagslied
Naturgenuss
Nebensonnen, Die
Neugierige, Der
Night And Dreams
None But The Lonely Heart
Nonne, Die
Normans Gesang
Now Love Has Falsely Played Me
O God The Rock Of Ages
Ode To Music
Oft In The Stilly Night
Ondine Et Le Pecheur, L'
Orest Auf Tauris
Organ Grinder, The
Orpheus
Ossians Lied Nach Dem Falle Nathos
Owls
Pastorella, La
Pause
Pax Vobiscum
Pensa Che Questo Istante
Perle, Die
Pflugerlied
Phidile
Philoktet
Pilgerweise
Pilgrim, Der
Pool, The
Post, Die
Post, The
Praise Of Tears
Prometheus
Punschlied
Questioner, The
Quiet Night, The
Rast
Raste Krieger Krieg Ist Aus
Rastlose Liebe
Rattenfanger, Der
Raven, The
Restless Love
Ritter Toggenburg
Romance
Romanze
Romanze Des Richard Lowenherz
Rose, Die
Rosebud, The
Rosenband, Das
Rosula In Parato
Ruckblick
Ruckweg
Ruhe Schonstes Gluck Der Erde
Sailor, The
Salve Regina
Sanctus
Sanger Am Felsen, Der
Sanger, Der
Sangers Habe, Des

Schubert *(Cont.)*

Sangers Morgenlied
Scene Aus Faust
Scene Aus Goethe's Faust
Schafer Und Der Reiter, Der
Schafers Klagelied
Schatten, Die
Schatzgraber, Der
Schatzgrabers Begehr
Schiffer, Der
Schiffers Scheidelied
Schlachtgesang
Schlaflied
Schlummerlied
Schmetterling, Der
Schubert
Schwager Kronos, An
Schwanengesang
Schwangesang
Schweizerlied
Schwertlied
Schwestergruss
Sehnen, Das
Sehnsucht
Sehnsucht Der Liebe
Sei Mir Gegrusst
Selige Welt
Seligkeit
Selma Und Selmar
Serenade
Serenata, La
Seufzer
Shilrik Und Vinvela
Sieg, Der
Skolie
Slumber Song
So Lasst Mich Scheinen
Sommernacht, Die
Son Fra L'Onde
Sonett I
Sonett II
Sonett III
Spinnerin, Die
Sprache Der Liebe
Spring Dreams
Springtide Longings
Stadt, Die
Standchen
Stars, The
Sterbende, Die
Sterne, Die
Sternennachte
Sternenwelten, Die
Stimme Der Liebe
Stormy Morning, The
Strom, Der
Sturmische Morgen, Der
Suleika
Suleika I
Suleika II
Suleika's Zweiter Gesang
Taglich Zu Singen
Taucher, Der
Tauschung, Die

Schubert (*Cont.*)
Thankfulness
Taubenpost, Die
Thee Love I Greet
Thekla
Think Me The Angel I Soon Shall Be
Tiefes Leid
Tischlerlied
Tischlied
To Be Sung On The Water
To His Lute
To Music
To The Eternal
To The Lyre
To The Moon
To The Nightingale
To Wander
Tod Oscars, Der
Tod Und Das Madchen, Der
Tod Und Der Jugling, Der
Todesmusik
Todtengraberlied
Todtengrabers Heimwehe
Todtengraberweise
Todtenkranz Fur Ein Kind
Todtenopfer
Town, The
Tranenregen
Trauer Der Liebe
Trauergesang
Traum, Der
Trinklied
Trinklied Aus Dem 14. Jahrhundert
Trinklied Vor Der Schlacht
Trockne Blumen
Trost
Trost An Elisa
Trost Im Liede
Trost In Thranen
Trout, The
Uber Wildemann
Um Mitternacht
Unfinished Symphony, The
Ungeduld
Ungluckliche, Der
Unterscheidung
Unterscheidung, Die
Uraniens Flucht
Vater Mit Dem Kind, Der
Vaterlandslied
Vatermorder, Der
Verfehlte Stunde, Die
Vergebliche Liebe
Vergissmeinnicht
Verklarung
Versunken
Vier Canzonen I
Vier Canzonen II
Vier Canzonen III
Vier Canzonen IV
Vier Weltalter, Die
Viola
Vogel, Die
Voice Of God Is Calling, The

Schubert (*Cont.*)
Vom Mitleiden Maria
Von Ida
Vor Meiner Wiege
Wachtelschlag, Der
Wallensteiner Lanzknecht Beim
    Trunk, Der
Wanderer An Den Mond, Der
Wanderer, Der
Wanderer, The
Wanderer An Den Mond, Der
Wanderer's Nachtlied
Wanderer's Night Song
Wandering
Wandern, Das
Wandrers Nachtlied
War Ich, Das
Warrior's Foreboding
Was Ist Sylvia
Wasserflut
Wegweiser, Der
Wehmut
Wehmuth, Die
Weiberfreund, Der
Weinen, Das
Welcome To All
Wer Kauft Liebesgotter
Wer Nie Sein Brod Mit Thranen Ass
Wer Sich Der Einsamkeit Ergiebt
Wetterfahne, Die
Where Are Those Who Long Have
    Striven
Whispering Breezes O'er The
    Mountain
Whither
Who Is Silvia
Who Is Sylvia
Who Ne'er With Tears Has Eaten
    Bread
Widerschein
Widerspruch
Wie Ulfru Fischt
Wiedersehn
Wiegenlied
Willkommen Und Abschied
Winterabend, Der
Winterlied
Wohin
Wonne Der Wehmuth
Young Nun, The
Ziehe Hin In Frieden
Zufriedene, Der
Zugenglocklein, Das
Zum Punsche
Zur Guten Nacht
Zurende Barde, Der
Zurnende Diana, Die
Zurnenden Diana, Der
Zwei Scenen
Zwerg, Der

Schucht
And Now Beloved Lord Thy Soul
    Resigning

Schuck
Glockenruf, Der
Mein Kamerad
Meinen Heiland Seh' Ich Gehen
Nur Mit Jesu Will Ich Pilger
    Wandern

Schuett
Spring's Awakening

Schuler
Keep The Love Of God In Your
    Heart
Make Me A Blessing
Oh What A Glory
Overshadowed
Praise Ye The Lord
To The Glory Land

Schulman
When You're Ugly Like Us

Schultes
Lambeth
Pray'r Is The Soul's Sincere Desire
Prayer Is The Soul's Sincere Desire

Schulthes
Jerusalem My Happy Home
Lamp Of Our Feet Whereby We
    Trace
Spirit Divine Attend Our Prayer
Thou To Whom The Sick And Dying

Schultz
Ihr Kinderlein Kommet
In Life's Earnest Morning
Praise The Lord Of Heaven
Purple And Gold, The

Schultze
Lili Marlene
Lilli Marlene

Schulz
Danket Dem Herrn
Das Ist Unbeschreiblich
Geist Vom Vater Taue Taue
Her Kommer Dine Armesma
Ihr Kinderlein Kommet
Lovely Evening
Meum Est Propositum
Meum Est Propostium
Neujahrslied
O Come Little Children
O Seht Auf Leisen Flugeln
Oh Come Little Children
Out-Of-Doors
Regina Caeli
Trost Fur Mancherei Tranen
We Plough The Fields
We Plough The Fields And Scatter
We Plow The Fields
We Plow The Fields And Scatter
Winterlied
Wir Pflugen Und Wir Streuen
Wirtshau, Das

Schumann
Abendlied
Abendstern, Der
All Praise To Thee Eternal Lord
Allnachtlich Im Traume

Schumann *(Cont.)*

Almond Tree, The
Alte Laute
Alten Bosen Lieder, Die
Amour Pour Amour
An Den Abendstern
An Den Sonnenschein
An Die Nachtigall
An Meinem Herzen An Meiner Brust
Anden Mond
Answer, The
Ant And The Grasshopper, The
Arbor Day
Arme Peter, Der
Attente
Auf Dem Rhein
Auftrage
Aurore De La Vie
Aus Den Ostlichen Rosen
Aus Meinen Thranen Spriessen
Autumn
Awake My Soul And With The Sun
Bedeckt Mich Mit Blumen
Beiden Grenadiere, Die
Bless Thou The Gifts
Blondel's Lied
Botschaft
Butterflies
By The Fireside
Capelle, Die
Carthage
Chant De Jeunes Filles
Child's Prayer
Christmas Song
Commit Thou All Thy Griefs
Confession
Cradle-Song
Das Ist Ein Floten Und Geigen
Declaration
Dedication
Dein Angesicht
Dem Helden
Dem Rothen Roslein Gleicht Mein
    Lieb
Der Bleicherin Nachtlied
Des Abends
Deserted Farm, The
Deutsche Rhein, Der
Devotion
Dragnet March, The
Du Bist Wie Eine Blume
Du Ring An Meinen Finger
Er Der Herrlichste Von Allen
Er Ist's
Er Und Sie
Erste Begegnung
Erstes Grun
Es Treibt Mich Hin
Evening Song
Evening Star, The
Failien-Gemalde
Fleur Mourante
Forth In Thy Name O Lord I Go
From Heaven Above

Schumann *(Cont.)*

From The Eastern Roses
Fruhlings Aukunft
Fruhlingsfahrt
Fruhlingsgruss
Fruhlingslied
Fruhlingsnacht
Garden Melody
Gluck, Das
Gratitude
Green Hat, The
Greenfinch, The
Guardian Angels
Guardians
Gypsy Life
Hail To The Sabbath Day
Happy Farmer, The
Highland Lullaby
Hinaus In's Freie
How Beauteous Were The Marks
    Divine
Hunting Song
I Liken Thee To A Flower
I Love The Quietness Of Prayer
I'll Ay Ca' In By Yon Toon
I'll Not Complain
Ich Denke Dein
Ich Grolle Nicht
Ich Hab' Im Traum Geweinet
Ich Kann Nicht Von Dir Lan
Ich Kann's Nicht Fassen Nicht
    Glauben
Ich Wand're Nicht
Ich Wandelte Unter Der Baumen
Im Walde
Im Westen
Im Wunderschonen Monat Mai
In Der Fremde
In Der Nacht
In Meeres Mitten
In The Woods
Intermezzo
Jager Wohlgemuth
Jasminenstrauch
Jung Volkers Lied
Jungling Liebt Ein Madchen, Ein
Kennst Du Das Land
Kinderwacht
King Of Kings
Klosterfraulein
Kuckucks Tod
Ladybird
Landliches Lied
Lasst Lautenspiel Und Becherklang
Let Us Be Thankful For Our Books
Lieb' Liebchen Leg's Handchen
Liebesgarten
Liebesgram
Liebeskummer
Liebhabers Standchen
Liesbte Was Kann Denn Uns
    Scheiden
Little Folk Song
Lord Speak To Me

Schumann *(Cont.)*

Lord Speak To Me That I May Speak
Loreley, The
Lotosblume, Die
Lotus Flower, The
Lotus Mystique
Lov'st Thou For Beauty
Mailied
Marienwurmchen
Marzveilchen
May-Dew, The
Meerfey
Mein Herz Ist Schwer
Minnesanger, Die
Mir Ist Ein Schons Brauns Maidelein
Mirage
Mit Myrthen Und Rosen
Mondnacht
Moonlight
Morning
My William
N'es-Tu Pas Le Regard De Dieu
Nachtbesuch
Nachtigall, Die
New Every Morning Is The Love
New Every Morning Is Thy Love
Nun Hast Du Mir Den Ersten
    Schmerz Gethan
Nussbaum, Der
O God Thy World Is Sweet With
    Prayer
O Golden Ray
O How Lovely Is My Darling
O Ihr Herren
O Master Let Me Walk With Thee
O Morning Light
O Thou Whose Glory Shone Like
    Fire
O Wie Lieblich Ist Das Madchen
O Ye Lordlings
Our Glorious Country
Out In The Open Air
Parade, The
Pitie
Plainte, La
Red Red Rose, A
Requiem
Ring, Der
Romanze
Rose And The Lily, The
Rose Die Lilie Die Taube, Die
Rose Die Lilie Die Taube Die Sonne,
    Die
Rose Stand Im Tau, Die
Rosebud Of The Wildwood
Rosmarien
'S Ist Nichts Mit Den Alten Weibern
Sandmann, Der
Schlachtgesang
Schlemmer, Der
Schlusslied Des Narren
Schmetterling
Schneeglockchen
Schon Blumelein
Schone Fremde

Schumann *(Cont.)*
Schone Wiege Meiner Leiden
Seit Ich Ihn Gesehen
Snowbells
So Wahr Die Sonne Scheinet
Soldatenbraut, Die
Soldier Song
Soldier's March
Soldier's Song
Song Of The Nightingale, The
Sonntags Am Rhein
Spring's Messenger
Springs Of Song
Standchen
Stille, Die
Stille Liebe
Stille Thranen
Summits Of Our Time
Sunday On The Rhine
Susser Freund Du Blickest
Swallows, The
Tamburinschlagerin
Tanzlied
Thou Art A Tender Blossom
Thou Art Like A Flower
Thou Art So Like A Flower
Thou 'rt Like Unto A Flower
Thou 'rt Lovely As A Flower
'Tis Spring
To The Sunshine
Ton Image
Traumerei
Two Grenadiers, The
Und Wussten's Die Blumen
Verlassene Magdlein, Das
Verrathene Liebe
Verschmitze, Die
Vetter Michel
Volksliedchen
Votum
Waise, Die
Waldesgesprach
Waldmadchen
Walnut Tree, The
Wanderlied
Was Will Die Einsame Thrane
Wassermann, Der
We Give Thee But Thine Own
We Lay Us Down To Sleep
Weihnachtlied
Wenn Ich Ein Voglein War
Wenn Ich In Deine Augen Seh'
Wha Is That At My Bower Door
When Gentle Winds
When May Has Blossomed Into
    Bloom
When That I Was A Little Boy
Widmung
Wiegenlied
Wind In The Cherry Tree
You Are Like A Lovely Flower

Schumer
Lipton Whistle Song

Schurbert
Kolma's Klage

Schuster
I'm Alone Because I Love You

Schuster & Cunningham & Whitcup
I Am An American

Schuster & Nelson
Ten Little Fingers And Ten Little
    Toes

Schutz
From Earthly Tasks Lift Up Thine
    Eyes
Glorious The Day When Christ Was
    Born
How Vain The Cruel Herod's Fear
Immortal Babe
O God The King Of Glory
Rejoice Ye Christians Loudly
Since Christ Our Lord Was Crucified
There Comes A Barque Full-Laden

Schuyler
16th Avenue
I Don't Know Where To Start
Love Out Loud
My Old Yellow Car

Schuyler & Knobloch
Little More Love, A

Schuyler & Overstreet
I Fell In Love Again Last Night
Long Line Of Love, A
You Can't Stop Love

Schvedov
With Heart Uplifted

Schwandt & Andree
Dream A Little Dream Of Me

Schwartz
All Good Gifts
Alone Together
Baby Talk
Beautiful City
Bedelia
Birds Fly Delightfully
Butterflies Are Free
By Myself
Chinatown My Chinatown
Corner Of The Sky
Dancing In The Dark
Day By Day
Flower Garden Ball, The
Gal In Calico, A
Ghost That Never Walked, The
Good-Bye Jonah
Hat My Father Wore Upon St
    Patrick's Day, The
Haunted Heart
Hello Hawaii How Are You
I Guess I'll Have To Change My
    Plans
I Love The Ladies
I See Your Face Before Me
I'm All Bound 'Round With The
    Mason Dixon Line
I'm Simply Crazy Over You

Schwartz *(Cont.)*
If There Is Someone Lovelier Than
    You
Ja Schon Ist Mein Schatz Nicht
Jour Et Nuit
Lady Be Good I See Your Face
    Before Me
Learn Your Lessons Well
Lion Tamer
Magic To Do
Mister Dooley
Oh But I Do
Prepare Ye
Prepare Ye The Way Of The Lord
Rainy Night In Rio, A
Rip Van Winkle Was A Lucky Man
Rock-A-Bye Your Baby With A Dixie
    Melody
Rum Tum Tiddle
Save The People
Something To Remember You By
That's Entertainment
Then I'll Be Tired Of You
They're Either Too Young Or Too
    Old
Through A Thousand Dreams
Triplets
Turn Back O Man
West End Avenue
Where The Red Red Roses Grow
With You
You And The Night And The Music

Schwartz & Friedman
Don't Shed A Tear

Schwartz & Prizant
Greene Kuzine, Di

Schwartz & Wyle
Ballad Of Gilligan's Island
Ballad Of Gilligan's Isle, The

Schwatz
That's Entertainment

Schweers
No One Mends A Broken Heart Like
    You

Schweers & Hicks & Murrah
That's What Her Memory Is For

Schweikert
Color The Children

Schweitzer
Sancta Maria
Tribulationes

Schweiz
Mir Ist Erbarmung Widerfahren

Schwind
Bonnie Flag
Flag Of Honor And Renown, The
Flag Raising Song
Land Imperial
My Home-Land Dear
Our Country's Flag
Our Lincoln Grant And Washington
Our Whole Country
Proudly Wave

Schwind *(Cont.)*
Reign Of Right And Education
Sleep Comrade Gently Sleep
Sciapiro
Columbus Day
SCLC
We Got A Thing Going
Scofield
Aileron
Beatles, The
Cassidae
Looks Like Meringue
Rough House
Spoons
V
Scoggin
Enter Into His Gates
Score & Reynolds & Maudsley
Space Age Love Song
Score & Reynolds & Score & Maudsley
I Ran So Far Away
Scott
Annie Laurie
Believe In Stevenson
Burning Bridges
Douglas Tender And True
Efficiency Rag
Evergreen Rag
Fascinator, The
Frog Legs Rag
God Is A Spirit
Gold M C, The
Great Scott Rag
Half The World
He Ain't Heavy He's My Brother
Honey Moon Rag
I've Got Rings On My Fingers
Jack Frost
Johnny Appleseed
Kansas City Rag
Lullaby
March Winds
My True Love
Now Is The Hour
On The Pike
On The Seashore
Open My Eyes That I May See
Ophelia Rag
Paramount Rag
Pop Muzik
Princess Rag, The
Prosperity Rag
Quality Rag
Red And Black, The
Ship Ahoy
Starsky And Hutch Theme
Summer Breeze, A
Sunburst Rag
Swing Me Higher Obadiah
Tarzan's Theme
Taste Of Honey, A
Thank You Lord
Theme From Sanchez Of Bel Air
Think On Me

Scott *(Cont.)*
Toy Trumpet, The
Tweedle Dee
Villanelle
What In The World's Come Over
    You
When The Heathen Trumpets Clang
Without Us
You're Not Alone
Zip Bang It Hit The Mark
Scott & De Koven
Oh Promise Me
**Scott & Dickerson & Brown & Miller &
    Jordan & Allen & Oskar**
Spill The Wine
Scott & Griffin
Love Is Like Oxygen
Scott & Jay & Seidman
Dancing Under A Latin Moon
Scott & Tucker & Priest & Connolly
California Nights
Scott & Wolfe
It's A Heartache
Scott-Gatty
All Things Are Thine
I Cannot Find Thee
Now Once Again For Help That
    Never Faileth
O Brother Man Fold To Thy Heart
O God Of Light Thy Word A Lamp
O Perfect Love All Human Thought
    Transcending
Scotto
It's Delightful To Be Married
Scriven & Converse
What A Friend We Have In Jesus
Scruggs
Call On Me
Foggy Mountain Breakdown
Hey Little Sister
Scruggs & Schuyler
Small Small World
Scruggs & Thompson
Count The Cost
Sea
Christ Alone Is Saviour
Christ Has Risen
Comforted
Counted Worthy
Following Fully
God's Bounty
I Belong To Jesus
I Wait For Thee O Lord
Make Me Willing
More Of Jesus
Up Yonder
Seal
Sea Song, A
Seals
I Dream Of Women Like You
One Friend
Two Old Cats Like Us

Seals & Barnes
Drinkin' And Dreamin'
Everybody Needs A Hero
I Won't Need You Anymore
Who's Gonna Fill Their Shoes
Seals & Barnes & Lyle
Joe Knows How To Live
Seals & Crofts
Diamond Girl
Get Closer
Summer Breeze
We May Never Pass This Way Again
Seals & Fritts
We Had It All
Seals & Kirby
No More One More Time
Seals & Lyle
Didn't We
Maybe Your Baby's Got The Blues
Seals & Meyer
Early In The Morning And Late At
    Night
Seals & Raven & Meyers
Bayou Boys
Seals & Setser
Seven Spanish Angels
Seals & Setser
Beyond Those Years
Country Girls
Let The Music Lift You Up
Seals & Setser & Diamond
I've Got A Rock N' Roll Heart
Seals & Sherrill & Barnes
Ten Feet Away
Seals & Williams
When We Make Love
Sealy
My Love And I
Seaman
Eternal Father God Of Grace
Safe In The Shadow Of The Lord
Surely God Loves Upright Men
Sears
Play On Love
Sears & Willis
It Came Upon The Midnight Clear
Seaton
Those Who Wait On The Lord
Seaver
Solomon Levi
Sebastian
Darling Be Home Soon
Daydream
Did You Ever Have To Make Up
    Your Mind
Do You Believe In Magic
Six O'Clock
Welcome Back Kotter
You And I
Sebastian & Boone & Sebastian
Summer In The City

Secunda
  Bei Mir Bist Du Schon
  Bei Mir Bist Du Schon Means That
      You're Grand
  Chazonim Oif Probe
  Donna Donna
Secunda & Schorr
  Mein Yiddishe Medele
Sedaka
  Oh Carol
  Where The Boys Are
Sedaka & Cody
  Laughter In The Rain
  Should've Never Let You Go
Sedaka & Greenfield
  Breaking Up Is Hard To Do
  Calendar Girl
  Love Will Keep Us Together
  Next Door To An Angel
  Oh Carol
Sedgwick
  Buckleys Sleighing Song
  Little Katy
Seeger
  All My Children Of The Son
  Bells Of Rhymney
  How Are We Going To Save
      Tomorrow
  I Want To Go To Andorra
  I'm Gonna Be An Engineer
  If You Love Your Uncle Sam
  If You Love Your Uncle Sam Bring
      Them Home
  Living In The Country
  My Dirty Stream
  One Man's Hands
  River Of My People
  Sailing Down My Golden River
  Song Of Myself
  Talkin' Union
  This Is A Land
  To My Old Brown Earth
  Turn Turn Turn
  Waist Deep In The Big Muddy
  Where Have All The Flowers Gone
  Who Killed Norma Jean
Seeger & Angula
  Guantanamera
Seeger & Hays
  Hammer Song, The
  If I Had A Hammer
Seeger & Hays & Lampell
  Union Train
Seeger & Hickerson
  Where Have All The Flowers Gone
Seely
  Leavin' And Sayin' Goodbye
Segal
  Melancholy Cow-Boy, The
Segal & Danzig
  Scarlet Ribbons
Seger
  Against The Wind
  American Storm

Seger *(Cont.)*
  Even Now
  Fire Lake
  Hollywood Nights
  Like A Rock
  Mainstreet
  Night Moves
  Roll Me Away
  Still The Same
  Understanding
  We've Got Tonight
  You'll Accomp'ny Me
Segur
  Dartmouth Song
Segura
  Telegrama, Un
Seidel
  Names Of Other Days, The
Seifert
  Ah If I Could But See Her
  More And More
Seismit-Doda
  Querida
Seitz & Lewis & Denny
  Before I Met You
Sekaric & Perren
  Reunited
Selby
  Widow Bird Sat Mourning , A
Selington
  Times Are Sadly Out Of Joint, The
Sellers
  Jesus Is Calling Thee
  Thy Word Is A Lamp To My Feet
Selnecker
  Awake My Heart And Render
  My Soul Awake And Render
  My Soul Awake And Render To God
Seltzer
  Eten Bamidbar
Sembello & Matkosky
  Maniac
Sembello & Sembello
  Automatic Man
Sembello & Willis
  Neutron Dance
  Stir It Up
Semmann
  Hail Alma Mater
Senesh & Zehavi
  Ashre Hagafrur
  Eli Eli
Senffel
  O Lord I Pray
Senicker
  Awake My Heart
Sergei & Whitol
  My God And I
Sering
  Was Verlangst Du Warum Bangst
      Du
Serling & Mills
  Meet Me In St Louis

Sermisy
  Jouissance Vous Donnerai
  Martin Menait Son Pourceau
  Tant Que Vivrai
Serpentini
  Land Of Our Fathers
Serradell
  Golondrina, La
  Song Of Mexico, A
  Swallow, The
Serrano
  Cancion Del Olvido, La
  Carro Del Sol, El
  Marinela
  Roca Fria Del Calvario, La
  Te Quiero Morena
Session
  How Much I Owe
Sessions
  On The Beach Of Fontana
Setchell
  Train That's Going West, The
Setser & Morris
  Why Lady Why
Setser & Seals & Miller
  Forget About Me
Settle
  But You Know I Love You
  Sing Hallelujah
Setzer
  Rock This Town
Severn
  May First
  Union Town
Sevison
  Give Me Oil In My Lamp
Sexton
  Salvation's Plan
Sexton & Wilk
  In Deep
Seymour
  Clover Leaf Rag
  Holy Moses
  Panama Rag
Sgambati
  Separazione
Shade
  Show Me The Ways O Lord
Shade & Williamson
  Sun Brimmer's Blues
Shafer
  All My Ex's Live In Texas
  I Never Knew What That Song
      Meant Before
  I Wonder Do You Think Of Me
  I've Got My Baby On My Mind
  Overnight Success
  You Babe
Shafer & Frizzel
  I Can't Get Over You To Save My
      Life
  Lucky Arms
  That's The Way Love Goes

Shafer & Owens
Honky Tonk Amnesia
Shafer & Shafer
All My Ex's Live In Texas
Shakespeare
St Valentine's Day
Shaley
Abendglocken, Die
Shamblin
He Walked On Water
Shanahan
Clear The Way For USC
Shand & Eaton & Leader
Dance With A Dolly
Dance With A Dolly With A Hole In
Her Stockin'
Dance With A Dolly With A Hole In
Her Stocking
Shane & Drake
White Snows Of Winter, The
Shankar & Fenton
Theme From Gandhi
Shanklin
Chanson D'amour
Shannon
Hats Off To Larry
I Go To Pieces
Keep Searchin'
Loyal Juniors
Sweet The Bells Are Ringing
That's An Irish Lullaby
Too-Ra-Loo-Ra-Loo-Ral
Too-Ra-Loo-Ra-Loo-Ral That's An
Irish Lullaby
Shannon & Crook
Runaway
Shannon & McKenzie
Little Town Flirt
Shapira & Hirsh
Bo B'Shalom
Shapiro & Campbell & Connelly
If I Had You
Shapiro & Stallman
Treasure Of Love
Sharp
Come Back When You Grow Up
Could It Be Love
Japanese Death Song
Locked In The Atom
You Can't Blame The Train
Sharp & James
Unchain My Heart
Sharp & Lowery
Why Does It Have To Be
Why Does It Have To Be Wrong Or
Right
Sharpe
Linda Lu
Voices Of The Angels
When The Great Red Dawn Is
Shining
Sharples
Felix The Wonderful Cat
Little Audrey Says

Shaver
Honky Tonk Heroes
I Couldn't Be Me Without You
Jesus Was Our Savior
LA Turnaround
Ride Me Down Easy
Willy The Wandering Gypsy And
Me
Shavers
Undecided
Shaw
All Bells In Paradise
Animal Voices
Autumn Days
Bees
Beetle, The
Birds' Homes
Birds-Nesting
Birthday Celebrations
By The Sea
Caterpillar
Cherry Tree, The
Cold Days
Columbia The Gem Of The Ocean
Corn
Country Evenings
Country Mornings
Cow, The
Crow, The
Cuckoo
Day And Night
Days Of The Months
Doggies Way
Donkey, The
Dragonfly, The
Ducks
Faithful Riding Horse, The
Father Eternal Ruler Of Creation
Fish, The
Fishing-Boat, The
Four Seasons, The
Fox, The
Frog And Toad
Frost
Girls With Guns
Glad That I Live Am I
Glory Be To Jesus
God Deigning Man To Be
God Is Love
God Is Working His Purpose
God Is Working His Purpose Out
God Whose Name Is Love
Gracious Spirit Holy Ghost
Green St Caper
Handwriting On The Wall, The
Hay, The
Holly
Holy Father In Thy Mercy
Holy Holy Holy Lord Thy Disciples
Home Pets
Horse Shoeing
I Heard A Sound Of Voices
I Sing Of A Maiden
In Excelsis Gloria

Shaw *(Cont.)*
In The Cross Of Christ I Glory
Insect Friends
It's A Right Little Tight Little
College
Jesu Meek And Gentle
Jesus Calls Us O'Er The Tumult
Kingfisher, The
Kings In Glory
Ladybird
Lamb Of God I Look To Thee
Lambing Time
Let All The World In Ev'ry Corner
Sing
Let All The World In Every Corner
Sing
Little Trotty Wagtail
Lou'siana Young
Loving Shepherd Of Thy Sheep
Make We Merry
Many Trees
Mary's Tears
Merry Christmas
Months, The
Mother Hen
Nesting Time
New Rhyme
Now Quit Your Care And Anxious
Fear
O Lady Moon
O Sisters Too How May We Do
Oak, The
Out Of Your Sleep
Owl, The
Pet Cow, The
Pet Hen, The
Pet Pig, The
Praise The Lord Ye Heavens Adore
Him
Purple And The Gold, The
Pussy And Doggie
Rainbow And Clouds
Rainbow, The
Red And The Black, The
Riddle, A
Rivulet, The
Rosewood
Scarecrow, The
Seahorses And Land Horses
Silk Worm, The
Sing For The Day
Snow Lies Thick, The
Song Of Harvest, A
Song Of September
Songs Of Praise The Angels Sang
Songs Of Praise The Angels Sing
Sparrow's Nest, The
Spring
Squirrel, The
Stars' Work, The
Summer
Sun, The
Swallow, The

Shaw *(Cont.)*
    Through The Night Of Doubt And
       Sorrow
    Thy Name
    Tide, The
    To Birds
    To Robin Redbreast
    Too Much Time On My Hands
    Town And Country Mice
    Unto Us A Boy Is Born
    Wasp, The
    Western Wagons
    Wild Birds Trapped
    Wind's Home, The
    Winter Rain
    Woody I On The New Ark
    Work Of Trees, The
    Worm, The
Shaw & Beckett
    Columbia The Gem Of The Ocean
Shaw & Clark
    Give Me Back My Cool Clean Water
Shaw & Minor
    Bringing In The Sheaves
Shayne
    Men In My Little Girl's Life, The
    Sinner Kissed An Angel, A
Shayne & Deane & Candy
    Men In My Little Girl's Life, The
Shayne & Regney
    Rain Rain Go Away
Shea
    Notre Dame Victory March
    Princeton Chorale
    Wonder Of It All, The
Shear
    All Through The Night
    If She Knew What She Wants
Shear & Lauper
    Steady
Shearing
    Lullaby Of Birdland
Sheehan
    Carillon
Sheeles
    Spacious Firmament On High, The
Sheeley
    Poor Little Fool
Sheeley & De Shannon
    Dum Dum
Sheets
    Morning Glory Starlit Sky
Sheila E
    Belle Of St Mark, The
    Glamorous Life, The
Shelb & King & Southard
    Tag Along
Sheldon
    Marching Soldiers
Sheldon & Fournier
    Love And Let Love
    Wheels Keep On Turning
Sheldon & Land & Hert
    Mashed Potato Time

Shelem
    Ptsach Bazemer
    Roeh Veroah
    Tall Corn Grows
Shelem & Shelem
    Ro-E V 'Ro-A
    Shibolet Ba-Sa-De
Shelley
    Hark Hark My Soul
    Power
Shelton & Shelton & Robin
    Just Because
Shemer
    Y'Rushalayim Shel Zahav
Shenhar & Zeira
    Ma Omrot Enayich
Shepard
    Alma Mater
    Brave Mother Yale
    Breathe Upon Us Blessed Spirit
    God's Loving Hand
    Little Knot Of Blue
    Old Brick Row, The
Shepherd
    Jesus Soll Die Losung Sein
Sheppard
    I've Waited A Lifetime
    This Is My Father's World
Sheppard & Miller
    Daddy's Home
    Thousand Miles Away, A
Shepperd
    Marie
    Some One
    This Is My Dream
Shepstone & Dibbens
    Please Tell Her That I Said Hello
    Please Tell Him That I Said Hello
Sheridan & Chiten
    Can't Wait Another Minute
Sherman
    Galilee Bright Galilee
    Governor's Pardon, The
    Graduation Day
    New Lebanon
    No No A Thousand Times No
    Protection
    Ramblin' Rose
    Save Your Sorrow For Tomorrow
    You're Sixteen
Sherman & Lewis & Silver
    No No A Thousand Times No
    Santa Claus Express, The
Sherman & Loeb
    Merry Christmas
Sherman & Sherman
    Age Of Not Believing, The
    Aristocats, The
    Beautiful Briny, The
    Chim Chim Cher-Ee
    Chitty Chitty Bang Bang
    Feed The Birds
    Feed The Birds Tuppence A Bag
    Follow Me Boys

Sherman & Sherman *(Cont.)*
    Fortuosity
    Higitus Figitus
    I Love To Laugh
    I Wanna Be Like You
    I'll Always Be Irish
    It's A Small World
    Jolly Holiday
    Let's Get Together
    Let's Go Fly A Kite
    Old Home Guard, The
    Pink Of Perfection, The
    Portobello Road
    Ramblin' Rose
    Rumbly In My Tumbly
    Scales And Arpeggios
    Spoonful Of Sugar, A
    Stay Awake
    Step In Time
    Supercalifragilisticexpialidocious
    When You're Loved
    Winnie The Pooh
    Wonderful Thing About Tiggers, The
    You're Sixteen
Sherrill
    Good Lovin'
    Good Lovin' Makes It Right
    Wild And Blue
    Woman Always Knows, A
Sherrill & Dalton
    Losing Kind Of Love
Sherrill & Davis
    Put Your Clothes Back On
Sherrill & Dipiero
    That Rock Won't Roll
Sherrill & Earle
    When You Fall In Love
Sherrill & Hall
    Sweet And Innocent
Sherrill & Mitchell & Wilson
    Lovin' Kind, The
Sherrill & Putman
    If You Think I Love You Now
    My Elusive Dreams
Sherrill & Seals & Barnes
    Ten Feet Away
Sherrill & Sherrill & Dalton
    Slow Down
Sherrill & Sutton
    Almost Persuaded
    Already It's Heaven
    Bedtime Story
    Good
    Have A Little Faith
    I Don't Wanna Play House
    I'm Down To My Last I Love You
    Kids Say The Darndest Things
    Kiss Away
    Livin' In A House Full Of Love
    Loser's Cathedral, A
    Marriage On The Rocks
    My Woman's Good To Me

Sherrill & Sutton *(Cont.)*
Take Me To Your World
There's A Party Goin' On
We Can Make It
With One Exception
You Mean The World To Me
Your Good Girl's Gonna Go Bad

Sherrill & Taylor & Strickland
Ceremony, The

Sherrill & Wilson
Door, The
I Love My Friend
Very Special Love Song, A

Sherrill & Wilson & Taylor
He Loves Me All The Way

Sherrill & Wilson & Mitchell
Safe In These Lovin' Arms Of Mine

Sherrill & Wilson & Walls
I Wish I Had A Mommy Like You

Sherrill & Wynette
Reach Out Your Hand
Reach Out Your Hand And Touch
   Somebody
Stand By Your Man
We Sure Can Love Each Other

Sherrod
Nothing But A Soldier

Sherwin
Beautiful Valley Of Eden
Break Thou The Bread Of Life
Christ For The World We Sing
Day Is Dying In The West
Floating On The Morning Breezes
Galilee Bright Galilee
God Of The Glorious Sunshine
Nightingale Sang In Berkeley Square,
   A
Sound The Battle Cry
Twilight
Worship The Lord In The Beauty Of
   Holiness

Sherwin & Katzman
California Ball, A
Clementine
Crossing The Plains
Days Of 'Forty-Nine, The
Dirty Miner, The
Down Among The Sheltering Pines
Fools Of Forty Nine, The
Gambler's Life, A
Going To The Mines
Gold Hunting
Hangtown Girls
Honest Miner, The
Leave You Miners Leave
Miner's Dream, The
Miner's Lament, The
Oh What A Miner
Poker Jim
Sailing For San Francisco
Sailing 'round The Horn
Sweet Betsey From Pike
We'll Strike It

Sherwin & Klickmann
Biscuit Shootin Susie
Chisholm Trail, The
Home On The Range
I Ride An Old Paint
Little Cowgirl
Lonesome Cowboy
Old Six Gun
When The Work Is Done This Fall
Whoopee Ti Yi Yo
Why The Westerner Went Wild

Sherwin & Powell
Cole Younger

Sherwood
Church Is Moving On, The
What Made Robin Sad

Shield
Arethusa, The
Before You Make A Promise
Bud Of The Rose, The
Ere Around The Huge Oak
Friar Of Orders Gray, The
Light As Thistledown
O Maiden Fair
On Life
Plough Boy, The
Way I Feel Tonight, The
Whene'er You Make A Promise
Wisdom Riches And Greatness

Shields
O Davidson
Waltz Me Around Again Willie
When William At Eve
Where The Belfry Looms

Shields & Evans
In The Good Old Summertime

Shiflett
Called Out

Shilkret
Jeannine
Jeannine I Dream Of Lilac Time
Lonesome Road, The

Shine
Sugarland Blues

Shipton
Call And Answer
Campbell's Jig
Classical Capers
Down By The Brook
Flight Of The Frisbee
G Wizz
Goin' Places
Gone Fishing
Little Ben
Madeleine
Marco
Money's The Word
MTA
Night Breeze
On The Run
Only Hopes Returning
Out Near Alice
Passing Note Waltz
Plumstones

Shipton *(Cont.)*
Rag Of Yer Own
Ridin' Blind
Road To Nowhere
Rollerball
Royal Dance
Skateboarding In The Park
Skimatics
Skyline
Snowmobiling
Squeaker's Prowl
Sunday Blues
Third Waltz, The
Thursday's Theme
TT's Blues
Two-Step Promenade
Waltz Of Love, The
Watermelon
Weekend Shuffle

Shire
Go For It
I Chose Right
I Don't Remember Christmas
It Goes Like It Goes
Only When I Laugh
Promise, The
Starting Here Starting Now
Theme From Lucas Tanner
Theres A New Girl In Town
With You I'm Born Again

Shondell
Still Loving You

Shooford & Williams
Rockin' Chair Daddy

Shorrock
Cool Change

Shorter
Children Of The Night
Elegant People
Infant Eyes
Lester Left Town
Lusitanos
One By One
Palladium
Pinocchio
Suspended Sentence
This Is For Albert
When It Was Now
Witch Hunt

Shostakovitch
Song Of Greeting
Wiegenlied

Showalter
Leaning On The Everlasting Arms
Standing By The Cross
What A Fellowship What A Joy
   Divine

Shrubsole
All Hail The Power
All Hail The Power Of Jesus' Name
Behold The Glories Of The Lamb
Miles Lane

Shueh
Chang Cheung Yiao

Shuman & Carr
Hey There Lonely Girl
Shuman & Carr & Lane
Clinging Vine
Shuman & Shuman & Brown
Seven Lonely Days
Shumann
Harvesting
Shumway
Schenectady
Shurtleff & Smart
Lead On O King Eternal
Shuster
Lo The Morn Is Splendor
Shuster & Nelson
Ten Little Fingers And Ten Little
Toes
Shuyler & Knobloch
American Me
Shvedoff
Dark Eyes
Sibelius
Accept Our Thanks
Be Still My Soul
Be Still My Soul The Lord Is On Thy
Side
Cavalry Catch, A
Chant Of The Reeds
Christmas Prayer, A
Finlandia
From The North
Home Port
Patriot's Prayer
Span Auf Den Wellen
This Is My Song
We Praise Our God
We Would Be Building
Sibelius-Mayer
O Capital
Sicardi
Arrorro
Ausenencia
Berceuse
Cancio Resucitado, La
Cancion De Los Sapos Entristecidos,
La
Cancion Del Beso Robado, La
Cancion Del Canario Resucitado, La
Juierio
Meciendo
Nuit De Montagne
Pajarito Chino
Rancho Solo, El
Salmo XXII
Sieczynski
Vienna My City Of Dreams
Wien Du Stadt Meiner Traume
Siegel
Little Peace, A
Love Is A Simple Thing
Siegmeister
Dreamy Kid, The
Funny Bone Song, The
Johnny Appleseed

Siegmeister (Cont.)
Lazy Afternoon
Lonely Star
Sieng
To Free Our Land
Sigler
Love Can Make You Happy
Sigler & Felder
Let Me Make Love To You
Sigler & Mann
Lolly Lolly Loo
Sigler & Tyson
Free Man
Sigman
Ballerina
Crazy He Calls Me
Dream Along With Me I'm On My
Way To A Star
Enjoy Yourself
Enjoy Yourself It's Later Than You
Think
Robin Hood
Sigman & Faith
My Heart Cries For You
Swedish Rhapsody
Sigman & Legrand & Barclay
Saddest Thing Of All, The
Sigman & Rayburn & Whitlock
Hop-Scotch Polka
Sikes
Carry Me Home
Silbar & Robbins & Stephenson
All My Life
Til I Loved You
Silberta
Who Wants A Drink
Silcher
Abendgebet
Annchen Von Tharau
Annie Of Tharaw
Blumen Und Das Laub, Die
Choosing, The
Daybreak
Far Out On The Desolate Billow
Farewell
Frisch Gesungen
Gold And Crimson Leaves Grow
Sere
Hand In Hand With Angels
Hark The Lilies Whisper
Ich Bin Klein Mein Herz Ist Rein
In Der Ferne
Kindness
Lebewohl
Liebesqual
Little Drops Of Water
Lorelei, Die
Lorelei, The
Loreleia
Loreley
Loreley, The
Mag Auch Die Liebe Weinen
Mei Maidle
Mein Heiland Ist Mein Steuermann

Silcher (Cont.)
Morning Bright, The
Prager Schlacht, Die
Prayer For Peace
Schweizer, Der
So Nimm Denn Meine Hande
Vale
Voglein Im Hohen Baum
Wohin Mit Der Freud
Silhouettes, The
Get A Job
Siloy
Das Hat Kein Goethe G'Schrieb 'n
Das Hat Kein Schil
Silva
Ouviram Do Ipiranga As Margens
Placidas
United States Of Brazil, The
Silver
Doodlin'
How Did He Look
Preacher, The
Song For My Father
There Goes My Heart
With These Hands
Silver & Cohn
Yes We Have No Bananas
Silver & Sherman & Meskill
On The Beach At Bali Bali
Silverman
Liberated Woman's Husband's
Talking Blues, The
Mancornadora, La
Trip On The River, A
Silvers
April Showers
I'll Bring You A Rainbow
Learnin' The Blues
Silversher
Happy Birthday
Silverstein
Boy Named Sue, A
Silverstein & Gibson
New Frankie And Johnnie Song, The
Silverwood
Just Tell Him Now
Silvestri
Back To The Future
Simeone
God Bless Us Everyone
Simien
My Toot Toot
Simmons
Around The Great White Throne
Black Water
Simmons & Baxter & McDonald
Carry Me Away
Simmons & Hawes & Jefferson
They Just Can't Stop It
Simmons & Taylor & Wilson
Early In The Morning
Simon
Ace In The Hole
Allergies

Simon (*Cont.*)
Armistice Day
Church Is Burning, A
Cloudy
Coming Around Again
Congratulations
Dangling Conversation, The
Everything Put Together Falls Apart
Hey Schoolgirl
Hobo's Blues
How The Heart Approaches What It
    Yearns
Il Pleut Bergere
Istanbul Not Constantinople
Jonah
Late Great Johnny Ace, The
Legend In Your Own Time
Let The River Run
Little Lady Make Believe
Oh Marion
Old Lamplighter, The
One-Trick Pony
Papa Hobo
Paranoia Blues
Patterns
Peace Like A River
Poem On The Underground Wall, A
Poinciana
Run That Body Down
Simple Desultory Phillippic, A
Sparrow
Wednesday Morning 3 Am
You Don't Know Where Your
    Interest Lies

Simon & Brackman
Haven't Got Time For The Pain
That's The Way I've Always Heard
    It Should Be

Simon & Kaplan
Harmony

Simon & Kirkpatrick
Wise Up

Simon & Mainieri
Jesse

Simon & Marks
All Of Me

Simon & McMahon
Give Me All Night

Simon & Shabalala
Diamonds On The Soles Of Her
    Shoes

Simon & Woodley
Red Rubber Ball

Simon, Carly
Anticipation
Right Thing to Do, The
You're So Vain
You've Got A Friend

Simon, Paul
59th Street Bridge Song, The
America
American Tune
April Come She Will
At The Zoo

Simon, Paul (*Cont.*)
Baby Driver
Big Bright Green Pleasure Machine,
    The
Blessed
Bookends
Boxer, The
Boy In The Bubble, The
Bridge Over Troubled Water
Cecilia
Condor Pasa, El
Duncan
Fakin' It
Fifty Ways To Leave Your Lover
Flowers Never Bend With The
    Rainfall
For Emily Whenever I May Find Her
Gone At Last
Graceland
Have A Good Time
Hazy Shade Of Winter, A
Hearts And Bones
Homeward Bound
I Am A Rock
I Do It For Your Love
I Know What I Know
Kathy's Song
Keep The Customer Satisfied
Kodachrome
Late In The Evening
Learn How To Fall
Leaves That Are Green
Loves Me Like A Rock
Me And Julio Down By The
    Schoolyard
Most Peculiar Man, A
Mother And Child Reunion
Mrs Robinson
My Little Town
Night Game
Old Friends
One Man's Ceiling Is Another Man's
    Floor
Only Living Boy In New York, The
Overs
Punky's Dilemma
Rene And Georgette Magritte With
    Their Dog After T
Richard Cory
Save The Life Of My Child
Scarborough Fair
Scarborough Fair Canticle
Silent Eyes
Slip Slidin' Away
So Long Frank Lloyd Wright
Some Folks' Lives Roll Easy
Something So Right
Somewhere They Can't Find Me
Song For The Asking
Sound Of Silence, The
St Judy's Comet
Still Crazy After All These Years
Stranded In A Limousine

Simon, Paul (*Cont.*)
Take Me To The Mardi Gras
Tenderness
That Was Your Mother
Train In The Distance
Under African Skies
Was A Sunny Day
We've Got A Groovy Thing Goin'
Why Don't You Write Me
You're Kind

Simone
Mississippi Goddam

Simonetti
Madrigale

Simonffy
This Is My Brown Eyed Girl

**Simonon & Headon & Strummer &
Jones**
Rock The Casbah
Should I Stay Or Should I Go

Simons
Marta
Peanut Vendor, The

Simons & Marks
All Of Me

Simonson & Hosman
Now Or Never

Simper
Fear Not O Land
Let The Whole Creation Cry
Praise The Lord O My Soul
Sing Unto The Lord

Simpkins
Drifting Away From God
Make Me White As Snow
When God Speaks

Simpson
Come Holy Spirit Heavenly Dove
Come Trembling Sinner In Whose
    Breast
Eternal Spirit God Of Truth
How Bright These Glorious Spirits
    Shine
O For A Closer Walk With God
Seek Ye The Lord

Simpson & Ashford
Your Precious Love

Simpson & Ashford & Armstead
Let's Go Get Stoned

Simpson & Burke
Yesterday Today Forever

Simpson & Simpson
To The Regions Beyond

Sims
Unseen Hand, The

Sinclair
Alleluia
Johnny Sands
Kookaburra

Sindici
Oh Gloria Inmarcesible

Sinding
Song Of Freedom
Sylvelin

Sineone
God Bless Us Everyone
Sing-Hai
China Will Be Free
Taihong Mountain
Singer
It Could Be A Wonderful World
Whither Thou Goest
Singer & Medora & White
At The Hop
Singh
Time Is Right
Singleton
Apple Green
Fool For Your Love
Sioly
Heut' Hab'i Schop Mei' Fahn'l
Weil I A Alter Drahrer Bin
Sion
One Common Purpose Bring Us
Here
Sissle & Blake
Daddy Won't You Please Come
Home
I'm Just Wild About Harry
Sisson
Alphabet, The
Bird And Flower
Sister Maris Stella
CSC
Sister Teresa Mary
Misericordia
Sixx
Looks That Kill
Piece Of Your Action
Shout At The Devil
Too Young To Fall In Love
Sixx & Lee & Mars
Girls Girls Girls
Sixx & Mars
Dr Feelgood
Without You
Sizemore
Climbers, The
Skelly
Boy's Best Friend Is His Mother, A
Strolling O'er The Brooklyn Bridge
Skillings
Bond Of Love, The
Born Again
He Is The Way He Is The Truth He
Is The Life
He Is The Way The Truth The Life
Jesus I Love You
Jesus Is Lord
Jesus Please Pray For Me
Lord We Praise You
Now Walk With God
This Our Hope
Whatever Is True
You Are My Father
Skinner
It Happened In Kaloha

Skinner & McElhone & Travers &
Honeythief, The
Skinner & Wallace
Lyin' In His Arms Again
Mama's Never Seen Those Eyes
Skinner & Wallace & Bell
Touch Me When We're Dancing
We've Got To Start Meeting Like
This
Skinner & Wallace & Ledford
He Rolled Away The Stone
Skinner & Wallace & Nathan
I'm Glad You Couldn't Sleep Last
Night
Let's Live This Dream Together
Sklerov & Kunin
Don't Plan On Sleeping Tonight
Skroup
Kde Domov Muj
Where Is My Home
Skylar
Gotta Be This Or That
Skylar & Cannon & Shaftel
Just A Little Bit South Of North
Carolina
Skylar & Kapp
Let's All Sing A Song For Christmas
Slack
Committed
Slagle & Slagle
Jesus Said It
Slate & Morrison & Keith
Blaze Of Glory
Everytime You Cross My Mind
Slate & Morrison & Ryles
Drinkin' Them Long Necks
Slate & Pippin
Sharing
Slate & Pippin & Keith
Let Me In
Slater
Jesu The Very Thought Of Thee
We Walk By Faith And Not By Sight
When Christ Was Lifted From The
Earth
Slates
Everyday Things
Skip Rope
Winter Fun
Slavit
Freedom Is A Constant Struggle
Slawson
Airplane Ride, An
Daniel Boone
Ohio River, The
Prairie Schooners
Ride Of Paul Revere, The
Snake Dance Song
Sleeper
America The Beautiful
Grit
Oh Fairest Alma Mater

Sleeper & Stebbins
Jesus I Come
Ye Must Be Born Again
Slicher
Soldat, Der
Slick
White Rabbit
Sloan & Barri
Secret Agent Man
You Baby Nobody But You
Sloane
Heaven Will Protect The Working
Girl
Slonov
Timmy
Small
Fifty-Nine Cents
Hanover Loyalty Song
Mothers Daughters Wives
Theme From Marathon Man
You Can Get Used
Small & Stebbins
I've Found A Friend
Smalls
Believe In Yourself
Ease On Down The Road
Home
Smart
Angels From The Realms Of Glory
Blessed Saviour Who Hast Taught
Me
Brightly Gleams Our Banner
Christ Is Made The Sure Foundation
Christ Thou Art The Sure
Foundation
Come Thou Now And Be Among Us
Day Is Gently Sinking To A Close,
The
Day Of Resurrection, The
Day Of The Resurrection, The
Evening
Faint Not Fear Not God Is Near
Thee
For The Beauty Of The Earth
For Thy Mercy Aye Pursuing
Forward Be Our Watchword
Glory Be To God The Father
Glory To The King Of Angels
Go Forward Christian Soldier
Go Make Of All Disciples
God Of Grace And God Of Glory
God Of Mercy God Of Grace
God That To The Fathers, The
God The Lord A King Remaineth
Hail Thou Source Of Every Blessing
Hark Hark My Soul
Hark Hark My Soul Angelic Songs
Hark Hark My Soul Angelic Songs
Are Swelling
Hark Hark My Soul Thy Father's
Voice Is Calling
Hark My Soul
Hasten The Time Appointed
Holy Father Great Creator

Smart *(Cont.)*

How Shall Come The Kingdom Holy
I Bind My Heart This Tide
I Know Not What The Future Hath
Land Of The Setting Sun, The
Lead On O King Eternal
Lead On Oh King Eternal
Lead Us Heavenly Father
Light's Abode Celestial Salem
Look Ye Saints The Sight Is Glorious
Lord Her Watch Thy Church Is
    Keeping
Lord Is My Shepherd, The
Lord Thou Lovist The Cheerful
    Giver
Lord Through Changing Days
O Brothers Lift Your Voices
O Day Of Light And Gladness
O For A Faith That Will Not Shrink
O Love That Casts Out Fear
O Thou God Of My Salvation
Praise My Soul The King Of Heaven
Rejoice All Ye Believers
Sabbath Bell, The
See The Conqu'ror Mounts In
    Triumph
See The Conqueror Mounts In
    Triumph
Speed Thy Servants Saviour Speed
    Them
Stars Of The Morning
Stars Of The Morning So Gloriously
    Bright
There Was Joy In Heaven
Through All The Changing Scenes
    Of Life
Through Love To Light
Vox Matutina
Welcome Happy Morning
What Our Father Does Is Well
When Brighter Suns And Milder
    Skies
Where The Weary Are At Rest
Winter Reigns O'er Many A Region

Smart & Lang

Holy Father Great Creator

Smetana

Haying Time
I Know A Maiden
Now In Joy Or Sorrow
Now's The Time
See The Budding Flowers Springing
Themes
To Music
Valka Valka
War Song
Where Is John

Smiley & Farrell

Because Of Who You Are

Smiley & Gersmehl & Farrell

Shine On

Smiley & Gersmehl & Huff & Lunn

Vital Signs

Smith

Adams And Liberty
All Labor Gained New Dignity
Amazing Grace Used To Be Her
    Favorite Song
America
Baby Doll
Backwater Blues
Ballin' The Jack
Be Strong We Are Not Here To Play
Be Thou My Guardian And My
    Guide
Blest Land Of Judea
Blow Blow Thou Winter Wind
Blue Bells
Blue Blues
Boat Song
By Shady Woods
Bye Baby Night Has Come
Campin' On De Ole Suwanee
Careful Look Within Your Heart, A
Careless Love
Carolina's Day
Christ The Lord Is Risen Today
Christmas Time
Colgate Fight Song, The
Come Noble Lads
Come Risen Lord And Deign To Be
    Our Guest
Come Sound His Praise
Come Sound His Praise Abroad
Conquering Kings Their Titles Take
Crown Him King Of Kings
Deulling Banjos
Dirty No-Gooder's Blues
Duelling Banjos
Easter Ode
Emmanuel
Fight Fight Fight
Fireman's Song, The
For You
Good Morning Carrie
Goodbye To You
Grace Tis A Charming Sound
Great Speckled Bird, The
Guitar Boogie
Guitar Boogie Shuffle
Hail Stanford Hail
Happy Birthday Baby Jesus
Happy Birthday Little Lord, A
Hard Time Blues
Harvard's Day
Harvest Song
He Met Me There
He's Got Everything Under Control
Himself He Slew
Holy Spirit
How Majestic Is Your Name
I Believe Jesus
I Can't Wait
In February
In The House Blues
It Makes My Love Come Down
Jailhouse Blues

Smith *(Cont.)*

Jessie The Flower O' Dumblane
Jesus Is A Rock In A Weary Land
Jesus Is Able
Jesus These Eyes Have Never Seen
Jing-A-Ling Jing-A-Ling
Joy Fills Our Inmost Hearts Today
Joy Of The Lord, The
Jude Doxology
Let Every Mortal Ear Attend
Lift Up Your Hearts
Long Road
Love Lifted Me
Lynchburg Town
Morning And Night
Most High Omnipotent
Most High Omnipotent Good Lord
My Man Blues
National Hymn
Nightingale's Lay
No More Dams I'll Make For Fish
Not Costly Domes Nor Marble
    Tow'rs
Now That I've Found Your Love
O Lord Our God Almighty King
O Master Let Me Walk With Thee
O Say Can You See
O That We Two Were Maying
O Thou Who Hast At Thy Command
Oak, The
Oh Say Can You See By The Dawn's
    Early Light
Old College Days
Olive Shade
One Night When Sorrow Burdened
Only The Strong Survive
Pickpocket Blues
Pinetop's Blues
Pirate Gold
Please Help Me Get Him Off My
    Mind
Poor Man's Blues
Poor Sally
Prodigal Comes Home, The
Psalm Of Life
Pussy Willow's Secret
Ranchero, The
Reckless Blues
Revolutionary Tea
River Shannon Moon
Safety Mamma
Secrets
September
September Gale, The
Shimmy Shimmy Ko-Ko Bop
Ships That Pass In The Night
Shipwreck Blues
Sing Unto Him
Slaves Are They
Soldiers Of Christ Arise
Solicitude
Son Is Coming Down, The
Song Of May, A

Smith (Cont.)
Song To Teachers College, A
Spirit Of Life In This New Dawn
Sprague
Stand Up And Bless The Lord
Standin' In The Rain Blues
Star-Spangled Banner, The
Statue, The
Summer Suns Are Glowing
Sweeter As The Days To By
Swinging
Talking Want Ad
Tennessee Central
That Lucky Old Sun
That Lucky Old Sun Just Rolls
    Around Heaven All Day
There Came Three Kings Ere Break
    Of Day
There's A Friend For Little Children
There's A Quiet Understanding
Third Rate Romance
This Child We Dedicate To Thee
This Is The Day The Lord Hath
    Made
Those Songs My Mother Used To
    Sing
Three Children Sliding
To Anacreon In Heaven
To Be Free
To Day
Toast To Harvard, A
Tres Pueri Ludentes
Under The Greenwood Tree
Velvet Shoes
Victory Song
Walk Don't Run
Wasted Life Blues
What A Difference Jesus Makes
When Daphne Sails With Me
When I'm Safe With Mother By
Where Is God
Why Don't You Pray
Wreck On The C And O, The
Young Woman's Blues
Smith & Abair
Everything To Me
Smith & Ackley
Joy In Serving Jesus
Smith & Bannister & Meece
And You Know It's Right
Smith & Brown
What A Morning
What I Learned From Loving You
Smith & Carey
America
Smith & Chapman & Bannister & Grant
Angels
Smith & Chapman & Grant
All I Needed To Say
Arms Of Love
Straight Ahead
Smith & Chapman & Marsh
Way, A

Smith & Chapman & Towner & Grant
Stubborn Love
Smith & Dixon
Big Boss Man
Smith & Faust
Angels Listened In, The
Smith & Fearis
Little Sir Echo
Smith & Gaither & Gaither
Unshakable Kingdom
Smith & Goldsmith
Hully Gully
Western Movies
Smith & Goldsmith & Barnum &
    Cooper
Peanut Butter
Smith & Hein
He's A Cousin Of Mine
Smith & Hooven & Winn
Gimme Little Sign
Smith & Hudson
End Of The Book
Find A Way
I Am Sure
I'm Up
New Heart, A
Smith & Johnson & Curry
Stranded In The Jungle
Smith & Johnson & Woods
When The Moon Comes Over The
    Mountain
Smith & Kirkpatrick
I Know
Smith & Kirkpatrick & Grant
Stay For Awhile
Smith & Lee
Hound Dog
Smith & Lee & Colton
Country Boy
Smith & Martin
Don't Go To Strangers
Smith & Miner
Rescue Me
Smith & Peters & Grant
Saved By Love
Smith & Pinkard
Gimme A Little Kiss Will Ya Huh
Smith & Rodeheaver
Then Jesus Came
Smith & Simon & Ett
I'm That Type Of Guy
Smith & Smith
Friends
Great Is The Lord
Hosanna
Not To Us O Lord
Race Is On, The
To The Praise Of His Glorious Grace
Smith & Smith & Bannister & Bannister
Holy Holy
Smith & Smith & Hudson
Jericho
Smith & Springsteen
Because The Night

Smith & Taylor
Down By The Old Mill Stream
Smith & Taylor & Kool & The Gang
Joanna
Stone Love
Smith & Thomas
Make My Heart Your Home
Right Where You Are
Smith & Troy & Williams
Cake Walking Babies From Home
Smith & Vincent
Don't You Just Know It
Rocking Pneumonia And The Boogie
    Woogie Flu
Sea Cruise
Smith & Wiener
To The Aisle
Smith & Williams
Jailhouse Blues
Smith & Wilson & David
Shuffle Song, The
Smith & Woods & Johnson
When The Moon Comes Over The
    Mountain
Smithe
Balder The Beautiful
Smither
Western
Smity & Smyth & Mack
Beat Of A Heart
Smoldon
April Song
Smotherman
Tomb Of The Unknown Love
Smucker
O Thou Joyful Day
Smurthwaite
Rain
Smurthwaite & Curtis
On Halloween Night
Smyth
Jesus The Best Friend Of All
Make Me A Channel Of Blessing
Smyth & Foreman
Our House
Snider
We're Not Gonna Take It
Snow
All The Right Moves
Crazy Like A Fox
Desperate Times
Don't Call It Love
Hart To Hart
I'm Movin' On
Let's Hear It For The Boy
Moving On
Poetry Man
Somewhere Down The Road
State Of Maine Song
TJ Hooker
You
You Should Hear How She Talks
    About You

Snow & Dunne
Main Title Theme From Lottery $

Snow & Golde
Gettin' Ready For Love

Snow & Kimball
Pledge, The

Snow & Weil
So Far So Good

Snowalter
Be A Blessing

Snuffer
March Of The Signaleers

Snyder
My Wife's Gone To The Country
Sheik Of Araby, The
Superman
Who's Sorry Now

Snyder & Kahan & Vallee
Talk To Me

Soderman
Peasants' Wedding March

Sodermann
Swedish Wedding March

Soechtig
Come Thou Weary One

Soeur Sourire
Dominique

Sohren
Give Praise And Glory Unto God
Praise To The Lord
Sing Praise To God Who Spoke
   Through Man

Solar
Chanson De Tous Les Jours, La

Solie
Femmes Voulez-Vous Eprouver
Parisien, Le

Solman
Bird On Nellie's Hat, The
Hymns Of The Old Church Choir,
   The
If I Had A Thousand Lives To Live
Oh Say Doctor
She Was Alright At Night
We're Ready For Teddy Again
When The Bell In The Lighthouse
   Rings
When The Evening Breeze Is Sighing
   Home Sweet Home
When The Snow Birds Cross The
   Valley

Solomon
All On Account Of Eliza
Land Without A Storm, A
Let's Have An Old Fashioned
   Christmas

Solovyev-Sedoy
Moscow Nights

Somerset
Dawn
Echo

Somervell
Every Morning The Red Sun
Forward Through The Ages

Somervell *(Cont.)*
In Summertime On Bredon
Lads In Their Hundreds, The
Shepherd's Cradle Song
Under The Greenwood Tree
We Give Thee But Thine Own
When Wilt Thou Save The People
White In The Moon
Young Love Lies Sleeping

Somerville
On The Idle Hill Of Summer
When Wilt Thou Save The People

Sommers
River Of Love
Thank God I'm A Country Boy

Sommerset
Dawn

Sondheim
Ah Paree
Another Hundred People
Anyone Can Whistle
Ballad Of Sweeney Todd, The
Barcelona
Beautiful Girls
Being Alive
Broadway Baby
By The Sea
Can That Boy Fox-Trot
Comedy Tonight
Company
Could I Leave You
Every Day A Little Death
Everybody Ought To Have A Maid
Everybody Says Don't
Getting Married Today
God-Why-Don't-You-Love-Me-Oh-Y
   ou-Do-I'll-See-You-Later Blues
Good Thing Going
Goodbye For Now
Green Finch And Linnet Bird
I Never Do Anything Twice
I Remember
I'm Still Here
Into The Woods
Johanna
Ladies Who Lunch, The
Little Things You Do Together, The
Losing My Mind
Love I Hear
Love Is In The Air
Lovely
Miller's Son, The
No One Is Alone
Not A Day Goes By
Not While I'm Around
One More Kiss
Our Time
Parade In Town, A
Pretty Lady
Pretty Women
Putting It Together
Remember
Send In The Clowns

Sondheim *(Cont.)*
Side By Side By Side
Sorry Grateful
Take Me To The World
That Dirty Old Man
You Must Meet My Wife

Sor
Air In C
Study

Sordill
Please Tip Your Waitress

Sorensen
Gott Ich Trete Hin Und Bete

Sorrels
Mother's Day Song

Sosebee
Mediation
Prosperity

Sosenko
Darling Je Vous Aime Beaucoup

Souffrain
Linda Mujer

Sour & Manners
We Could Make Such Beautiful
   Music

Sousa
Always Faithful
Be Kind To Your Web-Footed
   Friends
Capitan, El
Capitan's Song, The
Gladiator March
Hands Across The Sea
High School Cadets
King Cotton
Liberty Bell, The
Liberty Bell March
Semper Fidelis
Sound Off
Stars And Stripes Forever
Thunderer, The
Washington Post March, The
We Love The USA
We'll Follow Where The White
   Plume Waves

South
Down In The Boondocks
Games People Play
Rose Garden, A
Walk A Mile In My Shoes

South & Meaders & Brown
Old Bridges Burn Slow

Southard
Fountain, The

Souther
Faithless Love
You're Only Lonely

Souther & Kortchmar
If Anybody Had A Heart

Southern
Hallelujah Train

Southgate
Another Six Days' Work Is Done
He Lives The Great Redeemer Lives

Southgate *(Cont.)*
O Son Of Man Thou Madest Known
Thou Gracious Pow'r Whose Mercy

Sowerby
Beneath The Forms Of Outward Rite
Come Risen Lord And Deign To Be
Our Guest
Hush My Dear Lie Still And Slumber
I Will Lift Up Mine Eyes
O Be Joyful In The Lord
Peace In Our Time O Lord
People Who In Darkness Walked,
The
Strong Son Of God Immortal Love
Whoso Dwelleth

Spaeth
I Want To Harmonize
O Son Of God In Co-Eternal Might
Snow, The
Spebsqsa
There Was A Little Girl
Wind, The

Spafford & Bliss
It Is Well With My Soul

Spalding
Rock Of Rubies And The Quarrie Of
Pearls, The

Span
Matilda
Matilda Matilda

Sparks
Saturday Night
Today

Sparks & McGuire
Green Green

Spath
Es Regnet Gott Segnet Die Erde

Spazier
Ich Sag Es Jedem Dass Er Lebt

Speaks
April Rain
Day Is Past And Over, The
In Maytime
On The Road To Mandalay
Sylvia
When The Boys Come Home

Spear
Butterfly, The
Grocery Man, The
Indian Mother's Song
Rocking Chair
Streamliner, The
Winter And Summer

Speck
It's A Joy

Spector
Sally Go Round The Roses
Smoky Places
To Know Him Is To Love Him
To Know You Is To Love You

Spector & Bates
There's No Other Like My Baby

Spector & Greenwich & Barry
Be My Baby
Chapel Of Love
Then He Kissed Me

Speer
I Feel It In My Soul
I Just Began To Live
I Never Shall Forget The Day
Old Gospel Ship, The
Sun Is Sinking Fast, The

Speilman
Longest Walk, The

Spence
Barter
Half As Lovely Twice As True
Nice 'N' Easy
Outta My Mind

Spencer
All The World
Carelesss Kisses
Cavalcade
Cigareetes Whusky And Wild Wild
Women
Down On Old Mac Donald's Farm
Floating Skiff, The
In The Attic
Pirtate Crew, The
Room Full Of Roses
Then We'll Be Glad
This School Of Ours
Time Flies
Vocations
When Poppies Close Their Eyes
Wonderful Army Of God

Spenser
Love Comes Like A Summer Sigh

Speratus
We See Not Know Not All Our Way

Speroy
Let's Keep The Glow In Old Glory
There's An Angel Missing From
Heaven

Speyer
Au Rhin
Freedom Truth And Love

Spezier
Little Night Wind

Spickard & Carman
Pipeline

Spicer
Evening And Morning

Spielman
It Only Hurts For A Little While
Merry Christmas
Paper Roses

Spier
Put Your Little Foot Right Out

Spier & Conrad
Memory Lane

Spiess
Breathe On Me Breath Of God
Rise Up O Men Of God
This Is The Day Of Light
We Give Thee But Thine Own

Spilman
Afton Water
Away In A Manger
Cradle Hymn
Flow Gently Sweet Afton
Go Labor On Spend And Be Spent

Spina
It's So Nice To Have A Man Around
The House

Spinning
My Homestead 'Neath The Hill

Spivey
Moanin' The Blues

Splittard
Oh Cindy

Spofforth
Hail Smiling Morn

Spohr
All Things Bright And Beautiful
Amazing Grace
As Pants The Hart
As Pants The Hart For Cooling
Streams
Bible Is A Treasure Book, The
Blessed Forever
Chant Du Papillon, Le
Dear Jesus Ever At My Side
Forsake Me Not
Good Night
I Want A Principle Within
I Would Not Reach The Mountain's
Crest
Kriegerchor
Let God The Father God The Son
Let The Whole Creation Cry
Lied, Das
My Saviour On The Word Of Truth
O For A Heart To Praise My God
Proudly As The Eagle
Selig Sind Die Toten
Speak Gently
Voice Of Jesus
We Bear The Strain Of Earthly Care
While Thee I Seek Protecting Power
Who Are These Arrayed In White
Wood-Bird, The

Spoliansky
Hour Of Parting, The

Spooner
Answer Us Now
Sometime Somewhere

Sporle
Harrison Song, The
Long Time Ago, A

Spoth
Benedictus

Spotti
I Want To Be Wanted

Sprague
Catastrophe, A
Cowboy Love Song
Last Longhorn, The
Red River Valley

Sprague & Borop
Via Dolorosa
Sprague & Kirkpatrick
What A Way To Go
Sprague & Parks
Heavenly Father
Sprague & Weber
Can You Reach My Friend
Spratt
No Not Despairingly
Spriggs & Newton & Tyler & Noble
Twenty Years Ago
Springer
How Little We Know
Springfield
Celebrate Youth
Don't Talk To Strangers
Georgy Girl
Heaven Bound
I'll Never Find Another You
Jessie's Girl
Let's Get It While The Gettin's Good
Love Somebody
Some Memories Just Won't Die
That's What I Get For Loving You
World Of Our Own, A
Springfield & Tosti & Tate
Affair Of The Heart
Springsteen
Adam Raised A Cain
Angel, The
Atlantic City
Backstreets
Badlands
Be True
Blinded By The Light
Bobby Jean
Born In The USA
Born To Run
Brilliant Disguise
Cadillac Ranch
Candy's Room
Cover Me
Crush On You
Dancing In The Dark
Darkness Of The Edge Of Town
Darlington Country
Does This Bus Stop At 82nd Street
Downbound Train
Drive All Night
E Street Shuffle, The
Factory
Fade Away
Fever, The
Fire
For You
Fourth Of July
From Small Things Big Things One
    Day Come
Glory Days
Growin' Up
Held Up Without A Gun
Highway Patrol Man

Springsteen *(Cont.)*
Hungry Heart
I Wanna Marry You
I'm A Rocker
I'm Goin' Down
I'm On Fire
Incident On 57th Street
Independence Day
It's Hard To Be A Saint In The City
Jackson Cage
Janey Don't You Lose Heart
Johnny 99
Johnny Bye Bye
Jungleland
Kitty's Back
Lost In The Flood
Mansion On The Hill
Mary Queen Of Arkansas
Meeting Across The River
My Father's House
My Hometown
Nebraska
New York City Serenade
Night
No Surrender
One Step Up
Open All Night
Out In The Street
Out Of Work
Pink Cadillac
Point Blank
Price You Pay, The
Promised Land, The
Protection
Prove It All Night
Racing In The Street
Ramrod
Reason To Believe
Rendezvous
River, The
Rosalita
Savin' Up
She's The One
Sherry Darling
Shut Out The Light
Something In The Night
Spirit In The Night
Stand On It
State Trooper
Stolen Car
Streets Of Fire
Tenth Avenue Freeze Out
This Little Girl
Thunder Road
Ties That Bind, The
Tunnel Of Love
Two Hearts
Used Cars
Wild Billy's Circus Song
Working On The Highway
Wreck On The Highway

Springsteen *(Cont.)*
You Can Look But You Better Not
    Touch
Springsteen & Zevon
Jeannie Needs A Shooter
Spross
Great Tents Sleep, The
I Cannot Dance For You My Lord
Lindy
Little House, The
Love Calls Me
Oasis
Zohra It Is The Morning
Spry & Blea & Sands & Ruiz
Fanatic, The
Spurr
First Place
Squire
All Good People
In An Old Fashioned Town
Squire & Rabin & Horn
Leave It
St Aldegonde
Wilhelmus Of Nassau
St Clair
Ida May
St Claire & Goldie
He Is Love
St John
Cole Smoak
St Lewis & Perren
Who Done It
Staab
Beautiful Isle Of Make Believe
In The Fields Of Oklahoma
Love Is Like A Dream
Violets Sweet
Stade
Hark The Glad Sound
Welcome Thou Victor In The Strife
Staedtler
Fire I Can't Put Out, A
Stafford
Cow Patti
My Girl Bill
Stafford & Bowman
Wildwood Weed
Stafford & Fraser
Amarillo By Morning
Stagg
Robert La Follette Is The Man Of My
    Heart
Stainer
Amen
Amens
And Let This Feeble Body Fail
Beauteous Are The Flowers Of Earth
Behold A Sower From Afar
Child's Evensong, A
Christ The Lord Is Risen Today
Christ Who Once Among Us
Come Oh Come In Pious Lays
Cradle Song Of The Blessed Virgin,
    A

Stainer *(Cont.)*
  Creator Spirit By Whose Aid
  Cross Of Jesus Cross Of Sorrow
  God And Father Great And Holy
  God Is My Strong Salvation
  God Of Abraham Praise, The
  God Of Our Fathers Known Of Old
  God So Loved By The World
  God So Loved The World
  I Could Not Do Without Thee
  In The Cross Of Christ I Glory
  Jesus Tender Shepherd Hear Me
  Jesus The Very Thought Of Thee
  Leader Of Faithful Sould
  Long Ago The Lilies Faded
  Lord Jesus Son Of Mary
  Love Divine All Love Excelling
  My Hope Is In The Everlasting
  My Lord My Master At Thy Feet
    Adoring
  Now When The Dusky Shades Of
    Night
  O God The Rock Of Ages
  O King Of Kings O Lord Of Hosts
  O Word Of God Incarnate
  One Holy Church Of God Appears
  Saints Of God Their Conflict Past,
    The
  Sevenfold Amen
  Shine Thou Upon Us Lord
  Sow In The Morn Thy Seed
  Sun Declines O'Er Land And Sea,
    The
  Thank You God For All I Have
  There's A Wideness In God's Mercy
  Thy Kingdom Come O Lord
  Thy Way Not Mine O Lord
  We O Lord Are Little Pilgrims
Stalling
  Minnie's Yoo-Hoo
Stallings
  Calm This Storm For Me
  I've Been Redeemed
  Learning To Lean
  Touching Jesus
  You Make It Rain For Me
Stallone & Dicola
  Far From Home
  Far From Over
Stallone & Schless & Goldsmith
  Peace In Our Life
Stalls
  Stepping On The Clouds
Stalls & Price & Wilburn
  Set Another Place At The Table
Stampley & Rosson
  I'll Still Be Loving You
Stamps
  God And Man At Table Are Sat
    Down
  When All Of God's Singers Get
    Home

Stanford
  All Praise To Thee For Thou
  All Praise To Thee For Thou O King
    Divine
  Answer To A Child's Question
  Cuttin' Rushes
  Day By Day
  Drake's Drum
  I Bind This Day To Me Forever
  Little Red Lark, The
  Lullaby, A
  My Love's An Arbutus
  O Praise God In His Holiness
  Old Superb, The
  Outward Bound
  Peaceful Western Wind, The
  Rain It Raineth Every Day, The
  Virtue
  We Know That Christ Is Raised And
    Dies No More
  When In Our Music God Is Glorified
  Winds Of Bethlehem, The
  Winter Storms, The
  Wishes
Stange
  Bekehrte, Die
  Damon
Staniforth
  O Mother Dear Jerusalem
Stankey & West & Candelaria
  Honest I Do
Stanley
  Amazing Grace
  Amazing Grace How Sweet The
    Sound
  April Girl, An
  Bluebell Polka
  Caracas
  Cat And The Dog, The
  Come Ye That Know And Fear The
    Lord
  Cradle Song
  Handel
  Little Elsie
  Little John Bottlejohn
  Lord In The Morning Thou Shalt
    Hear
  Lord Of Life And King Of Glory
  My God And Is Thy Table Spread
  Punkydoodle And Jollapin
  Queen O'May, The
  Rah Rah
  These Things Shall Be
  Three Wise Women, The
  To God Your Every Want
  Warwick
  Whenever A Little Child Is Born
Stanley & Child
  Reason To Live
Stanley & Mitchell
  Crazy Crazy Nights
Stanphill
  Follow Me
  God Can Do Anything But Fail

Stanphill *(Cont.)*
  Happiness Is The Lord
  I Know Who Holds Tomorrow
  Mansion Over The Hilltop
  Room At The Cross
  Room At The Cross For You
  Supper Time
  There's Room At The Cross For You
Stansfield & Devaney & Morris
  All Around The World
Stanziale & Larusso
  Dress You Up
Starkey
  Don't Pass Me By
  Octopus's Garden
Starling & Cooler
  Catch Me I'm Falling
Starr
  Cover Girl
  Hangin' Tough
  Happy Radio
  I'll Be Loving You
  I'll Be Loving You Forever
  Iou
  Ooh La La I Can't Get Over You
  Right Stuff, The
  Somebody Loves Me
  Step By Step
  This One's For The Children
Starr & Bristol & Fuqua
  Twenty-Five Miles
Starr & Dickerson & Pullman
  Contact
Starr & Lancellotti
  Tonight
Statham
  Arm Of The Lord Awake Awake
  Jesus Wept Those Tears Are Over
  Mizpah
  O Life That Maketh All Things New
  Pass On The Torch
Steadman
  At Evening-Time
Stearman
  Call My Name
  Gloria
  There Is A Way
  When I Left My Hands To You In
    Praise
Stearns
  Balloon, The
  Train, The
Stebbin
  Some Day The Silver Cord Will
    Break
Stebbins
  Abide With Me Ever
  After
  All Will Be Well
  All's Clear Up Aloft
  Be Still O Heart
  Behold Him
  Believe And Receive

Stebbins *(Cont.)*

Believe On The Lord
Beyond The Smiling And The
    Weeping
Blessed Saviour Hear My Prayer
By Grace Are Ye Saved
Christ Hath Redeemed Us
Christ Is Coming
Christ Is Risen
Christ My All
Christian Walk Carefully
Closer Lord To Thee
Come Come Away
Come To The Fountain
Come Unto Me
Come Unto Me Ye Weary
Comfort Ye One Another
Crown Him
Day-Star Hath Risen, The
Do Unto Others
Early Seeking
Easter Flowers Are Blooming Bright
Evening Prayer
Eye Hath Not Seen
Fly To The Refuge
Fountain Of Mercy
Gather Them In
Give Your Heart To Jesus
Go On Your Way Rejoicing
Go Work Today
God Holds The Key
God Is Love
God Lives
Gospel Call, The
Gray Hills Taught Me Patience, The
Hand Of God, The
Have Thine Own Way Lord
He Feedeth His Flock
He Holds The Key
He Is Near
I Know That My Redeemer Lives
I'm A Pilgrim
I've Found A Friend
Impatient Heart Be Still
In The Hollow Of His Hand
In The Secret Of His Presence
In The Shadow Of The Rock
Jesus Beloved Of My Heart
Jesus I Come
Jesus Is Calling
Jesus Is Tenderly Calling
Jesus Is Tenderly Calling Thee Home
Jesus Only
Joint Heirs With Christ
Let Us Be Sure
Little While, A
Look To Jesus
Look Unto Me
Master Is Calling Thee, The
Meet Me There
Mighty To Save
Music Of God's Word, The
O Beautiful Land
O Let Us All Endeavor

Stebbins *(Cont.)*

O Sing Of My Redeemer
Oh To Be Over Yonder
Other Sheep I Have
Out Of My Bondage Sorrow And
    Night
Pass It On
Prex
Rejoice My Soul Rejoice
Rest In Heaven
Saviour Breathe An Evening Blessing
Some Day The Silver Cord Will
    Break
Take Time To Be Holy
There Is A Green Hill Far Away
Throw Out The Life Line
True-Hearted Whole-Hearted
True-Hearted Whole-Hearted
    Faithful And Loyal
Trust In The Lord
Trusting In Thee
Trusting The Promise
We Shall Meet And Rest
What Will You Do With Jesus
Where My Redeemer Leads Me
Who Are These
Whosoever Cometh
Work For The Time Is Flying
Ye Must Be Born Again
Yielded To God
Young Men In Christ The Lord

**Steel & Holliday & Christoforou &
Zekavica**

Shake For The Sheik
Wild Wild West

Steele

America Our Heritage
Garbage
Good Thing
How Firm A Foundation
I Love You Lord
Mikado's Daughter, The
On Tom-Big-Bee River
Rose Of Alabama, The
Shut That Door
Tom-Big-Bee-River
Walk Jaw Bone

Steele & Elliott

Here And Now

Steele & Gift

Don't Look Back
I'm Not Satisfied
Johnny Come Home
She Drives Me Crazy

Steenberg

My Pictures

Steffe

Battle Hymn Of The Republic, The
John Brown's Body
Keep Them Rolling
Lucretia Mott Song, The
Mine Eyes Have Seen The Glory
Mine Eyes Have Seen The Glory Of
    The Coming Of The Lord

Steffe *(Cont.)*

Move On Over
Queen's College Colours
S-M-I-L-E
Solidarity Forever

Stegall

Jerusalem On High

Stegall & Craig

All American Country Boy
I Think I'm In Love

Stegall & Morrow

Have I Got A Heart For You

Stegall & Murrah

Love Is What We Make It
Stranger Things Have Happened
We're In This Love Together

Stegall & Weatherley

Lady Like You, A

Steggall

Believe Not Those Who Say
Great King Of Glory Come
O Holy City Seen Of John
Our Church Helps Us To Worship
    God
Rejoice The Lord Is King
Songs Of Thankfulness And Praise
Virgin And The Child, The

Stehle

Plange Quasi Virgo

Steibelt

Es Ist Ein Sel'ges Leben

Stein

Furchte Dich Nicht
We Are With You

Stein & Loesser

Wave To Me My Lady

Steinbach

My Love Has Golden Hair

Steinberg

How Do I Make You

Steinberg & Kelly

Alone
I Drove All Night
I Want You So Bad
Like A Virgin
Listen To Your Heart
Sex As A Weapon
So Emotional
True Colors

Steinberg & Kelly & Hoffs

Eternal Flame
In Your Room

Steinberg & McLaughlin

It May Be Lon Chaney Don't Step
    On It

Steinel

My Heart Is A Haven

Steiner

Dark At The Top Of The Stairs, The
Honey-Babe
It Can't Be Wrong
My Own True Love
O Most Mighty O Most Holy

Steiner *(Cont.)*
Perry Mason Theme
Rome Adventure
Summer Place, A
Theme From A Summer Place
Steiner & Hawes
MTA, The
Steininger
Marching Along Together
Steinman
Holding Out For A Hero
Left In The Dark
Making Love Out Of Nothing At All
Read 'Em And Weep
Total Eclipse Of The Heart
Stelljes
Maroon Victory
Stem
Promise To Meet Me There
Stennett
On Jordan's Stormy Banks
Stenson
Prayer Perfect, The
Stentoft
Dyrene I Afrika
Stephens
Daddy Don't You Walk So Fast
Have Faith In God
Party Lights
Utah We Love Thee
Winchester Cathedral
Stephenson
Columbia
Stephenson & Dubois & McDill
Heartbreak Kid
Stephenson & Lorber & Robbins
If The Fall Don't Get You
Stept & Tobias & Brown
Comes Love
Don't Sit Under The Apple Tree
Don't Sit Under The Apple Tree
   With Anyone Else But Me
Sterling
On The Right Road With Roosevelt
Sing To The Lord
Sterling & Grossman & Lange
We're Going Over
Sterling & Ward
Strike Up The Band Here Comes A
   Sailor
Stern
Daddy Get Your Baby Out Of Jail
I Was Lucky
Little Lost Child, The
Mother Was A Lady
Teacher And The Boy, The
Stern & Caine
Happy Landin' With Landon
Sternberg
Walk Like An Egyptian
Sterndale-Bennett
Carol Singers, The
Sterry & Zatorski
Send Me An Angel '89

Steurlein
Liebeswerbung
Stevens
Ahab The Arab
Alma Mater
Bow Wow
Bridget The Midget The Queen Of
   The Blues
Clown, The
Come Back Again In June
Cornhusker, The
Cradle Song
Everything Is Beautiful
Farther Along
Father And Son
Frozen Logger
Frozen Logger, The
Funny Echo, The
Greedy Boy, The
Hail St Mary's
Hawaii Five-O
He Found It
He Whistled Just The Same
Here Comes My Baby
In Fourteen Hundred Ninety-Two
Lady D'Arbanville
Moon Shadow
Morning Has Broken
O Little Town Of Bethlehem
Oh Julie
Oh Very Young
Oregon Trail, The
Paul Bunyan
Santa Claus Is Watching You
Saucy Sue, The
Shakespeare's Carol
Shoo Fly
Shriner's Convention
Side Show, The
Sigh No More Ladies
Streak, The
Theme From Police Woman
Tinker And Cobbler
'Tis Song That Scatters Roses In The
   Heart
Wild World
Stevens & Davis
Somewhere In America
Stevens & Everette
Gitarzan
Stevens & Kanter
Black Coffee
Lovin' Only Me
Stevens & McCormick
Crazy In Love
Stevens & Rabbitt
I Can't Help Myself
Warning Sign
Stevens & Rabbitt & Galdston
World Without Love, A
Stevens & Rabbitt & Malloy
Drivin' My Life Away
Gone Too Far
Good Night For Falling In Love

Stevens & Rabbitt & Malloy *(Cont.)*
I Love A Rainy Night
Pour Me Another Tequila
Someone Could Lose A Heart
   Tonight
Step By Step
You Can't Run From Love
Stevens & Rabbitt & Walker
B-B-B-Burnin' Up With Love
Stevens & Ridgwell
I'm Shy Mary Ellen I'm Shy
Stevens & Scarbury
No Matter How High
Stevenson
Believe Me If All Those Endearing
   Young Charms
Come Buy My Cherries
Depth Of Mercy
Depth Of Mercy Can There Be
God Is Love
Harp That Once Through Tara's
   Halls, The
I'm Sad And Lonely Here
Oft In The Stilly Night
Row Our Bark
Stevenson & Gaye & Gordy
Beechwood 4-5789
Stevenson & Gaye & Hunter
Dancing In The Street
Stevenson & Long
Devil With A Blue Dress
Devil With A Blue Dress On
Stevenson & Moy
It Takes Two
Stevenson & O'Day
Rock 'n' Roll Heaven
Stevie B
In My Eyes
Stewart
Angel Gabriel
Church Of God Is Established, The
Cover Them Over With Beautiful
   Flowers
Hark Ten Thousand Harps And
   Voices
How Sweet How Heavenly Is The
   Sight
I Want To See The Old Home
Let Him To Whom We Now Belong
My Master Was A Worker
My New Life I Owe To Thee
O Beautiful My Country
O Still In Accents Sweet And Strong
Salvation O The Joyful Sound
Seven Wonders
With Joy We Hail The Sacred Day
Stewart & Appice
Da Ya Think I'm Sexy
Stewart & Cregan & Savigar & Dylan
Forever Young
Stewart & Gouldman
I'm Not In Love

Stewart & King
Bonaparte's Retreat
Tennessee Waltz
Stewart & Quittenton
Maggie May
Stewart & Walden & Cohen
Jody
Stewart & White
Time Passages
Stewart & Wood
Cindy Incidentally
Heart's Been Broken, A
Stay With Me
Year Of The Cat
Stewart, John
Daydream Believer
Stewart, Rod
Hot Legs
Tonight's The Night
You're In My Heart
Stewart, Sandy
Nightbird
Stewart, Sly
Dance To The Music
Everyday People
Family Affair
Hot Fun In The Summertime
I Want To Take You Higher
Thank You Falletin Me Be Mice Elf
Again
Stichl
Jager, De
Stickland
Fountain
Stier
In Front Old Pardee
Way Down In Easton
We'll Gather By The Twilight's
Glow
Stiffler
Healer Of Broken Hearts
Stigelli
Rayon De Tes Yeux, Un
Stiles
We're Men Of The Navy
Still
Breath Of A Rose, The
Grief
Lament
Up There
Stillman
Badger Song
Juke Box Saturday Night
Stillman & Allen
Home For The Holidays
Stillman & Block & Simon
Wide Open Places, The
Stillman & Lewis & Silver
No No A Thousand Times No
Stillman-Kelley
Eldorado
Stills
4 + 20
49 Bye-Byes

Stills (Cont.)
Carry On
Change Partners
Dark Star
For What It's Worth
Helplessly Hoping
Love The One You're With
Suite Judy Blue Eyes
War Games
You Don't Have To Cry
Stills & Curtis & Curtis
Southern Cross
Stills & Young
Everybody I Love You
Sting
Be Still My Beating Heart
De Do Do Do De Da Da Da
Don't Stand So Close To Me
Every Breath You Take
Every Little Thing She Does Is Magic
Fortress Around Your Heart
If You Love Somebody Set Them
Free
Invisible Sun
Love Is The Seventh Wave
Message In A Bottle
Roxanne
Russians
Spirits In The Material World
We'll Be Together
Wrapped Around Your Finger
Stinson & Waldman & Welch
Time's Up
Stiter
Brothers Cheer
Stock & Aitken & Waterman
Breakaway
Especially For You
Hand On Your Heart
Harder I Try, The
He Ain't No Competition
I Don't Wanna Get Hurt
I Heard A Rumour
I Should Be So Lucky
It Would Take A Strong Strong Man
It's No Secret
Love's About To Change My Heart
Never Gonna Give You Up
Nothing Can Divide Us
Nothing's Gonna Stop Me Now
Respectable
Say I'm Your Number One
Showin' Out
Take Me To Your Heart
Together Forever
Too Many Broken Hearts
Whatever I Do Wherever I Go
Whenever You Need Somebody
Stock & Aitken & Waterman & Dallin
I Can't Help It
Love In The First Degree

Stock & Aitken & Waterman & Dallin
& Fahey & Woodward
I Heard A Rumour
Stock & Aitken & Waterman & Summer
This Time I Know It's For Real
Stocks
Let It Be Now
Maker Of The Sun And Moon, The
What Will You Do With Jesus
Stockton
Come Every Soul By Sin Oppressed
Glory To His Name
Great Physician, The
Only Trust Him
Stoddard
New England New England
Twilight On Sumter
Stoeckel
Billy Buttercup
Little Squirrels
Pope, The
Stoecklin
Hymn To St Joseph
Stoerl
Father Whose Will Is Life And Good
Spirit Divine
Stokes
O Could I Speak The Matchless
Worth
Sweetheart Of Sigma Chi
Stole & Del Roma
I Will Follow Him
Stoloff & Sidney
To Love Again
Stolz
Im Prater Bluh'n Wieder Die Baume
Just For A Kiss Or Two
Two Hearts In 3-4 Time
Stolzel & Bach
Bist Du Bei Mir
Stonard
Oh Cruel Death
Stone
Are You Happy Baby
Gypsys Tramps And Theves
Hail The Night All Hail The Morn
Look Who Loves You Now
Lullaby Of Life
Ma Rag Time Baby
Sutton New
Stone & Bonime
Let's Dance
Stone & Shannon
So Good So Rare So Fine
Stone & Stapp
Chattanoogie Shoe Shine Boy
Stone & Wesley
Church's One Foundation, The
Stoneback
Lonesome Mountain Streams
Stonehill
Hymn
Just Plain Folks

Stookey
Apologize
Christmas Dinner
Early In The Morning
Good Times We Had, The
Irish Blessing
Love City
No Other Name
Norman Normal
Tender Hands
There Is Love
Wedding Song
Winner, The

Stookey & Bannard
House Song, The

Stookey & Batteast & Mezzetti
A 'Soalin

Stookey & Kniss
On A Desert Island With You In My
Dreams

Stookey & Mason & Dixon
I Dig Rock And Roll Music

Stookey & Milstein
There Was A Boy
You're The Only One

Stookey & Yarrow
Autumn To May
Cruel War, The
Man Of Constant Sorrow
This Train
Very Last Day

Stookey & Yarrow & Chandler
It's Raining

**Stookey & Yarrow & Travers & Dixon
& Kniss**
Song Is Love, The

Storace
Lullaby
Peaceful Slumb'ring On The Ocean

Storch
Greeting At Night

Storer
I Heard A Sound Of Voices

Storl
Alleluia Fairest Morning
Scorn Not The Slightest Word Or
Deed

Story
John W Davis

**Story & Jacobsen & Yarrow & Stookey
& Travers & Okun**
Cuckoo, The

Stothart
Cuban Love Song
March Of The Old Guard
Rogue Song, The
Sweetheart Darlin'

Stothart & Cugat
Santiago

Stothart & Ruby
I Wanna Be Loved By You

Stoughton
Cotton Gin, The
Great Adventure, The

Stoughton *(Cont.)*
Huckleberry Sal
Lord Is My Light, The
Paul Revere
PT Barnum
We Give Thanks
Yankee Hill

Stover
I'm Back For More
Sometimes You Just Can't Win

Strachey & Link
These Foolish Things
These Foolish Things Remind Me Of
You

Stradella
Col Mio Sangue Comprerei
O Lord Have Mercy
Pieta Signore
Se I Miei Sospiri

Straight
Lay My Head Beneath A Rose

Strals
Lord's Prayer, The

Strandlund & Pinkard
I Can Tell By The Way You Dance
I Can Tell By The Way You Dance
How You're Gonna Love Me
Tonight

Strange
Ballad Of Martin Luther King, The

Strange & Davis
Charro
Memories

Stranks & Strachey
No Orchids For My Lady

Strategier
Lord's Prayer, The

Stratta
Forget The Woman

Strattner
For Thy Mercy And Thy Grace
Life Of Ages Richly Poured
Lord What Off'ring Shall We Bring
Saviour Teach Me Day By Day
There's A Strife We All Must Wage
We Are Building Every Day

Straub
Gather The Sheaves

Straus
Love's Roundelay
Love's The Tune
Make A Wish
Music In My Heart
My Hero
Piccolo Piccolo
Walzertraum
While Hearts Are Singing

Strauss
All Souls' Day
Allerseelen
Allmachtige, Die
Aus Den Liedern Der Trauer
Barkarole

Strauss *(Cont.)*
Bell Song
Das Geheimnis
Dedication
Drittes Lied Der Ophelia
Erstes Lied Der Ophelia
For You
Fortune Teller, The
Geduld
Georgine, Die
Golden Sun, The
Hab Ich Euch Denn Je Geraten
Hail To Our Monarch
Hut Du Dich
Ihre Augen
Kuckuck
Liebe
Liebesgeschenke
Lob Des Leidens
Love And Mirth
Madrigal
Melody Of Spring
Mit Deinen Blauen Augen
My Hero
Nacht, Die
Night, The
Nur Mut
Old Vienna
Schwung
Seitdem Dein Aug' In Meines
Schaute
Serenade
Theme From 2001 A Space Odyssey
To You
Truffle Song, The
Truffles
Tyrolienne
Verschwiegenen, Die
Vienna Life
Wachterlied
Wanderers Gemutsruhe
Wer Wird Von Der Welt
While You Are Gone
Wild Rose Song
Wild Rose, The
Winternacht
Zeitlose, Die
Zweites Lied Der Ophelia

Strauss & Strauss
Pizzicato Polka

Strauss, Johann, Fils
Artists' Life
Beautiful Blue Danube
Blue Danube, The
Blue Danube Waltz
Emperor Waltz
My Blue Danube
Roses From The South
Tales From The Vienna Woods
Voci Di Primavera
Voices Of Spring

Strauss, Johann, Pere
Huldigung

Styne *(Cont.)*

How Do You Speak To An Angel
I Begged Her
I Believe
I Don't Want To Walk Without You
I Don't Want To Walk Without You
    Baby
I Fall In Love Too Easily
I Still Get Jealous
I Yes Me That's Who
I'll Walk Alone
I'm Glad I Waited For You
I'm Just Taking My Time
I'm The Greatest Star
I'm With You
I've Got A Rainbow Working For
    Me
I've Heard That Song Before
Individual Thing
It's Been A Long Long Time
It's Magic
It's The Same Old Dream
It's You Or No One
Just In Time
Killing Time
Let It Snow Let It Snow Let It Snow
Let Me Entertain You
Let's See What Happens
Little Girl From Little Rock
Long Before I Knew You
Lorelei
Make Someone Happy
Mu-Cha-Cha
Music That Makes Me Dance
Music That Makes Me Dance, The
My Own Morning
Never Never Land
On A Sunday By The Sea
Papa Won't You Dance With Me
Party's Over, The
People
Poor Little Rhode Island
Put 'Em In A Box Tie 'Em With A
    Ribbon
Put 'Em In A Box Tie 'Em With A
    Ribbon And Throw 'Em In The
    Deep Blue Sea
Ride On A Rainbow, A
Sadie Sadie
Saturday Night
Saturday Night Is The Loneliest
    Night Of The Week
Small World
Some Other Time
Some People
Song's Gotta Come From The Heart,
    The
Sugar
Talking To Yourself
There Goes That Song Again
Things We Did Last Summer, The
Three Coins In A Fountain

Styne *(Cont.)*

Three Coins In The Fountain
Time After Time
To A Small Degree
Together Wherever We Go
Under The Sunset Tree
Vict'ry Polka
What Makes The Sunset
Who Are You Now
You Are Woman I Am Man
You Gotta Get A Gimmick
You Gotta Have A Gimmick
You Mustn't Feel Discouraged
You'll Never Get Away From Me
You're My Girl

Su Yin-Lan

Bread Of Life For All Men Broken,
    The

Subway

Chinese Kung Fu

Sucher

Springtide Of Love, The

Suck

Cradle Song
Dandelions

Sudano & Esposito

Make It Last

Sudderth

Born Again
Perfect Example, The

Sudds

O That We Two Were Maying

Suessdorf

Moonlight In Vermont

Suesse

My Silent Love
Night Is Young And You're So
    Beautiful, The
You Oughta Be In Pictures

Suessmayer

April

Sufaris

Wipe Out

Suffield

Little Is Much When God Is In It

Sugar

Be A Man
Sit Down
We Are The Guys

Suitor

Light From Heaven Shone Around,
    A
Spirit Of Mercy Truth And Love

Sulivan

Carol For Christmas Day

Sullavan & Baron

Rum And Coca-Cola

Sullivan

After Much Debate Internal
Ah Leave Me Not
Ah Leave Me Not To Pine
Ah Me
Alas That Lovers Thus Should Meet
All The Legal Furies Seize You

Sullivan *(Cont.)*

Alleluia Alleluia
Alleluia Alleluia Hearts And Voices
Alleluiah Alleluiah
Alone And Yet Alive
Am I Alone And Unobserved
And God Shall Wipe Away All Tears
Angel Voices Ever Singing
Ape And The Lady, The
Appeal, An
As Some Day It May Happen
At The Crossroads
Autumn Woods
Bachelor Song
Battle's Roar Is Over, The
Believe It Or Not
Bell Trio
Birds In The Night
Blue Blood
Blue Juniata, The
Bow Bow Ye Lower Middle Classes
Brightly Dawns Our Wedding Day
Brightly Gleams Our Banner
British Tar, A
British Tar Is A Soaring Soul, A
Buttercup, The
By Christ Redeemed In Christ
    Restored
Call Of Samuel, The
Carefully On Tiptoe Stealing
Cheerily Carols The Lark Over The
    Cot
Chorister, The
Christ Is Risen
Climbing Over Rocky Mountain
Come Friends Who Plough The Sea
Come Ye Faithful Raise The Strain
Comes The Broken Flower
Coming Bye And Bye, The
Contemplative Sentry, The
Courage Brother Do Not Stumble
Criminal Cried, The
Dance A Cachucha
Darned Mounseer, The
Dear Friends Take Pity
Dear Friends Take Pity On My Lot
Dear John
Dickey Bird And The Owl, The
Draw Nigh And Take The Body Of
    Your Lord
Draw Thou My Soul
Draw Thou My Soul O Christ
Duke And The Duchess, The
Duke Of Plaza-Toro
Echo
Eheu Fugaces
Englishman, The
Ev'ry One Is Now A Fairy
Every Year At Easter Time
Expressive Glances
Faint Heart Never Won Fair Lady
Farewell My Own
For Love Alone
For Some Ridiculous Reason

Sullivan *(Cont.)*

For Thee O Dear Dear Country
Forward All Ye Faithful
Forward Be Our Watchword
Forward Through The Ages
Free From His Fetters Grim
From Every Kind Of Man
Funeral March, The
Ghost's High Noon, The
Girl Graduates
God The Father God The Son
Golden Harps Are Sounding
Good Morrow Good Lover
Good Queen Bess
Great Oak Tree, The
Hail Hail The Gang's All Here
Hail Poetry
Hail The Cross Of Jesus
Hail The Hero Workers
Happy Young Hearts
Hark The Hour Of Ten Is Sounding
Hark The Voice Of Jesus Calling
He And She
He Is Gone A Cloud Of Light
He Loves
Heaven Is My Home
Homeland O The Homeland, The
How Sweet The Answer Echo Makes
Hush'd Is The Bacon
Hushed Was The Evening Hymn
I Am A Courtier
I Am A Courtier Grave
I Am A Courtier Grave And Serious
I Am A Maiden
I Cannot Tell
I Cannot Tell What This Love May
    Be
I Hear The Soft Note
I Know A Youth
I Love Him I Love Him
I May Be Wrong
I May Be Wrong But I Think You're
    Wonderful
I Once Was A Very Abandoned
    Person
I Shipp'd D'Ye See
I Shipped D'Ye See
I Stole The Prince
I'm Called Little Buttercup
I've Found A Friend
I've Got A Little List
I've Jibe And Joke
Ida Was A Twelvemonth Old
If Life A Boon
If Somebody There Chanced To Be
If We're Weak Enough To Tarry
If You Give Me Your Attention
If You Go In
If You Want A Receipt
If You Want To Know Who We Are
If You're Anxious For To Shine
In Enterprise Of Martial Kind
In Ev're Mental Lore

Sullivan *(Cont.)*

In Good Queen Bess's Glorious Days
In Life A Boon
Into Parliament He Shall Go
Is Life A Boon
It Came Upon The Midnight Clear
It Is Not Love
Jesus I My Cross Have Taken
Jesus In Thy Dying Woes
Jesus My Saviour Look On Me
Joyous Life That Year By Year, The
Judge's Song, The
Kind Captain I've Important
    Information
Kind Goodheart
King Of The Jungle, The
Lady Fair, A
Lady Fair Of Lineage High, A
Law Is The True Embodiment, The
Law, The
Let Us Choral Anthems Raise
Life Is Lovely All The Year
Listen I Solemnly Walk'd
Living I, The
Little Maid Of Arcadee
Long Day Closes, The
Lord Chancellor's Song, The
Loudly Let The Trumpet Bray
Love Is A Plaintive Song
Love Unrequited
Lullaby Baby
Madrigal And Gavotte
Magnet And The Churn, The
Magnet Hung In A Hardware Shop,
    A
Maiden Fair To See, A
Man Who Would Woo A Fair Maid,
    A
Merrily Ring The Luncheon Bell
Merry Little Brooklet
Merry Madrigal, A
Merry Maiden And The Tar, The
Merryman And His Maid, The
Mighty Must, The
Minuet
Mirage, A
Miya-Sama
Moon And I, The
More Humane Mikado, A
More Love To Thee O Christ
My Boy You May Take It From Me
My Dearest Heart
My God And Father While I Stray
My God My Father While I Stray
My Master Is Punctual
My Name Is John Wellington Wells
My Object All Sublime
Never Mind The Why And
    Wherefore
Never Mind The Why Or Wherefore
Nice Young Girl, The
Nightmare, A
None Shall Part Us

Sullivan *(Cont.)*

Now Hearken To My Strict
    Command
Now Here's A First-Rate
    Opportunity
Now Praise We Great And Famous
    Men
Now To The Banquet We Press
O Better Far To Live And Die
O Gentlemen Listen I Pray
O Gladsome Light
O God Our Dwelling Place
O Hush Thee My Babie
O King Of Mercy
O List While We A Love Confess
O My Charmer
O My Darling O My Pet
Odd Old Man, An
Of All The Myriad Moods Of Mind
Of All The Young Ladies I Know
Oh A Private Buffoon
Oh Better Far To Live And Die
Oh Foolish Fay
Oh Gentlemen Listen
Oh Goddess Wise
Oh Is There Not One Maiden
Oh Is There Not One Maiden Breast
Oh Leave Me Not To Pine
Oh List While We A Love Confess
Oh Why Am I Moody And Sad
On A Tree By A River
Once Again
Once More Gondolieri
One Sole Baptismal Sign
Only Roses
Onward Onward Children
Our Fathers Were High-Minded Men
Out Of My Need You Come To Me
    O Father
Over The Bright Blue Sea
Philosophic Pill, The
Pirate King, The
Poor Wand'ring One
Poor Wandering One
Pour O King
Praise God For John Evangelist
Praise Ye The Lord
Printer Printer Take A Hinter
Prithee Pretty Maiden
Private Buffoon, A
Proper Pride
Queen Of The Holy Rosary
Rataplan
Recipe, A
Refrain Audacious Tar
Ring Forth Ye Bells
Rising Early In The Morning
Roses White And Roses Red
Rover's Apology, The
Sad Is That Woman's Lot
Said I To Myself
Said I To Myself Said I
Sans Souci
Saviour Sprinkle Many Nations

Sullivan (Cont.)

Saviour Teach Me Day By Day
Sigh No More Ladies
Silver'd Is The Raven Hair
Silvered Is The Raven Hair
Snow Lies White, The
So Ends My Dream
So Go To Him
So Please You Sir
Society Has Quite Forsaken All Her
  Wicked Courses
Solatium
Soon As We May
Speculation
Spirit Blest Who Art Adored
Spurn Not The Nobly Born
Strange Adventure
Suicide's Grave, The
Sun Whose Rays, The
Taken From The County Jail
Tangled Skein, The
Tarantara Tarantara
Then One Of Us Will Be A Queen
There Is Beauty
There Is Beauty In The Bellow Of
  The Blast
There Lived A King
There Was A Time
There's A Wideness In God's Mercy
Things Are Seldom What They Seem
This Helmet I Suppose
Though Tear And Long-Drawn Sigh
Through Good Report And Evil Lord
Through The Night Of Doubt And
  Sorrow
Time Was When Love And I
To Thee O Lord Our Hearts We
  Raise
To Thee O Lord Our Hearts We
  Raise In Hymns Of Adoration
Tripping Hither
Tripping Hither Tripping Thither
True Diffidence
Twenty Love-Sick Maidens We
Usher's Charge, The
Vorwarts Christi Streiter
Waterloo House Young Man, A
We Are Dainty Little Fairies
We Are Warriors Three
Welcome Happy Morning
Welcome Happy Morning Age To
  Age Shall Say
Welcome Joy Adieu To Sadness
Welcome To Our Hearts Again
Were I Thy Bride
What Does Little Birdie Say
When A Maiden Loves
When A Man Has Been A Naughty
  Baronet
When A Merry Maiden Marries
When A Wooer Goes A Wooing
When All Night Long
When All Night Long A Chap
  Remains

Sullivan (Cont.)

When Did You Get That Hat
When First My Old Old Love I
  Knew
When He Is Here
When I First Put This Uniform On
When I Go Out Of Door
When I Good Friends Was Call'd To
  The Bar
When I Good Friends Was Called To
  The Bar
When I Went To The Bar
When Maiden Loves
When Merry Maiden Marries
When Our Gallant Norman Foes
When The Buds Are Blossoming
When The Foeman Bares His Steel
When The Night Wind Howls
When You Had Left Our Pirate Fold
When You're Lying Awake
Whene'er I Spoke
Where Did You Get That Hat
Where Is Another Sweet
Who Are We
Who Trusts In God A Strong Abode
Whom Thou Hast Chained
Wild Roved An Indian Girl
Willow Waly
Witch's Curse, The
With A Sense Of Deep Emotion
With Catlike Tread
With Joy Abiding
With Joyous Shout
Woman Of The Wisest Wit, The
Working Monarch, The
Would You Know
Would You Know The Kind Of Maid
Ye Fair Green Hills Of Galilee
You're As Welcome As The Flowers
  In May
Young Strephon Is The Kind Of Lout

Sullivan, Arthur

Aesthete, The
Baffled Grumbler, The
Behold The Lord High Executioner
Braid The Raven Hair
Entrance And March Of Peers
Entrance Of Mikado
Flowers That Bloom In The Spring,
  The
For He Loves Little Buttercup
For He's Going To Marry Yum-Yum
He Is An Englishman
He's Going To Marry Yum Yum
Here's A How-De-Do
House Of Peers, The
Humane Mikado, A
I Am The Captain Of The Pinafore
I Am The Monarch Of The Sea
I Am The Ruler Of The Queen's
  Navee
I Am The Very Model

Sullivan, Arthur (Cont.)

I Am The Very Model Of A Modern
  Major-General
I Have A Song
I Have A Song To Sing
I Have A Song To Sing O
Lord High Executioner, The
Lost Chord, The
March Of The Peers
Model Of A Modern Major-General
Modern Major General, The
Monarch Of The Sea
My Eyes Are Fully Open
Nearer My God To Thee
Onward Christian Soldiers
Orpheus With His Lute
Pirate Chorus
Policeman's Lot, A
Policeman's Lot Is Not A Happy
  One, A
Policemen's Chorus
Sorcerer's Song, The
Sorry Her Lot
Sorry Her Lot Who Loves Too Well
Take A Pair Of Sparkling Eyes
They'll None Of 'Em Be Missed
They'll None Of Them Be Missed
Three Little Maids
Three Little Maids From School
Tit Willow
Wand'ring Minstrel, A
Wand'ring Minstrel I, A
Wandering Minstrel, A
We Sail The Ocean Blue
We're Called Gondolieri
Were You Not To Koko Plighted
What The **** Do We Care
When A Felon's Not Engaged
When A Felon's Not Engaged In His
  Employment
When Britain Really Rul'd The
  Waves
When Britain Really Ruled The
  Waves
When Fred'ric Was A Little Lad
When Frederic Was A Little Lad
When I Was A Lad
Willow Tit-Willow

Summer

Child Of A King, The
Dim All The Lights
Hey Baby
I Wish I Had A Girl

Summer & Moroder & Bellotte

Spring Affair
Winter Melody

**Summer & Moroder & Bellotte &
Mathieson**

Heaven Knows

Summer & Omartian

She Works Hard For The Money
Unconditional Love

Summers
In Christ I Feel The Heart Of God
Sumner
I Can Feel The Touch Of His Hand
Keep Me
Lord Teach Me To Pray
My Father Is Rich In Houses And
Lands
Ode On Science
Old Country Church, The
Shadow Of His Wings, The
Things That Matter, The
Sumner & Friend
Night Before Easter, The
**Sumner & Gilbert & Hook & Morris &
Hague**
True Faith
Sundberg & Ayres
Blessed Be The Children
Sunderwirth
What If
Suni
Hokis Murmoor
Hoontzk
Indz Mi Khuntrir
Miayn Kez
Sunshine
Tattooed Lady
Suppe
Light Cavalry Overture
Onward To Victory
Poet And Peasant Overture
Surfaris
Wipe Out
Surrey
Fall Softly Snow
Surrey & Surrey
Teen Angel
Susato
Douce Memoire
Suskind
Sororite
Suso
In Dulci Jubilio
Sussmayer
'Tis Springtime
Sutherland
Sailing
Sutter
Members Of One Mystic Body
O God All Knowing And Just
Sutton
Ain't Got Time To Be Unhappy
And The World Goes On
I Don't Care
Mail Day
O Bud
Thirty Days In Jail
What Made Milwaukee Famous
You're My Man
Sutton & Brown & Brody
Stop
Sutton & Lewis
He'd Still Love Me

Sutton & Wilson & Taylor
It's A Man's World
Sutzel
Power Of Song, The
Sveinbjornsson
Iceland The Millennial Hymn Of
1874
Millennial Hymn Of 1874
Swain
Home's Not Merely Four Square
Walls
Swain & Jolley
Trick Of The Night, A
Swan
China
Come Ye Disconsolate
Greenland
I Can Help
Lover Please
Ocean
Rapture
Summer
Trail Of Dreams
When Your Lover Has Gone
Swan & Lauridsen
Give Us A Song
Swander
Deep In The Heart Of Texas
Swann
Clock Carol, The
Swanson
Death Song, A
I Will Lie Down In Autumn
Negro Speaks Of Rivers, The
Swanstone & Carron & Morgan
Blues My Naughty Sweetie Gives To
Me
Swanstone & McCarron & Morgan
Blues
Swanstrom
Argentines The Portuguese And The
Greeks, The
Swartz
Colorado Home
Swayze & Widelitz
She's Like The Wind
Sweat
Counting
Sweelinck
Arise O Ye Servants Of God
Sweeney
Beulah Land
Buff And Blue, The
Happy Thought, A
Let's Be Little Leaves
When Little Ones Pray
Sweet
All Of Me
Go Mustangs Go
Honestly
Sweet & Grant
Fight On

Sweetser
Blest Are The Pure In Heart
Give To The Winds Thy Fear
It Is Not Death To Die
Lord In The Strength Of Grace
Mourn For The Thousands Slain
Since Jesus Is My Friend
Sweney
Awake Awake O Heart Of Mine
Beautiful Light, The
Beulah Land
Calling You And Me
Calvary
Coming Today
Conquering Now And Still To
Conquer
Freely And Forever
Glory All Is Glory
Golden Key
He Is My Portion Forever
He Will Come And Save You
Hour Of Prayer, The
I Will Shout His Praise In Glory
I've Been To The Fountain
I've Reached The Land Of Corn And
Wine
It's Just Like My Saviour
Jesus Is Passing By
Jesus Is With Me
Jesus Leads
Jesus Will Give You Rest
Led By The Hand Of Faith
Lord I Am Thine
More About Jesus
My Savior First Of All
My Saviour First Of All
Only A Beam Of Sunshine
Sunshine In The Soul
Tell Me The Story Of Jesus
Unsearchable Riches
Victory In Jesus
Victory Through Grace
When My Life-Work Is Ended
When We All Get Home
Whosoever Means Me
Why Cling To Earth
Why Not Catch The Sunbeams
Will There Be Any Stars
Wonderful Love
Swengle
Hail To Mac Murray
Swenson
Here O My Lord I See Thee Face To
Face
Swerdlow
Temple Battle Song
Swift
Can This Be Love
Can't We Be Friends
Dames
Dames Fine And Dandy
Easter
Fine And Dandy
Onward To Battle

Swift *(Cont.)*
Over In The Meadow
Pioneer Pioneer
Poor Mister Morgan
Poor Mr Morgan
Red Election Round
Sawing A Woman In Half
Scottsboro Boys Shall Not Die, The
Silver Rain
Swing Out Sister
Breakout
Twilight World
Swirsky & Gold
Tell It To My Heart
Sydenham
Believe Not Those Who Say
Maiden Of The Fleur De Lys, The
Sykes
Eternal Father Strong To Save
Thank You Lord
Yea Alabama
Sykes & Hunter
Running Over
Sylvers & Shelby
Second Time Around, The
Sylvers & Shelby & Shockley
And The Beat Goes On
Sylvers & Spencer
Take That To The Bank
Sylvia & Lopez
Happy Happy Birthday Baby
Syre
Praise The Lord
Szabo
Song Of Wrath
Szentirmay
To The Whippoorwill
Szentirmay & Nemeth
In My Whole Life Happy
There's But One Girl Underneath
The Sun
This Girl
Szymanowski
Song Of The Girl At The Window
Tabb-West
Cradle Song, A
Tableporter
Come What May
Tabrar
Daddy Wouldn't Buy Me A Bow
Wow
He's Going To Marry Mary Ann
Taccani
Chella Lla
Taccani & Dipaola
Come Prima
Tafelkonfekt
Gute Gewissen, Das
Taff & Taff
Be Still My Soul
Eagle Song
Taff & Taff & Hollihan
We Will Stand

Taft
Our Country
Tagliaferri
Piscatore 'E Pusilleco
Tahar-Lev & Hirsh
Hamishpacha Sheli
Malach Misulam Yaakov
Takacs
Psalm 23
Psalm 4
Talavera
Mexican Lullaby
Talbot
Child's Hymn To St Joseph
Fairies And Elves
Holy Is His Name
I Am He
Little Red Sled, The
My Gift
Our Songs
Talbot & Excell
I'll Be A Sunbeam
Talley
Behold That Star
Step Into The Water
Tallis
According To They Gracious Word
All Praise To Thee
All Praise To Thee My God
All Praise To Thee My God This
Night
Audivi Media Nocte
Awake My Soul And With The Sun
Behold The Bridegroom Cometh
Child's Wish, A
Come Now And Praise The Humble
Saint Of David's House
From All That Dwell Below The
Skies
Glory Be To The Father
Glory To Thee My God This Night
Great Creator Of The Worlds, The
Great Shepherd Of Your People Hear
I Heard The Voice Of Jesus Say
Lord Have Mercy Upon Us
Lord It Belongs Not To My Care
Lord's Prayer, The
Man Who Once Has Found Abode,
The
O God Our Refuge And Our
Strength
O God Whose Will Is Life
O Holy Spirit Come To Us
O Holy Spirit Lord Of Grace
O Lord Give Thy Holy Spirit
O Mean May Seem This House Of
Clay
O Thou Whose Feet Have Climbed
Life's Hill
O Where Are Kings And Empires
Now
Our Father Who Art In Heaven

Tallis *(Cont.)*
Tallis' Canon
Tallis' Ordinal
Thanks Be To Thee
To God Who Gives Us Daily Bread
To Mock Your Reign
When Rising From The Bed Of
Death
Tampa Red
Poor Stranger Blues
Tan'sur
Give Ear Ye Children
Tanner
Evergreen
Tans'ur
Alone Thou Goest Forth
Alone Thou Goest Forth O Lord
O Very God Of Very God
Tans'ur's
O Love Divine
O Thou In All Thy Might So Far
Tansur
According To They Gracious Word
He Lives The Great Redeemer Lives
While Shepherds Watched Their
Flocks
Tapp
Let Your Light So Shine
Promise Is Unto You, The
Tappan & Roth
Fool's Gold
Tapper
Cardinal, The
Grace Before Meat
Tar
Night Song
Targett
Sing My Fiddle
Slumber Slumber
Tarner
Ford It's The Going Thing
Let There Be Planters
Only Mustang Makes It Happen
This Is The L&M Moment
Tarney
Little In Love, A
We Don't Talk Anymore
Tarney & Sayer
Dreamin'
Tarney & Spencer
No Time To Lose
Tartaglia
Pennzoil Please
Tate
If I Should Plant A Tiny Seed Of
Love
Somewhere A Voice Is Calling
Tate & Handel
While Shepherds Watched
Tate & Morris
Anytime Anyplace Anywhere
Tatum
These Are The Best Times

Taub
Santa Fe Blues
Taubert
Bees, The
Cradle Song, A
Ever Near Ever Near
Gute Nacht Gute Nacht
Lullaby
Night
Oiseau Messager, L'
Sleep Beloved Sleep
Soldatenlied
Taupin
Dan Dare
Taupin & Page
These Dreams
Taupin & Page & Wolf & Lambert
We Built This City
Taverner
Rex Amabilis
Tawney
Ballad Of Sammy's Bar, The
Chicken On A Raft
Taylor
Ah Why Will My Dear Little Child
   Be So Cross
America Eternal
Angel In The Morning
Angel Of The Morning
Band Of Gold
Bartender's Blues
Boy From New York City, The
Broken Heart My God My King, A
Calling All Girls
Calvary Covers It All
Candido
Carolina In My Mind
Christ Up On The Mountain Peak
Country Road
Don't Go Away Without Jesus
Don't Let Me Be Lonely Tonight
Down By The Old Mill Stream
Everybody Loves Somebody
Fire And Rain
Funny
Glorious Things Of Thee Are Spoken
God Is Love Let Heaven Adore Him
Holy Spirit Ever Living
I Want To Be A Clone
Indiana Wants Me
Jesus From Whom All Blessings
   Flow
Jesus Lives Thy Terrors Now
Jesus The Calm That Fills My Breast
Just Gets Better With Time
Kookie Kookie Lend Me Your Comb
Little Jack
Lord Of All Being
Lord Of All Being Throned Afar
Lord Of Our Life God Whom We
   Fear
Meltdown At Madame Tussaud's
Mexico

Taylor (*Cont.*)
Miller's Song, The
My Shepherd Is The Lord
O God In Whom We Live
O Lord All Gorious Life Of Life
O Wrap The Flag Around Me Boys
Our Helper God We Bless Thy
   Name
Our Team
Radio Ga Ga
Sanctus
Service Of Supplies, The
Shelter
Shower The People
Something In The Way She Moves
Sparkling Rill, The
Stars On Summer Evenings Glow,
   The
Steam Roller
Sweet Baby James
Tell My People
Ten Thousand Men Of Harvard
This Day
Thou Source Divine
Three Ships, The
Walking Man
We Walk By Faith
Wild Thing
Your Smiling Face
Zachary Taylor
Taylor & Dallas
I Wish I Knew How It Would Feel
   To Be Free
Taylor & Davis
Boy From New York City, The
Taylor & Elias & Des Barres
I Do What I Do
Taylor & Hilliard
Battle Is The Lord's, The
Taylor & Jones
Take It Easy
Taylor & Kramer & Altman
Miss O'Leary's Irish Fruit Cake
Taylor & Linzer & Kool & The Gang
Fresh
Taylor & Rhodes & Lebon
Election Day
Goodbye Is Forever
I Don't Want Your Love
Notorious
Taylor & Wilson
Right Track Wrong Train
Soft Sweet And Warm
Taylor & Wilson & Richey
You're Gonna Hurt Me One More
   Time
Taylor & Wilson & Stampley
If You Touch Me
Tchaikovsky
An Den Schalf
Andante Cantabile
At The Ball
Call Of The Dance, The

Tchaikovsky (*Cont.*)
Canary, The
Capriccio Italien Theme
Cherubim Song
Christ When A Child A Garden
   Made
Cradle Song
Crown Of Roses, The
Cuckoo, The
Dance Of The Sugar-Plum Fairy
Death
Deception
Did My Mother Give Me Life
Disappointment
Don Juan's Serenade
Einst Zum Narren Jemand Spricht
Einzig Wortchen, Ein
Endless Love
Er Liebte Mich So Sehr
Es War Zur Ersten Fruhlingszeit
Fahrt Hin Ihr Traume
Farewell
Florentiner Lied
Hat Die Mutter Zu So Schwerem
   Leide
He Truly Loved Me So
Holy Blessed Trinity
Holy Holy Holy
If You But Knew
Inmitten Des Balles
It Was In Early Days Of Spring
Kanarienvogel, Der
Kein Wort Von Dir
Kuckuk, Der
Larmes, Les
Lebewohl
Legen
Legend, A
Legende
Lied Der Zigeunerin
Linger Yet
Lord I Cry Unto Thee
Lord Is My Shepherd, The
Love Theme From Romeo And Juliet
Lullaby During A Storm
March Slav
Mignon's Lied
Mignon's Song
Morning Hymn
My Heart Is Yours
Nein Wen Ich Liebe
Nicht Sogleich Hat Mich Liebe
   Erfullet
Nicht Worte Geliebter
Night Of Stars, A
Nightingale, The
No Whom I Love I'll Ne'er Reveal
No Word From Thee
None But The Lonely Heart
None But The Lonely Know
None But Who Yearning Know
Not At Once Did I Yield To Love's
   Yearning
Nur Du Allein

Tchaikovsky *(Cont.)*
Nur Wer Die Sehnsucht Kennt
Nutcracker Sweets
O Blessed And Ever Gracious Lord
O Geh' Nicht Von Mir Mein Freund
O Leave Me Not Friend Of Mine
O Mein Kind Durch Die
   Schweigende Nacht
O Mochtest Du Einmal Noch Singen
O My Child In The Silence Of Night
Ob Heller Tag
Oh Thou From Whom All Blessings
   Flow
Old Legend, An
On The Isle Of May
One Small Word
Only The Lonely Heart
Organ Grinder, The
Pauline's Romance
Pilgrim's Song
Pimpinella
Praise Ye The Lord
Praise Ye The Name Of The Lord
Romeo And Juliet
Serenade
Si Vous Saviez
Sleeping Beauty
Sleeping Beauty Waltz
Some One Said Unto The Fool
Song Of The Gipsy Girl
Song Tschaikowsky Wrote, The
Speak Not O Beloved
Spring
Standchen Des Don Juan
Sternennacht
Swear Not By The Inconstant Moon
Tears
Tell Me Why
That Simple Old Ballad O Sing Me
Thornrose Waltz
Thrane Bebt, Die
To Sleep
To Thee We Call
Tod, Der
'Twas You Alone
Waltz Of The Flowers
War Ich Nicht Ein Halm Auf
   Frischem Wiesengrund
Warte Noch
Warum
Was I Not A Blade Of Grass In
   Meadow Green
Was Nun
We Praise Thee
Weil' Ich Wie Einstmals Allein
What Care I
Wherefore
Whether Day Dawns
Why
Wiegenlied
Ye Who Have Yearned Alone
Yearning I Wait Now Alone
Yes I Love You

Tcherepnin
To Music
Tchesnokov
Adoration
Salvation Belongeth To Our God
Tead
I Hear A Sweet Voice Calling Me
Tedesco
Plaisir D'amour
Tegner
Bae Bae Lille Lam
Teifer
Full Time Job, A
Teitelbaum
Shprayz Ich Mir
Tejada
Faithless
Perjura
Tekple
In Sweet September
Teleman
Vergesserne Phillis, Die
Telson
Calling You
Tempchin
Peaceful Easy Feeling
Swayin' To The Music
Tempchin & Strandlund
Already Gone
Temperton
Always And Forever
Baby Come To Me
Boogie Nights
Do You Love Me
Give Me The Night
Man Size Love
Mystery
Rock With You
Someone In The Dark
Sweet Freedom
Thriller
Temperton & Garrett & Jones &
   Debarge
Secret Garden, The
Tempest
Cherokee
Final Countdown, The
Rock The Night
Superstitious
Tempest & Michaeli
Carrie
Temple
In Sweet September
Memories
My Lady's Bower
Old Garden, An
'Tis All That I Can Say
'Twas Surely Fate
Temple & Cotes
Prehistoric Man
Templeton
Old Macdonald Farms With Brahms
Ten Eyck
All The Way With Jesus

Tenaglia
Take Pity Sweet Eyes
Tenille
Do That To Me One More Time
Tennant & Lowe
Domino Dancing
It's A Sin
Opportunities
Suburbia
West End Girls
Tennant & Lowe & Hague
Love Comes Quickly
Tenney
Beneath Thy Shadow Hiding
Bird With A Broken Wing, The
Broad Is The Opening Field
Calvary's Stream Is Flowing
Children Of The Heavenly King
Crown Him Today
Draw Me Closer To Thee
Ever Will I Pray
Gird On The Sword And Armor
Hallowed Hour Of Prayer
Have You Told It All To Jesus
He Blessed Me There
I'll Lend A Hand
In Me Ye Shall Have Peace
In The Shadow Of The Cross
Jesus Is Able To Save
Jesus Is Passing This Way
Keep A Light In The Window
Lead Us Heavenly Father
Mansions Yonder, The
Mexicali Rose
My Old Country Home
My Sins Are Taken Away
We'll Never Say Good By
Where Will You Spend Eternity
Whosoever Will May Come
Tennille
Do That To Me One More Time
Way I Want To Touch You, The
Tepper
No Easy Way Out
Tepper & Bennett
All That I Am
Angel
Beach Boy Blues
Beginner's Luck
Boy Like Me A Girl Like You, A
G I Blues
Island Of Love
It's A Wonderful World
Just For Old Time's Sake
Lonesome Cowboy
Nuttin' For Christmas
Once Is Enough
Puppet On A String
Red Roses For A Blue Lady
Relax
Slicin' Sand
Smorgasbord
Suzy Snowflake

Tepper & Bennett *(Cont.)*
Walls Have Ears, The
Wheels On My Heels
Wonderful World Of The Young,
The
Tepper & Bennett & Schroeder
Shoppin' Around
Tepper & Brodsky
Busybody
Red Roses For A Blue Lady
Suzy Snowflake
Tepper & Marshall
Bel Age, Le
Terentiev
Regimental Polka
Terhune
Two Little Crabs
Terreaux
Let The Hills Resound
Terry
Gabriel's Message Does Away
Heart Of His Will, The
Heavenly Rest
Home Where I Belong
Our Sacred Pledge
Praise To The Holiest In The Height
Teschemacher & D'Hardelot
Because
Teschner
Advent
All Glory Laud And Honor
All Glory Praise And Honor
Blest Be The King Whose Coming
For Stories Fine And True
From Bethany
From Every Clime And Country
God Is My Strong Salvation
If God Himself Be For Me
Morning Light Is Breaking, The
O Bold O Foolish Peasants
O Enter Lord Thy Temple
O How Shall I Receive Thee
O Lord How Shall I Meet Thee
Our Dwelling Place
St Theodulph
With Happy Voices Ringing
Teschner & Bach
All Glory Laud And Honor
Tessier
Non Vous N'etes Pas Yeux
To Woodland Glades I Must Fare
Tex
Show Me
Thacker
Sunrise In The Morning
Thalberg
Wenn All Untreu Werden
Thatch
Lord Speak To Me That I May Speak
Thatcher
Creating God Your Fingers Trace
Jesus Redeemer Of The World
Lord Speak To Me That I May Speak

Thayer
Courtship
Phantom Band, The
'Twas A Bluebird
Theard
You Rascal You
Theard & Moore
Let The Good Times Roll
Theodorakis
Beyond Tomorrow
Theme From Zorba The Greek
Thibault
As The Sun Doth Daily Rise
My Life Is Like The Summer Rose
Thibaut
If This Be Love
Lament
Thicke & Loring & Burton
Facts Of Life, The
Thielemans
Bluesette
Thigpen
Lost And Found
Thiman
Dandelion, The
Easter Prayer, An
Ladybird, The
My Bonny Lass She Smileth
Sing We And Chant It
Spring Wind
Sun Doth Shine, The
We Shepherds Sing
Thom
Bubble Pipe Dream
Halloween
My Kite
Our Family
Skipping
Thomas
A Vos Jeux Mes Amis
Annie Of The Vale
Anyplace Is Paradise
Beautiful Isle Of The Sea
Behold Titania
Bells Of Christmas, The
Bonnie Eloise
Bonny Eloise
Connais Tu Le Pays
Contentment
Cottage By The Sea, The
Croquet
Dance Little Bird
Dost Thou Know That Sweet Land
Eternal God Whose Power Upholds
Evening
Fishing Blues
Gee Whiz
Gee Whiz Look At His Eyes
Girl Of My Dreams
Hold 'Em Joe
Hold On
I Am Titania
Jolly Good Laugh, A
King Of Rock And Roll

Thomas *(Cont.)*
Know'st Thou That Fair Land
Knowest Thou That Dear Land
Knowest Thou Younder Land
Lux Et Veritas
Matilda
May God Protect Columbia
Me Voici Dans Son Boudoir
My Neighbor
New Orleans Hop Scop Blues
Night-Hymn At Sea
Old Time, The
One Morning Oh So Early
Only For The Love Of The Lord
Part Time Servant
Parting
Perfect Mountain, A
Rings Of Gold
Rockin' Robin
Rose Of Killarney
Runner, The
Sing With Joy
Sioux City Sue
Sous Les Etoiles
Spinning Wheel
Summer Night, A
Sweet Thing
This Is That Time Of The Year
'Tis But A Little Faded Flower
Tis Said That Absence Conquers
Love
Two Roads
Walking The Dog
Winds In The Trees
Woman In Me, The
You Can't Hurry God
Zion's Joy
Thomas & McLollie
Hey Boy Hey Girl
Thomas & Ogden
Bring Them In
Thomas & Roberts
Notre Dame
Thomas & Ross
Just The Way I Planned It
Thomas & Thomas & Stevenson
I Need A Miracle
Thomas & Vikki
Gee Whiz
Thomason
Bible Tells Me So, The
Thome
Good Day Suzon
Pearls Of Gold
Thomerson
Behold How Good And Pleasant It Is
I Want To Walk As A Child Of The
Light
Thompson
Ain't No Way
Amici
Annie Lisle
Black Bawl, A
Bobbie Shaftoe's Gone To Sea

Thompson *(Cont.)*
Come Where The Lilies Bloom
Cornell Song
Cousin Jedediah
Do It Again A Little Bit Slower
Don't Go Out Tonight Dear Father
El Shaddai
Epigram Upon Handel And
    Buononcini
Far Above Cayuga's Waters
For Ah The Master Is So Fair
For Lincoln We Will Ever Stand
Fount Of Glory
Great Day Coming, The
He Was Nervous
Hoodoo, The
How Happy Every Child Of Grace
Humpty Dumpty Heart
I Will Praise Him
Jesus Bids You Come
Jesus Is All The World To Me
Lead Me Gently Home Father
Letter, The
Lift Your Heart In Prayer
Lilly Dale
Lines From The Ancient Mariner
Mighty To Save
Miner's Lament I, The
Quack Quack Said The Duck
Sinner And The Song, The
Softly And Tenderly
Softly And Tenderly Jesus Is Calling
Soldiers Of The Cross Arise
Spring Bursts Today
Tear-Stained Letter
There's A Great Day Coming
Wake Not But Hear Love
Whole Wide World For Jesus, The
World Must Be Taken, The

Thompson & Card
El Shaddai

Thompson & Card & Scruggs
Count Me In

Thompson & Davis
When We Wind Up The Watch On
    The Rhine

Thompson & Fleming
Cross My Broken Heart

Thompson & Jacquet
Robbin's Nest

Thompson & James & Christopher
Always On My Mind

Thompson & Scruggs & Card
Count Me In

Thomson
Agnus Dei
Bell Doth Toll, The
Bugle Song, The
Live Every Minute
Preciosilla
Sung By The Shepherds
Susie Asado
Take A Little Rhythm
Take O Take Those Lips Away

Thorne
Go U Northwestern

Thornton
Don't Give Up The Old Love For
    The New
It Don't Seem Like The Same Old
    Smile
My Sweetheart's The Man In The
    Moon
She May Have Seen Better Days
Streets Of Cairo
When You Were Sweet Sixteen

Thorpe & Brown
War Of The Worlds

Thouret
I Know Two Eyes That Fondly
There Are Loyal Hearts

Throckmorton
I Wish I Was Eighteen Again
I Wish You Could Have Turned My
    Head And Left My Heart Alone
I'm Knee Deep In Loving You
Last Cheater's Waltz, The
Middle Age Crazy
Papa's Sugar
Safely In The Arms Of Jesus
Trying To Love Two Women
Way I Am, The

Throckmorton & Braddock
Thinking Of A Rendezvous

Throckmorton & Fischer
One Of A Kind

Throckmorton & Vanhoy
Friday Night Bliues
I Don't Do Like That No More

Thrupp
Brightest And Best
Brightest And Best Of The Sons Of
    The Morning

Thrupp & Bradbury
Savior Like A Shepherd Lead Us

Thuille
Vom Scheiden

Thurman
Chaparral, The
Jehovah
Owl, The
Woodpecker, The

Thurman & Sorrells
Praise To The King

Thurman & Thurman & Peters
First Stone, The

Thurston
Remember The Nights

Tibbles & Idriss
Woody Woodpecker
Woody Woodpecker Song, The

Tiddeman
Flung To The Heedless Winds
Thy Way Not Mine O Lord

Tierney
Alice Blue Gown
M-I-S-S-I-S-S-I-P-P-I

Tiger & Vallance
Someday

Til Tuesday
Voices Carry

Tilbrook & Difford
853-5937
Goodbye Girl
Hourglass
Pulling Mussels From The Shell
Take Me I'm Yours

Tilden
One Hour More

Tilleard
Lo He Comes With Clouds
    Descending

Tillett
John Reilly
Jolly Thresher, The
My Parents Raised Me Tenderly
Paul Jones
Poor Little Sailor Boy, A
Prince Boys, The
Sailor's Grave, A
Seventy Two Today
Southern Girl's Reply, The

Tillis
Heart Over Mind
Honey
Ruby Don't Take Your Love To
    Town

Tillis & Kearney
Emotions

Tillis & Peddy
Honky Tonk Song

Tillman
House I Live In, The
I Love You So Much It Hurts
I'll Never Slip Around Again
If Only
Life's Railway To Heaven
Listen
My Mother's Bible
New Life
Old Time Power
Slipping Around
Unanswered Yet
When I Get To The End Of The Way

Tillotson
It Keeps Right On A-Hurtin'

Tilton
Bay Bye Here's A Fly

Timberg & Sharples
It's A Hap-Hap-Happy Day

Tindley
Go Wash In The Beautiful Stream
I'll Overcome Some Day
Nothing Between
Some Day
Stand By Me
We'll Understand It Better By And
    By
When The Storms Of Life Are
    Raging

Tiomkin
 Ballad Of The Alamo
 Blowing Wild
 Friendly Persuasion
 Giant
 Green Leaves Of Summer, The
 High And The Mighty, The
 High Noon
 Rio Bravo
 Town Without Pity

Tiomkin & Washington
 Rawhide

Tippin & Collie
 Something With A Ring To It

Tipton
 Soap TV Theme
 Theme From Soap, The

Tirana
 Zingarella

Titcomb
 Jesus Name Of Wondrous Love

Tobani
 Hearts And Flowers

Tobias
 In The Valley Of The Moon
 Jesus Saves
 Keep On Praying
 Miss You
 Sing
 We Did It Before And We Can Do It
  Again

Tobias & Burke
 In The Valley Of The Moon

Tobias & Lewis
 Rose O'Day

Tobias & Simon & Tobias
 Wait For Me Mary

Tobias & Turk
 Just Another Day Wasted Away

Todd & Lombardo
 Oooh Look-A There Ain't She Pretty

Toler
 New Day
 Thinkin' About Home

Tolhurst & Grombacher & Giraldo
 All Fired Up

Tomer
 God Be With You
 God Be With You Till We Meet
 God Be With You Till We Meet
  Again
 Gott Mit Euch Bis Wir Uns
  Wiederseh'n

Tomkins
 O Pray For The Peace Of Jerusalem

Tomlin & Poe & Grier
 Object Of My Affection, The

Tompkins & Pace & Speer
 Old Gospel Ship, The

Toms
 Billiken Song
 I Kind O' Like Ann Arbor

Toni C.
 Love Will Save The Day

Tonnessen
 Himmellske Lovsang, Den

Toolan
 I Am The Bread Of Life

Toombs
 5-10-15 Hours
 Daddy Daddy
 One Mint Julep

Toplady & Hastings
 Rock Of Ages

Torelli
 Thou Knowest Well
 Tu Lo Sai

Torme
 Lament To Love
 Stranger In Town, A

Torme & Wells
 Christmas Song, The

Torre & Spielman
 Paper Roses

Toselli
 Serenade

Tosh
 Days Are Gliding Swiftly By, The
 Lord Of Our Life

Tosti
 A Vucchella
 Alba Separa Dalla Luce L'Ombra, L'
 Aprile
 At The Convent Gate
 Ave Maria
 Beauty's Eyes
 Bid Me Good-Bye
 Chanson D L'adieu
 Could I
 Forever And Forever
 Forgetfulness
 Good-Bye
 Ideale
 Luna D'estate
 Malia
 Marechiare
 Mattinata
 Mia Canzone, La
 Morning
 My Ideal
 Ninon
 Non T'amo Piu
 O Voice Of Music
 Only A Year Ago
 Penso
 Pescatore Canta, Il
 Pour Un Baiser
 Quisiera Morir
 Ridonami La Calma
 Serenade, The
 Serenata, La
 Si Tu Le Voulais
 Sogno
 Thinking
 Tormento
 Tristezza
 Ultima Canzone, L'

Tosti (*Cont.*)
 Ultimo Bacio, L'
 Venetian Song
 Vorrei
 Vorrei Morire

Toto
 Mala Femmena

Tourison
 Big Red Team, The

Tourjee
 One Sweetly Solemn Thought
 There's A Wideness In God's Mercy
 Where The Dark Comes Most

Tours
 Am I A Soldier Of The Cross
 Day Of Resurrection, The
 Dear Lord Who Sought At Dawn Of
  Day
 Great God Beneath Whose Piercing
  Eye
 Jesus Lover Of My Soul
 Light Along The Ages, The
 Mother O' Mine
 O Day Of Rest And Gladness
 O Thou Who Sealest Up The Past
 Saw You Never In The Twilight
 Sky Can Still Remember, The
 There Is Never A Day So Dreary
 Thou Lord Of Light Across The
  Years
 Thy Kingdom Lord We Long For
 Voice Within, The
 We Journey Through A Vale Of
  Tears
 When His Salvation Bringing
 With Happy Voices Singing
 Year Ago, A

Tourtellot
 I Arise From Dreams Of Thee
 Serenade

Toussaint
 I Like It Like That
 Mother-In-Law
 Pulgas Freeway, Las
 Southern Nights
 Sunset At Sunset
 Working In The Coal Mine

Tovey
 Pure As The Dawn

Towne
 My Darling's Little Shoes

Towner
 All Is Forgiven
 All The Way Home
 Anywhere With Jesus
 Are You A Reaper
 At Calvary
 At Even Ere The Sun Was Set
 Baptise Me With The Spirit
 Be Not Deceived
 Better Land, The
 Bugle Call, The
 Changeless Word, The
 Christ Is Thy Light

Towner *(Cont.)*

Christ Jesus Hath The Power
Cleansed By Grace Divine
Cling To The Bible My Boy
Debt Unknown, The
Full Surrender
Give Me Thy Heart
Glory All The Way
God Sets A Still Small Voice
Grace Greater Than Our Sin
Hand That Was Wounded For Me,
    The
Hark Hark My Soul
He Died In My Place
He Is Knocking
He Suffered For You
How Sweet To Trust In Jesus
How They Sing Up Yonder
I Am Satisfied With Jesus
I Do Love Jesus With All My Heart
I Will Rejoice
I Would Not Have Thee Come
If I May But See Him
Immanuel Prince Of Peace
In Everything Give Thanks
Jesus Is Living Again
Jesus Knows Your Sorrow
King Of Kings
Let Everybody Sing
Life Is Mine
Lift Up Your Heads
Lift Your Nieghbor's Burden
Light In The Eastern Sky
Like Christ In Every Thing
Looking On You
Lord's My Shepherd, The
Love Found A Way
Make Me Like Thee
Man Of Galilee, The
Meeting In The Air, The
Move Forward
My Anchor Holds
My Offering
O Blessed Day
O Heavenly Love
O Lord Send A Revival
O Wonderful Love Of My God
O Wonderful Wonderful Story
O Word Of God
Oh Wanderer Rejoice
Old Fireside, The
Old Ship Zion, The
Only A Sinner
Onward Upward
Open The Windows Of Heaven
Paul And Silas
Trust And Obey
Trusting Heart, The
Victor's Crown, The
Weighed In The Balance
When We Walk With The Lord .
Who'll Be The Next
Why Will Ye Die

Towner *(Cont.)*

Worth Of A Soul, The
Would You Believe

Townsend

Blessed Are The Poor In Spirit
Come Ye That Love The Lord
Do Lord Remember Me
Done With Sin And Sorrow
For Your Love
He Arose
I Am Bound For The Promised Land
I Can't Stay Away
I'm Going Home
In Bright Mansions Above
In The River Of Jordan
Isle Of Mann
It's Me
Lord Bless Thee, The
My Lord's Writing All The Time
My Shepherd
New Hiding Place, A
No Hiding Place
Oh Freedom
On Calvary
Rise Shine For Thy Light Is
    A-Coming
There Is A Green Hill Far Away
There Is A Light Shining
Thine Arm O Lord In Days Of Old
Wade In The Water
We Shall Walk Through The Valley
When The Lord Shall Appear
Whiskey-Still
Will The Lighthouse Shine On Me
Witness For The Lord

Townsend & Smith

For God So Loved The World

Townshend

I Can See For Miles
My Generation
Pinball Wizard

Toy

Hip Hip Hooray

Tozer

Thou Son Of God Whose Flamin
    Eyes

Trabar & Adair

Just A Little Just A Little

Trader

Fool Such As I, A

Traditional

12th Of July, The
1815-1915
1881 Rent Agitation
900 Miles
999, The
A' Bhean Iadach
A Bholagan A Bho Chiuin
A Canoa Virou
A' Chaora Chrom
A Chaorain A Chaorain
A Chasen'dl Oif Shabos
A Chazandl Oyf Shabes
A Din-Toire Mit Gott

Traditional *(Cont.)*

A Dudele
A G'Naive
A Geneyve
A' Ghaoil Lig Dhachaigh Gu M'
    Mhathair Mi
A Kjore Vatten
A L'oree Du Buis De Chenes
A La Claire Fontaine
A La Coulee De Mines
A La Huella
A La Media Noche
A La Montanas Ire
A La Nanita Nana
A La Nuit Tombante
A La Orilla Del Palmar
A La Peche Des Moules
A La Rue
A La Rurru Nino
A La Volette
A Mare Encheu
A Mhor Thromanach
A Spalpeen Aroon
A Theanga Na Ri
A Tisket A Tasket
A Tu Nino En Este Dia
A-Cruising We Will Go
A-Hunting We Will Go
A-Jogging Along
A-Roving
A-Walking And A-Talking
ABC
ABC Tumble Down D
Abdul The Bulbul Ameer
Aberffraw Eisteddvod
Abgel Done Changed My Name
Abide With Me
Abiding In The Fields
Abilene
Abilene Rose
Abiyoyo
Aboard Of The Kangaroo
Abolitionist Hymn, The
Above The Plain
According To My Lord's Command
According To The Act
Account Of A Little Girl Who Was
    Burnt For Her Religion
Ach Du Lieber Augustin
Ach Gott Wie Weh Tut Scheiden
Ach Lieber Herre Jesu Christ
Ach The Moon Climbs High
Ach Wie Ist's Moglich Dann
Achachau
Achtsik Er Un Zibetsik Zi
Acre Of Land, An
Across The Western Ocean
Ad Cantum Leticie
Adams And Liberty
Addio La Caserma
Adelita
Adeste Fideles
Adieu Sweet Amaryllis

Traditional *(Cont.)*

Adieu To Bon County
Adieu To Dark Weather
Adieu To Old England
Adios
Adios Me Sueno
Adios Te Digo
Adir Hu
Adon Olom
Adorar Al Nino
Advent Tells Us Christ Is Near
Ae Fond Kiss
Aeroplane, The
Af Di Felder Grine Felder
African Counting Song
After 'While
Afterword
Afton Water
Aged Pilot Man, The
Agincourt Song, The
Aguinaldo No. 1
Aguinaldo No. 2
Ah Holy Jesus How Has Thou
   Offended
Ah Holy Jesus How Hast Thou
   Offended
Ah How The Moon Is Shining
Ah La Prune Au Jardin Va Ondulant
Ah La Sa Wu
Ah Mon Dieu Qu'est-Il Donc Arrive
Ah Si Mon Moine Voulait Danser
Ah Vous Dirai-Je Maman
Ah Where's The Miller's Daughter
Ah's De Man
Ahavat Hadassah
Aherlow
Ahora Voy A Cantarles
Ai Ai Der Rebe Geit
Aiken Drum
Ailein Ailein 'S Fhad Do Chadal
Ailein Duinn
Ailie Bain
Ailie Bain O' The Glen
Aimee McPherson
Ain' Gonna Grieve My Lord
Ain' No Mo' Cane On De Brazis
Ain't Goin' A Study War No More
Ain't Goin' To Study War No Mo'
Ain't Going To Rain No More
Ain't Gonna Let Nobody Turn Me
   Round
Ain't Gonna Rain
Ain't Got Long To Stay Heah
Ain't Gwine Study War No More
Ain't Gwine To Work No More
Ain't I Glad I've Got Out The
   Wilderness
Ain't It A Shame
Ain't It Hard To Be A Nigger
Ain't No Use O' My Workin' So
   Hard
Ain't That Good News

Traditional *(Cont.)*

Ain't You Glad You Got Good
   Religion
Airplanes
Akanamandla
Al Alimon
Al Amanecer Del Dia
Al Canto De Una Laguna
Al Chante Il Gial
Al Ha-Nisim
Al Ha-Sela Hah
Alabado
Alabado Al Nino Dios
Alabama
Alabama-Bound
Alabamy Bound
Alberts Tune
Ale Ale Glorious Ale
Ale Mentshen Tantzendik
Ale Vasserlech Flisn Avek
Ale-Wife And Her Barrel, The
Alec Orth's Waltz
Alegria
Aleluia
Alf Fran Jern
All Alone
All And Some
All Around The Maypole
All Beauty Within You
All Day On The Prairie
All Day While I'm At Work
All For Me Grog
All God's Children Got Shoes
All God's Chillun Got Wings
All Hail To The Days
All Heaven On A Maiden
All I Do The People Keep
   A-Grumbeling
All In A Stable Cold And Bare
All In The Morning
All Ireland Championship 1912, The
All Is Silent
All Is Well
All Mein Gedanken Die Ich Hab
All My Hope On God Is Founded
All My Trials
All Over This World
All Round My Hat
All That
All The Flowers On The Meadow
All The Pretty Li'l Horses
All The Pretty Little Horses
All Things Are Quite Silent
All Things Are Thine No Gift Have
   We
All Things Bright And Beautiful
All This Night
All This Night Shrill Chanticleer
All Through The Ale
All Through The Night
All Throughout The Great Wide
   World I Wandered
All Thru The Night
All We Do

Traditional *(Cont.)*

All Who Love And Serve Your City
All You That In This House
All's Well That Ends Well
Alla En El Rancho Grande
Allan Offa's Schottische
Alle Fugler Sna De Er
Allea Alleo
Alleluia
Alleluia Song Of Gladness
Allentown Ambulance
Allhallows Eve
Allons A Lafayette
Allouette
Alma Mater
Almfahren
Aloha No Wau I Ko Maka
Alone
Alone I Wait
Along The Peterskaya Road
Alonzo The Brave And The Fair
   Imogene
Alouette
Alouette Chanta Le Jour, L'
Alouette Gentille Alouette
Alouette, L'
Alphabet, The
Alphabet Song
Alphabet Song, The
Alpine Rose, The
Alpine Shepherds
Als Aus Der Heimat Ich Fortging
Als Ich Bei Meinen Schafen Wacht
Alte Guggisberger Lied, Das
Although You Are So Tiny
Altoona Freight Wreck, The
Alverson
Always Gay
Always Happy Can We Say
Am I A Soldier Of The Cross
Am I My Brother's Keeper
Am I Not Fondly Thine Own
Am I The Doctor
Am Lomand-See
Am Schonen Sommerabend
Am Weihnachtsbaum Die Lichter
   Brennen
Ama Birjinaren Bestez
Amalfi
Amalfi Bay
Amalia Rosa
Amapola Dol Camino
Amapola La Creole-A
Amapolita
Amar Amar
Amar Rabi Akiva
Amar Rabi Elazer
Amaryllis
Amazing Grace
Amazing Grace How Sweet The
   Sound
Amen
Amen Amen
Amens

Traditional *(Cont.)*

Amens-Fourfold
Amens-Sevenfold
Amens-Threefold
America
America Forever Or A Defiance To
    The Bulwark Of Religion
America The Anchor And Hope Of
    The World
American Army Hymn
American Constitution Frigate's
    Engagement With The British
    Frigate Guerrier
American Folk Trilogy, An
American History
American Spirit
American Star
American Trilogy
American Trilogy, An
American Volunteer, The
American Woods
Amo Amas
Amo Amas I Love A Lass
Amol Iz Geven A Mayse
Among Us In Holy Russia
Among Us On The Sea
Amor Que Te Tenia, El
Amour De Moi, L'
Amsterdam
An Bunnan Buide
An Bunnanan Bui
An Der Eisenbahn
An Gille Donn
An' He Never Said A Mumblin'
    Word
An' I Cry
An Racan A Bh'againne
An T-Each Odhar
An Tamhran Dochais
Anach Cuain
Anansi Play For Ma Dogma
Ancien Noel
Ancient Tune
And All That Hope In Thee For Stay
And Are We Yet Alive
And If You Don't Believe Me
And Thus He Spoke
And Wasn't That A Tidy One
And When I Die
And When The Leaves
And Who Pray Is Martin Van Buren
Andrew Bardeen
Andrew Battan
Andrew Rose
Andulka
Andulko
Angel Gabriel, The
Angel Roll De Stone Away, De
Angel Rolled The Stone Away, The
Angel, The
Angel's Message, The
Angel's Waitin' At De Tomb, De
Angel's Whisper, The

Traditional *(Cont.)*

Angeline
Angelique O
Angels And Ministers Spirits Of
    Grace
Angels And Shepherds
Angels And The Shepherds, The
Angels At Christmas Tide
Angels Done Bowed Down, The
Angels Fair We Heard On High
Angels From Heaven
Angels From The Realms
Angels From The Realms Of Glory
Angels Holy
Angels Lookin' At Me, De
Angels Rolled De Stone Away
Angels, The
Angels Waiting At The Door
Angels We Have Heard On High
Angels' Whisper
Angelus Ad Virginem
Anges Dans Nos Campagnes, Les
Angiolina
Ani Maamin
Animal Fair, The
Animal Song
Anitchka
Anna Maria
Anna's Rosy Cheeks
Annabel Lee
Anne Knutsdotter
Annette And Brother John
Annie
Annie Laurie
Annie Of Tharaw
Annie Shaw's Tune
Anniebelle
Another Day's Journey
Another Little Drink
Another Man Done Gone
Another Of Seafarers Describing Evil
    Fortune
Anson Best
Antonio
Anyam Szive
Apple Picking
Apple-Cheeked Rider, The
Apprends-Moi Ton Langage
Approach Of Winter, The
April
April Antics
April Warning, An
Apron Of Flowers, The
Arabs On The March
Aransom Shansom Through Yander
Arbol Y La Hoja, El
Arbrisseau Tout Tortu, Un
Archie O' Cawfield
Ardeleana
Are You Sleeping
Are You There Moriarity
Arima Konbertitu Baten
    Sentimendiak Khurutxiaren A

Traditional *(Cont.)*

Arise And Bar The Door-O
Arise Arise
Arizona
Arizona Killer, The
Arkansas Boys, The
Arkansas Traveler
Arkansas Traveler, The
Arkansas Traveller, The
Arkansaw Traveler
Arkumshaw's Farewell
Armored Cruiser Squadron, The
Army Blue
Army Chair Corps Song, The
Around Cape Horn
Around Her Neck She Wore A
    Yellow Ribbon
Around The Throne Of God A Band
Aroys Iz In Vilue A Nayer Bafel
Arroro
Arroz Con Leche
Arthur McBride
Arthur Nolan
Artillery Song
Artsa Alinu
Arum Di Lichtelach
Arvoles Yoran
As I Come 'Long De New-Cut Road
As I Me Walked
As I Roll My Rolling Ball
As I Roved Out
As I Sat On A Sunny Bank
As I Sat On The Sunny Bank
As I Set Down To Play Tin-Can
As I Sit Here Alone
As I Walked By Myself
As I Walked Out
As I Was A-Walking
As I Was Coming Back From Treves
As I Was Going To Banbury
As I Was Going Up A New-Cut
    Road
As I Was Walkin' Along The
    New-Out Road
As I Was Walking
As I Went Down To Port Jervis
As I Went Out For A Ramble
As I Went Out One Morning To
    Take The Morning Air
As I Went Out Walking For Pleasure
    One Day
As I Went Over The Water
As I Went To Bonner
As Jacky Was Trudging The
    Meadow Along
As Jacob With Travel Was Weary
As Joseph Was A-Walking
As Lately We Watched
As Now We Are Sailing
As One Day I Chance'd To Rove
As Out In The Fields
As Rhyming's The Rage
As The Storm Retreating Leaves
As Tommy Was Walking

Traditional *(Cont.)*

As We Were On The Ice And Snow
As When In Far Samaria
As William And Mary Stood By The
    Seashore
As With Gladness Men Of Old
As-Tu Vu La Casquette?
Ash Grove
Ash-Grove, The
Asi Amo Yo
Asikhatali
Astri Mi Astri
At Avignon
At Christmas Time When All Is Gay
At Corientes Lies A Fleet
At Dawn Of Day
At Father's Door
At Length There Dawns The
    Glorious Day
At Pierrot's Door
At Summer Morn
At Sunset
At The Bar Of God
At The Cherry Tree
At The Coming Of Spring
At The Cross Her Station Keeping
At The Fireplace
At The Foot Of Yonders Mountain
At The Fountain
At The Gate Of Heaven
At The Green Gate
At The Halt On The Left
At The Nativity
At The Pasture Bars
At The Sign Of The Barber
At Turners Hill
At Work Beside His Father's Bench
Athens
Atin Cu Pung Singsing
Atonement
Attend All Ye Drivers
Au Bois Du Rossignolet
Au Bois Rossignolet
Au Cabaret
Au Clair De La Lune
Au Creaux De Rocher
Au Jardin
Au Loin Sonnent Les Cloches
Au Point De Jour Quand Brille Au
    Ciel L'Aurore
Au Pont Des Vues
Auburn Haired Bonny Dey, The
Auf Auf Ihr Reichsgenossen
Auf Den Nebel Folgt Die Sonne
Auf Die Verteidigung Von Bergen
    Zoom
Auf Freien Bergeshohen
Auf Seele Auf
Auf Singet Und Trinket
Auld House, The
Auld Lang Syne
Auld Man He Courted Me, An
Auld Man He Courted Me, The
Auld Man's Mare's Deid, The

Traditional *(Cont.)*

Auld Robin Gray
Auld Soldier, The
Auld Uncle Watty
Aunt Dinah's Quilting Party
Aunt Rhody
Aunt Tabbie
Auntie Mina's Cooking The Sirup
Aupres De Ma Blonde
Aura Lee
Aurore Prader
Aurore Pradere
Aus Meines Herzens
Auserwahlte, Die
Ausgeflogen
Australia
Australia And The Amazon
Australia For Me
Australia's On The Wallaby
Australian Girls
Austrian Landler, An
Autauga
Autumn Sun
Avadim Hayinu
Ave Maris Stella
Avenging And Bright
Aviator's Hymn, The
Avinu Malkenu
Avondale Disaster, The
Avondale Mine Disaster, The
Avridme Galanica
Awake Awake To Love And Work
Awake Awake Ye Drowsy Sleepers
Awake My Soul In Joyful Lays
Awake Thou Spirit Of The
    Watchmen
Away Away At Break Of Day
Away Down East
Away For Rio
Away Idaho
Away In A Manger
Away My Soul
Away Rio
Away To Rio
Away To The Wars
Ay Caramba
Ay Linda Amiga
Ay Te Tsi Nye Te
Ay Tituy
Ay Waukin O
Ay-Ay-Ay
Aye Drink A Little Longer
Aye Lord Time Is Drawin' Nigh
Aye The Birks A-Bowing Or Lord
    Dingwall
Ayil Ayil
Aylye Lyulye Lyulye
Azov Gull, The
B'yond The Tisza
Ba Ba Mo Leanabh Beag
Baa Baa Black Sheep
Babcock Bedtime Story, The
Babe, The

Traditional *(Cont.)*

Babe In Bethlehem's Manger Laid,
    The
Babe In Bethlehem's Manger, The
Babe Is Born, A
Babe Is Born All Of A Maid, A
Babe Is Born All Of A May, A
Babe Is Born In Bethlehem, A
Babe Of Bethlehem
Babe Of Bethlehem, The
Babe So Tender, A
Babes In The Wood
Babes In The Wood, The
Babes In The Woods, The
Baby Baby Bunting
Baby Boy, The
Baby Brother Mine
Baby Bunting
Baby Bye Here's A Fly
Baby Did You Hear
Babylon Is Fallen
Babylon's Fallin
Bachelor Bold And Young, A
Bachelor's Fare
Bachelor's Hall
Bachelor's Lay, The
Bachelor's Song
Bachelor's Song, The
Bachelor's Walk
Back Again
Back Bay Hill
Back Side Albany Stan' Lake
    Champlain
Back To De Jail
Back To Larkins' Bar
Backblock Shearer, The
Backslider
Backwoodsman, The
Bad Companions
Bad Company
Bad Girl
Bad Girl's Lament
Bad Man Ballad
Badger Hill
Badouma Paddlers
Baffled Knight, The
Bagpipe Carol, The
Bagpipers' Carol
Bagpipers, The
Bagpipes
Bagpipes Playing
Bailiff's Daughter Of Islington, The
Bailiff's Daughter, The
Bainbridge Tragedy, The
Baintown
Bake A Cake
Bald Ist Es Wieder Nacht
Bald Knobber Song, The
Bald-Headed End Of The Broom,
    The
Bald-Headed Woman
Balena, The
Ball Games

Traditional *(Cont.)*

Ball, The
Ball Of The Seasons, The
Ball The Jack
Ballad, A
Ballad For Bill Moore
Ballad Of Blue Mountain Lake, The
Ballad Of Captain Kidd, The
Ballad Of Davy Crockett, The
Ballad Of Hennery White, The
Ballad Of Henry Green
Ballad Of Herbert Lee
Ballad Of Macneil Of Barra, The
Ballad Of Major Andre, The
Ballad Of Montcalm And Wolfe, The
Ballad Of Naomi Wise, The
Ballad Of Peter Gray, The
Ballad Of The Boll Weevil
Ballad Of The Boll Weevil, The
Ballad Of The Braswell Boys
Ballad Of The Clearwater, The
Ballad Of The Drover
Ballad Of The Erie Canal
Ballad Of The Pirate Wench
Ballad Of The Waterfall, The
Ballad On The Death Of Nathan
    Hale
Ballade De Jesus-Christ
Ballade Of Ivan Petrovsky Skevar, Ye
Ballinamona
Ballit Of De Boll Weevil, De
Ballit Of The Boll Weevil, The
Balls Of Simplicity
Ballymonan Brae
Balm In Gilead
Balm Of Gilead
Baloo Lammy
Balzamina
Bamba, La
Bamba-Lele
Bambambulele
Bamboo Screen, The
Bamthatha
Ban, Di
Banana Boat Song
Banana Boat Song, The
Band O'Gideon, De
Band Of Angels
Band Of Children, The
Band, The
Bangee Rang An-An-Ah Song
Bangidero
Banished Defender, The
Bank Of The Arkansaw, The
Banks O' Skene, The
Banks Of Allan Water, The
Banks Of Brandywine
Banks Of Brandywine, The
Banks Of Claudie, The
Banks Of Claudy, The
Banks Of Green Willow, The
Banks Of Kilrea, The
Banks Of Marble
Banks Of Newfoundland

Traditional *(Cont.)*

Banks Of Newfoundland, The
Banks Of Ohio
Banks Of Schuylkill, The
Banks Of Sweet Dundee, The
Banks Of Sweet Loch Ray, The
Banks Of Sweet Primeroses
Banks Of The Bann, The
Banks Of The Brandywine, The
Banks Of The Condamine, The
Banks Of The Dee, The
Banks Of The Esk, The
Banks Of The Little Eau Pleine, The
Banks Of The Murray, The
Banks Of The Nile, The
Banks Of The Ohio
Banks Of The Ohio, The
Banks Of The Old Raritan, The
Banks Of The Pamanow, The
Banks Of The River Dee, The
Banks Of The Riverine, The
Banks Of The Sacramento, The
Banks Of The Sacramento
Banks Of The Sweet Dundee, The
Banks Of The Towy, The
Bann Water Side, The
Banner Of The Sea, The
Bannity Dan
Bannocks O'Barley Meal
Banquet Song
Banshee, The
Bantama Kra Kro
Baptism
Baquine
Barb'ra Ellen
Barb'ry Allen
Barbara Allan
Barbara Allan's Cruelty
Barbara Allen
Barbara Ellen
Barbara Polka
Barbara Totally High
Barbaree
Barbary
Barbary Allen
Barbary Ellen
Barber Shaved The Mason, The
Bard Of Armagh, The
Bard's Dying Request, The
Bardy Train , The
Bare Mountain Top, The
Barefoot Boy, The
Bargeman's Abc, The
Barley Grain
Barley Mow, The
Barley Straw, The
Barnacle Bill The Sailor
Barney
Barney And Katie
Barney Buntline
Barney Graham
Barney Leave The Girls Alone
Barney McCoy
Barney O'Lean

Traditional *(Cont.)*

Barnyard Glee Club, The
Barnyard Song, The
Barnyards O'Delgaty, The
Baron Of Brackley, The
Baron Turned Ploughman, The
Barrack Street
Barrin' O' Our Door Weel
Barry Grenadiers, The
Barrymore Tithe Victory, The
Bartimeus
Bartolillo
Basket Of Eggs, The
Basket Of Onions, The
Basket Of Treasures
Basket-Maker's Child, The
Basque Lullaby, A
Basque Song
Bastard King Of England, The
Bates
Batson
Battle Between The Chesapeake And
    Shannon, The
Battle Cry Of Freedom
Battle Hymn Of The Hussites
Battle Hymn Of The Republic, The
Battle Of Alma
Battle Of Bunker Hill
Battle Of Erie, The
Battle Of Gettysburg, The
Battle Of Harlaw
Battle Of Jericho, The
Battle Of Lake Champlain, The
Battle Of Lake Erie, The
Battle Of Plattsburg, The
Battle Of Point Pleasant, The
Battle Of Shiloh Hill
Battle Of Shiloh Hill, The
Battle Of Shiloh, The
Battle Of Stonington
Battle Of The Kegs, The
Battle Of The Potomac With The
    Malays
Battle Of The Shannon And
    Chesapeake
Battle Of Tippecanoe
Battle Of Valparaiso, The
Battle Song
Battle With The Ladle
Bauernklage
Bauernstanz
Baumlein Steigen
Bavarian Folk Carol
Bavarian Hunting Song
Bay Dem Shtetl Shteyt A Shtibl
Bay Of Biscay Oh
Bay Of Biscay, The
Bay Of Mexico, The
Bayt Zhe Mir Oys A
    Finfuntsvantsiker
Bayt-Zhe Mir Oys A
    Finf-Un-Tsvantsiger
Be Home Early Tonight My Dear
    Boy

Traditional (*Cont.*)

Be Kind To Your Web-Footed
    Friends
Be On Your Guard
Be Silent Heaven Be Silent Earth
Be Thou My Vision
Be Thou My Vision O Lord
Be With Me
Bean Porridge Hot
Beans And Hard-Tack
Beans Bacon And Gravy
Beans I To The Mill
Bear In The Hill, The
Bear The News Mary
Bear Went Over The Mountain, A
Bear Went Over The Mountain, The
Beardiville Planting
Bears' Lullaby, The
Beau Galant, Le
Beau Matin Mo Contre Manette
Beautiful
Beautiful Beautiful Brown Eyes
Beautiful Bill
Beautiful Brown Eyes
Beautiful China
Beautiful Kahana
Beautiful Savior
Beauty Beauty Bride, The
Beauty Of Garmouth, The
Beaver Dam Road
Beaver Island Boys, The
Because She Ain't Built That Way
Bee, The
Bee Tree, The
Beech Tree's Petition, The
Been A Listening
Been Down Into The South
Been In De Pen So Long
Been To De Gypsy To Get Mah
    Fortune Tole
Beer Please
Beer Waltz
Beetle's Wedding, The
Before Dawn
Before I Had Found A Sweetheart
Before The Ending Of The Day
Before The Lord Jehovah's Throne
Before This Time Another Year
Beggar
Beggar Maid, The
Beggar Wench Of Wales, The
Beggarman's Song, The
Beggars' Chorus In The Jovial Crew,
    The
Beggin', The
Begone Dull Care
Behind The Great Wall
Behold A Lovely Flower
Behold That Star
Behold The Great Creator Makers
Behold The Savior Of Mankind
Behy Eviction, The
Bei Der Linde
Bei Meines Bulen Haupte

Traditional (*Cont.*)

Believe Me Dearest Susan
Believe Me If All Those Endearing
    Young Charms
Believer I Know
Bell, The
Bell Carol
Bell Done Ring, The
Bell Doth Toll, The
Bell Gordon Of Portmore
Bell Is Ringing, The
Bell Ringer, The
Bell Song
Bell-Bottom Trousers
Bella Pastorcita, Una
Bellaghy Fair
Bellamina
Belle
Belle A Pris L'epee, La
Belle Enfant S'en Par Les Grand
    Bois, Une
Belle Est Au Jardin D'amour, La
Belle Of Long Lake, The
Belle Of The Ball
Belle Plaine
Bellman's Song, The
Bells, The
Bells Of Aberdovey, The
Bells Of Hell, The
Bells Of Shandon, The
Belmont Stopes, The
Beloved
Belshazza' Had A Feas'
Belt Red As Flame
Belt Wi' Colours Three, The
Ben Backstay
Ben Bolt
Ben Dewberry's Final Run
Ben Fisher
Ben Hall
Ben Zoble's Jig
Bendemeer's Stream
Beneath A Roof Of Tiling
Benediction
Beneditzioneko
Benjamins' Lamentation For Their
    Sad Loss At Sea By Storms And
    Tempests
Benny Havens Oh
Bens Of Jura, The
Benton Country Arkansas
Berceuse
Bereaved Bird, The
Berg Op Zoom
Berger Secoue Ton Sommeil Profond
Bergere Aux Champs, La
Bergere Legere
Berlin Polka
Berlin Wall
Bervie's Bowers Are Bonny
Beryuzoviye Kalyechke
Beside The Brewery At St Mihiel
Besom Maker, The

Traditional (*Cont.*)

Bessie Beauty
Bessie Of Ballydubray
Bessy Bell
Best Old Feller In The World, The
Best Thing We Can Do, The
Bet On Stuball
Beth 'lem Night
Bethany
Bethlehem
Bethlehem Carol
Bethlehem Folk, The
Bethlehem Thou Happy City
Bethlehem's Stall
Betsey
Betsy B
Betsy Baker
Betsy From Pike
Betsy Of Dramoor
Better Git Yo' Ticket
Better Walk Steady
Betty And Dupree
Betty Anne
Beulah Land Mazurka
Beware Oh Beware
Beyond The Mountains
Bezem, De
Bibautzemann
Biddy Biddy
Bidh Sior-Chaoineadh
Big Corral, The
Big Hole In The Ground, The
Big Jim
Big Rock Candy Mountain, The
Big Rock Candy Mountains, The
Big Sunflower
Bigler, The
Bilbilicos, Los
Bile Dem Cabbage Down
Bile Them Cabbage Down
Bill Bailey
Bill Hopkin's Colt
Bill Large's First Waltz
Bill Large's Jig
Bill Large's Second Waltz
Bill Large's Waltz
Bill Martin And Ella Speed
Bill Painter's Waltz
Bill Peters The Stage Driver
Bill The Weaver
Bill Vanero
Billy Barlow
Billy Barlow On The Times
Billy Boiled Over, The
Billy Boy
Billy Collins' Schottische
Billy Dunn's Varsoviana
Billy McGee McGaw
Billy O'Rourke
Billy Pitt And The Union
Billy Richardson's Last Ride
Billy Taylor
Billy The Kid

Traditional *(Cont.)*

Billy Venero
Billy White
Bim-Bom
Bimba Mia
Bin Ich Mir A Schnayderl
Bin Ich Mir A Shnayderl
Bin Ich Mir Gegangen Fishelech
    Koyfn
Bingo
Binnorie
Binnorie O Binnorie
Birch Splinter, The
Birch Tree, The
Birchen Tree, The
Bird Dreams
Bird In A Cage
Bird Song, The
Birds' Courting Song
Birds, The
Biritullera, La
Birks Of Aberfeldy, The
Birmingham Sunday
Birobidjan
Birth Of Robin Hood, The
Biztu Mit Mir Broygez
Bizzoms
Black Ball Line, The
Black Betty
Black Bill's Wonderment
Black Cat, The
Black Cat Piddled In The White
    Cat's Eye, The
Black Gal, De
Black Is The Color
Black Is The Color Of My True
    Love's Hair
Black Is The Colour
Black Jack Davy
Black Rock Pork
Black Sheep Black Sheep
Black Troops Of Florian Geyer, The
Black Velvet Band, The
Black-Eyed Susan
Black-Eyed Susie
Blackberries
Blackbird, The
Blacksmith's Apprentice, The
Blackwell Merry Night
Blanche Comme La Neige
Blaydon Races, The
Bles' My Soul An' Gone
Bless You Bless You Bumble Bee
Blessed Be That Maid Marie
Blessed City Heav'nly Salem
Blessed City Heavenly Salem
Blessed Feasts Of Blessed Martyrs
Blessed Zulu War, The
Blessings Of Mary, The
Blessings Of The Hanuka Candles
Blin' Man Stood On De Road An'
    Cried, De

Traditional *(Cont.)*

Blin' Man Stood On De Way An'
    Cried
Blind Beggar's Daughter Of Bednall
    Green, The
Blind Child, The
Blind Child's Prayer, The
Blind Man
Blind Man Stood On The Road And
    Cried
Blind Man Stood On The Way And
    Cried
Blood
Blood Done Signed My Name
Blood On The Saddle
Blood Red Roses
Blood-Strained Banders, The
Bloody Waterloo
Blow Away The Morning Dew
Blow Blow Bully Boys Blow
Blow Boy Blow
Blow Boys Blow
Blow Bullies Blow
Blow Gabriel
Blow On The Sea Shell
Blow Th' Man Down
Blow The Candles Out
Blow The Man Down
Blow The Wind Southerly
Blow The Winds Southerly
Blow The Winds Southrly
Blow Ye Winds
Blow Ye Winds Heigh-Ho
Blow Ye Winds In The Morning
Blue
Blue Alsatian Mountains, The
Blue Bell Of Scotland, The
Blue Bells Of Scotland
Blue Bonnets, The
Blue Bottle
Blue Flowers And The Yellow, The
Blue Grotto, The
Blue Mountain
Blue Mountain Lake
Blue Sky Soft And Clear
Blue-Eyed Mary
Blue-Haired Jimmy
Blue-Tail Fly
Blue-Tail Fly, The
Blue-Tailed Fly, The
Bluebells Of Scotland, The
Blueberries
Blues
Blues Ain' Nothin', The
Blues For Cisco Houston
Bo Asi Me Nsa
Boar's Head Carol
Boar's Head Carol, The
Boar's Head In Hand Bear I, The
Boardinghouse, The
Boasting
Boat My Good Companion
Boatie Rows, The

Traditional *(Cont.)*

Boatin' Up Sandy
Boating
Boating On A Bullhead
Boating Song
Boatman Dance, De
Boatman, The
Boatswain's Call, The
Bob Dunn's Schottische
Bob O'Dunblane
Bob Thompson's Schottische
Bobbie Shaftoe
Bobby Shafto
Bodachan A Mhill Anna
Bohemian Carol
Bohemian Lullaby
Bohunkus
Boil Dem Cabbage Down
Bolamkin
Bold Adventures Of Captain Ross
Bold Ben Hall
Bold Brave Bonair, A
Bold Brennan On The Moor
Bold Carter
Bold Cockney
Bold Damosel
Bold Daniels
Bold Dickie
Bold Dickie And Bold Archie
Bold Dighton
Bold Fisherman, The
Bold Hunter, The
Bold Jack Donahoe
Bold Nelson's Praise
Bold Pedlar And Robin Hood
Bold Princess Royal
Bold Privateer, The
Bold Reynard
Bold Robing Hood
Bold Sailor, The
Bold Soldier, The
Bold Tenant Farmer
Bold Trellitee, The
Bold Wolfe
Bolero
Boll Weevil
Boll Weevil Blues
Boll Weevil, De
Boll Weevil Song, The
Boll Weevil, The
Bombed
Bombed Last Night
Bon Soir Dames
Bon Soir Ma Cherie
Bon Voyage Monsieur Dumollet
Bonavista Harbor
Bondsey And Maisry
Boney
Boney Is Down
Bonfires
Bonhomme Que Sais-Tu Faire
Bonne Aventure, La
Bonnes Gens Prenez Pitie D'un
    Dolent Mari

Traditional *(Cont.)*

Bonnie
Bonnie Banks O' Loch Lomond, The
Bonnie Blue Eyes
Bonnie Blue Flag, The
Bonnie Bonnie Banks O' Loch
    Lomon', The
Bonnie Bunch Of Roses, A
Bonnie Cravat, The
Bonnie Doon
Bonnie Dundee
Bonnie George Campbell
Bonnie Jean O' Bethelnie
Bonnie Lass O' Bennochie
Bonnie Lizzie Lindsay
Bonnie Mary Of Argyle
Bonnie Milk-White Lammie
Bonnie Pit Laddie, The
Bonnie Streets Of Fyve-Io
Bonnie Susie Cleland
Bonnie Wee Thing
Bonniest Lass In A' The Land
Bonny Banks Of Loch Lomond
Bonny Banks Of The Virgie O, The
Bonny Barbara Allan
Bonny Barbara Allen
Bonny Bay Of Biscay-O, The
Bonny Blue Handkerchief
Bonny Bonny Banks O' The Lomand
Bonny Bows O' London
Bonny Bows The Birks 'been The
    Waters O'Dee
Bonny Boy, The
Bonny Brier Bush, The
Bonny Brown Hen, The
Bonny Bunch Of Roses, The
Bonny Bunch Of Roses-O, The
Bonny Earl O' Moray, The
Bonny Earl Of Murray, The
Bonny House O' Airlie, The
Bonny Laboring Boy, The
Bonny Lady Jean O' Keith-Hall
Bonny Lass O' Fyvie, The
Bonny Lass O'Fyvie-O, The
Bonny Lass Of Aberdeen
Bonny Lass Of Anglesey, The
Bonny Light Horseman
Bonny Moorhen, The
Bonny Robin
Bonny Saint Johnston Stands Fair
    Upon Tay
Bonny Streets Of Fyvie-O, The
Bonny Wee Lass, The
Bonny Wee Thing
Bony On The Isle Of St Helen
Bony's Lament
Bonyparte
Boogie-Woogie On St Louis Blues
Book Of Books Our People's
    Stregnth
Boomba
Boomer Johnson
Booth Killed Lincoln

Traditional *(Cont.)*

Boozin'
Boquita Colorada
Bord, Di
Border Affair, A
Borinquena, La
Born Is He This Child Divine
Born Is He This Holy Child
Born Is Little Jesus
Borrachito, El
Boruh Elohenu
Bos'n John
Bosky Steer, The
Boston
Boston Burglar
Boston Burglar, The
Boston Burgular, The
Boston City
Boston Come-All-Ye, The
Boston Frigate's Engagement, The
Boston Post Office, The
Boston Privateering
Boston Tea Party, The
Boston Tea Tax Song
Boston Town
Boston's
Botany Bay
Bottle O
Bottles Of Black Porter
Bought A Rooster
Boulavogue
Bould Tadhy Quill, The
Boule's Ball
Bounce Aroun'
Bound For Charlers Town
Bound For Sydney Town
Bound For The Stormy Main
Bound To Alabama
Bound To Go
Bound To Ride
Bound Upon The Accursed Tree
Boundless Expanse Of The Sea, The
Boundless Mercy
Bounty Jumper, The
Bow And Balance
Bow Low Elder
Bower In My Breast, The
Bowers
Boys And Girls Come Away
Boys And Girls Come Out To Play
Boys From Company A, The
Boys From County Cork, The
Boys In The Bowery Pit, The
Boys Of Cold Water, The
Boys Of Scotland
Boys Of Wexford, The
Bozrah
Bra' Rabbit
Brabanconne, La
Braddock's Defeat
Braes O' Balquhidder, The
Braes Of Boyndlie, The
Bramble Briar, The

Traditional *(Cont.)*

Bramble Brier, The
Brandolina
Brandy Leave Me Alone
Brass-Mounted Army, The
Brats Of Jeremiah, The
Brave Engineer, The
Brave Old Donnely
Brave Soldier
Brave Wolfe
Brazilian Banter
Brazilian Rose
Bread In The Oven
Bread Of The World
Breaking Of Omagh Jail, The
Breelong Blacks, The
Breezer, The
Breezes Are Blowing
Breezes, The
Brennan On The Moor
Bressan Noel
Breton Noel
Brian Og And Molly Bawn
Bridge Of Avignon
Bridge Of Avignon, The
Bridget Donahue
Bridget Donohue
Bridget Maguire
Bridle And The Saddle, The
Brief Life Is Here Our Portion
Brigadier, Le
Brigantine Sinorca
Brigham Young
Bright And Joyful Is The Morn
Bright Diamond
Bright Morning Stars Are Rising
Bright Shades Of Blue, The
Bright Sparkles In De Churchyard
Bright Sparkles In The Churchyard
Brighter Days In Store
Brightest And Best Of The Stars Of
    The Morning
Brilliant Victory
Brinca La Tablita
Bring A Torch
Bring A Torch Jeanette Isabella
Bring A Torch Jeannette Isabella
Bring Back My Bonnie
Bring Back My Bonnie To Me
Bring Me A Little Water Silvy
Bring Your Torches
Brisk Young Lad, The
Brisk Young Sailor, A
British Grenadier, The
British Grenadiers, The
Brivele Der Mamen, A
Broad-Striped Trousers
Broken-Down Merry Go Round, The
Broken Engagement, The
Broken Heart, The
Broken Ring
Broken Ring, The
Broken Troth, The
Broken-Down Squatter, The
Broken-Hearted Boy, The

Traditional (*Cont.*)

Bronwen
Brook, The
Brooklet, The
Broom Man, The
Broom O' The Cowdenknowes
Brother Ephrum Got De Coon And
  Gone
Brother Green
Brother James' Air
Brother Noah
Brother Rabbit
Brothers
Brothers All
Brouillard Dans La Vallee
Brown Eyes
Brown Girl, The
Brown Hair'd Maiden, The
Brown October
Brown-Eyed Lee
Brown-Skin Gal
Brown-Skinned Woman, A
Brudstassen
Brunnlein Die Do Fliessen, Die
Bub-A-Dub-A-Dub
Buck Passing
Buckeye Jim
Bucking Broncho
Bucking Bronco, The
Budget A New Song, The
Buffalo, The
Buffalo Boy
Buffalo Driver's Song
Buffalo Gals
Buffalo Girls
Buffalo Skinner, The
Buffalo Skinners, The
Bugle, The
Bugle Call, The
Builders, The
Buked And Scorned
Bulbes
Bull-Dog, The
Bull-Whacker, The
Bulldog On The Bank
Bulldog On The Bank, The
Bullet Proof
Bullfight On The San Pedro, The
Bullfrog
Bullfrog Hop, The
Bullockies' Ball, The
Bullshit Bill
Bullyin' Jack-A-Diamonds
Bum Song, The
Bumpkin, The
Bung Yer Eye
Bung Your Eye
Burges
Burgess Varsoviana
Burgundian Carol
Burke And Hare
Burly Coon You Know, A
Burriquita, La
Burro, El

Traditional (*Cont.*)

Bury Me Beneath The Willow
Bury Me Not On The Lone Prairie
Buses Are A-Comin' Oh Yes
Bush Christening, The
Bushes And Briars
Bushman's Song, A
Busy Day, A
Butcher Boy, The
Butcher's Boy, The
Butcher's Frolic, The
Buttermilk Boy, The
Buttermilk Hill
Button You Must Wander
Buxom Lass, The
Buxom Lassies
Buy A Broom
Buy Me A China Doll
Buy My Tortillas
By An' By
By And By
By My Window
By Our Cottage
By The Light Of The Moon
By The Silver Rio Grande
By The Stream
By The Waters Of The Dee
By The Zuider Zee
By This Sacrament Sweet Jesus
By You Castle Wa
By'm By
Bye And Bye
Bye Baby Bunting
Bye-Bye Fedora
Byum Bye
C'est Aujourd'hui La Fete
  Printaniere
C'est Hip Puis Taiaut
C'est La Belle Francoise
C'est La Mon Doux Plaisir
C'est La Poulette Blanche
C'est Le Vent Frivolant
C'est Pas La Bague
Ca Ca Geschmauset
Ca' The Ewes
Ca' The Ewes To The Fauld Jamie
  Wi' Me
Ca' The Yowes
Ca' The Yowes To The Knowes
Cabbage Pie, The
Cabellito Rubio
Cabin Boy
Cabin Boy, The
Cacaki Sapico
Cacaki Sapicu
Cacaki Sapijatica
Cachucha, La
Cadet Lament
Cadet Rousselle
Cadrill
Caesar's Legion
Caesar's Victory, The
Cahin Of Love, The

Traditional (*Cont.*)

Caillette
Caisson Song
Cajeme
Cake, The
Calais Disaster, The
Calder Braes
Caledonia
Caledonio
Caleno Custure Me
Calico Pie
California
Call Dat Religion No No No No No
  No
Call Me Hangin' Johnny
Call Of Erin, The
Call Of The North
Call The Roll
Callahan
Caller Herrin
Calmly Flow Thy Streams
Calomel
Calvary
Cambria
Cambria's Tongue
Cambrian Eisteddvod, The
Cambrian Emigrant, The
Cambric Shirt, The
Came A-Riding
Camp Meetin'
Campamento Cerro Leon
Campana, La
Campanero, The
Campbells Are Comin', The
Campbells Are Coming, The
Camper's Life, The
Campfire Meeting, The
Can I Sleep In Your Barn Tonight
Can I Sleep In Your Barn Tonight
  Mister
Can The Circle Be Unbroken
Can Ye Sew Cushions
Can You Count The Star That
  Brightly
Can You Plant Cabbage
Can You Play
Can't Hide Sinner
Can't You Dance The Polka
Can't You Live Humble
Canada I O
Canaday-I-O
Canadian Boat Song
Canadien Errant, Un
Canal Boat Wedding
Canal Dance, The
Canal Sweethearts
Cancion De Navidad India
Candlelight Fisherman, The
Candlemas Eve
Candy Man Blues
Canella
Canette Va Flottant Sur L'Onde
  Bleue

Traditional *(Cont.)*

Cansado Estoy De Vivir
Canso Strait
Cant Dels Ocells, El
Cantemos
Canto De Cuna
Canto Dei Gondolieri
Canto Para Cosechar La Papa
Canzone D'i Zamponari
Cap 'n Baker
Cape Cod Chantey
Cape Cod Girls
Cape Cod Chanty
Capetown Girls, The
Capital Ship, A
Capitalism's Endless Chain
Captain Barton's Distress On Board
    The Lichfield
Captain Burke
Captain Conrod
Captain Glen
Captain Glen's Unhappy Boyage To
    New Barbary
Captain Hull's Victory
Captain James
Captain Jinks
Captain Jinks Of The Horse Marines
Captain John
Captain Jones's Invitation
Captain Kidd
Captain Kidd's Farewell To The Seas
Captain Mansfield's Fight With The
    Turks At Sea
Captain Morgan's March
Captain O Captain
Captain Robert Kidd
Captain Says Hurry
Captain Ward
Captain Ward And The Rainbow
Captain Wedderburn
Captain Wedderburn's Courtship
Captain With His Whiskers, The
Captain's Apprentice, The
Capture Of Little York
Capture Of The Essex
Caput Apri Defero
Cara Mamma Io Sono Malata
Cara Nina
Caramel Lady
Carbonerita, La
Card Song, The
Careful
Careless Love
Caresses
Carite, El
Carlson's Raiders
Carmagnole, La
Carme
Carmela
Carmen Carmela
Carnal And The Crane, The
Carnaval C'est Le Temps
    D'abondance

Traditional *(Cont.)*

Carnival Of Venice
Carnival Time
Carol Children Carol
Carol For Christingle
Carol For Christmas Eve, A
Carol For Easter Saturday, A
Carol For Everyman, A
Carol For New Year's Day
Carol Of Beauty
Carol Of Joy
Carol Of Saint Staffan
Carol Of Service
Carol Of The Advent
Carol Of The Bagpipers, The
Carol Of The Birds
Carol Of The Flowers
Carol Of The Flowers, The
Carol Of The Kingdom
Carol Of The Nuns At Chester
Carol Of The Village Musicians
Carolin'
Carolina
Caroline
Caroline Akaro
Caroline And Her Young Sailor Bold
Caroline Of Edinboro Town
Caroline Of Edinburgh Town
Caroline Of Edingburgh Town
Caroll Of Bryngyng In The Bore's
    Heed
Carolune Of Edinburgh Town
Carpenter, The
Carpenter's Wife, The
Carrier Dove, The
Carrier Pigeon, The
Carrion Crow, A
Carrion Crow Sat On An Oak, A
Carrion Crow, The
Carrosse Bien Attele, Un
Carry Him Along
Carry Me Back To Old Virginny
Carry Me Home
Cart-Driver, The
Cartagena, La
Carter
Carter, The
Cas Na Caora Hiortiach O
Cascabel, El
Casey Jones
Casey Jones Parody
Casey Jones The Miner
Casey Jones The Union Scab
Casey's Whiskey
Cash In Hand
Cashel Green
Casinha Pequenina, A
Casita, La
Castelreigh In Seventy-Four, The
Castle By The Sea, The
Castle Gardens
Castle Ha's Daughter
Castle Tower, The
Castleroe Mill

Traditional *(Cont.)*

Castles In Spain
Castles In The Air
Cat Came Back, The
Cat In The Sack
Catalonian Christman Carol
Cathedrales De France
Catholic Rent
Cats Of The Isle Of Man, The
Catskill Valley
Catskin's Garland
Cause I'm A Nigger
Cavadenti, Il
Cavalier's Glee
Cavaliers, The
Caviar
Cawsand Bay
Cc Rider
Ce N'est Pas Un Reve Qui Me
    Trouble
Cecil Waltz, The
Cefiro, El
Celebrated Workingman, A
Celebrons La Naissance
Celimene
Celos
Census Of 1891, The
'Cepting Ike
Cerro Adentro, El
Cert'nly Lord
Certainly Lord
Certinly Lawd
Ceux Qui S'Aiment Sont Toujours
    Malheureux
Ceylon
Ch'bin A Bocher A Hultay
Cha Bhi Mi 'Gad Thaladh
Cha Deid Mi Liom Fhin 'na
    Mhointich
Cha Labhair Mi 'N T-Oran
Cha N-Eil A' Chuis A' Cordadh
    Rium
Cha Yang Wu
Chad Gadyo
Chaidh Mi Dha 'n Bheinn
Chain Gang Blues
Chain Gang, De
Chain Gang, The
Chairs To Mend
Chakkiri-Bushi
Challenge Of Youth, The
Champagne Charlie
Champagne Charlie Waltz
Changes
Changing Her Mind
Changing Moods
Chanson Autrichienne
Chanson De La Foire
Chanson Du Tambourineur, La
Chanson Espagnole
Chanson Normande
Chanson Triste
Chant Huguenot
Chant Of The Short Ags

Traditional *(Cont.)*

Chant Of The Volga Boatmen
Chanticleer
Chanties
Chantons Les Amours De Jean
Chanty Song
Chaparrita, La
Chapter Of Good Things, A
Chapter Of Kings, The
Charbonnier Mon Ami
Charcoal Man, The
Charge The Can Cheerily
Charge To Keep, A
Chariot Of Mercy
Charles G Anderson
Charles Guiteau
Charles John Our Brave King
Charles Stewart Parnell's Grand
    Triumphant Process
Charleston Gals
Charlestown
Charley Brooks
Charley Hill's Old Slope
Charley Snyder
Charley Will You Come Out
    To-Night
Charley's Escape
Charlicou Charlicou
Charlie Blackman's Waltz
Charlie Condemned
Charlie Is My Darlin'
Charlie Is My Darling
Charlie Rutlage
Charlie Rutledge
Charm
Charmant Billie
Charmante Marguerite, La
Charming Beauty Bright
Charming Betsey
Charming Marguerite
Charming Moll Boy, The
Charming Molly O
Charming Name
Charming Shepherds, The
Charming Valley, The
Charming Young Widow I Met In
    The Train, The
Charro, El
Chase The Buffalo
Chatigo Chinyi
Chatskele
Chatskele Chatskele
Chatsworth Wreck, The
Chatter With The Angels
Chawe Chidyo Chem'chero
Che Lucero Aguai-I
Cheer Boys Cheer
Cheer For Navy, A
Cheer For The Purple
Cheer Up Old Woman
Cheer'ly Man
Cheer'ly O
Cheerful Hope
Chef De Gare, Le

Traditional *(Cont.)*

Chere Grand 'maman
Chere Patrie
Cherokee Indian Harvest Song
Cherries Are Ripe
Cherries Ripe
Cherry Bloom
Cherry Gathering
Cherry Tree
Cherry Tree Carol
Cherry-Tree Carol, The
Cherry-Tree, The
Chesapeake And Shannon
Cheshire Gate, The
Cheshire Hunt, The
Chevaliers De La Table Ronde, Les
Chevre Vient, La
Cheyenne
Chi Chi Bud
Chi Lai
Chi Mi Bhuam Air Bruaich An
    Lochain
Chiapanecas
Chicago
Chicamy Chickamy Crany Crow
Chichester Boys, The
Chicka-Hanka
Chicken And The Bone, The
Chicken Reel
Chickens Are A-Crowing, The
Chickens In De Bread Tray
Chickens They Are A Crowing, The
Chickens They Are Crowing, The
Chidings Of A Maiden Bright
Chien, Le
Chiflido, El
Chiggers
Chil Ether
Child And The Star, The
Child Divine
Child In The Manger
Child Is Born, A
Child Is Born In Bethlehem, A
Child Jesus Sleeps
Child Jesus, The
Child Of Beauty Was Born To Us, A
Child Of God
Child This Day, A
Child This Day Is Born, A
Child Was Born In Bethlehem, A
Child's Hymn
Child's Prayer, A
Children At The Manger, The
Children Go Where I Send Thee
Children In The Wood, The
Children Of The Free Woman
Children Of The Heavenly Father
Children Of The Heavenly King
Children Of The Hebrews, The
Children Pray This Love To Cherish
Children Sing A Carol Splendid
Children Who Walk In Jesus' Way
Children's Angel, The
Children's Carol

Traditional *(Cont.)*

Children's Song Of The Nativity
Chilly Water
Chilly Winds
Chimbley Sweeper
Chimes
Chiming Church Bells
Chimney Sweep, The
Chimney Sweeper, The
Chinese
Chinese Baby Song
Chinese Girls
Chinese National Anthem
Chinese Street Scene
Ching-A-Ling
Chiquirriquitin
Chirk Castle
Chiro Chacho
Chirstofo Columbo
Chisholm Trail, The
Cho Kurima Woye
Choctaw And Cherokee
Chodzil Sennek
Choice Of A Wife, The
Cholla Mo Ruin
Cholly Blues, The
Choose You A Seat 'n' Set Down
Choose Yourself A Partner
Choosing
Choosing A Career
Choosing A Husband
Chopping The Cane
Chossid Beim Bojn Di Suke, Die
Chouconne
Choucoune
Christ Be With Me
Christ Before Th' Eleven
Christ Beside Me
Christ Child's Lullaby, The
Christ Enthroned In Highest Heaven
Christ From Whom All Blessings
    Flow
Christ Has Arisen
Christ In The Garden
Christ Is Born
Christ Is Born Of Maiden Fair
Christ Is Gone Up Yet Ere He Passed
Christ Is Made The Sure Foundation
Christ Ist Erstanden
Christ Jesus Lay In Death's Strong
    Bands
Christ Superior To Moses
Christ The Fair Glory Of The Holy
    Angels
Christ The Life Of All The Living
Christ The Lord Hath Risen
Christ The Lord Is Ris'n Today
Christ The Lord Is Risen
Christ The Lord Is Risen Again
Christ The Lord Is Risen Today
Christ The Object Of Love
Christ The Worker Christ The
    Worker
Christ Was Born In Bethlehem

Traditional *(Cont.)*

Christ Was Born On Christmas Day
Christ When For Us You Were
    Baptized
Christ Who Died But Rose Again,
    The
Christ Whose Glory Fills The Skies
Christ-Child Is Born, The
Christbaum Is Der Schonate Baum,
    Des
Christbaum Ist Der Schonste Baum,
    Des
Christen Schmuck Und Ordensband,
    Des
Christi Himmelfahrt
Christian Dost Thou See Them
Christian Love
Christian Men Look Up On High
Christian Prospect
Christian Race
Christian Race, The
Christian Rise And Act The Creed
Christian Rise And Act Thy Creed
Christian Soldier
Christian Song
Christian's Farewell, The
Christian's Hope
Christians Awake
Christians Hark
Christians Lo The Star Appeareth
Christians Sound The Name That
    Saved Us
Christians To The Paschal Victim
Christine Leroy
Christkindlein Ich Preise Dich
Christkindleins Wiegenlied
Christmas
Christmas Bells
Christmas Candle
Christmas Carol
Christmas Child, The
Christmas Comes Anew
Christmas Day In The Morning
Christmas Day Is Come
Christmas Day Joyous
Christmas Duanag
Christmas Echoes
Christmas Eve
Christmas Eve Is Here
Christmas Eve Lullaby
Christmas Fantasy
Christmas Greeting
Christmas Hymn
Christmas In Rome
Christmas Invocation
Christmas Is Coming
Christmas Is Here
Christmas Joy
Christmas Luau
Christmas Lullaby
Christmas Nightingale, The
Christmas Of Old
Christmas Polka
Christmas Song

Traditional *(Cont.)*

Christmas Song, A
Christmas Spring
Christmas Stars
Christmas Tree With The Candles
    Glowing, The
Christmas Windows
Christmas's Lamentation
Christmasse Of Olde
Christofo Clumbo
Christus Am Kreuz
Christus Factus Est
Christus Gottes Ein'ger Sohn
Christus Herr Und Meister
Chtic Aby Spal Tak Zpivala
Chua-Ay
Chuir Iad Mise A Dh'eilein Liom
    Fhin
Chumbara
Church Bell Tollin' Ding Dong, De
Church In The Wildwood
Church Of God, De
Church Of God A Kingdom Is, The
Church Of God Is Everywhere, The
Church Of My Youth
Churning Lilt, A
Churning Song
Cicerenella
Cicirinella
Cielito Lindo
Cinderella
Cindy
Ciobane
Circle Dance
Circus Clown
Circus Day
Ciribiribin
City Called Heaven
City Council
City Not Made With Hands
City O' Babylon
City Of Baltimore, The
City Of Refuge
City Rat And The Country Rat, The
Civil Defense Sign
Clamanda
Clanking Spurs
Clanranald's Sweethearting
Clap Clap Handies
Clap Hands
Clara And Corydon
Clare's Dragoons
Clarence McFaden
Clarinet Polka
Clarington
Claud Allen
Claude Allen
Clay And Frelinghuysen
Clear The Kitchen
Clear The Track
Clear The Track Let The Bullgine
    Run
Clefs De La Prison, Les
Clem Murphy's Door

Traditional *(Cont.)*

Clementine
Clementine Mazurka
Clerk Sandy
Clerk Tamas And Fair Annie
Clerk's Twa Sons O' Owsenford
Click Click That's How The Shears
    Go
Click Go The Shears
Click Goes The Shears
Cliff, The
Cliff On The Volga, The
Climate, The
Climb Up Ye Chillun Climb
Climbin' Up The Mountain
Climbing Up The Golden Stairs
Clime Beneath Whose Genial Sun
Clinch Mountain
Cling Clang
Clo Nan Gillean
Clocks
Clocks And Watches
Clocks, The
Cloddy Banks
Close Beside Cuyahoga's Waters
Close Beside The Winding Cedar's
Closet Key, The
Clouds Are Sinking
Clover So White
Cluck Old Hen
Clucking Hen, The
Co Siod Thall Air Ceann Mo Ropa
Co-Ca-Che-Lunk
Coachman Small And Big
Coal Fatigue
Coal Miner's Child, The
Coal Owner And The Pitman's Wife,
    The
Coast Artillery Song
Coast Of Peru
Coasts Of Barbary
Coasts Of High Barbary, The
Cobbler And The Crow, The
Cobbler, The
Cocaine
Cocaine Bill
Cocaine Joe And Morphine Sue
Cocaine Lil
Cocaine Lil And Morphine Sue
Cock Robin
Cock Robin And Jenny Wren
Cock-A-Doodle-Doo
Cockchafer
Cockie-Leerie-La
Cockies Of Bungaree, The
Cockles And Mussels
Cocky Doodle Doodle Doo
Cocky Robin
Coco De Los Santos
Coco Do Engenho Novo
Cocoanut Grove
Coconut Woman
Cod Liver Ile
Codfish Shanty

Traditional (*Cont.*)

Coenam Cum Discipulis
Coffee Grows In White Oak Trees
Cohabs
Coin I Need
Coin To Spend, A
Coish Ariglen
Coisich Agus Faigh Dhomh Ceile
Coisire, Un
Colby
Cold Blows The Wind
Cold Is The Morning
Cold The Winds Of March
Cold Water
Cole Younger
Coleraine Girl, The
Coleraine Regatta
Coleshill
College Days Of Old
College Friendships
College Of Dreams
College On The Hill, The
College Pump, The
Collier Laddie, The
Colombo
Colonia Usina Catende
Colorado Trail, The
Coloured Girl From The South
Columbia Rules The Sea
Columbia The Gem Of The Ocean
Columbian Independence
Columbiana
Columbo
Columbus
Come A' Ye Tramps An' Hawkers
Come All Of God's Children
Come All Ye Fair And Tender Ladies
Come All Ye Fair And Tender
  Maidens
Come All Ye Jolly Soldiers
Come All Ye Of Tender Years
Come All Ye Old Comrades
Come All Ye Pretty Maids
Come All Ye Roving Rangers
Come All Ye Shepards
Come All Ye Toiling Millions
Come All Ye Valiant Soldiers
Come All You Bold Undaunted Men
Come All You Fair And Tender
  Ladies
Come All You Fellows For I Want
  You To Hear
Come All You People My Stour To
  Hear
Come All You Rounders If You
  Want To Hear
Come All You Tender-Hearted
  People
Come All You Texas Cowboys
Come All You Worthy Christian
  Men
Come All You Worthy Gentlemen
Come All You Young Maidens That
  Are Crossed In Love

Traditional (*Cont.*)

Come All You Young Men
Come All You Youth's Companions
Come All You Youths Of Evry State
Come All Young Men
Come Along And Shout Along
Come Along With Me Pretty Polly
Come An' Go With Me
Come And Go With Me
Come And Go With Me To That
  Land
Come And Let Us Rove Jamie
Come And See The Holy One
Come Back To Me
Come Boys Unsaddle The Horses
Come Brothers Drive Dull Care
  Away
Come Butter Come
Come Buy My Flowers
Come By Here
Come Children And Join In Our
  Festival Song
Come Christians Join And Sing
Come Christians Join To Sing
Come Classmates Gather Round Us
  Now
Come Come Quickly Away
Come Come Ye Saints
Come Dance And Sing
Come Dance My Chiquita
Come Dear Brother
Come Don't Hesitate
Come Down
Come Down Angels
Come Down To Tennessee
Come Fill Your Glasses
Come Fill Your Glasses Up
Come Follow
Come Friends Go With Me
Come Good Wind
Come Gracious Spirit Heavenly
  Dove
Come Hasten Ye Shepherds
Come Here Elisabette
Come Here Jesus If You Please
Come Here Lord
Come Hither Tom
Come Holy Ghost
Come Holy Ghost Creator Blest
Come Holy Ghost Our Souls Inspire
Come Holy Ghost With God The Son
Come In
Come Into My Arms
Come Leave Your Work
Come Let Us Sweetly Join
Come Life Shaker Life
Come Love We God
Come Mad Boys Be Glad Boys
Come Mother's Sons And Daughters
Come My Dove
Come My Lads
Come My Little Roving Sailor
Come My Ponies

Traditional (*Cont.*)

Come O Come Our Voices Raise
Come O God Abide Among Us
Come O Thou Traveler
Come O Thou Traveler Unknown
Come O'er The Sea
Come O'er The Stream Charlie
Come Oh Brothers
Come Oh Come With Me
Come On And Join The Air Corps
Come On Blue
Come Polly Pretty Polly
Come Pretty
Come Pretty Polly
Come Raise Me In Your Arms Dear
  Brother
Come Rally Youth
Come Rest In This Bosom
Come Riddle Come Riddle My Old
  Mother Dear
Come Riddle To Me My Dear
  Mother
Come Rock The Christ Child
Come Rock The Cradle For Him
Come Rouse Ye Lads And Lasses
Come Seniors Come
Come Shepherds
Come Shepherds Rise
Come Sing Now
Come Thou Almighty King
Come Thou Fount
Come Thou Fount Of Every Blessing
Come Thou Holy Paraclete
Come Thou Holy Spirit Bright
Come Thou Holy Spirit Come
Come Thou Redeemer Of The Earth
Come To Bethlehem
Come To Jesus
Come To Me
Come To Me All Ye Who Labor
Come To My Garden
Come To The Bower
Come To The Land
Come To The Old Oak Tree
Come To The Sea
Come Under My Plaidie
Come Unto Me
Come Unto Me Ye Weary
Come With Hearts Afire
Come With Thy Lute
Come Ye Who Are Pure And Holy
Come You Not From Newcastle
Come Young Men Pray Lend
  Attention
Come Young People And Listen To
  My Song
Comely Youth, The
Comin' Back To Kansas
Comin' Thri' The Rye
Comin' Thro' The Ry
Comin' Thro' The Rye
Comin' Through The Rye
Comin' Thru The Rye
Coming Around The Horn

Traditional *(Cont.)*

Coming Down A Little
Coming Down The Mountain
Comment Vouloir Qu'une Personne
    Chante
Commilito Optimus
Commodore Rodgers
Common Bill
Common Sailor, The
Communion
Communion Hymn
Como Busca El Tierno Infante
Como Pode O Peixe
Como Pode Vivir O Peixe
Companions All Sing Loudly
Companions Draw Nigh
Company Cook, The
Compere Guilleri
Comrades The Bugles Are Sounding
Con Las Abejas
Concerning Crocuses
Concert-Goer's Carol, A
Condescension
Condor Pasa, El
Confess Jehovah
Conga Passes, The
Congaudeat
Connaught Man's Ramble Jig, The
Connecticut Peddler, The
Conquering Kings Their Titles Take
Constant Farmer's Son, The
Constant Johnny
Constant Lover, The
Constant Lovers, The
Constitution And Guerriere, The
Constitution And The Guerriere, The
Constitution's Last Fight, The
Contrabandistas De Ronda, Los
Contrary Owl, The
Conundrum Song
Convention, The
Converted Thief, The
Convict Of Clonmel, The
Convict Song
Convict's Lamentation, The
Convict's Return, The
Conviction Of The Wise Men In
    Jerusalem
Coolgardie Miner, The
Coon-Can Game, The
Copihue Rojo, El
Coplas
Copper Kettle
Copper Strike Of '17, The
Copy Of Verses Composed By
    Captain Henry, A
Copy Of Verses On Jefferys The
    Seaman, A
Coquette
Coquito, El
Corbeille Dons Magnifiques Ladou
    Ladou
Corbleu Marion
Corde Natus Ex Parentis

Traditional *(Cont.)*

Cordelia Brown
Cordial Advice
Cordwood Cutter, The
Corn Riggs
Corn Rigs
Cornfield Holler
Cornflower Waltz, The
Cornish May Song
Corona, La
Corporal, The
Corporal Tim
Corrido De Bartolo Negro, El
Corrido De La Campana
    Reeleccionista
Corrido De La Miseria
Corrido De Las Tres Pelonas
Corrido De Los Oprimidos
Corrina Corrina
Cossack Rider, The
Cossack's Farewell
Cossack's Love Song
Cottage Door, The
Cottage In The Wood, The
Cottage Maiden, The
Cottager To Her Infant, The
Cotton Eye Joe
Cotton Field Song
Cotton Fields
Cotton Mill Girls
Cotton Needs A-Pickin'
Cotton Needs Pickin'
Cotton-Eyed Joe
Cotton-Mill Colic
Coughing
Could You Not Come
Couldn't Hear Nobody Pray
Couldn't Keep It To Myself
Couldn't Stand The Press
Count And Nun
Countersigns, The
Counting Sheep
Counting Song
Country Blues
Country Clod Hoppers
Country Dance, A
Country Gardens
Country Waltz
Countryman's Visit To Bartholomew
    Fair
County Jail, The
County Of Mayo, The
County Tyrone, The
Court House
Courte Paille, La
Courtin' In The Kitchen
Courtin' The Farmer's Daughter
Courting Of Molly Moore, The
Courting Song, The
Courting Susan Jane
Courting Winnie
Courtship
Courtship Of Billy Grimes

Traditional *(Cont.)*

Courtship Of Willie Riley
Cousin Jack
Coventry
Coventry Carol, The
Coverdale's Carol
Covered Wagon Days
Cow, The
Cowboy And The Maiden, The
Cowboy At Church, The
Cowboy Dance
Cowboy Jack
Cowboy Lullaby
Cowboy Meditations
Cowboy Reverie
Cowboy, The
Cowboy To Pitching Bronco
Cowboy's Christmas Ball, The
Cowboy's Dance Song
Cowboy's Dream, The
Cowboy's Gettin' Up Holler
Cowboy's Lament, The
Cowboy's Love Song, The
Cowboy's Meditation
Cowboy's Meditation, The
Cowboy's Prayer, A
Cowboy's Ride, The
Cowboy's Stroll, The
Cowboy's Sweet Bye And Bye, The
Cowboys' New Year's Dance, The
Cowherd's Song
Cowman's Prayer, The
Cowman's Troubles, The
Crab, The
Crabe Dans Calalou
Crabfish, The
Crack The Whip
Cradle All Lowly
Cradle Song
Cradle Song For A Young Warrior
Cradle Song Of The Infant Jesus
Cradle, The
Crafty Lover, The
Craw's Ta'en The Poussie, The
Crawdad
Crawdad Song, The
Crawfish
Crawfish Runnin' Down De Stream
Creation's Lord We Give Thee
    Thanks
Creator Of The Earth And Sky
Creator Of The Stars Of Night
Creator Spirit
Creator-Spirit All-Divine
Cree-Mo-Cri-Mo-Dorro-Wah
Creek Ribbon Dance
Creeping Jane
Creole Christmas Carol
Cresol
Crest And Crowning Of All Good,
    The
Crew Of The Whirlwind, The
Cribisse Cribisse

Traditional *(Cont.)*

Cricket Song, The
Cricket, The
Crickets For Luck
Cricketty Wee
Crimean War
Crimson Kerchief, The
Crimson Sarafan, The
Criole Candjo
Cripple Creek
Cristofor Colombo
Crocodile Song
Crocodile, The
Crodh Chailein
Crook And Plaid
Crooked Gun, The
Croppers' Song, The
Croppies Lie Down
Croppy Boy, The
Cross Of Christ
Cross Of Jesus Cross Of Sorrow
'Cross The Wide Missouri
Cross Where Thou My Saviour
Crossing The Plains
Crossroads
Crow Fish Man, The
Crow Song, The
Crow, The
Crown Him With Many Crowns
Crows In The Garden
Crucifixion
Cruel Brother, The
Cruel Mother, The
Cruel Shadow, The
Cruel Ship's Carpenter, The
Cruel War, The
Cruel War Is Raging, The
Cruel Youth, The
Cruiscin Lan
Cruise Of The Bigler, The
Cruise Of The Fair American, The
Cruise Of The Tiger, The
Cruising Boys Of Subdivision Nine,
    The
Crusader's Farewell
Crusader's Hymn
Crusaders A War Song
Cruz De Palo Bonito, La
Cryderville Jail
Crying Family, The
Crystal Fountain
Cshebogar
Cuando, El
Cuando El Rey Nimrod
Cuando Yo Me Muera
Cuatro Generales, Los
Cuatro Milpas
Cuatro Muleros, Los
Cuatro Palomitas Blancas
Cuba
Cucaracha, La
Cuckoo
Cuckoo Calls, The
Cuckoo Is A Pretty Bird, The

Traditional *(Cont.)*

Cuckoo Of The Grove
Cuckoo She's A Pretty Bird, The
Cuckoo Sings, The
Cuckoo Song, The
Cuckoo, The
Cuckoo Yodel, The
Cuckoo's Advice, The
Cuckoo's Spring Song, The
Cuckoo's Welcome, The
Cudgel Song, The
Cueca
Cuigeal Na Maghdin
Cuisiniere, La
Cumberland And The Merrimac, The
Cumberland Crew, The
Cumberland Gap
Cumberland's Crew, The
Cunningham Schottische, The
Cup Of Cold Poison, The
Cup Of Rejoicing, A
Cupid The Ploughboy
Cura No Va A La Iglesia, El
Curly Head Of Hair
Curly Joe
Curly Locks
Curly Locks Curly Locks
Curs'd Be The Wretch
Curse Of The Bigaler, The
Curse, The
Curtains Of Night, The
Custer's Last Charge
Cuszmy Sie
Cute Little Car, The
Cutting Down The Pines
Cutting Machine, The
Cutting Of The Turf, The
Czardas, The
Czech Dance Song
Czechoslovakian Dance Song
D And H Canal Song
D And H Canal, The
D'Arcy Farrow
D'ou Reviens-Tu Mon Fils Jacques
D'ou Veins-Tu Bergere
D'ou Venez-Vous Fillette
D'ou Viens-Tu Bergere
D'Ror Yikra
Da Bahia Me Mandaram
Da Droben Vom Berge
Da Laimh Sa Phiob
Da's All Right Baby
Dabbling In The Dew
Dad's Jig
Daddy
Daddy Shot A Bear
Daghela Avanti Passo
Daily Daily Sing The Praises
Daisy, The
Dale Una Posada
Dame Durden
Dame Get Up And Bake You Pies
Dame Get Up And Bake Your Pies

Traditional *(Cont.)*

Dame Hilda
Dame Joan
Damn And Blast And Bugger A Cat
Damn The Filipinos
Damper Song
Damsel Possessed Of Great Beauty,
    A
Damsel's Tragedy, The
Dan D'Irisleabhar Na Gaeilge
Dan McCole
Danbury Mare, The
Dance
Dance A Baby Diddy
Dance Me A Jig
Dance Of Greeting
Dance Of The Fairies
Dance Song
Dance, The
Dance To Your Daddy
Dancin' On De Green
Dancing Around
Dancing In The Barn
Dancing Maiden, The
Dancing Song
Dancing Together
Dancing With Rosa
Dandansoy
Dandelion
Dandoo
Dandy Jim Of Caroline
Dandy Man Oh
Danger Waters
Daniel Monroe
Daniel Saw De Stone
Daniel Saw The Stone
Danish Baby Song
Dankgebet
Dannebrog, The
Danns' A Bhrigi Danns' A Bhocai
Danny Boy
Danny Winters
Dans Kiev La Capitale
Dans La Chambrette Gaie
Dans La Cour De Ma Grand'mere
Dans La Prairie Verte Et Fleurie
Dans La Ville Au Jour Levant
Dans Le Village Ou Je Restais
Dans Les Chantiers Nous
    Hivernerons
Dans Les Haubans
Dans Les Prisons De Nantes
Dans Notre Village Qui Est Le Plus
    Sage
Dansez Calinda
Dansons La Capucine
Danville Chariot, The
Danville Girl
Dar Was A Gal In Our Town
Dara
Darby Ram, The
Darf I's Dirndel Lieben
Daria La Belle S'en Va Par Les
    Champs

Traditional *(Cont.)*

Dark Eyes
Dark Hollow, The
Dark Is The Even
Dark Was The Night
Dark-Eyed Canaller
Dark-Eyed Sailor, The
Darky Sunday School
Darlin'
Darlin' Corey
Darling Come Early
Darling Cora
Darling Corey
Darling Cory
Darling Go To Rest
Darling Little Joe
Darogoy Dal'noyu
Dartmouth Our Dartmouth
Darwin
Dashing Away With The Smoothing
  Iron
Dashing White Sergeant
Dass Es Auf Armen Erde
Dat Lonesome Stream
Dat Suits Me
Dat Water-Million
Dat's All Right
Date Of Thirty-Nine, The
Daughter Of The Rock, The
Daughters Of Erin, The
Daughters Will You Marry
David Meleh Yisrael
David Of The White Rock
David Ward
Davisson's Retirement
Davy Crockett
Dawn Is Sprinkling In The East, The
Dawn Of Jacob's Star Inciteth
Dawning Day, The
Day A Day Of Glory, A
Day Bomber's Lament
Day Bright Day Of Glory, A
Day Dah Light
Day Draws On With Golden Light,
  The
Day Has Come, The
Day Is Done
Day Is Past And Gone, The
Day Of Departure Is Come, The
Day Of Joy And Feasting, A
Day Of Resurrection, The
Day Of Wrath And Doom Pending
Day Of Wrath O Day Of Mourning
Day Thou Gavest, The
Day We Packed The Hamper For
  The Coast, The
Day's Farewell
Dayenu
Daylight
Days And Moments Quickly Flying
Days Are Gane That I Hae Seen, The
Days Grow Longer Sunbeams
  Stronger
Days Of Forty Nine, The

Traditional *(Cont.)*

Days Of My Childhood, The
Days Of Old, The
Days Of The Months, The
Dayspring Of Eternity
De Aquel Cerro Verde
De Las Montanas Venimos
De Mexico Ha Venido
De Morgensterne Hefft Sich
  Upgedrungen
De Nazaret Unos Huespedes
De Nederige Geboorte
De Tierra Lejana Venimos
De Tolv Hellige Ting
De Vita Hominis
De Volga Et Mikoula
Deacon Went Down , The
Dead Horse
Dead Horse Chanty, The
Dead Horse, The
Deaf Old Woman, The
Deaf Woman's Courtship, The
Dear Baby Jesus Now Rest In Sleep
Dear Bucknell
Dear Companion, The
Dear Evelina
Dear God We Like To Come To
  Church
Dear Harp Of My Country
Dear Irish Boy, The
Dear Katie
Dear Little Shamrock, The
Dear Master In Whose Life I See
Dear Old City By The Lee
Dear Old Home, The
Dear Old Number Six
Dear Old Pals
Dear Old Spc
Dear Prairie Home
Dear Sweet Little Isle Of Mann
Dear-A-Wee Lass, The
Death Ain't Nothin' But A Robber
Death Ain't You Got No Shame
Death Come To My House He
  Didn't Stay Long
Death Croon, The
Death Farewell, The
Death Of A Maiden Fair
Death Of A Romish Lady
Death Of Admiral Benbow, The
Death Of Crockett, The
Death Of Fred Lowry, The
Death Of General Warren
Death Of General Wolfe, The
Death Of Jerry Damron, The
Death Of Mary, The
Death Of Movitz' Fiancee, The
Death Of Mrs Lydia Woodburn, The
Death Of Oscar, The
Death Of Queen Jane, The
Death Of Robin Hood, The
Death Of The Brave, The
Death's Goin' To Lay His Hand On
  Me

Traditional *(Cont.)*

Death's Gwineter Lay His Cold Icy
  Hands On Me
Debka Daluna
Debka Rafiach
Debt I Owe
Decatur's Victory
Decisive Work
Deck The Hall
Deck The Hall With Boughs Of
  Holly
Deck The Halls
Deck The Halls With Boughs Of
  Holly
Declaration Of Independence
Decree, The
Deemster's Daughter, The
Deep Blue Sea
Deep Blue Sea, The
Deep Deep In Yonder Valley
Deep In The Forest
Deep River
Deep Sea Tug
Deep Spring
Deep's The Rima
Defeat And Victory
Deil's Awa Wi Th' Exciseman, The
Deilig Er Den Himmel Bla
Deilig Er Den Himmel Blaa
Deilig Er Jorden
Dein Konig Kommt
Deitch Company, The
Dejenme Paso Que Voy
Delhi Jail, The
Delia
Delia Gone
Delia's Gone
Delicieuses Cimes
Dem Bones
Dem Golden Slippers
Dem Milners Treren
Denke An Mich O Herr
Dennis O'Reilly
Dens Of Ireland, The
Dens Of Yarrow, The
Depouille Complete, La
Depth Of Mercy
Derby Ram, The
Derby Shed Ram, The
Dere's A Han' Writin' On De Wall
Dere's A Meetin' Here Tonight
Dere's An Old Camp-Meetin'
Dere's No Hidin' Place
Dere's No Hidin' Place Down Dere
Derelict
Dermot Hide Not Thy Anguish
Derniere Rose, La
Derrett
Derriere Chez Nous
Derry Gaol
Descend From Heav'n Ye Angels
  Come
Descend O Spirit Purging Flame

Traditional *(Cont.)*

Desde Mexico He Vinido
Dese Bones Am Gwineter Rise Again
Dese Bones Gonna Rise Again
Dese Bones Gwine To Rise Again
Desembre Congelat, El
Desperado, The
Despierta Mi Palomita
Destroyer Life
Destroyer Song
Desventurado
Det Star Ein Friar
Detroit
Deutschland Deutschland Uber Alles
Devant Chez Belfort
Devil And Bonaparte, The
Devil And The Farmer's Wife, The
Devil On Every Post Schottische, The
Devilish Mary
Devotion
Dew From Heaven, A
Dew Is On The Grass, The
Dewy Dens Of Yarrow, The
Dewy Dewy Dens Of Yarrow, The
Dewy Is The Grass
Dey All Got A Mate But Me
Dey Tell Me Joe Turner's Come To
    Town
Dh'eirich Mi Moch Maduinn Alainn
Dh'eirich Mi Ro' Bhial An Latha
Dhianainn Sugradh Ris An Nighinn
    Duibh
Di Zun Vet Arunter Geyn
Dia De Tu Santo, El
Dia Que Yo Naci, El
Diamanto
Diamond Joe
Dian Cadalan
Diana
Diana And Sweet William
Dicen Que Las Heladas
Dicen Que No Me Quiere
Dich Mutter Gottes Rufn Wir An
Dick German The Cobbler
Dick Whittington
Dickory Dickory Dare
Dickory Dickory Dock
Dicky Johnston
Did Not Old Pharaoh Get Lost
Did You Ever See A Lassie
Did You Ever See De Devil
Did You Ever See The Equal
Did You Hear My Jesus
Did You Play Gipsy
Did You See My Betsy
Didn't My Lord Deliver Daniel
Didn't Old John
Didn't Old Noah Build Him An Ark
Die In De Fiel'
Diesel And Shale
Dieu Quel Mariage
Different Dances

Traditional *(Cont.)*

Dig Din Don Dig Din Don Aux
    Oeufs Rouges Courons
Dig My Grave
Dig My Grave Long An' Narrow
Dillar A Dollar, A
Diller A Dollar, A
Dime Lluvia Si Ya Se Divisan
Din Plaiurile Romanei
Dinah Won't You Blow
Ding Dong
Ding Dong Bell
Ding Dong Merrily
Ding Dong Merrily On High
Dink's Blues
Dink's Song
Dios Os Guarde Gente Honrada
Dipsycola, The
Dire Gelt
Diridh Mi Stuc Nan Creag
Dirty Mistreatin' Women
Dis Am De Hammer
Disappointed Lover, The
Disappointed Sailor, The
Disappointed Serenader, The
Disappointed Suitor, The
Disconsolate Judy's Lamentation
Dishonest Miller, The
Dismiss Us With Thy Blessing Lord
Dismission Of Great I
Dismission Of The Devil
Distress
Distressed Men Of War
Dites Que Faut-Il Faire
Divers Never Gave Nothing To The
    Poor
Diverus And Lazarus
Dives And Laz'us
Dives And Lazarus
Divinuum Mysterium
Dixie
Dixieland
Dixon And Johnson
Do An' Nannie
Do Chrochadh A Thoill Thu
Do Do Pity My Case
Do Don't Touch-A My Garment
    Good Lord I'm Gwine Home
Do Lord Remember Me
Do My Johnny Booker
Do Not Awaken My Memories
Do Not Care
Do Not Grumble
Do Not Scold Me And Do Not
    Reproach Me
Do Remember
Do Trunken Sie Die Liebe Lange
    Nacht
Do What The Spirit Say
Dobe Bill
Dockers' Strike, The
Dockyard Gate, The
Dodger Song, The
Doffing Mistress, The

Traditional *(Cont.)*

Dog
Dog And Gun
Dog And The Gun, The
Dog In The Wood
Dogie Song
Dogs' Meeting, The
Dollar Down, A
Dolly
Dolly Grey
Dolly's Brae
Dolores Sweet And True
Dolphin's Return, The
Dolphy's Set Tune
Domina Maria
Domine Salvum Fac Regum
Don Cher Look At Me Caline
Don Francisco
Don Simon De Mi Vida
Don't Be Weary Traveler
Don't Ever Love Me
Don't Forget Me Little Darling
Don't Get Married
Don't Hesitate
Don't Let Nobody Turn Yer Roun'
Don't Let Yo' Watch Run Down
Don't Let Your Deal Go Down
Don't Let Your Watch Run Down
    Cap'n
Don't Marry The Mormon Boys
Don't Sell Any More Rum
Don't Stub Your Toe On Friday
Don't Tell A Lie
Don't Want To Go Home
Don't Ye View Dat Ship A Come A
    Sailin'
Don't You Go
Don't You Grieve After Me
Don't You Have Everybody For
    Your Friend
Don't You Hurry Worry With Me
Don't You Leave Me Here
Don't You Let Nobody Turn You
    Roun'
Don't You Like It
Don't You Weep When I'm Gone
Dona Ana
Dona Nobis
Dona Nobis Pacem
Donald Campbell
Donald Munro
Donald Of Glencoe
Done Esta La Ma' Teodora
Done Foun' My Los' Sheep
Done Made My Vow
Done Made My Vow To The Lord
Done With The World
Done Written Down My Name
Doney Gal
Donkey Music
Donkey Named Pete, A
Donkey, The

Traditional (*Cont.*)

Donkeys Love Carrots
Donnelly And Cooper
Doo Ma
Doodle Dandy
Doom Of Campbell Kelly And Doyle
Doon The Moor
Doraji
Doran Polka, The
Doran's Ass
Dormi Dormi O Bel Bambin
Dormi Iesu
Dornroschen
Dorotka
Dors Ma Colombe
Dort Unten In Der Muhle
Dos Fertsnte Yor
Dos Puntas Tiene El Camino
Dost Thou In A Manger Lie
Doubtful Shepherd
Dove Has Twin White Feet Fair, The
Dove, The
Dove's Song, The
Dover Road, The
Dowie Dens Of Yarrow, The
Down Along The Mother Volga
Down Among The Dead Men
Down By My Garden Pool
Down By The Embarras
Down By The Greenwood Shady
Down By The Greenwood Sidey
Down By The River
Down By The Riverside
Down By The Salley Gardens
Down By The Sally Gardens
Down By The Tan-Yard Side
Down Came An Angel
Down Down Down
Down Fell The Old Nag
Down In A Coal Mine
Down In A Lonely Graveyard
Down In A Village Where I Did
    Dwell
Down In Charleston Jail
Down In De Place Whar I Come
    From
Down In Dear Old Greenwich
    Village
Down In Lehigh Valley
Down In Mobile
Down In That Valley
Down In The Coal Mine
Down In The Garden
Down In The Lehigh Valley
Down In The Valley
Down In The Willow Garden
Down In Yon Forest
Down Mobile
Down On Me
Down The River
Down The Road
Down The Village Street
Down The Volga River
Down To De Mire

Traditional (*Cont.*)

Down To The Lime Kilns Come
Down Went McGinty
Down With It
Downfall Of Paris
Downfall Of Tythes At Slievenamon
Downward Road Is Crowded, The
Downward Roads
Downy Cheek, The
Dowry Song, The
Doxology
Doyle's Pastime On St Patrick's Day
Draftee, The
Dragon, The
Draw A Bucket Of Water
Draw Near O Lord
Draw Nigh And Take The Body Of
    The Lord
Draw Nigh Draw Nigh Emmanuel
Dreadnaught, The
Dreadnought, The
Dream, A
Dream Of Napolean, A
Dream, The
Dreaming By The Handmill
Dreamland
Dreary Black Hills, The
Dreary Dreary Life, The
Dreadful Ghost, The
Drei Fraulein
Drei Grossen Christlichen Feste, Die
Drei Laub Auf Einer Linden
Drei Lilien Drei Lilien
Drei Reiter Am Thor
Drei Roselein, Die
Dremlen Feygl Oyf Di Tsvagn
Dressmaker's Lament
Drill Ye Tarriers
Drill Ye Tarriers Drill
Drink A Highball
Drink Boys Drink
Drink It Down
Drink That Rot Gut
Drink To Me Only
Drink To Me Only With Thine Airs
Drink To Me Only With Thine Eyes
Drink Ye Of Mother's Wine
Drinkin' Of The Wine
Drinking Song
Drive Dull Care Away
Drive It On
Drive The Cold Winter Away
Driver Boy, The
Driver Boys Of Wadesville Shaft, The
Drivin' Steel
Driving On Bald Mountain
Driving Saw-Logs On The Plover
Driving Steel
Drooping Souls
Drop Down Ye Heavens From
    Above
Drought, The
Drover's Dream, The

Traditional (*Cont.*)

Drowned Lovers, The
Drowned Sailor, The
Drowsy Sleeper
Drowsy Sleeper, The
Drum Major, The
Drumdelgie
Drummer Boy
Drummer Boy Of Shiloh, The
Drummer Boy Of Waterloo, The
Drummer Man, The
Drunkard John
Drunkard's Doom, The
Drunkard's Dream, The
Drunkard's Hell, The
Drunkard's Hiccoughs, The
Drunkard's Home Made Sweet, The
Drunkard's Horse, The
Drunkard's Lone Child, The
Drunkard's Warning, A
Drunken Sailor, The
Dry Bones
Dry Dock Omnibus, The
Du Bist Mein
Du Bois Fleuri Viennent
Du Dobrinia
Du Du Liegst Mir Im Herzen
Du Guter Hirt Auf Zions Auen
Du Lieber Heilger Frommer Christ
Du Liebes Schiffermadchen
Du Mein Einzig Licht
Du Meydele Du Fayns Du Meydele
    Du Sheyns
Dubinushka
Duck Dance
Duckfoot Sue
Ducks Amongst The Rush
Dude Wrangler, The
Duermete Nino Lindo
Duke A-Riding
Duke Of Malb'rough, The
Duke Of York, The
Duke William
Dukke Lisse
Dulcimer
Dumb Wife, The
Dummy Line, De
Dummy Line, The
Duncan Gray
Dundai
Dundee
Dungiven Cricket March
Dunkle Wolke
Dunlap's Creek
Dunlavin Green
Dunvegan Dirge, A
Dupree
Duralaydeo
Durchs Oberland Auf
Dust An' Ashes
Dust Dust And Ashes
Dutch Carol
Dutch Company, The
Dutch Warbler

Traditional (*Cont.*)

Dutchman's Song
Duteous Day Now Closeth, The
Dve Gitari
Dweley
Dying Aviator
Dying Aviator, The
Dying Bagman, The
Dying Boy, The
Dying Californian, The
Dying Cowboy, The
Dying Cowgirl, The
Dying Day, The
Dying Drunkard, The
Dying Engineer, The
Dying Fisherman's Song, The
Dying Girl's Song, The
Dying Hobo, The
Dying Knight's Farewell, The
Dying Miller, The
Dying Minstrel, The
Dying Nun, The
Dying Outfit, The
Dying Ranger, The
Dying Robber Raised His Aching
  Brow, The
Dying Sergeant, The
Dying Soldier, The
Dying Soldier's Adieu, The
Dying Stockman, The
Dziasiaj W Betlejem
Dzisiaj W Betlejem
E Ben Ver, L'
E-R-I-E
Each Camp Fire Lights Anew
Each Little Flower That Opens
Eadie
Eamann An Chnoic
Earl Brand
Earl Crawford
Earl Lithgow
Earl Of Douglas And Dame
  Oliphant, The
Earl Of Mar's Daughter, The
Earl Of Moray, The
Early Dawn
Early Early In The Spring
Early In The Morning
Early In The Spring
Early My Dear
Early One Morning
Early This Spring We'll Leave
  Nauvoo
Early To Bed
Early To Bed And Early To Rise
Earth Has Many A Noble City
Earth Today Rejoices
Earth's Mighty Maker Whose
  Command
Earthly Friends
Earthly Friends Will Change And
  Falter
East Is Red, The

Traditional (*Cont.*)

East St Louis
East Virginia
Easter Alleluya
Easter Carol, An
Easter Day Carol
Easter Eggs
Easter Eggs Are Rolling
Easter Hymn
Eastern Monarchs Sages Three
Eating Goober Peas
Ecce Quam Bonum
Eccles Wakes
Echen Confites
Echo
Echo Canyon
Echo Carol, The
Echo Des Montagnes De Bethleem,
  L'
Echo Des Ravines, L'
Echo Sweet
Echoes Are Sounding
Ecstacy
Eddystone Light, The
Edelweiss
Edgefield
Edinburgh Town
Edward
Edward Jorgen
Ee-Rye-Ee Canal
Eensy Weensy Spider
Ef I Had A Ribbon Bow
Ef Ye Want To See Jesus
Ef Your Gal Gits Mad An' Tries To
  Bully You-U-U
Eg Gjaette Tulla
Eggleston Hall
Eggs And Marrowbone
Eguberriz
Eh Bi Nango
Eho Eho
Ehre Sei Gott
Ei Du Feiner Reuter
Eia Eia
Eifersuchtige Knabe, Der
Eight Bells
Eileadh 'S Na Huraibh O Ho
Eileen Aroon
Elanoy
Elder Blooming
Electric Tram, The
Elegance And Simplicity
Elegy Of Ivor Of Keri
Elend Hat Mich Umfangen
Elephant And The Flea, The
Elfin Knight, The
Eli Ah Can't Stan'
Eli Eli
Eli Yale
Elimeleh Of Gilhofen
Eliyahu Ha-Navi
Eliza
Eliza Jane
Eliza Or When I Landed In Glasgow

Traditional (*Cont.*)

Eliza's Flight
Elizabeth Elspeth Betsy And Bess
Elle Est Mal Batie La Maison
Ellen Smith
Ellen Smith Ballet, The
Eloquent Bells In Every Steeple
Elwina Of Waterloo
Emancipation
Embargo A New Song, The
Embargo, The
Emcompassed In An Angel's Frame
Emer's Farewell
Emigrant From Pike
Emigrant's Dying Child, The
Emigrant's Farewell, The
Emigrant's Farewell To Donegal,
  The
Emigrant's Song
Emma
Emma You My Darlin'
Emmigrant's Farewell, The
Empire Of The West, The
Empty Cot In The Bunkhouse
En Avant Poum Poum
En Belen A Media Noche
En Belen Tocan A Fuego
En Blancos Panales
En El Portal A Belen
En Kelohenu
En La Cordillera Ilueve
En Montant La Riviere
En Nombre Del Cielo
En Nombre Du Cielo
En Roulant Ma Boule
Enchanted Wood, The
End Of Mourning, The
End Of The Rainbow, The
Enfants Au Saloir, Les
Engel Sprach Ihr Hirtenleut, Der
Engineer Ocs Song
Engineer's Song
Engineers, The
England's Great Loss By A Storm Of
  Wind
Englische Jager, Der
English Courage Displayed
English Round, An
Enquirer
Enrame De La Fuente, El
Enseignez-Moi Donc
Enter In The Wilderness
Enterprise And Boxer
Enterre-Moi Dans La Cour
Enterrement Du Bossu, L'
Entre Le Boeuf Et L'ane Gris
Entreaty
Equinoctial And Phoebe
Equinoxial
Equinoxial And Phoebe
Er-I-E, The
Era Ya Tiempo
Eres Alta Y Delgada

Traditional (*Cont.*)

Eres Noche De Navidad
Erie Canal Ballad, The
Erie Canal Song, The
Erie Canal, The
Erin Far Away
Erin Is My Home
Erin On The Rhine
Erin The Green
Erin The Tear And The Smile
Erin The Tear And The Smile In
    Thine Eyes
Erin's Green Shore
Erin's Green Shores
Erinnre Dich Mein Geist
Eriskay Love Lilt, An
Eriskay Lullaby, An
Eriskay Melody
Erlaube Mir Fein's Madchen
Ermak Timofeievitch
Ernie Goodman's Waltz
Ernie James Schottische, The
Erwahlte, Die
Erwahlte Schatzchen, Das
Es Dunkelt Schon In Der Heide
Es Fiel Ein Himmelstaue
Es Fiel Ein Reif
Es Fur Ein Baur Ins Holz
Es Fur Gut Schiffmann Ubern Rhein
Es Geht Durch Alle Lande
Es Get Ein Dunkle Wolk Herein
Es Isch Kei Soliger Stamme
Es Ist Auf Erd Kein Schwerer Leid
Es Ist Ein Reis Entsprungen
Es Ist Ein' Ros'
Es Ist Ein Ros Entsprungen
Es Ist Ein Schnitter
Es Ist In Keinem Andern Heil
Es Ist Noch Eine Ruh' Vorhanden
Es Ist So Still Geworden
Es Ist So Still Im Kammerlein
Es Ist Vollbracht
Es Iz Gefloygn Di Gilderne Pave
Es Kam Ein Herr Zum Schloessli
Es Klingen Die Hammer
Es Legt Der Soldner Rotte
Es Reit Ein Herr Und Auch Sein
    Knecht
Es Ritten Drei Reiter
Es Stet Ein Lind In Jenem Tal
Es Sungen Drei Engel
Es Taget Vor Dem Walde
Es War 'Mal Eine Schaf'rin
Es Wird Scho Glei Dumpa
Es Wird So Hell
Es Wolt Ein Jager Jagen
Es Wolt Ein Maidlin Wasser Holn
Escondido
Escriveto, L'
Essence Of Ole Virginny, The
Est Ce Un Aigle Qui S'envole
Est-Ce Le Bonheur Joyeux Destin
Esta Calle Es Un Jardin
Esta Noche Es Noche Buena

Traditional (*Cont.*)

Esta Noche Nace Un Nino
Esta Noche Serena
Este Nino Hechicero
Ester
Estilo
Estudiantina
Et Barn Er Fodt I Betlehem
Et Ou C'est Que Tu Es Parti
Eternal Gifts Of Christ The King, The
Eternal Glory Of The Sky
Eternal God And Sovereign Lord
Eternal Monarch King Most High
Eternal Power Whose High Abode
Eternal Right
Eternal Ruler Of The Ceaseless
    Round
Eternity
Ethiopia
Eton Boating Song
Eu Na Wawae Iki
Eumerella Shore, The
Eureka
Ev'ry Day 'll Be Sunday
Ev'ry Night When The Sun Goes In
Ev'ry Time I Feel De Spirit
Ev'ry Time I Feel The Spirit
Ev'rybody Loves Saturday Night
Eva Toole
Evalina
Evening Bell, The
Evening Bells, The
Evening Hour, The
Evening Hymn
Evening In Port
Evening Prayer
Evening Song
Evening Song At Cornell
Evening Star
Evening Thoughts
Ever After On
Ever Faithful
Everlasting Absence Of God
    Intolerable
Every Little Step Goes Higher
Every Night When The Sun Goes In
Every Time I Feel The Spirit
Every Year As Round Comes
    Christmas
Every Year At Christmas
Everybody Loves Saturday Night
Everybody Sing Freedom
Everybody's Crackers On PT
Evil Hearted Me
Ewing Brooks
Execution Of Five Pirates For
    Murder
Exhilaration
Exile, The
Exile's Dream, The
Exiles, The
Experience

Traditional (*Cont.*)

Explosions From A Tropical
    Language
Express Office, The
Eyder Ich Leyg Mich Shlofn
Eyes Of Blue
Eyes Of Texas Are Upon You, The
Eyes Of Texas, The
Eyes Of The Fleet
Eyn Kol Eyn Kol Eyn Kol Vayn
Eyn Zach Vel Ich
Ezekiel Said Here Was A Wheel In A
    Wheel
Ezekiel Saw De Wheel
Ezekiel Saw The Wheel
Ezekiel's Wheel
F 2 A And The H S One, The
Fa-Le-Well Shisha Maley
Fable, A
Faca Sibh Oighrig
Face On The Bar Room Floor, The
Factor's Song, The
Factory Girl, The
Faded Coat Of Blue, The
Fader Jakob
Fading Youth
Fahre Fort Fahre Fort
Fahrende Handler, Der
Fai Ogoun
Fail O Ro Mar Dh'fhag Sinn
Fain Waterloo
Fair And Free Elections
Fair Annet
Fair Annie
Fair Caroline
Fair Charlotte
Fair Christmas Day Has Come
Fair Damsel
Fair Damsel From London, The
Fair Devorgill
Fair Ellender
Fair Fannie Moore
Fair Fannie More
Fair Flo-Ella, The
Fair Florella
Fair Harvard
Fair Hebe
Fair Hills And Valleys
Fair Hills Of Eire O, The
Fair Is My Lot
Fair Is The Summer
Fair Is Their Fame
Fair Julian Bond
Fair Lady Of London
Fair Lady Of The Plains, A
Fair Maid On The Shore
Fair Maids Of Mann
Fair Margaret And Sweet William
Fair Mary
Fair Napoli
Fair Princess Royal, The
Fair Reed
Fair Rosamond
Fair Rosanna

Traditional *(Cont.)*

Fair Sally
Fair Smith
Fair Una
Fair Waved The Golden Corn
Fair Wells
Fair William And Lady Maisry
Fair Wind's Blowing, A
Fairest Lord Jesus
Fairest Lord Jesus Ruler Of All
Fairest Lord Jesus Ruler Of All
    Nature
Fairies, The
Fairy Palace
Fais Do Do
Fais Dodo Colin
Faites Bouillir La Marmite
Faites-Moi Un Homme Sans Tete
Faith Of Our Fathers
Faithful Bird, The
Faithful Johnnie
Faithful Sailorboy Waltz, The
Faithless Smile, The
Falan-Tiding
Fall Of The Year, The
Falling Dew, The
False Knight Upon The Road, The
False Young Man, The
Falt Trom Trom Dualach
Fanchon
Fanny
Far Above Us Sails The Heron
Far Away O'er The Sea
Far Green Hill, The
Far-Away Valley
Fare The Well
Fare Thee Well
Fare Ye Well Lovely Nancy
Farewell
Farewell Manchester
Farewell To Bohemia
Farewell To Happiness
Farmer And His Wife, The
Farmer And The Crow, The
Farmer Boy, The
Farmer In The Dell, The
Farmer Is The Man, The
Farmer, The
Farmer's Curst Wife, The
Farmer's In The Dell, The
Farmyard, The
Farther Along
Farvel Gamle Rokken
Fatal Run
Fatal Wedding, The
Fate Of Talmadge Osborne, The
Father Abraham
Father And I Went Down To Camp
Father And Mother Dear
Father Grumble
Father In Heav'n Who Lovest All
Father James' Song
Father Kossuth Word Is Sending
Father Noah

Traditional *(Cont.)*

Father Of Mercy
Father She Said Varsoviana
Father We Praise Thee Now The
    Night Is Over
Father's Light And Splendor, The
Father's Old Grey Whiskers
Father's Waltz
Father's Whiskers
Faughanvale
Fee Fee Fiddle
Female Highwayman, The
Female Smuggler, The
Feng Yang Drum, The
Fennario
Ferner Klang, Ein
Festival Carol
Feuille-O
Fhuair Mi Liom Thu Mhairi
Fiddle-Dee-Dee
Fiddler, The
Fidler, A
Fighting Song
Fileuse
Fille De Parthenay
Finnegan's Wake
Fire Down Below
Fire Ship, The
Fireship, The
Firolera, La
First Christmas Day, The
First Cork Brigade, The
First Love
First Noel, The
First Nowel, The
First Nowele, The
First Nowell, The
First Nowell The Angel Did Say, The
First Set Of Quadrilles, The
First Set Tune
First Thanksgiving, The
Fish And Tea
Fish In The Sea, The
Fisher Lad Of Whitby, The
Fisher Maiden, The
Fisher Song, A
Fisherman Peter
Fisherman, The
Fisherman's Boy, The
Fisherman's Daughter, The
Fisherman's Girl, The
Fisherman's Love, The
Fisherman's Night Song
Fisherman's Song
Fisherman's Wife, The
Fishermen's Evening Song
Fishes' Lamentation, The
Fishing Song
Fitter The Rigger The Mech, The
Fitter's Song, The
Five And Twenty Years Ago
Five Bob To Four
Five Dollars A Day

Traditional *(Cont.)*

Five Fingers In The Boll
Five Hills
Five Hundred Miles
Five Times Five
Fix Me Jesus
Flag, The
Flag Of The Free
Flambeau D'Amour, Le
Flambeau Jeanette Isabelle, Un
Flapjacks Tree, The
Flash Frigate, The
Flat River Girl
Flat River Girl, The
Flat River Raftsman, The
Flee As A Bird
Flemish Carol
Flemmings Of Torbay, The
Fleur De L'Olivier, La
Flicka Will You Dance With Me
Flier, The
Flight
Flight Of The Earls, The
Flight Of Time, The
Fling Dat Hook In De Middle Of De
    Pon'
Flirting
Floating Scow Ob Ole Virginia, De
Floating Scow Of Old Virginny
Flora
Flora Lily Of The West
Flora Macdonald's Love Song
Florence
Flores De Mime
Flow Gently Sweet Afton
Flow Oh Water Flow On
Flow River
Flow River Flow
Flow Thou Regal Purple Stream
Flower Carol
Flower Drum
Flower Gardens
Flower Girl
Flower Girl, The
Flower O' Northumberland, The
Flower Of Changunga
Flower Of Corby Mill, The
Flower Of France And England O,
    The
Flower Of Gortade, The
Flower Of Magherally, The
Flower Of Sweet Dunmull, The
Flower Of Sweet Strabane, The
Flower Seeds
Flowers In May
Flowers In The Valley, The
Flowers O' The Forest, The
Flowers Of Edinburgh, The
Flowers Of Peace
Flowers Of Spring, The
Flowers Of The West, The
Flowing River
Floyd Collins
Flug Der Liebe, Der

Traditional (*Cont.*)

Flute And The Trumpet, The
Fly Song, The
Flying Cloud, The
Flying Cranes
Flying Dutchman, The
Flying Pieman, The
Flying U Twister
Fod
Foggy Dew, The
Foggy Foggy Dew, The
Foglia Di Fiore
Foller De Drinkin' Gou'd
Follow Me
Follow Me Full Of Glee
Follow The Drinkin' Gourd
Follow The Drinking Gourd
Follow The Kings
Followers Of The Lamb
Fond Of Chewing Gum
Fontaine Est Profonde, La
Fonye Dinen Iz Zeyer Biter
Fonye Ganev
Fooba Wooba John
Foolish Boy, The
Foolish Frog, The
Foom Foom Foom
Foot Of The Mountain Bow, The
Foot Prints
Footstool, The
For All The Saints
For Atti Dai
For Christmas Day
For He's A Jolly Good Fellow
For I Ain' Goin' T' Die No Mo'
For I'm A Good Old Rebel
For July 1816
For Me The Savior Died
For The Beauty Of The Earth
For The Brave Of Ev'ry Race
For The Fourth Of July
For The Might Of Thine Arm
For Those We Love Within The Veil
For Those Who Wrought With
    Loving Heart
Forest Nightingale, The
Forest Ranger, The
Forget Na' Dear Lassie
Forget The World
Forget Them Not
Forgive Our Sins As We Forgive
Forgotten Yesterdays
Forsaken
Forsaken Lover
Forsaken Maiden, The
Fortune My Foe
Forty Acre Farm, The
Forty Days And Forty Nights
Forty Years Ago
Forty-Eight Bottles
Forty-Nine Bottles
Foster's Lancers Tune
Foster's Varsoviana
Foundling Baby

Traditional (*Cont.*)

Fountain, The
Fountains Flowing
Four And Twenty Elders
Four And Twenty Lawyers
Four Balows
Four Generals, The
Four Grains Of Corn
Four In A Boat
Four Maries, The
Four Marys, The
Four Nights Drunk
Four O'Clock
Four-And-Twenty Tailors
Four-Step Schottische
Fourty Years I Worked With Pick
    And Drill
Fox And Goose
Fox And The Goose, The
Fox And The Lawyer Was Different
    In Kind, The
Fox, The
Fox Walked Out, The
Fox Went Out On A Starry Night, A
Fox Went Out One Starry Night, A
Fragment Of An Irish Ditty
Fragments Of Irish Songs
Frailach
Frank Collins' First Polka
Frank Collins' Second Polka
Frank Collins' Waltz
Frank Gardiner
Frankie
Frankie And Albert
Frankie And Johnnie
Frankie And Johnny
Frankie Was A Good Girl
Franklin's Crew
Frappe Et Puis Frappe
Fraytik In Der Fri
Fred Holland Schottische
Fred Karno's Air Corps
Free America
Free Americay
Free At Last
Free Salvation
Freedom And Dignity
Freedom Is Coming
Freedom Of Cuba, The
Freedom Train A' Comin'
Freedom's Comin' And It Won't Be
    Long
Freight Train
Frelich Zain
French Blues
French Canadian Rowing Song
French Cathedrals
French Privateer, The
Frenchman's Ball, The
Frere Jacques
Fresh Beautiful Flower
Fresh Fish Today
Fresh Peanuts
Friendly Beasts, The

Traditional (*Cont.*)

Friendly Toad, The
Friends And Neighbors
Friends Of Freedom
Friends Of Jesus
Friends We Left Behind Us, The
Friendship
Friendship And Love
Frisco
Frisky Jim
Frog And The Mouse, The
Frog He Would A-Wooing Go, A
Frog In A Cocked Hat
Frog In The Middle
Frog In The Spring, The
Frog In The Well
Frog Puddles
Frog Went A Courtin', A
Frog Went A-Courtin'
Frog Went A-Courting, A
Frog Went Co'tin', The
Frog Went-A-Courtin' He Did Ride
Frog's Courting, The
Frog's Courtship
Frog's Courtship, The
Froggie Went A-Courtin'
Froggie Went A-Courting
Froggy Went A-Courtin'
Frolicsome Sea Captain, The
From Beyond The Island
From Buffalo To Troy
From Church To Church
From East To West
From East To West From Shore To
    Shore
From Every Graveyard
From Great-Grandmother's Album
From Heaven High I Come To You
From O'er The Hills Of Fair Judea
From Siberia
From Sky Above
From The Chuck Wagon
From The Farm Back There Comes
    My Rose
From The Hills
From The Moon
From The Well
From The White Earth
From Thee All Skill And Science
    Flow
From Yon Mountain Verdant
Frosina Sings
Frost, The
Frozen Charlotte
Fuchs Du Hast Die Gans Gestohlen
Fuhng Yahng Flower Drum
Fuhng Yang Wha Gu
Fui No Itororo
Full Melodies All Hearts Will Please
Full Moon
Fuller And Warren
Fum Fum Fum
Fun Vanen Heybt Zich On A Libe
Funeral Chant

Traditional *(Cont.)*

Funeral Hymn
Funeral Train, The
Funf Sohne
Furman, Der
Furry Day Carol
Furusato
Fyfe's Noel
Gaberlunzie Laddie
Gaberlunzie Man, The
Gaberlunzie, The
Gabi Gabi
Gabriel Of High Degree
Gabriel's Message
Gabriel's Trumpet's Going To Blow
Gaines
Gal I Left Behind Me, The
Gale, The
Gallant Brigantine
Gallant Peter Clark
Gallant Poacher, The
Gallant Rainbow, The
Gallant Soldier, The
Gallant Victory, The
Gallery Carol, A
Gallito, El
Gallows Pole, The
Gallows Tree, The
Galway City
Galway Piper, The
Gambler's Blues
Gambling On The Sabbath Day
Game Chaoui, Une
Game Farm
Ganka
Gaol A' Chruidh
Gar Lieblich Hat Sich Gesellet
Garden Gate, The
Garden Hunter, The
Garden Hymn
Garden Of Jesus, The
Gardens In The Sea
Gardez Piti Milatt 'la
Gargal Machree
Garibaldi War Hymn
Garrawilla
Garry Owen
Gaudeamus Igitur
Gay Goss-Hawk, The
Gay Jemmie The Miller
Gay Old Man, The
Gay Spanish Maid, A
Gay Spanish Maid, The
Gay Young Lads
Gdy Sie Chrystus Rodzi
Geant, Le
Gebet Fur Das Vaterland
Gedanken Sind Frei, Die
Gee But I Want To Go Home
Geiterams
'Gelique O
Gems Of The Day
General Armstrong, The
General Monk's March

Traditional *(Cont.)*

General Munroe
General Roll Call
General Roll, The
General Scott And The Veteran
General Toast, The
General Wolfe
Generous Fiddler, The
Gentil Coquelicot
Gentle Jesus Meek And Mild
Gentle Julia
Gentle Mary Laid Her Child
Gentleman Froggie
Gentleman Of Exeter, A
Gentlemen Of Ireland, The
Genugsamkeit
Geography Song, The
Geordie
Geordie Gill
George Bond's Polka
George Collins
George Collum
George Jones
George Large Polka, The
George Large's First Step Dance
George Large's Second Step Dance
George Large's Waltz
George Promer
George Reilly
Georgia Boy
Georgia Land
Georgie
Georgie Porgie
Georgy
German Clockwinder, The
German Lullaby
German Peasants' Dance
German Tune
Germine
Gerry's Rocks
Gertjie
Gesu Bambin L'e Nato
Get Along Little Dogies
Get Away From Dis Co'nfiel
Get On Board
Get On Board Little Children
Get Out Of The Way Roll On Lucky
Get Out Yellow-Skins Get Out
Get Right Stay Right
Get Right With God
Get That Boat
Get Up And Go
Get Up Jack John Sit Down
Gettin' Up Holler
Getting Ready To Die
Gey Ich Mir Shpatsirn
Ghost Dance Song
Ghost Song
Ghostly Sailors, The
GI Blues
GI Insomnia
GI Joe
GI March
Gi Missue

Traditional *(Cont.)*

Gibn Dir Mayn Tochter
Gideon's Band
Gift Of God, The
Gift To Be Simple, The
Gifts From Over The Sea
Gil Morice
Gila Monster Route, The
Gilderne Pave, Di
Gilea Collins
Gilgarra Mountain
Gilgarrah Mountain
Gille Beag O Gille Lag O
Gille Beag O Leanabh Lag O
Gimme Dat Ol'-Time Religion
Gimme Dat Old Time Religion
Gimme Him
Gimme Yo' Han'
Gimme Your Hand
Gimmie That Old Time Religion
Gipsum Davy, The
Gipsy Tinker
Girl Fifteen, A
Girl From Scilla, The
Girl From Yewdall's Mill, The
Girl I Left Behind Me, The
Girl I Left Behind, The
Girl In The Wood, The
Girl Of Constant Sorrow
Girl Of The Shamrock Shore, The
Girl That Wore A Waterfall, The
Girl With The Flowing Hair, The
Girls And Boys Come Out To Play
Girls Around Cape Horn, The
Girls Of Today
Girls Of Valparaiso, The
Girofle Girofla
Git Along Josie
Git Along Little Doggies
Git Along Little Dogies
Git On Bo'd Little Child'en
Git On Board
Git On Board Little Children
Git On Board O'Ship O'Zion
Git Yo' Ticket
Give Me Jesus
Give Me That Old Time Religion
Give Me Three Grains Of Corn
   Mother
Give Me Your Hand
Give Rest Of Christ To Your
   Servants
Give To The Winds Thy Fears
Glad Christmas Bells
Glad News
Glad Tidings
Glasgow Peggy
Glasses Sparkle On The Board, The
Gloucestershire Wassailers' Song
Glee Reigns In Galilee
Glen-Orra
Glenarm Bay
Glencoe
Glendower's Warcry

Traditional *(Cont.)*

Glider Ride
Gloire Au Maitre Qui Regne Aux
    Creux
Glon's Alice Waltz
Gloria
Glorious Naval Victory
Glorious Prospect
Glorious Repeal Meeting Held At
    Tara Hill
Glorious Tidings
Glory And Honor
Glory Be To God On High
Glory Hallelujah
Glory Hallelujah To De New-Born
    King
Glory Of These Forty Days, The
Glory To God
Glory To That Newborn King
Glory Trail, The
Gloucester Wassail
Gloucestershire Wassail
Gluck Auf
Glunk-A-Runk
Go Ahead
Go And Tell That Little Maiden
Go Ask Of The Stars
Go Away From My Window
Go Away You Wicked Fellows
Go Chain The Lion Down
Go Down Death
Go Down In De Lonesome Valley
Go Down Moses
Go Down 'n The Valley And Pray
Go Down Ol' Hannah
Go Down Old Hannah
Go Down You Little Red Rising Sun
Go Forth To Life
Go Get The Ax
Go Get The Axe
Go In And Out The Window
Go Labour On Spend And Be Spent
Go Magi On Your Way
Go No More A-Rushing
Go Preachers
Go Roun' The Border Susie
Go Tell Aunt Patsey
Go Tell Aunt Rhodey
Go Tell Aunt Rhodie
Go Tell Aunt Rhody
Go Tell Aunt Tabbie
Go Tell It On De Mountain
Go Tell It On De Mountains
Go Tell It On The Mountain
Go Tell It On The Mountains
Go Ter Sleep
Go To Him Then
Go To Saint Pether
Go To Sea No More
Go To Sleep
Go To Sleep Little Baby Daddy Run
    Away
Go To Sleep Minette
Go To Sleepy

Traditional *(Cont.)*

Go To Sleepy Little Baby
Go Way F'om Mah Window
Go 'Way From My Window
Go 'Way Old Man
Go Where I Send Thee
Goat Kid, The
Goat, The
Goatherd's Call
Goblins Of The Lake, The
God Bless Our Native Land
God Bless The Master
God Bless The Master Of This House
God Give Ye Merry Christmas
God Himself Is With Us
God Is A God
God Is Ascended
God Is Born
God Is Everywhere
God Is The Loving Father
God Is The Refuge Of His Saints
God Knows All
God Loved The World
God Made Man Man Made Money
God Moves In A Mysterious Way
God My King Thy Might Confessing
God Of Abraham
God Of Abraham Praise, The
God Of Abraham Who Reigns
    Enthroned, The
God Of Bethel
God Of Grace And God Of Glory
God Of Our Fathers Known Of Old
God Of The Living In Whose Eyes
God Oo Ges
God Rest Ye Merry Gentlemen
God Rest You Merry
God Rest You Merry Gentlemen
God Save Ireland
God Save The King
God That Madest Earth And Heaven
God The Father All Things Created
God The Father God The Son
God The Father Son And Spirit
God Who Made The Earth
God Who Stretched The Spangled
    Heaven
God Whom Earth And Sea And Sky,
    The
God You Have Given Us Power
God's Dear Son
God's Dear Son Without Beginning
God's Goin' To Straighten Them
Godamighty Drag
Gods Of The Heathen
Goin' Back To Arizona
Goin' 'Cross The Mountain
Goin' Down The Road Feelin' Bad
Goin' Down The Road Feeling Bad
Goin' Home
Goin' Home On A Cloud
Goin' Keep My Skillet Greasy
Goin' To Boston

Traditional *(Cont.)*

Goin' To Ride Up In The Chariot
Goin' To See My Mother
Goin' To Shout
Goin' To Shout All Over God's
    Heab'n
Goin' To Shout All Over God's
    Heav'n
Going Home In The Chariot
Going Home Song
Going Home With The Milk In The
    Morning
Going Round The Horn
Going To Boston
Going To Heaven
Going To My Old Home
Going To Pull My War-Clothes
Going To Shout All Over God's
    Heav'n
Going To The Fair
Going To The Mexican War
Gol' Ring
Gold Band, The
Gold Digger's Lament, The
Gold Lake And Gold Bluff
Golden And The Blue
Golden Ball, The
Golden Butterflies
Golden Carol, The
Golden Glove, The
Golden Harp
Golden Mornings
Golden Rule, The
Golden Sheaves
Golden Slumbers
Golden Slumbers Kiss Your Eyes
Golden Stair, The
Golden Tresses
Golden Vanity, The
Golden Voyage, The
Golden Willow Tree, The
Gollycully, The
Gonna Keep My Skillet Greasy
Gonna Lay Down My Sword And
    Shield
Gonna Leave Big Rock Behind
Goober Peas
Good Adventure, The
Good Ale
Good Bye Old Paint
Good Christian Men Rejoice
Good Comrade, The
Good Dagobert
Good Evening
Good Evening My Pretty
Good For A Rush Or A Rally
Good King Wencelas
Good King Wenceslas
Good Lord I Done Done
Good Morning Brother Pilgrim
Good Morning Everybody
Good Morning Merry Sunshine
Good Morning Song

Traditional *(Cont.)*

Good Morrow Gossip Joan
Good Morrow 'Tis Saint Valentine's Day
Good Neighbor
Good News
Good News De Chariot's Comin'
Good News The Chariot's Coming
Good Night
Good Night An' Joy Be Wi' Ye A 'A
Good Night Prayer
Good Night To You All
Good Ol' Mountain Dew
Good Old Chariot
Good Old Man, The
Good Old Rebel
Good Ship Calabar, The
Good Ship Mary Cochrane, The
Good Wine Good Health
Good-By Mother
Good-By My Lover Good-By
Good-By Old Paint
Good-By Pretty Mama
Good-Bye Broadway Hello France
Good-Bye Brothers
Good-Bye Everybody
Good-Bye Fare You Well
Good-Bye Liza Jane
Good-Bye My Lover Good-Bye
Good-Bye My Riley O
Good-Bye Ol' Paint
Good-Morning My Pretty Little Miss
Good-Morrow To You Valentine
Goodby City O 'Babylon
Goodbye Brother
Goodbye Little Bonnie Goodbye
Goodbye My Love Goodbye
Goodbye Venezuela
Goodnight Irene
Goodnight Ladies
Goorianawa
Goose Girl, The
Goosey Goosey Gander
Gorosumako
Gospel Train Am Leabin', De
Gospel Train, De
Gospel Train, The
Got A Home At Las'
Got A Train In Cairo
Got Glory An' Honor
Got My Letter
Got No Money
Got Religion All Around The World
Got To Be Baptized
Got To Go To Judgment
Gott Gnad Dem Grossmechtigen Kaiser Frumme
Gott Gsegn Dich Laub
Grace
Grace Darling
Grand Old Maid Britainnia Reel Tune
Grandfather And Grandmother

Traditional *(Cont.)*

Grandma Grunts
Grandma's Advice
Granny's Old Armchair
Grant Us O God A Single Aim
Grass Of Uncle Sam, The
Grasshopper And The Ant, The
Grasshopper Settin' On A Sweet 'tater
Grasshoppers Three
Grassy Islands
Grave Of Wolfe Tone, The
Gray Goose
Great American Bum, The
Great American Flood Disaster, The
Great And Mighty Wonder, A
Great Are The Mercies
Great Big Dog
Great Big Nigger Sittin' On A Log
Great Big Stars
Great Big Tie An' Little Bitty Man
Great Camp Meetin', A
Great Camp-Meetin' In De Promised Land, A
Great Camp-Meeting In The Promised Land, A
Great Campmeeting
Great Day
Great Day For Me
Great Forerunner Of The Morn, The
Great Fun Run From Newcastle To Shields, The
Great God Of Heaven Is Come Down To Earth, The
Great God-A 'Mighty
Great Grand-Dad
Great July Jones
Great Meat Pie, The
Great Round-Up, The
Great Silkie, The
Great Speckled Bird, The
Great Tom Is Cast
Greedy Ducks
Green Bed, The
Green Beds, The
Green Besoms
Green Bushes, The
Green Cockade, The
Green Fields And Meadows, The
Green Fields Of America, The
Green Grass Growing All Around, The
Green Green Green
Green Grow The Lilacs
Green Grow The Rashes O
Green Grow The Rushes
Green Grow The Rushes O
Green Grow The Rushes Oh
Green Grow The Rushes-Ho
Green Grow 'th The Holly
Green Grows The Laurel
Green Linnet, The
Green Mossy Banks Of The Lea, The
Green Mountains

Traditional *(Cont.)*

Green Pidgeon
Green Willow
Green Willow Tree, The
Greenfields
Greenland Fishery
Greenland Men, The
Greenland Voyage, The
Greenland Whale Fishery
Greenland Whale Fishery, The
Greensleeves
Greer County
Greeting Song
Grenadier And The Lady, The
Grey Goose, De
Grey Goose, The
Grey Old Stone, The
Grimmig Tod, Der
Grimsby Fisherman, The
Grimsby Lads, The
Grinding
Grinding Corn
Gringalet
Grizzly Bear
Groun' Hog
Ground Hog
Ground Hog, The
Ground-Hog, The
Grouse Grouse Grouse
Grove Song, The
Grumbellin' People
Grun Grun Grun
Guairenita, La
Guajito
Guantanamera
Guaracha, The
Guardian Angel, The
Guerilla Man, The
Guerilla Song
Guess What I've Got
Guide Me O Thou Great Jehovah
Guide My Feet While I Run This Race
Guillannee, La
Guillenle
Gum Tree Canoe
Gun Canecutter, The
Gung Ho
Gur Tu Mo Nighean Donn Bhoidheach
Gura Mise Tha Fo Eislein
Gura Mise Tha Fo Mhulad
Gura Muladach A Tha Mi
Gute Nacht
Gwine To Lay Down My Burden
Gwine To Lay Me On A Cooling Board One Of Dese Mor
Gwine To Ride Up In The Chariot
Gwine Up
Gwineter Harness In De Mornin' Soon
Gwineter Ride Up In De Chariot Soon-A In De Mornin
Gwinter Sing All Along De Way

Traditional *(Cont.)*

Gypsy Dance
Gypsy Dancer
Gypsy Dave, The
Gypsy Davy, The
Gypsy Davy The Gypsy Laddie
Gypsy In Da Moonlight
Gypsy Laddie, The
Gypsy Rover, The
Gypsy Song
Gypsy, The
Gypsy Weather
Gypsy's Warning, The
Gypsy's Wedding Day, The
Ha Ha My Darlin' Chile
Ha L'aurore Qui Rayonne
Ha Nacido En Un Portal
Ha'k 'E Angels
Hackin's Too Tiresome, The
Had A Little Fight In Mexico
Had Gadyo
Had I A Castle Stately Built Love
Had To Get Up This Mornin'
Hadan
Hag Etsim Higia
Hail Babe Of God The Very Son
Hail Glorious St Patrick
Hail Hail
Hail Hail Hail
Hail Holy Holy Holy Lord
Hail Holy Queen Enthroned Above
Hail Pennsylvania
Hail The Glorious Golden City
Hail This Joyful Day's Return
Hail Thou Once Despised Jesus
Hail To The Chief
Hail To The Lord's Anointed
Hair Trigger Newt
Haiti Cherie
Hajej Nynej Jezisku
Hal Far Biss
Hal 'luyah
Hal-Le-Lu
Haleluya Pelo Tsa Rona
Half Has Never Been Told, The
Hallelujah
Hallelujah Bum Again
Hallelujah I'm A Bum
Hallelujah I'm A-Travelin'
Hallelujah To De Lam'
Hallowe'en
Hallowed Be Thy Name
Halloween Party
Ham Bone Ham Bone
Hamentashn
Hamlet Wreck, The
Hammer Man
Hammer Song, The
Hammering
Han' Me Down Yo' Silvah Trumpet
    Gabriel
Han Skal Leve Hojt
Hanan And Aliza

Traditional *(Cont.)*

Hand A' Bowl
Hand Me Down
Hand Me Down My Walkin' Cane
Hand Me Down My Walking Cane
Hand Me Down The Silver Trumpet
Hand O'er Hand
Handcart Song, The
Handful Of Gospel Love, A
Handkerchief Dance
Handsome Cabin Boy, The
Handsome Harry
Handsome Molly
Handsome Young Airman, The
Handy Andy
Hangin' Johnnie
Hanging Johnny
Hangman
Hangman Hangman Hangman
    Loosen Your Rope
Hangman Hangman Slack Your
    Rope
Hangman Slack On The Line
Hanka
Hannukkah O Hannukkah
Hanuka
Hanukkah Hanukkah
Hanukkah Song
Happiness The Sun Is Bringing
Happy Birthday
Happy Bride
Happy Christmas Morning
Happy Easter Day
Happy In The Lord
Happy Journey, The
Happy Meeting, A
Happy Night O Night Of Splendor
Harbour Le Cou
Hard Ain't It Hard
Hard By The Crystal Fountain
Hard Times
Hard Times In Ole Virginny
Hard Times In The Country
Hard To Be A Nigger
Hard Traveling
Hard Trials
Hard-Working Miner, The
Hardly Think I Will
Hardy Norseman, The
Hardy Northman, The
Hare's Dream, The
Hark Christian People
Hark Hark My Soul
Hark Hark The Dogs Do Bark
Hark Hark What News
Hark Hark What News The Angels
    Bring
Hark How All The Welkin Rings
Hark My Soul
Hark Now O Shepherds
Hark The Bells Are Ringing
Hark The Cock Do'th Crown
Hark The Glad Sound The Saviour
    Comes

Traditional *(Cont.)*

Hark The Summons
Hark The Voice Of Jesus Calling
Hark To Her Mighty Voice
Hark What Mean Those Holy Voices
Harmonika
Harmony Grove
Harp Of Wales, The
Harp That Once Thro' Tara's Hall,
    The
Harp That Once Thro' Tara's Halls,
    The
Harp That Once Through Tara's
    Hall, The
Harp That Once Through Tara's
    Halls, The
Harrende Braut, Die
Harris Love Lament
Harrison
Harrison Town
Harry Axford's Tune
Harry Bail
Harry Bluff
Harry Clay
Harry Dunn
Harry Parry
Harry Schulz's Schottische
Harry Schulz's Waltz
Harry Simms
Hartford Wreck
Harvard Student, The
Harvest Dance
Harvest Home
Harvest Hymn
Harvest Is Done, The
Harvest Is Over
Harvest Land
Harvest Moon Schottische, The
Harvest Song
Harvest Time
Harvest War Song, The
Harvesting
Harvey Logan
Has Sorrow Thy Young Days
    Shaded
Hasidic Prayer
Hatikvah
Haughs O' Newe Or The Downie,
    The
Haughty Maid Of Amsterdam, The
Haul Away I'm A Rollin' King
Haul Away Joe
Haul Away My Rosy
Haul In Your Bowline
Haul On Th' Bowlin'
Haul On The Bow-Line
Haul On The Bowlin'
Haul The Bowline
Hauling On The Bowline
Haunting Tune, The
Haur Gaixua Lo Eta Lo
Haur Komuniantek Batheiarriala
    Votoen Arraberritze
Hausel Am Rhein, Das

Traditional *(Cont.)*

Haut Haut Peyrot
Haut Sur La Montagne, La
Hava Nageela
Hava Nagila
Hava Nagilah
Hava Netse Bimholot
Havah Nagilah
Havdala
Have You A Girl Billy Boy
Have You Seen
Havu Godel
Havu Ladonai
Hawkie Is A Schemin' Bird
Hay Aqui Madre Un Jardin
Haymakers, The
Haymaking
He Arose
He Christine
He Has Silver
He Hey Why Do We Pay
He Is Born
He Is Born The Divine Christ Child
He Is King Of Kings
He Is Sleeping In A Manger
He Lies In The American Land
He Liveth Long Who Liveth Well
He Looked Beyond My Fault
He Looked Beyond My Fault And
    Saw My Need
He Menons La Danse
He Mounted The Girl On The
    Milk-White Steed
He Never Came Back
He Never Said A Mumblin' Word
He Ought To Know
He Passed
He Plowed The Lowlands Low
He Rose From The Dead
He Said Think Na Long Lassie
He Scarcely Thinks As Children
    Think
He Venido Palomita
He Wants Not Friends That Hath
    Thy Love
He Was Boasting Of His Shearing
He Was Sorry That He Did It
He Wears A Bonnet For A Hat
He Who Would Valiant Be
He Whom Joyous Shepherds Praised
He's A Mighty Good Leader
He's A-Choppin' In De New Groun'
He's All I Need
He's Got His Eyes On You
He's Got The Whole World In His
    Hand
He's Got The Whole World In His
    Hands
He's Jus' De Same Today
He's The Lily Of The Valley
Head That Once Was Crowned With
    Thorns, The
Heah I Am In Dis Low-Down Jail

Traditional *(Cont.)*

Healin' Waters
Hear A Word A Word In Season
Hear De Angels Singin'
Hear De Lambs A Cryin'
Hear Me Praying
Hear O Shepards
Hear Our Call
Hear The Glad Tidings
Hear Them Bells
Hear Us O Lamb
Hear What Great News We Bring
Hearken Ye Children
Hearken Ye Shepherds
Hearse Song, The
Heart Of The Mountains, The
Heart's Ease
Heav'n Bound Soldier
Heav'n Heav'n
Heaven Is A Beautiful Place
Heaven Is So High
Heavenly March, The
Hebrew Children, The
Heeia
Heel And Toe Polka
Hei-Di-Li-Dom
Heigh-Ho For A Husband
Heir Of Gogerddan, The
Hej Pada Pada
Hela Grand Pere
Heligoland
Hello Susie Brown
Hen Wlad Fy Nhadao
Henry Martin
Henry The Sailor Boy
Her Contended Farmer's Son
Her Dimpled Cheek
Herb's Jig
Herd, The
Herdboy, The
Here Betwixt Ass And Oxen Mild
Here Is Joy For Every Age
Here O My Lord I See Thee Face To
    Face
Here Rattler Here
Here We Come A-Caroling
Here We Come A-Wassailing
Here's To
Here's To Old Bohemia
Here's To The Couple
Here's To The Maiden
Here's To Thee Old Apple Tree
Hereford Carol
Herioz
Hermit And The Shepherds, The
Heroes
Herrick's Carol
Heveni Shalom Alehem
Hew 'round The Tree
Hey Betty Martin
Hey Diddle Diddle
Hey Ho Nobody Home
Hey Ho To The Greenwood

Traditional *(Cont.)*

Hey Hum Diddle Um Day
Hey Li Lee Lo
Hey Lollee
Hey Lolly Lolly
Hey You Gypsy
Hi Daughter Ho Daughter
Hi Ho Jerum
Hi Ho The Preacher Man
Hi Yi
Hi-Ne Ma Tov
Hiawatha's Wooing
Hickety Tickety
Hickory Dickory Dock
Hieland Laddie
High Barbaree
High Barbaree, The
High Barbary
High Betty Martin
High Germany
High Moon, The
High Mountain Stands, A
High The Cranes Are Flying
High The Waves Of Lake Balaton
Highland Laddie
Highland Mary
Highway Man
Hijo Del Conde, El
Hiking Song
Hilariter
Hilawe
Hildin Buildin'
Hills Of Tyrone, The
Hillside, The
Hilo Verde
Hinky Dinky Parlee Vou
Hinky Dinky Parley-Voo
Hirondelle Messagere Des Amours,
    Li
His Eye Is On The Sparrow
His Head Is Big
History Of The World
Hms Pique
Ho Every One That Thirsts
Ho Every Sleeper Waken
Ho Ro Gur Toil Linn Anna
Ho Slavonians
Hob Ich A Por Oksn
Hobo Bill
Hobo's Lullaby
Hodie Christus Natus Est
Hoggedee Boggedee How Now
Hokey Pokey, The
Hokey-Pokey, The
Hol' De Win' Don't Let It Blow
Hold In My Bucket, A
Hold Men Hold
Hold On
Hold The Wind
Hold Up Your Light
Hole In My Bucket
Holiday
Holiday Song
Holland's National Song

Traditional *(Cont.)*

Holly And Ivy
Holly And The Ivy, The
Holly Twig, The
Holy Bible
Holy Child, The
Holy God We Praise Thy Name
Holy Manna
Holy Mother Give To Me
Holy Mother Sings, The
Holy Order
Holy Power
Holy Savior Call
Holy Season, The
Holy Spirit Truth Divine
Holy Well, The
Home Boys Home
Home Dearie Home
Home Home Can I Forget Thee
Home On The Range
Home Sweet Home
Homeward Bound
Honespun Dress, The
Honey Bees Schottische, The
Honey Take One On Me
Honey'd Lip, The
Honza I Love You
Hoops My Dears
Hop Mayne Homentashn
Hop Up And Jump Up
Hope Of The World
Hopsa Lisella
Hor Mein Freund
Horn Fair
Hors Du Bois Du Grand Bois
 Tenebreox
Horse Race Song
Hosanna
Hosanna Loud Hosanna
Host And His Guests, The
Host Done Trabelling
Hostess's Daughter
Hot Boilin' Sun Comin' Over
Hot Cross Buns
Hot Zick Mir Di Zip Tsezipt
Houblons Au Vent On Dulant, Les
House Carpenter, The
House Of The Risin' Sun, The
House Of The Rising Sun, The
House On The Hill, The
Housewife's Lament, The
How Brightly Beams
How Can I Keep From Singing
How Can I Leave Thee
How D' You Do Schottische
How Did You Feel
How Firm A Foundation
How Great Thou Art
How Happy Every Child Of Grace
How I Wish I Was Single Again
How I Would Plough
How Little I Am In It All
How Long Brethren
How Long Train Been Gone

Traditional *(Cont.)*

How Long You'll Be Gone Lord
 Lovel
How Sad Was The Death Of My
 Sweetheart
How Should I Your True Love Know
How Slowly Move The Hours
How Stands The Glass Around
How Tedious And Tasteless
How Tedious And Tasteless The
 Hours
How Times Have Changed
How To Keep Store
How To Win
How Wondrous And Great Thy
 Works
How Wondrous And Great Thy
 Works God Of Praise
Hoya Hoya
Hsiao
Huchage
Hugh Hill The Ramoan Smuggler
Hughie Martin's Schottische
Hulyet Hulyet Kinderlech
Humahuaqueno, El
Humble Heart, The
Humble Humble I've Been Tryin' To
 Live Humble Humble
Humble Yo'self De Bell Done Ring
Humbly I Adore Thee
Humour Os Donnybrook
Humping Old Bluey
Humpty Dumpty
Hunchbacky Man, The
Hundred Lit'l Angels In The Ban', A
Hundred Pipers, The
Hundred Years Ago, A
Hundred Years On The Eastern
 Shore, A
Hungarian Dance
Hunter, The
Hunters Of Kentucky, The
Hunting Morn, The
Hunting The Hare
Hunting-Song
Huntsman, The
Hurdy-Gurdy, The
Huron Christmas Chant, A
Hurrah Sing Fare You Well
Hurricane Wind
Hurry Up Fellows
Husband And Wife
Hush A Bye Baby
Hush Hush
Hush Li'l' Baby
Hush Little Baby
Hush Little Jesus Boy
Hush My Babe Lie Still And Slumber
Hush Now My Children
Hush Somebody Callin' My Name
Hush Still
Hush-A-Ba Birdie
Hush-A-Baby-Bye
Hush-A-By Baby

Traditional *(Cont.)*

Hushaby
Hushaby Don't You Cry
Hushabye
Hussar, The
Hut Is Burning
Hut That's Upside Down, The
Hymn Of Glory Let Us Sing, A
Hymn Of Love, A
Hymn Of St Francis
Hymn Of Thanksgiving, A
Hymn Of The Slavs
Hymn To The Sun
I Ain't Going T' Study War No
 More
I Ain't Going To Die No More
I Ain't Gonna Grieve My Lord No
 More
I Ain't Got No Home
I Ain't Got Weary Yet
I Ain't Gwine Study War No More
I Ain't Gwine To Grieve My Lord
 No More
I Ain't Scared A' Your Jail
I Am A Ancient Mariner
I Am A Brisk And Sprightly Lad
I Am A Girl Of Constant Sorrow
I Am A Jolly Old Cowboy
I Am A Little Christian
I Am A Lone Cowboy
I Am A Maid That Sleeps In Love
I Am A Pilgrim
I Am A Poor Girl
I Am A Poor Wayfaring Stranger
I Am A Young Maiden
I Am Bound For The Kingdom
I Am Coming To A King
I Am Seeking For A City
I Am Sitting By The Bedroom
 Window
I Am Sure You Have Heard My
 Story
I Am The True Vine
I Am Tipsy
I Been A Bad Bad Girl
I Been 'Buked An' I Been Scorned
I Been In De Storm So Long
I Been In The Storm So Long
I Been Workin' On De Levee
I Been Wukkin' On De Railroad
I Beg Your Leave
I Believe I'll Go Back Home
I Believe This Is Jesus
I Belong To This Band
I Bind Unto Myself Today
I Bless The Lawd I'm Born To Die
I Bought Me A Rooster
I Call On Thee Lord Jesus Christ
I Came To The Sport
I Came To This Country In 1865
I Came To This Country In
 Eighteen-Forty-Nine
I Can Love Little

Traditional *(Cont.)*

I Can Not Tarry Here
I Can See
I Can Tell The World
I Can Whip The Scoundrel
I Can't Stay Away
I Can't Stay Behind
I Come From Salem City
I Come From Salem City Parody
I Come To The City Boys
I Come With Joy To Meet My Lord
I Could Not Do Without Thee
I Couldn' Hear Nobody Pray
I Couldn't Hear Nobody Pray
I Courted An Old Man
I Do Not Think His Light Blue Eyes
I Don't Care If I Do
I Don't Care To Stay Here Long
I Don't Expect To Stay
I Don't Feel Noways Tired
I Don't Intend To Die In Egypt Land
I Don't Mind Marrying
I Don't Want No More Army
I Don't Want No More Of Army Life
I Don't Want To Be Lost In The
  Slums
I Don't Work For A Living
I Done Done What Ya' Tol' Me To
  Do
I Dreamed Last Night Of My True
  Love
I Dreamt Last Night I Was Walkin'
  Around
I Dreamt Last Night Of My True
  Love
I Feel Like My Time Ain't Long
I Fell In Love With An Oxford Girl
I Fight Mit Sigel
I Fold Up My Arms And I Wonder
I Found A Little Blind Boy
I Found A Little Boll Weevil
I Found Jesus Over In Zion
I Gave My Love A Cherry
I Go Out At The Gate
I Goes To Fight Mit Sigel
I Got A Gal Her Name Is Maude
I Got A Hidin' Place
I Got A Home In The Rock
I Got A Home In-A Dat Rock
I Got A House In Baltimo
I Got A Key Tot The Kingdom
I Got A Mother In De Heavenly Lan'
I Got A Robe You Got A Robe
I Got Mah Swoad In Mah Han'
I Got Shoes
I Got To Lay In Yonder Graveyard
I Got To Roll
I Got Two Wings
I Gwine T' Beat Dis Rice
I Had A Little Dog
I Had A Little Nag
I Had A Little Nut Tree
I Had A Little Pony

Traditional *(Cont.)*

I Had A Sister Susan
I Had And Old Dog His Name Was
  Blue
I Had One Man
I Had Two Pigeons
I Hae Laid A Herrin In Saut
I Hasten Early
I Have A Little Drum
I Have A Little Union Bell
I Have Always Heard Of These Old
  Men
I Have Another Building
I Have Good Tobacco
I Have House And Land In Kent
I Have No Loving Mother Now
I Have Torn My Sunday Jacket
I Have Traveled This Wide World
  All Over
I Hear Upon The Highway
I Heard A Scythe
I Heard De Preachin' Of De Word
  O' God
I Heard From Heaven Today
I Heard The Angels Singin'
I Heard The Bells On Christmas Day
I Heard The Preaching Of The Elder
I Heard The Voice Of Jesus Say
I Heard The Whistle Blowing
I Himmelen I Himmelen
I Hope My Mother Will Be There
I Into The House Was Turning
I Jes' Come From De Fountain
I Jesu Navn
I Jing-A-Ling
I Just Now From Paris Came
I Kann Eams Net Feind Sein
I Know A Flower
I Know A Lass
I Know A Place Where Bluebells
  Grow
I Know De Lord's Laid His Hands
  On Me
I Know My Love
I Know O Blessed Mary
I Know That My Redeemer Lives
I Know The Lord's Laid His Hands
  On Me
I Know Where I'm Goin'
I Know Where I'm Going
I Learned About Horses From Her
I Learned It In The Meadow Path
I Liab Di So Fest
I Live On The Corner
I Lo'e Na A Laddie But Ane
I Love A Nobody
I Love Everybody
I Love Him Still Though He's Far
  Awa'
I Love Jesus
I Love Little Pussy
I Love Little Willie
I Love My Love In The Morning
I Love My Rooster

Traditional *(Cont.)*

I Love The Mountains
I Love Thee
I Love Thee O Mary
I Love Thee O Thou Lords Most
  High
I Love To Hear The Story
I Married A Wife
I Mean To Lift Up A Standard For
  My King
I Mourned In De Valley
I Must And I Will Get Married
I Must Go Gather Comfort
I Must Walk My Lonesome Valley
I Never Felt Such Love In My Soul
  Befo'
I Never Shall Marry
I Never Will Marry
I Once Loved A Boy
I Rejoice In The Cross
I Ride An Old Paint
I Rode My Little Horse
I Rode To Church Last Sunday
I Said The Donkey
I Saw Three Ships
I Saw You
I Stood On De Ribber Ob Jerdon
I Stood Outside The Gate
I Thank God I'm Free At Last
I Think By This Time He's Forgot
  Her
I Think When I Read That Sweet
  Story Of Old
I Thought To The Bottom We Would
  Go
I To The Hills Will Lift Mine Eyes
I Walk The Road Again
I Walked The Road Again
I Want A Seat In Paradise
I Want God's Heab'n To Be Mine
I Want Such A Wife
I Want To Be Ready
I Want To Be Ready I Want To Be
  Ready
I Want To Climb Up Jacob's Ladder
I Want To Die Easy When I Die
I Want To Go Home
I Want To Go There Too
I Want To Go To Glory
I Want To Have A Little Bomb Like
  You
I Wanta Go Home
I Wanta Live So God Can Use Me
I Wanted Wings
I Was Born About 10000 Years Ago
I Was Born About Ten Thousand
  Years Ago
I Was Born Almost Ten Thousand
  Years Ago
I Was On The Drive In 'eighty
I Was Sixteen Years Of Age
I Wash My Face In A Golden Vase
I Went Down In The Valley
I Went Down To The Old Depot

Traditional (*Cont.*)

I Went Down To The Valley
I Went Home One Night
I Went Out One Evening Just At The
   Close Of Day
I Went Out To Worldy Wiggy
   Waggy
I Went To Atlanta
I Went To My Sweetheart's House
I Went To Old Napper's House
I Went To The Fair At Bonlaghy
I Went To The Hop-Joint
I Went Up On The Mountain Top
I Whipped My Horse
I Will A Rise
I Will Be True The Livelong Day
I Will Bow And Be Simple
I Will Overcome
I Will Pray
I Will Put My Ship In Order
I Will Sing A Lullaby
I Will Tell You
I Winna Hae Tailor Nor Sutor
I Wish I Had Died In Egypt Lan'
I Wish I Had Died In Egypt Land
I Wish I Had Someone To Call My
   Own
I Wish I Have Had An Eagle Wing
I Wish I Was A Mole In The Ground
I Wish I Was Single
I Wish I Was Single Again
I Wish I Were A Bird Waltz
I Wish I Were A Crank
I Wish I Wuz A Little Rock
I Wish I'd Stayed In The Wagon
   Yard
I Wish They'd Do It Now
I Wish You Good Evening
I Wok Om A Mona
I Won't Stop Praying
I Wonder As I Wander
I Wonder When I Shall Be Married
I Wonder Why
I Woudn't Have An Old Man
I Would Not Be Alone
I Wrote My Love A Letter
I'd Like To Be In Texas
I'd Like To Be In Texas For The
   Round-Up In The Spring
I'll Ay Ca In By You Toun
I'll Be A Sergeant
I'll Be All Right
I'll Be All Smiles Tonight
I'll Be Beside You
I'll Be Ready When De Great Day
   Come
I'll Be Sleepin' In Mah Grave
I'll Be There
I'll Be There In The Morning
I'll Be With You When The Roses
   Bloom Again

Traditional (*Cont.*)

I'll Hang My Harp On A Willow
   Tree
I'll Hear De Trumpet Soun'
I'll Hear The Trumpet Sound
I'll Meet You In The Evening
I'll Not Marry At All
I'll Praise My Maker While I've
   Breath
I'll Remember You Love In My
   Prayers
I'll Tell Me Ma
I'll Tell You Where They Were
I'm A Dandy
I'm A Fisher
I'm A Goin' Down This Road
I'm A Going To Do All I Can
I'm A Going To Eat At The
   Welcome Table
I'm A Good Old Rebel
I'm A Little Teapot
I'm A Nachel-Bawn Reacher
I'm A Nut
I'm A Po' Lil' Orphan
I'm A Poor Stranger And Far From
   My Home
I'm A Rollin'
I'm A Scotch Bonny Wee One
I'm A Shepherd Of The Valley
I'm A Soldier Of The Cross
I'm A Stranger Here
I'm A Tight Little Irishman
I'm A Trav'ling To The Grave
I'm A-Looking For A Home
I'm A-Rolling
I'm Afloat
I'm Agoing To Join The Band
I'm An Everyday Witness
I'm Butt'ning
I'm Dying For Someone To Love Me
I'm Goin' Away
I'm Goin' Down To The River To Be
   Baptized
I'm Goin' Home On A Cloud
I'm Goin' To Sing
I'm Going Away To Texas
I'm Going Back With Jesus
I'm Going Down This Road Feeling
   Bad
I'm Going To Live With Jesus
I'm Going To Sing All The Way
I'm Gonna Leave Old Texas Now
I'm Gonna Sing When The Spirit
   Says Sing
I'm Gonna Sit At The Table Of The
   Lord
I'm Gonna Sit At The Welcome
   Table
I'm Gwine Down To Jordan Hallelu

Traditional (*Cont.*)

I'm Gwine See My Friends Agin
I'm Gwine Up To Heab'n Anyhow
I'm Just A-Goin' Over There
I'm Lookin' For My Jesus
I'm Nobody's Darling On Earth
I'm On My Way
I'm On My Way To The Freedom
   Land
I'm Rolling
I'm Runnin' On
I'm Seventeen Come Sunday
I'm So Glad
I'm The Man From Krakow
I'm Trampin'
I'm Troubled In Mind
I'm Troubled Lord
I'm Walkin' On Borrow'd Lan'
I'm Walking Wide
I'm Working On The Buildin'
I'm Worried Now But I Won't Be
   Worried Long
I'se Going' To Say Good-Bye
I'se Gwine Back To Dixie
I'se Gwine To Stan'
I'se Gwine To Weep No More
I'se Mighty Tired
I'se The B'y
I've A Jolly Sixpence
I've A Purse
I've Been A Wild Boy
I've Been A-List'ning All De Night
   Long
I've Been In De Storm So Long
I've Been In The Storm So Long
I've Been Lying In A Foxhole
I've Been Redeemed
I've Been Workin' On The Railroad
I've Been Working On The Railroad
I've Been Wukkin' On De Railroad
I've Been Wukkin' On The Railroad
I've Done What You Told Me To Do
I've Got A Home In The Rock Don't
   You See
I've Got A Robe
I've Got A Saviour That's Mighty To
   Keep
I've Got No Use For The Women
I've Got Sixpence
I've Got To Know
I've Heard Of A City Called Heaven
I've Just Come From The Fountain
I've Rambled This Country Both
   Earlye And Late
I've Set My Face For Zion's
   Kingdom
Iain Duinn Beir Orm
Ich Armes Kauzlein Kleine
Ich Armes Maidlein
Ich Far Dahin

Traditional (*Cont.*)

Ich Hort Ein Fraulein Klagen
Ich Hort Ein Sichelin Rauschen
Ich Kehre Wiederum
Ich Ritt Einmal Spazieren
Ich Schell Mein Horn In Jammers Ton
Ich Steh' An Deiner Krippe Hier
Ich Stund Auf Hohem Berge
Ida Red
Idaho Cowboy Dance, An
Idaho Jack
If A Donkey Comes To Tea
If Anybody Axes You Who Writ This Song
If Ever I Go A-Huntin'
If God Has Come
If He'd Be A Buckaroo
If Human Kindness Meets Return
If I Could
If I Got My Ticket Can I Ride
If I Had A Dog
If I Had Died When I Was A Babe
If I Had The Gov 'ner
If I Had The Wings
If I Have Mah Tickit Lawd
If I Sing Ahead Of You
If I Was A Blackbird
If I'd As Much Money As I Could Spend
If That High World
If Ye Would Hear
If You Can't Come Send One Angel Down
If You Catch Me Stealin'
If You Hit Me
If You Miss Me From The Back Of The Bus
If You Want To Know Where The Privates Are
If You Want To Write To Me
If You Were King
If Your Saddle Is Good And Tight
Il Court Il Court Le Furet
Il Est Ne Le Divin Enfant
Il Est Quelqu'un Sur Terre
Il Est Temps Cher Coeur De Me Marier
Il Est Un Boubeau Dans La Plaine
Il Etait Un' Bergere
Il Etait Un Petit Navire
Il Etait Une Bergere
Il Etait Une Fille
Il Etait Une Fille Une Fille D'Honneur
Il Nous Faut Des Tondeurs
Ilkley Moor Baht Hat
Ils Etaient Trois Petits Enfants
Im Himmel
Imaginary Trouble
Immaculate Mary
Immigration Song
Immortal Babe

Traditional (*Cont.*)

Immortal Invisible God Only Wise
In A Gondola
In A Manger
In A Manger He Is Sleeping
In A Rosebush
In A Seaport Town There Lived A Wealthy Merchant
In A Strange Land
In Amsterdam There Dwelt A Maid
In And Out The Dirty Windows
In Arkansas
In Autumn We Should Drink Boys
In Bahia
In Bed With The Major
In Bethlehem
In Bethlehem City
In Bethlehem City On Christmas-Day Morn
In Bethlehem That Fair City
In Bethlem's Manger
In Bibberly Town
In Bodmin Town
In Bright Mansions Above
In Dat Great Gittin-Up Mornin'
In De Mornin'
In Der Nacht
In Derry Vale
In Dulci Jubilo
In Evil Long I Took Delight
In Excelsis Deo
In Excelsis Gloria
In Exile
In Fading Light
In Filipino Land
In Good Old Colony Times
In Hawaii
In Heav'nly Love Abiding
In Heaven's Vault Above Me
In Heavenly Love Abiding
In Honor Of The Day
In Jersey City
In Jesus' Blood
In Joseph's Lovely Garden
In Kansas
In London Town Whar I Was Raised
In Memory Of James Lawrence Esquire
In Middle Winter They Set Out
In Midnight From Sleep
In My Bark Canoe
In My Little Cabin
In My Window Three Pots
In My Yard Violets
In October
In Old Kentuck In De Arternoon
In Old Pod-Auger Times
In Our Garden
In Our Little Park
In Oxford City
In Paradise Reposing
In Praise Of Music
In Praise Of Seafaring Men In Hope Of Good Fortune

Traditional (*Cont.*)

In Rome
In Some Lady's Garden
In Some Lonesome Graveyard
In Stiller Nacht
In Switzerland
In That New Jerusalem
In That Old Field
In The Army Of The Lord
In The Barracks
In The Bond
In The Church Yard
In The Days Of '76
In The Days When I Was Hard Up
In The Desert
In The Early Morning
In The Ending Of The Year
In The Evenin' Mama
In The Evening
In The Far East
In The Field So Early
In The Good Old Colony Days
In The Hills
In The Lane
In The Louisiana Lowlands
In The Meadow
In The Meadow Stood A Little Birch Tree
In The Merry Month Of May
In The Month Of October
In The Night Of Dark Eyes' Wonder
In The Parson's Yeard
In The Pines
In The Pit From Sin Set Free
In The Plaza
In The Shadow Of The Pines
In The Silence Of The Night
In The Silv'ry Moonlight
In The Stable
In The Styrian Land
In The Town
In The Town Of Oxford
In The Township Of Danville
In The Valley
In The Whole Town
In The Wint'ry Moonlight
In This Field
In This Lan'
In Those Twelve Days
In Town
In Vernali Tempore
In Vossevangen
In Yon Garden
In Yon Garden Fine An' Gay
Inca Pa Ta
Inchin' Along
Inching Along
Indeed Pretty Polly
Independence Day
Independent Lover, The
India, La
India's Burning Sands
Indian Brave, The

Traditional *(Cont.)*

Indian Flute, The
Indian March
Indian Song, An
Indian Song, The
Indian Tune, An
Indian War Song
Indignant Shake, An
Ine Vine Violet
Infant Holy Infant Lowly
Infant Lay Within A Shed, An
Infant So Gentle
Infantry, The
Infinite Light
Ingen Er Sa Trygg I Fare
Ingle Side, The
Ingo-Ango Fay
Ingrato Ya No Me Quieres
Inky Dinky Derby Town
Inn At Bethlehem, The
Inn, The
Innisfail
Innocent Maid
Ins Herz Gezinnt
Insbruck Ich Muss Dich Lassen
Inspired Bard, The
Instead Of Getting Married
Internationale, The
Into Paradise May The Angels Lead
Intoxicated Rat, The
Invitation
Invitation Of Love, The
Iowa Love Song
Ipharadisi
Ireland Poor Ireland
Ireland's Hurling Men
Irene
Irish Barber
Irish Carol
Irish Girl, The
Irish Jubilee, The
Irish Labourer
Irish Lady, The
Irish Mail Robber, The
Irish Molly-O
Irish Sixty-Ninth, The
Irish Trot, The
Irish Tune
Irish Wake, The
Irish Washerwoman, The
Irishman's Goldmine, The
Irishman's Observation On British
    Politics, An
Irishman's Observations On British
    Politics, An
Irishtown Crew, The
Is It To The Fields You're Going
Is It True
Is There Anybody Here
Is This The Way To Bethlehem
Isabeau S'y Promene
Island Sheiling Song, An
Islands Of Jamaica, The
Isle Of Beauty

Traditional *(Cont.)*

Issac-A-Bell And Hugh The Graeme
It Ain't Gonna Rain
It Builds Its Coral Palaces
It Came Upon A Midnight Clear
It Can't Be Done
It Cannot Be
It Happened On A Night In May
It Is A Thing Most Wonderful
It Is Finished Christ Hath Known
It Is Of A Rich Lady
It May Be De Las' Time
It Rains And It Hails
It Was A Mouse
It Was A 'for Our Rightfu King
It Was In The Moon Of Wintertime
It Was Poor Little Jesus
It Will Come It Will Come
It's A Lie
It's A Me O Lord
It's A Mean Old Scene
It's All The Same To Me
It's Cold Frosty Mornin'
It's Hard To Love
It's Lookin' Fer Railroad Bill
It's Me
It's Me O Lord
It's Raining It's Pouring
It's The Old Ship Of Zion
It's The Same The Whole World
    Over
It's The Syme The Whole World
    Over
It's Time To Stir Yourselves
Itabaiana
Itiskit Itasket
Ivon My Delight
Ivrogne Et Le Penitent, L'
Ivy And Holly
J A G Song
J'ai Cueilli La Belle Rose
J'ai Descendu Dans Mon Jardin
J'ai Du Bon Tabac
J'ai Entendu Le Rossignol Chanter
J'ai Fait Une Belle Trois Jours Trois
    Jours
J'ai Fait Tout Le Tour Du Grand
    Bois
J'ai Fait Trois Tours Du Grand Bois
J'ai Passe Devant La Porte
J'ai Un Beau Poisson D'or
J'ai Vu Le Loup Le Renard Le Lievre
J'entends Le Moulin
J'irai Vers Votre Ville
Ja Posejah Lubenice
Jack And Jill
Jack And Joe
Jack Be Nimble
Jack Dowling
Jack Haggerty
Jack Hall
Jack O'Diamonds

Traditional *(Cont.)*

Jack Robson
Jack Spratt
Jack Tar
Jack The Guinea Pig
Jack The Sailor
Jack The Sailor Boy
Jack Went A-Sailing
Jack Williams
Jack Wrack
Jack's Waltz
Jack-O'-Lantern
Jackaroe
Jackarse Eat It On The Way, The
Jackfish, The
Jackie Frazier
Jackie Jackie
Jackie Tar
Jacksons
Jacky Me Lad
Jacob Drink
Jacob Wolfe's Varsoviana
Jacob's Ladder
Jailer's Slumber Song, The
Jam Factory, The
Jam On Gerry's Rock, The
Jam On Gerry's Rocks
Jamaica Farewell
Jamais De La Vie
Jambalaya Gate
Jamele
James Bird
James Ervin
James Harris
James Herries
James Macdonald
James McDonald
James Munks's Confession
James Wayland
Jamestown Homeward Bound, The
Jamie Raeburn's Farewell
Jan Pieriewiet
Jane Jane
Jane Jess Jollander
Japanese Garden, A
Jardin D'amour, Le
Jarsey Jane
Jasmine Flower, The
Jawbone Song, The
Jawbone Walk, De
Jay Gould's Daughter
Jay-Bird Sittin' On A Hickory Limb
Jaycee Line, The
Je Caresserai La Belle Par Amitie
Je Le Mene Bien Mon Devidoir
Je M'ai Mis Aller Voir Une Jolie
    Brune
Je Me Leve A L'aurore Du Jour
Je Suis Un Jeune Homme
Je Te Donnerai Un Papier
    D'Aiguilles
Je Te Ferai Demoiselle

Traditional *(Cont.)*

Je Vais Mourir Sans Revoir A Mes
    Vieux Peres
Je Veux Me Marier
Je Voudrais Bien Me Marier
Jealous Lover, The
Jean Sur Son Divan
Jeanneton Prend Sa Faucille
Jeannette Isabella
Jeelie Piece Song, The
Jeepers
Jefferson And Liberty
Jeg Gikk En Tur
Jeg Gikk Meg Over Sjo Og Land
Jeg Synger Julekvad
Jehovah Has Triumph Messiah Is
    King
Jennie Jenkins
Jennie Johnson
Jenny Flow Gentle Rosemary
Jenny Jenkins
Jenny Jones
Jeorico
Jerusalem My Happy Home
Jerusalem The Golden
Jervis Bay, The
Jes' Lemme Tell You Whut De
    'Gator Done
Jesse James
Jessie Munroe
Jessie Of Ballington Brae
Jesu Dulcis Memoria
Jesu Lord Of Life And Glory
Jesu Tender Shepherd Hear Me
Jesucita, La
Jesus Ahatonhia
Jesus Born In Bethlea
Jesus Calls Us O'er The Tumult
Jesus Christ Is Ris'n Today
Jesus Christ S'habille En Pauvre
Jesus For Thee I Live
Jesus Goin' To Make Up My Dyin'
    Bed
Jesus Goin' To Make Up My Dying
    Bed
Jesus Gon Tuh Make Up My Dyin'
    Bed
Jesus Good Above All Other
Jesus Has Conquered Death
Jesus In Thy Dying Woes
Jesus In Thy Love Excelling
Jesus Is Crying
Jesus Is Risen From The Dead
Jesus Met The Woman
Jesus Name Of Wondrous Love
Jesus Of The Manger
Jesus Precioso
Jesus Rides That Milk-White Horse
Jesus Son Of God Most High
Jesus Son Of Mary Fount Of Life
Jesus Son Of Mary Fount Of Life
    Alone
Jesus The Very Thought Of Thee
Jesus Thou Divine Companion

Traditional *(Cont.)*

Jesus Walked
Jesus Was Born To Mary
Jeune Fille Au Gai Minois
Jew's Garden, The
Jiffery James And John
Jig
Jig Set Tune
Jim Along Jo
Jim Along Josey
Jim Along Josie
Jim Crow
Jim Haggerty's Story
Jim Jeffries' Schottische
Jim Oxford And His Salt Creek Girl
Jim Strange Killed Lula
Jimmie And Nancy
Jimmie Judd
Jimmie-Ma-Riley-Oh
Jimmy Loud
Jimmy Randal
Jimmy Randall
Jimmy Rose
Jimmy Sago Jackeroo
Jimmy Whalen
Jingle At The Window
Jingle Bells
Jinny Get Around
Jinny Git Around
Jinny Go Round And Around
Jinny Jan
Jinny Jenkins
Joan Come Kiss Me Now
Job
Jock O'Hazeldean
Jock O'Hazelgreen
Jock The Leg And The Merry
    Merchant
Jockey And Jenny
Jockey To The Fair
Jockey's Lament, The
Jocky Said To Jenny
Jocky Said To Jinnie
Joe Bowers
Joe Ferail Est Un Petit Negre
Joe Hill
Joe Livermore
Joe Turner Blues
Joe Yates' First Varsoviana
Joe Yates' Jig
Joe Yates Reel
Joe Yates' Second Varsoviana
Joe's Polka
Joe's Second Reel
Jog Along Till Shearing
Jog On Jog On
John Anderson My Jo
John B Sails
John Barleycorn
John Bramble
John Brown
John Brown Had A Little Indian
John Brown's Body

Traditional *(Cont.)*

John Bull's Taxes
John Cherokee
John Done Saw Dat Numbuh
John Done Saw That Number
John Doolan
John Dory
John Funston
John Gilbert
John Hardy
John Harty
John Henry
John Henry Blues
John Henry's Dead
John Hunter
John Jacob Jingleheimer Schmidt
John John
John Johnson's Wedding
John Of Hazelgreen
John Paul Jones
John Peel
John Randolph
John Reilly
John Riley
John Saw
John Saw De Angels
John Saw De Holy Numbah
John Saw The Holy Number
John Sold The Cow Well
John Thomas
John Was A-Writin
John's Gone Down On De Island
John's Gone To Hilo
Johnnie Bought A Ham
Johnnie Cope
Johnnie Go Milk The Bull
Johnnie Hopalong Varsoviana
Johnnie I Hardly Knew You
Johnnie Sands
Johnny And Betsy
Johnny Boker
Johnny Booker
Johnny Come A Long Time
Johnny Come Down To Hilo
Johnny Doolan's Cat
Johnny Doyle
Johnny Faa
Johnny Foran Mazurka
Johnny German
Johnny Graw
Johnny Has Gone For A Soldier
Johnny I Hardly Knew Ye
Johnny I Hardly Knew You
Johnny Is Gone For A Soldier
Johnny McCardner
Johnny Morgan
Johnny Must Fight
Johnny Of Hazelgreen
Johnny Riley
Johnny Ringo
Johnny Schmoker
Johnny Shall Have A New Bonnet
Johnny Stiles
Johnny The Sailor

Traditional *(Cont.)*

Johnny Troy
Johnny Won't You Ramble
Johnny's My Boy
Johnny's So Long At The Fair
Johnson Boys
Johnson Jinkson
Johnson's Mule
Johnston's Army Song
Johsua Fit De Battle Ob Jericho
Johsua Fit The Battle Of Jericho
Joli Tambour, Le
Jolie Blonde
Jolie Cane Cane Grise
Jolly Boatman
Jolly Farmer, The
Jolly Fisherman
Jolly Harrin', The
Jolly Jester, The
Jolly Miller Promenade
Jolly Miller, The
Jolly Old Roger
Jolly Old Saint Nicholas
Jolly Old St Nicholas
Jolly Pilote, The
Jolly Roving Tar
Jolly Sailor's True Description Of A
   Man-Of-War, The
Jolly Tune, A
Jolly Waggoner
Jongo
Jordan Am A Hard Road To Trabbel
Jornada, La
Jose And Rosita
Jose Cuervo
Josef Lieber Josef Mein
Joseph And Mary
Joseph Dearest
Joseph Dearest Joseph Mild
Joseph Dearest Joseph Mine
Joseph Mica Was Good Engineer
Joseph O Dear Joseph Mine
Joseph Was An Old Man
Josephine A Eu La Coqueluche
Joshua Ebenezer Fry
Joshua Fit De Battle
Joshua Fit De Battle Ob Jerico
Joshua Fit De Battle Of Jericho
Joshua Fit The Battle
Joshua Fit The Battle Of Jericho
Joshua Fought The Battle Of Jericho
Josua Fit De Battle 'roun' Jerico's
   Wall
Journeyman Tailor, The
Joy Dawned Again On Easter Day
Joy In Heaven
Joy In The Gates
Joy To The World
Joyful Blossoms
Joyful New Ballad, A
Joys Seven
Juanita
Juba
Juba Dis An' Juba Dat

Traditional *(Cont.)*

Jubalee
Jubilee
Judge Eternal Throned In Splendor
Judge Eternal Throned In Splendour
Judgment Day Is A Rollin' Around
Judgment Day Is Rolling Round
Judgment Will Find You So
Jug Of Punch, The
Juice Of The Forbidden Fruit, The
Juley
Julia
Julie Ann Johnson
Juliska
July Ann Johnson
Jump Jim Crow
Jumpin' Judy
June Lovely June
Jungle Rhythm
Just A Closer Walk With Thee
Just A Wee Doch-An-Dorris
Just As The Tide Was Flowing
Just From Dawson
Just One Girl For Me
Just One Girl Waltz
Just Set A Light
Jutlandish Dance Song
Kagda Ya Pyann
Kalinka
Kalioda Malioda
Kangaroo, The
Kanila
Kansas Boys
Kansas City #3
Karabli
Kari And Ola
Karo Song
Kate And The Cowhide
Katey Morey
Katherine Janfarie
Katherine Joffray
Katie Kearney
Katie Moore
Katy Cruel
Katy Dorey
Kedron
Keel Row, The
Keemo Kimo
Keep A Inchin' Along
Keep A-Inchin' Along Inchin' Along
Keep In The Middle Of The Road
Keep It Clean
Keep Me F'om Sinkin' Down
Keep Me From Sinkin' Down
Keep Me From Sinking Down
Keep My Skillet Good And Greasy
Keep That 'Possum Warm
Keep Thou Thine Image
Keep Yore Hand Upon The Chariot
Keep Your Eyes On The Prize
Keep Your Feet Still Geordie Hinney
Keep Your Garden Clean
Keep Your Hands On That Plow
Keep Your Lamps Trimmed

Traditional *(Cont.)*

Keeper, The
Keeper Would A Hunting Go, The
Keepers And Poachers
Kein Grosser Frend Auf Erden Ist
Kellswater
Kelly Gang, The
Kelly Gang Were Strong, The
Kelly Song
Kelly's Irish Brigade
Kelvingrove
Kemo Kimo
Kenny Wagner
Kenny Wagner's Surrender
Kentucky Feud Song, A
Kentucky Moonshiner
Kerrs Creek Varsoviana
Kerry Eviction, The
Kerry Recruit, The
Keshenever Pogrom
Ketzad M'Rakdin
Kevin Barry
Keys Of Canterbury, The
Keys Of Heaven, The
Keys Of My Heart, The
Ki Eshn'ra Shabbat
Ki-Wi Song, The
Kilkenny And The Giant Bodegh
Killer, The
Kind Maker Of The World
Kind Robin Loes Me
King And Queen
King Arthur Had Three Sons
King Beats The Drum, The
King Christian
King Emanuel
King George The 3rd's Minuet
King Herod And The Cock
King Jesus Built Me A House Above
King Jesus Is A Lis'enin'
King Jesus Is A-Listening
King John And The Bishop
King Of England
King Of France, The
King Of Love My Shepherd Is, The
King Of Names, The
King Of The Martyr's Noble Band
King Of The River
King Roger
King Rooster
King William Was King George's
   Son
King William Was King James's Son
Kingdom, The
Kings And The Shepherds, The
Kings Mountain
Kiso-Bushi
Kiss At The Door, A
Kiss Me Quick And Go
Kissing Lasses Of Yarmouth, The
Kitchen Kops
Kitchen Police
Kites Are Flying
Kitty Clover

Traditional *(Cont.)*

Kitty Gray
Kitty Kitty Casket
Kitty Magee
Kitty My Love Will You Marry Me
Kitty O'Noory
Kjaere Du Me Randi
Kjaere Gud
Kjaerlighet Fra Gud
Kjerringa Med Staven
Klein Klein Kleuterken
Kling Glockchen
Klokkene Sma
Knee-Bone
Kneels At The Feet Of His Friends
Knick Knack Cadillac
Knickerbocker Line, The
Knight And The Maiden, The
Knight's Appeal, The
Knock A Man Down
Knocking
Knoxville Girl, The
Koa-Lia
Kobesioniaz
Kol Dodi
Kol Nidre
Kola Run, The
Kolo
Kolyada
Konfirmazioniaz
Kookaburra
KP Guy, The
KP's Are Scrubbing Along, The
Kristallen Den Fina
Kuckaburro
Kuhreigen
Kum Aher Du Filizof
Kum Aher Du Filozof
Kum Ba Yah
Kum Bachur Atzel
Kum-Bah-Yah
Kumbaya
Kume Fum Geselle Min
Kurikinga
Kwan Tsen Tsen
Kye Kye Kule
Kyerem
Kyrie
Kyrie Eleison
L'Dovid Boruch
La'le Padraic 1913
La-Bas Sur Ces Montagnes
La-Haut Sur Ces Montagnes
Laang Barn Dance, The
Lace Maker, The
Ladie Gay, A
Ladies In The Dinin' Room
Lads Of Kilkenny, The
Lady And Her Page, The
Lady And The Dragoon, The
Lady Anne Bothwell's Lament
Lady Coventry's Minuet
Lady Elspat

Traditional *(Cont.)*

Lady Franklin's Lament For Her
 Husband
Lady Gay
Lady Isabel And The Elf Knight
Lady Ishbel And The Elfin-Knight
Lady Leroy
Lady Leroy, The
Lady Margaret
Lady Mary
Lady O'Gight, The
Lady Of Carlisle, The
Lady Of Carlysle
Lady Of The Lake, The
Lady Tartina, The
Lady Who Loved A Swine, The
Laird Abeen The Dee, The
Laird O' Drum, The
Laird O'Linne, The
Laird O'Meldrum And Tibbie
 Douglas
Laird Of Drum, The
Laird Of Southland's Courtship, The
Laissez-Moi Cha La Lise
Lake Of Pontchartrain, The
Lam' Done Been Down Here An'
 Died, De
Lamb Of God, The
Lambkin
Lame Soldier, The
Lament
Lament For An Absent Lover
Lament Of The Border Widow
Lamkin
Lammen Har Jag
Lamp Of Our Feet Whereby We
 Trace
Lancers Tune
Land League's Advice To The
 Tenant Farmers Of Ireland
Land O' The Leal, The
Land Of Liberty
Land Of Pleasure
Land Of The Midnight Sun
Landlord Fill The Flowing Bowl
Lane Country Bachelor, The
Lane County Bachelor, The
Lang Johnny More
Langt Udi Skoven
Lanky Long Legs Mazurka
Lannigan's Ball
Lanterns Glowing
Laquelle Marierons-Nous
Laredo
Laredo Mexican Folk Song
Larga Jornada, De
Largy Line, The
Lark In The Clear Air, The
Lark In The Morn
Lark In The Morning
Lark In The Morning, The
Lasca
Lass From The Low Countree, The

Traditional *(Cont.)*

Lass O'Glenshee
Lass O' Isla, The
Lass Of Glenshee, The
Lass Of Merthyr, The
Lass Of Mohee, The
Lass Of Richmond Hill, The
Lass Of Roch Royal
Lasst Uns Alle Froehlich Sein
Lasst Uns Singen
Last Band, The
Last Call For Assistance
Last Call, The
Last Fairy, The
Last Farewell, The
Last Fierce Charge, The
Last Rose Of Summer, The
Last Rumba, The
Last Sunday Morning Last Sunday
 Morning
Last Trip In The Fall
Last Wagon, The
Last Whig Song, The
Last Year Was A Fine Crap Year
Late Last Night
Latzika And Marishka
Laughing Ho Ho
Laughing Lisa
Laundry Song, A
Lauriger Horatius
Lauterbach
Lauterbach Song
Lavender Company, The
Lavender Cowboy, The
Lavender's Blue
Lavinia's Parlour
Lawd I Want Two Wings
Lawlan' Jenny
Lawyer, The
Lay Dis Body Down
Lay Down Late
Lay Down Your Staffs O Shepherds
Lay Me Low
Lay Ten Dollars Down
Lazy Cat, The
Lazy Farmer, The
Lazy John
Lazy Mary Will You Get Up
Lea Rig, The
Lead A Man Di Dee O Lead A Man
Lead Me To The Rock
Lead Us Heavenly Father
Lead Us Lord
Leaf By Leaf The Roses Fall
Leanin' On Dat Lamb
Leanin' On De Lord
Leaning On The Lamb
Learned Judge
Leather Breeches
Leave Her Johnnie Leave Her
Leave Her Johnny
Leaver Her Johnny Leave Her
Leaves Oh

Traditional *(Cont.)*

Leaving Of Liverpool
Leaving Old England
Lechayim
Leddle Bit A Niggeh An' Great Big
    Toe
Leezie Lindsay
Left Or Right
Legend Of Fair Eleanor And The
    Brown Gal, The
Legende Du Saint Livre, La
Leggo Me Han'
Lenachan's Farewell
Leo Frank And Mary Phagan
Leprechaun, The
Leron Leron Sinta
Lesbia Hath A Beaming Eye
Lesser Joys Of Mary, The
Let All Mortal Flesh Keep Silence
Let All Mortal Flesh Keep Silence
    And With Fear And Trembling
Let All That Are Mirth Inclined
Let All That Are To Mirth Inclined
Let All Things Now Living
Let De Heb'n-Light Shine On Me
Let Erin Remember
Let Erin Remember The Days Of Old
Let Me Carry Your Cross For Ireland
    Lord
Let Me Cross Your Threshold
Let Me Fly
Let Me Have Mother's Gospel
Let Me Keep Faith
Let Me Ride
Let My Little Light Shine
Let Our Gladness Know No End
Let Saints On Earth In Concert Sing
Let The Church Roll On
Let The Heaven Light Shine On Me
Let The Milk-Pail Stand Still
Let The Song Go Round The Earth
Let Thy Blood In Mercy Poured
Let Us Be Glad Because Of Words
Let Us Break Bread Together
Let Us Cheer The Weary Traveler
Let Us Cheer The Weary Traveller
Let Us Go O Shepherds
Let Us Now Our Voices Raise
Let Us Praise Thee
Let Us Quaff
Let Us Sing To The God Of Salvation
Let Us Sing Together
Let Us With A Gladsome Mind
Let Your Back And Side Go Bare
Let's Build A Bungalow
Let's Go To De Buryin'
Let's Go To The Woods
Letania Del Nino Dios
Lets Be Merry
Letter Edged In Black, The
Letter Writer, The
Levee Camp Blues
Levee Camp Holler
Levee Moan

Traditional *(Cont.)*

Levee Song
Lewie Gordon
Lexington Murder, The
Li Fal La And Li Fal Li
Li'l Boy Name David
Li'l Liza Jane
Li'l Liza Loves You
Libe A Libe, A
Liberty Song, The
Lice In Jail
Lie Low
Lieb Heimatland Ade
Lieb Nachtigall Wach Auf
Liebe Maienzeit, Die
Liebesklage
Liebeskummer
Liebesstolz
Liebste Bule Den Ich Han, Der
Lied Vom Feldmarschall, Das
Lied Zum Einzug Der Braut
Life In California
Life Is A Toil
Life Let Us Cherish
Life Of Georgie, The
Life On The Ocean Wave, A
Life On The Raging Canal, A
Life That's Free, The
Lift A Glass
Lift Up Your Heads Ye Mighty Gates
Lift Up Your Hearts
Lift Your Eyes Men Of Greece
Light As A Swallow
Light Of Other Days, The
Lights Of London Town, The
Light's Abode Celestial Salem
Lighten The Darkness Of Our Life's
    Long Night
Lightly Row
Lights In The Quarters Burnin'
    Mighty Dim
'Ligion So Sweet
Like A Nightingale
Like Pretty Birds
Lilies Are White
Lille Petter Edderkopp
Lille Postbud
Lilli Burlero
Lillibullero
Lily Lee
Lily Of Arkansas, The
Lily Of The Valley, The
Lily Of The West, The
Lily Song, The
Limber Zeal
Limey Sailor Song
Lincoln
Lincoln And Liberty
Lincolnshire Dance
Lincolnshire Poacher, The
Link O'Day
Linstead Market
Lion's Den
Lippai

Traditional *(Cont.)*

Liptitou, La
Lipto
Lis'en To De Lam's
Lisette
List To The Bells
Listen Lordlings
Listen Lordlings Unto Me
Listen Partner Listen
Listen To The Angel's Shoutin'
Listen To The Angels
Listen To The Cuckoo
Listen To The Lambs
Little Baby Hear Me Singing
Little Bee, The
Little Bell, The
Little Betty Blue
Little Billee
Little Bingo
Little Bird At My Window
Little Bird Little Bird
Little Bird, The
Little Birdie
Little Birds' Ball, The
Little Bit Of Sugar
Little Black Train Is A Comin'
Little Black Train, The
Little Blossom
Little Blue Ben
Little Bo-Peep
Little Boxes
Little Boy Blue
Little Brass Wagon
Little Brown Bulls, The
Little Brown Jug
Little Brown Jug Polka
Little Child In Manger Bare
Little Child On Earth Was Born, A
Little Children Wake And Listen
Little Cottage, The
Little David
Little David Play On Yo' Harp
Little David Play On Your Harp
Little Eskimo, The
Little Family, The
Little Farmer, The
Little Fish, The
Little Gal At Our House
Little Girl
Little Girl Don't You Cry
Little Gobbelin
Little Grove All In Green
Little Horse Of Mine
Little Jack Horner
Little Jack Horner And Little Miss
    Muffet
Little Jesus, The
Little Joe The Wrangler
Little Joe The Wrangler's Sister Nell
Little Johnny
Little Johnny Green
Little Lady Rose
Little Lady Water, The
Little Lame Girl

Traditional *(Cont.)*
Little Maggie
Little Maid Milking Her Cow, The
Little Mary Phagan
Little Massie Grove
Little Matthy Groves
Little Miss Muffet
Little Miss Muffett
Little Mohee
Little Mohee, The
Little More Cider Too, A
Little More Faith In Jesus, A
Little Moses
Little Musgrave And Lady Barnard
Little Nightingale
Little Nut Tree, The
Little Old Log Cabin In The Lane,
 The
Little Old Sod Shanty
Little Old Sod Shanty On My Claim
Little One Waltz, The
Little Pappoose Song, A
Little Pigs, The
Little Pine Tree
Little Place I Love, The
Little Polly Flinders
Little Red Hen, The
Little Red Lark, The
Little Robin Redbreast
Little Rosebud Casket
Little Rosewood Casket, The
Little Sailboat, The
Little Sally Waters
Little Seaside Villages, The
Little Ship
Little Ship, The
Little Shoe Black, The
Little Short Legs
Little Sir William
Little Snowball Bush
Little Son Hugh
Little Streak O' Lean An' A Little
 Streak O' Fat
Little Sweet One
Little Talk Wid Jesus Makes It Right,
 A
Little Talk With Jesus, A
Little Things
Little Tom Tinker
Little Tommy Tinker
Little Tommy Tittlemouse
Little Tommy Tucker
Little Trumpet
Little Turtle Dove, The
Little Vanny
Little Vessel, A
Little Wales
Little Wat Ye Wha's A-Comin'
Little Wee Croodin Doo
Little Wheel A-Turnin' In My Heart
Little Wheel A-Turning In My Heart
Little White Dove
Little Willie
Little Willie And Mary

Traditional *(Cont.)*
Little Wood, The
Little Wooden Shoes
Live A Humble
Liverpool Girls, The
Liverpool John
Liverpool Lullaby
Liverpool Play
Liverpool Song, The
Livin' Humble
Living Out Of Doors
Liza Anne
Liza Jane
Liza Lee
Llewelyn's Grave
Llewelyn's Last Appeal
Llorona, La
Lluvia, La
Lo How A Rose E'Er Blooming
Lo The Earth Is Ris'n Again
Loakie's Boat
Lobby-Loo
Loch Lomond
Loch Tay Boat Song
Locks And Bolts
Lofty Giant, The
Log Cabin And Hard Cider
 Candidate, The
Logger's Boast, The
Logie O'Buchan
Lolita
Lolly Too Dum
Lolly-Too-Dum-Day
Lolotte
Lomir Ale Zingen A Zemerl
Lomir Zich Iberbetn
London Bridge
London Street Call
London Town
Londonderry Air
Londonderry Love Song, A
Lone Star Trail, The
Lonely Banna Strand
Lonely Castle
Lonely Is The Hogan
Lonely Louisa
Lonely Shepherd, The
Lonesome Dove, The
Lonesome Grove, The
Lonesome Road, The
Lonesome Roving Wolves, The
Lonesome Scenes Of Winter
Lonesome Valley
Long Black Veil
Long De La Mer Jolie, Le
Long Des Rives, Le
Long Gone
Long Gone Blues
Long I Have Woven
Long John
Long Lankin Or Young Lambkin
Long Live The Girls Of Canada
Long Lonesome Road
Long Long Ago

Traditional *(Cont.)*
Long Summer Day
Long Tail Blue, The
Long Time Ago
Long Time Ago, A
Long Years Ago In Palestine
Longing For Home
Looby Loo
Look At That Darky There Mr Banjo
Look At The Sun
Look Away In The Heaven
Look Away Into Heaven
Look Down That Lonesome Road
Look Down To Us St Joseph
Look Hussars Are Marching
Look Mister Cuckoo
Look Where De Train Done Gone
Look-A How Dey Done My Lord
Looking For A Ship
Lookit Here
Looky There Now
Looky Yonder Where De Sun Done
 Gone
Loom, The
Lord Aboyne
Lord At First Did Adam Make, The
Lord Bateman
Lord Bateman's Castle
Lord Batesman
Lord Beichan
Lord Bless Thee, The
Lord Christ When First Thou Cam'st
 To Earth
Lord Christ When First Thou
 Came'st To Men
Lord Dismiss Us With Thy Blessing
Lord Ellenwater
Lord Gregory
Lord Heal Him
Lord Henry And Lady Margaret
Lord I Want To Be A Christian
Lord I Want To Be A Christian In-A
 My Heart
Lord I Wish I Had A Come
Lord I Would Own Thy Tender Care
Lord In His Righteousness Judgeth
 The People, The
Lord In His Righteousness, The
Lord Is My Shepherd, The
Lord It's All Almost Done
Lord Jesus From Thy Throne Above
Lord Jesus Think On Me
Lord John's Murder
Lord Lord You've Been So Good To
 Me
Lord Lovel
Lord Lovell
Lord Lover
Lord Make Me More Holy
Lord Of All Being Throned Afar
Lord Of All Hopefulness
Lord Of Gordon's Three Daughters,
 The
Lord Of Life And All Creation

Traditional *(Cont.)*

Lord Of The Dance
Lord Of The Sunlight
Lord Randal
Lord Rendal Song Of Somerset
Lord Rendall
Lord Saltoun And Annachie
Lord Thomas And Fair Ellender
Lord Thou Hast Searched Me
Lord To Thy Dear Cross We Flee
Lord Ullin's Daughter
Lord We Have Come At Your Own
Lord Who Throughout These Forty
    Days
Lord Whose Love Through Humble
    Service
Lord Will Come And Not Be Slow,
    The
Lord's Been Here, The
Lord's My Shepherd, The
Lord's Prayer, The
Lorde Natus Ex Parentis
Lorito Lorito
Loss Of The Amphitrite
Loss Of The Earl Of Moira
Loss Of The Evelyn Marie, The
Loss Of The Philosophy
Loss Of The Ramillies, The
Lost Jimmie Whalen, The
Lost Johnny Doyle, The
Lost Love Waltz
Lost On The Lady Elgin
Lost Youth, The
Lou Baylero
Loudly Proclaim
Louis Kossuth
Louisiana Girls
Louisiana Lowlands
Louse Song
Lousy Tailor, The
Love
Love An' Serve De Lord
Love And Blessing
Love By The Day
Love Came Down At Christmas
Love Divine All Love Excelling
Love Divine All Loves Excelling
Love Feast In Heaven
Love Henry
Love I Come Again
Love In Old Age
Love Is Come Again
Love Love Love
Love Me Little Love Me Long
Love Of God Shave, The
Love Oracle
Love Robbie
Love Somebody
Love Somebody Yes I Do
Love Song
Love Thoughts
Love Unto Death
Love Will Find Out The Way
Love's Lament In Mid-Autumn

Traditional *(Cont.)*

Love's My Permit
Love's Parting Or Jamie And Mary
Love's Reply
Love's Request
Lovely Ann
Lovely Annie
Lovely April
Lovely Banks Of Mourne, The
Lovely Evening
Lovely Evening, The
Lovely Glenshesk
Lovely Infant Dearest Saviour
Lovely Joan
Lovely Lace Weaver, The
Lovely Maiden
Lovely Meadows
Lovely Molly
Lovely Moon
Lovely Nancy
Lovely On The Water
Lovely Rose, The
Lovely Rosebush
Lovely Sky Of Christmas Eve
Lovely Willie
Lovely Willie's Sweetheart
Lover's Cuckoo, The
Lover's Farewell, A
Lover's Ghost, The
Lover's Tasks, The
Lover's Wishes, The
Loving Kindness
Low Back'd Car, The
Low Bridge Everybody Down
Low Down Chariot
Low In The Lowlands Low
Low-Backed Car, The
Low-Down Lonesome Low, The
Lower The Boat Down
Lowlands
Lowlands Low, The
Lowlands O' Holland, The
Lowlands Of Holland, The
Lowly Bethlehem
Lucky Jim
Lucky Sailor, The
Lucumi
Lucy Clark's Exaltation
Lucy Locket
Lucy Long
Lucy Neal
Luisella's Garden
Luke Oakley's Polka
Lula Gal
Lulajze Jezuniu
Lullabies
Lullaby
Lullaby Jesu
Lullaby Little One
Lullaby Of Mary And The Angels
Lullay Thou Little Tiny Child
Lully Lullay
Lully Lully Lu

Traditional *(Cont.)*

Lulu
Lumber Camp Song, The
Lumbering Boy
Lumberman's Alphabet, The
Lustily Lustily
Lustukru
Lute-Book Lullaby
Lydia Pinkham
Lying Tale, A
Lynchburg Town
'M Faca Sibh A' Mhaighdean
    Bheusach
M'amie Que J'Aime Tant
M'iteagan Is M'eoin Is M'uighean
Ma Belle M'a Donne Un Capot
Ma Belle Marianne
Ma Belle Si Tu Voulais
Ma Is J'ai Une Belle Ici
Ma Nish Tana
Ma Normandie
Ma Rosalie M'est Infidele
Ma Teodora
Ma Y'Didus
Ma Yafim Halelot
Macdonald's Farm
Machine-Guns They Rattle
Macpherson's Lament
Mad 'moiselle From Armentieres
Madam I Have Come A-Courting
Madame Arnaud Ape Donner Bal
Madame Baptiste Tirez-Moi Pas
Madame Donnez-Moi Lida, La
Maddalena
Madeleine
Madeline
Mademoiselle From Armentieres
Maggic Mac
Maggie Lauder
Maggie Mae
Maggie Was A Lady
Magi Draw Near
Magic
Magic Jug, The
Magpie's Jig, The
Magyar Leaders
Maid And The Magpie, The
Maid And The Soldier, The
Maid Freed From The Gallows, The
Maid I Love, The
Maid I Would Marry, The
Maid In Bedlam, The
Maid In Sorrow, The
Maid Of Aghadowey, The
Maid Of Amsterdam
Maid Of Fainey, The
Maid Of Leko, The
Maid Of Mourne Shore, The
Maid Of Sker, The
Maid Of The Cowdenknowes, The
Maid Of The Mill, The
Maid Of The Oaks
Maid On The Shore, The

Traditional (*Cont.*)

Maid's Complaint, The
Maiden And I, A
Maiden In The Garden, The
Maiden Tell Me
Maiden's Initiation
Maiden's Lament, The
Maiden's Lamentation, The
Maiden's Prayer, The
Maiden's Romance
Maids At Eighteen
Mail Boat Leinster, The
Mainsail Haul
Mairi Nic A Phi
Majestic Sweetness Sits Enthroned
Major Andrews' Execution
Make Me A Cowboy Again
Make Me A Pallet Down On Your
    Floor
Make New Friends
Make The Rafters Ring
Make We Joy
Maker Of The Sun And Moon, The
Mal D'amour Est Une Maladie, Le
Malaguena, La
Malaguena Salerosa
Malbrouck
Malbrough
Malbrough S'en Va-T-En Guerre
Malhaya La Concina
Maliseet Love-Song
Mama Gave Me A Little Husband
Mama I Saw A Sailboat
Mama Send Me
Maman Les P'tits Bateaux
Maman M'a Donnee En Mariage
Mambru
Mamma Dinah
Mamma's Gone To The Mail Boat
Mamma's Love
Mamman Donne Moi Un Pitit Mari
Mammy Loves
Mammy's Little Boy
Mampulorio, El
Man From Mullingar, The
Man Goin' Round
Man In The Moon, The
Man Lives Not For Himself Alone
Man Of Birmingham Town, The
Man Of Constant Sorrow
Man On The Flying Trapeze, The
Man Smart Woman Smarter
Man With The Big Hat, The
Man Without A Woman, A
Man You Don't Meet Every Day, A
Man's A Man For A' That, A
Mananitas, Las
Mandandiran
Mandolin Song, The
Mangoe Vert
Mangwani Mpulele
Mantle Of Green, The
Mantle So Green

Traditional (*Cont.*)

Mantle So Green, The
Many And Great O God
Many And Great O God Are Thy
    Works
Many Roads
Many Surprises
Many T'ousands Go
Many Thousan' Gone
Many Thousand Gone
Maple Leaf Forever, The
Marais Bouleur Waltz
Marbhrann Do Dh'fhear Airigh
    Mhuilinn
March, A
March Down To Jerdon
March Down To Jordan
March March Comrades All
March Of The Kings, The
March Of The Men Of Harlech, The
March Of The Three Kings
March On
March Song Of The Workers
March Wind
March Winds
Marche Des Rois, La
Marching On Georgia
Marching Saints, The
Marching Song
Marching Through Georgia
Marching Through Georgia Parody
Marching To Pretoria
Marching Together
Marching Tune
Marching Up The Heavenly Road
Margaritkes
Margot Dress The Vines
Mari Debarrasse De Sa Femme, Le
Maria Bewell
Maria Della Glisch
Maria Durch Ein Dornwald Ging
Maria Mari
Maria Und Joseph
Maria Wandered Through A Wood
Maria-La-O
Mariage Anglais, Le
Mariage Du Papillon, Le
Marianina
Marianne Goes To The Mill
Marianne's Loves
Marianni
Maricutana, La
Marie Mine
Marine Corps Flying Song
Marine Hymn
Marine Song
Mariner, The
Marines' Hymn
Marines' Hymn, The
Marion Lee
Mariposita
Market Day
Marko And The Three Germans
Marlborough

Traditional (*Cont.*)

Marlbrouk
Marlene
Maros Rivers Water
Marquise Empoisonnee
Married Man Gonna Keep Your
    Secret
Married Man, The
Married Me A Wife
Marrowbone Itch, The
Marthy Had A Baby
Martin Prit Sa Serpe
Martin Said To His Man
Martin Tim And Dan
Martyre De Sainte Catherine, La
Martyre De Sainte Catherine, Le
Mary An' Martha Jes' Gone 'long
    To Ring Dem Charmi
Mary And Martha
Mary Ann
Mary Blane
Mary Contrary And Little Boy Blue
Mary Dear Mother Of Jesus
Mary Dear Mother Of Jesus Divine
Mary Golden Tree, The
Mary Griffin
Mary Had A Baby
Mary Had A Baby Yes Lord
Mary Had A Boychild
Mary Had A Little Lamb
Mary Had A William Goat
Mary Hamilton
Mary Jane Waltz, The
Mary L Mackay, The
Mary Mary Quite Contrary
Mary Nail
Mary O' The Dee
Mary Of The Glacier
Mary Of The Wild Moor
Mary On The Mountain
Mary On The Wild Moor
Mary See Our Woe
Mary She Did Dream A Dream
Mary Was A Red Bird
Mary Wept An' Marthy Moaned
Mary What's The Matter
Mary Wore Three Links Of Chain
Mary's Ass
Mary's Farewell
Mary's Lamb
Mary's Lullaby
Mary's Resting Place
Mary's Wandering
Maryland My Maryland
Massa Gwine To Sell Us Tomorrow
Massa Had A Yaller Gal
Massacre Of The Monks, The
Master McGrath
Masters In The Hall
Masters In This Hall
Matilda
Matin En Me Levant, Le
Matrimonio Desigual, El

Traditional (*Cont.*)

Matt Hyland
Matthew Mark Luke And John
Matthy Groves
Matty Grove
Matty Groves
Matvise
Maumariee Vengee Par Son Frere, La
May Be The Las' Time I Don't
   Know
May Be The Last Time I Don't Know
   Time
May Breezes
May Carol
May Day Carol
May Day Garland
May I Woo The Lassie
May Morning Dew, The
May Our Poland Never Perish
May Pole Song
May Pole, The
May Queen, The
May Song
May The Grace Of Christ Our
   Saviour
May The Longtime Sun Shine
Mayday
Mayday Weather
Maykomashmalon
Mayn Yingele
Mazlim's Mill
Mazurek
Mazurka
McAfee's Confession
McCaffery
McCarthy's Song
McNab's Island
McSorley's Twins
Me And My Captain
Me Bless The Cross
Me Father Is A Lawyer In England
Me Gustan Todas I'm Fond Of All
   Girls
Me One Man
Me Voici Me Voila
Me 'n' My Baby An' My Baby's
   Frien'
Meadowland
Meadowlands
Meadows And Woods
Meadows Green
Meagher's Children
Meda Wawa Ase
Medics' Chant, The
Medrcy Swiata
Meek Old Crow, The
Meeks Murder, The
Meet Me Tonight
Meeting And Parting
Meeting Of The Waters Of The
   Hudson And Erie
Meeting Of The Waters, The
Megan's Daughter

Traditional (*Cont.*)

Mein Madel Hat Einen Rosenmund
Meisiesfontein
Melchior And Balthazar
Melissa
Mellom Bakkar Og Berg
Mellow Gal
Members Don't Git Weary
Memorial Song
Memories
Men And Children Everywhere
Men Of Harlech
Men's Clothes I Will Put On
Mending Shoes
Meng Chiang Nyu's Lament
Menteries, Les
Menybol Ar Angyal
Merchant Shipping Act, The
Merchant's Carol, The
Merchant's Only Son, The
Mercy Beauty
Mere Michel, La
Mermaid, The
Merrily Merrily
Merrily We Roll Along
Merry Christmas
Merry Go The Bells
Merry Golden Tree, The
Merry Green Broom Fields
Merry Lark
Merry Music
Merry-Go-Round, The
Merrymaking
Mess Call
Message
Message Came To A Maiden Young
Message, The
Messenger, The
Messiah Is Born
Metamorphosis
Methodist Pie
Meunier Tu Dors
Mexican Hat Dance
Mezinke Oysgegebn, Di
Mi Caballo Blanco
Mi Chacra
Mi Compadre Mono
Mi Escuelita
Mi Nenito Nene
Mi Pollera
Mi Y'Malel
Mi Yitneni Of
Michael
Michael Davitt 1881
Michael Finnigin
Michael Row De Boat Ashore
Michael Row The Boat
Michael Row The Boat Ashore
Michael Roy
Michalku
Michie Banjo
Michie Baziro
Michie Preval
Michigan-I-O

Traditional (*Cont.*)

Mick Murphy's Hornpipe
Mick Pilley's Schottische
Mickey Free On The Fashions
'Mid Ox And Ass
Midnight On The Ocean
Midnight Special, De
Midnight Special, The
Midnight Star, The
Midnight Train And 'Fo' Day Train,
   The
Midnight Waltz
Midsummer Eve
Midsummer Night
Migrant's Letter To His Mother
Mike
Mikkel Rev
Milatraisse Courri Dans Bal
Milk And De Veal
Milking Croon, A
Milking Croon I
Milking Croon II
Milkmaid, The
Milkmaids, The
Milky White Way
Mill In The Forest, The
Mill O' Tiftie's Annie
Mill, The
Mill-Wheel, The
Miller Of Devon, The
Miller Of The Dee, The
Miller, The
Miller You Sleep
Miller's Daughter, The
Miller's Daughters, The
Miller's Three Sons, The
Miller's Will, The
Million Stars Are Shining
Mince Pie Or A Pudding, A
Mind Your Bittnet
Mind Your Eye
Miner's Lifeguard
Minerva, The
Mingo Mountain
Minka
Minnesinger's Lied
Minstrel Boy, The
Minstrel's Return, The
Minuet De La Cour
Minum Kultani
Mir Gliebt Im Grunen Maien
Mirabeau
Miracle Of Saint Nicholas, The
Miracle Of The Cock, The
Miraculous Harvest, The
Miren Cuantas Luces
Mirror, The
Mis Flores Negras
Misere, La
Misere Qui Mene Le Negre Dans
   Bois
Miserere
Mishito, El
Miska And Panni

Traditional *(Cont.)*

Miss Bailey
Miss Dinah
Miss Gordon Of Gight
Miss Lucy Long
Miss Mary Belle
Miss Mary Jane
Missee Hopalong Varsoviana
Missionary Baptist Song
Missy Mouse And Mister Frog
Mistaken Thought
Mistenlaire, The
Mister Banjo
Mister Brown
Mister Congressman
Mister Frog
Mister Rabbit
Mister Stormalong
Mistletoe Bough, The
Mistletoe Carol, A
Mistress Mary Quite Contrary
Mistress More
Mit A Nodl On A Nodl
Mit Lieb Bin Ich Umfangen
Mit Lust Tet Ich Ausreiten
Mitchel's Address
Mitherless Bairn, The
Mitten Wir Im Leben Sind
Mixed-Up Old Man
Mizerna Cicha
Mizmor L'David
Mo Chubhrachan
Mo Ghaol An Te Nach Diobair Mi
Mo Run Ailein Ho Ho
Mo Thaobh Fodham
Mo-Oz Tsur Y'Shuoisi
Mo-Te-A-Pe Promene Sur La Rue
    Commune
Moanfully In Tarjan
Moanin'
Mobile Bay
Mocking Bird, The
Mockingbird
Mold Me Lord
Mole In The Ground
Mollie Vaughn
Molly And I
Molly And Me And The Baby
Molly Baun
Molly Baun Lavery
Molly Brannigan
Molly Lovely Molly
Molly Malone
Molly My Dear
Molly Put The Kettle On
Molly Van
Moluron He
Mon Abeille Volage
Mon Amour Est Barre Dans
    L'armoire
Mon Bebe Est Malade
Mon Coq Est Mort
Mon Mari Est Bien Malade

Traditional *(Cont.)*

Mon Mari Le Sot Est Un Buveur
    D'Eau
Mon Per' M'envoi-T'a L'herbe
Mon Pere Avait Cinq Cents Moutons
Mon Pere M'a Donne Un Mari
Mon Pere M'a Mariee A Un
    Vieillard
Monastary Legend
Mond Der Stet Am Hochsten, Der
Monday Mornin' Way 'fo' Day
Monday Morning
Mone Member Mone
Money In Both Pockets
Money Is King
Monkey And The Baboon, The
Monkey Married The Baboon's Sister
Monkey Motions
Monkey Settin' On De End Of A
    Rail
Monkey's Wedding, The
Monks' March, The
Monks Of Bangor's March, The
Monsieur Le Cure
Montezuma
Months Of The Year
Moo-Lee Flower, The
Moo-Lee-Hua
Moon, The
Moon Behind The Hill, The
Moon Shines Bright, The
Moonan Mazurka, The
Moonan Polka, The
Moonlight
Moonlight Attack On Curtin's House
    1885
Moonlight Walk, The
Moonshiner
Moorlough Mary
Moree Spider, The
Moreton's Bay
Mormon Battalion Song, The
Mormon Crossing, The
Morning Has Broken
Morning In Marken
Morning In Tyrol
Morning Song
Morning Star
Morning Train
Mornington Football Tragedy
    Fragment
Morris Dance, The
Morrissey Again The Field
Morrissey And The Buffalo Boy
Morrissey And The Russian Sailor
Mortar Song, The
Morvudd
Mos' Done Toilin' Here
Mossback, The
Most Done Ling'rin Here
Mot'l
Mother
Mother Ann's Plum Cake

Traditional *(Cont.)*

Mother Ann's Song
Mother Dear
Mother Lucy's Birthday Song
Mother Says Go On Dear Children
Mother Stop Grumbling
Mother Take In Your Service Flag
Mother The Bells Are Ringing
Mother's Child
Mother's Day
Mother's Letter To Her Son
Mother's Little Eye
Mother's Love
Mother's Love, The
Mothering Sunday
Motherless Child
Motherless Children Have A Hard
    Time
Mothers Golden Trumpet
Mottos On The Wall
Moulin, Le
Mount Agrafa
Mountain Maid, A
Mountain Ranger, The
Mountain Tow'ring High Before Me
Mountains
Mountains Of Mourne, The
Mourn Not The Pain Of Loving
Mournful Serenade, The
Mouser, The
Move Along
Move Members Move Dan-U-El
Move On Over
Mowers' Song, The
Mowing The Barley
MP, The
Mr Bancks' Tune
Mr Boll Weevil
Mr Turner's Academy Cotillion
Mr Woodburn's Courtship
Mr Woodbury's Courtship
Mrs McGrath
Mu Asapru
Much Ado O'Er Nothing
Muchachitos, Los
Mucho Te Quiero
Muckin' Of Geordie's Byre
Mudgee Schottische, The
Mudgee Waltz, The
Mudion River
Muffin Man, The
Mukiki Wai
Mul Ha'ohel
Mulberry Bush, The
Mule On The Mount
Mule Skinner Blues
Mule Skinner's Holler
Mule Song
Mullingar Heifer, The
Mum's Mazurka
Mum's Waltz
Mummer's Song

Traditional *(Cont.)*

Murdered Brother, The
Murdered Girl, The
Murm'ring Word
Musevisa
Mush A Doody
Mush Mush
Music
Music Box, The
Music Of The Brook
Musical Alphabet
Musici, Die
Musieu Bainjo
Muss I Denn
Muss I Denn Zum Stadtele 'naus
Musselin Aus Indien
Mustang Gray
My Ain Fireside
My Airplane And I
My All For Your Daughter
My Baby In A Guinea Blue Gown
My Baby's Blue Eyes
My Baby's In Memphis Layin'
    Aroun'
My Ball Flew Over In A Jew's
    Garden
My Bambino
My Bark Canoe
My Beautiful Muff
My Blue Heaven
My Bonnie
My Bonnie Is Over The Ocean
My Bonnie Lies Over The Ocean
My Bonnie Mary
My Bonnie Wee Hen
My Bonny Black Bess
My Bonny Cuckoo
My Bonny Love Is Young
My Boy Tammie
My Boy Willie
My Boyhood Happy Days Down On
    The Farm
My Bretheren Don't Get Weary
My Brother I Do Wonder
My Carnal Life I Will Lay Down
My Children Are Laughing Behind
    My Back
My Dame Hath A Lame Tame Crane
My Dancing Day
My Dearest Dear
My Dove
My Dream
My Dreydel
My Emmet's No More
My Ev'ry Thought
My Faith It Is An Oaken Staff
My Faith Looks Up To Thee
My Father How Long
My Father Is A Dutchman
My Father Was Born In Killarney
My Father's Gray Mare
My First Love
My Friend
My Friends Do Not Worry

Traditional *(Cont.)*

My Garden
My Garden Sleeps
My Gentle Harp
My God Accept My Heart This Day
My God He Is A Man Of War
My God How Wonderful Thou Art
My God Is A Rock In A Weary Land
My Good Lord Done Been Here
My Good Lord Has Been Here
My Good Lord Have Been Here
My Good Lord's Been Here
My Good Lord's Done Been Here
My Good Old Dog
My Good-Lookin' Man
My Government Claim
My Heart's In The Highlands
My Home's Across The Smokey
    Mountains
My Home's Across The Smoky
    Mountains
My Home's In Montana
My Homeland
My Homestead
My Horses Ain't Hungry
My Irish Polly
My Island
My Joy Would Grow In Measure
My Lady Greensleeves
My Lagan Love
My Last Cigar
My Last Gold Dollar
My Li'l John Henry
My Little German Home Across The
    Sea
My Little Heart Is Sighing
My Little Mohee
My Little Pretty One
My Little Silver Ribbon
My Little Yaller Coon
My Lord Delibered Daniel
My Lord Delivered Daniel
My Lord Says He's Gwineter Rain
    Down Fire
My Lord What A Mornin'
My Lord What A Morning
My Lord What A Mourning
My Lord's A-Writin' All De Time
My Lord's Goin' Move This Wicked
    Race
My Lord's Riding All The Time
My Lord's Writing All The Time
My Love Is A Rider
My Love Is But A Lassie Yet
My Love Is Like A Red Red Rose
My Love Is On The Ocean
My Love She Sits On The Campus
My Love She's But A Lassie Yet
My Love She's Like A Lassie Yet
My Love's An Arbutus
My Love's In Germany
My Lovely Annina
My Lovyer Is A Sailor Boy

Traditional *(Cont.)*

My Mammy Stoled A Cow
My Man John
My Marguerite
My Marianne
My Mary
My Mither She Feed Me When I Was
    O'er Young
My Mother Chose My Husband
My Mother Said Polka
My Mother's Voice
My Name Is Anna
My Name's Written On High
My Nellie's Blue Eyes
My Old Canal Mule
My Ole Mistis
My Own Delightful Hearth
My Parents' Grave
My Pigeon House
My Polly
My Polly Waltz
My Pretty Cabocla
My Pretty Maid
My Rose
My Sailor Lad
My Shepherd Will Supply My Need
My Ship Is On De Ocean
My Ship Is On The Ocean
My Sins Been Taken Away
My Sister Ain't You Mighty Glad
My Sister She Works In A Laundry
My Son Ted
My Soul Be At Res'
My Soul Rock On Jubilee
My Soul Wants To Go Home To
    Glory
My Soul's Been Anchored In De
    Lord
My Soul's Been Anchored In The
    Lord
My Sweetheart
My Sweetheart's The Mule In The
    Mines
My Top
My Trooper
My True Love's Gone A-Sailing
My Way's Cloudy
My Wild Eyed Cadet
My Yellow Gal
Mysteries Of A Hobo's Life
Mystic Night, The
N 'Ra-N 'Na
Na Corda Da Viola
Nach Gruner Farb Mein Berz
    Verlangt
Nachtwachterlied
Nachul-Born Easman
Naci En La Cumbre
Nae Bonnie Laddie Tae Tak' Me
    Awa'
Nae Luck About The House
Name In The Sand, The
Nan Of Logie Green

Traditional *(Cont.)*

Nancy Lee
Nancy Till
Nanette
Nanny
Nantucket Skipper, The
Naples
Napoleon Bonaparte
Napoleon's Farewell To Paris
Nar Juldagsmorgon Glimmar
Naranjas Dulces
Naranjo, El
Nat Goodwin
Native Mate
Nau Catarineta, La
Naughty Man
Navajo Happiness Song
Navidava Puri Nihua
Navire De Bayonee, Le
Navo La-Ohalim
Navvy On The Line
Navy Boys, The
Navy Fragment
Naw I Don't
Ne L'oserai Je Dire
Ne Pleure Pas Jeannette
Ne Pleure Pas Tant Charmante
  Blonde
Neapolitan Fisher's Song
Near Krakow
Near Woodstock Town
'Neath The Elms
Necken's Polska
Negro Ballads
Neha-Neha
Neighbor What Has You So Excited
Nell Flaherty's Drake
Nelson's Death And Victory
Nelson's Monument
Neptune
Nesem Vam Noviny
Nesta Rua
Net For A Night Raven, A
Netherlands Prayer Of Thanksgiving
Neumerella Shore, The
Never A Sound
Never Get A Lickin' Till I Go Down
  To Bimini
Never Leave Me Alone
Never Said A Mumbalin' Word
Never Said A Mumblin' Word
Never Take The Hindshoe From A
  Mule
Never Was A Child So Lovely
New Born Again
New Dial, A
New Ev'ry Morning Is The Love
New Garden Fields
New Hat, The
New Market Wreck, The
New Massachusetts Liberty Song,
  The
New Oysters

Traditional *(Cont.)*

New River Train
New Sea Song
New Song Against Rack Renting, A
New Song Called The Victory, A
New Song In Home Rule
  Association, A
New Song Of The Races Of
  Roscommon, A
New Song On The Blandford
  Privateer, A
New Song On The Hiring Of The
  Servants, A
New Song On The Rotten Potatoes,
  A
New Song On The Taxes, A
New Song On The Total Defeat Of
  The French Fleet
New Song Sympathising With The
  Fenian Exiles, A
New Year
New Year's Wish
New Years Bells, The
New York City
New-Born Babe, The
New-Born Baby, De
Newlyn Town
Next Market Day, The
Neyn Neyn Neyn
Nice Girls Don't Chase The Boys
Nice Little Window, The
Nick And A Nock, A
Nick Nack Paddy Whack
Nicolas And Marie
Nighean Dubh's A Nighean Donn
Night
Night Before Larry Was Stretched,
  The
Night Herding Song
Night I Stole Old Sammy Morgan's
  Gin, The
Night In Spring, A
Night In The Desert
Night Is Falling
Night-Herder's Song
Night The Goat Broke Loose On
  Grand Parade, The
Nightengal, The
Nightingale
Nightingale O Nightingale
Nightingale, The
Nightingales
Nights Of Gladness Waltz
Nine Hundred Miles
Nine Joys Of Mary, The
Nine Men Slept In A Boardinghouse
  Bed
Nine Pound Hammer
Nineteen Hundred And Ten
Ninos En Espana Cantan, Los
Nitra's Bells
Nixie Dixie
No Baia Tem
No Condemnation In My Soul

Traditional *(Cont.)*

No Fooling
No Hidin' Place
No Hidin' Place Down There
No Hiding Place
No Irish Need Apply
No Is My Answer
No L'aime Toi Chere
No More Auction Block For Me
No More Slaves
No More War
No Navy For Mine
No One Kills The College Scholar
No Room In The Inn
No Se Nino Hermoso
No Sir
No Sounds From The City Are
  Heard
No Surrender
No Use For The Women
Noah Hist The Windah
Noah's Ark
Noble Duke Of York, The
Noble Man, The
Noble Ribbon Boys, The
Noble Skewball, The
Nobleza India
Nobody Is Too Young
Nobody Know De Trouble I See
Nobody Knows
Nobody Knows De Trouble I See
Nobody Knows De Trouble I See
  Lord
Nobody Knows De Trouble I've Had
Nobody Knows De Trouble I've
  Seen
Nobody Knows The Trouble I See
Nobody Knows The Trouble I See
  Lord
Nobody Knows The Trouble I've
  Had
Nobody Knows The Trouble I've See
Nobody Knows The Trouble I've
  Seen
Nobody Knows The Trouble 'Ob
  Seen
Nobody Knows Who I Am
Nobody's Business
Nobosy Knows The Trouble I've
  Seen
Noches De Luna
Noel Bourguignon
Noel De Cour
Noel De Thevet
Noel Des Ausels
Noel Girl, The
Noel Noel
Noel Nouvelet
Noel Pour L'amour De Marie
Noel Raise The Roof
Noi De La Mare, El
None But The Righteous

Traditional *(Cont.)*

None Can Preach The Gospel Like
    The Mormons Do
Noomanally Shore, The
Norah Hist The Windah
Norfolk Girls, The
Noriu Miego
Norm McConnell's Mazurka
North Country Collier, The
North Wind Doth Blow, The
Northern Swans
Northfield
Nos Galan
Not A Rush This Lad
Not Always On The Mount May We
Not In Dumb Resignation
Not Long Upon The Mountain's
    Height
Nottamun Town
Nottingham Ale
Nourrice Du Roi, La
Nous Avons Crible Le Bon Grain
Nous Etions Dix Filles Dans Un Pre
Nous Irons A Valparaiso
Nous N'irons Plus Au Bois
November Days
Novgorod's Bells
Now Christ Is Risen
Now Glad Of Heart
Now I Am Married
Now I Lay Me Down To Sleep
Now In The Days Of Youth
Now Is Born The Child Divine
Now Let Me Fly
Now Let Us All Right Merry Be
Now Let Us All With One Accord
Now Light One Thousand Christmas
    Light
Now My Bonny Bonny Boy
Now My Dear Companions
Now My Tongue The Myst'ry
    Telling
Now My Tongue The Mystery
    Telling
Now Nature Hangs Her Mantle
    Green
Now Our Meeting's Over
Now Praise We Great And Famous
    Men
Now Right Now
Now Sing Your Songs Of Easter
Now Thank We All Our God
Now That The Daylight Fills The Sky
Now The Day Is Over
Now The Green Blade Riseth
Now The Holy Child Is Born
Now The Laborer's Task Is O'Er
Now We Must Part
Now We'll Make The Rafters Ring
Nsa Ni O
Nuar Det Jul Igen
Nummer Me One
Nuns In Frigid Cells

Traditional *(Cont.)*

Nur Du
Nurse Pinched The Baby, The
Nut Brown Maiden
O A-Hunting We Will Go
O All Ye Works Of God
O Ba Mo Leanabh O Ba O Ba
O Ba O I O Mo Leanabh
O Baby Thee I Love
O Be Joyful In The Lord
O Beau Soir Tombant
O Belinda
O Bethlehem Thou Holy Place
O Blanche Est La Neige
O Blessed St Joseph
O Blest Creator Of The Light
O Bury Me Beneath The Willow
O Bury Me Not On The Lone Prairie
O Caitanne
O Can Ye Sew Cushions
O Charlie Is My Darling
O Christ The Word Incarnate
O Christmas Pine
O Christmas Tree
O Christmas Tree Oh Tannenbaum
O Co Bheir Mi Liom
O Come All Ye Christians
O Come All Ye Faithful
O Come All Ye Faithful
    Triumphantly Sing
O Come Creator Spirit
O Come Little Children
O Come O Come Emmanuel
O Come O Come Immanuel
O Come Ye Shepherds
O Day Of Rest And Gladness
O De Robe
O Dear O
O Dearest Lord
O Death
O Desayo
O Dormi Iesu
O Du Frohliche
O Du Lieber Augustin
O Du Som Metter
O Eadar An Da Chraicionn
O Eveline
O Faithful Pine
O Father Thou Who Givest All
O Food To Pilgrims Given
O For A Closer Walk With God
O Gambler Git Up Off O' Yo' Knees
O Gato
O Gentle Savior
O Gimmie De Wings For To Move
    Along
O Gin I Were A Baron's Heir
O Gin I Were Where Gadie Rins
O Gin My Love Were Yon Red Rose
O Give Thanks
O Glorious Easter Morn
O God Before Whose Altar
O God Creation's Secret Force
O God May Your Face

Traditional *(Cont.)*

O God Of Bethel
O God Of Bethel By Whose Hand
O God Of Earth And Altar
O God Of Every Nation
O God Of Mercy God Of Might
O God Of Truth O Lord Of Might
O God Of Truth Whose Living Word
O God Our Help In Ages Past
O God To Those Who Here Profess
O God Unseen Yet Ever Near
O Gracious Father Of Mankind
O Gum B'Aotrom Linn An T-Astar
O Gur Trom Tha Mo Bhean-Sa
O Gwiazdo Betlejemska
O Happy Day
O Happy Joyful Day
O Hark To The Bells Glad Song
O Ho Na Ribeinean
O Ho Nighean E Ho Nighean
O Holy Lord
O Holy Savior
O Holy Spirit By Whose Breath
O How Lovely Is The Evening
O I Got A Light
O I Love Mother
O I'm A Good Old Rebel
O Ir Kleyne Lichtelech
O It's Goin' To Be A Mighty Day
O Ivan Hola Ivan
O J'Ai Passe Le Long Du Bois
O Jesus I Have Promised
O Jesus I Have Promised To Serve
    Thee
O Jesus Joy Of Loving Hearts
O Jesus Once A Nazareth Boy
O Jesus So Sweet
O Jesus Tender Shepherd Hear
O Jeunes Gens
O Josephine
O Kenmure's On And Awa Willie
O Lamb Beautiful Lamb
O Laufet Ihr Hirten
O Lawd Ain't Dey Rest Fo' De
    Weary One
O Lay Thy Loof In Mine Lass
O Leave Your Sheep
O Life That Maketh All Things New
O Light Of Light
O Little Flower
O Little One
O Little Town Of Bethlehem
O Lord A Strange Event
O Lord And Master Of Us All
O Lord How Long
O Lord I Am Not Worthy
O Lord I Want Two Wings
O Lord I'm Hungry
O Lord Most High Eternal King
O Love How Deep How Broad How
    High
O M'Ulaidh M'Ulaidh Ort
O Ma Petite Bergere
O Ma Tete Folle

Traditional (*Cont.*)

O Madam I Have Come A Courtin'
O Madame Fardeuil
O Make Me Holy
O Mary Dear
O Mary Don't You Weep
O Mary Don't You Weep Don't You Mourn
O Mary What You Weeping About
O Mary Where Is Your Baby
O Me O My
O Mo Dhuthaich
O Mon Beau Vignoble
O Month Of May
O Mother Don't You Weep
O My Little Soul
O My Lord What Shall I Do
O Night Peaceful And Blest
O Nightingale
O Nightingale Awake
O No John
O Petite Tete Folle
O Po' Little Jesus
O Pretty Polly
O Rocks Don't Fall On Me
O Saintly Joseph
O Sally My Dear
O San-Nisk-A-Na
O Sanctissima
O Saving Victim Opening Wide
O Shenandoah
O Shepherd Of The Nameless Fold
O Sinner Man
O Sinner Now Is De Time For To Pray
O Soldier Soldier
O Sole Mio
O Sons And Daughters Let Us Sing
O Sorrow Deep Who Would Not Weep
O Splendor Of God's Glory Bright
O Spirit Of The Living God
O Spirit Sweet Of Summer Time
O Store Gud
O Take Me Back To Switzerland
O Tannenbaum
O Tempora O Mores
O The Simple Gifts Of God
O The Sweet Dreams Of Nancy
O This Is No' My Ain Lassie
O Thou At Thy Eucharist Didst Pray
O Thou Eternal Christ Of God
O Thou In All Thy Might So Far
O Thou Joyful Day
O Thou Joyful O Thou Blessed
O Traurigkeit O Herzelied
O Trinity Of Blessed Light
O Vermeland
O Very God Of Very God
O Waly Waly
O Wasn't That A Mighty Day
O Wasnt Dat A Wide River
O Weel May The Boatie Row

Traditional (*Cont.*)

O Where Are You Going Billy Boy
O Where Have You Been Lord Randall My Son
O Whistle And I'll Come To You My Lad
O Whistle And I'll Come To Ye My Lad
O Whistle And I'll Come To You
O Who Is That
O Who Would Be A Shepherd Boy
O Who's Going To Shoe Your Little Feet
O Willie Was A Wanton Wag
O Willo Willo Willo
O Willow Willow
O Willy's Rare And Willy's Fair
O Wondrous Type O Vision Fair
O Word Of God Incarnate
O Word That Goest Forth On High
O Wretched Man
O Ye Young And Gay And Proud
O You Santy
O'Connell's New Song On Emancipation
O'Donnell Abu
O'Donnell's March
O'Donovan Rossa's Farewell To Dublin
O'er Continent And Ocean
O'er Tatra
O'er The Horizon
O'Houlihan
O-O-Oh Sistren An' Bred'ren
Oakum In The Woods, The
Oats And Beans
Oats And Beans And Barley Grow
Oats Peas Beans And Barley Grow
Observer's Lament
Obstruction
Occasion Manquee, L'
Ocean Burial, The
Ocean King, The
Ocean Queen
Ocean-Fight, The
Och Och Och Och Och Mar A Tha Mi
Ochy Chornia
October Days
Ode For The Fourth Of July 1827
Ode To Ben Perkins
Ode To New Jersey
Of All The Causes East And West
Of The Father's Love Begotten
Of These Four Letters Sing Will I
Of Thin Lath's
Off To Philadelphia
Off To Sea Once More
Offset For The Chesapeake
Oft In The Stilly Night
Oft-Told Tale, An
Often Jesus' Friends Remembered
Og Hor Lille Moer

Traditional (*Cont.*)

Ogallaly Song, The
Oh A-Rock-A My Soul
Oh Ba-By Ugh What You Gwine To Do
Oh Be Ready When The Train Comes In
Oh Bedad Then Says I
Oh Breathe On Me Breath Of God
Oh Bury Me Not On The Lone Prairie
Oh Christmas Tree
Oh Close To My Sweetheart
Oh Come All Ye Faithful
Oh Come Oh Come Emmanuel
Oh Come Shepherds
Oh Dat Low Bridge
Oh De Hebben Is Shinin'
Oh Dear Mama I'm Feeling So Badly
Oh Dear What Can The Matter Be
Oh Death
Oh Den My Little Soul's Gwine To Shine
Oh Didn't He Ramble
Oh Didn't It Rain
Oh Enter Dear Shepherds
Oh Eve Where Is Adam
Oh Freedom
Oh Fret Not For Tomorrow
Oh Give Me The Wings
Oh Give Thanks
Oh Give Way Jordan
Oh Graveyard
Oh Had I A Golden Thread
Oh Hanuka
Oh Happy Day
Oh Hear Me Prayin'
Oh Hear The Heav'nly Angels
Oh Ho Baby Take A One One Me
Oh Holy Lord
Oh How He Scolded
Oh How Joyfully
Oh How Lofty
Oh How Lovely Is The Evening
Oh I Have A Sweetheart
Oh I Should Like To Marry
Oh I Want Two Wings
Oh I've Been Tempted
Oh Lawd How Long
Oh Leave Your Flocks
Oh Limerick Is Beautiful
Oh Lord Oh My Lord
Oh Louisiana Gal Won't You Come Out To Night
Oh Mah Kitty Co Co
Oh Make A Me Holy
Oh Maman Qui Vient Sur La Route
Oh Mary Don't You Weep
Oh Mary Oh Marthy
Oh Miss Liza Oh Mah Darlin' Hoo
Oh Mister Moon
Oh Molly Reilly
Oh My Bonny Hightland Laddie

Traditional (*Cont.*)

Oh My Good Lord Show Me De
Way
Oh My Little Darling
Oh My Love
Oh My Lovin' Brother
Oh My Pretty Crowing Cock
Oh Night Among The Thousands
Oh Oh Oh It's A Lovely War
Oh Peter Go Ring-A Dem Bells
Oh Pritchett Oh Kelly
Oh Rock My Soul
Oh Rock-A My Soul
Oh Roll Your Leg Over
Oh Sacred Heart Of Jesus
Oh Say Do You Know The Way To
Selin
Oh Selina
Oh Show Me How The Gentlemen
Ride
Oh Sinner
Oh Sinner Man
Oh Sinner You'd Better Get Ready
Oh Soldier Soldier
Oh Tell Me How To Woo Thee
Oh The Beautiful Treasures
Oh The Sailor Looked And Looked
And Looked
Oh The Times Are Hard
Oh Them Golden Slippers
Oh Wans't Dat A Wide Ribber
Oh Wasn't Dat A Wide Riber
Oh Wasn't That A Wide River
Oh What A Horrible Morning
Oh What A Night
Oh What A Treat
Oh When I Come To Die
Oh Where Have You Been Come
Randall My Son
Oh Where Oh Where Has My Little
Dog Gone
Oh Who Can Compare Thee
Oh Who Is At My Bedroom Window
Oh Who Will Shoe My Foot
Oh Who Would Be A Shepherd Boy
Oh Who's Goin' To Shoe Your
Pretty Little Foot
Oh Why Camest Thou Before Me
Oh Woe To You Udny
Oh Won't You Sit Down
Oh Would You Be A Sunbeam
Oh Yea
Oh Yes
Oh Yes Oh Yes
Oh Yes Oh Yes Wait 'Til I Git On
My Robe
Oh You Bettah Mind
Oh You Dear Little Night
Ohio
Oi Bethlehem
Oid Den Oireachtas Mor I Mbaile
Ath Cliath 1897
Oifin Pripetshik
Ojul Med Din Glede

Traditional (*Cont.*)

Ol' A'k's A-Movin'
Ol' Ark's A-Moverin'
Ol' Ark's A-Moverin' An' I'm
Goin' Home, De
Ol' Elder Brown's
Ol' Hag You See Mammy
Ol' Joe Clark
Ol' Mickey Brannigan's Pup
Ol' Mother Hare
Ol' Rattler
Ol' Sheep Done Know De Road, De
Ol' Texas
Ol' Virginny Never Tire
Olas De La Laguna, Las
Old Abe Lincoln
Old Abe Lincoln Came Out Of The
Wilderness
Old Arizona
Old Arizona Again
Old Ark, The
Old Ark A Moverin' Along, The
Old Ark A-Movering Along, The
Old Ark's A-Moverin', De
Old Ark's A-Moverin', The
Old Ark's A-Movering Along, The
Old Ark's A-Movering, The
Old Aunt Jemima
Old Aunt Kate
Old Bach
Old Bachelor, The
Old Bachelor's Apology, The
Old Bang 'em
Old Bangam
Old Bangum
Old Bark Hut, The
Old Bee Make De Honeycomb
Old Bill
Old Bill Edwards' Schottische
Old Billygoat Waltz
Old Black Booger, The
Old Blind Drunk John
Old Blue
Old Bob Ridley
Old Brass Wagon
Old Bullock Dray, The
Old Bumpy
Old Butler's
Old Cabin Home, The
Old Chariot, The
Old Chestnut Tree, The
Old Chisholm Trail, The
Old Chizzum Trail, The
Old Circus Songs
Old Coat
Old Colony Times
Old Couple, The
Old Cow Died, The
Old Dan Tucker
Old Derry Air, An
Old Donegal
Old Dunn Cow, The

Traditional (*Cont.*)

Old England Forty Years Ago
Old Farm Gate, The
Old Farmer's Song, The
Old Father Hudson
Old Forty Nine
Old Garden, An
Old Garden Gate, The
Old Geezer, The
Old Gospel Ship, The
Old Grampus
Old Grampus Is Dead
Old Granddaddy's Dead
Old Granite State, The
Old Gray Goose, The
Old Gray Horse Come Tearin' Out
O' De Wilderness
Old Gray Horse, The
Old Gray Mare, The
Old Grey Beard
Old Grey Mare Come A Tearin' Out
O' The Wilderness
Old Grimes
Old Grumble
Old Hewson The Cobbler
Old Home, The
Old Horse
Old House At Home, The
Old Howard
Old Hundred
Old Hundredth
Old Hundreth
Old Indian, An
Old Irish March
Old Ironsides
Old Jeff Has Gone To Rest
Old Jesse
Old Jig Jog, The
Old Joe Clark
Old Joe Clarke
Old John Brown Had A Little Indian
Old King Buzzard Floating Hit
Old King Cole
Old King Coul
Old King Crow
Old Lady Who Swallowed A Fly,
The
Old Leather Breeches, The
Old Ma Bell
Old Macdonald
Old Macdonald Had A Farm
Old Maid And The Burglar, The
Old Maid Song, The
Old Maid's Song
Old Maid's Song, The
Old Man And A Young Man, An
Old Man At His Grave, An
Old Man In The Wood, The
Old Man Kangaroo, The
Old Man Noah
Old Man, The
Old Man Under The Hill, The
Old Man Who Came Over The
Moor, An

Traditional *(Cont.)*

Old Man Who Lived In The West,
The
Old Man Who Lived In The Wood,
The
Old Man's Comforts, The
Old Man's Courtship, The
Old McDonald Had A Farm
Old Miner's Refrain, The
Old Minstrel, The
Old Molly Hare
Old Mother Hubbard
Old Mountain Dew
Old Mule, De
Old Napper
Old Navy, The
Old Ned's A Rare Strong Chap
Old Neptune The God Of The Ocean
Old Noah
Old Noel
Old Norway
Old Oak Tree, The
Old Orange Flute, The
Old Paint
Old Pod Auger Times
Old Ponto Is Dead
Old Rattler
Old Reilly
Old Rosin The Beau
Old Rosin The Bow
Old Sailor, The
Old Sailor's Song
Old Sailors Never Die
Old Sam Fanny
Old Scotch Air, The
Old Settler, The
Old Settler's Song, The
Old Sheep Went To Sleep
Old Ship Of Zion
Old Shoes And Leggin's
Old Shoes And Leggings
Old Skibbereen
Old Skipper, The
Old Slew Foot
Old Smoky
Old Soldier's Prayer, The
Old Sow Song, The
Old Spotted Cow, The
Old Strawberry Roan, The
Old Tar River
Old Tikhvin Melody
Old Time Cowboy
Old Time Religion, The
Old Tippecanoe
Old Tobacco Box, The
Old Tombolin
Old Troy
Old Uncle Noah
Old Union Wagon, The
Old Unreconstructed, An
Old Welshwoman, The
Old Wether's Skin, The
Old White Mare, The
Old Woman

Traditional *(Cont.)*

Old Woman All Skin And Bones,
The
Old Woman And Her Little Pig, The
Old Woman And The Little Pig, The
Old Woman And The Peddler
Old Woman And The Pedlar, The
Old Woman From Boston, The
Old Woman In Dover, The
Old Woman Old Woman
Old Woman Who Went To Market,
The
Old Woman With A Cane
Old Woman's Courtship
Old Woman's Story, An
Old Yorkshire Gooding Carol
Old Zion's Children Marchin' Along
Old Zip Coon
Ole Ark A Moverin' Along, De
Ole Aunt Dinah Sick In Bed
Ole Aunt Kate
Ole Cow
Ole Dan Tucker
Ole Egypt
Ole Grey Goose, The
Ole Mars'r Had A Yaller Gal
Ole Marse John
Ole Massa
Ole Mister Rabbit
Ole Pee Dee
Ole Sheep Done Know De Road, De
Ole Ship O' Zion
Ole Ship Of Zion
Ole Smoky
Ole Tar River
Ole Tare River
Ole Zip Coon
Oleana
Oleanna
Olenu
Oli Aloha
Olive Tree, The
Oliver Cromwell
Olivette Warble
Omie Wise
On A Bank Of Flowers
On A Beau Dire
On A Delft Tile
On A Dry Branch
On A May Morning
On A Reste Six Ans Sur Mer
On Always Onward
On And On
On Board A Ninety Eight
On Board The Leicester Castle
On Board The Steamer
On Children's Day We Sweetly Sing
On Christmas Day
On Christmas Night
On Christmas Night All Angels Sing
On De Moun Tain Ugh O-Ver You
Der Ugh Killed Nah
On Friday Evening
On Friday Morning We Set Sail

Traditional *(Cont.)*

On Good Friday Raven Gives His
Young One A Bath
On His Bronco The Gay Caballero
On Jordan's Bank The Baptist's Cry
On Jordan's Stormy Banks I Stand
On Leaving Ireland
On Meesh E Gan
On No John
On Red River Shore
On Saturday Night
On Saturday Night When The Red
Wine
On Springfield Mountain
On That Most Blessed Night
On That Sabbath Morn
On The Baltic
On The Banks Of Allan Water
On The Banks Of Jordan
On The Banks Of Sweet Dundee
On The Banks Of Sweet Loch Rae
On The Banks Of The Little Eau
Pleine
On The Banks Of The Murray
On The Banks Of The Ohio
On The Banks Of The Old Omaha
On The Banks Of The Old Pee Dee
On The Banks Of The Old Raritan
On The Banks Of The Old Tennessee
On The Birthday Of The Lord
On The Bridge Of Avignon
On The British Blockade
On The Capture Of The Guerriere
On The Capture Of The United
States Frigate Essex
On The Corner
On The Death Of A Little Child
After A Very Short Illness
On The Death Of Augustine C
Ludlow
On The Death Of Captain Nicholas
Biddle
On The Eighth Day Of November
On The First Thanksgiving Day
On The Hike
On The Kama On The River
On The Lake Expeditions
On The Lakes Of Ponchartrain
On The Late Engagement In Charles
Town River
On The Late Royal Sloop Of War
General Monk
On The Launching Of The Frigate
Constitution
On The Launching Of The
Seventy-Four Gun Ship
Independence
On The Loss Of The Privateer
Brigantine General Armstrong
On The Memorable Victory
On The Merry-Go-Round
On The Mountain
On The Naval Attack Near Baltimore

Traditional *(Cont.)*

On The New American Frigate
    Alliance
On The Other Side Of Jordan
On The Picket Line
On The Roof A Magpie
On The Shores Of Havana
On The Shores Of South Carolina
On The Steps Of The Dole Office
    Door
On The Top Of The Hill
On The Village End
On The Way To California
On This Hill
On This Night
On To The Mountain
On Top Of Old Smokey
On Top Of Old Smoky
On Top Of Spaghetti
On Vicksburg's Bloody Battlefield
Once I Had A Sweetheart
Once I Had Plenty Of Thyme
Once I Knew A Pretty Girl
Once I Lived In Cottonwood
Once I Loved A Maiden Fair
Once I Saw A Sweet Briar-Rose
Once I Was A Trav'ller
Once More A Lumbering Go
Once On A Time There Lived A
    Lady
Once There Were Three Fishermen
Once To Every Man And Nation
Once Upon A Time Long Long Ago
Once When I Awoke
One And Twenty
One At A Time
One Button Two Buttons
One Christmas Morning
One Day For Recreation
One Day More
One Fine Day
One Fine Summer's Morning Or The
    Banks Of The Clyde
One Grain Of Sand
One Is High And One Is Low
One Kind Favor
One Man Shall Mow My Meadow
One Man's Hands
One Mo' Mile To Go
One More Day
One More Masur Today
One More River
One More River To Cross
One Morn As I Rambled
One Morning Clear
One Morning In May
One Night In Mexico
One Quiet Night
One Starlit Night
One Straw Swims
One Summer Evening
One Two Buckle My Shoe
One Two Three Steps
One-A These Days

Traditional *(Cont.)*

One-Tune Piper, The
Onions And Potatoes
Only A Cowboy
Only A Leaf
Only Begotten Word Of God
Only Begotten Word Of God Eternal
Ons Is Geboren Een Kindekin
Open Road, The
Open The Door
Open The Gates As High As The Sky
Open The Window Noah
Open Your Ears O Faithful People
Opossum, The
Opp Lille Hans
Oran Loch Sloy
Oran Na Politician
Oran Sniomhaidh
Orange And Blue, The
Orchestra
Orchestra, The
Organ Grinder, The
Organ Man, The
Original Barn Dance, The
Original Barn Dance Schottische
Original Coventry Carol, The
Original Talking Blues
Oriole
Orley's Jig
Orphan Blues
Orphan Boy Waltz
Orphan Girl, The
Orphan Maid, The
Orphelin, L'
Os Escravos De Job
Osborn Snare's Courtship
Ot Azoy Neyt A Shnayder
Other Cowboy Boasting Chants
Other Night, The
Other Shore, The
Ou Som Souroucou
Our Baby
Our Beautiful Valley
Our Bill
Our Blest Redeemer Ere He Breathed
Our Cherries
Our Father Who Art In Heaven
Our Father You Have Given Me
Our Freedom Is Immortal
Our God To Whom We Turn
Our Goodman
Our Land
Our Pure Virgin Was Going
Our Saintly Rabbis
Our Saviour Has Arisen
Our Song Of Gratitude
Our Trip
Out In De Rain
Out In Our Meadow
Out Of The Orient Crystal Skies
Out Of The Window
Out On The Meadow
Out On The Silvery Tide

Traditional *(Cont.)*

Out With Winter Push It Out
Outlandish Knight, The
Over And Over
Over Bethlehem A Star Shines
Over Hill Over Dale
Over In The Meadow
Over Jordan
Over London Bridge
Over My Head
Over Tatra
Over The Border
Over The Hills
Over The Hills And Far Away
Over The Meadows
Over The Mountians
Over The River And Through The
    Wood
Over The River And Through The
    Woods
Over The Water Over The Lee
Over The Water To Charlie
Over Yonder
Ovinu Ho'ov Horahamon
Ovinu Malkenu
Owl, The
Ox-Driving Song
Ox-Team Trail, The
Oxen And Sheep
Oxen Come
Oxford City
Oy A Nacht A Sheyne
Oy Dortn Dortn
Oy Dortn Dortn Ibern Vasserl
Oyfn Barg Un Ibern Barg
Oyfn Pripetshok
Oyfn Yam Veyet A Vintele
Oyster Fishers' Song, The
Ozi V'Zimras Yo
Pa Laven Sitter Nissen
Paal Paa Haugen
Pace-Egging Song
Paddy Backwards
Paddy Doyle
Paddy Doyle's Boots
Paddy Get Back
Paddy Malone
Paddy On The Canal
Paddy Sheahan
Paddy West
Paddy Works On The Erie
Paddy Works On The Railroad
Paddy Works On The Railway
Paddy's Own Good Irish Stew
Pagka-Tao
Pains In My Fingers
Painting A Fence
Pal Sine Honer
Palapala
Palisse, La
Palms Of Victory
Paloma, La
Paloma Mia
Palomita, Una

Traditional *(Cont.)*

Panama Tombe
Panama 'm Tombe
Papanulan
Papaya Tree, The
Paper Of Pins, A
Paper Of Pins, The
Papir Iz Doch Vays
Par La Cour Je Galope Je Trottine
Par Les Gais Jardins Remplis De
    Roses
Par Les Sentes
Para Los Caficultores
Paratroopers' Lament, The
Paresseuses Abeilles
Parlez-Nous A Boire
Parlor, The
Parnell And His Band
Partant Pour La Syrie
Parthenia Carol
Parting
Parting Friends
Parting Glass, The
Parting Me And My Bonny Lad, The
Parting Of Burns And His Highland
    Mary, The
Partners From Poland
Pas Loin De Chez Moi
Pass Around The Bottle
Pass Around Your Bottle
Pass Me Not
Passant Par Paris
Passing Once Thru Fair Lorraine
Passing Through
Passing Through Lorraine
Passion De Jesus-Christ, La
Passion De Notre Seigneur Jesus
    Christ, La
Past Three O'Clock
Pastime With Good Company
Pastora, La
Pastores A Belen, Los
Pastourelle De Thibaut De
    Champagne
Pastures Of Plenty
Pat Murphy Of The Irish Brigade
Pat On The Railway
Pat Works On The Railway
Pat's Wedding
Pat-A-Pan
Patrick O'Neal
Patrick Saintly Father
Patriots, The
Patton
Paul And Silas Layin' In Jail
Paul And The Chickens
Paul Jones' Victory
Paul Said To The Corinthians
Pauline
Pauvre Hobo, Un
Pauvre Jacques
Pauvre Paysan, Le
Paw-Paw Patch
Pawpaw Patch, The

Traditional *(Cont.)*

Pay Day At Coal Creek
Pay Me My Money Down
Pay With A Smile
Pea Ridge Battle, The
Pea Straw
Peace
Peace Be With You
Peace Pipe Song
Peace To All
Peaceful Evening
Peaceful Night
Peach Trees Waltz, The
Peanut Song
Peanut-Pickin' Song
Pearl, The
Peas An' Rice
Peas An' The Rice
Peas And Rice
Peas Beans Oats And Barley
Peasant Girl, The
Pease Porridge Hot
Peat Bog Soldiers, The
Peau La Peau La Peau Et Les Os, La
Peckerwood Peckerwood
Peddler Man, The
Peddler, The
Pedlar, The
Pedler, The
Peek-A-Boo
Peeler And The Goat, The
Peep Squirrel Peep
Peggy Gordon
Peggy O'Neill Schottische, The
Peigin Leitir Mor
Pelot De Betton
Penitence De Marie Madeleine, La
Penitent's Prayer, The
Pensive Minstrel, The
Peon Named Pancho, A
People Called Christians, A
Peppinetta
Pequen, El
Per Spelmann
Perche Vezzosi Rai
Perfect Rose, The
Perhaps When Lilies Bloom
Perica
Pernette, La
Peronnelle, La
Perrine Etait Servante
Persia's Crew, The
Personent Hodie
Persuassion
Pesky Serpent, The
Pete Fiddler
Pete Pete
Peter
Peter And Paul
Peter And The Swan
Peter Go Ring Dem Bells
Peter Go Ring Them Bells
Peter Go Ring-A Dem Bells
Peter Gray

Traditional *(Cont.)*

Peter On De Sea Sea Sea Sea
Peter On The Sea
Peter Piper
Peter Rambelay
Peter Street
Peterloo
Petit Bonhomme, Un
Petit Bonhomme Vit Encore
Petit Mari, Le
Petit Papa C'est Aujourd'hui Ta Fete
Petit Pauvre Et Le Mauvais Riche, Le
Petit Poisson Se Cache, Le
Petite Camuson
Petite Galiote, La
Petite Hirondelle, La
Petites Marionettes, Les
Pharoah's Army Got Drowned
Philadelphia Riots
Phillis On The New Made Hay
Pibole, La
Pick A Bale A Day
Pick A Bale O' Cotton
Pick A Bale Of Cotton
Pickin' Off De Cotton
Picnic, A
Picture From Life's Other Side, A
Piddlin' Pup, The
Pie In The Sky
Pierlala
Pierre De Grenoble
Pietro's Hat
Pigeons And Fairies
Pilgrim's Song
Pilgrimage To Compostella, The
Pilot, The
Pinchosl Un Chantschele
Pinery Boy, The
Pioneer Day 1870
Pioneer Song
Pipe Us The Songs Of Freedom
Piper Of Dundee, The
Piper, The
Pipers Of Balmoral, The
Pippin Hill
Pique La Baleine
Pirusa
Pitcher, The
Place Congo, La
Place Where My Love Johnny
    Dwells, The
Place Where The Old Horse Died,
    The
Plains Of Waterloo, The
Plainte Du Coureur De Bois, La
Plainte Du Coureur-Des-Bois, La
Planting Rice
Plantons La Vigne
Plastic Jesus
Play Ball
Playing Cowboy
Playing Cowboys
Pleasant And Delightful
Please Mister Conductor

Traditional (*Cont.*)

Pleased To Meet You
Pledged Horse, The
Plenty Good Room
Plongeur Noye, Le
Ploughboy's Dream, The
Ploughboys' Song
Pluie Tombe, La
Plumb De Line
Plus Superbe Qu'un Paon
Po' Boy
Po Laz'us
Po' Li'l Ella
Po' Mo'ner Got A Home At Las'
Po' Mournah
Po' Mourner's Got A Home At Las'
Po' Ol' Lazrus
Poacher, The
Pobre Corazon
Pochvalen Bud' Jezis Kristus
Poet's Delight, The
Poet's Loss, The
Point Maid, The
Pojdzmy Wszyscy
Polish Lullaby
Polish National Dance
Polk Dallas And Texas
Polka
Polka, The
Polka-Mazurka
Pollerita
Pollitos, Los
Polly Come With Me To Paarl
Polly Kimo
Polly Parrot
Polly Put The Kettle On
Polly Von
Polly Williams
Polly-Wolly-Doodle
Pommier Doux, Le
Pommy's Lament, The
Pompiers, Les
Ponce Muir's Suns
Pont De Morlaix, Le
Poodle-Noddle Nonsense
Poor And Single Sailor, The
Poor Auld Maidens, The
Poor Aunt, The
Poor Aviator Lay Dying, A
Poor Beggar's Daughter, A
Poor Little Jesus
Poor Lonesome Cowboy
Poor Man's Family, The
Poor Man's Labour
Poor Me
Poor Mourner's Got A Home
Poor Old Horse
Poor Old Maids
Poor Old Man, The
Poor Old Slave, The
Poor Oma Wise
Poor Omie
Poor Prince Charlie

Traditional (*Cont.*)

Poor Sinner
Poor Stranger, The
Poor Wayfarin' Stranger
Poor Wayfaring Man Of Grief, A
Poor Wayfaring Stranger, A
Poor Working Girl, The
Pop Goes The Question
Pop Goes The Weasel
'Por Un Beso De Tu Boca
Porcheronne, La
Pore Mournah
Port Of Embarkation
Portrait, Le
Portrush Fishing Disaster, The
Posadas, Las
Possum Song, The
Possum Valley
Postman, The
Potato, The
Poteen Good Luck To Ye Dear
Pourquoi Toutes Ces Tentures Et Ces
　　Rouges Tapis
Poverty
Prairie Flower
Prairie Grove
Praise And Thanks
Praise Of Christmas, The
Praise Of Love, The
Praise Of Sailors, The
Praise The Saviour
Praise To God
Praise To God For Things We See
Praise To The Living God
Praise To The Lord
Praise To The Lord The Almighty
Praise Ye The Lord
Praties, The
Pray God Bless
Pray On
Pray On The Way
Prayer
Prayer For Peace
Prayer Is De Key
Prayer Of Thanks
Prayer Of Thanksgiving
Preab San Ol
Preacher And The Bear, The
Preacher And The Slave, The
Preacher's Belly
Precept And Line
Preguntale A Las Estrellas
Premier Jour De Mai, Le
Prendr' Un P'tit Coup
Prentice Boy
Prepare Us
Pres Du Mur Un Vert Frene Ondule
　　Au Vent
Present Enjoyment
President Parker
Presidents, The
Prettiest Little Girl
Prettiest Song Of All, The
Pretty Boy Floyd

Traditional (*Cont.*)

Pretty Fair Maid, A
Pretty Girl Milking Her Cow, The
Pretty Girls And The Shoemaker
Pretty Girls Of Cork, The
Pretty Green Shawl
Pretty Jeannette
Pretty Jennee
Pretty Lips Schottische
Pretty Little Baby
Pretty Little Deer
Pretty Maid
Pretty Mary
Pretty Miller's Daughter
Pretty Mohee, The
Pretty Nancy
Pretty Ploughboy, The
Pretty Polly
Pretty Polly Ann
Pretty Polly Oliver
Pretty Sally
Pretty Sally Of London
Pretty Saro
Pretty Shepherdess
Pretty White Lily Waltz
Prickly Rose, The
Pride Of Glencoe, The
Pride Of Kildare, The
Primavera
Primitive Dance Tune
Primrose Blooms, The
Primus Lan'
Prince Charlie
Prince D'Orange, Le
Prince Des Ormeaux, Le
Prince Eugene
Prince Eugene, Le
Prince Of Wales Schottische
Prince Robert
Princeton Marines' Hymn
Priosun Chluain Meala
Prise De Mantoue, La
Prison Du Roi Francois, La
Prisoner For Life, A
Prisoner To The Swallow, The
Prisoner's Song
Private's Lament, The
Privateering, The
Procession, The
Proctors' Song
Prodigal Daughter, The
Promise, The
Promised Land, The
Proshchay
Prospecting Dream
Proud Lady Margaret
Przybiezeli Do Betlejem
Psalm 42
Psalm 51
Psalm 68
Psalm Of Sion
Puer Natus
Puer Natus In Bethlehem
Puer Nobis

Traditional (*Cont.*)

Pues Ques Es Lo Que Me Dices
Punchin' Dough
Punchinello
Pupil's Song
Pupu O Ewa
Puquito, El
Purim Day
Purlewaugh Mazurka, The
Purple Bamboo Flute
Purple Bamboo, The
Push Boat
Push Boat Song, The
Push The Business On
Pussy-Cat Pussy-Cat
Put John On The Islan'
Put Me In My Little Bed
Put My Little Shoes Away
Put On The Skillet
Put The Traffic Down
Put Yo' Honey Lovin' Mind On Me
Put Your Little Foot
Putman's Hill
Putney Hymn
Putney Hymn, The
Puttin' On The Style
Putting On The Style
Pye Sate On A Pear Tree, A
Qu'il Est Dru Ah Qu'il Est Dru Le
    Grand Chene Feuillu
Quail, The
Quaker Song, The
Quaker's Courtship
Quaker's Wooing, The
Quand Biron Voulut Danser
Quand J'etais Chez Mon Pere
Quand Je Suis Parti Pour Le Texas
Quand L'amour N'y Est Pas
Quand L'aurore Brille Au Ciel
Quand La Bergere Vient Des
    Champs
Quand La Guerre Est Fini
Quand La Mer Rouge Apparut
Quand Le Gai Gaillard Entend
Quand Mo Te Piti
Quand Vient L'aurore Vermeille
Quantrell
Quantrell Song
Que Bonita Bandera
Que El Cantar Tiene Sentido
Que Lejos Estoy
Que Nous Veulent Ils Cet Abbe
Que Tobaco Malo
Queen Astrid Comes No More
Queen Jane
Queen Of Hearts
Queen's Maries, The
Queer Business, A
Quelele, El
Quelle Est Cette Odeur Agreable
Quem Pastores
Quem Pastores Laudavere
Quest, The

Traditional (*Cont.*)

Qui Est Ce Qui Passe
Qui Est Le Meilleur Des Maitres
Qui N'a Pas D'amour
Qui Veut Ouir Chanson
Quick Dance
Quiero Jugar Con El Nino
Quiet Night
Quilting Party, The
Quite Different
Quittez Pasteurs
Quodlibet
Quoi Je T'ai Fait Malheureuse
Quoi Ma Voisine Es Tu Fachee
Quoique Soyez Petit Encore
Raatikkoon
Rabbit Hash
Raccoon And Possum
Raccoon Up In De 'simmon Tree
Radiant Morn Hath Passed Away,
    The
Rag-'O-Muffin Schottische
Ragged Leevy
Raggedy
Raggedy Man, De
Raggedy-Assed Cadets, The
Raging Can-All, The
Raging Canal, The
Ragupati Ra Gava Rajah Ram
Raiders' Lament, The
Raiders Song, The
Railroad Bill
Railroad Bill Cut A Mighty Big Dash
Railroad Blues
Railroad Boy
Railroad Corral, The
Railroad Song
Railroader For Me, A
Railroader, The
Railway, The
Rainbow Roun' My Shoulder
Rainbow Willow
Raise A Ruckus
Raise A Ruckus Tonight
Raise A Rukus Tonight
Raisins And Almonds
Rake And Rambling Boy
Rake's Lament, The
Rakes Of Mallow, The
Rallialei
Rally Round The Standard Boys
Rally Song
Ram Of Darby, The
Ramble Away
Rambler Gambler
Rambler, The
Ramblin' Gamblin' Man
Rambling Gambler
Rambling Gambling Man
Rambling Rover
Rambling Sailor, The
Rambling Shoemaker
Rambling Suiler, The
Ramenez Vos Moutons Du Champ

Traditional (*Cont.*)

Rana, La
Randonnee De Biquette
Range Of The Buffalo, The
Ranger, The
Ranger's Command
Ransomed Soldier, The
Ransum Scansum
Ranter Parson, The
Rantin' Rovin' Robin
Ranz Des Vaches, Le
Ranzo
Rap-A-Tap-Tap
Rare Willie Drowned In Yarrow
Raspberry Tart
Ratcatcher's Daughter, The
Ratcliffe Highway
Rattle Snake
Rattlin Roarin Willie
Ray Doran's Jig
Raz-Ma-Taz-A-Ma-Tee
Read In De Bible
Real Cowboy Life
Real Old Mountain Dew
Reapers' Song
Reason I Stay On Job So Long
Reb Dovid'l
Rebe Elimelech, Der
Rebel Soldier, The
Reborn Again
Recece
Recollections
Recruit, The
Recruiting Party, The
Red Flag, The
Red Fly The Banners O
Red Haired Man's Wife, The
Red Herring, The
Red Iron Ore
Red River Valley
Red Rose Top, The
Red Rosy Bush
Red Running Rue, The
Redwings
Reel Tune
Rei Herodes, El
Rejoice And Be Merry
Rejoice Thee O Heaven
Rejoice With Delight
Religion Is A Fortune
Religion Is A Fortune I Really Do
    Believe
Religion That My Lord Gave Me,
    The
Remarks On The Times
Remember
Remember All The People
Remember Your Servants Lord
Remon
Renaud
Renaud Le Tueur De Femmes
Repandons Sur Le Seuil Feuilles
    Vertes

Traditional *(Cont.)*

Repeal Of The Union
Resignation
Rest Of The Weary
Resurrection
Retour Du Marin, Le
Reuben And Rachel
Reuben Banzo
Reuben Ranzo
Reunion Song, A
Reveille
Reveillez Vous Belle Endormie
Revenge
Revolutionary Tea
Reynold's Letter On The American
   War
Rhinossorheeaguss, The
Rhymes And Chimes
Rich And Rare Were The Gems She
   Wore
Rich Mazurka, The
Rich Merchant's Daughter, The
Rich Mongolia
Rich Nobleman
Rich Old Farmer, The
Rich Old Lady, The
Rich Old Miser, A
Rich Old Miser Courted Me, The
Rich Ship Owner's Daughter, The
Rich Young Farmer, The
Richard Of Taunton Dean
Richard's Mary
Riddle Song, The
Riddle, The
Riddles Wisely Expounded
Ride A Cock-Horse
Ride In The Creel, The
Ride On Jesus
Ride On King Jesus
Ride On Moses
Ride On Ride On In Majesty
Ridin' Round The Range
Riding A Raid
Riding Down To Portsmouth
Riding In The Buggy
Riding On A Load Of Hay
Riding Through The Snow
Riflemen Of Bennington, The
Rig-A-Jig-Jig
Righ Gur Muladach Tha Mi
Righteous Joseph
Righteous Ones, The
Ring Around Her Finger, A
Ring Around The Rosie
Ring Around The Rosy
Ring My Mother Wore, The
Ring Out Wild Bells
Ring Out Ye Bells
Ring The Bell Watchman
Ring The Bells
Ring-A-Round-A-Rosy
Rinn Mi Mocheirigh Gu Eirigh
Rinordine
Rio Grande, The

Traditional *(Cont.)*

Rio Rio
Riqui Ran
Riqui Riqui Riquirran
Rise And Shine
Rise And Stretch
Rise Mourner Rise
Rise Mourners
Rise Shine For Thy Light Is
   A-Comin'
Rise Shine For Thy Light Is
   A-Coming
Rise Up Shepherd
Rise Up Shepherd An' Foller
Rise Up Shepherd An' Follow
Rise Up Shepherd And Foller
Rise Up Shepherd And Follow
Rise Up Shepherds An' Foller
Rises The Sun
Rising Of The Lark, The
Rising Of The Moon, The
Rising Of The Sun, The
Rita's Mazurka
Ritsch Ratsch Filibom
River Blues
River Of Life
River Of My People
River River
River's Side, The
Ro Ro Ro Din Bat
Road Gang Song
Road Is Rugged But I Must Go
Road Mender, The
Road To The Isles, The
Roamer, The
Roaming Gambler, The
Roast Beef Of Old England, The
Robin Adair
Robin And Richard
Robin Hood And Little John
Robin Hood And The Pedlar
Robin Hood And The Tanner
Robin Hood And The Three Squires
Robin Hood Robin Hood Said Little
   John
Robin Hood's Progress To
   Nottingham
Robin Tamson's Smiddy
Robins Last Will, The
Robinson Crusoe
Rock, The
Rock About My Saro Jane
Rock All Our Babies
Rock Island Line, The
Rock Of Ages
Rock Of Ages Let Our Song
Rock-A My Soul
Rock-A-By Baby
Rockabye Baby
Rockah Mh Moomba
Rockets
Rockin' Jerusalem
Rocking
Rocking Schottische, The

Traditional *(Cont.)*

Rocking Song
Rocks And The Mountains, The
Rocks In De Mountains
Rocks Of Scilly, The
Rocky Road
Rocky Road To Dublin, The
Rodda's Mazurka
Rodda's Polka
Rodeo Rider's Lament
Roi A Fait Battre Tambour, Le
Roi Dagobert, Le
Roi Des Amoureux, Le
Roi Renaud, Le
Roi S'en Va-T'en Chasse, Le
Roisin Dubh
Roland's Call
Roll Alabama Roll
Roll De Cotton Down
Roll De Ol' Chariot Along
Roll In My Sweet Baby's Arms
Roll Jordan Roll
Roll On
Roll On Columbia
Roll On Silver Moon
Roll Out Heave That Cotton
Roll Th' Cotton Down
Roll The Cotton Down
Roll The Old Chariot Along
Rollicking Bill The Sailor
Rolling Down To Old Maui
Rolling Home
Rolling King
Rolling Sailor, The
Rolling Stone, The
Rolly Trudum
Rom's Lament, The
Roman Castillo
Romanza
Romish Lady, The
Ronda Del Comte Arnau
Ronde Du Rosier, La
Rookie, The
Rookie's Lament, A
Room Enough
Rooster's Crowing
Root Hog Or Die
Rorate
Rorro, El
Rory O'More
Rosa
Rosa Lee
Rosa Vermelha, A
Rosa Y El Clavel, La
Rosa-Becka-Lina
Rosalinda
Rose D'en Bois, La
Rose Garden
Rose In The Air, The
Rose Ob Alabama, The
Rose Of Tralee, The
Rose Rose
Rose, The

Traditional *(Cont.)*

Rose Tree, The
Rose's Age, The
Roseanna
Rosebush, The
Roselil
Roselil Og Hendes Moder
Rosemary And Thyme
Rosemary Fair
Rosemary Lane
Rosemary Lovely Garland
Roses Blanches, Les
Roses From Fyn
Roses Tulips Gold And Pearl
Rosie
Rosier D'argent, Le
Rosika
Rosin The Bow
Rosina
Rossignol Du Vert Bocage
Rossignol Qui Vole, Le
Rossignolet Console Moi
Rossignolet Du Bois Rossignolet
    Sauvage
Rossignolet Sauvage Toi Qui Vas Au
    Village
Rosy Boy Posy Boy
Rosy Rosy Rosy
Rothesay Bay
Rough And Rolling Sea
'Round Her Neck She Wears A
    Yeller Ribbon
'Round Her Neck She Wears A
    Yellow Ribbon
Round The Bay Of Mexico
Round The Mulberry Bush
Round The Village
Round-Dance
Rounding The Horn
Roundup Lullaby
Rousabout Holler
Rousie's Song
Rovers Meet The Winders, The
Roving
Roving Cowboy, The
Roving Gambler, The
Roving Journeyman
Row De Dow De Dunfer
Row Row Row Your Boat
Row Your Boat
Roy Bean
Royal Banners Forward Go, The
Royal George, The
Royal Oak, The
Royal Proclamation
Royal Rose, The
Rozhinkes Mit Mandlen
Ruach M'Vaderet
Ruban Ruban Ruban
Ruben Ranzo
Rue
Rules Of The Road
Run Along You Little Dogies
Run Chillen Run

Traditional *(Cont.)*

Run Come See
Run Mary Run
Run Mourner Run
Run Nigger Run
Run To De City Of Refuge
Run To Jesus
Run To My Lord
Run With The Bullgine
Rune, A
Runnin' Runnin'
Runo
Russia Sings
Russian Dance
Russian Night Scene
Russian Twelfth Night Song
Russian Weaving Song, A
Rustic Miller, The
Rustler, The
Rusty Old Rover
Rye Whiskey
Rye Whiskey Rye Whiskey
Rye Whisky
Ryebuck Shearer, The
'S Ann Aig Port Taigh Na Hairigh
'S Ann Di-Luain Ro' La Fheill
    Micheil
'S Coma Liom Buntata Carrach
'S E Diuram 'S E Diuram
'S E M'Aghan Fhin Thu
'S E Mo Leannan Calum Gaolach
'S Moch An Diu Gun D'Rinn Mi
    Eirigh
'S Muladach Mi Ho I A Bho
'S Muladach Mi 's Mi Air M'Aineoil
'S Trom Mo Cheum Cha N-Eil Mi
    Sunndach
S 'Vivon
Sa Lately We Watxhed
Sa Parure En Main
Sa-Enu
Sabbath Has No End
Sable Island Song
Sacajawea
Sacramento
Sad Message, A
Sad Song, The
Said The Spider To The Fly
Sailing In The Boat
Sailing Song
Sailing Trade, The
Sailor, The
Sailor And His Bride, The
Sailor Bold, The
Sailor Boy, The
Sailor Courted, A
Sailor In The Ale House, The
Sailor In The Boat
Sailor Lad, The
Sailor Likes His Bottle O, The
Sailor Maid, The
Sailor Who Loved The Spankin' Gals
Sailor's Alphabet, The
Sailor's Christmas Day, The

Traditional *(Cont.)*

Sailor's Complaint, The
Sailor's Farewell, The
Sailor's Grave, The
Sailor's Hornpipe, The
Sailor's Lamentation, The
Sailor's Life, A
Sailor's Only Delight, The
Sailor's Return, The
Sailor's Sweetheart, The
Sailor's Wives, The
Sailors For My Money
Saint Nicolas Et Les Trois Petits
    Enfants
Saint Patrick's Day
Saint Stephen
Saint's Delight, The
Sainte Marguerite
Sainte Vierge Aux Cheveux
    Pendants, La
Saints Of God Lo Jesu's People
Saints Of God Their Conflict Past,
    The
Sairy Ann
Sakura
Sal Oge Ruadh
Salangadou
Salerno Fisherman
Sally Anne
Sally Brown
Sally Buck, The
Sally Come Up
Sally Go Round The Sunshine
Sally Go Up
Sally Goodin
Sally In Our Alley
Sally Munro
Sally My Dear
Sally Racket
Sally Waters
Sallys Flat Waltz
Saltarella
Salty Dog
Salutation Carol, The
Sam Bass
Sam Griffith
Sam Hall
Samba Lele
Same House As Me, The
Same Train
Samiotissa
Sammy Soapsuds
Samson
San Juantito
San Sereni
San Serenin
Sandman, The
Sandy Anna
Sandy Lan'
Sandy Land
Sandy Sam And Rusty Jiggs
Sandy's Mill
Sangaree

Traditional (*Cont.*)

Sangueo
Sanguree
Sankt Raphael
Sano Duso
Sans Day Carol
Sansa Kroma
Sant Josep I La Mare De Deu
Santa Anna
Santa Claus
Santa Claus Blues
Santa Fe Trail, The
Santa Lucia
Santa Maria
Santo Nino, El
Santo San Juanito
Santy Ana
Santy Anna
Santy Anno
Sapins Mes Sapins
Sapo, El
Sarah Williamson's Lament
Sarie Marais
Saro Jane
Satisfied
Saucy Bold Robber, The
Saucy Sailor
Saute Crapaud
Saute Petit Levraut
Save Me Lord Save Me
Save My Father's Picture From The
   Sale
Savez-Vois Plantez Les Choux
Savez-Vous Planter Les Choux
Savin Rock
Savior Like A Shepherd Lead Us
Saviour Blessed Saviour
Saviour For Us Now Is Born, A
Saviour Like A Shepherd Lead Us
Saviour When In Dust To Thee
Saviour's Universal Prayer, The
Saviour's Work, The
Savoyard, The
Saw The Timber
Saw You Never In The Twilight
Sawmill, The
Sawmill Song, The
Sawyer's Exit
Says I'm Boun'
Scabs Crawl In, The
Scalerica D'oro
Scandalize My Name
Scarborough Fair
Scarce Is Barley
Scarecrow, The
Scarlet Sarafan, The
Schlof Bobbeli
Schnitter Tod
Schnitzelbank
Schottische
Schwere Traum, Der
Scissors Grinder, The
Scolding Geese, The
Scolding Wife, A

Traditional (*Cont.*)

Scolding Wife, The
Scotland The Brave
Scotland's Burning
Scots Wha Hae
Scots Wha Hae Wi' Wallace Bled
Scottsboro
Scour And Scrub
Scratch A Match
Scratch Scratch
Screw This Cotton
Se Canto
Se Fue Volando
Se Norges Blomsterdal
Sea Fight In '92, The
Sea Gull
Sea Horses
Sea Martyrs, The
Sea Song, A
Sea's Lullaby, The
Seagulls And The Crickets, The
Seaman And His Love, A
Seaman's Compass, The
Seaman's Hymn
Seamen And Soldier's Last Farewell
   To Their Dearest Jewels, The
Seamen's Distress, The
Seamen's Wives' Vindication, The
Sean Van Voght
Seann Oran Seilge
Search Ye Your Camps
Searching For Lambs
Seated One Day In A Beautiful Cafe
Seben Times
Second Of August
Secret, A
Secret Flower, The
Secret Love
See Alaila Dip Her Feet
See Can't You Jump For Joy
See Him In Raiment Rent
See How Great A Flame Aspires
See See Rider
See See The Cape's In View
See That My Grave Is Kept Clean
See The Conqu'ror Mounts In
   Triumph
See The Conqueror Mounts In
   Triumph
See The Destined Day Arise
See The Signs Of Judgment
See-Saw Margery Daw
See-Saw Sacradown
Seed I Planted
Seeds Of Love, The
Seein' The Elephant
Seeing Nellie Home
Seek And Ye Shall Find
Seguidilla From La Mancha
Seguidillas Manchegas
Sel Bych Rad K Betlemu
Seldom Shines The Stars
Send A Tiket

Traditional (*Cont.*)

Sender Of Dreams
Senhora Of San Benito
Seno Wreck, The
Senora Duena De Casa
Senora Santa Ana
Senores Duenos De Casa
Sent Forth By God's Blessing
Sentry, The
Serenade
Serenade, A
Serenade In Vain
Serene Is The Night
Sergeant, The
Sergeant's Face, The
Servant Of Rosemary Lane, The
Servian National Hymn
Set Down Servant
Setenta Semanas, Las
Sett Deg Oppi Korja
Seule A Ma Fenetre
Seven Daughters, The
Seven Days' Pass, A
Seven Irishmen, The
Seven Joys Of Christmas, The
Seven Joys Of Mary, The
Seven Long Years
Seven Long Years In State Prison
Seven Steps
Seven Virgins, The
Seven White Stars
Sh Ta-Ra-Dah-Day
Sha Shtil
Shabat Shalom
Shabida Rudy
Shack Bully Holler
Shadow Of The Pines, The
Shadows
Shadows O'er The Forest
Shady Grove
Shake Off The Flesh
Shake That Little Foot
Shall I Ever Be The One
Shall I Wasting In Despair
Shallo Brown
Shalom Chaverim
Shalom My Friends Shalom
Shamrock And The Heather, The
Shamrock Shore, The
Shamus O'Brien
Shan Van Vocht, The
Shan Van Voght, The
Shanadoan
Shango
Shannon And The Chesapeake, The
Shanty Boy
Shanty Boys, The
Shanty-Boy And The Farmer's Son,
   The
Shanty-Boy And The Pine, The
Shantyman's Life, A
Shantyman's Life, The
Shaoil Liom Nach Robh Poll No
   Eabar

Traditional *(Cont.)*

Shark, The
Shavua Tov
She Moved Through The Fair
She Was Poor But She Was Honest
She Wore A Yellow Ribbon
She'll Be Comin' 'Round The
  Mountain
She'll Be Comin' Round The The
  Mountain
She'll Be Coming Around The
  Mountain
She'll Be Coming 'Round The
  Mountain
She's Like A Swallow
Shearer And The Swaggie, The
Shearer's Dream, The
Shearing At Castlereagh
Sheepskin And Beeswax
Shenandoah
Shenandoah, The
Shepherd And His Fife, The
Shepherd Boy, The
Shepherd In Love, A
Shepherd Of Cader, The
Shepherd Shepherd
Shepherd, The
Shepherd's Boy, The
Shepherd's Christmas Song
Shepherd's Song, The
Shepherd's Story, The
Shepherdess Be Kind
Shepherdess One Morning, A
Shepherdess Song
Shepherdess, The
Shepherds And The Star
Shepherds Are Singing
Shepherds At The Cradle
Shepherds Be Joyful
Shepherds Come A-Running
Shepherds Fear The Magi, The
Shepherds Hurried To Bethlehem
Shepherds In The Field Abiding
Shepherds Now Are You
Shepherds O Tell Your Story
Shepherds Of The Mountains
Shepherds' Pipes
Shepherds Rejoice
Shepherds Shake Off Your Drowsy
Shepherds Shake Off Your Drowsy
  Sleep
Shepherds Shake Off Your Sleep
Shepherds, The
Shepherds The Day Is Breaking
Shepherds Their Flocks A-Keeping
Shepherds To Bethlehem
Shepherds Watched Their Flocks By
  Night
Shepherds Watching
Shepherds Went Their Hasty Way,
  The
Sherfield Apprentice, The
Sheyn Bin Ich Sheyn

Traditional *(Cont.)*

Shilean Dance Song
Shilling A Night, The
Shilo Brown
Shine Along
Shine On Me
Shine Shine
Shiny Dew
Ship A-Sailing, A
Ship Carpenter, The
Ship In Distress, The
Ship Is All Laden, The
Ship Is At De Landin'
Ship Of Zion, The
Ship Sailed Away For Old England,
  The
Ship That Never Returned, The
Ship, The
Ship's Carpenter, The
Ships On De Oceans
Shir Ha-Ma'alos
Shlof Main Kind
Shlof Mayn Feygele
Shlof Mayn Kind Mayn Treyst Mayn
  Sheyner
Shlof Mayn Kind Shlof Keseyder
Sho 'Nough Steamboats
Shoals Of Herring, The
Shoemaker, The
Shoemaker's Son, The
Shoemaker's Song, The
Shon Ap Evan
Shoo Fly
Shoo Fly Don't Bother Me
Shoo Fly, The
Shoo Shoo Barata
Shoo-Shoo-Shoo-Lye
Shoot The Buffalo
Shooting Of His Dear
Shopping
Shore Navy, The
Shores Of Botany Bay, The
Short Life Of Trouble
Short Rations
Short 'nin 'bread
Shortenin' Bread
Shortening Bread
Shorty George
Shoshanat Ya'akov
Shot My Pistol In De Heart Of Town
Should You See My Love So True
Shoulder Blankets, The
Shout Alleluia To The Savior
Shout For Joy
Shout Josephine Shout
Shout On Pray On
Shout To The Lord With Joy
Shout Yankee Doodle
Shouting Pilgrim
Show Me The Way
Show Mercy Lord
Showing The Flag
Shplitz-Zhe Mir Dem Nayem Sher
Shuckin' Of The Corn

Traditional *(Cont.)*

Shuckin' The Corn
Shuffling Song
Shule Agra
Shule Aron
Shumayela
Shusti Fiddli
Shusti-Fidli
Shvartse Karshelech
Shvartse Karshelech Raysn Mir
Shy Incognita
Shy Violet, The
Si And I
Si J'etais Petite Mere
Si La Paille Ne Coutait Pas Si Cher
Si Nanay Si Tatay
Si Tu Avais Alexandrouchka
Sibdivided Cowboy, The
Sich A Gitting Up Stairs
Sicilian Mariners' Hymn
Sick Call
Sidney Allen
Siege Of Plattsburg
Siege Of Tripoli, The
Siembamba
Siembambe
Sierry Petes, The
Silent Devotion
Silent Kiss, The
Silent Night
Silk Merchant's Daughter, The
Silkie
Silver Bells Of Memory
Silver Cup
Silver Dagger
Silver Dagger, The
Silver Fountain, The
Silver Tide, The
Silvy
Sim Courted The Widow
Sim Shalom
Sim's Flotilla
Siman Tov
Simhat Torah
Simon Brodie Had A Cow
Simon Slick
Simple Birth, The
Simple Gifts
Simple Little Nancy Brown
Simple Simon
Sinbad
Since Love Can Enter An Iron Door
Since The Love Of Christ Has Joined
  Us
Since There's No One Come To Lead
  Me
Sing A Merry New Song
Sing A Song
Sing A Song Of Sixpence
Sing A-Ho That I Had The Wings Of
  A Dove
Sing Heigh Ho
Sing I Pray You
Sing My Tongue The Glorious Battle

Traditional (*Cont.*)

Sing Nightingale
Sing No More Creole-Free Nation
Sing Not Sing Not Nightingale
Sing O Sing This Blessed Morn
Sing Of The Land
Sing Ovy Sing Ivy
Sing Praise To God Who Reigns
    Above
Sing Ron Ron Ron
Sing Sally
Sing Sing
Sing Sing Darkies Sing
Sing Sing Sing
Sing The Universal Glory
Sing Till The Power Of The Lord
    Comes Down
Sing To Lord And King
Sing To The Lord The Children's
    Hymn
Sing We Noel
Sing We Now Of Christmas
Sing We Now The Life Within Us
Sing Your Way Home
Sing-A-Ling-A-Ling
Singabahambayo
Singin' Johnny
Singin' Wid A Sword In Ma Han'
Singing
Singing And Dancing
Singing For Jesus
Single Girl
Single Girl Married Girl
Single Girl, The
Single Life's The Rarest, A
Single Sailor, The
Sinking Of The Graf Spee, The
Sinless One To Jordan Came, The
Sinner Man
Sinner Please Doan Let Dis Harves'
    Pass
Sinner Please Don't Let Dis Harves'
    Pass
Sinner Please Don't Let This Harvest
    Pass
Sinner You Better Get Ready
Sinner's Call
Sinner's Invitation
Sinner-Man So Hard To Believe
Sinners' Redemption, The
Sinners Turn Why Will You Die
Sion Praise Thy Saviour Singing
    Hymns With Exultat
Sion's Daughter
Sioux Indians, The
Sioux Love Song
Sioux Night Dance Song
Sioux War Song
Siph' Amandla
Sippin' Cider Thru A Straw
Sipping Cider From A Straw
Sipping Cider Through A Straw
Sir Arthur And Lady Anne

Traditional (*Cont.*)

Sir Christemas
Sir Eglamore
Sir Francis Drake
Sir Harry Ddu
Sir Herbert Went A-Wooing
Sir Hugh
Sir James The Rose
Sir Niel And Mac Van
Sir Patrick Spens
Sir Walter Raleigh Sailing In The
    Lowlands
Sirdar Janko
Sire Andre S'en Va Chassant
Sire De Framboisy, Le
Sirup Is So Sweet
Sissy In The Bond
Sister Susan
Sister The Sun Is Rising
Sister Thou Wast Mild
Sistern And Brethern
Sisters
Sistren An' Brethren
Sit Down Servant Sit Down
Sit Down Sister
Sit Down Sister Sit Down
Sittin' Down Beside O' The Lamb
Sittin' In De Cotton
Six Hand Reel
Six Kings' Daughters
Six Little Ducks
Six Sweethearts, The
Six-Bit Express, De
Sixteen Thousand Miles From Home
Sixteen Thousand Miles Jig
Siyahamba
Sizewell Abc, The
Skate With Me
Skeptic's Daughter, The
Skibbereen
Skin And Bone Lady, The
Skip To M'Lou
Skip To My Lou
Skye Boat Song
Slack Your Rope
Slav Ho
Slavery Chain Done Broke At Last
Sledge, The
Sleep Baby Brother
Sleep Baby Sleep
Sleep Holy Babe
Sleep Little Angel
Sleep Little Jesus
Sleep Little Lord
Sleep My Child Jesus
Sleep No More The Glad Heavens
    Are Blazing
Sleep O Holy Child Of Mine
Sleep O Sleep
Sleep O Sleep My Lovely Child
Sleep Of The Infant Jesus
Sleep Oh Sleep Little Baby
Sleep Song
Sleeping Princess, The

Traditional (*Cont.*)

Sleepy Latrine, A
Sleepy Song, A
Slender Mountain Ash, The
Sliczna Panienka
Sloe Berry, The
Sloop John B, The
Slovak, The
Slow Song, A
Slum And Beans
Slumber Song
Slyseli Jsme V Betleme
Smacksman, The
Smashing Of The Van, The
Smiles
Smiling Little Lass, The
Smiling Spring
Smoking The Peace Pipe
Smuggler's Song, The
Smuggler's Victory, The
Snagtooth Sal
Snail Snail Come Out Of Your Hole
Snake Baked A Hoecake
Snake Dance Song
Snapoo
Sneel Snaul
Snow
Snow Feathers
Snow Flakes White And Downy
Snow Flakes White And Feathery
Snow Flurries
Snow Is On The Ground, The
Snow Lay On The Ground, The
Snow Time
Snowy-Breasted Pearl, The
Snyezhnaya Kolibellnaya
So Brother
So Dear Is My Charlie To Me
So Deep I Love
So Early In The Morning
So Handy
So Handy My Boys So Handy
So I Can Write My Name
So Wunsch Ich Ir Ein Gute Nacht
Sober Quaker, The
Soche, Di
Sodger Laddie, The
Soft Falls The Dew
Soft Music Is Stealing
Softly Calls The Cuckoo
Softly Now The Light Of Day
Soir Au Clair De Lune, Un
Soir Me Promenant, Un
Sois Nous Propice Danube
Soldier Boy
Soldier Boy For Me
Soldier Boy, The
Soldier From Missouri, A
Soldier Man Blues
Soldier Rest
Soldier Soldier Will You Marry Me
Soldier Soldier Won't You Marry Me
Soldier, The
Soldier Will You Marry Me

Traditional *(Cont.)*

Soldier Won't You Marry Me
Soldier's Grave, The
Soldier's Poor Little Boy, A
Soldier's Poor Little Boy, The
Soldier's Song, The
Soldier's Tear, The
Soldier's Wish, The
Soldier's Wooing, The
Soldiers Of The Cross Arise
Soleares
Solemn Address To Young People
Solemn Song
Solemn Thought
Solidarity
Solomon Levi
Solovei Budimirowitch
Som-Som Beni
Some Day
Some Mother's Child
Some O Dese Mornin's
Some O' These Days
Some Of These Days
Some Of These Mornings
Some Say That Love Is A Blessing
Somebody
Somebody Got Lost In A Storm
Somebody Got Lost In De Storm
Somebody's Buried In The
 Graveyard
Somebody's Calling My Name
Somebody's Knockin' At Yo' Do'
Somebody's Knockin' At Your Door
Somebody's Knocking At Your Door
Somebody's Tall And Handsome
Somebody's Waiting For Me
Someone
Someone's Smiles
Somerset Carol
Somerset Wassail
Something In Your Ear
Something New
Sometimes A Light Surprises
Sometimes I Feel Like A Motherless
 Child
Sometimes I Feel Like A Motherless
 Chile
Somewhere Far
Somewhere In New Guinea
Somm Eilles-Tu Me Petite Louison
Sommeil De L'Enfant Jesus, Le
Somos Dos Esposos
Son Of A Gambolier, A
Son Of Consolation, The
Son Of God Is Born For All
Son Of The Beach, The
Sonccuiman
Song And The Sigh, The
Song Before Christmas
Song For Freedom
Song For Our Times, A
Song Of A Lost Hunter, A

Traditional *(Cont.)*

Song Of A Soldier
Song Of Birds
Song Of Brother Green, The
Song Of China, A
Song Of Co-Lo-Vin
Song Of Hope
Song Of Iowa
Song Of John Hawkins And
 Comrades
Song Of John Henry
Song Of La Palisse
Song Of Praise, A
Song Of Sixpence, A
Song Of Song Titles
Song Of States, The
Song Of Swedish Patriots
Song Of The '41 Date
Song Of The Campus Commandos,
 The
Song Of The Canal
Song Of The Crib
Song Of The Croppy Boy
Song Of The Delhi Tongawallah
Song Of The Drummer, The
Song Of The Eleven Slash Slash
 Eleven
Song Of The Exile
Song Of The Fisherman
Song Of The Fishes
Song Of The Frogs
Song Of The Herb Gatherers
Song Of The Homefront
Song Of The Infant Jesus
Song Of The Kansas Emigrant
Song Of The Life-Boat Men
Song Of The Maremma
Song Of The Marines, The
Song Of The Miners
Song Of The Nuns Of Chester
Song Of The Officers' Torpedo Class
Song Of The Olindha Gatherers
Song Of The Open Air, A
Song Of The Pigeon
Song Of The Rebel Soldier, The
Song Of The Reed-Birds
Song Of The Rooster, The
Song Of The Rose, The
Song Of The Sea, A
Song Of The Seamen And Land
 Soldiers, A
Song Of The Ship
Song Of The Spirit
Song Of The Stamford Bullards
Song Of The Tailor
Song Of The Vermonters 1799, The
Song Of The Volga Boatman
Song Of The Volga Boatmen
Song On The Death Of Colonel
 Crafford, A
Song On The Duke's Late Glorious
 Success Over The
Song To Oshima
Song To The Birds

Traditional *(Cont.)*

Songs
Songs About Animals
Songs Of My Country, The
Songs Of Praise The Angels Sang
Sono Tre Giorni
Soon A Will Be Done
Soon May The Last Glad Song Arise
Soon One Mawnin' Death Come
 Creepin' In Yo' Room
Soon One Mornin' Death Come
 Creepin'
Sorida
Sorrowful Lament For Callaghan
 Greally And Mullen
Sorrows Of Memory, The
Soul Of Jesus Make Me Whole
Sounds I Like
Soup Song
Sourwood Mountain
Sous Les Branches D'Un Tilleul
South Australia
South Coast, The
Southerly Wind And A Cloudy Sky,
 A
Southern Encampment, The
Southern Soldier, The
Southwark Rebolution, De
Southwood Girls, The
Sow Took The Measles, The
Spanish Cachucha
Spanish Carol
Spanish Is The Loving Tongue
Spanish Johnny
Spanish Ladies
Spanish Lady
Spanish Maid, A
Spanish National Hymn
Spanish Waltz, The
Spanish War March
Spanking Maggie From The Ross
Sparrow, The
Special Aging Of Finance Contacts
Speckled Fish, The
Speed My Reindeers
Spin Maiden Spin
Spin Spin
Spinner, The
Spinning Song
Spinning Song, The
Spinning-Top
Spirit Blest Who Art Adored
Spirit Divine Attend Our Prayers
Spirit O' The Lord Done Fell On Me
Spirit Of God Like A Fire Is Burning,
 The
Spirit Of God Unleashed On Earth
Spirit, The
Splinter McLeod's Tune
Spookendyke's Waltz
Sporting Races Of Galway, The
Spread O Spread Thou Might Word
Sprig Of Thyme
Spring

Traditional *(Cont.)*

Spring Again Is Here, The
Spring Awakes
Spring Breezes Playing
Spring Calls
Spring Carol
Spring Farming
Spring Fever
Spring Has Come
Spring Has Now Unwrapped The
     Flowers
Spring Messages
Spring Morning
Spring Plowing
Spring's Acoming, The
Spring's Arrival
Spring's Message
Springfield Mountain
Springtime In Alaska
Springtime Is Here
Springtime It Brings On The
     Shearing, The
Spurn Point
Square Order Shuffle
Squaw Song
Squirrel, The
Squirrel Loves A Pleasant Chase,
     The
St George And The Drag-On
St James Hospital
St James Infirmary
St Patrick Was A Gentleman
St Patrick's Breastplate
St Patrick's Day
St Patrick's Potato Race
St Valentine's Day
Stable Call
Stagalee
Stagolee
Stagolee Done Kill De Bully
Stampede, The
Stan' Steady
Stan' Still Jordan
Stan'in' In De Need Of Prayer
Stancutza
Stand And Be Counted
Stand On The Sea Of Glass
Stand The Ground's Your Own
Stand The Storm
Stand Up Like Soldiers
Standard Of A Nation's Pride
Standin' In The Need Of Prayer
Standin' On De Corner
Standing In The Need Of Prayer
Standing On The Mountain
Stands A Maple
Star Carol, The
Star In Heaven, A
Star In The East, The
Star Of Christmas Morning, The
Star Of The Evening
Star Spangled Banner, The
Starlaw Disaster, The

Traditional *(Cont.)*

Starry Night For A Ramble, A
Stars Are Shining, The
Stars In The Elements
Stars Of Glory
Stars Of The Summer Night
State Fair
State Of Arkansas, The
Stately Southerner, The
Stavin' Chain
Stay In De Field
Stay In The Field
Stay On The Farm
Steady Jesus Listenin'
Steal Away
Steal Away And Pray
Steal Away To Jesus
Steal Away To Mah Fathuh's
     Kingdom
Steam From The Whistle Smoke
     From The Stack
Steel-Linin' Chant
Steeple Bells
Steer Roper, The
Stefan Was A Stable Boy
Stenka Razin
Step Tune
Step-Dance
Stev Fra Telemarken
Stewball
Stickin' Out A Mile From Blarney
Stickit Ball A Hack
Still Still Still
Stir The Pudding
Stitch In Time, A
Stockman's Last Bed, The
Stodola Pumpa
Stodum Tvau I Tuni
Stone Outside Dan Murphy's Door,
     The
Stonewall Jackson's Way
Stony Point
Stop Breaking Down
Stor Ola Lill' Ola
Store Hvite Flokk, Den
Stories Of Travel
Stork's Nest, The
Storks In Autumn
Stormalong
Stormy Scenes Of Winter, The
Stormy Weather Boys
Story Of George Mann
Story Of Gustave Ohr
Story Of The Coachman, The
Stranger
Strathspey
Strawberry Roan, The
Street Cry
Street Organ, The
Street Song
Street Vendors, The
Streets Of Laredo, The
Strength Of The Lion, The

Traditional *(Cont.)*

Strike The Bell
Strolling Fiddler, The
Strolling Minstrel, The
Strolling Through Norfolk
Stromming Boats, The
Student's Way, The
Study War No More
Subo Subo
Sucking Cider Through A Straw
Suckling Pig, The
Sugar Babe
Sugar Babe Blues
Sugar Hill
Sugarbush
Suliram
Sumer Is Icumen In
Summer Afternoon
Summer Carol
Summer Evening
Summer In Winter
Summer Is A-Comin' In
Summer Is A-Coming In
Summer Picture, A
Summer Time
Sun Gonna Shine In My Door Some
     Day
Sun Had Sunk Behind The Hill, The
Sun Is Burning, The
Sun May Be Shining Tomorrow
     Although It Is Cloudy Today
     Waltz, The
Sun Mows Down, The
Sun Of My Soul Thou Saviour Dear
Sun Of Suns, The
Sun Rises Bright In France, The
Sun Worshippers, The
Sunday Mornin' Ban
Sunday Morning
Sundown
Sundown Below
Sung At Harvest Time
Sunny Bank
Sunny Holiday, A
Sunny Naples
Sunrise Dance
Sunrise Serenade
Sunset
Sunset To Sunrise Changes Now
Supplication
Suppose
Sur L'herbette Verte
Sur La Route
Sur La Route De Dijon
Sur Le Bord Du Lac Un Saule
Sur Le Fleuve Daria
Sur Le Joli Vent
Sur Le Mont Un Chene
Sur Le Pont D'Avignon
Sur Le Pont La-Bas
Sur Les Champs La Brume
Sur Les Flots Canette Allait
Sur Les Flots Canette Blanche
Sur Les Marches Du Palais

Traditional (*Cont.*)

Sur Mon Pere
Sure He Has
Sus In Poarta Rai Ului
Susan Jane
Susan Van Dusan
Susani
Susanni
Susie Q
Sussex Carol
Sussex Mummers' Carol
Sussex Toast
Suvla Bay
Suzanne Pretty Maid
Suzette La Bonne Enfant
Swabian Trooper's Song
Swallows Are Flying
Swan Sings, The
Swansea Town
Swapping Song, The
Swedish Cradle Song
Swedish Lullaby
Sweep As I Go
Sweep Sweep And Cleanse Your
    Floor
Sweet And Precious Jesus
Sweet Anthems Sing
Sweet As The Song
Sweet Baby Sleep
Sweet Betsey From Pike
Sweet Betsy From Pike
Sweet Canaan
Sweet Evelina
Sweet Fa's The Eve
Sweet Hope
Sweet Jane
Sweet Little Birdie, The
Sweet Lone Vale, The
Sweet Marie
Sweet Memories Of Thee
Sweet Molly Malone
Sweet Molly-O
Sweet Nightingale
Sweet Oranges
Sweet Patate
Sweet Potatoes
Sweet Saviour Bless Us Ere We Go
Sweet Sugar Cane
Sweet Sunny South, The
Sweet The Evening Air
Sweet The Moments Rich In Blessing
Sweet Thing
Sweet Trinity
Sweet Turtle Dove
Sweet Was The Song The Virgin
    Sang
Sweet William
Sweet William And Lady Margaret
Sweet William's Ghost
Sweetest Sound I Ever Heard
Sweetheart Good Night
Sweetheart Out A-Hunting
Sweethearts And Wives
Sweetly Sings The Donkey

Traditional (*Cont.*)

Swell My Net Full
Swiftly Flowing Labe
Swiftly Flowing Waters
Swing A Lady Round
Swing Low
Swing Low Sweet Chariot
Swingin' On A Scab
Switzer, The
Switzer's Farewell, The
Sydney Cup Day
Sydney Flash, The
Sylvie
Szilvas Village
T For Texas
T'es Petite Mais T'es Mignonne
T'other Side Of Jordan
Ta Na La
Ta Ra Limavady
Ta-Ra-Ra Boom-De-Ay
Tachanka
Tactful Peddler, The
Tailor Boy, The
Take A Whiff On Me
Take Me Down The Harbour
Take Me Earth
Take This Hammer
Take Up The Courses
Take Up Your Cross The Savior Said
Take Yo' Time Miss Lucy
Taking Gair In The Night
Taking His Chance
Taladh Ar Slanair
Taladh Choinnich Oig
Tale Of A Little Pig
Tale Of A Sailor
Talking Atom
Talking Rent
Talking Union
Tall Angel At The Bar
Tallow-Candle
Tally Ho Hark Away
Tallyho
Tam Glen
Tam O' The Lin
Tambaroora Gold
Tambour, Le
Tambourine Dance
Tammany
Tan Patate-La' Tchuite
Taney County
Tanglefoot Sue
Tanker Song, The
Tante Monika
Tanz Fraylach
Tap Tap Tap
Tappe Jambes Fines
Taps
Tapscott We're All Bound To Go
Taquircapuscaiqui Ari
Tarantella
Tarde Era Triste, La
Tarde Fresquita De Mayo, Una
Tarde Fresquita, Una

Traditional (*Cont.*)

Taripai-Cha-Cucharata
Tarpaulin Jacket
Tarry Sailor, The
Tars Of The Blanche, The
Tattie Jock
Tatties An Herrin'
Te Quiero Nino Besar
Te Quiero Porque Te Quiero
Teach Me My God And King
Tearin' Out-A Wilderness
Tecolote, El
Tell All The World John
Tell 'Em I'm Gone
Tell It On De Mountain
Tell It On The Mountain
Tell Jesus I Done Done All I Can
Tell John Don' Call Duh Roll
Tell John Don' Call The Roll
Tell John Don't Call De Roll
Tell Me Dear
Tell Me Fair One
Tell Me Now
Tell Me Why
Tell O Shepherds
Tell Old Bill
Tell Out My Soul The Greatness Of
    The Lord
Tell Us Shepherds
Tell Us Wise Men
Tell-A-Me True
Temperance Call, The
Temperance River, The
Temperance Song
Temporal Temporal
Temps File, Le
Tempus Adest Floridum
Ten Brothers
Ten Green Bottles
Ten Little Devils
Ten Little Indians
Ten Little Niggers
Ten Miles From Home
Ten Poun' Ten
Ten Thousand Cattle
Ten Thousand Dollars For The
    Home Folks
Ten Thousand Men Were Going On
    Manoeuvres
Ten Thousand Miles
Ten Thousand Miles Away
Ten Thousand Miles From Home
Ten Virgins, The
Tender Care
Tender Child Was Born This Day, A
Tender Love
Tenderfoot, The
Tenes La De Pres
Tenho Um Vestido Novo
Tennessee
Terek, The
Terrible Inmensidad, La
Terrier Dog, The
Terry Collins' Waltz

Traditional *(Cont.)*

Texas
Texas Cowboy, The
Texas Ranger
Texas Rangers, The
Texian Boys
Tha Ghaoth An Iar A' Gobachadh
Tha Mi Sgith 'M Onaran
Tha Mile Long Air Cuan Eirinn
Tha Mo Dhuil Tha Mo Dhuil
Tha T'Athair Air An Daoraich
Thalaidhinn Thu
Thank God I'm On My Way To
   Heaven
Thank You
Thank You No
Thanksgiving Carol
Thanksgiving Hymn
Thanksgiving Prayer
That Big Rock Candy Mountain
That Cause Can Neither Be Lost Nor
   Stayed
That Is Even So
That Lonesome Valley
That Old Time Religion
That Pretty Little Girl
That Silly Song
That Suits Me
That's A Lie
That's Me
That's My Girl
That's Where The Money Goes
Thee Fairest Star
Themes From Processional To
   Calvary
Then My Little Sou's Gonna Shine
Then My Troubles Will Be Over
Then The Work's All Done This Fall
There Are Pits
There Are Twa Bonny Maidens
There Came A Little Stranger
There Came Three Kings
There Is A Balm In Gilead
There Is A Fountain Filled With
   Blood
There Is A Land Of Pure Delight
There Is A Ship
There Is A Tavern In The Town
There Is Joy In Ev'ry Day
There Is No Cradle Ready
There Is No Rose
There She Blows
There Was A Crooked Man
There Was A Jolly Miller
There Was A Little Boy
There Was A Little Girl
There Was A Little Hen
There Was A Little Man
There Was A Man And He Was Mad
There Was A Pig
There Was An Old Frog
There Was An Old Miller
There Was An Old Soldier
There Was An Old Witch

Traditional *(Cont.)*

There Was An Old Woman Had
   Three Cows
There Was An Old Woman Lived
   Under The Hill
There Was An Old Woman Who
   Lived In A Shoe
There Was An Old Women
There Was None Who Loved Her
   More Than I
There Was Once A Little Ship
There Was One There Was Two
   There Was Three Little
There Were Ten Virgins
There Were Three Kings
There's A House
There's A Little Dog At Our House
There's A Little Wheel A-Turnin'
There's A Little Wheel A-Turnin' In
   My Heart
There's A Man Goin' Round Takin'
   Names
There's A Meeting Here Tonight
There's A Wideness In God's Mercy
There's Born In Bethlehem's Manger
There's Fire Down Below
There's Nae Laddie Coming
There's Nae Luck About The House
There's No Hiding Place
There's No Room For You
There's Nothing Can Equal A Good
   Woman Still
There's The Cape-Cart
Therefore We Before Him Bending
These Things Shall Be
They Come God's Messengers Of
   Love
They Led My Lord Away
They Were Very Good To Me
Thief, The
Thine Arm O Lord In Days Of Old
Thine Forever God Of Love
Things About Goin' My Way
Things Impossible
Things That Are Mine
Think Dear Maiden
Thinnest Man I Ever Saw, The
Third Cavalry Song
This Be The Way
This Enders Nyzgt
This Endris Night
This Glad Easter Day
This Is A Sin-Trying World
This Is Christmas Eve
This Is De Healin' Water
This Is My Father's World
This Is The House That Jack Built
This Is The Man
This Is The Place
This Little Light Of Mine
This May Be The Last Time
This New Christmas Carol
This Ol' Hammer

Traditional *(Cont.)*

This Ol' Time Religion
This Old Man
This Old Time Religion
This Ole Hammer
This Time Another Year
This Train
Tho The Last Glimpse Of Erin
Thogail A' Bhuntat'
Thomas O' Yonderdale
Thomas O'Winesberrie
Thomas The Rhymer
Thornymoor Fields
Those Evening Bells
Thou Art My Shepherd
Thou Gracious God Whose Mercy
   Lends
Thou Lord Hast Power To Heal
Thou Lord Of Life Our Saving
   Health
Thou Lovest Me So Dearly
Thought I Heard Dat K C Whistle
   Blow
Thoughts At Evening
Three Acre O' Coffee
Three Blind Mice
Three Brothers, The
Three Children Sliding On The Ice
Three Craw
Three Crows
Three Drunken Maidens
Three Farmers Went A-Hunting
Three Gallant Huntsmen, The
Three Girls Drowned
Three Grains Of Corn
Three Green Lettuce Heads
Three Hand Reel
Three Holy Women
Three Horsemen, The
Three Hundred Pounds
Three Huntsmen, The
Three Jews, The
Three Jolly Fisherman
Three Jolly Frenchmen
Three King's Song, The
Three Kings, The
Three Kings Song
Three Little Babes, The
Three Little Kittens
Three Lovers
Three Men Went A-Hunting
Three Nights Drunk
Three Pigs
Three Pirates
Three Ponies
Three Ravens
Three Ravens, The
Three Rogues, The
Three Roses, The
Three Sailors, The
Three Score And Ten
Three Scotch Robbers, The
Three Sisters
Three Tailors, The

Traditional *(Cont.)*

Three Thousand Texas Steers
Three Times Around
Three Times Over
Three Traitors, The
Three White Doves
Three Wise Men Of Gotham
Threefold Amens
Thrice The Blackbird
Thrifty Miss
Thro' The Love Of God Our Saviour
Throned Upon The Awful Tree
Through Moorfields
Through Ormod's Graveyard
Through The Groves
Through The Shadows Of The Night
Through The Wood
Throw Me Anywhere
Thuirt An Gobha 'fuiricheamaid
Thuma Mina
Thumbs Up
Thuringian Folk Song
Thy Kingdom Come O Lord
Thy Kingdom Come On Bended
 Knee
Thy Kingdom Lord We Long For
Thy Lovely Bright Eyes
Ti Ayat Ti Meysa Nga Ubing
Tibbie Dunbar
Tic-E-Tic-E-Toc
Tic-Tac Du Moulin, Le
Tico Tico
Tidy-O
Tie-Shuffing Chant
Tie-Tamping Chant
Tiger Bay
Tiggy Tiggy Touchwood
Tilinka, The
Till An Crodh Faigh An Crodh
Tim
Tim Finnegan's Wake
Tim Finnigan's Wake
Timber Song
Timbrook
Time Is Drawin' Nigh
Time To Leave Her
Times Gettin' Hard
Timid Maiden, The
Timmy Tyes
Tingalayo
Tiny Sparrow
Tip And Ty
Tippecanoe And Tyler Too
Tipperary Christening, The
Tippi Canoo
Tiritomba
'Tis Jordan's River
'Tis Me O Lord
'Tis No Wind
'Tis So Sweet To Trust In Jesus
'Tis The Old Ship Of Zion
'Tis Winter Now The Fallen Snow
Tisserands Sont Pires Que Des
 Eveques, Les
Titanic, The

Traditional *(Cont.)*

Titles Of Songs
Tittery-Irie-Aye
To A Tiny Cottage
To All You Ladies
To An Inn So Lowly
To Bethle'm I Would Go
To Bethlehem Singing
To Gey Zich Lernen Tantsn
To Lauterbach
To Mary In Her Garden
To My Humble Supplication
To Noel
To Norway Mother Of The Brave
To Old Norway
To Rosella
To See God's Bleedin' Lam'
To Tarnoca I Went
To The Camel Man
To The Door I Strolled
To The Garden Annie Went
To The Home Of My Beloved
To The Memory Of Havlicek
To The Moon
To The Name Of Our Salvation
To The West Awhile To Stay
To Thee Before The Close Of Day
To Thee O Lord Our Hearts We
 Raise
To Tsobanopoulo
To Us Is Born A Little Child
To War Has Gone Duke
 Marlborough
Toast
Tobacco Union
Today The Light Of Angels Bright
Toi Qui Chantes Le Jour Et La Nuit
Toll The Bell Angel I Just Got Over
Tolosa Fair
Tom Big-Bee River
Tom Bolyn
Tom Bolynn
Tom Brown's Indian Boys
Tom Cat
Tom Corrigan
Tom Dooley
Tom Halyard
Tom O'Neil
Tom Queer
Tom Tom The Piper's Son
Tom's Gone T' Hilo
Tom's Gone To Ilo
Tom's Polka
Tomlin
Tommy Robin
Tommy's Gone To Hilo
Tomorrow Shall Be My Dancing Day
Ton Ti Bec Est Doux
Tone De Bell Easy
Tongue Twisters
Tono De Velorio De Cruz
Too Late
Toom-Balalaika
Toomba Toomba

Traditional *(Cont.)*

Torches
Toro Pinto, El
Tote Knabe, Der
Totenamt
Touch Not The Cup
Touching Grace We Princes Three
Toucouyoute
Tough Luck
Tour Prends Garde, La
Tourelay
Tourelay Tourelay
Touro-Louro-Louro
Tous Les Bourgeois De Chastres
Tout Autour Des Beaux Cytises
Tout Mon Or Est Bien Cache
Tout Pitit Negresse
Toutes Les Larmes Que J'Ai Versees
Tower On Guard, The
Towpath Circus
Toy Dance
Tra La La
Trader, The
Tragedia De Heraclio Bernal
Trail Herding Song, The
Trail To Mexico, The
Train Is A-Comin'
Train Is A-Coming, The
Train Pulled In The Station, The
Train That Will Never Be Found,
 The
Train To Kimberley
Tram Ride, The
Tramp The Bushes Of Australia
Trampin'
Transformations, Les
Traveler, The
Traveling
Traveling Down The Castlereagh
Treasure, The
Treasury Of Hope, The
Treasury Rats
Tree In The Wood, The
Tree, The
Tree Toad, The
Trees Are Getting High, The
Trees They Do Grow High, The
Trees They Grow So High, The
Trench Blues
Trente Et Un Du Mois D'Aout, Le
Trimousette
Trink Bruder Trink Oys
Trip On The Erie, A
Triste
Triste Vida E Do Marujo
Tristes Noces, Les
Troika
Troika Rushing
Troika, The
Trois Bons Droles, Les
Trois Filles D'un Prince, Les
Trois Jeunes Tambours
Trois Petits Tours Et Puis S'en Vont
Trois Roses Empoisonnees, Les

Traditional (*Cont.*)

Troll Of The Hill, The
Trooper And The Maid, The
Troopers, The
Trot Away
Troubles Was Hard
Trubadurvise
True And Trembling Brakeman, The
True Love On My Mind
True Lover Of Mine, A
True Lover's Farewell, The
True Lovers' Departure, The
True Yankee Sailor, The
Trump Of Freedom
Trumpeter Blow
Trusty Lariat
Truth From Above, The
Try Try Again
Tryin' To Cross The Red Sea
Tryin' To Get Home
Tshiribim
Tsvey Taybelech
Tu-Ru-Ru-Ru
Tuba
Tuba And The Alto Horn, The
Tuljak
Tum-Balalayka
Tumbalalaika
Tune Of Morvudd's Pipes, The
Tune The Old Cow Died Of, The
Tune The Old Cow Died On, The
Tuneful Guitar, The
Tuoll On Mun Kultani
Turbid Is The Bodrog
Turfman From Ardee, The
Turk Song
Turkey In The Straw
Turkey Shivaree, The
Turkish Lady, The
Turkish Round
Turkish Rover
Turn Again Whittington
Turn Back Pharoah's Army
Turn The Glasses Over
Turn Ye To Me
Turning Song
Turnip Greens
Turtle Dove, The
Tuscan Serenade
Tuta Maramba
Tutu Maramba
Tva Song, The
Twa Brothers, The
Twa Corbies, The
Twa Sisters, The
Twankidillo
Twankydillo
'Twas A Love Of Adventure
'Twas At The Back O' Bennochie
'Twas In The Moon Of Wintertime
'Twas On De Bluff
'Twas On One Sunday Morning
'Twas Summer And 'twas Evening
'Tween The Mount And Deep Deep
   Vale

Traditional (*Cont.*)

Tweed, The
Twelfth Night Comes
Twelfth Night Song
Twelve Apostles, The
Twelve Commandments, The
Twelve Days Of Christmas
Twelve Days Of Christmas, The
Twelve Gates To The City
Twelve Little Rabbits
Twelve O'Clock Is Striking
Twenty Years Ago
Twenty-Four Robbers
Twenty-One
Twenty-One Years
Twice Bloom The Acacia Trees
Twilight
Twilight Shadows Fall
Twin Ballots, The
Twinkle Little Star
Twinkle Twinkle Little Star
Twinkling Stars
'Twixt Gentle Ox And Ass So Gray
Two Banana
Two Brothers, The
Two By Two
Two Crows, The
Two Ducks On A Pond
Two Guitars
Two Jims Mazurka, The
Two Little Children
Two Little Dogs Sat By The Fire
Two Little Girls In Blue
Two Magicians, The
Two Mile Flat Varsoviana
Two Rabbits, The
Two Rigs Of Rye
Two Sisters, The
Two Sisters That Loved One Man,
   The
Two Stalwart Trees Both Rooted In
   The Faith
Two Wings
Tying A Knot In The Devil's Tail
Tying Knots In The Devil's Tail
Tyroleans, The
Tyrolese Mountain Song
Tyven Tyven
Tzur Mishelo
Ufaratzta
Uh-Uh No
Uibhist Nam Beann Arda
Ukranian Carol
Ulan Girls
Ule-Ule
Ulster Won't Have It
Umerella Shore, The
Un Canadien Errant
Un Deux Trois
Un Du Akerst
Uncle Charlie
Uncle Joe
Uncle Ned
Uncle Reuben

Traditional (*Cont.*)

Uncle Sam Simmie
Uncle Sam's Farm
Uncle Sammy He's Got The Artillery
Unconstant Lover, The
Und Unser Lieben Frauen Der
   Traumete
Under Eaves
Under Our Cottage Window
Under The Spreading Chestnut Tree
Under The Willow She's Sleeping
Under The Willow Waltz
Underneath The Forest Tree
Unfortunate Man, The
Unfortunate Miss Bailey
Unfortunate Wife, The
Union Boy, The
Union Girl, The
Union Maid
United Nations Make A Chain
United States And Macedonian, The
Unkle Johnnie
Unquiet Grave, The
Unseaworthy Ship, The
Unser Hans
Unser Liebe Fraue Vom Kalten
   Brunnen
Unter A Kleyn Beymele
Unter Dem Kinds Vigele
Until I Die
Until I Reach-A Ma Home
Unto The Cross Of Jesus
Unto Us A Boy Is Born
Unzer Rebenyu
Up On The House-Top
Up Over My Head
Up The Mountain
Upidee
Upon De Mountain
Upon Sir Francis Drak's Return
   From His Voyage About The
   World
Upon The Frosty Meadows
Upper California, The
Upside Down
Us Poor Fish
Ut Etter Ol
Utah Carroll
Utah Iron Horse, The
Ute Mountain Air
Utsu Etsa
Uy Tara La La
V'Hi Sheomdo
V'La Le Bon Vent
V'Nomar L'Fonov
V'Samachta B'Chagecha
V'Taher Libenu
Vacht Oyf
Vagabond's Song
Vahlsing Pollutes It
Vain Regrets
Valencianita
Valentine
Valiant Marine

Traditional *(Cont.)*

Valiant Sailor, The
Valiant Soldier, The
Valparaiso
Valse De La Grand'chenier, La
Valse Des Creoles, La
Vamos A Belen
Vamos A La Mar
Vamos Pastorcitos
Vamudara
Vamuroyi Woye
Van Cantando Por La Sierra
Van Dieman's Land
Van Diemen's Land
Vangeline
Varmeland
Varsoviana
Varsovienna
Vem Ca Cabeleria
Venadito, El
Vendor's Call
Venetian Waters
Venezuela
Veni Emmanuel
Venice Night
Venid Esposos Santos
Venid Pastorcitos
Venture Gwen
Vera Lee's Mazurka
Vera Lee's Polka-Mazurka
Verbum Caro
Verdant Groves
Vermeland
Very Bread Good Shepherd Tend Us
Very Little Negress Down On The
    Bayou, A
Vesper
Vesper Bells
Vesper Hymn
Vesuvian Shore, The
Vez Clavelina, Una
Vi Azoy Trinkt A Keyser Tey
Vi Zenen Mayne Yunge Yoren
Vic Large's Set Tune
Vicar Of Bray, The
Victory
Vidala
Vidalita, La
Viennese Refrain
Viennese Waltz
Viens Commere Viens Nous
    Bavarderons Bien
Vigndig A Fremd Kind
Vigne Au Vin, La
Vigolin
Vihuda L'Olam Teshev
Viking Lullaby
Vilikens And His Dinah
Village Bells, The
Village Bride's Trip To Mother, A
Village On The Road, The
Village Pride, The
Village Talk
Village-Evening It Is Late

Traditional *(Cont.)*

Villancico
Villancico Vasco
Villikins And His Dinah
Vintage Song, The
Violet, The
Virgen Lava Panales, La
Virgin Mary
Virgin Mary Had-A One Son, The
Virgin Most Pure, A
Virgin Unspotted, A
Virginia Reel
Virginia's Bloody Soil
Virginie
Vision Of Columbus, The
Vision Song
Vision, The
Vitamins
Viva Jujuy
Viva La Musica
Viva La Quince Brigada
Viva Panama
Vive Henri IV
Vive L'amour
Vive La Canadienne
Vive La Compagnie
Vive La Senior Class
Vive Les Matelots
Vive Vum
Vogelhochzeit, Die
Voice Of God, The
Voice Of One We Love, The
Voici La Saint Jean
Voici Le Mois De Mai
Voici Le Printemps
Voici Noel
Voila La Recompense
Volga Boat Song
Volga Boatmen
Volga, The
Vom Heiligen Martyrer Emmerano
Vom Himmel Hoch
Von Edler Art
Voreema
Voulez Vous Que Je Vous Chante
Vous Conne 'Tite La Maison
Voyage, The
Voyageur's Song
Voyez Ce Mulet La
Vreneli
Vula Botha
Vuszhe Vils Tu
W Zlobie Lezy
W-Nfa Nyem
Wabash Cannon Ball, The
Wabash Cannonball
Wach Auf Meins Herzens Schone
Wach Auf Wach Auf Mit Heller
    Stimm
Wade In De Water
Wade In Nuh Watuh Childun
Wade In The Water
Wagoner's Lad
Wai Bamba

Traditional *(Cont.)*

Wait A Little While
Wait For The Wagon
Waitress And The Sailor, The
Waits, The
Wake Me
Wake Nightingale
Wake Thee Now Dearest
Wake Up
Wake Up Boys
Wake Up Jacob
Wake Up Jacob Day Is A Breakin'
Wake Up Stur About
Wake Young Shepherds
Waking-Time
Wakken
Walk About Elders
Walk Her 'round
Walk In Jerusalem Jus' Like John
Walk In Jerusalem Just Like John
Walk Mary Down De Lane
Walk Softly
Walk Together Children
Walk You In De Light
Walkin' John
Walking At Night
Walking In De Light
Walking Song
Walks On The Heath, The
Wallaby Track, The
Walloping Window Blind, The
Walnut Harvest
Waltz From Calcasieu Parish, A
Waltz Of Vienna
Waltz Song
Waltz Song, A
Waltzing Matilda
Waltzing With Anya
Wanderer's Soliloquy, The
Wanderin'
Wandering Cowboy, The
Want To Go To Heaven When I Die
War Correspondent, The
War Department
War No More
War Song
Waratah Mazurka, The
Warbling Blackbird, The
Ward The Pirate
Waring Of Sonora Town
Wark Of The Weavers, The
Warm Boots
Warning, The
Warod Nocnej Ciszy
Warranted Love
Warranty Deed, The
Warrego Lament, The
Warrenton
Wars Of Germany, The
Was Wolln Wir Auf Den Abend Tun
Wash And Be Clean
Washing Day
Washington
Wasn' That A Wonder

Traditional *(Cont.)*

Wasn' That Hard Trials
Wasn't That A Mighty Day
Wasn't That A Time
Wasp Bite Nobi On Her Conch-Eye,
    A
Wassail Song, The
Wassail Wassail
Wassail Wassail All Over The Town
Waste Not Want Not
Watching The Sky
Watching The Wheat
Water Boy
Water Come A Me Eye
Water Is Wide, The
Water Me From De Lime Rock
Water Running
Water Sprites' Dance
Water Wheel, The
Water-Cresses, The
Waterbound
Watermelons
Waters Ripple And Flow
Watts' Cradle Song
Waulking Song
'Way Down In Cuba
'Way Down In Ole Virginia
Way Down In The Old Peedee
Way Down In The Ole Peedee
Way Down South
Way Down Yonder In The Cornfield
Way In The Heaven Bye-And-Bye
'Way In The Kingdom
Way Is Jesus, The
Way Of The Lord, The
Way Out In Idaho
Way Out There
'Way Out West In Kansas
Way Over In The Blooming Garden
Way Over Jordan
Way To Kerry, The
Wayfarin' Stranger
Wayfaring Stranger, The
We Are All Noddin'
We Are Building A Strong Union
We Are Building On A Rock
We Are Climbing Jacob's Ladder
We Are Climbing The Hills Of Zion
We Are Climin' Jacob's Ladder
We Are Crossing Jordan River
We Are God's Stewards
We Are Poor
We Are Soldiers
We Are The Romans
We Be Three Mariners
We Be Three Poor Mariners
We Celebrate The Birth
We Come From The Mountains
We Come To Greet You In Peace
We Do Squads Left
We Don't Get No Justice Here In
    Atlanta
We Fought Like The Divil
We Gather Together

Traditional *(Cont.)*

We Gather Together To Ask The
    Lord's Blessing
We Give Thee But Thine Own
We Got A Lot For Christmas
We Greet Thee Heavenly Dove
We Greet You Jesus
We Have From The Lord Received
    Grace
We Have Heard In Bethlehem
We Love Mrs Jones
We May Roam Thro' This World
We Must Go To Debrecen
We Must Part
We Plough The Fields
We See Not Know Not
We Shall Not Be Moved
We Shall Not Give Up The Fight
We Shall Overcome
We Shall Rise
We Shall Walk Thro' The Valley
We Shall Walk Through The Valley
We Sing The Glorious Conquest
We Sing The Praise Of Him Who
    Died
We Thank Thee Father For Our
    Homes
We Thank You Father
We Three Kings Of Orient Are
We Three Shepherds
We Will Be Merry Far And Wide
We Will Extol You Ever Blessed
    Lord
We Will March Through The Valley
We Will Overcome
We Will Send The Message Far
We Wish You A Merry Christmas
We'll All Go Down The Meadow
We'll All Go Together
We'll All Pull Through
We'll Be Ridin'
We'll Die In The Field
We'll End This War
We'll Get There All The Same
We'll Hunt The Buffalo
We'll Never Turn Back
We'll Overtake The Army
We'll Stand The Storm
We're All Bound To Go
We're All Nodding
We're Going To March In Augustine
    Tonight My Lord
We're Going To Pump Out Lake
    Erie
We're Going To Pump Out Old Lake
    Erie
We're The Raiders
We've Been A While A Wandering
We've Been Told Jesus Is Coming
We've Done Our Hitch In Hell
We've Had A Dance
Wealthy Merchant, The

Traditional *(Cont.)*

Wearin' O' The Green, The
Wearin' Of The Green
Wearing Of The Green, The
Wearing Of The Grey
Weary Of Earth And Laden With My
    Sin
Weary Traveler
Weaver Is Handsome, The
Weaving
Wedding Above In Glencree, The
Wedding Of Paddy O'Carroll, The
Wedding Prayer, A
Wedding Song
Wedding, The
Wedding Dress Song, The
Wedding Of Lochan McGraw, The
Wedlock
Wee Article, The
Wee Cooper O'Fife, The
Wee Cooper Of Fife, The
Wee Croodin' Doo, The
Wee Drappie O'T, A
Wee Magic Stane, The
Wee One, The
Wee Willie Gray
Wee Willie Winkie
Weel May The Keel Row
Weep No More
Weep No More For Baby
Weep-Willow Tree, The
Weepin' Mary
Weeping Willow Tree, The
Weevily Wheat
Weiber Mit Den Flohen, Die
Welcome Here Again
Welcome Of The Hostess, The
Welcome Summer
Welcome To Spring
Welcum To Scotland
Well Ah Looked Down De Railroad
    Fuh As Ah Could Se
Well Below The Valley, The
Well Sold The Cow
Welsh Carol
Welsh Lullaby
Went Up To The Mountain
Were You Ever In Rio Grand
Were You Ever In Rio Grande
Were You There
Were You There When They
    Crucified My Lord
Western Ocean
Western Plains, The
Westlyne Waltz
Westminster Carol
Westward
Wet Sheet And A Flowing Sea, A
Wexford Carol
Wha Wadna Fecht For Charlie
Whale, The
Whar You Gwine Buzzard
What A Court Hath Old England
What A Friend We Have In Jesus

Traditional (*Cont.*)

What A Mornin'
What A World
What Ails This Heart O' Mine
What Are These That Glow From Afar
What Are You Going To Do With A Drunken Sailor
What Can The Matter Be
What Child Is This
What Child Is This Who Laid To Rest
What Colour's Grass
What Do The Colonels And The Generals Do
What Does Little Birdie Say
What Folks Are Made Of
What Have You Lost
What Is The Meaning
What Kind Of Shoes Are You Going To Wear
What Light Is That
What Maidens Want
What Month Was My Jesus Born In
What Shall He Have That Killed The Deer
What Shall I Do
What Shall I Say
What Shall We Do With A Drunken Sailor
What Shall We Do With The Drunken Sailor
What Star Is This With Beams So Bright
What Thanks And Praise To Thee We Owe
What Tidings Brigest Thou
What Tongue Can Tell Thy Greatness Lord
What Will You Do
What Wondrous Love Is This
What Wondrous Love Is This O My Soul
What Yo' Gwine To Do When Yo' Lamp Burn Down
What You Going T' Do When The Lamp Burns Down
What You Gonna Call Your Pretty Little Baby
What's Little Babies Made Of
What's The Matter With Our School
Wheel Of Fortune, The
When Adam Was Created
When All Thy Mercies O My God
When April Comes
When Cheer Fills The Hearts Of My Friends
When Christ Was Born
When Christ Was Born In Bethlehem
When Christ Was Born Of Mary Free
When Christ Was Born To Set Us Free

Traditional (*Cont.*)

When Christ's Appearing Was Made Known
When Christmas Morn Is Dawning
When De Good Lord Sets You Free
When De Whale Get Strike
When E'er To The Clergyman's House
When First To This Country A Stranger I Came
When First Unto This Country
When Fortune Turns Her Wheel
When He Cometh Mazurka
When I Am A Man
When I Am Gone
When I Come
When I Die
When I Fall On My Knees
When I Lay My Burden Down
When I Lays Down
When I Lays Down And I Do Die
When I Raise My Eyes
When I Rise Crying' Holy
When I Survey The Wondrous Cross
When I Was A Young Man
When I Was In My Prime
When I Was Single
When I'm Dead
When I'm Dead An' Buried
When I'm Dead Don't You Grieve After Me
When I'm Gone
When I'm Gone To Come No Mo'
When Israel Was In Egypt's Land
When Jack Frost Comes
When Jesus Comes
When Jesus Left His Father's Throne
When Jesus Walked In Old Judea
When Jesus Was A Little Boy
When Jesus Went To Jordan's Stream
When Johnny Comes Down To Hilo
When Johnny Comes Marching Home
When Johnny Comes Marching Home Again
When Jones' Ale Was New
When Jones's Ale Was New
When Love Is Kind
When Moses Smote De Water
When Moses Smote The Water
When My Blood Runs Chilly And Col'
When My Lord Calls Me I Must Go
When Shall I Get There
When Sherman Marched Down To The Sea
When Spring Unlocks The Flowers To Paint The Laugh
When Stephen Full Of Power And Grace
When Summer Goes
When That I Was

Traditional (*Cont.*)

When The Bright God Of Day
When The Chestnut Leaves Are Falling
When The Infant Jesus
When The King Enjoys His Own Again
When The New York Boat Comes Down
When The Postman Comes
When The Revolution Comes
When The Saints Go Marching In
When The Swallows Homeward Fly
When The Train Comes Along
When The Work's All Done This Fall
When The World Around Us Throws
When They Laid The Body
When This Bloody War Is Over
When This Old Hat Was New
When Will You Come Again
When Will You Wed Me Wi' A Ring
When You Go To Get Your Shears
When You Hear My Coffin Sound
When Your Potato's Done
Whence Come Ye
Whence Comes This Rush Of Wings
Where Are You Going Abe Lincoln
Where Are You Going My Kind Pretty Maid
Where Are You Going To My Pretty Maid
Where Charity And Love Prevail
Where Cross The Crowded Ways Of Life
Where Did You Leave Your Lamb
Where Do You Worka John
Where Have All The Flowers Gone
Where Have You Been My Good Old Man
Where Have You Been Walking Shepherdess
Where Is My Little Dog Gone
Where Is Old Elijah
Where Is The True Man's Fatherland
Where Shall I Be When De Firs' Trumpet Soun'
Where Shall I Go
Where Shall I Go To Ease My Tremblin' Mind
Where The Gay Dreams Of Childhood
Where The Gentian Blows
Where The Grass Is Growing
Where The Wattles Are Blooming
Where They Were
Where Was Moses When The Light Went Out
Where Was Peter
Where Were You Oh Maiden
Where Wuz You
Where's Your Licence
Which Side Are You On

Traditional (*Cont.*)

While By My Sheep
While By My Sheep I Watched At
  Night
While London Sleeps
While Shepherds Watched
While Shepherds Watched Their
  Flocks
While Shepherds Watched Their
  Flocks By Night
While Strolling Thru The Park One
  Day
Whilst Landmen Wander Though
  Controlled
Whip And The Spurs, The
Whip Jamboree
Whipple's Mill
Whippoorwill
Whirling Maiden
Whiskey For My Johnny
Whiskey In The Jar
Whiskey Johnnie
Whiskey Johnny
Whiskey Seller, The
Whisky
Whisky In The Jar
Whisky Johnnie
Whisky Johnny
Whispering Willow, The
Whistle And Hoe
Whistle Daughter Whistle
Whistled Schottische, The
Whistling Gypsy Rover
Whistling Rufus
White Cockade
White Cockade, The
White Coral Bells
White Horse Pawin' In The Valley,
  The
White House Blues, The
White Lent
White Man Let Me Go
White Mantilla, The
White Pilgrim, The
Whitewashed Army Of The Lord,
  The
Who Are These Like Stars Appearing
Who Built De Ark
Who Built The Ark
Who Can Retell
Who Can Think To Find A Diamond
Who Comes Laughing
Who Dat
Who Dat A Comin Ovah Yondah
Who Did
Who Ever Loved
Who Fears To Speak Of Easter Week
Who Is Crying
Who Is Dat Yondah
Who Is He In Yonder Cot
Who Is The Man
Who Is This So Weak And Helpless
Who Is This With Garments Gory

Traditional (*Cont.*)

Who Made Ocean Earth And Sky
Who Owns The Game
Who Shall Deliver Po' Me
Who Was Here
Who Will Bow And Bend Like A
  Willow
Who Will Shoe
Who Will Shoe Your Pretty Little
  Foot
Who Will Sing Me One
Who'll Be A Witness For My Lord
Who'll Buy
Who'll Jine De Union
Who's Goin' To Close My Dyin'
  Eyes
Who's That A Calling
Whoa Haw Buck And Jerry Boy
Whoa Mule
Whoa Mule Whoa
Whoopee Ti Yo Git Along Little
  Dogies
Whoopee Ti-Yi-Yo
Whoopee Ti-Yi-Yo Git Along Little
  Dogies
Whoopie Ti Yi Yo
Why Did She Leave Killarney
Why Do You Bob Your Hair Girls
Why Do You Gaze At The Road
Why Shouldn't My Goose
Why Soldiers Why
Why Was The Darkie Born
Wi' A Hundred Pipers
Wi' A Hundred Pipers An' A'
Wi'a A Hundred Pipers An' A'
Wicked Polly
Widdecombe Fair
Widdicombe Fair
Widdy Widdy Way
Wide Missouri, The
Widow And The Orphan, The
Widow In The Cottage By The Sea,
  The
Widow Of Donaghadee, The
Widow Woman's Daughter, The
Widow's Plea, The
Wiegenlied Der Hirten
Wiewol Ich Arm Und Elend Bin
Wife Of Usher's Well, The
Wife Wrapt In Wether's Skin, The
Wild And Wicked Youth
Wild And Wicked Youth, The
Wild Bill Jones
Wild Colloina Boy, The
Wild Colonial Boy, The
Wild Goose Grasses
Wild Miz-Zou-Rye, The
Wild Moor, The
Wild Mountain Thyme
Wild Mustard River, The
Wild Rippling Water
Wild Rover
Wild Rover, The

Traditional (*Cont.*)

Wild Rover No More
Wild Winds
Wildwood Flower, The
Wilhelmus Of Nassau
Will The Circle Be Unbroken
Will Ye Go Lassie
Will Ye No Come Back Again
Will You Come To The Bow'r
Will You Come To The Bower
Will You Go Out West
Will You Miss Me
Will You Wear Red
William And Margaret
William And Nancy
William And Polly
William Glen
William Hall
William Taylor
William The Handsome Cabin Boy
Willie Moore
Willie Take Your Little Drum
Willie The Weeper
Willie Wastle Dwalls On Tweed
Willie's Drowned At Gamery
Willie's Drowned In Yarrow
Willie's Fatal Visit
Willie's Gane To Melville Castle
Willie's Lyke Wake
Willow And The Oak, The
Willow Tree, The
Willows By The River
Willy Boy Willy Boy
Willy Foster
Willy Reilly
Willy The Weeper
Willy-Willy-Will
Wilt Thou Soon Return
Wimoweh
Wind Blow East, The
Wind Mill, The
Wind Of Night
Wind Through The Olive Trees
Wind Up The May Tree
Wind'ard Car'line
Winds Through The Olive Trees
Windy Bill
Windy Old Weather
Wine I Drink
Wine Testers, The
Wings Of A Gull, The
Winnie's Primrose
Winning Of Cales, The
Winter By The Dnieper
Winter It Is Past, The
Winter Sat Lang, The
Winter Song
Winter'll Soon Be Over, De
Winter'll Soon Be Over, The
Winter's Farewell
Winter's Night
Winter's Sleep Was Long And Deep,
  The

Traditional (*Cont.*)

Wir Zogen In Das Feld
Wise Men Traveled From The East
Wish I Had A Jug O'Rum
Wish I Was In Heabum Settin'
 Down
Wish I's In Heaven Settin' Down
Wish You A Good Evening
Witch On The Brae, The
With A Hundred Pipers
With A Poom Poom Poom And A
 Doodle Doodle Det
With Her Dog And Gun
With His Pair The Bird Flies
With My Mind Stayed On Freedom
With Sound Of Fife
With The Dawn
With Triumph Has Our Lord
Within A Mile Of Edinboro'
Within The Town Of Bethl'em
Witner's Gone And Past, The
Witness, A
Witnin A Mile Of Edinboro' Town
Witty Lass Of London, The
Wives Aren't Like Maidens
Wo Warst Du
Woe Be Unto You
Woe Woe Mother Mine
Woke Up This Morning With My
 Mind On Freedom
Wol Auf Wir Wollen Jagen
Wol Uff Ir Lieben Gsellen
Wollust In Den Maien, Die
Woman Blue
Woman Blues
Woman Running The Farm, A
Woman Sweeter Than Man
Woman's Love
Woman's Rights
Woman's Sad Lot
Won't You Buy My Pretty Flowers
Won't You Go Down Old Hannah
Won't You Sit Down
Wonder Tidings
Wonder Where Is Good Ole Daniel
Wonderful Crocodile, The
Wonders Still The World Shall
 Witness
Wondrous Love
Wondrous Works
Woodchopper's Song
Wooden Leg'd Parson, The
Woodland Flowers Schottische
Woods Of Trugh, The
Woodsman's Alphabet, The
Woodsmen's Alphabet, The
Wooing, The
Wor Nanny's A Mazer
Word Whom Earth And Sea And
 Sky, The
Work All De Summer
Work And Play
Work Songs

Traditional (*Cont.*)

Work's Being Done, The
Workers' Carmagnole, The
Workers Of The World
Workin' On De Chain Gang
Workin' On De Levee
Workin' On De Railroad
Workin' On The Railroad
Workin' On The Railroad Line
World Has Waited Long
World Is Very Very Big, The
World Itself, The
World Turned Upside Down, The
World's Desire, The
Worried Man, A
Worried Man Blues
Worthy The Lamb
Would God I Were The Tender
 Apple Blossom
Would I Were A Pigeon
Wouldn't Drive So Hard But I
 Needs De Arns
Wounded Nancy's Return
Wraggle Taggle Gypsies, The
Wraggle-Taggle Gypsies O, The
Wreath Token, The
Wreck Between New Hope And
 Gethsemane, The
Wreck Of 36, The
Wreck Of 444, The
Wreck Of No 52, The
Wreck Of Number Nine, The
Wreck Of Old 97, The
Wreck Of Old Number Nine, The
Wreck Of The 1256, The
Wreck Of The C And O No 5, The
Wreck Of The Dandenogg
Wreck Of The Enterprise, The
Wreck Of The Flyer Duquesne, The
Wreck Of The Herring Fleet, The
Wreck Of The John B, The
Wreck Of The N And W Cannonball,
 The
Wreck Of The Northfleet, The
Wreck Of The Old 97, The
Wreck Of The Old Ninety Seven,
 The
Wreck Of The Rambler
Wreck Of The Royal Charter, The
Wreck Of The Royal Palm, The
Wreck Of The Six-Wheel Driver, The
Wreck Of The Southern Old 97, The
Wreck Of The Sportsman, The
Wreck Of The Titanic, The
Wreck Off Scilly, The
Wreck On The C And O, The
Wreck On The Hunnicut Curve, The
Wreck On The Somerset Road, The
Wren Boys, The
Wren Boy's Song, The
Wren Song, The
Wrestling Jacob
Wring My Hands And Cry

Traditional (*Cont.*)

Write Me A Letter From Home
Write Me A Letter From Home
 Waltz
Wsrod Nocnej Ciszy
Wunst I Had An Old Gray Mare
Wyandotte's Farewell Song, The
Wyoming Nester, The
Xtoles, Los
Ya He Na Ya Ya
Ya Ribon
Ya Viene La Vieja
Yankee Chronology
Yankee Doodle
Yankee Doodle For Lincoln
Yankee Man-Of-War, The
Yankee Ship Came Down The River,
 A
Yankele
Yanko
Yaravi
Yard Of Pudding, The
Yarn Of The Deep Blue Sea, A
Ye Banks And Braes
Ye Banks And Braes O' Bonnie
 Doon
Ye Gentlemen Of England
Ye Guardian Powers
Ye Lanlords Of Ireland
Ye Mariners All
Ye Mariners Of England
Ye Parliament Of England
Ye Parliaments Of England
Ye Servants Of God Your Master
Ye Sons Of Australia
Ye Watchers And Ye Holy Ones
Ye're Sair Dung Annie Or Bervie's
 Braes
Yea The Heavenly Child Is Born
Year Begins Of Joy And Grace, A
Year Is Swiftly Waning, The
Year Of Jubilo, The
Yearning For Homeland
Years Of Peace
Years Of Youth, The
Yeder Ruft Mich Ziamele
Yelenka
Yellow Girl Goes To The Ball
Yellow Haired Laddie, The
Yellow Meal
Yellow Rose Of Texas, The
Yellow Rose, The
Yenitchku
Yeo Heave Ho
Yeoman's Carols
Yerakina
Yes They Tell Me
Yet The Heavenly Child Is Born
Yi Mung Shan
Yigdal Elohim
Yis-M'Hu
Yisrael V'Oraita
Yo Heave Ho
Yo' Low Down Ways

Traditional *(Cont.)*

Yo M'Enamori D'Un Aire
Yo No Canto Por Cantar
Yo' Sins Are Gonna Find You Out
Yo Soy Indiecito
Yo Te Llevo En El Alma
Yodel Song
Yom Shabbaton
Yom Ze L'Yisrael
Yomi Yomi
Yona Paamona
Yonder Comes The High Sheriff
York
York Tune
Yorkshire Pigs, The
Yoshke Fort Avek
You And I Must Sunder
You Are A Bride
You Better Min'
You Better Mind
You Call Me Dog I Don' Ker
You Came Down From Heaven
You Dear Live In My Heart
You Didn't Do No Wrong
You Fair And Pretty Ladies
You Gentlemen Of England
You Go I'll Go Wid You
You Got A Right
You Got To Die
You Gotta Bus' Dis Rock
You Hear The Lambs A-Crying
You Lord We Praise In Songs Of
   Celebration
You May Bury Me In De Eas'
You May Bury Me In The East
You Might Easy Know A Doffer
You Mus' Hab Dat True Religion
You Never Miss The Water Till The
   Well Runs Dry
You Shall Never Have The Ring
You Shall Reap
You Should Have Been There
You Turn For Sugar An' Tea
You Wonder Why I'm A Hobo
You'd Better Min'
You'd Better Run
You're A Friend Of Mine
You're Going To Reap Just What
   You Sow
You're In The Army Now
You're My Brother So Give Me Your
   Han'
You've Got To Go Down
Youn Tou Tou
Young Akin
Young Alanthia
Young Alban And Amandy
Young Allan
Young And Old Must Raise The Lay
Young Beichan
Young Beichen
Young Bekie
Young But Daily Growing

Traditional *(Cont.)*

Young Charlotte
Young Collins
Young Constantine
Young Counselor, The
Young Craigston
Young Diana
Young Edmon Bold
Young Edmund In The Lowlands
   Low
Young George Washington
Young Girl Was Married Off, The
Young Guards, The
Young Henry Green
Young Henry The Poacher
Young Hunting
Young Indian Lass
Young John Riley
Young John's Been A Cruising
Young Johnnie
Young Johnny
Young Ladies
Young Ladies In Town
Young Les Darcy
Young Maid A-Milking Did Go, A
Young Man Shun That Cup
Young Man Who Couldn't Hoe
   Corn, The
Young Man Who Didn't Hoe Corn,
   The
Young Man Who Wouldn't Hoe
   Corn
Young Man Who Wouldn't Hoe
   Corn, The
Young Man's Love, A
Young May Moon, The
Young Men's Song, The
Young Mind Thus, The
Young Monroe At Gerry's Rock
Young Peggy
Young Prince Of Spain, The
Young Sailor Cut Down In His
   Prime, The
Young Servant Man, The
Young Strongbow
Young Voyageur, The
Young Widow
Young William
Youpe Youpe Sur La Riviere
Your Friends Are My Friends
Your Home And Mine
Youth And Age
Youth's Companions
Youth's Stick Dance
Yowe Lamb, The
Yuk Mei Yun
Yule Feast, A
Yule Nisse
Zaccheus Climbed The Sycamo' Tree
Zack The Mormon Engineer
Zancudo, El
Zandunga, La
Zangaiwa Chakatanga Pano

Traditional *(Cont.)*

Zayzhe Mir Gezunt
Zeb Tunney's Girl
Zebra Dun, The
Zebra Dunn
'Zekiel Saw De Wheel
Zerzlich Tut Mich Erfreuen
Zezulka Z Lesa Vylitla
Zhamele
Zhankoye
Zillertal Du Bist Mei Freud
Zinch Oo Zinch
Zinga-Za
Zion
Zion Praise Thy Savior Singing
Zion Weep A-Low
Zion's Children
Zion's Soldier
Zip Coon
Zither And I
Zits Ich Mir Oyfn Benkele
Zog Nit Keynmol
Zol Ich Zayn A Rov
Zolst Azoy Lebn Zayn Gezint
Zorra Astuta, La
Zu Bethlehem Geboren
Zum Gali
Zum Gali Gali
Zum-Zum
Zwei Konigskinder
Zweisiedler, Der

Trapani & Lange
Cara Mia

Traveling Wilburys, The
End Of The Line
Handle With Care

Travers
Life Is A Jest

Travers & Dorough & Popper
Yesterday's Tomorrow

Travis
I Told You So
Sixteen Tons
Teacher's Lament, The

Travis & Lindley
It's Out Of My Hands
Promises

Tredinnick
Born By The Holy Spirit's Breath
Come Rejoice Before Your Maker
He Walks Among The Golden
   Lamps
Heavenly Hosts In Ceaseless
   Worship
Lord Now Lettest Thou Thy Servant
May God Be Gracious To Us
No Weight Of Gold Or Silver
O All Ye Works Of The Lord
O How Amiable Are Thy Dwellings
O Praise The God Of Israel
Our God Has Turned To His People
We Praise Thee O God

Tredinnick & Hopkins & Warren
I Will Give Thanks Unto The Lord

Tredinnick & Turle & Warren
When The Lord Turned Again
Tregina
Hail Glorious Land Of Love And
Peace
Treharne
Corals
Trejo
Rogaciano El Huapanguero
Trembath
From The Eastern Mountains
Hail The Hero Workers
Trench
Flag Of Our Union, The
Trenet
Beyond The Sea
Fleur Bleue
Grand Cafe, Le
Hop Hop
I Wish You Love
Il Pleut Dans Ma Chambre
J'Ai Ta Main
Jardin Du Mois De Mai
Menilmontant
Mer, La
Pic Pic Pic
Polka Du Roi
Serenade
Serenade Portugaise
Vie Qui Va, La
Trenet & Lasry
Soleil Et La Lune, La
Trenet & Matas
Papa Pique Et Maman Coud
Sainte-Catherine
Trent
We Praise Thee O God
Trent & Carmichael
In The Still Of The Night
Trevathan
Bully Song
May Irwin's Bully Song
Trevor
When It's Apple Blossom Time In
Normandy
Trigg
Joy In The Lord
Trimachi & Kasenetz & Katz
Free As The Wind
Trimingham
To Sea To Sea
Trinkaus
God Made You Mine
Triplett
How About Your Heart
Jesus Heal The People
Jesus Is Precious
Tripp
After Calvary
Tripp & Laverne
It's Worth It All
That Day Is Almost Here
Tripp & Paris
Cryin'

Tristano
Lennie's Pennies
Trotere
En El Madrid De Anos Atras
In Old Madrid
Leonore
Trotere & Bingham
Changeless
Trounstine
Give Me A Kiss By The Numbers
Troup
Daddy
Girl Can't Help It, The
Route 66
Snootie Little Cutie
Troutman & Beck
As We Lay
Troutman & Troutman
I Want To Be Your Man
Trovajoli
Why
Trowbridge
American Prayer, An
Blest Of God The God Of Nations
Christ Alone Has Power To Save
Ev'rybody Laugh
Jesus Is Coming
Jesus Is Coming Again
Lead On
Prayer, A
Troxel & Christopher & Ellis
Come Softly To Me
Troyte
Strain Upraise Of Joy And Praise,
The
True & Lindsay & Hogin
Too Many Lovers
Trueg
Eyeballing
Heigh Ho Nobody's Home
Loose Change
Truh
Twilight
Truhart
Wabash Cannon Ball, The
Truhn
Three Bumble Bees, The
Three Chafers, The
Trzetrzelewska & White
Baby You're Mine
Cruising For Bruising
Time And Tide
Trzetrzelewska & White & Ross
New Day For You
Promises
Tschesnokoff
Salvation Is Created
Tschesnokov
Cherubic Hymn
Tschirch
Flowers For The Brave
Forest, The
Tuama
John Twomey's Drinking Song

Tubb
Take A Letter Miss Gray
Walking The Floor Over You
Waltz Across Texas
Tubb & West & Benedict & Sanders
I'm Bitin' My Fingernails And
Thinking Of You
Tuck
Threshold, The
Tucker
General Grant's The Man
I Don't Know How They Do It But
They Do
Oh Girls Get A Home Of Your Own
Stand By The Flag
Sweet Genevieve
Weeping Sad And Lonely
What Shall I Render To My God
When The Cruel War Is Over
When This Cruel War Is Over
Tuckerman
Bunker Hill
God Bless Our Native Land
Lift Up Your Heads Ye Mighty Gates
Lord From Far-Severed Climes We
Come
Tufts
American Flag, The
Cradle Song
Tullar
Face To Face
Face To Face With Christ
Nailed To The Cross
Tunick
Tattinger's
Tunney
How Excellent In Thy Name
Sound His Praise
Undivided
Tunney & Tunney
Let There Be Praise
O Magnify The Lord
Tunney & Tunney & Darnall
For Unto Us
Tunney & Tunney & Smith
How Excellent Is Thy Name
Turk
After My Laughter Came Tears
Turk & Ahlert & Richman
Walkin' My Baby Back Home
Turk & Handman
Are You Lonesome Tonight
Turk & Smith & Pinkard
Gimme A Little Kiss Will Ya Huh
Turle
According To They Gracious Word
Head Of The Church Triumphant
My God How Wonderful Thou Art
O Lord Our Fathers Oft Have Told
O Still In Accents Sweet And Strong
We Praise Thee Lord For Hours Of
Bliss

Turner
Breakfast Bell
Carry It On
Confidence
Dancing Heart, The
Goodbye So Long
Hallelujah I Want To Sing All About
    It
Hey Doll Baby
Honey Hush
Nutbush City Limits
Pray Maiden Pray
Roll On Silver Moon
We Would See Jesus
When I Am Gone
Turner & McGranahan
Christ Returneth
Turner & Parsons & Chaplin
Smile
Turpin
St Louis Rag, The
Turrin
Theme From A New Life
Turton
Glory Gilds The Sacred Page, A
Turunen
My Home
Tveitt
Vi Skal Ikkje Sove
Tweel & Dyer
Every Time Two Fools Collide
Twiggs
Money Am A Hard Thing To
    Borrow
Twilley
Girls
Twitty
It's Only Make Believe
Linda On My Mind
You've Never Been This Far Before
Twynham
Lo Our Savior King Is Here
Tye
Go To Dark Gethsemane
O God Be Merciful
Sing Unto The Lord
While Shepherds Watched Their
    Flocks
Tyler
Diamonds And Pearls
Dream On
Deck Of Cards, The
Tyler & Hamilton
Janie's Got A Gun
Tyler & Perry
Draw The Line
Love In An Elevator
Walk This Way
Tyler & Perry & Child
What It Takes
Tyler & Perry & Vallance & Knight
Rag Doll
Tyler & Vallance
Other Side, The

Tyner
Aisha
Fly With The Wind
In Search Of My Heart
Peresina
Senor Carlos
Utopia
Tyrell
Famous Teddy Z Theme, The
Tyson
Debutante Ball, The
Four Strong Winds
Sea Moods
Someday Soon
Tyte
My Mary Anne
U2
Angel Of Harlem
Desire
I Still Haven't Found What I'm
    Looking For
Pride
Pride In The Name Of Love
With Or Without You
Ubela
Fruhling Der Die Welt Verklart
Udall
Stay In Your Own Back Yard
Udell & Geld
Freedom
Uehlein
Solidarnosc
Ufford
Throw Out The Life Line
Uglow
O Saving Victim Opening Wide
Uhland & Mendelssohn
Sabbath Morn, The
Uhr
Tears For Souvenirs
Ulmer
Pigalle
Umiliani
Mah-Na Mah-Na
Unde & Rush
Natural Attraction
Underdahl
Mitt Bu Min Heim
Ungerer
Jerusalem Surge
Passio Domini N J Christi
Unseld
God Of Love, The
Launch Out
Praise Him Again
Twilight Is Falling
Updegraff
No Room In The Inn
Upham
Olban Or The White Captive
Upton
More Today Than Yesterday
Uranga
Alla En El Rancho Grande

Urbont
One Life To Live
Theme From General Hospital
Ure & Geldof
Do They Know It's Christmas
Urguhart
Far Above Cayuga's Waters
Urhan
O God In Restless Living
Urwin
Surely It Is God Who Saves Me
Utcheson
O For A Thousand Tongues To Sing
Vacek
Hunter
Innocent
Lark Was Singing, The
Oh No
Owl, The
Polka For Two
Vagnetti
Gleaners' Song
Vail
Alone With Jesus
Close To Thee
He Died For Thee
Nothing But Leaves The Spirit
    Grieves
O The Beloved City
Scatter Seeds Of Kindness
Thou My Everlasting Portion
Valderrabano
Argimina Cancion De Las Reynas De
    Espana
Ay De Mi Dize El Buen Padre
Bracos Traygo Cansados, Los
Como Puedo Yo Bivir
Donde Son Estas Serranas
Eulalia Borgonela
Jamas Cosa
O Que En La Cumbre
Quid Prodest
Rugier Qual Sempre Fui
Senora Si Te Olvidare
Tristes Lagrimas Mias, Las
Y Arded Coracon Arded
Valdez
Sol Que Tu Eres, El
Vale
Hail Thee Spirit Lord Eternal
Joy Of The Lord, The
Vale & Leeson
Take Me Home Tonight
Valens
Bamba, La
Come On Let's Go
Donna
Ooh My Head
Valentine & Valentine & Wiggins
Moneys Too Tight To Mention
Valerius
William Of Nassau
Vallance & Bettis & Barnes & Carlisi
Like No Other Night

Vallance & Carlisi & Vanzant & Steele & Barnes
Somebody Like You
Vallance & Reid & Parker & Connelly & Hanson & Frew
Someday
Vallance & Reid & Parker Et Al
Don't Forget Me When I'm Gone
Valle
Face I Love, The
If You Went Away
Valle & Valle
So Nice
Vallee & Carmichael
Old Man Harlem
Vallee & Noble & Campbell & Connelly
Good Night Sweetheart
Valverde
Clavelitos
Van Alstyne
Cheyenne
For Your Boy And My Boy
Good Mornin'
I'm Afraid To Come Home In The Dark
In The Shade Of The Old Apple Tree
It Looks Like A Big Night To-Night
Memories
Navajo
Rag-Time Chimes
San Antonio
That Old Girl Of Mine
What Are You Going To Do To Help The Boys
What's The Matter With Father
Won't You Come Over To My House
Van Alstyne & Schmidt & Curtis
Drifting And Dreaming
Van Boskerck
Semper Paratus
Van Campenhout
Brabanconne, La
Van De Venter
Jesus My Saviour
Looking This Way
Over The River Faces I See
We Shall Shine As The Stars
Van De Venter & Weeden
I Surrender All
Sunlight
Van De Water
Apart
Gloria Patria
Good Shepherd, The
Lord Is My Shepherd, The
Night Of Nights
Van Dyke
We're All For You Uncle Sam
Van Dyke & Black
Auctioneer
Van Etten
Go Northwestern Go
Go U Northwestern

Van Halen & Anthony & Roth
And The Cradle Will Rock
Van Halen & Hagar & Anthony & Van Halen
When It's Love
Why Can't This Be Love
Van Halen & Van Halen & Anthony & Roth
Dance The Night Away
Hot For Teacher
I'll Wait
Jamie's Cryin'
Jump
Panama
Van Heusen
All My Tomorrows
All The Way
All This And Heaven Too
Aren't You Glad You're You
But Beautiful
Call Me Irresponsible
Christmas Is For Children
Close To Christmas
Come Blow Your Horn
Come Dance With Me
Come Fly With Me
Country Style
Darn That Dream
Deep In A Dream
Ev'rybody Has The Right To Be Wrong
Ev'rybody Has The Right To Be Wrong At Least Once
Fancy Meeting You Here
Going My Way
Heaven Can Wait
Here's That Rainy Day
High Hopes
High Hopes Campaign Version
I Thought About You
I'll Only Miss Her When I Think Of Her
Imagination
Impatient Years, The
Incurably Romantic
It Could Happen To You
It's Always You
It's Nice To Go Trav'ling
Last Dance, The
Let's Not Be Sensible
Like Someone In Love
Look To Your Heart
Love And Marriage
Love Is A Bore
Moonlight Becomes You
My Kind Of Town
My Kind Of Town Chicago Is
Nancy
Nancy With The Laughing Face
Not As A Stranger
Oh You Crazy Moon
Only The Lonely

Van Heusen (Cont.)
Opposites
Opposites Opposites Opposites
Our Town
Personality
Pocketful Of Miracles
Polka Dots And Moonbeams
Road To Morocco, The
Second Time Around, The
Secret Of Christmas, The
Song From Some Came Running
Straight Down The Middle
Style
Sunday Monday Or Always
Swinging On A Star
Teamwork
Tender Trap, The
That Christmas Feeling
Thoroughly Modern Millie
To Love And Be Loved
Walking Happy
Warmer Than A Whisper
When No One Cares
Where Love Has Gone
Van Pelt
Foggy Mountain Top
Van Ronk
Bamboo
Van & Schenck & Lodge
That Red Head Gal
Van Steeden & Clarkson & Clarkson
Home
Van Warmer
I Will Whisper Your Name
Van Zandt
Pancho And Lefty
Vance
Catch A Falling Star
God Bless The King
Vance & Carr
Gina
Vance & Pockriss
Catch A Falling Star
Itsy Bitsy Teenie Weenie Yellow Polkadot Bikini
Run Sally Run
What Is Love
Vance & Snyder
What Will My Mary Say
Vancheri
Sicilia Bedda
Vandell & Ingles
Now I Have Everything
Vanderpool
Dear To The Heart Of God
Vandevere
Autumn Wind, The
Busy Birds
Carol For Christmas, A
Christopher Columbus
Cobbler, The
From Sheep To Sweater
From Wheat To Bread
God Of The Out-Of-Doors

Vandevere *(Cont.)*
Hear The Wind
Here And There
I'm Happy
Junior Safety Patrol, The
Liner And The Tug, The
Pets
Play Suits
Rhythmical Rain
Salute The Flag
Saturday Morning
Singing Strings
Something Silly
Song For Columbus, A
Team Work
To Greet The May
Trim Trig Trailer, The
Tuneful Twaddle
Valentine, The
Valley Forge
Washer, The
Why

Vandiver & Ramos
Don't Waste It On The Blues

Vandross
So Amazing

Vandross & Adderley
Give Me The Reason
Stop To Love

Vandross & Anderson
There's Nothing Better Than Love

Vandross & Miller
It's Over Now
'Til My Baby Comes Home
You're My Choice Tonight

Vangelis
Chariots Of Fire
Hymne
Missing
Race To The End
State Of Independence

Vanhoose
Green Pastures

Vanhoy
Sail Away
What's Forever For

Vanhoy & Allen & Cook
I've Been Wrong Before

Vanhoy & Cook & Putman
I Wish That I Could Hurt That Way
Again

Vanhoy & Putman & Cook
Baby You're Something

Vannah
Flag, The

Vannata & Goddard
You

Vannelli
Wheels Of Life

Varlamov
Red Sarafan, The
Snow Flurries

Vars
Flipper

Vatro
Anna

Vaughan
Good By
If I Could Hear My Mother Pray
Again
My Loved Ones Are Waiting For Me
There's No Depression In Heaven

Vaughan Williams
All Beautiful The March Of Days
All Creatures Of Our God And King
All Praise To Thee For Thou O King
Divine
Amour De Moy, L'
As Those Of Old Their First Fruits
Brought
At The Name Of Jesus
Blackmwore By The Stour
Blake's Cradle Song
Bright Is The Ring Of Words
By All Your Saints Still Striving
Claribel
Come Down O Love Divine
Come My Way My Truth My Life
Dream-Land
Eternal Ruler Of The Ceaseless
Round
Father All Loving Who Rulest
Father We Praise Thee Now The
Night Is Over
For All The Saints
God Be With You Till We Meet
Again
Golden Carol, The
Great Forerunner Of The Morn, The
Hail Thee Festival Day
Hail To The Lord Who Comes
He Who Was Nailed To The Cross Is
Lord
He Who Would Valiant Be 'gainst
I Come The Great Redeemer Cries
I Sing The Almighty Power Of God
Jesus Our Might Lord
Joseph Dearest Joseph Mine
Lift Up Your Hearts
Lo In The Likeness Of Fire
Lord God You Now Have Set Your
Servant Free
Master Of Eager Youth
O God Of Earth And Altar
O Jesus Crowned With All Renown
O Jesus Crowned With All
Renowned
O Little Town Of Bethlehem
Saviour Again To Thy Dear Name
We Raise
She's Like The Swallow
Silent Noon
Sky Above The Roof, The
Snow In The Street
Spanish Ladies, The
Take O Take
Thou Who At Thy First Eucharist
When Icicles Hang By The Wall

Vaughan Williams *(Cont.)*
When Jesus Left His Father's Throne
Winter's Willow, The
Ye Watchers And Ye Holy Ones

Vaughan Williams
All Saints Hymn
For All Saints
Wassail Wassail All Over The Town
Wither's Rocking Hymn

Vaughn
My Heroes Have Always Been
Cowboys
Peace On Earth This Christmas
Rags
May There Be Peace On Earth This
Christmas

Vaught
Band, The
Bedtime
How Creatures Move
Mother's Call
Mother's Song
Night Time

Vautor
Sweet Suffolk Owl

Vecchi
Fummo Felici Un Tempo
So Well I Know Who's Happy

Vega
Gypsy
Luka
Solitude Standing

Veit
Kafer Und Die Blume, Der
Schone Rohtraut

Vejvoda
She Likes To Dance
Where Is My Youth

Veksler
Yisrolik

Velazquez
Besame Mucho

Velona
Lollipops And Roses

Vene
Attesa Del Sogno
Attesa Vana, L'O
Musica E Luce
Stornello Lunigiano

Venna
And Will The Great Eternal God

Venosa & Picone
Little Star

Venua
Before Jehovah's Awful Throne
Come O My Soul In Sacred Lays
God Send Us Men Whose Aim
'Twill Be
Great God Attend While Zion Sings
Jesus Shall Reign Where'er The Sun

Venya
All Ye That Fear God's Holy Name

Vera
At This Moment
Veran
Je Hais Les Dimanches
Verdelot
I Vosta Acuti Dardi
Verdi
Ah Fors' E Lui
Ah Fors' E Luieful Prime
Ah I Have Sighed To Rest Me
Ah Was It He
Ah Why Recall
Aida March
Anvil Chorus
At My Mercy
Ave Maria
Bella Figlia Dell'amore
By The Firelight
Calm The Tempest
Canzone
Caro Nome
Carved Upon My Heart
Celeste Aida
Celestial Aida
Chorus Of The Hebrew Captives
Come Away
Consecration Of Rhadames
Cross Crown And Throne
Di Mie Discolpe
Di Provenza
Donna E Mobile, La
Emerald Isle
Ernani Fly With Me
Ev'ry Flower
Ever Free
Fairest Daughter Of The Graces
Fierce Flames Are Soaring
Gloria All' Egitto
Glory To Egypt
God Of The Nations
Grand March
Grand Opera
Gypsy Song
Heavenly Aida
Home To Our Mountains
In My Heart
Just As I Am
Libiamo Libiamo
Look Thee O Heav'n Tis Over
Ma Tu Re
Mastery
May In Venice
Miserere
Most Beloved Name Of All
My Sword In Vengeance
Narrative
Now Hope Renewed
O Patria Mia
O Terra Addio
Of That Dark Scaffold
Oh I Have Sighed To Rest Me
Oh Love Immortal
Ol Tale Amor
Our Flag O'er Us Waving

Verdi (Cont.)
Over The Summer Sea
Padre A Costoro
Peace To Thy Spirit
Pity Kind Heaven
Possente Ftha
Praise Ye
Pura Siccome
Quartette
Rigoletto Quartet
Sempre Libera
Sempre Libre
Sleep My Sweet Baby
Soldiers Chorus
Someone's Last Call
Song Of The Soldiers
Speed Your Journey
Su Del Nilo
Tempest Of The Heart
Thou Art A Mystery
Tra Foreste Vergini, La
Triumphal March
Up Ye Brave Egyptian Soldiers
Vergilian Cento, A
Was This The Man My Fancy Saw
We Are Equal
We'll Fly These Walls
When She Smiles
Woman Is Fickle
Vermulst
Joseph Patron Saint Of Workers
O Sing To God With Joy
Psalm 22
Trust In God And Come Before Him
We Come To You With Longing
Vernon
Robin Hood
When That I Was A Little Tiny Boy
Vernor
Girl I Love, The
Sweetheart Of Sigma Chi, The
Veroli
Let's Live For Love
Verrall
Ah Come Sweet Night
Vest & Chamberlain
Land Of Cotton
Vestuti
Chinese Maiden
Night Sky
Vetter
Come Holy Ghost With God The Son
Let There Be Light
O God Creation's Secret Force
O God Of Truth O Lord Of Might
Vezner & Henry
Where've You Been
Viadana
Exsulatate Justi
O Sacrum Convivium
Vian
Luna Rosa

Vibbard
Glad That I Live Am I
Vicenti
Bolivia
Vickery
Honky Tonk Wine
Vickery & Borchers
Jamestown Ferry, The
Vickery & Kemp
Fireman, The
Vickery & Kilgore
Let Somebody Else Drive
She Went A Little Bit Farther
Victoria
Jesu Dulcis Memoria
Kyrie
Of The Glorious Body Telling
Vidal
If I Were A Ray Of Light
Printemps Nouveau
Returning Spring
Vilinsky & Snyder & Norman
One In A Million
Villa-Lobos
Chapel Of St John, The
Villard
A L'enseigne De La Fille Sans Coeur
Three Bells, The
Trois Cloches, Les
Villiera
Union Of South Africa
Villiers
Pourtant Si Je Suis Brunette
Si Vous Voulez
Stem Van Suid-Afrika, Die
Voice Of South Africa, The
Villoldo
Choclo, El
Vincent
Blow Soft Winds
Bright Summer
Little Soldier, The
Night Bells, The
Spring Day
Vincent & Caldbeck
Peace Perfect Peace
Peace Perfect Peace In This Dark
World Of Sin
Vincent & Davis
Be-Bop-A-Lula
Vincent & Smith
Rockin' Pneumonia And The Boogie
Woogie Flu
Vincenti
Bolivia
O Bolivians We're Blessed By Good
Fortune
Viner
Lord Behold Us With Thy Blessing
Lord Dismiss Us With Thy Blessing
Violinsky
Honolulu Eyes
When Francis Dances With Me

Vittoria
Jesu Dulcis
O Vos Omnes
Popule Meus
Tanquam Agnus

Vitz
Bist Du Fern Auch Von Bekannten
Du Klagst Und Fuhlest Die
Beschwerden
Fremdling Auf Erden, Ein
Gott Sprach Zu Dir
Ich Trat Zur Sabbatstunde
O Mein Jesu Reich An Gnaden
Teures Wort Aus Gottes Munde
Weihnacht Ist Heut'
Wetter Zieht Hernieder, Das
Wie Der Hirsh Nach Frischen
Quellen

Vivaldi
Domine Deus
Vivaldi Concerto In C Major

Vizzard
Wake The Echoes

Vleck
Lehigh's Pride

Voborsky
Little Huts Under The Mountains

Vogel
Apple Gatherers, The
Baby Mine
Beech Nuts
Chatterboxes
Dogs And Cats
Dollies' Mamma, The
Ducklings
Lazy Bones
Lizzie Let Us Sledging Go
Mother's Birthday
O What Shall I Do
Path Through The Lilac Trees, The
Saturday Night
Waltz, The

Vogelweide
My Song Is From Franconia

Vogrich
Confession
Love

Voice & Yellowstone
On The Shelf

Voigt
Mother-Love

Voigtlander
Geist Des Herrn
Gotteslamm
Unter Lilien Jener Freuden
Vor Meines Herzens Konig

Volinkaty
Satin Sheets

Volkman
Ich Halte Ihr Die Augen Zu

Volkmann
Im Gewittersturm

Volkoviski
Shtiler Shtiler

Voll
Pals Of The Little Red School

Volpe
Ours Is The Future

Von La Hache
Conquered Banner, The

Von Tilzer
Alexander
Bird In A Gilded Cage, A
Down At The Old Bull And Bush
Down Where The Wurzburger Flows
Go On And Coax Me
I Love I Love I Love My Wife But
Oh You Kid
I Want A Girl
I Want A Girl Just Like The Girl
I Want A Girl Just Like The Girl
That Married Dear Old Dad
I'd Leave Ma Happy Home For You
I'm The Lonesomest Gal In Town
It's A Long Long Way To The USA
And The Girl I Left Behind
Mansion Of Aching Hearts, The
On A Sunday Afternoon
Put Your Arms Around Me Honey
Rufus Rastus Johnson Brown
Somebody's Waiting For Me
Spider And The Fly, The
Take Me Out To The Ball Game
Teasing
That Old Irish Mother Of Mine
Under The Anheuser Bush
Wait Till The Sun Shines Nellie
What You Goin' To Do When The
Rent Comes Round
What You Gonna Do When The Rent
Comes 'round
When The Harvest Days Are Over
Where The Morning Glories Twine
Around The Door
Where The Sweet Magnolias Grow

Von Tilzer & Brown
He's Our Al

**Von Tilzer & Sterling & Munro &
Lewis**
When My Baby Smiles At Me

Vorzon & Conlan
Just Our Luck

Voss
Keep In Mind That I Love You
Standing Behind A Man

Vousden
Bonnie Blue Flag, The

Vulpius
Abide O Dearest Jesus
Abide With Us Our Saviour
Another Year Is Dawning
Baptized In Water Sealed By The
Spirit
Bid The Din Of Battle Cease
Christ's Holy Morn
Christus Der Ist Mein Leben
Easter Hallelujah, An

Vulpius (Cont.)
From Age To Age How Grandly
Rise
Gentle Mary Laid Her Child
Good Christian Men Rejoice And
Sing
Good Christians All Rejoice And
Sing
I Like To Think Of Jesus
I Worship Thee Lord Jesus
Into Our Hearts O Spirit Come
Let Our Choir New Anthems Raise
Lord Who Shall Sit Beside Thee
May Choirs Of Angels Lead You To
Paradise
My God My God And Can It Be
Nuthatch, The
O God Of Truth
O Heavenly Jerusalem
O Lord Our Lord In All The Earth
Praise We Our God
Say Not They Die
Sing Praise To Our Creator
This Is Our Accepted Time
To Us Is Born A Little Child
We Pray No More
What Grace O Lord And Beauty
Shone
What Sweet Of Life Endureth

Waaktaar & Furuholmen
Take On Me

Wachsmann
Awake
Join In Singing
Morning Round
Rooster Now Crows
To Market

Wade
Adeste Fideles
Another Year Of Setting Suns
Hours That Were
How Firm A Foundation
I've Got A Pain In My Sawdust
Lo He Comes With Clouds
Descending
Meet Me By Moonlight Alone
O Come All Ye Faithful

Wade & Gill
Heart Breaker

Wade & Mar
God Cared Enough

Wadhams
Let Him Go

Wadhams & Neigher
I Want You

Waelrant
D'amours Me Va

Wagenheim
Intoxique
Moi J'Fais Mon Rond
Parce Que

Waghorne
All Things Bright And Beautiful

Wagner
Arie Der Elisabeth
Athmest Du Nicht
Awake
Awake Draws Nigh The Break Of
    Day
Bacchanale
Ballade Der Senta
Beloved One Come
Bridal Chorus
Bridal March
Bridal Procession
Bridal Song
Brunnhilde's War-Cry
Chorale Meister Singer Von
    Nurnberg, Die
Dors Mon Enfant
Dreams
Du Armste
Einsam In Truben Tagen
Elizabeth's Prayer
Elsa's Dream
Elsas Gesang An Die Lufte
Elsas Traum
Euch Luften Die Mein Klagen
Evening Star
Faithful And True
Flag Of The Free
Fuhl 'ich Zu Dir
Gebet Der Elisabeth
Grand March
Here Comes The Bride
In Fernem Land
In God We Trust
King Of Kings
King's Prayer
Legend Of The Holy Grail, The
Lied Des Steuermanns
Little Gray Donkey
Lohengrin's Entrance
Lohengrin's Farewell
Mein Herr Und Gott
My Harp Shall Praise Thee
Nun Sei Bedankt
O Du Mein Holder Abendstern
O King Most High Of Earth And Sky
O Thou Sublime Sweet Evening Star
Oh Star Of Eve
Pilgrim Chorus
Pilgrims Chorus, The
Pilgrims' Song
Praise To Minstrelsy
Processional
Rest Here With Me
Ride Of The Valkyries
Schlachthymne
Should He Return
Siegmund's Love Song
Song Of Venus
Spinning Chorus
Swan Song
To The Evening Star
Traume
Under The Double Eagle

Wagner *(Cont.)*
Walter's Prize Song
Was't Magic
When Thou Dost Gaze At Me
Ye Wand'ring Breezes
Wagoner
Wild Mustang
Wahlberg
Dansen Pa Makeskjaer
Johan Pa Snippen
Wainer
Varshe
Wainright
Christians Awake
Christians Awake Salute The Happy
    Morn
Wainwright
Christians Awake
Christians Awake Salute The Happy
    Morn
Earth O Lord Is One Great Field, The
Eternal Ruler Of The Ceaseless
    Round
Father We Thank Thee For The
    Night
Life's A Bumper
Now Comes The Light
Out Of The Dark
Where Ancient Forests Widely
    Spread
Wait
When Clinton Was The Governor
Waite
Battle Cry
Waite & Cain & Schon & Spiro
Heaven Is A 4 Letter Word
Waite & Sandford & Leonard
Missing You
Wakefield
Drummond
No Sir
Polly And I
Wakely
Song Of The Sierras
Too Late
Wakely & Bond
Those Gone And Left Me Blues
Wakely & Rivers & Rogers
Walkin' The Sidewalks Of Shame
Wakely & White
I'm Casting My Lasso Towards The
    Sky
If You Knew What It Meant To Be
    Lonesome
Wakeman
Six Wives Of Henry VIII, The
Wakenius
Cutting Edge
Walch
For Thee O Dear Dear Country
God Of The Nations Near And Far
Jesus My Lord How Rich Thy Grace
Jesus The Very Thought Of Thee

Walch *(Cont.)*
Lord Will Come And Not Be Slow,
    The
My Father For Another Night
My Sins My Sins My Saviour
O Christian Haste Thy Mission High
    Fulfilling
O God Who Workest Hitherto
O How The Thought Of God
    Attracts
O Sion Haste Thy Mission High
    Fulfilling
O Zion Haste
O Zion Haste Thy Mission High
O Zion Haste Thy Mission High
    Fulfilling
There Is A Land Of Pure Delight
Walden
How 'Bout Us
Walden & Hull
Let Me Be Your Angel
Waldis
Pleasure It Is
When I In Pain And Sorrow Moan
Waldman
Letter Home
Waldman & Bickhardt
That's How You Know When Love's
    Right
Waldman & Photoglo
Fishin' In The Dark
You Can't Run Away From Your
    Heart
Waldmann
Little Fishermaiden
Waldorf
Masquerade
Waldron
Duquility
Left Alone
Soul Eyes
Waldrup
Solid Comfort
Waldteufel
Dolores
Espana
Estudiantina
September Breeze
Skaters, The
Skaters' Waltz, The
Walford
O King Enthroned On High
Walford & Bradbury
Sweet Hour Of Prayer
Walker
Address For All, An
Are You Sincere
Babe Of Bethlehem, The
Believer
Bereaved Maid, The
Breaker
Bruce's Address
Burning Lamp

Walker (*Cont.*)
Call It Stormy Monday
Christian Prospect
Christian Warfare, The
Christian's Conflicts, The
Christian's Hope, The
Come And Taste With Me
Complainer
Contented Soldier
Corinna's Going A-Maying
Distant Drums
Distress
Don't Be Afraid Of The Dark
Dream Baby
Dream Baby How Long Must I
    Dream
Dudley
Faithful Soldier
French Broad
Good Old Way, The
Good Physician, The
Hallelujah
Heavenly Armor
Heavenly Armour
Heavenly March, The
Hebrew Children
Hicks' Farewell
Humble Penitent
I Went To Heaven
I'm Still In Love With You
In That Morning
In The Misty Moonlight
In The Morning
Indian's Farewell
Invitation
Jerusalem
King Of Glory King Of Peace
Lament
Light Of The World We Hail Thee
Lone Pilgrim, The
Long Boy
Louisiana
Mercy Seat
Millennium
Missionary Farewell
Mourner's Lamentation
Mr Bojangles
My God Accept My Heart This Day
Never Borrow Money Needlessly
Nocturne
O Love O Life Our Faith And Sight
Pardoning Love
Parting Hand
Pilgrim Song
Pleading Saviour
Red Red Rose, A
Sing The Glory Of His Name
Social Bank
Sufferings Of Christ
Sweet Harmony
Sweet Let Me Go
Sweet Prospect
Thorny Desert

Walker (*Cont.*)
True Happiness
Walk With God
Watchman's Call, The
Weeping Saviour
Zion's Light
Walker & Arnold
You Don't Know Me
Walker & Pierce
I Don't Care
Leavin' On Your Mind
Walker & Sullivan
When My Blue Moon Turns To Gold
    Again
Walker & Wilkin
Fallen Angel
Wallace
Ah Let Me Like A Soldier Fall
Alone With Thee
City By The Bay
Flag Of Our Union, The
Flag Of Our Union Forever, The
Following The Leader
Good Night And Pleasant Dreams
How D'Ye Do And Shake Hands
I Wish I Had My Old Girl Back
    Again
Immortal Love
Immortal Love Forever Full
In Happy Moments
In Happy Moments Day By Day
Missing Link, The
Pink Elephants
Pink Elephants On Parade
Scenes That Are Brightest
See Israel's Gentle Shepherd Stand
Sleeping I Dream'd Love
Speak Gently
Sweet Spirit Hear My Prayer
Trust Only In The Lord
We Bear The Strain Of Earthly Care
We May Not Climb The Heavenly
    Steps
When I See An Elephant Fly
Why Do I Weep For Thee
Yes Let Me Like A Soldier Fall
Wallace & Skinner & Bell
Even The Nights Are Better
Wallace & Weeks
Hindustan
Waller
Haaka Hula Hickey Dula
Happy As The Day Is Long
How Come You Do Me Like You Do
Jealous
Just Try To Picture Me Down Home
    In Tennessee
Love Divine
Shiloah
Shoe Shine Boy
Waller & Brooks
Ain't Misbehavin
Black And Blue

Waller & Turnbridge
Got A Date With An Angel
Waller & Williams
Squeeze Me
Waller, Fats
Alligator Crawl
Blue Turning Grey Over You
Cash For Your Trash
Honeysuckle Rose
Joint Is Jumpin', The
Keepin' Out Of Mischief Now
Viper's Drag
Walls
Mizpah
Walsh
All Night Long
Jesus The Very Thought Of Thee
Walsh & Goldenberg
Automatic
Walsh & Henley & Frey
Life In The Fast Lane
Walter
As Men Of Old Their First Fruits
    Brought
Hail To Georgia
Rise Up O Men Of God
Rise Up Ye Saints Of God
Stand Soldier Of The Cross
Walter & Peek
I Would Be True
Walters
Beautiful Brown Eyes
Walther
Christ Jesus Lay In Death's Strong
    Bands
Mit Fried Und Freud Fahr Ich Dahin
Out Of The Depths I Cry To Thee
Walthers
Come In Out Of The Draft
Walthew
Mistress Mine
Splendour Falls, The
Walton
Creator Spirit By Whose Aid
O Jesus Christ Our Lord Most Dear
Wambold
Little Church Around The Corner,
    The
Wand
Dallas Blues
Wansel & Biggs
Forever I Do
Wansel & Biggs & Gamble
If Only You Knew
Warburton
Christ Of The Upward Way
O Holy Spirit Gracious Gift Divine
Onward Christian Soldiers
Thy Kingdom Come O Lord
Ward
Aeterna California
America Forever
America The Beautiful
Band Played On, The

Ward *(Cont.)*
Dear Webster
Faith Takes A Vision
Forward Go
George Of The Jungle
How Happy Every Child Of Grace
Must I Say Adios
New-Born King Who Comes Today,
  The
O Beautiful For Spacious Skies
O Mother Dear Jerusalem
Purple Orchid, The
Sorrow Of Mydath
Strike Up The Band
Strike Up The Band Here Comes A
  Sailor
Think Of Your Head In The Morning
Whitestown
Your Boy Is On The Coal Pile Now
Ward & Gersmehl
I Belong To You
Ward & Tyson
Black Velvet
Ward-Jackson
Erk's Lament, The
Ward-Steinman
Season
Wardell
We Want A Man Like Roosevelt
Warden & Beavers
Here I Am Drunk Again
Warden & Palermo
Sit A Little Closer
Ware
Boy In The Gallery, The
I Want You
Mammy's Song
Rover
Warfield & Williams
Baby Won't You Please Come Home
Wariner
Where Did I Go Wrong
Wariner & Hart
Hold On
Wariner & Labounty
I Got Dreams
Wariner & McAnally
Precious Thing
Wariner & Murrah
When I Could Come Home To You
Warlamoff
Ah Tell Me Why
Warlock
Adam Lay Ybounden
Balulalow
Bayly Beareth The Bell Away, The
I Have A Garden
Little Trotty Wagtail
My Little Sweet Darling
Rest Sweet Nymphs
Sleep
Sweet Content
Take Oh Take Those Lips Away

Warlock *(Cont.)*
Tyrley Tyrlow
Whenas The Rye
Warner
Hail Pacific Hail
Warner & Bradbury
Jesus Loves Me
Warner & Lomax & Lomax
Tom Dooley
Warnick
Dogs Kids Love To Bite, The
Warnke
Come To Me
Warnock
Song Of Dedication
Warrack
Eternal God Whose Power Upholds
When Stephen Full Of Pow'r And
  Grace
Warrell
We Saw Thee Not When Thou Didst
  Come
Warren
All I Want Is Forever
Angels Praise Him
April Snow
Be Gracious To Me Lord
Blame It On The Rain
Christ Is Risen From The Dead
Clothed In Kingly Majesty
Cobbler And Tinker
Coffee Time
Come Holy Spirit
Darkness Turns To Dawn, The
Daydreaming All Night Long
Empty He Came
Everybody's Got To Learn Sometime
Fool Has Said, The
Friendly Star
Glory To God In His Holy Place
God Of Heaven Thunders, The
God Of Our Father Whose Almighty
  Hand
God Of Our Fathers
God Of Our Fathers Whose
  Almighty Hand
God Of The Nations
Gold Digger's Song, The
Gold Diggers' Song
Great Is The Lord
He Walks Among The Golden
  Lamps
He Who Stands In Awe Of God
Heart Is So Smart, The
Heralds Of Christ Who Bear
Honeymoon Hotel
How Could You
How Good A Thing It Is
I Get Weak
I Know Why And So Do You
I Love My Baby My Baby Loves Me
I Wanna Be A Dancin' Man
I Wanna Go Back To Bali
I Was Glad When I Heard Them Say

Warren *(Cont.)*
I Worship You O Lord
I'll Be Your Shelter
I'm Goin' Shoppin' With You
I've Got To Sing A Torch Song
If I Could Turn Back Time
If You Feel Like Singing Sing
In Majesty And Splendour
In The Days Of Need
Innamorata
Ironing Song
Land Of Our Hearts
Lands Of The Earth
Legend Of Wyatt Earp
Lift Up Your Hearts
Listen To My Prayer Lord
Look Away
Lord Is King, The
Lord Is My Shepherd, The
Lord Now Let Your Servant
Lord Who Is He That Shall Dwell
Lord You've Tested Me
Love Will Lead You Back
Marjorie's Almanac
Merciful And Gracious Be
My Soul Proclaims The Greatness Of
  The Lord
Nagasaki
Night And Day
No Weight Of Gold Or Silver
Now Sing My Soul
O Lord Be Gracious
O Lord Of Life Where'er They Be
Past Are The Cross The Scourge
Praise Him
Praise O Praise The Lord Our God
Praise The Lord Of Heaven
Praise To The Lord
Put That Down In Writing
Queen O'May, The
Remember My Forgotten Man
Rhythm Of The Night
Rise Crowned With Light Imperial
  Salem Rise
Rubberneckin'
Safe In The Hands Of God
Safe In The Shadow Of The Lord
Seeing's Believing
Separate Tables
Since Our Great High Priest
Sing A New Song
Sing We Praise
Snow Towards Evening
Spirit Came As Promised, The
Stranger In Paree, A
Sweetgrass Range
Swing Your Partner Round And
  Round
Then I Saw A New Heaven And
  Earth
There Was A Little Girl
These Are The Facts

Warren (*Cont.*)

This World Has Great Rewards To
    Give
Timeless Love
To Everyone Whom God Has Made
To Our Musical Club
To The Praise Of God The Father
To This We Have Been Called
Two Dreams Met
We Praise You O Father
When God Delivered Israel
When I See You Smile
When I'm Back On My Feet Again
When Lawless Men Succeed
When The Sun Is Darkened
Who Will You Run To
Will Of God, The
Will O' The Wisp, The
Wings Over The Navy
You Say The Sweetest Things Baby
You're An Education
Your Baby Never Looked Good In
    Blue

Warren & Carter

Wild Side Of Life, The

Warren & Gorman

Rose Of The Rio Grande

Warren & Vallance & Adams

When The Night Comes

Warren & Verissimo & Silva & Sagle

Where The Blue And Lonely Go

Warren, Harry

About A Quarter To Nine
Affair To Remember, An
Am I In Love
At Last
Boulevard Of Broken Dreams, The
By The River Sainte Marie
Chattanooga Choo Choo
Cheerful Little Earful
Chica Chica Boom Chic
Coffee In The Morning
Dames
Don't Give Up The Ship
Down Argentina Way
Forty-Second Street
Girlfriend Of The Whirling Dervish,
    The
Go Into Your Dance
Have A Little Faith In Me
I Found A Million Dollar Baby
I Found A Million Dollar Baby In A
    Five And Ten Cent Store
I Had The Craziest Dream
I Had The Craziest Dream Last
    Night
I Know Now
I Only Have Eyes For You
I Wish I Knew
I Yi Yi Yi Yi I Like You Very Much
I'll Sing You A Thousand Love
    Songs
I'll String Along With You
I've Got A Gal In Kalamazoo

Warren, Harry (*Cont.*)

It Happened In Sun Valley
Jeepers Creepers
Latin Quarter, The
Lullaby Of Broadway
Lulu's Back In Town
More I See You, The
My Dream Is Yours
My Heart Tells Me
No Love No Nothin'
On The Atchison Topeka And The
    Sante Fe
Pettin' In The Park
Remember Me
September In The Rain
Serenade In Blue
Shadow Waltz
Shanghai Lil
She's A Latin From Manhattan
Shuffle Off To Buffalo
That's Amore
There Will Never Be Another You
This Heart Of Mine
This Is Always
Wait And See
Where Do You Worka John
With Plenty Of Money And You
Words Are In My Heart, The
Would You Like To Take A Walk
You May Not Be An Angel But I'll
    String Along With You
You Must Have Been A Beautiful
    Baby
You Wonderful You
You'll Never Know
You're Getting To Be A Habit With
    Me
You're My Everything
Young And Healthy
Zing A Little Zong

Warshawsky

Briv Fun Amerike, A
By The Fireside
Kesl Gardn
Lidl Fun Broyt, Dos
Mechutonim Geyen, Di
Milners Trern, Dem
Oyfn Pripitchik

Wartensee

Come Says Jesus' Sacred Voice
Horton

Washburn

Lord Of Health Thou Life Within Us
Wave High The Red Bandana

Washington & Crosby & Young

Ghost Of A Chance, A

Washington & Karger

Gidget

Washington & Lewis

I'll Be Home

Washington & Young

Stella By Starlight

Wasilkowsky

Al Tiro

Waterman

Red And Black, The

Waters

Another Brick In The Wall Part 1
Belle Of Avenoo A, The
Money
Rollin' Stone

Waters & Dunn

Strangers Again

Waters & King

I've Cried My Last Tear For You

Waters & Shapiro & Dunn

Are You Ever Gonna Love Me
Only When I Love

Waters & Stuart

Partners With God

Wathall

Break New-Born Year On Glad Eyes
    Break
I Little See I Little Know
Long Years Ago O'Er Bethlehem's
    Hills
Not Only When Ascends The Song
Our Highest Joys Succeed Our Griefs
R-E-M-O-R-S-E
Slowly Slowly Dark'ning
There's A Song In The Air

Watkins

Raise Your Hands

Watkinson & Alder

Back Of My Hand

Watley & Cymone

Friends
Looking For A New Love
Real Love

Watson

All In A Garden Fair
Anchored
Babylon
Five Japanese Love Poems
John Chinaman My Jo
Light Of The World We Hail Thee
Little One
Lookin' Out For Number One
O Beautiful My Country
Passing Away
Racing With The Moon
Spanish Gypsy, The
This Is The Hour Of The Banquet
We're Madly For Adlai

Watson & Edmonds & Ladd & Ladd

Rock Steady

Watt

Thanksgiving Hymn

Watts

Addio
Blue Are Her Eyes
Capri
From A Roman Hill
Isle Of Beauty
Naples
Night Song At Amalfi

Watts *(Cont.)*
Ponte Vecchio Florence
Ruins Of Paestum
Stresa
There's No Room For Heaven Here
Villa Serbelloni Bellaggio
Wings Of Night
Watts & Croft
O God Our Help In Ages Past
Watts & Hatton
Jesus Shall Reign
Lord Thou Shalt Reign Where'er The
Sun
Watts & Lowry
We're Marching To Zion
Watts & Ryerson & Eaton
Blue Champagne
Waxman
Cimarron
Katsumi Love Theme
Place In The Sun, A
Theme From Peyton Place
Wonderful Season Of Love, The
Wayne
Country Bumpkin
Don't Let 'em Take It Away
Dreamer's Holiday, A
I Understand
In A Little Spanish Town
Laughing On The Outside Crying
On The Inside
Miss America
Ramona
There She Is Miss America
Wayne & Anderson
Saginaw Michigan
Wayne & Edwards
See You In September
Wayne & Moore
One Little Step At A Time
Wayne & Morris
Blue Velvet
Wayne & Reichner
I Need Your Love Tonight
Wayne & Weisman & Fuller
Spinout
Weale
O Help Us Lord Each Hour Of Need
Weatherly
I'll Still Love You
If You Ever Change Your Mind
Midnight Train To Georgia
Roses And Love Songs
Weatherly & Adams
Holy City, The
Weatherly & Knobloch
Hot Nights
Weatherspoon & Bowden & Dean
I'll Say Forever My Love
Weatherspoon & Dean
It's Wonderful To Be Loved By You
Weatherspoon & Dean & Goga
Farewell Is A Lonely Sound

Weatherspoon & Johnson & Dean
I'll Pick A Rose For My Rose
Weaver
Camel, The
I Walked Into The Garden
Moon-Marketing
Only God
What Will You Do In That Day
Webb
All I Know
Be A Hero
Beth
By The Time I Get To Phoenix
Children's Hosanna
Clowns Exit Laughing
Dancing Girl
Debout Sainte Cohorte
Didn't We
Everybody Gets To Go To The Moon
Fair Weather Lover
First Hymn From Grand Terrace
From All Thy Saints In Warfare
From Ocean Unto Ocean
Galveston
Girl Who Needs Me, The
God Is My Strong Salvation
God Our Strength
Gospel Morning
Hail To The Lord's Anointed
Halfway In The Middle
Here I'll Stand
How Can You Do It
Hymn From Grand Terrace
I Can't Get It
I Can't Leave You All Alone
I Can't Quit
I Don't Need You
I Think We're Gonna Make It Baby
I'll Be Back When Winter's Gone
If I'd Been A Different Man
If These Walls Could Speak
If Thou Art An Honest Friend
If You Leave Me
In Heavenly Love Abiding
In My Wildest Dreams
Lift Up The People's Banner
Light Pours Down From Heaven,
The
Little Family, The
Lost Generation
Love Now
Lovers Such As I
Macarthur Park
Mainliner
Midnight Mail
Mirror Mind
Moon Is A Harsh Mistress, The
Morning Light
Morning Light Is Breaking, The
Moving On
Name Of My Sorrow, The
Now Host With Host Assembling

Webb *(Cont.)*
Now Is The Time Approaching
O Love Divine
One Summer Night
Our Wedding Prayer
Parenthesis
Plow This Ground
Psalms For The Semi-Living
Shadows Of Summer
She Never Smiles Anymore
Smartest Fool, The
Stand Up For Jesus
Stand Up Stand Up For Jesus
Summer Lovers, The
Take It Easy
There Ain't No Doubt
There He Goes
This Is Where I Came In
This Is Your Life
Up Up And Away
Wassail Song
What No Pretzels
Whatever Happened To Christmas
When Eddie Comes Home
When I'm Dead
When It Was Done
Where's The Playground Susie
Wichita Lineman
Will Men E'er Dwell Together
World Made Of Windows
Webb & Watkins
Roar Lion Roar
Webbe
Ask Me Why I Do Not Sing
Benevento
Brightest And Best
Come Thou Holy Spirit Come
Come Ye Disconsolate
Come Ye Disconsolate Where'er Ye
Languish
Cure A Lass A Dram, The
Glorious Apollo
Holy Spirit Font Of Light
Judge Eternal Throned In Splendor
Let Me Sleep This Night Away
Lo He Comes With Clouds
Descending
Look From Thy Sphere Of Endless
Day
Lord's My Shepherd, The
Mansion Of Peace
Me Knows Is Cold
My God Thy Table Now Is Spread
Nazareth
New Ev'ry Morning Is The Love
New Every Morning Is The Love
New Every Morning Is Thy Love
Not Giv'n To Us From Out The
Skies
Now I Am Married
Now My Soul Thy Voice Upraising
Now We Are Met
Now With The Rising Golden Dawn

Webbe (Cont.)
O For That Flame Of Living Fire
O God Above The Drifting Years
O God In Whom We Live And Move
O Salutaris
O Saving Victim Opening Wide
O Spirit Of The Living God
O What Amazing Words Of Grace
Old Giles
Our Gifts Of Money
Song Of The Reaper
Spirit Of Mercy Truth And Love
Swell The Anthem
Tantum Ergo Sacramentum
Thou Rulest Lord
When Israel Of The Lord Beloved
While With Ceaseless Course The
    Sun

Webber
Constancy

Weber
Arabien Mein Heimatland
As A Little Child
As The Sun Doth Daily Rise
Berceuse
Boat Song, The
Cast Thy Burden On The Lord
Cradle Song
Day By Day The Manna Fell
Days Of Summer Glory
Declining Day
Dein Wille Herr Gescheh'
Depth Of Mercy
Depth Of Mercy Can There Be
Echoing Bell Tones
Einst Traumte Meiner Selgen Base
Elfin Song
Euriante
Evening Prayer
Fais Do Do
From All They Saints In Warfare
Fruhlingslied
Gebet Vor Der Schlacht
God Of Mercy God Of Grace
Gottes Sternlein Glanzen Wieder
Grablied
Grosser Schopfer Herr Der Welt
Hail To The Lord's Anointed
Heart Of The Seeker, The
Huntsmen's Chorus
I Saw A Rosebud
Immortals, The
Invitation To The Dance
Jagerchor
Jesus Calls Us O'er The Tumult
Kommt Ein Schlanker Bursch
    Gegangen
Lord I Cannot Let Thee Go
Lord Of Hosts To Thee We Raise
Lord We Come Before Thee Now
Lutzow's Wild Hunt
Lutzows Wilde Jagd
Mes Yeux Ne Savent Te Le Dire
Mit Dem Pfeil Dem Bogen

Weber (Cont.)
Morning Song
My Jesus As Thou Wilt
O Fatima Etereo Dono
Our Prayer
Ozean Du Ungeheuer
Pain Of Love
Prayer
Prayer For Each Day
Prayer From Der Freischutz
Round, A
Schwertlied
Shepherd, The
Shopping
Singing A Love Song
Sleep Dearest Baby
Softly Now The Light Of Day
Softly Sighs The Voice Of Evening
Song Of Freedom
Sword Song
Thy Way Not Mine
Thy Way Not Mine O Lord
Toujours Adieu
Tyrolienne De Sylvana
Und Ob Die Wolke Sie Verhulle
Wedding Chorus
Wie Naht Mir Der Schlummer
Wir Wollen Naus In Garten

Weber & Borop
It Is Good

Weber & Sprague & Bannister
Carry On

Weber & Thurman & Thurman
Flawless

Webster
Army Bean, The
Come To The Savior Just Now
Do You Know The Friend Of Sinners
Get Out Of Mexico
God Leads To Victory
I'll Walk With God
In The Sweet By And By
In The Sweet Bye And Bye
It Shall Be Well
Joy In Sorrow
Lorena
Love Song From Mutiny On The
    Bounty
Man In A Raincoat
O For A Closer Walk With God
O Holy Spirit
Preacher And The Slave, The
Precious Word Of Jesus
Sweet By And By
Sweet Bye And Bye
There's A Land That Is Fairer Than
    Day
Toil Of Brain Or Heart Or Hand, The
Underneath The Banner
Where The Blessed Savior Leads

Webster & Burke
Black Coffee

Webster & Livingston
Twelfth Of Never, The

Webster & Tiomkin
Green Leaves Of Summer, The

Wechter
Spanish Flea

Weckerly
Glory To God
I For Thee Was Crucified

Weeden
God Give Us Homes
He Saves Me
I Surrender All
Inner Circle, The
My Mother's Prayer
Will The Will Of Christ, The
Yes He Will

Weekes
Slowly By Thy Hand Unfurled

Weeks
Joan Of Arc
Navy Wings

Weeks & Fazioli
Navy Wings

Weelkes
Grace My Lovely One Fair Beauties
Hark All Ye Lovely Saints Above
Lady Your Eye My Love Enforced
Lo Country Sports
Nightingale, The
O Rose So Brightly Glowing
On The Plains Fairy Trains
Since Robin Hood
Strike It Up Tabor
Welcome Sweet Pleasure

Weersma
Penny Serenade

Weidt
How Fair Thou Art

Weigle
No One Ever Cared For Me Like
    Jesus

Weigle & Muller
I Have Found A Hiding Place

Weil
Spring Song

Weiland
Will You Love Me Then As Now

Weill
Bilbao Song, The
Green-Up Time
It Never Was You
Lonely House
Lost In The Stars
Love Song
Mack The Knife
My Ship
September Song
Speak Low
Stay Well
Tripoli
Tschaikowsky And Other Russians

Weimar
Children Of The Heav'nly King
Children Of The Heavenly King

Weimar *(Cont.)*
Lo The Easter Tide Is Here
O Love Divine How Sweet Thou Art
Weinberg & Marks & Warren
Where Do You Work-A John
Weinkranz
Y'Varech'cha
Weinrich
Sail Along Silv'ry Moon
Weir
Born Cross-Eyed
Cassidy
Estimated Prophet
Jack Straw
Music Never Stopped, The
One More Saturday Night
Sugar Magnolia
Weirick
Makin' Love Ukulele Style
Weisberg
Christmas For Cowboys
Weise
Passionslied
Rezept Wider Die Melancholei
Weisenthal
Ingle Side, The
Weisgall
Dying Airman, The
Dying Soldier, The
Fife Tune
Leveller, The
Lord I Have Seen Too Much
My Sweet Old Etcetera
Shiloh
Suicide In Trenches
Weisman
As Long As I Have You
Change Of Habit
Danny
Don't Ask Me Why
Fame And Fortune
Follow That Dream
Fun In Acapulco
How Can You Lose
How Can You Lose What You Never
    Had
I Slipped I Stumbled I Fell
I'll Be Back
Let Us Pray
Miracle Happened To Me, A
Miracle Happened To Me It Could
    Happen To You, A
Ridin' The Rainbow
Slowly But Surely
There's So Much World To See
This Is Living
What Can I Give Him
Weisman & Wayne
Hard Luck
Weisman & Wayne & Garrett
Night Has A Thousand Eyes, The
Weisman & Wayne & Karger
We Call On Him

Weisman & Wise & Fuller
I Got Lucky
Steppin' Out Of Line
Weiss
Can't Give You Anything
Disco Baby
Love Is The Answer
Maggie Flynn
Rhinestone Cowboy
Thank You Song, The
Vertraue Ihm
While You Danced Danced Danced
Why Can't I Walk Away
Weiss & Deshannon
Bette Davis Eyes
Weiss & Mann
Put Your Dreams Away
Weiss & Peretti & Creatore
Can't Help Falling In Love
Wild In The Country
Weiss & Sherman
That Sunday That Summer
Weiss & Thiele
What A Wonderful World
Weisse
God Of All Grace Thy Mercy Send
Once He Came In Blessing
Wekerlin
At The Village Dance
My Friend
Welch
Faithful Pipe To Smoke, A
I'm Awfully Glad To Be Popular
Just Look Wise
Michigan Field Song, The
Oh Alma Mater
Sentimental Lady
Ta-Dum Ta-Dum
When Night Falls Dear
When We Were In College
Wishing Just Wishing
Welch & Hostill
Please Mr Please
Welch & Stinson
Let It Be You
Weldon
I Like Mountain Music
Outskirts Of Town
Weller
Jam Up And Jelly Tight
My Ever Changing Moods
Weller & Oldham
Lonely Women Make Good Lovers
Welles
Connecticut
Wellesley
Come Holy Spirit Come
For All Thy Saints
Forever With The Lord (First Tune)
God Of The Searching Mind
I Love Thy Church
Teach Me My God And King

Wellings
Dreaming
Forget Forgive
Someday
Wellman
Men Of Dartmouth
Wells
Casual Look, A
Guide
Holy Spirit Faithful Guide
Joan Of Arc
Place In The Sun, A
We Got It Made
WKRP In Cincinnati
Yester-Me Yester-You Yesterday
Wells & Heath
Living By Faith
Wells & Terry & Gill
One Of The Deathless Army
Wells & Torme
Born To Be Blue
Welsh
Advent Candles
Musical Alphabet
Welz
Am Weihnachtsbaum Die Lichter
    Brennen
Weman
Sion Praise Thy Saviour
Sion Praise Thy Saviour Singing
Wendling
Oh How I Wish I Could Sleep
Oh What A Pal Was Mary
Yacka Hula Hickey Dula
Wendling & Kortlander
Felix The Cat
Wendte
All Things Bless Thee
Come Forth O Christian Children
Come Friends The World Wants
    Mending
Forward Children Forward
God Make My Life A Little Light
Happy Christmas
Happy Days Are Gliding
Hast Thou Heard It O My Brother
Lead Us Heavenly Father
Rouse Up To Work
Softly Now On Angel Pinions
Still Small Voice, The
When Twilight Falls
Wenrich
I Ain't Got Weary Yet
Moonlight Bay
Peaches And Cream
Put On Your Old Grey Bonnet
Silver Bell
Sweet Cider Time When You Were
    Mine
Tulip And The Rose
When It's Moonlight In Mayo
When You Wore A Tulip
When You Wore A Tulip And I
    Wore A Big Red Rose

Wenrich *(Cont.)*
Where Do We Go From Here
Where Do We Go From Here Boys

Wents
Allerschonster Menschensohn

Wentworth
Big Big Sky, The
Choice Colors
Harvest Song
Seesaw
Storm Clouds
Sun And Moon
Waves
Yoo-Hoo

Wentz
Blumelein O Blumelein
Englein Verlassen Im Himmel Die
    Bracht, Die
Englein Verlassen Im Himmel Die
    Pracht, Die
Frieden Ach Frieden
Ich Lobe Dich
Im Himmel Wo Mein Heiland
    Wohnet
In Deinem Namen O Herr
Jauchzet Ihr Himmel
Jesu Meine Wunden
Kommt Lasst Uns Knie'n
Mein Loffen Steht Zum Himmel
O Herr Der Mut Entsinket Mir
O Tag Der Auferstehung
So Weit So Weit Die Wolken Gehn
Sterne Funkeln, Die
Wach' Auf Mein Herz
Welch' Susse Worte

Wenzlik
Papa Come Back To Mamma

Werner
All United
Christ Whose Glory Fills The Skies
Heidenroslein, Das
O Salutaris
Praise Our Great And Gracious Lord
Rosula In Prato
Sah Ein Knab Ein Roslein Stehn
Two Roses, The
We Believe In One True God
Wondering

Werner & Idol
Cradle Of Love

Wert
Ah Dolente Partita

Wesigall
Futility

Wesley
Advent Of Our God, The
Alleluia Sing To Jesus
Another Year Is Dawning
Behold The Lamb Of God
Can We By Searching Find Out God
Christ The Lord Is Risen Today
Church's One Foundation Is Jesus
    Christ, The
Church's One Foundation, The

Wesley *(Cont.)*
Come Sound His Praise Abroad
Dies Irae
Father Whate'er Of Earthly Bliss
God Is My Strong Salvation
God Of The Strong God Of The
    Weak
Hail To The Lord's Anointed
I Lay My Sins On Jesus
Jesus Lover Of My Soul
Joyful Joyful We Adore Thee
Lead Me Lord
Lord What A Change In One Short
    Hour
My God My Father While I Stray
Not Far Beyond The Sea
O Bless The Lord My Soul
O Day Of Rest And Gladness
O God Most Merciful And True
O God The Rock Of Ages
O God The Son Eternal Thy Dread
    Might
O God To Us Show Mercy
O Living Bread From Heaven
O Thou Who Camest From Above
O Thou Who Through This Holy
    Week
Oh For A Thousand Tongues
Praise The Lord Ye Heavens Adore
    Him
Praise Waits For Thee
Show Me The Way
Since Jesus Is My Friend
Sons Of Men Behold
Sunday Bells Are Calling, The
There Is A Blessed Home
Thou'rt With Me O My Father
We Sing Of God The Mighty Source
What Cheering Words Are These
Wie Konnt' Ich Sein Vergessen

Wesley & Campbell
And Can It Be That I Should Gain

Wesley & Darwall
Rejoice The Lord Is King

Wesley & Elvey
Soldiers Of Christ Arise

Wesley & Glaser
O For A Thousand Tongues To Sing

Wesley & Marsh
Jesus Lover Of My Soul

Wesley & Prichard
Come Thou Long Expected Jesus

West
As Comes The Breath Of Spring
Bugle Song
Daffodils
Everything At Reilly's Must Be Done
    In Irish Style
Five Hundred Miles
Friend O Mine
Good Morning
Halloween
Jenny Lind Mania, The

West *(Cont.)*
Marching With The Heroes
Milkweed
Mystery, A
North Wind, The
Our Court Ball
Saviour Blessed Saviour
Shining Days Of May, The
Shining Ship, The
Snowflakes
Spring Rain
Today
Triple Cheer, The
Tulips
Upside Down

West & Mainegra
Separate Ways

West & Ornadel
Portrait Of My Love, A

West & Spreen
Holly Leaves And Christmas Trees
Seeing Is Believing

West & West
There's Anger In The Land

Westbrook
Glory Love And Praise And Honor

Westendorf
I'll Take You Home Again Kathleen

Westerberg
I'll Be You

Westlake
It's A Matter Of Time

Westlake & Most
How The Web Was Woven

Weston
All In The Tree
Autumn In Rome
Bugle Blow
Dancing Is Fun
Good Wishes
Making Music
Morning At Camp
Row Burnie Row
Spanish Dance
Sun's Looking Glass, The
Tailors
Tax The Bachelors
Wandering
When Bands Begin To Play

Weston & Barnes
When Father Papered The Parlour

Weston & Lee
Good-Bye-Ee

Westra
Jesus Christ Is Born Today

Wetmore
My Mountain Home
Uncle Tom's Cabin

Wetton
Smile Has Left Your Eyes, The

Wetton & Downes
Don't Cry
Go

Whitfield & Strong & Penzabene
End Of Our Road, The
I Could Never Love Another
I Wish It Would Rain
Whitford
On A Rugged Hill
Whiting
Ain't We Got Fun
And They Called It Dixieland
For Those In Peril On The Sea
Have You Got Any Castles Baby
Hooray For Hollywood
I Wonder Where My Buddies Are
   To-Night
I've Hitched My Wagon To A Star
Japanese Sandman, The
Louise
Silhouetted In The Moonlight
Till We Meet Again
Too Marvelous For Words
Whiting & Brown
You're An Old Smoothie
Whiting & Brown & Desylva
Eadie Was A Lady
Whiting & Chase
My Ideal
Whiting & Harling
Beyond The Blue Horizon
Whitley
What Kind Of Fool Do You Think I
   Am
Whitlock
California Bloomer
Lucy Song
Thorn Tree In The Garden
Whitmer
Backward We Look O God Of All
   Days
Blow Golden Trumpets Sweet And
   Clear
We Know The Paths
Whitmore
America
Whitney
Jesus Tender Saviour
Mosquitos' Parade, The
Soldiers' Song
Whitney & Kramer
Far Away Places
No Man Is An Island
That's The Last Tear
Whitsett
Jesus Christ The Same
Whitsett & Mateer
Dear Me
Whittaker
Blaweary
Girl Sings, A
New World In The Morning
Oh Hush Thee My Baby
Song Of Shadows, The
Spring
Where Is Thy Crown Of Beauty

Whittemore
Brothers Come
My Lord Is Leading Me On
Seek Only Thy Perfect Way
Shout With Joy
Too Precious
We Shall Rise
Whitten
I Don't Want To Talk About It
Whitter & Noell & Lewey
Wreck Of The Old 97, The
Whittle
Moment By Moment
Whittle & McGranahan
There Shall Be Showers Of Blessings
Whittle & Moody
Moment By Moment
Whittler
Merry Song, A
Whitwell
Hail The Sign The Sign Of Jesus
Whitworth
He Will Pilot Me
Whyte
Behold The Bridegroom Comes
Wichern
Gesang Verschont Das Leben
Nacht Vergeht, Die
Weihnacht Weihnacht Kehret Wieder
Wickede
Heart's Spring-Time, The
Wickes
Our Father Which Art In Heaven
Wicklow
I Know That In The Holy Name
Widmann
Awake And Rub Your Clouded Eyes
Zu Miltenberg Am Maine
Widmer
Evening Rest
Widmeyer
Come And Dine
Widor
Ah Can You Tell Me Why
Albayde
And Did They Not Move You To
   Feel
April
Aurora
Ave Maria
Bee, The
Bouquet, The
Broken Vase, The
Captive, The
Contemplation
Contentment
Diver, The
Do You Ever Think Beloved
Find Me But A Meadow Clear
Give Me Alone Every Hour
Hunter Dreams Within The Wood,
   The
I Think Of Thee
In The Plain

Widor *(Cont.)*
Indian Song
Invocation
Is There Some Fair Meadow Green
Let Us Love On
Mon Bras Pressait
Morning Song
My Soul Its Secret Has
Never To See Or To Hear Her
Old Song, The
On This Sad Earth
Prayer
Serenade
Sigh For Sigh I Falter Near Thee
Sigh, The
Slumbering Cathedral, The
Springtime Prayer
Starry Night
Stars, The
Sunset
Sweet Appeal, The
Tears Of The Past
To Thee
When To Me You Show A Rose
Within My Arms
Wiechard
Jack O'Lantern
Wiedlin & Hall
Our Lips Are Sealed
Wiehelm
Watch On The Rhine
Wiener & Gold & Gluck
It's My Party
Wiggin
I Know Not Why
Lover's Song, The
Lullaby
My Laddie
O'er The Moor Amang The Heather
Phoebe
Plantation Christmas Carol
She Is So Fair
To Electra
Wiggins
Mill Mother's Lament, The
Wilayto
Organize The South
Wilburn
Born To Fly
Conversation Peace
Didn't We Papa
For Loving Me
God's Little People
Resident Power
Run With The Power
Satan You're A Liar
Wilburn & Crook
Just Any Day Now
What A Beautiful Day For The Lord
   To Come Again
Wilburn & Goodman
I'm Gonna Go Higher
Wilburn & Graham & Richardson
My House Is Your House

Wilburn & Huffman
  Put Something Back
Wilburn & Lehman
  Heartmender
  Miracle Man
Wilburn & Thomas
  Teach Me To See
Wilburn & Thomas & Thomas
  Pray For Me
Wilbye
  Adew Sweet Amarillis
  Adieu Sweet Amarillis
  Adieu Sweet Amaryllis
  As Matchless Beauty
  Away Thou Shalt Not Love
  Change Me O Heavens Into The
    Ruby Stone
  Flora Gave Me Fairest Flowers
  Lady When I Behold The Roses
  Thus Saith My Cloris Bright
  Weep O Mine Eyes
Wilcox
  Dreaming All Day
  We Connect
  Worth While
Wild
  Easter Carol
  Little Cares That Fretted Me, The
  Prayer
Wilde & Wilde
  Kids In America
Wilder
  Alabama And Kearsarge, The
  Answers, The
  April Age, The
  Baby Bunting
  Baggage Room Blues, The
  Bingo
  Bobby Shaftoe
  Buckee Bene
  Cradle Song
  Crazy In The Heart
  Crocodile, The
  Cuckoo Is A Pretty Bird, The
  Do Do L'enfant Do
  Don't Deny
  Douglas Mountain
  Elephant Present, The
  Ellen
  Evening Is A Little Boy
  From Every Stormy Wind
  From Every Stormy Wind That
    Blows
  Golux's Song, The
  Good Night
  Hark Hark The Dogs Do Bark
  How Are You Conscript
  How Lovely Is Christmas
  Huntsmen, The
  Hush Little Baby
  I Like It Here
  I Like It Here And This Is Where I'll
    Stay
  I See It Now

Wilder *(Cont.)*
  I'd Gladly Walk To Alaska
  I'll Be Around
  If Love's Like A Lark
  Infant Innocence
  Invalid Corps, The
  It All Depends
  It's A Fine Day For Walkin' Country
    Style
  Journey, The
  Lady Sings The Blues, The
  Listen To Your Heart
  Love Is When
  Love Means
  Lovers And Losers
  Many Million Years Ago
  Mimosa And Me
  Minnie And Winnie
  My Christmas Coloring Book
  Night
  Night Talk
  Night Will Never Stay, The
  Nut Tree, The
  Rain Rain Don't Go 'Way
  Remember My Child
  Seal Lullaby
  Star Wish
  Starlighter, The
  Such A Lonely Girl Am I
  Summer Is A-Comin' In
  Telephone Book Lullaby, The
  That's My Girl
  Tiptoe Night
  Turn Left At Monday
  Unbelievable
  Walk Pretty
  Wee Willie Winkie
  When A Robin Leaves Chicago
  Where Do You Go
  Where Do You Sleep
  Winds Are Hushed, The
  Windy Nights
  Winter Of My Discontent, The
  Wrong Blues, The
Wilder & Palitz
  While We're Young
Wilder & Prestopino
  Break My Stride
Wildermere
  I Know That My Redeemer Lives
  There's Only One Mother
Wildhorn
  I Do
Wildhorn & Jackson
  Where Do Broken Hearts Go
Wilensky
  Uri Tsiyon
Wiley
  Car-Barlick-Acid
Wilh
  Trumpet, The

Wilhelm
  Bright College Years
  Christmas
  Custodia Rhenana
  First Christmas Night, The
  Fruhlingszeit
  O Land Beloved
  Our Flag
  Rheni Excubiae
  Wacht Am Rhein, Der
  Wacht Am Rhein, Die
  Watch By The Rhine, The
  Watch On The Rhine, The
Wilhelmj
  Fishermaiden
Wilkerson
  Touchdown Song
Wilkes
  Jesus I Live To Thee
  Jesus My Truth My Way
  Let Us With A Gladsome Mind
  Lo The Earth Is Risen Again
  Lo We Stand Before Thee
  Praise To God And Thanksgiving
Wilkie
  I've Seen My Valley Filled With
    Springtime
  Storm King
Wilkin
  Behold The Man
  Gto
  I Have Returned
  Lord Let Me Leave A Song
  Reach Up And Touch God's Hand
  Scars In The Hands Of Jesus, The
  Where I'm Going
Wilkin & Dill
  Long Black Veil, The
Wilkins
  Hail To Old Oac
  Hail To Old Osc
  Prodigal Son
Wilkinson
  Because Of You
  Victory
  When The Green Goes Forth To
    Battle
Wilkinson & Gross
  Honor Your Parents
Willaert
  Allons Allons Gay Gayement Ma
    Mignonne
  Madrigal
  Qui La Dira
  Si Je Ne Voy M'amie
  Sur Le Joli Jonc
Willan
  Isabeau S'y Promene
  Laquelle Marierons-Nous
  Navire De Bayonne, Le
  Only Begotten Word Of God Eternal
  Petite Hirondelle, La
  Rossignol Du Vert Bocage

Willan *(Cont.)*
Saint Marguerite
Si J'etais Petite Mere

Willard
Cares Chorus

Willensky
Got To Be There
If You Say My Eyes Are Beautiful

Willet
Don't Let The Stars Get In Your
Eyes

Willet & Pryor & Trammel
Don't Let The Stars Get In Your
Eyes

Willi
To Music

William & Ames
Brother's Theme, The

Williams
Alabama Waltz
All My Rowdy Friends Are Coming
Over Tonight
Alone And Forsaken
America The Dream Goes On
Angel Of Death, The
Are You Lonely Too
Are You Walking And A-Talking For
The Lord
At The Name Of Jesus
Attitude Adjustment
Autumn Picture, An
Baby Please Don't Go
Bad Boy
Basin Street Blues
Bayou Pon Pon
Benedictus
Big C
Bind Us Together Lord
Blues Come Around, The
Bony Moronie
Bucket's Got A Hole In It, The
California Zephyr
Calling You
Christ Is All
Christ Is King
Christ Is The King
Classical Gas
Come Down O Love Divine
Come Pretty Wag
Come We That Love The Lord
Come Ye Faithful
Come Ye That Love The Lord
Cossack's Song, The
Country Boy Can Survive, A
Countryfied
Dalston
Day Is Rolling On, The
Dear Brother
Dizzy Miss Lizzie
Don't Give Us A Reason
Down In The Licensed Saloon
Earth Angel
Easter

Williams *(Cont.)*
Emperor, The
Exsultate Justi
Fanfare For Ten Year Olds
Finders Are Keepers
Fool About You
For All The Saints
For Me There Is No Place
Forest Battle, The
Forever Man
Forever's A Long Long Time
Fraulein
Give Us The Wings Of Faith
Givin' It Up For Your Love
God Hath Spoken By His Prophets
Good Friends Good Whiskey And
Good Lovin'
Gospel Changes
Great Is The Lord Our God
Gulf Coast Blues
Hail The Day That Sees Him Rise
Hail Thee Festival Day
Hast Thou Heard It
Have You Any Room For Jesus
He Who Would Valiant Be
Here's That Sunny Day
Home In Heaven, A
Homesick
Honey Do You Love Me Huh
Honky Tonkin'
Hooking Cow Blues
House Of Gold, A
How Can You Refuse Him Now
How Did My Heart Rejoice To Hear
How Far Is It To Bethlehem
Hymn To New England, A
I Ain't Got Nothing But Time
I Can't Escape From You
I Don't Care If Tomorrow Never
Comes
I Heard You Crying In Your Sleep
I Just Didn't Have The Heart To Say
Goodbye
I Lost The Only Love I Knew
I Love Thy Kingdom Lord
I Love Thy Zion Lord
I Love You Honey
I Loved A Lass A Fair One
I Want To Spend My Life With You
I Wish You Didn't Love Me So
Much
I'll Be A Bach'lor Till I Die
I'm A Long Gone Daddy
I'm Going Home
I'm Gonna Sing
I'm Just Crying Cause I Care
I'm So Tired Of It All
I'm Yvonne Of The Bayou
If The South Woulda Won
If We Were In Love
If You'll Be A Baby To Me
In The Waves

Williams *(Cont.)*
Is This Goodbye
It's A Long Long Way To Tipperary
Jesus Christ Is Risen Today
Jesus Died For Me
Jesus Remembered Me
Just Me And My Broken Heart
Just Now
Just Talk With Him A Little While
Key To Love, The
Kindness
Land Of The Giants
Lapti Nek
Larboard Watch
Last Night I Dreamed Of Heaven
Let The Earth Rejoice And Sing
Let Your Love Flow
Let's Be 'Plane Engines
Liberty Fanfare
Lift Up Your Heads Ye Mighty Gates
Lift Up Your Hearts
Little Bosephus
Little Darlin'
Little Robin Redbreast
Lo The Earth Is Ris'n Again
Lo The Earth Is Risen Again
Long Live The Nation
Lord God The Holy Ghost
Lost On The River
Low Down Blues
Machine Gun
Major Moves
Man Without A Woman, A
Me And My Broken Heart
Memories Of Mother
Message To My Mother, A
Mother Is Gone
Mr Smith
My Cold Cold Heart Is Melted Now
My Heart Won't Let Me Go
My Love For You Has Turned To
Hate
Never Again Will I Knock On Your
Door
Never Been So Lonesome
Nice To Be Around
Night Owl
Nite Owl
Nobody
Non Nobis Domine
O Bless The Lord My Soul
O Come And Mourn With Me
O Lord Our God Arise
Old Fashioned Love Song, An
Olympic Spirit, The
On A Poet's Lips
On Parade
Once To Ev'ry Man And Nation
Once To Every Man And Nation
Orchestra
Ozymandias
Pan American
Parade Of The Ewoks
Perfect Love, A

Williams, Hank *(Cont.)*
Jambalaya On The Bayou
Let's Turn Back The Years
Long Gone Lonesome Blues
May You Never Be Alone
Men With Broken Hearts
Mind Your Own Business
Moanin The Blues
Move It On Over
My Bucket's Got A Hole In It
My Heart Would Know
My Sweet Love Ain't Around
Nobody's Lonesome For Me
Ramblin' Man
There'll Be No Teardrops Tonight
There's A Tear In My Beer
There's Nothing As Sweet As My
    Baby
Weary Blues From Waitin
Why Don't You Love Me
Why Should We Try Anymore
You Win Again
You're Gonna Change Or I'm
    Gonna Leave
Your Cheatin' Heart

Williams, Hank Jr.
All My Rowdy Friends Have Settled
    Down
Born To Boogie
Cajun Baby
Dixie On My Mind
Family Tradition
Heaven Can't Be Found
I'm For Love
Man Of Steel
Texas Woman
Young Country

Williams, John
Can You Read My Mind
Cantina Band
Celebration Fanfare
Close Encounters Of The Third Kind
Empire Strikes Back Medley, The
Ewok Celebration
Fanfare For Michael Dukakis
Han Solo And The Princess
Han Solo Returns
Imperial March, The
Luke And Leia
Marion's Theme
May The Force Be With You
Mission Theme, The
Olympic Fanfare And Theme
Raiders March
Star Wars
Theme From Aftermash
Theme From Close Encounters Of
    The Third Kind
Theme From ET
Theme From ET The Extra-Terrestrial
Theme From Jaws

Williams, John *(Cont.)*
Theme From Superman
Theme From The Accidental Tourist
Theme From The Apartment
Theme From The Cowboys
Theme From The Magician
Winter Games Fanfare
Yoda's Theme

Williamson
This Is My Father's World
Welfare Store Blues

Willing
Bliss For Which Our Spirits Pine,
    The
Goodness Of God, The
On Jordan's Banks The Herald's Cry
Starry Firmament On High, The

Willis
Calm On The Listening Ear Of Night
CC Rider
Come O Lord Like Morning Sunlight
Door Is Still Open To My Heart, The
Fairest Lord Jesus
Fairest Lord Jesus Ruler Of All
    Nature
Hang Up My Rock And Roll Shoes
It Came Upon A Midnight Clear
It Come Upon The Midnight Clear
Raggy Rag
There Is A Green Hill Far Away
While Shepherds Watch'd Their
    Flocks By Night
While Shepherds Watched Their
    Flocks By Night

Willis & Lasley
Love Me Again

Wills
Bad Company
Cindy
I Wonder If You Feel The Way I Do
San Antonio Rose

Wills & Anderson
Rag Mop

Wills & Duncan
Take Me Back To Tulsa

Wills & Pfrimmer
You're The Last Thing I Needed
    Tonight

Wills & Quillen
They Never Lost You

Wills & Shore
Lady In Waiting
Leona
Woman Your Love

Wills & Wills
Faded Love

Willson
Dogies' Lullaby, The
Goodnight My Someone
I Ain't Down Yet
It's Beginning To Look Like
    Christmas
Lida Rose

Willson *(Cont.)*
May The Good Lord Bless And Keep
    You
Seventy Six Trombones
Smokey The Bear Is A Wise Bear
Till There Was You
Will You Be Saved Tonight
Ya Got Trouble

Wilm
Before The Sun Awakes

Wilmore
Florida

Wilson
Ain't Dat A Shame
Airman's Song, The
Alas And Did My Saviour Bleed
Alas Did My Saviour Bleed
All Authority And Power
And Must I Be To Judgment Brouth
Angels Bright Heavens High
Any Time's The Time For Prayer
As Longs The Deer For Cooling
    Streams
As Pants The Hart
As Pants The Hart For Cooling
    Streams
Avon
Bang Bang
Beautiful City, The
Behold The Saviour Of Mankind
Bells
Beneath His Wings
Blessed Be The Lord God Of Israel
Bow Down To Washington
Brave Pure And True
Bugle Round, The
Carmena
Chained
Christmas Morn
Circus, The
Clock, The
Clouds
Come Rejoice Before Your Maker
Dandelions
Down In The Dumps
Easter Bells
Faithful Vigil Ended
Flag Of Liberty
Flies
Forever Here My Rest
Forever Here My Rest Shall Be
Forgotten For Eternity
From The Depths Of My Soul
Frost Pictures
Gimme A Pigfoot
Gimme A Pigfoot And A Bottle Of
    Beer
Glory Of Conquest, The
Glory To God In The Highest
God Has Been Gracious
Gordon For Me, A
Grace
Happy Is He Whose Offence Is
    Forgiven

Wilson *(Cont.)*
Have Mercy Lord
How Are Thy Servants Blest O Lord
How Happy Are Thy Servants Lord
How Lovely How Lovely The Place
   Of Your Dwelling
How Sweet And Silent Is The Place
I Found Him In My Heart
I Love My Lord
I Talk To God Wherever I May Be
I Will Pilot Thee
If The Building Is Not Of The Lord
Indian Summer
Jericho Road, The
Joke, The
Kick It Out
Lilacs In The Rain
Listen To The Chorus
Lord I Delight To Recall
Lord When We Bend Before Thy
   Throne
Lord's My Shepherd, The
Mail Bags
Marching Song, A
Memorial Hymn
Mercy Blessing Favour Grace
Moon Balloon
My Friends
My God I Love Thee
My Soul Sing The Praise Of God For
   Ever
Naughty Soap Song
Noisy March
O Bless The God Of Israel
O Come Let Us Sing To The Lord
O For A Closer Walk With God
O God Whose Smile Is In The Sky
O Righteous Lord
Our God Has Turned To His People
Owl, The
Pro Patria
Questions
Quit You Like Men
Round Of Laughter, A
Set The Flag On Their Graves
Sing A New Song To The Lord
Sing A Song Of Waving Flags
Sing The Wondrous Love Of Jesus
Sing To The Lord
Snowbird, The
Song Of The Brook
Stand Up O God
Streamliner, The
Swinging
Take Me For A Buggy Ride
Take O Take Those Lips Away
Telephone Man
Tenor And Baritone
Thanks To God
Thanksgiving Day
Theme From Alfred Hitchcock, The
There's A Beautiful Flag
Tilda Jane And Samuel
Train For Poppyland, The

Wilson *(Cont.)*
Traveler, The
Tuff Enuff
Unto Thee O Lord
Upon The Dawn Of Easter Day
Was There Ever A Friend So True
We Give You Praise O' God
What Kind Of Man
When I Survey The Wondrous Cross
When The Flowers Are Brightest
When We All Get To Heaven
Won't You Charleston With Me
Wry Fragments
Year's At The Spring, The
Wilson & Bomar
Cheatin' On A Cheater
Wilson & Brennan
Down By The Old Apple Tree
Wilson & Caston & Poree
Keep On Truckin'
Wilson & Christian
Don't Worry Baby
Wilson & Ennis & Wilson
Down On Me
Even It Up
Wilson & Fuller & Berryhill & Conno
Wipe Out
Wilson & Harvey
Baby Baby
Wilson & Jones
On The Road Again
Wilson & Love
Do It Again
Fun Fun Fun
Girls On The Beach
Good Vibrations
Surfin'
Surfin' Safari
Wilson & Mitchell
Love's The Answer
Make Me Your Kind Of Woman
Wilson & Morrison
Love The World Away
Make Believe It's Your First Time
When A Love Ain't Right
Wilson & Porter & Levy
Ko Ko Mo I Love You So
Wilson & Ritchie
Picture Of Me, A
Wilson & Robinson
Still Water
Wilson & Schuler
Make Me A Blessing
Wilson & Sherrill
I'll See Him Through
Wilson & Sherrill & Bourke
Most Beautiful Girl, The
Wilson & Sherrill & Davis
I Don't Want To Lose You
Wilson & Sherrill & Taylor
He Loves Me All The Way
My Man

Wilson & Sherrill & Walls
After Closing Time
Wilson & Smith
My Weakness
Wilson & Tucker
Baby Workout
Wilson & Usher
409
In My Room
Wilson & Wilson & Ennis
Dog And Butterfly
Wilson & Wilson & Ennis & Fisher
Mistral Wind
Wilson & Wilson & Fisher & Derosier
Barracuda
Wilson & Wilson & Leese & Andes &
   Carmassi & Ennis
How Can I Refuse
Wilson & Wilson & Phillips
Release Me
Wilson, Brian
All Summer Long
Be True To Your School
California Girls
Catch A Wave
Help Me Rhonda
I Get Around
Little Deuce Coupe
Little Saint Nick
Shut Down
Surfer Girl
Wouldn't It Be Nice
Wilton
Hallelujah For The Cross
Winans
Make It Like It Was
Tomorrow
Winbush
Something In The Way You Make
   Me Feel
Winch
Memorial Hymn
Winchell
Niagara Falls
Windisch
Marching On With Jesus
Sinner's Friend, The
Soul Garden, The
Walking With Jesus
Wine & Levine
Candida
Wine & Sager
Groovy Kind Of Love, A
Winfree & Boutelie
China Boy
Wingate & Petrie
I Don't Want To Play In Your Yard
Winge
To My Mother
Winger & Beach
Hungry
Winger & Beach & Hill
Seventeen

Wingfield
Making A Good Thing Better
Winkler
Welcome To My World
Winkler & Hathcock
Welcome To My World
Winkler & Rauch
Answer Me My Love
Winkler & Rauch & Sigman
Answer Me My Love
Winkless
Snap Crackle And Pop
Winn
Not What These Hands Have Done
Winnemore
Stop That Knocking At The Door
Winner
Abraham's Daughter
Ellie Rhee
God Save Our President
He's Gone To The Arms Of
   Abraham
How The Gates Came Ajar
Listen To The Mocking Bird
Little Brown Jug
Oil On The Brain
Out Of Work
Rosalie Schottische
'Twas At The Siege Of Vicksburg
Whispering Hope
Winsett
Jesus Is Coming Soon
Winslow
Dancin' With The Devil
Hey Looka Yonder
Winter
Sure Is Good To Know We're Ready
   For A Nuclear War
Wedding Banquet, The
White Wings
Winther & Kjerulf
Last Night
Wintherow
Houseful, A
Winwood
Sea Of Joy
Talking Back To The Night
Winwood & Davis & Winwood
Gimme Some Lovin'
Winwood & Jennings
Back In The High Life Again
Don't You Know What The Night
   Can Do
Finer Things, The
Higher Love
Holding On
Roll With It
Valerie
While You See A Chance
Wipo
Victimae Paschali Laudes
Wirth & Howard
Together
Together Theme From Silver Spoons

Wise
Beguine, The
Choo-Choo Honeymoon
Dames At Sea
It's You
Raining In My Heart
Sailor Of My Dreams, The
Shenandoah Waltz
Singapore Sue
Son Of God
Strange News From The Rose
There's Something About You
Torn Was One Day
Wise & Starr
Kissin' Cousins
Wise & Twomey & Blagman
Put The Blame On Me
Wise & Weisman & Fuller
Rock-A-Hula Baby
Wise & Weisman & Twomey &
Kaempfert
Wooden Heart
Wiseman
Have I Told You Lately That I Love
   You
Tenderly He Watches
Witherow
'Tis The Night Of Halloween
Withers
Ain't No Sunshine
Lean On Me
Witmore
Florida
Witt
Come Thou Long Expected Jesus
Earth Has Many A Noble City
Earth Has Many Noble Cities
Eyes Of Azure
God Is In His Holy Temple
God My King Thy Might Confessing
Improperium Exspectavit Cor Meun
Moth And The Flame, The
My Dear Jesus I'll Not Leave
My Heart's Tonight In Texas
Onward Onward
Slowly By Thy Hand Unfurled
Tear, The
Veni Creator Spiritus
When Angels Watch
Witthauer
Glocklein Hell Vom Turme Da
Stars And Dewdrops
Witty
Jesus Wept
When I Survey The Cross
Wizell & Melsher
I May Never Pass This Way Again
Wllington & Tizol
Caravan
Wohlfarth-Grille
My Present
Wohlfeil
I Will Extol Thee
Jesus Thou Art Mine Forever

Wohlfeil *(Cont.)*
Liebe Die Fuer Mich Gestorben
Lord's Prayer, The
Wolcott
Saludos Amigos
Woldin
He Come Down This Morning
Man Say
Measure The Valleys
Whole Lotta Sunlight, A
Whose Little Angry Man
Wolf
Abschied
Ach Des Knaben Augen
Ach Im Maien War's
Ach Wie Lang Die Seele Schlummert
Alle Gingen Herz Zur Ruh
An Die Geliebte
Anacreon's Grave
Anakreons Grab
Auch Kleine Dinge
Auf Dem Grunen Balcon
Auf Dem Grunen Balkon
Auf Ein Altes Bild
Autumn Holiday
Bedeckt Mich Mit Blumen
Benedeit Die Sel'ge Mutter
Biterolf
Bitt' Ihn O Mutter Bitte Den Knaben
Blindes Schauen Dunkle Leuchte
Come Within Noble Warrior
Commission, A
Convalescent's Song To Hope, The
Cophtisches Lied
Da Nur Leid Und Leidenschaft
Dass Doch Gemalt All' Deine Reize
   Waren
Deine Mutter Susses Kind
Dereinst Dereinst Gedanke Mein
Drummer, The
Drunken Must We Be
Du Denkst Mit Einem Fadchen Mich
   Zu Fangen
Du Gott Gebarst Du Reine, Die
Du Sagst Mir Dass Ich Keine Furstin
   Sei
E 'En Little Things
Eide So Die Liebe Schwur
Elfenlied
Forsaken Maiden, The
Freund, Der
From Her Balcony Green
Fuhr Mich Kind Nach Bethlehem
Fussreise
Gardener, The
Gebet
Geh Geliebter Geh Jetzt
Genesene An Die Hoffnung, Der
Gesang Weylas
Gesegnet Sei Das Grun
Gesegnet Sei Durch Den Die Welt
   Entstund

Wolf *(Cont.)*
Geselle Woll'n Wir Uns In Kutten
    Hullen
Harfesnpieler
He Who On Solitude Is Bent
Heb' Auf Dein Blondes Haupt
Heimweh
Herr Was Tragt Der Boden Hier
Herz Verzage Nicht Geschwind
Heut Nacht Erhob Ich Mich Um
    Mitternacht
Hoffahrtig Seid Ihr Schones Kind
How Many Hours I've Wasted
Hunter, The
I'm Always Drunk In San Francisco
Ich Esse Nun Mein Brod Nicht
    Trocken Mehr
Ich Fuhr Uber Meer
Ich Hab' In Penna Einen Liebsten
    Wohnen
Ich Liess Sagen Und Mir Ward
    Erzahlt
Ihr Jungen Leute
Ihr Schwebet Um Diese Palmen, Die
Ihr Seid Die Allerschonste
In Dem Schatten Meiner Locken
Insatiable Love
Jager, Der
Klinge Klinge Mein Pandero
Komm O Tod Von Nacht Umgeben
Koniglich Gebet
Kopfchen Kopfchen Nicht
    Gewimmert
Lass Sie Nur Gehn Die So Die Stolze
    Spielt
Lebe Wohl
Liebe Mir Im Busen Zundet Einen
    Brand
Lied Eines Verliebten
Love Within My Bosom
Maiden's First Love-Song, A
Man Sagt Mir Deine Mutter Woll' Es
    Nicht
Mein Leibster Ist So Klein
Mein Liebster Hat Zu Tische Mich
    Geladen
Mein Liebster Singt Am Haus
Mir Ward Gesagt
Mogen Alle Bosen Zungen
Mond Hat Eine Schwere Klag
    Erhoben, Der
Morgenthau
Morning
Mouse Trap, The
Muhvoll Komm Ich Und Beladen
Musikant, Der
My Native Land
Nachtzauber
Nein Junger Herr
New Love
Nicht Langer Kann Ich Singen
Nimmersatte Liebe
Now I Am Thine

Wolf *(Cont.)*
Nun Bin Ich Dein
Nun Lass Uns Frieden Schliessen
Nun Wandre Maria
O War' Dein Haus Durchsichtig Wie
    Ein Glas
O Wusstest Du Wie Viel Ich
    Deinetwegen
Ob Auch Finstre Blicke Glitten
Play My Love With Love Your Game
Prayer
Rattenfanger, Der
Sad I Come And Bending Lowly
Sagt Ihm Dass Er Zu Mir Komme
Sagt Seid Ihr Es Feiner Herr
Sailor's Farewell, The
Sara
Schmerzliche Wonnen Und Wonnige
    Schmerzen
Schon Streckt' Ich Aus Im Bett
Schweig' Einmal Still
Secrecy
Seemanns Abschied
Selig Ihr Blinden
Seltsam Ist Juanas Weise
Serenade, The
Seufzer
Sie Blasen Zum Abmarsch
Soldier I, The
Soldier II, The
Song To Spring
Spring Can Really Hang You Up The
    Most
Standchen, Das
Standchen Euch Zu Bringen, Ein
Sterb' Ich So Hullt In Blumen Meine
    Glieder
Tambour, Der
Thieves Are Not Made By Occasion
Think Me The Angel I Soon Shall Be
Thou Art The Lovliest Maiden
Thro' Thy Dear Love Fortuned
    Highly
Tief Im Herzen Trag' Ich Pein
Tinkle Gaily My Pandero
'Tis Spring
To An Ancient Picture
To Rest To Rest
Tramping
Trau Nicht Der Liebe
Treibe Nur Mit Lieben Spott
Und Schlafst Du Mein Madchen
Und Steht Ihr Fruh Am Morgen Auf
Und Willst Du Deinen Liebsten
    Sterben Sehen
Verborgenheit
Verlassene Magdlein, Das
Verschling' Der Abgrund Meines
    Liebsten Hutte
Verschwiegene Liebe
Verzweifelte Liebhaber, Der
Wachterlied Auf Der Wartburg
Wandering

Wolf *(Cont.)*
Was Fur Ein Lied Soll Dir Gesungen
    Werden
Was Soll Der Zorn Mein Schatz
Wehe Der Die Mir Verstricke
Weint Nicht Ihr Auglein
Wenn Du Mein Liebster Steigst Zum
    Himmel Auf
Wenn Du Mich Mit Den Augen
    Streifst Und Lachst
Wenn Du Zu Den Blumen Gehst
Wer Rief Dich Denn
Wer Sein Holdes Lieb Verloren
Wer That Deinem Fusslein Weh
Weyla's Song
When Thou Goest To Thy Flowers
When Thou My Loved One
    Mountest Up To Heaven
While You Sober Dwell, The
Wie Lange Schon War Immer Mein
    Verlangen
Wie Soll Ich Frohlich Sein
Wie Viele Zeit Verlor Ich Dich Zu
    Lieben
Wir Haben Beide Lange Zeit
    Geschwiegen
Wohl Kenn' Ich Eueren Stand
Wouldst Thou Behold Thy Lover
    Sadly Dying
Wunden Tragst Du Mein Geliebter
Zur Ruh Zur Ruh
Wolf & Greene
Until I Met You
Wolf & Herron & Sinatra
I'm A Fool To Want You
Wolf & Justman
Freeze-Frame
Must Of Got Lost
Wolf & Wolf
Sara
Who's Johnny
Wolf-Ferrari
Angiolo Delicato Fresco E Bello
E Tanto C'e Pericol Ch'io Ti Lasci
Jo Dei Saluati Ve Ne Mando Mille
O Guarda Guarda Quel Nobile
    Augello
O Si Che Non Sapevo Sospirare
Quando Ti Vidi A Quel Canto
    Apparire
Sia Benedetto Chi Fece Lo Mondo
Verde Praticello Senza Piante, Un
Wolfarth-Grille
Cherries
Rain Or Shine
Wolfe
Christmas Is For Children
Cold-Hearted
Genialisch Treiben
Glory Road, De
God's Wonderful People
Greater Is He That Is In Me
Grenzen Der Menschheit
Have A Nice Day With Jesus

Wolfe *(Cont.)*
I Keep Falling In Love With Him
Jesus Be The Lord Of All
Jesus Made A Believer Out Of Me
Jesus Will Be What Makes It Heaven
        For Me
Just Suppose
Let Them Know
More Than Wonderful
One Day Too Late
Only Jesus Can Satisfy Your Soul
Play Ball
Prometheus
Rockies, The
Shortnin' Bread
Straight Up
Surely The Presence Of The Lord Is
        In This Place
There's Something In The Air
Valentine Surprise
We Thank God
Wonderful Feeling, A

Wolfe & Wolfe
Jesus Be The Lord Of All

Wolfer
Dancing In The Sheets

Wolfert & Nelson
Songbird

Wolfert & Sager
Heart Breaker

Wolff
Cold-Hearted
Crooked Boss, The
Follow My Heartbeat
Jakie And Andy
March Of The Garment Workers
Old Chiseller, The
Straight Up
Ten Little Sweatshops

Wolff & Roman
Whole Wide World

Wolfrum
Osterlied
Pfingsttag

Wolfsohn
May God Save The Union

Wolfson & Warrington
Texas Christmas Is A Lone Star
        Christmas, A

Wolinski
Ain't Nobody

Wolinski & Hewett & Free
Don't Get Stopped In Beverly Hills

Wolkenstein
Ave Mater O Maria

Wolle
Fling Out The Banner

Wolley
Purple People Eater

Woloshin
Mutual Of Omaha People You Can
        Count On
Take Life A Little Easier

Woloshin & Gavin
We're Together
You Deserve A Break Today

Wolverton
Bouncing Ball
Forest Music
Freight Boats
George Washington
Minor Scales
Mist, The
Moving Day
My Flag
My Kitty
My Swing
New Highway, The
Nobody Knows
One Two Three
Raindrop, The
Riddle, A
Sad Mother Nature
Scarecrow, The
Schoolroom Helpers
Sea Shell
Spring Song
Surprise
Tiny Snowflakes
Tommy Stout
Trees In Autumn
Winter
Winter Visitor, The
Witch, The

Womack
Breezin'
Love Has Finally Come At Last

Womack & Womack
It's All Over Now

Wonder
Do I Do
Golden Lady
Land Of La La
Lately
My Eyes Don't Cry
My Love
Outside My Window
Overjoyed
Ribbon In The Sky
Send One Your Love
Sir Duke
Skeletons
With Each Beat Of My Heart
You And I
You're Supposed To Keep Your
        Love For Me

Wonder & Cosby & Hardaway & Moy
I Was Made To Love Her

Wonder & Cosby & Moy
I'm Wondering
My Cherie Amour
Never Had A Dream Come True
Shoo-Be-Doo-Be-Doo-Da-Day
Uptight
Uptight Everything's Alright

Wonder & Garrett
Let's Get Serious

Wonder & Garrett & Wright
It's A Shame

Wonder & Hunter
Loving You Is Sweeter Than Ever

Wonder & Riser & Hunter & Hardaway
Don't Know Why I Love You
I Don't Know Why

Wonder & Wright
If You Really Love Me
Your Kiss Is Sweet

**Wonder & Wright & Harraway &
Garrett**
Signed Sealed Delivered
Signed Sealed Delivered I'm Yours

Wonder, Stevie
All In Love Is Fair
Boogie On Reggae Woman
Don't You Worry 'bout A Thing
Go Home
Higher Ground
I Just Called To Say I Love You
I Wish
Isn't She Lovely
Living For The City
Love Light In Flight
Master Blaster
Part-Time Lover
Superstition
Tell Me Something Good
That Girl
Too High
You Are The Sunshine Of My Life
You Haven't Done Nothin'

Wonn
Parade, The
Thanking God

Wonnberger
Gen Himmel Aufgefahren Ist

Wood
Ants Will Not Eat Your Fingers
Bells Of Washington
Father We Come With Youth And
        Vigor
First Christmas, The
Granger's Yankeedoodle, The
Jerusalem High Tower Thy Glorious
        Walls
My One And Only Love
O Strength And Stay Upholding All
        Creation
Peace Of The River
Roses Of Picardy
Shoo Fly Pie And Apple Pan Dowdy
Somebody Stole My Gal
This Joyful Eastertide

Wood & Bibo & Conrad
Good Night

Wood & Holmes
One Way Flight

Wood & Mueller & Johnson & Busse
Wang Wang Blues, The

Wood & Seiler & Marcus
Till Then
Woodard
When You Decide To Follow Jesus
Woodbury
And Am I Born To Die
Be Kind To The Loved Ones At
    Home
By Cool Siloam's Shady Rill
Jesus Calls Us
Lest We Forget
Long Have I Sat Beneath The Sound
Merry Bells Are Ringing, The
O Love Divine What Hast Thou
    Done
Old Oaken Bucket, The
Servant Of God Well Done
Speed Away
Stars In The Summer Night
Stars Of A Summer Night
Stars Of The Summer Night
Strike The Harp Gently
Sweet The Moments Rich In Blessing
Take My Heart O Father O Take It
When I Survey The Wondrous Cross
When Time Seems Short And Death
    Is Near
Woodforde-Finden
At Sea
Eyes Like The Sea
Her Words Come To Me
Kashmiri Song
Kashmiri Songs
Less Than The Dust
Temple Bells, The
There Is An Orchard
Till I Wake
Woodman
And Can I Yet Delay
Behold What Wondrous Grace
Down To The Sacred Wave
I Am Thy Harp
I Love Thy Kingdom Lord
If On A Quiet Sea
It Singeth Low In Every Heart
Lend Me Thy Lance
Ring Out Ring Out O Christmas
    Bells
Savior Kindly Calls, The
State Street
Welcome Sweet Day Of Rest
Woodruff
With Spirits Light
Woods
College Years
Cool Aide
God Defend New Zealand
Going Down Jordan
I'll Never Say Never Again Again
I'm Looking Over A Four Leaf
    Clover
Just Like A Butterfly
Little Street Where Old Friends Meet,
    A

Woods (*Cont.*)
New Zealand
Paddlin' Madelin' Home
River Stay 'way From My Door
Side By Side
Voice In The Old Village Choir, The
What A Little Moonlight Can Do
When The Moon Comes Over The
    Mountain
When The Red Red Robin Comes
    Bob Bob Bobbin' Along
Woods & Brown
Clouds Will Soon Roll By, The
Woods & Campbell & Connelly
Just An Echo In The Valley
Old Kitchen Kettle, The
Try A Little Tenderness
Woods & Crockett
Lord Is Lifted Up, The
Woods & Kirkland & James
Something's Got A Hold On Me
Woodward
Joe Bowers
Now It Is Evening Time To Rest
    From Labor
O Day Of Radiant Gladness
Woodward & Chestnut
Harvest John
Woodworth
Hunters Of Kentucky, The
Old Oaken Bucket, The
Wooldridge
We Give Thee But Thine Own
Wooler
Let God Arise
Woolery & Darlow
Slave To The Rhythm
Wooley
Blue Guitar
Purple People Eater, The
Woolfson & Parsons
Don't Answer Me
Eye In The Sky
Prime Time
Stereotomy
Time
Woolley & Horn & Downes
Video Killed The Radio Star
Woolsey
Mashed Potatoes
Saved To Tell Others
Wooster & Smith
Black Cat Rag, The
Worden
Crossing The Bar
O Precious Seal Of Love
We Will Stand The Storm
Worf
Mis'ry River
Worgan
Christ The Lord Is Ris'n Today
Christ The Lord Is Risen Today
Jesus Christ Is Risen To-Day

Work
All Are Talking Of Utah
Babylon Is Fallen
Battle Hymn, The
Brave Boys Are They
Columbia's Guardian Angels
Come Home Father
Corporal Schnapps
Crossing The Grand Sierras
Dancing In The Sun
Father Dear Father Come Home
    With Me Now
God Save The Nation
Grafted Into The Army
Grandfather's Clock
Grandfather's Hat
Great Day
His Grandfather's Hat
How I Love To Sing
Kingdom Come
Kingdom Comin'
Kingdom Coming
Little Major
Making Believe
Marching For Justice And Freedom
Marching Thro' Georgia
Marching Through Georgia
Marching Thru' Georgia
Our Captain's Last Word
Paint 'er Red
Rag Man
Ship That Never Returned, The
Sleeping For The Flag
Soliloquy
Somebody's Knocking At Your Door
Song Of A Thousand Years
'Tis Finished 't Is Ended
Turn To The One You Love
Uncle Joe's Hail Columbia
Vote For Me
Wake Nicodemus
Washington And Lincoln
When I Was A Water Boy
When Our Boys Come Home
When Sherman Marched Down To
    The Sea
When We Go Marching Home
Year Of Jubilo
Work & Clay
Grafted Into The Army
Worrall
Disco Mickey Mouse
Macho Duck
Worrell
Don't Stop Praying
Worsing
Hils Fra Meg Der Hjemme
Worth
Don't You Know
Super Chicken
Worth & Cowan
Do I Worry

Wortsman
Nursery Rhyme For Dead Children
Wostenholm
Not In Vain The Distance Beacons
There's A Light Upon The
Mountains
Wotawa
Hail Purdue
Wrede
School March
Wren
O Son Of Man Thou Madest Know
Wright
Cinco Robles
Dream Weaver
I Am Thine O Christ
Love Is Alive
O For A Heart To Praise My God
Precious Memories
Red And Black
Valentine
Wright & Forrest
And This Is My Beloved
Baubles Bangles And Beads
It's A Blue World
Night Of My Nights
Sands Of Time
Strange Music
Stranger In Paradise
Wright & Leigh
Why Goodbye
Wright & Nielson
Repetitive Regret
Wrighton
Dearest Spot Of Earth To Me
Dearest Spot, The
Her Bright Smile
Her Bright Smile Haunts Me Still
Only A Lock Of Her Hair
Wrubel
Flirtation Walk
I Can't Love You Any More
I'm Afraid The Masquerade Is Over
I'm Stepping Out With A Memory
Tonight
Lady In Red, The
Masquerade Is Over, The
Music Maestro Please
My Own America
Zip-A-Dee-Doo-Dah
Wuerthner
My Girl At Michigan
We Will Not Forget Our Alma Mater
Wurm
Eleazar Wheelock
Wyatt
Once A Boat Has Broken From The
Shore
Wyche
Woman A Lover A Friend, A
Wyche & Watts
Alright Okay You Win
Wycliffe-Jones
Not To Us Be Glory Given

Wyeth
Come Thou Fount
Come Thou Fount Of Every Blessing
Wyman
Downtown Suzie
In Another Land
Wyner
Exeunt
Wynette & Sherrill & Richey
'Til I Can Make It On My Own
Wynette & Sherrill & Sutton
Singing My Song
Ways To Love A Man, The
Wynn
Save Lord
Wyrick
In My Eyes
Wyrtzen
Celebrate
Worthy Is The Lamb
Wyrtzen & Fischer
Woman's Prayer, A
Wyrtzen & Wyrtzen
Yesterday Today And Tomorrow
Wyton
Ancient Of Days Who Sittest
Throned
How Wondrous Great How Glorious
Bright
Lord You Give The Great
Commission
Mighty Sound From Heaven At
Pentecost, A
Where Is This Stupendous Stranger
Wyvill
God Of Our Fathers Known Of Old
Xanroff & Sablon
Fiacre, Le
Xavier
My God I Love Thee
Yablokoff
Papirosen
Yananda
Singing Kites
Yancey & Yancey
Make Me A Pallet On The Floor
Yandell & Ingles
Now I Have Everything
Yantis
Turn It Over To Jesus He Cares
Yaokley
Jesus Thy Boundless Love To Me
Yarrow
Day Is Done
Gilgarra Mountain
Moments Of The Soft Persuasion
Weep For Jamie
Yarrow & Grossman & Travers
Great Mandella, The
Great Mandella The Wheel Of Life,
The
Yarrow & Jarrell
Torn Between Two Lovers

Yarrow & Lipton
Puff The Magic Dragon
Yarrow & Mezzetti
Make-Believe Town
Yarrow & Stookey & Chandler
It's Raining
Yarrow & Stookey & Travers & Okun
Come And Go With Me
Gone The Rainbow
Mon Vrai Destin
Monday Morning
She Dreams
**Yarrow & Stookey & Travers & Okun &
Story & Jacobs**
Cuckoo, The
Yarrow & Yardley
If I Had Wings
Yarrow & Zimmel
Rich Man Poor Man
Yates & Sankey
Faith Is The Victory
Yates & Small & Paul
Only Because
Yeats
Florida Our Alma Mater
Yellen & Ager & Bigelow & Bates
Hard Hearted Hannah
Hard Hearted Hannah The Vamp Of
Savannah
Yellen & Ager & Pollack
I Wish I Had My Old Gal Back
Again
Yellen & Pollack
Yiddishe Ma-Me
Yerbury
Blue And Gold, The
Yerkins & Siegle
Ghost On The Beach
Yeston
Be On Your Own
Nine
Till I Loved You
Unusual Way
Yetter
Noel Noel
Yin-Lan
O Bread Of Life For Sinners Broken
Yoakam
Guitars Cadillacs
I Got You
I Sang Dixie
It Won't Hurt
Little Ways
Yomen
Libster Mayner
Zun Vet Arunter Geyn, Di
Yon
Ave Maria
Gesu Bambino
Lacrymosa Dies Illa
Yonathan & Amariglio
Yesh P'Rachim
Yonathan & Heiman
Chofim

Youmans
Carioca
Flying Down To Rio
Great Day
Hallelujah
I Know That You Know
I Want To Be Happy
More Than You Know
No No Nanette
Orchids In The Moonlight
Sometimes I'm Happy
Tea For Two
Tea For Two Cha Cha
Through The Years
Time On My Hands
Time On My Hands You In My
  Arms
Too Many Rings Around Rosie
Without A Song

Young
Alabama
At The Cross
Birds
Bridge, The
Broken Arrow
Brown Cheering Song, The
Burned
Cinnamon Girl
Crazy Love
Cripple Creek Ferry
Dance Dance Dance
Do I Have To Come Right Out And
  Say It
Don't Be Denied
Don't Go Out Into The Rain
Don't Let It Bring You Down
Down By The River
Everybody Knows This Is Nowhere
Expecting To Fly
Flying On The Ground Is Wrong
Ghost Of A Chance, A
Half-Penny Two-Penny
Here We Are In The Years
Hey Hey My My
I Am A Child
I Believe In You
I'm Alone Because I Love You
I've Been Waiting For You
If I Could Have Her Tonight
Journey Thru The Past
Keep On Dancing
La
Last Dance
Last Trip To Tulsa, The
Lawd You Made The Night Too
  Long
Loner, The
Lookin' For A Love
Lord Is In His Holy Temple, The
Losing End, The
Lotta Love
Love In Mind
Love Is A Rose

Young (Cont.)
Love Is The Thing
Love Me To-Night
Miss You Kiss, A
Morning Lights
Now Sing We Joyfully Unto God
Nowadays Clancy Can't Even Sing
Old Laughing Lady, The
On The Way Home
Out Of My Mind
Out On The Weekend
Round And Round And Round
Running Dry
Sea Of Madness
Slide, The
Soldier
Street Of Dreams
Sugar Mountain
Summertime
Sweetest Thing I've Ever Known,
  The
Sweetest Thing, The
'Tain't What You Do
Tea Party Talk
Tell Me Why
There's A World
Till The Morning Comes
Time Fades Away
What Did You Do To My Life
Where Can I Go Without You
Whistle
Wonderin'
Words
Written On The Wind
Yonder Stands The Sinner
You Don't Bring Me Flowers

Young & Adamson
Around The World

Young & Cavanaugh
Let There Be You

Young & Deaton
Wine Me Up

Young & Feyne
Jumpin With Symphony Sid

Young & Guerriero & Bates
Lion's Loose Again, The

Young & Kewley
Everything Must Change
Some People

Young & King & Van Alstyne
Beautiful Love

Young & Pierce
Don't You

Young & Schwartz & Ager
In A Little Red Barn On A Farm
  Down In Indiana

Young & Vanda
Friday On My Mind
Good Times
Love Is In The Air

Young & Wilson
Run Home Girl

Young & Young
Pump Up The Volume

Young, Neil
After The Gold Rush
Are You Ready For The Country
Country Girl
Cowgirl In The Sand
Harvest
Heart Of Gold
Helpless
Like A Hurricane
Long May You Run
Man Needs A Maid, A
Mr Soul
Needle And The Damage Done, The
Ohio
Old Man
Only Love Can Break Your Heart
Rockin' In The Free World
Southern Man
Walk On
When You Dance I Can Really Love

Young, Victor
Around The World
Golden Earrings
I Don't Stand A Ghost Of A Chance
  With You
Love Letters
My Foolish Heart
Stella By Starlight
Sweet Madness
Sweet Sue
Sweet Sue Just You
When I Fall In Love

Yradier
Curro Marinero, El
Dove, The
Paloma, La

Yrapani & Lange
Cara Mia

Yresne
C'est Liu Que Mon Coeura Choisi

Yuill
Song Of The Illinois Legionaire

Yvain
My Man

Zaballos
Pues Ya Las Claras Fuentes

Zabka & Upton
Christmas Eve In My Home Town

Zachary
Peace

Zachary & Zachary
I'm Riding The Tide

Zahn
Reiterlied

Zaimont
Fox, The
Soliloquy

Zakharov
Strolling Home
Through The Village
Who Knows Why

Zamir
Ma Tovu

Zappa
Valley Girl
Zaqinul
Mercy Mercy Mercy
Zaret & Singer
One Meat Ball
Zaret & Whitney & Kramer
High On A Windy Hill
It All Comes Back To Me Now
My Sister And I
Zarin
Blue Bolero
Zaritsky
Little White Duck, The
Zart
Sing Praise To God Who Reigns
Above
Zarzycki
Woodland Gossip
Zatino
Holly Boy, The
Zawinul
Birdland
Cannonball
Gibraltar
Mercy Mercy Mercy
Remark You Made, A
Young And Fine
Zehavi
Barren Land
Caravan, A
Zeigler & Zeigler
Say Amen
Zeiler & James
I'm The One Mama Warned You
About
Zeiner
Alike Are Life And Death
Merry Archers, The
Morning Song, A
Night Song, A
Owl And The Pussy-Cat, The
Scarlet And The Gray, The
Serenade, A
Sleep Comrades Sleep
Still Still With Thee
Sun Awakes, The
Zeira
L'Cha Dodi
Night's Bright, The
Zeitlin
Carole's Garden
I Thou
Quiet Now
Zeller
I Can't Believe I'm Losing You
Nightingale Song
Nightingale's Song, The
On The South Side Of Chicago
Zelter
Bundeslied
Dead Soldier, The
King In Thule
Konig In Thule, Der

Zelter *(Cont.)*
Meister Und Gesell
Musensohn, Der
Rex Thulae
Um Mitternacht
Zerface & Zerface & Morrison & Macrae
Up To Heaven
Zero
All This And More
I Won't Look Back
Zero & Chrome & Bators & Blitz & Thomas & Magnum
Sonic Reducer
Zeunder
Ye Christian Heralds
Zeuner
Again The Angel Song We Hear
At Eventide
Behold The Christian Warrior Stand
Go Forth To Life
Go Labor On Spend And Be Spent
Go Preach My Gospel Saith The
Lord
Great God The Nations Of The Earth
Let Man Be Free
Lift Up Your Hearts To Things
Above
O God The Darkness Roll Away
O What Amazing Words Of Grace
Press On Press On
Voice Of Old, The
What Equal Honors Shall We Bring
Ye Christian Heralds
Ye Christian Heralds Go
Ye Christian Heralds Go Proclaim
Zevon
Carmelita
Hasten Down The Wind
Poor Poor Pitiful Me
Ziegler
Praise We The Lord Who Made All
Beauty
Zigman & Zigman
Elad
Zilberts
Haneros Halolu
Zilch
Once In The End Of The World
Zim
I Must Survive
Never Again
Papa
Z'Chor Remember
Zog Nit Kenmol
Zimmer
Auferstanden Ist Der Herr
Zimmerman
Anchors Aweigh
Carmen Case
Golden Rule, The
Zindars
Elsa
Sareen Jurer

Zinn
Reach For Your Faith
Zinnen
Ons Hemecht
Zintheo
We Cheer For The U Of M
Zoeller & Bernhard
Cinnamon Cake
Zollner
Cycle Song
Happy Wanderer, The
Secret, The
Wanderschaft
Where Would I Be
Wohin
Zolotarieff
Gipsy, The
Zoob
Let's Cheer Again For Temple
Zschavitz
Winds, The
Zsigmond
Szep Tavaszi Almok
Szep Vagy Gyonyoru Vagy
Zuccalmaglio
Baurin Und Der Ritter, Die
Jagerlied
Letzte Tanz, Der
Liebesentzucken
Schlechte Besserung
Spannung
Verstohlen Geht Der Mond Auf
Zuener
Build Up An Altar To The Lord
Great God We Sing That Mighty
Hand
Zumsteeg
Jesus Ist Kommen
Zundel
Beyond The Smiling
Beyond The Smiling And The
Weeping
I Was A Wandering Sheep
Jesus I My Cross Have Taken
Know My Soul Thy Full Salvation
Lebanon
Lord Whose Love Through Humble
Service
Love Divine
Love Divine All Love Excelling
Love Divine All Loves Excelling
There's A Wideness In God's Mercy
Zweig & Zweig
Y'Did Nefesh
Zwyssig
Lasst Jehovah Uns Erheben

THE SOURCES
(OPERAS, MUSICALS, MOVIES
AND OTHER SOURCES OF SONGS)

SOURCES OF SONGS

10
It's Easy To Say
100 Cards
Rock Island Line
101 Dalmations
Cruella De Ville
107
Leander
110 In The Shade
Everything Beautiful Happens At
Night
Gonna Be Another Hot Day
Is It Really Me
Love Don't Turn Away
Man And A Woman, A
Raunchy
Simple Little Things
13 Days To Broadway
You There In The Back Row
1600 Pennsylvania Avenue
Take Care Of This House
20 20
ABC 20 20
20000 Leagues Under The Sea
Whale Of A Tale, A
2001 A Space Odyssey
Also Sprach Zarathustra
Theme From 2001 A Space Odyssey
227
There's No Place Like Home
3rd Man, The
(*see* **Third Man, The**)
42nd Street
About A Quarter To Nine
Forty-Second Street
Gold Digger's Song, The
Lullaby Of Broadway
Shadow Waltz
Shuffle Off To Buffalo
You're Getting To Be A Habit With
Me
45 Minutes From Broadway
Forty-Five Minutes From Broadway
Mary's Grand Old Name
So Long Mary
48 Hours
Back In Town
70 Girls 70
Home
Yes
76 Nashville
Country Comfort
77 Sunset Strip
77 Sunset Strip
9 1/2 Weeks
I Do What I Do
9 To 5
Nine To Five
9:15 Revue, The
Get Happy

A Team, The
Theme From The A Team
A To Z
Limehouse Blues
ABC Monday Night Baseball
Slugger Theme, The
ABC Monday Night Football
ABC Monday Night Football
All My Rowdy Friends Are Coming
Over Tonight
About Face
One Little WAC
About Last Night
So Far So Good
Absence Of Malice
Absence Of Malice
Accidental Tourist, The
Theme From The Accidental Tourist
Accused, The
Theme From The Accused
Ace In The Hole
Ace In The Hole
Acis And Galatea
Would You Gain The Tender
Creature
Act, The
City Lights
My Own Space
Adam 12
Theme From Adam 12
Addams Family, The
Addams Family, The
Adler, Der
Eagle, The
Adolphe Et Clara
D'un Epoux Cheri
Advance To The Rear
Today
Adventures In Paradise
Adventures In Paradise
Adventures Of Don Quixote
Rose In The Snow, A
Affair To Remember, An
Affair To Remember, An
After The Ball
Jolly Good Luck To The Girl Who
Loves A Soldier
Aftermash
Theme From Aftermash
Against All Odds
Against All Odds
Agony And The Ecstasy, The
Agony And The Ecstasy Theme, The
Aida
Aida March
Celeste Aida
Celestial Aida
Consecration Of Rhadames
Di Mie Discolpe
Triumphal March

Ain't Misbehavin'
Ain't Misbehavin
Alligator Crawl
Cash For Your Trash
Honeysuckle Rose
I'm Gonna Sit Right Down And
Write Myself A Letter
Joint Is Jumpin', The
Mean To Me
Airport
Airport Love Theme
Aladdin (1958)
Wouldn't It Be Fun
Alamo, The
Green Leaves Of Summer, The
Alaskans, The
Alaskans, The
Alceste
Arie Der Alceste
Divinites Du Styx
Heros Que Jiattends, Le
Non Ce N'Est Point Un Sacrifice
Ye Awful Stygian Powers
Alcina
Tornami A Vagheggiar
Verdant Meadows
Verdi Prati
Alexander's Feast
Revenge Timotheus Cries
Alf
Theme From Alf
Alfie
Alfie
Alfred Hitchcock Presents
Funeral March Of The Marionettes
Theme From Alfred Hitchcock, The
Algeria
Ask Her While The Band Is Playing
Love Is Like A Cigarette
Rose Of The World
Alias Smith And Jones
Theme From Alias Smith And Jones
Alice
There's A New Girl In Town
Alice In Wonderland (1951)
Beautiful Soup
Crocodile, The
How D'Ye Do And Shake Hands
I'm Late
Unbirthday Song, The
Very Good Advice
Alice's Adventures In Wonderland
(1933)
Voice Of The Lobster, The
You Are Old Father William
Alice's Restaurant
Alice's Restaurant
All American
If I Were You

All American *(Cont.)*
  Old Immigration And Naturalization
    Rag, The
  Once Upon A Time
  Our Children
  What A Country
All In The Family
  Remembering You
  Those Were The Days
All My Children
  All My Children
All That Jazz
  And All That Jazz
All The King's Horses
  Little White Gardenia, A
All The Right Moves
  All The Right Moves
All This And Heaven Too
  All This And Heaven Too
All-American, The
  Once Upon A Time
Allegro
  Gentleman Is A Dope, The
  So Far
  You Are Never Away
Allegro, L'
  Hide Me From Day's Garish Eye
  Let Me Wander Not Unseen
  Oft In A Plat Of Rising Ground
  Or Let The Merry Bells Ring Round
  These Delights If Thou Canst Give
Allessandro
  Allurements The Dearest
Amadigi
  My Hope-Star Royal
Amadis
  Bois Epais
  Bois Epais Redouble Ton Ombre
  Close Thee Now And For Aye
  Forest Gloom Lend Darkness To
    Hold Me
  Gloomy Woods
  Shaded Grove
  Suivons L'amour
Amant Jaloux, L'
  Tandis Que Tout Sommeille
Ameer, The
  Cupid Will Guide
American Bandstand
  Bandstand Boogie
American Dream, An
  Time For Love, A
American Gigolo
  Call Me
American Tail, An
  Somewhere Out There
Americana
  Brother Can You Spare A Dime
  Satan's Li'l Lamb
Americanization Of Emily, The
  Emily
Amphion Anglicus
  Self Banished, The

Anacreon
  De Ma Barque Legere
  Laisse En Paix Le Dieu Des Combats
  Si Des Tristescypres
Anchors Aweigh
  Charm Of You, The
  I Begged Her
  I Fall In Love Too Easily
  What Makes The Sunset
And Justice For All
  There's Something Funny Going On
And The Angels Sing
  It Could Happen To You
Andre Charlot's Revue
  Cup Of Coffee A Sandwich and You,
    A
  Limehouse Blues
Andrea Chenier
  O Pastorelle Addio
  Parting Chorus
Andy Griffith Show, The
  Andy Griffith Show, The
  Theme From The Andy Griffith
    Show, The
Andy Hardy Meets A Debutante
  I'm Nobody's Baby
Angel Face
  I Might Be Your Once In A While
Angel In The Wings
  Civilization
Angie
  Different Worlds
Animal Crackers
  Hooray For Captain Spaulding
Ankles Aweigh
  Eleven O'Clock Song, An
Anna
  Anna
  Non Dimenticar
Anna Bolena
  Oh That I Never More Might See
Annie
  Easy Street
  It's The Hard Knock Life
  Little Girls
  Maybe
  Tomorrow
  You're Never Fully Dressed Without
    A Smile
Annie Get Your Gun
  Anything You Can Do
  Doin' What Comes Naturally
  Girl That I Marry
  I Got The Sun In The Morning
  I'm An Indian Too
  My Defenses Are Down
  There's No Business Like Show
    Business
  They Say It's Wonderful
  Who Do You Love I Hope
  You Can't Get A Man With A Gun
Annie McGuire
  Annie McGuire

Another World
  Another World
  Another World Theme
Anyone Can Whistle
  Anyone Can Whistle
  Everybody Says Don't
  Parade In Town, A
Anything Goes
  All Through The Night
  Anything Goes
  Blow Gabriel Blow
  Buddie Beware
  I Get A Kick Out Of You
  Moonburn
  You're The Top
Apartment, The
  Key To Love, The
  Theme From The Apartment
Applause
  Applause
  But Alive
  One Of A Kind
  Something Greater
  Think How It's Gonna Be
  Welcome To The Theater
April Fools, The
  April Fools, The
April In Paris
  April In Paris
  That's What Makes Paris Paree
April Love
  April Love
Arabesque
  Arabesque
  We've Loved Before
Arianna, L'
  Lasciatemi Morire
  O Death Pray Come And Save Me
  O Let Me Perish
Ariodante
  I Press Thee To My Bosom
Aristocats, The
  Ev'rybody Wants To Be A Cat
  Scales And Arpeggios
Arlesienne, L'
  Thine The Glory
  Three Kings, The
Armide
  Ah Si La Liberte
  On S'Etonnerait Moins
  Voici La Charmante Retraite
Arms And The Girl
  Nothin' For Nothin'
  There Must Be Somethin' Better
    Than This
Around The World In 80 Days
  Around The World
Arsenio Hall Show, The
  Hall Or Nothing
Artaxerxes
  Soldier Tir'd, The
Arthur
  Arthur's Theme

Arthur 2 On The Rocks
Love Is My Decision
Artists And Models
Innamorata
As The World Turns
World Turns On And On, The
As Thousands Cheer
Easter Parade
Heat Wave
As You Like It
Blow Blow Thou Winter Wind
It Was A Lover And His Lass
Spring Song, A
Under The Greenwood Tree
As You Were
Washington Square
Astarte
Esperto Nocchiero, L'
Atalanta
Care Selve
Go Call Irene
Athalia
Gentle Airs Melodious Strains
Will God Whose Mercies Ever Flow
Athalie
Oh Praise The Lord
Attila
Praise Ye
Automan
Automan
Ave Maria
Otello
Away Down Souf
Away Down South
Axe An Apple And A Buckskin Jacket, An
How Lovely Is Christmas
Azara
Azara
Babes In Arms
I Wish I Were In Love Again
Johnny One Note
Lady Is A Tramp, The
My Funny Valentine
Where Or When
Babes In Toyland
Go To Sleep Slumber Deep
I Can't Do The Sum
Jane
March Of The Toys
Toyland
Toyland March
Babes On Broadway
Hoe Down
How About You
Babette
Baby
I Chose Right
Baby Doll
Theme From Baby Doll
Back Roads
Ask Me No Questions
Back To The Future
Back To The Future

Back To The Future III
Doubleback
Bagdad Cafe
Calling You
Ballad Of Baby Doe, The
Lettersong
Willow Song
Ballet Ballads
I've Got Me
Ballet For A Girl In Buchanan
Colour My World
Bamba, La
Bamba, La
Come On Let's Go
Who Do You Love
Bambi
Little April Shower
Love Is A Song
Banacek
Theme From Banacek
Band Wagon, The
Dancing In The Dark
Shine On Your Shoes, A
That's Entertainment
You And The Night And The Music
Barber Of Bagdad
Salamaleikum
Barber Of Seville, The
(*see* **Barbiere de Siviglia**)
Barbiere Di Siviglia, Il
Cavatina
Frag Ich Mein Beklommnes Herz
Je Suis Lindor
There's A Voice That I Enshrine
Tyrant Soon I'll Burst Thy Chains
Voce Poco Fa, Una
Bare Essence
In Finding You I Found Love
Baretta
Baretta's Theme
Barnum
Colors Of My Life, The
Come Follow The Band
I Like Your Style
Love Makes Such Fools Of Us All
There Is A Sucker Born Ev'ry Minute
Bartered Bride, The
I Know A Maiden
Now In Joy Or Sorrow
See The Budding Flowers Springing
Batman
Arms Of Orion, The
Batdance
Batman Theme
Battle Cry
Honey-Babe
Beaches
Wind Beneath My Wings, The
Beany And Cecil
Beany And Cecil
Bears And I, The
Sweet Surrender

Beatlemania
She Loves You
Beauty And The Beast
First Time I Loved Forever, The
Theme From Beauty And The Beast
Because You're Mine
Because You're Mine
Bedknobs And Broomsticks
Age Of Not Believing, The
Beautiful Briny, The
Old Home Guard, The
Portobello Road
Beggar Student, The
Belles Of Poland
Entrance Song
Beggar's Holiday
Take Love Easy
Tomorrow Mountain
Beggar's Opera
Before The Barn-Door Crowing
Come Sweet Lass
How Happy Could I Be With Either
Youth's The Season
Were I Laid On Greenland's Coast
Bella Molinara, La
Why Is My Heart So Heavy
Belle Of New York, The
I Wanna Be A Dancin' Man
Purity Brigade, The
Seeing's Believing
She Is The Belle Of New York
Belle Of The Nineties
My Old Flame
Belletti
In Thee In Gladness
Bells Are Ringing
Drop That Name
Just In Time
Long Before I Knew You
Party's Over, The
Bells Of Capistrano
Don't Bite The Hand That's Feeding You
Bells Of Heaven
Soldier's Song, The
Bells Of St Mary's
Aren't You Glad You're You
Belmont And Constance
Of Selim Mighty Great And Powerful
Belshazzar
Great God Who Yet But Darkly Known
O Sacred Oracles Of Truth
Rejoice My Countrymen
Ben
Ben
Ben Hur
Love Theme From Ben-Hur
Benny Goodman Story, The
And The Angels Sing
I Got It Bad And That Ain't Good

Berenice
 Come See Where Golden-Hearted
  Spring
 Yea Mid Chains
Best Foot Forward
 Buckle Down Winsocki
 Ev'ry Time
 Just A Little Joint With A Juke Box
Best Friends
 How Do You Keep The Music
  Playing
Best Little Whorehouse In Texas, The
 I Will Always Love You
Best Of Everything, The
 Best Of Everything, The
Best Things In Life Are Free, The
 Button Up Your Overcoat
 It All Depends On You
 Sonny Boy
Best Years Of Our Lives
 Lazy River
Better Days
 Better Days
Between The Devil
 By Myself
 I See Your Face Before Me
 Triplets
Beverly Hillbillies
 Ballad Of Jed Clampett, The
Beverly Hills Cop
 Axel F
 Don't Get Stopped In Beverly Hills
 Heat Is On, The
 Neutron Dance
 New Attitude
 Stir It Up
Beverly Hills Cop II
 Be There
 Better Way
 Cross My Broken Heart
 In Deep
 Shakedown
Bewitched
 Bewitched
Big
 Heart And Soul
Big Broadcast Of 1933, The
 Please
Big Broadcast Of 1936
 Miss Brown To You
Big Broadcast Of 1938, The
 Thanks For The Memory
Big Pond, The
 You Brought A New Kind Of Love
  To Me
Big River
 River In The Rain
 Worlds Apart
Big Show, The
 May The Good Lord Bless And Keep
  You
 Our Time
 Poor Butterfly

Billion Dollar Baby
 I Got A One Track Mind
Billy Jack
 One Tin Soldier
Billy Rose's Diamond Horseshoe
 More I See You, The
Bing Boys Are Here, The
 If You Were The Only Girl In The
  World
Bionic Woman, The
 Theme From The Bionic Woman
Birth Of The Blues
 Birth Of The Blues, The
Bitter Sweet
 I'll See You Again
 If Love Were All
 Zigeuner
Black Crook, The
 You Naughty Naughty Men
Blackbirds Of 1928
 Diga Diga Doo
Blackbirds Of 1930
 Memories Of You
Blackbirds Of 1934
 Moonglow
Blackboard Jungle, The
 Rock Around The Clock
Blame It On Rio
 Blame It On Rio
Blanche Of Provence
 Cradle Song
Blazing Saddles
 Theme From Blazing Saddles
Bless The Beasts And Children
 Bless The Beasts And Children
Blind Date
 Simply Meant To Be
Blodwen
 My Blodwen
Blonde Crazy
 When Your Lover Has Gone
Bloomer Girl
 Eagle And Me, TheEvelina
 Right As The Rain
 When The Boys Come Home
Blossom Time
 Song Of Love
Blowing Wild
 Blowing Wild
Blue And The Gray, The
 Theme From The Blue And The
  Gray
Blue Gardenia
 Blue Gardenia
Blue Hawaii
 Can't Help Falling In Love
Blue Kitten, The
 Madeleine
Blue Skies
 You Keep Coming Back Like A Song
Blue Thunder
 Theme From Blue Thunder
Bluebeard
 Rondo

Blues In The Night
 Blues In The Night
 This Time The Dream's On Me
Bob Newhart Show
 Home To Emily
Bobo, The
 Imagine
Body And Soul
 Body And Soul
Boheme, La
 Donde Lieta
 Musetta's Waltz
 Quando Men Vo
 Si Me Chiamano Mimi
Bohemian Girl
 Come With The Gipsy Bride
 Galop
 Gipsy Song
 Gypsy Life
 Happy And Light
 Heart Bowed Down, The
 I Dreamt That I Dwelt In Marble
  Halls
 In The Gypsy's Life
 Oh What Full Delight
 See At Your Feet
 Soldier's Life, A
 Then You'll Remember Me
 When The Fair Land Of Poland
Bolero
 All My Love
Bombo
 April Showers
 California Here I Come
 Toot Toot Tootsie Good-Bye
Bonanza
 Bonanza
Bone Room, The
 Postcards
 Wonderful Way To Die, A
Bonita
 Ranger's Song
Bonne Cuisine, La
 Civet A Toute Vitesse
 Plum Pudding
 Queues De Boeuf
 Tavouk Gueunksis
Boon
 Rock With Me
Boris Godunov
 Coronation Scene
 Long Live And Reign Great Boris
 Marina's Song
Born Free
 Born Free
Born To Dance
 Easy To Love
 I've Got You Under My Skin
Born To Love
 Easy To Love
Bouffe Et Le Tailleur, Le
 Conservez Bien La Paix Du Coeur
Boy Friend, The
 Won't You Charleston With Me

Boys From Syracuse, The
Falling In Love With Love
Sing For Your Supper
This Can't Be Love
Brady Bunch, The
Brady Bunch, The
Brady Bunch Theme, The
Bran Pie
Ja-Da
Branded
Branded
Breakfast At Tiffany's
Breakfast At Tiffany's (Play)
Moon River (Movie)
Breakfast Club, The
Don't You Forget About Me
Breezy
Breezy's Song
Brian's Song
Brian's Song
Hands Of Time, The
Bridge On The River Kwai
River Kwai March, The
Brigadoon
Almost Like Being In Love
Brigadoon
Come To Me Bend To Me
Heather On The Hill, The
I'll Go Home With Bonnie Jean
Waitin' For My Dearie
Bright Eyes
On The Good Ship Lollipop
Bring 'Em Back Alive
Bring 'Em Back Alive
Broadcast News
Theme From Broadcast News
Broadway Gondolier
Lulu's Back In Town
Broadway Melody Of 1928
Wedding Of The Painted Doll
You Were Meant For Me
Broadway Melody Of 1936
Broadway Rhythm
You Are My Lucky Star
Broadway Melody Of 1938
Dear Mr Gable
Broadway Melody Of 1940
Between You And Me
I Concentrate On You
Bronco Billy
Misery Loves Company
Brother Sun Sister Moon
Brother Sun Sister Moon
Brothers
Brother's Theme, The
Bruderlein Fein
Unter Dem Bluhenden Lindenbaum
Buck Privates
Boogie Woogie Bugle Boy
Buddy System, The
Here's That Sunny Day
Bugs Bunny Show, The
This Is It

Buster
Two Hearts
Butch Cassidy And The Sundance Kid
Raindrops Keep Fallin' On My Head
By Jupiter
Wait Till You See Her
Bye Bye Birdie
Kids
Lot Of Livin' To Do, A
Put On A Happy Face
Cabaret
Cabaret (Play)
Married (Play)
Maybe This Time (Movie)
Money Money (Play)
Willkommen (Play)
Cabin In The Sky
Cabin In The Sky (Play)
Happiness Is A Thing Called Joe
(Movie)
Life's Full Of Consequence (Movie)
Taking A Chance On Love (Play)
Things Ain't What They Used To Be
(Movie)
Caddy, The
That's Amore
Caddyshack
I'm Alright
Caddyshack II
Nobody's Fool
Cades County
Theme From Cades County
Cage Aux Folles, La
Best Of Times, The
Look Over There
Song On The Sand
Cagney And Lacey
Cagney And Lacey Theme
Cain And Mable
I'll Sing You A Thousand Love
Songs
Calamity Jane
Secret Love
Call Me Madam
It's A Lovely Day Today
Marrying For Love
Ocarina
You're Just In Love
Camelot
Camelot
How To Handle A Woman
I Loved You Once In Silence
If Ever I Would Leave You
Simple Joys Of Maidenhood, The
Camille Du Le Souterrain
Notre Meunier Charge D'Argent
On Nous Dit Que Dans L'Mariage
Can't Help Singing
Can't Help Singing
Can-Can
Allez-Vous-En Go Away
C'Est Magnifique

Can-Can (Cont.)
I Love Paris
It's All Right With Me
Candide
Ballad Of Eldorado, The
Best Of All Possible Worlds, The
Glitter And Be Gay
I Am Easily Assimilated
It Must Be So
Make Our Garden Grow
My Love
Oh Happy We
What's The Use
You Were Dead You Know
Cantata No. 3 (Bach)
Ach Gott Wie Manches Herzeleid
Cantata No. 4 (Bach)
Christ Lag In Todesbanden
Cantata No. 9 (Bach)
Es Ist Das Heil Uns Kommen Her
Cantata No. 10 (Bach)
Meine Seel' Erhebt Den Herren
Cantata No. 12 (Bach)
Was Gott Thut Das Ist Wohlgethan
Cantata No. 13 (Bach)
Meine Seufzer Meine Tranen
Cantata No. 14 (Bach)
War' Gott Nicht Mit Uns Diese Zeit
Cantata No. 16 (Bach)
Helft Mir Gott's Gute Preisen
Cantata No. 17 (Bach)
Nun Lob' Hein' Seel' Den Herren
Cantata No. 18 (Bach)
Durch Adams Fall Ist Ganz Verderbt
Cantata No. 23 (Bach)
Christe Du Lamm Gottes
Cantata No. 26 (Bach)
Ach Wie Fluchtig, Ach Wie Nichtig
Cantata No. 27 (Bach)
Welt Ade Ich Bin Dein Mude
Wer Weiss Wie Nahe Mir Mein Ende
Cantata No. 29 (Bach)
Nun Lob' Mein' Seel' Den Herren
Cantata No. 30 (Bach)
Freu' Dich Sehr O Meine Seele
Cantata No. 33 (Bach)
Allein Zu Dir Herr Jesu Christ
Cantata No. 37 (Bach)
Ich Dank' Dir Lieber Herre
Cantata No. 38 (Bach)
Aus Tiefer Noth Schrei Ich Zu Dir
Cantata No. 40 (Bach)
Darzu Ist Erschienen Der Sohn
Gottes
Freuet Euch Ihr Christen
Schwing' Dich Zu Deinem Gott
Wir Christenleut'
Cantata No. 41 (Bach)
Jesu Nun Sei Gepreiset
To Thee Alone Be Glory
Cantata No. 42 (Bach)
Verleih Uns Frieden Gnadiglich

Cantata No. 45 (Bach)
  O Gott Du Frommer Gott
  O Love That Casts Out Fear
Cantata No. 46 (Bach)
  O Grosser Gott Von Macht
  Schauet Doch Und Sehet
Cantata No. 47 (Bach)
  Warum Betrubst Du Dich Mein Herz
Cantata No. 48 (Bach)
  Ach Gott Und Herr
  Herr Jesu Christ Du Hochstes Gut
Cantata No. 52 (Bach)
  In Dich Hab' Ich Gehoffet Herr
Cantata No. 59 (Bach)
  Komm Heiliger Geist Herre Gott
Cantata No. 60 (Bach)
  Come Thou O Come
  Es Ist Genung Herr Wenn Es Dir
    Gefallt
Cantata No. 64 (Bach)
  Gelobet Seist Du Jesu Christ
  Nun Komm, Der Heiden Heiland
Cantata No. 65 (Bach)
  Puer Natus In Bethlehem
Cantata No. 66 (Bach)
  Christ Ist Erstanden
  Erfreut Euch Ihr Herzen
Cantata No. 67 (Bach)
  Erschienen Ist Der Herrlich' Tag
Cantata No. 69 (Bach)
  Es Woll' Uns Gott Genadig Sein
Cantata No. 70 (Bach)
  Meinen Jesum Lass' Ich Nicht
  Wachet Beter
Cantata No. 72 (Bach)
  Was Mein Gott Will Das G'Scheh'
    Allzeit
Cantata No. 73 (Bach)
  Herr Wie Du Willt
  Von Gott Will Ich Nicht Lassen
Cantata No. 74 (Bach)
  Kommt Her Zu Mir Spricht Gottes
    Sohn
Cantata No. 78 (Bach)
  Jeus Der Du Meine Seele
Cantata No. 79 (Bach)
  Nun Danket Alle Gott
Cantata No. 81 (Bach)
  Jesus Schlaft Was Soll Ich Hoffen
Cantata No. 82 (Bach)
  Ich Habe Genug
Cantata No. 83 (Bach)
  Mit Fried' Und Freud' Ich Fahr'
    Dahin
Cantata No. 85 (Bach)
  Ist Gott Mein Schild Und
    Helfersmann
Cantata No. 93 (Bach)
  Wer Nur Den Lieben Gott Lasst
    Walten
Cantata No. 95 (Bach)
  Mit Fried' Und Freud' Ich Fahr'
    Dahin
  Wenn Mein Stundlein Vorhanden Ist

Cantata No. 96 (Bach)
  Herr Christ Der Ein'ge Gottes-Sohn
Cantata No. 97 (Bach)
  O Welt Ich Muss Dich Lassen
Cantata No. 104 (Bach)
  Begluckte Heerde
  Du Hirte Israel
Cantata No. 112 (Bach)
  Allein Gott In Der Hoh' Sei Ehr'
Cantata No. 114 (Bach)
  Ach Lieben Christen Seid Getrost
Cantata No. 115 (Bach)
  Straf Mich Nicht In Deinem Zorn
Cantata No. 120 (Bach)
  Herr Gott Dich Loben Wir
Cantata No. 121 (Bach)
  Christum Wir Sollen Loben Schon
Cantata No. 122 (Bach)
  Neugebor'ne Kindelein, Das
Cantata No. 123 (Bach)
  Liebster Immanuel Herzog Der
    Frommen
Cantata No. 127 (Bach)
  Herr Jesu Christ Wahr'r Mensch
    Und Gott
Cantata No. 128 (Bach)
  Auf Christi Himmelfahrt Allein
Cantata No. 130 (Bach)
  Herr Gott Dich Loben Alle Wir
Cantata No. 133 (Bach)
  Ich Freue Mich In Dir
Cantata No. 137 (Bach)
  Lobe Den Herren Den Machtigen
    Konig Der Ehren
Cantata No. 140 (Bach)
  Now Let All The Heavens Adore
    Thee
  Wachet Auf Ruft Uns Die Stimme
Cantata No. 144 (Bach)
  Was Gott Thut Das Ist Wohlgethan
Cantata No. 145 (Bach)
  Jesus Meine Zuversicht
  So Du Mit Deinem Munde Bekennest
    Jesum
Cantata No. 146 (Bach)
  My Spirit Be Joyful
Cantata No. 147 (Bach)
  Jesu Joy Of Man's Desiring
  Jesu Meiner Seele Wonne
Cantata No. 151 (Bach)
  Lobt Gott Ihr Christen Alle Gleich
Cantata No. 153 (Bach)
  Ach Gott Vom Himmel Sieh' Darein
Cantata No. 156 (Bach)
  Herr Wie Du Will't So Schick's Mit
    Mir
Cantata No. 159 (Bach)
  Sehet Wir Gehn Hinauf Gen
    Jerusalem
Cantata No. 161 (Bach)
  Herzlich Thut Mich Verlangen
  My Soul There Is A Country
Cantata No. 162 (Bach)
  Alle Menschen Mussen Sterben

Cantata No. 165 (Bach)
  Nun Lasst Uns Gott Dem Herren
Cantata No. 174 (Bach)
  Herzlich Lieb Hab' Dich O Herr
Cantata No. 176 (Bach)
  Christ Unser Herr Zum Jordan Kam
Cantata No. 180 (Bach)
  Schmucke Dich O Liebe Seele
Cantata No. 184 (Bach)
  O Herre Gott Dein Gottlich Wort
Cantata No. 185 (Bach)
  Ich Ruf' Zu Dir Herr Jesu Christ
Cantata No. 187 (Bach)
  Singen Wir Aus Herzensgrund
Cantata No. 188 (Bach)
  Auf Meinen Lieben Gott
Cantata No. 196 (Bach)
  Herr Segne Euch, Der
Cantata No. 197 (Bach)
  Nun Bitten Wir Den Heiligen Geist
Cantata No. 208 (Bach)
  Jesus Shepherd Be Thou Near Me
  Schafe Konnen Sicher Weiden
  Sheep May Safely Graze
Cantata No. 212 (Bach)
  And Now To The Drone Of The
    Dudelsack
  Come One And All With Right Good
    Will
Capital News
  Capital News
Capitan, El
  Capitan's Song, The
Captain Carey USA
  Mona Lisa
Captain Horatio Hornblower
  Captain Hornblower Theme
Capuleti Ed I Montecchi, I
  Ascolta
  Deh Tu
Car Wash
  Car Wash
Carefree
  Change Partners
Carmen
  Boys' Chorus
  Carmen's Song And Dance
  Castanet Song
  Changing The Guard
  Draussen Am Wall Von Sevilla
  En Vain Pour Eviter
  Fleur Que Tu M'Avais Jetee, La
  Gypsy Girls
  Habanera
  Halte-La
  I Say That By Fear I'm Not Haunted
  I Vow I'll Do All In My Power
  If You Love Me
  If You Love Me Carmen
  Ja Die Liebe Hat Bunte Flugel
  Je Dia Que Rien Ne M'epouvante
  Love Is Like A Bird Rebellious
  March Of The Toreadors

Cinderella *(Cont.)*
Lovely Night, A (Rodgers)
So This Is Love (Disney)
Ten Minutes Ago (Rodgers)
Work Song, The (Disney)
Cinderella Liberty
Nice To Be Around
Clair Or The Maid Of Milan
Home Sweet Home
Close Encounters Of The Third Kind
Close Encounters Of The Third Kind
Theme From Close Encounters Of
The Third Kind
Clowns, The
Ebb Tide
Clowns In Clover
Don't Blame Me
Clue
Theme From Clue
Cocktail
Kokomo
Coco
Coco
Money Rings Out Like Freedom, The
Cocoanut Grove
Cocoanut Grove
You Leave Me Breathless
Cocoon
Dream
Colette
Earthly Paradise
Colette Collage
Room Is Filled With You, The
College Humor
Learn To Croon
College Rhythm
Stay As Sweet As You Are
College Swing
College Swing
How'dja Like To Love Me
Moments Like This
Color Purple, The
Color Purple, The
Don't Make Me No Never Mind
Mailbox
Maybe God Is Tryin' To Tell You
Somethin'
Miss Celie's Blues
Sisters Theme
Colt 45
Colt 45
Columbo
Theme From Columbo
Come Blow Your Horn
Come Blow Your Horn
Come Dance With Me
Come Dance With Me
Last Dance, The
Come Fly With Me
Come Fly With Me
Come Together
Holy Holy
Come Ye Sons Of Art
Sound The Trumpet

Coming To America
Come Into My Life
Coming To America
Company
Another Hundred People
Barcelona
Being Alive
Company
Little Things You Do Together, The
Side By Side
Sorry Grateful
Competition, The
Love Theme From The Competition
Comus
Sweet Echo
Connecticut Yankee, A
To Keep My Love Alive
Connie's Hot Chocolates
(*see* **Hot Chocolates**)
Contes D'Hoffman, Les
Barcarolle
Belle Nuit O Nuit D'Amour
Child Of Mine
Fellowship
Little Doll With China Eyes
Lovely Night
Lovely Night O Night Of Love
Waltz Song
Conversation Piece
I'll Follow My Secret Heart
Regency Rakes
There's Always Something Fishy
About The French
Cool Hand Luke
Down Here On The Ground
Coq D'or, Le
Hymn To The Sun
Cosby Show, The
Kiss Me
Cosi Fan Tutte
Loser Dieb Ist Amor, Ein
Schon Ein Madchen Von Funfzehn
Jahren
Cotton Club Parade
As Long As I Live (1934)
Happy As The Day Is Long (1933)
I've Got The World On A String
(1932)
Ill Wind (1934)
Stormy Weather (1933)
Wail Of The Reefer Man (1932)
Cotton Club Revue
I Love A Parade
Shoe Shine Boy
Countess From Hong Kong, A
This Is My Song
Countess Maritza
Play Gypsies Dance Gypsies
Country Girl, The
Dissertation On The State Of Bliss
Courted Into Court
Mister Johnson
Courtship Of Eddie's Father, The
My Best Friend

Cousins
Love Theme From Cousins
Cover Girl
Long Ago And Far Away
Sure Thing
Cowboys, The
Theme From The Cowboys
Cox And Box
Buttercup, The
Hush'd Is The Bacon
Listen I Solemnly Walk'd
My Master Is Punctual
Printer Printer Take A Hinter
Rataplan
Cradle Will Rock, The
Cradle Will Rock, The
Nickel Under The Foot
Crazy Like A Fox
Crazy Like A Fox
Crazy Quilt
I Found A Million Dollar Baby In A
Five & Ten Cent Store
Creation, The
(*see* **Schopfung, Die**)
Crime Story
Runaway
Cristoforo Colombo
Lesson In Love, A
Crucifixion, The
As Pants The Hart
God So Loved The World
Crusaders, The
O Zion Blest City
Cuban Love Song, The
Cuban Love Song
Cunning Man
Had I Heard Each Am'rous Ditty
Cutter To Houston
Cutter To Houston
Cymbeline
Hark Hark The Lark
Czar And The Carpenter, The
With Dark Suspicions
Daddy Long Legs
Something's Gotta Give
Dallas
Dallas
Dames
Dames
I Only Have Eyes For You
Dames At Sea
Beguine, The
Choo-Choo Honeymoon
Dames At Sea
It's You
Raining In My Heart
Sailor Of My Dreams, The
Singapore Sue
There's Something About You
Damn Yankees
Heart
Shoeless Joe From Hannibal Mo
Two Lost Souls
Whatever Lola Wants Lola Gets

Don Giovanni (Cont.)
Finch Han Dal Vino
Ich Grausam O Nein Geliebter
Il Mio Tesoro
Joy Flies Away
Nay Bid Me Not
Non Mi Dir
Now With Our Hands United
Pledge Now Thy Hand
Schmale Tobe Lieber Junge
Spring The Charmer
Vedrai Carino
Wenn Du Fein Artig Bist

Don't Bother Me I Can't Cope
Thank Heaven For You

Doogie Howser MD
Doogie Howser MD

Down Among The Sheltering Palms
Who Will It Be When The Time
Comes

Down Argentine Way
Down Argentina Way
Two Dreams Met

Dr Kildare
Theme From Dr Kildare

Dr Strangelove
Theme From Dr Strangelove

Dr Zhivago
(*see* **Doctor Zhivago**)

Dragnet
Dragnet March, The
Just The Facts

Dragonslayer
Dragonslayer Romantic Theme
Romantic Theme

Drat The Cat
I Like Him
She Touched Me

Dream A Little Dream
Dream A Little Dream Of Me

Dream Girl, The
At The Rain-Bow's End
My Dream Girl

Dreamer
Reach For The Top

Dreamgirls
And I Am Telling You I'm Not
Going
Dreamgirls

Drum Crazy
I Love My Baby My Baby Loves Me

Dubarry Was A Lady
But In The Morning No
Do I Love You
Friendship
Katie Went To Haiti
Well Did You Evah

Duet
Duet Theme

Dukes Of Hazzard, The
Good Ol' Boys

Dumbo
Baby Mine
Casey Junior

Dumbo (*Cont.*)
Pink Elephants On Parade
When I See An Elephant Fly

Dune
Dune

Dynasty
Dynasty
Theme From Dynasty

E.T.
Someone In The Dark
Theme From E.T.

Earl And The Girl, The
How'd You Like To Spoon With Me

Earl Carroll's Vanities of 1932
I Gotta Right To Sing The Blues

East Of Eden
Theme From East Of Eden

Easter Parade
Couple Of Swells, A
Fella With An Umbrella
It Only Happens When I Dance With
You
Steppin' Out With My Baby

Easy Living
Easy Living

Eclair, L'
Call Me Thine Own

Eddie And The Cruisers
On The Dark Side
Tender Years

Eddy Duchin Story, The
To Love Again

Egmont
Liebe, Die

Eight Is Enough
Eight Is Enough

Eileen
Irish Have A Great Day Tonight, The
Thine Alone
When Shall I Again See Ireland

Elijah
Be Not Afraid
Blessed Are The Men
Cast Thy Burden Upon The Lord
If With All Your Hearts
It Is Enough
Lift Thine Eyes
Lift Thine Eyes To The Mountains
O Rest In The Lord
Petition
Wirf Dein Anliegen Auf Den Herrn
Ye People Rend Your Hearts

Elisir D'Amore, L'
Down Her Soft Cheek A Pearly Tear
Furtiva Lagrima, Una
Furtive Tear, A

Ellery Queen
Theme From Ellery Queen

Elvira Madigan
Elvira
Elvira's Theme

Emerald Point NAS
Emerald Point NAS

Emergency
Theme From Emergency

Emmanuelle
Emmanuelle

Empire Of The Sun
Exsultate Justi
Toyplanes Home And Hearth

Empire Revue
Everybody's Doing It Now

Empire Strikes Back, The
Han Solo And The Princess
Imperial March, The
May The Force Be With You
Yoda's Theme

Enchantress, The
Come Little Fishes
To The Land Of My Own Romance

Endless Love
Endless Love

Enea Nel Lazio
Come Opprima

Enfant Prodigue, L'
Dieu D'Israel Calme Mon Desespoir

Entertainment Tonight
Entertainment Tonight

Entfuhrung Aus Dem Serail
Arie Der Constanze
Welche Wonne Welche Lust

Epreuve Villageoise, L'
Bon Dieu Bon Dieu Comme A C'Te
Fete

Erminie
Birds Of A Feather
Good Night
Lullaby
Parade, The

Ernani
Ernani Fly With Me

Espanola
One Hour More

Esther
I'll Hear No More
O Beauteous Queen
Pluck Root And Branch
Sing Songs Of Praise
Turn Not O Queen Thy Face Away

Eteolle
Che Fiero Costume

Eubie
I'm Just Wild About Harry
Memories Of You

Eugene Onegin
Yes I Love You

Euryanthe
Echoing Bell Tones
Euriante
Romance

Eurydice
Invocation Of Orpheus

Evangeline
Golden Chains
Thinking Love Of Thee

Fliegende Hollander, Der
Ballade Der Senta
Sailors' Chorus
Santa's Ballad
Flipper
Flipper
Flintstones, The
Flintstones, The
Flirtation Walk
Flirtation Walk
FloraDora
I Want To Be A Military Man
Flora The Red Menace
Quiet Thing, A
Sing Happy
Floridante
Crushed By Fate
Flower Drum Song
Don't Marry Me
I Enjoy Being A Girl
My Best Love
Sunday
You Are Beautiful
Flying Colors
Alone Together
Shine On Your Shoes, A
Flying Down To Rio
Carioca
Flying Dutchman, The
(see **Fliegende Hollander, Der**)
FM
It Keeps You Runnin'
Lido Shuffle
Life In The Fast Lane
Fol-De-Rol
Can It Be True
Follies
Ah Paree
Beautiful Girls
Broadway Baby
Could I Leave You
I'm Still Here
Losing My Mind
One More Kiss
Follow Me
Oh Johnny Oh
Follow The Boys
I'll Walk Alone
Follow The Fleet
Get Thee Behind Me Satan
I'm Putting All My Eggs In One
Basket
Let Yourself Go
Let's Face The Music And Dance
We Saw The Sea
Follow Thru
Button Up Your Overcoat
Fools
Someone Who Cares
Footlight Parade
By A Waterfall
Honeymoon Hotel
Shanghai Lil

Footloose
Almost Paradise
Dancing In The Sheets
Footloose
Holding Out For A Hero
Let's Hear It For The Boy
For Me And My Gal
For Me And My Gal
When You Wore A Tulip And I
Wore A Big Red Rose
For Your Eyes Only
For Your Eyes Only
Forest Rangers, The
Jingle Jangle Jingle
Fortune Teller, The
Always Do As People Say You
Should
Gypsy Love Song
Romany Life
Forty Second Street
(see **42nd Street**)
Forty-Five Minutes From Broadway
(see **45 Minutes from Broadway**)
Foul Play
Ready To Take A Chance Again
Fox, The
Fox, The
That Night
Fox And The Hound, The
Best Of Friends
Fra Diavolo
On Yonder Rock
On Yonder Rock Reclining
Romanze Der Zerline
Frasquita
My Little Nest Of Heavenly Blue
Frauenliebe Und Leben
Du Ring An Meinem Finger
Er Der Herrlichste Von Allen
Ich Kann's Nicht Fassen Nicht
Glauben
Nun Hast Du Mir Den Ersten
Schmerz Gethan
Seit Ich Ihn Gesehen
Susser Freund Du Blickest
Free Spirit
Free Spirit Theme
Freischutz, Der
Einst Traumte Maeiner Selgen Base
How Friendly Sleep Was To Me
Kommt Ein Schlanker Bursch
Gegangen
Leise Leise
Prayer
Softly Sighs The Voice Of Evening
Thy Way Not Mine
Und Ob Die Wolke Sie Verhulle
Wie Nahte Mir Der Schlummer
French Connection, The
French Connection Theme, The
French Doll, The
Do It Again
French Girl, The
A Frangesa Costa

Friday The 13th The Series
Friday The 13th The Series
Friend And Foe
Moonlight At Killarney
Over The Mountain
Peek-A-Boo
There's Always A Seat In The Parlor
For You
Friendly Persuasion
Friendly Persuasion
Fritz
Lullaby
Fritz Among The Gypsies
Emmet's Cuckoo Song
From Here To Eternity
From Here To Eternity
From Russia With Love
From Russia With Love
Fugitive, The (Television)
Fugitive, The
Funny Face
Babbitt And The Bromide, The (Play)
Clap Yo' Hands (Movie)
Funny Face (Play)
He Loves And She Loves (Play)
High Hat (Play)
How Long Has This Been Going On
(Play)
Let's Kiss And Make Up (Play)
My One And Only (Play)
's Wonderful (Play)
Funny Girl
Don't Rain On My Parade (Play)
Funny Girl (Play)
Music That Makes Me Dance, The
(Play)
My Man (Movie)
People (Play)
Sadie Sadie (Play)
Who Are You Now (Play)
You Are Woman I Am Man (Play)
Funny Lady
How Lucky Can You Get
Isn't This Better
**Funny Thing Happened On The Way
To The Forum, A**
Comedy Tonight
Everybody Ought To Have A Maid
Love I Hear
Lovely
That Dirty Old Man
Gaily Gaily
There's Enough To Go Around
Tomorrow Is My Friend
Gambler, The
Gambler, The
Gandhi
Theme From Gandhi
Gang's All Here, The
No Love No Nothin'
Garden Of Kama, The
Kashmiri Song
Less Than The Duet

Garden Of Kama, The *(Cont.)*
    Temple Bells, The
    Till I Wake
Garden Of The Moon
    Girlfriend Of The Whirling Dervish,
      The
Garrick Gaities
    Manhattan (1925)
    Mountain Greenery (1926)
    Sentimental Me (1925)
Gaudeamus
    Departure
    Old Assyrian Song
Gay Divorce
    After You
    Continental, The
    I've Got You On My Mind
    Mister And Missus Fitch
    Night And Day
Gay Divorce, The
    Night And Day
Gay Life, The
    For The First Time
Gay Purr-Ee
    Little Drops Of Rain
    Money Cat, The
    Paris Is A Lonely Town
Gazza Ladra, La
    Di Piacer Mi Balza Il Cor
Geisha, The
    Amorous Goldfish, The
    Jewel Of Asia, The
General Hospital
    Theme From General Hospital
Gentlemen Prefer Blondes
    Bye Bye Baby
    Diamonds Are A Girl's Best Friend
    Little Girl From Little Rock
George M
    Give My Regards To Broadway
    You're A Grand Old Flag
George Washington Jr
    Ethel Levey's Virginia Song
    You're A Grand Old Flag
George White's Scandals
    Black Bottom (1926)
    Cinderelatives (1922)
    I Need A Garden (1924)
    Life Is Just A Bowl Of Cherries
      (1931)
    Thrill Is Gone, The (1931)
    You And I (1923)
George White's Scandals 1920
    My Lady
George White's Scandals 1921
    I Love You
    South Sea Isles
George White's Scandals 1922
    I'll Build A Stairway To Paradise
    She Hangs Out In Our Alley
George White's Scandals 1923
    Let's Be Lonesome Together
    There Is Nothing Too Good For You

George White's Scandals 1924
    Kongo Kate
    Night Time In Araby
    Somebody Loves Me
George White's Scandals 1926
    Birth Of The Blues, The
George White's Scandals Of 1939
    Are You Havin' Any Fun
Georgy Girl
    Georgy Girl
Get Hep To Love
    Siboney
Get Into Your Dance
    About A Quarter To Nine
Ghostbusters
    Ghostbusters
Ghostbusters II
    On Our Own
Giant
    Giant
Gidget
    My Gidget
Gift To Be Simple
    Lord Of The Dance
Gigi
    A Toujours (Play)
    Gigi (Movie)
    I Remember It Well (Movie)
    Night They Invented Champagne,
      The (Movie)
    Thank Heaven For Little Girls
      (Movie)
Gilligan's Island
    Ballad Of Gilligan's Island
    Ballad Of Gilligan's Isle
    Ballad Of Gilligan's Isle, The
Gimme A Break
    Ready For Anything
Gioconda, La
    Blind Girl's Song, The
    Cielo A Mar
    Dance Of The Hours
Girl Behind The Counter, The
    Glow-Worm, The
Girl Crazy
    Bidin' My Time (Play)
    Boy What Love Has Done To Me
      (Play)
    But Not For Me (Play)
    Could You Use Me (Play)
    Embraceable You (Play)
    I Got Rhythm (Play)
    Sam And Delilah (Play)
    Treat Me Rough (Play)
    You've Got What Gets Me (Movie,
      1932)
Girl Friend, The
    Blue Room, The
Girl From UNCLE, The
    Theme From The Girl From UNCLE
Girl From Utah, The
    They Didn't Believe Me

Girl In Pink Tights, The
    Lost In Loveliness
Girl Who Came To Supper, The
    I'll Remember Her
Girls, Les
    Ca C'est L'amour
Girls Just Want To Have Fun
    Dancing In The Street
Girofle Girofla
    Song At Dawn
Girofle-Girofla
    Morning Serenade
    Son Of A Wealthy House, The
Giulio Cesare
    By This Falchion Lighting-Garnished
    Da Tempeste
    Piangero La Sorte Mia
    Tempeste, Da
Giulio Sabino
    Lungi Dal Caro Bene
Give My Regards To Broadway
    When Francis Dances With Me
Glad To See You
    Guess I'll Hang My Tears Out To
      Dry
Glass Menagerie, The
    Blue Roses
    Tom's Theme
Glass Slipper, The
    Take My Love
Glenn Miller Story, The
    I Want To Be Happy
    Tuxedo Junction
Glockchen Des Eremiten, Das
    Arie Der Rose
Gloria
    Domine Deus
    Gloria
Gloriana
    I Love You Dear
Go Into Your Dance
    About A Quarter To Nine
    Go Into Your Dance
    She's A Latin From Manhattan
Godfather, The
    Godfather Waltz, The
    Speak Softly Love
Godfather II, The
    Love Said Goodbye
    Theme From Godfather II
Godspell
    All Good Gifts (Play)
    Beautiful City (Movie)
    Day By Day (Play)
    Prepare Ye The Way Of The Lord
      (Play)
    Save The People (Play)
Going Hollywood
    Going Hollywood
    Temptation
Going My Way
    Going My Way
    Swinging On A Star
    That's An Irish Lullaby

Going Places
Jeepers Creepers
Gold Diggers In Paris
Daydreaming
I Wanna Go Back To Bali
Latin Quarter, The
Put That Down In Writing
Stranger In Paree, A
Gold Diggers Of 1933
Gold Digger's Song, The
I've Got To Sing A Torch Song
Pettin' In The Park
Remember My Forgotten Man
Shadow Waltz
Gold Diggers Of 1935
I'm Going Shopping With You
Lullaby Of Broadway
Words Are In My Heart
Gold Diggers Of 1937
With Plenty Of Money And You
Gold Diggers Of Broadway
Lullaby Of Broadway
Painting The Clouds With Sunshine
Tip-Toe Thru' The Tulips With Me
Golden Apple, The
It's The Going Home Together
Lazy Afternoon
Windflowers
Golden Boy
Golden Boy
I Want To Be With You
This Is The Life
Golden Child, The
Best Man In The World, The
Golden Dog, The
Living On Love
Golden Earrings
Golden Earrings
Golden Girls, The
Thank You For Being A Friend
Golden Legend, The
O Gladsome Light
Golden Rainbow
For Once In Your Life
Golden Room, The
Girl Sings, A
Goldfinger
Goldfinger
Goldwyn Follies
Love Is Here To Stay
Love Walked In
Spring Again
Gomer Pyle USMC
Gomer Pyle
Gondoliers, The
Dance A Cachucha
Duke And The Duchess, The
Duke Of Plaza-Toro
Finale
I Am A Courtier
I Am A Courtier Grave
I Am A Courtier Grave And Serious
I Stole The Prince

Gondoliers, The *(Cont.)*
In Enterprise Of Martial Kind
Kind Goodheart
O My Darling O My Pet
Once More Gondolieri
Recipe, A
Rising Early In The Morning
Roses White And Roses Red
Take A Pair Of Sparkling Eyes
Tangled Skein, The
Then One Of Us Will Be A Queen
There Lived A King
There Was A Time
We're Called Gondolieri
When A Merry Maiden Marries
Working Monarch, The
Gone With The Wind
My Own True Love
Good Boy
I Wanna Be Loved By You
Good Morning Dearie
Ka-Lu-A
Good Morning Judge
I Was So Young
Good News
Best Things In Life Are Free, The
Good News
Just Imagine
Lucky In Love
Varsity Drag, The
Goodbye Girl, The
Goodbye Girl
Goodbye Mr Chips (1969)
Fill The World With Love
You And I
Goonies, The
Goonies 'r' Good Enough, The
Theme From The Goonies
Gott Der Hoffnung Erfulle Euch
Komm Gott Schopfer Heiliger Geist
Bach
Goya
Till I Loved You
Graduate, The
Mrs Robinson
Scarborough Fair
Grande Duchesse, La
Letters From Lovers
Sabre Of My Father, The
Song Of General Boom, The
Song Of The Saber
Grand Duke, The
So Ends My Dream
Grasshopper And The Ants, The
World Owes Me A Living, The
Grease
Freddy My Love (Play)
Hopelessly Devoted To You (Movie)
Look At Me I'm Sandra Dee (Play)
Summer Nights (Play)
We Go Together (Play)
Great Caruso, The
Loveliest Night Of The Year, The

Great Day
Great Day
More Than You Know
Without A Song
Great Magoo, The
It's Only A Paper Moon
Great Mouse Detective, The
Great Mouse Detective, The
Great Race, The
Sweetheart Tree, The
Great Ziegfeld, The
It's Been So Long
Greatest, The
Greatest Love Of All, The
Greatest American Hero, The
Theme From The Greatest American
Hero, The
Green Acres
Green Acres
Green Dolphin Street
On Green Dolphin Street
Greenwich Village Follies (1924)
My Long Ago Girl
Wait For The Moon
Greenwillow
Faraway Boy
Gideon Briggs I Love You
Greenwillow Christmas
Music Of Home, The
Never Will I Marry
Summertime Love
Walking Away Whistling
Gregorian Mass For Doctors
Alleluia Justus Germinabit
Gremlins
Gizmo
Grey Sonnets
Soliloquy
Greystone The Legend Of Tarzan
Tarzan's Theme
Griselda
For The Glory
Per La Gloria D'adorarvi
Since 'Tis Glory
Since 'Tis Glory To Adore You
Growing Pains
As Long As We Got Each Other
Guess Who's Coming To Dinner
Glory Of Love, The
Guiding Light
Theme From Guiding Light
Gulliver's Travels (1939)
It's A Hap-Hap-Happy Day
Gunn
I Like The Look
Guy Named Joe, A
I'll Get By As Long As I Have You
Guys And Dolls
Adelaide's Lament (Play)
Bushel And A Peck, A (Play)
Follow The Fold (Play)
Fugue For Tinhorns (Play)

Guys And Dolls *(Cont.)*
Guys And Dolls (Play)
I'll Know (Play)
I've Never Been In Love Before
   (Play)
If I Were A Bell (Play)
Luck Be A Lady (Play)
Marry The Man Today (Play)
More I Cannot Wish You (Play)
My Time Of Day (Play)
Oldest Established, The (Play)
Pet Me Poppa (Movie)
Sit Down You're Rockin' The Boat
   (Play)
Sue Me (Play)
Take Back Your Mink (Play)
Three Cornered Tune (Play)
Woman In Love, A (Movie)
Gypsy
All I Need Is The Girl
Everything's Coming Up Roses
Let Me Entertain You
Small World
Some People
Together Wherever We Go
You Gotta Have A Gimmick
You'll Never Get Away From Me
HMS Pinafore
Bell Trio
British Tar, A
British Tar Is A Soaring Soul, A
Buttercup
Carefully On Tiptoe Stealing
Choruses From Pinafore
Englishman, The
Farewell My Own
Finale
For He Loves Little Buttercup
Gaily Tripping
He Is An Englishman
I Am The Captain Of The Pinafore
I Am The Monarch Of The Sea
I Am The Ruler Of The Queen's
   Navee
I'm Called Little Buttercup
Kind Captain I've Important
   Information
Maiden Fair To See, A
Merry Maiden And The Tar, The
Monarch Of The Sea
Never Mind The Why And
   Wherefore
Never Mind The Why Or Wherefore
Over The Bright Blue Sea
Pinafore Sequence
Refrain Audacious Tar
Sorry Her Lot
Sorry Her Lot Who Loves Too Well
Things Are Seldom What They Seem
We Sail The Ocean Blue
When Fred'ric Was A Little Lad
When Frederic Was A Little Lad
When I Was A Lad

Hair
Aquarius
Aquarius, Let The Sunshine In
Easy To Be Hard
Frank Mills
Good Morning Starshine
Hair
Let The Sunshine In
Manchester England
Half A Sixpence
If The Rain's Got To Fall
Money To Burn
Hallelujah Baby
My Own Morning
Hallelujah I'm A Bum
You Are Too Beautiful
Hamlet
A Vos Jeux Mes Amis
Hang 'em High
Hang 'em High
Hans Christian Andersen
Anywhere I Wander
I'm Hans Christian Andersen
Inch Worm, The
King's New Clothes, The
No Two People
Thumbelina
Ugly Duckling, The
Wonderful Copenhagen
Hansel And Gretel
Brother Come And Dance
Children's Prayer, The
Dance With Me
Dancing Lesson, The
Evening Prayer
Lied Des Sandmannchens
Little Man Stands Silent Within The
   Wood, A
O Magic Cast-Le
Sandman's Lullaby
Sandman's Song
Susy Little Susy
Tiny Little Man, A
Happiest Millionaire, The
Fortuosity
Happy Birthday To Me
Happy Birthday To Me
Happy Days
Happy Days
Happy Ending, The
What Are You Doing The Rest Of
   Your Life
Happy Hunting
Mutual Admiration Society
Happy Time, The
Happy Time, The
I Don't Remember You
Hard Day's Night, A
Hard Day's Night, A
Hard To Get
You Must Have Been A Beautiful
   Baby

Hard To Hold
Love Somebody
Harlow
Girl Talk
Harry And Son
Harry's Theme
Hart To Hart
Hart To Hart
Harvey Girls, The
On The Atchison Topeka And The
   Santa Fe
Swing Your Partner Round And
   Round
Wait And See
Hatari
Baby Elephant Walk
Having A Wild Weekend
Catch Us If You Can
Hawaii
Hawaii
Wishing Doll, The
Hawaii Five-O
Hawaii Five-O
Hawaiian Eye
Hawaiian Eye
Hazel Flagg
Ev'ry Street's A Boulevard In Old
   New York
How Do You Speak To An Angel
Heads Up
Ship Without A Sail, A
Heartburn
Coming Around Again
Heavy Metal
Heavy Metal
Hee Haw
Hee Haw
Hello Dolly
Before The Parade Passes By
Hello Dolly
It Only Takes A Moment
Hello Frisco Hello
You'll Never Know
Help
Help
Her Highness And The Bell
Dream When You're Feeling Blue
Her Regiment
Someday
Here Come The Waves
Ac-Cent-Tchu-Ate The Positive
Let's Take The Long Way Home
Here Comes The Groom
In The Cool Cool Cool Of The
   Evening
Here Is My Heart
June In January
Love Is Just Around The Corner
Here's Howe
Crazy Rhythm
Herman And Katnip
Skiddle Diddle Dee-Skiddle Diddle
   Dey
Herodiade
He Is Kind He Is Good

High And The Mighty, The
  High And The Mighty, The
High Button Shoes
  Can't You Just See Yourself
  I Still Get Jealous
  On A Sunday By The Sea
  Papa Won't You Dance With Me
  You're My Girl
High Jinks
  Bubble, The
  Something Seems Tingle Ingleing
High Noon
  High Noon
High Society
  Mind If I Make Love To You
  True Love
  You're Sensational
High Spirits
  You'd Better Love Me
High Time
  Second Time Around, The
High Wide And Handsome
  Can I Forget You
  Folks Who Live On The Hill, The
Higher And Higher
  I Couldn't Sleep A Wink Last Night
    (Movie)
  It Never Entered My Mind (Play)
Hill Street Blues
  Hill Street Blues Theme, The
Hippolyte Et Aricie
  A L'amour Rendez Les Armes
  Nightingales Passion-Stirred
His And Hers
  Love Crazy
His Brother's Wife
  Can't We Fall In Love
Hit The Deck
  Hallelujah
  Sometimes I'm Happy
Hitchy Koo Of 1919
  Old Fashioned Garden
Hitchy Koo Of 1922
  Love Letter Words
Hold Everything (Play)
  You're The Cream In My Coffee
Hold On To Your Hats
  Don't Let It Get You Down
  There's A Great Day Coming
    Manana
  World Is In My Arms
Hole In The Head, A
  All My Tomorrows
  High Hopes
Holiday Inn
  Abraham
  Be Careful It's My Heart
Hollywood Canteen
  Don't Fence Me In
  Hollywood Canteen
  Sweet Dreams Sweetheart

Hollywood Hotel
  Hooray For Hollywood
Hollywood Revue Of 1929
  Singin' In The Rain
Holy City
  No Shadows Yonder
Hondo
  Theme From Hondo
Honeysuckle Rose
  On The Road Again
Hooperman
  Theme From Hooperman
Hooray For What
  Buds Won't Bud
  Down With Love
  God's Country
  In The Shade Of The New Apple
    Tree
  Moanin' In The Mornin'
Hot Chocolates (1929)
  Ain't Misbehavin
  Black And Blue
Hotel
  Theme From Hotel
House I Live In, The
  House I Live In, The
House Of Flowers
  Don't Like Goodbyes
  House Of Flowers
  I Never Has Seen Snow
  Sleepin' Bee, A
  Two Ladies In De Shade Of De
    Banana Tree
Houston Knights
  Houston Knights
How Now Dow Jones
  Step To The Rear
How To Succeed In Business Without
** Really Trying**
  Brotherhood Of Man
  Cinderella Darling
  Coffee Break
  Company Way, The
  Grand Old Ivy
  Happy To Keep His Dinner Warm
  How To Succeed In Business
    Without Really Trying
  I Believe In You
  Love From A Heart Of Gold
  Paris Original
  Rosemary
  Secretary Is Not A Toy, A
Howdy Doody
  It's Howdy Doody Time
Huguenots, Les
  Page's Song, The
Hullo Ragtime
  Alexander's Ragtime Band
Hunter
  Hunter
Hurricane, The
  Moon Of Manakoora, The
Hymn Of Praise
  Ich Harrete Des Herrn

Hymn Of The Nativity, A
  Sung By The Shepherds
I Can Get It For You Wholesale
  Miss Marmelstein
I Could Go On Singing
  Hello Bluebird
I Cover The Waterfront
  I Cover The Waterfront
I Do I Do
  Honeymoon Is Over, The
  I Do I Do
  Love Isn't Everything
  My Cup Runneth Over
  Roll Up The Ribbons
  Together Forever
  What Is A Woman
  Where Are The Snows
I Dream Of Jeannie
  Jeannie
I Dream Too Much
  I Dream Too Much
I Love Lucy
  I Love Lucy
I Love My Wife
  Hey There Good Times
  I Love My Wife
I Married An Angel
  I Married An Angel
  Spring Is Here
I Married Joan
  I Married Joan
I Ought To Be In Pictures
  One Hello
I Spy
  I Spy
I'd Rather Be Right
  Have You Met Miss Jones
I'll Get By
  Once In A While
I'll Never Say Goodbye
  Promise, The
I'll See You In My Dreams
  It Had To Be You
I'll Take Romance
  I'll Take Romance
I'm Getting My Act Together
  In A Simple Way I Love You
Ice Castles
  Theme From Ice Castles
  Through The Eyes Of Love
Iceland
  There Will Never Be Another You
Ich Hatte Viel Bekummerni
  Seufzer Tranen Kummer Not
Idol's Eye, The
  Fairy Tales
  Tattooed Man, The
If Ever I See You Again
  California
Imenen
  Chi Scherza Colle Rose
Immensee
  My Fate I Cannot Banish
  Song Of The Harp-Girl

Immortal, The
Theme From The Immortal
In A Persian Garden
Myself When Young
In Caliente
Lady In Red, The
In DaHomey
I'm A Jonah Man
In London
By The Sycamore Tree
In Society
My Dreams Are Getting Better All
The Time
In The Good Old Summertime
I Don't Care
Last Night When We Were Young
In The Heat Of The Night
In The Heat Of The Night
In Wall Street
Belle Of Murray Hill, The
Indian Princess
I Attempt From Love's Sickness To
Fly
Indigo Und Die Vierzig Rauber
Tyrolienne
Indiscretion Of An American Wife
Autumn In Rome
Innisfallen
Killarney
Innocents Of Paris
Louise
Inside Daisy Clover
You're Gonna Hear From Me
Inside U.S.A.
Haunted Heart
Intermezzo
Intermezzo
International Revue
Exactly Like You
On The Sunny Side Of The Street
Into The Woods
Into The Woods
No One Is Alone
Invitation
Invitation
Iolanthe
Autumn Woods
Blue Blood
Bow Bow Ye Lower Middle Classes
Contemplative Sentry, The
Entrance And March Of Peers
Ev'ry One Is Now A Fairy
Faint Heart Never Won Fair Lady
Fal Lal La
Finale
Good Morrow Good Lover
He Loves
House Of Peers, The
If We're Weak Enough To Tarry
If You Go In
In Good Queen Bess's Glorious Days
Into Parliament He Shall Go
Law Is The True Embodiment, The

Iolanthe *(Cont.)*
Law, The
Lord Chancellor's Song, The
Loudly Let The Trumpet Bray
Love Unrequited
March Of The Peers
None Shall Part Us
Of All The Young Ladies I Know
Oh Foolish Fay
Said I To Myself Said I
Soon As We May
Spurn Not The Nobly Born
Tripping Hither
Tripping Hither Tripping Hither
We Are Dainty Little Fairies
Welcome To Our Hearts Again
When All Night Long
When All Night Long A Chap
Remains
When Britain Really Rul'd The
Waves
When Britain Really Ruled The
Waves
When I Went To The Bar
When You're Lying Awake
Young Strephon Is The Kind Of Lout
Iphigenie En Aulide
Par Un Pere Cruel
Unis Des La Plus Tendre Enfance
Iphigenie Auf Tauris
O Du Die Mir Einst Hilfe Gab
O Lasst Mich Tiefgebeugte
Par Un Pere Cruel
Prayer
Unis Des La Plus Tendre Enfance
Irato, L'
O Ciel Que Faire
Irene
Alice Blue Gown
World Must Be Bigger Than An
Avenue, The
Irish Minstrel, The
Bye Bye Baby Bye Bye
I Love Music
My Nelly's Blue Eyes
Scanlan's Rose Song
What's In A Kiss
Irma La Douce
From A Prison Cell
Irma La Douce
Our Language Of Love
Iron Eagle II
Enemies Like You And Me
Ironside
Theme From Ironside
Ishtar
Little Darlin'
Island In The Sun
Island In The Sun
Lead Man Holler
Isle O' Dreams, The
When Irish Eyes Are Smiling
Isle Of Dreams, The
(see **Isle O' Dreams, The**)

Isle Of Surprise, The
Claribel
Orient
Israel In Egypt
Thou Shalt Bring Them In
It Happened In Brooklyn
Brooklyn Bridge, The
I Believe
It's The Same Old Dream
Song's Gotta Come From The Heart,
The
Time After Time
It Happened In Nordland
Absinthe Frappe
Knot Of Blue, The
It Takes A Thief
Theme From It Takes A Thief
It's A Bird It's A Plane It's Superman
It's Superman
You've Got Possibilities
It's Garry Shandling's Show
Garry's Closing Theme
It's Garry's Theme
It's My Turn
It's My Turn
Italian Job, The
On Days Like These
Ivanhoe
Romanze Des Richard Lowenherz
Jahreszeiten, Die
Schon Eilet Froh Der Akkersmann
Welche Labung Fur Die Sinne
Jailhouse Rock
Jailhouse Rock
Jamaica
Ain' It De Truth
Cocoanut Sweet
Little Biscuit
Pretty To Walk With
Push De Button
What Good Does It Do Now
Jaws
Theme From Jaws
Jazz Singer, The
America (1980)
Hello Again (1980)
My Mammy (1921)
This Is A Very Special Day (1953)
Toot Toot Tootsie (1927)
Toot Toot Tootsie Goodbye (1927)
Jeffersons, The
Movin' On Up
Jennifer
Angel Eyes
Jeopardy
Jeopardy Theme
Jephtha
Deeper And Deeper Still
Farewell Ye Limpid Springs
First Perish Thou
For Ever Blessed
In Gentle Murmurs
Let Other Creatures Die

Jephtha *(Cont.)*
Pour Forth No More
Scenes Of Horror
Smiling Dawn, The
Twill Be A Painful Separation
Waft Her Angels
When His Loud Voice In Thunder
   Spoke
Jersey Lily, The
Bedelia
Jesu Nostra Redemptio
Ipsa Te Cogat Pietas
Jesus Christ Superstar
Herod's Song
I Don't Know How To Love Him
Jesus Christ Superstar
Superstar
Jewel Of The Nile, The
When The Going Gets Tough The
   Tough Get Going
Joan Of Arc
On To The Battle
Joan Rivers Show, The
Theme From The Joan Rivers Show
Joanie Loves Chachi
You Look At Me
Joanna
I'll Catch The Sun
Jocelyn
Berceuse
Lullaby
Johnny Angel
Memphis In June
Joker Is Wild, The
All The Way
Jolly Miller
Miller Of The Dee, The
Jolson Story, The
Anniversary Song
April Showers
Liza
**Joseph And The Amazing Technicolor
Dreamcoat**
Any Dream Will Do
Close Every Door
Joshua
Aria
Heroes When With Glory Burning
My Cup Is Full
O Hatt Ich Jubals Harf
Oh Had I Jubal's Lyre
See The Raging Flames Arise
Shall I In Mamre's Fertile Plain
Joy Of Living
Just Let Me Look At You
You Couldn't Be Cuter
Jubilee
Begin The Beguine
Just One Of Those Things
Kling-Kling Bird On Top Of The
   Divi-Divi Tree, The
Me And Marie
Picture Of Me Without You, A

Jubilee *(Cont.)*
When Love Comes Your Way
Why Shouldn't I
Judas Maccabaeus
Arm Arm Ye Brave
Come Ever Smiling Liberty
Father Of Heaven
Hallelujah Amen
How Vain Is Man
Lord Worketh Wonders, The
My Arms Against This Gorgias Will
   I Go
O Liberty Thy Choicest Treasure
O Lovely Peace
See The Conquering Hero Comes
Sound An Alarm
Thanks To My Brethren
Judd For The Defense
Theme From Judd For The Defense
Jugement De Midas
Du Destin Qui T'Accable
Jumbo
Little Girl Blue
Most Beautiful Girl In The World,
   The
My Romance
Jump For Joy
I Got It Bad And That Ain't Good
Jungle Book, The
Bare Necessities, The
I Wan'na Be Like You
Jungle Princess
Moonlight And Shadows
Juno
I Wish It So
My True Heart
Just For You
Zing A Little Zong
Karate Kid
Moment Of Truth
Karate Kid II
Glory Of Love
This Is The Time
Karate Kid III
Listen To Your Heart
Kate And Allie
Friends
Kate McShane
Kate McShane
Katinka
Allah's Holiday
Katinka
Rackety Coo
Kelly
I'll Never Go There Anymore
Kelly's Heroes
Burning Bridges
Kerry Gow
Handful Of Earth, A
Kill That Story
Two Cigarettes In The Dark
Kinderlieder
Fruhlings Aukunft

King And I, The
Getting To Know You
Hello Young Lovers
I Have Dreamed
I Whistle A Happy Tune
My Lord And My Master
Shall We Dance
We Kiss In A Shadow
King Arthur
Fairest Isle
Invitation
Shepherd Shepherd Leave Decoying
Two Daughters Of This Aged Stream
King Creole
Don't Ask Me Why
King Lear
Come Over The Born Bessy
King Of Burlesque
Spreadin' Rhythm Around
King Of Jazz, The
Happy Feet
King Olaf
As Torrents In Summer
Kings Crossing
King's Crossing
Kings Go Forth
Song From Kings Go Forth, The
Kismet
And This Is My Beloved
Baubles Bangles And Beads
Night Of My Nights
Sands Of Time
Stranger In Paradise
Kiss Me Kate
Another Op'nin' Another Show
   (Play)
Brush Up Your Shakespeare (Play)
From This Moment On (Movie)
So In Love (Play)
Wunderbar (Play)
Kittiwake Island
I'd Gladly Walk To Alaska
If Love's Like A Lark
When A Robin Leaves Chicago
Knickerbocker Holiday
It Never Was You
September Song
Knommt Dir Manchmal In Den Sinn
Do You Often Call To Mind
Knot's Landing
Knot's Landing
Kojak
Theme From Kojak
Kramer Vs. Kramer
Vivaldi Concerto In C Major
Kreuzzug, Der
Crusade, The
Crusaders
Kwamina
Nothing More To Look Forward To
What's Wrong With Me

Little Old New York
Little Old New York
Little Prince, The (Movie)
Little Prince
Little Shop Of Horrors
Prologue
Suddenly Seymour
Little Show, The
Can't We Be Friends
I Guess I'll Have To Change My
Plan
Moanin' Low
Little Tycoon Waltz, The
Love Comes Like A Summer Sigh
Little Whopper, The
We'll Build A Cute Little Nest
Liturgy Of St John Chrysostum
Cherubim Song
Live And Let Die
Live And Let Die
Live To Tell
Live To Tell
Load Of Coal
Honeysuckle Rose
Lohengrin
Armste, Du
Athmest Du Nicht
Bridal Chorus
Bridal March
Bridal Procession
Bridal Song
Du Armste
Einsam In Truben Tagen
Elsa's Dream
Elsas Gesang An Die Lufte
Elsas Traum
Euch Luften Die Mein Klagen
Faithful And True
Flag Of The Free
Fuhl Ich Zu Dir
Here Comes The Bride
I Give Thee Thanks
If He Returns
In Distant Land
In Fernem Land
King Of Kings
King's Prayer
Legend Of The Holy Grail, The
Lohengrin's Entrance
Mein Herr Und Gott
Nun Sei Bedankt
O King Of Kings
Rest Here With Me
Should He Return
Swan Song
When Thou Dost Gaze On Me
Ye Wand'ring Breezes
Long Hot Summer, The
Long Hot Summer, The
Long Voyage Home, The
Harbor Lights
Longest Day, The
Longest Day, The

Look Ma I'm Dancin'
I'm Not So Bright
Looney Tunes
Merry-Go-Round Broke Down, The
Lord Byron Of Broadway
Should I
Lord Is A Sun And Shield, The
Now Thank We All Our God
Lost In The Stars
Lost In The Stars
Stay Well
Lotario
Now Behold The Car Advances
Lottery
Main Title Theme From Lottery
Turn Of The Cards
Louisiana Purchase
It's A Lovely Day Tomorrow
Love Affair
Wishing
Love American Style
Love Amercian Style
Love Boat, The
Love Boat, The
Love Finds Andy Hardy
In-Between
Meet The Heat Of My Heart
Love In A Village
Gentle Youth Ah Tell Me Why
Love In The Afternoon
Fascination
Love Is A Many-Splendored Thing
Love Is A Many-Splendored Thing
Love Letters
Love Letters
Love Life
Green Up Time
Love Song
Love Me Or Leave Me
I'll Never Stop Loving You
Love Me Tender
Love Me Tender
Love Me Tonight
Isn't It Romantic
Lover
Mimi
Love Sidney
Friends Forever
Love Story
Love Story
Theme From Love Story
Where Do I Begin
Love's Labour's Lost
When Daisies Pied
When Daisies Pied And Violets
Lovely Griselda, The
Hawthorn Buds Are Springing, The
Lovely To Look At
Lovely To Look At
Lovers And Other Strangers
For All We Know
Loving You
Let Me Be Your Teddy Bear

Lucas Tanner
Theme From Lucas Tanner
Lucia Di Lammermoor
Ardon Gl'incensi
At Last I'm Thine
Chi Mi Frena
Dolce Suono Mi Colpi Mi Sua Voce,
Il
Ensanguined And Lurid
Finale
Hail Rosy Morn
Hail To The Happy Bridal Day
I Hear The Breathing
If Thou Plead'st
Sea, The
Sextet
Sextette
Thou Hast Spread Thy Wings To
Heaven
What From Vengeance Now
Restrains Me
What Restrains Me
When He Is Here
When Twlight Shadows
Where He But Here
Lucrezia Borgia
It Is Better To Laugh Than Be
Sighing
Lullaby Of Broadway
Lullaby Of Broadway
Lustigen Weiber
Arie Der Anna
Arie Der Frau Fluth
M*A*S*H
Song From M*A*S*H
Suicide Is Painless
M-Squad
Theme From M-Squad
Macgyver
Macgyver
Mack And Mabel
I Won't Send Roses
Time Heals Everything
Mad Max Beyond The Thunderdome
One Of The Living
We Don't Need Another Hero
Mad Show
Boy From..., The
Madama Butterfly
Bel Di Vedremo, Un
Entrata De Butterfly
Humming Chorus
Madame Sherry
Birth Of Passion, The
Madcap Duchess, The
Love Is A Story That's Old
Star Of Love
Madwoman Of Central Park
My New Friends
Magic Christian, The
Come And Get It
Magic Flute, The
(*see* **Zauberflote, Die**)

Magic Show, The
  Lion Tamer
  West End Avenue
Magician, The
  Theme From The Magician
Magnificat
  Freut Euch Und Jubilirt
  Gloria In Excelsis Deo
  Vom Himmel Hoch Da Komm Ich
    Her
Magnificent Seven, The
  Magnificent Seven, The
Mahmound
  Toll Toll The Knell
Mahogany
  Do You Know Where You're Going
    To
  Theme From Mahogany
Maid Of Pskov, The
  Cradle Song
Main Event, The
  Main Event, The
Main Street
  Meet Me Mamie On Main Street
Make A Wish
  Make A Wish
Make It Snappy
  Yes We Have No Bananas
Make Mine Music
  All The Cats Join In
Makin' Whoopee
  Love Me Or Leave Me
Making Love
  Making Love
Mame
  If He Walked Into My Life
  Mame
  We Need A Little Christmas
Man And A Woman, A
  Man And A Woman, A
Man Could Get Killed, A
  Strangers In The Night
Man From Snowy River, The
  Jessica's Theme
  Man From Snowy River, The
Man From UNCLE, The
  Theme From The Man From UNCLE
Man Of La Mancha
  Dulcinea
  Impossible Dream, The
  Man Of La Mancha
Man Who Knew Too Much, The
  Que Sera Sera
Man Who Loved Women, The
  Blackie's Tune
  Little Boys
Man Who Shot Libert Valance
  Man Who Shot Liberty Valance, The
Man Woman And Child
  Never Gone
Manhattan
  But Not For Me
  Do-Do-Do
  Embraceable You

Manhattan *(Cont.)*
  I've Got A Crush On You
  Oh Lady Be Good
  'S Wonderful
  Someone To Watch Over Me
Mannix
  Mannix
Manon
  Come Let's Obey
  Dream Song
  Gavotte
  Instant Charmant
  Reve, Le
Manon Lescaut
  Ora O Tirsi, L'
Many Loves Of Dobie Gillis
  Dobie
Marathon Man
  Theme From Marathon Man
Marcus Welby M.D.
  Theme From Marcus Welby M.D.
Marechal Ferrant, Le
  Brillant Dans Mon Emploi
Margie
  Margie
Marianne
  Just You Just Me
Mariano
  Slumbering In The Dusky Twilight
Maritana
  Ah Let Me Like A Soldier Fall
  In Happy Moments
  In Happy Moments Day By Day
  Scenes That Are Brightest
  Yes Let Me Like A Soldier Fall
Marjorie Morningstar
  Very Precious Love, A
Marriage Of Figaro, The
  (see **Nozze di Figaro, Le**)
Marriage Market, The
  You're Here And I'm Here
Martha
  Ah So Pure
  Dawn Of Peace, The
  Heav'n May To You Grant Pardon
  Heaven May To You Grant Pardon
  How So Fair
  Last Rose Of Summer, The
  Like A Dream
  M'appari
  Maidens Bright And Fair
  Night So Fair
  Nightingale, The
  O'er My Head
  Volkslied
Mary Hartman Mary Hartman
  Premiere Occasion
Mary Poppins
  Chim Chim Cher-Ee
  Feed The Birds Tuppence A Bag
  I Love To Laugh
  Jolly Holiday
  Let's Go Fly A Kite
  Spoonful Of Sugar, A

Mary Poppins *(Cont.)*
  Step In Time
  Supercalifragilisticexpialidocious
Mary Tyler Moore Show
  Love Is All Around
Masaniello
  Fishermen's Chorus
Mascot, The
  Coaching Song
  Gobble Duet
  Legend Of The Mascots
  Now All Is Safely Over
  When In Your Eyes I Look
Masque Of Comus
  Sweet Echo
Mass (Bernstein)
  I Go On
  Simple Song, A
Mass Ecce Sacerdos Magnus (Palestrina)
  Agnus Dei
Mass First In C (Mozart)
  Song Of Praise
Mass For Maundy Thursday
  (Traditional)
  Christus Factus Est
Mass In A-Flat (Schubert)
  Credo
Mass In B Minor (Bach)
  Crucifixus
  Cum Sancto Spiritu
Mass L'homme Aime (Ockeghem)
  Kyrie
Mass No. 1 Lux Et Origo
  Agnus Dei
  Gloria
  Kyrie
  Sanctus
Mass Quam Pulchri Sunt (Victoria)
  Kyrie
Mass VII (Lotti)
  Kyrie
Masterpiece Theatre
  Masterpiece, The
Matthaus-Passion
  Aus Liebe Will Mein Heiland
    Sterben
  Commit Thy Ways O Pilgrim
  Herzlich Thut Mich Verlangen
  Herzliebster Jesu Was Hast Du
    Verbrochen
  O Lord Do Not Forget Me
  O Welt Ich Muss Dich Lassen
  Werde Munter Mein Gemuthe
Matthew Passion
  (see **Matthaus-Passion**)
Maverick
  Maverick
Mavourneen
  Molly O
Maybe
  Maybe
Mayor
  Good Times
  Mayor

Maytime
  Road To Paradise, The
  Will You Remember
McCloud
  Theme From McCloud
McCoy
  Theme From McCoy
McMillan And Wife
  Theme From McMillan And Wife
Me And Juliet
  Big Black Giant, The
  I'm Your Girl
  No Other Love
  Very Special Day, A
Me And My Girl
  Lambeth Walk
  Leaning On A Lamp-Post
Me Natalie
  Natalie
  We
Measure For Measure
  Take O Take Those Lips Away
Meet Danny Wilson
  When You're Smiling
Meet Me In St Louis
  Boy Next Door, The
  Have Yourself A Merry Little
    Christmas
  Meet Me In St Louis Louis
  Trolley Song, The
Meistersinger Von Nurnberg, Die
  Awake
  Awake Draws Nigh The Break Of
    Day
  Chorale
  Prize Song
  Walter's Prize Song
Melancholy Knight, The
  Sir Eglamore
Melismata
  Remember O Thou Man
  Three Ravens, The
Melody For Two
  September In The Rain
Melody Time
  Blue Shadows On The Trail
  Lord Is Good To Me, The
Melusina
  In Bressilia's Forest Shade
Mentira, La
  Yellow Days
Merrily We Roll Along
  Good Thing Going
  Not A Day Goes By
  Our Time
Merry Widow, The
  I Love You So
  Merry Widow Waltz
  Study Of Woman, The
  Vilia
  Waltz Song
Meslanges, Les
  Good-Day Dear Heart
  Good-Day Sweetheart

Messe Solennelle
  Blessed Is He Who Cometh
  Lord God Omnipotent
  O Bread Of Life From Heaven
Messiah
  And The Glory Of The Lord
  Behold A Virgin Shall Conceive
  But Thou Didst Not Leave His Soul
    In Hell
  But Who May Abide The Day Of His
    Coming
  Come Unto Him
  Comfort Ye Comfort Ye My People
  Comfort Ye My People
  Er Weidet Seine Herde
  Ev'ry Valley Shall Be Exhalted
  Every Valley Shall Be Exalted
  For Unto Us A Child Is Born
  Hallelujah Chorus
  He Shall Feed His Flock
  He Was Despised
  He Was Despised And Rejected
  How Beautiful Are The Feet
  How Beautiful Are The Feet Of Him
  I Know That My Redeemer Liveth
  Ich Weiss Dass Mein Erloser Lebet
  If God Be For Us Who Can Be
    Against Us
  O Thou That Tellest
  Overture
  Pastoral Symphony
  People That Walked In Darkness,
    The
  Thus Saith The Lord
  Trumpet Shall Sound, The
  Why Do The Nations
  Wie Lieblich Ist Der Boten Schritt
Mexican Hayride
  I Love You
Miami Vice
  Evan
  Flashback
  Miami Vice
  Smuggler's Blues
  Vice
  You Belong To The City
Mickey Mouse Club
  Mickey Mouse Alma Mater
  Mickey Mouse Club March
  Mickey Mouse March, The
Mickey Mouse Disco
  Macho Duck
Mickey Spillane's Mike Hammer
  Harlem Nocturne
Midas
  In These Greasy Old Tatters His
    Charms Brighter Shine
  Jove In His Chair
  Lovely Nymph Assuage My Anguish
Midnight Cowboy
  Everybody's Talkin'
  Midnight Cowboy

Midnight Express
  Love's Theme
  Theme From Midnight Express
Midnight Rounders Of 1921
  Ma He's Making Eyes At Me
Midnight Suns, The
  I've Got Rings On My Fingers
Midsummer Night's Dream, A
  Fairies
  Nocturne
  Wedding March
Mighty Mouse
  Mighty Mouse Theme Song, The
Mignon
  Behold Titania
  Connais Tu Le Pays
  Dost Thou Know That Sweet Land
  I Am Titania
  Je Suis Titania
  Know'st Thou That Fair Land
  Know'st Thou Yonder Land
  Knowest Thou That Dear Land
  Me Voici Dans Son Boudoir
Mikado, The
  Alone And Yet Alive
  As Some Day It May Happen
  At The Crossroads
  Behold The Lord High Executioner
  Braid The Raven Hair
  Brightly Dawns Our Wedding Day
  Choruses From The Mikado
  Criminal Cried, The
  Entrance Of Mikado
  Flowers That Bloom In The Spring,
    The
  For He's Going To Marry Yum-Yum
  From Every Kind Of Man
  He's Going To Marry Yum-Yum
  Here's A How-De-Do
  Humane Mikado, A
  I've Got A Little List
  If You Want To Know Who We Are
  Lord High Executioner, The
  Merry Madrigal, A
  Mi-Ya Sa-Ma
  Miya Sama
  Moon And I, The
  My Object All Sublime
  On A Tree By A River
  Proper Pride
  So Please You Sir
  Speculation
  Sun Whose Rays, The
  Taken From The County Jail
  There Is Beauty In The Bellow Of
    The Blast
  They'll None Of Them Be Missed
  Three Little Maids
  Three Little Maids From School
  Tit Willow
  Tit-Willow
  Wand'ring Minstrel, A

Mikado, The *(Cont.)*
Wand'ring Minstrel I, A
Wandering Minstrel, A
Were You Not To Koko Plighted
Willow Tit-Willow
With Joyous Shout
Milk And Honey
Milk And Honey
Shalom
Million Dollar Baby
I Found A Million Dollar Baby In A
Five And Ten Cent Store
Millions D'Arlequin, Les
Serenade
Millions Of Harlequin, The
(*see* **Millions D'Arlequin, Les**)
Minuet In G
In Autumn
Miss 1917
Go Little Boat
Miss Chicken Little
Don't Deny
It's A Fine Day For Walkin' Country
Style
Miss Dolly Dollars
Woman Is Only A Woman, A
Miss Jones
Miss Jones
Miss Liberty
You Can Have Him
Miss Molly Dollars
Good Cigar Is A Smoke, A
Missing
Missing
Mission, The
Mission Theme, The
Mission Impossible
Mission Impossible Theme
Mississippi
Down By The River
It's Easy To Remember
Mississippi Suite
Mardi Gras
Mister Ed
Mister Ed
Mister Roger's Neighborhood
Won't You Be My Neighbor
Mlle Modiste
I Want What I Want When I Want It
If I Were On The Stage
Kiss Me Again
Mod Squad, The
Mod Squad, The
Modern Times
Smile
Molly Maguires, The
Theme Song From The Molly
Maguires
Mommie Dearest
Mommie Dearest
Theme From Mommie Dearest
Mondo Cane
More

Moneychangers, The
Love Theme From The
Moneychangers
Monkees, The
Monkees, The
Theme From The Monkees
Monroes, The
Theme From The Monroes
Monte Carlo
Beyond The Blue Horizon
Moo-Lee Chwa
Moo-Lee Flower, The
Moonlighting
Moonlighting
Moonstruck
That's Amore
Mork And Mindy
Mork And Mindy Theme
Theme From Mork And Mindy
Morris Gest Midnight Whirl
Limehouse Nights
Poppyland
Mort De Jeanne D'Arc, La
Arioso
Moscow On The Hudson
Freedom
People Up In Texas
Most Happy Fella, The
Abbondanza
Big D
Don't Cry
Happy To Make Your Acquaintance
I Like Ev'rybody
Joey Joey Joey
Most Happy Fella, The
My Heart Is So Full Of You
Somebody Somewhere
Standing On The Corner
Warm All Over
Moulin Rouge
Boulevard Of Broken Dreams, The
Coffee In The Morning
Song From Moulin Rouge, The
Mount Of Olives
Hallelujah Chorus
O Triumph All Ye Ransom'd
Mountaineers, The
Wayworn Traveller, The
Mr Bug Goes To Town
I'll Dance At Your Wedding Honey
Dear
We're The Couple In The Castle
Mr Dodd Takes The Air
Am I In Love
Remember Me
Mr Imperium
Andiamo
Mr Lucky
Mr Lucky
Softly
Mr Wonderful
Mr Wonderful
Too Close For Comfort

Mulligan Guard Ball, The
Babies On Our Block, The
Mulligan Guard Pic-Nic
Mary Kelly's Beau
Mum's The Word
River Stay 'Way From My Door
Mummy Monarch, The
I'm Saving A Place For You
Muppet Movie, The
Rainbow Connection, The
Muppet Show, The
Muppet Show Theme, The
Murder At The Vanities (Movie)
Cocktails For Two
Murder On The Orient Express
Orient Express, The
Murray Anderson's Almanac (1929)
I May Be Wrong
Musette, La
Musette, The
Music In My Heart (Movie)
It's A Blue World
Music In The Air
I've Told Ev'ry Little Star
In Egern On The Tegern See
Song Is You, The
Music Man, The
Goodnight My Someone
Lida Rose
Seventy Six Trombones
Till There Was You
Ya Got Trouble
Musical Lady
Cease Ye Fountains Cease To
Murmur
Mutiny On The Bounty (1963)
Love Song From Mutiny On The
Bounty
My Blue Heaven
Halloween
I Love A New Yorker
My Dad Can't Be Crazy Can He
Theme From My Dad Can't Be
Crazy Can He
My Dream Is Yours
My Dream Is Yours
My Fair Lady
Get Me To The Church On Time
I Could Have Danced All Night
I've Grown Accustomed To Her
Face
Just You Wait
On The Street Where You Live
Rain In Spain, The
Show Me
With A Little Bit Of Luck
Without You
Wouldn't It Be Loverly
My Foolish Heart
My Foolish Heart
My Last Farewell
My Dreams

My Maryland
Mother
Silver Moon
Your Land And My Land
My Mother The Car
My Mother The Car
My Sister Sam
Room Enough For Two
My Stepmother Is An Alien
Room To Move
My Two Dads
You Can Count On Me
Myles Aroon
Live My Love Oh Live
My Maggie
Scanlan's Swing Song
Myrthen
Im Westen
Mein Herz Ist Schwer
Nussbaum, Der
Widmung
Mystery Of Edwin Drood, The
Moonfall
There You Are
Nabucco
Chorus Of The Hebrew Captives
Naked City
New Naked City Theme
Naked Gun, The
Theme From The Naked Gun From
The Files Of Police Squad
Name Of The Game
Theme From Name Of The Game
Napoleon Passes
You Know Who
Nashville
I'm Easy
National Lampoon's Vacation
Holiday Road
National Velvet (Television)
Theme From National Velvet
Natoma
Dagger Dance
Natural, The
Natural, The
Naughty Marietta
Ah Sweet Mystery Of Life
Dance Of The Marionettes
I'm Falling In Love With Someone
Italian Street Song
Naughty Marietta
'Neath The Southern Moon
Tramp Tramp Tramp
NBC News
Mission Theme, The
NBC Theme
Olympic Spirit, The
Neptune's Daughter
Baby It's Cold Outside
Nero Wolfe
Nero Wolfe
Nervous Set, The
Ballad Of The Sad Young Men

Neverending Story, The
Neverending Story
Never On Sunday
Never On Sunday
New Gidget, The
One In A Million
New Girl In Town
If That Was Love
It's Good To Be Alive
Sunshine Girl
New Life, A
Theme From A New Life
New Moon, The
Girl On The Prow, The
Lover Come Back To Me
Marianne
One Kiss
Softly As In A Morning Sunrise
Stouthearted Men
Wanting You
New World Symphony
Massa Dear
Requiem For Yesterday
New York New York
But The World Goes 'Round
Do Nothin' Till You Hear From Me
Don't Get Around Much Anymore
Happy Ending
Theme From New York New York
There Goes The Ball Game
You Are My Lucky Star
New Yorkers, The (1930)
Great Indoors, The
I Happen To Like New York
I'm Getting Myself Ready For You
Love For Sale
Take Me Back To Manhattan
Where Have You Been
Newhart
Newhart
Nicholas And Alexandra
Nicholas And Alexandra
Theme From Nicholas And
Alexandra
Too Beautiful To Last
Night And Day
Begin The Beguine
Just One Of Those Things
Let's Do It Let's Fall In Love
Night And Day
What Is This Thing Called Love
Night At The Opera, A
Alone
Cosi Cosa
Night In Heaven, A
Heaven
Night Is Young, The
When I Grow Too Old To Dream
Night Shift
That's What Friends Are For
Night Song
Who Killed 'er
Nina
Quand Le Bien-Aime Reviendra

Nine
Be On Your Own
Unusual Way
Nine O'Clock Revue, The (1931)
Penthouse Serenade
Niobe
Beneath The Ocean's Swelling Wave
No No Nanette
I Want To Be Happy
No No Nanette
Tea For Two
No Small Affair
Love Makes You Blind
No Strings
Sweetest Sounds, The
Nobody's Perfekt
Nobody's Perfekt
Norma
Arie Der Norma
Casta Diva
Chaste Enchantress
Flowers For The Brave
Lady Awake
Norma Rae
It Goes Like It Goes
North And South
North And South
Norwood
I'll Paint You A Song
Not As A Stranger
Not As A Stranger
Now Like The Holy Host
Cherubic Hymn
Now Voyager
It Can't Be Wrong
Nozze Di Figaro, Le
Cherubino's Song
Deh Vieni No Tardar
Dove Sono
Endlich Naht Sich Die Stunde
Hor Mein Flehn
Ich Weiss Nicht Wo Ich Bin Was Ich
Tue
In The Army
Non So Piu
Porgi Amor
Sagt Holde Frauen
Silently Blending
Tell Me O Fair Ones
Voi Che Sapete
What Is This Splendor
Wohin Flohen Die Wonndestunden
Ye Who Love's Power
Nutcracker
Dance Of The Sugar Plum Fairy
Waltz Of The Flowers
O Come Let Us Sing
O Come Let Us Worship
Oberon
Arabien Mein Heimatland
Ozean Du Ungeheuer
Obispah
Wine And Woman

Occasional Oratorio
Then Will I Jehovah's Praise
Octopussy
All Time High
Odd Couple, The
Odd Couple, The
Odessa File, The
Christmas Dream
Oedipe A Colonne
Dieux Ce N'est Pas Pour Moi
Elle M'a Prodigue Sa Tendresse
Of Thee I Sing
Because Because
Love Is Sweeping The Country
Of Thee I Sing
Who Cares
Wintergreen For President
Officer And A Gentleman, An
Up Where We Belong
Oh Boy
Old-Fashioned Wife, An
Till The Clouds Roll By
Oh Calcutta
Ballerina
I Like The Look
Oh God
Theme From Oh God
Oh Kay
Clap Yo' Hands
Do Do Do
Fidgety Feet
Maybe
Oh Kay
Someone To Watch Over Me
Oh Please
I Know That You Know
Oies De Frere Philippe, Les
Je Sais Attacher Des Rubans
Ojello
Ave Maria
Oklahoma
I Cain't Say No
Lonely Room
Many A New Day
Oh What A Beautiful Mornin'
Oklahoma
People Will Say We're In Love
Pore Jud
Surrey With The Fringe On Top, The
Oklahoma Crude
Oklahoma Crude
Send A Little Love My Way
Oliver
As Long As He Needs Me
Consider Yourself
I'd Do Anything
Oliver
Where Is Love
Who Will Buy
Olivette
All On Account Of Eliza
Bob Up Serenely
Torpedo And The Whale, The

On A Clear Day You Can See Forever
Come Back To Me
Hurry It's Lovely Up Here
Love With All The Trimmings
(Movie)
Melinda
On A Clear Day You Can See
Forever
On The SS Bernard Cohn
She Wasn't You
Wait Till We're Sixty-Five
What Did I Have That I Don't Have
On The Avenue
He Ain't Got Rhythm
I've Got My Love To Keep Me
Warm
On The Town
Carried Away
I Can Cook Too
I Feel Like I'm Not Out Of Bed Yet
Lonely Town
Lucky To Be Me
New York New York
On The Town (Movie)
Some Other Time
You're Awful (Movie)
On The Twentieth Century
I Rise Again
On The Twentieth Century
Our Private World
On With The Show (Movie)
Am I Blue
On Your Toes (Play)
Heart Is Quicker Than The Eye, The
There's A Small Hotel
Once In A Hundred Years
I Like To Flop In The Waves That
Slop
Once Is Not Enough
Once Is Not Enough
Once Over Lightly
Just Because
Once Upon A Mattress
Yesterday I Loved You
Once Upon A Time In America
Once Upon A Time In America
Theme From Once Upon A Time In
America
One Day At A Time
One Day At A Time
One Flew Over The Cuckoo's Nest
One Flew Over The Cuckoo's Nest
One Life To Live
One Life To Live
One Minute To Zero
When I Fall In Love
One Night In The Tropics
Remind Me
One On One
My Fair Share
One Touch Of Venus
Speak Low

One-Trick Pony
Late In The Evening
One-Trick Pony
Only A Rose
Only A Rose
Only Girl, The
When You're Away
When You're Wearing The Ball And
Chain
Only When I Laugh
Only When I Laugh
Open House
Theme From Open House
Open The Door And See All The People
I See It Now
Love Is When
Mimosa And Me
Remember My Child
Such A Lonely Girl Am I
That's My Girl
Unbelievable
Operette
Dearest Love
Orange Blossoms
Kiss In The Dark, A
Orchestra Wives
At Last
I've Got A Gal In Kalamazoo
Serenade In Blue
Ordinary People
Theme From Ordinary People
Orelgroschenoper, Der
Mack The Knife
Orfeo (Gluck)
Che Faro
Che Faro Senza Euridice
From The Realm Of Souls Departed
I Have Lost My Euridice
I Have Lost My Eurydice
If Here Where All Is Dark And
Silent
Orphee Dux Enfers (Offenbach)
Can Can
Otello
Assisa Aun Pie D'Un Salice
Ave Maria
Deh Calma O Ciel
Othello
And Let Me The Canakin Clink
Other Side Of Midnight
Noelle's Theme
Our House
Our House
Our Nell
Innocent Ingenue Baby
Walking Home With Angeline
Our Town
Impatient Years, The
Look To Your Heart
Love And Marriage
Our Town
Out Of Africa
Music Of Goodbye, The

Out Of This World
From This Moment On (Play)
I Am Loved (Play)
June Comes Around Every Year
(Movie)
Out Of This World (Movie)
Use Your Imagination (Play)
Where Oh Where (Play)
You Don't Remind Me (Play)
Over The Top
Meet Me Half Way
Winner Takes It All
Pacific Overtures
Pretty Lady
Pagan, The
Pagan Love Song
Pageant Of The Holy Nativity, The
To Bethlehem
Pagliacci, I
Arioso
E Allor Perche
Guarda Amor Mio
Mattinata
O Colombina
Recitar
Serenade
Si Puo
Stridono Lassu
Vesti La Giubba
Paint Your Wagon
Another Autumn
I Still See Elisa
I Talk To The Trees
They Call The Wind Maria
Wandrin' Star
Pajama Game
Hernando's Hideaway
Hey There
I'm Not At All In Love
Small Talk
Steam Heat
Pal Joey
Bewitched
I Could Write A Book
Lady Is A Tramp, The
Zip
Palais Royal Revue
Thank You For A Lovely Day
Paleface
Buttons And Bows
Panama Hattie
I've Still Got My Health
Let's Be Buddies
Make It Another Old Fashioned
Please
Papa's Delicate Condition
Call Me Irresponsible
Paper Chase
I Want To Spend My Life With You
Papillon
Free As The Wind
Paradise Lost
Chorus Of Seraphim

Pardon De Ploermel, Le
Light-Flitting Shadow
Pardon My English
Isn't It A Pity
Lorelei
My Cousin In Milwaukee
Parent Trap, The
Let's Get Together
Paride Ed Elena
O Del Mio Doce Ardor
Paris
Don't Look At Me That Way
Let's Do It Let's Fall In Love
Let's Misbehave
Paris And Helen
Beloved Strand
Thou Art My Dear Beloved
Paris In Spring
Paris In The Spring
Parisian Model, The
It's Delightful To Be Married
Park Avenue Fantasy
Stairway To The Stars
Partridge Family, The
Come On Get Happy
Party, The
Nothing To Lose
Pary Satis
Nightingale And The Rose, The
Pasblavem
Go Lovely Rose
Passing Show
I'm Forever Blowing Bubbles
Passing Show, The
Old Before His Time
Passing Show Of 1912, The
Ragtime Jockey Man, The
Passing Show Of 1916, The
Pretty Baby
Passing Show Of 1918, The
Smiles
Passing Show Of 1922, The
Carolina In The Morning
Patience
Aesthete, The
After Much Debate Internal
Am I Alone And Unobserved
Coming Bye And Bye, The
Finale
I Cannot Tell
I Cannot Tell What Love May Be
I Cannot Tell What This Love May
Be
I Hear The Soft Note
If You Want A Receipt
If You're Anxious For To Shine
Love Is A Plaintive Song
Magnet And The Churn, The
Magnet Hung In A Hardware Shop,
A
Oh List While We A Love Confess
Prithee Pretty Maiden
Sad Is That Woman's Lot

Patience (Cont.)
Silver'd Is The Raven Hair
Silvered Is The Raven Hair
So Go To Him
Twenty Love Sick Maidens We
Waterloo House Young Man, A
When I First Put This Uniform On
When I Go Out Of Door
Patron, The
How Stands The Glass Around
Patton
Patton Theme, The
Patty Duke Show, The
Patty Duke Theme, The
Peaceable Kingdom
Peaceable Kingdom Theme
Peanuts
Linus And Lucy
Pearl Fishers, The
Notte Di Carezze
Romance De Nadir
Peasant Cantata, The
Bagpipe Chorus
Come Sing With Us
Where The Bagpipes Play
Pecheurs De Perles
Romance
Peer Gynt
Morning
Solvejg's Song
Peggy Sue Got Married
He Don't Love You Like I Love You
Pennies From Heaven
Pennies From Heaven
Per Lontananza Di Donna Crudele
Bela Dea
Perfect Strangers
Nothing's Gonna Stop Me Now
Peri, The
Home Of My Youth
Thoughts That Have For Years Been
Sleeping
Perichole, La
Tu N'est Pas Beau
Perils Of Pauline, The
I Wish I Didn't Love You So Much
Perle Du Bresil, La
Charmant Oiseau
Delightful Bird
Perry Mason
Perry Mason Theme
Pete's Dragon
Candle On The Water
It's Not Easy
Peter Gunn
Brothers Go To Mother's, The
Dreamsville
Joanna
Little Man Theme, The
Peter Gunn
Timothy

Presidio, The
Theme From The Presidio
Pretty In Pink
If You Leave
Pretty In Pink
Pretty Woman
King Of Wishful Thinking
Prettybelle
To A Small Degree
Prime Of Miss Jean Brodie, The
Jean
Primerose
Quand De La Nuit Le Voile Tutelaire
Prince Igor
Prince Igor's Song
Song Of The Slave Girls
Summer Star
Prince Of Pilsen, The
Heidelberg
Message Of The Violet, The
Prince Of Tonight, The
I Wonder Who's Kissing Her Now
Princess, The
Sweet And Low
Princess Bride, The
Storybook Love
Princess Ida
Ape And The Lady, The
Baffled Grumbler, The
Come Mighty Must
Expressive Glances
Girl Graduates
I Am A Maiden
Ida Was A Twelvemonth Old
If You Give Me Your Attention
Lady Fair, A
Lady Fair Of Lineage High, A
Merrily Ring The Luncheon Bell
Mighty Must, The
Now Hearken To My Strict
Command
Oh Goddess Wise
This Helmet I Suppose
We Are Warriors Three
Whene'er I Spoke
Whom Thou Hast Chained
With Joy Abiding
Woman Of The Wisest Wit, The
Would You Know
Would You Know The Kind Of Maid
Princess Pat
All For You
Love Is The Best Of All
Neapolitan Love Song
Princesse D'Elide, La
Ariette De La Princesse D'Elide
Princesse Endormie, La
Sleeping Princess, The
Prinz Methusalem
Bell Song
Prisonnier, Le
Oh Ciel Dois-Je En Croire Mes Yeux
Private Buckaroo
Don't Sit Under The Apple Tree

Private Lives
Someday I'll Find You
Private's Affair, A
Warm And Willing
Prizefighter And The Lady
You've Got Ev'rything
Promenade
Promenade Theme
Promises Promises
I'll Never Fall In Love Again
Promises Promises
Whoever You Are I Love You
Prophete, Le
Ah My Son
Provincetown Follies
Red Sails In The Sunset
Pskovitianka
River Of Sleep
Punky Brewster
Every Time I Turn Around
Puritani, I
Lauriger Horatius
O Rendetemi La Speme
Son Vergin Vezzosa
Vien Diletto
Purple Rain
Purple Rain
When Doves Cry
Pyrrhus And Demetrius
Fortune
Quare Fella, The
Oul' Triangle, The
Quark
Theme From Quark
Queen's Lace Handkerchief, The
Hail To Our Monarch
Truffles
Truffle Song, The
Wild Roses
Wild Rose Song
Quicksilver
One Sunny Day
Quiero Llenarme De Ti
Greatest Performance Of My Life,
The
Quo Vadis
Lygia
Racing With The Moon
Theme From Racing With The Moon
Radamisto
Shade Departed
Vessel Storm Driven, The
Raiders Of The Lost Ark
Marion's Theme
Raiders March
Raisin
He Come Down This Morning
Man Say
Measure The Valleys
Whole Lotta Sunlight, A
Whose Little Angry Man
Rambo
Peace In Our Life

Rambo First Blood Part II
Peace In Our Life
Raoul De Crequi
Jour Lisette Allait Au Champ, Un
Rascal
Summer Sweet
Ratto Di Proserpina, Il
Lieti Fiori Ombrose Piante
Razor's Edge, The
Mam'selle
Ready Willing And Able
Too Marvelous For Words
Real McCoys, The
Real McCoys, The
Rebecca
Chorus Of Camel-Drivers
Rebel Without A Cause
Theme From Rebel Without A Cause
Red Hot And Blue
Down In The Depths On The
Ninetieth Floor
Goodbye Little Dream Goodbye
It's De Lovely
Ours
Ridin' High
Red Mill, The
Because You're You
Every Day Is Ladies' Day With Me
In Old New York
Isle Of Our Dreams, The
Moonbeams
Streets Of New York, The
When You're Pretty And The World
Is Fair
Redemption, The
Lovely Appear
Unfold Ye Portals
Redhead
'Erbie Fitch's Twitch
My Girl Is Just Enough Woman For
Me
Reds
Goodbye For Now
Reilly Ace Of Spies
Reilly
Reilly And The 400
Maggie Murphy's Home
Remington Steele
Remington Steele
Theme For Laura
Renaud
Barbare Amour
Requiem
Pie Jesu
Requiem Mass
Sanctus
Rescuers, The
Someone's Waiting For You
Return Of The Jedi
Emperor, The
Ewok Celebration
Forest Battle, The
Han Solo Returns

Return Of The Jedi *(Cont.)*
Lapti Nek
Luke And Leia
Parade Of The Ewoks
Return Of The Pink Panther
Greatest Gift, The
Reuben Reuben
Hills Of Amalfi, The
Revenge Of The Nerds II
Back To Paradise
Revenge With Music
You And The Night And The Music
Rhapsody In Blue
American In Paris, An
But Not For Me
Embraceable You
Rhinestone
Tennessee Homesick Blues
Rhythm On The Range
I'm An Old Cowhand From The Rio
Grande
Rhythm On The River
Only Forever
Rhythmania
Between The Devil And The Deep
Blue Sea
Rich Man Poor Man
Theme From Rich Man Poor Man
Rich Young And Pretty
Wonder Why
Richard Boone Show, The
How Soon
Richard Coeur De Lion
Danse N'est Pas Ce Que J'aime, La
Fievre Brulante, Une
Je Crains De Lui Parler La Nuit
Ride 'em Cowboy (1942)
I'll Remember April
Right Stuff, The
Right Stuff, The
Right This Way
I Can Dream Can't I
I'll Be Seeing You
Rigoletto
Ah Why Recall
Bella Figlia Dell'amore
Caro Nome
Carved Upon My Heart
Donna E Mobile, La
Emerald Isle
Ev'ry Flower
Fairest Daughter Of The Graces
Over The Summer Sea
Thou Art A Mystery
We Are Equal
Woman Is Fickle
Rinaldo
Lascia Ch'io Pianga
Lass Mich Mit Tranen
Leave Me In Sorrow
Ring Up The Curtain
Are You There Moriarity

Rink, The
After All These Years
Marry Me
We Can Make It
Rio Bravo
Rio Bravo
Rip Van Winkle
Who Are All These Folks I See
Ripley's Believe It Or Not
Theme From Ripley's Believe It Or
Not
Riptide
Riptide
River Rat
Billy's Home
Boat, The
Halfway Right
In One Ear
Maybe Next Time
Murder, The
River's Song, The
Rock On The Bayou
Take No Prisoners
Wherever You Are
Road House
Again
Road To Hong Kong, The
Let's Not Be Sensible
Teamwork
Warmer Than A Whisper
Road To Morocco, The
Moonlight Becomes You
Road To Morocco, The
Road To Rio, The
But Beautiful
Road To Utopia
Personality
**Roar Of The Greasepaint The Smell Of
The Crowd, The**
Feeling Good
Joker, The
Look At That Face
Nothing Can Stop Me Now
Who Can I Turn To When Nobody
Needs Me
Wonderful Day Like Today, A
Robe, The
Love Theme From The Robe
Roberta
I Won't Dance (Movie)
Lovely To Look At (Movie)
Smoke Gets In Your Eyes (Play)
Touch Of Your Hand, The (Play)
Yesterdays (Movie)
Robin And The 7 Hoods
My Kind Of Town Chicago Is
Style
Robin Hood
Love
Oo-De-Lally
Song Of The Brown October Ale
Tinkers' Song
Robinson Crusoe Jr
Yacka Hula Hickey Dula

Rockford Files, The
Theme From The Rockford Files
Rocky
Gonna Fly Now
Rocky II
Redemption
Rocky III
Eye Of The Tiger
Rocky IV
Burning Heart
Double Or Nothing
Living In America
Rodelinda
Art Thou Troubled
Dove Sei
Dove Sei Amato Bene
Where Now Art Thou My Own
Beloved One
With Mournful Sounds Of Weeping
Rodrigo
Heard The Command And I Obey
When Golden Sunbeams
Roi Et Le Fermier, Le
Ce N'est Qu'ici Ce N'est Qu'au
Village
Il Regardait Mon Bouquet
Non Vous Ne M'Avez Jamais
Traitee Ainsi
Roi Malgre Lui, Le
Fete Polonaise
Roland
Je Mourrai
Romance Of Athlone, A
My Wild Irish Rose
Romance On The High Seas
It's Magic
It's You Or No One
Put 'em In A Box Tie 'em With A
Ribbon
Put 'em In A Box Tie 'em With A
Ribbon And Throw 'Em In The
Deep Blue Sea
Romantic Comedy
Maybe
Rome Adventure
Al Di La
Rome Adventure
Romeo And Juliet
Romeo And Juliet
Time For Us, A
Romeo Et Juliette
Ah Je Veux Vivre
Cavatina
J'aimerai Toute Ma Vie
Song Jest Perfume And Dances
Waltz Song
Room 222
Theme From Room 222
Roots
Roots
Rosalie
How Long Has This Been Going On
In The Still Of The Night (Movie)
Rosalie

Show Is On, The
By Strauss
Little Old Lady
Shuffle Along
I'm Just Wild About Harry
Siehe Es Hat Uberwunden Der Lowe
Wo Gott Der Herr Nicht Bei Uns
Halt Bach
Sierra
Theme From Sierra
Silk Stockings
All Of You
As On Through The Seasons We Sail
Paris Loves Lovers
Silk Stockings
Stereophonic Sound
Silver Spoons
Together
Together Theme From Silver Spoons
Silverado
Main Theme From Silverado
Simple Simon
Cottage In The Country That's The
Thing, A
Dancing On The Ceiling
Ten Cents A Dance
Sinbad
Rock-A-Bye Your Baby With A Dixie
Melody
Swanee
Since You Went Away
Together
Sing
Birthday Suit
Romance
Sing
Singin' In The Rain
Fit As A Fiddle
Make 'em Laugh
Singin' In The Rain
Singing Fool, The
I'm Sitting On Top Of The World
Singing Kid, The
You're The Cure For What Ails Me
Singing Marine, The
I Know Now
Singing Nun, The
Dominique
Singing Pilgrim
Home Of The Soul
Sinner Take All
I'd Be Lost Without You
Sitting Pretty
Did You Ever See A Dream Walking
Six Million Dollar Man, The
Theme From Six Million Dollar Man
Six Pack
Love Will Turn You Around
Skidmore Fancy Ball, The
Babies On Our Block, The
Sky's The Limit, The
My Shining Hour
One For My Baby

Sky's The Limit, The *(Cont.)*
One For My Baby And One More
For The Road
Skyscraper
Ev'rybody Has The Right To Be
Wrong
Ev'rybody Has The Right To Be
Wrong At Least Once
I'll Only Miss Her When I Think Of
Her
Opposites
Sleepers Awake
(*see* **Wachet Auf** [Bach])
Sleeping Beauty
I Wonder
Once Upon A Dream
Sleeping Beauty Waltz
Sleeping Beauty And The Beast, The
Rip Van Winkle Was A Lucky Man
Smiles
Time On My Hands
Time On My Hands You In My
Arms
Smiling Lieutenant, The
While Hearts Are Singing
Smothers Brothers Comedy
Brothers' Theme, The
Snegourotchka
Song Of The Shepherd Lehl
Snoopy
Just One Person
Snow White And The Seven Dwarfs
Heigh Ho Heigh Ho
Heigh-Ho
I'm Wishing
One Song
Silly Song
Someday My Prince Will Come
Whistle While You Work
With A Smile And A Song
So Dear To My Heart
Lavender Blue
Lavender Blue Dilly Dilly
Soap
Theme From Soap, The
Society Circus, A
Moon Dear
Soldier In The Rain
Soldier In The Rain
Solid Gold
Solid Gold
Solomon
What Though I Trace
What Though I Trace Each Herb
And Flower
With Thee Th' Unsheltered Moor I'd
Tread
Some Came Running
Song From Some Came Running
To Love And Be Loved

Some Like It Hot
I Wanna Be Loved By You
Lady's In Love With You, The
Stairway To The Stars
Someone In April
It's Time For A Love Song
One More Walk Around The Garden
Something For The Boys
Could It Be You
I'm In Love With A Soldier Boy
Something To Shout About
You'd Be So Nice To Come Home
To
Sometimes A Great Notion
All His Children
Somewhere In Time
Somewhere In Time
Son Of Paleface
Am I In Love
Son The Highest
He Shall Be Great
Song And Dance
Last Man In My Life, The
Take That Look Off Your Face
Take That Look Off Your Face
Reprise
Tell Me On A Sunday
Unexpected Song
Song Is Born, A
Heart And Soul
Song Of Norway
Strange Music
Song Of The Flame
Signal, The
Song Of The Flame
Song Of The South
Zip-A-Dee-Doo-Dah
Songwriter, The
Songwriter
Sonnambula, La
Ah Must Ye Fade
Ah Non Credea Mirarti
Ah Non Credea Mirarti Ah Non
Giunge
Gentle Maiden
Oh Recall Not
Sophie's Choice
Theme From Sophie's Choice
Sophisticated Ladies
It Don't Mean A Thing
It Don't Mean A Thing If It Ain't
Got That Swing
Mood Indigo
Perdido
Satin Doll
Solitude
Sophisticated Lady
Take The A Train
Sorcerer, The
Alas That Lovers Thus Should Meet
Dear Friends Take Pity
Dear Friends Take Pity On My Lot
Eheu Fugaces
For Love Alone

Sorcerer, The (Cont.)
Happy Young Hearts
It Is Not Love
Minuet
My Name Is John Wellington Wells
Now To The Banquet We Press
Ring Forth Ye Bells
Sorcerer's Song, The
Time Was When Love And I
Welcome Joy Adieu To Sadness
When He Is Here
Sosarme
Grace Thy Fair Brow
Sound Of Music, The
Climb Ev'ry Mountain
Do-Re-Mi
Edelweiss (Movie)
My Favorite Things
Sound Of Music, The
Wedding Processional (Movie)
Source, La
Regrets
South American Way
South American Way
South Pacific
Bali Ha'i
Cock-Eyed Optimist, A
Happy Talk
Honey Bun
Some Enchanted Evening
There Is Nothing Like A Dame
This Nearly Was Mine
Wonderful Guy, A
Younger Than Springtime
Space 1999
Theme From Space 1999
Space Hunter Adventures In The Forbidden Zone
Space Hunter Adventures In The Forbidden Zone
Spanish Blades
Day After Day
Spanish Student, The
Stars Of The Summer Night
Spenser For Hire
Spenser For Hire Theme
Spice Of 1922
Way Down Yonder In New Orleans
Splash
Love Came For Me
Splashdance
Happy Birthday
Splendor In The Grass
Theme From Splendor In The Grass
Spring Break
Spring Break
Spring Is Here
Have A Little Faith In Me (Movie)
Spring Is Here
With A Song In My Heart
Springtime In The Rockies (1942)
I Had The Craziest Dream
I Had The Craziest Dream Last Night

Spy Who Loved Me, The
Nobody Does It Better
Squatter Sovereignty
Paddy Duffy's Cart
Widow Nolan's Goat, The
St Elmo's Fire
Love Theme From St Elmo's Fire
St Elmo's Fire
St Elsewhere
St Elsewhere
St John Passion
Christus Der Uns Selig Macht
Jesu Leiden Pein Und Tod
Mach's Mit Mir Gott Nach Deiner Gut
Thy Will O Lord Be Done
Valet Will Ich Dir Geben
Vater Unser Im Himmelreich
St Louis Woman
Any Place I Hang My Hat Is Home
Come Rain Or Come Shine
I Had Myself A True Love
I Wonder What Became Of Me
Legalize My Name
Lullaby
Woman's Prerogative, A
St Matthew Passion
(see **Matthaus-Passion**)
St Patrick's Breastplate
Christ Beside Me
St Paul
But The Lord Is Mindful
But The Lord Is Mindful Of His Own
How Lovely Are The Messengers
Jerusalem Thou That Killest The Prophets
Stabat Mater
Cuius Animam
Inflammatus
Saviour Breathe Forgiveness O'Er Me
When To Danger Duty Calls Me
Stage Struck
Fancy Meeting You
Stags At Bay
East Of The Sun
East Of The Sun And West Of The Moon
East Of The Sun West Of The Moon
Stand By Me
Book Of Love
Everyday
Stand By Me
Star Is Born, A
Born In A Trunk (1954)
Evergreen (1976)
I Believe In Love (1976)
Lose That Long Face (1954)
Man That Got Away, The (1954)
Swanee (1954)
Star Search
Theme From Star Search

Star Spangled Rhythm
Hit The Road To Dreamland
That Old Black Magic
Star Trek
Star Trek
Theme From Star Trek
Star Trek II The Wrath Of Kahn
Main Theme From Star Trek II
Wrath Of Khan, The
Star Trek III The Search For Spock
Search For Spock, The
Star Trek IV The Voyage Home
Theme From Star Trek IV The Voyage Home
Star Trek V The Final Frontier
Moon's A Window To Heaven, The
Star Trek The Next Generation
Star Trek The Next Generation
Star Wars
Cantina Band
Imperial March, The
Princess Leia's Theme
Star Wars
Starlight Express
Make Up My Heart
Only You
Starlight Express
There's Me
Starman
Starman
Stars On Ice
Juke Box Saturday Night
Stars Over Broadway
Carry Me Back To The Lone Prairie
September In The Rain
Starting Here Starting Now
I Don't Remember Christmas
Starting Here Starting Now
Starting Over
Better Than Ever
State Fair (1945)
It Might As Well Be Spring
It's A Grand Night For Singing
Staying Alive
Far From Over
Stellidaura Vendicata, La
Deh Rendetemi
Step Lively
As Long As There's Music
Come Out Come Out Wherever Are
Some Other Time
Sterile Cuckoo, The
Come Saturday Morning
Sting, The
Entertainer, The
Stir Crazy
Crazy
Stop Look Listen
I Love A Piano
Stop The World I Want To Get Off
Gonna Build A Mountain
Once In A Lifetime
What Kind Of Fool Am I

To Have And Have Not
Baltimore Oriole
How Little We Know
To Live And Die In LA
To Live And Die In LA
To Sir With Love
To Sir With Love
Toast Of New Orleans, The
Be My Love
Tom Jones
A Chanter Rire Et Boire
Tonight At 8:30
You Were There
Tonight Show
Johnny's Theme
Too Many Girls
I Didn't Know What Time It Was
Tootsie
It Might Be You
That's All
Top Gun
Danger Zone
Take My Breath Away
Top Gun Anthem
Top Hat
Cheek To Cheek
Isn't This A Lovely Day
No Strings
Piccolino
Top Hat White Tie And Tails
Top Of The Town
Where Are You
Torrid Zone
Mi Caballero
Touch Of Class, A
All That Love Went To Waste
Touch Of Class, A
Tower Of Babel, The
Three Pictures
Towering Inferno, The
We May Never Love Like This
Again
Trail Of The Lonesome Pine, The
Twilight On The Trail
Traviata, La
Ah Fors' E Lui
Ah Was It He
Come Away
Di Provenza
Drinking Song
Ever Free
Libiamo Libiamo
Parigi O Cara
Pura Siccome
Sempre Libera
Was This The Man My Fancy Saw
Treasure Girl
Feeling I'm Falling
I Don't Think I'll Fall In Love Today
I've Got A Crush On You
K-Ra-Zy For You
Tresor Suppose, Le
En Vain Le Coeur Veut Se Defendre

Trial By Jury
All The Legal Furies Seize You
Comes The Broken Flower
Hark The Hour Of Ten Is Sounding
I Love Him I Love Him
Judge's Song, The
Lovesick Boy, The
O Gentlemen Listen I Pray
Oh Gentlemen Listen
Solatium
When First My Old Old Love I
Knew
When I Good Friends Was Call'd To
The Bar
When I Good Friends Was Called To
The Bar
With A Sense Of Deep Emotion
Trip To Chinatown, A
Push Dem Clouds Away
Tristan Und Isolde
Dreams
Triumph Of Time And Truth, The
False Destructive Ways Of Pleasure
Loathsome Urns Disclose Your
Treasure
Trompeter Von Sakkingen, Der
It Was Not So To Be
Trovatore, Il
Ah I Have Sighed To Rest Me
Anvil Chorus
Aria
At My Mercy
Calm The Tempest
Canzone
Duel, The
Fierce Flames Are Soaring
Finale
God Of The Nations
Gypsy Song
Home To Our Mountains
Look Thee O Heav'n Tis Over
Mastery
Miserere
My Sword In Vengeance
Narrative
Of That Dark Scaffold
Our Flag O'er Us Waving
Sleep My Sweet Baby
Soldiers Chorus
Song Of The Soldiers
Tempest Of The Heart
When She Smiles
True Grit
True Grit
True To Life
Old Music Master, The
Tucker The Man And His Dream
Captain Of Industry
Tumble Inn
Trousseau Ball
Twelfth Night
Come Away Come Away Death
Come Away Death
Farewell Dear Love

Twelfth Night *(Cont.)*
O Mistress Mine
She Never Told Her Love
Song From Shakespeare's Twelfth
Night
Thou Knave
When That I Was A Little Tiny Boy
When That I Was And A Little Tiny
Boy
Twenty Million Sweethearts
I'll String Along With You
Twilight Zone
Nights Are Forever
Twilight Zone
Twirly Whirly
Come Down Ma Evenin' Star
Two For The Show
How High The Moon
Two Gentlemen Of Verona
An Silvia
Who Is Sylvia
Two Girls And A Sailor
Sweet And Lovely
Two Marriages
We're Home Here
Two Of A Kind
Desperate Times
Take A Chance
Two Weeks With Love
Aba Daba Honeymoon, The
Two's Company
Good Little Girls Go To Heaven
Tyrolean, The
Nightingale Song
Umbrellas Of Cherbourg, The
I Will Wait For You
Watch What Happens
Unchained
Unchained Melody
Uncommon Love, An
Lucky One, The
Undine
Arie Der Undine
Uninvited, The
Stella By Starlight
Unmarried Woman, An
Theme From An Unmarried Woman
Unmarried Woman, An
Unsinkable Molly Brown, The
I Ain't Down Yet
Untouchables, The
Untouchables Theme, The
Up In Central Park
Carousel In The Park
Close As Pages In A Book
Urban Cowboy
All Night Long
Could I Have This Dance
Look What You've Done To Me
Lookin' For Love
Love The World Away
Used Cars
Used Cars

White Lady, The
Ballade Of The White Lady
With Joy My Flowing Cup I Bring
White Nights
Say You Say Me
Separate Lives
Who Is Killing The Great Chefs Of Europe
Natasha's Theme
Who's That Girl
Causing A Commotion
Who's That Girl
Who's The Boss
Brand New Life
Whoopee
I'm Bringing A Red Red Rose
Love Me Or Leave Me
Makin' Whoopee
My Baby Just Cares For Me
Widow Jones
May Irwin's Bully Song
Wild Rose, The
We'll Have A Kingdom
Wildcat
Hey Look Me Over
Wilhelm Meister
Lied Der Mignon
Mignon Und Der Harfner
Will O' The Whispers
My Blue Heaven
William Tell
Pull Away Brave Boys
Rossini
Vesper Bells
Willy Wonka And The Chocolate Factory
Candy Man, The
Winds Of War, The
Love Theme From The Winds Of War
Winnie The Pooh
Winnie The Pooh
Winnie The Pooh And The Blustery Day
Wonderful Thing About Tiggers, The
Winnie The Pooh And The Honey Tree
Winnie The Pooh
Winter's Tale, A
Autolycus' Song
But Shall I Go Mourn For That
Get You Hence For I Must Go
Lawn As White As Driven Snow
When Daffodils Begin To Peer
Winterreise
Auf Dem Flusse
Das Wirtshau
Einsamkeit
Erstarrung
Fruhlingstraum
Gefror'ne Tranen
Greise Kopf, Der
Gute Nacht
Im Dorfe

Winterreise *(Cont.)*
Irrlicht
Krahe, Die
Leiermann, Der
Letzte Hoffnung
Lindenbaum, Der
Mut
Nebensonnen, Die
Post, Die
Rast
Ruckblick
Spring Dreams
Sturmische Morgen, Der
Tauschung
Wasserflut
Wegweiser, Der
Wetterfahne, Die
Wirtshaus, Das
Wipeout
Peter's Theme
Wish You Were Here
Wish You Were Here
Wit And Drollery
Saylor's Song, The
Witness
Main Theme From Witness
Wives And Lovers
Wives And Lovers
Wiz, The
Believe In Yourself (Movie)
Ease On Down The Road
Home
Wizard Of Oz, The
Ding Dong The Witch Is Dead (Movie)
Hurrah For Baffin's Bay (Movie)
If I Only Had A Brain (Movie)
Over The Rainbow (Movie)
We're Off To See The Wizard (Movie)
Wizard Of The Nile, The
In Dreamland
My Angeline
Star Light Star Bright
WKRP In Cincinnati
WKRP In Cincinnati
Woman In Red, The
I Just Called To Say I Love You
Love Light In Flight
Woman Of Samaria, The
God Is A Spirit
Woman Of The Year
Grass Is Always Greener, The
I Wrote The Book
One Of The Girls
Sometimes A Day Goes By
Woman's Love
I Would Live In Your Life
To One Away
Wonderful Town
It's Love
Little Bit In Love, A
My Darlin' Eileen

Wonderful Town *(Cont.)*
Ohio
One Hundred Easy Ways
Pass That Football
Quiet Girl, A
Swing
Wrong Note Rag, The
Wonderland
Only One, The
Woodland
Tale Of The Turtle Dove, The
Woodman, The
Streamlet, The
Words And Music
Blue Moon
Blue Room, The
I Wish I Were In Love Again
Mountain Greenery
Thou Swell
With A Song In My Heart
Working
If I Could've Been
Working Girl
Let The River Run
Written On The Wind
Written On The Wind
Wuthering Heights
I Was Born In Love With You
Wyatt Earp
Legend Of Wyatt Earp
Xanadu
Magic
Suddenly
Xanadu
Xerxes
(see **Serse**)
Yankee Consul, The
Ain't It Funny What Difference Just A Few Hours Make
Yankee Girl, The
I've Got Rings On My Fingers
Yellow Submarine
Yellow Submarine
Yentl
Papa Can You Hear Me
Way He Makes Me Feel, The
Yeomen Of The Guard, The
Ah Me
Finale
Free From His Fetters Grim
Funeral March
I Have A Song
I Have A Song To Sing O
I've Jibe And Joke
Is Life A Boon
Man Who Would Woo A Fair Maid, A
Mirage, A
Oh A Private Buffoon
Oh A Private Buffoon Is A Light Hearted Loon
Philosophic Pill, The
Private Buffoon, A
Strange Adventure